Psychology 2e

SENIOR CONTRIBUTING AUTHORS
ROSE M. SPIELMAN, FORMERLY OF QUINNIPIAC UNIVERSITY
WILLIAM J. JENKINS, MERCER UNIVERSITY
MARILYN D. LOVETT, SPELMAN COLLEGE

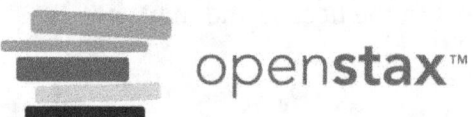

To learn more about OpenStax, visit openstaxtextbooks.com
Individual print copies and bulk orders can be purchased through our website.

Books and Cover Design © 2022 Open Stax Textbooks.
Textbook content produced by OpenStax is licensed under a CCA4

For questions regarding this licensing, please contact

info@openstaxtextbooks.com

Trademarks
The OpenStax name, OpenStax logo, OpenStax book covers, OpenStax CNX name, OpenStax CNX logo, OpenStax Tutor name, Openstax Tutor logo, Connexions name, Connexions logo, Rice University name, and Rice University logo are not subject to the license and may not be reproduced without the prior and express written consent

OpenStax

OpenStax provides free, peer-reviewed, openly licensed textbooks for introductory college and Advanced Placement® courses and low-cost, personalized courseware that helps students learn. A nonprofit ed tech initiative based at Rice University, we're committed to helping students access the tools they need to complete their courses and meet their educational goals.

Rice University

OpenStax, OpenStax CNX, and OpenStax Tutor are initiatives of Rice University. As a leading research university with a distinctive commitment to undergraduate education, Rice University aspires to path-breaking research, unsurpassed teaching, and contributions to the betterment of our world. It seeks to fulfill this mission by cultivating a diverse community of learning and discovery that produces leaders across the spectrum of human endeavor.

Philanthropic Support

OpenStax is grateful for our generous philanthropic partners, who support our vision to improve educational opportunities for all learners.

Laura and John Arnold Foundation	The Maxfield Foundation
Arthur and Carlyse Ciocca Charitable Foundation	Burt and Deedee McMurtry
Ann and John Doerr	Michelson 20MM Foundation
Bill & Melinda Gates Foundation	National Science Foundation
Girard Foundation	The Open Society Foundations
Google Inc.	Jumee Yhu and David E. Park III
The William and Flora Hewlett Foundation	Brian D. Patterson USA-International Foundation
Rusty and John Jaggers	The Bill and Stephanie Sick Fund
The Calvin K. Kazanjian Economics Foundation	Robin and Sandy Stuart Foundation
Charles Koch Foundation	The Stuart Family Foundation
Leon Lowenstein Foundation, Inc.	Tammy and Guillermo Treviño

Table of Contents

Preface 1
Chapter 1: Introduction to Psychology 7
    1.1 What Is Psychology? 8
    1.2 History of Psychology 9
    1.3 Contemporary Psychology 19
    1.4 Careers in Psychology 27
Chapter 2: Psychological Research 37
    2.1 Why Is Research Important? 38
    2.2 Approaches to Research 44
    2.3 Analyzing Findings 52
    2.4 Ethics 63
Chapter 3: Biopsychology 75
    3.1 Human Genetics 76
    3.2 Cells of the Nervous System 83
    3.3 Parts of the Nervous System 89
    3.4 The Brain and Spinal Cord 92
    3.5 The Endocrine System 104
Chapter 4: States of Consciousness 115
    4.1 What Is Consciousness? 116
    4.2 Sleep and Why We Sleep 122
    4.3 Stages of Sleep 124
    4.4 Sleep Problems and Disorders 129
    4.5 Substance Use and Abuse 134
    4.6 Other States of Consciousness 143
Chapter 5: Sensation and Perception 155
    5.1 Sensation versus Perception 156
    5.2 Waves and Wavelengths 160
    5.3 Vision 163
    5.4 Hearing 171
    5.5 The Other Senses 175
    5.6 Gestalt Principles of Perception 179
Chapter 6: Learning 191
    6.1 What Is Learning? 192
    6.2 Classical Conditioning 193
    6.3 Operant Conditioning 203
    6.4 Observational Learning (Modeling) 214
Chapter 7: Thinking and Intelligence 225
    7.1 What Is Cognition? 226
    7.2 Language 230
    7.3 Problem Solving 234
    7.4 What Are Intelligence and Creativity? 241
    7.5 Measures of Intelligence 245
    7.6 The Source of Intelligence 252
Chapter 8: Memory 263
    8.1 How Memory Functions 264
    8.2 Parts of the Brain Involved with Memory 272
    8.3 Problems with Memory 276
    8.4 Ways to Enhance Memory 286
Chapter 9: Lifespan Development 295
    9.1 What Is Lifespan Development? 296

    9.2 Lifespan Theories 300
    9.3 Stages of Development 310
    9.4 Death and Dying 331

Chapter 10: Emotion and Motivation 341
    10.1 Motivation 342
    10.2 Hunger and Eating 348
    10.3 Sexual Behavior 354
    10.4 Emotion 362

Chapter 11: Personality 379
    11.1 What Is Personality? 380
    11.2 Freud and the Psychodynamic Perspective 383
    11.3 Neo-Freudians: Adler, Erikson, Jung, and Horney 389
    11.4 Learning Approaches 395
    11.5 Humanistic Approaches 399
    11.6 Biological Approaches 400
    11.7 Trait Theorists 401
    11.8 Cultural Understandings of Personality 406
    11.9 Personality Assessment 408

Chapter 12: Social Psychology 421
    12.1 What Is Social Psychology? 422
    12.2 Self-presentation 428
    12.3 Attitudes and Persuasion 432
    12.4 Conformity, Compliance, and Obedience 438
    12.5 Prejudice and Discrimination 446
    12.6 Aggression 452
    12.7 Prosocial Behavior 455

Chapter 13: Industrial-Organizational Psychology 471
    13.1 What Is Industrial and Organizational Psychology? 472
    13.2 Industrial Psychology: Selecting and Evaluating Employees 481
    13.3 Organizational Psychology: The Social Dimension of Work 493
    13.4 Human Factors Psychology and Workplace Design 503

Chapter 14: Stress, Lifestyle, and Health 511
    14.1 What Is Stress? 512
    14.2 Stressors 522
    14.3 Stress and Illness 528
    14.4 Regulation of Stress 541
    14.5 The Pursuit of Happiness 548

Chapter 15: Psychological Disorders 563
    15.1 What Are Psychological Disorders? 564
    15.2 Diagnosing and Classifying Psychological Disorders 568
    15.3 Perspectives on Psychological Disorders 571
    15.4 Anxiety Disorders 575
    15.5 Obsessive-Compulsive and Related Disorders 581
    15.6 Posttraumatic Stress Disorder 585
    15.7 Mood Disorders 588
    15.8 Schizophrenia 598
    15.9 Dissociative Disorders 603
    15.10 Disorders in Childhood 604
    15.11 Personality Disorders 611

Chapter 16: Therapy and Treatment 629
    16.1 Mental Health Treatment: Past and Present 630
    16.2 Types of Treatment 636

16.3 Treatment Modalities	648
16.4 Substance-Related and Addictive Disorders: A Special Case	652
16.5 The Sociocultural Model and Therapy Utilization	655

Index 759

Preface

Welcome to *Psychology 2e*, an OpenStax resource. This textbook was written to increase student access to high-quality learning materials, maintaining highest standards of academic rigor at little to no cost.

ABOUT OPENSTAX

OpenStax is a nonprofit based at Rice University, and it's our mission to improve student access to education. Our first openly licensed college textbook was published in 2012, and our library has since scaled to over 35 books for college and AP® courses used by hundreds of thousands of students. OpenStax Tutor, our low-cost personalized learning tool, is being piloted in college courses throughout the country. Through our partnerships with philanthropic foundations and our alliance with other educational resource organizations, OpenStax is breaking down the most common barriers to learning and empowering students and instructors to succeed.

ABOUT OPENSTAX RESOURCES

Customization

You are free to use the entire book or pick and choose the sections that are most relevant to the needs of your course. Feel free to remix the content by assigning your students certain chapters and sections in your syllabus, in the order that you prefer. You can even provide a direct link in your syllabus to the sections in the web view of your book.

Instructors also have the option of creating a customized version of this book. The custom version can be made available to students in low-cost print or digital form through their campus bookstore.

Art Attribution in *Psychology 2e*

In *Psychology 2e*, most art contains attribution to its title, creator or rights holder, host platform, and license within the caption. Because the art is openly licensed, anyone may reuse the art as long as they provide the same attribution to its original source.

To maximize readability and content flow, some art does not include attribution in the text. If you reuse art from *Psychology 2e* that does not have attribution provided, use the following attribution: Copyright Rice University, OpenStax.

Errata

All OpenStax textbooks undergo a rigorous review process. However, like any professional-grade textbook, errors sometimes occur. Since our books are web based, we can make updates periodically when deemed pedagogically necessary. If you have a correction to suggest, submit it through the link on your book page on openstax.org. Subject matter experts review all errata suggestions. OpenStax is committed to remaining transparent about all updates, so you will also find a list of past errata changes on your book page on openstax.org.

ABOUT *PSYCHOLOGY 2E*

Psychology 2e is designed to meet scope and sequence requirements for the single-semester introduction to psychology course. The book offers a comprehensive treatment of core concepts, grounded in both classic studies and current and emerging research. The text also includes coverage of the DSM-5 in examinations of psychological disorders. *Psychology 2e* incorporates discussions that reflect the diversity within the discipline, as well as the diversity of cultures and communities across the globe.

Coverage and scope

The first edition of *Psychology* has been used by thousands of faculty and hundreds of thousands of students since its publication in 2015. OpenStax mined our adopters' extensive and helpful feedback to identify the most significant revision needs while maintaining the organization that many instructors had incorporated into their courses. Specific surveys, pre-revision reviews, and customization analysis, as well as analytical data from OpenStax partners and online learning environments, all aided in planning the revision.

The result is a book that thoroughly treats psychology's foundational concepts while adding current and meaningful coverage in specific areas. *Psychology 2e* retains its manageable scope and contains ample features to draw learners into the discipline.

Structurally, the textbook remains similar to the first edition, with no chapter reorganization and very targeted changes at the section level.

- Chapter 1: Introduction to Psychology
- Chapter 2: Psychological Research
- Chapter 3: Biopsychology
- Chapter 4: States of Consciousness
- Chapter 5: Sensation and Perception
- Chapter 6: Learning
- Chapter 7: Thinking and Intelligence
- Chapter 8: Memory
- Chapter 9: Lifespan Development
- Chapter 10: Motivation and Emotion
- Chapter 11: Personality
- Chapter 12: Social Psychology
- Chapter 13: Industrial-Organizational Psychology
- Chapter 14: Stress, Lifestyle, and Health
- Chapter 15: Psychological Disorders
- Chapter 16: Therapy and Treatment

CHANGES TO THE SECOND EDITION

OpenStax only undertakes second editions when significant modifications to the text are necessary. In the case of *Psychology 2e*, user feedback indicated that we needed to focus on a few key areas, which we have done in the following ways.

Content revisions for clarity, accuracy, and currency

The revision plan varied by chapter based on need. Some chapters were significantly updated for conceptual coverage, research-informed data, and clearer language. In other chapters, the revisions focused mostly on currency of examples and updates to statistics.

Over 210 new research references have been added or updated in order to improve the scholarly underpinnings of the material and broaden the perspective for students. Dozens of examples and feature boxes have been changed or added to better explain concepts and/or increase relevance for students.

Research replication and validity

To engage students in stronger critical analysis and inform them about research reproducibility, substantial coverage has been added to the research chapter and strategically throughout the textbook whenever key studies are discussed. This material is presented in a balanced way and provides instructors with ample opportunity to discuss the importance of replication in a manner that best suits their course.

Diversity, representation, and inclusion

With the help of researchers and teachers who focus on diversity- and identity-related issues, OpenStax has engaged in detailed diversity reviews to identify opportunities to improve the textbook. Reviewers were asked to follow a framework to evaluate the book's terminology, research citations, key contributors to the field, photos and illustrations, and related aspects, commenting on the representation and consideration of diverse groups. Significant additions and revisions were made in this regard, and the review framework itself is available among the OpenStax *Psychology 2e* instructor resources.

Art and illustrations

Under the guidance of the authors and expert scientific illustrators, especially those well versed in creating accessible art, the OpenStax team made changes throughout the art program in *Psychology 2e*.

Accessibility improvements

As with all OpenStax books, the first edition of *Psychology* was created with a focus on accessibility. We have emphasized and improved that approach in the second edition. Our goal is to ensure that all OpenStax websites and the web view versions of our learning materials follow accessible web design best practices, so that they will meet the W3C-WAI Web Content Accessibility Guidelines (WCAG) 2.0 at Level AA and Section 508 of the Rehabilitation Act. The WCAG 2.0 guidelines explain ways to make web content more accessible for people with disabilities and more user-friendly for everyone.

> To accommodate users of specific assistive technologies, all alternative text was reviewed and revised for comprehensiveness and clarity.

> All illustrations were revised to improve the color contrast, which is important for some visually impaired students.

> Overall, the OpenStax platform has been continually upgraded to improve accessibility.

To learn more about our commitment and progress, please view our accessibility statement (https://openstax.org/accessibility-statement).

A transition guide will be available on openstax.org to highlight the specific chapter-level changes to the second edition.

Pedagogical foundation

Psychology 2e engages students through inquiry, self-reflection, and investigation. Features in the second edition have been carefully updated to remain topical and relevant while deepening students' relationship to the material. They include the following:

> **Everyday Connection** features tie psychological topics to everyday issues and behaviors that students encounter in their lives and the world. Topics include the validity of scores on college

entrance exams, the opioid crisis, the impact of social status on stress and healthcare, and cognitive mapping.

What Do You Think? features provide research-based information and ask students their views on controversial issues. Topics include "Brain Dead and on Life Support," "Violent Media and Aggression," and "Capital Punishment and Criminals with Intellectual Disabilities."

Dig Deeper features discuss one specific aspect of a topic in greater depth so students can dig more deeply into the concept. Examples include discussions on the distinction between evolutionary psychology and behavioral genetics, recent findings on neuroplasticity, the field of forensic psychology, and a presentation of research on strategies for coping with prejudice and discrimination.

Connect the Concepts features revisit a concept learned in another chapter, expanding upon it within a different context. Features include "Emotional Expression and Emotional Regulation," "Tweens, Teens, and Social Norms," and "Conditioning and OCD."

Art, interactives, and assessments that engage

Our art program is designed to enhance students' understanding of psychological concepts through simple, effective graphs, diagrams, and photographs. *Psychology 2e* also incorporates links to relevant interactive exercises and animations that help bring topics to life. Selected assessment items touch directly on students' lives.

Link to Learning features direct students to online interactive exercises and animations that add a fuller context to core content and provide an opportunity for application.

Personal Application Questions engage students in topics at a personal level to encourage reflection and promote discussion.

ADDITIONAL RESOURCES
Student and Instructor Resources

We've compiled additional resources for both students and instructors, including Getting Started Guides, an instructor solution guide, a test bank, and PowerPoint slides. Instructor resources require a verified instructor account, which you can apply for when you log in or create your account on openstax.org. Take advantage of these resources to supplement your OpenStax book.

Community Hubs

OpenStax partners with the Institute for the Study of Knowledge Management in Education (ISKME) to offer Community Hubs on OER Commons—a platform for instructors to share community-created resources that support OpenStax books, free of charge. Through our Community Hubs, instructors can upload their own materials or download resources to use in their own courses, including additional ancillaries, teaching material, multimedia, and relevant course content. We encourage instructors to join the hubs for the subjects most relevant to your teaching and research as an opportunity both to enrich your courses and to engage with other faculty.

To reach the Community Hubs, visit www.oercommons.org/hubs/openstax.

Technology partners

As allies in making high-quality learning materials accessible, our technology partners offer optional low-cost tools that are integrated with OpenStax books. To access the technology options for your text, visit your book page on openstax.org.

ABOUT THE AUTHORS
Senior contributing authors

Rose M. Spielman (Content Lead)
Dr. Rose Spielman has been teaching psychology and working as a licensed clinical psychologist for 20 years. Her academic career has included positions at Quinnipiac University, Housatonic Community College, and Goodwin College. As a licensed clinical psychologist, educator, and volunteer director, Rose is able to connect with people from diverse backgrounds and facilitate treatment, advocacy, and education. In her years of work as a teacher, therapist, and administrator, she has helped thousands of students and clients and taught them to advocate for themselves and move their lives forward to become more productive citizens and family members.

William J. Jenkins, Mercer University
Marilyn D. Lovett, Spelman College

Contributing Authors

Mara Aruguete, Lincoln University
Laura Bryant, Eastern Gateway Community College
Barbara Chappell, Walden University
Kathryn Dumper, Bainbridge State College
Arlene Lacombe, Saint Joseph's University
Julie Lazzara, Paradise Valley Community College
Tammy McClain, West Liberty University
Barbara B. Oswald, Miami University
Marion Perlmutter, University of Michigan
Mark D. Thomas, Albany State University

Reviewers

Patricia G. Adams, Pitt Community College
Daniel Bellack, Trident Technical College
Christopher M. Bloom, Providence College
Jerimy Blowers, Cayuga Community College
Salena Brody, Collin College
David A. Caicedo, Borough of Manhattan Community College, CUNY
Bettina Casad, University of Missouri–St. Louis
Sharon Chacon, Northeast Wisconsin Technical College
James Corpening
Frank Eyetsemitan, Roger Williams University
Tamara Ferguson, Utah State University
Kathleen Flannery, Saint Anselm College
Johnathan Forbey, Ball State University
Laura Gaudet, Chadron State College
William Goggin, University of Southern Mississippi
Jeffery K. Gray, Charleston Southern University
Heather Griffiths, Fayetteville State University
Mark Holder, University of British Columbia
Rita Houge, Des Moines Area Community College
Colette Jacquot, Strayer University
John Johanson, Winona State University
Andrew Johnson, Park University
Shaila Khan, Tougaloo College

Cynthia Kreutzer, Georgia State University Perimeter College at Clarkston Campus
Carol Laman, Houston Community College
Dana C. Leighton, Texas A&M University—Texarkana
Thomas Malloy, Rhode Island College
Jan Mendoza, Golden West College
Christopher Miller, University of Minnesota
Lisa Moeller, Beckfield College
Amy T. Nusbaum, Heritage University
Jody Resko, Queensborough Community College (CUNY)
Hugh Riley, Baylor University
Juan Salinas, University of Texas at Austin
Brittney Schrick, Southern Arkansas University
Phoebe Scotland, College of the Rockies
Christine Selby, Husson University
Sally B. Seraphin, Centre College
Brian Sexton, Kean University
Nancy Simpson, Trident Technical College
Jason M. Smith, Federal Bureau of Prisons – FCC Hazelton
Robert Stennett, University of Georgia
Jennifer Stevenson, Ursinus College
Eric Weiser, Curry College
Jay L. Wenger, Harrisburg Area Community College
Alan Whitehead, Southern Virginia University
Valjean Whitlow, American Public University
Rachel Wu, University of California, Riverside
Alexandra Zelin, University of Tennessee at Chattanooga

Chapter 1
Introduction to Psychology

Figure 1.1 Psychology is the scientific study of mind and behavior. (credit "background": modification of work by Nattachai Noogure; credit "top left": modification of work by U.S. Navy; credit "top middle-left": modification of work by Peter Shanks; credit "top middle-right": modification of work by "devinf"/Flickr; credit "top right": modification of work by Alejandra Quintero Sinisterra; credit "bottom left": modification of work by Gabriel Rocha; credit "bottom middle-left": modification of work by Caleb Roenigk; credit "bottom middle-right": modification of work by Staffan Scherz; credit "bottom right": modification of work by Czech Provincial Reconstruction Team)

Chapter Outline

1.1 What Is Psychology?
1.2 History of Psychology
1.3 Contemporary Psychology
1.4 Careers in Psychology

Introduction

Clive Wearing is an accomplished musician who lost his ability to form new memories when he became sick at the age of 46. While he can remember how to play the piano perfectly, he cannot remember what he ate for breakfast just an hour ago (Sacks, 2007). James Wannerton experiences a taste sensation that is associated with the sound of words. His former girlfriend's name tastes like rhubarb (Mundasad, 2013). John Nash is a brilliant mathematician and Nobel Prize winner. However, while he was a professor at MIT, he would tell people that the *New York Times* contained coded messages from extraterrestrial beings that were intended for him. He also began to hear voices and became suspicious of the people around him. Soon thereafter, Nash was diagnosed with schizophrenia and admitted to a state-run mental institution (O'Connor & Robertson, 2002). Nash was the subject of the 2001 movie *A Beautiful Mind*. Why did these people have these experiences? How does the human brain work? And what is the connection between the brain's internal processes and people's external behaviors? This textbook will introduce you to various ways that the field of psychology has explored these questions.

1.1 What Is Psychology?

Learning Objectives

By the end of this section, you will be able to:
- Define psychology
- Understand the merits of an education in psychology

What is creativity? Why do some people become homeless? What are prejudice and discrimination? What is consciousness? The field of psychology explores questions like these. **Psychology** refers to the scientific study of the mind and behavior. Psychologists use the scientific method to acquire knowledge. To apply the scientific method, a researcher with a question about how or why something happens will propose a tentative explanation, called a hypothesis, to explain the phenomenon. A hypothesis should fit into the context of a scientific theory, which is a broad explanation or group of explanations for some aspect of the natural world that is consistently supported by evidence over time. A theory is the best understanding we have of that part of the natural world. The researcher then makes observations or carries out an experiment to test the validity of the hypothesis. Those results are then published or presented at research conferences so that others can replicate or build on the results.

Scientists test that which is perceivable and measurable. For example, the hypothesis that a bird sings because it is happy is not a hypothesis that can be tested since we have no way to measure the happiness of a bird. We must ask a different question, perhaps about the brain state of the bird, since this can be measured. However, we can ask individuals about whether they sing because they are happy since they are able to tell us. Thus, psychological science is empirical, based on measurable data.

In general, science deals only with matter and energy, that is, those things that can be measured, and it cannot arrive at knowledge about values and morality. This is one reason why our scientific understanding of the mind is so limited, since thoughts, at least as we experience them, are neither matter nor energy. The scientific method is also a form of empiricism. An **empirical method** for acquiring knowledge is one based on observation, including experimentation, rather than a method based only on forms of logical argument or previous authorities.

It was not until the late 1800s that psychology became accepted as its own academic discipline. Before this time, the workings of the mind were considered under the auspices of philosophy. Given that any behavior is, at its roots, biological, some areas of psychology take on aspects of a natural science like biology. No biological organism exists in isolation, and our behavior is influenced by our interactions with others. Therefore, psychology is also a social science.

WHY STUDY PSYCHOLOGY?

Often, students take their first psychology course because they are interested in helping others and want to learn more about themselves and why they act the way they do. Sometimes, students take a psychology course because it either satisfies a general education requirement or is required for a program of study such as nursing or pre-med. Many of these students develop such an interest in the area that they go on to declare psychology as their major. As a result, psychology is one of the most popular majors on college campuses across the United States (Johnson & Lubin, 2011). A number of well-known individuals were psychology majors. Just a few famous names on this list are Facebook's creator Mark Zuckerberg, television personality and political satirist Jon Stewart, actress Natalie Portman, and filmmaker Wes Craven (Halonen, 2011). About 6 percent of all bachelor degrees granted in the United States are in the discipline of psychology (U.S. Department of Education, 2016).

An education in psychology is valuable for a number of reasons. Psychology students hone critical thinking skills and are trained in the use of the scientific method. Critical thinking is the active application of a set of skills to information for the understanding and evaluation of that information. The evaluation of information—assessing its reliability and usefulness— is an important skill in a world full of competing "facts," many of which are designed to be misleading. For example, critical thinking involves maintaining an attitude of skepticism, recognizing internal biases, making use of logical thinking, asking appropriate questions, and making observations. Psychology students also can develop better communication skills during the course of their undergraduate coursework (American Psychological Association, 2011). Together, these factors increase students' scientific literacy and prepare students to critically evaluate the various sources of information they encounter.

In addition to these broad-based skills, psychology students come to understand the complex factors that shape one's behavior. They appreciate the interaction of our biology, our environment, and our experiences in determining who we are and how we will behave. They learn about basic principles that guide how we think and behave, and they come to recognize the tremendous diversity that exists across individuals and across cultural boundaries (American Psychological Association, 2011).

> **LINK TO LEARNING**
>
> Watch a brief video about some questions to consider before deciding to major in psychology (http://openstax.org/l/psycmajor) to learn more.

1.2 History of Psychology

Learning Objectives

By the end of this section, you will be able to:
- Understand the importance of Wundt and James in the development of psychology
- Appreciate Freud's influence on psychology
- Understand the basic tenets of Gestalt psychology
- Appreciate the important role that behaviorism played in psychology's history
- Understand basic tenets of humanism
- Understand how the cognitive revolution shifted psychology's focus back to the mind

Psychology is a relatively young science with its experimental roots in the 19th century, compared, for example, to human physiology, which dates much earlier. As mentioned, anyone interested in exploring issues related to the mind generally did so in a philosophical context prior to the 19th century. Two 19th century scholars, Wilhelm Wundt and William James, are generally credited as being the founders of psychology as a science and academic discipline that was distinct from philosophy. This section will provide an overview of the shifts in paradigms that have influenced psychology from Wundt and James through today.

WUNDT AND STRUCTURALISM

Wilhelm Wundt (1832–1920) was a German scientist who was the first person to be referred to as a psychologist. His famous book entitled *Principles of Physiological Psychology* was published in 1873. Wundt viewed psychology as a scientific study of conscious experience, and he believed that the goal of psychology was to identify components of consciousness and how those components combined to result in our conscious experience. Wundt used **introspection** (he called it "internal perception"), a process by which someone examines their own conscious experience as objectively as possible, making the human mind like any other aspect of nature that a scientist observed. He believed in the notion of voluntarism—that people have free will and should know the intentions of a psychological experiment if they were participating (Danziger, 1980). Wundt considered his version experimental introspection; he used instruments such as those that measured reaction time. He also wrote *Volkerpsychologie* in 1904 in which he suggested that psychology should include the study of culture, as it involves the study of people. Edward Titchener, one of his students, went on to develop **structuralism**. Its focus was on the contents of mental processes rather than their function (Pickren & Rutherford, 2010). Wundt established his psychology laboratory at the University at Leipzig in 1879 (Figure 1.2). In this laboratory, Wundt and his students conducted experiments on, for example, reaction times. A subject, sometimes in a room isolated from the scientist, would receive a stimulus such as a light, image, or sound. The subject's reaction to the stimulus would be to push a button, and an apparatus would record the time to reaction. Wundt could measure reaction time to one-thousandth of a second (Nicolas & Ferrand, 1999).

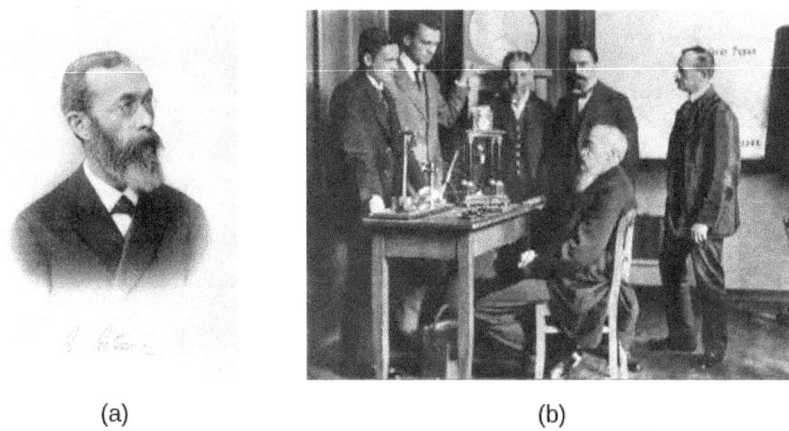

(a) (b)

Figure 1.2 (a) Wilhelm Wundt is credited as one of the founders of psychology. He created the first laboratory for psychological research. (b) This photo shows him seated and surrounded by fellow researchers and equipment in his laboratory in Germany.

However, despite his efforts to train individuals in the process of introspection, this process remained highly subjective, and there was very little agreement between individuals.

JAMES AND FUNCTIONALISM

William James (1842–1910) was the first American psychologist who espoused a different perspective on how psychology should operate (Figure 1.3). James was introduced to Darwin's theory of evolution by natural selection and accepted it as an explanation of an organism's characteristics. Key to that theory is the idea that natural selection leads to organisms that are adapted to their environment, including their behavior. Adaptation means that a trait of an organism has a function for the survival and reproduction of the individual, because it has been naturally selected. As James saw it, psychology's purpose was to study the function of behavior in the world, and as such, his perspective was known as **functionalism**. Functionalism focused on how mental activities helped an organism fit into its environment. Functionalism has a second, more subtle meaning in that functionalists were more interested in the operation of the whole mind rather than of its individual parts, which were the focus of structuralism. Like Wundt, James believed that introspection could serve as one means by which someone might study mental activities, but James also relied on more objective measures, including the use of various recording devices, and examinations of concrete products of mental activities and of anatomy and physiology (Gordon, 1995).

Figure 1.3 William James, shown here in a self-portrait, was the first American psychologist.

FREUD AND PSYCHOANALYTIC THEORY

Perhaps one of the most influential and well-known figures in psychology's history was Sigmund Freud (Figure 1.4). Freud (1856–1939) was an Austrian neurologist who was fascinated by patients suffering from "hysteria" and neurosis. Hysteria was an ancient diagnosis for disorders, primarily of women with a wide variety of symptoms, including physical symptoms and emotional disturbances, none of which had an apparent physical cause. Freud theorized that many of his patients' problems arose from the unconscious mind. In Freud's view, the unconscious mind was a repository of feelings and urges of which we have no awareness. Gaining access to the unconscious, then, was crucial to the successful resolution of the patient's problems. According to Freud, the unconscious mind could be accessed through dream analysis, by examinations of the first words that came to people's minds, and through seemingly innocent slips of the tongue. **Psychoanalytic theory** focuses on the role of a person's unconscious, as well as early childhood experiences, and this particular perspective dominated clinical psychology for several decades (Thorne & Henley, 2005).

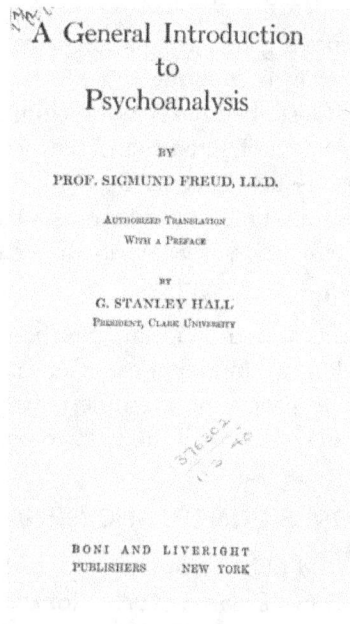

(a) (b)

Figure 1.4 (a) Sigmund Freud was a highly influential figure in the history of psychology. (b) One of his many books, *A General Introduction to Psychoanalysis*, shared his ideas about psychoanalytical therapy; it was published in 1922.

Freud's ideas were influential, and you will learn more about them when you study lifespan development, personality, and therapy. For instance, many therapists believe strongly in the unconscious and the impact of early childhood experiences on the rest of a person's life. The method of psychoanalysis, which involves the patient talking about their experiences and selves, while not invented by Freud, was certainly popularized by him and is still used today. Many of Freud's other ideas, however, are controversial. Drew Westen (1998) argues that many of the criticisms of Freud's ideas are misplaced, in that they attack his older ideas without taking into account later writings. Westen also argues that critics fail to consider the success of the broad ideas that Freud introduced or developed, such as the importance of childhood experiences in adult motivations, the role of unconscious versus conscious motivations in driving our behavior, the fact that motivations can cause conflicts that affect behavior, the effects of mental representations of ourselves and others in guiding our interactions, and the development of personality over time. Westen identifies subsequent research support for all of these ideas.

More modern iterations of Freud's clinical approach have been empirically demonstrated to be effective (Knekt et al., 2008; Shedler, 2010). Some current practices in psychotherapy involve examining unconscious aspects of the self and relationships, often through the relationship between the therapist and the client. Freud's historical significance and contributions to clinical practice merit his inclusion in a discussion of the historical movements within psychology.

WERTHEIMER, KOFFKA, KÖHLER, AND GESTALT PSYCHOLOGY

Max Wertheimer (1880–1943), Kurt Koffka (1886–1941), and Wolfgang Köhler (1887–1967) were three German psychologists who immigrated to the United States in the early 20th century to escape Nazi Germany. These scholars are credited with introducing psychologists in the United States to various Gestalt principles. The word Gestalt roughly translates to "whole;" a major emphasis of Gestalt psychology deals with the fact that although a sensory experience can be broken down into individual parts, how those parts relate to each other as a whole is often what the individual responds to in perception. For example, a song may be made up of individual notes played by different instruments, but the real nature of the song is perceived in the combinations of these notes as they form the melody, rhythm, and harmony. In many ways, this particular perspective would have directly contradicted Wundt's ideas of structuralism (Thorne & Henley, 2005).

Unfortunately, in moving to the United States, these scientists were forced to abandon much of their work and were unable to continue to conduct research on a large scale. These factors along with the rise of behaviorism (described next) in the United States prevented principles of Gestalt psychology from being as influential in the United States as they had been in their native Germany (Thorne & Henley, 2005). Despite these issues, several Gestalt principles are still very influential today. Considering the human individual as a whole rather than as a sum of individually measured parts became an important foundation in humanistic theory late in the century. The ideas of Gestalt have continued to influence research on sensation and perception.

Structuralism, Freud, and the Gestalt psychologists were all concerned in one way or another with describing and understanding inner experience. But other researchers had concerns that inner experience could be a legitimate subject of scientific inquiry and chose instead to exclusively study behavior, the objectively observable outcome of mental processes.

PAVLOV, WATSON, SKINNER, AND BEHAVIORISM

Early work in the field of behavior was conducted by the Russian physiologist Ivan Pavlov (1849–1936). Pavlov studied a form of learning behavior called a conditioned reflex, in which an animal or human produced a reflex (unconscious) response to a stimulus and, over time, was conditioned to produce the response to a different stimulus that the experimenter associated with the original stimulus. The reflex Pavlov worked with was salivation in response to the presence of food. The salivation reflex could be elicited using a second stimulus, such as a specific sound, that was presented in association with the initial food stimulus several times. Once the response to the second stimulus was "learned," the food stimulus could be omitted. Pavlov's "classical conditioning" is only one form of learning behavior studied by behaviorists.

John B. Watson (1878–1958) was an influential American psychologist whose most famous work occurred during the early 20th century at Johns Hopkins University (Figure 1.5). While Wundt and James were concerned with understanding conscious experience, Watson thought that the study of consciousness was flawed. Because he believed that objective analysis of the mind was impossible, Watson preferred to focus directly on observable behavior and try to bring that behavior under control. Watson was a major proponent of shifting the focus of psychology from the mind to behavior, and this approach of observing and controlling behavior came to be known as **behaviorism**. A major object of study by behaviorists was learned behavior and its interaction with inborn qualities of the organism. Behaviorism commonly used animals in experiments under the assumption that what was learned using animal models could, to some degree, be applied to human behavior. Indeed, Tolman (1938) stated, "I believe that everything important in psychology (except … such matters as involve society and words) can be investigated in essence through the continued experimental and theoretical analysis of the determiners of rat behavior at a choice-point in a maze."

Figure 1.5 John B. Watson is known as the father of behaviorism within psychology.

Behaviorism dominated experimental psychology for several decades, and its influence can still be felt today (Thorne & Henley, 2005). Behaviorism is largely responsible for establishing psychology as a scientific discipline through its objective methods and especially experimentation. In addition, it is used in behavioral and cognitive-behavioral therapy. Behavior modification is commonly used in classroom settings. Behaviorism has also led to research on environmental influences on human behavior.

B. F. Skinner (1904–1990) was an American psychologist (Figure 1.6). Like Watson, Skinner was a behaviorist, and he concentrated on how behavior was affected by its consequences. Therefore, Skinner spoke of reinforcement and punishment as major factors in driving behavior. As a part of his research, Skinner developed a chamber that allowed the careful study of the principles of modifying behavior through reinforcement and punishment. This device, known as an operant conditioning chamber (or more familiarly, a Skinner box), has remained a crucial resource for researchers studying behavior (Thorne & Henley, 2005).

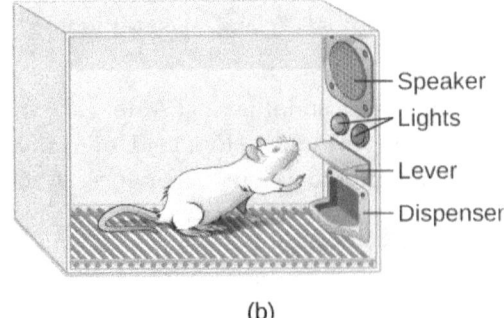

Figure 1.6 (a) B. F. Skinner is famous for his research on operant conditioning. (b) Modified versions of the operant conditioning chamber, or Skinner box, are still widely used in research settings today. (credit a: modification of work by "Silly rabbit"/Wikimedia Commons)

The Skinner box is a chamber that isolates the subject from the external environment and has a behavior indicator such as a lever or a button. When the animal pushes the button or lever, the box is able to deliver a positive reinforcement of the behavior (such as food) or a punishment (such as a noise) or a token conditioner (such as a light) that is correlated with either the positive reinforcement or punishment.

Skinner's focus on positive and negative reinforcement of learned behaviors had a lasting influence in psychology that has waned somewhat since the growth of research in cognitive psychology. Despite this, conditioned learning is still used in human behavioral modification. Skinner's two widely read and controversial popular science books about the value of operant conditioning for creating happier lives remain as thought-provoking arguments for his approach (Greengrass, 2004).

MASLOW, ROGERS, AND HUMANISM

During the early 20th century, American psychology was dominated by behaviorism and psychoanalysis. However, some psychologists were uncomfortable with what they viewed as limited perspectives being so influential to the field. They objected to the pessimism and determinism (all actions driven by the unconscious) of Freud. They also disliked the reductionism, or simplifying nature, of behaviorism. Behaviorism is also deterministic at its core, because it sees human behavior as entirely determined by a combination of genetics and environment. Some psychologists began to form their own ideas that emphasized personal control, intentionality, and a true predisposition for "good" as important for our self-concept and our behavior. Thus, humanism emerged. **Humanism** is a perspective within psychology that emphasizes the potential for good that is innate to all humans. Two of the most well-known proponents of humanistic psychology are Abraham Maslow and Carl Rogers (O'Hara, n.d.).

Abraham Maslow (1908–1970) was an American psychologist who is best known for proposing a hierarchy of human needs in motivating behavior (Figure 1.7). Although this concept will be discussed in more detail in a later chapter, a brief overview will be provided here. Maslow asserted that so long as basic needs necessary for survival were met (e.g., food, water, shelter), higher-level needs (e.g., social needs) would begin to motivate behavior. According to Maslow, the highest-level needs relate to self-actualization, a process by which we achieve our full potential. Obviously, the focus on the positive aspects of human nature that are characteristic of the humanistic perspective is evident (Thorne & Henley, 2005). Humanistic psychologists rejected, on principle, the research approach based on reductionist experimentation in the tradition of the physical and biological sciences, because it missed the "whole" human being. Beginning with Maslow and Rogers, there was an insistence on a humanistic research program. This program has been largely qualitative (not measurement-based), but there exist a number of quantitative research strains within humanistic psychology, including research on happiness, self-concept, meditation, and the outcomes of humanistic psychotherapy (Friedman, 2008).

Figure 1.7 Maslow's hierarchy of needs is shown.

Carl Rogers (1902–1987) was also an American psychologist who, like Maslow, emphasized the potential for good that exists within all people (Figure 1.8). Rogers used a therapeutic technique known as client-centered therapy in helping his clients deal with problematic issues that resulted in their seeking psychotherapy. Unlike a psychoanalytic approach in which the therapist plays an important role in interpreting what conscious behavior reveals about the unconscious mind, client-centered therapy involves the patient taking a lead role in the therapy session. Rogers believed that a therapist needed to display three features to maximize the effectiveness of this particular approach: unconditional positive regard, genuineness, and empathy. Unconditional positive regard refers to the fact that the therapist accepts their client for who they are, no matter what he or she might say. Provided these factors, Rogers believed that people were more than capable of dealing with and working through their own issues (Thorne & Henley, 2005).

Figure 1.8 Carl Rogers, shown in this portrait, developed a client-centered therapy method that has been influential in clinical settings. (credit: "Didius"/Wikimedia Commons)

Humanism has been influential to psychology as a whole. Both Maslow and Rogers are well-known names among students of psychology (you will read more about both later in this text), and their ideas have influenced many scholars. Furthermore, Rogers' client-centered approach to therapy is still commonly used in psychotherapeutic settings today (O'hara, n.d.)

> **LINK TO LEARNING**
>
> View a brief **video of Carl Rogers describing his therapeutic approach (http://openstax.org/l/crogers1)** to learn more.

THE COGNITIVE REVOLUTION

Behaviorism's emphasis on objectivity and focus on external behavior had pulled psychologists' attention away from the mind for a prolonged period of time. The early work of the humanistic psychologists redirected attention to the individual human as a whole, and as a conscious and self-aware being. By the 1950s, new disciplinary perspectives in linguistics, neuroscience, and computer science were emerging, and these areas revived interest in the mind as a focus of scientific inquiry. This particular perspective has come to be known as the cognitive revolution (Miller, 2003). By 1967, Ulric Neisser published the first textbook entitled *Cognitive Psychology*, which served as a core text in cognitive psychology courses around the country (Thorne & Henley, 2005).

Although no one person is entirely responsible for starting the cognitive revolution, Noam Chomsky was very influential in the early days of this movement (**Figure 1.9**). Chomsky (1928–), an American linguist, was dissatisfied with the influence that behaviorism had had on psychology. He believed that psychology's focus on behavior was short-sighted and that the field had to re-incorporate mental functioning into its purview if it were to offer any meaningful contributions to understanding behavior (Miller, 2003).

Figure 1.9 Noam Chomsky was very influential in beginning the cognitive revolution. In 2010, this mural honoring him was put up in Philadelphia, Pennsylvania. (credit: Robert Moran)

European psychology had never really been as influenced by behaviorism as had American psychology; and thus, the cognitive revolution helped reestablish lines of communication between European psychologists and their American counterparts. Furthermore, psychologists began to cooperate with scientists in other fields, like anthropology, linguistics, computer science, and neuroscience, among others. This interdisciplinary approach often was referred to as the cognitive sciences, and the influence and prominence of this particular perspective resonates in modern-day psychology (Miller, 2003).

> ### DIG DEEPER
>
> **Feminist Psychology**
>
> The science of psychology has had an impact on human wellbeing, both positive and negative. The dominant influence of Western, white, and male academics in the early history of psychology meant that psychology developed with the biases inherent in those individuals, which often had negative consequences for members of society who were not white or male. Women, members of ethnic minorities in both the United States and other countries, and individuals with sexual orientations other than straight had difficulties entering the field of psychology and therefore influencing its development. They also suffered from the attitudes of white male psychologists who were not immune to the nonscientific attitudes prevalent in the society in which they developed and worked. Until the 1960s, the science of psychology was largely a "womanless" psychology (Crawford & Marecek, 1989), meaning that few women were able to practice psychology, so they had little influence on what was studied. In addition, the experimental subjects of psychology were mostly men, which resulted from underlying assumptions that gender had no influence on psychology and that women were not of sufficient interest to study.
>
> An article by Naomi Weisstein, first published in 1968 (Weisstein, 1993), stimulated a feminist revolution in psychology by presenting a critique of psychology as a science. She also specifically criticized male psychologists for constructing the psychology of women entirely out of their own cultural biases and without careful experimental tests to verify any of their characterizations of women. Weisstein used, as examples, statements by prominent psychologists in the 1960s, such as this quote by Bruno Bettleheim: "We must start with the realization that, as much as women want to be good scientists or engineers, they want first and foremost to be womanly companions of men and to be mothers." Weisstein's critique formed the foundation for the subsequent development of a feminist psychology that attempted to be free of the influence of male cultural biases on our knowledge of the psychology of women.
>
> Crawford & Marecek (1989) identify several feminist approaches to psychology that can be described as feminist psychology. These include re-evaluating and discovering the contributions of women to the history of psychology, studying psychological gender differences, and questioning the male bias present across the practice of the scientific approach to knowledge.

MULTICULTURAL AND CROSS-CULTURAL PSYCHOLOGY

Culture has important impacts on individuals and social psychology, yet the effects of culture on psychology are under-studied. There is a risk that psychological theories and data derived from white, American settings could be assumed to apply to individuals and social groups from other cultures and this is unlikely to be true (Betancourt & López, 1993). One weakness in the field of cross-cultural psychology is that in looking for differences in psychological attributes across cultures, there remains a need to go beyond simple descriptive statistics (Betancourt & López, 1993). In this sense, it has remained a descriptive science, rather than one seeking to determine cause and effect. For example, a study of characteristics of individuals seeking treatment for a binge eating disorder in Hispanic American, African American, and Caucasian American individuals found significant differences between groups (Franko et al., 2012). The study concluded that results from studying any one of the groups could not be extended to the other groups, and yet potential causes of the differences were not measured. Multicultural psychologists develop theories and conduct research with diverse populations, typically within one country. Cross-cultural psychologists compare populations across countries, such as participants from the United States compared to participants from China.

In 1920, Francis Cecil Sumner was the first African American to receive a PhD in psychology in the United States. Sumner established a psychology degree program at Howard University, leading to the education of a new generation of African American psychologists (Black, Spence, and Omari, 2004). Much of the work of early psychologists from diverse backgrounds was dedicated to challenging intelligence testing and promoting innovative educational methods for children. George I. Sanchez contested such testing with

Mexican American children. As a psychologist of Mexican heritage, he pointed out that the language and cultural barriers in testing were keeping children from equal opportunities (Guthrie, 1998). By 1940, he was teaching with his doctoral degree at University of Texas at Austin and challenging segregated educational practices (Romo, 1986).

Two famous African American researchers and psychologists are Mamie Phipps Clark and her husband, Kenneth Clark. They are best known for their studies conducted on African American children and doll preference, research that was instrumental in the *Brown v. Board of Education* Supreme Court desegregation case. The Clarks applied their research to social services and opened the first child guidance center in Harlem (American Psychological Association, 2019).

Listen to the podcast below describing the Clarks' research and impact on the Supreme Court decision.

LINK TO LEARNING

Listen to a podcast about the influence of an African American's psychology research on the historic Brown v. Board of Education civil rights case (http://openstax.org/l/crogers2) to learn more.

The American Psychological Association has several ethnically based organizations for professional psychologists that facilitate interactions among members. Since psychologists belonging to specific ethnic groups or cultures have the most interest in studying the psychology of their communities, these organizations provide an opportunity for the growth of research on the interplay between culture and psychology.

WOMEN IN PSYCHOLOGY

Although rarely given credit, women have been contributing to psychology since its inception as a field of study. In 1894, Margaret Floy Washburn was the first woman awarded the doctoral degree in psychology. She wrote *The Animal Mind: A Textbook of Comparative Psychology*, and it was the standard in the field for over 20 years. In the mid 1890s, Mary Whiton Calkins completed all requirements toward the PhD in psychology, but Harvard University refused to award her that degree because she was a woman. She had been taught and mentored by William James, who tried and failed to convince Harvard to award her the doctoral degree. Her memory research studied primacy and recency (Madigan & O'Hara, 1992), and she also wrote about how structuralism and functionalism both explained self-psychology (Calkins, 1906).

Another influential woman, Mary Cover Jones, conducted a study she considered to be a sequel to John B. Watson's study of Little Albert (you'll learn about this study in the chapter on Learning). Jones unconditioned fear in Little Peter, who had been afraid of rabbits (Jones, 1924).

Ethnic minority women contributing to the field of psychology include Martha Bernal and Inez Beverly Prosser; their studies were related to education. Bernal, the first Latina to earn her doctoral degree in psychology (1962) conducted much of her research with Mexican American children. Prosser was the first African American woman awarded the PhD in 1933 at the University of Cincinnati (Benjamin, Henry, & McMahon, 2005).

1.3 Contemporary Psychology

Learning Objectives

By the end of this section, you will be able to:
- Appreciate the diversity of interests and foci within psychology
- Understand basic interests and applications in each of the described areas of psychology
- Demonstrate familiarity with some of the major concepts or important figures in each of the described areas of psychology

Contemporary psychology is a diverse field that is influenced by all of the historical perspectives described in the preceding section. Reflective of the discipline's diversity is the diversity seen within the **American Psychological Association (APA)**. The APA is a professional organization representing psychologists in the United States. The APA is the largest organization of psychologists in the world, and its mission is to advance and disseminate psychological knowledge for the betterment of people. There are 56 divisions within the APA, representing a wide variety of specialties that range from Societies for the Psychology of Religion and Spirituality to Exercise and Sport Psychology to Behavioral Neuroscience and Comparative Psychology. Reflecting the diversity of the field of psychology itself, members, affiliate members, and associate members span the spectrum from students to doctoral-level psychologists, and come from a variety of places including educational settings, criminal justice, hospitals, the armed forces, and industry (American Psychological Association, 2014). G. Stanley Hall was the first president of the APA. Before he earned his doctoral degree, he was an adjunct instructor at Wilberforce University, a historically black college/university (HBCU), while serving as faculty at Antioch College. Hall went on to work under William James, earning his PhD. Eventually, he became the first president of Clark University in Massachusetts when it was founded (Pickren & Rutherford, 2010).

The Association for Psychological Science (APS) was founded in 1988 and seeks to advance the scientific orientation of psychology. Its founding resulted from disagreements between members of the scientific and clinical branches of psychology within the APA. The APS publishes five research journals and engages in education and advocacy with funding agencies. A significant proportion of its members are international, although the majority is located in the United States. Other organizations provide networking and collaboration opportunities for professionals of several ethnic or racial groups working in psychology, such as the National Latina/o Psychological Association (NLPA), the Asian American Psychological Association (AAPA), the Association of Black Psychologists (ABPsi), and the Society of Indian Psychologists (SIP). Most of these groups are also dedicated to studying psychological and social issues within their specific communities.

This section will provide an overview of the major subdivisions within psychology today in the order in which they are introduced throughout the remainder of this textbook. This is not meant to be an exhaustive listing, but it will provide insight into the major areas of research and practice of modern-day psychologists.

LINK TO LEARNING

Please visit this **website about the divisions within the APA (http://openstax.org/l/biopsychology)** to learn more.

View these **student resources (http://openstax.org/l/studentresource)** also provided by the APA.

BIOPSYCHOLOGY AND EVOLUTIONARY PSYCHOLOGY

As the name suggests, **biopsychology** explores how our biology influences our behavior. While biological psychology is a broad field, many biological psychologists want to understand how the structure and function of the nervous system is related to behavior (Figure 1.10). As such, they often combine the research strategies of both psychologists and physiologists to accomplish this goal (as discussed in Carlson, 2013).

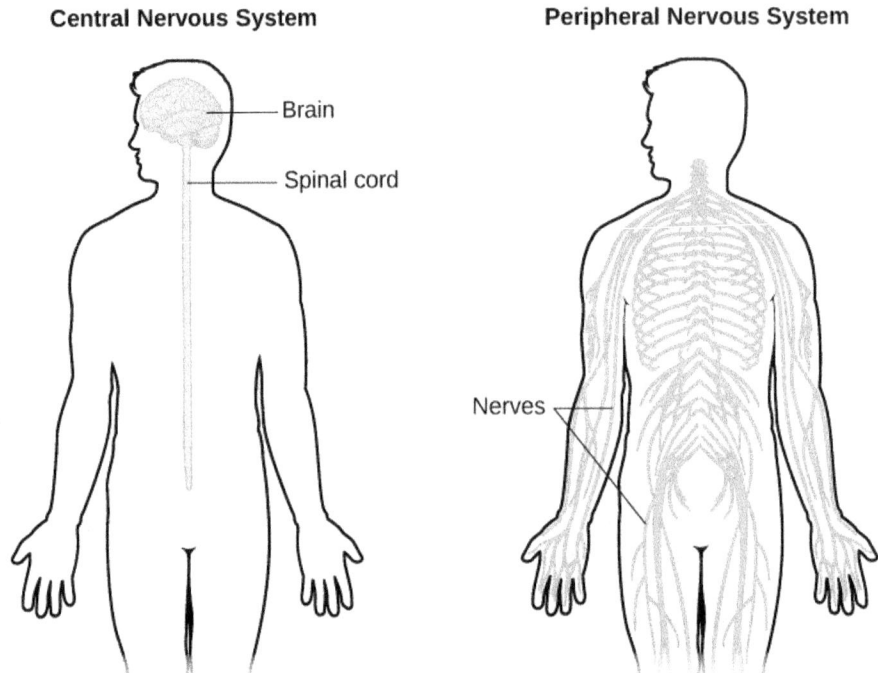

Figure 1.10 Biological psychologists study how the structure and function of the nervous system generate behavior.

The research interests of biological psychologists span a number of domains, including but not limited to, sensory and motor systems, sleep, drug use and abuse, ingestive behavior, reproductive behavior, neurodevelopment, plasticity of the nervous system, and biological correlates of psychological disorders. Given the broad areas of interest falling under the purview of biological psychology, it will probably come as no surprise that individuals from all sorts of backgrounds are involved in this research, including biologists, medical professionals, physiologists, and chemists. This interdisciplinary approach is often referred to as neuroscience, of which biological psychology is a component (Carlson, 2013).

While biopsychology typically focuses on the immediate causes of behavior based in the physiology of a human or other animal, evolutionary psychology seeks to study the ultimate biological causes of behavior. To the extent that a behavior is impacted by genetics, a behavior, like any anatomical characteristic of a human or animal, will demonstrate adaption to its surroundings. These surroundings include the physical environment and, since interactions between organisms can be important to survival and reproduction, the social environment. The study of behavior in the context of evolution has its origins with Charles Darwin, the co-discoverer of the theory of evolution by natural selection. Darwin was well aware that behaviors should be adaptive and wrote books titled, *The Descent of Man* (1871) and *The Expression of the Emotions in Man and Animals* (1872), to explore this field.

Evolutionary psychology, and specifically, the evolutionary psychology of humans, has enjoyed a resurgence in recent decades. To be subject to evolution by natural selection, a behavior must have a significant genetic cause. In general, we expect all human cultures to express a behavior if it is caused genetically, since the genetic differences among human groups are small. The approach taken by most evolutionary psychologists is to predict the outcome of a behavior in a particular situation based on evolutionary theory and then to make observations, or conduct experiments, to determine whether the results match the theory. It is important to recognize that these types of studies are not strong evidence that a behavior is adaptive, since they lack information that the behavior is in some part genetic and not entirely cultural (Endler, 1986). Demonstrating that a trait, especially in humans, is naturally selected is extraordinarily difficult; perhaps for this reason, some evolutionary psychologists are content to assume the behaviors they study have genetic determinants (Confer et al., 2010).

One other drawback of evolutionary psychology is that the traits that we possess now evolved under environmental and social conditions far back in human history, and we have a poor understanding of what these conditions were. This makes predictions about what is adaptive for a behavior difficult. Behavioral traits need not be adaptive under current conditions, only under the conditions of the past when they evolved, about which we can only hypothesize.

There are many areas of human behavior for which evolution can make predictions. Examples include memory, mate choice, relationships between kin, friendship and cooperation, parenting, social organization, and status (Confer et al., 2010).

Evolutionary psychologists have had success in finding experimental correspondence between observations and expectations. In one example, in a study of mate preference differences between men and women that spanned 37 cultures, Buss (1989) found that women valued earning potential factors greater than men, and men valued potential reproductive factors (youth and attractiveness) greater than women in their prospective mates. In general, the predictions were in line with the predictions of evolution, although there were deviations in some cultures.

SENSATION AND PERCEPTION

Scientists interested in both physiological aspects of sensory systems as well as in the psychological experience of sensory information work within the area of sensation and perception (Figure 1.11). As such, sensation and perception research is also quite interdisciplinary. Imagine walking between buildings as you move from one class to another. You are inundated with sights, sounds, touch sensations, and smells. You also experience the temperature of the air around you and maintain your balance as you make your way. These are all factors of interest to someone working in the domain of sensation and perception.

Figure 1.11 When you look at this image, you may see a duck or a rabbit. The sensory information remains the same, but your perception can vary dramatically.

As described in a later chapter that focuses on the results of studies in sensation and perception, our experience of our world is not as simple as the sum total of all of the sensory information (or sensations) together. Rather, our experience (or perception) is complex and is influenced by where we focus our attention, our previous experiences, and even our cultural backgrounds.

COGNITIVE PSYCHOLOGY

As mentioned in the previous section, the cognitive revolution created an impetus for psychologists to focus their attention on better understanding the mind and mental processes that underlie behavior. Thus, **cognitive psychology** is the area of psychology that focuses on studying cognitions, or thoughts, and their relationship to our experiences and our actions. Like biological psychology, cognitive psychology is broad in its scope and often involves collaborations among people from a diverse range of disciplinary backgrounds. This has led some to coin the term cognitive science to describe the interdisciplinary nature of this area of research (Miller, 2003).

Cognitive psychologists have research interests that span a spectrum of topics, ranging from attention to problem solving to language to memory. The approaches used in studying these topics are equally diverse. Given such diversity, cognitive psychology is not captured in one chapter of this text per se; rather, various concepts related to cognitive psychology will be covered in relevant portions of the chapters in this text on sensation and perception, thinking and intelligence, memory, lifespan development, social psychology, and therapy.

DEVELOPMENTAL PSYCHOLOGY

Developmental psychology is the scientific study of development across a lifespan. Developmental psychologists are interested in processes related to physical maturation. However, their focus is not limited to the physical changes associated with aging, as they also focus on changes in cognitive skills, moral reasoning, social behavior, and other psychological attributes.

Early developmental psychologists focused primarily on changes that occurred through reaching adulthood, providing enormous insight into the differences in physical, cognitive, and social capacities that exist between very young children and adults. For instance, research by Jean Piaget (**Figure 1.12**) demonstrated that very young children do not demonstrate object permanence. Object permanence refers to the understanding that physical things continue to exist, even if they are hidden from us. If you were to show an adult a toy, and then hide it behind a curtain, the adult knows that the toy still exists. However, very young infants act as if a hidden object no longer exists. The age at which object permanence is achieved is somewhat controversial (Munakata, McClelland, Johnson, and Siegler, 1997).

Figure 1.12 Jean Piaget is famous for his theories regarding changes in cognitive ability that occur as we move from infancy to adulthood.

While Piaget was focused on cognitive changes during infancy and childhood as we move to adulthood, there is an increasing interest in extending research into the changes that occur much later in life. This may be reflective of changing population demographics of developed nations as a whole. As more and more people live longer lives, the number of people of advanced age will continue to increase. Indeed, it is estimated that there were just over 40 million people aged 65 or older living in the United States in 2010. However, by 2020, this number is expected to increase to about 55 million. By the year 2050, it is estimated that nearly 90 million people in this country will be 65 or older (Department of Health and

Human Services, n.d.).

PERSONALITY PSYCHOLOGY

Personality psychology focuses on patterns of thoughts and behaviors that make each individual unique. Several individuals (e.g., Freud and Maslow) that we have already discussed in our historical overview of psychology, and the American psychologist Gordon Allport, contributed to early theories of personality. These early theorists attempted to explain how an individual's personality develops from his or her given perspective. For example, Freud proposed that personality arose as conflicts between the conscious and unconscious parts of the mind were carried out over the lifespan. Specifically, Freud theorized that an individual went through various psychosexual stages of development. According to Freud, adult personality would result from the resolution of various conflicts that centered on the migration of erogenous (or sexual pleasure-producing) zones from the oral (mouth) to the anus to the phallus to the genitals. Like many of Freud's theories, this particular idea was controversial and did not lend itself to experimental tests (Person, 1980).

More recently, the study of personality has taken on a more quantitative approach. Rather than explaining how personality arises, research is focused on identifying **personality traits**, measuring these traits, and determining how these traits interact in a particular context to determine how a person will behave in any given situation. Personality traits are relatively consistent patterns of thought and behavior, and many have proposed that five trait dimensions are sufficient to capture the variations in personality seen across individuals. These five dimensions are known as the "Big Five" or the Five Factor model, and include dimensions of conscientiousness, agreeableness, neuroticism, openness, and extraversion (**Figure 1.13**). Each of these traits has been demonstrated to be relatively stable over the lifespan (e.g., Rantanen, Metsäpelto, Feldt, Pulkinnen, and Kokko, 2007; Soldz & Vaillant, 1999; McCrae & Costa, 2008) and is influenced by genetics (e.g., Jang, Livesly, and Vernon, 1996).

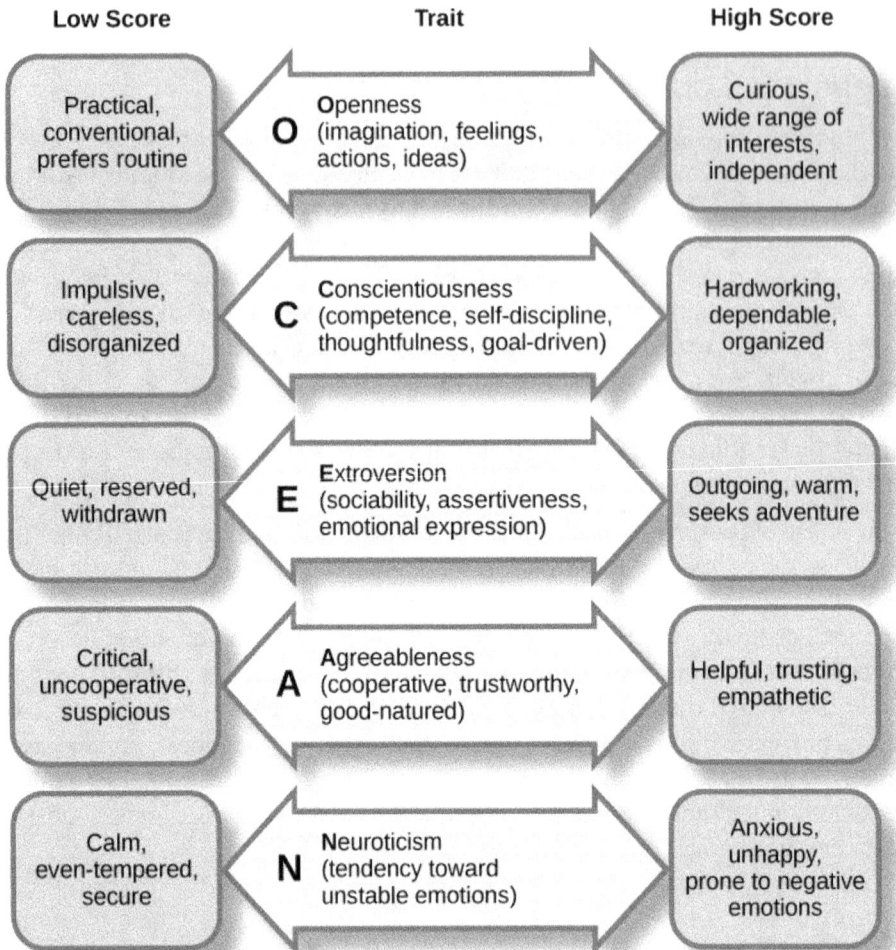

Figure 1.13 Each of the dimensions of the Five Factor model is shown in this figure. The provided description would describe someone who scored highly on that given dimension. Someone with a lower score on a given dimension could be described in opposite terms.

SOCIAL PSYCHOLOGY

Social psychology focuses on how we interact with and relate to others. Social psychologists conduct research on a wide variety of topics that include differences in how we explain our own behavior versus how we explain the behaviors of others, prejudice, and attraction, and how we resolve interpersonal conflicts. Social psychologists have also sought to determine how being among other people changes our own behavior and patterns of thinking.

There are many interesting examples of social psychological research, and you will read about many of these in a later chapter of this textbook. Until then, you will be introduced to one of the most controversial psychological studies ever conducted. Stanley Milgram was an American social psychologist who is most famous for research that he conducted on obedience. After the holocaust, in 1961, a Nazi war criminal, Adolf Eichmann, who was accused of committing mass atrocities, was put on trial. Many people wondered how German soldiers were capable of torturing prisoners in concentration camps, and they were unsatisfied with the excuses given by soldiers that they were simply following orders. At the time, most psychologists agreed that few people would be willing to inflict such extraordinary pain and suffering, simply because they were obeying orders. Milgram decided to conduct research to determine whether or not this was true (Figure 1.14). As you will read later in the text, Milgram found that nearly two-thirds of his participants were willing to deliver what they believed to be lethal shocks to another person, simply because they were instructed to do so by an authority figure (in this case, a man dressed in a lab coat). This was in spite of the fact that participants received payment for simply showing up for the research study and could have chosen not to inflict pain or more serious consequences on another person by withdrawing from the study. No one was actually hurt or harmed in any way, Milgram's experiment was a clever ruse that took advantage of research confederates, those who pretend to be participants in a research study who are actually working for the researcher and have clear, specific directions on how to behave during the research study (Hock, 2009). Milgram's and others' studies that involved deception and potential emotional harm to study participants catalyzed the development of ethical guidelines for conducting psychological research that discourage the use of deception of research subjects, unless it can be argued not to cause harm and, in general, requiring informed consent of participants.

Public Announcement

WE WILL PAY YOU $4.00 FOR ONE HOUR OF YOUR TIME

Persons Needed for a Study of Memory

*We will pay five hundred New Haven men to help us complete a scientific study of memory and learning. The study is being done at Yale University.

*Each person who participates will be paid $4.00 (plus 50c carfare) for approximately 1 hour's time. We need you for only one hour; there are no further obligations. You may choose the time you would like to come (evenings, weekdays, or weekends).

*No special training, education, or experience is needed. We want:

Factory workers	Businessmen	Construction workers
City employees	Clerks	Salespeople
Laborers	Professional people	White-collar workers
Barbers	Telephone workers	Others

All persons must be between the ages of 20 and 50. High school and college students cannot be used.

*If you meet these qualifications, fill out the coupon below and mail it now to Professor Stanley Milgram, Department of Psychology, Yale University, New Haven. You will be notified later of the specific time and place of the study. We reserve the right to decline any application.

*You will be paid $4.00 (plus 50c carfare) as soon as you arrive at the laboratory.

TO:
PROF. STANLEY MILGRAM, DEPARTMENT OF PSYCHOLOGY, YALE UNIVERSITY, NEW HAVEN, CONN. I want to take part in this study of memory and learning. I am between the ages of 20 and 50. I will be paid $4.00 (plus 50c carfare) if I participate.

NAME (Please Print).................................
ADDRESS..
TELEPHONE NO. .... Best time to call you ....
AGE........OCCUPATION................... SEX......
CAN YOU COME:
WEEKDAYS .... EVENINGS ......WEEKENDS.........

Figure 1.14 Stanley Milgram's research demonstrated just how far people will go in obeying orders from an authority figure. This advertisement was used to recruit subjects for his research.

INDUSTRIAL-ORGANIZATIONAL PSYCHOLOGY

Industrial-Organizational psychology (I-O psychology) is a subfield of psychology that applies psychological theories, principles, and research findings in industrial and organizational settings. I-O psychologists are often involved in issues related to personnel management, organizational structure, and workplace environment. Businesses often seek the aid of I-O psychologists to make the best hiring decisions as well as to create an environment that results in high levels of employee productivity and efficiency. In addition to its applied nature, I-O psychology also involves conducting scientific research on behavior within I-O settings (Riggio, 2013).

HEALTH PSYCHOLOGY

Health psychology focuses on how health is affected by the interaction of biological, psychological, and sociocultural factors. This particular approach is known as the **biopsychosocial model** (Figure 1.15). Health psychologists are interested in helping individuals achieve better health through public policy, education, intervention, and research. Health psychologists might conduct research that explores the relationship between one's genetic makeup, patterns of behavior, relationships, psychological stress, and health. They may research effective ways to motivate people to address patterns of behavior that contribute to poorer health (MacDonald, 2013).

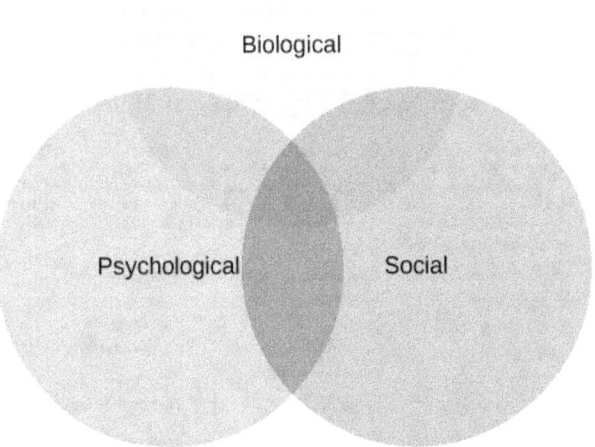

Figure 1.15 The biopsychosocial model suggests that health/illness is determined by an interaction of these three factors.

SPORT AND EXERCISE PSYCHOLOGY

Researchers in **sport and exercise psychology** study the psychological aspects of sport performance, including motivation and performance anxiety, and the effects of sport on mental and emotional wellbeing. Research is also conducted on similar topics as they relate to physical exercise in general. The discipline also includes topics that are broader than sport and exercise but that are related to interactions between mental and physical performance under demanding conditions, such as fire fighting, military operations, artistic performance, and surgery.

CLINICAL PSYCHOLOGY

Clinical psychology is the area of psychology that focuses on the diagnosis and treatment of psychological disorders and other problematic patterns of behavior. As such, it is generally considered to be a more applied area within psychology; however, some clinicians are also actively engaged in scientific research. **Counseling psychology** is a similar discipline that focuses on emotional, social, vocational, and health-related outcomes in individuals who are considered psychologically healthy.

As mentioned earlier, both Freud and Rogers provided perspectives that have been influential in shaping how clinicians interact with people seeking psychotherapy. While aspects of the psychoanalytic theory are still found among some of today's therapists who are trained from a psychodynamic perspective, Roger's ideas about client-centered therapy have been especially influential in shaping how many clinicians operate. Furthermore, both behaviorism and the cognitive revolution have shaped clinical practice in the forms of behavioral therapy, cognitive therapy, and cognitive-behavioral therapy (Figure 1.16). Issues related to the diagnosis and treatment of psychological disorders and problematic patterns of behavior will be discussed in detail in later chapters of this textbook.

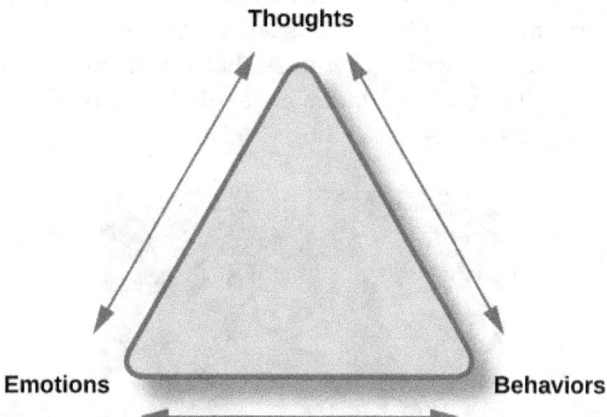

Figure 1.16 Cognitive-behavioral therapists take cognitive processes and behaviors into account when providing psychotherapy. This is one of several strategies that may be used by practicing clinical psychologists.

By far, this is the area of psychology that receives the most attention in popular media, and many people mistakenly assume that all psychology is clinical psychology.

FORENSIC PSYCHOLOGY

Forensic psychology is a branch of psychology that deals questions of psychology as they arise in the context of the justice system. For example, forensic psychologists (and forensic psychiatrists) will assess a person's competency to stand trial, assess the state of mind of a defendant, act as consultants on child custody cases, consult on sentencing and treatment recommendations, and advise on issues such as eyewitness testimony and children's testimony (American Board of Forensic Psychology, 2014). In these capacities, they will typically act as expert witnesses, called by either side in a court case to provide their research- or experience-based opinions. As expert witnesses, forensic psychologists must have a good understanding of the law and provide information in the context of the legal system rather than just within the realm of psychology. Forensic psychologists are also used in the jury selection process and witness preparation. They may also be involved in providing psychological treatment within the criminal justice system. Criminal profilers are a relatively small proportion of psychologists that act as consultants to law enforcement.

1.4 Careers in Psychology

Learning Objectives

By the end of this section, you will be able to:
- Understand educational requirements for careers in academic settings
- Understand the demands of a career in an academic setting
- Understand career options outside of academic settings

Psychologists can work in many different places doing many different things. In general, anyone wishing to continue a career in psychology at a 4-year institution of higher education will have to earn a doctoral degree in psychology for some specialties and at least a master's degree for others. In most areas of psychology, this means earning a PhD in a relevant area of psychology. Literally, **PhD** refers to a doctor of philosophy degree, but here, philosophy does not refer to the field of philosophy per se. Rather, philosophy in this context refers to many different disciplinary perspectives that would be housed in a traditional college of liberal arts and sciences.

The requirements to earn a PhD vary from country to country and even from school to school, but usually, individuals earning this degree must complete a dissertation. A **dissertation** is essentially a long research paper or bundled published articles describing research that was conducted as a part of the candidate's doctoral training. In the United States, a dissertation generally has to be defended before a committee of expert reviewers before the degree is conferred (Figure 1.17).

Figure 1.17 Doctoral degrees are generally conferred in formal ceremonies involving special attire and rites. (credit: Public Affairs Office Fort Wainwright)

Once someone earns a PhD, they may seek a faculty appointment at a college or university. Being on the faculty of a college or university often involves dividing time between teaching, research, and service to the institution and profession. The amount of time spent on each of these primary responsibilities varies dramatically from school to school, and it is not uncommon for faculty to move from place to place in search of the best personal fit among various academic environments. The previous section detailed some of the major areas that are commonly represented in psychology departments around the country; thus, depending on the training received, an individual could be anything from a biological psychologist to a clinical psychologist in an academic setting (Figure 1.18).

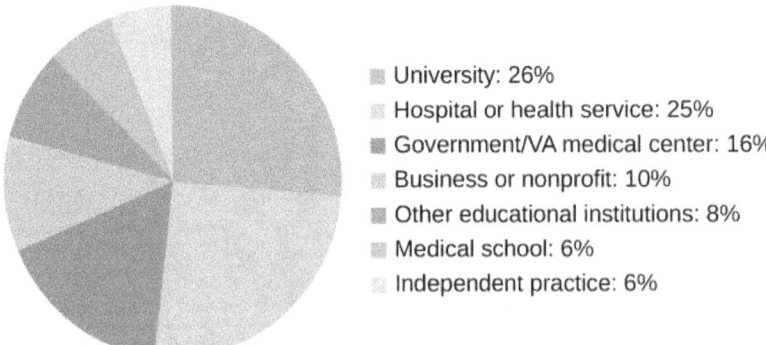

Figure 1.18 Individuals earning a PhD in psychology have a range of employment options.

> **LINK TO LEARNING**
>
> Use this interactive tool and explore different careers in psychology based on degree levels (http://openstax.org/l/degreecareer) to learn more.

OTHER CAREERS IN ACADEMIC SETTINGS

Often times, schools offer more courses in psychology than their full-time faculty can teach. In these cases, it is not uncommon to bring in an adjunct faculty member or instructor. Adjunct faculty members and instructors usually have an advanced degree in psychology, but they often have primary careers outside of academia and serve in this role as a secondary job. Alternatively, they may not hold the doctoral degree required by most 4-year institutions and use these opportunities to gain experience in teaching. Furthermore, many 2-year colleges and schools need faculty to teach their courses in psychology. In general, many of the people who pursue careers at these institutions have master's degrees in psychology, although some PhDs make careers at these institutions as well.

Some people earning PhDs may enjoy research in an academic setting. However, they may not be interested in teaching. These individuals might take on faculty positions that are exclusively devoted to conducting research. This type of position would be more likely an option at large, research-focused universities.

In some areas in psychology, it is common for individuals who have recently earned their PhD to seek out positions in **postdoctoral training programs** that are available before going on to serve as faculty. In most cases, young scientists will complete one or two postdoctoral programs before applying for a full-time faculty position. Postdoctoral training programs allow young scientists to further develop their research programs and broaden their research skills under the supervision of other professionals in the field.

CAREER OPTIONS OUTSIDE OF ACADEMIC SETTINGS

Individuals who wish to become practicing clinical psychologists have another option for earning a doctoral degree, which is known as a PsyD. A **PsyD** is a doctor of psychology degree that is increasingly popular among individuals interested in pursuing careers in clinical psychology. PsyD programs generally place less emphasis on research-oriented skills and focus more on application of psychological principles in the clinical context (Norcorss & Castle, 2002).

Regardless of whether earning a PhD or PsyD, in most states, an individual wishing to practice as a licensed clinical or counseling psychologist may complete postdoctoral work under the supervision of a licensed psychologist. Within the last few years, however, several states have begun to remove this requirement, which would allow people to get an earlier start in their careers (Munsey, 2009). After an individual has met the state requirements, their credentials are evaluated to determine whether they can sit for the licensure exam. Only individuals that pass this exam can call themselves licensed clinical or counseling psychologists (Norcross, n.d.). Licensed clinical or counseling psychologists can then work in a number of settings, ranging from private clinical practice to hospital settings. It should be noted that clinical psychologists and psychiatrists do different things and receive different types of education. While both can conduct therapy and counseling, clinical psychologists have a PhD or a PsyD, whereas psychiatrists have a doctor of medicine degree (MD). As such, licensed clinical psychologists can administer and interpret psychological tests, while psychiatrists can prescribe medications.

Individuals earning a PhD can work in a variety of settings, depending on their areas of specialization. For example, someone trained as a biopsychologist might work in a pharmaceutical company to help test the efficacy of a new drug. Someone with a clinical background might become a forensic psychologist and work within the legal system to make recommendations during criminal trials and parole hearings, or serve as an expert in a court case.

While earning a doctoral degree in psychology is a lengthy process, usually taking between 5–6 years of graduate study (DeAngelis, 2010), there are a number of careers that can be attained with a master's degree in psychology. People who wish to provide psychotherapy can become licensed to serve as various types of professional counselors (Hoffman, 2012). Relevant master's degrees are also sufficient for individuals seeking careers as school psychologists (National Association of School Psychologists, n.d.), in some capacities related to sport psychology (American Psychological Association, 2014), or as consultants in various industrial settings (Landers, 2011, June 14). Undergraduate coursework in psychology may be applicable to other careers such as psychiatric social work or psychiatric nursing, where assessments and therapy may be a part of the job.

As mentioned in the opening section of this chapter, an undergraduate education in psychology is associated with a knowledge base and skill set that many employers find quite attractive. It should come as no surprise, then, that individuals earning bachelor's degrees in psychology find themselves in a number of different careers, as shown in Table 1.1. Examples of a few such careers can involve serving as case managers, working in sales, working in human resource departments, and teaching in high schools. The rapidly growing realm of healthcare professions is another field in which an education in psychology is helpful and sometimes required. For example, the Medical College Admission Test (MCAT) exam that people must take to be admitted to medical school now includes a section on the psychological foundations of behavior.

Top Occupations Employing Graduates with a BA in Psychology (Fogg, Harrington, Harrington, & Shatkin, 2012)

Ranking	Occupation
1	Mid- and top-level management (executive, administrator)
2	Sales
3	Social work
4	Other management positions
5	Human resources (personnel, training)
6	Other administrative positions
7	Insurance, real estate, business
8	Marketing and sales
9	Healthcare (nurse, pharmacist, therapist)
10	Finance (accountant, auditor)

Table 1.1

> **LINK TO LEARNING**
>
> The APA provides career information (http://openstax.org/l/careers) about various areas of psychology.

Key Terms

American Psychological Association (APA) professional organization representing psychologists in the United States

behaviorism focus on observing and controlling behavior

biopsychology study of how biology influences behavior

biopsychosocial model perspective that asserts that biology, psychology, and social factors interact to determine an individual's health

clinical psychology area of psychology that focuses on the diagnosis and treatment of psychological disorders and other problematic patterns of behavior

cognitive psychology study of cognitions, or thoughts, and their relationship to experiences and actions

counseling psychology area of psychology that focuses on improving emotional, social, vocational, and other aspects of the lives of psychologically healthy individuals

developmental psychology scientific study of development across a lifespan

dissertation long research paper about research that was conducted as a part of the candidate's doctoral training

empirical method method for acquiring knowledge based on observation, including experimentation, rather than a method based only on forms of logical argument or previous authorities

forensic psychology area of psychology that applies the science and practice of psychology to issues within and related to the justice system

functionalism focused on how mental activities helped an organism adapt to its environment

humanism perspective within psychology that emphasizes the potential for good that is innate to all humans

introspection process by which someone examines their own conscious experience in an attempt to break it into its component parts

ology suffix that denotes "scientific study of"

personality psychology study of patterns of thoughts and behaviors that make each individual unique

personality trait consistent pattern of thought and behavior

PhD (doctor of philosophy) doctoral degree conferred in many disciplinary perspectives housed in a traditional college of liberal arts and sciences

postdoctoral training program allows programs and broaden their research skills under the supervision of other professionals in the field

psychoanalytic theory focus on the role of the unconscious in affecting conscious behavior

psychology scientific study of the mind and behavior

PsyD (doctor of psychology) doctoral degree that places less emphasis on research-oriented skills and focuses more on application of psychological principles in the clinical context

sport and exercise psychology area of psychology that focuses on the interactions between mental and emotional factors and physical performance in sports, exercise, and other activities

structuralism understanding the conscious experience through introspection

Summary

1.1 What Is Psychology?
Psychology is defined as the scientific study of mind and behavior. Students of psychology develop critical thinking skills, become familiar with the scientific method, and recognize the complexity of behavior.

1.2 History of Psychology
Before the time of Wundt and James, questions about the mind were considered by philosophers. However, both Wundt and James helped create psychology as a distinct scientific discipline. Wundt was a structuralist, which meant he believed that our cognitive experience was best understood by breaking that experience into its component parts. He thought this was best accomplished by introspection.

William James was the first American psychologist, and he was a proponent of functionalism. This particular perspective focused on how mental activities served as adaptive responses to an organism's environment. Like Wundt, James also relied on introspection; however, his research approach also incorporated more objective measures as well.

Sigmund Freud believed that understanding the unconscious mind was absolutely critical to understand conscious behavior. This was especially true for individuals that he saw who suffered from various hysterias and neuroses. Freud relied on dream analysis, slips of the tongue, and free association as means to access the unconscious. Psychoanalytic theory remained a dominant force in clinical psychology for several decades.

Gestalt psychology was very influential in Europe. Gestalt psychology takes a holistic view of an individual and his experiences. As the Nazis came to power in Germany, Wertheimer, Koffka, and Köhler immigrated to the United States. Although they left their laboratories and their research behind, they did introduce America to Gestalt ideas. Some of the principles of Gestalt psychology are still very influential in the study of sensation and perception.

One of the most influential schools of thought within psychology's history was behaviorism. Behaviorism focused on making psychology an objective science by studying overt behavior and deemphasizing the importance of unobservable mental processes. John Watson is often considered the father of behaviorism, and B. F. Skinner's contributions to our understanding of principles of operant conditioning cannot be underestimated.

As behaviorism and psychoanalytic theory took hold of so many aspects of psychology, some began to become dissatisfied with psychology's picture of human nature. Thus, a humanistic movement within psychology began to take hold. Humanism focuses on the potential of all people for good. Both Maslow and Rogers were influential in shaping humanistic psychology.

During the 1950s, the landscape of psychology began to change. A science of behavior began to shift back to its roots of focus on mental processes. The emergence of neuroscience and computer science aided this transition. Ultimately, the cognitive revolution took hold, and people came to realize that cognition was crucial to a true appreciation and understanding of behavior.

1.3 Contemporary Psychology
Psychology is a diverse discipline that is made up of several major subdivisions with unique perspectives. Biological psychology involves the study of the biological bases of behavior. Sensation and perception refer to the area of psychology that is focused on how information from our sensory modalities is received, and how this information is transformed into our perceptual experiences of the world around us. Cognitive psychology is concerned with the relationship that exists between thought and behavior,

and developmental psychologists study the physical and cognitive changes that occur throughout one's lifespan. Personality psychology focuses on individuals' unique patterns of behavior, thought, and emotion. Industrial and organizational psychology, health psychology, sport and exercise psychology, forensic psychology, and clinical psychology are all considered applied areas of psychology. Industrial and organizational psychologists apply psychological concepts to I-O settings. Health psychologists look for ways to help people live healthier lives, and clinical psychology involves the diagnosis and treatment of psychological disorders and other problematic behavioral patterns. Sport and exercise psychologists study the interactions between thoughts, emotions, and physical performance in sports, exercise, and other activities. Forensic psychologists carry out activities related to psychology in association with the justice system.

1.4 Careers in Psychology

Generally, academic careers in psychology require doctoral degrees. However, there are a number of nonacademic career options for people who have master's degrees in psychology. While people with bachelor's degrees in psychology have more limited psychology-related career options, the skills acquired as a function of an undergraduate education in psychology are useful in a variety of work contexts.

Review Questions

1. Which of the following was mentioned as a skill to which psychology students would be exposed?
   a. critical thinking
   b. use of the scientific method
   c. critical evaluation of sources of information
   d. all of the above

2. Before psychology became a recognized academic discipline, matters of the mind were undertaken by those in _____.
   a. biology
   b. chemistry
   c. philosophy
   d. physics

3. In the scientific method, a hypothesis is a(n) _____.
   a. observation
   b. measurement
   c. test
   d. proposed explanation

4. Based on your reading, which theorist would have been most likely to agree with this statement: Perceptual phenomena are best understood as a combination of their components.
   a. William James
   b. Max Wertheimer
   c. Carl Rogers
   d. Noam Chomsky

5. _____ is most well-known for proposing his hierarchy of needs.
   a. Noam Chomsky
   b. Carl Rogers
   c. Abraham Maslow
   d. Sigmund Freud

6. Rogers believed that providing genuineness, empathy, and _____ in the therapeutic environment for his clients was critical to their being able to deal with their problems.
   a. structuralism
   b. functionalism
   c. Gestalt
   d. unconditional positive regard

7. The operant conditioning chamber (aka _____ box) is a device used to study the principles of operant conditioning.
   a. Skinner
   b. Watson
   c. James
   d. Koffka

8. A researcher interested in how changes in the cells of the hippocampus (a structure in the brain related to learning and memory) are related to memory formation would be most likely to identify as a(n) _____ psychologist.
    a. biological
    b. health
    c. clinical
    d. social

9. An individual's consistent pattern of thought and behavior is known as a(n) _____.
    a. psychosexual stage
    b. object permanence
    c. personality
    d. perception

10. In Milgram's controversial study on obedience, nearly _____ of the participants were willing to administer what appeared to be lethal electrical shocks to another person because they were told to do so by an authority figure.
    a. 1/3
    b. 2/3
    c. 3/4
    d. 4/5

11. A researcher interested in what factors make an employee best suited for a given job would most likely identify as a(n) _____ psychologist.
    a. personality
    b. clinical
    c. social
    d. I-O

12. If someone wanted to become a psychology professor at a 4-year college, they would probably need a _____ degree in psychology.
    a. bachelor of science
    b. bachelor of art
    c. master's
    d. PhD

13. The _____ places less emphasis on research and more emphasis on application of therapeutic skills.
    a. PhD
    b. PsyD
    c. postdoctoral training program
    d. dissertation

14. Which of the following degrees would be the minimum required to teach psychology courses in high school?
    a. PhD
    b. PsyD
    c. master's degree
    d. bachelor's degree

15. One would need at least a(n) _____ degree to serve as a school psychologist.
    a. associate's
    b. bachelor's
    c. master's
    d. doctoral

Critical Thinking Questions

16. Why do you think psychology courses like this one are often requirements of so many different programs of study?

17. Why do you think many people might be skeptical about psychology being a science?

18. How did the object of study in psychology change over the history of the field since the 19th century?

19. In part, what aspect of psychology was the behaviorist approach to psychology a reaction to?

20. Given the incredible diversity among the various areas of psychology that were described in this section, how do they all fit together?

21. What are the potential ethical concerns associated with Milgram's research on obedience?

22. Why is an undergraduate education in psychology so helpful in a number of different lines of work?

23. Other than a potentially greater salary, what would be the reasons an individual would continue on to get a graduate degree in psychology?

Personal Application Questions

24. Why are you taking this course? What do you hope to learn about during this course?

25. Freud is probably one of the most well-known historical figures in psychology. Where have you encountered references to Freud or his ideas about the role that the unconscious mind plays in determining conscious behavior?

26. Now that you've been briefly introduced to some of the major areas within psychology, which are you most interested in learning more about? Why?

27. Which of the career options in the field of psychology is most appealing to you?

Chapter 2
Psychological Research

Figure 2.1 How does television content impact children's behavior? (credit: modification of work by "antisocialtory"/Flickr)

Chapter Outline

2.1 Why Is Research Important?
2.2 Approaches to Research
2.3 Analyzing Findings
2.4 Ethics

Introduction

Have you ever wondered whether the violence you see on television affects your behavior? Are you more likely to behave aggressively in real life after watching people behave violently in dramatic situations on the screen? Or, could seeing fictional violence actually get aggression out of your system, causing you to be more peaceful? How are children influenced by the media they are exposed to? A psychologist interested in the relationship between behavior and exposure to violent images might ask these very questions.

Since ancient times, humans have been concerned about the effects of new technologies on our behaviors and thinking processes. The Greek philosopher Socrates, for example, worried that writing—a new technology at that time—would diminish people's ability to remember because they could rely on written records rather than committing information to memory. In our world of rapidly changing technologies, questions about their effects on our daily lives and their resulting long-term impacts continue to emerge. In addition to the impact of screen time (on smartphones, tablets, computers, and gaming), technology is emerging in our vehicles (such as GPS and smart cars) and residences (with devices like Alexa or Google Home and doorbell cameras). As these technologies become integrated into our lives, we are faced with questions about their positive and negative impacts. Many of us find ourselves with a strong opinion on these issues, only to find the person next to us bristling with the opposite view.

How can we go about finding answers that are supported not by mere opinion, but by evidence that we can all agree on? The findings of psychological research can help us navigate issues like this.

2.1 Why Is Research Important?

Learning Objectives

By the end of this section, you will be able to:
- Explain how scientific research addresses questions about behavior
- Discuss how scientific research guides public policy
- Appreciate how scientific research can be important in making personal decisions

Scientific research is a critical tool for successfully navigating our complex world. Without it, we would be forced to rely solely on intuition, other people's authority, and blind luck. While many of us feel confident in our abilities to decipher and interact with the world around us, history is filled with examples of how very wrong we can be when we fail to recognize the need for evidence in supporting claims. At various times in history, we would have been certain that the sun revolved around a flat earth, that the earth's continents did not move, and that mental illness was caused by possession (Figure 2.2). It is through systematic scientific research that we divest ourselves of our preconceived notions and superstitions and gain an objective understanding of ourselves and our world.

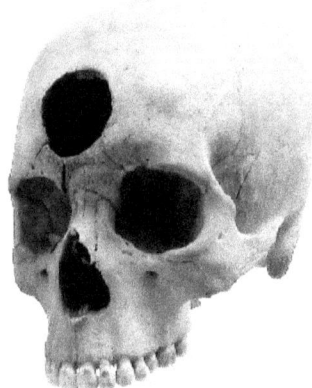

Figure 2.2 Some of our ancestors, across the world and over the centuries, believed that trephination—the practice of making a hole in the skull, as shown here—allowed evil spirits to leave the body, thus curing mental illness and other disorders. (credit: "taiproject"/Flickr)

The goal of all scientists is to better understand the world around them. Psychologists focus their attention on understanding behavior, as well as the cognitive (mental) and physiological (body) processes that underlie behavior. In contrast to other methods that people use to understand the behavior of others, such as intuition and personal experience, the hallmark of scientific research is that there is evidence to support a claim. Scientific knowledge is empirical: It is grounded in objective, tangible evidence that can be observed time and time again, regardless of who is observing.

While behavior is observable, the mind is not. If someone is crying, we can see behavior. However, the reason for the behavior is more difficult to determine. Is the person crying due to being sad, in pain, or happy? Sometimes we can learn the reason for someone's behavior by simply asking a question, like "Why are you crying?" However, there are situations in which an individual is either uncomfortable or unwilling to answer the question honestly, or is incapable of answering. For example, infants would not be able to explain why they are crying. In such circumstances, the psychologist must be creative in finding ways to better understand behavior. This chapter explores how scientific knowledge is generated, and how important that knowledge is in forming decisions in our personal lives and in the public domain.

USE OF RESEARCH INFORMATION

Trying to determine which theories are and are not accepted by the scientific community can be difficult, especially in an area of research as broad as psychology. More than ever before, we have an incredible amount of information at our fingertips, and a simple internet search on any given research topic might result in a number of contradictory studies. In these cases, we are witnessing the scientific community going through the process of reaching a consensus, and it could be quite some time before a consensus emerges. For example, the explosion in our use of technology has led researchers to question whether this ultimately helps or hinders us. The use and implementation of technology in educational settings has become widespread over the last few decades. Researchers are coming to different conclusions regarding the use of technology. To illustrate this point, a study investigating a smartphone app targeting surgery residents (graduate students in surgery training) found that the use of this app can increase student engagement and raise test scores (Shaw & Tan, 2015). Conversely, another study found that the use of technology in undergraduate student populations had negative impacts on sleep, communication, and time management skills (Massimini & Peterson, 2009). Until sufficient amounts of research have been conducted, there will be no clear consensus on the effects that technology has on a student's acquisition of knowledge, study skills, and mental health.

In the meantime, we should strive to think critically about the information we encounter by exercising a degree of healthy skepticism. When someone makes a claim, we should examine the claim from a number of different perspectives: what is the expertise of the person making the claim, what might they gain if the claim is valid, does the claim seem justified given the evidence, and what do other researchers think of the claim? This is especially important when we consider how much information in advertising campaigns and on the internet claims to be based on "scientific evidence" when in actuality it is a belief or perspective of just a few individuals trying to sell a product or draw attention to their perspectives.

We should be informed consumers of the information made available to us because decisions based on this information have significant consequences. One such consequence can be seen in politics and public policy. Imagine that you have been elected as the governor of your state. One of your responsibilities is to manage the state budget and determine how to best spend your constituents' tax dollars. As the new governor, you need to decide whether to continue funding early intervention programs. These programs are designed to help children who come from low-income backgrounds, have special needs, or face other disadvantages. These programs may involve providing a wide variety of services to maximize the children's development and position them for optimal levels of success in school and later in life (Blann, 2005). While such programs sound appealing, you would want to be sure that they also proved effective before investing additional money in these programs. Fortunately, psychologists and other scientists have conducted vast amounts of research on such programs and, in general, the programs are found to be effective (Neil & Christensen, 2009; Peters-Scheffer, Didden, Korzilius, & Sturmey, 2011). While not all programs are equally effective, and the short-term effects of many such programs are more pronounced, there is reason to believe that many of these programs produce long-term benefits for participants (Barnett, 2011). If you are committed to being a good steward of taxpayer money, you would want to look at research. Which programs are most effective? What characteristics of these programs make them effective? Which programs promote the best outcomes? After examining the research, you would be best equipped to make decisions about which programs to fund.

> **LINK TO LEARNING**
>
> Watch this video about early childhood program effectiveness (http://openstax.org/l/programeffect) to learn how scientists evaluate effectiveness and how best to invest money into programs that are most effective.

Ultimately, it is not just politicians who can benefit from using research in guiding their decisions. We all might look to research from time to time when making decisions in our lives. Imagine you just found out that a close friend has breast cancer or that one of your young relatives has recently been diagnosed with autism. In either case, you want to know which treatment options are most successful with the fewest side effects. How would you find that out? You would probably talk with your doctor and personally review the research that has been done on various treatment options—always with a critical eye to ensure that you are as informed as possible.

In the end, research is what makes the difference between facts and opinions. **Facts** are observable realities, and **opinions** are personal judgments, conclusions, or attitudes that may or may not be accurate. In the scientific community, facts can be established only using evidence collected through empirical research.

NOTABLE RESEARCHERS

Psychological research has a long history involving important figures from diverse backgrounds. While the introductory chapter discussed several researchers who made significant contributions to the discipline, there are many more individuals who deserve attention in considering how psychology has advanced as a science through their work (Figure 2.3). For instance, Margaret Floy Washburn (1871–1939) was the first woman to earn a PhD in psychology. Her research focused on animal behavior and cognition (Margaret Floy Washburn, PhD, n.d.). Mary Whiton Calkins (1863–1930) was a preeminent first-generation American psychologist who opposed the behaviorist movement, conducted significant research into memory, and established one of the earliest experimental psychology labs in the United States (Mary Whiton Calkins, n.d.).

Francis Sumner (1895–1954) was the first African American to receive a PhD in psychology in 1920. His dissertation focused on issues related to psychoanalysis. Sumner also had research interests in racial bias and educational justice. Sumner was one of the founders of Howard University's department of psychology, and because of his accomplishments, he is sometimes referred to as the "Father of Black Psychology." Thirteen years later, Inez Beverly Prosser (1895–1934) became the first African American woman to receive a PhD in psychology. Prosser's research highlighted issues related to education in segregated versus integrated schools, and ultimately, her work was very influential in the hallmark *Brown v. Board of Education* Supreme Court ruling that segregation of public schools was unconstitutional (Ethnicity and Health in America Series: Featured Psychologists, n.d.).

 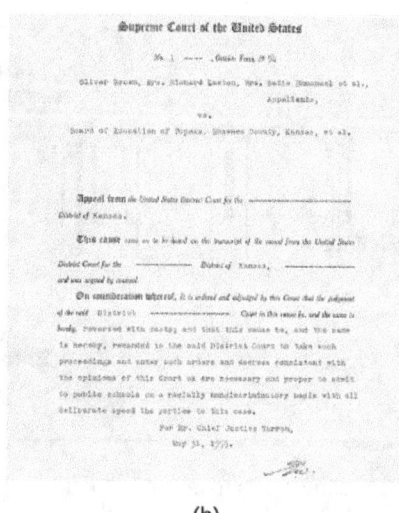

Figure 2.3 (a) Margaret Floy Washburn was the first woman to earn a doctorate degree in psychology. (b) The outcome of *Brown v. Board of Education* was influenced by the research of psychologist Inez Beverly Prosser, who was the first African American woman to earn a PhD in psychology.

Although the establishment of psychology's scientific roots occurred first in Europe and the United States, it did not take much time until researchers from around the world began to establish their own laboratories and research programs. For example, some of the first experimental psychology laboratories in South America were founded by Horatio Piñero (1869–1919) at two institutions in Buenos Aires, Argentina (Godoy & Brussino, 2010). In India, Gunamudian David Boaz (1908–1965) and Narendra Nath Sen Gupta (1889–1944) established the first independent departments of psychology at the University of Madras and the University of Calcutta, respectively. These developments provided an opportunity for Indian researchers to make important contributions to the field (Gunamudian David Boaz, n.d.; Narendra Nath Sen Gupta, n.d.).

When the American Psychological Association (APA) was first founded in 1892, all of the members were white males (Women and Minorities in Psychology, n.d.). However, by 1905, Mary Whiton Calkins was elected as the first female president of the APA, and by 1946, nearly one-quarter of American psychologists were female. Psychology became a popular degree option for students enrolled in the nation's historically black higher education institutions, increasing the number of black Americans who went on to become psychologists. Given demographic shifts occurring in the United States and increased access to higher educational opportunities among historically underrepresented populations, there is reason to hope that the diversity of the field will increasingly match the larger population, and that the research contributions made by the psychologists of the future will better serve people of all backgrounds (Women and Minorities in Psychology, n.d.).

THE PROCESS OF SCIENTIFIC RESEARCH

Scientific knowledge is advanced through a process known as the scientific method. Basically, ideas (in the form of theories and hypotheses) are tested against the real world (in the form of empirical observations), and those empirical observations lead to more ideas that are tested against the real world, and so on. In this sense, the scientific process is circular. The types of reasoning within the circle are called deductive and inductive. In **deductive reasoning**, ideas are tested in the real world; in **inductive reasoning**, real-world observations lead to new ideas (Figure 2.4). These processes are inseparable, like inhaling and exhaling, but different research approaches place different emphasis on the deductive and inductive aspects.

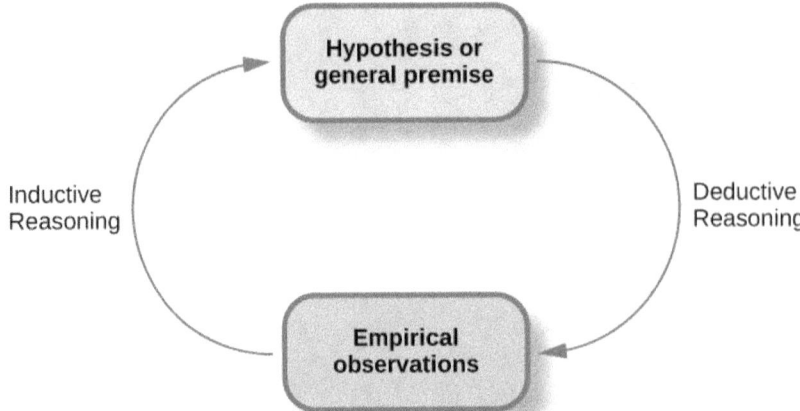

Figure 2.4 Psychological research relies on both inductive and deductive reasoning.

In the scientific context, deductive reasoning begins with a generalization—one hypothesis—that is then used to reach logical conclusions about the real world. If the hypothesis is correct, then the logical conclusions reached through deductive reasoning should also be correct. A deductive reasoning argument might go something like this: All living things require energy to survive (this would be your hypothesis). Ducks are living things. Therefore, ducks require energy to survive (logical conclusion). In this example, the hypothesis is correct; therefore, the conclusion is correct as well. Sometimes, however, an incorrect hypothesis may lead to a logical but incorrect conclusion. Consider this argument: all ducks are born with the ability to see. Quackers is a duck. Therefore, Quackers was born with the ability to see. Scientists use deductive reasoning to empirically test their hypotheses. Returning to the example of the ducks, researchers might design a study to test the hypothesis that if all living things require energy to survive, then ducks will be found to require energy to survive.

Deductive reasoning starts with a generalization that is tested against real-world observations; however, inductive reasoning moves in the opposite direction. Inductive reasoning uses empirical observations to construct broad generalizations. Unlike deductive reasoning, conclusions drawn from inductive reasoning may or may not be correct, regardless of the observations on which they are based. For instance, you may notice that your favorite fruits—apples, bananas, and oranges—all grow on trees; therefore, you assume that all fruit must grow on trees. This would be an example of inductive reasoning, and, clearly, the existence of strawberries, blueberries, and kiwi demonstrate that this generalization is not correct despite it being based on a number of direct observations. Scientists use inductive reasoning to formulate theories, which in turn generate hypotheses that are tested with deductive reasoning. In the end, science involves both deductive and inductive processes.

For example, case studies, which you will read about in the next section, are heavily weighted on the side of empirical observations. Thus, case studies are closely associated with inductive processes as researchers gather massive amounts of observations and seek interesting patterns (new ideas) in the data. Experimental research, on the other hand, puts great emphasis on deductive reasoning.

We've stated that theories and hypotheses are ideas, but what sort of ideas are they, exactly? A **theory** is a well-developed set of ideas that propose an explanation for observed phenomena. Theories are repeatedly checked against the world, but they tend to be too complex to be tested all at once; instead, researchers create hypotheses to test specific aspects of a theory.

A **hypothesis** is a testable prediction about how the world will behave if our idea is correct, and it is often worded as an if-then statement (e.g., if I study all night, I will get a passing grade on the test). The hypothesis is extremely important because it bridges the gap between the realm of ideas and the real world. As specific hypotheses are tested, theories are modified and refined to reflect and incorporate the result of these tests **Figure 2.5**.

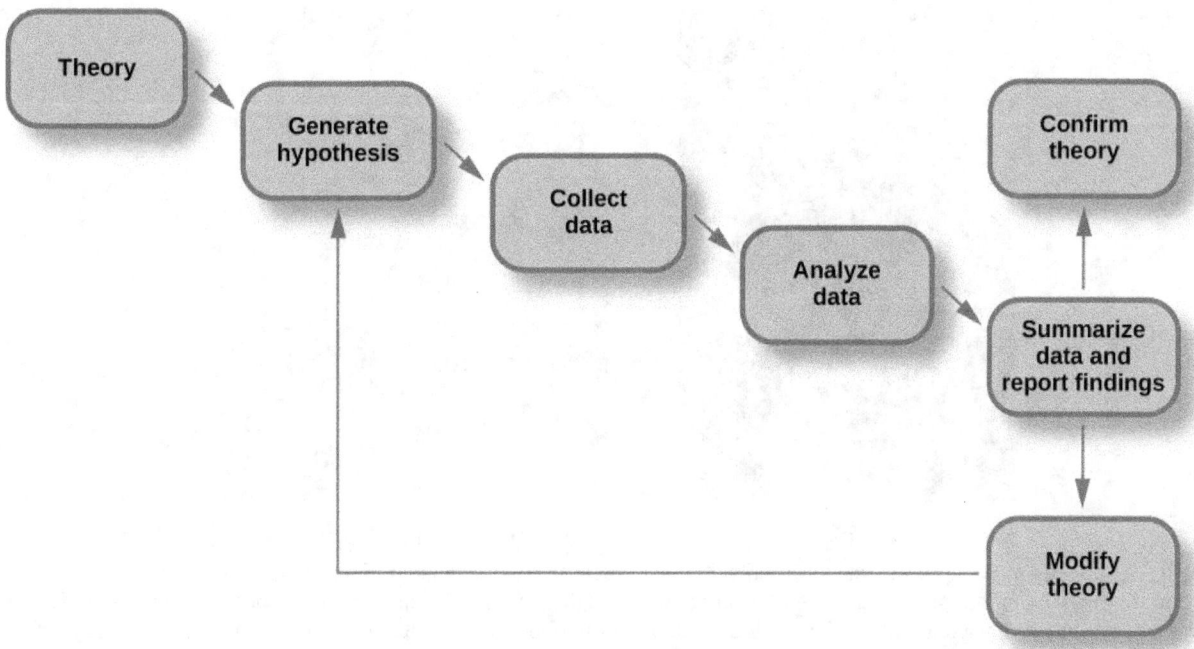

Figure 2.5 The scientific method involves deriving hypotheses from theories and then testing those hypotheses. If the results are consistent with the theory, then the theory is supported. If the results are not consistent, then the theory should be modified and new hypotheses will be generated.

To see how this process works, let's consider a specific theory and a hypothesis that might be generated from that theory. As you'll learn in a later chapter, the James-Lange theory of emotion asserts that emotional experience relies on the physiological arousal associated with the emotional state. If you walked out of your home and discovered a very aggressive snake waiting on your doorstep, your heart would begin to race and your stomach churn. According to the James-Lange theory, these physiological changes would result in your feeling of fear. A hypothesis that could be derived from this theory might be that a person who is unaware of the physiological arousal that the sight of the snake elicits will not feel fear.

A scientific hypothesis is also **falsifiable**, or capable of being shown to be incorrect. Recall from the introductory chapter that Sigmund Freud had lots of interesting ideas to explain various human behaviors (**Figure 2.6**). However, a major criticism of Freud's theories is that many of his ideas are not falsifiable; for example, it is impossible to imagine empirical observations that would disprove the existence of the id, the ego, and the superego—the three elements of personality described in Freud's theories. Despite this, Freud's theories are widely taught in introductory psychology texts because of their historical significance for personality psychology and psychotherapy, and these remain the root of all modern forms of therapy.

 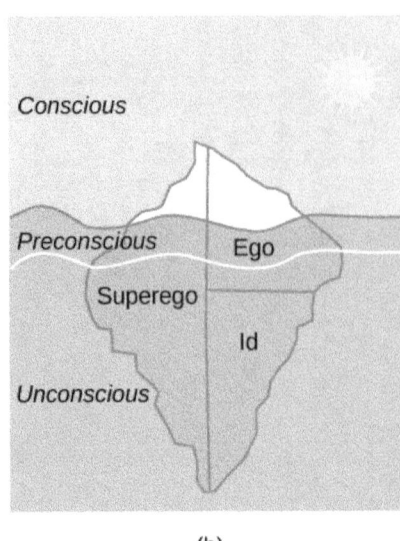

(a) (b)

Figure 2.6 Many of the specifics of (a) Freud's theories, such as (b) his division of the mind into id, ego, and superego, have fallen out of favor in recent decades because they are not falsifiable. In broader strokes, his views set the stage for much of psychological thinking today, such as the unconscious nature of the majority of psychological processes.

In contrast, the James-Lange theory does generate falsifiable hypotheses, such as the one described above. Some individuals who suffer significant injuries to their spinal columns are unable to feel the bodily changes that often accompany emotional experiences. Therefore, we could test the hypothesis by determining how emotional experiences differ between individuals who have the ability to detect these changes in their physiological arousal and those who do not. In fact, this research has been conducted and while the emotional experiences of people deprived of an awareness of their physiological arousal may be less intense, they still experience emotion (Chwalisz, Diener, & Gallagher, 1988).

Scientific research's dependence on falsifiability allows for great confidence in the information that it produces. Typically, by the time information is accepted by the scientific community, it has been tested repeatedly.

2.2 Approaches to Research

Learning Objectives

By the end of this section, you will be able to:
- Describe the different research methods used by psychologists
- Discuss the strengths and weaknesses of case studies, naturalistic observation, surveys, and archival research
- Compare longitudinal and cross-sectional approaches to research
- Compare and contrast correlation and causation

There are many research methods available to psychologists in their efforts to understand, describe, and explain behavior and the cognitive and biological processes that underlie it. Some methods rely on observational techniques. Other approaches involve interactions between the researcher and the individuals who are being studied—ranging from a series of simple questions to extensive, in-depth interviews—to well-controlled experiments.

Each of these research methods has unique strengths and weaknesses, and each method may only be appropriate for certain types of research questions. For example, studies that rely primarily on observation produce incredible amounts of information, but the ability to apply this information to the larger population is somewhat limited because of small sample sizes. Survey research, on the other hand, allows researchers to easily collect data from relatively large samples. While this allows for results to be generalized to the larger population more easily, the information that can be collected on any given survey is somewhat limited and subject to problems associated with any type of self-reported data. Some researchers conduct archival research by using existing records. While this can be a fairly inexpensive way to collect data that can provide insight into a number of research questions, researchers using this approach have no control on how or what kind of data was collected. All of the methods described thus far are correlational in nature. This means that researchers can speak to important relationships that might exist between two or more variables of interest. However, correlational data cannot be used to make claims about cause-and-effect relationships.

Correlational research can find a relationship between two variables, but the only way a researcher can claim that the relationship between the variables is cause and effect is to perform an experiment. In experimental research, which will be discussed later in this chapter, there is a tremendous amount of control over variables of interest. While this is a powerful approach, experiments are often conducted in very artificial settings. This calls into question the validity of experimental findings with regard to how they would apply in real-world settings. In addition, many of the questions that psychologists would like to answer cannot be pursued through experimental research because of ethical concerns.

CLINICAL OR CASE STUDIES

In 2011, the *New York Times* published a feature story on Krista and Tatiana Hogan, Canadian twin girls. These particular twins are unique because Krista and Tatiana are conjoined twins, connected at the head. There is evidence that the two girls are connected in a part of the brain called the thalamus, which is a major sensory relay center. Most incoming sensory information is sent through the thalamus before reaching higher regions of the cerebral cortex for processing.

> **LINK TO LEARNING**
>
> Watch this **CBC video about Krista's and Tatiana's lives (http://openstax.org/l/hogans)** to learn more.

The implications of this potential connection mean that it might be possible for one twin to experience the sensations of the other twin. For instance, if Krista is watching a particularly funny television program, Tatiana might smile or laugh even if she is not watching the program. This particular possibility has piqued the interest of many neuroscientists who seek to understand how the brain uses sensory information.

These twins represent an enormous resource in the study of the brain, and since their condition is very rare, it is likely that as long as their family agrees, scientists will follow these girls very closely throughout their lives to gain as much information as possible (Dominus, 2011).

Over time, it has become clear that while Krista and Tatiana share some sensory experiences and motor control, they remain two distinct individuals, which provides tremendous insight into researchers interested in the mind and the brain (Egnor, 2017).

In observational research, scientists are conducting a **clinical** or **case study** when they focus on one person or just a few individuals. Indeed, some scientists spend their entire careers studying just 10–20 individuals. Why would they do this? Obviously, when they focus their attention on a very small number of people, they can gain a tremendous amount of insight into those cases. The richness of information that is collected in clinical or case studies is unmatched by any other single research method. This allows the researcher to have a very deep understanding of the individuals and the particular phenomenon being studied.

If clinical or case studies provide so much information, why are they not more frequent among researchers? As it turns out, the major benefit of this particular approach is also a weakness. As mentioned earlier, this approach is often used when studying individuals who are interesting to researchers because they have a rare characteristic. Therefore, the individuals who serve as the focus of case studies are not like most other people. If scientists ultimately want to explain all behavior, focusing attention on such a special group of people can make it difficult to generalize any observations to the larger population as a whole. **Generalizing** refers to the ability to apply the findings of a particular research project to larger segments of society. Again, case studies provide enormous amounts of information, but since the cases are so specific, the potential to apply what's learned to the average person may be very limited.

NATURALISTIC OBSERVATION

If you want to understand how behavior occurs, one of the best ways to gain information is to simply observe the behavior in its natural context. However, people might change their behavior in unexpected ways if they know they are being observed. How do researchers obtain accurate information when people tend to hide their natural behavior? As an example, imagine that your professor asks everyone in your class to raise their hand if they always wash their hands after using the restroom. Chances are that almost everyone in the classroom will raise their hand, but do you think hand washing after every trip to the restroom is really that universal?

This is very similar to the phenomenon mentioned earlier in this chapter: many individuals do not feel comfortable answering a question honestly. But if we are committed to finding out the facts about hand washing, we have other options available to us.

Suppose we send a classmate into the restroom to actually watch whether everyone washes their hands after using the restroom. Will our observer blend into the restroom environment by wearing a white lab coat, sitting with a clipboard, and staring at the sinks? We want our researcher to be inconspicuous—perhaps standing at one of the sinks pretending to put in contact lenses while secretly recording the relevant information. This type of observational study is called **naturalistic observation**: observing behavior in its natural setting. To better understand peer exclusion, Suzanne Fanger collaborated with colleagues at the University of Texas to observe the behavior of preschool children on a playground. How did the observers remain inconspicuous over the duration of the study? They equipped a few of the children with wireless microphones (which the children quickly forgot about) and observed while taking notes from a distance. Also, the children in that particular preschool (a "laboratory preschool") were accustomed to having observers on the playground (Fanger, Frankel, & Hazen, 2012).

It is critical that the observer be as unobtrusive and as inconspicuous as possible: when people know they are being watched, they are less likely to behave naturally. If you have any doubt about this, ask yourself how your driving behavior might differ in two situations: In the first situation, you are driving down a deserted highway during the middle of the day; in the second situation, you are being followed by a police car down the same deserted highway (Figure 2.7).

Figure 2.7 Seeing a police car behind you would probably affect your driving behavior. (credit: Michael Gil)

It should be pointed out that naturalistic observation is not limited to research involving humans. Indeed, some of the best-known examples of naturalistic observation involve researchers going into the field to observe various kinds of animals in their own environments. As with human studies, the researchers maintain their distance and avoid interfering with the animal subjects so as not to influence their natural behaviors. Scientists have used this technique to study social hierarchies and interactions among animals ranging from ground squirrels to gorillas. The information provided by these studies is invaluable in understanding how those animals organize socially and communicate with one another. The anthropologist Jane Goodall, for example, spent nearly five decades observing the behavior of chimpanzees in Africa (**Figure 2.8**). As an illustration of the types of concerns that a researcher might encounter in naturalistic observation, some scientists criticized Goodall for giving the chimps names instead of referring to them by numbers—using names was thought to undermine the emotional detachment required for the objectivity of the study (McKie, 2010).

(a)　　　　　　　　　　　　　　(b)

Figure 2.8 (a) Jane Goodall made a career of conducting naturalistic observations of (b) chimpanzee behavior. (credit "Jane Goodall": modification of work by Erik Hersman; "chimpanzee": modification of work by "Afrika Force"/Flickr.com)

The greatest benefit of naturalistic observation is the validity, or accuracy, of information collected unobtrusively in a natural setting. Having individuals behave as they normally would in a given situation means that we have a higher degree of ecological validity, or realism, than we might achieve with other research approaches. Therefore, our ability to generalize the findings of the research to real-world situations is enhanced. If done correctly, we need not worry about people or animals modifying their behavior simply because they are being observed. Sometimes, people may assume that reality programs give us a glimpse into authentic human behavior. However, the principle of inconspicuous observation is violated as reality stars are followed by camera crews and are interviewed on camera for personal confessionals. Given that environment, we must doubt how natural and realistic their behaviors are.

The major downside of naturalistic observation is that they are often difficult to set up and control. In our restroom study, what if you stood in the restroom all day prepared to record people's hand washing behavior and no one came in? Or, what if you have been closely observing a troop of gorillas for weeks only to find that they migrated to a new place while you were sleeping in your tent? The benefit of realistic data comes at a cost. As a researcher you have no control of when (or if) you have behavior to observe. In addition, this type of observational research often requires significant investments of time, money, and a good dose of luck.

Sometimes studies involve structured observation. In these cases, people are observed while engaging in set, specific tasks. An excellent example of structured observation comes from Strange Situation by Mary Ainsworth (you will read more about this in the chapter on lifespan development). The Strange Situation is a procedure used to evaluate attachment styles that exist between an infant and caregiver. In this scenario, caregivers bring their infants into a room filled with toys. The Strange Situation involves a number of phases, including a stranger coming into the room, the caregiver leaving the room, and the caregiver's return to the room. The infant's behavior is closely monitored at each phase, but it is the behavior of the infant upon being reunited with the caregiver that is most telling in terms of characterizing the infant's attachment style with the caregiver.

Another potential problem in observational research is **observer bias**. Generally, people who act as observers are closely involved in the research project and may unconsciously skew their observations to fit their research goals or expectations. To protect against this type of bias, researchers should have clear criteria established for the types of behaviors recorded and how those behaviors should be classified. In addition, researchers often compare observations of the same event by multiple observers, in order to test **inter-rater reliability**: a measure of reliability that assesses the consistency of observations by different observers.

SURVEYS

Often, psychologists develop surveys as a means of gathering data. **Surveys** are lists of questions to be answered by research participants, and can be delivered as paper-and-pencil questionnaires, administered electronically, or conducted verbally (**Figure 2.9**). Generally, the survey itself can be completed in a short time, and the ease of administering a survey makes it easy to collect data from a large number of people.

Surveys allow researchers to gather data from larger samples than may be afforded by other research methods. A **sample** is a subset of individuals selected from a **population**, which is the overall group of individuals that the researchers are interested in. Researchers study the sample and seek to generalize their findings to the population. Generally, researchers will begin this process by calculating various measures of central tendency from the data they have collected. These measures provide an overall summary of what a typical response looks like. There are three measures of central tendency: mode, median, and mean. The mode is the most frequently occurring response, the median lies at the middle of a given data set, and the mean is the arithmetic average of all data points. Means tend to be most useful in conducting additional analyses like those described below; however, means are very sensitive to the effects of outliers, and so one must be aware of those effects when making assessments of what measures of central tendency tell us about a data set in question.

Figure 2.9 Surveys can be administered in a number of ways, including electronically administered research, like the survey shown here. (credit: Robert Nyman)

There is both strength and weakness of the survey in comparison to case studies. By using surveys, we can collect information from a larger sample of people. A larger sample is better able to reflect the actual diversity of the population, thus allowing better generalizability. Therefore, if our sample is sufficiently large and diverse, we can assume that the data we collect from the survey can be generalized to the larger population with more certainty than the information collected through a case study. However, given the greater number of people involved, we are not able to collect the same depth of information on each person that would be collected in a case study.

Another potential weakness of surveys is something we touched on earlier in this chapter: People don't always give accurate responses. They may lie, misremember, or answer questions in a way that they think makes them look good. For example, people may report drinking less alcohol than is actually the case.

Any number of research questions can be answered through the use of surveys. One real-world example is the research conducted by Jenkins, Ruppel, Kizer, Yehl, and Griffin (2012) about the backlash against the US Arab-American community following the terrorist attacks of September 11, 2001. Jenkins and colleagues wanted to determine to what extent these negative attitudes toward Arab-Americans still existed nearly a decade after the attacks occurred. In one study, 140 research participants filled out a survey with 10 questions, including questions asking directly about the participant's overt prejudicial attitudes toward people of various ethnicities. The survey also asked indirect questions about how likely the participant would be to interact with a person of a given ethnicity in a variety of settings (such as, "How likely do you think it is that you would introduce yourself to a person of Arab-American descent?"). The results of the research suggested that participants were unwilling to report prejudicial attitudes toward any ethnic group. However, there were significant differences between their pattern of responses to questions about social interaction with Arab-Americans compared to other ethnic groups: they indicated less willingness for social interaction with Arab-Americans compared to the other ethnic groups. This suggested that the participants harbored subtle forms of prejudice against Arab-Americans, despite their assertions that this was not the case (Jenkins et al., 2012).

ARCHIVAL RESEARCH

Some researchers gain access to large amounts of data without interacting with a single research participant. Instead, they use existing records to answer various research questions. This type of research approach is known as **archival research**. Archival research relies on looking at past records or data sets to look for interesting patterns or relationships.

For example, a researcher might access the academic records of all individuals who enrolled in college within the past ten years and calculate how long it took them to complete their degrees, as well as course loads, grades, and extracurricular involvement. Archival research could provide important information about who is most likely to complete their education, and it could help identify important risk factors for struggling students (Figure 2.10).

Figure 2.10 A researcher doing archival research examines records, whether archived as a (a) hardcopy or (b) electronically. (credit "paper files": modification of work by "Newtown graffiti"/Flickr; "computer": modification of work by INPIVIC Family/Flickr)

In comparing archival research to other research methods, there are several important distinctions. For one, the researcher employing archival research never directly interacts with research participants. Therefore, the investment of time and money to collect data is considerably less with archival research. Additionally, researchers have no control over what information was originally collected. Therefore, research questions have to be tailored so they can be answered within the structure of the existing data sets. There is also no guarantee of consistency between the records from one source to another, which might make comparing and contrasting different data sets problematic.

LONGITUDINAL AND CROSS-SECTIONAL RESEARCH

Sometimes we want to see how people change over time, as in studies of human development and lifespan. When we test the same group of individuals repeatedly over an extended period of time, we are conducting longitudinal research. **Longitudinal research** is a research design in which data-gathering is administered repeatedly over an extended period of time. For example, we may survey a group of individuals about their dietary habits at age 20, retest them a decade later at age 30, and then again at age 40.

Another approach is cross-sectional research. In **cross-sectional research**, a researcher compares multiple segments of the population at the same time. Using the dietary habits example above, the researcher might directly compare different groups of people by age. Instead of studying a group of people for 20 years to see how their dietary habits changed from decade to decade, the researcher would study a group of 20-year-old individuals and compare them to a group of 30-year-old individuals and a group of 40-year-old individuals. While cross-sectional research requires a shorter-term investment, it is also limited by differences that exist between the different generations (or cohorts) that have nothing to do with age per se, but rather reflect the social and cultural experiences of different generations of individuals make them different from one another.

To illustrate this concept, consider the following survey findings. In recent years there has been significant growth in the popular support of same-sex marriage. Many studies on this topic break down survey participants into different age groups. In general, younger people are more supportive of same-sex marriage than are those who are older (Jones, 2013). Does this mean that as we age we become less open to the idea of same-sex marriage, or does this mean that older individuals have different perspectives because of the social climates in which they grew up? Longitudinal research is a powerful approach because the same individuals are involved in the research project over time, which means that the researchers need to be less concerned with differences among cohorts affecting the results of their study.

Often longitudinal studies are employed when researching various diseases in an effort to understand particular risk factors. Such studies often involve tens of thousands of individuals who are followed for several decades. Given the enormous number of people involved in these studies, researchers can feel confident that their findings can be generalized to the larger population. The Cancer Prevention Study-3 (CPS-3) is one of a series of longitudinal studies sponsored by the American Cancer Society aimed at determining predictive risk factors associated with cancer. When participants enter the study, they complete a survey about their lives and family histories, providing information on factors that might cause or prevent the development of cancer. Then every few years the participants receive additional surveys to complete. In the end, hundreds of thousands of participants will be tracked over 20 years to determine which of them develop cancer and which do not.

Clearly, this type of research is important and potentially very informative. For instance, earlier longitudinal studies sponsored by the American Cancer Society provided some of the first scientific demonstrations of the now well-established links between increased rates of cancer and smoking (American Cancer Society, n.d.) (**Figure 2.11**).

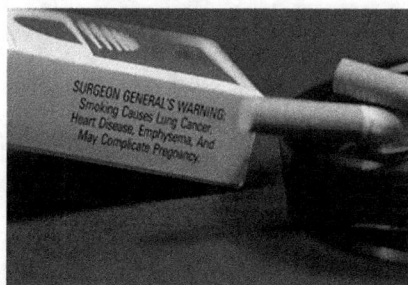

Figure 2.11 Longitudinal research like the CPS-3 help us to better understand how smoking is associated with cancer and other diseases. (credit: CDC/Debora Cartagena)

As with any research strategy, longitudinal research is not without limitations. For one, these studies require an incredible time investment by the researcher and research participants. Given that some longitudinal studies take years, if not decades, to complete, the results will not be known for a considerable period of time. In addition to the time demands, these studies also require a substantial financial investment. Many researchers are unable to commit the resources necessary to see a longitudinal project through to the end.

Research participants must also be willing to continue their participation for an extended period of time, and this can be problematic. People move, get married and take new names, get ill, and eventually die. Even without significant life changes, some people may simply choose to discontinue their participation in the project. As a result, the **attrition** rates, or reduction in the number of research participants due to dropouts, in longitudinal studies are quite high and increases over the course of a project. For this reason, researchers using this approach typically recruit many participants fully expecting that a substantial number will drop out before the end. As the study progresses, they continually check whether the sample still represents the larger population, and make adjustments as necessary.

2.3 Analyzing Findings

Learning Objectives

By the end of this section, you will be able to:
- Explain what a correlation coefficient tells us about the relationship between variables
- Recognize that correlation does not indicate a cause-and-effect relationship between variables
- Discuss our tendency to look for relationships between variables that do not really exist
- Explain random sampling and assignment of participants into experimental and control groups
- Discuss how experimenter or participant bias could affect the results of an experiment
- Identify independent and dependent variables

Did you know that as sales in ice cream increase, so does the overall rate of crime? Is it possible that indulging in your favorite flavor of ice cream could send you on a crime spree? Or, after committing crime do you think you might decide to treat yourself to a cone? There is no question that a relationship exists between ice cream and crime (e.g., Harper, 2013), but it would be pretty foolish to decide that one thing actually caused the other to occur.

It is much more likely that both ice cream sales and crime rates are related to the temperature outside. When the temperature is warm, there are lots of people out of their houses, interacting with each other, getting annoyed with one another, and sometimes committing crimes. Also, when it is warm outside, we are more likely to seek a cool treat like ice cream. How do we determine if there is indeed a relationship between two things? And when there is a relationship, how can we discern whether it is attributable to coincidence or causation?

CORRELATIONAL RESEARCH

Correlation means that there is a relationship between two or more variables (such as ice cream consumption and crime), but this relationship does not necessarily imply cause and effect. When two variables are correlated, it simply means that as one variable changes, so does the other. We can measure correlation by calculating a statistic known as a correlation coefficient. A **correlation coefficient** is a number from -1 to +1 that indicates the strength and direction of the relationship between variables. The correlation coefficient is usually represented by the letter r.

The number portion of the correlation coefficient indicates the strength of the relationship. The closer the number is to 1 (be it negative or positive), the more strongly related the variables are, and the more predictable changes in one variable will be as the other variable changes. The closer the number is to zero, the weaker the relationship, and the less predictable the relationships between the variables becomes. For instance, a correlation coefficient of 0.9 indicates a far stronger relationship than a correlation coefficient of 0.3. If the variables are not related to one another at all, the correlation coefficient is 0. The example above about ice cream and crime is an example of two variables that we might expect to have no relationship to each other.

The sign—positive or negative—of the correlation coefficient indicates the direction of the relationship (**Figure 2.12**). A **positive correlation** means that the variables move in the same direction. Put another way, it means that as one variable increases so does the other, and conversely, when one variable decreases so does the other. A **negative correlation** means that the variables move in opposite directions. If two variables are negatively correlated, a decrease in one variable is associated with an increase in the other and vice versa.

The example of ice cream and crime rates is a positive correlation because both variables increase when temperatures are warmer. Other examples of positive correlations are the relationship between an individual's height and weight or the relationship between a person's age and number of wrinkles. One might expect a negative correlation to exist between someone's tiredness during the day and the number of hours they slept the previous night: the amount of sleep decreases as the feelings of tiredness increase. In a real-world example of negative correlation, student researchers at the University of Minnesota found a weak negative correlation ($r = -0.29$) between the average number of days per week that students got fewer than 5 hours of sleep and their GPA (Lowry, Dean, & Manders, 2010). Keep in mind that a negative correlation is not the same as no correlation. For example, we would probably find no correlation between hours of sleep and shoe size.

As mentioned earlier, correlations have predictive value. Imagine that you are on the admissions committee of a major university. You are faced with a huge number of applications, but you are able to accommodate only a small percentage of the applicant pool. How might you decide who should be admitted? You might try to correlate your current students' college GPA with their scores on standardized tests like the SAT or ACT. By observing which correlations were strongest for your current students, you could use this information to predict relative success of those students who have applied for admission into the university.

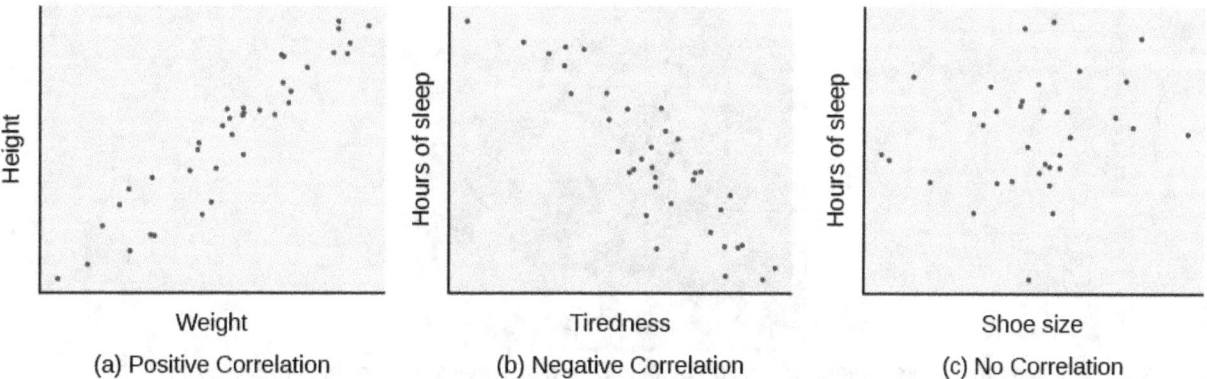

Figure 2.12 Scatterplots are a graphical view of the strength and direction of correlations. The stronger the correlation, the closer the data points are to a straight line. In these examples, we see that there is (a) a positive correlation between weight and height, (b) a negative correlation between tiredness and hours of sleep, and (c) no correlation between shoe size and hours of sleep.

LINK TO LEARNING

Manipulate this **interactive scatterplot (http://openstax.org/l/scatplot)** to practice your understanding of positive and negative correlation.

Correlation Does Not Indicate Causation

Correlational research is useful because it allows us to discover the strength and direction of relationships that exist between two variables. However, correlation is limited because establishing the existence of a relationship tells us little about **cause and effect**. While variables are sometimes correlated because one does cause the other, it could also be that some other factor, a **confounding variable**, is actually causing the systematic movement in our variables of interest. In the ice cream/crime rate example mentioned earlier, temperature is a confounding variable that could account for the relationship between the two variables.

Even when we cannot point to clear confounding variables, we should not assume that a correlation between two variables implies that one variable causes changes in another. This can be frustrating when a cause-and-effect relationship seems clear and intuitive. Think back to our discussion of the research done by the American Cancer Society and how their research projects were some of the first demonstrations of the link between smoking and cancer. It seems reasonable to assume that smoking causes cancer, but if we were limited to correlational research, we would be overstepping our bounds by making this assumption.

Unfortunately, people mistakenly make claims of causation as a function of correlations all the time. Such claims are especially common in advertisements and news stories. For example, recent research found that people who eat cereal on a regular basis achieve healthier weights than those who rarely eat cereal (Frantzen, Treviño, Echon, Garcia-Dominic, & DiMarco, 2013; Barton et al., 2005). Guess how the cereal companies report this finding. Does eating cereal really cause an individual to maintain a healthy weight, or are there other possible explanations, such as, someone at a healthy weight is more likely to regularly eat a healthy breakfast than someone who is obese or someone who avoids meals in an attempt to diet (**Figure 2.13**)? While correlational research is invaluable in identifying relationships among variables, a major limitation is the inability to establish causality. Psychologists want to make statements about cause and effect, but the only way to do that is to conduct an experiment to answer a research question. The next section describes how scientific experiments incorporate methods that eliminate, or control for, alternative explanations, which allow researchers to explore how changes in one variable cause changes in another variable.

Figure 2.13 Does eating cereal really cause someone to be a healthy weight? (credit: Tim Skillern)

Illusory Correlations

The temptation to make erroneous cause-and-effect statements based on correlational research is not the only way we tend to misinterpret data. We also tend to make the mistake of illusory correlations, especially with unsystematic observations. **Illusory correlations**, or false correlations, occur when people believe that relationships exist between two things when no such relationship exists. One well-known illusory correlation is the supposed effect that the moon's phases have on human behavior. Many people passionately assert that human behavior is affected by the phase of the moon, and specifically, that people act strangely when the moon is full (**Figure 2.14**).

Figure 2.14 Many people believe that a full moon makes people behave oddly. (credit: Cory Zanker)

There is no denying that the moon exerts a powerful influence on our planet. The ebb and flow of the ocean's tides are tightly tied to the gravitational forces of the moon. Many people believe, therefore, that it is logical that we are affected by the moon as well. After all, our bodies are largely made up of water. A meta-analysis of nearly 40 studies consistently demonstrated, however, that the relationship between the moon and our behavior does not exist (Rotton & Kelly, 1985). While we may pay more attention to odd behavior during the full phase of the moon, the rates of odd behavior remain constant throughout the lunar cycle.

Why are we so apt to believe in illusory correlations like this? Often we read or hear about them and simply accept the information as valid. Or, we have a hunch about how something works and then look for evidence to support that hunch, ignoring evidence that would tell us our hunch is false; this is known as **confirmation bias**. Other times, we find illusory correlations based on the information that comes most easily to mind, even if that information is severely limited. And while we may feel confident that we can use these relationships to better understand and predict the world around us, illusory correlations can have significant drawbacks. For example, research suggests that illusory correlations—in which certain behaviors are inaccurately attributed to certain groups—are involved in the formation of prejudicial attitudes that can ultimately lead to discriminatory behavior (Fiedler, 2004).

CAUSALITY: CONDUCTING EXPERIMENTS AND USING THE DATA

As you've learned, the only way to establish that there is a cause-and-effect relationship between two variables is to conduct a scientific experiment. Experiment has a different meaning in the scientific context than in everyday life. In everyday conversation, we often use it to describe trying something for the first time, such as experimenting with a new hair style or a new food. However, in the scientific context, an experiment has precise requirements for design and implementation.

The Experimental Hypothesis

In order to conduct an experiment, a researcher must have a specific hypothesis to be tested. As you've learned, hypotheses can be formulated either through direct observation of the real world or after careful review of previous research. For example, if you think that the use of technology in the classroom has negative impacts on learning, then you have basically formulated a hypothesis—namely, that the use of technology in the classroom should be limited because it decreases learning. How might you have arrived at this particular hypothesis? You may have noticed that your classmates who take notes on their laptops perform at lower levels on class exams than those who take notes by hand, or those who receive a lesson via a computer program versus via an in-person teacher have different levels of performance when tested (**Figure 2.15**).

Figure 2.15 How might the use of technology in the classroom impact learning? (credit: modification of work by Nikolay Georgiev/Pixabay)

These sorts of personal observations are what often lead us to formulate a specific hypothesis, but we cannot use limited personal observations and anecdotal evidence to rigorously test our hypothesis. Instead, to find out if real-world data supports our hypothesis, we have to conduct an experiment.

Designing an Experiment

The most basic experimental design involves two groups: the experimental group and the control group. The two groups are designed to be the same except for one difference— experimental manipulation. The **experimental group** gets the experimental manipulation—that is, the treatment or variable being tested (in this case, the use of technology)—and the **control group** does not. Since experimental manipulation is the only difference between the experimental and control groups, we can be sure that any differences between the two are due to experimental manipulation rather than chance.

In our example of how the use of technology should be limited in the classroom, we have the experimental group learn algebra using a computer program and then test their learning. We measure the learning in our control group after they are taught algebra by a teacher in a traditional classroom. It is important for the control group to be treated similarly to the experimental group, with the exception that the control group does not receive the experimental manipulation.

We also need to precisely define, or operationalize, how we measure learning of algebra. An **operational definition** is a precise description of our variables, and it is important in allowing others to understand exactly how and what a researcher measures in a particular experiment. In operationalizing learning, we might choose to look at performance on a test covering the material on which the individuals were taught by the teacher or the computer program. We might also ask our participants to summarize the information that was just presented in some way. Whatever we determine, it is important that we operationalize learning in such a way that anyone who hears about our study for the first time knows exactly what we mean by learning. This aids peoples' ability to interpret our data as well as their capacity to repeat our experiment should they choose to do so.

Once we have operationalized what is considered use of technology and what is considered learning in our experiment participants, we need to establish how we will run our experiment. In this case, we might have participants spend 45 minutes learning algebra (either through a computer program or with an in-person math teacher) and then give them a test on the material covered during the 45 minutes.

Ideally, the people who score the tests are unaware of who was assigned to the experimental or control group, in order to control for experimenter bias. **Experimenter bias** refers to the possibility that a researcher's expectations might skew the results of the study. Remember, conducting an experiment requires a lot of planning, and the people involved in the research project have a vested interest in supporting their hypotheses. If the observers knew which child was in which group, it might influence how they interpret ambiguous responses, such as sloppy handwriting or minor computational mistakes. By being blind to which child is in which group, we protect against those biases. This situation is a **single-blind study**, meaning that one of the groups (participants) are unaware as to which group they are in (experiment or control group) while the researcher who developed the experiment knows which participants are in each group.

In a **double-blind study**, both the researchers and the participants are blind to group assignments. Why would a researcher want to run a study where no one knows who is in which group? Because by doing so, we can control for both experimenter and participant expectations. If you are familiar with the phrase **placebo effect**, you already have some idea as to why this is an important consideration. The placebo effect occurs when people's expectations or beliefs influence or determine their experience in a given situation. In other words, simply expecting something to happen can actually make it happen.

The placebo effect is commonly described in terms of testing the effectiveness of a new medication. Imagine that you work in a pharmaceutical company, and you think you have a new drug that is effective in treating depression. To demonstrate that your medication is effective, you run an experiment with two groups: The experimental group receives the medication, and the control group does not. But you don't want participants to know whether they received the drug or not.

Why is that? Imagine that you are a participant in this study, and you have just taken a pill that you think will improve your mood. Because you expect the pill to have an effect, you might feel better simply because you took the pill and not because of any drug actually contained in the pill—this is the placebo effect.

To make sure that any effects on mood are due to the drug and not due to expectations, the control group receives a placebo (in this case a sugar pill). Now everyone gets a pill, and once again neither the researcher nor the experimental participants know who got the drug and who got the sugar pill. Any differences in mood between the experimental and control groups can now be attributed to the drug itself rather than to experimenter bias or participant expectations (**Figure 2.16**).

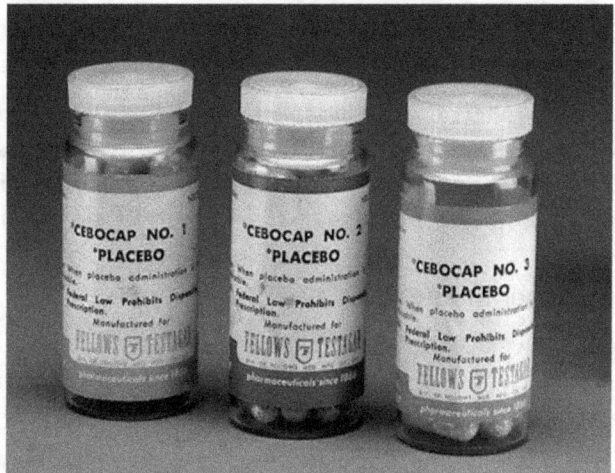

Figure 2.16 Providing the control group with a placebo treatment protects against bias caused by expectancy. (credit: Elaine and Arthur Shapiro)

Independent and Dependent Variables

In a research experiment, we strive to study whether changes in one thing cause changes in another. To achieve this, we must pay attention to two important variables, or things that can be changed, in any experimental study: the independent variable and the dependent variable. An **independent variable** is manipulated or controlled by the experimenter. In a well-designed experimental study, the independent variable is the only important difference between the experimental and control groups. In our example of how technology use in the classroom affects learning, the independent variable is the type of learning by participants in the study (**Figure 2.17**). A **dependent variable** is what the researcher measures to see how much effect the independent variable had. In our example, the dependent variable is the learning exhibited by our participants.

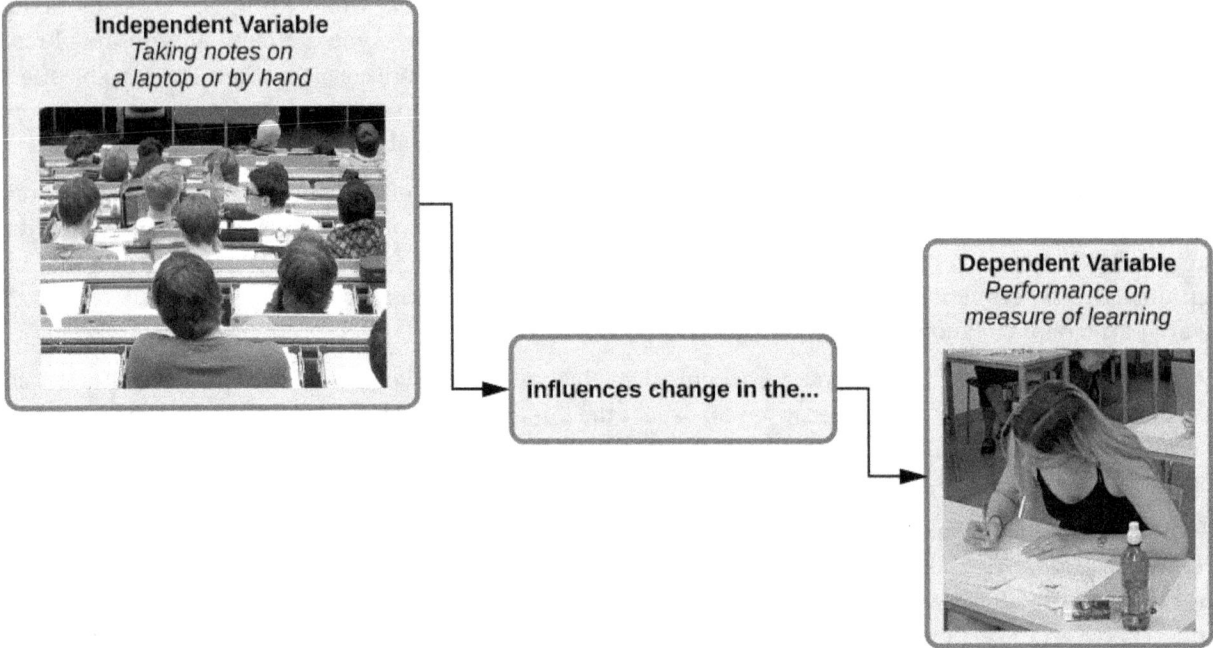

Figure 2.17 In an experiment, manipulations of the independent variable are expected to result in changes in the dependent variable. (credit: "classroom" modification of work by Nikolay Georgiev/Pixabay; credit "note taking": modification of work by KF/Wikimedia)

We expect that the dependent variable will change as a function of the independent variable. In other words, the dependent variable *depends* on the independent variable. A good way to think about the relationship between the independent and dependent variables is with this question: What effect does the independent variable have on the dependent variable? Returning to our example, what is the effect of being taught a lesson through a computer program versus through an in-person instructor?

Selecting and Assigning Experimental Participants

Now that our study is designed, we need to obtain a sample of individuals to include in our experiment. Our study involves human participants so we need to determine who to include. **Participants** are the subjects of psychological research, and as the name implies, individuals who are involved in psychological research actively participate in the process. Often, psychological research projects rely on college students to serve as participants. In fact, the vast majority of research in psychology subfields has historically involved students as research participants (Sears, 1986; Arnett, 2008). But are college students truly representative of the general population? College students tend to be younger, more educated, more liberal, and less diverse than the general population. Although using students as test subjects is an accepted practice, relying on such a limited pool of research participants can be problematic because it is difficult to generalize findings to the larger population.

Our hypothetical experiment involves high school students, and we must first generate a sample of students. Samples are used because populations are usually too large to reasonably involve every member in our particular experiment (Figure 2.18). If possible, we should use a random sample (there are other types of samples, but for the purposes of this chapter, we will focus on random samples). A **random sample** is a subset of a larger population in which every member of the population has an equal chance of being selected. Random samples are preferred because if the sample is large enough we can be reasonably sure that the participating individuals are representative of the larger population. This means that the percentages of characteristics in the sample—sex, ethnicity, socioeconomic level, and any other characteristics that might affect the results—are close to those percentages in the larger population.

In our example, let's say we decide our population of interest is algebra students. But all algebra students is a very large population, so we need to be more specific; instead we might say our population of interest is all algebra students in a particular city. We should include students from various income brackets, family situations, races, ethnicities, religions, and geographic areas of town. With this more manageable population, we can work with the local schools in selecting a random sample of around 200 algebra students who we want to participate in our experiment.

In summary, because we cannot test all of the algebra students in a city, we want to find a group of about 200 that reflects the composition of that city. With a representative group, we can generalize our findings to the larger population without fear of our sample being biased in some way.

Figure 2.18 Researchers may work with (a) a large population or (b) a sample group that is a subset of the larger population. (credit "crowd": modification of work by James Cridland; credit "students": modification of work by Laurie Sullivan)

Now that we have a sample, the next step of the experimental process is to split the participants into experimental and control groups through random assignment. With **random assignment**, all participants have an equal chance of being assigned to either group. There is statistical software that will randomly assign each of the algebra students in the sample to either the experimental or the control group.

Random assignment is critical for sound experimental design. With sufficiently large samples, random assignment makes it unlikely that there are systematic differences between the groups. So, for instance, it would be very unlikely that we would get one group composed entirely of males, a given ethnic identity, or a given religious ideology. This is important because if the groups were systematically different before the experiment began, we would not know the origin of any differences we find between the groups: Were the differences preexisting, or were they caused by manipulation of the independent variable? Random assignment allows us to assume that any differences observed between experimental and control groups result from the manipulation of the independent variable.

> **LINK TO LEARNING**
>
> Use this online random number generator (http://openstax.org/l/rannumbers) to learn more about random sampling and assignments.

Issues to Consider

While experiments allow scientists to make cause-and-effect claims, they are not without problems. True experiments require the experimenter to manipulate an independent variable, and that can complicate many questions that psychologists might want to address. For instance, imagine that you want to know what effect sex (the independent variable) has on spatial memory (the dependent variable). Although you can certainly look for differences between males and females on a task that taps into spatial memory, you cannot directly control a person's sex. We categorize this type of research approach as quasi-experimental and recognize that we cannot make cause-and-effect claims in these circumstances.

Experimenters are also limited by ethical constraints. For instance, you would not be able to conduct an experiment designed to determine if experiencing abuse as a child leads to lower levels of self-esteem among adults. To conduct such an experiment, you would need to randomly assign some experimental participants to a group that receives abuse, and that experiment would be unethical.

Interpreting Experimental Findings

Once data is collected from both the experimental and the control groups, a **statistical analysis** is conducted to find out if there are meaningful differences between the two groups. A statistical analysis determines how likely any difference found is due to chance (and thus not meaningful). For example, if an experiment is done on the effectiveness of a nutritional supplement, and those taking a placebo pill (and not the supplement) have the same result as those taking the supplement, then the experiment has shown that the nutritional supplement is not effective. Generally, psychologists consider differences to be statistically significant if there is less than a five percent chance of observing them if the groups did not actually differ from one another. Stated another way, psychologists want to limit the chances of making "false positive" claims to five percent or less.

The greatest strength of experiments is the ability to assert that any significant differences in the findings are caused by the independent variable. This occurs because random selection, random assignment, and a design that limits the effects of both experimenter bias and participant expectancy should create groups that are similar in composition and treatment. Therefore, any difference between the groups is attributable to the independent variable, and now we can finally make a causal statement. If we find that watching a violent television program results in more violent behavior than watching a nonviolent program, we can safely say that watching violent television programs causes an increase in the display of violent behavior.

Reporting Research

When psychologists complete a research project, they generally want to share their findings with other scientists. The American Psychological Association (APA) publishes a manual detailing how to write a paper for submission to scientific journals. Unlike an article that might be published in a magazine like *Psychology Today*, which targets a general audience with an interest in psychology, scientific journals generally publish **peer-reviewed journal articles** aimed at an audience of professionals and scholars who are actively involved in research themselves.

> **LINK TO LEARNING**
>
> The **Online Writing Lab (OWL) (http://openstax.org/l/owl)** at Purdue University can walk you through the APA writing guidelines.

A peer-reviewed journal article is read by several other scientists (generally anonymously) with expertise in the subject matter. These peer reviewers provide feedback—to both the author and the journal editor—regarding the quality of the draft. Peer reviewers look for a strong rationale for the research being described, a clear description of how the research was conducted, and evidence that the research was conducted in an ethical manner. They also look for flaws in the study's design, methods, and statistical analyses. They check that the conclusions drawn by the authors seem reasonable given the observations made during the research. Peer reviewers also comment on how valuable the research is in advancing the discipline's knowledge. This helps prevent unnecessary duplication of research findings in the scientific literature and, to some extent, ensures that each research article provides new information. Ultimately, the journal editor will compile all of the peer reviewer feedback and determine whether the article will be published in its current state (a rare occurrence), published with revisions, or not accepted for publication.

Peer review provides some degree of quality control for psychological research. Poorly conceived or executed studies can be weeded out, and even well-designed research can be improved by the revisions suggested. Peer review also ensures that the research is described clearly enough to allow other scientists to **replicate** it, meaning they can repeat the experiment using different samples to determine reliability. Sometimes replications involve additional measures that expand on the original finding. In any case, each replication serves to provide more evidence to support the original research findings. Successful replications of published research make scientists more apt to adopt those findings, while repeated failures tend to cast doubt on the legitimacy of the original article and lead scientists to look elsewhere. For example, it would be a major advancement in the medical field if a published study indicated that taking a new drug helped individuals achieve a healthy weight without changing their diet. But if other scientists could not replicate the results, the original study's claims would be questioned.

In recent years, there has been increasing concern about a "replication crisis" that has affected a number of scientific fields, including psychology. Some of the most well-known studies and scientists have produced research that has failed to be replicated by others (as discussed in Shrout & Rodgers, 2018). In fact, even a famous Nobel Prize-winning scientist has recently retracted a published paper because she had difficulty replicating her results (Nobel Prize-winning scientist Frances Arnold retracts paper, 2020 January 3). These kinds of outcomes have prompted some scientists to begin to work together and more openly, and some would argue that the current "crisis" is actually improving the ways in which science is conducted and in how its results are shared with others (Aschwanden, 2018).

> **DIG DEEPER**
>
> **The Vaccine-Autism Myth and Retraction of Published Studies**
>
> Some scientists have claimed that routine childhood vaccines cause some children to develop autism, and, in fact, several peer-reviewed publications published research making these claims. Since the initial reports, large-scale epidemiological research has suggested that vaccinations are not responsible for causing autism and that it is much safer to have your child vaccinated than not. Furthermore, several of the original studies making this claim have since been retracted.
>
> A published piece of work can be rescinded when data is called into question because of falsification,

fabrication, or serious research design problems. Once rescinded, the scientific community is informed that there are serious problems with the original publication. Retractions can be initiated by the researcher who led the study, by research collaborators, by the institution that employed the researcher, or by the editorial board of the journal in which the article was originally published. In the vaccine-autism case, the retraction was made because of a significant conflict of interest in which the leading researcher had a financial interest in establishing a link between childhood vaccines and autism (Offit, 2008). Unfortunately, the initial studies received so much media attention that many parents around the world became hesitant to have their children vaccinated (Figure 2.19). Continued reliance on such debunked studies has significant consequences. For instance, between January and October of 2019, there were 22 measles outbreaks across the United States and more than a thousand cases of individuals contracting measles (Patel et al., 2019). This is likely due to the anti-vaccination movements that have risen from the debunked research. For more information about how the vaccine/autism story unfolded, as well as the repercussions of this story, take a look at Paul Offit's book, *Autism's False Prophets: Bad Science, Risky Medicine, and the Search for a Cure.*

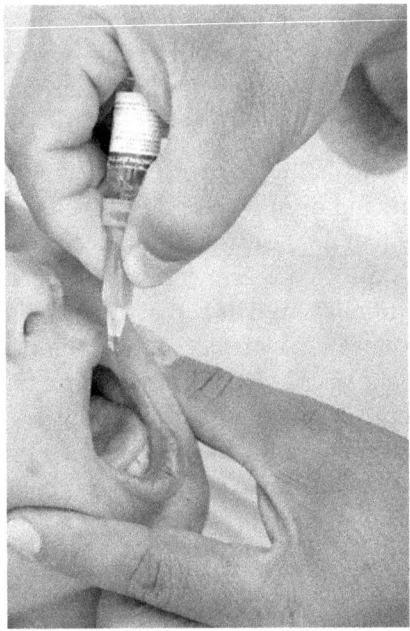

Figure 2.19 Some people still think vaccinations cause autism. (credit: modification of work by UNICEF Sverige)

RELIABILITY AND VALIDITY

Reliability and validity are two important considerations that must be made with any type of data collection. **Reliability** refers to the ability to consistently produce a given result. In the context of psychological research, this would mean that any instruments or tools used to collect data do so in consistent, reproducible ways. There are a number of different types of reliability. Some of these include inter-rater reliability (the degree to which two or more different observers agree on what has been observed), internal consistency (the degree to which different items on a survey that measure the same thing correlate with one another), and test-retest reliability (the degree to which the outcomes of a particular measure remain consistent over multiple administrations).

Unfortunately, being consistent in measurement does not necessarily mean that you have measured something correctly. To illustrate this concept, consider a kitchen scale that would be used to measure the weight of cereal that you eat in the morning. If the scale is not properly calibrated, it may consistently under- or overestimate the amount of cereal that's being measured. While the scale is highly reliable in producing consistent results (e.g., the same amount of cereal poured onto the scale produces the same reading each time), those results are incorrect. This is where validity comes into play. **Validity** refers to the extent to which a given instrument or tool accurately measures what it's supposed to measure, and once again, there are a number of ways in which validity can be expressed. Ecological validity (the degree to which research results generalize to real-world applications), construct validity (the degree to which a given variable actually captures or measures what it is intended to measure), and face validity (the degree to which a given variable seems valid on the surface) are just a few types that researchers consider. While any valid measure is by necessity reliable, the reverse is not necessarily true. Researchers strive to use instruments that are both highly reliable and valid.

EVERYDAY CONNECTION

How Valid Are the SAT and ACT?

Standardized tests like the SAT and ACT are supposed to measure an individual's aptitude for a college education, but how reliable and valid are such tests? Research conducted by the College Board suggests that scores on the SAT have high predictive validity for first-year college students' GPA (Kobrin, Patterson, Shaw, Mattern, & Barbuti, 2008). In this context, predictive validity refers to the test's ability to effectively predict the GPA of college freshmen. Given that many institutions of higher education require the SAT or ACT for admission, this high degree of predictive validity might be comforting.

However, the emphasis placed on SAT or ACT scores in college admissions has generated some controversy on a number of fronts. For one, some researchers assert that these tests are biased and place minority students at a disadvantage and unfairly reduces the likelihood of being admitted into a college (Santelices & Wilson, 2010). Additionally, some research has suggested that the predictive validity of these tests is grossly exaggerated in how well they are able to predict the GPA of first-year college students. In fact, it has been suggested that the SAT's predictive validity may be overestimated by as much as 150% (Rothstein, 2004). Many institutions of higher education are beginning to consider de-emphasizing the significance of SAT scores in making admission decisions (Rimer, 2008).

Recent examples of high profile cheating scandals both domestically and abroad have only increased the scrutiny being placed on these types of tests, and as of March 2019, more than 1000 institutions of higher education have either relaxed or eliminated the requirements for SAT or ACT testing for admissions (Strauss, 2019, March 19).

2.4 Ethics

Learning Objectives

By the end of this section, you will be able to:
- Discuss how research involving human subjects is regulated
- Summarize the processes of informed consent and debriefing
- Explain how research involving animal subjects is regulated

Today, scientists agree that good research is ethical in nature and is guided by a basic respect for human dignity and safety. However, as you will read in the feature box, this has not always been the case. Modern researchers must demonstrate that the research they perform is ethically sound. This section presents how ethical considerations affect the design and implementation of research conducted today.

RESEARCH INVOLVING HUMAN PARTICIPANTS

Any experiment involving the participation of human subjects is governed by extensive, strict guidelines designed to ensure that the experiment does not result in harm. Any research institution that receives federal support for research involving human participants must have access to an **institutional review board (IRB)**. The IRB is a committee of individuals often made up of members of the institution's administration, scientists, and community members (Figure 2.20). The purpose of the IRB is to review proposals for research that involves human participants. The IRB reviews these proposals with the principles mentioned above in mind, and generally, approval from the IRB is required in order for the experiment to proceed.

Figure 2.20 An institution's IRB meets regularly to review experimental proposals that involve human participants. (credit: International Hydropower Association/Flickr)

An institution's IRB requires several components in any experiment it approves. For one, each participant must sign an informed consent form before they can participate in the experiment. An **informed consent** form provides a written description of what participants can expect during the experiment, including potential risks and implications of the research. It also lets participants know that their involvement is completely voluntary and can be discontinued without penalty at any time. Furthermore, the informed consent guarantees that any data collected in the experiment will remain completely confidential. In cases where research participants are under the age of 18, the parents or legal guardians are required to sign the informed consent form.

LINK TO LEARNING

View this example of a consent form (http://openstax.org/l/consentform) to learn more.

While the informed consent form should be as honest as possible in describing exactly what participants will be doing, sometimes deception is necessary to prevent participants' knowledge of the exact research question from affecting the results of the study. **Deception** involves purposely misleading experiment participants in order to maintain the integrity of the experiment, but not to the point where the deception could be considered harmful. For example, if we are interested in how our opinion of someone is affected by their attire, we might use deception in describing the experiment to prevent that knowledge from affecting participants' responses. In cases where deception is involved, participants must receive a full **debriefing** upon conclusion of the study—complete, honest information about the purpose of the experiment, how the data collected will be used, the reasons why deception was necessary, and information about how to obtain additional information about the study.

DIG DEEPER

Ethics and the Tuskegee Syphilis Study

Unfortunately, the ethical guidelines that exist for research today were not always applied in the past. In 1932, poor, rural, black, male sharecroppers from Tuskegee, Alabama, were recruited to participate in an experiment conducted by the U.S. Public Health Service, with the aim of studying syphilis in black men (Figure 2.21). In exchange for free medical care, meals, and burial insurance, 600 men agreed to participate in the study. A little more than half of the men tested positive for syphilis, and they served as the experimental group (given that the researchers could not randomly assign participants to groups, this represents a quasi-experiment). The remaining syphilis-free individuals served as the control group. However, those individuals that tested positive for syphilis were never informed that they had the disease.

While there was no treatment for syphilis when the study began, by 1947 penicillin was recognized as an effective treatment for the disease. Despite this, no penicillin was administered to the participants in this study, and the participants were not allowed to seek treatment at any other facilities if they continued in the study. Over the course of 40 years, many of the participants unknowingly spread syphilis to their wives (and subsequently their children born from their wives) and eventually died because they never received treatment for the disease. This study was discontinued in 1972 when the experiment was discovered by the national press (Tuskegee University, n.d.). The resulting outrage over the experiment led directly to the National Research Act of 1974 and the strict ethical guidelines for research on humans described in this chapter. Why is this study unethical? How were the men who participated and their families harmed as a function of this research?

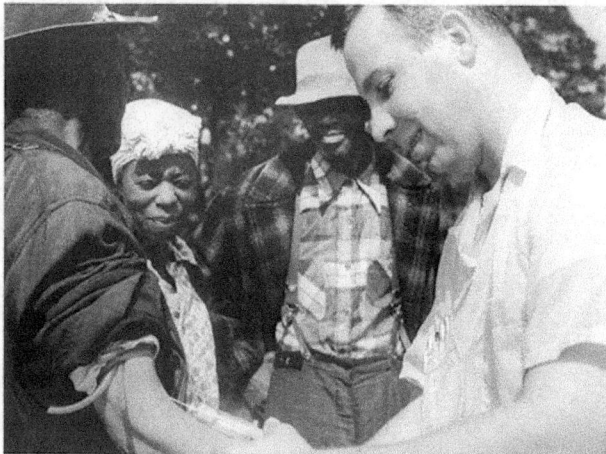

Figure 2.21 A participant in the Tuskegee Syphilis Study receives an injection.

LINK TO LEARNING

Visit this website about the Tuskegee Syphilis Study (http://openstax.org/l/tuskegee) to learn more.

RESEARCH INVOLVING ANIMAL SUBJECTS

Many psychologists conduct research involving animal subjects. Often, these researchers use rodents (Figure 2.22) or birds as the subjects of their experiments—the APA estimates that 90% of all animal research in psychology uses these species (American Psychological Association, n.d.). Because many basic processes in animals are sufficiently similar to those in humans, these animals are acceptable substitutes for research that would be considered unethical in human participants.

Figure 2.22 Rats, like the one shown here, often serve as the subjects of animal research.

This does not mean that animal researchers are immune to ethical concerns. Indeed, the humane and ethical treatment of animal research subjects is a critical aspect of this type of research. Researchers must design their experiments to minimize any pain or distress experienced by animals serving as research subjects.

Whereas IRBs review research proposals that involve human participants, animal experimental proposals are reviewed by an **Institutional Animal Care and Use Committee (IACUC)**. An IACUC consists of institutional administrators, scientists, veterinarians, and community members. This committee is charged with ensuring that all experimental proposals require the humane treatment of animal research subjects. It also conducts semi-annual inspections of all animal facilities to ensure that the research protocols are being followed. No animal research project can proceed without the committee's approval.

Key Terms

archival research method of research using past records or data sets to answer various research questions, or to search for interesting patterns or relationships

attrition reduction in number of research participants as some drop out of the study over time

cause-and-effect relationship changes in one variable cause the changes in the other variable; can be determined only through an experimental research design

clinical or case study observational research study focusing on one or a few people

confirmation bias tendency to ignore evidence that disproves ideas or beliefs

confounding variable unanticipated outside factor that affects both variables of interest, often giving the false impression that changes in one variable causes changes in the other variable, when, in actuality, the outside factor causes changes in both variables

control group serves as a basis for comparison and controls for chance factors that might influence the results of the study—by holding such factors constant across groups so that the experimental manipulation is the only difference between groups

correlation relationship between two or more variables; when two variables are correlated, one variable changes as the other does

correlation coefficient number from -1 to +1, indicating the strength and direction of the relationship between variables, and usually represented by r

cross-sectional research compares multiple segments of a population at a single time

debriefing when an experiment involved deception, participants are told complete and truthful information about the experiment at its conclusion

deception purposely misleading experiment participants in order to maintain the integrity of the experiment

deductive reasoning results are predicted based on a general premise

dependent variable variable that the researcher measures to see how much effect the independent variable had

double-blind study experiment in which both the researchers and the participants are blind to group assignments

empirical grounded in objective, tangible evidence that can be observed time and time again, regardless of who is observing

experimental group group designed to answer the research question; experimental manipulation is the only difference between the experimental and control groups, so any differences between the two are due to experimental manipulation rather than chance

experimenter bias researcher expectations skew the results of the study

fact objective and verifiable observation, established using evidence collected through empirical research

falsifiable able to be disproven by experimental results

generalize inferring that the results for a sample apply to the larger population

hypothesis (plural: hypotheses) tentative and testable statement about the relationship between two or more variables

illusory correlation seeing relationships between two things when in reality no such relationship exists

independent variable variable that is influenced or controlled by the experimenter; in a sound experimental study, the independent variable is the only important difference between the experimental and control group

inductive reasoning conclusions are drawn from observations

informed consent process of informing a research participant about what to expect during an experiment, any risks involved, and the implications of the research, and then obtaining the person's consent to participate

Institutional Animal Care and Use Committee (IACUC) committee of administrators, scientists, veterinarians, and community members that reviews proposals for research involving non-human animals

Institutional Review Board (IRB) committee of administrators, scientists, and community members that reviews proposals for research involving human participants

inter-rater reliability measure of agreement among observers on how they record and classify a particular event

longitudinal research studies in which the same group of individuals is surveyed or measured repeatedly over an extended period of time

naturalistic observation observation of behavior in its natural setting

negative correlation two variables change in different directions, with one becoming larger as the other becomes smaller; a negative correlation is not the same thing as no correlation

observer bias when observations may be skewed to align with observer expectations

operational definition description of what actions and operations will be used to measure the dependent variables and manipulate the independent variables

opinion personal judgments, conclusions, or attitudes that may or may not be accurate

participants subjects of psychological research

peer-reviewed journal article article read by several other scientists (usually anonymously) with expertise in the subject matter, who provide feedback regarding the quality of the manuscript before it is accepted for publication

placebo effect people's expectations or beliefs influencing or determining their experience in a given situation

population overall group of individuals that the researchers are interested in

positive correlation two variables change in the same direction, both becoming either larger or smaller

random assignment method of experimental group assignment in which all participants have an equal chance of being assigned to either group

random sample subset of a larger population in which every member of the population has an equal chance of being selected

reliability consistency and reproducibility of a given result

replicate repeating an experiment using different samples to determine the research's reliability

sample subset of individuals selected from the larger population

single-blind study experiment in which the researcher knows which participants are in the experimental group and which are in the control group

statistical analysis determines how likely any difference between experimental groups is due to chance

survey list of questions to be answered by research participants—given as paper-and-pencil questionnaires, administered electronically, or conducted verbally—allowing researchers to collect data from a large number of people

theory well-developed set of ideas that propose an explanation for observed phenomena

validity accuracy of a given result in measuring what it is designed to measure

Summary

2.1 Why Is Research Important?
Scientists are engaged in explaining and understanding how the world around them works, and they are able to do so by coming up with theories that generate hypotheses that are testable and falsifiable. Theories that stand up to their tests are retained and refined, while those that do not are discarded or modified. In this way, research enables scientists to separate fact from simple opinion. Having good information generated from research aids in making wise decisions both in public policy and in our personal lives.

2.2 Approaches to Research
The clinical or case study involves studying just a few individuals for an extended period of time. While this approach provides an incredible depth of information, the ability to generalize these observations to the larger population is problematic. Naturalistic observation involves observing behavior in a natural setting and allows for the collection of valid, true-to-life information from realistic situations. However, naturalistic observation does not allow for much control and often requires quite a bit of time and money to perform. Researchers strive to ensure that their tools for collecting data are both reliable (consistent and replicable) and valid (accurate).

Surveys can be administered in a number of ways and make it possible to collect large amounts of data quickly. However, the depth of information that can be collected through surveys is somewhat limited compared to a clinical or case study.

Archival research involves studying existing data sets to answer research questions.

Longitudinal research has been incredibly helpful to researchers who need to collect data on how people change over time. Cross-sectional research compares multiple segments of a population at a single time.

2.3 Analyzing Findings
A correlation is described with a correlation coefficient, r, which ranges from -1 to 1. The correlation coefficient tells us about the nature (positive or negative) and the strength of the relationship between two or more variables. Correlations do not tell us anything about causation—regardless of how strong the relationship is between variables. In fact, the only way to demonstrate causation is by conducting an experiment. People often make the mistake of claiming that correlations exist when they really do not.

Researchers can test cause-and-effect hypotheses by conducting experiments. Ideally, experimental participants are randomly selected from the population of interest. Then, the participants are randomly assigned to their respective groups. Sometimes, the researcher and the participants are blind to group membership to prevent their expectations from influencing the results.

In ideal experimental design, the only difference between the experimental and control groups is whether participants are exposed to the experimental manipulation. Each group goes through all phases of the experiment, but each group will experience a different level of the independent variable: the experimental group is exposed to the experimental manipulation, and the control group is not exposed to the experimental manipulation. The researcher then measures the changes that are produced in the dependent variable in each group. Once data is collected from both groups, it is analyzed statistically to determine if there are meaningful differences between the groups.

Psychologists report their research findings in peer-reviewed journal articles. Research published in this format is checked by several other psychologists who serve as a filter separating ideas that are supported by evidence from ideas that are not. Replication has an important role in ensuring the legitimacy of published research. In the long run, only those findings that are capable of being replicated consistently will achieve consensus in the scientific community.

2.4 Ethics

Ethics in research is an evolving field, and some practices that were accepted or tolerated in the past would be considered unethical today. Researchers are expected to adhere to basic ethical guidelines when conducting experiments that involve human participants. Any experiment involving human participants must be approved by an IRB. Participation in experiments is voluntary and requires informed consent of the participants. If any deception is involved in the experiment, each participant must be fully debriefed upon the conclusion of the study.

Animal research is also held to a high ethical standard. Researchers who use animals as experimental subjects must design their projects so that pain and distress are minimized. Animal research requires the approval of an IACUC, and all animal facilities are subject to regular inspections to ensure that animals are being treated humanely.

Review Questions

1. Scientific hypotheses are _____ and falsifiable.
   a. observable
   b. original
   c. provable
   d. testable

2. _____ are defined as observable realities.
   a. behaviors
   b. facts
   c. opinions
   d. theories

3. Scientific knowledge is _____.
   a. intuitive
   b. empirical
   c. permanent
   d. subjective

4. A major criticism of Freud's early theories involves the fact that his theories _____.
   a. were too limited in scope
   b. were too outrageous
   c. were too broad
   d. were not testable

5. Sigmund Freud developed his theory of human personality by conducting in-depth interviews over an extended period of time with a few clients. This type of research approach is known as a(n): _____.
   a. archival research
   b. case study
   c. naturalistic observation
   d. survey

6. _____ involves observing behavior in individuals in their natural environments.
   a. archival research
   b. case study
   c. naturalistic observation
   d. survey

7. The major limitation of case studies is _____.
   a. the superficial nature of the information collected in this approach
   b. the lack of control that the researcher has in this approach
   c. the inability to generalize the findings from this approach to the larger population
   d. the absence of inter-rater reliability

8. The benefit of naturalistic observation studies is _____.
   a. the honesty of the data that is collected in a realistic setting
   b. how quick and easy these studies are to perform
   c. the researcher's capacity to make sure that data is collected as efficiently as possible
   d. the ability to determine cause and effect in this particular approach

9. Using existing records to try to answer a research question is known as _____.
   a. naturalistic observation
   b. survey research
   c. longitudinal research
   d. archival research

10. _____ involves following a group of research participants for an extended period of time.
    a. archival research
    b. longitudinal research
    c. naturalistic observation
    d. cross-sectional research

11. A(n) _____ is a list of questions developed by a researcher that can be administered in paper form.
    a. archive
    b. case Study
    c. naturalistic observation
    d. survey

12. Longitudinal research is complicated by high rates of _____.
    a. deception
    b. observation
    c. attrition
    d. generalization

13. Height and weight are positively correlated. This means that:
    a. There is no relationship between height and weight.
    b. Usually, the taller someone is, the thinner they are.
    c. Usually, the shorter someone is, the heavier they are.
    d. As height increases, typically weight increases.

14. Which of the following correlation coefficients indicates the strongest relationship between two variables?
    a. −.90
    b. −.50
    c. +.80
    d. +.25

15. Which statement best illustrates a negative correlation between the number of hours spent watching TV the week before an exam and the grade on that exam?
    a. Watching too much television leads to poor exam performance.
    b. Smart students watch less television.
    c. Viewing television interferes with a student's ability to prepare for the upcoming exam.
    d. Students who watch more television perform more poorly on their exams.

16. The correlation coefficient indicates the weakest relationship when _____.
    a. it is closest to 0
    b. it is closest to -1
    c. it is positive
    d. it is negative

17. _____ means that everyone in the population has the same likelihood of being asked to participate in the study.
    a. operationalizing
    b. placebo effect
    c. random assignment
    d. random sampling

18. The _____ is controlled by the experimenter, while the _____ represents the information collected and statistically analyzed by the experimenter.
    a. dependent variable; independent variable
    b. independent variable; dependent variable
    c. placebo effect; experimenter bias
    d. experiment bias; placebo effect

19. Researchers must _____ important concepts in their studies so others would have a clear understanding of exactly how those concepts were defined.
    a. randomly assign
    b. randomly select
    c. operationalize
    d. generalize

20. Sometimes, researchers will administer a(n) _____ to participants in the control group to control for the effects that participant expectation might have on the experiment.
    a. dependent variable
    b. independent variable
    c. statistical analysis
    d. placebo

21. _____ is to animal research as _____ is to human research.
    a. informed consent; deception
    b. IACUC; IRB
    c. IRB; IACUC
    d. deception; debriefing

22. Researchers might use _____ when providing participants with the full details of the experiment could skew their responses.
    a. informed consent
    b. deception
    c. ethics
    d. debriefing

23. A person's participation in a research project must be _____.
    a. random
    b. rewarded
    c. voluntary
    d. public

24. Before participating in an experiment, individuals should read and sign the _____ form.
    a. informed consent
    b. debriefing
    c. IRB
    d. ethics

Critical Thinking Questions

25. In this section, the D.A.R.E. program was described as an incredibly popular program in schools across the United States despite the fact that research consistently suggests that this program is largely ineffective. How might one explain this discrepancy?

26. The scientific method is often described as self-correcting and cyclical. Briefly describe your understanding of the scientific method with regard to these concepts.

27. In this section, conjoined twins, Krista and Tatiana, were described as being potential participants in a case study. In what other circumstances would you think that this particular research approach would be especially helpful and why?

28. Presumably, reality television programs aim to provide a realistic portrayal of the behavior displayed by the characters featured in such programs. This section pointed out why this is not really the case. What changes could be made in the way that these programs are produced that would result in more honest portrayals of realistic behavior?

29. Which of the research methods discussed in this section would be best suited to research the effectiveness of the D.A.R.E. program in preventing the use of alcohol and other drugs? Why?

30. Aside from biomedical research, what other areas of research could greatly benefit by both longitudinal and archival research?

31. Earlier in this section, we read about research suggesting that there is a correlation between eating cereal and weight. Cereal companies that present this information in their advertisements could lead someone to believe that eating more cereal causes healthy weight. Why would they make such a claim and what arguments could you make to counter this cause-and-effect claim?

32. Recently a study was published in the journal, *Nutrition and Cancer*, which established a negative correlation between coffee consumption and breast cancer. Specifically, it was found that women consuming more than 5 cups of coffee a day were less likely to develop breast cancer than women who never consumed coffee (Lowcock, Cotterchio, Anderson, Boucher, & El-Sohemy, 2013). Imagine you see a newspaper story about this research that says, "Coffee Protects Against Cancer." Why is this headline misleading and why would a more accurate headline draw less interest?

33. Sometimes, true random sampling can be very difficult to obtain. Many researchers make use of convenience samples as an alternative. For example, one popular convenience sample would involve students enrolled in Introduction to Psychology courses. What are the implications of using this sampling technique?

34. Peer review is an important part of publishing research findings in many scientific disciplines. This process is normally conducted anonymously; in other words, the author of the article being reviewed does not know who is reviewing the article, and the reviewers are unaware of the author's identity. Why would this be an important part of this process?

35. Some argue that animal research is inherently flawed in terms of being ethical because unlike human participants, animals do not consent to be involved in research. Do you agree with this perspective? Given that animals do not consent to be involved in research projects, what sorts of extra precautions should be taken to ensure that they receive the most humane treatment possible?

36. At the end of the last section, you were asked to design a basic experiment to answer some question of interest. What ethical considerations should be made with the study you proposed to ensure that your experiment would conform to the scientific community's expectations of ethical research?

Personal Application Questions

37. Healthcare professionals cite an enormous number of health problems related to obesity, and many people have an understandable desire to attain a healthy weight. There are many diet programs, services, and products on the market to aid those who wish to lose weight. If a close friend was considering purchasing or participating in one of these products, programs, or services, how would you make sure your friend was fully aware of the potential consequences of this decision? What sort of information would you want to review before making such an investment or lifestyle change yourself?

38. A friend of yours is working part-time in a local pet store. Your friend has become increasingly interested in how dogs normally communicate and interact with each other, and is thinking of visiting a local veterinary clinic to see how dogs interact in the waiting room. After reading this section, do you think this is the best way to better understand such interactions? Do you have any suggestions that might result in more valid data?

39. As a college student, you are no doubt concerned about the grades that you earn while completing your coursework. If you wanted to know how overall GPA is related to success in life after college, how would you choose to approach this question and what kind of resources would you need to conduct this research?

40. We all have a tendency to make illusory correlations from time to time. Try to think of an illusory correlation that is held by you, a family member, or a close friend. How do you think this illusory correlation came about and what can be done in the future to combat them?

41. Are there any questions about human or animal behavior that you would really like to answer? Generate a hypothesis and briefly describe how you would conduct an experiment to answer your question.

42. Take a few minutes to think about all of the advancements that our society has achieved as a function of research involving animal subjects. How have you, a friend, or a family member benefited directly from this kind of research?

Chapter 3
Biopsychology

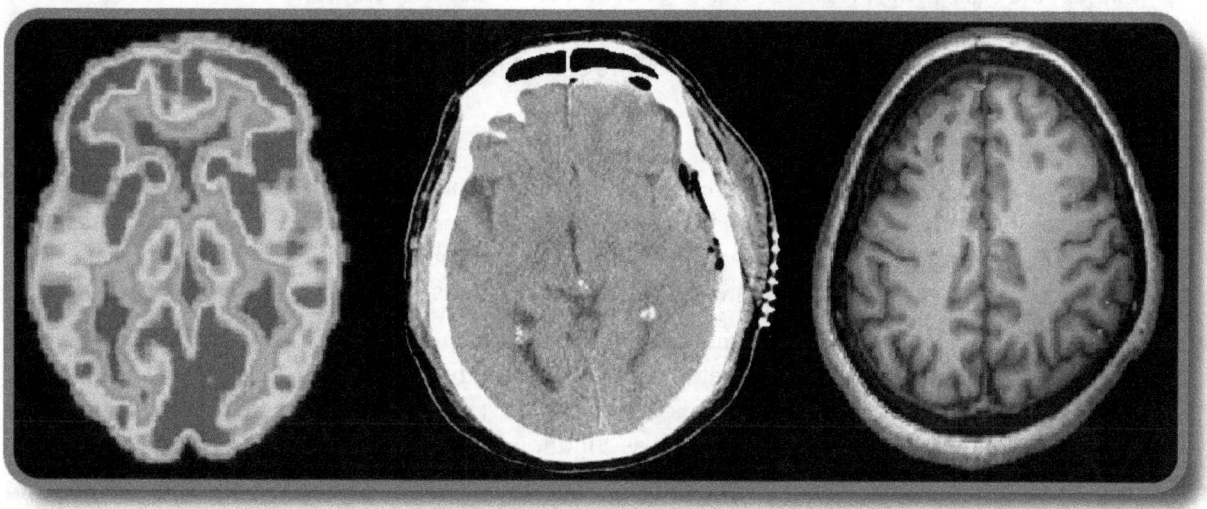

Figure 3.1 Different brain imaging techniques provide scientists with insight into different aspects of how the human brain functions. Left to right, PET scan (positron emission tomography), CT scan (computerized tomography), and fMRI (functional magnetic resonance imaging) are three types of scans. (credit "left": modification of work by Health and Human Services Department, National Institutes of Health; credit "center": modification of work by "Aceofhearts1968"/Wikimedia Commons; credit "right": modification of work by Kim J, Matthews NL, Park S.)

Chapter Outline

3.1 Human Genetics
3.2 Cells of the Nervous System
3.3 Parts of the Nervous System
3.4 The Brain and Spinal Cord
3.5 The Endocrine System

Introduction

Have you ever taken a device apart to find out how it works? Many of us have done so, whether to attempt a repair or simply to satisfy our curiosity. A device's internal workings are often distinct from its user interface on the outside. For example, we don't think about microchips and circuits when we turn up the volume on a mobile phone; instead, we think about getting the volume just right. Similarly, the inner workings of the human body are often distinct from the external expression of those workings. It is the job of psychologists to find the connection between these—for example, to figure out how the firings of millions of neurons become a thought.

This chapter strives to explain the biological mechanisms that underlie behavior. These physiological and anatomical foundations are the basis for many areas of psychology. In this chapter, you will learn how genetics influence both physiological and psychological traits. You will become familiar with the structure and function of the nervous system. And, finally, you will learn how the nervous system interacts with the endocrine system.

3.1 Human Genetics

Learning Objectives

By the end of this section, you will be able to:
- Explain the basic principles of the theory of evolution by natural selection
- Describe the differences between genotype and phenotype
- Discuss how gene-environment interactions are critical for expression of physical and psychological characteristics

Psychological researchers study genetics in order to better understand the biological factors that contribute to certain behaviors. While all humans share certain biological mechanisms, we are each unique. And while our bodies have many of the same parts—brains and hormones and cells with genetic codes—these are expressed in a wide variety of behaviors, thoughts, and reactions.

Why do two people infected by the same disease have different outcomes: one surviving and one succumbing to the ailment? How are genetic diseases passed through family lines? Are there genetic components to psychological disorders, such as depression or schizophrenia? To what extent might there be a psychological basis to health conditions such as childhood obesity?

To explore these questions, let's start by focusing on a specific genetic disorder, sickle cell anemia, and how it might manifest in two affected sisters. Sickle-cell anemia is a genetic condition in which red blood cells, which are normally round, take on a crescent-like shape (Figure 3.2). The changed shape of these cells affects how they function: sickle-shaped cells can clog blood vessels and block blood flow, leading to high fever, severe pain, swelling, and tissue damage.

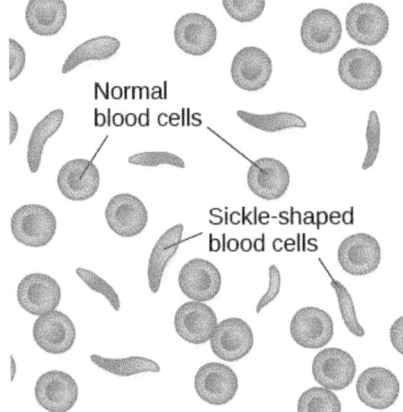

Figure 3.2 Normal blood cells travel freely through the blood vessels, while sickle-shaped cells form blockages preventing blood flow.

Many people with sickle-cell anemia—and the particular genetic mutation that causes it—die at an early age. While the notion of "survival of the fittest" may suggest that people suffering from this disorder have a low survival rate and therefore the disorder will become less common, this is not the case. Despite the negative evolutionary effects associated with this genetic mutation, the sickle-cell gene remains relatively common among people of African descent. Why is this? The explanation is illustrated with the following scenario.

Imagine two young women—Luwi and Sena—sisters in rural Zambia, Africa. Luwi carries the gene for sickle-cell anemia; Sena does not carry the gene. Sickle-cell carriers have one copy of the sickle-cell gene but do not have full-blown sickle-cell anemia. They experience symptoms only if they are severely dehydrated or are deprived of oxygen (as in mountain climbing). Carriers are thought to be immune from malaria (an often deadly disease that is widespread in tropical climates) because changes in their blood chemistry and immune functioning prevent the malaria parasite from having its effects (Gong, Parikh, Rosenthal, & Greenhouse, 2013). However, full-blown sickle-cell anemia, with two copies of the sickle-cell gene, does not provide immunity to malaria.

While walking home from school, both sisters are bitten by mosquitos carrying the malaria parasite. Luwi is protected against malaria because she carries the sickle-cell mutation. Sena, on the other hand, develops malaria and dies just two weeks later. Luwi survives and eventually has children, to whom she may pass on the sickle-cell mutation.

> **LINK TO LEARNING**
>
> Visit this **website about how a mutation in DNA leads to sickle cell anemia (http://openstax.org/l/sickle1)** to learn more.

Malaria is rare in the United States, so the sickle-cell gene benefits nobody: the gene manifests primarily in minor health problems for carriers with one copy, or a severe full-blown disease with no health benefits for carriers with two copies. However, the situation is quite different in other parts of the world. In parts of Africa where malaria is prevalent, having the sickle-cell mutation does provide health benefits for carriers (protection from malaria).

The story of malaria fits with Charles Darwin's **theory of evolution by natural selection** (Figure 3.3). In simple terms, the theory states that organisms that are better suited for their environment will survive and reproduce, while those that are poorly suited for their environment will die off. In our example, we can see that, as a carrier, Luwi's mutation is highly adaptive in her African homeland; however, if she resided in the United States (where malaria is rare), her mutation could prove costly—with a high probability of the disease in her descendants and minor health problems of her own.

 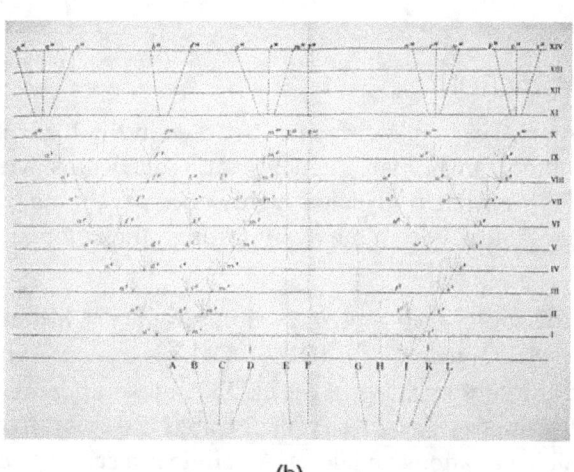

(a) (b)

Figure 3.3 (a) In 1859, Charles Darwin proposed his theory of evolution by natural selection in his book, *On the Origin of Species*. (b) The book contains just one illustration: this diagram that shows how species evolve over time through natural selection.

DIG DEEPER

Two Perspectives on Genetics and Behavior

It's easy to get confused about two fields that study the interaction of genes and the environment, such as the fields of evolutionary psychology and behavioral genetics. How can we tell them apart?

In both fields, it is understood that genes not only code for particular traits, but also contribute to certain patterns of cognition and behavior. Evolutionary psychology focuses on how universal patterns of behavior and cognitive processes have evolved over time. Therefore, variations in cognition and behavior would make individuals more or less successful in reproducing and passing those genes on to their offspring. Evolutionary psychologists study a variety of psychological phenomena that may have evolved as adaptations, including fear response, food preferences, mate selection, and cooperative behaviors (Confer et al., 2010).

Whereas evolutionary psychologists focus on universal patterns that evolved over millions of years, behavioral geneticists study how individual differences arise, in the present, through the interaction of genes and the environment. When studying human behavior, behavioral geneticists often employ twin and adoption studies to research questions of interest. Twin studies compare the likelihood that a given behavioral trait is shared among identical and fraternal twins; adoption studies compare those rates among biologically related relatives and adopted relatives. Both approaches provide some insight into the relative importance of genes and environment for the expression of a given trait.

LINK TO LEARNING

Watch this interview with renowned evolutionary psychologist David Buss (http://openstax.org/l/buss) to learn more about how a psychologist approaches evolution and how this approach fits within the social sciences.

GENETIC VARIATION

Genetic variation, the genetic difference between individuals, is what contributes to a species' adaptation to its environment. In humans, genetic variation begins with an egg, about 100 million sperm, and fertilization. Fertile women ovulate roughly once per month, releasing an egg from follicles in the ovary. During the egg's journey from the ovary through the fallopian tubes, to the uterus, a sperm may fertilize the egg.

The egg and the sperm each contain 23 chromosomes. **Chromosomes** are long strings of genetic material known as **deoxyribonucleic acid (DNA)**. DNA is a helix-shaped molecule made up of nucleotide base pairs. In each chromosome, sequences of DNA make up **genes** that control or partially control a number of visible characteristics, known as traits, such as eye color, hair color, and so on. A single gene may have multiple possible variations, or alleles. An **allele** is a specific version of a gene. So, a given gene may code for the trait of hair color, and the different alleles of that gene affect which hair color an individual has.

When a sperm and egg fuse, their 23 chromosomes combine to create a zygote with 46 chromosomes (23 pairs). Therefore, each parent contributes half the genetic information carried by the offspring; the resulting physical characteristics of the offspring (called the phenotype) are determined by the interaction of genetic material supplied by the parents (called the genotype). A person's **genotype** is the genetic makeup of that individual. **Phenotype**, on the other hand, refers to the individual's inherited physical characteristics, which are a combination of genetic and environmental influences (Figure 3.4).

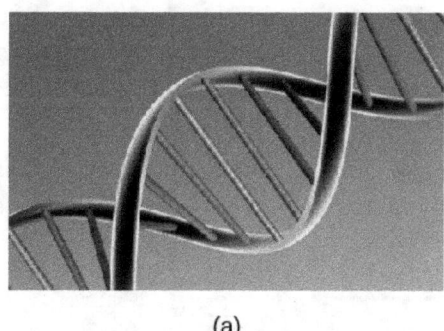

(a) (b)

Figure 3.4 (a) Genotype refers to the genetic makeup of an individual based on the genetic material (DNA) inherited from one's parents. (b) Phenotype describes an individual's observable characteristics, such as hair color, skin color, height, and build. (credit a: modification of work by Caroline Davis; credit b: modification of work by Cory Zanker)

Most traits are controlled by multiple genes, but some traits are controlled by one gene. A characteristic like cleft chin, for example, is influenced by a single gene from each parent. In this example, we will call the gene for cleft chin "B," and the gene for smooth chin "b." Cleft chin is a dominant trait, which means that having the **dominant allele** either from one parent (Bb) or both parents (BB) will always result in the phenotype associated with the dominant allele. When someone has two copies of the same allele, they are said to be **homozygous** for that allele. When someone has a combination of alleles for a given gene, they are said to be **heterozygous**. For example, smooth chin is a recessive trait, which means that an individual will only display the smooth chin phenotype if they are homozygous for that **recessive allele** (bb).

Imagine that a woman with a cleft chin mates with a man with a smooth chin. What type of chin will their child have? The answer to that depends on which alleles each parent carries. If the woman is homozygous for cleft chin (BB), her offspring will always have cleft chin. It gets a little more complicated, however, if the mother is heterozygous for this gene (Bb). Since the father has a smooth chin—therefore homozygous for the recessive allele (bb)—we can expect the offspring to have a 50% chance of having a cleft chin and a 50% chance of having a smooth chin (**Figure 3.5**).

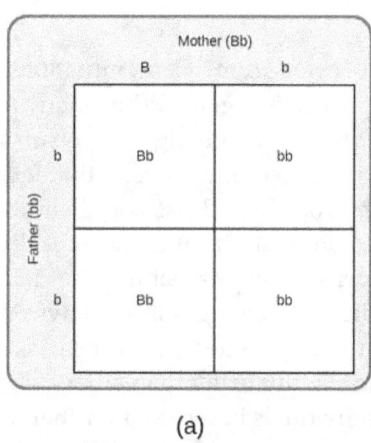
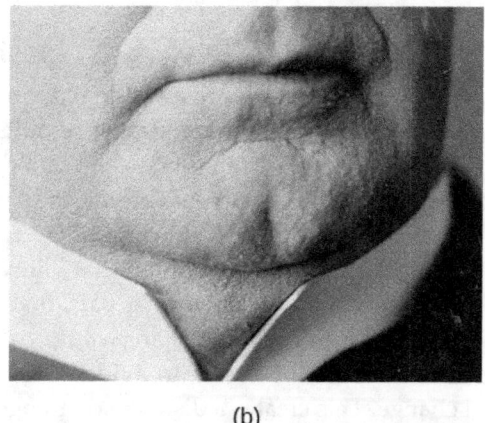

(a) (b)

Figure 3.5 (a) A Punnett square is a tool used to predict how genes will interact in the production of offspring. The capital B represents the dominant allele, and the lowercase b represents the recessive allele. In the example of the cleft chin, where B is cleft chin (dominant allele), wherever a pair contains the dominant allele, B, you can expect a cleft chin phenotype. You can expect a smooth chin phenotype only when there are two copies of the recessive allele, bb. (b) A cleft chin, shown here, is an inherited trait.

In sickle cell anemia, heterozygous carriers (like Luwi from the example) can develop blood resistance to malaria infection while those who are homozygous (like Sena) have a potentially lethal blood disorder. Sickle-cell anemia is just one of many genetic disorders caused by the pairing of two recessive genes. For example, phenylketonuria (PKU) is a condition in which individuals lack an enzyme that normally converts harmful amino acids into harmless byproducts. If someone with this condition goes untreated, he or she will experience significant deficits in cognitive function, seizures, and an increased risk of various psychiatric disorders. Because PKU is a recessive trait, each parent must have at least one copy of the recessive allele in order to produce a child with the condition (Figure 3.6).

So far, we have discussed traits that involve just one gene, but few human characteristics are controlled by a single gene. Most traits are **polygenic**: controlled by more than one gene. Height is one example of a polygenic trait, as are skin color and weight.

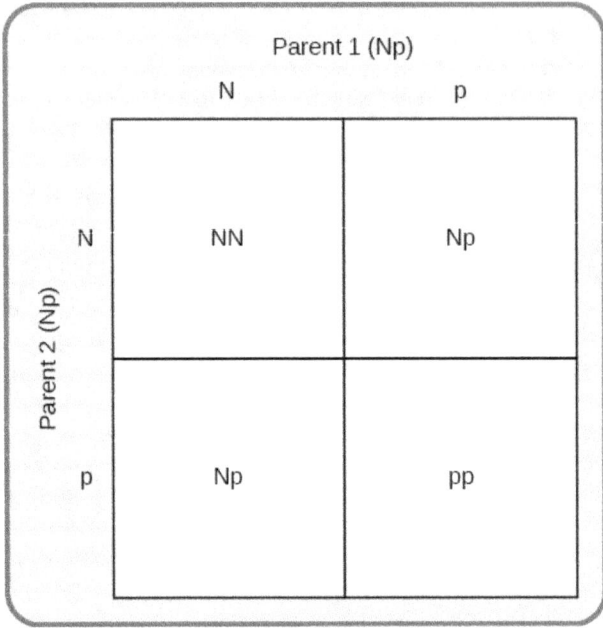

Figure 3.6 In this Punnett square, N represents the normal allele, and p represents the recessive allele that is associated with PKU. If two individuals mate who are both heterozygous for the allele associated with PKU, their offspring have a 25% chance of expressing the PKU phenotype.

Where do harmful genes that contribute to diseases like PKU come from? Gene mutations provide one source of harmful genes. A **mutation** is a sudden, permanent change in a gene. While many mutations can be harmful or lethal, once in a while, a mutation benefits an individual by giving that person an advantage over those who do not have the mutation. Recall that the theory of evolution asserts that individuals best adapted to their particular environments are more likely to reproduce and pass on their genes to future generations. In order for this process to occur, there must be competition—more technically, there must be variability in genes (and resultant traits) that allow for variation in adaptability to the environment. If a population consisted of identical individuals, then any dramatic changes in the environment would affect everyone in the same way, and there would be no variation in selection. In contrast, diversity in genes and associated traits allows some individuals to perform slightly better than others when faced with environmental change. This creates a distinct advantage for individuals best suited for their environments in terms of successful reproduction and genetic transmission.

DIG DEEPER

Human Diversity

This chapter focuses on biology. Later in this course you will learn about social psychology and issues of race, prejudice, and discrimination. When we focus strictly on biology, race becomes a weak construct. After the sequencing of the human genome at the turn of the millennium, many scientists began to argue that race was not a useful variable in genetic research and that its continued use represents a potential source of confusion and harm. The racial categories that some believed to be helpful in studying genetic diversity in humans are largely irrelevant. A person's skin tone, eye color, and hair texture are functions of their genetic makeups, but there is actually more genetic variation within a given racial category than there is between racial categories. In some cases, focus on race has led to difficulties with misdiagnoses and/or under-diagnoses of diseases ranging from sickle cell anemia to cystic fibrosis. Some argue that we need to distinguish between ancestry and race and then focus on ancestry. This approach would facilitate greater understanding of human genetic diversity (Yudell, Roberts, DeSalle, & Tishkoff, 2016).

GENE-ENVIRONMENT INTERACTIONS

Genes do not exist in a vacuum. Although we are all biological organisms, we also exist in an environment that is incredibly important in determining not only when and how our genes express themselves, but also in what combination. Each of us represents a unique interaction between our genetic makeup and our environment; range of reaction is one way to describe this interaction. **Range of reaction** asserts that our genes set the boundaries within which we can operate, and our environment interacts with the genes to determine where in that range we will fall. For example, if an individual's genetic makeup predisposes her to high levels of intellectual potential and she is reared in a rich, stimulating environment, then she will be more likely to achieve her full potential than if she were raised under conditions of significant deprivation. According to the concept of range of reaction, genes set definite limits on potential, and environment determines how much of that potential is achieved. Some disagree with this theory and argue that genes do not set a limit on a person's potential with reaction norms being determined by the environment. For example, when individuals experience neglect or abuse early in life, they are more likely to exhibit adverse psychological and/or physical conditions that can last throughout their lives. These conditions may develop as a function of the negative environmental experiences in individuals from dissimilar genetic backgrounds (Miguel, Pereira, Silveira, & Meaney, 2019; Short & Baram, 2019).

Another perspective on the interaction between genes and the environment is the concept of **genetic environmental correlation**. Stated simply, our genes influence our environment, and our environment influences the expression of our genes (Figure 3.7). Not only do our genes and environment interact, as in range of reaction, but they also influence one another bidirectionally. For example, the child of an NBA player would probably be exposed to basketball from an early age. Such exposure might allow the child to realize his or her full genetic, athletic potential. Thus, the parents' genes, which the child shares, influence the child's environment, and that environment, in turn, is well suited to support the child's genetic potential.

Figure 3.7 Nature and nurture work together like complex pieces of a human puzzle. The interaction of our environment and genes makes us the individuals we are. (credit "puzzle": modification of work by Cory Zanker; credit "houses": modification of work by Ben Salter; credit "DNA": modification of work by NHGRI)

In another approach to gene-environment interactions, the field of **epigenetics** looks beyond the genotype itself and studies how the same genotype can be expressed in different ways. In other words, researchers study how the same genotype can lead to very different phenotypes. As mentioned earlier, gene expression is often influenced by environmental context in ways that are not entirely obvious. For instance, identical twins share the same genetic information (**identical twins** develop from a single fertilized egg that split, so the genetic material is exactly the same in each; in contrast, **fraternal twins** usually result from two different eggs fertilized by different sperm, so the genetic material varies as with non-twin siblings). But even with identical genes, there remains an incredible amount of variability in how gene expression can unfold over the course of each twin's life. Sometimes, one twin will develop a disease and the other will not. In one example, Aliya, an identical twin, died from cancer at age 7, but her twin, now 19 years old, has never had cancer. Although these individuals share an identical genotype, their phenotypes differ as a result of how that genetic information is expressed over time and through their unique environmental interactions. The epigenetic perspective is very different from range of reaction, because here the genotype is not fixed and limited.

LINK TO LEARNING

Watch this video about the epigenetics of twin studies (http://openstax.org/l/twinstudy) to learn more.

Genes affect more than our physical characteristics. Indeed, scientists have found genetic linkages to a number of behavioral characteristics, ranging from basic personality traits to sexual orientation to spirituality (for examples, see Mustanski et al., 2005; Comings, Gonzales, Saucier, Johnson, & MacMurray, 2000). Genes are also associated with temperament and a number of psychological disorders, such as depression and schizophrenia. So while it is true that genes provide the biological blueprints for our cells, tissues, organs, and body, they also have a significant impact on our experiences and our behaviors.

Let's look at the following findings regarding schizophrenia in light of our three views of gene-environment interactions. Which view do you think best explains this evidence?

In a 2004 study by Tienari and colleagues, of people who were given up for adoption, adoptees whose biological mothers had schizophrenia *and* who had been raised in a disturbed family environment were much more likely to develop schizophrenia or another psychotic disorder than were any of the other groups in the study:

- Of adoptees whose biological mothers had schizophrenia (high genetic risk) and who were raised in disturbed family environments, 36.8% were likely to develop schizophrenia.
- Of adoptees whose biological mothers had schizophrenia (high genetic risk) and who were raised in healthy family environments, 5.8% were likely to develop schizophrenia.
- Of adoptees with a low genetic risk (whose mothers did not have schizophrenia) and who were raised in disturbed family environments, 5.3% were likely to develop schizophrenia.
- Of adoptees with a low genetic risk (whose mothers did not have schizophrenia) and who were raised in healthy family environments, 4.8% were likely to develop schizophrenia.

The study shows that adoptees with high genetic risk were most likely to develop schizophrenia if they were raised in disturbed home environments. This research lends credibility to the notion that both genetic vulnerability and environmental stress are necessary for schizophrenia to develop, and that genes alone do not tell the full tale.

3.2 Cells of the Nervous System

Learning Objectives

By the end of this section, you will be able to:
- Identify the basic parts of a neuron
- Describe how neurons communicate with each other
- Explain how drugs act as agonists or antagonists for a given neurotransmitter system

Psychologists striving to understand the human mind may study the nervous system. Learning how the body's cells and organs function can help us understand the biological basis of human psychology. The **nervous system** is composed of two basic cell types: glial cells (also known as glia) and neurons. Glial cells are traditionally thought to play a supportive role to neurons, both physically and metabolically. **Glial cells** provide scaffolding on which the nervous system is built, help neurons line up closely with each other to allow neuronal communication, provide insulation to neurons, transport nutrients and waste products, and mediate immune responses. For years, researchers believed that there were many more glial cells than neurons; however, more recent work from Suzanna Herculano-Houzel's laboratory has called this long-standing assumption into question and has provided important evidence that there may be a nearly 1:1 ratio of glia cells to neurons. This is important because it suggests that human brains are more similar to other primate brains than previously thought (Azevedo et al, 2009; Hercaulano-Houzel, 2012; Herculano-Houzel, 2009). **Neurons**, on the other hand, serve as interconnected information processors that are essential for all of the tasks of the nervous system. This section briefly describes the structure and function of neurons.

NEURON STRUCTURE

Neurons are the central building blocks of the nervous system, 100 billion strong at birth. Like all cells, neurons consist of several different parts, each serving a specialized function (**Figure 3.8**). A neuron's outer surface is made up of a **semipermeable membrane**. This membrane allows smaller molecules and molecules without an electrical charge to pass through it, while stopping larger or highly charged molecules.

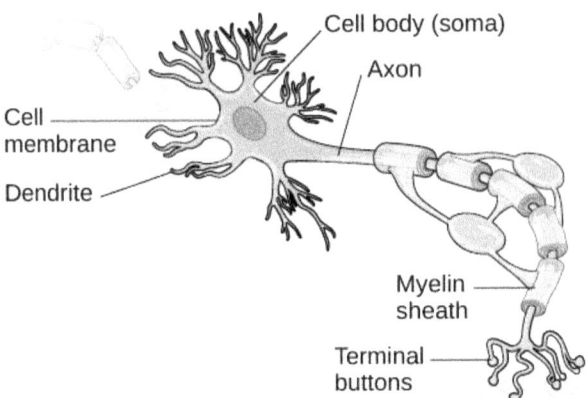

Figure 3.8 This illustration shows a prototypical neuron, which is being myelinated by a glial cell.

The nucleus of the neuron is located in the **soma**, or cell body. The soma has branching extensions known as **dendrites**. The neuron is a small information processor, and dendrites serve as input sites where signals are received from other neurons. These signals are transmitted electrically across the soma and down a major extension from the soma known as the **axon**, which ends at multiple **terminal buttons**. The terminal buttons contain **synaptic vesicles** that house **neurotransmitters**, the chemical messengers of the nervous system.

Axons range in length from a fraction of an inch to several feet. In some axons, glial cells form a fatty substance known as the **myelin sheath**, which coats the axon and acts as an insulator, increasing the speed at which the signal travels. The myelin sheath is not continuous and there are small gaps that occur down the length of the axon. These gaps in the myelin sheath are known as the **Nodes of Ranvier**. The myelin sheath is crucial for the normal operation of the neurons within the nervous system: the loss of the insulation it provides can be detrimental to normal function. To understand how this works, let's consider an example. PKU, a genetic disorder discussed earlier, causes a reduction in myelin and abnormalities in white matter cortical and subcortical structures. The disorder is associated with a variety of issues including severe cognitive deficits, exaggerated reflexes, and seizures (Anderson & Leuzzi, 2010; Huttenlocher, 2000). Another disorder, multiple sclerosis (MS), an autoimmune disorder, involves a large-scale loss of the myelin sheath on axons throughout the nervous system. The resulting interference in the electrical signal prevents the quick transmittal of information by neurons and can lead to a number of symptoms, such as dizziness, fatigue, loss of motor control, and sexual dysfunction. While some treatments may help to modify the course of the disease and manage certain symptoms, there is currently no known cure for multiple sclerosis.

In healthy individuals, the neuronal signal moves rapidly down the axon to the terminal buttons, where synaptic vesicles release neurotransmitters into the synaptic cleft (Figure 3.9). The **synaptic cleft** is a very small space between two neurons and is an important site where communication between neurons occurs. Once neurotransmitters are released into the synaptic cleft, they travel across it and bind with corresponding receptors on the dendrite of an adjacent neuron. **Receptors**, proteins on the cell surface where neurotransmitters attach, vary in shape, with different shapes "matching" different neurotransmitters.

How does a neurotransmitter "know" which receptor to bind to? The neurotransmitter and the receptor have what is referred to as a lock-and-key relationship—specific neurotransmitters fit specific receptors similar to how a key fits a lock. The neurotransmitter binds to any receptor that it fits.

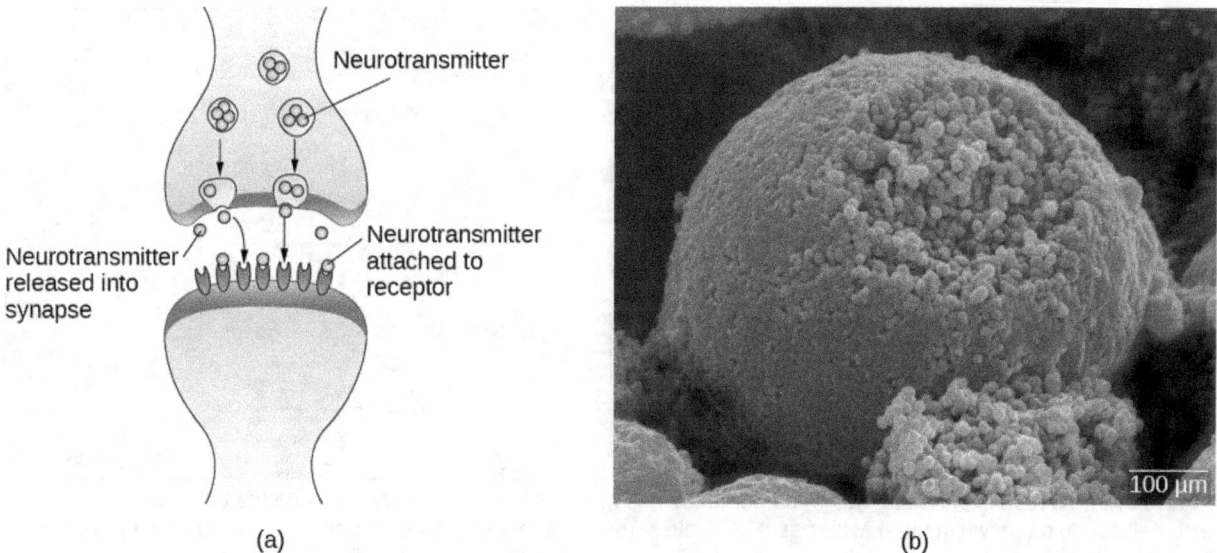

Figure 3.9 (a) The synaptic cleft is the space between the terminal button of one neuron and the dendrite of another neuron. (b) In this pseudo-colored image from a scanning electron microscope, a terminal button (green) has been opened to reveal the synaptic vesicles (orange and blue) inside. Each vesicle contains about 10,000 neurotransmitter molecules. (credit b: modification of work by Tina Carvalho, NIH-NIGMS; scale-bar data from Matt Russell)

NEURONAL COMMUNICATION

Now that we have learned about the basic structures of the neuron and the role that these structures play in neuronal communication, let's take a closer look at the signal itself—how it moves through the neuron and then jumps to the next neuron, where the process is repeated.

We begin at the neuronal membrane. The neuron exists in a fluid environment—it is surrounded by extracellular fluid and contains intracellular fluid (i.e., cytoplasm). The neuronal membrane keeps these two fluids separate—a critical role because the electrical signal that passes through the neuron depends on the intra- and extracellular fluids being electrically different. This difference in charge across the membrane, called the **membrane potential**, provides energy for the signal.

The electrical charge of the fluids is caused by charged molecules (ions) dissolved in the fluid. The semipermeable nature of the neuronal membrane somewhat restricts the movement of these charged molecules, and, as a result, some of the charged particles tend to become more concentrated either inside or outside the cell.

Between signals, the neuron membrane's potential is held in a state of readiness, called the **resting potential**. Like a rubber band stretched out and waiting to spring into action, ions line up on either side of the cell membrane, ready to rush across the membrane when the neuron goes active and the membrane opens its gates (i.e., a sodium-potassium pump that allows movement of ions across the membrane). Ions in high-concentration areas are ready to move to low-concentration areas, and positive ions are ready to move to areas with a negative charge.

In the resting state, sodium (Na^+) is at higher concentrations outside the cell, so it will tend to move into the cell. Potassium (K^+), on the other hand, is more concentrated inside the cell, and will tend to move out of the cell (Figure 3.10). In addition, the inside of the cell is slightly negatively charged compared to the outside. This provides an additional force on sodium, causing it to move into the cell.

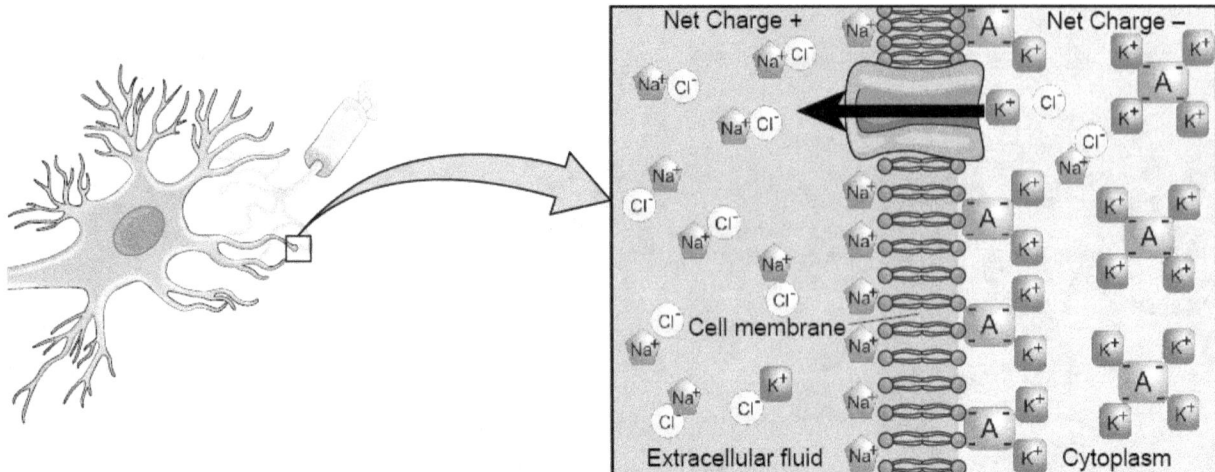

Figure 3.10 At resting potential, Na⁺ (blue pentagons) is more highly concentrated outside the cell in the extracellular fluid (shown in blue), whereas K⁺ (purple squares) is more highly concentrated near the membrane in the cytoplasm or intracellular fluid. Other molecules, such as chloride ions (yellow circles) and negatively charged proteins (brown squares), help contribute to a positive net charge in the extracellular fluid and a negative net charge in the intracellular fluid.

From this resting potential state, the neuron receives a signal and its state changes abruptly (Figure 3.11). When a neuron receives signals at the dendrites—due to neurotransmitters from an adjacent neuron binding to its receptors—small pores, or gates, open on the neuronal membrane, allowing Na⁺ ions, propelled by both charge and concentration differences, to move into the cell. With this influx of positive ions, the internal charge of the cell becomes more positive. If that charge reaches a certain level, called the **threshold of excitation**, the neuron becomes active and the action potential begins.

Many additional pores open, causing a massive influx of Na⁺ ions and a huge positive spike in the membrane potential, the peak action potential. At the peak of the spike, the sodium gates close and the potassium gates open. As positively charged potassium ions leave, the cell quickly begins repolarization. At first, it hyperpolarizes, becoming slightly more negative than the resting potential, and then it levels off, returning to the resting potential.

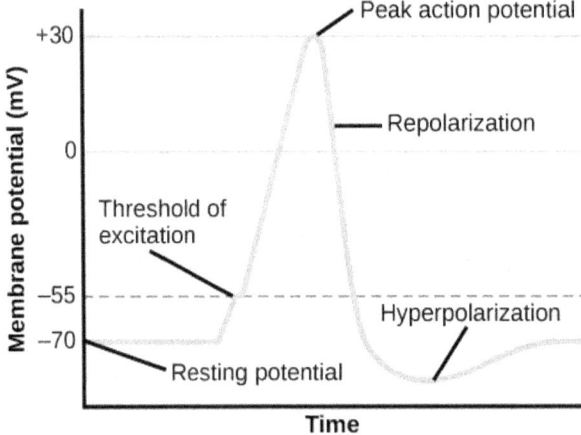

Figure 3.11 During the action potential, the electrical charge across the membrane changes dramatically.

This positive spike constitutes the **action potential**: the electrical signal that typically moves from the cell body down the axon to the axon terminals. The electrical signal moves down the axon with the impulses jumping in a leapfrog fashion between the Nodes of Ranvier. The Nodes of Ranvier are natural gaps in the myelin sheath. At each point, some of the sodium ions that enter the cell diffuse to the next section of the axon, raising the charge past the threshold of excitation and triggering a new influx of sodium ions. The action potential moves all the way down the axon in this fashion until reaching the terminal buttons.

The action potential is an **all-or-none** phenomenon. In simple terms, this means that an incoming signal from another neuron is either sufficient or insufficient to reach the threshold of excitation. There is no in-between, and there is no turning off an action potential once it starts. Think of it like sending an email or a text message. You can think about sending it all you want, but the message is not sent until you hit the send button. Furthermore, once you send the message, there is no stopping it.

Because it is all or none, the action potential is recreated, or propagated, at its full strength at every point along the axon. Much like the lit fuse of a firecracker, it does not fade away as it travels down the axon. It is this all-or-none property that explains the fact that your brain perceives an injury to a distant body part like your toe as equally painful as one to your nose.

As noted earlier, when the action potential arrives at the terminal button, the synaptic vesicles release their neurotransmitters into the synaptic cleft. The neurotransmitters travel across the synapse and bind to receptors on the dendrites of the adjacent neuron, and the process repeats itself in the new neuron (assuming the signal is sufficiently strong to trigger an action potential). Once the signal is delivered, excess neurotransmitters in the synaptic cleft drift away, are broken down into inactive fragments, or are reabsorbed in a process known as **reuptake**. Reuptake involves the neurotransmitter being pumped back into the neuron that released it, in order to clear the synapse (**Figure 3.12**). Clearing the synapse serves both to provide a clear "on" and "off" state between signals and to regulate the production of neurotransmitter (full synaptic vesicles provide signals that no additional neurotransmitters need to be produced).

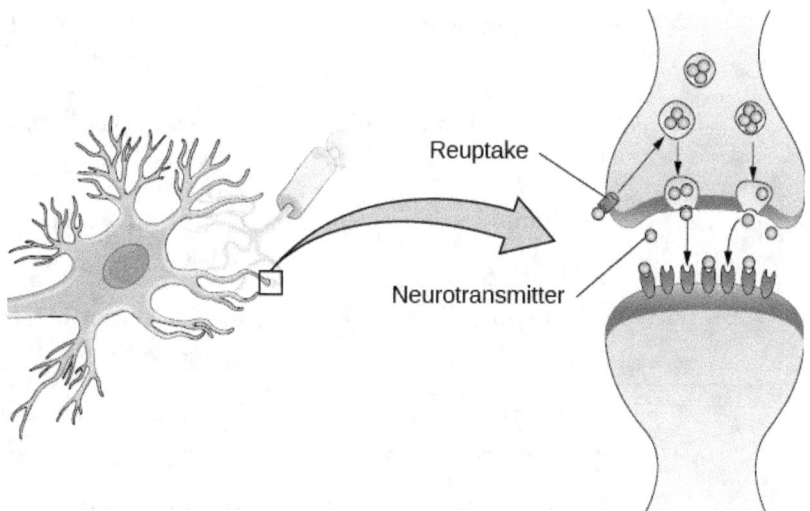

Figure 3.12 Reuptake involves moving a neurotransmitter from the synapse back into the axon terminal from which it was released.

Neuronal communication is often referred to as an electrochemical event. The movement of the action potential down the length of the axon is an electrical event, and movement of the neurotransmitter across the synaptic space represents the chemical portion of the process. However, there are some specialized connections between neurons that are entirely electrical. In such cases, the neurons are said to communicate via an electrical synapse. In these cases, two neurons physically connect to one another via gap junctions, which allows the current from one cell to pass into the next. There are far fewer electrical synapses in the brain, but those that do exist are much faster than the chemical synapses that have been described above (Connors & Long, 2004).

LINK TO LEARNING

Watch this video about neuronal communication (http://openstax.org/l/neuroncom) to learn more.

NEUROTRANSMITTERS AND DRUGS

There are several different types of neurotransmitters released by different neurons, and we can speak in broad terms about the kinds of functions associated with different neurotransmitters (Table 3.1). Much of what psychologists know about the functions of neurotransmitters comes from research on the effects of drugs in psychological disorders. Psychologists who take a **biological perspective** and focus on the physiological causes of behavior assert that psychological disorders like depression and schizophrenia are associated with imbalances in one or more neurotransmitter systems. In this perspective, psychotropic medications can help improve the symptoms associated with these disorders. **Psychotropic medications** are drugs that treat psychiatric symptoms by restoring neurotransmitter balance.

Major Neurotransmitters and How They Affect Behavior

Neurotransmitter	Involved in	Potential Effect on Behavior
Acetylcholine	Muscle action, memory	Increased arousal, enhanced cognition
Beta-endorphin	Pain, pleasure	Decreased anxiety, decreased tension
Dopamine	Mood, sleep, learning	Increased pleasure, suppressed appetite
Gamma-aminobutyric acid (GABA)	Brain function, sleep	Decreased anxiety, decreased tension
Glutamate	Memory, learning	Increased learning, enhanced memory
Norepinephrine	Heart, intestines, alertness	Increased arousal, suppressed appetite
Serotonin	Mood, sleep	Modulated mood, suppressed appetite

Table 3.1

Psychoactive drugs can act as agonists or antagonists for a given neurotransmitter system. **Agonists** are chemicals that mimic a neurotransmitter at the receptor site. An **antagonist**, on the other hand, blocks or impedes the normal activity of a neurotransmitter at the receptor. Agonists and antagonists represent drugs that are prescribed to correct the specific neurotransmitter imbalances underlying a person's condition. For example, Parkinson's disease, a progressive nervous system disorder, is associated with low levels of dopamine. Therefore, a common treatment strategy for Parkinson's disease involves using dopamine agonists, which mimic the effects of dopamine by binding to dopamine receptors.

Certain symptoms of schizophrenia are associated with overactive dopamine neurotransmission. The antipsychotics used to treat these symptoms are antagonists for dopamine—they block dopamine's effects by binding its receptors without activating them. Thus, they prevent dopamine released by one neuron from signaling information to adjacent neurons.

In contrast to agonists and antagonists, which both operate by binding to receptor sites, reuptake inhibitors prevent unused neurotransmitters from being transported back to the neuron. This allows neurotransmitters to remain active in the synaptic cleft for longer durations, increasing their effectiveness. Depression, which has been consistently linked with reduced serotonin levels, is commonly treated with selective serotonin reuptake inhibitors (SSRIs). By preventing reuptake, SSRIs strengthen the effect of serotonin, giving it more time to interact with serotonin receptors on dendrites. Common SSRIs on the market today include Prozac, Paxil, and Zoloft. The drug LSD is structurally very similar to serotonin, and it affects the same neurons and receptors as serotonin. Psychotropic drugs are not instant solutions for people suffering from psychological disorders. Often, an individual must take a drug for several weeks before seeing improvement, and many psychoactive drugs have significant negative side effects. Furthermore, individuals vary dramatically in how they respond to the drugs. To improve chances for success, it is not uncommon for people receiving pharmacotherapy to undergo psychological and/or behavioral therapies as well. Some research suggests that combining drug therapy with other forms of therapy tends to be more effective than any one treatment alone (for one such example, see March et al., 2007).

3.3 Parts of the Nervous System

Learning Objectives

By the end of this section, you will be able to:
- Describe the difference between the central and peripheral nervous systems
- Explain the difference between the somatic and autonomic nervous systems
- Differentiate between the sympathetic and parasympathetic divisions of the autonomic nervous system

The nervous system can be divided into two major subdivisions: the **central nervous system (CNS)** and the **peripheral nervous system (PNS)**, shown in Figure 3.13. The CNS is comprised of the brain and spinal cord; the PNS connects the CNS to the rest of the body. In this section, we focus on the peripheral nervous system; later, we look at the brain and spinal cord.

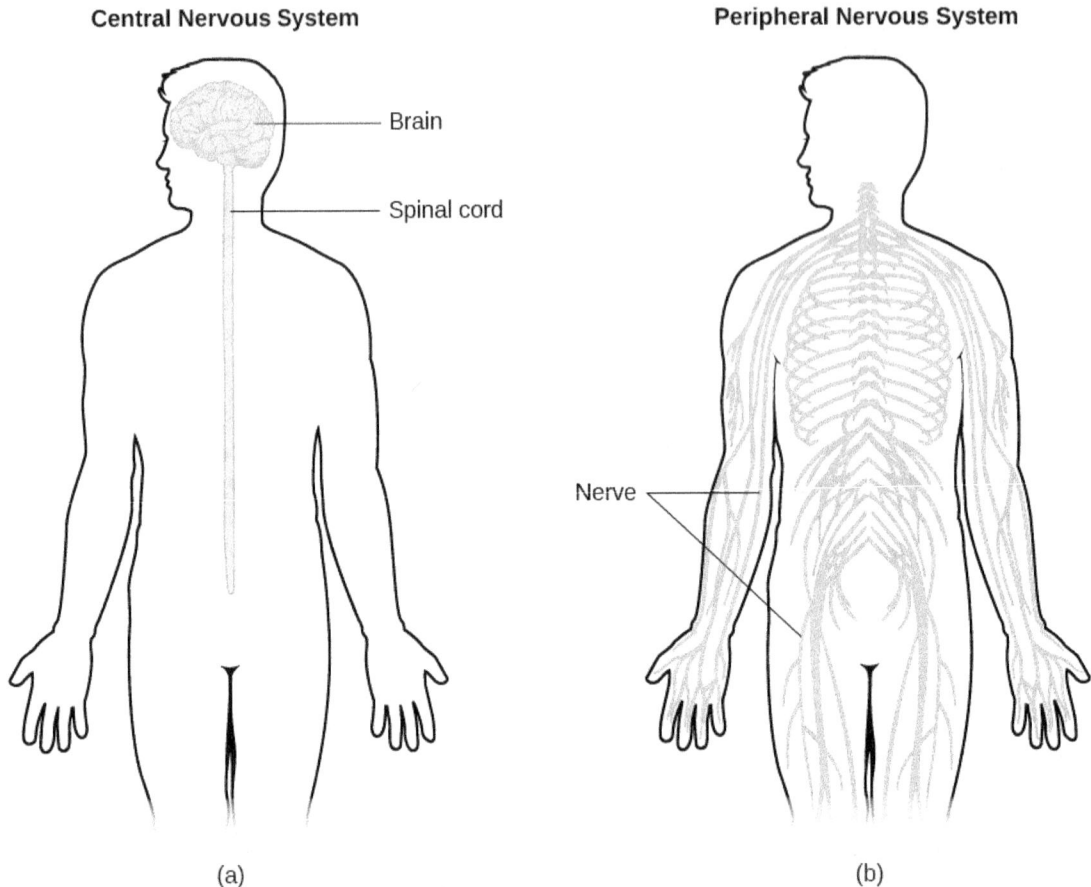

Figure 3.13 The nervous system is divided into two major parts: (a) the Central Nervous System and (b) the Peripheral Nervous System.

PERIPHERAL NERVOUS SYSTEM

The peripheral nervous system is made up of thick bundles of axons, called nerves, carrying messages back and forth between the CNS and the muscles, organs, and senses in the periphery of the body (i.e., everything outside the CNS). The PNS has two major subdivisions: the somatic nervous system and the autonomic nervous system.

The **somatic nervous system** is associated with activities traditionally thought of as conscious or voluntary. It is involved in the relay of sensory and motor information to and from the CNS; therefore, it consists of motor neurons and sensory neurons. Motor neurons, carrying instructions from the CNS to the muscles, are efferent fibers (efferent means "moving away from"). Sensory neurons, carrying sensory information to the CNS, are afferent fibers (afferent means "moving toward"). A helpful way to remember this is that **e**fferent = **e**xit and **a**fferent = **a**rrive. Each nerve is basically a bundle of neurons forming a two-way superhighway, containing thousands of axons, both efferent and afferent.

The **autonomic nervous system** controls our internal organs and glands and is generally considered to be outside the realm of voluntary control. It can be further subdivided into the sympathetic and parasympathetic divisions (Figure 3.14). The **sympathetic nervous system** is involved in preparing the body for stress-related activities; the **parasympathetic nervous system** is associated with returning the body to routine, day-to-day operations. The two systems have complementary functions, operating in tandem to maintain the body's homeostasis. **Homeostasis** is a state of equilibrium, or balance, in which biological conditions (such as body temperature) are maintained at optimal levels.

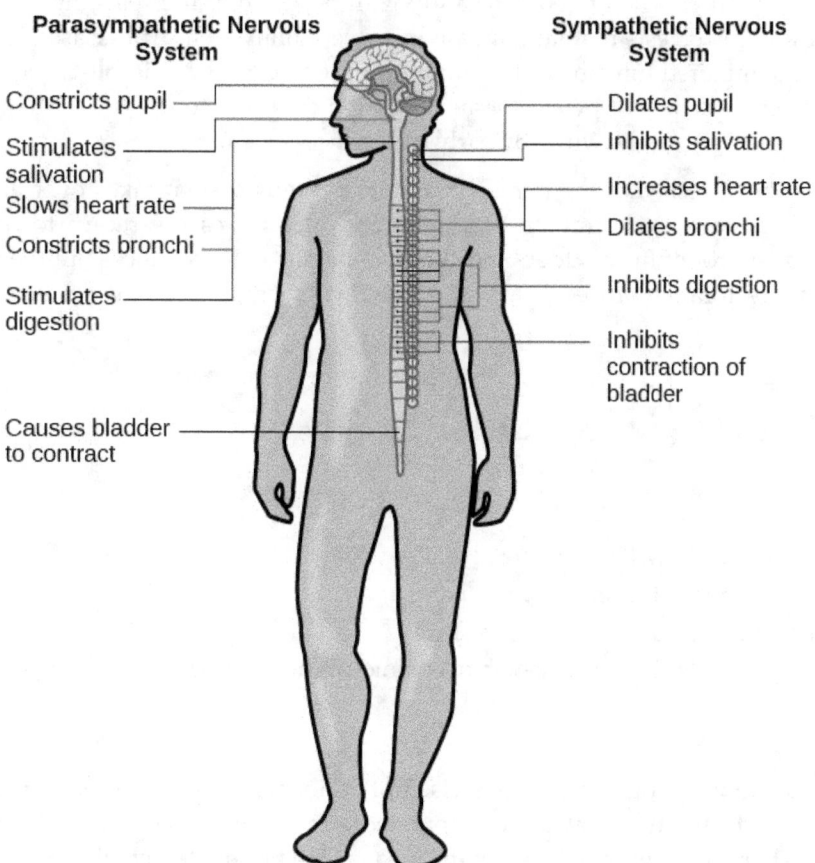

Figure 3.14 The sympathetic and parasympathetic divisions of the autonomic nervous system have the opposite effects on various systems.

The sympathetic nervous system is activated when we are faced with stressful or high-arousal situations. The activity of this system was adaptive for our ancestors, increasing their chances of survival. Imagine, for example, that one of our early ancestors, out hunting small game, suddenly disturbs a large bear with her cubs. At that moment, his body undergoes a series of changes—a direct function of sympathetic activation—preparing him to face the threat. His pupils dilate, his heart rate and blood pressure increase, his bladder relaxes, his liver releases glucose, and adrenaline surges into his bloodstream. This constellation of physiological changes, known as the **fight or flight response,** allows the body access to energy reserves and heightened sensory capacity so that it might fight off a threat or run away to safety.

LINK TO LEARNING

Watch this **video about the Fight Flight Freeze response** (http://openstax.org/l/response) to learn more.

While it is clear that such a response would be critical for survival for our ancestors, who lived in a world full of real physical threats, many of the high-arousal situations we face in the modern world are more psychological in nature. For example, think about how you feel when you have to stand up and give a presentation in front of a roomful of people, or right before taking a big test. You are in no real physical danger in those situations, and yet you have evolved to respond to a perceived threat with the fight or flight response. This kind of response is not nearly as adaptive in the modern world; in fact, we suffer negative health consequences when faced constantly with psychological threats that we can neither fight nor flee. Recent research suggests that an increase in susceptibility to heart disease (Chandola, Brunner, & Marmot, 2006) and impaired function of the immune system (Glaser & Kiecolt-Glaser, 2005) are among the many negative consequences of persistent and repeated exposure to stressful situations. Some of this tendency for stress reactivity can be wired by early experiences of trauma.

Once the threat has been resolved, the parasympathetic nervous system takes over and returns bodily functions to a relaxed state. Our hunter's heart rate and blood pressure return to normal, his pupils constrict, he regains control of his bladder, and the liver begins to store glucose in the form of glycogen for future use. These restorative processes are associated with activation of the parasympathetic nervous system.

3.4 The Brain and Spinal Cord

Learning Objectives

By the end of this section, you will be able to:
- Explain the functions of the spinal cord
- Identify the hemispheres and lobes of the brain
- Describe the types of techniques available to clinicians and researchers to image or scan the brain

The brain is a remarkably complex organ comprised of billions of interconnected neurons and glia. It is a bilateral, or two-sided, structure that can be separated into distinct lobes. Each lobe is associated with certain types of functions, but, ultimately, all of the areas of the brain interact with one another to provide the foundation for our thoughts and behaviors. In this section, we discuss the overall organization of the brain and the functions associated with different brain areas, beginning with what can be seen as an extension of the brain, the spinal cord.

THE SPINAL CORD

It can be said that the spinal cord is what connects the brain to the outside world. Because of it, the brain can act. The spinal cord is like a relay station, but a very smart one. It not only routes messages to and from the brain, but it also has its own system of automatic processes, called reflexes.

The top of the spinal cord is a bundle of nerves that merges with the brain stem, where the basic processes of life are controlled, such as breathing and digestion. In the opposite direction, the spinal cord ends just below the ribs—contrary to what we might expect, it does not extend all the way to the base of the spine.

The spinal cord is functionally organized in 30 segments, corresponding with the vertebrae. Each segment is connected to a specific part of the body through the peripheral nervous system. Nerves branch out from the spine at each vertebra. Sensory nerves bring messages in; motor nerves send messages out to the muscles and organs. Messages travel to and from the brain through every segment.

Some sensory messages are immediately acted on by the spinal cord, without any input from the brain. Withdrawal from a hot object and the knee jerk are two examples. When a sensory message meets certain parameters, the spinal cord initiates an automatic reflex. The signal passes from the sensory nerve to a simple processing center, which initiates a motor command. Seconds are saved, because messages don't have to go the brain, be processed, and get sent back. In matters of survival, the spinal reflexes allow the body to react extraordinarily fast.

The spinal cord is protected by bony vertebrae and cushioned in cerebrospinal fluid, but injuries still occur. When the spinal cord is damaged in a particular segment, all lower segments are cut off from the brain, causing paralysis. Therefore, the lower on the spine damage occurs, the fewer functions an injured individual will lose.

Neuroplasticity

Bob Woodruff, a reporter for ABC, suffered a traumatic brain injury after a bomb exploded next to the vehicle he was in while covering a news story in Iraq. As a consequence of these injuries, Woodruff experienced many cognitive deficits including difficulties with memory and language. However, over time and with the aid of intensive amounts of cognitive and speech therapy, Woodruff has shown an incredible recovery of function (Fernandez, 2008, October 16).

One of the factors that made this recovery possible was **neuroplasticity**. Neuroplasticity refers to how the nervous system can change and adapt. Neuroplasticity can occur in a variety of ways including personal experiences, developmental processes, or, as in Woodruff's case, in response to some sort of damage or injury that has occurred. Neuroplasticity can involve creation of new synapses, pruning of synapses that are no longer used, changes in glial cells, and even the birth of new neurons. Because of neuroplasticity, our brains are constantly changing and adapting, and while our nervous system is most plastic when we are very young, as Woodruff's case suggests, it is still capable of remarkable changes later in life.

THE TWO HEMISPHERES

The surface of the brain, known as the **cerebral cortex**, is very uneven, characterized by a distinctive pattern of folds or bumps, known as **gyri** (singular: gyrus), and grooves, known as **sulci** (singular: sulcus), shown in **Figure 3.15**. These gyri and sulci form important landmarks that allow us to separate the brain into functional centers. The most prominent sulcus, known as the **longitudinal fissure**, is the deep groove that separates the brain into two halves or **hemispheres**: the left hemisphere and the right hemisphere.

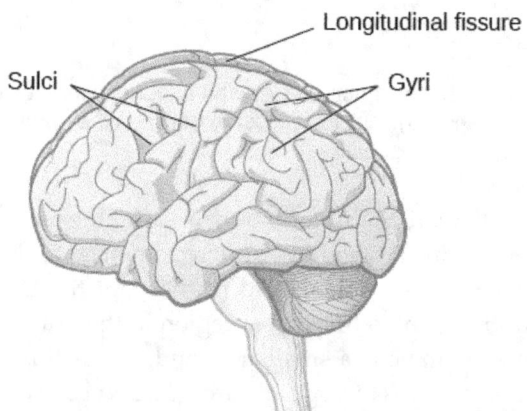

Figure 3.15 The surface of the brain is covered with gyri and sulci. A deep sulcus is called a fissure, such as the longitudinal fissure that divides the brain into left and right hemispheres. (credit: modification of work by Bruce Blaus)

There is evidence of specialization of function—referred to as **lateralization**—in each hemisphere, mainly regarding differences in language functions. The left hemisphere controls the right half of the body, and the right hemisphere controls the left half of the body. Decades of research on lateralization of function by Michael Gazzaniga and his colleagues suggest that a variety of functions ranging from cause-and-effect reasoning to self-recognition may follow patterns that suggest some degree of hemispheric dominance (Gazzaniga, 2005). For example, the left hemisphere has been shown to be superior for forming associations in memory, selective attention, and positive emotions. The right hemisphere, on the other hand, has been shown to be superior in pitch perception, arousal, and negative emotions (Ehret, 2006). However, it should be pointed out that research on which hemisphere is dominant in a variety of different behaviors has produced inconsistent results, and therefore, it is probably better to think of how the two hemispheres interact to produce a given behavior rather than attributing certain behaviors to one hemisphere versus the other (Banich & Heller, 1998).

The two hemispheres are connected by a thick band of neural fibers known as the **corpus callosum**, consisting of about 200 million axons. The corpus callosum allows the two hemispheres to communicate with each other and allows for information being processed on one side of the brain to be shared with the other side.

Normally, we are not aware of the different roles that our two hemispheres play in day-to-day functions, but there are people who come to know the capabilities and functions of their two hemispheres quite well. In some cases of severe epilepsy, doctors elect to sever the corpus callosum as a means of controlling the spread of seizures (**Figure 3.16**). While this is an effective treatment option, it results in individuals who have "split brains." After surgery, these split-brain patients show a variety of interesting behaviors. For instance, a split-brain patient is unable to name a picture that is shown in the patient's left visual field because the information is only available in the largely nonverbal right hemisphere. However, they are able to recreate the picture with their left hand, which is also controlled by the right hemisphere. When the more verbal left hemisphere sees the picture that the hand drew, the patient is able to name it (assuming the left hemisphere can interpret what was drawn by the left hand).

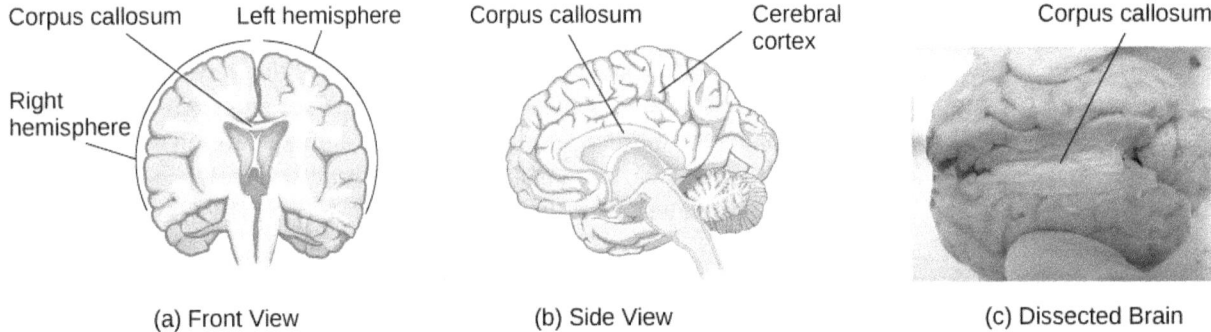

Figure 3.16 (a, b) The corpus callosum connects the left and right hemispheres of the brain. (c) A scientist spreads this dissected sheep brain apart to show the corpus callosum between the hemispheres. (credit c: modification of work by Aaron Bornstein)

Much of what we know about the functions of different areas of the brain comes from studying changes in the behavior and ability of individuals who have suffered damage to the brain. For example, researchers study the behavioral changes caused by strokes to learn about the functions of specific brain areas. A stroke, caused by an interruption of blood flow to a region in the brain, causes a loss of brain function in the affected region. The damage can be in a small area, and, if it is, this gives researchers the opportunity to link any resulting behavioral changes to a specific area. The types of deficits displayed after a stroke will be largely dependent on where in the brain the damage occurred.

Consider Theona, an intelligent, self-sufficient woman, who is 62 years old. Recently, she suffered a stroke in the front portion of her right hemisphere. As a result, she has great difficulty moving her left leg. (As you learned earlier, the right hemisphere controls the left side of the body; also, the brain's main motor centers are located at the front of the head, in the frontal lobe.) Theona has also experienced behavioral changes. For example, while in the produce section of the grocery store, she sometimes eats grapes, strawberries, and apples directly from their bins before paying for them. This behavior—which would have been very embarrassing to her before the stroke—is consistent with damage in another region in the frontal lobe—the prefrontal cortex, which is associated with judgment, reasoning, and impulse control.

FOREBRAIN STRUCTURES

The two hemispheres of the cerebral cortex are part of the **forebrain** (**Figure 3.17**), which is the largest part of the brain. The forebrain contains the cerebral cortex and a number of other structures that lie beneath the cortex (called subcortical structures): thalamus, hypothalamus, pituitary gland, and the limbic system (a collection of structures). The cerebral cortex, which is the outer surface of the brain, is associated with higher level processes such as consciousness, thought, emotion, reasoning, language, and memory. Each cerebral hemisphere can be subdivided into four lobes, each associated with different functions.

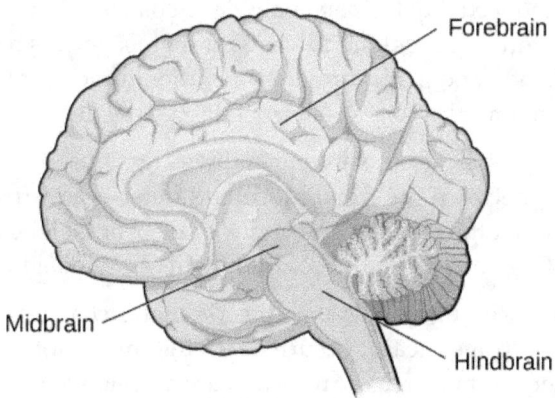

Figure 3.17 The brain and its parts can be divided into three main categories: the forebrain, midbrain, and hindbrain.

Lobes of the Brain

The four lobes of the brain are the frontal, parietal, temporal, and occipital lobes (Figure 3.18). The **frontal lobe** is located in the forward part of the brain, extending back to a fissure known as the central sulcus. The frontal lobe is involved in reasoning, motor control, emotion, and language. It contains the **motor cortex**, which is involved in planning and coordinating movement; the **prefrontal cortex**, which is responsible for higher-level cognitive functioning; and **Broca's area**, which is essential for language production.

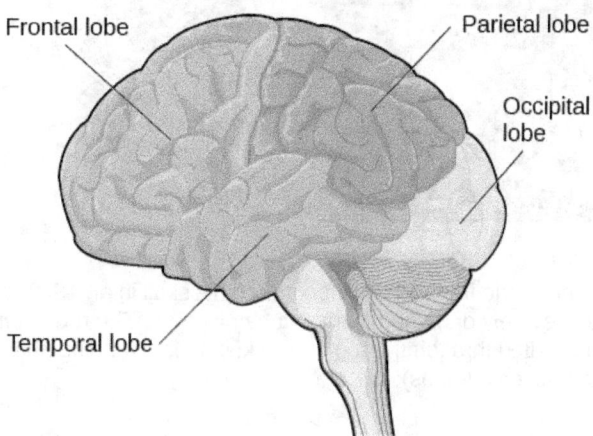

Figure 3.18 The lobes of the brain are shown.

People who suffer damage to Broca's area have great difficulty producing language of any form (Figure 3.18). For example, Padma was an electrical engineer who was socially active and a caring, involved parent. About twenty years ago, she was in a car accident and suffered damage to her Broca's area. She completely lost the ability to speak and form any kind of meaningful language. There is nothing wrong with her mouth or her vocal cords, but she is unable to produce words. She can follow directions but can't respond verbally, and she can read but no longer write. She can do routine tasks like running to the market to buy milk, but she could not communicate verbally if a situation called for it.

Probably the most famous case of frontal lobe damage is that of a man by the name of Phineas Gage. On September 13, 1848, Gage (age 25) was working as a railroad foreman in Vermont. He and his crew were using an iron rod to tamp explosives down into a blasting hole to remove rock along the railway's path. Unfortunately, the iron rod created a spark and caused the rod to explode out of the blasting hole, into Gage's face, and through his skull (**Figure 3.19**). Although lying in a pool of his own blood with brain matter emerging from his head, Gage was conscious and able to get up, walk, and speak. But in the months following his accident, people noticed that his personality had changed. Many of his friends described him as no longer being himself. Before the accident, it was said that Gage was a well-mannered, soft-spoken man, but he began to behave in odd and inappropriate ways after the accident. Such changes in personality would be consistent with loss of impulse control—a frontal lobe function.

Beyond the damage to the frontal lobe itself, subsequent investigations into the rod's path also identified probable damage to pathways between the frontal lobe and other brain structures, including the limbic system. With connections between the planning functions of the frontal lobe and the emotional processes of the limbic system severed, Gage had difficulty controlling his emotional impulses.

However, there is some evidence suggesting that the dramatic changes in Gage's personality were exaggerated and embellished. Gage's case occurred in the midst of a 19th century debate over localization—regarding whether certain areas of the brain are associated with particular functions. On the basis of extremely limited information about Gage, the extent of his injury, and his life before and after the accident, scientists tended to find support for their own views, on whichever side of the debate they fell (Macmillan, 1999).

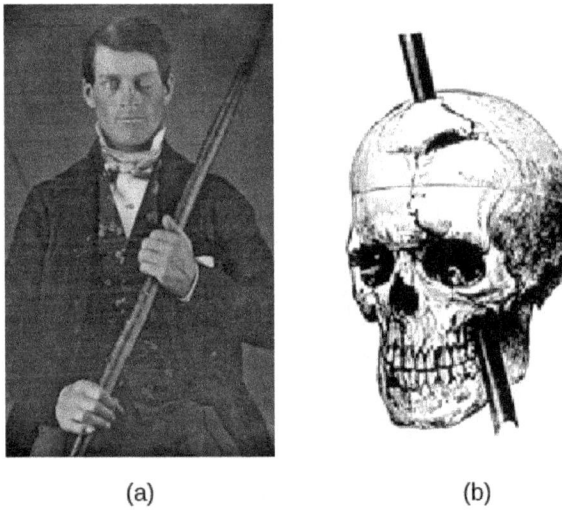

(a) (b)

Figure 3.19 (a) Phineas Gage holds the iron rod that penetrated his skull in an 1848 railroad construction accident. (b) Gage's prefrontal cortex was severely damaged in the left hemisphere. The rod entered Gage's face on the left side, passed behind his eye, and exited through the top of his skull, before landing about 80 feet away. (credit a: modification of work by Jack and Beverly Wilgus)

The brain's **parietal lobe** is located immediately behind the frontal lobe, and is involved in processing information from the body's senses. It contains the **somatosensory cortex**, which is essential for processing sensory information from across the body, such as touch, temperature, and pain. The somatosensory cortex is organized topographically, which means that spatial relationships that exist in the body are generally maintained on the surface of the somatosensory cortex (**Figure 3.20**). For example, the portion of the cortex that processes sensory information from the hand is adjacent to the portion that processes information from the wrist.

> **LINK TO LEARNING**
>
> One fascinating example of neuroplasticity involves reorganization of the somatosensory cortex following limb amputation. Check out this NPR segment about amputees' experiences of "phantom limbs" following amputation (http://openstax.org/l/phantomlimb) to learn more.

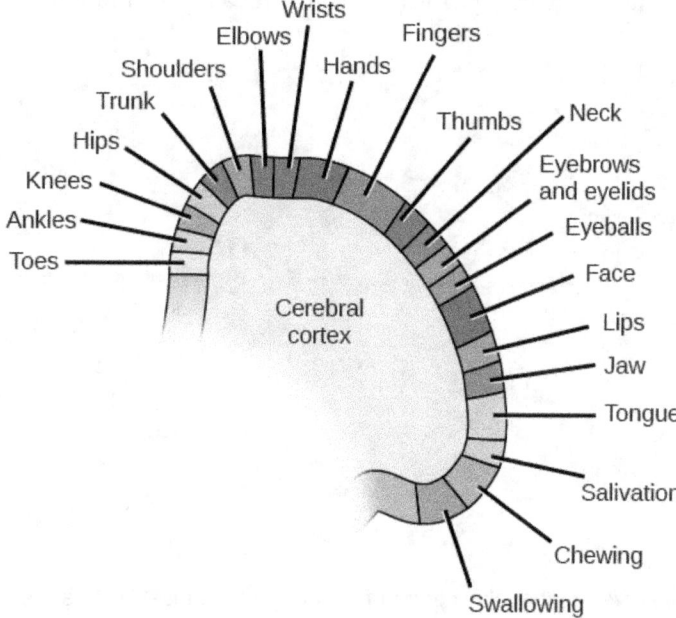

Figure 3.20 Spatial relationships in the body are mirrored in the organization of the somatosensory cortex.

The **temporal lobe** is located on the side of the head (temporal means "near the temples"), and is associated with hearing, memory, emotion, and some aspects of language. The **auditory cortex**, the main area responsible for processing auditory information, is located within the temporal lobe. **Wernicke's area**, important for speech comprehension, is also located here. Whereas individuals with damage to Broca's area have difficulty producing language, those with damage to Wernicke's area can produce sensible language, but they are unable to understand it (Figure 3.21).

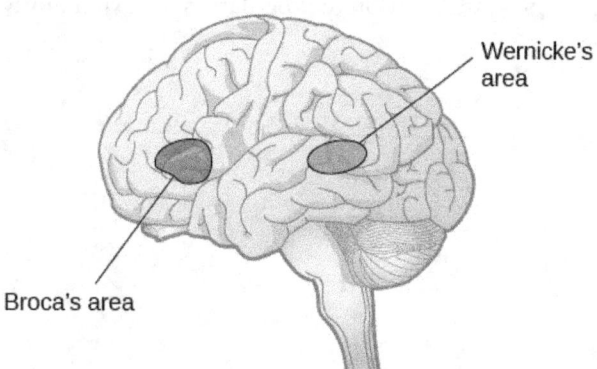

Figure 3.21 Damage to either Broca's area or Wernicke's area can result in language deficits. The types of deficits are very different, however, depending on which area is affected.

The **occipital lobe** is located at the very back of the brain, and contains the primary visual cortex, which is responsible for interpreting incoming visual information. The occipital cortex is organized retinotopically, which means there is a close relationship between the position of an object in a person's visual field and the position of that object's representation on the cortex. You will learn much more about how visual information is processed in the occipital lobe when you study sensation and perception.

Other Areas of the Forebrain

Other areas of the forebrain, located beneath the cerebral cortex, include the thalamus and the limbic system. The **thalamus** is a sensory relay for the brain. All of our senses, with the exception of smell, are routed through the thalamus before being directed to other areas of the brain for processing (**Figure 3.22**).

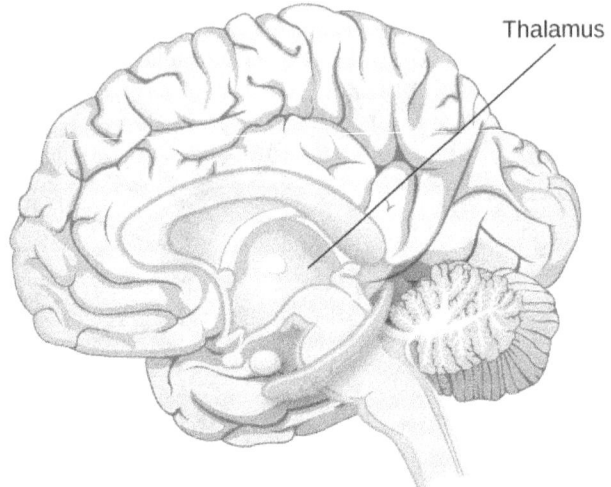

Figure 3.22 The thalamus serves as the relay center of the brain where most senses are routed for processing.

The **limbic system** is involved in processing both emotion and memory. Interestingly, the sense of smell projects directly to the limbic system; therefore, not surprisingly, smell can evoke emotional responses in ways that other sensory modalities cannot. The limbic system is made up of a number of different structures, but three of the most important are the hippocampus, the amygdala, and the hypothalamus (**Figure 3.23**). The **hippocampus** is an essential structure for learning and memory. The **amygdala** is involved in our experience of emotion and in tying emotional meaning to our memories. The **hypothalamus** regulates a number of homeostatic processes, including the regulation of body temperature, appetite, and blood pressure. The hypothalamus also serves as an interface between the nervous system and the endocrine system and in the regulation of sexual motivation and behavior.

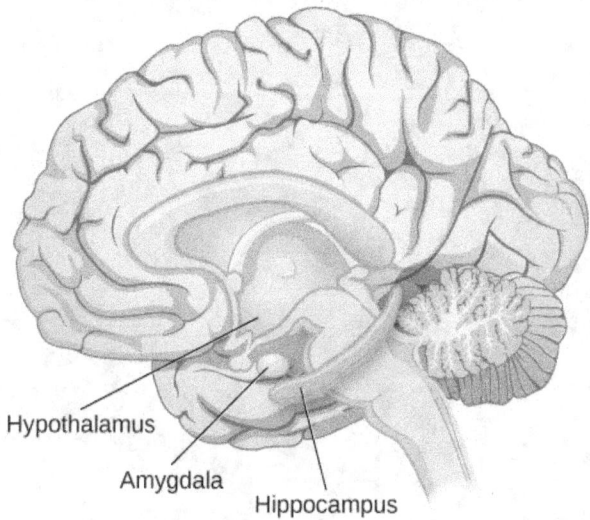

Figure 3.23 The limbic system is involved in mediating emotional response and memory.

The Case of Henry Molaison (H.M.)

In 1953, Henry Gustav Molaison (H. M.) was a 27-year-old man who experienced severe seizures. In an attempt to control his seizures, H. M. underwent brain surgery to remove his hippocampus and amygdala. Following the surgery, H.M's seizures became much less severe, but he also suffered some unexpected—and devastating—consequences of the surgery: he lost his ability to form many types of new memories. For example, he was unable to learn new facts, such as who was president of the United States. He was able to learn new skills, but afterward he had no recollection of learning them. For example, while he might learn to use a computer, he would have no conscious memory of ever having used one. He could not remember new faces, and he was unable to remember events, even immediately after they occurred. Researchers were fascinated by his experience, and he is considered one of the most studied cases in medical and psychological history (Hardt, Einarsson, & Nader, 2010; Squire, 2009). Indeed, his case has provided tremendous insight into the role that the hippocampus plays in the consolidation of new learning into explicit memory.

LINK TO LEARNING

Clive Wearing, an accomplished musician, lost the ability to form new memories when his hippocampus was damaged through illness. Check out the first few minutes of this documentary video about this man and his condition (http://openstax.org/l/wearing) to learn more.

MIDBRAIN AND HINDBRAIN STRUCTURES

The **midbrain** is comprised of structures located deep within the brain, between the forebrain and the hindbrain. The **reticular formation** is centered in the midbrain, but it actually extends up into the forebrain and down into the hindbrain. The reticular formation is important in regulating the sleep/wake cycle, arousal, alertness, and motor activity.

The **substantia nigra** (Latin for "black substance") and the **ventral tegmental area (VTA)** are also located in the midbrain (Figure 3.24). Both regions contain cell bodies that produce the neurotransmitter dopamine, and both are critical for movement. Degeneration of the substantia nigra and VTA is involved in Parkinson's disease. In addition, these structures are involved in mood, reward, and addiction (Berridge

& Robinson, 1998; Gardner, 2011; George, Le Moal, & Koob, 2012).

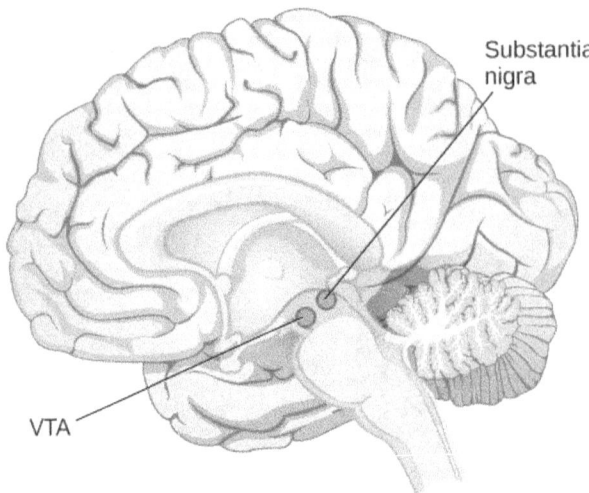

Figure 3.24 The substantia nigra and ventral tegmental area (VTA) are located in the midbrain.

The **hindbrain** is located at the back of the head and looks like an extension of the spinal cord. It contains the medulla, pons, and cerebellum (Figure 3.25). The **medulla** controls the automatic processes of the autonomic nervous system, such as breathing, blood pressure, and heart rate. The word pons literally means "bridge," and as the name suggests, the **pons** serves to connect the hindbrain to the rest of the brain. It also is involved in regulating brain activity during sleep. The medulla, pons, and various structures are known as the brainstem, and aspects of the brainstem span both the midbrain and the hindbrain.

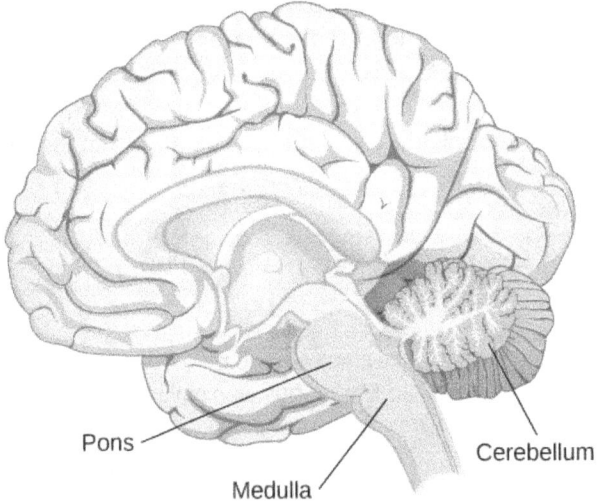

Figure 3.25 The pons, medulla, and cerebellum make up the hindbrain.

The **cerebellum** (Latin for "little brain") receives messages from muscles, tendons, joints, and structures in our ear to control balance, coordination, movement, and motor skills. The cerebellum is also thought to be an important area for processing some types of memories. In particular, procedural memory, or memory involved in learning and remembering how to perform tasks, is thought to be associated with the cerebellum. Recall that H. M. was unable to form new explicit memories, but he could learn new tasks. This is likely due to the fact that H. M.'s cerebellum remained intact.

Chapter 3 | Biopsychology

> ### WHAT DO YOU THINK?
>
> **Brain Dead and on Life Support**
>
> What would you do if your spouse or loved one was declared brain dead but his or her body was being kept alive by medical equipment? Whose decision should it be to remove a feeding tube? Should medical care costs be a factor?
>
> On February 25, 1990, a Florida woman named Terri Schiavo went into cardiac arrest, apparently triggered by a bulimic episode. She was eventually revived, but her brain had been deprived of oxygen for a long time. Brain scans indicated that there was no activity in her cerebral cortex, and she suffered from severe and permanent cerebral atrophy. Basically, Schiavo was in a vegetative state. Medical professionals determined that she would never again be able to move, talk, or respond in any way. To remain alive, she required a feeding tube, and there was no chance that her situation would ever improve.
>
> On occasion, Schiavo's eyes would move, and sometimes she would groan. Despite the doctors' insistence to the contrary, her parents believed that these were signs that she was trying to communicate with them.
>
> After 12 years, Schiavo's husband argued that his wife would not have wanted to be kept alive with no feelings, sensations, or brain activity. Her parents, however, were very much against removing her feeding tube. Eventually, the case made its way to the courts, both in the state of Florida and at the federal level. By 2005, the courts found in favor of Schiavo's husband, and the feeding tube was removed on March 18, 2005. Schiavo died 13 days later.
>
> Why did Schiavo's eyes sometimes move, and why did she groan? Although the parts of her brain that control thought, voluntary movement, and feeling were completely damaged, her brainstem was still intact. Her medulla and pons maintained her breathing and caused involuntary movements of her eyes and the occasional groans. Over the 15-year period that she was on a feeding tube, Schiavo's medical costs may have topped $7 million (Arnst, 2003).
>
> These questions were brought to popular conscience decades ago in the case of Terri Schiavo, and they have persisted. In 2013, a 13-year-old girl who suffered complications after tonsil surgery was declared brain dead. There was a battle between her family, who wanted her to remain on life support, and the hospital's policies regarding persons declared brain dead. In another complicated 2013–14 case in Texas, a pregnant EMT professional declared brain dead was kept alive for weeks, despite her spouse's directives, which were based on her wishes should this situation arise. In this case, state laws designed to protect an unborn fetus came into consideration until doctors determined the fetus unviable.
>
> Decisions surrounding the medical response to patients declared brain dead are complex. What do you think about these issues?

BRAIN IMAGING

You have learned how brain injury can provide information about the functions of different parts of the brain. Increasingly, however, we are able to obtain that information using brain imaging techniques on individuals who have not suffered brain injury. In this section, we take a more in-depth look at some of the techniques that are available for imaging the brain, including techniques that rely on radiation, magnetic fields, or electrical activity within the brain.

Techniques Involving Radiation

A **computerized tomography (CT) scan** involves taking a number of x-rays of a particular section of a person's body or brain (**Figure 3.26**). The x-rays pass through tissues of different densities at different rates, allowing a computer to construct an overall image of the area of the body being scanned. A CT scan is often used to determine whether someone has a tumor or significant brain atrophy.

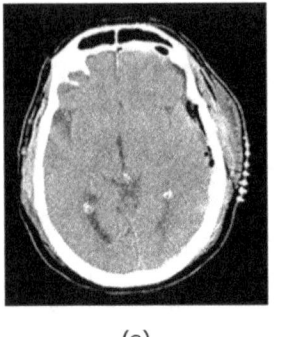
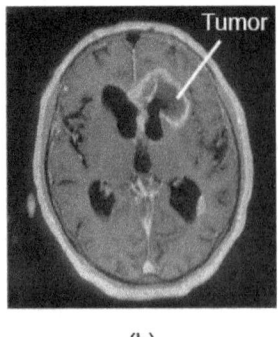

Figure 3.26 A CT scan can be used to show brain tumors. (a) The image on the left shows a healthy brain, whereas (b) the image on the right indicates a brain tumor in the left frontal lobe. (credit a: modification of work by "Aceofhearts1968"/Wikimedia Commons; credit b: modification of work by Roland Schmitt et al)

Positron emission tomography (PET) scans create pictures of the living, active brain (Figure 3.27). An individual receiving a PET scan drinks or is injected with a mildly radioactive substance, called a tracer. Once in the bloodstream, the amount of tracer in any given region of the brain can be monitored. As a brain area becomes more active, more blood flows to that area. A computer monitors the movement of the tracer and creates a rough map of active and inactive areas of the brain during a given behavior. PET scans show little detail, are unable to pinpoint events precisely in time, and require that the brain be exposed to radiation; therefore, this technique has been replaced by the fMRI as an alternative diagnostic tool. However, combined with CT, PET technology is still being used in certain contexts. For example, CT/PET scans allow better imaging of the activity of neurotransmitter receptors and open new avenues in schizophrenia research. In this hybrid CT/PET technology, CT contributes clear images of brain structures, while PET shows the brain's activity.

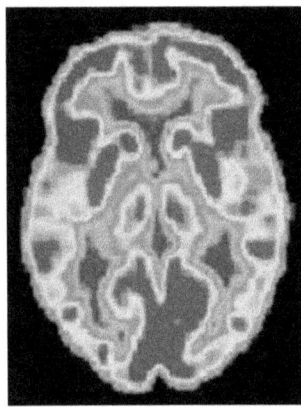

Figure 3.27 A PET scan is helpful for showing activity in different parts of the brain. (credit: Health and Human Services Department, National Institutes of Health)

Techniques Involving Magnetic Fields

In **magnetic resonance imaging (MRI)**, a person is placed inside a machine that generates a strong magnetic field. The magnetic field causes the hydrogen atoms in the body's cells to move. When the magnetic field is turned off, the hydrogen atoms emit electromagnetic signals as they return to their original positions. Tissues of different densities give off different signals, which a computer interprets and displays on a monitor. **Functional magnetic resonance imaging (fMRI)** operates on the same principles, but it shows changes in brain activity over time by tracking blood flow and oxygen levels. The fMRI provides more detailed images of the brain's structure, as well as better accuracy in time, than is possible in PET scans (Figure 3.28). With their high level of detail, MRI and fMRI are often used to compare the brains of healthy individuals to the brains of individuals diagnosed with psychological disorders. This comparison helps determine what structural and functional differences exist between these populations.

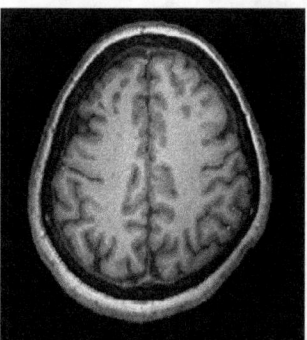

Figure 3.28 An fMRI shows activity in the brain over time. This image represents a single frame from an fMRI. (credit: modification of work by Kim J, Matthews NL, Park S.)

LINK TO LEARNING

Visit this **virtual lab about MRI and fMRI (http://openstax.org/l/mri)** to learn more.

Techniques Involving Electrical Activity

In some situations, it is helpful to gain an understanding of the overall activity of a person's brain, without needing information on the actual location of the activity. **Electroencephalography (EEG)** serves this purpose by providing a measure of a brain's electrical activity. An array of electrodes is placed around a person's head (Figure 3.29). The signals received by the electrodes result in a printout of the electrical activity of his or her brain, or brainwaves, showing both the frequency (number of waves per second) and amplitude (height) of the recorded brainwaves, with an accuracy within milliseconds. Such information is especially helpful to researchers studying sleep patterns among individuals with sleep disorders.

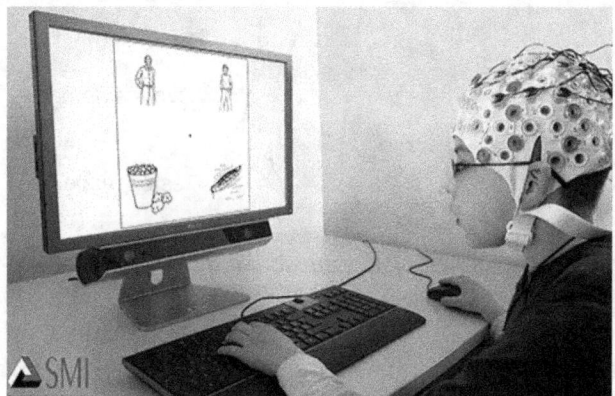

Figure 3.29 Using caps with electrodes, modern EEG research can study the precise timing of overall brain activities. (credit: SMI Eye Tracking)

3.5 The Endocrine System

Learning Objectives

By the end of this section, you will be able to:
- Identify the major glands of the endocrine system
- Identify the hormones secreted by each gland
- Describe each hormone's role in regulating bodily functions

The **endocrine system** consists of a series of glands that produce chemical substances known as **hormones** (**Figure 3.30**). Like neurotransmitters, hormones are chemical messengers that must bind to a receptor in order to send their signal. However, unlike neurotransmitters, which are released in close proximity to cells with their receptors, hormones are secreted into the bloodstream and travel throughout the body, affecting any cells that contain receptors for them. Thus, whereas neurotransmitters' effects are localized, the effects of hormones are widespread. Also, hormones are slower to take effect, and tend to be longer lasting.

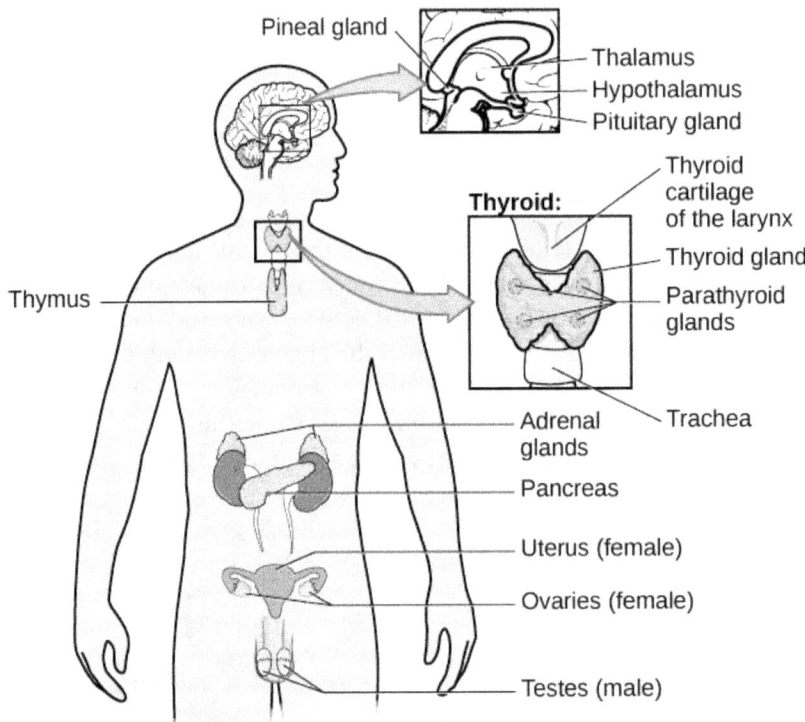

Figure 3.30 The major glands of the endocrine system are shown.

Hormones are involved in regulating all sorts of bodily functions, and they are ultimately controlled through interactions between the hypothalamus (in the central nervous system) and the pituitary gland (in the endocrine system). Imbalances in hormones are related to a number of disorders. This section explores some of the major glands that make up the endocrine system and the hormones secreted by these glands (**Table 3.2**).

MAJOR GLANDS

The **pituitary gland** descends from the hypothalamus at the base of the brain, and acts in close association with it. The pituitary is often referred to as the "master gland" because its messenger hormones control all the other glands in the endocrine system, although it mostly carries out instructions from the hypothalamus. In addition to messenger hormones, the pituitary also secretes growth hormone, endorphins for pain relief, and a number of key hormones that regulate fluid levels in the body.

Located in the neck, the **thyroid gland** releases hormones that regulate growth, metabolism, and appetite. In hyperthyroidism, or Grave's disease, the thyroid secretes too much of the hormone thyroxine, causing agitation, bulging eyes, and weight loss. In hypothyroidism, reduced hormone levels cause sufferers to experience tiredness, and they often complain of feeling cold. Fortunately, thyroid disorders are often treatable with medications that help reestablish a balance in the hormones secreted by the thyroid.

The **adrenal glands** sit atop our kidneys and secrete hormones involved in the stress response, such as epinephrine (adrenaline) and norepinephrine (noradrenaline). The **pancreas** is an internal organ that secretes hormones that regulate blood sugar levels: insulin and glucagon. These pancreatic hormones are essential for maintaining stable levels of blood sugar throughout the day by lowering blood glucose levels (insulin) or raising them (glucagon). People who suffer from **diabetes** do not produce enough insulin; therefore, they must take medications that stimulate or replace insulin production, and they must closely control the amount of sugars and carbohydrates they consume.

The **gonads** secrete sexual hormones, which are important in reproduction, and mediate both sexual motivation and behavior. The female gonads are the ovaries; the male gonads are the testes. Ovaries secrete estrogens and progesterone, and the testes secrete androgens, such as testosterone.

Major Endocrine Glands and Associated Hormone Functions

Endocrine Gland	Associated Hormones	Function
Hypothalamus	Releasing and inhibiting hormones, such as oxytocin	Regulate hormone release from pituitary gland
Pituitary	Growth hormone, releasing and inhibiting hormones (such as thyroid stimulating hormone)	Regulate growth, regulate hormone release
Thyroid	Thyroxine, triiodothyronine	Regulate metabolism and appetite
Pineal	Melatonin	Regulate some biological rhythms such as sleep cycles
Adrenal	Epinephrine, norepinephrine	Stress response, increase metabolic activities
Pancreas	Insulin, glucagon	Regulate blood sugar levels
Ovaries	Estrogen, progesterone	Mediate sexual motivation and behavior, reproduction
Testes	Androgens, such as testosterone	Mediate sexual motivation and behavior, reproduction

Table 3.2

DIG DEEPER

Athletes and Anabolic Steroids

Although it is against Federal laws and many professional athletic associations (The National Football League, for example) have banned their use, anabolic steroid drugs continue to be used by amateur and professional athletes. The drugs are believed to enhance athletic performance. Anabolic steroid drugs mimic the effects of the body's own steroid hormones, like testosterone and its derivatives. These drugs have the potential to provide a competitive edge by increasing muscle mass, strength, and endurance, although not all users may experience these results. Moreover, use of performance-enhancing drugs (PEDs) does not come without risks. Anabolic steroid use has been linked with a wide variety of potentially negative outcomes, ranging in severity from largely cosmetic (acne) to life threatening (heart attack). Furthermore, use of these substances can result in profound changes in mood and can increase aggressive behavior (National Institute on Drug Abuse, 2001).

Baseball player Alex Rodriguez (A-Rod) has been at the center of a media storm regarding his use of illegal PEDs. Rodriguez's performance on the field was unparalleled while using the drugs; his success played a large role in negotiating a contract that made him the highest paid player in professional baseball. Although Rodriguez maintains that he has not used PEDs for the several years, he received a substantial suspension in 2013 that, if upheld, will cost him more than 20 million dollars in earnings (Gaines, 2013). What are your thoughts on athletes and doping? Why or why not should the use of PEDs be banned? What advice would you give an athlete who was considering using PEDs?

Key Terms

action potential electrical signal that moves down the neuron's axon

adrenal gland sits atop our kidneys and secretes hormones involved in the stress response

agonist drug that mimics or strengthens the effects of a neurotransmitter

all-or-none phenomenon that incoming signal from another neuron is either sufficient or insufficient to reach the threshold of excitation

allele specific version of a gene

amygdala structure in the limbic system involved in our experience of emotion and tying emotional meaning to our memories

antagonist drug that blocks or impedes the normal activity of a given neurotransmitter

auditory cortex strip of cortex in the temporal lobe that is responsible for processing auditory information

autonomic nervous system controls our internal organs and glands

axon major extension of the soma

biological perspective view that psychological disorders like depression and schizophrenia are associated with imbalances in one or more neurotransmitter systems

Broca's area region in the left hemisphere that is essential for language production

central nervous system (CNS) brain and spinal cord

cerebellum hindbrain structure that controls our balance, coordination, movement, and motor skills, and it is thought to be important in processing some types of memory

cerebral cortex surface of the brain that is associated with our highest mental capabilities

chromosome long strand of genetic information

computerized tomography (CT) scan imaging technique in which a computer coordinates and integrates multiple x-rays of a given area

corpus callosum thick band of neural fibers connecting the brain's two hemispheres

dendrite branch-like extension of the soma that receives incoming signals from other neurons

deoxyribonucleic acid (DNA) helix-shaped molecule made of nucleotide base pairs

diabetes disease related to insufficient insulin production

dominant allele allele whose phenotype will be expressed in an individual that possesses that allele

electroencephalography (EEG) recording the electrical activity of the brain via electrodes on the scalp

endocrine system series of glands that produce chemical substances known as hormones

epigenetics study of gene-environment interactions, such as how the same genotype leads to different phenotypes

fight or flight response activation of the sympathetic division of the autonomic nervous system, allowing access to energy reserves and heightened sensory capacity so that we might fight off a given threat or run away to safety

forebrain largest part of the brain, containing the cerebral cortex, the thalamus, and the limbic system, among other structures

fraternal twins twins who develop from two different eggs fertilized by different sperm, so their genetic material varies the same as in non-twin siblings

frontal lobe part of the cerebral cortex involved in reasoning, motor control, emotion, and language; contains motor cortex

functional magnetic resonance imaging (fMRI) MRI that shows changes in metabolic activity over time

gene sequence of DNA that controls or partially controls physical characteristics

genetic environmental correlation view of gene-environment interaction that asserts our genes affect our environment, and our environment influences the expression of our genes

genotype genetic makeup of an individual

glial cell nervous system cell that provides physical and metabolic support to neurons, including neuronal insulation and communication, and nutrient and waste transport

gonad secretes sexual hormones, which are important for successful reproduction, and mediate both sexual motivation and behavior

gyrus (plural: gyri) bump or ridge on the cerebral cortex

hemisphere left or right half of the brain

heterozygous consisting of two different alleles

hindbrain division of the brain containing the medulla, pons, and cerebellum

hippocampus structure in the temporal lobe associated with learning and memory

homeostasis state of equilibrium—biological conditions, such as body temperature, are maintained at optimal levels

homozygous consisting of two identical alleles

hormone chemical messenger released by endocrine glands

hypothalamus forebrain structure that regulates sexual motivation and behavior and a number of homeostatic processes; serves as an interface between the nervous system and the endocrine system

identical twins twins that develop from the same sperm and egg

lateralization concept that each hemisphere of the brain is associated with specialized functions

limbic system collection of structures involved in processing emotion and memory

longitudinal fissure deep groove in the brain's cortex

magnetic resonance imaging (MRI) magnetic fields used to produce a picture of the tissue being imaged

medulla hindbrain structure that controls automated processes like breathing, blood pressure, and heart rate

membrane potential difference in charge across the neuronal membrane

midbrain division of the brain located between the forebrain and the hindbrain; contains the reticular formation

motor cortex strip of cortex involved in planning and coordinating movement

mutation sudden, permanent change in a gene

myelin sheath fatty substance that insulates axons

neuron cells in the nervous system that act as interconnected information processors, which are essential for all of the tasks of the nervous system

neuroplasticity nervous system's ability to change

neurotransmitter chemical messenger of the nervous system

Nodes of Ranvier open spaces that are found in the myelin sheath that encases the axon

occipital lobe part of the cerebral cortex associated with visual processing; contains the primary visual cortex

pancreas secretes hormones that regulate blood sugar

parasympathetic nervous system associated with routine, day-to-day operations of the body

parietal lobe part of the cerebral cortex involved in processing various sensory and perceptual information; contains the primary somatosensory cortex

peripheral nervous system (PNS) connects the brain and spinal cord to the muscles, organs and senses in the periphery of the body

phenotype individual's inheritable physical characteristics

pituitary gland secretes a number of key hormones, which regulate fluid levels in the body, and a number of messenger hormones, which direct the activity of other glands in the endocrine system

polygenic multiple genes affecting a given trait

pons hindbrain structure that connects the brain and spinal cord; involved in regulating brain activity during sleep

positron emission tomography (PET) scan involves injecting individuals with a mildly radioactive substance and monitoring changes in blood flow to different regions of the brain

prefrontal cortex area in the frontal lobe responsible for higher-level cognitive functioning

psychotropic medication drugs that treat psychiatric symptoms by restoring neurotransmitter balance

range of reaction asserts our genes set the boundaries within which we can operate, and our environment interacts with the genes to determine where in that range we will fall

receptor protein on the cell surface where neurotransmitters attach

recessive allele allele whose phenotype will be expressed only if an individual is homozygous for that allele

resting potential the state of readiness of a neuron membrane's potential between signals

reticular formation midbrain structure important in regulating the sleep/wake cycle, arousal, alertness, and motor activity

reuptake neurotransmitter is pumped back into the neuron that released it

semipermeable membrane cell membrane that allows smaller molecules or molecules without an electrical charge to pass through it, while stopping larger or highly charged molecules

soma cell body

somatic nervous system relays sensory and motor information to and from the CNS

somatosensory cortex essential for processing sensory information from across the body, such as touch, temperature, and pain

substantia nigra midbrain structure where dopamine is produced; involved in control of movement

sulcus (plural: sulci) depressions or grooves in the cerebral cortex

sympathetic nervous system involved in stress-related activities and functions

synaptic cleft small gap between two neurons where communication occurs

synaptic vesicle storage site for neurotransmitters

temporal lobe part of cerebral cortex associated with hearing, memory, emotion, and some aspects of language; contains primary auditory cortex

terminal button axon terminal containing synaptic vesicles

thalamus sensory relay for the brain

theory of evolution by natural selection states that organisms that are better suited for their environments will survive and reproduce compared to those that are poorly suited for their environments

threshold of excitation level of charge in the membrane that causes the neuron to become active

thyroid secretes hormones that regulate growth, metabolism, and appetite

ventral tegmental area (VTA) midbrain structure where dopamine is produced: associated with mood, reward, and addiction

Wernicke's area important for speech comprehension

Summary

3.1 Human Genetics
Genes are sequences of DNA that code for a particular trait. Different versions of a gene are called alleles—sometimes alleles can be classified as dominant or recessive. A dominant allele always results in the dominant phenotype. In order to exhibit a recessive phenotype, an individual must be homozygous

for the recessive allele. Genes affect both physical and psychological characteristics. Ultimately, how and when a gene is expressed, and what the outcome will be—in terms of both physical and psychological characteristics—is a function of the interaction between our genes and our environments.

3.2 Cells of the Nervous System

Glia and neurons are the two cell types that make up the nervous system. While glia generally play supporting roles, the communication between neurons is fundamental to all of the functions associated with the nervous system. Neuronal communication is made possible by the neuron's specialized structures. The soma contains the cell nucleus, and the dendrites extend from the soma in tree-like branches. The axon is another major extension of the cell body; axons are often covered by a myelin sheath, which increases the speed of transmission of neural impulses. At the end of the axon are terminal buttons that contain synaptic vesicles filled with neurotransmitters.

Neuronal communication is an electrochemical event. The dendrites contain receptors for neurotransmitters released by nearby neurons. If the signals received from other neurons are sufficiently strong, an action potential will travel down the length of the axon to the terminal buttons, resulting in the release of neurotransmitters into the synaptic cleft. Action potentials operate on the all-or-none principle and involve the movement of Na^+ and K^+ across the neuronal membrane.

Different neurotransmitters are associated with different functions. Often, psychological disorders involve imbalances in a given neurotransmitter system. Therefore, psychotropic drugs are prescribed in an attempt to bring the neurotransmitters back into balance. Drugs can act either as agonists or as antagonists for a given neurotransmitter system.

3.3 Parts of the Nervous System

The brain and spinal cord make up the central nervous system. The peripheral nervous system is comprised of the somatic and autonomic nervous systems. The somatic nervous system transmits sensory and motor signals to and from the central nervous system. The autonomic nervous system controls the function of our organs and glands, and can be divided into the sympathetic and parasympathetic divisions. Sympathetic activation prepares us for fight or flight, while parasympathetic activation is associated with normal functioning under relaxed conditions.

3.4 The Brain and Spinal Cord

The brain consists of two hemispheres, each controlling the opposite side of the body. Each hemisphere can be subdivided into different lobes: frontal, parietal, temporal, and occipital. In addition to the lobes of the cerebral cortex, the forebrain includes the thalamus (sensory relay) and limbic system (emotion and memory circuit). The midbrain contains the reticular formation, which is important for sleep and arousal, as well as the substantia nigra and ventral tegmental area. These structures are important for movement, reward, and addictive processes. The hindbrain contains the structures of the brainstem (medulla, pons, and midbrain), which control automatic functions like breathing and blood pressure. The hindbrain also contains the cerebellum, which helps coordinate movement and certain types of memories.

Individuals with brain damage have been studied extensively to provide information about the role of different areas of the brain, and recent advances in technology allow us to glean similar information by imaging brain structure and function. These techniques include CT, PET, MRI, fMRI, and EEG.

3.5 The Endocrine System

The glands of the endocrine system secrete hormones to regulate normal body functions. The hypothalamus serves as the interface between the nervous system and the endocrine system, and it controls the secretions of the pituitary. The pituitary serves as the master gland, controlling the secretions of all other glands. The thyroid secretes thyroxine, which is important for basic metabolic processes and growth; the adrenal glands secrete hormones involved in the stress response; the pancreas secretes hormones that regulate blood sugar levels; and the ovaries and testes produce sex hormones that regulate sexual motivation and behavior.

Review Questions

1. A(n) _____ is a sudden, permanent change in a sequence of DNA.
   a. allele
   b. chromosome
   c. epigenetic
   d. mutation

2. _____ refers to a person's genetic makeup, while _____ refers to a person's physical characteristics.
   a. Phenotype; genotype
   b. Genotype; phenotype
   c. DNA; gene
   d. Gene; DNA

3. _____ is the field of study that focuses on genes and their expression.
   a. Social psychology
   b. Evolutionary psychology
   c. Epigenetics
   d. Behavioral neuroscience

4. Humans have _____ pairs of chromosomes.
   a. 15
   b. 23
   c. 46
   d. 78

5. The _____ receive(s) incoming signals from other neurons.
   a. soma
   b. terminal buttons
   c. myelin sheath
   d. dendrites

6. A(n) _____ facilitates or mimics the activity of a given neurotransmitter system.
   a. axon
   b. SSRI
   c. agonist
   d. antagonist

7. Multiple sclerosis involves a breakdown of the _____.
   a. soma
   b. myelin sheath
   c. synaptic vesicles
   d. dendrites

8. An action potential involves Na^+ moving _____ the cell and K^+ moving _____ the cell.
   a. inside; outside
   b. outside; inside
   c. inside; inside
   d. outside; outside

9. Our ability to make our legs move as we walk across the room is controlled by the _____ nervous system.
   a. autonomic
   b. somatic
   c. sympathetic
   d. parasympathetic

10. If your _____ is activated, you will feel relatively at ease.
    a. somatic nervous system
    b. sympathetic nervous system
    c. parasympathetic nervous system
    d. spinal cord

11. The central nervous system is comprised of _____.
    a. sympathetic and parasympathetic nervous systems
    b. organs and glands
    c. somatic and autonomic nervous systems
    d. brain and spinal cord

12. Sympathetic activation is associated with _____.
    a. pupil dilation
    b. storage of glucose in the liver
    c. increased heart rate
    d. both A and C

13. The _____ is a sensory relay station where all sensory information, except for smell, goes before being sent to other areas of the brain for further processing.
    a. amygdala
    b. hippocampus
    c. hypothalamus
    d. thalamus

14. Damage to the _____ disrupts one's ability to comprehend language, but it leaves one's ability to produce words intact.
    a. amygdala
    b. Broca's Area
    c. Wernicke's Area
    d. occipital lobe

15. A(n) _____ uses magnetic fields to create pictures of a given tissue.
    a. EEG
    b. MRI
    c. PET scan
    d. CT scan

16. Which of the following is not a structure of the forebrain?
    a. thalamus
    b. hippocampus
    c. amygdala
    d. substantia nigra

17. The two major hormones secreted from the pancreas are:
    a. estrogen and progesterone
    b. norepinephrine and epinephrine
    c. thyroxine and oxytocin
    d. glucagon and insulin

18. The _____ secretes messenger hormones that direct the function of the rest of the endocrine glands.
    a. ovary
    b. thyroid
    c. pituitary
    d. pancreas

19. The _____ gland secretes epinephrine.
    a. adrenal
    b. thyroid
    c. pituitary
    d. master

20. The _____ secretes hormones that regulate the body's fluid levels.
    a. adrenal
    b. pituitary
    c. testes
    d. thyroid

Critical Thinking Questions

21. The theory of evolution by natural selection requires variability of a given trait. Why is variability necessary and where does it come from?

22. Cocaine has two effects on synaptic transmission: it impairs reuptake of dopamine and it causes more dopamine to be released into the synaptic cleft. Would cocaine be classified as an agonist or antagonist? Why?

23. Drugs such as lidocaine and novocaine act as Na^+ channel blockers. In other words, they prevent sodium from moving across the neuronal membrane. Why would this particular effect make these drugs such effective local anesthetics?

24. What are the implications of compromised immune function as a result of exposure to chronic stress?

25. Examine Figure 3.14, illustrating the effects of sympathetic nervous system activation. How would all of these things play into the fight or flight response?

26. Before the advent of modern imaging techniques, scientists and clinicians relied on autopsies of people who suffered brain injury with resultant change in behavior to determine how different areas of the brain were affected. What are some of the limitations associated with this kind of approach?

27. Which of the techniques discussed would be viable options for you to determine how activity in the reticular formation is related to sleep and wakefulness? Why?

28. Hormone secretion is often regulated through a negative feedback mechanism, which means that once a hormone is secreted it will cause the hypothalamus and pituitary to shut down the production of signals necessary to secrete the hormone in the first place. Most oral contraceptives are made of small doses of estrogen and/or progesterone. Why would this be an effective means of contraception?

29. Chemical messengers are used in both the nervous system and the endocrine system. What properties do these two systems share? What properties are different? Which one would be faster? Which one would result in long-lasting changes?

Personal Application Questions

30. You share half of your genetic makeup with each of your parents, but you are no doubt very different from both of them. Spend a few minutes jotting down the similarities and differences between you and your parents. How do you think your unique environment and experiences have contributed to some of the differences you see?

31. Have you or someone you know ever been prescribed a psychotropic medication? If so, what side effects were associated with the treatment?

32. Hopefully, you do not face real physical threats from potential predators on a daily basis. However, you probably have your fair share of stress. What situations are your most common sources of stress? What can you do to try to minimize the negative consequences of these particular stressors in your life?

33. You read about H. M.'s memory deficits following the bilateral removal of his hippocampus and amygdala. Have you encountered a character in a book, television program, or movie that suffered memory deficits? How was that character similar to and different from H. M.?

34. Given the negative health consequences associated with the use of anabolic steroids, what kinds of considerations might be involved in a person's decision to use them?

Chapter 4

States of Consciousness

Figure 4.1 Sleep, which we all experience, is a quiet and mysterious pause in our daily lives. Two sleeping children are depicted in this 1895 oil painting titled *Zwei schlafende Mädchen auf der Ofenbank*, which translates as "two sleeping girls on the stove," by Swiss painter Albert Anker.

Chapter Outline

4.1 What Is Consciousness?
4.2 Sleep and Why We Sleep
4.3 Stages of Sleep
4.4 Sleep Problems and Disorders
4.5 Substance Use and Abuse
4.6 Other States of Consciousness

Introduction

Our lives involve regular, dramatic changes in the degree to which we are aware of our surroundings and our internal states. While awake, we feel alert and aware of the many important things going on around us. Our experiences change dramatically while we are in deep sleep and once again when we are dreaming. Some people also experience altered states of consciousness through meditation, hypnosis, or alcohol and other drugs.

This chapter will discuss states of consciousness with a particular emphasis on sleep. The different stages of sleep will be identified, and sleep disorders will be described. The chapter will close with discussions of altered states of consciousness produced by psychoactive drugs, hypnosis, and meditation.

4.1 What Is Consciousness?

Learning Objectives

By the end of this section, you will be able to:
- Understand what is meant by consciousness
- Explain how circadian rhythms are involved in regulating the sleep-wake cycle, and how circadian cycles can be disrupted
- Discuss the concept of sleep debt

Consciousness describes our awareness of internal and external stimuli. Awareness of internal stimuli includes feeling pain, hunger, thirst, sleepiness, and being aware of our thoughts and emotions. Awareness of external stimuli includes experiences such as seeing the light from the sun, feeling the warmth of a room, and hearing the voice of a friend.

We experience different states of consciousness and different levels of awareness on a regular basis. We might even describe consciousness as a continuum that ranges from full awareness to a deep sleep. **Sleep** is a state marked by relatively low levels of physical activity and reduced sensory awareness that is distinct from periods of rest that occur during wakefulness. **Wakefulness** is characterized by high levels of sensory awareness, thought, and behavior. Beyond being awake or asleep, there are many other states of consciousness people experience. These include daydreaming, intoxication, and unconsciousness due to anesthesia. We might also experience unconscious states of being via drug-induced anesthesia for medical purposes. Often, we are not completely aware of our surroundings, even when we are fully awake. For instance, have you ever daydreamed while driving home from work or school without really thinking about the drive itself? You were capable of engaging in the all of the complex tasks involved with operating a motor vehicle even though you were not aware of doing so. Many of these processes, like much of psychological behavior, are rooted in our biology.

BIOLOGICAL RHYTHMS

Biological rhythms are internal rhythms of biological activity. A woman's menstrual cycle is an example of a biological rhythm—a recurring, cyclical pattern of bodily changes. One complete menstrual cycle takes about 28 days—a lunar month—but many biological cycles are much shorter. For example, body temperature fluctuates cyclically over a 24-hour period (**Figure 4.2**). Alertness is associated with higher body temperatures, and sleepiness with lower body temperatures.

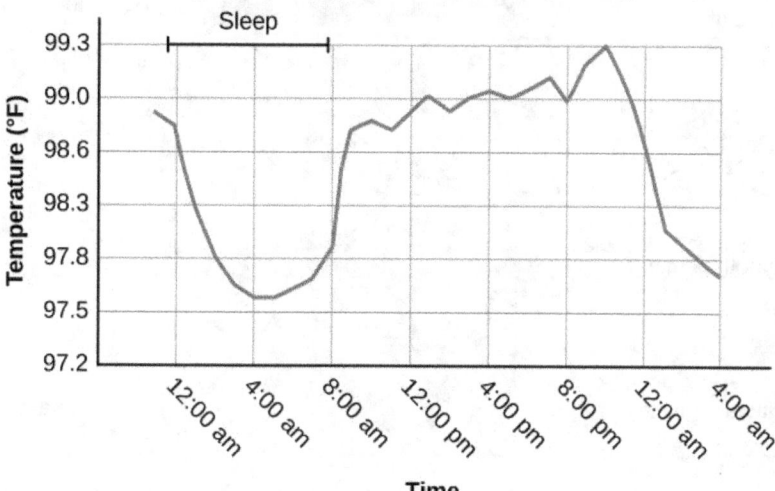

Figure 4.2 This chart illustrates the circadian change in body temperature over 28 hours in a group of eight young men. Body temperature rises throughout the waking day, peaking in the afternoon, and falls during sleep with the lowest point occurring during the very early morning hours.

This pattern of temperature fluctuation, which repeats every day, is one example of a circadian rhythm. A **circadian rhythm** is a biological rhythm that takes place over a period of about 24 hours. Our sleep-wake cycle, which is linked to our environment's natural light-dark cycle, is perhaps the most obvious example of a circadian rhythm, but we also have daily fluctuations in heart rate, blood pressure, blood sugar, and body temperature. Some circadian rhythms play a role in changes in our state of consciousness.

If we have biological rhythms, then is there some sort of biological clock? In the brain, the hypothalamus, which lies above the pituitary gland, is a main center of homeostasis. **Homeostasis** is the tendency to maintain a balance, or optimal level, within a biological system.

The brain's clock mechanism is located in an area of the hypothalamus known as the **suprachiasmatic nucleus (SCN)**. The axons of light-sensitive neurons in the retina provide information to the SCN based on the amount of light present, allowing this internal clock to be synchronized with the outside world (Klein, Moore, & Reppert, 1991; Welsh, Takahashi, & Kay, 2010) (**Figure 4.3**).

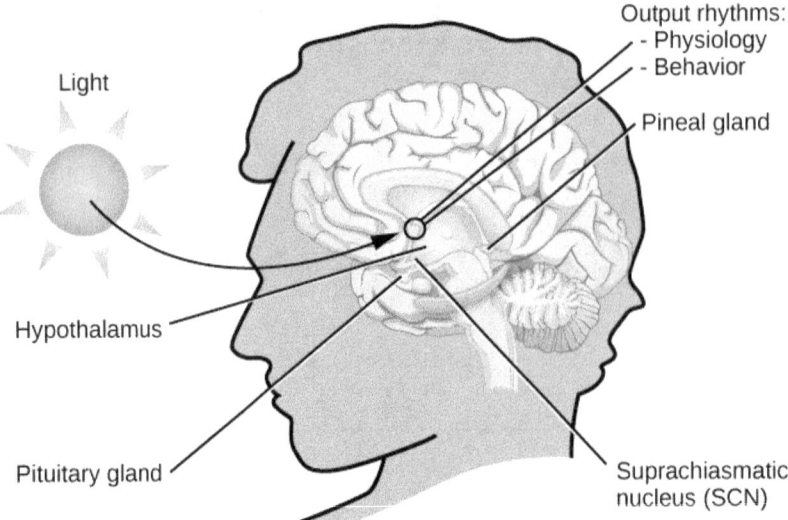

Figure 4.3 The suprachiasmatic nucleus (SCN) serves as the brain's clock mechanism. The clock sets itself with light information received through projections from the retina.

PROBLEMS WITH CIRCADIAN RHYTHMS

Generally, and for most people, our circadian cycles are aligned with the outside world. For example, most people sleep during the night and are awake during the day. One important regulator of sleep-wake cycles is the hormone **melatonin**. The **pineal gland**, an endocrine structure located inside the brain that releases melatonin, is thought to be involved in the regulation of various biological rhythms and of the immune system during sleep (Hardeland, Pandi-Perumal, & Cardinali, 2006). Melatonin release is stimulated by darkness and inhibited by light.

There are individual differences in regard to our sleep-wake cycle. For instance, some people would say they are morning people, while others would consider themselves to be night owls. These individual differences in circadian patterns of activity are known as a person's chronotype, and research demonstrates that morning larks and night owls differ with regard to sleep regulation (Taillard, Philip, Coste, Sagaspe, & Bioulac, 2003). **Sleep regulation** refers to the brain's control of switching between sleep and wakefulness as well as coordinating this cycle with the outside world.

LINK TO LEARNING

Watch this brief video about circadian rhythms and how they affect sleep (http://openstax.org/l/circadian) to learn more.

Disruptions of Normal Sleep

Whether lark, owl, or somewhere in between, there are situations in which a person's circadian clock gets out of synchrony with the external environment. One way that this happens involves traveling across multiple time zones. When we do this, we often experience jet lag. **Jet lag** is a collection of symptoms that results from the mismatch between our internal circadian cycles and our environment. These symptoms include fatigue, sluggishness, irritability, and **insomnia** (i.e., a consistent difficulty in falling or staying asleep for at least three nights a week over a month's time) (Roth, 2007).

Individuals who do rotating shift work are also likely to experience disruptions in circadian cycles.

Rotating shift work refers to a work schedule that changes from early to late on a daily or weekly basis. For example, a person may work from 7:00 a.m. to 3:00 p.m. on Monday, 3:00 a.m. to 11:00 a.m. on Tuesday, and 11:00 a.m. to 7:00 p.m. on Wednesday. In such instances, the individual's schedule changes so frequently that it becomes difficult for a normal circadian rhythm to be maintained. This often results in sleeping problems, and it can lead to signs of depression and anxiety. These kinds of schedules are common for individuals working in health care professions and service industries, and they are associated with persistent feelings of exhaustion and agitation that can make someone more prone to making mistakes on the job (Gold et al., 1992; Presser, 1995).

Rotating shift work has pervasive effects on the lives and experiences of individuals engaged in that kind of work, which is clearly illustrated in stories reported in a qualitative study that researched the experiences of middle-aged nurses who worked rotating shifts (West, Boughton & Byrnes, 2009). Several of the nurses interviewed commented that their work schedules affected their relationships with their family. One of the nurses said,

> If you've had a partner who does work regular job 9 to 5 office hours . . . the ability to spend time, good time with them when you're not feeling absolutely exhausted . . . that would be one of the problems that I've encountered. (West et al., 2009, p. 114)

While disruptions in circadian rhythms can have negative consequences, there are things we can do to help us realign our biological clocks with the external environment. Some of these approaches, such as using a bright light as shown in **Figure 4.4**, have been shown to alleviate some of the problems experienced by individuals suffering from jet lag or from the consequences of rotating shift work. Because the biological clock is driven by light, exposure to bright light during working shifts and dark exposure when not working can help combat insomnia and symptoms of anxiety and depression (Huang, Tsai, Chen, & Hsu, 2013).

Figure 4.4 Devices like this are designed to provide exposure to bright light to help people maintain a regular circadian cycle. They can be helpful for people working night shifts or for people affected by seasonal variations in light.

LINK TO LEARNING

Watch this **video about overcoming jet lag (http://openstax.org/l/jetlag)** to learn some tips.

Insufficient Sleep

When people have difficulty getting sleep due to their work or the demands of day-to-day life, they accumulate a sleep debt. A person with a **sleep debt** does not get sufficient sleep on a chronic basis. The consequences of sleep debt include decreased levels of alertness and mental efficiency. Interestingly, since the advent of electric light, the amount of sleep that people get has declined. While we certainly welcome the convenience of having the darkness lit up, we also suffer the consequences of reduced amounts of sleep because we are more active during the nighttime hours than our ancestors were. As a result, many of us sleep less than 7–8 hours a night and accrue a sleep debt. While there is tremendous variation in any given individual's sleep needs, the National Sleep Foundation (n.d.) cites research to estimate that newborns require the most sleep (between 12 and 18 hours a night) and that this amount declines to just 7–9 hours by the time we are adults.

If you lie down to take a nap and fall asleep very easily, chances are you may have sleep debt. Given that college students are notorious for suffering from significant sleep debt (Hicks, Fernandez, & Pelligrini, 2001; Hicks, Johnson, & Pelligrini, 1992; Miller, Shattuck, & Matsangas, 2010), chances are you and your classmates deal with sleep debt-related issues on a regular basis. In 2015, the National Sleep Foundation updated their sleep duration hours, to better accommodate individual differences. Table 4.1 shows the new recommendations, which describe sleep durations that are "recommended", "may be appropriate", and "not recommended".

Sleep Needs at Different Ages

Age	Recommended	May be appropriate	Not recommended
0–3 months	14–17 hours	11–13 hours 18–19 hours	Fewer than 11 hours More than 19 hours
4–11 months	12–15 hours	10–11 hours 16–18 hours	Fewer than 10 hours More than 18 hours
1–2 years	11–14 hours	9–10 hours 15–16 hours	Fewer than 9 hours More than 16 hours
3–5 years	10–13 hours	8–9 hours 14 hours	Fewer than 8 hours More than 14 hours
6–13 years	9–11 hours	7–8 hours 12 hours	Fewer than 7 hours More than 12 hours
14–17 years	8–10 hours	7 hours 11 hours	Fewer than 7 hours More than 11 hours
18–25 years	7–9 hours	6 hours 10–11 hours	Fewer than 6 hours More than 11 hours
26–64 years	7–9 hours	6 hours 10 hours	Fewer than 6 hours More than 10 hours
≥65 years	7–8 hours	5–6 hours 9 hours	Fewer than 5 hours More than 9 hours

Table 4.1

Sleep debt and sleep deprivation have significant negative psychological and physiological consequences Figure 4.5. As mentioned earlier, lack of sleep can result in decreased mental alertness and cognitive function. In addition, sleep deprivation often results in depression-like symptoms. These effects can occur as a function of accumulated sleep debt or in response to more acute periods of sleep deprivation. It may surprise you to know that sleep deprivation is associated with obesity, increased blood pressure, increased levels of stress hormones, and reduced immune functioning (Banks & Dinges, 2007). A sleep deprived individual generally will fall asleep more quickly than if she were not sleep deprived. Some sleep-deprived individuals have difficulty staying awake when they stop moving (example sitting and watching television or driving a car). That is why individuals suffering from sleep deprivation can also put themselves and others at risk when they put themselves behind the wheel of a car or work with dangerous machinery. Some research suggests that sleep deprivation affects cognitive and motor function as much as, if not more than, alcohol intoxication (Williamson & Feyer, 2000). Research shows that the most severe effects of sleep deprivation occur when a person stays awake for more than 24 hours (Killgore & Weber, 2014; Killgore et al., 2007), or following repeated nights with fewer than four hours in bed (Wickens, Hutchins, Lauk, Seebook, 2015). For example, irritability, distractibility, and impairments in cognitive and moral judgment can occur with fewer than four hours of sleep. If someone stays awake for 48 consecutive hours, they could start to hallucinate.

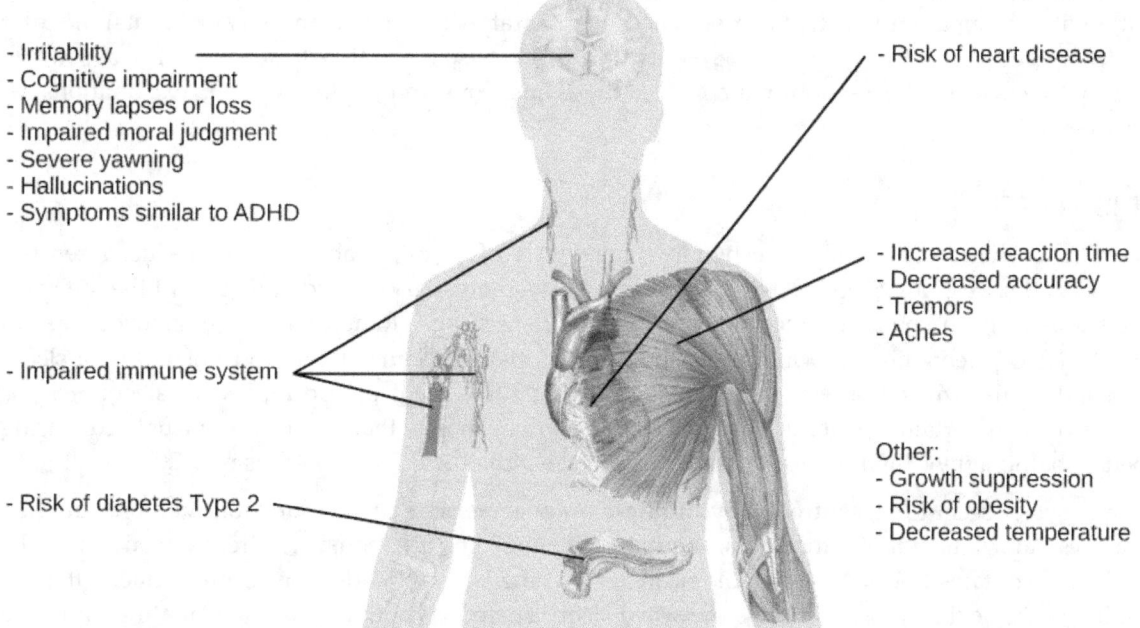

Figure 4.5 This figure illustrates some of the negative consequences of sleep deprivation. While cognitive deficits may be the most obvious, many body systems are negatively impacted by lack of sleep. (credit: modification of work by Mikael Häggström)

LINK TO LEARNING

Read this article about sleep needs (http://openstax.org/l/sleephabits) to assess your own sleeping habits.

The amount of sleep we get varies across the lifespan. When we are very young, we spend up to 16 hours a day sleeping. As we grow older, we sleep less. In fact, a **meta-analysis**, which is a study that combines the results of many related studies, conducted within the last decade indicates that by the time we are 65 years old, we average fewer than 7 hours of sleep per day (Ohayon, Carskadon, Guilleminault, & Vitiello, 2004).

4.2 Sleep and Why We Sleep

Learning Objectives

By the end of this section, you will be able to:
- Describe areas of the brain involved in sleep
- Understand hormone secretions associated with sleep
- Describe several theories aimed at explaining the function of sleep

We spend approximately one-third of our lives sleeping. Given the average life expectancy for U.S. citizens falls between 73 and 79 years old (Singh & Siahpush, 2006), we can expect to spend approximately 25 years of our lives sleeping. Some animals never sleep (e.g., some fish and amphibian species); other animals sleep very little without apparent negative consequences (e.g., giraffes); yet some animals (e.g., rats) die after two weeks of sleep deprivation (Siegel, 2008). Why do we devote so much time to sleeping? Is it absolutely essential that we sleep? This section will consider these questions and explore various explanations for why we sleep.

WHAT IS SLEEP?

You have read that sleep is distinguished by low levels of physical activity and reduced sensory awareness. As discussed by Siegel (2008), a definition of sleep must also include mention of the interplay of the circadian and homeostatic mechanisms that regulate sleep. Homeostatic regulation of sleep is evidenced by sleep rebound following sleep deprivation. **Sleep rebound** refers to the fact that a sleep-deprived individual will fall asleep more quickly during subsequent opportunities for sleep. Sleep is characterized by certain patterns of activity of the brain that can be visualized using electroencephalography (EEG), and different phases of sleep can be differentiated using EEG as well.

Sleep-wake cycles seem to be controlled by multiple brain areas acting in conjunction with one another. Some of these areas include the thalamus, the hypothalamus, and the pons. As already mentioned, the hypothalamus contains the SCN—the biological clock of the body—in addition to other nuclei that, in conjunction with the thalamus, regulate slow-wave sleep. The pons is important for regulating rapid eye movement (REM) sleep (National Institutes of Health, n.d.).

Sleep is also associated with the secretion and regulation of a number of hormones from several endocrine glands including: melatonin, follicle stimulating hormone (FSH), luteinizing hormone (LH), and growth hormone (National Institutes of Health, n.d.). You have read that the pineal gland releases melatonin during sleep (Figure 4.6). Melatonin is thought to be involved in the regulation of various biological rhythms and the immune system (Hardeland et al., 2006). During sleep, the pituitary gland secretes both FSH and LH which are important in regulating the reproductive system (Christensen et al., 2012; Sofikitis et al., 2008). The pituitary gland also secretes growth hormone, during sleep, which plays a role in physical growth and maturation as well as other metabolic processes (Bartke, Sun, & Longo, 2013).

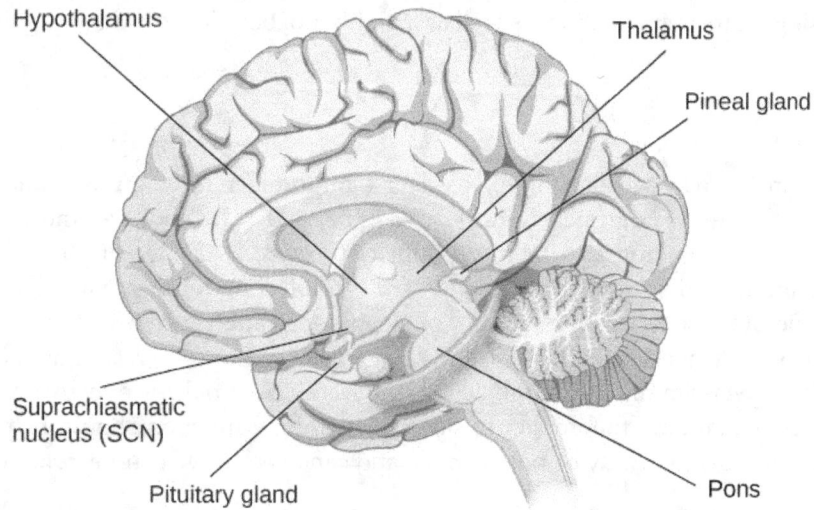

Figure 4.6 The pineal and pituitary glands secrete a number of hormones during sleep.

WHY DO WE SLEEP?

Given the central role that sleep plays in our lives and the number of adverse consequences that have been associated with sleep deprivation, one would think that we would have a clear understanding of why it is that we sleep. Unfortunately, this is not the case; however, several hypotheses have been proposed to explain the function of sleep.

Adaptive Function of Sleep

One popular hypothesis of sleep incorporates the perspective of evolutionary psychology. **Evolutionary psychology** is a discipline that studies how universal patterns of behavior and cognitive processes have evolved over time as a result of natural selection. Variations and adaptations in cognition and behavior make individuals more or less successful in reproducing and passing their genes to their offspring. One hypothesis from this perspective might argue that sleep is essential to restore resources that are expended during the day. Just as bears hibernate in the winter when resources are scarce, perhaps people sleep at night to reduce their energy expenditures. While this is an intuitive explanation of sleep, there is little research that supports this explanation. In fact, it has been suggested that there is no reason to think that energetic demands could not be addressed with periods of rest and inactivity (Frank, 2006; Rial et al., 2007), and some research has actually found a negative correlation between energetic demands and the amount of time spent sleeping (Capellini, Barton, McNamara, Preston, & Nunn, 2008).

Another evolutionary hypothesis of sleep holds that our sleep patterns evolved as an adaptive response to predatory risks, which increase in darkness. Thus we sleep in safe areas to reduce the chance of harm. Again, this is an intuitive and appealing explanation for why we sleep. Perhaps our ancestors spent extended periods of time asleep to reduce attention to themselves from potential predators. Comparative research indicates, however, that the relationship that exists between predatory risk and sleep is very complex and equivocal. Some research suggests that species that face higher predatory risks sleep fewer hours than other species (Capellini et al., 2008), while other researchers suggest there is no relationship between the amount of time a given species spends in deep sleep and its predation risk (Lesku, Roth, Amlaner, & Lima, 2006).

It is quite possible that sleep serves no single universally adaptive function, and different species have evolved different patterns of sleep in response to their unique evolutionary pressures. While we have discussed the negative outcomes associated with sleep deprivation, it should be pointed out that there are many benefits that are associated with adequate amounts of sleep. A few such benefits listed by the

National Sleep Foundation (n.d.) include maintaining healthy weight, lowering stress levels, improving mood, and increasing motor coordination, as well as a number of benefits related to cognition and memory formation.

Cognitive Function of Sleep

Another theory regarding why we sleep involves sleep's importance for cognitive function and memory formation (Rattenborg, Lesku, Martinez-Gonzalez, & Lima, 2007). Indeed, we know sleep deprivation results in disruptions in cognition and memory deficits (Brown, 2012), leading to impairments in our abilities to maintain attention, make decisions, and recall long-term memories. Moreover, these impairments become more severe as the amount of sleep deprivation increases (Alhola & Polo-Kantola, 2007). Furthermore, slow-wave sleep after learning a new task can improve resultant performance on that task (Huber, Ghilardi, Massimini, & Tononi, 2004) and seems essential for effective memory formation (Stickgold, 2005). Understanding the impact of sleep on cognitive function should help you understand that cramming all night for a test may be not effective and can even prove counterproductive.

> **LINK TO LEARNING**
>
> Watch this brief video that gives sleep tips for college students (http://openstax.org/l/sleeptips) to learn more.

Getting the optimal amount of sleep has also been associated with other cognitive benefits. Research indicates that included among these possible benefits are increased capacities for creative thinking (Cai, Mednick, Harrison, Kanady, & Mednick, 2009; Wagner, Gais, Haider, Verleger, & Born, 2004), language learning (Fenn, Nusbaum, & Margoliash, 2003; Gómez, Bootzin, & Nadel, 2006), and inferential judgments (Ellenbogen, Hu, Payne, Titone, & Walker, 2007). It is possible that even the processing of emotional information is influenced by certain aspects of sleep (Walker, 2009).

> **LINK TO LEARNING**
>
> Watch this brief video about the relationship between sleep and memory (http://openstax.org/l/sleepmemory) to learn more.

4.3 Stages of Sleep

Learning Objectives

By the end of this section, you will be able to:
- Differentiate between REM and non-REM sleep
- Describe the differences between the three stages of non-REM sleep
- Understand the role that REM and non-REM sleep play in learning and memory

Sleep is not a uniform state of being. Instead, sleep is composed of several different stages that can be differentiated from one another by the patterns of brain wave activity that occur during each stage. These changes in brain wave activity can be visualized using EEG and are distinguished from one another by both the frequency and amplitude of brain waves (Figure 4.7). Sleep can be divided into two different general phases: REM sleep and non-REM (NREM) sleep. **Rapid eye movement (REM)** sleep is characterized by darting movements of the eyes under closed eyelids. Brain waves during REM sleep appear very similar to brain waves during wakefulness. In contrast, **non-REM (NREM)** sleep is subdivided into four stages distinguished from each other and from wakefulness by characteristic patterns of brain waves. The first three stages of sleep are NREM sleep, while the fourth and final stage of sleep is REM sleep. In this section, we will discuss each of these stages of sleep and their associated patterns of brain wave activity.

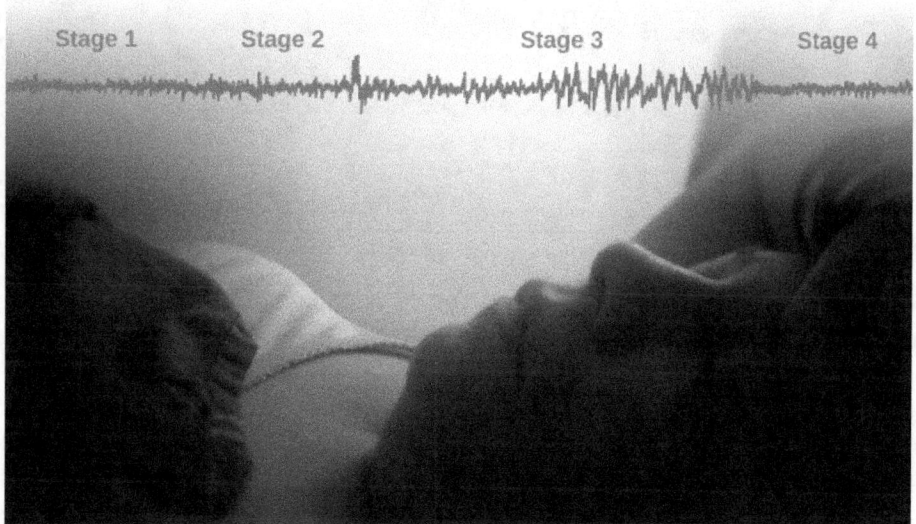

Figure 4.7 Brainwave activity changes dramatically across the different stages of sleep. (credit "sleeping": modification of work by Ryan Vaarsi)

NREM STAGES OF SLEEP

The first stage of NREM sleep is known as stage 1 sleep. **Stage 1 sleep** is a transitional phase that occurs between wakefulness and sleep, the period during which we drift off to sleep. During this time, there is a slowdown in both the rates of respiration and heartbeat. In addition, stage 1 sleep involves a marked decrease in both overall muscle tension and core body temperature.

In terms of brain wave activity, stage 1 sleep is associated with both alpha and theta waves. The early portion of stage 1 sleep produces **alpha waves**, which are relatively low frequency (8–13Hz), high amplitude patterns of electrical activity (waves) that become synchronized (Figure 4.8). This pattern of brain wave activity resembles that of someone who is very relaxed, yet awake. As an individual continues through stage 1 sleep, there is an increase in theta wave activity. **Theta waves** are even lower frequency (4–7 Hz), higher amplitude brain waves than alpha waves. It is relatively easy to wake someone from stage 1 sleep; in fact, people often report that they have not been asleep if they are awoken during stage 1 sleep.

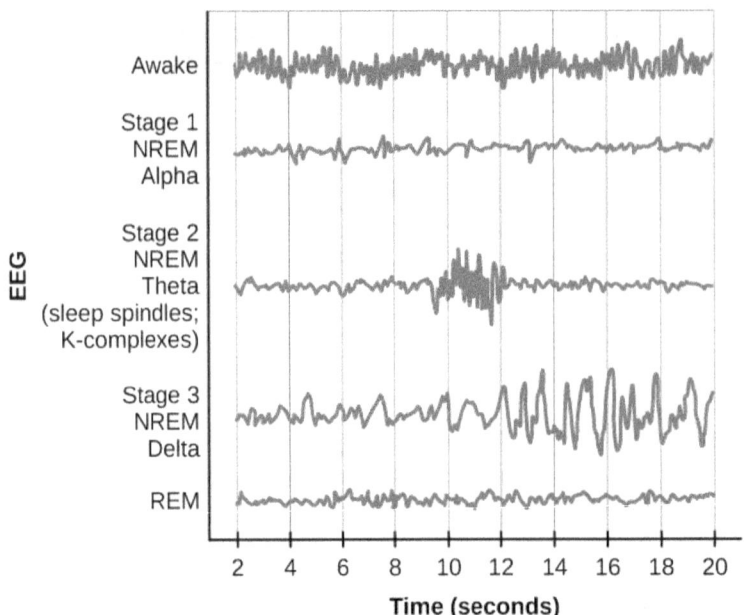

Figure 4.8 Brainwave activity changes dramatically across the different stages of sleep.

As we move into **stage 2 sleep**, the body goes into a state of deep relaxation. Theta waves still dominate the activity of the brain, but they are interrupted by brief bursts of activity known as sleep spindles (**Figure 4.9**). A **sleep spindle** is a rapid burst of higher frequency brain waves that may be important for learning and memory (Fogel & Smith, 2011; Poe, Walsh, & Bjorness, 2010). In addition, the appearance of K-complexes is often associated with stage 2 sleep. A **K-complex** is a very high amplitude pattern of brain activity that may in some cases occur in response to environmental stimuli. Thus, K-complexes might serve as a bridge to higher levels of arousal in response to what is going on in our environments (Halász, 1993; Steriade & Amzica, 1998).

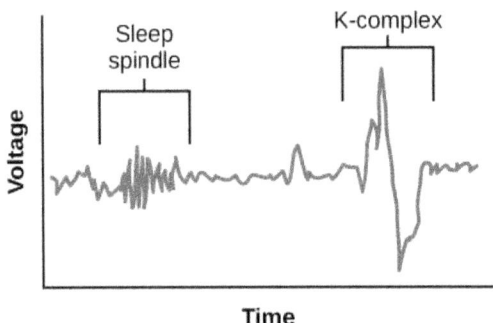

Figure 4.9 Stage 2 sleep is characterized by the appearance of both sleep spindles and K-complexes.

Stage 3 is often referred to as deep sleep or slow-wave sleep because this stage is characterized by low frequency (less than 3 Hz), high amplitude **delta waves** (**Figure 4.10**). During this time, an individual's heart rate and respiration slow dramatically. It is much more difficult to awaken someone from sleep during stage 3 than during earlier stages. Interestingly, individuals who have increased levels of alpha brain wave activity (more often associated with wakefulness and transition into stage 1 sleep) during stage 3 often report that they do not feel refreshed upon waking, regardless of how long they slept (Stone, Taylor, McCrae, Kalsekar, & Lichstein, 2008).

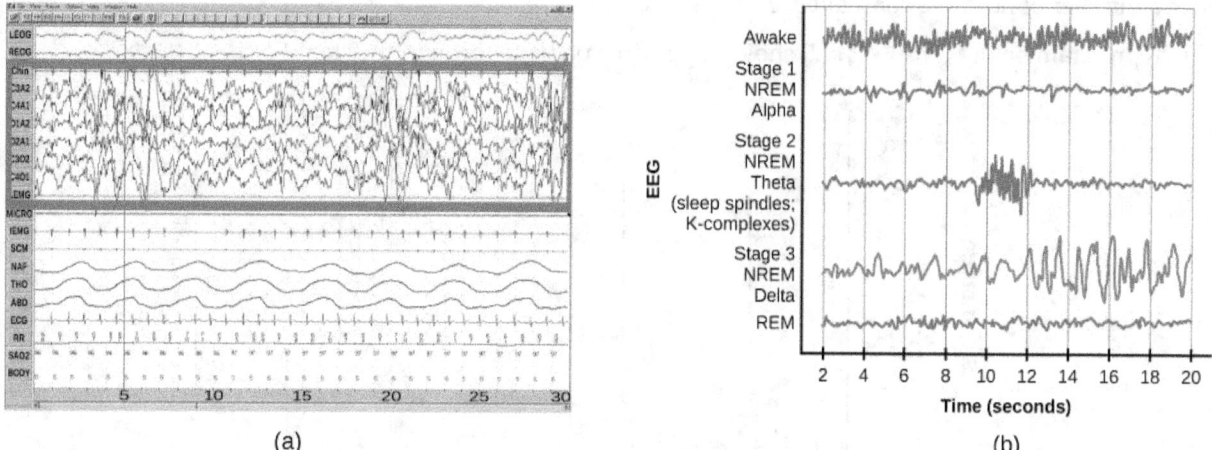

Figure 4.10 (a) Delta waves, which are low frequency and high amplitude, characterize (b) slow-wave stage 3 and stage 4 sleep.

REM SLEEP

As mentioned earlier, REM sleep is marked by rapid movements of the eyes. The brain waves associated with this stage of sleep are very similar to those observed when a person is awake, as shown in Figure 4.11, and this is the period of sleep in which dreaming occurs. It is also associated with paralysis of muscle systems in the body with the exception of those that make circulation and respiration possible. Therefore, no movement of voluntary muscles occurs during REM sleep in a normal individual; REM sleep is often referred to as paradoxical sleep because of this combination of high brain activity and lack of muscle tone. Like NREM sleep, REM has been implicated in various aspects of learning and memory (Wagner, Gais, & Born, 2001; Siegel, 2001).

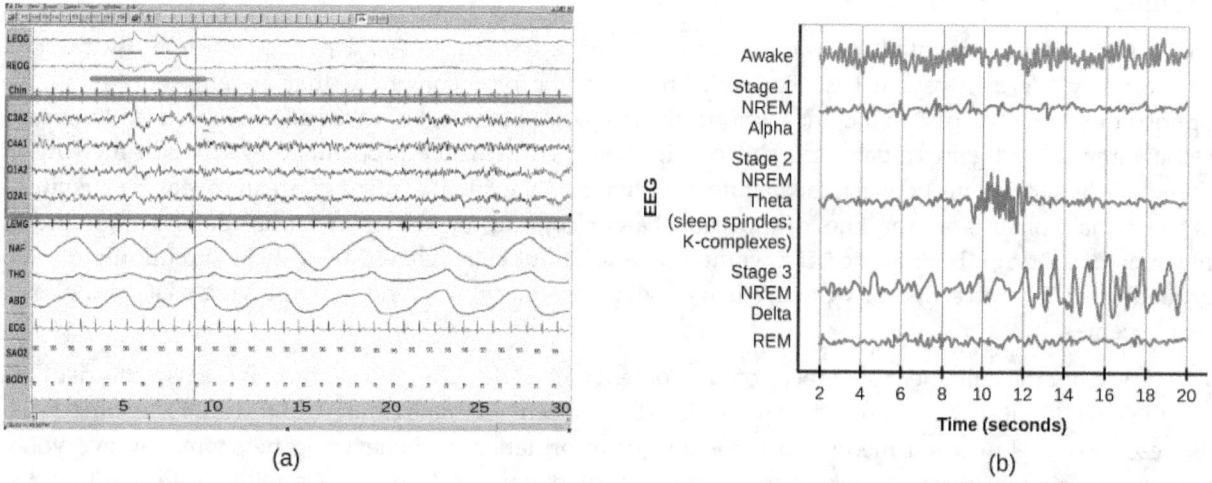

Figure 4.11 (a) A period of rapid eye movement is marked by the short red line segment. The brain waves associated with REM sleep, outlined in the red box in (a), look very similar to those seen (b) during wakefulness.

If people are deprived of REM sleep and then allowed to sleep without disturbance, they will spend more time in REM sleep in what would appear to be an effort to recoup the lost time in REM. This is known as the REM rebound, and it suggests that REM sleep is also homeostatically regulated. Aside from the role that REM sleep may play in processes related to learning and memory, REM sleep may also be involved in emotional processing and regulation. In such instances, REM rebound may actually represent an adaptive response to stress in nondepressed individuals by suppressing the emotional salience of aversive events that occurred in wakefulness (Suchecki, Tiba, & Machado, 2012). Sleep deprivation in general is associated with a number of negative consequences (Brown, 2012).

The hypnogram below (**Figure 4.12**) shows a person's passage through the stages of sleep.

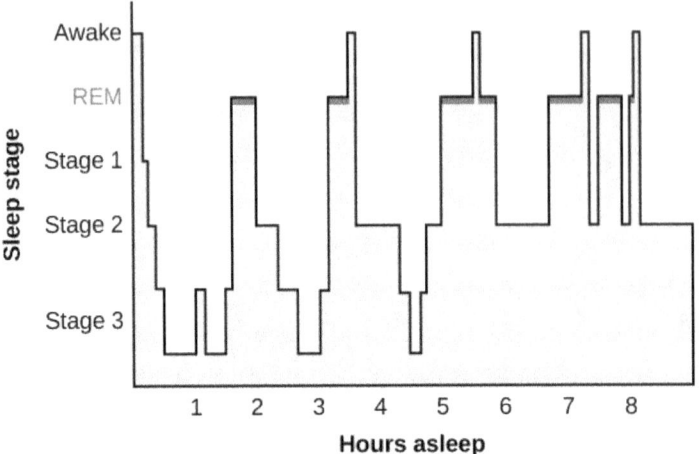

Figure 4.12 A hypnogram is a diagram of the stages of sleep as they occur during a period of sleep. This hypnogram illustrates how an individual moves through the various stages of sleep.

LINK TO LEARNING

View this **video about the various stages of sleep (http://openstax.org/l/sleepstages)** to learn more.

Dreams

Dreams and their associated meanings vary across different cultures and periods of time. By the late 19th century, German psychiatrist Sigmund Freud had become convinced that dreams represented an opportunity to gain access to the unconscious. By analyzing dreams, Freud thought people could increase self-awareness and gain valuable insight to help them deal with the problems they faced in their lives. Freud made distinctions between the manifest content and the latent content of dreams. **Manifest content** is the actual content, or storyline, of a dream. **Latent content**, on the other hand, refers to the hidden meaning of a dream. For instance, if a woman dreams about being chased by a snake, Freud might have argued that this represents the woman's fear of sexual intimacy, with the snake serving as a symbol of a man's penis.

Freud was not the only theorist to focus on the content of dreams. The 20th century Swiss psychiatrist Carl Jung believed that dreams allowed us to tap into the collective unconscious. The **collective unconscious**, as described by Jung, is a theoretical repository of information he believed to be shared by everyone. According to Jung, certain symbols in dreams reflected universal archetypes with meanings that are similar for all people regardless of culture or location.

The sleep and dreaming researcher Rosalind Cartwright, however, believes that dreams simply reflect life events that are important to the dreamer. Unlike Freud and Jung, Cartwright's ideas about dreaming have found empirical support. For example, she and her colleagues published a study in which women going through divorce were asked several times over a five month period to report the degree to which their former spouses were on their minds. These same women were awakened during REM sleep in order to provide a detailed account of their dream content. There was a significant positive correlation between the degree to which women thought about their former spouses during waking hours and the number of times their former spouses appeared as characters in their dreams (Cartwright, Agargun, Kirkby, & Friedman, 2006). Recent research (Horikawa, Tamaki, Miyawaki, & Kamitani, 2013) has uncovered new techniques by which researchers may effectively detect and classify the visual images that occur during dreaming by using fMRI for neural measurement of brain activity patterns, opening the way for additional research in this area.

Alan Hobson, a neuroscientist, is credited for developing activation-synthesis theory of dreaming. Early versions of this theory proposed that dreams were not the meaning-filled representations of angst proposed by Freud and others, but were rather the result of our brain attempting to make sense of ("synthesize") the neural activity ("activation") that was happening during REM sleep. Recent adaptations (e.g., Hobson, 2002) continue to update the theory based on accumulating evidence. For example, Hobson (2009) suggests that dreaming may represent a state of protoconsciousness. In other words, dreaming involves constructing a virtual reality in our heads that we might use to help us during wakefulness. Among a variety of neurobiological evidence, John Hobson cites research on lucid dreams as an opportunity to better understand dreaming in general. **Lucid dreams** are dreams in which certain aspects of wakefulness are maintained during a dream state. In a lucid dream, a person becomes aware of the fact that they are dreaming, and as such, they can control the dream's content (LaBerge, 1990).

4.4 Sleep Problems and Disorders

Learning Objectives

By the end of this section, you will be able to:
- Describe the symptoms and treatments of insomnia
- Recognize the symptoms of several parasomnias
- Describe the symptoms and treatments for sleep apnea
- Recognize risk factors associated with sudden infant death syndrome (SIDS) and steps to prevent it
- Describe the symptoms and treatments for narcolepsy

Many people experience disturbances in their sleep at some point in their lives. Depending on the population and sleep disorder being studied, between 30% and 50% of the population suffers from a sleep disorder at some point in their lives (Bixler, Kales, Soldatos, Kaels, & Healey, 1979; Hossain & Shapiro, 2002; Ohayon, 1997, 2002; Ohayon & Roth, 2002). This section will describe several sleep disorders as well as some of their treatment options.

INSOMNIA

Insomnia, a consistent difficulty in falling or staying asleep, is the most common of the sleep disorders. Individuals with insomnia often experience long delays between the times that they go to bed and actually fall asleep. In addition, these individuals may wake up several times during the night only to find that they have difficulty getting back to sleep. As mentioned earlier, one of the criteria for insomnia involves experiencing these symptoms for at least three nights a week for at least one month's time (Roth, 2007).

It is not uncommon for people suffering from insomnia to experience increased levels of anxiety about their inability to fall asleep. This becomes a self-perpetuating cycle because increased anxiety leads to increased arousal, and higher levels of arousal make the prospect of falling asleep even more unlikely. Chronic insomnia is almost always associated with feeling overtired and may be associated with symptoms of depression.

There may be many factors that contribute to insomnia, including age, drug use, exercise, mental status, and bedtime routines. Not surprisingly, insomnia treatment may take one of several different approaches.

People who suffer from insomnia might limit their use of stimulant drugs (such as caffeine) or increase their amount of physical exercise during the day. Some people might turn to over-the-counter (OTC) or prescribed sleep medications to help them sleep, but this should be done sparingly because many sleep medications result in dependence and alter the nature of the sleep cycle, and they can increase insomnia over time. Those who continue to have insomnia, particularly if it affects their quality of life, should seek professional treatment.

Some forms of psychotherapy, such as cognitive-behavioral therapy, can help sufferers of insomnia. **Cognitive-behavioral therapy** is a type of psychotherapy that focuses on cognitive processes and problem behaviors. The treatment of insomnia likely would include stress management techniques and changes in problematic behaviors that could contribute to insomnia (e.g., spending more waking time in bed). Cognitive-behavioral therapy has been demonstrated to be quite effective in treating insomnia (Savard, Simard, Ivers, & Morin, 2005; Williams, Roth, Vatthauer, & McCrae, 2013).

EVERYDAY CONNECTION

Solutions to Support Healthy Sleep

Has something like this ever happened to you? My sophomore college housemate got so stressed out during finals sophomore year he drank almost a whole bottle of Nyquil to try to fall asleep. When he told me, I made him go see the college therapist.

Many college students struggle getting the recommended 7–9 hours of sleep each night. However, for some, it's not because of all-night partying or late-night study sessions. It's simply that they feel so overwhelmed and stressed that they cannot fall asleep or stay asleep. One or two nights of sleep difficulty is not unusual, but if you experience anything more than that, you should seek a doctor's advice.

Here are some tips to maintain healthy sleep:

- Stick to a sleep schedule, even on the weekends. Try going to bed and waking up at the same time every day to keep your biological clock in sync so your body gets in the habit of sleeping every night.
- Avoid anything stimulating for an hour before bed. That includes exercise and bright light from devices.
- Exercise daily.
- Avoid naps.
- Keep your bedroom temperature between 60 and 67 degrees. People sleep better in cooler temperatures.
- Avoid alcohol, cigarettes, caffeine, and heavy meals before bed. It may feel like alcohol helps you sleep, but it actually disrupts REM sleep and leads to frequent awakenings. Heavy meals may make you sleepy, but they can also lead to frequent awakenings due to gastric distress.
- If you cannot fall asleep, leave your bed and do something else until you feel tired again. Train your body to associate the bed with sleeping rather than other activities like studying, eating, or watching television shows.

PARASOMNIAS

A **parasomnia** is one of a group of sleep disorders in which unwanted, disruptive motor activity and/or experiences during sleep play a role. Parasomnias can occur in either REM or NREM phases of sleep. Sleepwalking, restless leg syndrome, and night terrors are all examples of parasomnias (Mahowald & Schenck, 2000).

Sleepwalking

In **sleepwalking**, or somnambulism, the sleeper engages in relatively complex behaviors ranging from wandering about to driving an automobile. During periods of sleepwalking, sleepers often have their eyes open, but they are not responsive to attempts to communicate with them. Sleepwalking most often occurs during slow-wave sleep, but it can occur at any time during a sleep period in some affected individuals (Mahowald & Schenck, 2000).

Historically, somnambulism has been treated with a variety of pharmacotherapies ranging from benzodiazepines to antidepressants. However, the success rate of such treatments is questionable. Guilleminault et al. (2005) found that sleepwalking was not alleviated with the use of benzodiazepines. However, all of their somnambulistic patients who also suffered from sleep-related breathing problems showed a marked decrease in sleepwalking when their breathing problems were effectively treated.

DIG DEEPER

A Sleepwalking Defense?

On January 16, 1997, Scott Falater sat down to dinner with his wife and children and told them about difficulties he was experiencing on a project at work. After dinner, he prepared some materials to use in leading a church youth group the following morning, and then he attempted to repair the family's swimming pool pump before retiring to bed. The following morning, he awoke to barking dogs and unfamiliar voices from downstairs. As he went to investigate what was going on, he was met by a group of police officers who arrested him for the murder of his wife (Cartwright, 2004; CNN, 1999).

Yarmila Falater's body was found in the family's pool with 44 stab wounds. A neighbor called the police after witnessing Falater standing over his wife's body before dragging her into the pool. Upon a search of the premises, police found blood-stained clothes and a bloody knife in the trunk of Falater's car, and he had blood stains on his neck.

Remarkably, Falater insisted that he had no recollection of hurting his wife in any way. His children and his wife's parents all agreed that Falater had an excellent relationship with his wife and they couldn't think of a reason that would provide any sort of motive to murder her (Cartwright, 2004).

Scott Falater had a history of regular episodes of sleepwalking as a child, and he had even behaved violently toward his sister once when she tried to prevent him from leaving their home in his pajamas during a sleepwalking episode. He suffered from no apparent anatomical brain anomalies or psychological disorders. It appeared that Scott Falater had killed his wife in his sleep, or at least, that is the defense he used when he was tried for his wife's murder (Cartwright, 2004; CNN, 1999). In Falater's case, a jury found him guilty of first degree murder in June of 1999 (CNN, 1999); however, there are other murder cases where the sleepwalking defense has been used successfully. As scary as it sounds, many sleep researchers believe that homicidal sleepwalking is possible in individuals suffering from the types of sleep disorders described below (Broughton et al., 1994; Cartwright, 2004; Mahowald, Schenck, & Cramer Bornemann, 2005; Pressman, 2007).

REM Sleep Behavior Disorder (RBD)

REM sleep behavior disorder (RBD) occurs when the muscle paralysis associated with the REM sleep phase does not occur. Individuals who suffer from RBD have high levels of physical activity during REM sleep, especially during disturbing dreams. These behaviors vary widely, but they can include kicking, punching, scratching, yelling, and behaving like an animal that has been frightened or attacked. People who suffer from this disorder can injure themselves or their sleeping partners when engaging in these behaviors. Furthermore, these types of behaviors ultimately disrupt sleep, although affected individuals have no memories that these behaviors have occurred (Arnulf, 2012).

This disorder is associated with a number of neurodegenerative diseases such as Parkinson's disease. In fact, this relationship is so robust that some view the presence of RBD as a potential aid in the diagnosis and treatment of a number of neurodegenerative diseases (Ferini-Strambi, 2011). Clonazepam, an anti-anxiety medication with sedative properties, is most often used to treat RBD. It is administered alone or in conjunction with doses of melatonin (the hormone secreted by the pineal gland). As part of treatment, the sleeping environment is often modified to make it a safer place for those suffering from RBD (Zangini, Calandra-Buonaura, Grimaldi, & Cortelli, 2011).

Other Parasomnias

A person with **restless leg syndrome** has uncomfortable sensations in the legs during periods of inactivity or when trying to fall asleep. This discomfort is relieved by deliberately moving the legs, which, not surprisingly, contributes to difficulty in falling or staying asleep. Restless leg syndrome is quite common and has been associated with a number of other medical diagnoses, such as chronic kidney disease and diabetes (Mahowald & Schenck, 2000). There are a variety of drugs that treat restless leg syndrome: benzodiazepines, opiates, and anticonvulsants (Restless Legs Syndrome Foundation, n.d.).

Night terrors result in a sense of panic in the sufferer and are often accompanied by screams and attempts to escape from the immediate environment (Mahowald & Schenck, 2000). Although individuals suffering from night terrors appear to be awake, they generally have no memories of the events that occurred, and attempts to console them are ineffective. Typically, individuals suffering from night terrors will fall back asleep again within a short time. Night terrors apparently occur during the NREM phase of sleep (Provini, Tinuper, Bisulli, & Lagaresi, 2011). Generally, treatment for night terrors is unnecessary unless there is some underlying medical or psychological condition that is contributing to the night terrors (Mayo Clinic, n.d.).

SLEEP APNEA

Sleep apnea is defined by episodes during which a sleeper's breathing stops. These episodes can last 10–20 seconds or longer and often are associated with brief periods of arousal. While individuals suffering from sleep apnea may not be aware of these repeated disruptions in sleep, they do experience increased levels of fatigue. Many individuals diagnosed with sleep apnea first seek treatment because their sleeping partners indicate that they snore loudly and/or stop breathing for extended periods of time while sleeping (Henry & Rosenthal, 2013). Sleep apnea is much more common in overweight people and is often associated with loud snoring. Surprisingly, sleep apnea may exacerbate cardiovascular disease (Sánchez-de-la-Torre, Campos-Rodriguez, & Barbé, 2012). While sleep apnea is less common in thin people, anyone, regardless of their weight, who snores loudly or gasps for air while sleeping, should be checked for sleep apnea.

While people are often unaware of their sleep apnea, they are keenly aware of some of the adverse consequences of insufficient sleep. Consider a patient who believed that as a result of his sleep apnea he "had three car accidents in six weeks. They were ALL my fault. Two of them I didn't even know I was involved in until afterwards" (Henry & Rosenthal, 2013, p. 52). It is not uncommon for people suffering from undiagnosed or untreated sleep apnea to fear that their careers will be affected by the lack of sleep, illustrated by this statement from another patient, "I'm in a job where there's a premium on being mentally alert. I was really sleepy… and having trouble concentrating…. It was getting to the point where it was kind of scary" (Henry & Rosenthal, 2013, p. 52).

There are two types of sleep apnea: obstructive sleep apnea and central sleep apnea. **Obstructive sleep apnea** occurs when an individual's airway becomes blocked during sleep, and air is prevented from entering the lungs. In **central sleep apnea**, disruption in signals sent from the brain that regulate breathing cause periods of interrupted breathing (White, 2005).

One of the most common treatments for sleep apnea involves the use of a special device during sleep. A **continuous positive airway pressure (CPAP)** device includes a mask that fits over the sleeper's nose and mouth, which is connected to a pump that pumps air into the person's airways, forcing them to remain open, as shown in Figure 4.13. Some newer CPAP masks are smaller and cover only the nose. This treatment option has proven to be effective for people suffering from mild to severe cases of sleep apnea (McDaid et al., 2009). However, alternative treatment options are being explored because consistent compliance by users of CPAP devices is a problem. Recently, a new EPAP (expiratory positive air pressure) device has shown promise in double-blind trials as one such alternative (Berry, Kryger, & Massie, 2011).

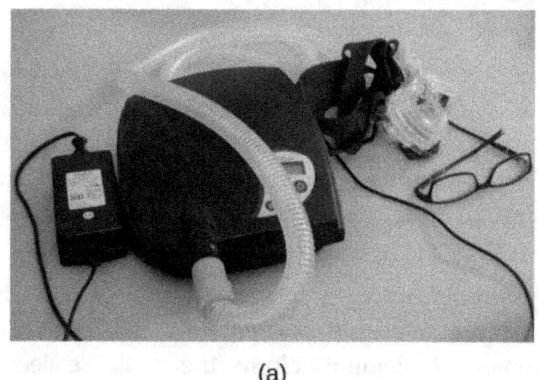
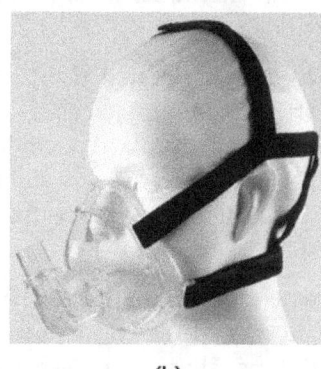

(a)   (b)

Figure 4.13   (a) A typical CPAP device used in the treatment of sleep apnea is (b) affixed to the head with straps, and a mask that covers the nose and mouth.

SIDS

In **sudden infant death syndrome (SIDS)** an infant stops breathing during sleep and dies. Infants younger than 12 months appear to be at the highest risk for SIDS, and boys have a greater risk than girls. A number of risk factors have been associated with SIDS including premature birth, smoking within the home, and hyperthermia. There may also be differences in both brain structure and function in infants that die from SIDS (Berkowitz, 2012; Mage & Donner, 2006; Thach, 2005).

The substantial amount of research on SIDS has led to a number of recommendations to parents to protect their children (Figure 4.14). For one, research suggests that infants should be placed on their backs when put down to sleep, and their cribs should not contain any items which pose suffocation threats, such as blankets, pillows or padded crib bumpers (cushions that cover the bars of a crib). Infants should not have caps placed on their heads when put down to sleep in order to prevent overheating, and people in the child's household should abstain from smoking in the home. Recommendations like these have helped to decrease the number of infant deaths from SIDS in recent years (Mitchell, 2009; Task Force on Sudden Infant Death Syndrome, 2011).

Figure 4.14   The Safe to Sleep campaign educates the public about how to minimize risk factors associated with SIDS. This campaign is sponsored in part by the National Institute of Child Health and Human Development.

NARCOLEPSY

Unlike the other sleep disorders described in this section, a person with **narcolepsy** cannot resist falling asleep at inopportune times. These sleep episodes are often associated with **cataplexy**, which is a lack of muscle tone or muscle weakness, and in some cases involves complete paralysis of the voluntary muscles. This is similar to the kind of paralysis experienced by healthy individuals during REM sleep (Burgess & Scammell, 2012; Hishikawa & Shimizu, 1995; Luppi et al., 2011). Narcoleptic episodes take on other features of REM sleep. For example, around one third of individuals diagnosed with narcolepsy experience vivid, dream-like hallucinations during narcoleptic attacks (Chokroverty, 2010).

Surprisingly, narcoleptic episodes are often triggered by states of heightened arousal or stress. The typical episode can last from a minute or two to half an hour. Once awakened from a narcoleptic attack, people report that they feel refreshed (Chokroverty, 2010). Obviously, regular narcoleptic episodes could interfere with the ability to perform one's job or complete schoolwork, and in some situations, narcolepsy can result in significant harm and injury (e.g., driving a car or operating machinery or other potentially dangerous equipment).

Generally, narcolepsy is treated using psychomotor stimulant drugs, such as amphetamines (Mignot, 2012). These drugs promote increased levels of neural activity. Narcolepsy is associated with reduced levels of the signaling molecule hypocretin in some areas of the brain (De la Herrán-Arita & Drucker-Colín, 2012; Han, 2012), and the traditional stimulant drugs do not have direct effects on this system. Therefore, it is quite likely that new medications that are developed to treat narcolepsy will be designed to target the hypocretin system.

There is a tremendous amount of variability among sufferers, both in terms of how symptoms of narcolepsy manifest and the effectiveness of currently available treatment options. This is illustrated by McCarty's (2010) case study of a 50-year-old woman who sought help for the excessive sleepiness during normal waking hours that she had experienced for several years. She indicated that she had fallen asleep at inappropriate or dangerous times, including while eating, while socializing with friends, and while driving her car. During periods of emotional arousal, the woman complained that she felt some weakness in the right side of her body. Although she did not experience any dream-like hallucinations, she was diagnosed with narcolepsy as a result of sleep testing. In her case, the fact that her cataplexy was confined to the right side of her body was quite unusual. Early attempts to treat her condition with a stimulant drug alone were unsuccessful. However, when a stimulant drug was used in conjunction with a popular antidepressant, her condition improved dramatically.

4.5 Substance Use and Abuse

Learning Objectives

By the end of this section, you will be able to:
- Describe the diagnostic criteria for substance use disorders
- Identify the neurotransmitter systems impacted by various categories of drugs
- Describe how different categories of drugs affect behavior and experience

While we all experience altered states of consciousness in the form of sleep on a regular basis, some people use drugs and other substances that result in altered states of consciousness as well. This section will present information relating to the use of various psychoactive drugs and problems associated with such use. This will be followed by brief descriptions of the effects of some of the more well-known drugs commonly used today.

SUBSTANCE USE DISORDERS

The fifth edition of the *Diagnostic and Statistical Manual of Mental Disorders, Fifth Edition* (DSM-5) is used by clinicians to diagnose individuals suffering from various psychological disorders. Drug use disorders are addictive disorders, and the criteria for specific substance (drug) use disorders are described in DSM-5. A person who has a substance use disorder often uses more of the substance than they originally intended to and continues to use that substance despite experiencing significant adverse consequences. In individuals diagnosed with a substance use disorder, there is a compulsive pattern of drug use that is often associated with both physical and psychological dependence.

Physical dependence involves changes in normal bodily functions—the user will experience withdrawal from the drug upon cessation of use. In contrast, a person who has **psychological dependence** has an emotional, rather than physical, need for the drug and may use the drug to relieve psychological distress. **Tolerance** is linked to physiological dependence, and it occurs when a person requires more and more drug to achieve effects previously experienced at lower doses. Tolerance can cause the user to increase the amount of drug used to a dangerous level—even to the point of overdose and death.

Drug **withdrawal** includes a variety of negative symptoms experienced when drug use is discontinued. These symptoms usually are opposite of the effects of the drug. For example, withdrawal from sedative drugs often produces unpleasant arousal and agitation. In addition to withdrawal, many individuals who are diagnosed with substance use disorders will also develop tolerance to these substances. Psychological dependence, or drug craving, is a recent addition to the diagnostic criteria for substance use disorder in DSM-5. This is an important factor because we can develop tolerance and experience withdrawal from any number of drugs that we do not abuse. In other words, physical dependence in and of itself is of limited utility in determining whether or not someone has a substance use disorder.

DRUG CATEGORIES

The effects of all psychoactive drugs occur through their interactions with our endogenous neurotransmitter systems. Many of these drugs, and their relationships, are shown in Table 4.2. As you have learned, drugs can act as agonists or antagonists of a given neurotransmitter system. An agonist facilitates the activity of a neurotransmitter system, and antagonists impede neurotransmitter activity.

Drugs and Their Effects

Class of Drug	Examples	Effects on the Body	Effects When Used	Psychologically Addicting?
Stimulants	Cocaine, amphetamines (including some ADHD medications such as Adderall), methamphetamines, MDMA ("Ecstasy" or "Molly")	Increased heart rate, blood pressure, body temperature	Increased alertness, mild euphoria, decreased appetite in low doses. High doses increase agitation, paranoia, can cause hallucinations. Some can cause heightened sensitivity to physical stimuli. High doses of MDMA can cause brain toxicity and death.	Yes
Sedative-Hypnotics ("Depressants")	Alcohol, barbiturates (e.g., secobarbital, pentobarbital), Benzodiazepines (e.g., Xanax)	Decreased heart rate, blood pressure	Low doses increase relaxation, decrease inhibitions. High doses can induce sleep, cause motor disturbance, memory loss, decreased respiratory function, and death.	Yes

Drugs and Their Effects

Class of Drug	Examples	Effects on the Body	Effects When Used	Psychologically Addicting?
Opiates	Opium, Heroin, Fentanyl, Morphine, Oxycodone, Vicoden, methadone, and other prescription pain relievers	Decreased pain, pupil dilation, decreased gut motility, decreased respiratory function	Pain relief, euphoria, sleepiness. High doses can cause death due to respiratory depression.	Yes
Hallucinogens	Marijuana, LSD, Peyote, mescaline, DMT, dissociative anesthetics including ketamine and PCP	Increased heart rate and blood pressure that may dissipate over time	Mild to intense perceptual changes with high variability in effects based on strain, method of ingestion, and individual differences	Yes

Table 4.2

Alcohol and Other Depressants

Ethanol, which we commonly refer to as alcohol, is in a class of psychoactive drugs known as depressants (Figure 4.15). A **depressant** is a drug that tends to suppress central nervous system activity. Other depressants include barbiturates and benzodiazepines. These drugs share in common their ability to serve as agonists of the gamma-Aminobutyric acid (GABA) neurotransmitter system. Because GABA has a quieting effect on the brain, GABA agonists also have a quieting effect; these types of drugs are often prescribed to treat both anxiety and insomnia.

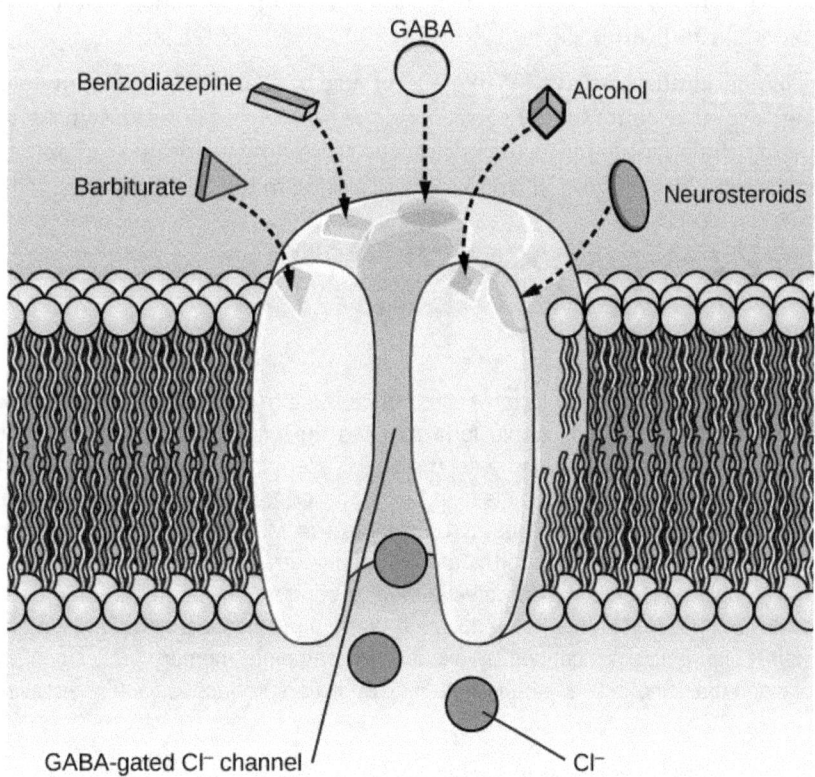

Figure 4.15 The GABA-gated chloride (Cl⁻) channel is embedded in the cell membrane of certain neurons. The channel has multiple receptor sites where alcohol, barbiturates, and benzodiazepines bind to exert their effects. The binding of these molecules opens the chloride channel, allowing negatively-charged chloride ions (Cl⁻) into the neuron's cell body. Changing its charge in a negative direction pushes the neuron *away* from firing; thus, activating a GABA neuron has a quieting effect on the brain.

Acute alcohol administration results in a variety of changes to consciousness. At rather low doses, alcohol use is associated with feelings of euphoria. As the dose increases, people report feeling sedated. Generally, alcohol is associated with decreases in reaction time and visual acuity, lowered levels of alertness, and reduction in behavioral control. With excessive alcohol use, a person might experience a complete loss of consciousness and/or difficulty remembering events that occurred during a period of intoxication (McKim & Hancock, 2013). In addition, if a pregnant woman consumes alcohol, her infant may be born with a cluster of birth defects and symptoms collectively called fetal alcohol spectrum disorder (FASD) or fetal alcohol syndrome (FAS).

With repeated use of many central nervous system depressants, such as alcohol, a person becomes physically dependent upon the substance and will exhibit signs of both tolerance and withdrawal. Psychological dependence on these drugs is also possible. Therefore, the abuse potential of central nervous system depressants is relatively high.

Drug withdrawal is usually an aversive experience, and it can be a life-threatening process in individuals who have a long history of very high doses of alcohol and/or barbiturates. This is of such concern that people who are trying to overcome addiction to these substances should only do so under medical supervision.

Stimulants

Stimulants are drugs that tend to increase overall levels of neural activity. Many of these drugs act as agonists of the dopamine neurotransmitter system. Dopamine activity is often associated with reward and craving; therefore, drugs that affect dopamine neurotransmission often have abuse liability. Drugs in this category include cocaine, amphetamines (including methamphetamine), cathinones (i.e., bath salts), MDMA (ecstasy), nicotine, and caffeine.

Cocaine can be taken in multiple ways. While many users snort cocaine, intravenous injection and inhalation (smoking) are also common. The freebase version of cocaine, known as crack, is a potent, smokable version of the drug. Like many other stimulants, cocaine agonizes the dopamine neurotransmitter system by blocking the reuptake of dopamine in the neuronal synapse.

> **DIG DEEPER**
>
> **Methamphetamine**
>
> Methamphetamine in its smokable form, often called "crystal meth" due to its resemblance to rock crystal formations, is highly addictive. The smokable form reaches the brain very quickly to produce an intense euphoria that dissipates almost as fast as it arrives, prompting users to continuing taking the drug. Users often consume the drug every few hours across days-long binges called "runs," in which the user forgoes food and sleep. In the wake of the opiate epidemic, many drug cartels in Mexico are shifting from producing heroin to producing highly potent but inexpensive forms of methamphetamine. The low cost coupled with lower risk of overdose than with opiate drugs is making crystal meth a popular choice among drug users today (NIDA, 2019). Using crystal meth poses a number of serious long-term health issues, including dental problems (often called "meth mouth"), skin abrasions caused by excessive scratching, memory loss, sleep problems, violent behavior, paranoia, and hallucinations. Methamphetamine addiction produces an intense craving that is difficult to treat.

Amphetamines have a mechanism of action quite similar to cocaine in that they block the reuptake of dopamine in addition to stimulating its release (Figure 4.16). While amphetamines are often abused, they are also commonly prescribed to children diagnosed with attention deficit hyperactivity disorder (ADHD). It may seem counterintuitive that stimulant medications are prescribed to treat a disorder that involves hyperactivity, but the therapeutic effect comes from increases in neurotransmitter activity within certain areas of the brain associated with impulse control. These brain areas include the prefrontal cortex and basal ganglia.

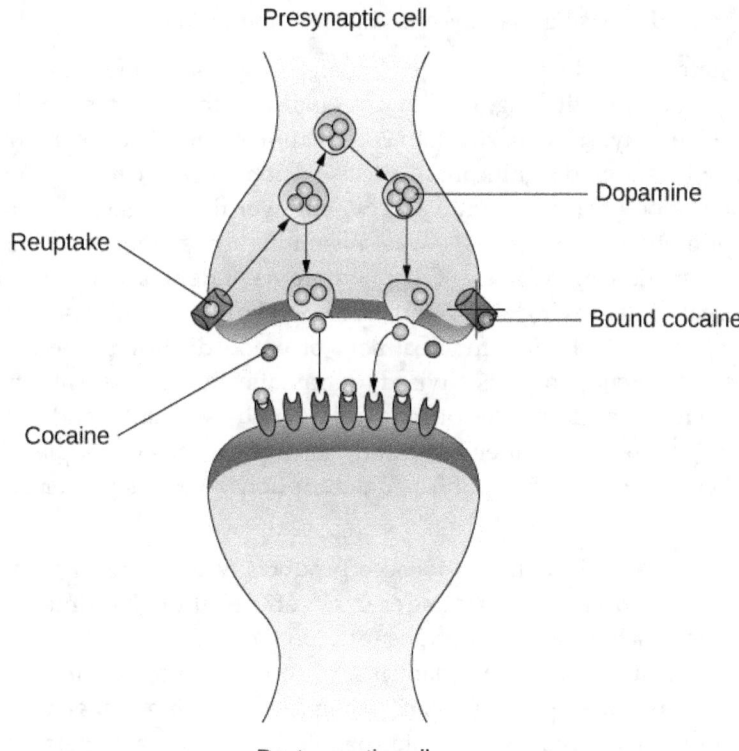

Figure 4.16 As one of their mechanisms of action, cocaine and amphetamines block the reuptake of dopamine from the synapse into the presynaptic cell.

In recent years, methamphetamine (meth) use has become increasingly widespread. **Methamphetamine** is a type of amphetamine that can be made from ingredients that are readily available (e.g., medications containing pseudoephedrine, a compound found in many over-the-counter cold and flu remedies). Despite recent changes in laws designed to make obtaining pseudoephedrine more difficult, methamphetamine continues to be an easily accessible and relatively inexpensive drug option (Shukla, Crump, & Chrisco, 2012).

Stimulant users seek a **euphoric high**, feelings of intense elation and pleasure, especially in those users who take the drug via intravenous injection or smoking. MDMA (3,4-methelynedioxy-methamphetamine, commonly known as "ecstasy" or "Molly") is a mild stimulant with perception-altering effects. It is typically consumed in pill form. Users experience increased energy, feelings of pleasure, and emotional warmth. Repeated use of these stimulants can have significant adverse consequences. Users can experience physical symptoms that include nausea, elevated blood pressure, and increased heart rate. In addition, these drugs can cause feelings of anxiety, hallucinations, and paranoia (Fiorentini et al., 2011). Normal brain functioning is altered after repeated use of these drugs. For example, repeated use can lead to overall depletion among the monoamine neurotransmitters (dopamine, norepinephrine, and serotonin). Depletion of certain neurotransmitters can lead to mood dysphoria, cognitive problems, and other factors. This can lead to people compulsively using stimulants such as cocaine and amphetamines, in part to try to reestablish the person's physical and psychological pre-use baseline. (Jayanthi & Ramamoorthy, 2005; Rothman, Blough, & Baumann, 2007).

Caffeine is another stimulant drug. While it is probably the most commonly used drug in the world, the potency of this particular drug pales in comparison to the other stimulant drugs described in this section. Generally, people use caffeine to maintain increased levels of alertness and arousal. Caffeine is found in many common medicines (such as weight loss drugs), beverages, foods, and even cosmetics (Herman & Herman, 2013). While caffeine may have some indirect effects on dopamine neurotransmission, its primary mechanism of action involves antagonizing adenosine activity (Porkka-Heiskanen, 2011). Adenosine is a neurotransmitter that promotes sleep. Caffeine is an adenosine antagonist, so caffeine inhibits the adenosine receptors, thus decreasing sleepiness and promoting wakefulness.

While caffeine is generally considered a relatively safe drug, high blood levels of caffeine can result in insomnia, agitation, muscle twitching, nausea, irregular heartbeat, and even death (Reissig, Strain, & Griffiths, 2009; Wolt, Ganetsky, & Babu, 2012). In 2012, Kromann and Nielson reported on a case study of a 40-year-old woman who suffered significant ill effects from her use of caffeine. The woman used caffeine in the past to boost her mood and to provide energy, but over the course of several years, she increased her caffeine consumption to the point that she was consuming three liters of soda each day. Although she had been taking a prescription antidepressant, her symptoms of depression continued to worsen and she began to suffer physically, displaying significant warning signs of cardiovascular disease and diabetes. Upon admission to an outpatient clinic for treatment of mood disorders, she met all of the diagnostic criteria for substance dependence and was advised to dramatically limit her caffeine intake. Once she was able to limit her use to less than 12 ounces of soda a day, both her mental and physical health gradually improved. Despite the prevalence of caffeine use and the large number of people who confess to suffering from caffeine addiction, this was the first published description of soda dependence appearing in scientific literature.

Nicotine is highly addictive, and the use of tobacco products is associated with increased risks of heart disease, stroke, and a variety of cancers. Nicotine exerts its effects through its interaction with acetylcholine receptors. Acetylcholine functions as a neurotransmitter in motor neurons. In the central nervous system, it plays a role in arousal and reward mechanisms. Nicotine is most commonly used in the form of tobacco products like cigarettes or chewing tobacco; therefore, there is a tremendous interest in developing effective smoking cessation techniques. To date, people have used a variety of nicotine replacement therapies in addition to various psychotherapeutic options in an attempt to discontinue their use of tobacco products. In general, smoking cessation programs may be effective in the short term, but it is unclear whether these effects persist (Cropley, Theadom, Pravettoni, & Webb, 2008; Levitt, Shaw, Wong, & Kaczorowski, 2007; Smedslund, Fisher, Boles, & Lichtenstein, 2004). Vaping as a means to deliver nicotine is becoming increasingly popular, especially among teens and young adults. Vaping uses battery-powered devices, sometimes called e-cigarettes, that deliver liquid nicotine and flavorings as a vapor. Originally reported as a safe alternative to the known cancer-causing agents found in cigarettes, vaping is now known to be very dangerous and has led to serious lung disease and death in users.

Opioids

An **opioid** is one of a category of drugs that includes heroin, morphine, methadone, and codeine. Opioids have analgesic properties; that is, they decrease pain. Humans have an endogenous opioid neurotransmitter system—the body makes small quantities of opioid compounds that bind to opioid receptors reducing pain and producing euphoria. Thus, opioid drugs, which mimic this endogenous painkilling mechanism, have an extremely high potential for abuse. Natural opioids, called **opiates**, are derivatives of opium, which is a naturally occurring compound found in the poppy plant. There are now several synthetic versions of opiate drugs (correctly called opioids) that have very potent painkilling effects, and they are often abused. For example, the National Institutes of Drug Abuse has sponsored research that suggests the misuse and abuse of the prescription pain killers hydrocodone and oxycodone are significant public health concerns (Maxwell, 2006). In 2013, the U.S. Food and Drug Administration recommended tighter controls on their medical use.

Historically, heroin has been a major opioid drug of abuse (Figure 4.17). Heroin can be snorted, smoked, or injected intravenously. Heroin produces intense feelings of euphoria and pleasure, which are amplified when the heroin is injected intravenously. Following the initial "rush," users experience 4–6 hours of "going on the nod," alternating between conscious and semiconscious states. Heroin users often shoot the drug directly into their veins. Some people who have injected many times into their arms will show "track marks," while other users will inject into areas between their fingers or between their toes, so as not to show obvious track marks and, like all abusers of intravenous drugs, have an increased risk for contraction of both tuberculosis and HIV.

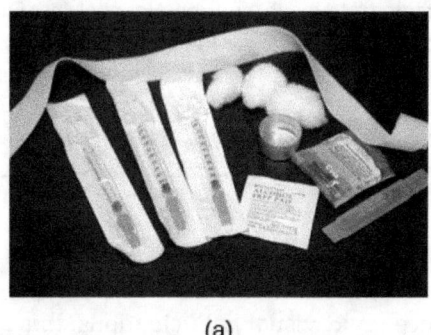 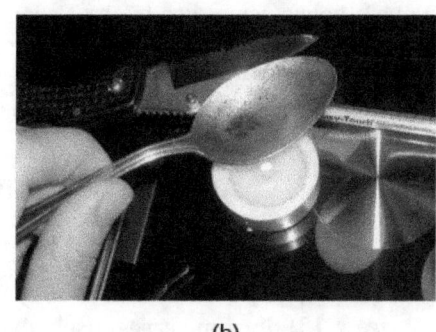

Figure 4.17 (a) Common paraphernalia for heroin preparation and use are shown here in a needle exchange kit. (b) Heroin is cooked on a spoon over a candle. (credit a: modification of work by Todd Huffman)

Aside from their utility as analgesic drugs, opioid-like compounds are often found in cough suppressants, anti-nausea, and anti-diarrhea medications. Given that withdrawal from a drug often involves an experience opposite to the effect of the drug, it should be no surprise that opioid withdrawal resembles a severe case of the flu. While opioid withdrawal can be extremely unpleasant, it is not life-threatening (Julien, 2005). Still, people experiencing opioid withdrawal may be given methadone to make withdrawal from the drug less difficult. **Methadone** is a synthetic opioid that is less euphorigenic than heroin and similar drugs. **Methadone clinics** help people who previously struggled with opioid addiction manage withdrawal symptoms through the use of methadone. Other drugs, including the opioid buprenorphine, have also been used to alleviate symptoms of opiate withdrawal.

Codeine is an opioid with relatively low potency. It is often prescribed for minor pain, and it is available over-the-counter in some other countries. Like all opioids, codeine does have abuse potential. In fact, abuse of prescription opioid medications is becoming a major concern worldwide (Aquina, Marques-Baptista, Bridgeman, & Merlin, 2009; Casati, Sedefov, & Pfeiffer-Gerschel, 2012).

EVERYDAY CONNECTION

The Opioid Crisis

Few people in the United States remain untouched by the recent opioid epidemic. It seems like everyone knows a friend, family member, or neighbor who has died of an overdose. Opioid addiction reached crisis levels in the United States such that by 2019, an average of 130 people died *each day* of an opioid overdose (NIDA, 2019).

The crisis actually began in the 1990s, when pharmaceutical companies began mass-marketing pain-relieving opioid drugs like OxyContin with the promise (now known to be false) that they were non-addictive. Increased prescriptions led to greater rates of misuse, along with greater incidence of addiction, even among patients who used these drugs as prescribed. Physiologically, the body can become addicted to opiate drugs in less than a week, including when taken as prescribed. Withdrawal from opioids includes pain, which patients often misinterpret as pain caused by the problem that led to the original prescription, and which motivates patients to continue using the drugs.

The FDA's 2013 recommendation for tighter controls on opiate prescriptions left many patients addicted to prescription drugs like OxyContin unable to obtain legitimate prescriptions. This created a black market for the drug, where prices soared to $80 or more for a single pill. To prevent withdrawal, many people turned to cheaper heroin, which could be bought for $5 a dose or less. To keep heroin affordable, many dealers began adding more potent synthetic opioids including fentanyl and carfentanyl to increase the effects of heroin. These synthetic drugs are so potent that even small doses can cause overdose and death.

Large-scale public health campaigns by the National Institutes of Health and the National Institute of Drug Abuse have led to recent declines in the opioid crisis. These initiatives include increasing access to treatment and recovery services, increasing access to overdose-reversal drugs like Naloxone, and implementing better public health monitoring systems (NIDA, 2019).

Hallucinogens

A **hallucinogen** is one of a class of drugs that results in profound alterations in sensory and perceptual experiences (Figure 4.18). In some cases, users experience vivid visual hallucinations. It is also common for these types of drugs to cause hallucinations of body sensations (e.g., feeling as if you are a giant) and a skewed perception of the passage of time.

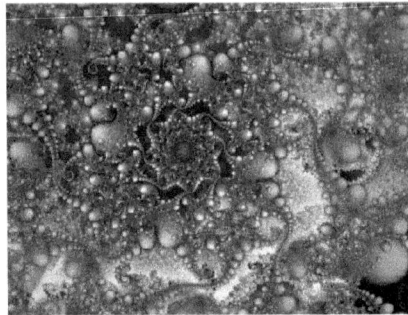

Figure 4.18 Psychedelic images like this are often associated with hallucinogenic compounds. (credit: modification of work by "new 1Illuminati"/Flickr)

As a group, hallucinogens are incredibly varied in terms of the neurotransmitter systems they affect. Mescaline and LSD are serotonin agonists, and PCP (angel dust) and ketamine (an animal anesthetic) act as antagonists of the NMDA glutamate receptor. In general, these drugs are not thought to possess the same sort of abuse potential as other classes of drugs discussed in this section.

LINK TO LEARNING

To learn more about some of the most commonly abused prescription and street drugs, check out the Commonly Abused Drugs Chart (http://openstax.org/l/drugabuse) and the Commonly Abused Prescription Drugs Chart (http://openstax.org/l/Rxabuse) from the National Institute on Drug Abuse.

DIG DEEPER

Medical Marijuana

The decade from 2010–2019 brought many changes in laws regarding marijuana. While the possession and use of marijuana remains illegal in many states, it is now legal to possess limited quantities of marijuana for recreational use in eleven states: Alaska, California, Colorado, Illinois, Maine, Massachusetts, Michigan, Nevada, Oregon, Vermont, and Washington. Medical marijuana is legal in over half of the United States and in the District of Columbia (Figure 4.19). Medical marijuana is marijuana that is prescribed by a doctor for the treatment of a health condition. For example, people who undergo chemotherapy will often be prescribed marijuana to stimulate their appetites and prevent excessive weight loss resulting from the side effects of chemotherapy treatment. Marijuana may also have some promise in the treatment of a variety of medical conditions (Mather, Rauwendaal, Moxham-Hall, & Wodak, 2013; Robson, 2014; Schicho & Storr, 2014).

Figure 4.19 Medical marijuana shops are becoming more and more common in the United States. (credit: Laurie Avocado)

While medical marijuana laws have been passed on a state-by-state basis, federal laws still classify this as an illicit substance, making conducting research on the potentially beneficial medicinal uses of marijuana problematic. There is quite a bit of controversy within the scientific community as to the extent to which marijuana might have medicinal benefits due to a lack of large-scale, controlled research (Bostwick, 2012). As a result, many scientists have urged the federal government to allow for relaxation of current marijuana laws and classifications in order to facilitate a more widespread study of the drug's effects (Aggarwal et al., 2009; Bostwick, 2012; Kogan & Mechoulam, 2007).

Until recently, the United States Department of Justice routinely arrested people involved and seized marijuana used in medicinal settings. In the latter part of 2013, however, the United States Department of Justice issued statements indicating that they would not continue to challenge state medical marijuana laws. This shift in policy may be in response to the scientific community's recommendations and/or reflect changing public opinion regarding marijuana.

4.6 Other States of Consciousness

Learning Objectives

By the end of this section, you will be able to:
- Define hypnosis and meditation
- Understand the similarities and differences of hypnosis and meditation

Our states of consciousness change as we move from wakefulness to sleep. We also alter our consciousness through the use of various psychoactive drugs. This final section will consider hypnotic and meditative states as additional examples of altered states of consciousness experienced by some individuals.

HYPNOSIS

Hypnosis is a state of extreme self-focus and attention in which minimal attention is given to external stimuli. In the therapeutic setting, a clinician may use relaxation and suggestion in an attempt to alter the thoughts and perceptions of a patient. Hypnosis has also been used to draw out information believed to be buried deeply in someone's memory. For individuals who are especially open to the power of suggestion, hypnosis can prove to be a very effective technique, and brain imaging studies have demonstrated that hypnotic states are associated with global changes in brain functioning (Del Casale et al., 2012; Guldenmund, Vanhaudenhuyse, Boly, Laureys, & Soddu, 2012).

Historically, hypnosis has been viewed with some suspicion because of its portrayal in popular media and entertainment (Figure 4.20). Therefore, it is important to make a distinction between hypnosis as an empirically based therapeutic approach versus as a form of entertainment. Contrary to popular belief, individuals undergoing hypnosis usually have clear memories of the hypnotic experience and are in control of their own behaviors. While hypnosis may be useful in enhancing memory or a skill, such enhancements are very modest in nature (Raz, 2011).

Figure 4.20 Popular portrayals of hypnosis have led to some widely-held misconceptions.

How exactly does a hypnotist bring a participant to a state of hypnosis? While there are variations, there are four parts that appear consistent in bringing people into the state of suggestibility associated with hypnosis (National Research Council, 1994). These components include:

- The participant is guided to focus on one thing, such as the hypnotist's words or a ticking watch.
- The participant is made comfortable and is directed to be relaxed and sleepy.
- The participant is told to be open to the process of hypnosis, trust the hypnotist and let go.
- The participant is encouraged to use his or her imagination.

These steps are conducive to being open to the heightened suggestibility of hypnosis.

People vary in terms of their ability to be hypnotized, but a review of available research suggests that most people are at least moderately hypnotizable (Kihlstrom, 2013). Hypnosis in conjunction with other techniques is used for a variety of therapeutic purposes and has shown to be at least somewhat effective for pain management, treatment of depression and anxiety, smoking cessation, and weight loss (Alladin, 2012; Elkins, Johnson, & Fisher, 2012; Golden, 2012; Montgomery, Schnur, & Kravits, 2012).

How does hypnosis work? Two theories attempt to answer this question: One theory views hypnosis as dissociation and the other theory views it as the performance of a social role. According to the dissociation view, hypnosis is effectively a dissociated state of consciousness, much like our earlier example where you may drive to work, but you are only minimally aware of the process of driving because your attention is focused elsewhere. This theory is supported by Ernest Hilgard's research into hypnosis and pain. In Hilgard's experiments, he induced participants into a state of hypnosis, and placed their arms into ice water. Participants were told they would not feel pain, but they could press a button if they did; while they reported not feeling pain, they did, in fact, press the button, suggesting a dissociation of consciousness while in the hypnotic state (Hilgard & Hilgard, 1994).

Taking a different approach to explain hypnosis, the social-cognitive theory of hypnosis sees people in hypnotic states as performing the social role of a hypnotized person. As you will learn when you study social roles, people's behavior can be shaped by their expectations of how they should act in a given situation. Some view a hypnotized person's behavior not as an altered or dissociated state of consciousness, but as their fulfillment of the social expectations for that role (Coe, 2009; Coe & Sarbin, 1966).

MEDITATION

Meditation is the act of focusing on a single target (such as the breath or a repeated sound) to increase awareness of the moment. While hypnosis is generally achieved through the interaction of a therapist and the person being treated, an individual can perform meditation alone. Often, however, people wishing to learn to meditate receive some training in techniques to achieve a meditative state.

Although there are a number of different techniques in use, the central feature of all meditation is clearing the mind in order to achieve a state of relaxed awareness and focus (Chen et al., 2013; Lang et al., 2012). Mindfulness meditation has recently become popular. In the variation of mindful meditation, the meditator's attention is focused on some internal process or an external object (Zeidan, Grant, Brown, McHaffie, & Coghill, 2012).

Meditative techniques have their roots in religious practices (Figure 4.21), but their use has grown in popularity among practitioners of alternative medicine. Research indicates that meditation may help reduce blood pressure, and the American Heart Association suggests that meditation might be used in conjunction with more traditional treatments as a way to manage hypertension, although there is not sufficient data for a recommendation to be made (Brook et al., 2013). Like hypnosis, meditation also shows promise in stress management, sleep quality (Caldwell, Harrison, Adams, Quin, & Greeson, 2010), treatment of mood and anxiety disorders (Chen et al., 2013; Freeman et al., 2010; Vøllestad, Nielsen, & Nielsen, 2012), and pain management (Reiner, Tibi, & Lipsitz, 2013).

(a) (b)

Figure 4.21 (a) This is a statue of a meditating Buddha, representing one of the many religious traditions of which meditation plays a part. (b) People practicing meditation may experience an alternate state of consciousness. (credit a: modification of work by Jim Epler; credit b: modification of work by Caleb Roenigk)

LINK TO LEARNING

Feeling stressed? Think meditation might help? Watch this **instructional video about using Buddhist meditation techniques to alleviate stress (http://openstax.org/l/meditate)** to learn more.

> **LINK TO LEARNING**
>
> Watch this video about the results of a brain imaging study in individuals who underwent specific mindfulness meditative techniques (http://openstax.org/l/brainimaging) to learn more.

Key Terms

alpha wave type of relatively low frequency, relatively high amplitude brain wave that becomes synchronized; characteristic of the beginning of stage 1 sleep

biological rhythm internal cycle of biological activity

cataplexy lack of muscle tone or muscle weakness, and in some cases complete paralysis of the voluntary muscles

central sleep apnea sleep disorder with periods of interrupted breathing due to a disruption in signals sent from the brain that regulate breathing

circadian rhythm biological rhythm that occurs over approximately 24 hours

codeine opiate with relatively low potency often prescribed for minor pain

cognitive-behavioral therapy psychotherapy that focuses on cognitive processes and problem behaviors that is sometimes used to treat sleep disorders such as insomnia

collective unconscious theoretical repository of information shared by all people across cultures, as described by Carl Jung

consciousness awareness of internal and external stimuli

continuous positive airway pressure (CPAP) device used to treat sleep apnea; includes a mask that fits over the sleeper's nose and mouth, which is connected to a pump that pumps air into the person's airways, forcing them to remain open

delta wave type of low frequency, high amplitude brain wave characteristic of stage 3 and stage 4 sleep

depressant drug that tends to suppress central nervous system activity

euphoric high feelings of intense elation and pleasure from drug use

evolutionary psychology discipline that studies how universal patterns of behavior and cognitive processes have evolved over time as a result of natural selection

hallucinogen one of a class of drugs that results in profound alterations in sensory and perceptual experiences, often with vivid hallucinations

homeostasis tendency to maintain a balance, or optimal level, within a biological system

hypnosis state of extreme self-focus and attention in which minimal attention is given to external stimuli

insomnia consistent difficulty in falling or staying asleep for at least three nights a week over a month's time

jet lag collection of symptoms brought on by travel from one time zone to another that results from the mismatch between our internal circadian cycles and our environment

K-complex very high amplitude pattern of brain activity associated with stage 2 sleep that may occur in response to environmental stimuli

latent content hidden meaning of a dream, per Sigmund Freud's view of the function of dreams

lucid dream people become aware that they are dreaming and can control the dream's content

manifest content storyline of events that occur during a dream, per Sigmund Freud's view of the function of dreams

meditation clearing the mind in order to achieve a state of relaxed awareness and focus

melatonin hormone secreted by the endocrine gland that serves as an important regulator of the sleep-wake cycle

meta-analysis study that combines the results of several related studies

methadone synthetic opioid that is less euphorogenic than heroin and similar drugs; used to manage withdrawal symptoms in opiate users

methadone clinic uses methadone to treat withdrawal symptoms in opiate users

methamphetamine type of amphetamine that can be made from pseudoephedrine, an over-the-counter drug; widely manufactured and abused

narcolepsy sleep disorder in which the sufferer cannot resist falling to sleep at inopportune times

night terror sleep disorder in which the sleeper experiences a sense of panic and may scream or attempt to escape from the immediate environment

non-REM (NREM) period of sleep outside periods of rapid eye movement (REM) sleep

obstructive sleep apnea sleep disorder defined by episodes when breathing stops during sleep as a result of blockage of the airway

opiate/opioid one of a category of drugs that has strong analgesic properties; opiates are produced from the resin of the opium poppy; includes heroin, morphine, methadone, and codeine

parinsomnia one of a group of sleep disorders characterized by unwanted, disruptive motor activity and/or experiences during sleep

physical dependence changes in normal bodily functions that cause a drug user to experience withdrawal symptoms upon cessation of use

pineal gland endocrine structure located inside the brain that releases melatonin

psychological dependence emotional, rather than a physical, need for a drug which may be used to relieve psychological distress

rapid eye movement (REM) sleep period of sleep characterized by brain waves very similar to those during wakefulness and by darting movements of the eyes under closed eyelids

REM sleep behavior disorder (RBD) sleep disorder in which the muscle paralysis associated with the REM sleep phase does not occur; sleepers have high levels of physical activity during REM sleep, especially during disturbing dreams

restless leg syndrome sleep disorder in which the sufferer has uncomfortable sensations in the legs when trying to fall asleep that are relieved by moving the legs

rotating shift work work schedule that changes from early to late on a daily or weekly basis

sleep state marked by relatively low levels of physical activity and reduced sensory awareness that is distinct from periods of rest that occur during wakefulness

sleep apnea sleep disorder defined by episodes during which breathing stops during sleep

sleep debt result of insufficient sleep on a chronic basis

sleep rebound sleep-deprived individuals will experience shorter sleep latencies during subsequent opportunities for sleep

sleep regulation brain's control of switching between sleep and wakefulness as well as coordinating this cycle with the outside world

sleep spindle rapid burst of high frequency brain waves during stage 2 sleep that may be important for learning and memory

sleepwalking (also, somnambulism) sleep disorder in which the sleeper engages in relatively complex behaviors

stage 1 sleep first stage of sleep; transitional phase that occurs between wakefulness and sleep; the period during which a person drifts off to sleep

stage 2 sleep second stage of sleep; the body goes into deep relaxation; characterized by the appearance of sleep spindles

stage 3 sleep third stage of sleep; deep sleep characterized by low frequency, high amplitude delta waves

stage 4 sleep fourth stage of sleep; deep sleep characterized by low frequency, high amplitude delta waves

stimulant drug that tends to increase overall levels of neural activity; includes caffeine, nicotine, amphetamines, and cocaine

sudden infant death syndrome (SIDS) infant (one year old or younger) with no apparent medical condition suddenly dies during sleep

suprachiasmatic nucleus (SCN) area of the hypothalamus in which the body's biological clock is located

theta wave type of low frequency, high amplitude brain wave characteristic of stage 1 and stage 2 sleep

tolerance state of requiring increasing quantities of the drug to gain the desired effect

wakefulness characterized by high levels of sensory awareness, thought, and behavior

withdrawal variety of negative symptoms experienced when drug use is discontinued

Summary

4.1 What Is Consciousness?
States of consciousness vary over the course of the day and throughout our lives. Important factors in these changes are the biological rhythms, and, more specifically, the circadian rhythms generated by the suprachiasmatic nucleus (SCN). Typically, our biological clocks are aligned with our external environment, and light tends to be an important cue in setting this clock. When people travel across multiple time zones or work rotating shifts, they can experience disruptions of their circadian cycles that can lead to insomnia, sleepiness, and decreased alertness. Bright light therapy has shown to be promising in dealing with circadian disruptions. If people go extended periods of time without sleep, they will accrue a sleep debt and potentially experience a number of adverse psychological and physiological consequences.

4.2 Sleep and Why We Sleep
We devote a very large portion of time to sleep, and our brains have complex systems that control various aspects of sleep. Several hormones important for physical growth and maturation are secreted during sleep. While the reason we sleep remains something of a mystery, there is some evidence to suggest that sleep is very important to learning and memory.

4.3 Stages of Sleep
The different stages of sleep are characterized by the patterns of brain waves associated with each stage. As a person transitions from being awake to falling asleep, alpha waves are replaced by theta waves. Sleep spindles and K-complexes emerge in stage 2 sleep. Stage 3 and stage 4 are described as slow-wave sleep that is marked by a predominance of delta waves. REM sleep involves rapid movements of the eyes, paralysis of voluntary muscles, and dreaming. Both NREM and REM sleep appear to play important roles in learning and memory. Dreams may represent life events that are important to the dreamer. Alternatively, dreaming may represent a state of protoconsciousness, or a virtual reality, in the mind that helps a person during consciousness.

4.4 Sleep Problems and Disorders
Many individuals suffer from some type of sleep disorder or disturbance at some point in their lives. Insomnia is a common experience in which people have difficulty falling or staying asleep. Parasomnias involve unwanted motor behavior or experiences throughout the sleep cycle and include RBD, sleepwalking, restless leg syndrome, and night terrors. Sleep apnea occurs when individuals stop breathing during their sleep, and in the case of sudden infant death syndrome, infants will stop breathing during sleep and die. Narcolepsy involves an irresistible urge to fall asleep during waking hours and is often associated with cataplexy and hallucination.

4.5 Substance Use and Abuse
Substance use disorder is defined in DSM-5 as a compulsive pattern of drug use despite negative consequences. Both physical and psychological dependence are important parts of this disorder. Alcohol, barbiturates, and benzodiazepines are central nervous system depressants that affect GABA neurotransmission. Cocaine, amphetamine, cathinones, and MDMA are all central nervous stimulants that agonize dopamine neurotransmission, while nicotine and caffeine affect acetylcholine and adenosine, respectively. Opiate drugs serve as powerful analgesics through their effects on the endogenous opioid neurotransmitter system, and hallucinogenic drugs cause pronounced changes in sensory and perceptual experiences. The hallucinogens are variable with regards to the specific neurotransmitter systems they affect.

4.6 Other States of Consciousness
Hypnosis is a focus on the self that involves suggested changes of behavior and experience. Meditation involves relaxed, yet focused, awareness. Both hypnotic and meditative states may involve altered states of consciousness that have potential application for the treatment of a variety of physical and psychological disorders.

Review Questions

1. The body's biological clock is located in the _____.
    a. hippocampus
    b. thalamus
    c. hypothalamus
    d. pituitary gland

2. _____ occurs when there is a chronic deficiency in sleep.
    a. jet lag
    b. rotating shift work
    c. circadian rhythm
    d. sleep debt

3. _____ cycles occur roughly once every 24 hours.
   a. biological
   b. circadian
   c. rotating
   d. conscious

4. _____ is one way in which people can help reset their biological clocks.
   a. Light-dark exposure
   b. coffee consumption
   c. alcohol consumption
   d. napping

5. Growth hormone is secreted by the _____ while we sleep.
   a. pineal gland
   b. thyroid
   c. pituitary gland
   d. pancreas

6. The _____ plays a role in controlling slow-wave sleep.
   a. hypothalamus
   b. thalamus
   c. pons
   d. both a and b

7. _____ is a hormone secreted by the pineal gland that plays a role in regulating biological rhythms and immune function.
   a. growth hormone
   b. melatonin
   c. LH
   d. FSH

8. _____ appears to be especially important for enhanced performance on recently learned tasks.
   a. melatonin
   b. slow-wave sleep
   c. sleep deprivation
   d. growth hormone

9. _____ is(are) described as slow-wave sleep.
   a. stage 1
   b. stage 2
   c. stage 3 and stage 4
   d. REM sleep

10. Sleep spindles and K-complexes are most often associated with _____ sleep.
    a. stage 1
    b. stage 2
    c. stage 3 and stage 4
    d. REM

11. Symptoms of _____ may be improved by REM deprivation.
    a. schizophrenia
    b. Parkinson's disease
    c. depression
    d. generalized anxiety disorder

12. The _____ content of a dream refers to the true meaning of the dream.
    a. latent
    b. manifest
    c. collective unconscious
    d. important

13. _____ is loss of muscle tone or control that is often associated with narcolepsy.
    a. RBD
    b. CPAP
    c. cataplexy
    d. insomnia

14. An individual may suffer from _____ if there is a disruption in the brain signals that are sent to the muscles that regulate breathing.
    a. central sleep apnea
    b. obstructive sleep apnea
    c. narcolepsy
    d. SIDS

15. The most common treatment for _____ involves the use of amphetamine-like medications.
    a. sleep apnea
    b. RBD
    c. SIDS
    d. narcolepsy

16. _____ is another word for sleepwalking.
    a. insomnia
    b. somnambulism
    c. cataplexy
    d. narcolepsy

17. _____ occurs when a drug user requires more and more of a given drug in order to experience the same effects of the drug.
    a. withdrawal
    b. psychological dependence
    c. tolerance
    d. reuptake

18. Cocaine blocks the reuptake of _____.
    a. GABA
    b. glutamate
    c. acetylcholine
    d. dopamine

19. _____ refers to drug craving.
    a. psychological dependence
    b. antagonism
    c. agonism
    d. physical dependence

20. LSD affects _____ neurotransmission.
    a. dopamine
    b. serotonin
    c. acetylcholine
    d. norepinephrine

21. _____ is most effective in individuals that are very open to the power of suggestion.
    a. hypnosis
    b. meditation
    c. mindful awareness
    d. cognitive therapy

22. _____ has its roots in religious practice.
    a. hypnosis
    b. meditation
    c. cognitive therapy
    d. behavioral therapy

23. Meditation may be helpful in _____.
    a. pain management
    b. stress control
    c. treating the flu
    d. both a and b

24. Research suggests that cognitive processes, such as learning, may be affected by _____.
    a. hypnosis
    b. meditation
    c. mindful awareness
    d. progressive relaxation

Critical Thinking Questions

25. Healthcare professionals often work rotating shifts. Why is this problematic? What can be done to deal with potential problems?

26. Generally, humans are considered diurnal which means we are awake during the day and asleep during the night. Many rodents, on the other hand, are nocturnal. Why do you think different animals have such different sleep-wake cycles?

27. If theories that assert sleep is necessary for restoration and recovery from daily energetic demands are correct, what do you predict about the relationship that would exist between individuals' total sleep duration and their level of activity?

28. How could researchers determine if given areas of the brain are involved in the regulation of sleep?

29. Differentiate the evolutionary theories of sleep and make a case for the one with the most compelling evidence.

30. Freud believed that dreams provide important insight into the unconscious mind. He maintained that a dream's manifest content could provide clues into an individual's unconscious. What potential criticisms exist for this particular perspective?

31. Some people claim that sleepwalking and talking in your sleep involve individuals acting out their dreams. Why is this particular explanation unlikely?

32. One of the recommendations that therapists will make to people who suffer from insomnia is to spend less waking time in bed. Why do you think spending waking time in bed might interfere with the ability to fall asleep later?

33. How is narcolepsy with cataplexy similar to and different from REM sleep?

34. The negative health consequences of both alcohol and tobacco products are well-documented. A drug like marijuana, on the other hand, is generally considered to be as safe, if not safer than these legal drugs. Why do you think marijuana use continues to be illegal in many parts of the United States?

35. Why are programs designed to educate people about the dangers of using tobacco products just as important as developing tobacco cessation programs?

36. What advantages exist for researching the potential health benefits of hypnosis?

37. What types of studies would be most convincing regarding the effectiveness of meditation in the treatment for some type of physical or mental disorder?

Personal Application Questions

38. We experience shifts in our circadian clocks in the fall and spring of each year with time changes associated with daylight saving time. Is springing ahead or falling back easier for you to adjust to, and why do you think that is?

39. What do you do to adjust to the differences in your daily schedule throughout the week? Are you running a sleep debt when daylight saving time begins or ends?

40. Have you (or someone you know) ever experienced significant periods of sleep deprivation because of simple insomnia, high levels of stress, or as a side effect from a medication? What were the consequences of missing out on sleep?

41. Researchers believe that one important function of sleep is to facilitate learning and memory. How does knowing this help you in your college studies? What changes could you make to your study and sleep habits to maximize your mastery of the material covered in class?

42. What factors might contribute to your own experiences with insomnia?

43. Many people experiment with some sort of psychoactive substance at some point in their lives. Why do you think people are motivated to use substances that alter consciousness?

44. Under what circumstances would you be willing to consider hypnosis and/or meditation as a treatment option? What kind of information would you need before you made a decision to use these techniques?

Chapter 5

Sensation and Perception

Figure 5.1 If you were standing in the midst of this street scene, you would be absorbing and processing numerous pieces of sensory input. (credit: modification of work by Cory Zanker)

Chapter Outline

5.1 Sensation versus Perception
5.2 Waves and Wavelengths
5.3 Vision
5.4 Hearing
5.5 The Other Senses
5.6 Gestalt Principles of Perception

Introduction

Imagine standing on a city street corner. You might be struck by movement everywhere as cars and people go about their business, by the sound of a street musician's melody or a horn honking in the distance, by the smell of exhaust fumes or of food being sold by a nearby vendor, and by the sensation of hard pavement under your feet.

We rely on our sensory systems to provide important information about our surroundings. We use this information to successfully navigate and interact with our environment so that we can find nourishment, seek shelter, maintain social relationships, and avoid potentially dangerous situations.

This chapter will provide an overview of how sensory information is received and processed by the nervous system and how that affects our conscious experience of the world. We begin by learning the distinction between sensation and perception. Then we consider the physical properties of light and sound stimuli, along with an overview of the basic structure and function of the major sensory systems. The chapter will close with a discussion of a historically important theory of perception called Gestalt.

5.1 Sensation versus Perception

Learning Objectives

By the end of this section, you will be able to:
- Distinguish between sensation and perception
- Describe the concepts of absolute threshold and difference threshold
- Discuss the roles attention, motivation, and sensory adaptation play in perception

SENSATION

What does it mean to sense something? Sensory receptors are specialized neurons that respond to specific types of stimuli. When sensory information is detected by a sensory receptor, **sensation** has occurred. For example, light that enters the eye causes chemical changes in cells that line the back of the eye. These cells relay messages, in the form of action potentials (as you learned when studying biopsychology), to the central nervous system. The conversion from sensory stimulus energy to action potential is known as **transduction**.

You have probably known since elementary school that we have five senses: vision, hearing (audition), smell (olfaction), taste (gustation), and touch (somatosensation). It turns out that this notion of five senses is oversimplified. We also have sensory systems that provide information about balance (the vestibular sense), body position and movement (proprioception and kinesthesia), pain (nociception), and temperature (thermoception).

The sensitivity of a given sensory system to the relevant stimuli can be expressed as an absolute threshold. **Absolute threshold** refers to the minimum amount of stimulus energy that must be present for the stimulus to be detected 50% of the time. Another way to think about this is by asking how dim can a light be or how soft can a sound be and still be detected half of the time. The sensitivity of our sensory receptors can be quite amazing. It has been estimated that on a clear night, the most sensitive sensory cells in the back of the eye can detect a candle flame 30 miles away (Okawa & Sampath, 2007). Under quiet conditions, the hair cells (the receptor cells of the inner ear) can detect the tick of a clock 20 feet away (Galanter, 1962).

It is also possible for us to get messages that are presented below the threshold for conscious awareness—these are called **subliminal messages**. A stimulus reaches a physiological threshold when it is strong enough to excite sensory receptors and send nerve impulses to the brain: This is an absolute threshold. A message below that threshold is said to be subliminal: We receive it, but we are not consciously aware of it. Over the years there has been a great deal of speculation about the use of subliminal messages in advertising, rock music, and self-help audio programs. Research evidence shows that in laboratory settings, people can process and respond to information outside of awareness. But this does not mean that we obey these messages like zombies; in fact, hidden messages have little effect on behavior outside the laboratory (Kunst-Wilson & Zajonc, 1980; Rensink, 2004; Nelson, 2008; Radel, Sarrazin, Legrain, & Gobancé, 2009; Loersch, Durso, & Petty, 2013).

Absolute thresholds are generally measured under incredibly controlled conditions in situations that are optimal for sensitivity. Sometimes, we are more interested in how much difference in stimuli is required to detect a difference between them. This is known as the **just noticeable difference (jnd)** or **difference threshold**. Unlike the absolute threshold, the difference threshold changes depending on the stimulus intensity. As an example, imagine yourself in a very dark movie theater. If an audience member were to receive a text message that caused the cell phone screen to light up, chances are that many people would notice the change in illumination in the theater. However, if the same thing happened in a brightly lit arena during a basketball game, very few people would notice. The cell phone brightness does not change, but its ability to be detected as a change in illumination varies dramatically between the two contexts. Ernst Weber proposed this theory of change in difference threshold in the 1830s, and it has become known as Weber's law: The difference threshold is a constant fraction of the original stimulus, as the example illustrates.

PERCEPTION

While our sensory receptors are constantly collecting information from the environment, it is ultimately how we interpret that information that affects how we interact with the world. **Perception** refers to the way sensory information is organized, interpreted, and consciously experienced. Perception involves both bottom-up and top-down processing. **Bottom-up processing** refers to sensory information from a stimulus in the environment driving a process, and **top-down processing** refers to knowledge and expectancy driving a process, as shown in **Figure 5.2** (Egeth & Yantis, 1997; Fine & Minnery, 2009; Yantis & Egeth, 1999).

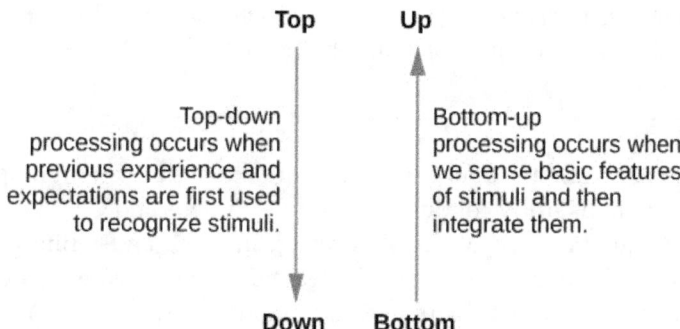

Figure 5.2 Top-down and bottom-up are ways we process our perceptions.

Imagine that you and some friends are sitting in a crowded restaurant eating lunch and talking. It is very noisy, and you are concentrating on your friend's face to hear what she is saying, then the sound of breaking glass and clang of metal pans hitting the floor rings out. The server dropped a large tray of food. Although you were attending to your meal and conversation, that crashing sound would likely get through your attentional filters and capture your attention. You would have no choice but to notice it. That attentional capture would be caused by the sound from the environment: it would be bottom-up.

Alternatively, top-down processes are generally goal directed, slow, deliberate, effortful, and under your control (Fine & Minnery, 2009; Miller & Cohen, 2001; Miller & D'Esposito, 2005). For instance, if you misplaced your keys, how would you look for them? If you had a yellow key fob, you would probably look for yellowness of a certain size in specific locations, such as on the counter, coffee table, and other similar places. You would not look for yellowness on your ceiling fan, because you know keys are not normally lying on top of a ceiling fan. That act of searching for a certain size of yellowness in some locations and not others would be top-down—under your control and based on your experience.

One way to think of this concept is that sensation is a physical process, whereas perception is psychological. For example, upon walking into a kitchen and smelling the scent of baking cinnamon rolls, the *sensation* is the scent receptors detecting the odor of cinnamon, but the *perception* may be "Mmm, this smells like the bread Grandma used to bake when the family gathered for holidays."

Although our perceptions are built from sensations, not all sensations result in perception. In fact, we often don't perceive stimuli that remain relatively constant over prolonged periods of time. This is known as **sensory adaptation**. Imagine going to a city that you have never visited. You check in to the hotel, but when you get to your room, there is a road construction sign with a bright flashing light outside your window. Unfortunately, there are no other rooms available, so you are stuck with a flashing light. You decide to watch television to unwind. The flashing light was extremely annoying when you first entered your room. It was as if someone was continually turning a bright yellow spotlight on and off in your room, but after watching television for a short while, you no longer notice the light flashing. The light is still flashing and filling your room with yellow light every few seconds, and the photoreceptors in your eyes still sense the light, but you no longer perceive the rapid changes in lighting conditions. That you no longer perceive the flashing light demonstrates sensory adaptation and shows that while closely associated, sensation and perception are different.

There is another factor that affects sensation and perception: attention. Attention plays a significant role in determining what is sensed versus what is perceived. Imagine you are at a party full of music, chatter, and laughter. You get involved in an interesting conversation with a friend, and you tune out all the background noise. If someone interrupted you to ask what song had just finished playing, you would probably be unable to answer that question.

> **LINK TO LEARNING**
>
> See for yourself how inattentional blindness works by checking out this selective attention test (http://openstax.org/l/blindness) from Simons and Chabris (1999).

One of the most interesting demonstrations of how important attention is in determining our perception of the environment occurred in a famous study conducted by Daniel Simons and Christopher Chabris (1999). In this study, participants watched a video of people dressed in black and white passing basketballs. Participants were asked to count the number of times the team dressed in white passed the ball. During the video, a person dressed in a black gorilla costume walks among the two teams. You would think that someone would notice the gorilla, right? Nearly half of the people who watched the video didn't notice the gorilla at all, despite the fact that he was clearly visible for nine seconds. Because participants were so focused on the number of times the team dressed in white was passing the ball, they completely tuned out other visual information. **Inattentional blindness** is the failure to notice something that is completely visible because the person was actively attending to something else and did not pay attention to other things (Mack & Rock, 1998; Simons & Chabris, 1999).

In a similar experiment, researchers tested inattentional blindness by asking participants to observe images moving across a computer screen. They were instructed to focus on either white or black objects, disregarding the other color. When a red cross passed across the screen, about one third of subjects did not notice it (Figure 5.3) (Most, Simons, Scholl, & Chabris, 2000).

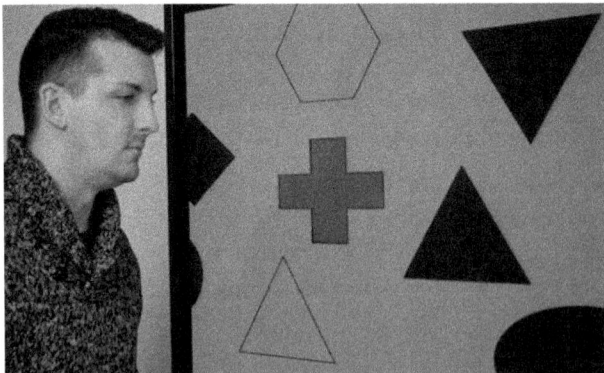

Figure 5.3 Nearly one third of participants in a study did not notice that a red cross passed on the screen because their attention was focused on the black or white figures. (credit: Cory Zanker)

Motivation can also affect perception. Have you ever been expecting a really important phone call and, while taking a shower, you think you hear the phone ringing, only to discover that it is not? If so, then you have experienced how motivation to detect a meaningful stimulus can shift our ability to discriminate between a true sensory stimulus and background noise. The ability to identify a stimulus when it is embedded in a distracting background is called **signal detection theory**. This might also explain why a mother is awakened by a quiet murmur from her baby but not by other sounds that occur while she is asleep. Signal detection theory has practical applications, such as increasing air traffic controller accuracy. Controllers need to be able to detect planes among many signals (blips) that appear on the radar screen and follow those planes as they move through the sky. In fact, the original work of the researcher who developed signal detection theory was focused on improving the sensitivity of air traffic controllers to plane blips (Swets, 1964).

Our perceptions can also be affected by our beliefs, values, prejudices, expectations, and life experiences. As you will see later in this chapter, individuals who are deprived of the experience of binocular vision during critical periods of development have trouble perceiving depth (Fawcett, Wang, & Birch, 2005). The shared experiences of people within a given cultural context can have pronounced effects on perception. For example, Marshall Segall, Donald Campbell, and Melville Herskovits (1963) published the results of a multinational study in which they demonstrated that individuals from Western cultures were more prone to experience certain types of visual illusions than individuals from non-Western cultures, and vice versa. One such illusion that Westerners were more likely to experience was the Müller-Lyer illusion (Figure 5.4): The lines appear to be different lengths, but they are actually the same length.

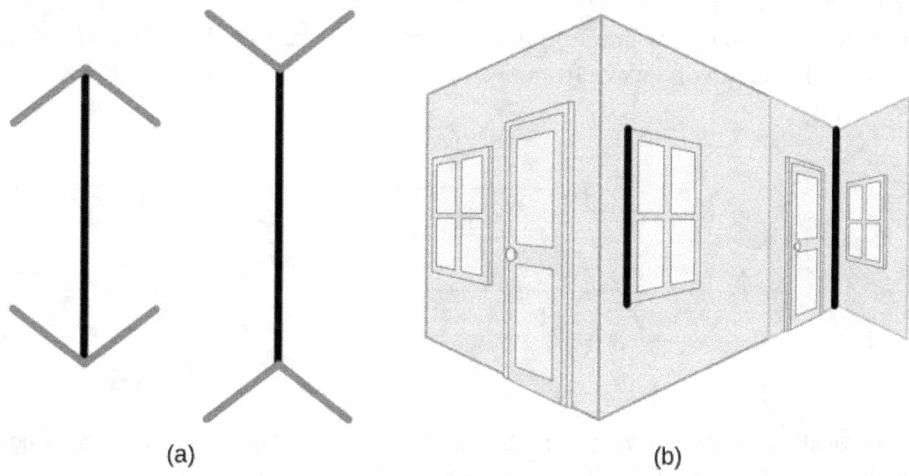

Figure 5.4 In the Müller-Lyer illusion, lines appear to be different lengths although they are identical. (a) Arrows at the ends of lines may make the line on the right appear longer, although the lines are the same length. (b) When applied to a three-dimensional image, the line on the right again may appear longer although both black lines are the same length.

These perceptual differences were consistent with differences in the types of environmental features experienced on a regular basis by people in a given cultural context. People in Western cultures, for example, have a perceptual context of buildings with straight lines, what Segall's study called a carpentered world (Segall et al., 1966). In contrast, people from certain non-Western cultures with an uncarpentered view, such as the Zulu of South Africa, whose villages are made up of round huts arranged in circles, are less susceptible to this illusion (Segall et al., 1999). It is not just vision that is affected by cultural factors. Indeed, research has demonstrated that the ability to identify an odor, and rate its pleasantness and its intensity, varies cross-culturally (Ayabe-Kanamura, Saito, Distel, Martínez-Gómez, & Hudson, 1998).

Children described as thrill seekers are more likely to show taste preferences for intense sour flavors (Liem, Westerbeek, Wolterink, Kok, & de Graaf, 2004), which suggests that basic aspects of personality might affect perception. Furthermore, individuals who hold positive attitudes toward reduced-fat foods are more likely to rate foods labeled as reduced fat as tasting better than people who have less positive attitudes about these products (Aaron, Mela, & Evans, 1994).

5.2 Waves and Wavelengths

Learning Objectives

By the end of this section, you will be able to:
- Describe important physical features of wave forms
- Show how physical properties of light waves are associated with perceptual experience
- Show how physical properties of sound waves are associated with perceptual experience

Visual and auditory stimuli both occur in the form of waves. Although the two stimuli are very different in terms of composition, wave forms share similar characteristics that are especially important to our visual and auditory perceptions. In this section, we describe the physical properties of the waves as well as the perceptual experiences associated with them.

AMPLITUDE AND WAVELENGTH

Two physical characteristics of a wave are amplitude and wavelength (**Figure 5.5**). The **amplitude** of a wave is the distance from the center line to the top point of the crest or the bottom point of the trough. **Wavelength** refers to the length of a wave from one peak to the next.

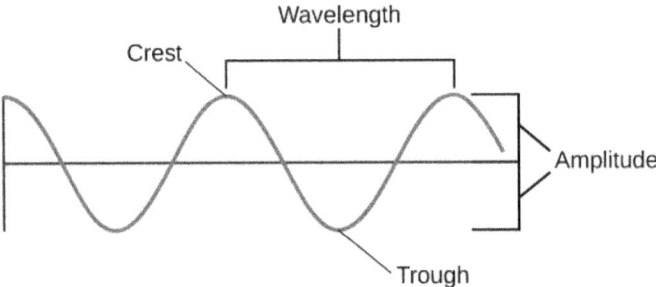

Figure 5.5 The amplitude or height of a wave is measured from the peak to the trough. The wavelength is measured from peak to peak.

Wavelength is directly related to the frequency of a given wave form. **Frequency** refers to the number of waves that pass a given point in a given time period and is often expressed in terms of **hertz (Hz)**, or cycles per second. Longer wavelengths will have lower frequencies, and shorter wavelengths will have higher frequencies (**Figure 5.6**).

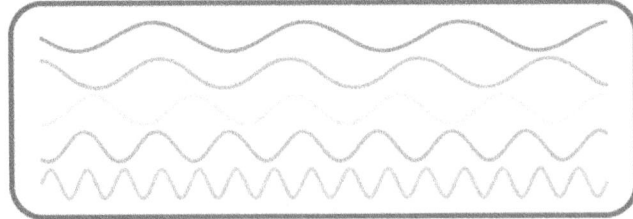

Figure 5.6 This figure illustrates waves of differing wavelengths/frequencies. At the top of the figure, the red wave has a long wavelength/short frequency. Moving from top to bottom, the wavelengths decrease and frequencies increase.

LIGHT WAVES

The **visible spectrum** is the portion of the larger **electromagnetic spectrum** that we can see. As **Figure 5.7** shows, the electromagnetic spectrum encompasses all of the electromagnetic radiation that occurs in our environment and includes gamma rays, x-rays, ultraviolet light, visible light, infrared light, microwaves, and radio waves. The visible spectrum in humans is associated with wavelengths that range from 380 to 740 nm—a very small distance, since a nanometer (nm) is one billionth of a meter. Other species can detect other portions of the electromagnetic spectrum. For instance, honeybees can see light in the ultraviolet range (Wakakuwa, Stavenga, & Arikawa, 2007), and some snakes can detect infrared radiation in addition to more traditional visual light cues (Chen, Deng, Brauth, Ding, & Tang, 2012; Hartline, Kass, & Loop, 1978).

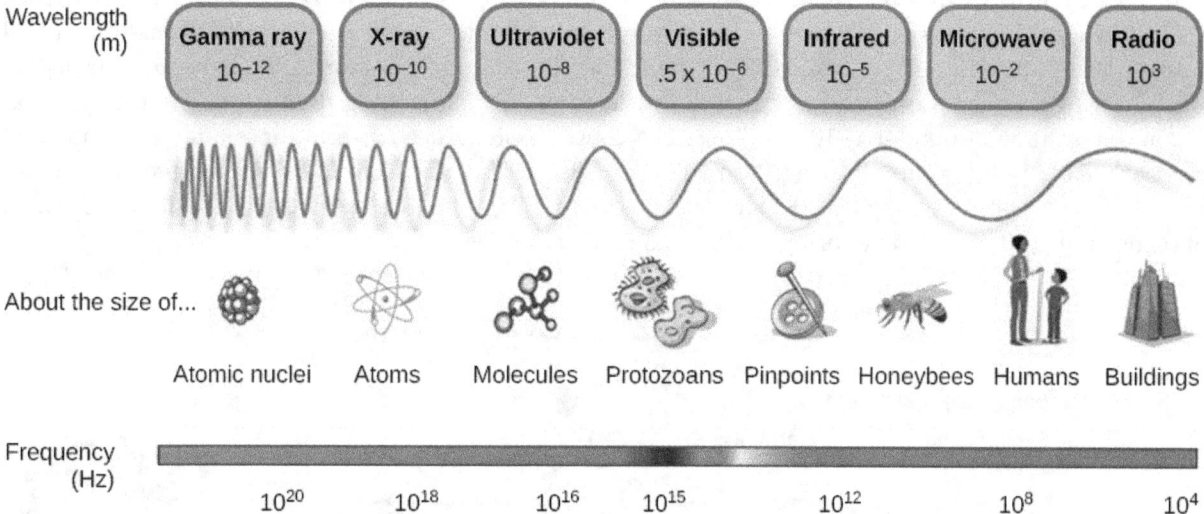

Figure 5.7 Light that is visible to humans makes up only a small portion of the electromagnetic spectrum.

In humans, light wavelength is associated with perception of color (Figure 5.8). Within the visible spectrum, our experience of red is associated with longer wavelengths, greens are intermediate, and blues and violets are shorter in wavelength. (An easy way to remember this is the mnemonic ROYGBIV: red, orange, yellow, green, blue, indigo, violet.) The amplitude of light waves is associated with our experience of brightness or intensity of color, with larger amplitudes appearing brighter.

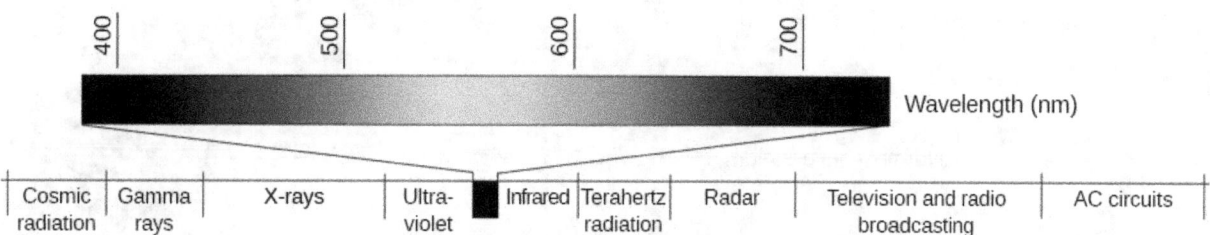

Figure 5.8 Different wavelengths of light are associated with our perception of different colors. (credit: modification of work by Johannes Ahlmann)

SOUND WAVES

Like light waves, the physical properties of sound waves are associated with various aspects of our perception of sound. The frequency of a sound wave is associated with our perception of that sound's **pitch**. High-frequency sound waves are perceived as high-pitched sounds, while low-frequency sound waves are perceived as low-pitched sounds. The audible range of sound frequencies is between 20 and 20000 Hz, with greatest sensitivity to those frequencies that fall in the middle of this range.

As was the case with the visible spectrum, other species show differences in their audible ranges. For instance, chickens have a very limited audible range, from 125 to 2000 Hz. Mice have an audible range from 1000 to 91000 Hz, and the beluga whale's audible range is from 1000 to 123000 Hz. Our pet dogs and cats have audible ranges of about 70–45000 Hz and 45–64000 Hz, respectively (Strain, 2003).

The loudness of a given sound is closely associated with the amplitude of the sound wave. Higher amplitudes are associated with louder sounds. Loudness is measured in terms of **decibels (dB)**, a logarithmic unit of sound intensity. A typical conversation would correlate with 60 dB; a rock concert might check in at 120 dB (**Figure 5.9**). A whisper 5 feet away or rustling leaves are at the low end of our hearing range; sounds like a window air conditioner, a normal conversation, and even heavy traffic or a vacuum cleaner are within a tolerable range. However, there is the potential for hearing damage from about 80 dB to 130 dB: These are sounds of a food processor, power lawnmower, heavy truck (25 feet away), subway train (20 feet away), live rock music, and a jackhammer. About one-third of all hearing loss is due to noise exposure, and the louder the sound, the shorter the exposure needed to cause hearing damage (Le, Straatman, Lea, & Westerberg, 2017). Listening to music through earbuds at maximum volume (around 100–105 decibels) can cause noise-induced hearing loss after 15 minutes of exposure. Although listening to music at maximum volume may not seem to cause damage, it increases the risk of age-related hearing loss (Kujawa & Liberman, 2006). The threshold for pain is about 130 dB, a jet plane taking off or a revolver firing at close range (Dunkle, 1982).

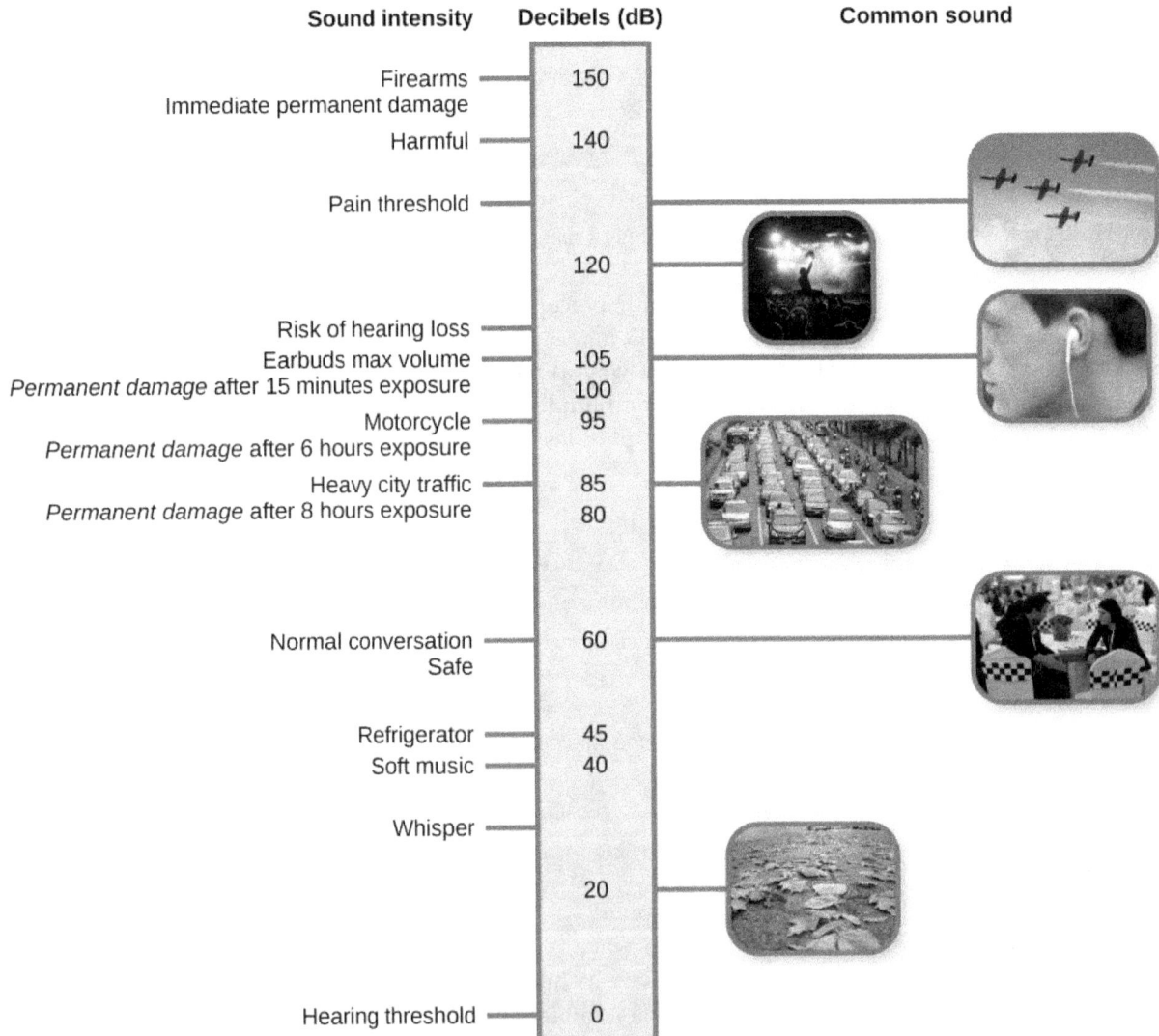

Figure 5.9 This figure illustrates the loudness of common sounds. (credit "planes": modification of work by Max Pfandl; credit "crowd": modification of work by Christian Holmér; credit: "earbuds": modification of work by "Skinny Guy Lover_Flickr"/Flickr; credit "traffic": modification of work by "quinntheislander_Pixabay"/Pixabay; credit "talking": modification of work by Joi Ito; credit "leaves": modification of work by Aurelijus Valeiša)

Although wave amplitude is generally associated with loudness, there is some interaction between frequency and amplitude in our perception of loudness within the audible range. For example, a 10 Hz sound wave is inaudible no matter the amplitude of the wave. A 1000 Hz sound wave, on the other hand, would vary dramatically in terms of perceived loudness as the amplitude of the wave increased.

> **LINK TO LEARNING**
>
> Watch this **brief video about our perception of frequency and amplitude (http://openstax.org/l/frequency)** to learn more.

Of course, different musical instruments can play the same musical note at the same level of loudness, yet they still sound quite different. This is known as the timbre of a sound. **Timbre** refers to a sound's purity, and it is affected by the complex interplay of frequency, amplitude, and timing of sound waves.

5.3 Vision

Learning Objectives

By the end of this section, you will be able to:
- Describe the basic anatomy of the visual system
- Discuss how rods and cones contribute to different aspects of vision
- Describe how monocular and binocular cues are used in the perception of depth

The visual system constructs a mental representation of the world around us (**Figure 5.10**). This contributes to our ability to successfully navigate through physical space and interact with important individuals and objects in our environments. This section will provide an overview of the basic anatomy and function of the visual system. In addition, we will explore our ability to perceive color and depth.

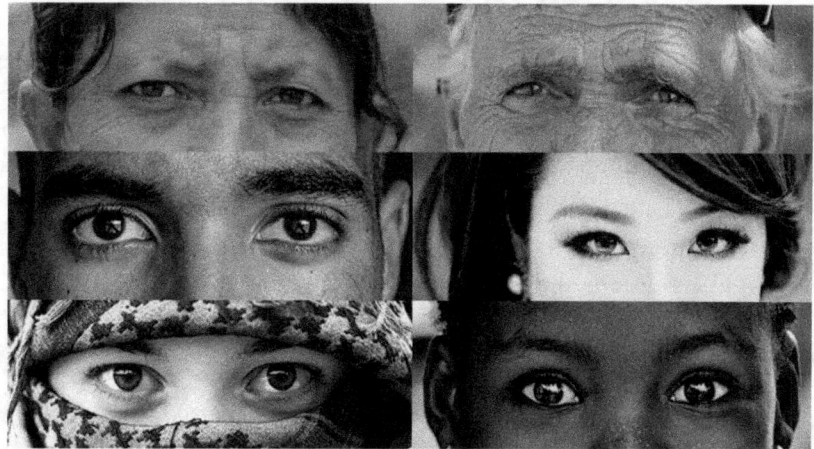

Figure 5.10 Our eyes take in sensory information that helps us understand the world around us. (credit "top left": modification of work by "rajkumar1220"/Flickr"; credit "top right": modification of work by Thomas Leuthard; credit "middle left": modification of work by Demietrich Baker; credit "middle right": modification of work by "kaybee07"/Flickr; credit "bottom left": modification of work by "Isengardt"/Flickr; credit "bottom right": modification of work by Willem Heerbaart)

ANATOMY OF THE VISUAL SYSTEM

The eye is the major sensory organ involved in vision (Figure 5.11). Light waves are transmitted across the cornea and enter the eye through the pupil. The **cornea** is the transparent covering over the eye. It serves as a barrier between the inner eye and the outside world, and it is involved in focusing light waves that enter the eye. The **pupil** is the small opening in the eye through which light passes, and the size of the pupil can change as a function of light levels as well as emotional arousal. When light levels are low, the pupil will become dilated, or expanded, to allow more light to enter the eye. When light levels are high, the pupil will constrict, or become smaller, to reduce the amount of light that enters the eye. The pupil's size is controlled by muscles that are connected to the **iris**, which is the colored portion of the eye.

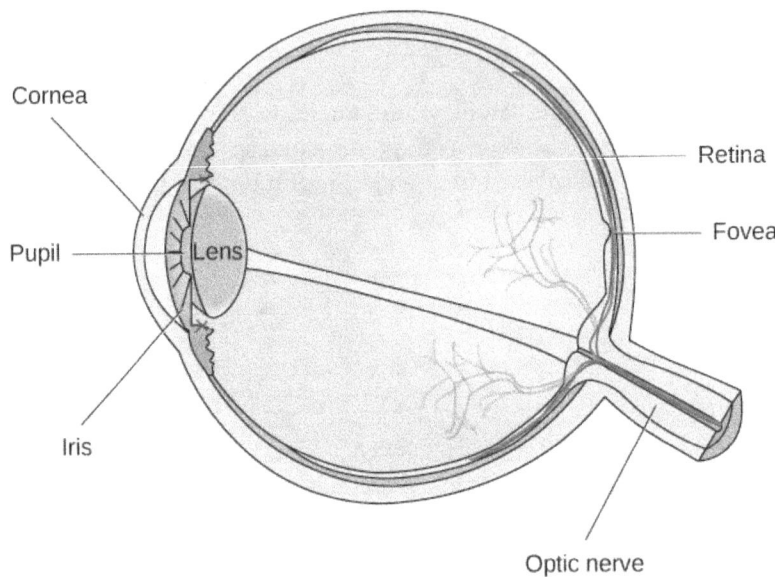

Figure 5.11 The anatomy of the eye is illustrated in this diagram.

After passing through the pupil, light crosses the **lens**, a curved, transparent structure that serves to provide additional focus. The lens is attached to muscles that can change its shape to aid in focusing light that is reflected from near or far objects. In a normal-sighted individual, the lens will focus images perfectly on a small indentation in the back of the eye known as the **fovea**, which is part of the **retina**, the light-sensitive lining of the eye. The fovea contains densely packed specialized photoreceptor cells (Figure 5.12). These **photoreceptor** cells, known as cones, are light-detecting cells. The **cones** are specialized types of photoreceptors that work best in bright light conditions. Cones are very sensitive to acute detail and provide tremendous spatial resolution. They also are directly involved in our ability to perceive color.

While cones are concentrated in the fovea, where images tend to be focused, rods, another type of photoreceptor, are located throughout the remainder of the retina. **Rods** are specialized photoreceptors that work well in low light conditions, and while they lack the spatial resolution and color function of the cones, they are involved in our vision in dimly lit environments as well as in our perception of movement on the periphery of our visual field.

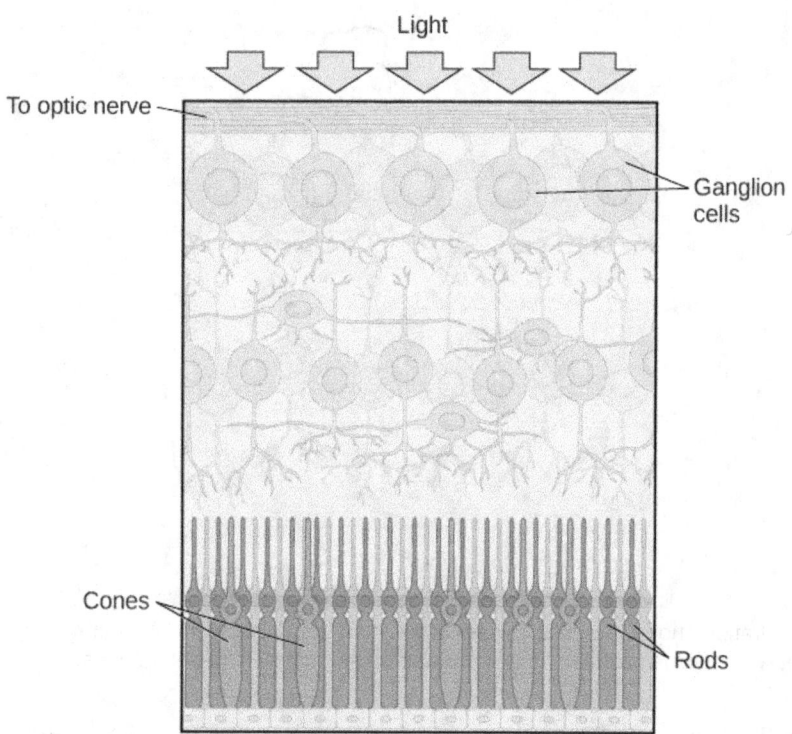

Figure 5.12 The two types of photoreceptors are shown in this image. Cones are colored green and rods are blue.

We have all experienced the different sensitivities of rods and cones when making the transition from a brightly lit environment to a dimly lit environment. Imagine going to see a blockbuster movie on a clear summer day. As you walk from the brightly lit lobby into the dark theater, you notice that you immediately have difficulty seeing much of anything. After a few minutes, you begin to adjust to the darkness and can see the interior of the theater. In the bright environment, your vision was dominated primarily by cone activity. As you move to the dark environment, rod activity dominates, but there is a delay in transitioning between the phases. If your rods do not transform light into nerve impulses as easily and efficiently as they should, you will have difficulty seeing in dim light, a condition known as night blindness.

Rods and cones are connected (via several interneurons) to retinal ganglion cells. Axons from the retinal ganglion cells converge and exit through the back of the eye to form the **optic nerve**. The optic nerve carries visual information from the retina to the brain. There is a point in the visual field called the **blind spot**: Even when light from a small object is focused on the blind spot, we do not see it. We are not consciously aware of our blind spots for two reasons: First, each eye gets a slightly different view of the visual field; therefore, the blind spots do not overlap. Second, our visual system fills in the blind spot so that although we cannot respond to visual information that occurs in that portion of the visual field, we are also not aware that information is missing.

The optic nerve from each eye merges just below the brain at a point called the **optic chiasm**. As Figure 5.13 shows, the optic chiasm is an X-shaped structure that sits just below the cerebral cortex at the front of the brain. At the point of the optic chiasm, information from the right visual field (which comes from both eyes) is sent to the left side of the brain, and information from the left visual field is sent to the right side of the brain.

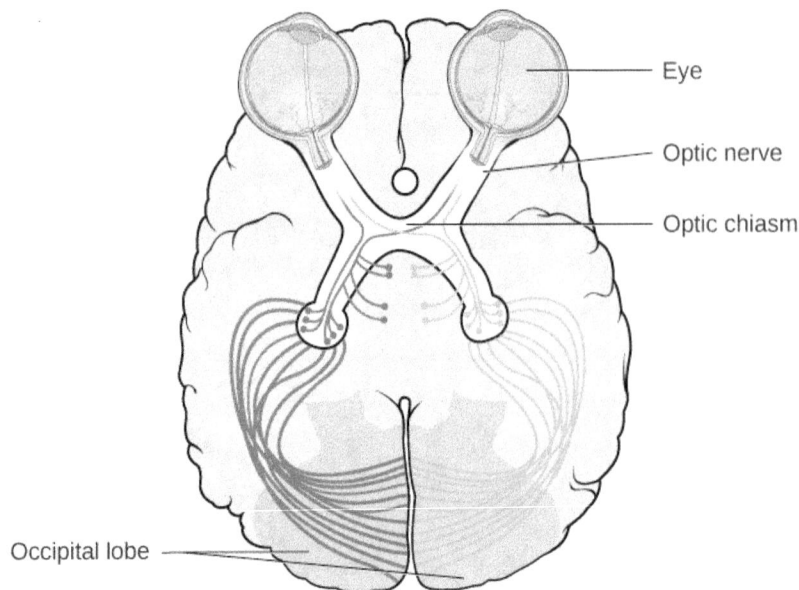

Figure 5.13 This illustration shows the optic chiasm at the front of the brain and the pathways to the occipital lobe at the back of the brain, where visual sensations are processed into meaningful perceptions.

Once inside the brain, visual information is sent via a number of structures to the occipital lobe at the back of the brain for processing. Visual information might be processed in parallel pathways which can generally be described as the "what pathway" and the "where/how" pathway. The "what pathway" is involved in object recognition and identification, while the "where/how pathway" is involved with location in space and how one might interact with a particular visual stimulus (Milner & Goodale, 2008; Ungerleider & Haxby, 1994). For example, when you see a ball rolling down the street, the "what pathway" identifies what the object is, and the "where/how pathway" identifies its location or movement in space.

WHAT DO YOU THINK?

The Ethics of Research Using Animals

David Hubel and Torsten Wiesel were awarded the Nobel Prize in Medicine in 1981 for their research on the visual system. They collaborated for more than twenty years and made significant discoveries about the neurology of visual perception (Hubel & Wiesel, 1959, 1962, 1963, 1970; Wiesel & Hubel, 1963). They studied animals, mostly cats and monkeys. Although they used several techniques, they did considerable single unit recordings, during which tiny electrodes were inserted in the animal's brain to determine when a single cell was activated. Among their many discoveries, they found that specific brain cells respond to lines with specific orientations (called ocular dominance), and they mapped the way those cells are arranged in areas of the visual cortex known as columns and hypercolumns.

In some of their research, they sutured one eye of newborn kittens closed and followed the development of the kittens' vision. They discovered there was a critical period of development for vision. If kittens were deprived of input from one eye, other areas of their visual cortex filled in the area that was normally used by the eye that was sewn closed. In other words, neural connections that exist at birth can be lost if they are deprived of sensory input.

What do you think about sewing a kitten's eye closed for research? To many animal advocates, this would seem brutal, abusive, and unethical. What if you could do research that would help ensure babies and children born with certain conditions could develop normal vision instead of becoming blind? Would you want that research done? Would you conduct that research, even if it meant causing some harm to cats? Would you think the same way if you were the parent of such a child? What if you worked at the animal shelter?

Like virtually every other industrialized nation, the United States permits medical experimentation on animals, with few limitations (assuming sufficient scientific justification). The goal of any laws that exist is not to ban such tests but rather to limit unnecessary animal suffering by establishing standards for the humane treatment and housing of animals in laboratories.

As explained by Stephen Latham, the director of the Interdisciplinary Center for Bioethics at Yale (2012), possible legal and regulatory approaches to animal testing vary on a continuum from strong government regulation and monitoring of all experimentation at one end, to a self-regulated approach that depends on the ethics of the researchers at the other end. The United Kingdom has the most significant regulatory scheme, whereas Japan uses the self-regulation approach. The U.S. approach is somewhere in the middle, the result of a gradual blending of the two approaches.

There is no question that medical research is a valuable and important practice. The question is whether the use of animals is a necessary or even best practice for producing the most reliable results. Alternatives include the use of patient-drug databases, virtual drug trials, computer models and simulations, and noninvasive imaging techniques such as magnetic resonance imaging and computed tomography scans ("Animals in Science/Alternatives," n.d.). Other techniques, such as microdosing, use humans not as test animals but as a means to improve the accuracy and reliability of test results. In vitro methods based on human cell and tissue cultures, stem cells, and genetic testing methods are also increasingly available.

Today, at the local level, any facility that uses animals and receives federal funding must have an Institutional Animal Care and Use Committee (IACUC) that ensures that the NIH guidelines are being followed. The IACUC must include researchers, administrators, a veterinarian, and at least one person with no ties to the institution: that is, a concerned citizen. This committee also performs inspections of laboratories and protocols.

COLOR AND DEPTH PERCEPTION

We do not see the world in black and white; neither do we see it as two-dimensional (2-D) or flat (just height and width, no depth). Let's look at how color vision works and how we perceive three dimensions (height, width, and depth).

Color Vision

Normal-sighted individuals have three different types of cones that mediate color vision. Each of these cone types is maximally sensitive to a slightly different wavelength of light. According to the **trichromatic theory of color vision**, shown in Figure 5.14, all colors in the spectrum can be produced by combining red, green, and blue. The three types of cones are each receptive to one of the colors.

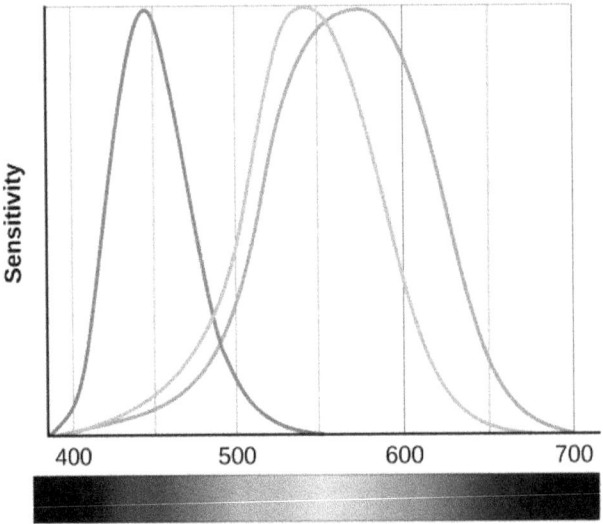

Figure 5.14 This figure illustrates the different sensitivities for the three cone types found in a normal-sighted individual. (credit: modification of work by Vanessa Ezekowitz)

CONNECT THE CONCEPTS

Colorblindness: A Personal Story

Several years ago, I dressed to go to a public function and walked into the kitchen where my 7-year-old daughter sat. She looked up at me, and in her most stern voice, said, "You can't wear that." I asked, "Why not?" and she informed me the colors of my clothes did not match. She had complained frequently that I was bad at matching my shirts, pants, and ties, but this time, she sounded especially alarmed. As a single father with no one else to ask at home, I drove us to the nearest convenience store and asked the store clerk if my clothes matched. She said my pants were a bright green color, my shirt was a reddish orange, and my tie was brown. She looked at my quizzically and said, "No way do your clothes match." Over the next few days, I started asking my coworkers and friends if my clothes matched. After several days of being told that my coworkers just thought I had "a really unique style," I made an appointment with an eye doctor and was tested (Figure 5.15). It was then that I found out that I was colorblind. I cannot differentiate between most greens, browns, and reds. Fortunately, other than unknowingly being badly dressed, my colorblindness rarely harms my day-to-day life.

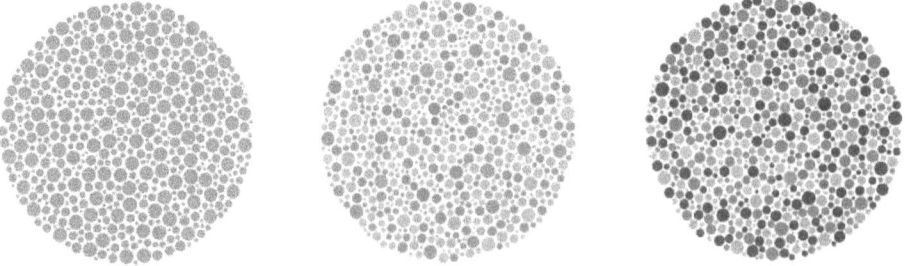

Figure 5.15 The Ishihara test evaluates color perception by assessing whether individuals can discern numbers that appear in a circle of dots of varying colors and sizes.

Some forms of color deficiency are rare. Seeing in grayscale (only shades of black and white) is extremely rare, and people who do so only have rods, which means they have very low visual acuity and cannot see very well. The most common X-linked inherited abnormality is red-green color blindness (Birch, 2012). Approximately 8% of males with European Caucasian decent, 5% of Asian males, 4% of African males, and less than 2% of indigenous American males, Australian males, and Polynesian males have red-green color deficiency (Birch, 2012). Comparatively, only about 0.4% in females from European Caucasian descent have red-green color deficiency (Birch, 2012).

The trichromatic theory of color vision is not the only theory—another major theory of color vision is known as the **opponent-process theory**. According to this theory, color is coded in opponent pairs: black-white, yellow-blue, and green-red. The basic idea is that some cells of the visual system are excited by one of the opponent colors and inhibited by the other. So, a cell that was excited by wavelengths associated with green would be inhibited by wavelengths associated with red, and vice versa. One of the implications of opponent processing is that we do not experience greenish-reds or yellowish-blues as colors. Another implication is that this leads to the experience of negative afterimages. An **afterimage** describes the continuation of a visual sensation after removal of the stimulus. For example, when you stare briefly at the sun and then look away from it, you may still perceive a spot of light although the stimulus (the sun) has been removed. When color is involved in the stimulus, the color pairings identified in the opponent-process theory lead to a negative afterimage. You can test this concept using the flag in Figure 5.16.

Figure 5.16 Stare at the white dot for 30–60 seconds and then move your eyes to a blank piece of white paper. What do you see? This is known as a negative afterimage, and it provides empirical support for the opponent-process theory of color vision.

But these two theories—the trichromatic theory of color vision and the opponent-process theory—are not mutually exclusive. Research has shown that they just apply to different levels of the nervous system. For visual processing on the retina, trichromatic theory applies: the cones are responsive to three different wavelengths that represent red, blue, and green. But once the signal moves past the retina on its way to the brain, the cells respond in a way consistent with opponent-process theory (Land, 1959; Kaiser, 1997).

LINK TO LEARNING

Watch this **video about color perception (http://openstax.org/l/colorvision)** to learn more.

Depth Perception

Our ability to perceive spatial relationships in three-dimensional (3-D) space is known as **depth perception**. With depth perception, we can describe things as being in front, behind, above, below, or to the side of other things.

Our world is three-dimensional, so it makes sense that our mental representation of the world has three-dimensional properties. We use a variety of cues in a visual scene to establish our sense of depth. Some of these are **binocular cues**, which means that they rely on the use of both eyes. One example of a binocular depth cue is **binocular disparity**, the slightly different view of the world that each of our eyes receives. To experience this slightly different view, do this simple exercise: extend your arm fully and extend one of your fingers and focus on that finger. Now, close your left eye without moving your head, then open your left eye and close your right eye without moving your head. You will notice that your finger seems to shift as you alternate between the two eyes because of the slightly different view each eye has of your finger.

A 3-D movie works on the same principle: the special glasses you wear allow the two slightly different images projected onto the screen to be seen separately by your left and your right eye. As your brain processes these images, you have the illusion that the leaping animal or running person is coming right toward you.

Although we rely on binocular cues to experience depth in our 3-D world, we can also perceive depth in 2-D arrays. Think about all the paintings and photographs you have seen. Generally, you pick up on depth in these images even though the visual stimulus is 2-D. When we do this, we are relying on a number of **monocular cues**, or cues that require only one eye. If you think you can't see depth with one eye, note that you don't bump into things when using only one eye while walking—and, in fact, we have more monocular cues than binocular cues.

An example of a monocular cue would be what is known as linear perspective. **Linear perspective** refers to the fact that we perceive depth when we see two parallel lines that seem to converge in an image (**Figure 5.17**). Some other monocular depth cues are interposition, the partial overlap of objects, and the relative size and closeness of images to the horizon.

Figure 5.17 We perceive depth in a two-dimensional figure like this one through the use of monocular cues like linear perspective, like the parallel lines converging as the road narrows in the distance. (credit: Marc Dalmulder)

DIG DEEPER

Stereoblindness

Bruce Bridgeman was born with an extreme case of lazy eye that resulted in him being stereoblind, or unable to respond to binocular cues of depth. He relied heavily on monocular depth cues, but he never had a true appreciation of the 3-D nature of the world around him. This all changed one night in 2012 while Bruce was seeing a movie with his wife.

The movie the couple was going to see was shot in 3-D, and even though he thought it was a waste of money, Bruce paid for the 3-D glasses when he purchased his ticket. As soon as the film began, Bruce put on the glasses and experienced something completely new. For the first time in his life he appreciated the true depth of the world around him. Remarkably, his ability to perceive depth persisted outside of the movie theater.

There are cells in the nervous system that respond to binocular depth cues. Normally, these cells require activation during early development in order to persist, so experts familiar with Bruce's case (and others like his) assume that at some point in his development, Bruce must have experienced at least a fleeting moment of binocular vision. It was enough to ensure the survival of the cells in the visual system tuned to binocular cues. The mystery now is why it took Bruce nearly 70 years to have these cells activated (Peck, 2012).

5.4 Hearing

Learning Objectives

By the end of this section, you will be able to:
- Describe the basic anatomy and function of the auditory system
- Explain how we encode and perceive pitch
- Discuss how we localize sound

Our auditory system converts pressure waves into meaningful sounds. This translates into our ability to hear the sounds of nature, to appreciate the beauty of music, and to communicate with one another through spoken language. This section will provide an overview of the basic anatomy and function of the auditory system. It will include a discussion of how the sensory stimulus is translated into neural impulses, where in the brain that information is processed, how we perceive pitch, and how we know where sound is coming from.

ANATOMY OF THE AUDITORY SYSTEM

The ear can be separated into multiple sections. The outer ear includes the **pinna**, which is the visible part of the ear that protrudes from our heads, the auditory canal, and the **tympanic membrane**, or eardrum. The middle ear contains three tiny bones known as the **ossicles**, which are named the **malleus** (or hammer), **incus** (or anvil), and the **stapes** (or stirrup). The inner ear contains the semi-circular canals, which are involved in balance and movement (the vestibular sense), and the cochlea. The **cochlea** is a fluid-filled, snail-shaped structure that contains the sensory receptor cells (hair cells) of the auditory system (**Figure 5.18**).

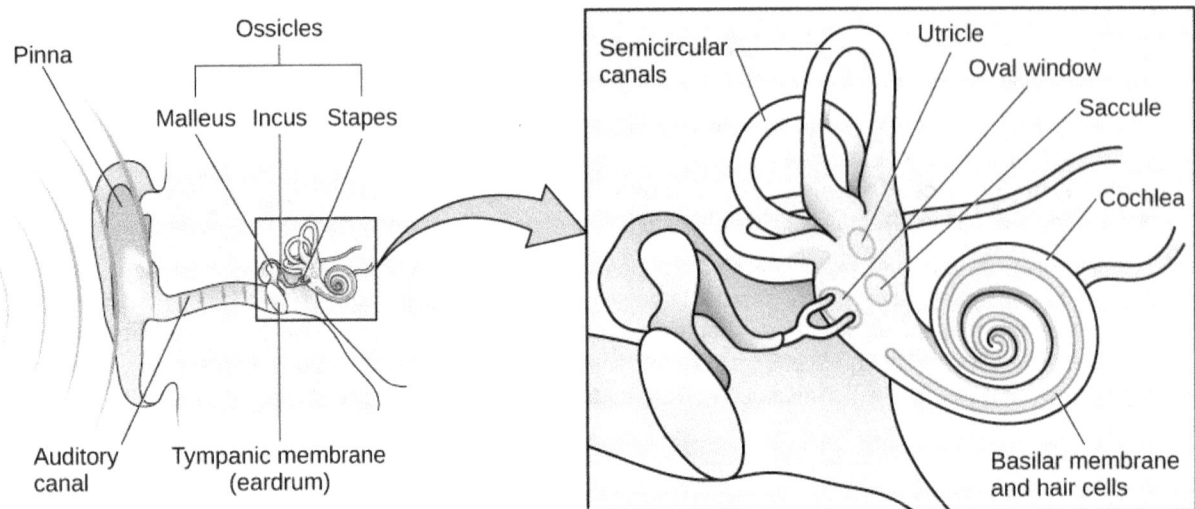

Figure 5.18 The ear is divided into outer (pinna and tympanic membrane), middle (the three ossicles: malleus, incus, and stapes), and inner (cochlea and basilar membrane) divisions.

Sound waves travel along the auditory canal and strike the tympanic membrane, causing it to vibrate. This vibration results in movement of the three ossicles. As the ossicles move, the stapes presses into a thin membrane of the cochlea known as the oval window. As the stapes presses into the oval window, the fluid inside the cochlea begins to move, which in turn stimulates **hair cells**, which are auditory receptor cells of the inner ear embedded in the basilar membrane. The **basilar membrane** is a thin strip of tissue within the cochlea.

The activation of hair cells is a mechanical process: the stimulation of the hair cell ultimately leads to activation of the cell. As hair cells become activated, they generate neural impulses that travel along the auditory nerve to the brain. Auditory information is shuttled to the inferior colliculus, the medial geniculate nucleus of the thalamus, and finally to the auditory cortex in the temporal lobe of the brain for processing. Like the visual system, there is also evidence suggesting that information about auditory recognition and localization is processed in parallel streams (Rauschecker & Tian, 2000; Renier et al., 2009).

PITCH PERCEPTION

Different frequencies of sound waves are associated with differences in our perception of the pitch of those sounds. Low-frequency sounds are lower pitched, and high-frequency sounds are higher pitched. How does the auditory system differentiate among various pitches?

Several theories have been proposed to account for pitch perception. We'll discuss two of them here: temporal theory and place theory. The **temporal theory** of pitch perception asserts that frequency is coded by the activity level of a sensory neuron. This would mean that a given hair cell would fire action potentials related to the frequency of the sound wave. While this is a very intuitive explanation, we detect such a broad range of frequencies (20–20,000 Hz) that the frequency of action potentials fired by hair cells cannot account for the entire range. Because of properties related to sodium channels on the neuronal membrane that are involved in action potentials, there is a point at which a cell cannot fire any faster (Shamma, 2001).

The **place theory** of pitch perception suggests that different portions of the basilar membrane are sensitive to sounds of different frequencies. More specifically, the base of the basilar membrane responds best to high frequencies and the tip of the basilar membrane responds best to low frequencies. Therefore, hair cells that are in the base portion would be labeled as high-pitch receptors, while those in the tip of basilar membrane would be labeled as low-pitch receptors (Shamma, 2001).

In reality, both theories explain different aspects of pitch perception. At frequencies up to about 4000 Hz, it is clear that both the rate of action potentials and place contribute to our perception of pitch. However, much higher frequency sounds can only be encoded using place cues (Shamma, 2001).

SOUND LOCALIZATION

The ability to locate sound in our environments is an important part of hearing. Localizing sound could be considered similar to the way that we perceive depth in our visual fields. Like the monocular and binocular cues that provided information about depth, the auditory system uses both **monaural** (one-eared) and **binaural** (two-eared) cues to localize sound.

Each pinna interacts with incoming sound waves differently, depending on the sound's source relative to our bodies. This interaction provides a monaural cue that is helpful in locating sounds that occur above or below and in front or behind us. The sound waves received by your two ears from sounds that come from directly above, below, in front, or behind you would be identical; therefore, monaural cues are essential (Grothe, Pecka, & McAlpine, 2010).

Binaural cues, on the other hand, provide information on the location of a sound along a horizontal axis by relying on differences in patterns of vibration of the eardrum between our two ears. If a sound comes from an off-center location, it creates two types of binaural cues: interaural level differences and interaural timing differences. **Interaural level difference** refers to the fact that a sound coming from the right side of your body is more intense at your right ear than at your left ear because of the attenuation of the sound wave as it passes through your head. **Interaural timing difference** refers to the small difference in the time at which a given sound wave arrives at each ear (Figure 5.19). Certain brain areas monitor these differences to construct where along a horizontal axis a sound originates (Grothe et al., 2010).

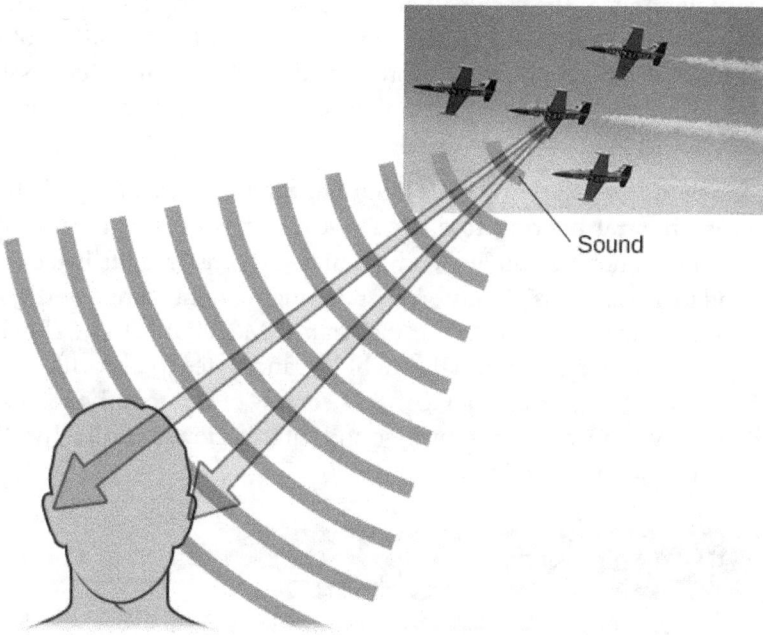

Figure 5.19 Localizing sound involves the use of both monaural and binaural cues. (credit "plane": modification of work by Max Pfandl)

HEARING LOSS

Deafness is the partial or complete inability to hear. Some people are born without hearing, which is known as **congenital deafness**. Other people suffer from **conductive hearing loss**, which is due to a problem delivering sound energy to the cochlea. Causes for conductive hearing loss include blockage of the ear canal, a hole in the tympanic membrane, problems with the ossicles, or fluid in the space between the eardrum and cochlea. Another group of people suffer from sensorineural hearing loss, which is the most common form of hearing loss. Sensorineural hearing loss can be caused by many factors, such as aging, head or acoustic trauma, infections and diseases (such as measles or mumps), medications, environmental effects such as noise exposure (noise-induced hearing loss, as shown in Figure 5.20), tumors, and toxins (such as those found in certain solvents and metals).

(a)   (b)

Figure 5.20 Environmental factors that can lead to sensorineural hearing loss include regular exposure to loud music or construction equipment. (a) Musical performers and (b) construction workers are at risk for this type of hearing loss. (credit a: modification of work by "GillyBerlin_Flickr"/Flickr; credit b: modification of work by Nick Allen)

Given the mechanical nature by which the sound wave stimulus is transmitted from the eardrum through the ossicles to the oval window of the cochlea, some degree of hearing loss is inevitable. With conductive hearing loss, hearing problems are associated with a failure in the vibration of the eardrum and/or movement of the ossicles. These problems are often dealt with through devices like hearing aids that amplify incoming sound waves to make vibration of the eardrum and movement of the ossicles more likely to occur.

When the hearing problem is associated with a failure to transmit neural signals from the cochlea to the brain, it is called **sensorineural hearing loss**. One disease that results in sensorineural hearing loss is **Ménière's disease**. Although not well understood, Ménière's disease results in a degeneration of inner ear structures that can lead to hearing loss, tinnitus (constant ringing or buzzing), **vertigo** (a sense of spinning), and an increase in pressure within the inner ear (Semaan & Megerian, 2011). This kind of loss cannot be treated with hearing aids, but some individuals might be candidates for a cochlear implant as a treatment option. **Cochlear implants** are electronic devices that consist of a microphone, a speech processor, and an electrode array. The device receives incoming sound information and directly stimulates the auditory nerve to transmit information to the brain.

LINK TO LEARNING

Watch this video about cochlear implant surgeries (http://openstax.org/l/cochlear) to learn more.

WHAT DO YOU THINK?

Deaf Culture

In the United States and other places around the world, deaf people have their own language, schools, and customs. This is called deaf culture. In the United States, deaf individuals often communicate using American Sign Language (ASL); ASL has no verbal component and is based entirely on visual signs and gestures. The primary mode of communication is signing. One of the values of deaf culture is to continue traditions like using sign language rather than teaching deaf children to try to speak, read lips, or have cochlear implant surgery.

When a child is diagnosed as deaf, parents have difficult decisions to make. Should the child be enrolled in mainstream schools and taught to verbalize and read lips? Or should the child be sent to a school for deaf children to learn ASL and have significant exposure to deaf culture? Do you think there might be differences in the way that parents approach these decisions depending on whether or not they are also deaf?

5.5 The Other Senses

Learning Objectives

By the end of this section, you will be able to:
- Describe the basic functions of the chemical senses
- Explain the basic functions of the somatosensory, nociceptive, and thermoceptive sensory systems
- Describe the basic functions of the vestibular, proprioceptive, and kinesthetic sensory systems

Vision and hearing have received an incredible amount of attention from researchers over the years. While there is still much to be learned about how these sensory systems work, we have a much better understanding of them than of our other sensory modalities. In this section, we will explore our chemical senses (taste and smell) and our body senses (touch, temperature, pain, balance, and body position).

THE CHEMICAL SENSES

Taste (gustation) and smell (olfaction) are called chemical senses because both have sensory receptors that respond to molecules in the food we eat or in the air we breathe. There is a pronounced interaction between our chemical senses. For example, when we describe the flavor of a given food, we are really referring to both gustatory and olfactory properties of the food working in combination.

Taste (Gustation)

You have learned since elementary school that there are four basic groupings of taste: sweet, salty, sour, and bitter. Research demonstrates, however, that we have at least six taste groupings. Umami is our fifth taste. **Umami** is actually a Japanese word that roughly translates to yummy, and it is associated with a taste for monosodium glutamate (Kinnamon & Vandenbeuch, 2009). There is also a growing body of experimental evidence suggesting that we possess a taste for the fatty content of a given food (Mizushige, Inoue, & Fushiki, 2007).

Molecules from the food and beverages we consume dissolve in our saliva and interact with taste receptors on our tongue and in our mouth and throat. **Taste buds** are formed by groupings of taste receptor cells with hair-like extensions that protrude into the central pore of the taste bud (**Figure 5.21**). Taste buds have a life cycle of ten days to two weeks, so even destroying some by burning your tongue won't have any long-term effect; they just grow right back. Taste molecules bind to receptors on this extension and cause chemical changes within the sensory cell that result in neural impulses being transmitted to the brain via different nerves, depending on where the receptor is located. Taste information is transmitted to the medulla, thalamus, and limbic system, and to the gustatory cortex, which is tucked underneath the overlap between the frontal and temporal lobes (Maffei, Haley, & Fontanini, 2012; Roper, 2013).

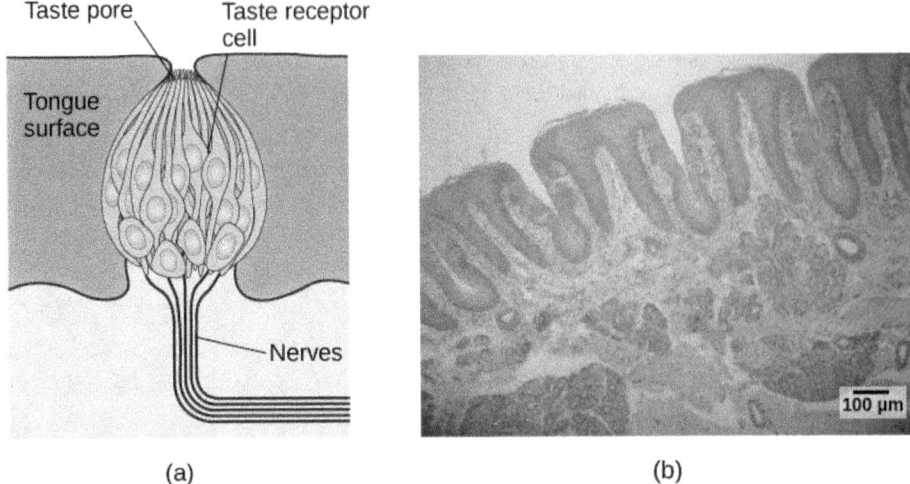

Figure 5.21 (a) Taste buds are composed of a number of individual taste receptors cells that transmit information to nerves. (b) This micrograph shows a close-up view of the tongue's surface. (credit a: modification of work by Jonas Töle; credit b: scale-bar data from Matt Russell)

Smell (Olfaction)

Olfactory receptor cells are located in a mucous membrane at the top of the nose. Small hair-like extensions from these receptors serve as the sites for odor molecules dissolved in the mucus to interact with chemical receptors located on these extensions (Figure 5.22). Once an odor molecule has bound a given receptor, chemical changes within the cell result in signals being sent to the **olfactory bulb**: a bulb-like structure at the tip of the frontal lobe where the olfactory nerves begin. From the olfactory bulb, information is sent to regions of the limbic system and to the primary olfactory cortex, which is located very near the gustatory cortex (Lodovichi & Belluscio, 2012; Spors et al., 2013).

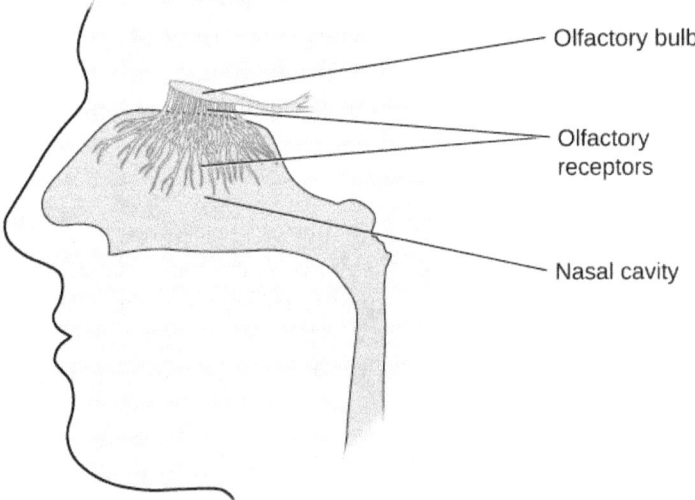

Figure 5.22 Olfactory receptors are the hair-like parts that extend from the olfactory bulb into the mucous membrane of the nasal cavity.

There is tremendous variation in the sensitivity of the olfactory systems of different species. We often think of dogs as having far superior olfactory systems than our own, and indeed, dogs can do some remarkable things with their noses. There is some evidence to suggest that dogs can "smell" dangerous drops in blood glucose levels as well as cancerous tumors (Wells, 2010). Dogs' extraordinary olfactory abilities may be due to the increased number of functional genes for olfactory receptors (between 800 and 1200), compared to the fewer than 400 observed in humans and other primates (Niimura & Nei, 2007).

Many species respond to chemical messages, known as **pheromones**, sent by another individual (Wysocki & Preti, 2004). Pheromonal communication often involves providing information about the reproductive status of a potential mate. So, for example, when a female rat is ready to mate, she secretes pheromonal signals that draw attention from nearby male rats. Pheromonal activation is actually an important component in eliciting sexual behavior in the male rat (Furlow, 1996, 2012; Purvis & Haynes, 1972; Sachs, 1997). There has also been a good deal of research (and controversy) about pheromones in humans (Comfort, 1971; Russell, 1976; Wolfgang-Kimball, 1992; Weller, 1998).

TOUCH, THERMOCEPTION, AND NOCICEPTION

A number of receptors are distributed throughout the skin to respond to various touch-related stimuli (**Figure 5.23**). These receptors include Meissner's corpuscles, Pacinian corpuscles, Merkel's disks, and Ruffini corpuscles. **Meissner's corpuscles** respond to pressure and lower frequency vibrations, and **Pacinian corpuscles** detect transient pressure and higher frequency vibrations. **Merkel's disks** respond to light pressure, while **Ruffini corpuscles** detect stretch (Abraira & Ginty, 2013).

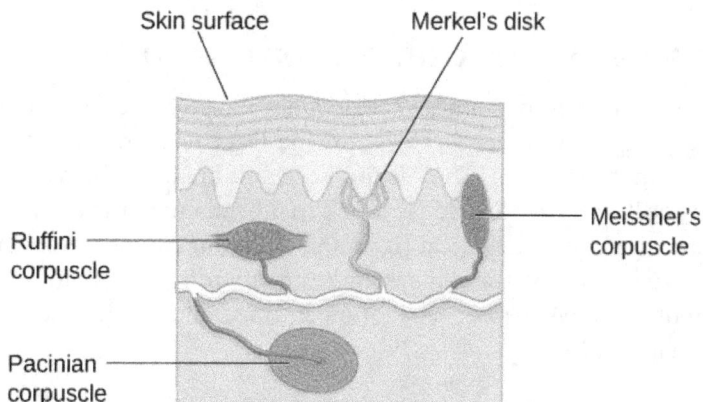

Figure 5.23 There are many types of sensory receptors located in the skin, each attuned to specific touch-related stimuli.

In addition to the receptors located in the skin, there are also a number of free nerve endings that serve sensory functions. These nerve endings respond to a variety of different types of touch-related stimuli and serve as sensory receptors for both **thermoception** (temperature perception) and **nociception** (a signal indicating potential harm and maybe pain) (Garland, 2012; Petho & Reeh, 2012; Spray, 1986). Sensory information collected from the receptors and free nerve endings travels up the spinal cord and is transmitted to regions of the medulla, thalamus, and ultimately to somatosensory cortex, which is located in the postcentral gyrus of the parietal lobe.

Pain Perception

Pain is an unpleasant experience that involves both physical and psychological components. Feeling pain is quite adaptive because it makes us aware of an injury, and it motivates us to remove ourselves from the cause of that injury. In addition, pain also makes us less likely to suffer additional injury because we will be gentler with our injured body parts.

Generally speaking, pain can be considered to be neuropathic or inflammatory in nature. Pain that signals some type of tissue damage is known as **inflammatory pain**. In some situations, pain results from damage to neurons of either the peripheral or central nervous system. As a result, pain signals that are sent to the brain get exaggerated. This type of pain is known as **neuropathic pain**. Multiple treatment options for pain relief range from relaxation therapy to the use of analgesic medications to deep brain stimulation. The most effective treatment option for a given individual will depend on a number of considerations, including the severity and persistence of the pain and any medical/psychological conditions.

Some individuals are born without the ability to feel pain. This very rare genetic disorder is known as **congenital insensitivity to pain** (or **congenital analgesia**). While those with congenital analgesia can detect differences in temperature and pressure, they cannot experience pain. As a result, they often suffer significant injuries. Young children have serious mouth and tongue injuries because they have bitten themselves repeatedly. Not surprisingly, individuals suffering from this disorder have much shorter life expectancies due to their injuries and secondary infections of injured sites (U.S. National Library of Medicine, 2013).

> **LINK TO LEARNING**
>
> Watch this video about congenital insensitivity to pain (http://openstax.org/l/congenital) to learn more.

THE VESTIBULAR SENSE, PROPRIOCEPTION, AND KINESTHESIA

The **vestibular sense** contributes to our ability to maintain balance and body posture. As Figure 5.24 shows, the major sensory organs (utricle, saccule, and the three semicircular canals) of this system are located next to the cochlea in the inner ear. The vestibular organs are fluid-filled and have hair cells, similar to the ones found in the auditory system, which respond to movement of the head and gravitational forces. When these hair cells are stimulated, they send signals to the brain via the vestibular nerve. Although we may not be consciously aware of our vestibular system's sensory information under normal circumstances, its importance is apparent when we experience motion sickness and/or dizziness related to infections of the inner ear (Khan & Chang, 2013).

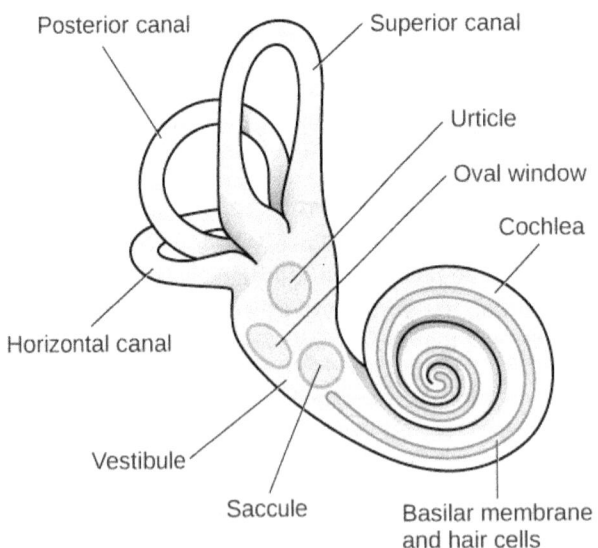

Figure 5.24 The major sensory organs of the vestibular system are located next to the cochlea in the inner ear. These include the utricle, saccule, and the three semicircular canals (posterior, superior, and horizontal).

In addition to maintaining balance, the vestibular system collects information critical for controlling movement and the reflexes that move various parts of our bodies to compensate for changes in body position. Therefore, both **proprioception** (perception of body position) and **kinesthesia** (perception of the body's movement through space) interact with information provided by the vestibular system.

These sensory systems also gather information from receptors that respond to stretch and tension in muscles, joints, skin, and tendons (Lackner & DiZio, 2005; Proske, 2006; Proske & Gandevia, 2012). Proprioceptive and kinesthetic information travels to the brain via the spinal column. Several cortical regions in addition to the cerebellum receive information from and send information to the sensory organs of the proprioceptive and kinesthetic systems.

5.6 Gestalt Principles of Perception

Learning Objectives

By the end of this section, you will be able to:
- Explain the figure-ground relationship
- Define Gestalt principles of grouping
- Describe how perceptual set is influenced by an individual's characteristics and mental state

In the early part of the 20th century, Max Wertheimer published a paper demonstrating that individuals perceived motion in rapidly flickering static images—an insight that came to him as he used a child's toy tachistoscope. Wertheimer, and his assistants Wolfgang Köhler and Kurt Koffka, who later became his partners, believed that perception involved more than simply combining sensory stimuli. This belief led to a new movement within the field of psychology known as **Gestalt psychology**. The word *gestalt* literally means form or pattern, but its use reflects the idea that the whole is different from the sum of its parts. In other words, the brain creates a perception that is more than simply the sum of available sensory inputs, and it does so in predictable ways. Gestalt psychologists translated these predictable ways into principles by which we organize sensory information. As a result, Gestalt psychology has been extremely influential in the area of sensation and perception (Rock & Palmer, 1990).

One Gestalt principle is the **figure-ground relationship**. According to this principle, we tend to segment our visual world into figure and ground. Figure is the object or person that is the focus of the visual field, while the ground is the background. As **Figure 5.25** shows, our perception can vary tremendously, depending on what is perceived as figure and what is perceived as ground. Presumably, our ability to interpret sensory information depends on what we label as figure and what we label as ground in any particular case, although this assumption has been called into question (Peterson & Gibson, 1994; Vecera & O'Reilly, 1998).

Figure 5.25 The concept of figure-ground relationship explains why this image can be perceived either as a vase or as a pair of faces.

Another Gestalt principle for organizing sensory stimuli into meaningful perception is **proximity**. This principle asserts that things that are close to one another tend to be grouped together, as Figure 5.26 illustrates.

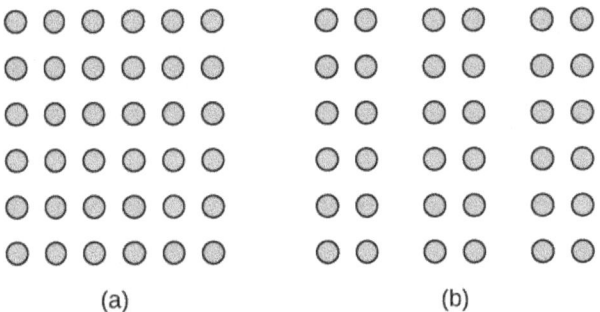

Figure 5.26 The Gestalt principle of proximity suggests that you see (a) one block of dots on the left side and (b) three columns on the right side.

How we read something provides another illustration of the proximity concept. For example, we read this sentence like this, notl iket hiso rt hat. We group the letters of a given word together because there are no spaces between the letters, and we perceive words because there are spaces between each word. Here are some more examples: Cany oum akes enseo ft hiss entence? What doth es e wor dsmea n?

We might also use the principle of **similarity** to group things in our visual fields. According to this principle, things that are alike tend to be grouped together (Figure 5.27). For example, when watching a football game, we tend to group individuals based on the colors of their uniforms. When watching an offensive drive, we can get a sense of the two teams simply by grouping along this dimension.

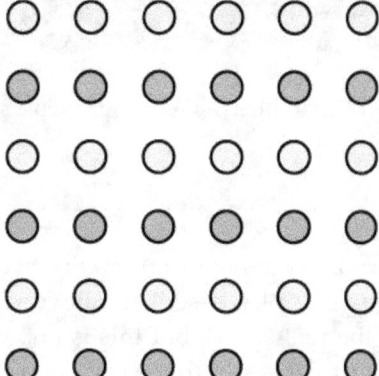

Figure 5.27 When looking at this array of dots, we likely perceive alternating rows of colors. We are grouping these dots according to the principle of similarity.

Two additional Gestalt principles are the law of **continuity** (or **good continuation**) and **closure**. The law of continuity suggests that we are more likely to perceive continuous, smooth flowing lines rather than jagged, broken lines (**Figure 5.28**). The **principle of closure** states that we organize our perceptions into complete objects rather than as a series of parts (**Figure 5.29**).

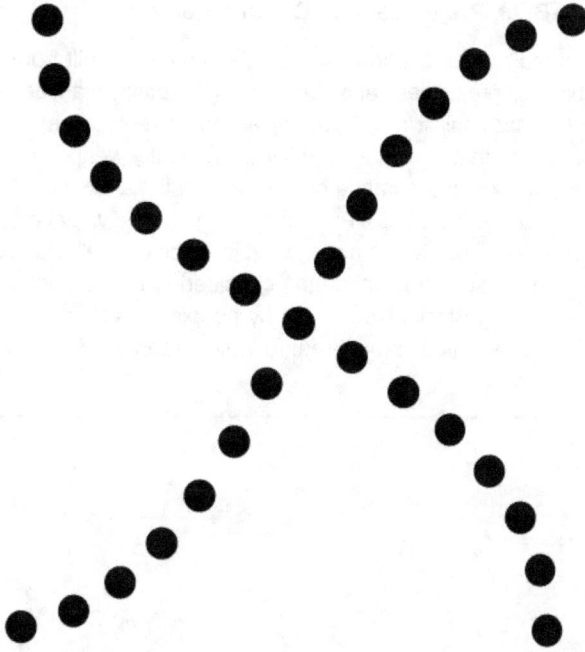

Figure 5.28 Good continuation would suggest that we are more likely to perceive this as two overlapping lines, rather than four lines meeting in the center.

Figure 5.29 Closure suggests that we will perceive a complete circle and rectangle rather than a series of segments.

LINK TO LEARNING

Watch this video showing real world examples of Gestalt principles (http://openstax.org/l/gestalt) to learn more.

According to Gestalt theorists, **pattern perception**, or our ability to discriminate among different figures and shapes, occurs by following the principles described above. You probably feel fairly certain that your perception accurately matches the real world, but this is not always the case. Our perceptions are based on **perceptual hypotheses**: educated guesses that we make while interpreting sensory information. These hypotheses are informed by a number of factors, including our personalities, experiences, and expectations. We use these hypotheses to generate our perceptual set. For instance, research has demonstrated that those who are given verbal priming produce a biased interpretation of complex ambiguous figures (Goolkasian & Woodbury, 2010).

DIG DEEPER

The Depths of Perception: Bias, Prejudice, and Cultural Factors

In this chapter, you have learned that perception is a complex process. Built from sensations, but influenced by our own experiences, biases, prejudices, and cultures, perceptions can be very different from person to person. Research suggests that implicit racial prejudice and stereotypes affect perception. For instance, several studies have demonstrated that non-Black participants identify weapons faster and are more likely to identify non-weapons as weapons when the image of the weapon is paired with the image of a Black person (Payne, 2001; Payne, Shimizu, & Jacoby, 2005). Furthermore, White individuals' decisions to shoot an armed target in a video game is made more quickly when the target is Black (Correll, Park, Judd, & Wittenbrink, 2002; Correll, Urland, & Ito, 2006). This research is important, considering the number of very high-profile cases in the last few decades in which young Blacks were killed by people who claimed to believe that the unarmed individuals were armed and/or represented some threat to their personal safety.

Key Terms

absolute threshold minimum amount of stimulus energy that must be present for the stimulus to be detected 50% of the time

afterimage continuation of a visual sensation after removal of the stimulus

amplitude height of a wave

basilar membrane thin strip of tissue within the cochlea that contains the hair cells which serve as the sensory receptors for the auditory system

binaural cue two-eared cue to localize sound

binocular cue cue that relies on the use of both eyes

binocular disparity slightly different view of the world that each eye receives

blind spot point where we cannot respond to visual information in that portion of the visual field

bottom-up processing system in which perceptions are built from sensory input

closure organizing our perceptions into complete objects rather than as a series of parts

cochlea fluid-filled, snail-shaped structure that contains the sensory receptor cells of the auditory system

cochlear implant electronic device that consists of a microphone, a speech processor, and an electrode array to directly stimulate the auditory nerve to transmit information to the brain

conductive hearing loss failure in the vibration of the eardrum and/or movement of the ossicles

cone specialized photoreceptor that works best in bright light conditions and detects color

congenital deafness deafness from birth

congenital insensitivity to pain (congenital analgesia) genetic disorder that results in the inability to experience pain

cornea transparent covering over the eye

deafness partial or complete inability to hear

decibel (dB) logarithmic unit of sound intensity

depth perception ability to perceive depth

electromagnetic spectrum all the electromagnetic radiation that occurs in our environment

figure-ground relationship segmenting our visual world into figure and ground

fovea small indentation in the retina that contains cones

frequency number of waves that pass a given point in a given time period

Gestalt psychology field of psychology based on the idea that the whole is different from the sum of its parts

good continuation (also, continuity) we are more likely to perceive continuous, smooth flowing lines rather than jagged, broken lines

hair cell auditory receptor cell of the inner ear

hertz (Hz) cycles per second; measure of frequency

inattentional blindness failure to notice something that is completely visible because of a lack of attention

incus middle ear ossicle; also known as the anvil

inflammatory pain signal that some type of tissue damage has occurred

interaural level difference sound coming from one side of the body is more intense at the closest ear because of the attenuation of the sound wave as it passes through the head

interaural timing difference small difference in the time at which a given sound wave arrives at each ear

iris colored portion of the eye

just noticeable difference difference in stimuli required to detect a difference between the stimuli

kinesthesia perception of the body's movement through space

lens curved, transparent structure that provides additional focus for light entering the eye

linear perspective perceive depth in an image when two parallel lines seem to converge

malleus middle ear ossicle; also known as the hammer

Meissner's corpuscle touch receptor that responds to pressure and lower frequency vibrations

Merkel's disk touch receptor that responds to light touch

monaural cue one-eared cue to localize sound

monocular cue cue that requires only one eye

Ménière's disease results in a degeneration of inner ear structures that can lead to hearing loss, tinnitus, vertigo, and an increase in pressure within the inner ear

neuropathic pain pain from damage to neurons of either the peripheral or central nervous system

nociception sensory signal indicating potential harm and maybe pain

olfactory bulb bulb-like structure at the tip of the frontal lobe, where the olfactory nerves begin

olfactory receptor sensory cell for the olfactory system

opponent-process theory of color perception color is coded in opponent pairs: black-white, yellow-blue, and red-green

optic chiasm X-shaped structure that sits just below the brain's ventral surface; represents the merging of the optic nerves from the two eyes and the separation of information from the two sides of the visual field to the opposite side of the brain

optic nerve carries visual information from the retina to the brain

Pacinian corpuscle touch receptor that detects transient pressure and higher frequency vibrations

pattern perception ability to discriminate among different figures and shapes

peak (also, crest) highest point of a wave

perception way that sensory information is interpreted and consciously experienced

perceptual hypothesis educated guess used to interpret sensory information

pheromone chemical message sent by another individual

photoreceptor light-detecting cell

pinna visible part of the ear that protrudes from the head

pitch perception of a sound's frequency

place theory of pitch perception different portions of the basilar membrane are sensitive to sounds of different frequencies

principle of closure organize perceptions into complete objects rather than as a series of parts

proprioception perception of body position

proximity things that are close to one another tend to be grouped together

pupil small opening in the eye through which light passes

retina light-sensitive lining of the eye

rod specialized photoreceptor that works well in low light conditions

Ruffini corpuscle touch receptor that detects stretch

sensation what happens when sensory information is detected by a sensory receptor

sensorineural hearing loss failure to transmit neural signals from the cochlea to the brain

sensory adaptation not perceiving stimuli that remain relatively constant over prolonged periods of time

signal detection theory change in stimulus detection as a function of current mental state

similarity things that are alike tend to be grouped together

stapes middle ear ossicle; also known as the stirrup

subliminal message message presented below the threshold of conscious awareness

taste bud grouping of taste receptor cells with hair-like extensions that protrude into the central pore of the taste bud

temporal theory of pitch perception sound's frequency is coded by the activity level of a sensory neuron

thermoception temperature perception

timbre sound's purity

top-down processing interpretation of sensations is influenced by available knowledge, experiences, and thoughts

transduction conversion from sensory stimulus energy to action potential

trichromatic theory of color perception color vision is mediated by the activity across the three groups of cones

trough lowest point of a wave

tympanic membrane eardrum

umami taste for monosodium glutamate

vertigo spinning sensation

vestibular sense contributes to our ability to maintain balance and body posture

visible spectrum portion of the electromagnetic spectrum that we can see

wavelength length of a wave from one peak to the next peak

Summary

5.1 Sensation versus Perception
Sensation occurs when sensory receptors detect sensory stimuli. Perception involves the organization, interpretation, and conscious experience of those sensations. All sensory systems have both absolute and difference thresholds, which refer to the minimum amount of stimulus energy or the minimum amount of difference in stimulus energy required to be detected about 50% of the time, respectively. Sensory adaptation, selective attention, and signal detection theory can help explain what is perceived and what is not. In addition, our perceptions are affected by a number of factors, including beliefs, values, prejudices, culture, and life experiences.

5.2 Waves and Wavelengths
Both light and sound can be described in terms of wave forms with physical characteristics like amplitude, wavelength, and timbre. Wavelength and frequency are inversely related so that longer waves have lower frequencies, and shorter waves have higher frequencies. In the visual system, a light wave's wavelength is generally associated with color, and its amplitude is associated with brightness. In the auditory system, a sound's frequency is associated with pitch, and its amplitude is associated with loudness.

5.3 Vision
Light waves cross the cornea and enter the eye at the pupil. The eye's lens focuses this light so that the image is focused on a region of the retina known as the fovea. The fovea contains cones that possess high levels of visual acuity and operate best in bright light conditions. Rods are located throughout the retina and operate best under dim light conditions. Visual information leaves the eye via the optic nerve. Information from each visual field is sent to the opposite side of the brain at the optic chiasm. Visual information then moves through a number of brain sites before reaching the occipital lobe, where it is processed.

Two theories explain color perception. The trichromatic theory asserts that three distinct cone groups are tuned to slightly different wavelengths of light, and it is the combination of activity across these cone types that results in our perception of all the colors we see. The opponent-process theory of color vision asserts that color is processed in opponent pairs and accounts for the interesting phenomenon of a negative afterimage. We perceive depth through a combination of monocular and binocular depth cues.

5.4 Hearing
Sound waves are funneled into the auditory canal and cause vibrations of the eardrum; these vibrations move the ossicles. As the ossicles move, the stapes presses against the oval window of the cochlea, which

causes fluid inside the cochlea to move. As a result, hair cells embedded in the basilar membrane become enlarged, which sends neural impulses to the brain via the auditory nerve.

Pitch perception and sound localization are important aspects of hearing. Our ability to perceive pitch relies on both the firing rate of the hair cells in the basilar membrane as well as their location within the membrane. In terms of sound localization, both monaural and binaural cues are used to locate where sounds originate in our environment.

Individuals can be born deaf, or they can develop deafness as a result of age, genetic predisposition, and/or environmental causes. Hearing loss that results from a failure of the vibration of the eardrum or the resultant movement of the ossicles is called conductive hearing loss. Hearing loss that involves a failure of the transmission of auditory nerve impulses to the brain is called sensorineural hearing loss.

5.5 The Other Senses
Taste (gustation) and smell (olfaction) are chemical senses that employ receptors on the tongue and in the nose that bind directly with taste and odor molecules in order to transmit information to the brain for processing. Our ability to perceive touch, temperature, and pain is mediated by a number of receptors and free nerve endings that are distributed throughout the skin and various tissues of the body. The vestibular sense helps us maintain a sense of balance through the response of hair cells in the utricle, saccule, and semi-circular canals that respond to changes in head position and gravity. Our proprioceptive and kinesthetic systems provide information about body position and body movement through receptors that detect stretch and tension in the muscles, joints, tendons, and skin of the body.

5.6 Gestalt Principles of Perception
Gestalt theorists have been incredibly influential in the areas of sensation and perception. Gestalt principles such as figure-ground relationship, grouping by proximity or similarity, the law of good continuation, and closure are all used to help explain how we organize sensory information. Our perceptions are not infallible, and they can be influenced by bias, prejudice, and other factors.

Review Questions

1. _____ refers to the minimum amount of stimulus energy required to be detected 50% of the time.
    a. absolute threshold
    b. difference threshold
    c. just noticeable difference
    d. transduction

2. Decreased sensitivity to an unchanging stimulus is known as _____.
    a. transduction
    b. difference threshold
    c. sensory adaptation
    d. inattentional blindness

3. _____ involves the conversion of sensory stimulus energy into neural impulses.
    a. sensory adaptation
    b. inattentional blindness
    c. difference threshold
    d. transduction

4. _____ occurs when sensory information is organized, interpreted, and consciously experienced.
    a. sensation
    b. perception
    c. transduction
    d. sensory adaptation

5. Which of the following correctly matches the pattern in our perception of color as we move from short wavelengths to long wavelengths?
    a. red to orange to yellow
    b. yellow to orange to red
    c. yellow to red to orange
    d. orange to yellow to red

6. The visible spectrum includes light that ranges from about _____.
    a. 400–700 nm
    b. 200–900 nm
    c. 20–20000 Hz
    d. 10–20 dB

7. The electromagnetic spectrum includes _____.
    a. radio waves
    b. x-rays
    c. infrared light
    d. all of the above

8. The audible range for humans is _____.
    a. 380–740 Hz
    b. 10–20 dB
    c. less than 300 dB
    d. 20-20,000 Hz

9. The quality of a sound that is affected by frequency, amplitude, and timing of the sound wave is known as _____.
    a. pitch
    b. tone
    c. electromagnetic
    d. timbre

10. The _____ is a small indentation of the retina that contains cones.
    a. optic chiasm
    b. optic nerve
    c. fovea
    d. iris

11. _____ operate best under bright light conditions.
    a. cones
    b. rods
    c. retinal ganglion cells
    d. striate cortex

12. _____ depth cues require the use of both eyes.
    a. monocular
    b. binocular
    c. linear perspective
    d. accommodating

13. If you were to stare at a green dot for a relatively long period of time and then shift your gaze to a blank white screen, you would see a _____ negative afterimage.
    a. blue
    b. yellow
    c. black
    d. red

14. Hair cells located near the base of the basilar membrane respond best to _____ sounds.
    a. low-frequency
    b. high-frequency
    c. low-amplitude
    d. high-amplitude

15. The three ossicles of the middle ear are known as _____.
    a. malleus, incus, and stapes
    b. hammer, anvil, and stirrup
    c. pinna, cochlea, and utricle
    d. both a and b

16. Hearing aids might be effective for treating _____.
    a. Ménière's disease
    b. sensorineural hearing loss
    c. conductive hearing loss
    d. interaural time differences

17. Cues that require two ears are referred to as _____ cues.
    a. monocular
    b. monaural
    c. binocular
    d. binaural

18. Chemical messages often sent between two members of a species to communicate something about reproductive status are called _____.
    a. hormones
    b. pheromones
    c. Merkel's disks
    d. Meissner's corpuscles

19. Which taste is associated with monosodium glutamate?
    a. sweet
    b. bitter
    c. umami
    d. sour

20. _____ serve as sensory receptors for temperature and pain stimuli.
    a. free nerve endings
    b. Pacinian corpuscles
    c. Ruffini corpuscles
    d. Meissner's corpuscles

21. Which of the following is involved in maintaining balance and body posture?
    a. auditory nerve
    b. nociceptors
    c. olfactory bulb
    d. vestibular system

22. According to the principle of _____, objects that occur close to one another tend to be grouped together.
    a. similarity
    b. good continuation
    c. proximity
    d. closure

23. Our tendency to perceive things as complete objects rather than as a series of parts is known as the principle of _____.
    a. closure
    b. good continuation
    c. proximity
    d. similarity

24. According to the law of _____, we are more likely to perceive smoothly flowing lines rather than choppy or jagged lines.
    a. closure
    b. good continuation
    c. proximity
    d. similarity

25. The main point of focus in a visual display is known as the _____.
    a. closure
    b. perceptual set
    c. ground
    d. figure

Critical Thinking Questions

26. Not everything that is sensed is perceived. Do you think there could ever be a case where something could be perceived without being sensed?

27. Please generate a novel example of how just noticeable difference can change as a function of stimulus intensity.

28. Why do you think other species have such different ranges of sensitivity for both visual and auditory stimuli compared to humans?

29. Why do you think humans are especially sensitive to sounds with frequencies that fall in the middle portion of the audible range?

30. Compare the two theories of color perception. Are they completely different?

31. Color is not a physical property of our environment. What function (if any) do you think color vision serves?

32. Given what you've read about sound localization, from an evolutionary perspective, how does sound localization facilitate survival?

33. How can temporal and place theories both be used to explain our ability to perceive the pitch of sound waves with frequencies up to 4000 Hz?

34. Many people experience nausea while traveling in a car, plane, or boat. How might you explain this as a function of sensory interaction?

35. If you heard someone say that they would do anything not to feel the pain associated with significant injury, how would you respond given what you've just read?

36. Do you think women experience pain differently than men? Why do you think this is?

37. The central tenet of Gestalt psychology is that the whole is different from the sum of its parts. What does this mean in the context of perception?

38. Take a look at the following figure. How might you influence whether people see a duck or a rabbit?

Figure 5.30

Personal Application Questions

39. Think about a time when you failed to notice something around you because your attention was focused elsewhere. If someone pointed it out, were you surprised that you hadn't noticed it right away?

40. If you grew up with a family pet, then you have surely noticed that they often seem to hear things that you don't hear. Now that you've read this section, you probably have some insight as to why this may be. How would you explain this to a friend who never had the opportunity to take a class like this?

41. Take a look at a few of your photos or personal works of art. Can you find examples of linear perspective as a potential depth cue?

42. If you had to choose to lose either your vision or your hearing, which would you choose and why?

43. As mentioned earlier, a food's flavor represents an interaction of both gustatory and olfactory information. Think about the last time you were seriously congested due to a cold or the flu. What changes did you notice in the flavors of the foods that you ate during this time?

44. Have you ever listened to a song on the radio and sung along only to find out later that you have been singing the wrong lyrics? Once you found the correct lyrics, did your perception of the song change?

Chapter 6
Learning

Figure 6.1 Loggerhead sea turtle hatchlings are born knowing how to find the ocean and how to swim. Unlike the sea turtle, humans must learn how to swim (and surf). (credit "turtle": modification of work by Becky Skiba, USFWS; credit "surfer": modification of work by Mike Baird)

Chapter Outline

6.1 What Is Learning?
6.2 Classical Conditioning
6.3 Operant Conditioning
6.4 Observational Learning (Modeling)

Introduction

The summer sun shines brightly on a deserted stretch of beach. Suddenly, a tiny grey head emerges from the sand, then another and another. Soon the beach is teeming with loggerhead sea turtle hatchlings (Figure 6.1). Although only minutes old, the hatchlings know exactly what to do. Their flippers are not very efficient for moving across the hot sand, yet they continue onward, instinctively. Some are quickly snapped up by gulls circling overhead and others become lunch for hungry ghost crabs that dart out of their holes. Despite these dangers, the hatchlings are driven to leave the safety of their nest and find the ocean.

Not far down this same beach, Ben and his son, Julian, paddle out into the ocean on surfboards. A wave approaches. Julian crouches on his board, then jumps up and rides the wave for a few seconds before losing his balance. He emerges from the water in time to watch his father ride the face of the wave.

Unlike baby sea turtles, which know how to find the ocean and swim with no help from their parents, we are not born knowing how to swim (or surf). Yet we humans pride ourselves on our ability to learn. In fact, over thousands of years and across cultures, we have created institutions devoted entirely to learning. But have you ever asked yourself how exactly it is that we learn? What processes are at work as we come to know what we know? This chapter focuses on the primary ways in which learning occurs.

6.1 What Is Learning?

Learning Objectives

By the end of this section, you will be able to:
- Explain how learned behaviors are different from instincts and reflexes
- Define learning
- Recognize and define three basic forms of learning—classical conditioning, operant conditioning, and observational learning

Birds build nests and migrate as winter approaches. Infants suckle at their mother's breast. Dogs shake water off wet fur. Salmon swim upstream to spawn, and spiders spin intricate webs. What do these seemingly unrelated behaviors have in common? They all are *unlearned* behaviors. Both instincts and reflexes are innate (unlearned) behaviors that organisms are born with. **Reflexes** are a motor or neural reaction to a specific stimulus in the environment. They tend to be simpler than instincts, involve the activity of specific body parts and systems (e.g., the knee-jerk reflex and the contraction of the pupil in bright light), and involve more primitive centers of the central nervous system (e.g., the spinal cord and the medulla). In contrast, **instincts** are innate behaviors that are triggered by a broader range of events, such as maturation and the change of seasons. They are more complex patterns of behavior, involve movement of the organism as a whole (e.g., sexual activity and migration), and involve higher brain centers.

Both reflexes and instincts help an organism adapt to its environment and do not have to be learned. For example, every healthy human baby has a sucking reflex, present at birth. Babies are born knowing how to suck on a nipple, whether artificial (from a bottle) or human. Nobody teaches the baby to suck, just as no one teaches a sea turtle hatchling to move toward the ocean. Learning, like reflexes and instincts, allows an organism to adapt to its environment. But unlike instincts and reflexes, learned behaviors involve change and experience: **learning** is a relatively permanent change in behavior or knowledge that results from experience. In contrast to the innate behaviors discussed above, learning involves acquiring knowledge and skills through experience. Looking back at our surfing scenario, Julian will have to spend much more time training with his surfboard before he learns how to ride the waves like his father.

Learning to surf, as well as any complex learning process (e.g., learning about the discipline of psychology), involves a complex interaction of conscious and unconscious processes. Learning has traditionally been studied in terms of its simplest components—the associations our minds automatically make between events. Our minds have a natural tendency to connect events that occur closely together or in sequence. **Associative learning** occurs when an organism makes connections between stimuli or events that occur together in the environment. You will see that associative learning is central to all three basic learning processes discussed in this chapter; classical conditioning tends to involve unconscious processes, operant conditioning tends to involve conscious processes, and observational learning adds social and cognitive layers to all the basic associative processes, both conscious and unconscious. These learning processes will be discussed in detail later in the chapter, but it is helpful to have a brief overview of each as you begin to explore how learning is understood from a psychological perspective.

In classical conditioning, also known as Pavlovian conditioning, organisms learn to associate events—or stimuli—that repeatedly happen together. We experience this process throughout our daily lives. For example, you might see a flash of lightning in the sky during a storm and then hear a loud boom of thunder. The sound of the thunder naturally makes you jump (loud noises have that effect by reflex). Because lightning reliably predicts the impending boom of thunder, you may associate the two and jump when you see lightning. Psychological researchers study this associative process by focusing on what can be seen and measured—behaviors. Researchers ask if one stimulus triggers a reflex, can we train a different stimulus to trigger that same reflex? In operant conditioning, organisms learn, again, to associate events—a behavior and its consequence (reinforcement or punishment). A pleasant consequence encourages more of that behavior in the future, whereas a punishment deters the behavior. Imagine you are teaching your dog, Hodor, to sit. You tell Hodor to sit, and give him a treat when he does. After repeated experiences, Hodor begins to associate the act of sitting with receiving a treat. He learns that the consequence of sitting is that he gets a doggie biscuit (**Figure 6.2**). Conversely, if the dog is punished when exhibiting a behavior, it becomes conditioned to avoid that behavior (e.g., receiving a small shock when crossing the boundary of an invisible electric fence).

Figure 6.2 In operant conditioning, a response is associated with a consequence. This dog has learned that certain behaviors result in receiving a treat. (credit: Crystal Rolfe)

Observational learning extends the effective range of both classical and operant conditioning. In contrast to classical and operant conditioning, in which learning occurs only through direct experience, observational learning is the process of watching others and then imitating what they do. A lot of learning among humans and other animals comes from observational learning. To get an idea of the extra effective range that observational learning brings, consider Ben and his son Julian from the introduction. How might observation help Julian learn to surf, as opposed to learning by trial and error alone? By watching his father, he can imitate the moves that bring success and avoid the moves that lead to failure. Can you think of something you have learned how to do after watching someone else?

All of the approaches covered in this chapter are part of a particular tradition in psychology, called behaviorism, which we discuss in the next section. However, these approaches do not represent the entire study of learning. Separate traditions of learning have taken shape within different fields of psychology, such as memory and cognition, so you will find that other chapters will round out your understanding of the topic. Over time these traditions tend to converge. For example, in this chapter you will see how cognition has come to play a larger role in behaviorism, whose more extreme adherents once insisted that behaviors are triggered by the environment with no intervening thought.

6.2 Classical Conditioning

Learning Objectives

By the end of this section, you will be able to:
- Explain how classical conditioning occurs
- Summarize the processes of acquisition, extinction, spontaneous recovery, generalization, and discrimination

Does the name Ivan Pavlov ring a bell? Even if you are new to the study of psychology, chances are that you have heard of Pavlov and his famous dogs.

Pavlov (1849–1936), a Russian scientist, performed extensive research on dogs and is best known for his experiments in classical conditioning (Figure 6.3). As we discussed briefly in the previous section, **classical conditioning** is a process by which we learn to associate stimuli and, consequently, to anticipate events.

Figure 6.3 Ivan Pavlov's research on the digestive system of dogs unexpectedly led to his discovery of the learning process now known as classical conditioning.

Pavlov came to his conclusions about how learning occurs completely by accident. Pavlov was a physiologist, not a psychologist. Physiologists study the life processes of organisms, from the molecular level to the level of cells, organ systems, and entire organisms. Pavlov's area of interest was the digestive system (Hunt, 2007). In his studies with dogs, Pavlov measured the amount of saliva produced in response to various foods. Over time, Pavlov (1927) observed that the dogs began to salivate not only at the taste of food, but also at the sight of food, at the sight of an empty food bowl, and even at the sound of the laboratory assistants' footsteps. Salivating to food in the mouth is reflexive, so no learning is involved. However, dogs don't naturally salivate at the sight of an empty bowl or the sound of footsteps.

These unusual responses intrigued Pavlov, and he wondered what accounted for what he called the dogs' "psychic secretions" (Pavlov, 1927). To explore this phenomenon in an objective manner, Pavlov designed a series of carefully controlled experiments to see which stimuli would cause the dogs to salivate. He was able to train the dogs to salivate in response to stimuli that clearly had nothing to do with food, such as the sound of a bell, a light, and a touch on the leg. Through his experiments, Pavlov realized that an organism has two types of responses to its environment: (1) unconditioned (unlearned) responses, or reflexes, and (2) conditioned (learned) responses.

In Pavlov's experiments, the dogs salivated each time meat powder was presented to them. The meat powder in this situation was an **unconditioned stimulus (UCS)**: a stimulus that elicits a reflexive response in an organism. The dogs' salivation was an **unconditioned response (UCR)**: a natural (unlearned) reaction to a given stimulus. Before conditioning, think of the dogs' stimulus and response like this:

$$\text{Meat powder (UCS)} \rightarrow \text{Salivation (UCR)}$$

In classical conditioning, a neutral stimulus is presented immediately before an unconditioned stimulus. Pavlov would sound a tone (like ringing a bell) and then give the dogs the meat powder (Figure 6.4). The tone was the **neutral stimulus (NS)**, which is a stimulus that does not naturally elicit a response. Prior to conditioning, the dogs did not salivate when they just heard the tone because the tone had no association for the dogs.

$$\text{Tone (NS) + Meat Powder (UCS)} \rightarrow \text{Salivation (UCR)}$$

When Pavlov paired the tone with the meat powder over and over again, the previously neutral stimulus (the tone) also began to elicit salivation from the dogs. Thus, the neutral stimulus became the **conditioned**

stimulus (CS), which is a stimulus that elicits a response after repeatedly being paired with an unconditioned stimulus. Eventually, the dogs began to salivate to the tone alone, just as they previously had salivated at the sound of the assistants' footsteps. The behavior caused by the conditioned stimulus is called the **conditioned response (CR)**. In the case of Pavlov's dogs, they had learned to associate the tone (CS) with being fed, and they began to salivate (CR) in anticipation of food.

Tone (CS) → Salivation (CR)

Before Conditioning

During Conditioning   **After Conditioning**

Figure 6.4 Before conditioning, an unconditioned stimulus (food) produces an unconditioned response (salivation), and a neutral stimulus (bell) does not produce a response. During conditioning, the unconditioned stimulus (food) is presented repeatedly just after the presentation of the neutral stimulus (bell). After conditioning, the neutral stimulus alone produces a conditioned response (salivation), thus becoming a conditioned stimulus.

LINK TO LEARNING

View this **video about Pavlov and his dogs (http://openstax.org/l/pavlov2)** to learn more.

REAL WORLD APPLICATION OF CLASSICAL CONDITIONING

How does classical conditioning work in the real world? Consider the case of Moisha, who was diagnosed with cancer. When she received her first chemotherapy treatment, she vomited shortly after the chemicals were injected. In fact, every trip to the doctor for chemotherapy treatment shortly after the drugs were injected, she vomited. Moisha's treatment was a success and her cancer went into remission. Now, when she visits her oncologist's office every 6 months for a check-up, she becomes nauseous. In this case, the chemotherapy drugs are the unconditioned stimulus (UCS), vomiting is the unconditioned response (UCR), the doctor's office is the conditioned stimulus (CS) after being paired with the UCS, and nausea is the conditioned response (CR). Let's assume that the chemotherapy drugs that Moisha takes are given through a syringe injection. After entering the doctor's office, Moisha sees a syringe, and then gets her medication. In addition to the doctor's office, Moisha will learn to associate the syringe will the medication and will respond to syringes with nausea. This is an example of higher-order (or second-order) conditioning, when the conditioned stimulus (the doctor's office) serves to condition another stimulus (the syringe). It is hard to achieve anything above second-order conditioning. For example, if someone rang a bell every time Moisha received a syringe injection of chemotherapy drugs in the doctor's office, Moisha likely will never get sick in response to the bell.

Consider another example of classical conditioning. Let's say you have a cat named Tiger, who is quite spoiled. You keep her food in a separate cabinet, and you also have a special electric can opener that you use only to open cans of cat food. For every meal, Tiger hears the distinctive sound of the electric can opener ("zzhzhz") and then gets her food. Tiger quickly learns that when she hears "zzhzhz" she is about to get fed. What do you think Tiger does when she hears the electric can opener? She will likely get excited and run to where you are preparing her food. This is an example of classical conditioning. In this case, what are the UCS, CS, UCR, and CR?

What if the cabinet holding Tiger's food becomes squeaky? In that case, Tiger hears "squeak" (the cabinet), "zzhzhz" (the electric can opener), and then she gets her food. Tiger will learn to get excited when she hears the "squeak" of the cabinet. Pairing a new neutral stimulus ("squeak") with the conditioned stimulus ("zzhzhz") is called **higher-order conditioning**, or **second-order conditioning**. This means you are using the conditioned stimulus of the can opener to condition another stimulus: the squeaky cabinet (Figure 6.5). It is hard to achieve anything above second-order conditioning. For example, if you ring a bell, open the cabinet ("squeak"), use the can opener ("zzhzhz"), and then feed Tiger, Tiger will likely never get excited when hearing the bell alone.

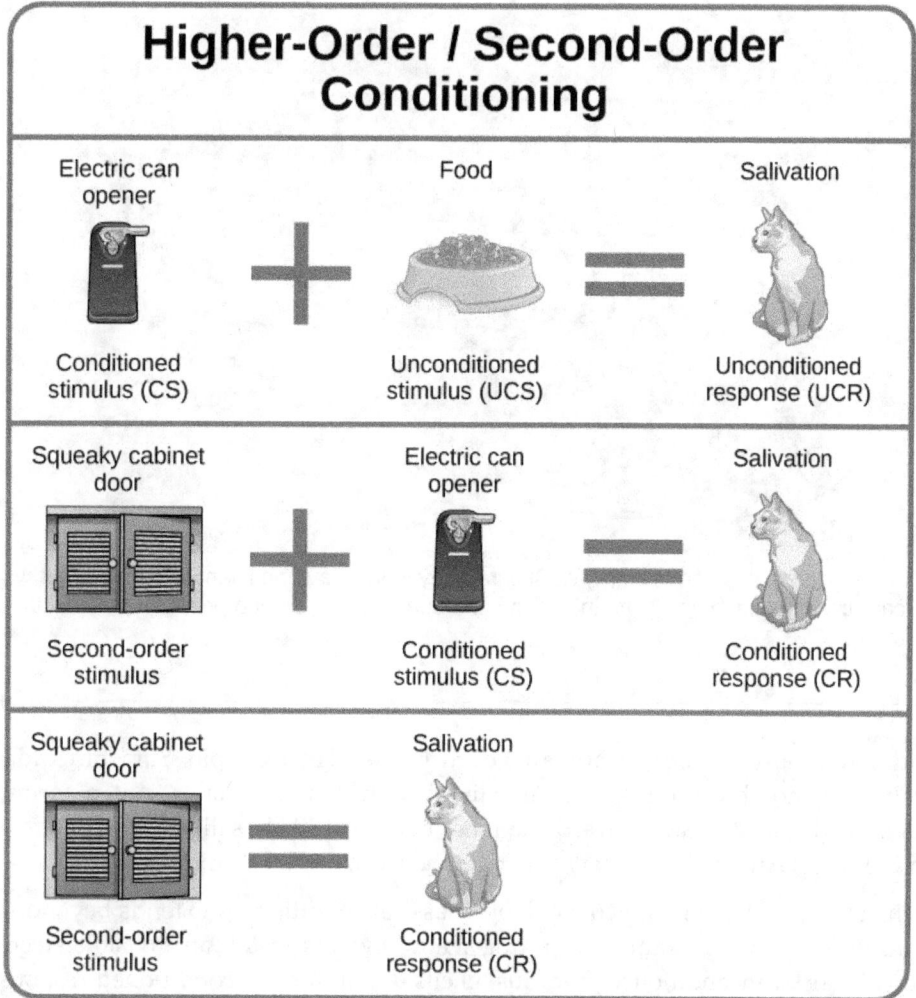

Figure 6.5 In higher-order conditioning, an established conditioned stimulus is paired with a new neutral stimulus (the second-order stimulus), so that eventually the new stimulus also elicits the conditioned response, without the initial conditioned stimulus being presented.

EVERYDAY CONNECTION

Classical Conditioning at Stingray City

Kate and her spouse recently vacationed in the Cayman Islands, and booked a boat tour to Stingray City, where they could feed and swim with the southern stingrays. The boat captain explained how the normally solitary stingrays have become accustomed to interacting with humans. About 40 years ago, fishermen began to clean fish and conch (unconditioned stimulus) at a particular sandbar near a barrier reef, and large numbers of stingrays would swim in to eat (unconditioned response) what the fishermen threw into the water; this continued for years. By the late 1980s, word of the large group of stingrays spread among scuba divers, who then started feeding them by hand. Over time, the southern stingrays in the area were classically conditioned much like Pavlov's dogs. When they hear the sound of a boat engine (neutral stimulus that becomes a conditioned stimulus), they know that they will get to eat (conditioned response).

As soon as they reached Stingray City, over two dozen stingrays surrounded their tour boat. The couple slipped into the water with bags of squid, the stingrays' favorite treat. The swarm of stingrays bumped and rubbed up against their legs like hungry cats (**Figure 6.6**). Kate was able to feed, pet, and even kiss (for luck) these amazing creatures. Then all the squid was gone, and so were the stingrays.

Figure 6.6 Kate holds a southern stingray at Stingray City in the Cayman Islands. These stingrays have been classically conditioned to associate the sound of a boat motor with food provided by tourists. (credit: Kathryn Dumper)

Classical conditioning also applies to humans, even babies. For example, Sara buys formula in blue canisters for her six-month-old daughter, Angelina. Whenever Sara takes out a formula container, Angelina gets excited, tries to reach toward the food, and most likely salivates. Why does Angelina get excited when she sees the formula canister? What are the UCS, CS, UCR, and CR here?

So far, all of the examples have involved food, but classical conditioning extends beyond the basic need to be fed. Consider our earlier example of a dog whose owners install an invisible electric dog fence. A small electrical shock (unconditioned stimulus) elicits discomfort (unconditioned response). When the unconditioned stimulus (shock) is paired with a neutral stimulus (the edge of a yard), the dog associates the discomfort (unconditioned response) with the edge of the yard (conditioned stimulus) and stays within the set boundaries. In this example, the edge of the yard elicits fear and anxiety in the dog. Fear and anxiety are the conditioned response.

LINK TO LEARNING

Watch this video clip from the television show, The Office, for a humorous look at conditioning (http://openstax.org/l/theoffice) in which Jim conditions Dwight to expect a breath mint every time Jim's computer makes a specific sound.

GENERAL PROCESSES IN CLASSICAL CONDITIONING

Now that you know how classical conditioning works and have seen several examples, let's take a look at some of the general processes involved. In classical conditioning, the initial period of learning is known as **acquisition**, when an organism learns to connect a neutral stimulus and an unconditioned stimulus. During acquisition, the neutral stimulus begins to elicit the conditioned response, and eventually the neutral stimulus becomes a conditioned stimulus capable of eliciting the conditioned response by itself. Timing is important for conditioning to occur. Typically, there should only be a brief interval between presentation of the conditioned stimulus and the unconditioned stimulus. Depending on what is being conditioned, sometimes this interval is as little as five seconds (Chance, 2009). However, with other types of conditioning, the interval can be up to several hours.

Taste aversion is a type of conditioning in which an interval of several hours may pass between the conditioned stimulus (something ingested) and the unconditioned stimulus (nausea or illness). Here's how it works. Between classes, you and a friend grab a quick lunch from a food cart on campus. You share a dish of chicken curry and head off to your next class. A few hours later, you feel nauseous and become ill. Although your friend is fine and you determine that you have intestinal flu (the food is not the culprit), you've developed a taste aversion; the next time you are at a restaurant and someone orders curry, you immediately feel ill. While the chicken dish is not what made you sick, you are experiencing taste aversion: you've been conditioned to be averse to a food after a single, bad experience.

How does this occur—conditioning based on a single instance and involving an extended time lapse between the event and the negative stimulus? Research into taste aversion suggests that this response may be an evolutionary adaptation designed to help organisms quickly learn to avoid harmful foods (Garcia & Rusiniak, 1980; Garcia & Koelling, 1966). Not only may this contribute to species survival via natural selection, but it may also help us develop strategies for challenges such as helping cancer patients through the nausea induced by certain treatments (Holmes, 1993; Jacobsen et al., 1993; Hutton, Baracos, & Wismer, 2007; Skolin et al., 2006). Garcia and Koelling (1966) showed not only that taste aversions could be conditioned, but also that there were biological constraints to learning. In their study, separate groups of rats were conditioned to associate either a flavor with illness, or lights and sounds with illness. Results showed that all rats exposed to flavor-illness pairings learned to avoid the flavor, but none of the rats exposed to lights and sounds with illness learned to avoid lights or sounds. This added evidence to the idea that classical conditioning could contribute to species survival by helping organisms learn to avoid stimuli that posed real dangers to health and welfare.

Robert Rescorla demonstrated how powerfully an organism can learn to predict the UCS from the CS. Take, for example, the following two situations. Ari's dad always has dinner on the table every day at 6:00. Soraya's mom switches it up so that some days they eat dinner at 6:00, some days they eat at 5:00, and other days they eat at 7:00. For Ari, 6:00 reliably and consistently predicts dinner, so Ari will likely start feeling hungry every day right before 6:00, even if he's had a late snack. Soraya, on the other hand, will be less likely to associate 6:00 with dinner, since 6:00 does not always predict that dinner is coming. Rescorla, along with his colleague at Yale University, Alan Wagner, developed a mathematical formula that could be used to calculate the probability that an association would be learned given the ability of a conditioned stimulus to predict the occurrence of an unconditioned stimulus and other factors; today this is known as the Rescorla-Wagner model (Rescorla & Wagner, 1972)

Once we have established the connection between the unconditioned stimulus and the conditioned stimulus, how do we break that connection and get the dog, cat, or child to stop responding? In Tiger's case, imagine what would happen if you stopped using the electric can opener for her food and began to use it only for human food. Now, Tiger would hear the can opener, but she would not get food. In classical conditioning terms, you would be giving the conditioned stimulus, but not the unconditioned stimulus. Pavlov explored this scenario in his experiments with dogs: sounding the tone without giving the dogs the meat powder. Soon the dogs stopped responding to the tone. **Extinction** is the decrease in the conditioned response when the unconditioned stimulus is no longer presented with the conditioned stimulus. When presented with the conditioned stimulus alone, the dog, cat, or other organism would show a weaker and weaker response, and finally no response. In classical conditioning terms, there is a gradual weakening and disappearance of the conditioned response.

What happens when learning is not used for a while—when what was learned lies dormant? As we just discussed, Pavlov found that when he repeatedly presented the bell (conditioned stimulus) without the meat powder (unconditioned stimulus), extinction occurred; the dogs stopped salivating to the bell. However, after a couple of hours of resting from this extinction training, the dogs again began to salivate when Pavlov rang the bell. What do you think would happen with Tiger's behavior if your electric can opener broke, and you did not use it for several months? When you finally got it fixed and started using it to open Tiger's food again, Tiger would remember the association between the can opener and her food—she would get excited and run to the kitchen when she heard the sound. The behavior of Pavlov's dogs and Tiger illustrates a concept Pavlov called **spontaneous recovery**: the return of a previously extinguished conditioned response following a rest period (Figure 6.7).

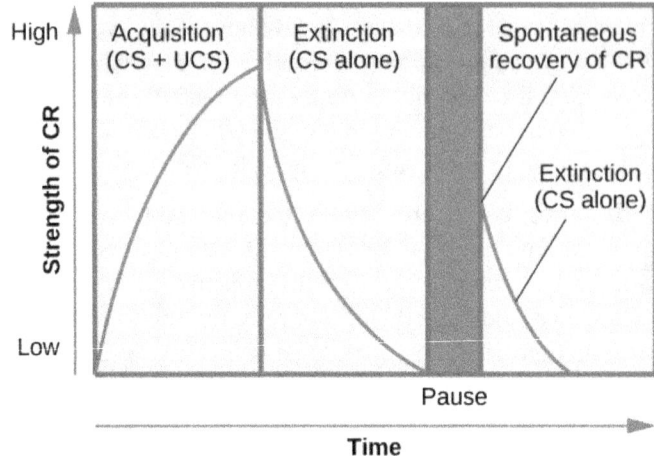

Figure 6.7 This is the curve of acquisition, extinction, and spontaneous recovery. The rising curve shows the conditioned response quickly getting stronger through the repeated pairing of the conditioned stimulus and the unconditioned stimulus (acquisition). Then the curve decreases, which shows how the conditioned response weakens when only the conditioned stimulus is presented (extinction). After a break or pause from conditioning, the conditioned response reappears (spontaneous recovery).

Of course, these processes also apply in humans. For example, let's say that every day when you walk to campus, an ice cream truck passes your route. Day after day, you hear the truck's music (neutral stimulus), so you finally stop and purchase a chocolate ice cream bar. You take a bite (unconditioned stimulus) and then your mouth waters (unconditioned response). This initial period of learning is known as acquisition, when you begin to connect the neutral stimulus (the sound of the truck) and the unconditioned stimulus (the taste of the chocolate ice cream in your mouth). During acquisition, the conditioned response gets stronger and stronger through repeated pairings of the conditioned stimulus and unconditioned stimulus. Several days (and ice cream bars) later, you notice that your mouth begins to water (conditioned response) as soon as you hear the truck's musical jingle—even before you bite into the ice cream bar. Then one day you head down the street. You hear the truck's music (conditioned stimulus), and your mouth waters (conditioned response). However, when you get to the truck, you discover that they are all out of ice cream. You leave disappointed. The next few days you pass by the truck and hear the music, but don't stop to get an ice cream bar because you're running late for class. You begin to salivate less and less when you hear the music, until by the end of the week, your mouth no longer waters when you hear the tune. This illustrates extinction. The conditioned response weakens when only the conditioned stimulus (the sound of the truck) is presented, without being followed by the unconditioned stimulus (chocolate ice cream in the mouth). Then the weekend comes. You don't have to go to class, so you don't pass the truck. Monday morning arrives and you take your usual route to campus. You round the corner and hear the truck again. What do you think happens? Your mouth begins to water again. Why? After a break from conditioning, the conditioned response reappears, which indicates spontaneous recovery.

Acquisition and extinction involve the strengthening and weakening, respectively, of a learned association. Two other learning processes—stimulus discrimination and stimulus generalization—are involved in determining which stimuli will trigger learned responses. Animals (including humans) need to distinguish between stimuli—for example, between sounds that predict a threatening event and sounds that do not—so that they can respond appropriately (such as running away if the sound is threatening). When an organism learns to respond differently to various stimuli that are similar, it is called **stimulus discrimination**. In classical conditioning terms, the organism demonstrates the conditioned response only to the conditioned stimulus. Pavlov's dogs discriminated between the basic tone that sounded before they were fed and other tones (e.g., the doorbell), because the other sounds did not predict the arrival of food. Similarly, Tiger, the cat, discriminated between the sound of the can opener and the sound of the electric mixer. When the electric mixer is going, Tiger is not about to be fed, so she does not come running to the kitchen looking for food. In our other example, Moisha, the cancer patient, discriminated between oncologists and other types of doctors. She learned not to feel ill when visiting doctors for other types of appointments, such as her annual physical.

On the other hand, when an organism demonstrates the conditioned response to stimuli that are similar to the condition stimulus, it is called **stimulus generalization**, the opposite of stimulus discrimination. The more similar a stimulus is to the condition stimulus, the more likely the organism is to give the conditioned response. For instance, if the electric mixer sounds very similar to the electric can opener, Tiger may come running after hearing its sound. But if you do not feed her following the electric mixer sound, and you continue to feed her consistently after the electric can opener sound, she will quickly learn to discriminate between the two sounds (provided they are sufficiently dissimilar that she can tell them apart). In our other example, Moisha continued to feel ill whenever visiting other oncologists or other doctors in the same building as her oncologist.

BEHAVIORISM

John B. Watson, shown in **Figure 6.8**, is considered the founder of behaviorism. Behaviorism is a school of thought that arose during the first part of the 20th century, which incorporates elements of Pavlov's classical conditioning (Hunt, 2007). In stark contrast with Freud, who considered the reasons for behavior to be hidden in the unconscious, Watson championed the idea that all behavior can be studied as a simple stimulus-response reaction, without regard for internal processes. Watson argued that in order for psychology to become a legitimate science, it must shift its concern away from internal mental processes because mental processes cannot be seen or measured. Instead, he asserted that psychology must focus on outward observable behavior that can be measured.

Figure 6.8 John B. Watson used the principles of classical conditioning in the study of human emotion.

Watson's ideas were influenced by Pavlov's work. According to Watson, human behavior, just like animal behavior, is primarily the result of conditioned responses. Whereas Pavlov's work with dogs involved the conditioning of reflexes, Watson believed the same principles could be extended to the conditioning of human emotions (Watson, 1919). Thus began Watson's work with his graduate student Rosalie Rayner and a baby called Little Albert. Through their experiments with Little Albert, Watson and Rayner (1920) demonstrated how fears can be conditioned.

In 1920, Watson was the chair of the psychology department at Johns Hopkins University. Through his position at the university he came to meet Little Albert's mother, Arvilla Merritte, who worked at a campus hospital (DeAngelis, 2010). Watson offered her a dollar to allow her son to be the subject of his experiments in classical conditioning. Through these experiments, Little Albert was exposed to and conditioned to fear certain things. Initially he was presented with various neutral stimuli, including a rabbit, a dog, a monkey, masks, cotton wool, and a white rat. He was not afraid of any of these things. Then Watson, with the help of Rayner, conditioned Little Albert to associate these stimuli with an emotion—fear. For example, Watson handed Little Albert the white rat, and Little Albert enjoyed playing with it. Then Watson made a loud sound, by striking a hammer against a metal bar hanging behind Little Albert's head, each time Little Albert touched the rat. Little Albert was frightened by the sound—demonstrating a reflexive fear of sudden loud noises—and began to cry. Watson repeatedly paired the loud sound with the white rat. Soon Little Albert became frightened by the white rat alone. In this case, what are the UCS, CS, UCR, and CR? Days later, Little Albert demonstrated stimulus generalization—he became afraid of other furry things: a rabbit, a furry coat, and even a Santa Claus mask (Figure 6.9). Watson had succeeded in conditioning a fear response in Little Albert, thus demonstrating that emotions could become conditioned responses. It had been Watson's intention to produce a phobia—a persistent, excessive fear of a specific object or situation— through conditioning alone, thus countering Freud's view that phobias are caused by deep, hidden conflicts in the mind. However, there is no evidence that Little Albert experienced phobias in later years. Little Albert's mother moved away, ending the experiment. While Watson's research provided new insight into conditioning, it would be considered unethical by today's standards.

Figure 6.9 Through stimulus generalization, Little Albert came to fear furry things, including Watson in a Santa Claus mask.

LINK TO LEARNING

View scenes from this **video on John Watson's experiment in which Little Albert was conditioned to respond in fear to furry objects (http://openstax.org/l/Watson1)** to learn more.

As you watch the video, look closely at Little Albert's reactions and the manner in which Watson and Rayner present the stimuli before and after conditioning. Based on what you see, would you come to the same conclusions as the researchers?

EVERYDAY CONNECTION

Advertising and Associative Learning

Advertising executives are pros at applying the principles of associative learning. Think about the car commercials you have seen on television. Many of them feature an attractive model. By associating the model with the car being advertised, you come to see the car as being desirable (Cialdini, 2008). You may be asking yourself, does this advertising technique actually work? According to Cialdini (2008), men who viewed a car commercial that included an attractive model later rated the car as being faster, more appealing, and better designed than did men who viewed an advertisement for the same car minus the model.

Have you ever noticed how quickly advertisers cancel contracts with a famous athlete following a scandal? As far as the advertiser is concerned, that athlete is no longer associated with positive feelings; therefore, the athlete cannot be used as an unconditioned stimulus to condition the public to associate positive feelings (the unconditioned response) with their product (the conditioned stimulus).

Now that you are aware of how associative learning works, see if you can find examples of these types of advertisements on television, in magazines, or on the Internet.

6.3 Operant Conditioning

Learning Objectives

By the end of this section, you will be able to:
- Define operant conditioning
- Explain the difference between reinforcement and punishment
- Distinguish between reinforcement schedules

The previous section of this chapter focused on the type of associative learning known as classical conditioning. Remember that in classical conditioning, something in the environment triggers a reflex automatically, and researchers train the organism to react to a different stimulus. Now we turn to the second type of associative learning, **operant conditioning**. In operant conditioning, organisms learn to associate a behavior and its consequence (Table 6.1). A pleasant consequence makes that behavior more likely to be repeated in the future. For example, Spirit, a dolphin at the National Aquarium in Baltimore, does a flip in the air when her trainer blows a whistle. The consequence is that she gets a fish.

Classical and Operant Conditioning Compared

	Classical Conditioning	Operant Conditioning
Conditioning approach	An unconditioned stimulus (such as food) is paired with a neutral stimulus (such as a bell). The neutral stimulus eventually becomes the conditioned stimulus, which brings about the conditioned response (salivation).	The target behavior is followed by reinforcement or punishment to either strengthen or weaken it, so that the learner is more likely to exhibit the desired behavior in the future.
Stimulus timing	The stimulus occurs immediately before the response.	The stimulus (either reinforcement or punishment) occurs soon after the response.

Table 6.1

Psychologist B. F. Skinner saw that classical conditioning is limited to existing behaviors that are reflexively elicited, and it doesn't account for new behaviors such as riding a bike. He proposed a theory about how such behaviors come about. Skinner believed that behavior is motivated by the consequences we receive for the behavior: the reinforcements and punishments. His idea that learning is the result of consequences is based on the law of effect, which was first proposed by psychologist Edward Thorndike. According to the **law of effect**, behaviors that are followed by consequences that are satisfying to the organism are more likely to be repeated, and behaviors that are followed by unpleasant consequences are less likely to be repeated (Thorndike, 1911). Essentially, if an organism does something that brings about a desired result, the organism is more likely to do it again. If an organism does something that does not bring about a desired result, the organism is less likely to do it again. An example of the law of effect is in employment. One of the reasons (and often the main reason) we show up for work is because we get paid to do so. If we stop getting paid, we will likely stop showing up—even if we love our job.

Working with Thorndike's law of effect as his foundation, Skinner began conducting scientific experiments on animals (mainly rats and pigeons) to determine how organisms learn through operant conditioning (Skinner, 1938). He placed these animals inside an operant conditioning chamber, which has come to be known as a "Skinner box" (Figure 6.10). A Skinner box contains a lever (for rats) or disk (for pigeons) that the animal can press or peck for a food reward via the dispenser. Speakers and lights can be associated with certain behaviors. A recorder counts the number of responses made by the animal.

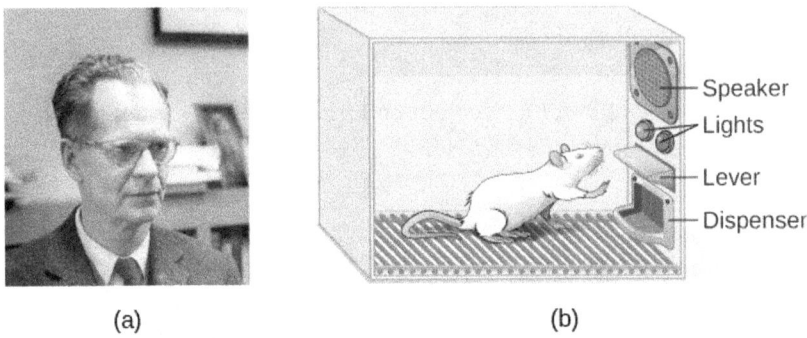

(a) (b)

Figure 6.10 (a) B. F. Skinner developed operant conditioning for systematic study of how behaviors are strengthened or weakened according to their consequences. (b) In a Skinner box, a rat presses a lever in an operant conditioning chamber to receive a food reward. (credit a: modification of work by "Silly rabbit"/Wikimedia Commons)

LINK TO LEARNING

Watch this brief video to see Skinner's interview and a demonstration of operant conditioning of pigeons (http://openstax.org/l/skinner1) to learn more.

In discussing operant conditioning, we use several everyday words—positive, negative, reinforcement, and punishment—in a specialized manner. In operant conditioning, positive and negative do not mean good and bad. Instead, *positive* means you are adding something, and *negative* means you are taking something away. *Reinforcement* means you are increasing a behavior, and *punishment* means you are decreasing a behavior. Reinforcement can be positive or negative, and punishment can also be positive or negative. All reinforcers (positive or negative) *increase* the likelihood of a behavioral response. All punishers (positive or negative) *decrease* the likelihood of a behavioral response. Now let's combine these four terms: positive reinforcement, negative reinforcement, positive punishment, and negative punishment (Table 6.2).

Positive and Negative Reinforcement and Punishment

	Reinforcement	**Punishment**
Positive	Something is *added* to *increase* the likelihood of a behavior.	Something is *added* to *decrease* the likelihood of a behavior.
Negative	Something is *removed* to *increase* the likelihood of a behavior.	Something is *removed* to *decrease* the likelihood of a behavior.

Table 6.2

REINFORCEMENT

The most effective way to teach a person or animal a new behavior is with positive reinforcement. In **positive reinforcement**, a desirable stimulus is added to increase a behavior.

For example, you tell your five-year-old son, Jerome, that if he cleans his room, he will get a toy. Jerome quickly cleans his room because he wants a new art set. Let's pause for a moment. Some people might say, "Why should I reward my child for doing what is expected?" But in fact we are constantly and consistently rewarded in our lives. Our paychecks are rewards, as are high grades and acceptance into our preferred school. Being praised for doing a good job and for passing a driver's test is also a reward. Positive reinforcement as a learning tool is extremely effective. It has been found that one of the most effective ways to increase achievement in school districts with below-average reading scores was to pay the children to read. Specifically, second-grade students in Dallas were paid $2 each time they read a book and passed a short quiz about the book. The result was a significant increase in reading comprehension (Fryer, 2010). What do you think about this program? If Skinner were alive today, he would probably think this was a great idea. He was a strong proponent of using operant conditioning principles to influence students' behavior at school. In fact, in addition to the Skinner box, he also invented what he called a teaching machine that was designed to reward small steps in learning (Skinner, 1961)—an early forerunner of computer-assisted learning. His teaching machine tested students' knowledge as they worked through various school subjects. If students answered questions correctly, they received immediate positive reinforcement and could continue; if they answered incorrectly, they did not receive any reinforcement. The idea was that students would spend additional time studying the material to increase their chance of being reinforced the next time (Skinner, 1961).

In **negative reinforcement**, an undesirable stimulus is removed to increase a behavior. For example, car manufacturers use the principles of negative reinforcement in their seatbelt systems, which go "beep, beep, beep" until you fasten your seatbelt. The annoying sound stops when you exhibit the desired behavior, increasing the likelihood that you will buckle up in the future. Negative reinforcement is also used frequently in horse training. Riders apply pressure—by pulling the reins or squeezing their legs—and then remove the pressure when the horse performs the desired behavior, such as turning or speeding up. The pressure is the negative stimulus that the horse wants to remove.

PUNISHMENT

Many people confuse negative reinforcement with punishment in operant conditioning, but they are two very different mechanisms. Remember that reinforcement, even when it is negative, always increases a behavior. In contrast, **punishment** always decreases a behavior. In **positive punishment**, you add an undesirable stimulus to decrease a behavior. An example of positive punishment is scolding a student to get the student to stop texting in class. In this case, a stimulus (the reprimand) is added in order to decrease the behavior (texting in class). In **negative punishment**, you remove a pleasant stimulus to decrease behavior. For example, when a child misbehaves, a parent can take away a favorite toy. In this case, a stimulus (the toy) is removed in order to decrease the behavior.

Punishment, especially when it is immediate, is one way to decrease undesirable behavior. For example, imagine your four-year-old son, Brandon, hit his younger brother. You have Brandon write 100 times "I will not hit my brother" (positive punishment). Chances are he won't repeat this behavior. While strategies like this are common today, in the past children were often subject to physical punishment, such as spanking. It's important to be aware of some of the drawbacks in using physical punishment on children. First, punishment may teach fear. Brandon may become fearful of the street, but he also may become fearful of the person who delivered the punishment—you, his parent. Similarly, children who are punished by teachers may come to fear the teacher and try to avoid school (Gershoff et al., 2010). Consequently, most schools in the United States have banned corporal punishment. Second, punishment may cause children to become more aggressive and prone to antisocial behavior and delinquency (Gershoff, 2002). They see their parents resort to spanking when they become angry and frustrated, so, in turn, they may act out this same behavior when they become angry and frustrated. For example, because you spank Brenda when you are angry with her for her misbehavior, she might start hitting her friends when they won't share their toys.

While positive punishment can be effective in some cases, Skinner suggested that the use of punishment should be weighed against the possible negative effects. Today's psychologists and parenting experts favor reinforcement over punishment—they recommend that you catch your child doing something good and reward her for it.

Shaping

In his operant conditioning experiments, Skinner often used an approach called shaping. Instead of rewarding only the target behavior, in **shaping**, we reward successive approximations of a target behavior. Why is shaping needed? Remember that in order for reinforcement to work, the organism must first display the behavior. Shaping is needed because it is extremely unlikely that an organism will display anything but the simplest of behaviors spontaneously. In shaping, behaviors are broken down into many small, achievable steps. The specific steps used in the process are the following:

1. Reinforce any response that resembles the desired behavior.
2. Then reinforce the response that more closely resembles the desired behavior. You will no longer reinforce the previously reinforced response.
3. Next, begin to reinforce the response that even more closely resembles the desired behavior.
4. Continue to reinforce closer and closer approximations of the desired behavior.
5. Finally, only reinforce the desired behavior.

Shaping is often used in teaching a complex behavior or chain of behaviors. Skinner used shaping to teach pigeons not only such relatively simple behaviors as pecking a disk in a Skinner box, but also many unusual and entertaining behaviors, such as turning in circles, walking in figure eights, and even playing ping pong; the technique is commonly used by animal trainers today. An important part of shaping is stimulus discrimination. Recall Pavlov's dogs—he trained them to respond to the tone of a bell, and not to similar tones or sounds. This discrimination is also important in operant conditioning and in shaping behavior.

LINK TO LEARNING

Watch this brief video of Skinner's pigeons playing ping pong (http://openstax.org/l/pingpong) to learn more.

It's easy to see how shaping is effective in teaching behaviors to animals, but how does shaping work with humans? Let's consider parents whose goal is to have their child learn to clean his room. They use shaping to help him master steps toward the goal. Instead of performing the entire task, they set up these steps and reinforce each step. First, he cleans up one toy. Second, he cleans up five toys. Third, he chooses whether to pick up ten toys or put his books and clothes away. Fourth, he cleans up everything except two toys. Finally, he cleans his entire room.

PRIMARY AND SECONDARY REINFORCERS

Rewards such as stickers, praise, money, toys, and more can be used to reinforce learning. Let's go back to Skinner's rats again. How did the rats learn to press the lever in the Skinner box? They were rewarded with food each time they pressed the lever. For animals, food would be an obvious reinforcer.

What would be a good reinforcer for humans? For your child Chris, it was the promise of a toy when they cleaned their room. How about Sydney, the soccer player? If you gave Sydney a piece of candy every time Sydney scored a goal, you would be using a **primary reinforcer**. Primary reinforcers are reinforcers that have innate reinforcing qualities. These kinds of reinforcers are not learned. Water, food, sleep, shelter, sex, and touch, among others, are primary reinforcers. Pleasure is also a primary reinforcer. Organisms do not lose their drive for these things. For most people, jumping in a cool lake on a very hot day would be reinforcing and the cool lake would be innately reinforcing—the water would cool the person off (a physical need), as well as provide pleasure.

A **secondary reinforcer** has no inherent value and only has reinforcing qualities when linked with a primary reinforcer. Praise, linked to affection, is one example of a secondary reinforcer, as when you called out "Great shot!" every time Sydney made a goal. Another example, money, is only worth something when you can use it to buy other things—either things that satisfy basic needs (food, water, shelter—all primary reinforcers) or other secondary reinforcers. If you were on a remote island in the middle of the Pacific Ocean and you had stacks of money, the money would not be useful if you could not spend it. What about the stickers on the behavior chart? They also are secondary reinforcers.

Sometimes, instead of stickers on a sticker chart, a token is used. Tokens, which are also secondary reinforcers, can then be traded in for rewards and prizes. Entire behavior management systems, known as token economies, are built around the use of these kinds of token reinforcers. Token economies have been found to be very effective at modifying behavior in a variety of settings such as schools, prisons, and mental hospitals. For example, a study by Cangi and Daly (2013) found that use of a token economy increased appropriate social behaviors and reduced inappropriate behaviors in a group of autistic school children. Autistic children tend to exhibit disruptive behaviors such as pinching and hitting. When the children in the study exhibited appropriate behavior (not hitting or pinching), they received a "quiet hands" token. When they hit or pinched, they lost a token. The children could then exchange specified amounts of tokens for minutes of playtime.

EVERYDAY CONNECTION

Behavior Modification in Children

Parents and teachers often use behavior modification to change a child's behavior. Behavior modification uses the principles of operant conditioning to accomplish behavior change so that undesirable behaviors are switched for more socially acceptable ones. Some teachers and parents create a sticker chart, in which several behaviors are listed (Figure 6.11). Sticker charts are a form of token economies, as described in the text. Each time children perform the behavior, they get a sticker, and after a certain number of stickers, they get a prize, or reinforcer. The goal is to increase acceptable behaviors and decrease misbehavior. Remember, it is best to reinforce desired behaviors, rather than to use punishment. In the classroom, the teacher can reinforce a wide range of behaviors, from students raising their hands, to walking quietly in the hall, to turning in their homework. At home, parents might create a behavior chart that rewards children for things such as putting away toys, brushing their teeth, and helping with dinner. In order for behavior modification to be effective, the reinforcement needs to be connected with the behavior; the reinforcement must matter to the child and be done consistently.

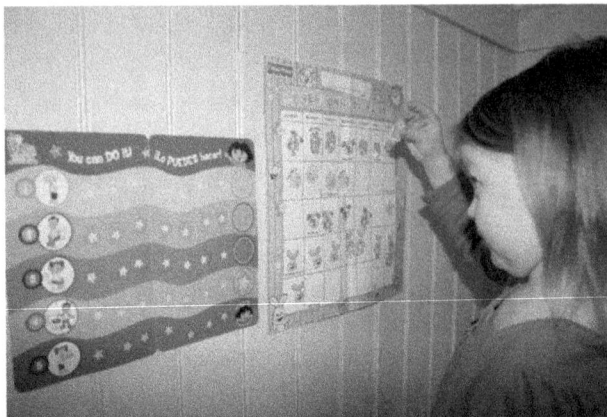

Figure 6.11 Sticker charts are a form of positive reinforcement and a tool for behavior modification. Once this child earns a certain number of stickers for demonstrating a desired behavior, she will be rewarded with a trip to the ice cream parlor. (credit: Abigail Batchelder)

Time-out is another popular technique used in behavior modification with children. It operates on the principle of negative punishment. When a child demonstrates an undesirable behavior, she is removed from the desirable activity at hand (Figure 6.12). For example, say that Sophia and her brother Mario are playing with building blocks. Sophia throws some blocks at her brother, so you give her a warning that she will go to time-out if she does it again. A few minutes later, she throws more blocks at Mario. You remove Sophia from the room for a few minutes. When she comes back, she doesn't throw blocks.

There are several important points that you should know if you plan to implement time-out as a behavior modification technique. First, make sure the child is being removed from a desirable activity and placed in a less desirable location. If the activity is something undesirable for the child, this technique will backfire because it is more enjoyable for the child to be removed from the activity. Second, the length of the time-out is important. The general rule of thumb is one minute for each year of the child's age. Sophia is five; therefore, she sits in a time-out for five minutes. Setting a timer helps children know how long they have to sit in time-out. Finally, as a caregiver, keep several guidelines in mind over the course of a time-out: remain calm when directing your child to time-out; ignore your child during time-out (because caregiver attention may reinforce misbehavior); and give the child a hug or a kind word when time-out is over.

(a)   (b)

Figure 6.12 Time-out is a popular form of negative punishment used by caregivers. When a child misbehaves, he or she is removed from a desirable activity in an effort to decrease the unwanted behavior. For example, (a) a child might be playing on the playground with friends and push another child; (b) the child who misbehaved would then be removed from the activity for a short period of time. (credit a: modification of work by Simone Ramella; credit b: modification of work by "Spring Dew"/Flickr)

REINFORCEMENT SCHEDULES

Remember, the best way to teach a person or animal a behavior is to use positive reinforcement. For example, Skinner used positive reinforcement to teach rats to press a lever in a Skinner box. At first, the rat might randomly hit the lever while exploring the box, and out would come a pellet of food. After eating the pellet, what do you think the hungry rat did next? It hit the lever again, and received another pellet of food. Each time the rat hit the lever, a pellet of food came out. When an organism receives a reinforcer each time it displays a behavior, it is called **continuous reinforcement**. This reinforcement schedule is the quickest way to teach someone a behavior, and it is especially effective in training a new behavior. Let's look back at the dog that was learning to sit earlier in the chapter. Now, each time he sits, you give him a treat. Timing is important here: you will be most successful if you present the reinforcer immediately after he sits, so that he can make an association between the target behavior (sitting) and the consequence (getting a treat).

LINK TO LEARNING

Watch this **video clip of veterinarian Dr. Sophia Yin shaping a dog's behavior using the steps outlined above (http://openstax.org/l/sueyin)** to learn more.

Once a behavior is trained, researchers and trainers often turn to another type of reinforcement schedule—partial reinforcement. In **partial reinforcement**, also referred to as intermittent reinforcement, the person or animal does not get reinforced every time they perform the desired behavior. There are several different types of partial reinforcement schedules (Table 6.3). These schedules are described as either fixed or variable, and as either interval or ratio. *Fixed* refers to the number of responses between reinforcements, or the amount of time between reinforcements, which is set and unchanging. *Variable* refers to the number of responses or amount of time between reinforcements, which varies or changes. *Interval* means the schedule is based on the time between reinforcements, and *ratio* means the schedule is based on the number of responses between reinforcements.

Reinforcement Schedules

Reinforcement Schedule	Description	Result	Example
Fixed interval	Reinforcement is delivered at predictable time intervals (e.g., after 5, 10, 15, and 20 minutes).	Moderate response rate with significant pauses after reinforcement	Hospital patient uses patient-controlled, doctor-timed pain relief
Variable interval	Reinforcement is delivered at unpredictable time intervals (e.g., after 5, 7, 10, and 20 minutes).	Moderate yet steady response rate	Checking Facebook
Fixed ratio	Reinforcement is delivered after a predictable number of responses (e.g., after 2, 4, 6, and 8 responses).	High response rate with pauses after reinforcement	Piecework—factory worker getting paid for every x number of items manufactured
Variable ratio	Reinforcement is delivered after an unpredictable number of responses (e.g., after 1, 4, 5, and 9 responses).	High and steady response rate	Gambling

Table 6.3

Now let's combine these four terms. A **fixed interval reinforcement schedule** is when behavior is rewarded after a set amount of time. For example, June undergoes major surgery in a hospital. During recovery, she is expected to experience pain and will require prescription medications for pain relief. June is given an IV drip with a patient-controlled painkiller. Her doctor sets a limit: one dose per hour. June pushes a button when pain becomes difficult, and she receives a dose of medication. Since the reward (pain relief) only occurs on a fixed interval, there is no point in exhibiting the behavior when it will not be rewarded.

With a **variable interval reinforcement schedule**, the person or animal gets the reinforcement based on varying amounts of time, which are unpredictable. Say that Manuel is the manager at a fast-food restaurant. Every once in a while someone from the quality control division comes to Manuel's restaurant. If the restaurant is clean and the service is fast, everyone on that shift earns a $20 bonus. Manuel never knows when the quality control person will show up, so he always tries to keep the restaurant clean and ensures that his employees provide prompt and courteous service. His productivity regarding prompt service and keeping a clean restaurant are steady because he wants his crew to earn the bonus.

With a **fixed ratio reinforcement schedule**, there are a set number of responses that must occur before the behavior is rewarded. Carla sells glasses at an eyeglass store, and she earns a commission every time she sells a pair of glasses. She always tries to sell people more pairs of glasses, including prescription sunglasses or a backup pair, so she can increase her commission. She does not care if the person really needs the prescription sunglasses, Carla just wants her bonus. The quality of what Carla sells does not matter because her commission is not based on quality; it's only based on the number of pairs sold. This distinction in the quality of performance can help determine which reinforcement method is most appropriate for a particular situation. Fixed ratios are better suited to optimize the quantity of output, whereas a fixed interval, in which the reward is not quantity based, can lead to a higher quality of output.

In a **variable ratio reinforcement schedule**, the number of responses needed for a reward varies. This is the most powerful partial reinforcement schedule. An example of the variable ratio reinforcement schedule is gambling. Imagine that Sarah—generally a smart, thrifty woman—visits Las Vegas for the first time. She is not a gambler, but out of curiosity she puts a quarter into the slot machine, and then another, and another. Nothing happens. Two dollars in quarters later, her curiosity is fading, and she is just about to quit. But then, the machine lights up, bells go off, and Sarah gets 50 quarters back. That's more like it! Sarah gets back to inserting quarters with renewed interest, and a few minutes later she has used up all her gains and is $10 in the hole. Now might be a sensible time to quit. And yet, she keeps putting money into the slot machine because she never knows when the next reinforcement is coming. She keeps thinking that with the next quarter she could win $50, or $100, or even more. Because the reinforcement schedule in most types of gambling has a variable ratio schedule, people keep trying and hoping that the next time they will win big. This is one of the reasons that gambling is so addictive—and so resistant to extinction.

In operant conditioning, extinction of a reinforced behavior occurs at some point after reinforcement stops, and the speed at which this happens depends on the reinforcement schedule. In a variable ratio schedule, the point of extinction comes very slowly, as described above. But in the other reinforcement schedules, extinction may come quickly. For example, if June presses the button for the pain relief medication before the allotted time her doctor has approved, no medication is administered. She is on a fixed interval reinforcement schedule (dosed hourly), so extinction occurs quickly when reinforcement doesn't come at the expected time. Among the reinforcement schedules, variable ratio is the most productive and the most resistant to extinction. Fixed interval is the least productive and the easiest to extinguish (**Figure 6.13**).

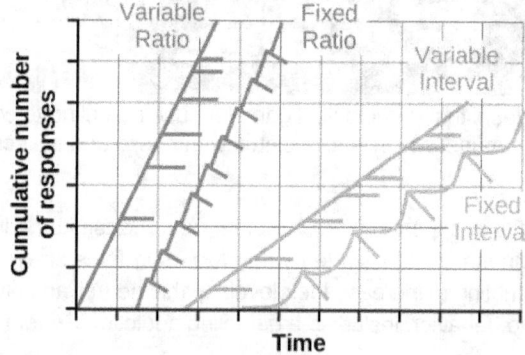

Figure 6.13 The four reinforcement schedules yield different response patterns. The variable ratio schedule is unpredictable and yields high and steady response rates, with little if any pause after reinforcement (e.g., gambler). A fixed ratio schedule is predictable and produces a high response rate, with a short pause after reinforcement (e.g., eyeglass saleswoman). The variable interval schedule is unpredictable and produces a moderate, steady response rate (e.g., restaurant manager). The fixed interval schedule yields a scallop-shaped response pattern, reflecting a significant pause after reinforcement (e.g., surgery patient).

CONNECT THE CONCEPTS

Gambling and the Brain

Skinner (1953) stated, "If the gambling establishment cannot persuade a patron to turn over money with no return, it may achieve the same effect by returning part of the patron's money on a variable-ratio schedule" (p. 397).

Skinner uses gambling as an example of the power of the variable-ratio reinforcement schedule for maintaining behavior even during long periods without any reinforcement. In fact, Skinner was so confident in his knowledge of gambling addiction that he even claimed he could turn a pigeon into a pathological gambler ("Skinner's Utopia," 1971). It is indeed true that variable-ratio schedules keep behavior quite persistent—just imagine the frequency of a child's tantrums if a parent gives in even once to the behavior. The occasional reward makes it almost impossible to stop the behavior.

Recent research in rats has failed to support Skinner's idea that training on variable-ratio schedules alone causes pathological gambling (Laskowski et al., 2019). However, other research suggests that gambling does seem to work on the brain in the same way as most addictive drugs, and so there may be some combination of brain chemistry and reinforcement schedule that could lead to problem gambling (Figure 6.14). Specifically, modern research shows the connection between gambling and the activation of the reward centers of the brain that use the neurotransmitter (brain chemical) dopamine (Murch & Clark, 2016). Interestingly, gamblers don't even have to win to experience the "rush" of dopamine in the brain. "Near misses," or almost winning but not actually winning, also have been shown to increase activity in the ventral striatum and other brain reward centers that use dopamine (Chase & Clark, 2010). These brain effects are almost identical to those produced by addictive drugs like cocaine and heroin (Murch & Clark, 2016). Based on the neuroscientific evidence showing these similarities, the DSM-5 now considers gambling an addiction, while earlier versions of the DSM classified gambling as an impulse control disorder.

Figure 6.14 Some research suggests that pathological gamblers use gambling to compensate for abnormally low levels of the hormone norepinephrine, which is associated with stress and is secreted in moments of arousal and thrill. (credit: Ted Murphy)

In addition to dopamine, gambling also appears to involve other neurotransmitters, including norepinephrine and serotonin (Potenza, 2013). Norepinephrine is secreted when a person feels stress, arousal, or thrill. It may be that pathological gamblers use gambling to increase their levels of this neurotransmitter. Deficiencies in serotonin might also contribute to compulsive behavior, including a gambling addiction (Potenza, 2013).

It may be that pathological gamblers' brains are different than those of other people, and perhaps this difference may somehow have led to their gambling addiction, as these studies seem to suggest. However, it is very difficult to ascertain the cause because it is impossible to conduct a true experiment (it would be unethical to try to turn randomly assigned participants into problem gamblers). Therefore, it may be that causation actually moves in the opposite direction—perhaps the act of gambling somehow changes neurotransmitter levels in some gamblers' brains. It also is possible that some overlooked factor, or confounding variable, played a role in both the gambling addiction and the differences in brain chemistry.

COGNITION AND LATENT LEARNING

Strict behaviorists like Watson and Skinner focused exclusively on studying behavior rather than cognition (such as thoughts and expectations). In fact, Skinner was such a staunch believer that cognition didn't matter that his ideas were considered **radical behaviorism**. Skinner considered the mind a "black box"—something completely unknowable—and, therefore, something not to be studied. However, another behaviorist, Edward C. Tolman, had a different opinion. Tolman's experiments with rats demonstrated that organisms can learn even if they do not receive immediate reinforcement (Tolman & Honzik, 1930; Tolman, Ritchie, & Kalish, 1946). This finding was in conflict with the prevailing idea at the time that reinforcement must be immediate in order for learning to occur, thus suggesting a cognitive aspect to learning.

In the experiments, Tolman placed hungry rats in a maze with no reward for finding their way through it. He also studied a comparison group that was rewarded with food at the end of the maze. As the unreinforced rats explored the maze, they developed a **cognitive map**: a mental picture of the layout of the maze (Figure 6.15). After 10 sessions in the maze without reinforcement, food was placed in a goal box at the end of the maze. As soon as the rats became aware of the food, they were able to find their way through the maze quickly, just as quickly as the comparison group, which had been rewarded with food all along. This is known as **latent learning**: learning that occurs but is not observable in behavior until there is a reason to demonstrate it.

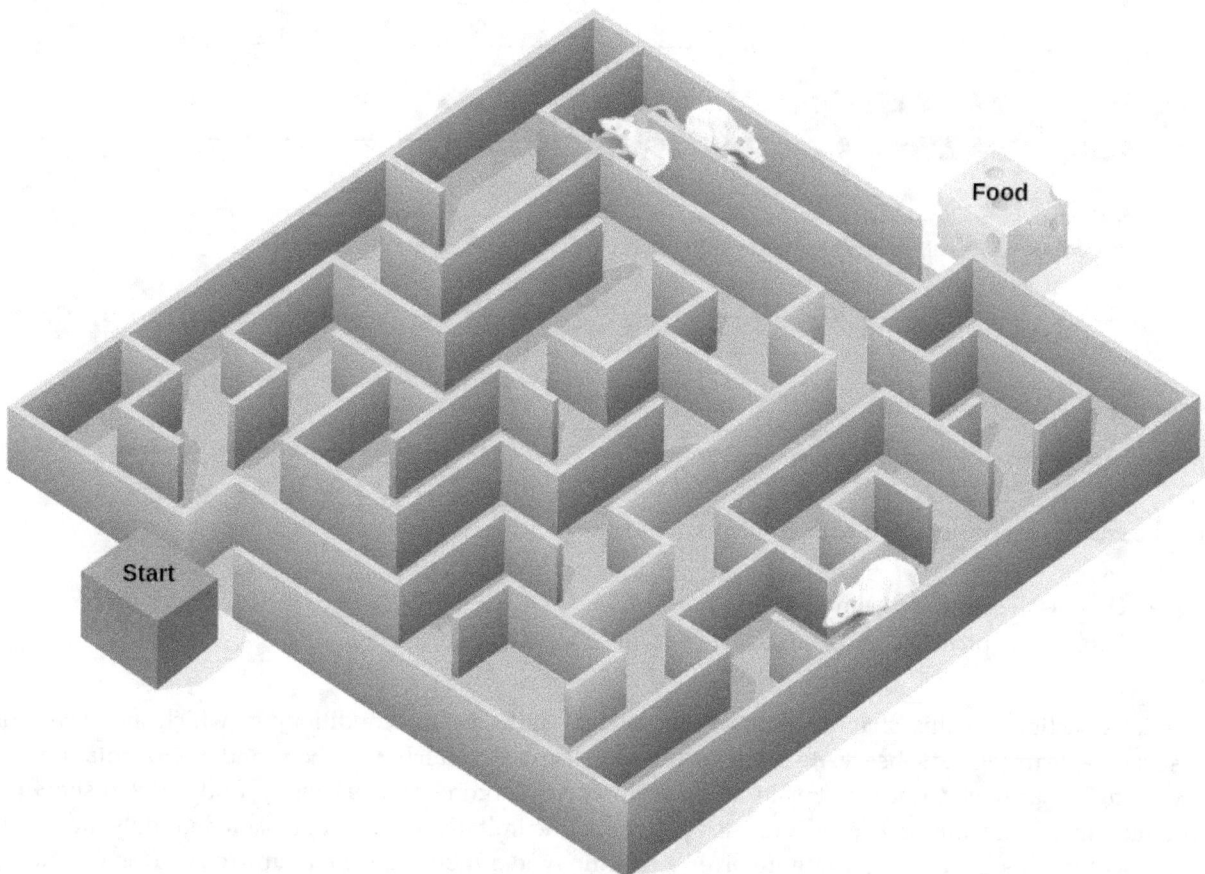

Figure 6.15 Psychologist Edward Tolman found that rats use cognitive maps to navigate through a maze. Have you ever worked your way through various levels on a video game? You learned when to turn left or right, move up or down. In that case you were relying on a cognitive map, just like the rats in a maze. (credit: modification of work by "FutUndBeidl"/Flickr)

Latent learning also occurs in humans. Children may learn by watching the actions of their parents but only demonstrate it at a later date, when the learned material is needed. For example, suppose that Ravi's dad drives him to school every day. In this way, Ravi learns the route from his house to his school, but he's never driven there himself, so he has not had a chance to demonstrate that he's learned the way. One morning Ravi's dad has to leave early for a meeting, so he can't drive Ravi to school. Instead, Ravi follows the same route on his bike that his dad would have taken in the car. This demonstrates latent learning. Ravi had learned the route to school, but had no need to demonstrate this knowledge earlier.

> **EVERYDAY CONNECTION**
>
> **This Place Is Like a Maze**
>
> Have you ever gotten lost in a building and couldn't find your way back out? While that can be frustrating, you're not alone. At one time or another we've all gotten lost in places like a museum, hospital, or university library. Whenever we go someplace new, we build a mental representation—or cognitive map—of the location, as Tolman's rats built a cognitive map of their maze. However, some buildings are confusing because they include many areas that look alike or have short lines of sight. Because of this, it's often difficult to predict what's around a corner or decide whether to turn left or right to get out of a building. Psychologist Laura Carlson (2010) suggests that what we place in our cognitive map can impact our success in navigating through the environment. She suggests that paying attention to specific features upon entering a building, such as a picture on the wall, a fountain, a statue, or an escalator, adds information to our cognitive map that can be used later to help find our way out of the building.

> **LINK TO LEARNING**
>
> Watch this video about Carlson's studies on cognitive maps and navigation in buildings (http://openstax.org/l/carlsonmaps) to learn more.

6.4 Observational Learning (Modeling)

Learning Objectives

By the end of this section, you will be able to:
- Define observational learning
- Discuss the steps in the modeling process
- Explain the prosocial and antisocial effects of observational learning

Previous sections of this chapter focused on classical and operant conditioning, which are forms of associative learning. In **observational learning**, we learn by watching others and then imitating, or modeling, what they do or say. For instance, have you ever gone to YouTube to find a video showing you how to do something? The individuals performing the imitated behavior are called **models**. Research suggests that this imitative learning involves a specific type of neuron, called a mirror neuron (Hickock, 2010; Rizzolatti, Fadiga, Fogassi, & Gallese, 2002; Rizzolatti, Fogassi, & Gallese, 2006).

Humans and other animals are capable of observational learning. As you will see, the phrase "monkey see, monkey do" really is accurate (Figure 6.16). The same could be said about other animals. For example, in a study of social learning in chimpanzees, researchers gave juice boxes with straws to two groups of captive chimpanzees. The first group dipped the straw into the juice box, and then sucked on the small amount of juice at the end of the straw. The second group sucked through the straw directly, getting much more juice. When the first group, the "dippers," observed the second group, "the suckers," what do you think happened? All of the "dippers" in the first group switched to sucking through the straws directly. By simply observing the other chimps and modeling their behavior, they learned that this was a more efficient method of getting juice (Yamamoto, Humle, and Tanaka, 2013).

Figure 6.16 This spider monkey learned to drink water from a plastic bottle by seeing the behavior modeled by a human. (credit: U.S. Air Force, Senior Airman Kasey Close)

Imitation is much more obvious in humans, but is imitation really the sincerest form of flattery? Consider Claire's experience with observational learning. Claire's nine-year-old son, Jay, was getting into trouble at school and was defiant at home. Claire feared that Jay would end up like her brothers, two of whom were in prison. One day, after yet another bad day at school and another negative note from the teacher, Claire, at her wit's end, beat her son with a belt to get him to behave. Later that night, as she put her children to bed, Claire witnessed her four-year-old daughter, Anna, take a belt to her teddy bear and whip it. Claire was horrified, realizing that Anna was imitating her mother. It was then that Claire knew she wanted to discipline her children in a different manner.

Like Tolman, whose experiments with rats suggested a cognitive component to learning, psychologist Albert Bandura's ideas about learning were different from those of strict behaviorists. Bandura and other researchers proposed a brand of behaviorism called social learning theory, which took cognitive processes into account. According to Bandura, pure behaviorism could not explain why learning can take place in the absence of external reinforcement. He felt that internal mental states must also have a role in learning and that observational learning involves much more than imitation. In imitation, a person simply copies what the model does. Observational learning is much more complex. According to Lefrançois (2012) there are several ways that observational learning can occur:

1. You learn a new response. After watching your coworker get chewed out by your boss for coming in late, you start leaving home 10 minutes earlier so that you won't be late.

2. You choose whether or not to imitate the model depending on what you saw happen to the model. Remember Julian and his father? When learning to surf, Julian might watch how his father pops up successfully on his surfboard and then attempt to do the same thing. On the other hand, Julian might learn not to touch a hot stove after watching his father get burned on a stove.

3. You learn a general rule that you can apply to other situations.

Bandura identified three kinds of models: live, verbal, and symbolic. A live model demonstrates a behavior in person, as when Ben stood up on his surfboard so that Julian could see how he did it. A verbal instructional model does not perform the behavior, but instead explains or describes the behavior, as when a soccer coach tells his young players to kick the ball with the side of the foot, not with the toe. A symbolic model can be fictional characters or real people who demonstrate behaviors in books, movies, television shows, video games, or Internet sources (Figure 6.17).

(a) (b)

Figure 6.17 (a) Yoga students learn by observation as their yoga instructor demonstrates the correct stance and movement for her students (live model). (b) Models don't have to be present for learning to occur: through symbolic modeling, this child can learn a behavior by watching someone demonstrate it on television. (credit a: modification of work by Tony Cecala; credit b: modification of work by Andrew Hyde)

LINK TO LEARNING

Latent learning and modeling are used all the time in the world of marketing and advertising. This Ford commercial starring Derek Jeter (http://openstax.org/l/jeter) played for months across the New York, New Jersey, and Connecticut areas. Jeter is an award-winning baseball player for the New York Yankees. The commercial aired in a part of the country where Jeter is an incredibly well-known athlete. He is wealthy, and considered very loyal and good looking. What message are the advertisers sending by having him featured in the ad? How effective do you think it is?

STEPS IN THE MODELING PROCESS

Of course, we don't learn a behavior simply by observing a model. Bandura described specific steps in the process of modeling that must be followed if learning is to be successful: attention, retention, reproduction, and motivation. First, you must be focused on what the model is doing—you have to pay attention. Next, you must be able to retain, or remember, what you observed; this is retention. Then, you must be able to perform the behavior that you observed and committed to memory; this is reproduction. Finally, you must have motivation. You need to want to copy the behavior, and whether or not you are motivated depends on what happened to the model. If you saw that the model was reinforced for her behavior, you will be more motivated to copy her. This is known as **vicarious reinforcement**. On the other hand, if you observed the model being punished, you would be less motivated to copy her. This is called **vicarious punishment**. For example, imagine that four-year-old Allison watched her older sister Kaitlyn playing in their mother's makeup, and then saw Kaitlyn get a time out when their mother came in. After their mother left the room, Allison was tempted to play in the make-up, but she did not want to get a time-out from her mother. What do you think she did? Once you actually demonstrate the new behavior, the reinforcement you receive plays a part in whether or not you will repeat the behavior.

Bandura researched modeling behavior, particularly children's modeling of adults' aggressive and violent behaviors (Bandura, Ross, & Ross, 1961). He conducted an experiment with a five-foot inflatable doll that he called a Bobo doll. In the experiment, children's aggressive behavior was influenced by whether the teacher was punished for her behavior. In one scenario, a teacher acted aggressively with the doll, hitting, throwing, and even punching the doll, while a child watched. There were two types of responses by the children to the teacher's behavior. When the teacher was punished for her bad behavior, the children decreased their tendency to act as she had. When the teacher was praised or ignored (and not punished for her behavior), the children imitated what she did, and even what she said. They punched, kicked, and yelled at the doll.

> **LINK TO LEARNING**
>
> Watch this **video clip about the famous Bobo doll experiment (http://openstax.org/l/bobodoll)** to see a portion of the experiment and an interview with Albert Bandura.

What are the implications of this study? Bandura concluded that we watch and learn, and that this learning can have both prosocial and antisocial effects. Prosocial (positive) models can be used to encourage socially acceptable behavior. Parents in particular should take note of this finding. If you want your children to read, then read to them. Let them see you reading. Keep books in your home. Talk about your favorite books. If you want your children to be healthy, then let them see you eat right and exercise, and spend time engaging in physical fitness activities together. The same holds true for qualities like kindness, courtesy, and honesty. The main idea is that children observe and learn from their parents, even their parents' morals, so be consistent and toss out the old adage "Do as I say, not as I do," because children tend to copy what you do instead of what you say. Besides parents, many public figures, such as Martin Luther King, Jr. and Mahatma Gandhi, are viewed as prosocial models who are able to inspire global social change. Can you think of someone who has been a prosocial model in your life?

The antisocial effects of observational learning are also worth mentioning. As you saw from the example of Claire at the beginning of this section, her daughter viewed Claire's aggressive behavior and copied it. Research suggests that this may help to explain why abused children often grow up to be abusers themselves (Murrell, Christoff, & Henning, 2007). In fact, about 30% of abused children become abusive parents (U.S. Department of Health & Human Services, 2013). We tend to do what we know. Abused children, who grow up witnessing their parents deal with anger and frustration through violent and aggressive acts, often learn to behave in that manner themselves. Sadly, it's a vicious cycle that's difficult to break.

Some studies suggest that violent television shows, movies, and video games may also have antisocial effects (Figure 6.18) although further research needs to be done to understand the correlational and causational aspects of media violence and behavior. Some studies have found a link between viewing violence and aggression seen in children (Anderson & Gentile, 2008; Kirsch, 2010; Miller, Grabell, Thomas, Bermann, & Graham-Bermann, 2012). These findings may not be surprising, given that a child graduating from high school has been exposed to around 200,000 violent acts including murder, robbery, torture, bombings, beatings, and rape through various forms of media (Huston et al., 1992). Not only might viewing media violence affect aggressive behavior by teaching people to act that way in real life situations, but it has also been suggested that repeated exposure to violent acts also desensitizes people to it. Psychologists are working to understand this dynamic.

Figure 6.18 Can video games make us violent? Psychological researchers study this topic. (credit: "woodleywonderworks"/Flickr)

LINK TO LEARNING

View this video about the connection between violent video games and violent behavior (http://openstax.org/l/videogamevio) to learn more.

WHAT DO YOU THINK?

Violent Media and Aggression

Does watching violent media or playing violent video games cause aggression? Albert Bandura's early studies suggested television violence increased aggression in children, and more recent studies support these findings. For example, research by Craig Anderson and colleagues (Anderson, Bushman, Donnerstein, Hummer, & Warbuten, 2015; Anderson et al., 2010; Bushman et al., 2016) found extensive evidence to suggest a causal link between hours of exposure to violent media and aggressive thoughts and behaviors. However, studies by Christopher Ferguson and others suggests that while there may be a link between violent media exposure and aggression, research to date has not accounted for other risk factors for aggression including mental health and family life (Ferguson, 2011; Gentile, 2016). What do think?

Key Terms

acquisition period of initial learning in classical conditioning in which a human or an animal begins to connect a neutral stimulus and an unconditioned stimulus so that the neutral stimulus will begin to elicit the conditioned response

associative learning form of learning that involves connecting certain stimuli or events that occur together in the environment (classical and operant conditioning)

classical conditioning learning in which the stimulus or experience occurs before the behavior and then gets paired or associated with the behavior

cognitive map mental picture of the layout of the environment

conditioned response (CR) response caused by the conditioned stimulus

conditioned stimulus (CS) stimulus that elicits a response due to its being paired with an unconditioned stimulus

continuous reinforcement rewarding a behavior every time it occurs

extinction decrease in the conditioned response when the unconditioned stimulus is no longer paired with the conditioned stimulus

fixed interval reinforcement schedule behavior is rewarded after a set amount of time

fixed ratio reinforcement schedule set number of responses must occur before a behavior is rewarded

higher-order conditioning (also, second-order conditioning) using a conditioned stimulus to condition a neutral stimulus

instinct unlearned knowledge, involving complex patterns of behavior; instincts are thought to be more prevalent in lower animals than in humans

latent learning learning that occurs, but it may not be evident until there is a reason to demonstrate it

law of effect behavior that is followed by consequences satisfying to the organism will be repeated and behaviors that are followed by unpleasant consequences will be discouraged

learning change in behavior or knowledge that is the result of experience

model person who performs a behavior that serves as an example (in observational learning)

negative punishment taking away a pleasant stimulus to decrease or stop a behavior

negative reinforcement taking away an undesirable stimulus to increase a behavior

neutral stimulus (NS) stimulus that does not initially elicit a response

observational learning type of learning that occurs by watching others

operant conditioning form of learning in which the stimulus/experience happens after the behavior is demonstrated

partial reinforcement rewarding behavior only some of the time

positive punishment adding an undesirable stimulus to stop or decrease a behavior

positive reinforcement adding a desirable stimulus to increase a behavior

primary reinforcer has innate reinforcing qualities (e.g., food, water, shelter, sex)

punishment implementation of a consequence in order to decrease a behavior

radical behaviorism staunch form of behaviorism developed by B. F. Skinner that suggested that even complex higher mental functions like human language are nothing more than stimulus-outcome associations

reflex unlearned, automatic response by an organism to a stimulus in the environment

reinforcement implementation of a consequence in order to increase a behavior

secondary reinforcer has no inherent value unto itself and only has reinforcing qualities when linked with something else (e.g., money, gold stars, poker chips)

shaping rewarding successive approximations toward a target behavior

spontaneous recovery return of a previously extinguished conditioned response

stimulus discrimination ability to respond differently to similar stimuli

stimulus generalization demonstrating the conditioned response to stimuli that are similar to the conditioned stimulus

unconditioned response (UCR) natural (unlearned) behavior to a given stimulus

unconditioned stimulus (UCS) stimulus that elicits a reflexive response

variable interval reinforcement schedule behavior is rewarded after unpredictable amounts of time have passed

variable ratio reinforcement schedule number of responses differ before a behavior is rewarded

vicarious punishment process where the observer sees the model punished, making the observer less likely to imitate the model's behavior

vicarious reinforcement process where the observer sees the model rewarded, making the observer more likely to imitate the model's behavior

Summary

6.1 What Is Learning?
Instincts and reflexes are innate behaviors—they occur naturally and do not involve learning. In contrast, learning is a change in behavior or knowledge that results from experience. There are three main types of learning: classical conditioning, operant conditioning, and observational learning. Both classical and operant conditioning are forms of associative learning where associations are made between events that occur together. Observational learning is just as it sounds: learning by observing others.

6.2 Classical Conditioning
Pavlov's pioneering work with dogs contributed greatly to what we know about learning. His experiments explored the type of associative learning we now call classical conditioning. In classical conditioning, organisms learn to associate events that repeatedly happen together, and researchers study how a reflexive response to a stimulus can be mapped to a different stimulus—by training an association between the two stimuli. Pavlov's experiments show how stimulus-response bonds are formed. Watson, the founder

of behaviorism, was greatly influenced by Pavlov's work. He tested humans by conditioning fear in an infant known as Little Albert. His findings suggest that classical conditioning can explain how some fears develop.

6.3 Operant Conditioning

Operant conditioning is based on the work of B. F. Skinner. Operant conditioning is a form of learning in which the motivation for a behavior happens *after* the behavior is demonstrated. An animal or a human receives a consequence after performing a specific behavior. The consequence is either a reinforcer or a punisher. All reinforcement (positive or negative) *increases* the likelihood of a behavioral response. All punishment (positive or negative) *decreases* the likelihood of a behavioral response. Several types of reinforcement schedules are used to reward behavior depending on either a set or variable period of time.

6.4 Observational Learning (Modeling)

According to Bandura, learning can occur by watching others and then modeling what they do or say. This is known as observational learning. There are specific steps in the process of modeling that must be followed if learning is to be successful. These steps include attention, retention, reproduction, and motivation. Through modeling, Bandura has shown that children learn many things both good and bad simply by watching their parents, siblings, and others.

Review Questions

1. Which of the following is an example of a reflex that occurs at some point in the development of a human being?
    a. child riding a bike
    b. teen socializing
    c. infant sucking on a nipple
    d. toddler walking

2. Learning is best defined as a relatively permanent change in behavior that _____.
    a. is innate
    b. occurs as a result of experience
    c. is found only in humans
    d. occurs by observing others

3. Two forms of associative learning are _____ and _____.
    a. classical conditioning; operant conditioning
    b. classical conditioning; Pavlovian conditioning
    c. operant conditioning; observational learning
    d. operant conditioning; learning conditioning

4. In _____ the stimulus or experience occurs before the behavior and then gets paired with the behavior.
    a. associative learning
    b. observational learning
    c. operant conditioning
    d. classical conditioning

5. A stimulus that does not initially elicit a response in an organism is a(n) _____.
    a. unconditioned stimulus
    b. neutral stimulus
    c. conditioned stimulus
    d. unconditioned response

6. In Watson and Rayner's experiments, Little Albert was conditioned to fear a white rat, and then he began to be afraid of other furry white objects. This demonstrates _____.
    a. higher order conditioning
    b. acquisition
    c. stimulus discrimination
    d. stimulus generalization

7. Extinction occurs when _____.
   a. the conditioned stimulus is presented repeatedly without being paired with an unconditioned stimulus
   b. the unconditioned stimulus is presented repeatedly without being paired with a conditioned stimulus
   c. the neutral stimulus is presented repeatedly without being paired with an unconditioned stimulus
   d. the neutral stimulus is presented repeatedly without being paired with a conditioned stimulus

8. In Pavlov's work with dogs, the psychic secretions were _____.
   a. unconditioned responses
   b. conditioned responses
   c. unconditioned stimuli
   d. conditioned stimuli

9. _____ is when you take away a pleasant stimulus to stop a behavior.
   a. positive reinforcement
   b. negative reinforcement
   c. positive punishment
   d. negative punishment

10. Which of the following is *not* an example of a primary reinforcer?
    a. food
    b. money
    c. water
    d. sex

11. Rewarding successive approximations toward a target behavior is _____.
    a. shaping
    b. extinction
    c. positive reinforcement
    d. negative reinforcement

12. Slot machines reward gamblers with money according to which reinforcement schedule?
    a. fixed ratio
    b. variable ratio
    c. fixed interval
    d. variable interval

13. The person who performs a behavior that serves as an example is called a _____.
    a. teacher
    b. model
    c. instructor
    d. coach

14. In Bandura's Bobo doll study, when the children who watched the aggressive model were placed in a room with the doll and other toys, they _____.
    a. ignored the doll
    b. played nicely with the doll
    c. played with tinker toys
    d. kicked and threw the doll

15. Which is the correct order of steps in the modeling process?
    a. attention, retention, reproduction, motivation
    b. motivation, attention, reproduction, retention
    c. attention, motivation, retention, reproduction
    d. motivation, attention, retention, reproduction

16. Who proposed observational learning?
    a. Ivan Pavlov
    b. John Watson
    c. Albert Bandura
    d. B. F. Skinner

Critical Thinking Questions

17. Compare and contrast classical and operant conditioning. How are they alike? How do they differ?

18. What is the difference between a reflex and a learned behavior?

19. If the sound of your toaster popping up toast causes your mouth to water, what are the UCS, CS, and CR?

20. Explain how the processes of stimulus generalization and stimulus discrimination are considered opposites.

21. How does a neutral stimulus become a conditioned stimulus?

22. What is a Skinner box and what is its purpose?

23. What is the difference between negative reinforcement and punishment?

24. What is shaping and how would you use shaping to teach a dog to roll over?

25. What is the effect of prosocial modeling and antisocial modeling?

26. Cara is 17 years old. Cara's mother and father both drink alcohol every night. They tell Cara that drinking is bad and she shouldn't do it. Cara goes to a party where beer is being served. What do you think Cara will do? Why?

Personal Application Questions

27. What is your personal definition of learning? How do your ideas about learning compare with the definition of learning presented in this text?

28. What kinds of things have you learned through the process of classical conditioning? Operant conditioning? Observational learning? How did you learn them?

29. Can you think of an example in your life of how classical conditioning has produced a positive emotional response, such as happiness or excitement? How about a negative emotional response, such as fear, anxiety, or anger?

30. Explain the difference between negative reinforcement and punishment, and provide several examples of each based on your own experiences.

31. Think of a behavior that you have that you would like to change. How could you use behavior modification, specifically positive reinforcement, to change your behavior? What is your positive reinforcer?

32. What is something you have learned how to do after watching someone else?

Chapter 7
Thinking and Intelligence

Figure 7.1 Thinking is an important part of our human experience, and one that has captivated people for centuries. Today, it is one area of psychological study. The 19th-century *Girl with a Book* by José Ferraz de Almeida Júnior, the 20th-century sculpture *The Thinker* by August Rodin, and Shi Ke's 10th-century painting *Huike Thinking* all reflect the fascination with the process of human thought. (credit "middle": modification of work by Jason Rogers; credit "right": modification of work by Tang Zu-Ming)

Chapter Outline
7.1 What Is Cognition?
7.2 Language
7.3 Problem Solving
7.4 What Are Intelligence and Creativity?
7.5 Measures of Intelligence
7.6 The Source of Intelligence

Introduction

What is the best way to solve a problem? How does a person who has never seen or touched snow in real life develop an understanding of the concept of snow? How do young children acquire the ability to learn language with no formal instruction? Psychologists who study thinking explore questions like these and are called cognitive psychologists.

Cognitive psychologists also study intelligence. What is intelligence, and how does it vary from person to person? Are "street smarts" a kind of intelligence, and if so, how do they relate to other types of intelligence? What does an IQ test really measure? These questions and more will be explored in this chapter as you study thinking and intelligence.

In other chapters, we discussed the cognitive processes of perception, learning, and memory. In this chapter, we will focus on high-level cognitive processes. As a part of this discussion, we will consider thinking and briefly explore the development and use of language. We will also discuss problem solving and creativity before ending with a discussion of how intelligence is measured and how our biology and environments interact to affect intelligence. After finishing this chapter, you will have a greater appreciation of the higher-level cognitive processes that contribute to our distinctiveness as a species.

7.1 What Is Cognition?

Learning Objectives

By the end of this section, you will be able to:
- Describe cognition
- Distinguish concepts and prototypes
- Explain the difference between natural and artificial concepts
- Describe how schemata are organized and constructed

Imagine all of your thoughts as if they were physical entities, swirling rapidly inside your mind. How is it possible that the brain is able to move from one thought to the next in an organized, orderly fashion? The brain is endlessly perceiving, processing, planning, organizing, and remembering—it is always active. Yet, you don't notice most of your brain's activity as you move throughout your daily routine. This is only one facet of the complex processes involved in cognition. Simply put, **cognition** is thinking, and it encompasses the processes associated with perception, knowledge, problem solving, judgment, language, and memory. Scientists who study cognition are searching for ways to understand how we integrate, organize, and utilize our conscious cognitive experiences without being aware of all of the unconscious work that our brains are doing (for example, Kahneman, 2011).

COGNITION

Upon waking each morning, you begin thinking—contemplating the tasks that you must complete that day. In what order should you run your errands? Should you go to the bank, the cleaners, or the grocery store first? Can you get these things done before you head to class or will they need to wait until school is done? These thoughts are one example of cognition at work. Exceptionally complex, cognition is an essential feature of human consciousness, yet not all aspects of cognition are consciously experienced.

Cognitive psychology is the field of psychology dedicated to examining how people think. It attempts to explain how and why we think the way we do by studying the interactions among human thinking, emotion, creativity, language, and problem solving, in addition to other cognitive processes. Cognitive psychologists strive to determine and measure different types of intelligence, why some people are better at problem solving than others, and how emotional intelligence affects success in the workplace, among countless other topics. They also sometimes focus on how we organize thoughts and information gathered from our environments into meaningful categories of thought, which will be discussed later.

CONCEPTS AND PROTOTYPES

The human nervous system is capable of handling endless streams of information. The senses serve as the interface between the mind and the external environment, receiving stimuli and translating it into nervous impulses that are transmitted to the brain. The brain then processes this information and uses the relevant pieces to create thoughts, which can then be expressed through language or stored in memory for future use. To make this process more complex, the brain does not gather information from external environments only. When thoughts are formed, the mind synthesizes information from emotions and memories (**Figure 7.2**). Emotion and memory are powerful influences on both our thoughts and behaviors.

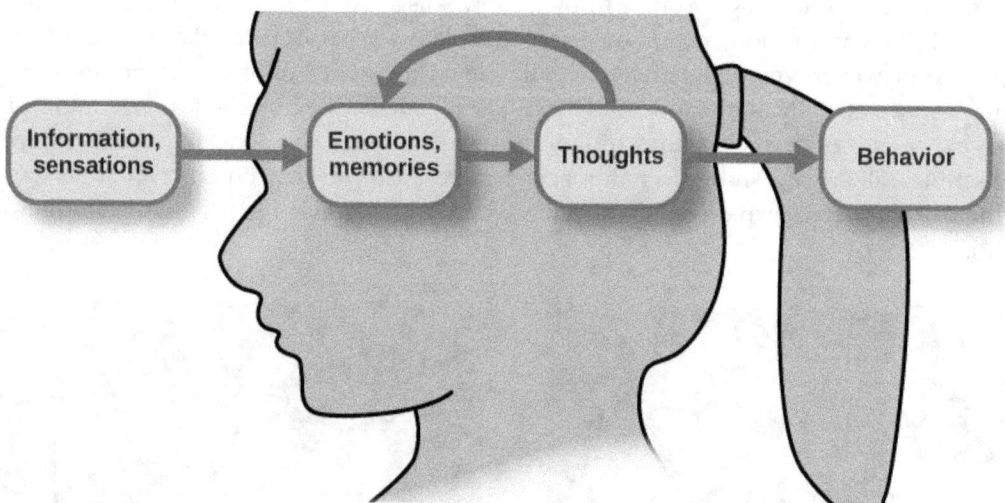

Figure 7.2 Sensations and information are received by our brains, filtered through emotions and memories, and processed to become thoughts.

In order to organize this staggering amount of information, the mind has developed a "file cabinet" of sorts in the mind. The different files stored in the file cabinet are called concepts. **Concepts** are categories or groupings of linguistic information, images, ideas, or memories, such as life experiences. Concepts are, in many ways, big ideas that are generated by observing details, and categorizing and combining these details into cognitive structures. You use concepts to see the relationships among the different elements of your experiences and to keep the information in your mind organized and accessible.

Concepts are informed by our semantic memory (you will learn more about semantic memory in a later chapter) and are present in every aspect of our lives; however, one of the easiest places to notice concepts is inside a classroom, where they are discussed explicitly. When you study United States history, for example, you learn about more than just individual events that have happened in America's past. You absorb a large quantity of information by listening to and participating in discussions, examining maps, and reading first-hand accounts of people's lives. Your brain analyzes these details and develops an overall understanding of American history. In the process, your brain gathers details that inform and refine your understanding of related concepts like democracy, power, and freedom.

Concepts can be complex and abstract, like justice, or more concrete, like types of birds. In psychology, for example, Piaget's stages of development are abstract concepts. Some concepts, like tolerance, are agreed upon by many people, because they have been used in various ways over many years. Other concepts, like the characteristics of your ideal friend or your family's birthday traditions, are personal and individualized. In this way, concepts touch every aspect of our lives, from our many daily routines to the guiding principles behind the way governments function.

Another technique used by your brain to organize information is the identification of prototypes for the concepts you have developed. A **prototype** is the best example or representation of a concept. For example, what comes to your mind when you think of a dog? Most likely your early experiences with dogs will shape what you imagine. If your first pet was a Golden Retriever, there is a good chance that this would be your prototype for the category of dogs.

NATURAL AND ARTIFICIAL CONCEPTS

In psychology, concepts can be divided into two categories, natural and artificial. **Natural concepts** are created "naturally" through your experiences and can be developed from either direct or indirect experiences. For example, if you live in Essex Junction, Vermont, you have probably had a lot of direct experience with snow. You've watched it fall from the sky, you've seen lightly falling snow that barely covers the windshield of your car, and you've shoveled out 18 inches of fluffy white snow as you've thought, "This is perfect for skiing." You've thrown snowballs at your best friend and gone sledding down the steepest hill in town. In short, you know snow. You know what it looks like, smells like, tastes like, and feels like. If, however, you've lived your whole life on the island of Saint Vincent in the Caribbean, you may never have actually seen snow, much less tasted, smelled, or touched it. You know snow from the indirect experience of seeing pictures of falling snow—or from watching films that feature snow as part of the setting. Either way, snow is a natural concept because you can construct an understanding of it through direct observations, experiences with snow, or indirect knowledge (such as from films or books) (**Figure 7.3**).

(a)

(b)

Figure 7.3 (a) Our concept of snow is an example of a natural concept—one that we understand through direct observation and experience. (b) In contrast, artificial concepts are ones that we know by a specific set of characteristics that they always exhibit, such as what defines different basic shapes. (credit a: modification of work by Maarten Takens; credit b: modification of work by "Shayan (USA)"/Flickr)

An **artificial concept**, on the other hand, is a concept that is defined by a specific set of characteristics. Various properties of geometric shapes, like squares and triangles, serve as useful examples of artificial concepts. A triangle always has three angles and three sides. A square always has four equal sides and four right angles. Mathematical formulas, like the equation for area (length × width) are artificial concepts defined by specific sets of characteristics that are always the same. Artificial concepts can enhance the understanding of a topic by building on one another. For example, before learning the concept of "area of a square" (and the formula to find it), you must understand what a square is. Once the concept of "area of a square" is understood, an understanding of area for other geometric shapes can be built upon the original understanding of area. The use of artificial concepts to define an idea is crucial to communicating with others and engaging in complex thought. According to Goldstone and Kersten (2003), concepts act as building blocks and can be connected in countless combinations to create complex thoughts.

SCHEMATA

A **schema** is a mental construct consisting of a cluster or collection of related concepts (Bartlett, 1932). There are many different types of schemata, and they all have one thing in common: schemata are a method of organizing information that allows the brain to work more efficiently. When a schema is activated, the brain makes immediate assumptions about the person or object being observed.

There are several types of schemata. A **role schema** makes assumptions about how individuals in certain roles will behave (Callero, 1994). For example, imagine you meet someone who introduces himself as a firefighter. When this happens, your brain automatically activates the "firefighter schema" and begins making assumptions that this person is brave, selfless, and community-oriented. Despite not knowing this person, already you have unknowingly made judgments about him. Schemata also help you fill in gaps in the information you receive from the world around you. While schemata allow for more efficient information processing, there can be problems with schemata, regardless of whether they are accurate: Perhaps this particular firefighter is not brave, he just works as a firefighter to pay the bills while studying to become a children's librarian.

An **event schema**, also known as a **cognitive script**, is a set of behaviors that can feel like a routine. Think about what you do when you walk into an elevator (Figure 7.4). First, the doors open and you wait to let exiting passengers leave the elevator car. Then, you step into the elevator and turn around to face the doors, looking for the correct button to push. You never face the back of the elevator, do you? And when you're riding in a crowded elevator and you can't face the front, it feels uncomfortable, doesn't it? Interestingly, event schemata can vary widely among different cultures and countries. For example, while it is quite common for people to greet one another with a handshake in the United States, in Tibet, you greet someone by sticking your tongue out at them, and in Belize, you bump fists (Cairns Regional Council, n.d.)

Figure 7.4 What event schema do you perform when riding in an elevator? (credit: "Gideon"/Flickr)

Because event schemata are automatic, they can be difficult to change. Imagine that you are driving home from work or school. This event schema involves getting in the car, shutting the door, and buckling your seatbelt before putting the key in the ignition. You might perform this script two or three times each day. As you drive home, you hear your phone's ring tone. Typically, the event schema that occurs when you hear your phone ringing involves locating the phone and answering it or responding to your latest text message. So without thinking, you reach for your phone, which could be in your pocket, in your bag, or on the passenger seat of the car. This powerful event schema is informed by your pattern of behavior and the pleasurable stimulation that a phone call or text message gives your brain. Because it is a schema, it is extremely challenging for us to stop reaching for the phone, even though we know that we endanger our own lives and the lives of others while we do it (Neyfakh, 2013) (Figure 7.5).

Figure 7.5 Texting while driving is dangerous, but it is a difficult event schema for some people to resist.

Remember the elevator? It feels almost impossible to walk in and *not* face the door. Our powerful event schema dictates our behavior in the elevator, and it is no different with our phones. Current research suggests that it is the habit, or event schema, of checking our phones in many different situations that makes refraining from checking them while driving especially difficult (Bayer & Campbell, 2012). Because texting and driving has become a dangerous epidemic in recent years, psychologists are looking at ways to help people interrupt the "phone schema" while driving. Event schemata like these are the reason why many habits are difficult to break once they have been acquired. As we continue to examine thinking, keep in mind how powerful the forces of concepts and schemata are to our understanding of the world.

7.2 Language

Learning Objectives

By the end of this section, you will be able to:
- Define language and demonstrate familiarity with the components of language
- Understand the development of language
- Explain the relationship between language and thinking

Language is a communication system that involves using words and systematic rules to organize those words to transmit information from one individual to another. While language is a form of communication, not all communication is language. Many species communicate with one another through their postures, movements, odors, or vocalizations. This communication is crucial for species that need to interact and develop social relationships with their conspecifics. However, many people have asserted that it is language that makes humans unique among all of the animal species (Corballis & Suddendorf, 2007; Tomasello & Rakoczy, 2003). This section will focus on what distinguishes language as a special form of communication, how the use of language develops, and how language affects the way we think.

COMPONENTS OF LANGUAGE

Language, be it spoken, signed, or written, has specific components: a lexicon and grammar. **Lexicon** refers to the words of a given language. Thus, lexicon is a language's vocabulary. **Grammar** refers to the set of rules that are used to convey meaning through the use of the lexicon (Fernández & Cairns, 2011). For instance, English grammar dictates that most verbs receive an "-ed" at the end to indicate past tense.

Words are formed by combining the various phonemes that make up the language. A **phoneme** (e.g., the sounds "ah" vs. "eh") is a basic sound unit of a given language, and different languages have different sets of phonemes. Phonemes are combined to form **morphemes**, which are the smallest units of language that convey some type of meaning (e.g., "I" is both a phoneme and a morpheme). We use semantics and syntax to construct language. Semantics and syntax are part of a language's grammar. **Semantics** refers to the process by which we derive meaning from morphemes and words. **Syntax** refers to the way words are organized into sentences (Chomsky, 1965; Fernández & Cairns, 2011).

We apply the rules of grammar to organize the lexicon in novel and creative ways, which allow us to communicate information about both concrete and abstract concepts. We can talk about our immediate and observable surroundings as well as the surface of unseen planets. We can share our innermost thoughts, our plans for the future, and debate the value of a college education. We can provide detailed instructions for cooking a meal, fixing a car, or building a fire. Through our use of words and language, we are able to form, organize, and express ideas, schema, and artificial concepts.

LANGUAGE DEVELOPMENT

Given the remarkable complexity of a language, one might expect that mastering a language would be an especially arduous task; indeed, for those of us trying to learn a second language as adults, this might seem to be true. However, young children master language very quickly with relative ease. B. F. Skinner (1957) proposed that language is learned through reinforcement. Noam Chomsky (1965) criticized this behaviorist approach, asserting instead that the mechanisms underlying language acquisition are biologically determined. The use of language develops in the absence of formal instruction and appears to follow a very similar pattern in children from vastly different cultures and backgrounds. It would seem, therefore, that we are born with a biological predisposition to acquire a language (Chomsky, 1965;

Fernández & Cairns, 2011). Moreover, it appears that there is a critical period for language acquisition, such that this proficiency at acquiring language is maximal early in life; generally, as people age, the ease with which they acquire and master new languages diminishes (Johnson & Newport, 1989; Lenneberg, 1967; Singleton, 1995).

Children begin to learn about language from a very early age (Table 7.1). In fact, it appears that this is occurring even before we are born. Newborns show preference for their mother's voice and appear to be able to discriminate between the language spoken by their mother and other languages. Babies are also attuned to the languages being used around them and show preferences for videos of faces that are moving in synchrony with the audio of spoken language versus videos that do not synchronize with the audio (Blossom & Morgan, 2006; Pickens, 1994; Spelke & Cortelyou, 1981).

Stages of Language and Communication Development

Stage	Age	Developmental Language and Communication
1	0–3 months	Reflexive communication
2	3–8 months	Reflexive communication; interest in others
3	8–13 months	Intentional communication; sociability
4	12–18 months	First words
5	18–24 months	Simple sentences of two words
6	2–3 years	Sentences of three or more words
7	3–5 years	Complex sentences; has conversations

Table 7.1

DIG DEEPER

The Case of Genie

In the fall of 1970, a social worker in the Los Angeles area found a 13-year-old girl who was being raised in extremely neglectful and abusive conditions. The girl, who came to be known as Genie, had lived most of her life tied to a potty chair or confined to a crib in a small room that was kept closed with the curtains drawn. For a little over a decade, Genie had virtually no social interaction and no access to the outside world. As a result of these conditions, Genie was unable to stand up, chew solid food, or speak (Fromkin, Krashen, Curtiss, Rigler, & Rigler, 1974; Rymer, 1993). The police took Genie into protective custody.

Genie's abilities improved dramatically following her removal from her abusive environment, and early on, it appeared she was acquiring language—much later than would be predicted by critical period hypotheses that had been posited at the time (Fromkin et al., 1974). Genie managed to amass an impressive vocabulary in a relatively short amount of time. However, she never developed a mastery of the grammatical aspects of language (Curtiss, 1981). Perhaps being deprived of the opportunity to learn language during a critical period impeded Genie's ability to fully acquire and use language.

You may recall that each language has its own set of phonemes that are used to generate morphemes, words, and so on. Babies can discriminate among the sounds that make up a language (for example, they can tell the difference between the "s" in vision and the "ss" in fission); early on, they can differentiate between the sounds of all human languages, even those that do not occur in the languages that are used in their environments. However, by the time that they are about 1 year old, they can only discriminate among those phonemes that are used in the language or languages in their environments (Jensen, 2011; Werker & Lalonde, 1988; Werker & Tees, 1984).

> **LINK TO LEARNING**
>
> Watch this video about how babies lose the ability to discriminate among all possible human phonemes as they age (http://openstax.org/l/language) to learn more.

After the first few months of life, babies enter what is known as the babbling stage, during which time they tend to produce single syllables that are repeated over and over. As time passes, more variations appear in the syllables that they produce. During this time, it is unlikely that the babies are trying to communicate; they are just as likely to babble when they are alone as when they are with their caregivers (Fernández & Cairns, 2011). Interestingly, babies who are raised in environments in which sign language is used will also begin to show babbling in the gestures of their hands during this stage (Petitto, Holowka, Sergio, Levy, & Ostry, 2004).

Generally, a child's first word is uttered sometime between the ages of 1 year to 18 months, and for the next few months, the child will remain in the "one word" stage of language development. During this time, children know a number of words, but they only produce one-word utterances. The child's early vocabulary is limited to familiar objects or events, often nouns. Although children in this stage only make one-word utterances, these words often carry larger meaning (Fernández & Cairns, 2011). So, for example, a child saying "cookie" could be identifying a cookie or asking for a cookie.

As a child's lexicon grows, she begins to utter simple sentences and to acquire new vocabulary at a very rapid pace. In addition, children begin to demonstrate a clear understanding of the specific rules that apply to their language(s). Even the mistakes that children sometimes make provide evidence of just how much they understand about those rules. This is sometimes seen in the form of **overgeneralization**. In this context, overgeneralization refers to an extension of a language rule to an exception to the rule. For example, in English, it is usually the case that an "s" is added to the end of a word to indicate plurality. For example, we speak of one dog versus two dogs. Young children will overgeneralize this rule to cases that are exceptions to the "add an s to the end of the word" rule and say things like "those two gooses" or "three mouses." Clearly, the rules of the language are understood, even if the exceptions to the rules are still being learned (Moskowitz, 1978).

LANGUAGE AND THOUGHT

When we speak one language, we agree that words are representations of ideas, people, places, and events. The given language that children learn is connected to their culture and surroundings. But can words themselves shape the way we think about things? Psychologists have long investigated the question of whether language shapes thoughts and actions, or whether our thoughts and beliefs shape our language. Two researchers, Edward Sapir and Benjamin Lee Whorf, began this investigation in the 1940s. They wanted to understand how the language habits of a community encourage members of that community to interpret language in a particular manner (Sapir, 1941/1964). Sapir and Whorf proposed that language determines thought. For example, in some languages there are many different words for love. However, in English we use the word love for all types of love. Does this affect how we think about love depending on the language that we speak (Whorf, 1956)? Researchers have since identified this view as too absolute, pointing out a lack of empiricism behind what Sapir and Whorf proposed (Abler, 2013; Boroditsky, 2011; van Troyer, 1994). Today, psychologists continue to study and debate the relationship between language and thought.

> **WHAT DO YOU THINK?**
>
> **The Meaning of Language**
>
> Think about what you know of other languages; perhaps you even speak multiple languages. Imagine for a moment that your closest friend fluently speaks more than one language. Do you think that friend thinks differently, depending on which language is being spoken? You may know a few words that are not translatable from their original language into English. For example, the Portuguese word *saudade* originated during the 15th century, when Portuguese sailors left home to explore the seas and travel to Africa or Asia. Those left behind described the emptiness and fondness they felt as *saudade* (Figure 7.6). The word came to express many meanings, including loss, nostalgia, yearning, warm memories, and hope. There is no single word in English that includes all of those emotions in a single description. Do words such as *saudade* indicate that different languages produce different patterns of thought in people? What do you think??
>
>
>
> (a)   (b)
>
> **Figure 7.6** These two works of art depict *saudade*. (a) *Saudade de Nápoles*, which is translated into "missing Naples," was painted by Bertha Worms in 1895. (b) Almeida Júnior painted *Saudade* in 1899.

Language may indeed influence the way that we think, an idea known as linguistic determinism. One recent demonstration of this phenomenon involved differences in the way that English and Mandarin Chinese speakers talk and think about time. English speakers tend to talk about time using terms that describe changes along a horizontal dimension, for example, saying something like "I'm running behind schedule" or "Don't get ahead of yourself." While Mandarin Chinese speakers also describe time in horizontal terms, it is not uncommon to also use terms associated with a vertical arrangement. For example, the past might be described as being "up" and the future as being "down." It turns out that these differences in language translate into differences in performance on cognitive tests designed to measure how quickly an individual can recognize temporal relationships. Specifically, when given a series of tasks with vertical priming, Mandarin Chinese speakers were faster at recognizing temporal relationships between months. Indeed, Boroditsky (2001) sees these results as suggesting that "habits in language encourage habits in thought" (p. 12).

One group of researchers who wanted to investigate how language influences thought compared how

English speakers and the Dani people of Papua New Guinea think and speak about color. The Dani have two words for color: one word for *light* and one word for *dark*. In contrast, the English language has 11 color words. Researchers hypothesized that the number of color terms could limit the ways that the Dani people conceptualized color. However, the Dani were able to distinguish colors with the same ability as English speakers, despite having fewer words at their disposal (Berlin & Kay, 1969). A recent review of research aimed at determining how language might affect something like color perception suggests that language can influence perceptual phenomena, especially in the left hemisphere of the brain. You may recall from earlier chapters that the left hemisphere is associated with language for most people. However, the right (less linguistic hemisphere) of the brain is less affected by linguistic influences on perception (Regier & Kay, 2009)

7.3 Problem Solving

Learning Objectives

By the end of this section, you will be able to:
- Describe problem solving strategies
- Define algorithm and heuristic
- Explain some common roadblocks to effective problem solving and decision making

People face problems every day—usually, multiple problems throughout the day. Sometimes these problems are straightforward: To double a recipe for pizza dough, for example, all that is required is that each ingredient in the recipe be doubled. Sometimes, however, the problems we encounter are more complex. For example, say you have a work deadline, and you must mail a printed copy of a report to your supervisor by the end of the business day. The report is time-sensitive and must be sent overnight. You finished the report last night, but your printer will not work today. What should you do? First, you need to identify the problem and then apply a strategy for solving the problem.

PROBLEM-SOLVING STRATEGIES

When you are presented with a problem—whether it is a complex mathematical problem or a broken printer, how do you solve it? Before finding a solution to the problem, the problem must first be clearly identified. After that, one of many problem solving strategies can be applied, hopefully resulting in a solution.

A **problem-solving strategy** is a plan of action used to find a solution. Different strategies have different action plans associated with them (Table 7.2). For example, a well-known strategy is **trial and error**. The old adage, "If at first you don't succeed, try, try again" describes trial and error. In terms of your broken printer, you could try checking the ink levels, and if that doesn't work, you could check to make sure the paper tray isn't jammed. Or maybe the printer isn't actually connected to your laptop. When using trial and error, you would continue to try different solutions until you solved your problem. Although trial and error is not typically one of the most time-efficient strategies, it is a commonly used one.

Problem-Solving Strategies

Method	Description	Example
Trial and error	Continue trying different solutions until problem is solved	Restarting phone, turning off WiFi, turning off bluetooth in order to determine why your phone is malfunctioning

Problem-Solving Strategies

Method	Description	Example
Algorithm	Step-by-step problem-solving formula	Instruction manual for installing new software on your computer
Heuristic	General problem-solving framework	Working backwards; breaking a task into steps

Table 7.2

Another type of strategy is an algorithm. An **algorithm** is a problem-solving formula that provides you with step-by-step instructions used to achieve a desired outcome (Kahneman, 2011). You can think of an algorithm as a recipe with highly detailed instructions that produce the same result every time they are performed. Algorithms are used frequently in our everyday lives, especially in computer science. When you run a search on the Internet, search engines like Google use algorithms to decide which entries will appear first in your list of results. Facebook also uses algorithms to decide which posts to display on your newsfeed. Can you identify other situations in which algorithms are used?

A heuristic is another type of problem solving strategy. While an algorithm must be followed exactly to produce a correct result, a **heuristic** is a general problem-solving framework (Tversky & Kahneman, 1974). You can think of these as mental shortcuts that are used to solve problems. A "rule of thumb" is an example of a heuristic. Such a rule saves the person time and energy when making a decision, but despite its time-saving characteristics, it is not always the best method for making a rational decision. Different types of heuristics are used in different types of situations, but the impulse to use a heuristic occurs when one of five conditions is met (Pratkanis, 1989):

- When one is faced with too much information
- When the time to make a decision is limited
- When the decision to be made is unimportant
- When there is access to very little information to use in making the decision
- When an appropriate heuristic happens to come to mind in the same moment

Working backwards is a useful heuristic in which you begin solving the problem by focusing on the end result. Consider this example: You live in Washington, D.C. and have been invited to a wedding at 4 PM on Saturday in Philadelphia. Knowing that Interstate 95 tends to back up any day of the week, you need to plan your route and time your departure accordingly. If you want to be at the wedding service by 3:30 PM, and it takes 2.5 hours to get to Philadelphia without traffic, what time should you leave your house? You use the working backwards heuristic to plan the events of your day on a regular basis, probably without even thinking about it.

Another useful heuristic is the practice of accomplishing a large goal or task by breaking it into a series of smaller steps. Students often use this common method to complete a large research project or long essay for school. For example, students typically brainstorm, develop a thesis or main topic, research the chosen topic, organize their information into an outline, write a rough draft, revise and edit the rough draft, develop a final draft, organize the references list, and proofread their work before turning in the project. The large task becomes less overwhelming when it is broken down into a series of small steps.

EVERYDAY CONNECTION

Solving Puzzles

Problem-solving abilities can improve with practice. Many people challenge themselves every day with puzzles and other mental exercises to sharpen their problem-solving skills. Sudoku puzzles appear daily in most newspapers. Typically, a sudoku puzzle is a 9×9 grid. The simple sudoku below (Figure 7.7) is a 4×4 grid. To solve the puzzle, fill in the empty boxes with a single digit: 1, 2, 3, or 4. Here are the rules: The numbers must total 10 in each bolded box, each row, and each column; however, each digit can only appear once in a bolded box, row, and column. Time yourself as you solve this puzzle and compare your time with a classmate.

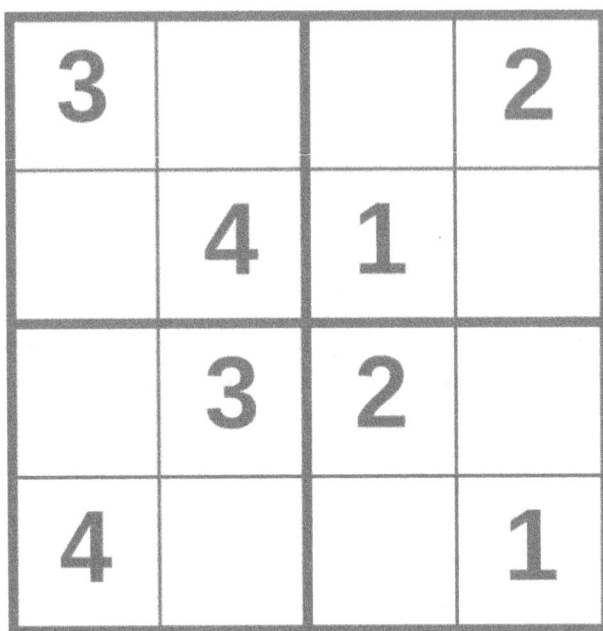

Figure 7.7 How long did it take you to solve this sudoku puzzle? (You can see the answer at the end of this section.)

Here is another popular type of puzzle (Figure 7.8) that challenges your spatial reasoning skills. Connect all nine dots with four connecting straight lines without lifting your pencil from the paper:

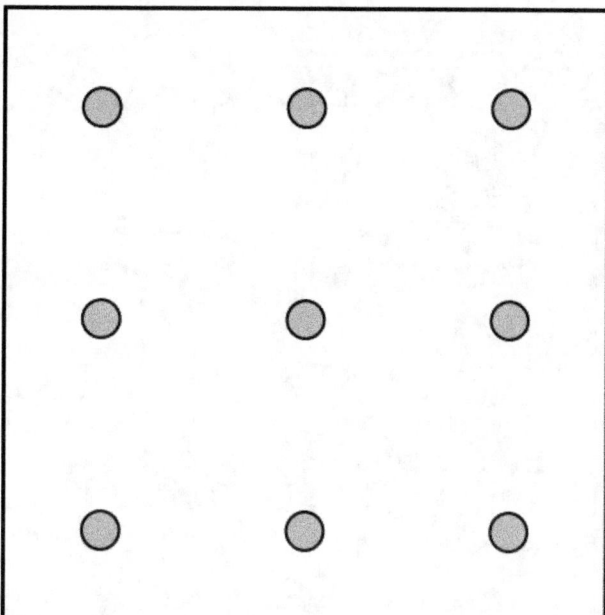

Figure 7.8 Did you figure it out? (The answer is at the end of this section.) Once you understand how to crack this puzzle, you won't forget.

Take a look at the "Puzzling Scales" logic puzzle below (Figure 7.9). Sam Loyd, a well-known puzzle master, created and refined countless puzzles throughout his lifetime (Cyclopedia of Puzzles, n.d.).

Figure 7.9 What steps did you take to solve this puzzle? You can read the solution at the end of this section.

PITFALLS TO PROBLEM SOLVING

Not all problems are successfully solved, however. What challenges stop us from successfully solving a problem? Albert Einstein once said, "Insanity is doing the same thing over and over again and expecting a different result." Imagine a person in a room that has four doorways. One doorway that has always been open in the past is now locked. The person, accustomed to exiting the room by that particular doorway, keeps trying to get out through the same doorway even though the other three doorways are open. The person is stuck—but she just needs to go to another doorway, instead of trying to get out through the locked doorway. A **mental set** is where you persist in approaching a problem in a way that has worked in the past but is clearly not working now.

Functional fixedness is a type of mental set where you cannot perceive an object being used for something other than what it was designed for. Duncker (1945) conducted foundational research on functional fixedness. He created an experiment in which participants were given a candle, a book of matches, and a box of thumbtacks. They were instructed to use those items to attach the candle to the wall so that it did not drip wax onto the table below. Participants had to use functional fixedness to solve the problem (**Figure 7.10**). During the *Apollo 13* mission to the moon, NASA engineers at Mission Control had to overcome functional fixedness to save the lives of the astronauts aboard the spacecraft. An explosion in a module of the spacecraft damaged multiple systems. The astronauts were in danger of being poisoned by rising levels of carbon dioxide because of problems with the carbon dioxide filters. The engineers found a way for the astronauts to use spare plastic bags, tape, and air hoses to create a makeshift air filter, which saved the lives of the astronauts.

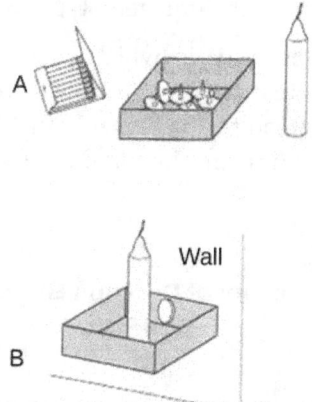

Figure 7.10 In Duncker's classic study, participants were provided the three objects in the top panel and asked to solve the problem. The solution is shown in the bottom portion.

LINK TO LEARNING

Check out this Apollo 13 scene about NASA engineers overcoming functional fixedness (http://openstax.org/l/Apollo13) to learn more.

Researchers have investigated whether functional fixedness is affected by culture. In one experiment, individuals from the Shuar group in Ecuador were asked to use an object for a purpose other than that for which the object was originally intended. For example, the participants were told a story about a bear and a rabbit that were separated by a river and asked to select among various objects, including a spoon, a cup, erasers, and so on, to help the animals. The spoon was the only object long enough to span the imaginary river, but if the spoon was presented in a way that reflected its normal usage, it took participants longer to choose the spoon to solve the problem. (German & Barrett, 2005). The researchers wanted to know if exposure to highly specialized tools, as occurs with individuals in industrialized nations, affects their ability to transcend functional fixedness. It was determined that functional fixedness is experienced in both industrialized and nonindustrialized cultures (German & Barrett, 2005).

In order to make good decisions, we use our knowledge and our reasoning. Often, this knowledge and reasoning is sound and solid. Sometimes, however, we are swayed by biases or by others manipulating a situation. For example, let's say you and three friends wanted to rent a house and had a combined target budget of $1,600. The realtor shows you only very run-down houses for $1,600 and then shows you a very nice house for $2,000. Might you ask each person to pay more in rent to get the $2,000 home? Why would the realtor show you the run-down houses and the nice house? The realtor may be challenging your anchoring bias. An **anchoring bias** occurs when you focus on one piece of information when making a decision or solving a problem. In this case, you're so focused on the amount of money you are willing to spend that you may not recognize what kinds of houses are available at that price point.

The **confirmation bias** is the tendency to focus on information that confirms your existing beliefs. For example, if you think that your professor is not very nice, you notice all of the instances of rude behavior exhibited by the professor while ignoring the countless pleasant interactions he is involved in on a daily basis. **Hindsight bias** leads you to believe that the event you just experienced was predictable, even though it really wasn't. In other words, you knew all along that things would turn out the way they did. **Representative bias** describes a faulty way of thinking, in which you unintentionally stereotype someone or something; for example, you may assume that your professors spend their free time reading books and engaging in intellectual conversation, because the idea of them spending their time playing volleyball or visiting an amusement park does not fit in with your stereotypes of professors.

Finally, the **availability heuristic** is a heuristic in which you make a decision based on an example, information, or recent experience that is that readily available to you, even though it may not be the best example to inform your decision. Biases tend to "preserve that which is already established—to maintain our preexisting knowledge, beliefs, attitudes, and hypotheses" (Aronson, 1995; Kahneman, 2011). These biases are summarized in Table 7.3.

Summary of Decision Biases

Bias	Description
Anchoring	Tendency to focus on one particular piece of information when making decisions or problem-solving
Confirmation	Focuses on information that confirms existing beliefs
Hindsight	Belief that the event just experienced was predictable
Representative	Unintentional stereotyping of someone or something
Availability	Decision is based upon either an available precedent or an example that may be faulty

Table 7.3

> **LINK TO LEARNING**
>
> Watch this teacher-made music video about cognitive biases (http://openstax.org/l/CogBias) to learn more.

Were you able to determine how many marbles are needed to balance the scales in Figure 7.9? You need nine. Were you able to solve the problems in Figure 7.7 and Figure 7.8? Here are the answers (Figure 7.11).

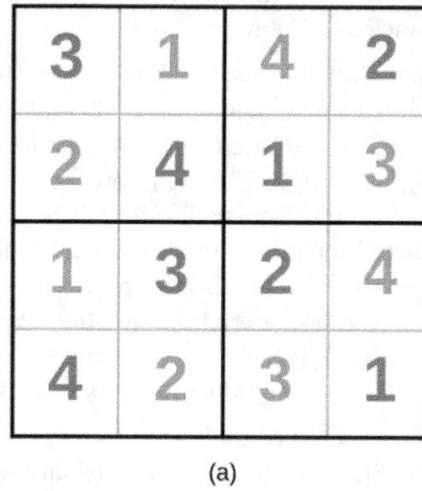
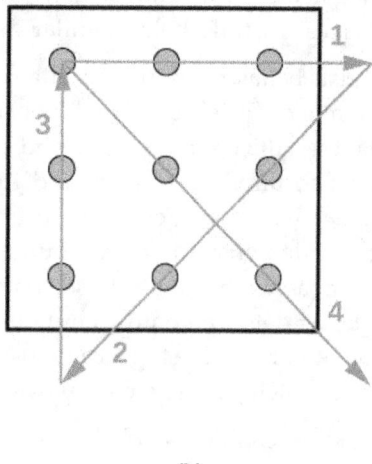

(a) (b)

Figure 7.11

7.4 What Are Intelligence and Creativity?

Learning Objectives

By the end of this section, you will be able to:
- Define intelligence
- Explain the triarchic theory of intelligence
- Identify the difference between intelligence theories
- Explain emotional intelligence
- Define creativity

A four-and-a-half-year-old boy sits at the kitchen table with his father, who is reading a new story aloud to him. He turns the page to continue reading, but before he can begin, the boy says, "Wait, Daddy!" He points to the words on the new page and reads aloud, "Go, Pig! Go!" The father stops and looks at his son. "Can you read that?" he asks. "Yes, Daddy!" And he points to the words and reads again, "Go, Pig! Go!"

This father was not actively teaching his son to read, even though the child constantly asked questions about letters, words, and symbols that they saw everywhere: in the car, in the store, on the television. The dad wondered about what else his son might understand and decided to try an experiment. Grabbing a sheet of blank paper, he wrote several simple words in a list: mom, dad, dog, bird, bed, truck, car, tree. He put the list down in front of the boy and asked him to read the words. "Mom, dad, dog, bird, bed, truck, car, tree," he read, slowing down to carefully pronounce *bird* and *truck*. Then, "Did I do it, Daddy?" "You sure did! That is very good." The father gave his little boy a warm hug and continued reading the story about the pig, all the while wondering if his son's abilities were an indication of exceptional intelligence or simply a normal pattern of linguistic development. Like the father in this example, psychologists have wondered what constitutes intelligence and how it can be measured.

CLASSIFYING INTELLIGENCE

What exactly is intelligence? The way that researchers have defined the concept of intelligence has been modified many times since the birth of psychology. British psychologist Charles Spearman believed intelligence consisted of one general factor, called g, which could be measured and compared among individuals. Spearman focused on the commonalities among various intellectual abilities and deemphasized what made each unique. Long before modern psychology developed, however, ancient philosophers, such as Aristotle, held a similar view (Cianciolo & Sternberg, 2004).

Others psychologists believe that instead of a single factor, intelligence is a collection of distinct abilities. In the 1940s, Raymond Cattell proposed a theory of intelligence that divided general intelligence into two components: crystallized intelligence and fluid intelligence (Cattell, 1963). **Crystallized intelligence** is characterized as acquired knowledge and the ability to retrieve it. When you learn, remember, and recall information, you are using crystallized intelligence. You use crystallized intelligence all the time in your coursework by demonstrating that you have mastered the information covered in the course. **Fluid intelligence** encompasses the ability to see complex relationships and solve problems. Navigating your way home after being detoured onto an unfamiliar route because of road construction would draw upon your fluid intelligence. Fluid intelligence helps you tackle complex, abstract challenges in your daily life, whereas crystallized intelligence helps you overcome concrete, straightforward problems (Cattell, 1963).

Other theorists and psychologists believe that intelligence should be defined in more practical terms. For example, what types of behaviors help you get ahead in life? Which skills promote success? Think about this for a moment. Being able to recite all 45 presidents of the United States in order is an excellent party trick, but will knowing this make you a better person?

Robert Sternberg developed another theory of intelligence, which he titled the **triarchic theory of intelligence** because it sees intelligence as comprised of three parts (Sternberg, 1988): practical, creative, and analytical intelligence (Figure 7.12).

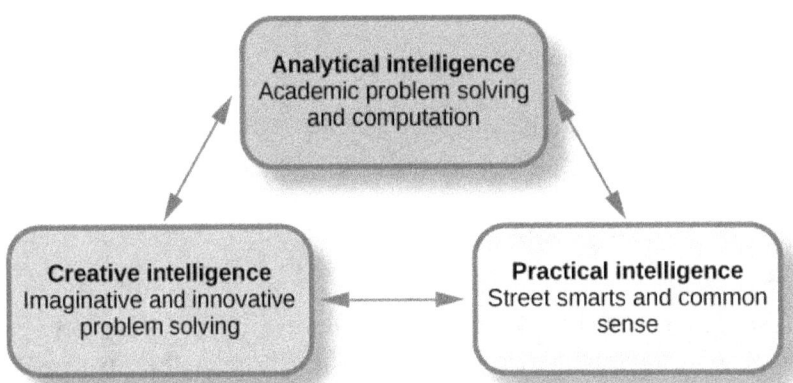

Figure 7.12 Sternberg's theory identifies three types of intelligence: practical, creative, and analytical.

Practical intelligence, as proposed by Sternberg, is sometimes compared to "street smarts." Being practical means you find solutions that work in your everyday life by applying knowledge based on your experiences. This type of intelligence appears to be separate from traditional understanding of IQ; individuals who score high in practical intelligence may or may not have comparable scores in creative and analytical intelligence (Sternberg, 1988).

This story about the 2007 Virginia Tech shootings illustrates both high and low practical intelligences. During the incident, one student left her class to go get a soda in an adjacent building. She planned to return to class, but when she returned to her building after getting her soda, she saw that the door she used to leave was now chained shut from the inside. Instead of thinking about why there was a chain around the door handles, she went to her class's window and crawled back into the room. She thus potentially exposed herself to the gunman. Thankfully, she was not shot. On the other hand, a pair of students was walking on campus when they heard gunshots nearby. One friend said, "Let's go check it out and see what is going on." The other student said, "No way, we need to run away from the gunshots." They did just that. As a result, both avoided harm. The student who crawled through the window demonstrated some creative intelligence but did not use common sense. She would have low practical intelligence. The student who encouraged his friend to run away from the sound of gunshots would have much higher practical intelligence.

Analytical intelligence is closely aligned with academic problem solving and computations. Sternberg says that analytical intelligence is demonstrated by an ability to analyze, evaluate, judge, compare, and contrast. When reading a classic novel for literature class, for example, it is usually necessary to compare the motives of the main characters of the book or analyze the historical context of the story. In a science course such as anatomy, you must study the processes by which the body uses various minerals in different human systems. In developing an understanding of this topic, you are using analytical intelligence. When solving a challenging math problem, you would apply analytical intelligence to analyze different aspects of the problem and then solve it section by section.

Creative intelligence is marked by inventing or imagining a solution to a problem or situation. Creativity in this realm can include finding a novel solution to an unexpected problem or producing a beautiful work of art or a well-developed short story. Imagine for a moment that you are camping in the woods with some friends and realize that you've forgotten your camp coffee pot. The person in your group who figures out a way to successfully brew coffee for everyone would be credited as having higher creative intelligence.

Multiple Intelligences Theory was developed by Howard Gardner, a Harvard psychologist and former student of Erik Erikson. Gardner's theory, which has been refined for more than 30 years, is a more recent development among theories of intelligence. In Gardner's theory, each person possesses at least eight intelligences. Among these eight intelligences, a person typically excels in some and falters in others (Gardner, 1983). **Table 7.4** describes each type of intelligence.

Multiple Intelligences

Intelligence Type	Characteristics	Representative Career
Linguistic intelligence	Perceives different functions of language, different sounds and meanings of words, may easily learn multiple languages	Journalist, novelist, poet, teacher
Logical-mathematical intelligence	Capable of seeing numerical patterns, strong ability to use reason and logic	Scientist, mathematician
Musical intelligence	Understands and appreciates rhythm, pitch, and tone; may play multiple instruments or perform as a vocalist	Composer, performer
Bodily kinesthetic intelligence	High ability to control the movements of the body and use the body to perform various physical tasks	Dancer, athlete, athletic coach, yoga instructor
Spatial intelligence	Ability to perceive the relationship between objects and how they move in space	Choreographer, sculptor, architect, aviator, sailor
Interpersonal intelligence	Ability to understand and be sensitive to the various emotional states of others	Counselor, social worker, salesperson
Intrapersonal intelligence	Ability to access personal feelings and motivations, and use them to direct behavior and reach personal goals	Key component of personal success over time

Multiple Intelligences

Intelligence Type	Characteristics	Representative Career
Naturalist intelligence	High capacity to appreciate the natural world and interact with the species within it	Biologist, ecologist, environmentalist

Table 7.4

Gardner's theory is relatively new and needs additional research to better establish empirical support. At the same time, his ideas challenge the traditional idea of intelligence to include a wider variety of abilities, although it has been suggested that Gardner simply relabeled what other theorists called "cognitive styles" as "intelligences" (Morgan, 1996). Furthermore, developing traditional measures of Gardner's intelligences is extremely difficult (Furnham, 2009; Gardner & Moran, 2006; Klein, 1997).

Gardner's inter- and intrapersonal intelligences are often combined into a single type: emotional intelligence. **Emotional intelligence** encompasses the ability to understand the emotions of yourself and others, show empathy, understand social relationships and cues, and regulate your own emotions and respond in culturally appropriate ways (Parker, Saklofske, & Stough, 2009). People with high emotional intelligence typically have well-developed social skills. Some researchers, including Daniel Goleman, the author of *Emotional Intelligence: Why It Can Matter More than IQ*, argue that emotional intelligence is a better predictor of success than traditional intelligence (Goleman, 1995). However, emotional intelligence has been widely debated, with researchers pointing out inconsistencies in how it is defined and described, as well as questioning results of studies on a subject that is difficulty to measure and study emperically (Locke, 2005; Mayer, Salovey, & Caruso, 2004)

The most comprehensive theory of intelligence to date is the Cattell-Horn-Carroll (CHC) theory of cognitive abilities (Schneider & McGrew, 2018). In this theory, abilities are related and arranged in a hierarchy with general abilities at the top, broad abilities in the middle, and narrow (specific) abilities at the bottom. The narrow abilities are the only ones that can be directly measured; however, they are integrated within the other abilities. At the general level is general intelligence. Next, the broad level consists of general abilities such as fluid reasoning, short-term memory, and processing speed. Finally, as the hierarchy continues, the narrow level includes specific forms of cognitive abilities. For example, short-term memory would further break down into memory span and working memory capacity.

Intelligence can also have different meanings and values in different cultures. If you live on a small island, where most people get their food by fishing from boats, it would be important to know how to fish and how to repair a boat. If you were an exceptional angler, your peers would probably consider you intelligent. If you were also skilled at repairing boats, your intelligence might be known across the whole island. Think about your own family's culture. What values are important for Latinx families? Italian families? In Irish families, hospitality and telling an entertaining story are marks of the culture. If you are a skilled storyteller, other members of Irish culture are likely to consider you intelligent.

Some cultures place a high value on working together as a collective. In these cultures, the importance of the group supersedes the importance of individual achievement. When you visit such a culture, how well you relate to the values of that culture exemplifies your **cultural intelligence**, sometimes referred to as cultural competence.

> **LINK TO LEARNING**
>
> Watch this video that compares different theories of intelligence (http://openstax.org/l/theoryintel) to learn more.

CREATIVITY

Creativity is the ability to generate, create, or discover new ideas, solutions, and possibilities. Very creative people often have intense knowledge about something, work on it for years, look at novel solutions, seek out the advice and help of other experts, and take risks. Although creativity is often associated with the arts, it is actually a vital form of intelligence that drives people in many disciplines to discover something new. Creativity can be found in every area of life, from the way you decorate your residence to a new way of understanding how a cell works.

Creativity is often assessed as a function of one's ability to engage in **divergent thinking**. Divergent thinking can be described as thinking "outside the box;" it allows an individual to arrive at unique, multiple solutions to a given problem. In contrast, **convergent thinking** describes the ability to provide a correct or well-established answer or solution to a problem (Cropley, 2006; Gilford, 1967)

> **EVERYDAY CONNECTION**
>
> **Creativity**
>
> Dr. Tom Steitz, former Sterling Professor of Biochemistry and Biophysics at Yale University, spent his career looking at the structure and specific aspects of RNA molecules and how their interactions could help produce antibiotics and ward off diseases. As a result of his lifetime of work, he won the Nobel Prize in Chemistry in 2009. He wrote, "Looking back over the development and progress of my career in science, I am reminded how vitally important good mentorship is in the early stages of one's career development and constant face-to-face conversations, debate and discussions with colleagues at all stages of research. Outstanding discoveries, insights and developments do not happen in a vacuum" (Steitz, 2010, para. 39). Based on Steitz's comment, it becomes clear that someone's creativity, although an individual strength, benefits from interactions with others. Think of a time when your creativity was sparked by a conversation with a friend or classmate. How did that person influence you and what problem did you solve using creativity?

7.5 Measures of Intelligence

Learning Objectives

By the end of this section, you will be able to:
- Explain how intelligence tests are developed
- Describe the history of the use of IQ tests
- Describe the purposes and benefits of intelligence testing

While you're likely familiar with the term "IQ" and associate it with the idea of intelligence, what does IQ really mean? IQ stands for **intelligence quotient** and describes a score earned on a test designed to measure intelligence. You've already learned that there are many ways psychologists describe intelligence (or more aptly, intelligences). Similarly, IQ tests—the tools designed to measure intelligence—have been the subject of debate throughout their development and use.

When might an IQ test be used? What do we learn from the results, and how might people use this information? While there are certainly many benefits to intelligence testing, it is important to also note the limitations and controversies surrounding these tests. For example, IQ tests have sometimes been used as arguments in support of insidious purposes, such as the eugenics movement (Severson, 2011). The infamous Supreme Court Case, *Buck v. Bell*, legalized the forced sterilization of some people deemed "feeble-minded" through this type of testing, resulting in about 65,000 sterilizations (*Buck v. Bell*, 274 U.S. 200; Ko, 2016). Today, only professionals trained in psychology can administer IQ tests, and the purchase of most tests requires an advanced degree in psychology. Other professionals in the field, such as social workers and psychiatrists, cannot administer IQ tests. In this section, we will explore what intelligence tests measure, how they are scored, and how they were developed.

MEASURING INTELLIGENCE

It seems that the human understanding of intelligence is somewhat limited when we focus on traditional or academic-type intelligence. How then, can intelligence be measured? And when we measure intelligence, how do we ensure that we capture what we're really trying to measure (in other words, that IQ tests function as valid measures of intelligence)? In the following paragraphs, we will explore the how intelligence tests were developed and the history of their use.

The IQ test has been synonymous with intelligence for over a century. In the late 1800s, Sir Francis Galton developed the first broad test of intelligence (Flanagan & Kaufman, 2004). Although he was not a psychologist, his contributions to the concepts of intelligence testing are still felt today (Gordon, 1995). Reliable intelligence testing (you may recall from earlier chapters that reliability refers to a test's ability to produce consistent results) began in earnest during the early 1900s with a researcher named Alfred Binet (**Figure 7.13**). Binet was asked by the French government to develop an intelligence test to use on children to determine which ones might have difficulty in school; it included many verbally based tasks. American researchers soon realized the value of such testing. Louis Terman, a Stanford professor, modified Binet's work by standardizing the administration of the test and tested thousands of different-aged children to establish an average score for each age. As a result, the test was normed and standardized, which means that the test was administered consistently to a large enough representative sample of the population that the range of scores resulted in a bell curve (bell curves will be discussed later). **Standardization** means that the manner of administration, scoring, and interpretation of results is consistent. **Norming** involves giving a test to a large population so data can be collected comparing groups, such as age groups. The resulting data provide norms, or referential scores, by which to interpret future scores. Norms are not expectations of what a given group *should* know but a demonstration of what that group *does* know. Norming and standardizing the test ensures that new scores are reliable. This new version of the test was called the Stanford-Binet Intelligence Scale (Terman, 1916). Remarkably, an updated version of this test is still widely used today.

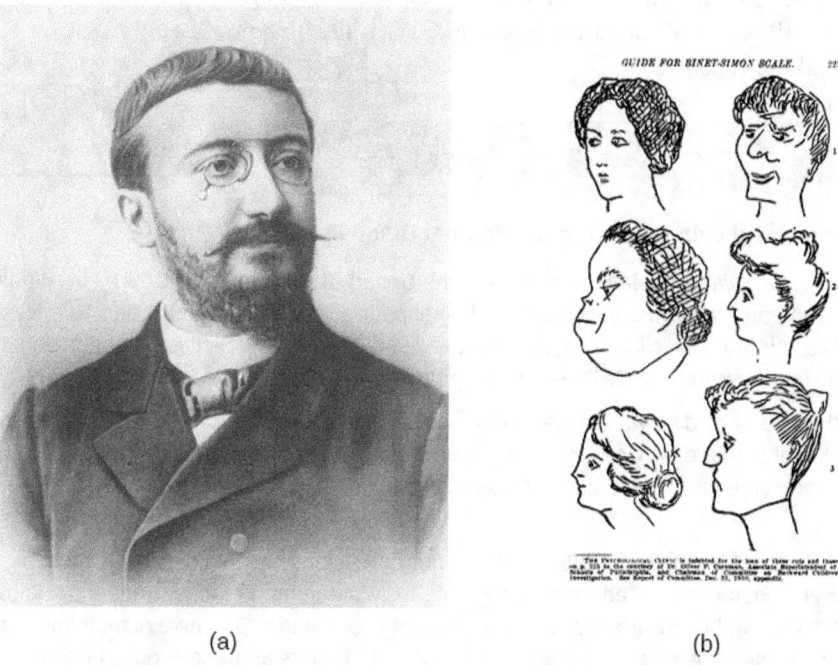

Figure 7.13 French psychologist Alfred Binet helped to develop intelligence testing. (b) This page is from a 1908 version of the Binet-Simon Intelligence Scale. Children being tested were asked which face, of each pair, was prettier.

In 1939, David Wechsler, a psychologist who spent part of his career working with World War I veterans, developed a new IQ test in the United States. Wechsler combined several subtests from other intelligence tests used between 1880 and World War I. These subtests tapped into a variety of verbal and nonverbal skills, because Wechsler believed that intelligence encompassed "the global capacity of a person to act purposefully, to think rationally, and to deal effectively with his environment" (Wechsler, 1958, p. 7). He named the test the Wechsler-Bellevue Intelligence Scale (Wechsler, 1981). This combination of subtests became one of the most extensively used intelligence tests in the history of psychology. Although its name was later changed to the Wechsler Adult Intelligence Scale (WAIS) and has been revised several times, the aims of the test remain virtually unchanged since its inception (Boake, 2002). Today, there are three intelligence tests credited to Wechsler, the Wechsler Adult Intelligence Scale-fourth edition (WAIS-IV), the Wechsler Intelligence Scale for Children (WISC-V), and the Wechsler Preschool and Primary Scale of Intelligence—IV (WPPSI-IV) (Wechsler, 2012). These tests are used widely in schools and communities throughout the United States, and they are periodically normed and standardized as a means of recalibration. As a part of the recalibration process, the WISC-V was given to thousands of children across the country, and children taking the test today are compared with their same-age peers (Figure 7.13).

The WISC-V is composed of 14 subtests, which comprise five indices, which then render an IQ score. The five indices are Verbal Comprehension, Visual Spatial, Fluid Reasoning, Working Memory, and Processing Speed. When the test is complete, individuals receive a score for each of the five indices and a Full Scale IQ score. The method of scoring reflects the understanding that intelligence is comprised of multiple abilities in several cognitive realms and focuses on the mental processes that the child used to arrive at his or her answers to each test item.

Interestingly, the periodic recalibrations have led to an interesting observation known as the Flynn effect. Named after James Flynn, who was among the first to describe this trend, the **Flynn effect** refers to the observation that each generation has a significantly higher IQ than the last. Flynn himself argues, however, that increased IQ scores do not necessarily mean that younger generations are more intelligent per se (Flynn, Shaughnessy, & Fulgham, 2012).

Ultimately, we are still left with the question of how valid intelligence tests are. Certainly, the most modern versions of these tests tap into more than verbal competencies, yet the specific skills that should be assessed in IQ testing, the degree to which any test can truly measure an individual's intelligence, and the use of the results of IQ tests are still issues of debate (Gresham & Witt, 1997; Flynn, Shaughnessy, & Fulgham, 2012; Richardson, 2002; Schlinger, 2003).

WHAT DO YOU THINK?

Capital Punishment and Criminals with Intellectual Disabilities

The case of *Atkins v. Virginia* was a landmark case in the United States Supreme Court. On August 16, 1996, two men, Daryl Atkins and William Jones, robbed, kidnapped, and then shot and killed Eric Nesbitt, a local airman from the U.S. Air Force. A clinical psychologist evaluated Atkins and testified at the trial that Atkins had an IQ of 59. The mean IQ score is 100. The psychologist concluded that Atkins was mildly mentally retarded.

The jury found Atkins guilty, and he was sentenced to death. Atkins and his attorneys appealed to the Supreme Court. In June 2002, the Supreme Court reversed a previous decision and ruled that executions of mentally retarded criminals are 'cruel and unusual punishments' prohibited by the Eighth Amendment. The court wrote in their decision:

> Clinical definitions of mental retardation require not only subaverage intellectual functioning, but also significant limitations in adaptive skills. Mentally retarded persons frequently know the difference between right and wrong and are competent to stand trial. Because of their impairments, however, by definition they have diminished capacities to understand and process information, to communicate, to abstract from mistakes and learn from experience, to engage in logical reasoning, to control impulses, and to understand others' reactions. Their deficiencies do not warrant an exemption from criminal sanctions, but diminish their personal culpability (*Atkins v. Virginia*, 2002, par. 5).

The court also decided that there was a state legislature consensus against the execution of the mentally retarded and that this consensus should stand for all of the states. The Supreme Court ruling left it up to the states to determine their own definitions of mental retardation and intellectual disability. The definitions vary among states as to who can be executed. In the Atkins case, a jury decided that because he had many contacts with his lawyers and thus was provided with intellectual stimulation, his IQ had reportedly increased, and he was now smart enough to be executed. He was given an execution date and then received a stay of execution after it was revealed that lawyers for co-defendant, William Jones, coached Jones to "produce a testimony against Mr. Atkins that did match the evidence" (Liptak, 2008). After the revelation of this misconduct, Atkins was re-sentenced to life imprisonment.

Atkins v. Virginia (2002) highlights several issues regarding society's beliefs around intelligence. In the Atkins case, the Supreme Court decided that intellectual disability *does* affect decision making and therefore should affect the nature of the punishment such criminals receive. Where, however, should the lines of intellectual disability be drawn? In May 2014, the Supreme Court ruled in a related case (*Hall v. Florida*) that IQ scores cannot be used as a final determination of a prisoner's eligibility for the death penalty (Roberts, 2014).

THE BELL CURVE

The results of intelligence tests follow the bell curve, a graph in the general shape of a bell. When the bell curve is used in psychological testing, the graph demonstrates a normal distribution of a trait, in this case, intelligence, in the human population. Many human traits naturally follow the bell curve. For example, if you lined up all your female schoolmates according to height, it is likely that a large cluster of them would be the average height for an American woman: 5'4"–5'6". This cluster would fall in the center of the bell curve, representing the average height for American women (Figure 7.14). There would be fewer women who stand closer to 4'11". The same would be true for women of above-average height: those who stand closer to 5'11". The trick to finding a bell curve in nature is to use a large sample size. Without a large sample size, it is less likely that the bell curve will represent the wider population. A **representative sample** is a subset of the population that accurately represents the general population. If, for example, you measured the height of the women in your classroom only, you might not actually have a representative sample. Perhaps the women's basketball team wanted to take this course together, and they are all in your class. Because basketball players tend to be taller than average, the women in your class may not be a good representative sample of the population of American women. But if your sample included all the women at your school, it is likely that their heights would form a natural bell curve.

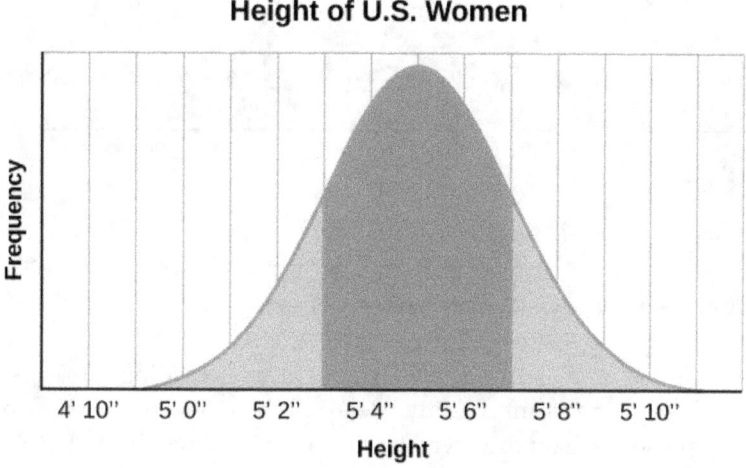

Figure 7.14 Are you of below-average, average, or above-average height?

The same principles apply to intelligence tests scores. Individuals earn a score called an intelligence quotient (IQ). Over the years, different types of IQ tests have evolved, but the way scores are interpreted remains the same. The average IQ score on an IQ test is 100. **Standard deviations** describe how data are dispersed in a population and give context to large data sets. The bell curve uses the standard deviation to show how all scores are dispersed from the average score (Figure 7.15). In modern IQ testing, one standard deviation is 15 points. So a score of 85 would be described as "one standard deviation below the mean." How would you describe a score of 115 and a score of 70? Any IQ score that falls within one standard deviation above and below the mean (between 85 and 115) is considered average, and 68% of the population has IQ scores in this range. An IQ score of 130 or above is considered a superior level.

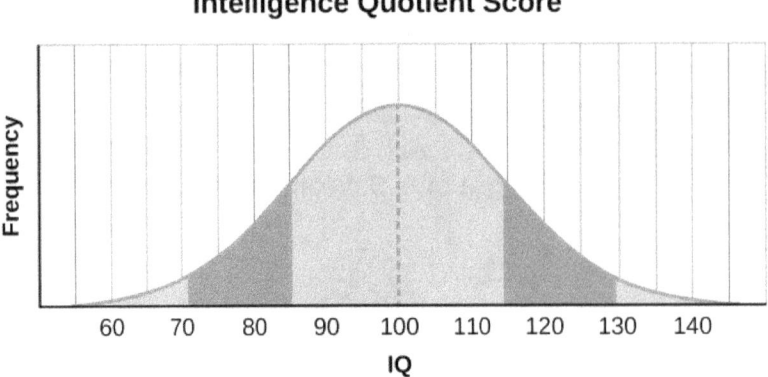

Figure 7.15 The majority of people have an IQ score between 85 and 115.

Only 2.2% of the population has an IQ score below 70 (American Psychological Association [APA], 2013). A score of 70 or below indicates significant cognitive delays. When these are combined with major deficits in adaptive functioning, a person is diagnosed with having an intellectual disability (American Association on Intellectual and Developmental Disabilities, 2013). Formerly known as mental retardation, the accepted term now is intellectual disability, and it has four subtypes: mild, moderate, severe, and profound (Table 7.5). *The Diagnostic and Statistical Manual of Psychological Disorders* lists criteria for each subgroup (APA, 2013).

Characteristics of Cognitive Disorders

Intellectual Disability Subtype	Percentage of Population with Intellectual Disabilities	Description
Mild	85%	3rd- to 6th-grade skill level in reading, writing, and math; may be employed and live independently
Moderate	10%	Basic reading and writing skills; functional self-care skills; requires some oversight
Severe	5%	Functional self-care skills; requires oversight of daily environment and activities
Profound	<1%	May be able to communicate verbally or nonverbally; requires intensive oversight

Table 7.5

On the other end of the intelligence spectrum are those individuals whose IQs fall into the highest ranges. Consistent with the bell curve, about 2% of the population falls into this category. People are considered gifted if they have an IQ score of 130 or higher, or superior intelligence in a particular area. Long ago, popular belief suggested that people of high intelligence were maladjusted. This idea was disproven through a groundbreaking study of gifted children. In 1921, Lewis Terman began a longitudinal study of over 1500 children with IQs over 135 (Terman, 1925). His findings showed that these children became well-educated, successful adults who were, in fact, well-adjusted (Terman & Oden, 1947). Additionally, Terman's study showed that the subjects were above average in physical build and attractiveness, dispelling an earlier popular notion that highly intelligent people were "weaklings." Some people with very high IQs elect to join Mensa, an organization dedicated to identifying, researching, and fostering intelligence. Members must have an IQ score in the top 2% of the population, and they may be required to pass other exams in their application to join the group.

DIG DEEPER

What's in a Name? Mental Retardation

In the past, individuals with IQ scores below 70 and significant adaptive and social functioning delays were diagnosed with mental retardation. When this diagnosis was first named, the title held no social stigma. In time, however, the degrading word "retard" sprang from this diagnostic term. "Retard" was frequently used as a taunt, especially among young people, until the words "mentally retarded" and "retard" became an insult. As such, the DSM-5 now labels this diagnosis as "intellectual disability." Many states once had a Department of Mental Retardation to serve those diagnosed with such cognitive delays, but most have changed their name to Department of Developmental Disabilities or something similar in language. The Social Security Administration still uses the term "mental retardation" but is considering eliminating it from its programming (Goad, 2013). Earlier in the chapter, we discussed how language affects how we think. Do you think changing the title of this department has any impact on how people regard those with developmental disabilities? Does a different name give people more dignity, and if so, how? Does it change the expectations for those with developmental or cognitive disabilities? Why or why not?

WHY MEASURE INTELLIGENCE?

The value of IQ testing is most evident in educational or clinical settings. Children who seem to be experiencing learning difficulties or severe behavioral problems can be tested to ascertain whether the child's difficulties can be partly attributed to an IQ score that is significantly different from the mean for her age group. Without IQ testing—or another measure of intelligence—children and adults needing extra support might not be identified effectively. In addition, IQ testing is used in courts to determine whether a defendant has special or extenuating circumstances that preclude him from participating in some way in a trial. People also use IQ testing results to seek disability benefits from the Social Security Administration.

The following case study demonstrates the usefulness and benefits of IQ testing. Candace, a 14-year-old girl experiencing problems at school in Connecticut, was referred for a court-ordered psychological evaluation. She was in regular education classes in ninth grade and was failing every subject. Candace had never been a stellar student but had always been passed to the next grade. Frequently, she would curse at any of her teachers who called on her in class. She also got into fights with other students and occasionally shoplifted. When she arrived for the evaluation, Candace immediately said that she hated everything about school, including the teachers, the rest of the staff, the building, and the homework. Her parents stated that they felt their daughter was picked on, because she was of a different race than the teachers and most of the other students. When asked why she cursed at her teachers, Candace replied, "They only call on me when I don't know the answer. I don't want to say, 'I don't know' all of the time and look like an idiot in front of my friends. The teachers embarrass me." She was given a battery of tests, including an IQ test. Her score on the IQ test was 68. What does Candace's score say about her ability to excel or even succeed in regular education classes without assistance? Why were her difficulties never noticed or addressed?

7.6 The Source of Intelligence

Learning Objectives

By the end of this section, you will be able to:
- Describe how genetics and environment affect intelligence
- Explain the relationship between IQ scores and socioeconomic status
- Describe the difference between a learning disability and a developmental disorder

A young girl, born of teenage parents, lives with her grandmother in rural Mississippi. They are poor—in serious poverty—but they do their best to get by with what they have. She learns to read when she is just 3 years old. As she grows older, she longs to live with her mother, who now resides in Wisconsin. She moves there at the age of 6 years. At 9 years of age, she is raped. During the next several years, several different male relatives repeatedly molest her. Her life unravels. She turns to drugs and sex to fill the deep, lonely void inside her. Her mother then sends her to Nashville to live with her father, who imposes strict behavioral expectations upon her, and over time, her wild life settles once again. She begins to experience success in school, and at 19 years old, becomes the youngest and first African-American female news anchor ("Dates and Events," n.d.). The woman—Oprah Winfrey—goes on to become a media giant known for both her intelligence and her empathy.

HIGH INTELLIGENCE: NATURE OR NURTURE?

Where does high intelligence come from? Some researchers believe that intelligence is a trait inherited from a person's parents. Scientists who research this topic typically use twin studies to determine the heritability of intelligence. The Minnesota Study of Twins Reared Apart is one of the most well-known twin studies. In this investigation, researchers found that identical twins raised together and identical twins raised apart exhibit a higher correlation between their IQ scores than siblings or fraternal twins raised together (Bouchard, Lykken, McGue, Segal, & Tellegen, 1990). The findings from this study reveal a genetic component to intelligence (Figure 7.15). At the same time, other psychologists believe that intelligence is shaped by a child's developmental environment. If parents were to provide their children with intellectual stimuli from before they are born, it is likely that they would absorb the benefits of that stimulation, and it would be reflected in intelligence levels.

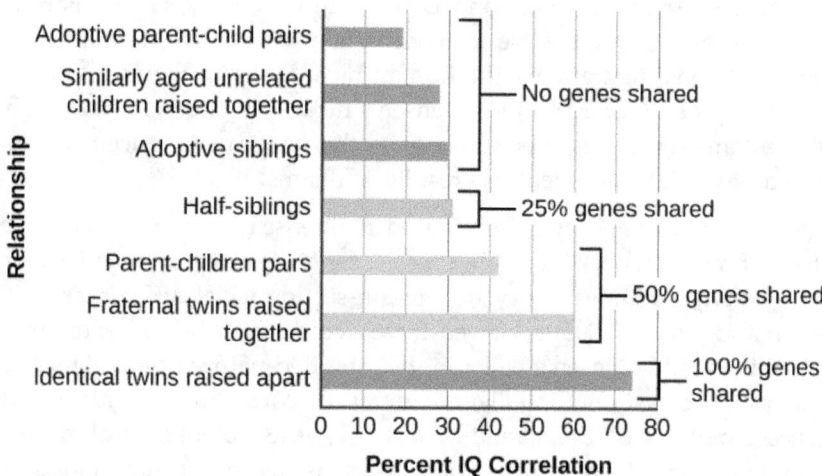

Figure 7.16 The correlations of IQs of unrelated versus related persons reared apart or together suggest a genetic component to intelligence.

The reality is that aspects of each idea are probably correct. In fact, one study suggests that although genetics seem to be in control of the level of intelligence, the environmental influences provide both stability and change to trigger manifestation of cognitive abilities (Bartels, Rietveld, Van Baal, & Boomsma, 2002). Certainly, there are behaviors that support the development of intelligence, but the genetic component of high intelligence should not be ignored. As with all heritable traits, however, it is not always possible to isolate how and when high intelligence is passed on to the next generation.

Range of Reaction is the theory that each person responds to the environment in a unique way based on his or her genetic makeup. According to this idea, your genetic potential is a fixed quantity, but whether you reach your full intellectual potential is dependent upon the environmental stimulation you experience, especially in childhood. Think about this scenario: A couple adopts a child who has average genetic intellectual potential. They raise her in an extremely stimulating environment. What will happen to the couple's new daughter? It is likely that the stimulating environment will improve her intellectual outcomes over the course of her life. But what happens if this experiment is reversed? If a child with an extremely strong genetic background is placed in an environment that does not stimulate him: What happens? Interestingly, according to a longitudinal study of highly gifted individuals, it was found that "the two extremes of optimal and pathological experience are both represented disproportionately in the backgrounds of creative individuals"; however, those who experienced supportive family environments were more likely to report being happy (Csikszentmihalyi & Csikszentmihalyi, 1993, p. 187).

Another challenge to determining origins of high intelligence is the confounding nature of our human social structures. It is troubling to note that some ethnic groups perform better on IQ tests than others—and it is likely that the results do not have much to do with the quality of each ethnic group's intellect. The same is true for socioeconomic status. Children who live in poverty experience more pervasive, daily stress than children who do not worry about the basic needs of safety, shelter, and food. These worries can negatively affect how the brain functions and develops, causing a dip in IQ scores. Mark Kishiyama and his colleagues determined that children living in poverty demonstrated reduced prefrontal brain functioning comparable to children with damage to the lateral prefrontal cortex (Kishyama, Boyce, Jimenez, Perry, & Knight, 2009).

The debate around the foundations and influences on intelligence exploded in 1969, when an educational psychologist named Arthur Jensen published the article "How Much Can We Boost I.Q. and Achievement" in the *Harvard Educational Review*. Jensen had administered IQ tests to diverse groups of students, and his results led him to the conclusion that IQ is determined by genetics. He also posited that intelligence was made up of two types of abilities: Level I and Level II. In his theory, Level I is responsible for rote memorization, whereas Level II is responsible for conceptual and analytical abilities. According to his findings, Level I remained consistent among the human race. Level II, however, exhibited differences among ethnic groups (Modgil & Routledge, 1987). Jensen's most controversial conclusion was that Level II intelligence is prevalent among Asians, then Caucasians, then African Americans. Robert Williams was among those who called out racial bias in Jensen's results (Williams, 1970).

Obviously, Jensen's interpretation of his own data caused an intense response in a nation that continued to grapple with the effects of racism (Fox, 2012). However, Jensen's ideas were not solitary or unique; rather, they represented one of many examples of psychologists asserting racial differences in IQ and cognitive ability. In fact, Rushton and Jensen (2005) reviewed three decades worth of research on the relationship between race and cognitive ability. Jensen's belief in the inherited nature of intelligence and the validity of the IQ test to be the truest measure of intelligence are at the core of his conclusions. If, however, you believe that intelligence is more than Levels I and II, or that IQ tests do not control for socioeconomic and cultural differences among people, then perhaps you can dismiss Jensen's conclusions as a single window that looks out on the complicated and varied landscape of human intelligence.

In a related story, parents of African American students filed a case against the State of California in 1979, because they believed that the testing method used to identify students with learning disabilities was culturally unfair as the tests were normed and standardized using white children (*Larry P. v. Riles*). The testing method used by the state disproportionately identified African American children as mentally retarded. This resulted in many students being incorrectly classified as "mentally retarded." According to a summary of the case, *Larry P. v. Riles*:

> In violation of Title VI of the Civil Rights Act of 1964, the Rehabilitation Act of 1973, and the Education for All Handicapped Children Act of 1975, defendants have utilized standardized intelligence tests that are racially and culturally biased, have a discriminatory impact against black children, and have not been validated for the purpose of essentially permanent placements of black children into educationally dead-end, isolated, and stigmatizing classes for the so-called educable mentally retarded. Further, these federal laws have been violated by defendants' general use of placement mechanisms that, taken together, have not been validated and result in a large over-representation of black children in the special E.M.R. classes. (*Larry P. v. Riles*, par. 6)

Once again, the limitations of intelligence testing were revealed.

WHAT ARE LEARNING DISABILITIES?

Learning disabilities are cognitive disorders that affect different areas of cognition, particularly language or reading. It should be pointed out that learning disabilities are not the same thing as intellectual disabilities. Learning disabilities are considered specific neurological impairments rather than global intellectual or developmental disabilities. A person with a language disability has difficulty understanding or using spoken language, whereas someone with a reading disability, such as dyslexia, has difficulty processing what he or she is reading.

Often, learning disabilities are not recognized until a child reaches school age. One confounding aspect of learning disabilities is that they most often affect children with average to above-average intelligence. In other words, the disability is specific to a particular area and not a measure of overall intellectual ability. At the same time, learning disabilities tend to exhibit comorbidity with other disorders, like attention-deficit hyperactivity disorder (ADHD). Anywhere between 30–70% of individuals with diagnosed cases of ADHD also have some sort of learning disability (Riccio, Gonzales, & Hynd, 1994). Let's take a look at three examples of common learning disabilities: dysgraphia, dyslexia, and dyscalculia.

Dysgraphia

Children with **dysgraphia** have a learning disability that results in a struggle to write legibly. The physical task of writing with a pen and paper is extremely challenging for the person. These children often have extreme difficulty putting their thoughts down on paper (Smits-Engelsman & Van Galen, 1997). This difficulty is inconsistent with a person's IQ. That is, based on the child's IQ and/or abilities in other areas, a child with dysgraphia should be able to write, but can't. Children with dysgraphia may also have problems with spatial abilities.

Students with dysgraphia need academic accommodations to help them succeed in school. These accommodations can provide students with alternative assessment opportunities to demonstrate what they know (Barton, 2003). For example, a student with dysgraphia might be permitted to take an oral exam rather than a traditional paper-and-pencil test. Treatment is usually provided by an occupational therapist, although there is some question as to how effective such treatment is (Zwicker, 2005).

Dyslexia

Dyslexia is the most common learning disability in children. An individual with **dyslexia** exhibits an inability to correctly process letters. The neurological mechanism for sound processing does not work properly in someone with dyslexia. As a result, dyslexic children may not understand sound-letter correspondence. A child with dyslexia may mix up letters within words and sentences—letter reversals, such as those shown in **Figure 7.17**, are a hallmark of this learning disability—or skip whole words while reading. A dyslexic child may have difficulty spelling words correctly while writing. Because of the disordered way that the brain processes letters and sound, learning to read is a frustrating experience. Some dyslexic individuals cope by memorizing the shapes of most words, but they never actually learn to read (Berninger, 2008).

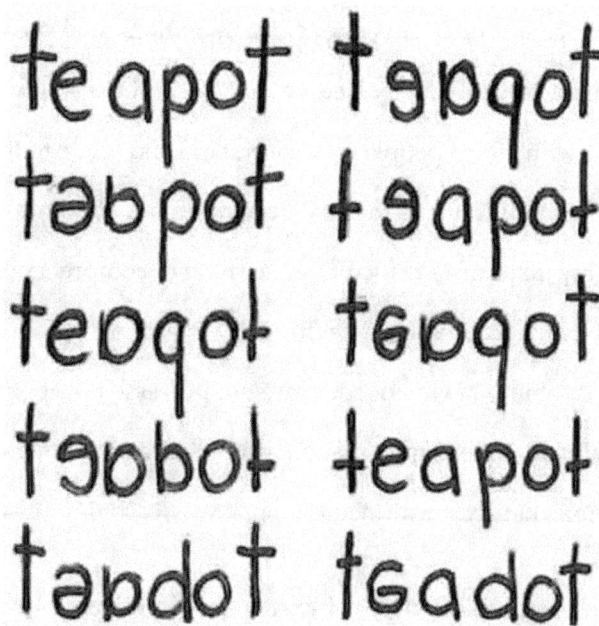

Figure 7.17 These written words show variations of the word "teapot" as written by individuals with dyslexia.

Dyscalculia

Dyscalculia is difficulty in learning or comprehending arithmetic. This learning disability is often first evident when children exhibit difficulty discerning how many objects are in a small group without counting them. Other symptoms may include struggling to memorize math facts, organize numbers, or fully differentiate between numerals, math symbols, and written numbers (such as "3" and "three").

Key Terms

algorithm problem-solving strategy characterized by a specific set of instructions

analytical intelligence aligned with academic problem solving and computations

anchoring bias faulty heuristic in which you fixate on a single aspect of a problem to find a solution

artificial concept concept that is defined by a very specific set of characteristics

availability heuristic faulty heuristic in which you make a decision based on information readily available to you

cognition thinking, including perception, learning, problem solving, judgment, and memory

cognitive psychology field of psychology dedicated to studying every aspect of how people think

cognitive script set of behaviors that are performed the same way each time; also referred to as an event schema

concept category or grouping of linguistic information, objects, ideas, or life experiences

confirmation bias faulty heuristic in which you focus on information that confirms your beliefs

convergent thinking providing correct or established answers to problems

creative intelligence ability to produce new products, ideas, or inventing a new, novel solution to a problem

creativity ability to generate, create, or discover new ideas, solutions, and possibilities

crystallized intelligence characterized by acquired knowledge and the ability to retrieve it

cultural intelligence ability with which people can understand and relate to those in another culture

divergent thinking ability to think "outside the box" to arrive at novel solutions to a problem

dyscalculia learning disability that causes difficulty in learning or comprehending mathematics

dysgraphia learning disability that causes extreme difficulty in writing legibly

dyslexia common learning disability in which letters are not processed properly by the brain

emotional intelligence ability to understand emotions and motivations in yourself and others

event schema set of behaviors that are performed the same way each time; also referred to as a cognitive script

fluid intelligence ability to see complex relationships and solve problems

Flynn effect observation that each generation has a significantly higher IQ than the previous generation

functional fixedness inability to see an object as useful for any other use other than the one for which it was intended

grammar set of rules that are used to convey meaning through the use of a lexicon

heuristic mental shortcut that saves time when solving a problem

hindsight bias belief that the event just experienced was predictable, even though it really wasn't

intelligence quotient (also, IQ) score on a test designed to measure intelligence

language communication system that involves using words to transmit information from one individual to another

lexicon the words of a given language

mental set continually using an old solution to a problem without results

morpheme smallest unit of language that conveys some type of meaning

Multiple Intelligences Theory Gardner's theory that each person possesses at least eight types of intelligence

natural concept mental groupings that are created "naturally" through your experiences

norming administering a test to a large population so data can be collected to reference the normal scores for a population and its groups

overgeneralization extension of a rule that exists in a given language to an exception to the rule

phoneme basic sound unit of a given language

practical intelligence aka "street smarts"

problem-solving strategy method for solving problems

prototype best representation of a concept

range of reaction each person's response to the environment is unique based on his or her genetic make-up

representative bias faulty heuristic in which you stereotype someone or something without a valid basis for your judgment

representative sample subset of the population that accurately represents the general population

role schema set of expectations that define the behaviors of a person occupying a particular role

schema (plural = schemata) mental construct consisting of a cluster or collection of related concepts

semantics process by which we derive meaning from morphemes and words

standard deviation measure of variability that describes the difference between a set of scores and their mean

standardization method of testing in which administration, scoring, and interpretation of results are consistent

syntax manner by which words are organized into sentences

trial and error problem-solving strategy in which multiple solutions are attempted until the correct one is found

triarchic theory of intelligence Sternberg's theory of intelligence; three facets of intelligence: practical, creative, and analytical

working backwards heuristic in which you begin to solve a problem by focusing on the end result

Summary

7.1 What Is Cognition?
In this section, you were introduced to cognitive psychology, which is the study of cognition, or the brain's ability to think, perceive, plan, analyze, and remember. Concepts and their corresponding prototypes help us quickly organize our thinking by creating categories into which we can sort new information. We also develop schemata, which are clusters of related concepts. Some schemata involve routines of thought and behavior, and these help us function properly in various situations without having to "think twice" about them. Schemata show up in social situations and routines of daily behavior.

7.2 Language
Language is a communication system that has both a lexicon and a system of grammar. Language acquisition occurs naturally and effortlessly during the early stages of life, and this acquisition occurs in a predictable sequence for individuals around the world. Language has a strong influence on thought, and the concept of how language may influence cognition remains an area of study and debate in psychology.

7.3 Problem Solving
Many different strategies exist for solving problems. Typical strategies include trial and error, applying algorithms, and using heuristics. To solve a large, complicated problem, it often helps to break the problem into smaller steps that can be accomplished individually, leading to an overall solution. Roadblocks to problem solving include a mental set, functional fixedness, and various biases that can cloud decision making skills.

7.4 What Are Intelligence and Creativity?
Intelligence is a complex characteristic of cognition. Many theories have been developed to explain what intelligence is and how it works. Sternberg generated his triarchic theory of intelligence, whereas Gardner posits that intelligence is comprised of many factors. Still others focus on the importance of emotional intelligence. Finally, creativity seems to be a facet of intelligence, but it is extremely difficult to measure objectively.

7.5 Measures of Intelligence
In this section, we learned about the history of intelligence testing and some of the challenges regarding intelligence testing. Intelligence tests began in earnest with Binet; Wechsler later developed intelligence tests that are still in use today: the WAIS-IV and WISC-V. The Bell curve shows the range of scores that encompass average intelligence as well as standard deviations.

7.6 The Source of Intelligence
Genetics and environment affect intelligence and the challenges of certain learning disabilities. The intelligence levels of all individuals seem to benefit from rich stimulation in their early environments. Highly intelligent individuals, however, may have a built-in resiliency that allows them to overcome difficult obstacles in their upbringing. Learning disabilities can cause major challenges for children who are learning to read and write. Unlike developmental disabilities, learning disabilities are strictly neurological in nature and are not related to intelligence levels. Students with dyslexia, for example, may have extreme difficulty learning to read, but their intelligence levels are typically average or above average.

Review Questions

1. Cognitive psychology is the branch of psychology that focuses on the study of _____.
   a. human development
   b. human thinking
   c. human behavior
   d. human society

2. Which of the following is an example of a prototype for the concept of leadership on an athletic team?
   a. the equipment manager
   b. the scorekeeper
   c. the team captain
   d. the quietest member of the team

3. Which of the following is an example of an artificial concept?
   a. mammals
   b. a triangle's area
   c. gemstones
   d. teachers

4. An event schema is also known as a cognitive _____.
   a. stereotype
   b. concept
   c. script
   d. prototype

5. _____ provides general principles for organizing words into meaningful sentences.
   a. Linguistic determinism
   b. Lexicon
   c. Semantics
   d. Syntax

6. _____ are the smallest unit of language that carry meaning.
   a. Lexicon
   b. Phonemes
   c. Morphemes
   d. Syntax

7. The meaning of words and phrases is determined by applying the rules of _____.
   a. lexicon
   b. phonemes
   c. overgeneralization
   d. semantics

8. _____ is (are) the basic sound units of a spoken language.
   a. Syntax
   b. Phonemes
   c. Morphemes
   d. Grammar

9. A specific formula for solving a problem is called _____.
   a. an algorithm
   b. a heuristic
   c. a mental set
   d. trial and error

10. A mental shortcut in the form of a general problem-solving framework is called _____.
    a. an algorithm
    b. a heuristic
    c. a mental set
    d. trial and error

11. Which type of bias involves becoming fixated on a single trait of a problem?
    a. anchoring bias
    b. confirmation bias
    c. representative bias
    d. availability bias

12. Which type of bias involves relying on a false stereotype to make a decision?
    a. anchoring bias
    b. confirmation bias
    c. representative bias
    d. availability bias

13. Fluid intelligence is characterized by _____.
    a. being able to recall information
    b. being able to create new products
    c. being able to understand and communicate with different cultures
    d. being able to see complex relationships and solve problems

14. Which of the following is not one of Gardner's Multiple Intelligences?
    a. creative
    b. spatial
    c. linguistic
    d. musical

15. Which theorist put forth the triarchic theory of intelligence?
    a. Goleman
    b. Gardner
    c. Sternberg
    d. Steitz

16. When you are examining data to look for trends, which type of intelligence are you using most?
    a. practical
    b. analytical
    c. emotional
    d. creative

17. In order for a test to be normed and standardized it must be tested on _____.
    a. a group of same-age peers
    b. a representative sample
    c. children with mental disabilities
    d. children of average intelligence

18. The mean score for a person with an average IQ is _____.
    a. 70
    b. 130
    c. 85
    d. 100

19. Who developed the IQ test most widely used today?
    a. Sir Francis Galton
    b. Alfred Binet
    c. Louis Terman
    d. David Wechsler

20. The DSM-5 now uses _____ as a diagnostic label for what was once referred to as mental retardation.
    a. autism and developmental disabilities
    b. lowered intelligence
    c. intellectual disability
    d. cognitive disruption

21. Where does high intelligence come from?
    a. genetics
    b. environment
    c. both A and B
    d. neither A nor B

22. Arthur Jensen believed that _____.
    a. genetics was solely responsible for intelligence
    b. environment was solely responsible for intelligence
    c. intelligence level was determined by race
    d. IQ tests do not take socioeconomic status into account

23. What is a learning disability?
    a. a developmental disorder
    b. a neurological disorder
    c. an emotional disorder
    d. an intellectual disorder

24. Which of the following statements is true?
    a. Poverty always affects whether individuals are able to reach their full intellectual potential.
    b. An individual's intelligence is determined solely by the intelligence levels of his siblings.
    c. The environment in which an individual is raised is the strongest predictor of her future intelligence
    d. There are many factors working together to influence an individual's intelligence level.

Critical Thinking Questions

25. Describe an event schema that you would notice at a sporting event.

26. Explain why event schemata have so much power over human behavior.

27. How do words not only represent our thoughts but also represent our values?

28. How could grammatical errors actually be indicative of language acquisition in children?

29. How do words not only represent our thoughts but also represent our values?

30. What is functional fixedness and how can overcoming it help you solve problems?

31. How does an algorithm save you time and energy when solving a problem?

32. Describe a situation in which you would need to use practical intelligence.

33. Describe a situation in which cultural intelligence would help you communicate better.

34. Why do you think different theorists have defined intelligence in different ways?

35. Compare and contrast the benefits of the Stanford-Binet IQ test and Wechsler's IQ tests.

36. What evidence exists for a genetic component to an individual's IQ?

37. Describe the relationship between learning disabilities and intellectual disabilities to intelligence.

Personal Application Questions

38. Describe a natural concept that you know fully but that would be difficult for someone else to understand and explain why it would be difficult.

39. Can you think of examples of how language affects cognition?

40. Which type of bias do you recognize in your own decision making processes? How has this bias affected how you've made decisions in the past and how can you use your awareness of it to improve your decisions making skills in the future?

41. What influence do you think emotional intelligence plays in your personal life?

42. In thinking about the case of Candace described earlier, do you think that Candace benefitted or suffered as a result of consistently being passed on to the next grade?

43. Do you believe your level of intelligence was improved because of the stimuli in your childhood environment? Why or why not?

Chapter 8
Memory

Figure 8.1 Photographs can trigger our memories and bring past experiences back to life. (credit: modification of work by Cory Zanker)

Chapter Outline

8.1 How Memory Functions
8.2 Parts of the Brain Involved with Memory
8.3 Problems with Memory
8.4 Ways to Enhance Memory

Introduction

We may be top-notch learners, but if we don't have a way to store what we've learned, what good is the knowledge we've gained?

Take a few minutes to imagine what your day might be like if you could not remember anything you had learned. You would have to figure out how to get dressed. What clothing should you wear, and how do buttons and zippers work? You would need someone to teach you how to brush your teeth and tie your shoes. Who would you ask for help with these tasks, since you wouldn't recognize the faces of these people in your house? Wait . . . is this even your house? Uh oh, your stomach begins to rumble and you feel hungry. You'd like something to eat, but you don't know where the food is kept or even how to prepare it. Oh dear, this is getting confusing. Maybe it would be best just go back to bed. A bed . . . what is a bed?

We have an amazing capacity for memory, but how, exactly, do we process and store information? Are there different kinds of memory, and if so, what characterizes the different types? How, exactly, do we retrieve our memories? And why do we forget? This chapter will explore these questions as we learn about memory.

8.1 How Memory Functions

Learning Objectives

By the end of this section, you will be able to:
- Discuss the three basic functions of memory
- Describe the three stages of memory storage
- Describe and distinguish between procedural and declarative memory and semantic and episodic memory

Memory is an information processing system; therefore, we often compare it to a computer. **Memory** is the set of processes used to encode, store, and retrieve information over different periods of time (Figure 8.2).

Figure 8.2 Encoding involves the input of information into the memory system. Storage is the retention of the encoded information. Retrieval, or getting the information out of memory and back into awareness, is the third function.

LINK TO LEARNING

Watch this **video of unexpected facts about memory (http://openstax.org/l/unexpectfact)** to learn more.

ENCODING

We get information into our brains through a process called **encoding**, which is the input of information into the memory system. Once we receive sensory information from the environment, our brains label or code it. We organize the information with other similar information and connect new concepts to existing concepts. Encoding information occurs through automatic processing and effortful processing.

If someone asks you what you ate for lunch today, more than likely you could recall this information quite easily. This is known as **automatic processing**, or the encoding of details like time, space, frequency, and the meaning of words. Automatic processing is usually done without any conscious awareness. Recalling the last time you studied for a test is another example of automatic processing. But what about the actual test material you studied? It probably required a lot of work and attention on your part in order to encode that information. This is known as **effortful processing** (Figure 8.3).

Figure 8.3 When you first learn new skills such as driving a car, you have to put forth effort and attention to encode information about how to start a car, how to brake, how to handle a turn, and so on. Once you know how to drive, you can encode additional information about this skill automatically. (credit: Robert Couse-Baker)

What are the most effective ways to ensure that important memories are well encoded? Even a simple sentence is easier to recall when it is meaningful (Anderson, 1984). Read the following sentences (Bransford & McCarrell, 1974), then look away and count backwards from 30 by threes to zero, and then try to write down the sentences (no peeking back at this page!).

1. The notes were sour because the seams split.
2. The voyage wasn't delayed because the bottle shattered.
3. The haystack was important because the cloth ripped.

How well did you do? By themselves, the statements that you wrote down were most likely confusing and difficult for you to recall. Now, try writing them again, using the following prompts: bagpipe, ship christening, and parachutist. Next count backwards from 40 by fours, then check yourself to see how well you recalled the sentences this time. You can see that the sentences are now much more memorable because each of the sentences was placed in context. Material is far better encoded when you make it meaningful.

There are three types of encoding. The encoding of words and their meaning is known as **semantic encoding**. It was first demonstrated by William Bousfield (1935) in an experiment in which he asked people to memorize words. The 60 words were actually divided into 4 categories of meaning, although the participants did not know this because the words were randomly presented. When they were asked to remember the words, they tended to recall them in categories, showing that they paid attention to the meanings of the words as they learned them.

Visual encoding is the encoding of images, and **acoustic encoding** is the encoding of sounds, words in particular. To see how visual encoding works, read over this list of words: *car, level, dog, truth, book, value*. If you were asked later to recall the words from this list, which ones do you think you'd most likely remember? You would probably have an easier time recalling the words *car, dog,* and *book*, and a more difficult time recalling the words *level, truth,* and *value*. Why is this? Because you can recall images (mental pictures) more easily than words alone. When you read the words *car, dog,* and *book* you created images of these things in your mind. These are concrete, high-imagery words. On the other hand, abstract words like *level, truth,* and *value* are low-imagery words. High-imagery words are encoded both visually and semantically (Paivio, 1986), thus building a stronger memory.

Now let's turn our attention to acoustic encoding. You are driving in your car and a song comes on the radio that you haven't heard in at least 10 years, but you sing along, recalling every word. In the United States, children often learn the alphabet through song, and they learn the number of days in each month through rhyme: "Thirty days hath September, / April, June, and November; / All the rest have thirty-one, / Save February, with twenty-eight days clear, / And twenty-nine each leap year." These lessons are easy to remember because of acoustic encoding. We encode the sounds the words make. This is one of the reasons why much of what we teach young children is done through song, rhyme, and rhythm.

Which of the three types of encoding do you think would give you the best memory of verbal information? Some years ago, psychologists Fergus Craik and Endel Tulving (1975) conducted a series of experiments to find out. Participants were given words along with questions about them. The questions required the participants to process the words at one of the three levels. The visual processing questions included such things as asking the participants about the font of the letters. The acoustic processing questions asked the participants about the sound or rhyming of the words, and the semantic processing questions asked the participants about the meaning of the words. After participants were presented with the words and questions, they were given an unexpected recall or recognition task.

Words that had been encoded semantically were better remembered than those encoded visually or acoustically. Semantic encoding involves a deeper level of processing than the shallower visual or acoustic encoding. Craik and Tulving concluded that we process verbal information best through semantic encoding, especially if we apply what is called the self-reference effect. The **self-reference effect** is the tendency for an individual to have better memory for information that relates to oneself in comparison to material that has less personal relevance (Rogers, Kuiper, & Kirker, 1977). Could semantic encoding be beneficial to you as you attempt to memorize the concepts in this chapter?

STORAGE

Once the information has been encoded, we have to somehow retain it. Our brains take the encoded information and place it in storage. **Storage** is the creation of a permanent record of information.

In order for a memory to go into storage (i.e., long-term memory), it has to pass through three distinct stages: Sensory Memory, Short-Term Memory, and finally Long-Term Memory. These stages were first proposed by Richard Atkinson and Richard Shiffrin (1968). Their model of human memory (**Figure 8.4**), called Atkinson and Shiffrin's model, is based on the belief that we process memories in the same way that a computer processes information.

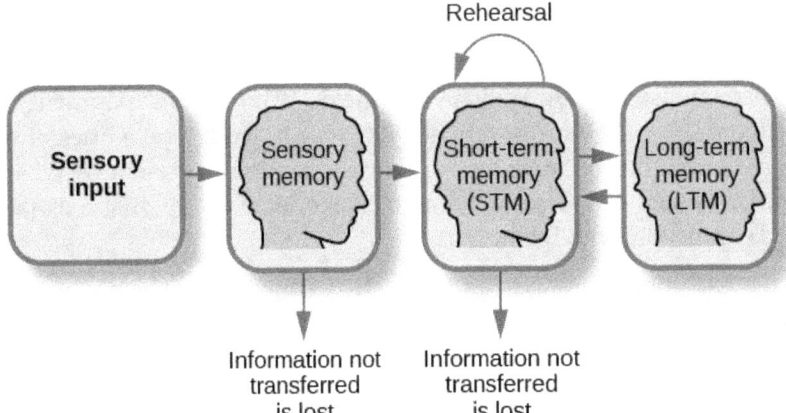

Figure 8.4 According to the Atkinson-Shiffrin model of memory, information passes through three distinct stages in order for it to be stored in long-term memory.

Atkinson and Shiffrin's model is not the only model of memory. Baddeley and Hitch (1974) proposed a working memory model in which short-term memory has different forms. In their model, storing memories in short-term memory is like opening different files on a computer and adding information. The working memory files hold a limited amount of information. The type of short-term memory (or computer file) depends on the type of information received. There are memories in visual-spatial form, as well as memories of spoken or written material, and they are stored in three short-term systems: a visuospatial sketchpad, an episodic buffer (Baddeley, 2000), and a phonological loop. According to Baddeley and

Hitch, a central executive part of memory supervises or controls the flow of information to and from the three short-term systems, and the central executive is responsible for moving information into long-term memory.

Sensory Memory

In the Atkinson-Shiffrin model, stimuli from the environment are processed first in **sensory memory**: storage of brief sensory events, such as sights, sounds, and tastes. It is very brief storage—up to a couple of seconds. We are constantly bombarded with sensory information. We cannot absorb all of it, or even most of it. And most of it has no impact on our lives. For example, what was your professor wearing the last class period? As long as the professor was dressed appropriately, it does not really matter what she was wearing. Sensory information about sights, sounds, smells, and even textures, which we do not view as valuable information, we discard. If we view something as valuable, the information will move into our short-term memory system.

Short-Term Memory

Short-term memory (STM) is a temporary storage system that processes incoming sensory memory. The terms short-term and working memory are sometimes used interchangeably, but they are not exactly the same. Short-term memory is more accurately described as a component of working memory. Short-term memory takes information from sensory memory and sometimes connects that memory to something already in long-term memory. Short-term memory storage lasts 15 to 30 seconds. Think of it as the information you have displayed on your computer screen, such as a document, spreadsheet, or website. Then, information in STM goes to long-term memory (you save it to your hard drive), or it is discarded (you delete a document or close a web browser).

Rehearsal moves information from short-term memory to long-term memory. Active rehearsal is a way of attending to information to move it from short-term to long-term memory. During active rehearsal, you repeat (practice) the information to be remembered. If you repeat it enough, it may be moved into long-term memory. For example, this type of active rehearsal is the way many children learn their ABCs by singing the alphabet song. Alternatively, elaborative rehearsal is the act of linking new information you are trying to learn to existing information that you already know. For example, if you meet someone at a party and your phone is dead but you want to remember his phone number, which starts with area code 203, you might remember that your uncle Abdul lives in Connecticut and has a 203 area code. This way, when you try to remember the phone number of your new prospective friend, you will easily remember the area code. Craik and Lockhart (1972) proposed the levels of processing hypothesis that states the deeper you think about something, the better you remember it.

You may find yourself asking, "How much information can our memory handle at once?" To explore the capacity and duration of your short-term memory, have a partner read the strings of random numbers (**Figure 8.5**) out loud to you, beginning each string by saying, "Ready?" and ending each by saying, "Recall," at which point you should try to write down the string of numbers from memory.

9754   68259   913825   5316842   86951372   719384273
6419   67148   648327   5963827   51739826   163875942

Figure 8.5 Work through this series of numbers using the recall exercise explained above to determine the longest string of digits that you can store.

Note the longest string at which you got the series correct. For most people, the capacity will probably be close to 7 plus or minus 2. In 1956, George Miller reviewed most of the research on the capacity of short-term memory and found that people can retain between 5 and 9 items, so he reported the capacity of short-term memory was the "magic number" 7 plus or minus 2. However, more contemporary research has found working memory capacity is 4 plus or minus 1 (Cowan, 2010). Generally, recall is somewhat better for random numbers than for random letters (Jacobs, 1887) and also often slightly better for information we hear (acoustic encoding) rather than information we see (visual encoding) (Anderson, 1969).

Memory trace decay and interference are two factors that affect short-term memory retention. Peterson and Peterson (1959) investigated short-term memory using the three letter sequences called trigrams (e.g., CLS) that had to be recalled after various time intervals between 3 and 18 seconds. Participants remembered about 80% of the trigrams after a 3-second delay, but only 10% after a delay of 18 seconds, which caused them to conclude that short-term memory decayed in 18 seconds. During decay, the memory trace becomes less activated over time, and the information is forgotten. However, Keppel and Underwood (1962) examined only the first trials of the trigram task and found that proactive interference also affected short-term memory retention. During proactive interference, previously learned information interferes with the ability to learn new information. Both memory trace decay and proactive interference affect short-term memory. Once the information reaches long-term memory, it has to be consolidated at both the synaptic level, which takes a few hours, and into the memory system, which can take weeks or longer.

Long-term Memory

Long-term memory (LTM) is the continuous storage of information. Unlike short-term memory, long-term memory storage capacity is believed to be unlimited. It encompasses all the things you can remember that happened more than just a few minutes ago. One cannot really consider long-term memory without thinking about the way it is organized. Really quickly, what is the first word that comes to mind when you hear "peanut butter"? Did you think of jelly? If you did, you probably have associated peanut butter and jelly in your mind. It is generally accepted that memories are organized in semantic (or associative) networks (Collins & Loftus, 1975). A semantic network consists of concepts, and as you may recall from what you've learned about memory, concepts are categories or groupings of linguistic information, images, ideas, or memories, such as life experiences. Although individual experiences and expertise can affect concept arrangement, concepts are believed to be arranged hierarchically in the mind (Anderson & Reder, 1999; Johnson & Mervis, 1997, 1998; Palmer, Jones, Hennessy, Unze, & Pick, 1989; Rosch, Mervis, Gray, Johnson, & Boyes-Braem, 1976; Tanaka & Taylor, 1991). Related concepts are linked, and the strength of the link depends on how often two concepts have been associated.

Semantic networks differ depending on personal experiences. Importantly for memory, activating any part of a semantic network also activates the concepts linked to that part to a lesser degree. The process is known as spreading activation (Collins & Loftus, 1975). If one part of a network is activated, it is easier to access the associated concepts because they are already partially activated. When you remember or recall something, you activate a concept, and the related concepts are more easily remembered because they are partially activated. However, the activations do not spread in just one direction. When you remember something, you usually have several routes to get the information you are trying to access, and the more links you have to a concept, the better your chances of remembering.

There are two types of long-term memory: *explicit* and *implicit* (Figure 8.6). Understanding the difference between explicit memory and implicit memory is important because aging, particular types of brain trauma, and certain disorders can impact explicit and implicit memory in different ways. **Explicit memories** are those we consciously try to remember, recall, and report. For example, if you are studying for your chemistry exam, the material you are learning will be part of your explicit memory. In keeping with the computer analogy, some information in your long-term memory would be like the information you have saved on the hard drive. It is not there on your desktop (your short-term memory), but most of the time you can pull up this information when you want it. Not all long-term memories are strong memories, and some memories can only be recalled using prompts. For example, you might easily recall a fact, such as the capital of the United States, but you might struggle to recall the name of the restaurant at which you had dinner when you visited a nearby city last summer. A prompt, such as that the restaurant was named after its owner, might help you recall the name of the restaurant. Explicit memory is sometimes referred to as declarative memory, because it can be put into words. Explicit memory is divided into episodic memory and semantic memory.

> **LINK TO LEARNING**
>
> View this **video that explains short-term and long-term memory** (http://openstax.org/l/HMbrain) to learn more about how memories are stored and retrieved.

Episodic memory is information about events we have personally experienced (i.e., an episode). For instance, the memory of your last birthday is an episodic memory. Usually, episodic memory is reported as a story. The concept of episodic memory was first proposed about in the 1970s (Tulving, 1972). Since then, Tulving and others have reformulated the theory, and currently scientists believe that episodic memory is memory about happenings in particular places at particular times—the what, where, and when of an event (Tulving, 2002). It involves recollection of visual imagery as well as the feeling of familiarity (Hassabis & Maguire, 2007). **Semantic memory** is knowledge about words, concepts, and language-based knowledge and facts. Semantic memory is typically reported as facts. Semantic means having to do with language and knowledge about language. For example, answers to the following questions like "what is the definition of psychology" and "who was the first African American president of the United States" are stored in your semantic memory.

Implicit memories are long-term memories that are not part of our consciousness. Although implicit memories are learned outside of our awareness and cannot be consciously recalled, implicit memory is demonstrated in the performance of some task (Roediger, 1990; Schacter, 1987). Implicit memory has been studied with cognitive demand tasks, such as performance on artificial grammars (Reber, 1976), word memory (Jacoby, 1983; Jacoby & Witherspoon, 1982), and learning unspoken and unwritten contingencies and rules (Greenspoon, 1955; Giddan & Eriksen, 1959; Krieckhaus & Eriksen, 1960). Returning to the computer metaphor, implicit memories are like a program running in the background, and you are not aware of their influence. Implicit memories can influence observable behaviors as well as cognitive tasks. In either case, you usually cannot put the memory into words that adequately describe the task. There are several types of implicit memories, including procedural, priming, and emotional conditioning.

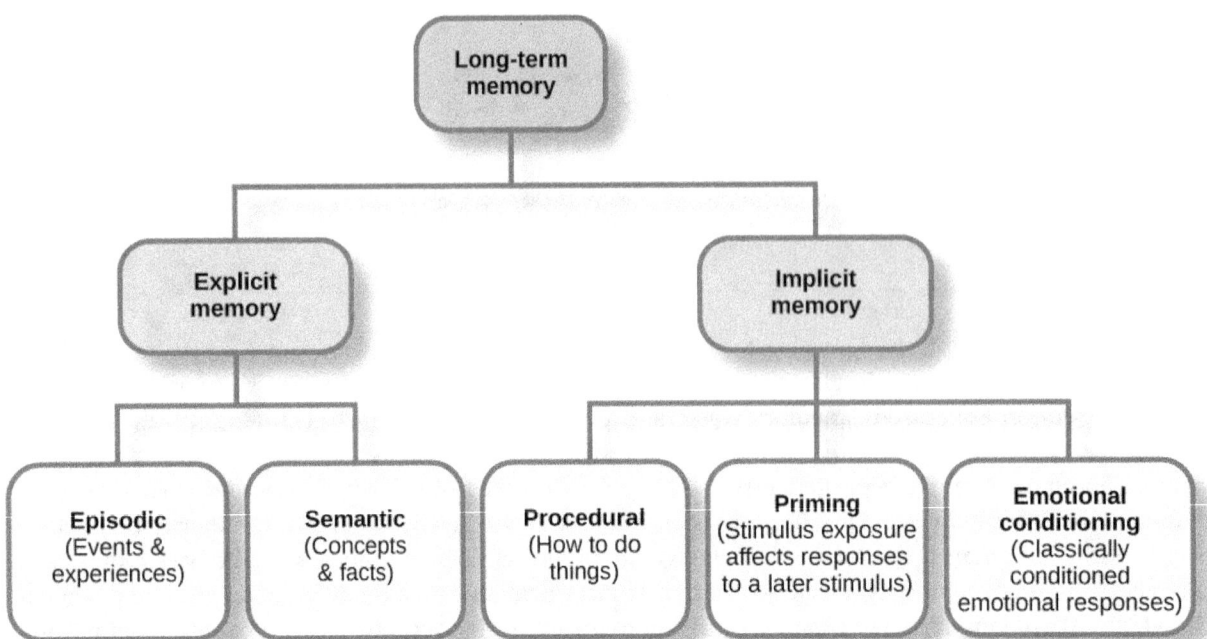

Figure 8.6 There are two components of long-term memory: explicit and implicit. Explicit memory includes episodic and semantic memory. Implicit memory includes procedural memory and things learned through conditioning.

Implicit **procedural memory** is often studied using observable behaviors (Adams, 1957; Lacey & Smith, 1954; Lazarus & McCleary, 1951). Implicit procedural memory stores information about the way to do something, and it is the memory for skilled actions, such as brushing your teeth, riding a bicycle, or driving a car. You were probably not that good at riding a bicycle or driving a car the first time you tried, but you were much better after doing those things for a year. Your improved bicycle riding was due to learning balancing abilities. You likely *thought* about staying upright in the beginning, but now you just *do* it. Moreover, you probably are good at staying balanced, but cannot tell someone the exact way you do it. Similarly, when you first learned to drive, you probably thought about a lot of things that you just do now without much thought. When you first learned to do these tasks, someone may have told you how to do them, but everything you learned since those instructions that you cannot readily explain to someone else as the way to do it is implicit memory.

Implicit priming is another type of implicit memory (Schacter, 1992). During priming exposure to a stimulus affects the response to a later stimulus. Stimuli can vary and may include words, pictures, and other stimuli to elicit a response or increase recognition. For instance, some people really enjoy picnics. They love going into nature, spreading a blanket on the ground, and eating a delicious meal. Now, unscramble the following letters to make a word.

AETPL

What word did you come up with? Chances are good that it was "plate."

Had you read, "Some people really enjoy growing flowers. They love going outside to their garden, fertilizing their plants, and watering their flowers," you probably would have come up with the word "petal" instead of plate.

Do you recall the earlier discussion of semantic networks? The reason people are more likely to come up with "plate" after reading about a picnic is that plate is associated (linked) with picnic. Plate was primed by activating the semantic network. Similarly, "petal" is linked to flower and is primed by flower. Priming is also the reason you probably said jelly in response to peanut butter.

Implicit emotional conditioning is the type of memory involved in classically conditioned emotion responses (Olson & Fazio, 2001). These emotional relationships cannot be reported or recalled but can be associated with different stimuli. For example, specific smells can cause specific emotional responses for some people. If there is a smell that makes you feel positive and nostalgic, and you don't know where that response comes from, it is an implicit emotional response. Similarly, most people have a song that causes a specific emotional response. That song's effect could be an implicit emotional memory (Yang, Xu, Du, Shi, & Fang, 2011).

EVERYDAY CONNECTION

Can You Remember Everything You Ever Did or Said?

Episodic memories are also called autobiographical memories. Let's quickly test your autobiographical memory. What were you wearing exactly five years ago today? What did you eat for lunch on April 10, 2009? You probably find it difficult, if not impossible, to answer these questions. Can you remember every event you have experienced over the course of your life—meals, conversations, clothing choices, weather conditions, and so on? Most likely none of us could even come close to answering these questions; however, American actress Marilu Henner, best known for the television show *Taxi*, can remember. She has an amazing and highly superior autobiographical memory (Figure 8.7).

Figure 8.7 Marilu Henner's super autobiographical memory is known as hyperthymesia. (credit: Mark Richardson)

Very few people can recall events in this way; right now, fewer than 20 have been identified as having this ability, and only a few have been studied (Parker, Cahill & McGaugh 2006). And although hyperthymesia normally appears in adolescence, two children in the United States appear to have memories from well before their tenth birthdays.

LINK TO LEARNING

Watch this **video about superior autobiographical memory (http://openstax.org/l/endlessmem)** from the television news show *60 Minutes* to learn more.

RETRIEVAL

So you have worked hard to encode (via effortful processing) and store some important information for your upcoming final exam. How do you get that information back out of storage when you need it? The act of getting information out of memory storage and back into conscious awareness is known as **retrieval**. This would be similar to finding and opening a paper you had previously saved on your computer's hard drive. Now it's back on your desktop, and you can work with it again. Our ability to retrieve information from long-term memory is vital to our everyday functioning. You must be able to retrieve information from memory in order to do everything from knowing how to brush your hair and teeth, to driving to work, to knowing how to perform your job once you get there.

There are three ways you can retrieve information out of your long-term memory storage system: recall, recognition, and relearning. **Recall** is what we most often think about when we talk about memory retrieval: it means you can access information without cues. For example, you would use recall for an essay test. **Recognition** happens when you identify information that you have previously learned after encountering it again. It involves a process of comparison. When you take a multiple-choice test, you are relying on recognition to help you choose the correct answer. Here is another example. Let's say you graduated from high school 10 years ago, and you have returned to your hometown for your 10-year reunion. You may not be able to recall all of your classmates, but you recognize many of them based on their yearbook photos.

The third form of retrieval is **relearning**, and it's just what it sounds like. It involves learning information that you previously learned. Whitney took Spanish in high school, but after high school she did not have the opportunity to speak Spanish. Whitney is now 31, and her company has offered her an opportunity to work in their Mexico City office. In order to prepare herself, she enrolls in a Spanish course at the local community center. She's surprised at how quickly she's able to pick up the language after not speaking it for 13 years; this is an example of relearning.

8.2 Parts of the Brain Involved with Memory

Learning Objectives

By the end of this section, you will be able to:
- Explain the brain functions involved in memory
- Recognize the roles of the hippocampus, amygdala, and cerebellum

Are memories stored in just one part of the brain, or are they stored in many different parts of the brain? Karl Lashley began exploring this problem, about 100 years ago, by making lesions in the brains of animals such as rats and monkeys. He was searching for evidence of the **engram**: the group of neurons that serve as the "physical representation of memory" (Josselyn, 2010). First, Lashley (1950) trained rats to find their way through a maze. Then, he used the tools available at the time—in this case a soldering iron—to create lesions in the rats' brains, specifically in the cerebral cortex. He did this because he was trying to erase the engram, or the original memory trace that the rats had of the maze.

Lashley did not find evidence of the engram, and the rats were still able to find their way through the maze, regardless of the size or location of the lesion. Based on his creation of lesions and the animals' reaction, he formulated the **equipotentiality hypothesis**: if part of one area of the brain involved in memory is damaged, another part of the same area can take over that memory function (Lashley, 1950). Although Lashley's early work did not confirm the existence of the engram, modern psychologists are making progress locating it. For example, Eric Kandel has spent decades studying the synapse and its role in controlling the flow of information through neural circuits needed to store memories (Mayford, Siegelbaum, & Kandel, 2012).

Many scientists believe that the entire brain is involved with memory. However, since Lashley's research, other scientists have been able to look more closely at the brain and memory. They have argued that memory is located in specific parts of the brain, and specific neurons can be recognized for their involvement in forming memories. The main parts of the brain involved with memory are the amygdala, the hippocampus, the cerebellum, and the prefrontal cortex (Figure 8.8).

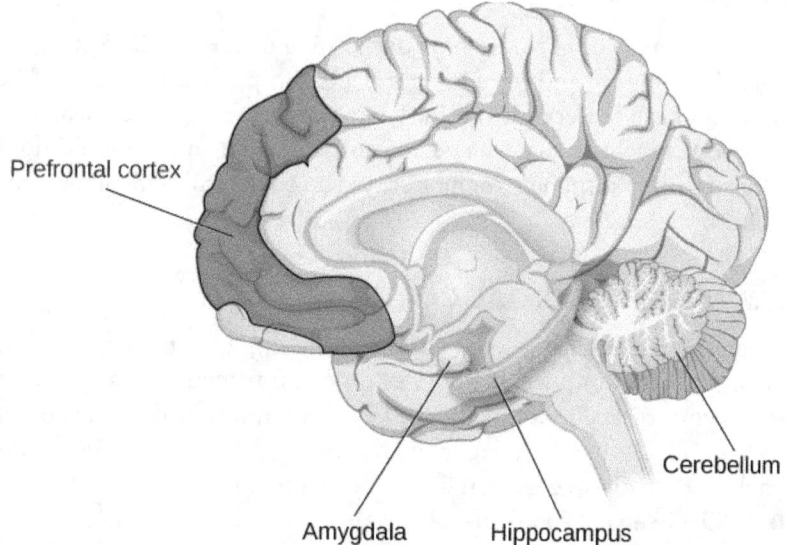

Figure 8.8 The amygdala is involved in fear and fear memories. The hippocampus is associated with declarative and episodic memory as well as recognition memory. The cerebellum plays a role in processing procedural memories, such as how to play the piano. The prefrontal cortex appears to be involved in remembering semantic tasks.

THE AMYGDALA

First, let's look at the role of the amygdala in memory formation. The main job of the amygdala is to regulate emotions, such as fear and aggression (Figure 8.8). The amygdala plays a part in how memories are stored because storage is influenced by stress hormones. For example, one researcher experimented with rats and the fear response (Josselyn, 2010). Using Pavlovian conditioning, a neutral tone was paired with a foot shock to the rats. This produced a fear memory in the rats. After being conditioned, each time they heard the tone, they would freeze (a defense response in rats), indicating a memory for the impending shock. Then the researchers induced cell death in neurons in the lateral amygdala, which is the specific area of the brain responsible for fear memories. They found the fear memory faded (became extinct). Because of its role in processing emotional information, the amygdala is also involved in memory consolidation: the process of transferring new learning into long-term memory. The amygdala seems to facilitate encoding memories at a deeper level when the event is emotionally arousing.

LINK TO LEARNING

In this TED Talk called "A Mouse. A Laser Beam. A Manipulated Memory," (http://openstax.org/l/mousebeam) Steve Ramirez and Xu Liu from MIT talk about using laser beams to manipulate fear memory in rats. Find out why their work caused a media frenzy once it was published in *Science*.

THE HIPPOCAMPUS

Another group of researchers also experimented with rats to learn how the hippocampus functions in memory processing (Figure 8.8). They created lesions in the hippocampi of the rats, and found that the rats demonstrated memory impairment on various tasks, such as object recognition and maze running. They concluded that the hippocampus is involved in memory, specifically normal recognition memory as well as spatial memory (when the memory tasks are like recall tests) (Clark, Zola, & Squire, 2000). Another job of the hippocampus is to project information to cortical regions that give memories meaning and connect them with other memories. It also plays a part in memory consolidation: the process of transferring new learning into long-term memory.

Injury to this area leaves us unable to process new declarative memories. One famous patient, known for years only as H. M., had both his left and right temporal lobes (hippocampi) removed in an attempt to help control the seizures he had been suffering from for years (Corkin, Amaral, González, Johnson, & Hyman, 1997). As a result, his declarative memory was significantly affected, and he could not form new semantic knowledge. He lost the ability to form new memories, yet he could still remember information and events that had occurred prior to the surgery.

THE CEREBELLUM AND PREFRONTAL CORTEX

Although the hippocampus seems to be more of a processing area for explicit memories, you could still lose it and be able to create implicit memories (procedural memory, motor learning, and classical conditioning), thanks to your cerebellum (Figure 8.8). For example, one classical conditioning experiment is to accustom subjects to blink when they are given a puff of air to the eyes. When researchers damaged the cerebellums of rabbits, they discovered that the rabbits were not able to learn the conditioned eye-blink response (Steinmetz, 1999; Green & Woodruff-Pak, 2000).

Other researchers have used brain scans, including positron emission tomography (PET) scans, to learn how people process and retain information. From these studies, it seems the prefrontal cortex is involved. In one study, participants had to complete two different tasks: either looking for the letter *a* in words (considered a perceptual task) or categorizing a noun as either living or non-living (considered a semantic task) (Kapur et al., 1994). Participants were then asked which words they had previously seen. Recall was much better for the semantic task than for the perceptual task. According to PET scans, there was much more activation in the left inferior prefrontal cortex in the semantic task. In another study, encoding was associated with left frontal activity, while retrieval of information was associated with the right frontal region (Craik et al., 1999).

NEUROTRANSMITTERS

There also appear to be specific neurotransmitters involved with the process of memory, such as epinephrine, dopamine, serotonin, glutamate, and acetylcholine (Myhrer, 2003). There continues to be discussion and debate among researchers as to which neurotransmitter plays which specific role (Blockland, 1996). Although we don't yet know which role each neurotransmitter plays in memory, we do know that communication among neurons via neurotransmitters is critical for developing new memories. Repeated activity by neurons leads to increased neurotransmitters in the synapses and more efficient and more synaptic connections. This is how memory consolidation occurs.

It is also believed that strong emotions trigger the formation of strong memories, and weaker emotional experiences form weaker memories; this is called **arousal theory** (Christianson, 1992). For example, strong emotional experiences can trigger the release of neurotransmitters, as well as hormones, which strengthen memory; therefore, our memory for an emotional event is usually better than our memory for a non-emotional event. When humans and animals are stressed, the brain secretes more of the neurotransmitter glutamate, which helps them remember the stressful event (McGaugh, 2003). This is clearly evidenced by what is known as the flashbulb memory phenomenon.

A **flashbulb memory** is an exceptionally clear recollection of an important event (Figure 8.9). Where were you when you first heard about the 9/11 terrorist attacks? Most likely you can remember where you were and what you were doing. In fact, a Pew Research Center (2011) survey found that for those Americans who were age 8 or older at the time of the event, 97% can recall the moment they learned of this event, even a decade after it happened.

Figure 8.9 Most people can remember where they were when they first heard about the 9/11 terrorist attacks. This is an example of a flashbulb memory: a record of an atypical and unusual event that has very strong emotional associations. (credit: Michael Foran)

DIG DEEPER

Inaccurate and False Memories

Even flashbulb memories for important events can have decreased accuracy with the passage of time. For example, on at least three occasions, when asked how he heard about the terrorist attacks of 9/11, President George W. Bush responded inaccurately. In January 2002, less than 4 months after the attacks, the then sitting President Bush was asked how he heard about the attacks. He responded:

> I was sitting there, and my Chief of Staff—well, first of all, when we walked into the classroom, I had seen this plane fly into the first building. There was a TV set on. And you know, I thought it was pilot error and I was amazed that anybody could make such a terrible mistake. (Greenberg, 2004, p. 2)

Contrary to what President Bush stated, no one saw the first plane hit, except people on the ground near the twin towers. Video footage of the first plane was not recorded because it was a normal Tuesday morning, until the first plane hit.

Memory is not like a video recording. Human memory, even flashbulb memories, can be frail. Different parts of them, such as the time, visual elements, and smells, are stored in different places. When something is remembered, these components have to be put back together for the complete memory, which is known as memory reconstruction. Each component creates a chance for an error to occur. False memory is remembering something that did not happen. Research participants have recalled hearing a word, even though they never heard the word (Roediger & McDermott, 2000).

Do you remember where you were when you heard about the school shooting at Marjorie Douglas High School? Who were you with and what were you doing? What did you talk about? Can you contact those people you were with? Do they have the same memories as you or do they have different memories?

8.3 Problems with Memory

Learning Objectives

By the end of this section, you will be able to:
- Compare and contrast the two types of amnesia
- Discuss the unreliability of eyewitness testimony
- Discuss encoding failure
- Discuss the various memory errors
- Compare and contrast the two types of interference

You may pride yourself on your amazing ability to remember the birthdates and ages of all of your friends and family members, or you may be able recall vivid details of your 5th birthday party at Chuck E. Cheese's. However, all of us have at times felt frustrated, and even embarrassed, when our memories have failed us. There are several reasons why this happens.

AMNESIA

Amnesia is the loss of long-term memory that occurs as the result of disease, physical trauma, or psychological trauma. Endel Tulving (2002) and his colleagues at the University of Toronto studied K. C. for years. K. C. suffered a traumatic head injury in a motorcycle accident and then had severe amnesia. Tulving writes,

> the outstanding fact about K.C.'s mental make-up is his utter inability to remember any events, circumstances, or situations from his own life. His episodic amnesia covers his whole life, from birth to the present. The only exception is the experiences that, at any time, he has had in the last minute or two. (Tulving, 2002, p. 14)

Anterograde Amnesia

There are two common types of amnesia: anterograde amnesia and retrograde amnesia (Figure 8.10). Anterograde amnesia is commonly caused by brain trauma, such as a blow to the head. With **anterograde amnesia**, you cannot remember new information, although you can remember information and events that happened prior to your injury. The hippocampus is usually affected (McLeod, 2011). This suggests that damage to the brain has resulted in the inability to transfer information from short-term to long-term memory; that is, the inability to consolidate memories.

Many people with this form of amnesia are unable to form new episodic or semantic memories, but are still able to form new procedural memories (Bayley & Squire, 2002). This was true of H. M., which was discussed earlier. The brain damage caused by his surgery resulted in anterograde amnesia. H. M. would read the same magazine over and over, having no memory of ever reading it—it was always new to him. He also could not remember people he had met after his surgery. If you were introduced to H. M. and then you left the room for a few minutes, he would not know you upon your return and would introduce himself to you again. However, when presented the same puzzle several days in a row, although he did not remember having seen the puzzle before, his speed at solving it became faster each day (because of relearning) (Corkin, 1965, 1968).

Figure 8.10 This diagram illustrates the timeline of retrograde and anterograde amnesia. Memory problems that extend back in time before the injury and prevent retrieval of information previously stored in long-term memory are known as retrograde amnesia. Conversely, memory problems that extend forward in time from the point of injury and prevent the formation of new memories are called anterograde amnesia.

Retrograde Amnesia

Retrograde amnesia is loss of memory for events that occurred prior to the trauma. People with retrograde amnesia cannot remember some or even all of their past. They have difficulty remembering episodic memories. What if you woke up in the hospital one day and there were people surrounding your bed claiming to be your spouse, your children, and your parents? The trouble is you don't recognize any of them. You were in a car accident, suffered a head injury, and now have retrograde amnesia. You don't remember anything about your life prior to waking up in the hospital. This may sound like the stuff of Hollywood movies, and Hollywood has been fascinated with the amnesia plot for nearly a century, going all the way back to the film *Garden of Lies* from 1915 to more recent movies such as the Jason Bourne spy thrillers. However, for real-life sufferers of retrograde amnesia, like former NFL football player Scott Bolzan, the story is not a Hollywood movie. Bolzan fell, hit his head, and deleted 46 years of his life in an instant. He is now living with one of the most extreme cases of retrograde amnesia on record.

> **LINK TO LEARNING**
>
> View the **video story about Scott Bolzan's amnesia and his attempts to get his life back (http://openstax.org/l/bolzan)** to learn more.

MEMORY CONSTRUCTION AND RECONSTRUCTION

The formulation of new memories is sometimes called **construction**, and the process of bringing up old memories is called **reconstruction**. Yet as we retrieve our memories, we also tend to alter and modify them. A memory pulled from long-term storage into short-term memory is flexible. New events can be added and we can change what we think we remember about past events, resulting in inaccuracies and distortions. People may not intend to distort facts, but it can happen in the process of retrieving old memories and combining them with new memories (Roediger & DeSoto, 2015).

Suggestibility

When someone witnesses a crime, that person's memory of the details of the crime is very important in catching the suspect. Because memory is so fragile, witnesses can be easily (and often accidentally) misled due to the problem of suggestibility. **Suggestibility** describes the effects of misinformation from external sources that leads to the creation of false memories. In the fall of 2002, a sniper in the DC area shot people at a gas station, leaving Home Depot, and walking down the street. These attacks went on in a variety of places for over three weeks and resulted in the deaths of ten people. During this time, as you can imagine, people were terrified to leave their homes, go shopping, or even walk through their neighborhoods. Police officers and the FBI worked frantically to solve the crimes, and a tip hotline was set up. Law enforcement received over 140,000 tips, which resulted in approximately 35,000 possible suspects (Newseum, n.d.).

Most of the tips were dead ends, until a white van was spotted at the site of one of the shootings. The police chief went on national television with a picture of the white van. After the news conference, several other eyewitnesses called to say that they too had seen a white van fleeing from the scene of the shooting. At the time, there were more than 70,000 white vans in the area. Police officers, as well as the general public, focused almost exclusively on white vans because they believed the eyewitnesses. Other tips were ignored. When the suspects were finally caught, they were driving a blue sedan.

As illustrated by this example, we are vulnerable to the power of suggestion, simply based on something we see on the news. Or we can claim to remember something that in fact is only a suggestion someone made. It is the suggestion that is the cause of the false memory.

Eyewitness Misidentification

Even though memory and the process of reconstruction can be fragile, police officers, prosecutors, and the courts often rely on eyewitness identification and testimony in the prosecution of criminals. However, faulty eyewitness identification and testimony can lead to wrongful convictions (Figure 8.11).

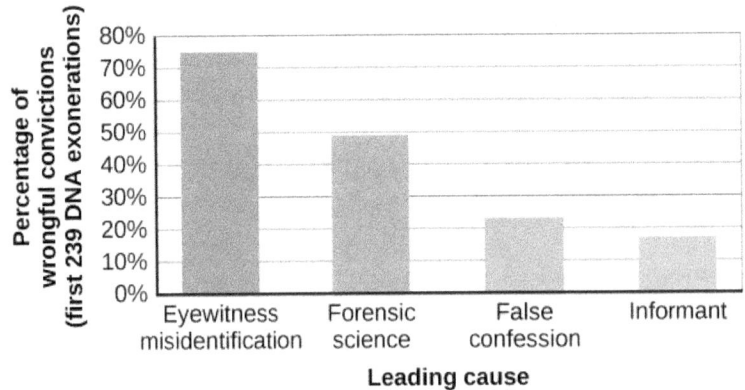

Figure 8.11 In studying cases where DNA evidence has exonerated people from crimes, the Innocence Project discovered that eyewitness misidentification is the leading cause of wrongful convictions (Benjamin N. Cardozo School of Law, Yeshiva University, 2009).

How does this happen? In 1984, Jennifer Thompson, then a 22-year-old college student in North Carolina, was brutally raped at knifepoint. As she was being raped, she tried to memorize every detail of her rapist's face and physical characteristics, vowing that if she survived, she would help get him convicted. After the police were contacted, a composite sketch was made of the suspect, and Jennifer was shown six photos. She chose two, one of which was of Ronald Cotton. After looking at the photos for 4–5 minutes, she said, "Yeah. This is the one," and then she added, "I think this is the guy." When questioned about this by the detective who asked, "You're sure? Positive?" She said that it was him. Then she asked the detective if she did OK, and he reinforced her choice by telling her she did great. These kinds of unintended cues and suggestions by police officers can lead witnesses to identify the wrong suspect. The district attorney was concerned about her lack of certainty the first time, so she viewed a lineup of seven men. She said she was trying to decide between numbers 4 and 5, finally deciding that Cotton, number 5, "Looks most like him." He was 22 years old.

By the time the trial began, Jennifer Thompson had absolutely no doubt that she was raped by Ronald Cotton. She testified at the court hearing, and her testimony was compelling enough that it helped convict him. How did she go from, "I think it's the guy" and it "Looks most like him," to such certainty? Gary Wells and Deah Quinlivan (2009) assert it's suggestive police identification procedures, such as stacking lineups to make the defendant stand out, telling the witness which person to identify, and confirming witnesses choices by telling them "Good choice," or "You picked the guy."

After Cotton was convicted of the rape, he was sent to prison for life plus 50 years. After 4 years in prison, he was able to get a new trial. Jennifer Thompson once again testified against him. This time Ronald Cotton was given two life sentences. After serving 11 years in prison, DNA evidence finally demonstrated that Ronald Cotton did not commit the rape, was innocent, and had served over a decade in prison for a crime he did not commit.

LINK TO LEARNING

Watch this **first video about Ronald Cotton who was falsely convicted (http://openstax.org/l/Cotton1)** and then watch this **second video about the task of his accuser (http://openstax.org/l/Cotton2)** to learn more about the fallibility of memory.

Ronald Cotton's story, unfortunately, is not unique. There are also people who were convicted and placed on death row, who were later exonerated. The Innocence Project is a non-profit group that works to exonerate falsely convicted people, including those convicted by eyewitness testimony. To learn more, you can visit http://www.innocenceproject.org.

DIG DEEPER

Preserving Eyewitness Memory: The Elizabeth Smart Case

Contrast the Cotton case with what happened in the Elizabeth Smart case. When Elizabeth was 14 years old and fast asleep in her bed at home, she was abducted at knifepoint. Her nine-year-old sister, Mary Katherine, was sleeping in the same bed and watched, terrified, as her beloved older sister was abducted. Mary Katherine was the sole eyewitness to this crime and was very fearful. In the coming weeks, the Salt Lake City police and the FBI proceeded with caution with Mary Katherine. They did not want to implant any false memories or mislead her in any way. They did not show her police line-ups or push her to do a composite sketch of the abductor. They knew if they corrupted her memory, Elizabeth might never be found. For several months, there was little or no progress on the case. Then, about 4 months after the kidnapping, Mary Katherine first recalled that she had heard the abductor's voice prior to that night (he had worked exactly one day as a handyman at the family's home) and then she was able to name the person whose voice it was. The family contacted the press and others recognized him—after a total of nine months, the suspect was caught and Elizabeth Smart was returned to her family.

The Misinformation Effect

Cognitive psychologist Elizabeth Loftus has conducted extensive research on memory. She has studied false memories as well as recovered memories of childhood sexual abuse. Loftus also developed the **misinformation effect paradigm**, which holds that after exposure to additional and possibly inaccurate information, a person may misremember the original event.

According to Loftus, an eyewitness's memory of an event is very flexible due to the misinformation effect. To test this theory, Loftus and John Palmer (1974) asked 45 U.S. college students to estimate the speed of cars using different forms of questions (Figure 8.12). The participants were shown films of car accidents and were asked to play the role of the eyewitness and describe what happened. They were asked, "About how fast were the cars going when they (smashed, collided, bumped, hit, contacted) each other?" The participants estimated the speed of the cars based on the verb used.

Participants who heard the word "smashed" estimated that the cars were traveling at a much higher speed than participants who heard the word "contacted." The implied information about speed, based on the verb they heard, had an effect on the participants' memory of the accident. In a follow-up one week later, participants were asked if they saw any broken glass (none was shown in the accident pictures). Participants who had been in the "smashed" group were more than twice as likely to indicate that they did remember seeing glass. Loftus and Palmer demonstrated that a leading question encouraged them to not only remember the cars were going faster, but to also falsely remember that they saw broken glass.

(a)

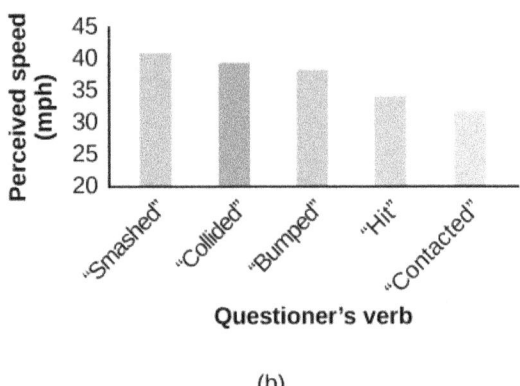
(b)

Figure 8.12 When people are asked leading questions about an event, their memory of the event may be altered. (credit a: modification of work by Rob Young)

Controversies over Repressed and Recovered Memories

Other researchers have described how whole events, not just words, can be falsely recalled, even when they did not happen. The idea that memories of traumatic events could be repressed has been a theme in the field of psychology, beginning with Sigmund Freud, and the controversy surrounding the idea continues today.

Recall of false autobiographical memories is called **false memory syndrome**. This syndrome has received a lot of publicity, particularly as it relates to memories of events that do not have independent witnesses—often the only witnesses to the abuse are the perpetrator and the victim (e.g., sexual abuse).

On one side of the debate are those who have recovered memories of childhood abuse years after it occurred. These researchers argue that some children's experiences have been so traumatizing and distressing that they must lock those memories away in order to lead some semblance of a normal life. They believe that repressed memories can be locked away for decades and later recalled intact through hypnosis and guided imagery techniques (Devilly, 2007).

Research suggests that having no memory of childhood sexual abuse is quite common in adults. For instance, one large-scale study conducted by John Briere and Jon Conte (1993) revealed that 59% of 450 men and women who were receiving treatment for sexual abuse that had occurred before age 18 had forgotten their experiences. Ross Cheit (2007) suggested that repressing these memories created psychological distress in adulthood. The Recovered Memory Project was created so that victims of childhood sexual abuse can recall these memories and allow the healing process to begin (Cheit, 2007; Devilly, 2007).

On the other side, Loftus has challenged the idea that individuals can repress memories of traumatic events from childhood, including sexual abuse, and then recover those memories years later through therapeutic techniques such as hypnosis, guided visualization, and age regression.

Loftus is not saying that childhood sexual abuse doesn't happen, but she does question whether or not those memories are accurate, and she is skeptical of the questioning process used to access these memories, given that even the slightest suggestion from the therapist can lead to misinformation effects. For example, researchers Stephen Ceci and Maggie Brucks (1993, 1995) asked three-year-old children to use an anatomically correct doll to show where their pediatricians had touched them during an exam. Fifty-five percent of the children pointed to the genital/anal area on the dolls, even when they had not received any form of genital exam.

Ever since Loftus published her first studies on the suggestibility of eyewitness testimony in the 1970s, social scientists, police officers, therapists, and legal practitioners have been aware of the flaws in interview practices. Consequently, steps have been taken to decrease suggestibility of witnesses. One way is to modify how witnesses are questioned. When interviewers use neutral and less leading language, children more accurately recall what happened and who was involved (Goodman, 2006; Pipe, 1996; Pipe, Lamb, Orbach, & Esplin, 2004). Another change is in how police lineups are conducted. It's recommended that a blind photo lineup be used. This way the person administering the lineup doesn't know which photo belongs to the suspect, minimizing the possibility of giving leading cues. Additionally, judges in some states now inform jurors about the possibility of misidentification. Judges can also suppress eyewitness testimony if they deem it unreliable.

FORGETTING

"I've a grand memory for forgetting," quipped Robert Louis Stevenson. **Forgetting** refers to loss of information from long-term memory. We all forget things, like a loved one's birthday, someone's name, or where we put our car keys. As you've come to see, memory is fragile, and forgetting can be frustrating and even embarrassing. But why do we forget? To answer this question, we will look at several perspectives on forgetting.

Encoding Failure

Sometimes memory loss happens before the actual memory process begins, which is encoding failure. We can't remember something if we never stored it in our memory in the first place. This would be like trying to find a book on your e-reader that you never actually purchased and downloaded. Often, in order to remember something, we must pay attention to the details and actively work to process the information (effortful encoding). Lots of times we don't do this. For instance, think of how many times in your life you've seen a penny. Can you accurately recall what the front of a U.S. penny looks like? When researchers Raymond Nickerson and Marilyn Adams (1979) asked this question, they found that most Americans don't know which one it is. The reason is most likely encoding failure. Most of us never encode the details of the penny. We only encode enough information to be able to distinguish it from other coins. If we don't encode the information, then it's not in our long-term memory, so we will not be able to remember it.

Figure 8.13 Can you tell which coin, (a), (b), (c), or (d) is the accurate depiction of a US nickel? The correct answer is (c).

Memory Errors

Psychologist Daniel Schacter (2001), a well-known memory researcher, offers seven ways our memories fail us. He calls them the seven sins of memory and categorizes them into three groups: forgetting, distortion, and intrusion (Table 8.1).

Schacter's Seven Sins of Memory

Sin	Type	Description	Example
Transience	Forgetting	Accessibility of memory decreases over time	Forget events that occurred long ago
absentmindedness	Forgetting	Forgetting caused by lapses in attention	Forget where your phone is
Blocking	Forgetting	Accessibility of information is temporarily blocked	Tip of the tongue
Misattribution	Distortion	Source of memory is confused	Recalling a dream memory as a waking memory
Suggestibility	Distortion	False memories	Result from leading questions
Bias	Distortion	Memories distorted by current belief system	Align memories to current beliefs
Persistence	Intrusion	Inability to forget undesirable memories	Traumatic events

Table 8.1

Let's look at the first sin of the forgetting errors: **transience**, which means that memories can fade over time. Here's an example of how this happens. Nathan's English teacher has assigned his students to read the novel *To Kill a Mockingbird*. Nathan comes home from school and tells his mom he has to read this book for class. "Oh, I loved that book!" she says. Nathan asks her what the book is about, and after some hesitation she says, "Well . . . I know I read the book in high school, and I remember that one of the main characters is named Scout, and her father is an attorney, but I honestly don't remember anything else." Nathan wonders if his mother actually read the book, and his mother is surprised she can't recall the plot. What is going on here is storage decay: unused information tends to fade with the passage of time.

In 1885, German psychologist Hermann Ebbinghaus analyzed the process of memorization. First, he memorized lists of nonsense syllables. Then he measured how much he learned (retained) when he attempted to relearn each list. He tested himself over different periods of time from 20 minutes later to 30 days later. The result is his famous forgetting curve (**Figure 8.14**). Due to storage decay, an average person will lose 50% of the memorized information after 20 minutes and 70% of the information after 24 hours (Ebbinghaus, 1885/1964). Your memory for new information decays quickly and then eventually levels out.

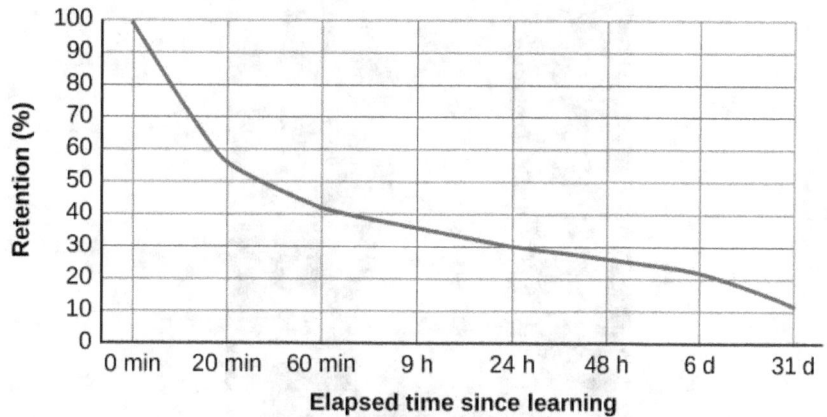

Figure 8.14 The Ebbinghaus forgetting curve shows how quickly memory for new information decays.

Are you constantly losing your cell phone? Have you ever driven back home to make sure you turned off the stove? Have you ever walked into a room for something, but forgotten what it was? You probably answered yes to at least one, if not all, of these examples—but don't worry, you are not alone. We are all prone to committing the memory error known as **absentmindedness**, which describes lapses in memory caused by breaks in attention or our focus being somewhere else.

Cynthia, a psychologist, recalls a time when she recently committed the memory error of absentmindedness.

> When I was completing court-ordered psychological evaluations, each time I went to the court, I was issued a temporary identification card with a magnetic strip which would open otherwise locked doors. As you can imagine, in a courtroom, this identification is valuable and important and no one wanted it to be lost or be picked up by a criminal. At the end of the day, I would hand in my temporary identification. One day, when I was almost done with an evaluation, my daughter's day care called and said she was sick and needed to be picked up. It was flu season, I didn't know how sick she was, and I was concerned. I finished up the evaluation in the next ten minutes, packed up my briefcase, and rushed to drive to my daughter's day care. After I picked up my daughter, I could not remember if I had handed back my identification or if I had left it sitting out on a table. I immediately called the court to check. It turned out that I had handed back my identification. Why could I not remember that? (personal communication, September 5, 2013)

When have you experienced absentmindedness?

"I just streamed this movie called *Oblivion*, and it had that famous actor in it. Oh, what's his name? He's been in all of those movies, like *The Shawshank Redemption* and *The Dark Knight* trilogy. I think he's even won an Oscar. Oh gosh, I can picture his face in my mind, and hear his distinctive voice, but I just can't think of his name! This is going to bug me until I can remember it!" This particular error can be so frustrating because you have the information right on the tip of your tongue. Have you ever experienced this? If so, you've committed the error known as **blocking**: you can't access stored information (**Figure 8.15**).

Figure 8.15 Blocking is also known as tip-of-the-tongue (TOT) phenomenon. The memory is right there, but you can't seem to recall it, just like not being able to remember the name of that very famous actor, Morgan Freeman. (credit: modification of work by D. Miller)

Now let's take a look at the three errors of distortion: misattribution, suggestibility, and bias. **Misattribution** happens when you confuse the source of your information. Let's say Alejandra was dating Lucia and they saw the first Hobbit movie together. Then they broke up and Alejandra saw the second Hobbit movie with someone else. Later that year, Alejandra and Lucia get back together. One day, they are discussing how the Hobbit books and movies are different and Alejandra says to Lucia, "I loved watching the second movie with you and seeing you jump out of your seat during that super scary part." When Lucia responded with a puzzled and then angry look, Alejandra realized she'd committed the error of misattribution.

What if someone is a victim of rape shortly after watching a television program? Is it possible that the victim could actually blame the rape on the person she saw on television because of misattribution? This is exactly what happened to Donald Thomson.

> Australian eyewitness expert Donald Thomson appeared on a live TV discussion about the unreliability of eyewitness memory. He was later arrested, placed in a lineup and identified by a victim as the man who had raped her. The police charged Thomson although the rape had occurred at the time he was on TV. They dismissed his alibi that he was in plain view of a TV audience and in the company of the other discussants, including an assistant commissioner of police.... Eventually, the investigators discovered that the rapist had attacked the woman as she was watching TV—the very program on which Thomson had appeared. Authorities eventually cleared Thomson. The woman had confused the rapist's face with the face that she had seen on TV. (Baddeley, 2004, p. 133)

The second distortion error is suggestibility. Suggestibility is similar to misattribution, since it also involves false memories, but it's different. With misattribution you create the false memory entirely on your own, which is what the victim did in the Donald Thomson case above. With suggestibility, it comes from someone else, such as a therapist or police interviewer asking leading questions of a witness during an interview.

Memories can also be affected by **bias**, which is the final distortion error. Schacter (2001) says that your feelings and view of the world can actually distort your memory of past events. There are several types of bias:

- Stereotypical bias involves racial and gender biases. For example, when Asian American and European American research participants were presented with a list of names, they more frequently incorrectly remembered typical African American names such as Jamal and Tyrone to be associated with the occupation basketball player, and they more frequently incorrectly remembered typical White names such as Greg and Howard to be associated with the occupation of politician (Payne, Jacoby, & Lambert, 2004).

- Egocentric bias involves enhancing our memories of the past (Payne et al., 2004). Did you really score the winning goal in that big soccer match, or did you just assist?

- Hindsight bias happens when we think an outcome was inevitable after the fact. This is the "I knew it all along" phenomenon. The reconstructive nature of memory contributes to hindsight bias (Carli, 1999). We remember untrue events that seem to confirm that we knew the outcome all along.

Have you ever had a song play over and over in your head? How about a memory of a traumatic event, something you really do not want to think about? When you keep remembering something, to the point where you can't "get it out of your head" and it interferes with your ability to concentrate on other things, it is called **persistence**. It's Schacter's seventh and last memory error. It's actually a failure of our memory system because we involuntarily recall unwanted memories, particularly unpleasant ones (Figure 8.16). For instance, you witness a horrific car accident on the way to work one morning, and you can't concentrate on work because you keep remembering the scene.

Figure 8.16 Many veterans of military conflicts involuntarily recall unwanted, unpleasant memories. (credit: Department of Defense photo by U.S. Air Force Tech. Sgt. Michael R. Holzworth)

Interference

Sometimes information is stored in our memory, but for some reason it is inaccessible. This is known as interference, and there are two types: proactive interference and retroactive interference (Figure 8.17). Have you ever gotten a new phone number or moved to a new address, but right after you tell people the old (and wrong) phone number or address? When the new year starts, do you find you accidentally write the previous year? These are examples of **proactive interference**: when old information hinders the recall of newly learned information. **Retroactive interference** happens when information learned more recently hinders the recall of older information. For example, this week you are studying about memory and learn about the Ebbinghaus forgetting curve. Next week you study lifespan development and learn about Erikson's theory of psychosocial development, but thereafter have trouble remembering Ebbinghaus's work because you can only remember Erickson's theory.

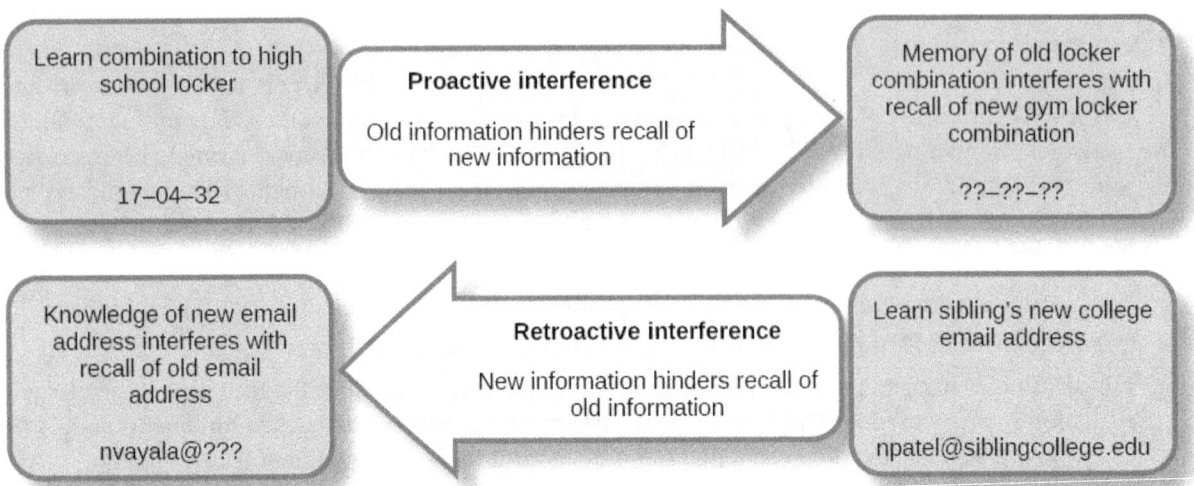

Figure 8.17 Sometimes forgetting is caused by a failure to retrieve information. This can be due to interference, either retroactive or proactive.

8.4 Ways to Enhance Memory

Learning Objectives

By the end of this section, you will be able to:
- Recognize and apply memory-enhancing strategies
- Recognize and apply effective study techniques

Most of us suffer from memory failures of one kind or another, and most of us would like to improve our memories so that we don't forget where we put the car keys or, more importantly, the material we need to know for an exam. In this section, we'll look at some ways to help you remember better, and at some strategies for more effective studying.

MEMORY-ENHANCING STRATEGIES

What are some everyday ways we can improve our memory, including recall? To help make sure information goes from short-term memory to long-term memory, you can use **memory-enhancing strategies**. One strategy is rehearsal, or the conscious repetition of information to be remembered (Craik & Watkins, 1973). Think about how you learned your multiplication tables as a child. You may recall that 6 x 6 = 36, 6 x 7 = 42, and 6 x 8 = 48. Memorizing these facts is rehearsal.

Another strategy is **chunking**: you organize information into manageable bits or chunks (Bodie, Powers, & Fitch-Hauser, 2006). Chunking is useful when trying to remember information like dates and phone numbers. Instead of trying to remember 5205550467, you remember the number as 520-555-0467. So, if you met an interesting person at a party and you wanted to remember his phone number, you would naturally chunk it, and you could repeat the number over and over, which is the rehearsal strategy.

> **LINK TO LEARNING**
>
> Try this **fun activity that employs a memory-enchancing strategy** (http://openstax.org/l/memgame) to learn more.

You could also enhance memory by using **elaborative rehearsal**: a technique in which you think about the meaning of new information and its relation to knowledge already stored in your memory (Tigner, 1999). Elaborative rehearsal involves both linking the information to knowledge already stored and repeating the information. For example, in this case, you could remember that 520 is an area code for Arizona and the person you met is from Arizona. This would help you better remember the 520 prefix. If the information is retained, it goes into long-term memory.

Mnemonic devices are memory aids that help us organize information for encoding (Figure 8.18). They are especially useful when we want to recall larger bits of information such as steps, stages, phases, and parts of a system (Bellezza, 1981). Brian needs to learn the order of the planets in the solar system, but he's having a hard time remembering the correct order. His friend Kelly suggests a mnemonic device that can help him remember. Kelly tells Brian to simply remember the name Mr. VEM J. SUN, and he can easily recall the correct order of the planets: **M**ercury, **V**enus, **E**arth, **M**ars, **J**upiter, **S**aturn, **U**ranus, and **N**eptune. You might use a mnemonic device to help you remember someone's name, a mathematical formula, or the order of mathematical operations.

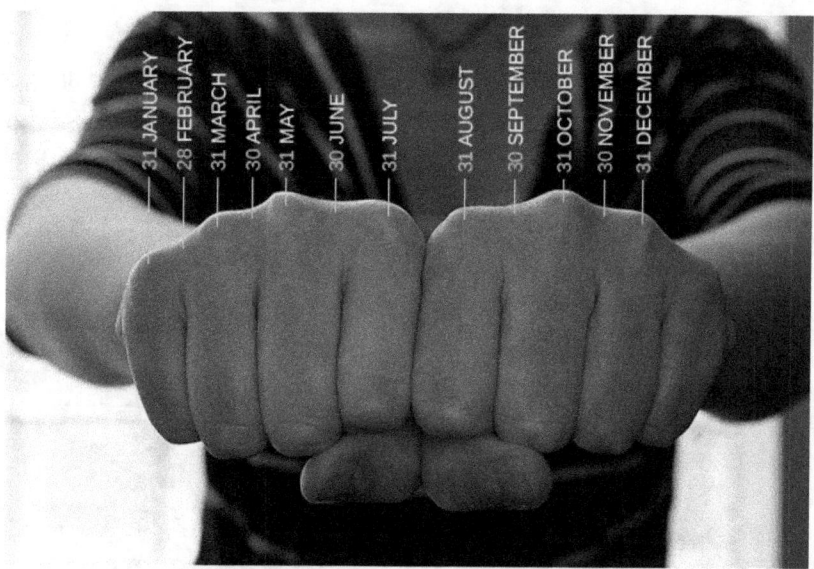

Figure 8.18 This is a knuckle mnemonic to help you remember the number of days in each month. Months with 31 days are represented by the protruding knuckles and shorter months fall in the spots between knuckles. (credit: modification of work by Cory Zanker)

If you have ever watched the television show *Modern Family*, you might have seen Phil Dunphy explain how he remembers names:

> The other day I met this guy named Carl. Now, I might forget that name, but he was wearing a Grateful Dead t-shirt. What's a band like the Grateful Dead? Phish. Where do fish live? The ocean. What else lives in the ocean? Coral. Hello, Co-arl. (Wrubel & Spiller, 2010)

It seems the more vivid or unusual the mnemonic, the easier it is to remember. The key to using any mnemonic successfully is to find a strategy that works for you.

> **LINK TO LEARNING**
>
> Joshua Foer is a science writer who "accidentally" won the U.S. Memory Championships. Watch his TEDTalk, titled "Feats of Memory Anyone Can Do," in which he explains a mnemonic device called the memory palace (http://openstax.org/l/foer) to learn more.

Some other strategies that are used to improve memory include expressive writing and saying words aloud. Expressive writing helps boost your short-term memory, particularly if you write about a traumatic experience in your life. Masao Yogo and Shuji Fujihara (2008) had participants write for 20-minute intervals several times per month. The participants were instructed to write about a traumatic experience, their best possible future selves, or a trivial topic. The researchers found that this simple writing task increased short-term memory capacity after five weeks, but only for the participants who wrote about traumatic experiences. Psychologists can't explain why this writing task works, but it does.

What if you want to remember items you need to pick up at the store? Simply say them out loud to yourself. A series of studies (MacLeod, Gopie, Hourihan, Neary, & Ozubko, 2010) found that saying a word out loud improves your memory for the word because it increases the word's distinctiveness. Feel silly, saying random grocery items aloud? This technique works equally well if you just mouth the words. Using these techniques increased participants' memory for the words by more than 10%. These techniques can also be used to help you study.

HOW TO STUDY EFFECTIVELY

Based on the information presented in this chapter, here are some strategies and suggestions to help you hone your study techniques (Figure 8.19). The key with any of these strategies is to figure out what works best for you.

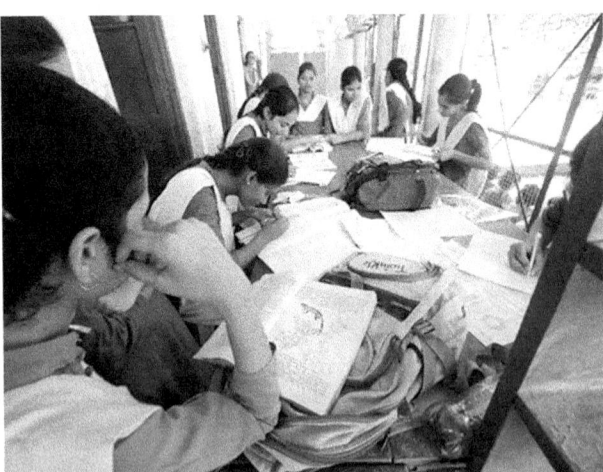

Figure 8.19 Memory techniques can be useful when studying for class. (credit: Barry Pousman)

- **Use elaborative rehearsal**: In a famous article, Fergus Craik and Robert Lockhart (1972) discussed their belief that information we process more deeply goes into long-term memory. Their theory is called **levels of processing**. If we want to remember a piece of information, we should think about it more deeply and link it to other information and memories to make it more meaningful. For example, if we are trying to remember that the hippocampus is involved with memory processing, we might envision a hippopotamus with excellent memory and then we could better remember the hippocampus.

- **Apply the self-reference effect**: As you go through the process of elaborative rehearsal, it would be even more beneficial to make the material you are trying to memorize personally meaningful to you. In other words, make use of the self-reference effect. Write notes in your own words. Write definitions from the text, and then rewrite them in your own words. Relate the material to something you have already learned for another class, or think how you can apply the concepts to your own life. When you do this, you are building a web of retrieval cues that will help you access the material when you want to remember it.

- **Use distributed practice**: Study across time in short durations rather than trying to cram it all in at once. Memory consolidation takes time, and studying across time allows time for memories to consolidate. In addition, cramming can cause the links between concepts to become so active that you get stuck in a link, and it prevents you from accessing the rest of the information that you learned.

- **Rehearse, rehearse, rehearse**: Review the material over time, in spaced and organized study sessions. Organize and study your notes, and take practice quizzes/exams. Link the new information to other information you already know well.

- **Study efficiently**: Students are great highlighters, but highlighting is not very efficient because students spend too much time studying the things they already learned. Instead of highlighting, use index cards. Write the question on one side and the answer on the other side. When you study, separate your cards into those you got right and those you got wrong. Study the ones you got wrong and keep sorting. Eventually, all your cards will be in the pile you answered correctly.

- **Be aware of interference**: To reduce the likelihood of interference, study during a quiet time without interruptions or distractions (like television or music).

- **Keep moving**: Of course you already know that exercise is good for your body, but did you also know it's also good for your mind? Research suggests that regular aerobic exercise (anything that gets your heart rate elevated) is beneficial for memory (van Praag, 2008). Aerobic exercise promotes neurogenesis: the growth of new brain cells in the hippocampus, an area of the brain known to play a role in memory and learning.

- **Get enough sleep**: While you are sleeping, your brain is still at work. During sleep the brain organizes and consolidates information to be stored in long-term memory (Abel & Bäuml, 2013).

- **Make use of mnemonic devices**: As you learned earlier in this chapter, mnemonic devices often help us to remember and recall information. There are different types of mnemonic devices, such as the acronym. An acronym is a word formed by the first letter of each of the words you want to remember. For example, even if you live near one, you might have difficulty recalling the names of all five Great Lakes. What if I told you to think of the word Homes? HOMES is an acronym that represents Huron, Ontario, Michigan, Erie, and Superior: the five Great Lakes. Another type of mnemonic device is an acrostic: you make a phrase of all the first letters of the words. For example, if you are taking a math test and you are having difficulty remembering *the order of operations*, recalling the following sentence will help you: "Please Excuse My Dear Aunt Sally," because the order of mathematical operations is Parentheses, Exponents, Multiplication, Division, Addition, Subtraction. There also are jingles, which are rhyming tunes that contain key words related to the concept, such as *i before e, except after c*.

Key Terms

absentmindedness lapses in memory that are caused by breaks in attention or our focus being somewhere else

acoustic encoding input of sounds, words, and music

amnesia loss of long-term memory that occurs as the result of disease, physical trauma, or psychological trauma

anterograde amnesia loss of memory for events that occur after the brain trauma

arousal theory strong emotions trigger the formation of strong memories and weaker emotional experiences form weaker memories

Atkinson-Shiffrin model memory model that states we process information through three systems: sensory memory, short-term memory, and long-term memory

automatic processing encoding of informational details like time, space, frequency, and the meaning of words

bias how feelings and view of the world distort memory of past events

blocking memory error in which you cannot access stored information

chunking organizing information into manageable bits or chunks

construction formulation of new memories

declarative memory type of long-term memory of facts and events we personally experience

effortful processing encoding of information that takes effort and attention

elaborative rehearsal thinking about the meaning of new information and its relation to knowledge already stored in your memory

encoding input of information into the memory system

engram physical trace of memory

episodic memory type of declarative memory that contains information about events we have personally experienced, also known as autobiographical memory

equipotentiality hypothesis some parts of the brain can take over for damaged parts in forming and storing memories

explicit memory memories we consciously try to remember and recall

false memory syndrome recall of false autobiographical memories

flashbulb memory exceptionally clear recollection of an important event

forgetting loss of information from long-term memory

implicit memory memories that are not part of our consciousness

levels of processing information that is thought of more deeply becomes more meaningful and thus better committed to memory

long-term memory (LTM) continuous storage of information

memory set of processes used to encode, store, and retrieve information over different periods of time

memory-enhancing strategy technique to help make sure information goes from short-term memory to long-term memory

misattribution memory error in which you confuse the source of your information

misinformation effect paradigm after exposure to additional and possibly inaccurate information, a person may misremember the original event

mnemonic device memory aids that help organize information for encoding

persistence failure of the memory system that involves the involuntary recall of unwanted memories, particularly unpleasant ones

proactive interference old information hinders the recall of newly learned information

procedural memory type of long-term memory for making skilled actions, such as how to brush your teeth, how to drive a car, and how to swim

recall accessing information without cues

recognition identifying previously learned information after encountering it again, usually in response to a cue

reconstruction process of bringing up old memories that might be distorted by new information

rehearsal repetition of information to be remembered

relearning learning information that was previously learned

retrieval act of getting information out of long-term memory storage and back into conscious awareness

retroactive interference information learned more recently hinders the recall of older information

retrograde amnesia loss of memory for events that occurred prior to brain trauma

self-reference effect tendency for an individual to have better memory for information that relates to oneself in comparison to material that has less personal relevance

semantic encoding input of words and their meaning

semantic memory type of declarative memory about words, concepts, and language-based knowledge and facts

sensory memory storage of brief sensory events, such as sights, sounds, and tastes

short-term memory (STM) holds about seven bits of information before it is forgotten or stored, as well as information that has been retrieved and is being used

storage creation of a permanent record of information

suggestibility effects of misinformation from external sources that leads to the creation of false memories

transience memory error in which unused memories fade with the passage of time

visual encoding input of images

Summary

8.1 How Memory Functions
Memory is a system or process that stores what we learn for future use.

Our memory has three basic functions: encoding, storing, and retrieving information. Encoding is the act of getting information into our memory system through automatic or effortful processing. Storage is retention of the information, and retrieval is the act of getting information out of storage and into conscious awareness through recall, recognition, and relearning. The idea that information is processed through three memory systems is called the Atkinson-Shiffrin model of memory. First, environmental stimuli enter our sensory memory for a period of less than a second to a few seconds. Those stimuli that we notice and pay attention to then move into short-term memory. According to the Atkinson-Shiffrin model, if we rehearse this information, then it moves into long-term memory for permanent storage. Other models like that of Baddeley and Hitch suggest there is more of a feedback loop between short-term memory and long-term memory. Long-term memory has a practically limitless storage capacity and is divided into implicit and explicit memory.

8.2 Parts of the Brain Involved with Memory
Beginning with Karl Lashley, researchers and psychologists have been searching for the engram, which is the physical trace of memory. Lashley did not find the engram, but he did suggest that memories are distributed throughout the entire brain rather than stored in one specific area. Now we know that three brain areas do play significant roles in the processing and storage of different types of memories: cerebellum, hippocampus, and amygdala. The cerebellum's job is to process procedural memories; the hippocampus is where new memories are encoded; the amygdala helps determine what memories to store, and it plays a part in determining where the memories are stored based on whether we have a strong or weak emotional response to the event. Strong emotional experiences can trigger the release of neurotransmitters, as well as hormones, which strengthen memory, so that memory for an emotional event is usually stronger than memory for a non-emotional event. This is shown by what is known as the flashbulb memory phenomenon: our ability to remember significant life events. However, our memory for life events (autobiographical memory) is not always accurate.

8.3 Problems with Memory
All of us at times have felt dismayed, frustrated, and even embarrassed when our memories have failed us. Our memory is flexible and prone to many errors, which is why eyewitness testimony has been found to be largely unreliable. There are several reasons why forgetting occurs. In cases of brain trauma or disease, forgetting may be due to amnesia. Another reason we forget is due to encoding failure. We can't remember something if we never stored it in our memory in the first place. Schacter presents seven memory errors that also contribute to forgetting. Sometimes, information is actually stored in our memory, but we cannot access it due to interference. Proactive interference happens when old information hinders the recall of newly learned information. Retroactive interference happens when information learned more recently hinders the recall of older information.

8.4 Ways to Enhance Memory
There are many ways to combat the inevitable failures of our memory system. Some common strategies that can be used in everyday situations include mnemonic devices, rehearsal, self-referencing, and adequate sleep. These same strategies also can help you to study more effectively.

Review Questions

1. _____ is a memory store with a phonological loop, visiospatial sketchpad, episodic buffer, and a central executive.
    a. sensory memory
    b. episodic memory
    c. working memory
    d. implicit memory

2. The storage capacity of long-term memory is _____.
    a. one or two bits of information
    b. seven bits, plus or minus two
    c. limited
    d. essentially limitless

3. The three functions of memory are _____.
    a. automatic processing, effortful processing, and storage
    b. encoding, processing, and storage
    c. automatic processing, effortful processing, and retrieval
    d. encoding, storage, and retrieval

4. This physical trace of memory is known as the _____.
    a. engram
    b. Lashley effect
    c. Deese-Roediger-McDermott Paradigm
    d. flashbulb memory effect

5. An exceptionally clear recollection of an important event is a (an) _____.
    a. engram
    b. arousal theory
    c. flashbulb memory
    d. equipotentiality hypothesis

6. _____ is when our recollections of the past are done in a self-enhancing manner.
    a. stereotypical bias
    b. egocentric bias
    c. hindsight bias
    d. enhancement bias

7. Tip-of-the-tongue phenomenon is also known as _____.
    a. persistence
    b. misattribution
    c. transience
    d. blocking

8. The formulation of new memories is sometimes called _____, and the process of bringing up old memories is called _____.
    a. construction; reconstruction
    b. reconstruction; construction
    c. production; reproduction
    d. reproduction; production

9. When you are learning how to play the piano, the statement "Every good boy does fine" can help you remember the notes E, G, B, D, and F for the lines of the treble clef. This is an example of a (an) _____.
    a. jingle
    b. acronym
    c. acrostic
    d. acoustic

10. According to a study by Yogo and Fujihara (2008), if you want to improve your short-term memory, you should spend time writing about _____.
    a. your best possible future self
    b. a traumatic life experience
    c. a trivial topic
    d. your grocery list

11. The self-referencing effect refers to _____.
    a. making the material you are trying to memorize personally meaningful to you
    b. making a phrase of all the first letters of the words you are trying to memorize
    c. making a word formed by the first letter of each of the words you are trying to memorize
    d. saying words you want to remember out loud to yourself

12. Memory aids that help organize information for encoding are _____.
    a. mnemonic devices
    b. memory-enhancing strategies
    c. elaborative rehearsal
    d. effortful processing

Critical Thinking Questions

13. Compare and contrast implicit and explicit memory.

14. According to the Atkinson-Shiffrin model, name and describe the three stages of memory.

15. Compare and contrast the two ways in which we encode information.

16. What might happen to your memory system if you sustained damage to your hippocampus?

17. Compare and contrast the two types of interference.

18. Compare and contrast the two types of amnesia.

19. What is the self-reference effect, and how can it help you study more effectively?

20. You and your roommate spent all of last night studying for your psychology test. You think you know the material; however, you suggest that you study again the next morning an hour prior to the test. Your roommate asks you to explain why you think this is a good idea. What do you tell her?

Personal Application Questions

21. Describe something you have learned that is now in your procedural memory. Discuss how you learned this information.

22. Describe something you learned in high school that is now in your semantic memory.

23. Describe a flashbulb memory of a significant event in your life.

24. Which of the seven memory errors presented by Schacter have you committed? Provide an example of each one.

25. Jurors place a lot of weight on eyewitness testimony. Imagine you are an attorney representing a defendant who is accused of robbing a convenience store. Several eyewitnesses have been called to testify against your client. What would you tell the jurors about the reliability of eyewitness testimony?

26. Create a mnemonic device to help you remember a term or concept from this chapter.

27. What is an effective study technique that you have used? How is it similar to/different from the strategies suggested in this chapter?

Chapter 9
Lifespan Development

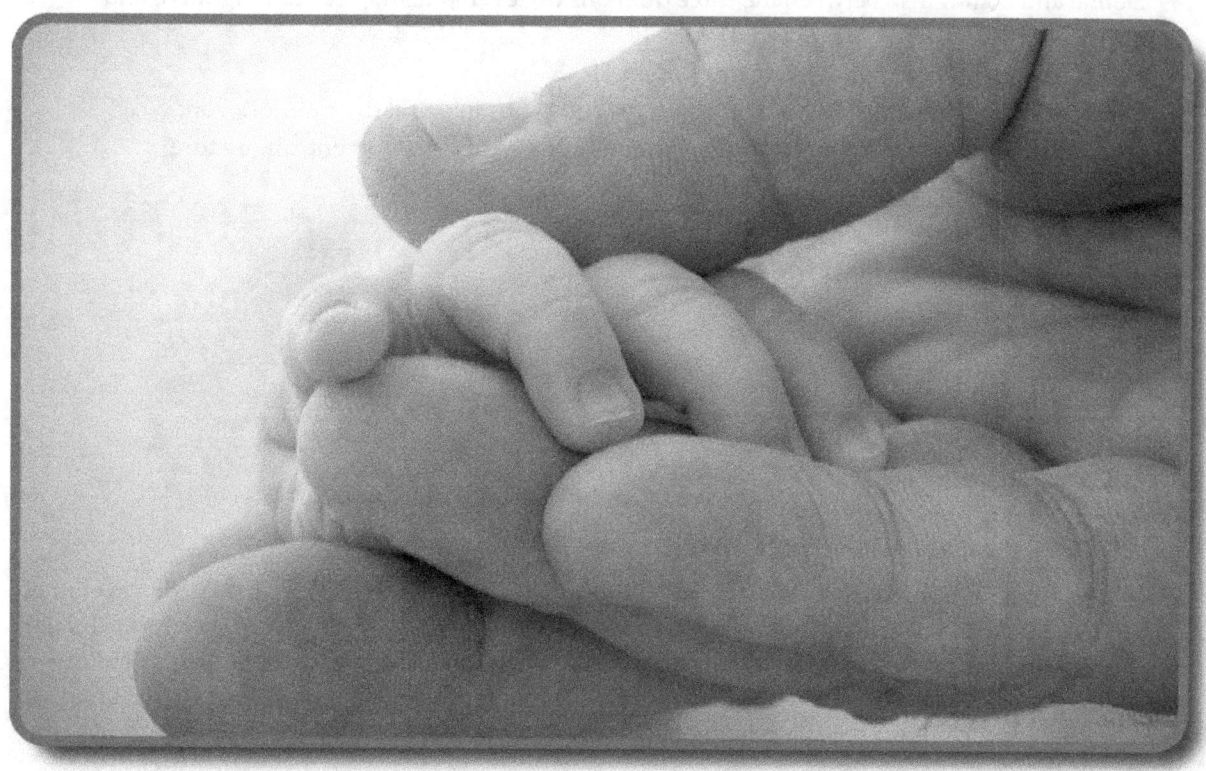

Figure 9.1 How have you changed since childhood? How are you the same? What will your life be like 25 years from now? Fifty years from now? Lifespan development studies how you change as well as how you remain the same over the course of your life. (credit: modification of work by Giles Cook)

Chapter Outline

9.1 What Is Lifespan Development?
9.2 Lifespan Theories
9.3 Stages of Development
9.4 Death and Dying

Introduction

Welcome to the story of your life. In this chapter we explore the fascinating tale of how you have grown and developed into the person you are today. We also look at some ideas about who you will grow into tomorrow. Yours is a story of lifespan development (Figure 9.1), from the start of life to the end.

The process of human growth and development is more obvious in infancy and childhood, yet your development is happening this moment and will continue, minute by minute, for the rest of your life. Who you are today and who you will be in the future depends on a blend of genetics, environment, culture, relationships, and more, as you continue through each phase of life. You have experienced firsthand much of what is discussed in this chapter. Now consider what psychological science has to say about your physical, cognitive, and psychosocial development, from the womb to the tomb.

9.1 What Is Lifespan Development?

Learning Objectives

By the end of this section, you will be able to:
- Define and distinguish between the three domains of development: physical, cognitive and psychosocial
- Discuss the normative approach to development
- Understand the three major issues in development: continuity and discontinuity, one common course of development or many unique courses of development, and nature versus nurture

> My heart leaps up when I behold
> A rainbow in the sky:
> So was it when my life began;
> So is it now I am a man;
> So be it when I shall grow old,
> Or let me die!
> The Child is father of the Man;
> I could wish my days to be
> Bound each to each by natural piety. (Wordsworth, 1802)

In this poem, William Wordsworth writes, "the child is father of the man." What does this seemingly incongruous statement mean, and what does it have to do with lifespan development? Wordsworth might be suggesting that the person he is as an adult depends largely on the experiences he had in childhood. Consider the following questions: To what extent is the adult you are today influenced by the child you once were? To what extent is a child fundamentally different from the adult he grows up to be?

These are the types of questions developmental psychologists try to answer, by studying how humans change and grow from conception through childhood, adolescence, adulthood, and death. They view development as a lifelong process that can be studied scientifically across three developmental domains—physical, cognitive, and psychosocial development. **Physical development** involves growth and changes in the body and brain, the senses, motor skills, and health and wellness. **Cognitive development** involves learning, attention, memory, language, thinking, reasoning, and creativity. **Psychosocial development** involves emotions, personality, and social relationships. We refer to these domains throughout the chapter.

CONNECT THE CONCEPTS

Research Methods in Developmental Psychology

You've learned about a variety of research methods used by psychologists. Developmental psychologists use many of these approaches in order to better understand how individuals change mentally and physically over time. These methods include naturalistic observations, case studies, surveys, and experiments, among others.

Naturalistic observations involve observing behavior in its natural context. A developmental psychologist might observe how children behave on a playground, at a daycare center, or in the child's own home. While this research approach provides a glimpse into how children behave in their natural settings, researchers have very little control over the types and/or frequencies of displayed behavior.

In a case study, developmental psychologists collect a great deal of information from one individual in order to better understand physical and psychological changes over the lifespan. This particular approach is an excellent way to better understand individuals, who are exceptional in some way, but it is especially prone to researcher bias in interpretation, and it is difficult to generalize conclusions to the larger population.

In one classic example of this research method being applied to a study of lifespan development Sigmund Freud analyzed the development of a child known as "Little Hans" (Freud, 1909/1949). Freud's findings helped inform his theories of psychosexual development in children, which you will learn about later in this chapter. Little Genie, the subject of a case study discussed in the chapter on thinking and intelligence, provides another example of how psychologists examine developmental milestones through detailed research on a single individual. In Genie's case, her neglectful and abusive upbringing led to her being unable to speak until, at age 13, she was removed from that harmful environment. As she learned to use language, psychologists were able to compare how her language acquisition abilities differed when occurring in her late-stage development compared to the typical acquisition of those skills during the ages of infancy through early childhood (Fromkin, Krashen, Curtiss, Rigler, & Rigler, 1974; Curtiss, 1981).

The survey method asks individuals to self-report important information about their thoughts, experiences, and beliefs. This particular method can provide large amounts of information in relatively short amounts of time; however, validity of data collected in this way relies on honest self-reporting, and the data is relatively shallow when compared to the depth of information collected in a case study. An example of comprehensive survey was the research done by Ruth W. Howard. In 1947, she obtained her doctorate by surveying 229 sets of triplets, the most comprehensive research of triplets completed at the time. This pioneering woman was also the first African-American woman to earn a PhD in psychology (American Psychological Association, 2019).

Experiments involve significant control over extraneous variables and manipulation of the independent variable. As such, experimental research allows developmental psychologists to make causal statements about certain variables that are important for the developmental process. Because experimental research must occur in a controlled environment, researchers must be cautious about whether behaviors observed in the laboratory translate to an individual's natural environment.

Later in this chapter, you will learn about several experiments in which toddlers and young children observe scenes or actions so that researchers can determine at what age specific cognitive abilities develop. For example, children may observe a quantity of liquid poured from a short, fat glass into a tall, skinny glass. As the experimenters question the children about what occurred, the subjects' answers help psychologists understand at what age a child begins to comprehend that the volume of liquid remained the same although the shapes of the containers differs.

Across these three domains—physical, cognitive, and psychosocial—the **normative approach** to development is also discussed. This approach asks, "What is normal development?" In the early decades of the 20th century, normative psychologists studied large numbers of children at various ages to determine norms (i.e., average ages) of when most children reach specific developmental milestones in each of the three domains (Gesell, 1933, 1939, 1940; Gesell & Ilg, 1946; Hall, 1904). Although children develop at slightly different rates, we can use these age-related averages as general guidelines to compare children with same-age peers to determine the approximate ages they should reach specific normative events called **developmental milestones** (e.g., crawling, walking, writing, dressing, naming colors, speaking in sentences, and starting puberty).

Not all normative events are universal, meaning they are not experienced by all individuals across all cultures. Biological milestones, such as puberty, tend to be universal, but social milestones, such as the age when children begin formal schooling, are not necessarily universal; instead, they affect most individuals in a particular culture (Gesell & Ilg, 1946). For example, in developed countries children begin school around 5 or 6 years old, but in developing countries, like Nigeria, children often enter school at an advanced age, if at all (Huebler, 2005; United Nations Educational, Scientific, and Cultural Organization [UNESCO], 2013).

To better understand the normative approach, imagine two new mothers, Louisa and Kimberly, who are close friends and have children around the same age. Louisa's daughter is 14 months old, and Kimberly's son is 12 months old. According to the normative approach, the average age a child starts to walk is 12 months. However, at 14 months Louisa's daughter still isn't walking. She tells Kimberly she is worried that something might be wrong with her baby. Kimberly is surprised because her son started walking when he was only 10 months old. Should Louisa be worried? Should she be concerned if her daughter is not walking by 15 months or 18 months?

> **LINK TO LEARNING**
>
> The Centers for Disease Control and Prevention (CDC) describes the developmental milestones for children from 2 months through 5 years old. After reviewing the information, take this Developmental Milestones Quiz (http://openstax.org/l/milestones) to see how well you recall what you've learned. If you are a parent with concerns about your child's development, contact your pediatrician.

ISSUES IN DEVELOPMENTAL PSYCHOLOGY

There are many different theoretical approaches regarding human development. As we evaluate them in this chapter, recall that developmental psychology focuses on how people change, and keep in mind that all the approaches that we present in this chapter address questions of change: Is the change smooth or uneven (continuous versus discontinuous)? Is this pattern of change the same for everyone, or are there many different patterns of change (one course of development versus many courses)? How do genetics and environment interact to influence development (nature versus nurture)?

Is Development Continuous or Discontinuous?

Continuous development views development as a cumulative process, gradually improving on existing skills (Figure 9.2). With this type of development, there is gradual change. Consider, for example, a child's physical growth: adding inches to height year by year. In contrast, theorists who view development as **discontinuous** believe that development takes place in unique stages: It occurs at specific times or ages. With this type of development, the change is more sudden, such as an infant's ability to conceive object permanence.

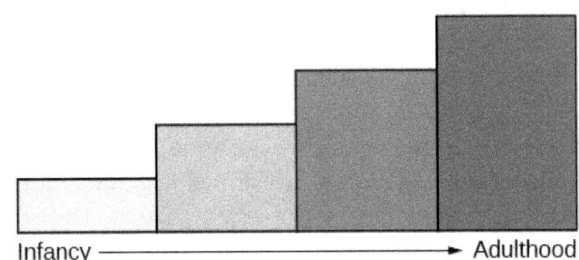

Figure 9.2 The concept of continuous development can be visualized as a smooth slope of progression, whereas discontinuous development sees growth in more discrete stages.

Is There One Course of Development or Many?

Is development essentially the same, or universal, for all children (i.e., there is one course of development) or does development follow a different course for each child, depending on the child's specific genetics and environment (i.e., there are many courses of development)? Do people across the world share more similarities or more differences in their development? How much do culture and genetics influence a child's behavior?

Stage theories hold that the sequence of development is universal. For example, in cross-cultural studies of language development, children from around the world reach language milestones in a similar sequence (Gleitman & Newport, 1995). Infants in all cultures coo before they babble. They begin babbling at about the same age and utter their first word around 12 months old. Yet we live in diverse contexts that have a unique effect on each of us. For example, researchers once believed that motor development follows one course for all children regardless of culture. However, child care practices vary by culture, and different practices have been found to accelerate or inhibit achievement of developmental milestones such as sitting, crawling, and walking (Karasik, Adolph, Tamis-LeMonda, & Bornstein, 2010).

For instance, let's look at the Aché society in Paraguay. They spend a significant amount of time foraging in forests. While foraging, Aché mothers carry their young children, rarely putting them down in order to protect them from getting hurt in the forest. Consequently, their children walk much later: They walk around 23–25 months old, in comparison to infants in Western cultures who begin to walk around 12 months old. However, as Aché children become older, they are allowed more freedom to move about, and by about age 9, their motor skills surpass those of U.S. children of the same age: Aché children are able to climb trees up to 25 feet tall and use machetes to chop their way through the forest (Kaplan & Dove, 1987). As you can see, our development is influenced by multiple contexts, so the timing of basic motor functions may vary across cultures. However, the functions themselves are present in all societies (Figure 9.3).

(a)   (b)

Figure 9.3 All children across the world love to play. Whether in (a) Florida or (b) South Africa, children enjoy exploring sand, sunshine, and the sea. (credit a: modification of work by "Visit St. Pete/Clearwater"/Flickr; credit b: modification of work by "stringer_bel"/Flickr)

How Do Nature and Nurture Influence Development?

Are we who we are because of **nature** (biology and genetics), or are we who we are because of **nurture** (our environment and culture)? This longstanding question is known in psychology as the nature versus nurture debate. It seeks to understand how our personalities and traits are the product of our genetic makeup and biological factors, and how they are shaped by our environment, including our parents, peers, and culture. For instance, why do biological children sometimes act like their parents—is it because of genetics or because of early childhood environment and what the child has learned from the parents? What about children who are adopted—are they more like their biological families or more like their adoptive families? And how can siblings from the same family be so different?

We are all born with specific genetic traits inherited from our parents, such as eye color, height, and certain personality traits. Beyond our basic genotype, however, there is a deep interaction between our genes and our environment: Our unique experiences in our environment influence whether and how particular traits are expressed, and at the same time, our genes influence how we interact with our environment (Diamond, 2009; Lobo, 2008). This chapter will show that there is a reciprocal interaction between nature and nurture as they both shape who we become, but the debate continues as to the relative contributions of each.

> **DIG DEEPER**
>
> **The Achievement Gap: How Does Socioeconomic Status Affect Development?**
>
> The achievement gap refers to the persistent difference in grades, test scores, and graduation rates that exist among students of different ethnicities, races, and—in certain subjects—sexes (Winerman, 2011). Research suggests that these achievement gaps are strongly influenced by differences in socioeconomic factors that exist among the families of these children. While the researchers acknowledge that programs aimed at reducing such socioeconomic discrepancies would likely aid in equalizing the aptitude and performance of children from different backgrounds, they recognize that such large-scale interventions would be difficult to achieve. Therefore, it is recommended that programs aimed at fostering aptitude and achievement among disadvantaged children may be the best option for dealing with issues related to academic achievement gaps (Duncan & Magnuson, 2005).
>
> Low-income children perform significantly more poorly than their middle- and high-income peers on a number of educational variables: They have significantly lower standardized test scores, graduation rates, and college entrance rates, and they have much higher school dropout rates. There have been attempts to correct the achievement gap through state and federal legislation, but what if the problems start before the children even enter school?
>
> Psychologists Betty Hart and Todd Risley (2006) spent their careers looking at early language ability and progression of children in various income levels. In one longitudinal study, they found that although all the parents in the study engaged and interacted with their children, middle- and high-income parents interacted with their children differently than low-income parents. After analyzing 1,300 hours of parent-child interactions, the researchers found that middle- and high-income parents talk to their children significantly more, starting when the children are infants. By 3 years old, high-income children knew almost double the number of words known by their low-income counterparts, and they had heard an estimated total of 30 million more words than the low-income counterparts (Hart & Risley, 2003). And the gaps only become more pronounced. Before entering kindergarten, high-income children score 60% higher on achievement tests than their low-income peers (Lee & Burkam, 2002).
>
> There are solutions to this problem. At the University of Chicago, experts are working with low-income families, visiting them at their homes, and encouraging them to speak more to their children on a daily and hourly basis. Other experts are designing preschools in which students from diverse economic backgrounds are placed in the same classroom. In this research, low-income children made significant gains in their language development, likely as a result of attending the specialized preschool (Schechter & Byeb, 2007). What other methods or interventions could be used to decrease the achievement gap? What types of activities could be implemented to help the children of your community or a neighboring community?

9.2 Lifespan Theories

Learning Objectives

By the end of this section, you will be able to:
- Discuss Freud's theory of psychosexual development
- Describe the major tasks of child and adult psychosocial development according to Erikson
- Discuss Piaget's view of cognitive development and apply the stages to understanding childhood cognition
- Describe Kohlberg's theory of moral development
- Compare and contrast the strengths and weaknesses of major developmental theories

There are many theories regarding how babies and children grow and develop into happy, healthy adults. We explore several of these theories in this section.

PSYCHOSEXUAL THEORY OF DEVELOPMENT

Sigmund Freud (1856–1939) believed that personality develops during early childhood. For Freud, childhood experiences shape our personalities and behavior as adults. Freud viewed development as discontinuous; he believed that each of us must pass through a series of stages during childhood, and that if we lack proper nurturance and parenting during a stage, we may become stuck, or fixated, in that stage. Freud's stages are called the stages of **psychosexual development**. According to Freud, children's pleasure-seeking urges are focused on a different area of the body, called an erogenous zone, at each of the five stages of development: oral, anal, phallic, latency, and genital.

While most of Freud's ideas have not found support in modern research, we cannot discount the contributions that Freud has made to the field of psychology. Psychologists today dispute Freud's psychosexual stages as a legitimate explanation for how one's personality develops, but what we can take away from Freud's theory is that personality is shaped, in some part, by experiences we have in childhood. These stages are discussed in detail in the chapter on personality.

PSYCHOSOCIAL THEORY OF DEVELOPMENT

Erik Erikson (1902–1994) (Figure 9.4), another stage theorist, took Freud's theory and modified it as psychosocial theory. Erikson's **psychosocial development** theory emphasizes the social nature of our development rather than its sexual nature. While Freud believed that personality is shaped only in childhood, Erikson proposed that personality development takes place all through the lifespan. Erikson suggested that how we interact with others is what affects our sense of self, or what he called the ego identity.

Figure 9.4 Erik Erikson proposed the psychosocial theory of development. In each stage of Erikson's theory, there is a psychosocial task that we must master in order to feel a sense of competence.

Erikson proposed that we are motivated by a need to achieve competence in certain areas of our lives. According to psychosocial theory, we experience eight stages of development over our lifespan, from infancy through late adulthood. At each stage there is a conflict, or task, that we need to resolve. Successful completion of each developmental task results in a sense of competence and a healthy personality. Failure to master these tasks leads to feelings of inadequacy.

According to Erikson (1963), trust is the basis of our development during infancy (birth to 12 months). Therefore, the primary task of this stage is trust versus mistrust. Infants are dependent upon their caregivers, so caregivers who are responsive and sensitive to their infant's needs help their baby to develop a sense of trust; their baby will see the world as a safe, predictable place. Unresponsive caregivers who do not meet their baby's needs can engender feelings of anxiety, fear, and mistrust; their baby may see the world as unpredictable.

As toddlers (ages 1–3 years) begin to explore their world, they learn that they can control their actions and act on the environment to get results. They begin to show clear preferences for certain elements of the environment, such as food, toys, and clothing. A toddler's main task is to resolve the issue of autonomy versus shame and doubt, by working to establish independence. This is the "me do it" stage. For example, we might observe a budding sense of autonomy in a 2-year-old child who wants to choose her clothes and dress herself. Although her outfits might not be appropriate for the situation, her input in such basic decisions has an effect on her sense of independence. If denied the opportunity to act on her environment, she may begin to doubt her abilities, which could lead to low self-esteem and feelings of shame.

Once children reach the preschool stage (ages 3–6 years), they are capable of initiating activities and asserting control over their world through social interactions and play. According to Erikson, preschool children must resolve the task of initiative versus guilt. By learning to plan and achieve goals while interacting with others, preschool children can master this task. Those who do will develop self-confidence and feel a sense of purpose. Those who are unsuccessful at this stage—with their initiative misfiring or stifled—may develop feelings of guilt. How might over-controlling parents stifle a child's initiative?

During the elementary school stage (ages 7–11), children face the task of industry versus inferiority. Children begin to compare themselves to their peers to see how they measure up. They either develop a sense of pride and accomplishment in their schoolwork, sports, social activities, and family life, or they feel inferior and inadequate when they don't measure up. What are some things parents and teachers can do to help children develop a sense of competence and a belief in themselves and their abilities?

In adolescence (ages 12–18), children face the task of identity versus role confusion. According to Erikson, an adolescent's main task is developing a sense of self. Adolescents struggle with questions such as "Who am I?" and "What do I want to do with my life?" Along the way, most adolescents try on many different selves to see which ones fit. Adolescents who are successful at this stage have a strong sense of identity and are able to remain true to their beliefs and values in the face of problems and other people's perspectives. What happens to apathetic adolescents, who do not make a conscious search for identity, or those who are pressured to conform to their parents' ideas for the future? These teens will have a weak sense of self and experience role confusion. They are unsure of their identity and confused about the future.

People in early adulthood (i.e., 20s through early 40s) are concerned with intimacy versus isolation. After we have developed a sense of self in adolescence, we are ready to share our life with others. Erikson said that we must have a strong sense of self before developing intimate relationships with others. Adults who do not develop a positive self-concept in adolescence may experience feelings of loneliness and emotional isolation.

When people reach their 40s, they enter the time known as middle adulthood, which extends to the mid-60s. The social task of middle adulthood is generativity versus stagnation. Generativity involves finding your life's work and contributing to the development of others, through activities such as volunteering, mentoring, and raising children. Those who do not master this task may experience stagnation, having little connection with others and little interest in productivity and self-improvement.

From the mid-60s to the end of life, we are in the period of development known as late adulthood. Erikson's task at this stage is called integrity versus despair. He said that people in late adulthood reflect on their lives and feel either a sense of satisfaction or a sense of failure. People who feel proud of their accomplishments feel a sense of integrity, and they can look back on their lives with few regrets. However, people who are not successful at this stage may feel as if their life has been wasted. They focus on what "would have," "should have," and "could have" been. They face the end of their lives with feelings of bitterness, depression, and despair. Table 9.1 summarizes the stages of Erikson's theory.

Erikson's Psychosocial Stages of Development

Stage	Age (years)	Developmental Task	Description
1	0–1	Trust vs. mistrust	Trust (or mistrust) that basic needs, such as nourishment and affection, will be met
2	1–3	Autonomy vs. shame/doubt	Develop a sense of independence in many tasks
3	3–6	Initiative vs. guilt	Take initiative on some activities—may develop guilt when unsuccessful or boundaries overstepped
4	7–11	Industry vs. inferiority	Develop self-confidence in abilities when competent or sense of inferiority when not
5	12–18	Identity vs. confusion	Experiment with and develop identity and roles
6	19–29	Intimacy vs. isolation	Establish intimacy and relationships with others
7	30–64	Generativity vs. stagnation	Contribute to society and be part of a family
8	65–	Integrity vs. despair	Assess and make sense of life and meaning of contributions

Table 9.1

COGNITIVE THEORY OF DEVELOPMENT

Jean Piaget (1896–1980) is another stage theorist who studied childhood development (**Figure 9.5**). Instead of approaching development from a psychoanalytical or psychosocial perspective, Piaget focused on children's cognitive growth. He believed that thinking is a central aspect of development and that children are naturally inquisitive. However, he said that children do not think and reason like adults (Piaget, 1930, 1932). His theory of cognitive development holds that our cognitive abilities develop through specific stages, which exemplifies the discontinuity approach to development. As we progress to a new stage, there is a distinct shift in how we think and reason.

Figure 9.5 Jean Piaget spent over 50 years studying children and how their minds develop.

Piaget said that children develop schemata to help them understand the world. **Schemata** are concepts (mental models) that are used to help us categorize and interpret information. By the time children have reached adulthood, they have created schemata for almost everything. When children learn new information, they adjust their schemata through two processes: assimilation and accommodation. First, they assimilate new information or experiences in terms of their current schemata: **assimilation** is when they take in information that is comparable to what they already know. **Accommodation** describes when they change their schemata based on new information. This process continues as children interact with their environment.

For example, 2-year-old Abdul learned the schema for dogs because his family has a Labrador retriever. When Abdul sees other dogs in his picture books, he says, "Look mommy, dog!" Thus, he has assimilated them into his schema for dogs. One day, Abdul sees a sheep for the first time and says, "Look mommy, dog!" Having a basic schema that a dog is an animal with four legs and fur, Abdul thinks all furry, four-legged creatures are dogs. When Abdul's mom tells him that the animal he sees is a sheep, not a dog, Abdul must accommodate his schema for dogs to include more information based on his new experiences. Abdul's schema for dog was too broad, since not all furry, four-legged creatures are dogs. He now modifies his schema for dogs and forms a new one for sheep.

Like Freud and Erikson, Piaget thought development unfolds in a series of stages approximately associated with age ranges. He proposed a theory of cognitive development that unfolds in four stages: sensorimotor, preoperational, concrete operational, and formal operational (Table 9.2).

Piaget's Stages of Cognitive Development

Age (years)	Stage	Description	Developmental issues
0–2	Sensorimotor	World experienced through senses and actions	Object permanence Stranger anxiety

Piaget's Stages of Cognitive Development

Age (years)	Stage	Description	Developmental issues
2–6	Preoperational	Use words and images to represent things, but lack logical reasoning	Pretend play Egocentrism Language development
7–11	Concrete operational	Understand concrete events and analogies logically; perform arithmetical operations	Conservation Mathematical transformations
12–	Formal operational	Formal operations Utilize abstract reasoning	Abstract logic Moral reasoning

Table 9.2

The first stage is the **sensorimotor** stage, which lasts from birth to about 2 years old. During this stage, children learn about the world through their senses and motor behavior. Young children put objects in their mouths to see if the items are edible, and once they can grasp objects, they may shake or bang them to see if they make sounds. Between 5 and 8 months old, the child develops **object permanence**, which is the understanding that even if something is out of sight, it still exists (Bogartz, Shinskey, & Schilling, 2000). According to Piaget, young infants do not remember an object after it has been removed from sight. Piaget studied infants' reactions when a toy was first shown to an infant and then hidden under a blanket. Infants who had already developed object permanence would reach for the hidden toy, indicating that they knew it still existed, whereas infants who had not developed object permanence would appear confused.

> **LINK TO LEARNING**
>
> Please take a few minutes and view this brief video demonstrating different children's abilities to understand object permanence (http://openstax.org/l/piaget) to learn more.

In Piaget's view, around the same time children develop object permanence, they also begin to exhibit stranger anxiety, which is a fear of unfamiliar people. Babies may demonstrate this by crying and turning away from a stranger, by clinging to a caregiver, or by attempting to reach their arms toward familiar faces such as parents. Stranger anxiety results when a child is unable to assimilate the stranger into an existing schema; therefore, she can't predict what her experience with that stranger will be like, which results in a fear response.

Piaget's second stage is the **preoperational stage**, which is from approximately 2 to 7 years old. In this stage, children can use symbols to represent words, images, and ideas, which is why children in this stage engage in pretend play. A child's arms might become airplane wings as he zooms around the room, or a child with a stick might become a brave knight with a sword. Children also begin to use language in the preoperational stage, but they cannot understand adult logic or mentally manipulate information (the term *operational* refers to logical manipulation of information, so children at this stage are considered to be *pre*-operational). Children's logic is based on their own personal knowledge of the world so far, rather than on conventional knowledge. For example, dad gave a slice of pizza to 10-year-old Keiko and another slice to her 3-year-old brother, Kenny. Kenny's pizza slice was cut into five pieces, so Kenny told his sister that he got more pizza than she did. Children in this stage cannot perform mental operations because they have not developed an understanding of **conservation**, which is the idea that even if you change the appearance of something, it is still equal in size as long as nothing has been removed or added.

> **LINK TO LEARNING**
>
> Watch this **video of a boy in the preoperational stage responding to Piaget's conservation tasks (http://openstax.org/l/piaget2)** to learn more.

During this stage, we also expect children to display **egocentrism**, which means that the child is not able to take the perspective of others. A child at this stage thinks that everyone sees, thinks, and feels just as they do. Let's look at Kenny and Keiko again. Keiko's birthday is coming up, so their mom takes Kenny to the toy store to choose a present for his sister. He selects an Iron Man action figure for her, thinking that if he likes the toy, his sister will too. An egocentric child is not able to infer the perspective of other people and instead attributes his own perspective.

> **LINK TO LEARNING**
>
> Piaget developed the Three-Mountain Task to determine the level of egocentrism displayed by children. Children view a 3-dimensional mountain scene from one viewpoint, and are asked what another person at a different viewpoint would see in the same scene. Watch this **short video of the Three Mountain Task in action (http://openstax.org/l/WonderYears)** from the University of Minnesota and the Science Museum of Minnesota.

Piaget's third stage is the **concrete operational stage**, which occurs from about 7 to 11 years old. In this stage, children can think logically about real (concrete) events; they have a firm grasp on the use of numbers and start to employ memory strategies. They can perform mathematical operations and understand transformations, such as addition is the opposite of subtraction, and multiplication is the opposite of division. In this stage, children also master the concept of conservation: Even if something changes shape, its mass, volume, and number stay the same. For example, if you pour water from a tall, thin glass to a short, fat glass, you still have the same amount of water. Remember Keiko and Kenny and the pizza? How did Keiko know that Kenny was wrong when he said that he had more pizza?

Children in the concrete operational stage also understand the principle of **reversibility**, which means that objects can be changed and then returned back to their original form or condition. Take, for example, water that you poured into the short, fat glass: You can pour water from the fat glass back to the thin glass and still have the same amount (minus a couple of drops).

The fourth, and last, stage in Piaget's theory is the **formal operational stage**, which is from about age 11 to adulthood. Whereas children in the concrete operational stage are able to think logically only about concrete events, children in the formal operational stage can also deal with abstract ideas and hypothetical situations. Children in this stage can use abstract thinking to problem solve, look at alternative solutions, and test these solutions. In adolescence, a renewed egocentrism occurs. For example, a 15-year-old with a very small pimple on her face might think it is huge and incredibly visible, under the mistaken impression that others must share her perceptions.

Beyond Formal Operational Thought

As with other major contributors of theories of development, several of Piaget's ideas have come under criticism based on the results of further research. For example, several contemporary studies support a model of development that is more continuous than Piaget's discrete stages (Courage & Howe, 2002; Siegler, 2005, 2006). Many others suggest that children reach cognitive milestones earlier than Piaget describes (Baillargeon, 2004; de Hevia & Spelke, 2010).

According to Piaget, the highest level of cognitive development is formal operational thought, which develops between 11 and 20 years old. However, many developmental psychologists disagree with Piaget, suggesting a fifth stage of cognitive development, known as the postformal stage (Basseches, 1984; Commons & Bresette, 2006; Sinnott, 1998). In postformal thinking, decisions are made based on situations and circumstances, and logic is integrated with emotion as adults develop principles that depend on contexts. One way that we can see the difference between an adult in postformal thought and an adolescent in formal operations is in terms of how they handle emotionally charged issues.

It seems that once we reach adulthood our problem solving abilities change: As we attempt to solve problems, we tend to think more deeply about many areas of our lives, such as relationships, work, and politics (Labouvie-Vief & Diehl, 1999). Because of this, postformal thinkers are able to draw on past experiences to help them solve new problems. Problem-solving strategies using postformal thought vary, depending on the situation. What does this mean? Adults can recognize, for example, that what seems to be an ideal solution to a problem at work involving a disagreement with a colleague may not be the best solution to a disagreement with a significant other.

CONNECT THE CONCEPTS

Neuroconstructivism

The genetic environmental correlation you've learned about concerning the bidirectional influence of genes and the environment has been explored in more recent theories (Newcombe, 2011). One such theory, neuroconstructivism, suggests that neural brain development influences cognitive development. Experiences that a child encounters can impact or change the way that neural pathways develop in response to the environment. An individual's behavior is based on how one understands the world. There is interaction between neural and cognitive networks at and between each level, consisting of these:

- genes
- neurons
- brain
- body
- social environment

These interactions shape mental representations in the brain and are dependent on context that individuals actively explore throughout their lifetimes (Westermann, Mareschal, Johnson, Sirois, Spratling, & Thomas, 2007).

An example of this would be a child who may be genetically predisposed to a difficult temperament. They may have parents who provide a social environment in which they are encouraged to express themselves in an optimal manner. The child's brain would form neural connections enhanced by that environment, thus influencing the brain. The brain gives information to the body about how it will experience the environment. Thus, neural and cognitive networks work together to influence genes (i.e., attenuating temperament), body (i.e., may be less prone to high blood pressure), and social environment (i.e., may seek people who are similar to them).

SOCIOCULTURAL THEORY OF DEVELOPMENT

Lev Vygotsky was a Russian psychologist who proposed a sociocultural theory of development. He suggested that human development is rooted in one's culture. A child's social world, for example, forms the basis for the formation of language and thought. The language one speaks and the ways a person thinks about things is dependent on one's cultural background. Vygotsky also considered historical influences as key to one's development. He was interested in the process of development and the individual's interactions with their environment (John-Steiner & Mahn, 1996).

MORAL THEORY OF DEVELOPMENT

A major task beginning in childhood and continuing into adolescence is discerning right from wrong. Psychologist Lawrence Kohlberg (1927–1987) extended upon the foundation that Piaget built regarding cognitive development. Kohlberg believed that moral development, like cognitive development, follows a series of stages. To develop this theory, Kohlberg posed moral dilemmas to people of all ages, and then he analyzed their answers to find evidence of their particular stage of moral development. Before reading about the stages, take a minute to consider how you would answer one of Kohlberg's best-known moral dilemmas, commonly known as the Heinz dilemma:

> In Europe, a woman was near death from a special kind of cancer. There was one drug that the doctors thought might save her. It was a form of radium that a druggist in the same town had recently discovered. The drug was expensive to make, but the druggist was charging ten times what the drug cost him to make. He paid $200 for the radium and charged $2,000 for a small dose of the drug. The sick woman's husband, Heinz, went to everyone he knew to borrow the money, but he could only get together about $1,000, which is half of what it cost. He told the druggist that his wife was dying and asked him to sell it cheaper or let him pay later. But the druggist said: "No, I discovered the drug and I'm going to make money from it." So Heinz got desperate and broke into the man's store to steal the drug for his wife. Should the husband have done that? (Kohlberg, 1969, p. 379)

How would you answer this dilemma? Kohlberg was not interested in whether you answer yes or no to the dilemma: Instead, he was interested in the reasoning behind your answer.

After presenting people with this and various other moral dilemmas, Kohlberg reviewed people's responses and placed them in different **stages of moral reasoning** (Figure 9.6). According to Kohlberg, an individual progresses from the capacity for pre-conventional morality (before age 9) to the capacity for conventional morality (early adolescence), and toward attaining post-conventional morality (once formal operational thought is attained), which only a few fully achieve. Kohlberg placed in the highest stage responses that reflected the reasoning that Heinz should steal the drug because his wife's life is more important than the pharmacist making money. The value of a human life overrides the pharmacist's greed.

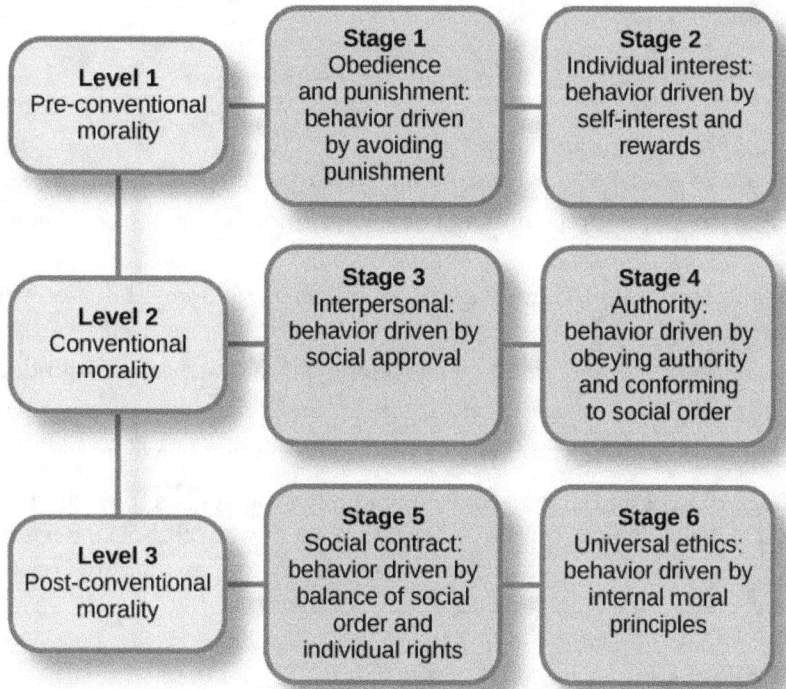

Figure 9.6 Kohlberg identified three levels of moral reasoning: pre-conventional, conventional, and post-conventional: Each level is associated with increasingly complex stages of moral development.

It is important to realize that even those people who have the most sophisticated, post-conventional reasons for some choices may make other choices for the simplest of pre-conventional reasons. Many psychologists agree with Kohlberg's theory of moral development but point out that moral reasoning is very different from moral behavior. Sometimes what we say we would do in a situation is not what we actually do in that situation. In other words, we might "talk the talk," but not "walk the walk."

How does this theory apply to males and females? Kohlberg (1969) felt that more males than females move past stage four in their moral development. He went on to note that women seem to be deficient in their moral reasoning abilities. These ideas were not well received by Carol Gilligan, a research assistant of Kohlberg, who consequently developed her own ideas of moral development. In her groundbreaking book, *In a Different Voice: Psychological Theory and Women's Development*, Gilligan (1982) criticized her former mentor's theory because it was based only on upper class White men and boys. She argued that women are not deficient in their moral reasoning—she proposed that males and females reason differently. Girls and women focus more on staying connected and the importance of interpersonal relationships. Therefore, in the Heinz dilemma, many girls and women respond that Heinz should not steal the medicine. Their reasoning is that if he steals the medicine, is arrested, and is put in jail, then he and his wife will be separated, and she could die while he is still in prison.

9.3 Stages of Development

Learning Objectives

By the end of this section, you will be able to:
- Describe the stages of prenatal development and recognize the importance of prenatal care
- Appraise physical, cognitive, and emotional development that occurs from infancy through childhood
- Compare and contrast physical, cognitive, and emotional development that occurs during adolescence
- Examine physical, cognitive, and emotional development that occurs in adulthood

From the moment we are born until the moment we die, we continue to develop.

As discussed at the beginning of this chapter, developmental psychologists often divide our development into three areas: physical development, cognitive development, and psychosocial development. Mirroring Erikson's stages, lifespan development is divided into different stages that are based on age. We will discuss prenatal, infant, child, adolescent, and adult development.

PRENATAL DEVELOPMENT

How did you come to be who you are? From beginning as a one-cell structure to your birth, your prenatal development occurred in an orderly and delicate sequence.

There are three stages of prenatal development: germinal, embryonic, and fetal. Let's take a look at what happens to the developing baby in each of these stages.

Germinal Stage (Weeks 1–2)

In the discussion of biopsychology earlier in the book, you learned about genetics and DNA. A mother and father's DNA is passed on to the child at the moment of conception. **Conception** occurs when sperm fertilizes an egg and forms a zygote (Figure 9.7). A **zygote** begins as a one-cell structure that is created when a sperm and egg merge. The genetic makeup and sex of the baby are set at this point. During the first week after conception, the zygote divides and multiplies, going from a one-cell structure to two cells, then four cells, then eight cells, and so on. This process of cell division is called **mitosis**. Mitosis is a fragile process, and fewer than one-half of all zygotes survive beyond the first two weeks (Hall, 2004). After 5 days of mitosis there are 100 cells, and after 9 months there are billions of cells. As the cells divide, they become more specialized, forming different organs and body parts. In the germinal stage, the mass of cells has yet to attach itself to the lining of the mother's uterus. Once it does, the next stage begins.

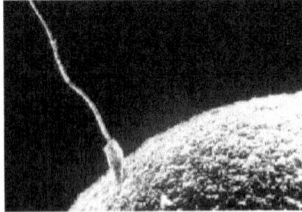

Figure 9.7 Sperm and ovum fuse at the point of conception.

Embryonic Stage (Weeks 3–8)

After the zygote divides for about 7–10 days and has 150 cells, it travels down the fallopian tubes and implants itself in the lining of the uterus. Upon implantation, this multi-cellular organism is called an

embryo. Now blood vessels grow, forming the placenta. The **placenta** is a structure connected to the uterus that provides nourishment and oxygen from the mother to the developing embryo via the umbilical cord. Basic structures of the embryo start to develop into areas that will become the head, chest, and abdomen. During the embryonic stage, the heart begins to beat and organs form and begin to function. The neural tube forms along the back of the embryo, developing into the spinal cord and brain.

Fetal Stage (Weeks 9–40)

When the organism is about nine weeks old, the embryo is called a fetus. At this stage, the fetus is about the size of a kidney bean and begins to take on the recognizable form of a human being as the "tail" begins to disappear.

From 9–12 weeks, the sex organs begin to differentiate. At about 16 weeks, the fetus is approximately 4.5 inches long. Fingers and toes are fully developed, and fingerprints are visible. By the time the fetus reaches the sixth month of development (24 weeks), it weighs up to 1.4 pounds. Hearing has developed, so the fetus can respond to sounds. The internal organs, such as the lungs, heart, stomach, and intestines, have formed enough that a fetus born prematurely at this point has a chance to survive outside of the mother's womb. Throughout the fetal stage the brain continues to grow and develop, nearly doubling in size from weeks 16 to 28. Around 36 weeks, the fetus is almost ready for birth. It weighs about 6 pounds and is about 18.5 inches long, and by week 37 all of the fetus's organ systems are developed enough that it could survive outside the mother's uterus without many of the risks associated with premature birth. The fetus continues to gain weight and grow in length until approximately 40 weeks. By then, the fetus has very little room to move around and birth becomes imminent. The progression through the stages is shown in **Figure 9.8**.

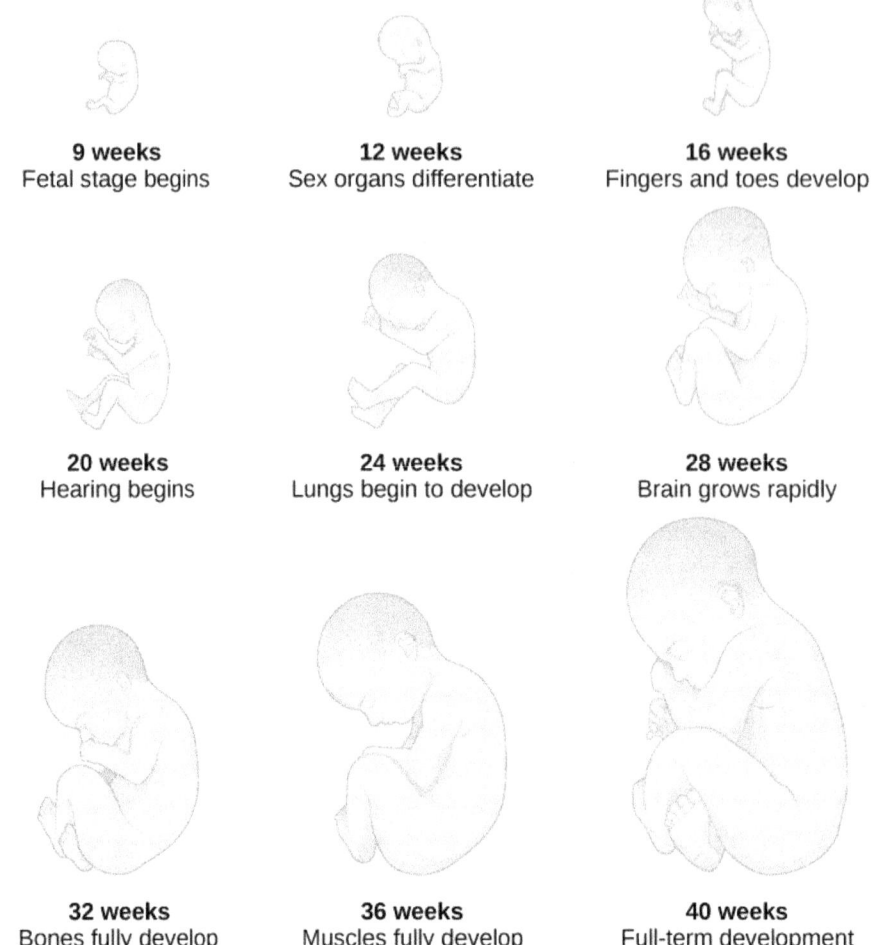

Figure 9.8 During the fetal stage, the baby's brain develops and the body adds size and weight, until the fetus reaches full-term development.

LINK TO LEARNING

For an amazing look at prenatal development and the process of birth, view the video Life's Greatest Miracle (http://openstax.org/l/miracle) from Nova and PBS.

Prenatal Influences

During each prenatal stage, genetic and environmental factors can affect development. The developing fetus is completely dependent on the mother for life. It is important that the mother takes good care of herself and receives **prenatal care**, which is medical care during pregnancy that monitors the health of both the mother and the fetus (Figure 9.9). According to the National Institutes of Health ([NIH], 2013), routine prenatal care is important because it can reduce the risk of complications to the mother and fetus during pregnancy. In fact, women who are trying to become pregnant or who may become pregnant should discuss pregnancy planning with their doctor. They may be advised, for example, to take a vitamin containing folic acid, which helps prevent certain birth defects, or to monitor aspects of their diet or exercise routines.

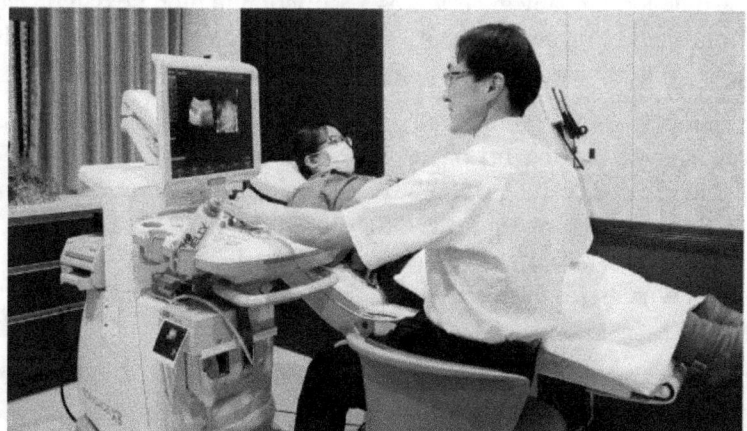

Figure 9.9 A pregnant woman receives an ultrasound as part of her prenatal care. (credit: "MIKI Yoshihito_Flickr"/Flickr)

Recall that when the zygote attaches to the wall of the mother's uterus, the placenta is formed. The placenta provides nourishment and oxygen to the fetus. Most everything the mother ingests, including food, liquid, and even medication, travels through the placenta to the fetus, hence the common phrase "eating for two." Anything the mother is exposed to in the environment affects the fetus; if the mother is exposed to something harmful, the child can show life-long effects.

A **teratogen** is any environmental agent—biological, chemical, or physical—that causes damage to the developing embryo or fetus. There are different types of teratogens. Alcohol and most drugs cross the placenta and affect the fetus. Alcohol is not safe to drink in any amount during pregnancy. Alcohol use during pregnancy has been found to be the leading preventable cause of mental retardation in children in the United States (Maier & West, 2001). Excessive maternal drinking while pregnant can cause fetal alcohol spectrum disorders with life-long consequences for the child ranging in severity from minor to major (Table 9.3). Fetal alcohol spectrum disorders (FASD) are a collection of birth defects associated with heavy consumption of alcohol during pregnancy. Physically, children with FASD may have a small head size and abnormal facial features. Cognitively, these children may have poor judgment, poor impulse control, higher rates of ADHD, learning issues, and lower IQ scores. These developmental problems and delays persist into adulthood (Streissguth et al., 2004). Based on studies conducted on animals, it also has been suggested that a mother's alcohol consumption during pregnancy may predispose her child to like alcohol (Youngentob et al., 2007).

Fetal Alcohol Syndrome Facial Features

Facial Feature	Potential Effect of Fetal Alcohol Syndrome
Head size	Below-average head circumference
Eyes	Smaller than average eye opening, skin folds at corners of eyes
Nose	Low nasal bridge, short nose
Midface	Smaller than average midface size
Lip and philtrum	Thin upper lip, indistinct philtrum

Table 9.3

Smoking is also considered a teratogen because nicotine travels through the placenta to the fetus. When the mother smokes, the developing baby experiences a reduction in blood oxygen levels. According to the Centers for Disease Control and Prevention (2013), smoking while pregnant can result in premature birth, low-birth-weight infants, stillbirth, and sudden infant death syndrome (SIDS).

Heroin, cocaine, methamphetamine, almost all prescription medicines, and most over-the counter medications are also considered teratogens. Babies born with a heroin addiction need heroin just like an adult addict. The child will need to be gradually weaned from the heroin under medical supervision; otherwise, the child could have seizures and die. Other teratogens include radiation, viruses such as HIV and herpes, and rubella (German measles). Women in the United States are much less likely to be afflicted with rubella because most women received childhood immunizations or vaccinations that protect the body from disease.

Each organ of the fetus develops during a specific period in the pregnancy, called the **critical or sensitive period** (Figure 9.8). For example, research with primate models of FASD has demonstrated that the time during which a developing fetus is exposed to alcohol can dramatically affect the appearance of facial characteristics associated with fetal alcohol syndrome. Specifically, this research suggests that alcohol exposure that is limited to day 19 or 20 of gestation can lead to significant facial abnormalities in the offspring (Ashley, Magnuson, Omnell, & Clarren, 1999). Given regions of the brain also show sensitive periods during which they are most susceptible to the teratogenic effects of alcohol (Tran & Kelly, 2003).

WHAT DO YOU THINK?

Should Women Who Use Drugs During Pregnancy Be Arrested and Jailed?

As you now know, women who use drugs or alcohol during pregnancy can cause serious lifelong harm to their child. Some people have advocated mandatory screenings for women who are pregnant and have a history of drug abuse, and if the women continue using, to arrest, prosecute, and incarcerate them (Figdor & Kaeser, 1998). This policy was tried in Charleston, South Carolina, as recently as 20 years ago. The policy was called the Interagency Policy on Management of Substance Abuse During Pregnancy, and had disastrous results.

> The Interagency Policy applied to patients attending the obstetrics clinic at MUSC, which primarily serves patients who are indigent or on Medicaid. It did not apply to private obstetrical patients. The policy required patient education about the harmful effects of substance abuse during pregnancy. . . . [A] statement also warned patients that protection of unborn and newborn children from the harms of illegal drug abuse could involve the Charleston police, the Solicitor of the Ninth Judicial Court, and the Protective Services Division of the Department of Social Services (DSS). (Jos, Marshall, & Perlmutter, 1995, pp. 120–121)

This policy seemed to deter women from seeking prenatal care, deterred them from seeking other social services, and was applied solely to low-income women, resulting in lawsuits. The program was canceled after 5 years, during which 42 women were arrested. A federal agency later determined that the program involved human experimentation without the approval and oversight of an institutional review board (IRB). What were the flaws in the program and how would you correct them? What are the ethical implications of charging pregnant women with child abuse?

INFANCY THROUGH CHILDHOOD

The average newborn weighs approximately 7.5 pounds. Although small, a newborn is not completely helpless because his reflexes and sensory capacities help him interact with the environment from the moment of birth. All healthy babies are born with **newborn reflexes**: inborn automatic responses to particular forms of stimulation. Reflexes help the newborn survive until it is capable of more complex behaviors—these reflexes are crucial to survival. They are present in babies whose brains are developing normally and usually disappear around 4–5 months old. Let's take a look at some of these newborn reflexes. The rooting reflex is the newborn's response to anything that touches her cheek: When you stroke a baby's cheek, she naturally turns her head in that direction and begins to suck. The sucking reflex is the automatic, unlearned, sucking motions that infants do with their mouths. Several other interesting newborn reflexes can be observed. For instance, if you put your finger into a newborn's hand, you will witness the grasping reflex, in which a baby automatically grasps anything that touches his palms. The Moro reflex is the newborn's response when she feels like she is falling. The baby spreads her arms, pulls them back in, and then (usually) cries. How do you think these reflexes promote survival in the first months of life?

LINK TO LEARNING

Take a few minutes to view this brief video clip about newborn reflexes (http://openstax.org/l/newflexes) to learn more.

What can young infants see, hear, and smell? Newborn infants' sensory abilities are significant, but their senses are not yet fully developed. Many of a newborn's innate preferences facilitate interaction with caregivers and other humans. Although vision is their least developed sense, newborns already show a preference for faces. Babies who are just a few days old also prefer human voices, they will listen to voices longer than sounds that do not involve speech (Vouloumanos & Werker, 2004), and they seem to prefer their mother's voice over a stranger's voice (Mills & Melhuish, 1974). In an interesting experiment, 3-week-old babies were given pacifiers that played a recording of the infant's mother's voice and of a stranger's voice. When the infants heard their mother's voice, they sucked more strongly at the pacifier (Mills & Melhuish, 1974). Newborns also have a strong sense of smell. For instance, newborn babies can distinguish the smell of their own mother from that of others. In a study by MacFarlane (1978), 1-week-old babies who were being breastfed were placed between two gauze pads. One gauze pad was from the bra of a nursing mother who was a stranger, and the other gauze pad was from the bra of the infant's own mother. More than two-thirds of the week-old babies turned toward the gauze pad with their mother's scent.

Physical Development

In infancy, toddlerhood, and early childhood, the body's physical development is rapid (Figure 9.10). On average, newborns weigh between 5 and 10 pounds, and a newborn's weight typically doubles in six months and triples in one year. By 2 years old the weight will have quadrupled, so we can expect that a 2 year old should weigh between 20 and 40 pounds. The average length of a newborn is 19.5 inches, increasing to 29.5 inches by 12 months and 34.4 inches by 2 years old (WHO Multicentre Growth Reference Study Group, 2006).

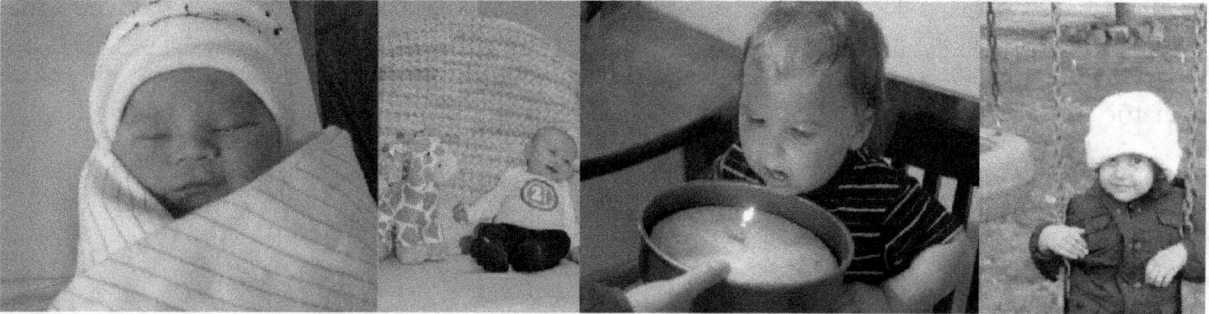

Figure 9.10 Children experience rapid physical changes through infancy and early childhood. (credit "left": modification of work by Kerry Ceszyk; credit "middle-left": modification of work by Kristi Fausel; credit "middle-right": modification of work by "devinf"/Flickr; credit "right": modification of work by Rose Spielman)

During infancy and childhood, growth does not occur at a steady rate (Carel, Lahlou, Roger, & Chaussain, 2004). Growth slows between 4 and 6 years old: During this time children gain 5–7 pounds and grow about 2–3 inches per year. Once girls reach 8–9 years old, their growth rate outpaces that of boys due to a pubertal growth spurt. This growth spurt continues until around 12 years old, coinciding with the start of the menstrual cycle. By 10 years old, the average girl weighs 88 pounds, and the average boy weighs 85 pounds.

We are born with all of the brain cells that we will ever have—about 100–200 billion neurons (nerve cells) whose function is to store and transmit information (Huttenlocher & Dabholkar, 1997). However, the nervous system continues to grow and develop. Each neural pathway forms thousands of new connections during infancy and toddlerhood. This period of rapid neural growth is called blooming. Neural pathways continue to develop through puberty. The blooming period of neural growth is then followed by a period of pruning, where neural connections are reduced. It is thought that pruning causes the brain to function more efficiently, allowing for mastery of more complex skills (Hutchinson, 2011). Blooming occurs during the first few years of life, and pruning continues through childhood and into adolescence in various areas of the brain.

The size of our brains increases rapidly. For example, the brain of a 2-year-old is 55% of its adult size, and by 6 years old the brain is about 90% of its adult size (Tanner, 1978). During early childhood (ages 3–6), the frontal lobes grow rapidly. Recalling our discussion of the 4 lobes of the brain earlier in this book, the frontal lobes are associated with planning, reasoning, memory, and impulse control. Therefore, by the time children reach school age, they are developmentally capable of controlling their attention and behavior. Through the elementary school years, the frontal, temporal, occipital, and parietal lobes all grow in size. The brain growth spurts experienced in childhood tend to follow Piaget's sequence of cognitive development, so that significant changes in neural functioning account for cognitive advances (Kolb & Whishaw, 2009; Overman, Bachevalier, Turner, & Peuster, 1992).

Motor development occurs in an orderly sequence as infants move from reflexive reactions (e.g., sucking and rooting) to more advanced motor functioning. For instance, babies first learn to hold their heads up, then to sit with assistance, and then to sit unassisted, followed later by crawling and then walking.

Motor skills refer to our ability to move our bodies and manipulate objects. **Fine motor skills** focus on the muscles in our fingers, toes, and eyes, and enable coordination of small actions (e.g., grasping a toy, writing with a pencil, and using a spoon). **Gross motor skills** focus on large muscle groups that control our arms and legs and involve larger movements (e.g., balancing, running, and jumping).

As motor skills develop, there are certain developmental milestones that young children should achieve (Table 9.4). For each milestone there is an average age, as well as a range of ages in which the milestone should be reached. An example of a developmental milestone is sitting. On average, most babies sit alone at 7 months old. Sitting involves both coordination and muscle strength, and 90% of babies achieve this milestone between 5 and 9 months old. In another example, babies on average are able to hold up their head at 6 weeks old, and 90% of babies achieve this between 3 weeks and 4 months old. If a baby is not holding up his head by 4 months old, he is showing a delay. If the child is displaying delays on several milestones, that is reason for concern, and the parent or caregiver should discuss this with the child's pediatrician. Some developmental delays can be identified and addressed through early intervention.

Developmental Milestones, Ages 2–5 Years

Age (years)	Physical	Personal/Social	Language	Cognitive
2	Kicks a ball; walks up and down stairs	Plays alongside other children; copies adults	Points to objects when named; puts 2–4 words together in a sentence	Sorts shapes and colors; follows 2-step instructions
3	Climbs and runs; pedals tricycle	Takes turns; expresses many emotions; dresses self	Names familiar things; uses pronouns	Plays make believe; works toys with parts (levers, handles)
4	Catches balls; uses scissors	Prefers social play to solo play; knows likes and interests	Knows songs and rhymes by memory	Names colors and numbers; begins writing letters
5	Hops and swings; uses fork and spoon	Distinguishes real from pretend; likes to please friends	Speaks clearly; uses full sentences	Counts to 10 or higher; prints some letters and copies basic shapes

Table 9.4

Cognitive Development

In addition to rapid physical growth, young children also exhibit significant development of their cognitive abilities. Piaget thought that children's ability to understand objects—such as learning that a rattle makes a noise when shaken—was a cognitive skill that develops slowly as a child matures and interacts with the environment. Today, developmental psychologists think Piaget was incorrect. Researchers have found that even very young children understand objects and how they work long before they have experience with those objects (Baillargeon, 1987; Baillargeon, Li, Gertner, & Wu, 2011). For example, children as young as 3 months old demonstrated knowledge of the properties of objects that they had only viewed and did not have prior experience with them. In one study, 3-month-old infants were shown a truck rolling down a track and behind a screen. The box, which appeared solid but was actually hollow, was placed next to the track. The truck rolled past the box as would be expected. Then the box was placed on the track to block the path of the truck. When the truck was rolled down the track this time, it continued unimpeded. The infants spent significantly more time looking at this impossible event (Figure 9.11). Baillargeon (1987) concluded that they knew solid objects cannot pass through each other. Baillargeon's findings suggest that very young children have an understanding of objects and how they work, which Piaget (1954) would have said is beyond their cognitive abilities due to their limited experiences in the world.

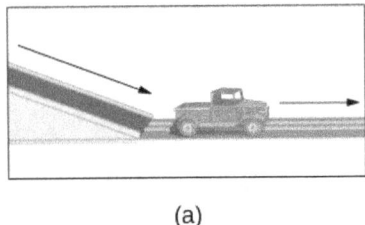 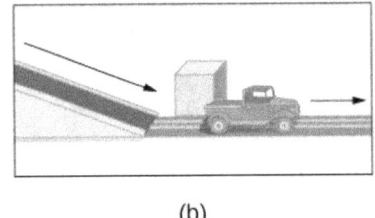 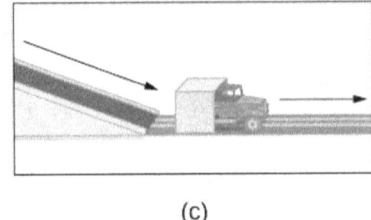

(a) (b) (c)

Figure 9.11 In Baillargeon's study, infants observed a truck (a) roll down an unobstructed track, (b) roll down an unobstructed track with an obstruction (box) beside it, and (c) roll down and pass through what appeared to be an obstruction.

Just as there are physical milestones that we expect children to reach, there are also cognitive milestones. It is helpful to be aware of these milestones as children gain new abilities to think, problem solve, and communicate. For example, infants shake their head "no" around 6–9 months, and they respond to verbal requests to do things like "wave bye-bye" or "blow a kiss" around 9–12 months. Remember Piaget's ideas about object permanence? We can expect children to grasp the concept that objects continue to exist even when they are not in sight by around 8 months old. Because toddlers (i.e., 12–24 months old) have mastered object permanence, they enjoy games like hide and seek, and they realize that when someone leaves the room they will come back (Loop, 2013). Toddlers also point to pictures in books and look in appropriate places when you ask them to find objects.

Preschool-age children (i.e., 3–5 years old) also make steady progress in cognitive development. Not only can they count, name colors, and tell you their name and age, but they can also make some decisions on their own, such as choosing an outfit to wear. Preschool-age children understand basic time concepts and sequencing (e.g., before and after), and they can predict what will happen next in a story. They also begin to enjoy the use of humor in stories. Because they can think symbolically, they enjoy pretend play and inventing elaborate characters and scenarios. One of the most common examples of their cognitive growth is their blossoming curiosity. Preschool-age children love to ask "Why?"

An important cognitive change occurs in children this age. Recall that Piaget described 2–3 year olds as egocentric, meaning that they do not have an awareness of others' points of view. Between 3 and 5 years old, children come to understand that people have thoughts, feelings, and beliefs that are different from their own. This is known as theory-of-mind (TOM). Children can use this skill to tease others, persuade their parents to purchase a candy bar, or understand why a sibling might be angry. When children develop TOM, they can recognize that others have false beliefs (Dennett, 1987; Callaghan et al., 2005).

LINK TO LEARNING

False-belief tasks are useful in determining a child's acquisition of theory-of-mind (TOM). Take a look at this video clip that shows a false belief task involving a box of crayons (http://openstax.org/l/crayons) to learn more.

Cognitive skills continue to expand in middle and late childhood (6–11 years old). Thought processes become more logical and organized when dealing with concrete information (Figure 9.12). Children at this age understand concepts such as the past, present, and future, giving them the ability to plan and work toward goals. Additionally, they can process complex ideas such as addition and subtraction and cause-and-effect relationships. However, children's attention spans tend to be very limited until they are around 11 years old. After that point, it begins to improve through adulthood.

Figure 9.12 Because they understand luck and fairness, children in middle and late childhood (6–11 years old) are able to follow rules for games. (credit: Edwin Martinez)

One well-researched aspect of cognitive development is language acquisition. As mentioned earlier, the order in which children learn language structures is consistent across children and cultures (Hatch, 1983). You've also learned that some psychological researchers have proposed that children possess a biological predisposition for language acquisition.

Starting before birth, babies begin to develop language and communication skills. At birth, babies apparently recognize their mother's voice and can discriminate between the language(s) spoken by their mothers and foreign languages, and they show preferences for faces that are moving in synchrony with audible language (Blossom & Morgan, 2006; Pickens, 1994; Spelke & Cortelyou, 1981).

Children communicate information through gesturing long before they speak, and there is some evidence that gesture usage predicts subsequent language development (Iverson & Goldin-Meadow, 2005). In terms of producing spoken language, babies begin to coo almost immediately. Cooing is a one-syllable combination of a consonant and a vowel sound (e.g., coo or ba). Interestingly, babies replicate sounds from their own languages. A baby whose parents speak French will coo in a different tone than a baby whose parents speak Spanish or Urdu. After cooing, the baby starts to babble. Babbling begins with repeating a syllable, such as ma-ma, da-da, or ba-ba. When a baby is about 12 months old, we expect her to say her first word for meaning, and to start combining words for meaning at about 18 months.

At about 2 years old, a toddler uses between 50 and 200 words; by 3 years old they have a vocabulary of up to 1,000 words and can speak in sentences. During the early childhood years, children's vocabulary increases at a rapid pace. This is sometimes referred to as the "vocabulary spurt" and has been claimed to involve an expansion in vocabulary at a rate of 10–20 new words per week. Recent research may indicate that while some children experience these spurts, it is far from universal (as discussed in Ganger & Brent, 2004). It has been estimated that, 5 year olds understand about 6,000 words, speak 2,000 words, and can define words and question their meanings. They can rhyme and name the days of the week. Seven year olds speak fluently and use slang and clichés (Stork & Widdowson, 1974).

What accounts for such dramatic language learning by children? Behaviorist B. F. Skinner thought that we learn language in response to reinforcement or feedback, such as through parental approval or through being understood. For example, when a two-year-old child asks for juice, he might say, "me juice," to which his mother might respond by giving him a cup of apple juice. Noam Chomsky (1957) criticized Skinner's theory and proposed that we are all born with an innate capacity to learn language. Chomsky called this mechanism a language acquisition device (LAD). Who is correct? Both Chomsky and Skinner are right. Remember that we are a product of both nature and nurture. Researchers now believe that language acquisition is partially inborn and partially learned through our interactions with our linguistic environment (Gleitman & Newport, 1995; Stork & Widdowson, 1974).

Attachment

Psychosocial development occurs as children form relationships, interact with others, and understand and manage their feelings. In social and emotional development, forming healthy attachments is very important and is the major social milestone of infancy. **Attachment** is a long-standing connection or bond with others. Developmental psychologists are interested in how infants reach this milestone. They ask such questions as: How do parent and infant attachment bonds form? How does neglect affect these bonds? What accounts for children's attachment differences?

Researchers Harry Harlow, John Bowlby, and Mary Ainsworth conducted studies designed to answer these questions. In the 1950s, Harlow conducted a series of experiments on monkeys. He separated newborn monkeys from their mothers. Each monkey was presented with two surrogate mothers. One surrogate monkey was made out of wire mesh, and she could dispense milk. The other monkey was softer and made from cloth: This monkey did not dispense milk. Research shows that the monkeys preferred the soft, cuddly cloth monkey, even though she did not provide any nourishment. The baby monkeys spent their time clinging to the cloth monkey and only went to the wire monkey when they needed to be fed. Prior to this study, the medical and scientific communities generally thought that babies become attached to the people who provide their nourishment. However, Harlow (1958) concluded that there was more to the mother-child bond than nourishment. Feelings of comfort and security are the critical components to maternal-infant bonding, which leads to healthy psychosocial development.

> **LINK TO LEARNING**
>
> Harlow's studies of monkeys were performed before modern ethics guidelines were in place, and today his experiments are widely considered to be unethical and even cruel. Watch this video of actual footage of Harlow's monkey studies (http://openstax.org/l/monkeystudy) to learn more.

Building on the work of Harlow and others, John Bowlby developed the concept of attachment theory. He defined attachment as the affectional bond or tie that an infant forms with the mother (Bowlby, 1969). An infant must form this bond with a primary caregiver in order to have normal social and emotional development. In addition, Bowlby proposed that this attachment bond is very powerful and continues throughout life. He used the concept of secure base to define a healthy attachment between parent and child (1988). A **secure base** is a parental presence that gives the child a sense of safety as he explores his surroundings. Bowlby said that two things are needed for a healthy attachment: The caregiver must be responsive to the child's physical, social, and emotional needs; and the caregiver and child must engage in mutually enjoyable interactions (Bowlby, 1969) (**Figure 9.13**).

Figure 9.13 Mutually enjoyable interactions promote the parent-infant bond. (credit: "balouriarajesh_Pixabay"/Pixabay)

While Bowlby thought attachment was an all-or-nothing process, Mary Ainsworth's (1970) research showed otherwise. Ainsworth wanted to know if children differ in the ways they bond, and if so, why.

To find the answers, she used the Strange Situation procedure to study attachment between mothers and their infants (1970). In the Strange Situation, the mother (or primary caregiver) and the infant (age 12-18 months) are placed in a room together. There are toys in the room, and the caregiver and child spend some time alone in the room. After the child has had time to explore her surroundings, a stranger enters the room. The mother then leaves her baby with the stranger. After a few minutes, she returns to comfort her child.

Based on how the infants/toddlers responded to the separation and reunion, Ainsworth identified three types of parent-child attachments: secure, avoidant, and resistant (Ainsworth & Bell, 1970). A fourth style, known as disorganized attachment, was later described (Main & Solomon, 1990). The most common type of attachment—also considered the healthiest—is called **secure attachment** (Figure 9.14). In this type of attachment, the toddler prefers his parent over a stranger. The attachment figure is used as a secure base to explore the environment and is sought out in times of stress. Securely attached children were distressed when their caregivers left the room in the Strange Situation experiment, but when their caregivers returned, the securely attached children were happy to see them. Securely attached children have caregivers who are sensitive and responsive to their needs.

Figure 9.14 In secure attachment, the parent provides a secure base for the toddler, allowing him to securely explore his environment. (credit: Kerry Ceszyk)

With **avoidant attachment**, the child is unresponsive to the parent, does not use the parent as a secure base, and does not care if the parent leaves. The toddler reacts to the parent the same way she reacts to a stranger. When the parent does return, the child is slow to show a positive reaction. Ainsworth theorized that these children were most likely to have a caregiver who was insensitive and inattentive to their needs (Ainsworth, Blehar, Waters, & Wall, 1978).

In cases of **resistant attachment**, children tend to show clingy behavior, but then they reject the attachment figure's attempts to interact with them (Ainsworth & Bell, 1970). These children do not explore the toys in the room, as they are too fearful. During separation in the Strange Situation, they became extremely disturbed and angry with the parent. When the parent returns, the children are difficult to comfort. Resistant attachment is the result of the caregivers' inconsistent level of response to their child.

Finally, children with **disorganized attachment** behaved oddly in the Strange Situation. They freeze, run around the room in an erratic manner, or try to run away when the caregiver returns (Main & Solomon, 1990). This type of attachment is seen most often in kids who have been abused. Research has shown that abuse disrupts a child's ability to regulate their emotions.

While Ainsworth's research has found support in subsequent studies, it has also met criticism. Some researchers have pointed out that a child's temperament may have a strong influence on attachment (Gervai, 2009; Harris, 2009), and others have noted that attachment varies from culture to culture, a factor not accounted for in Ainsworth's research (Rothbaum, Weisz, Pott, Miyake, & Morelli, 2000; van Ijzendoorn & Sagi-Schwartz, 2008).

> **LINK TO LEARNING**
>
> Watch this **video clip of the Strange Situation (http://openstax.org/l/strangesitu)** and try to identify which type of attachment baby Lisa exhibits.

Self-Concept

Just as attachment is the main psychosocial milestone of infancy, the primary psychosocial milestone of childhood is the development of a positive sense of self. How does self-awareness develop? Infants don't have a self-concept, which is an understanding of who they are. If you place a baby in front of a mirror, she will reach out to touch her image, thinking it is another baby. However, by about 18 months a toddler will recognize that the person in the mirror is herself. How do we know this? In a well-known experiment, a researcher placed a red dot of paint on children's noses before putting them in front of a mirror (Amsterdam, 1972). Commonly known as the mirror test, this behavior is demonstrated by humans and a few other species and is considered evidence of self-recognition (Archer, 1992). At 18 months old they would touch their own noses when they saw the paint, surprised to see a spot on their faces. By 24–36 months old children can name and/or point to themselves in pictures, clearly indicating self-recognition.

Children from 2–4 years old display a great increase in social behavior once they have established a self-concept. They enjoy playing with other children, but they have difficulty sharing their possessions. Also, through play children explore and come to understand their gender roles and can label themselves as a girl or boy (Chick, Heilman-Houser, & Hunter, 2002). By 4 years old, children can cooperate with other children, share when asked, and separate from parents with little anxiety. Children at this age also exhibit autonomy, initiate tasks, and carry out plans. Success in these areas contributes to a positive sense of self. Once children reach 6 years old, they can identify themselves in terms of group memberships: "I'm a first grader!" School-age children compare themselves to their peers and discover that they are competent in some areas and less so in others (recall Erikson's task of industry versus inferiority). At this age, children recognize their own personality traits as well as some other traits they would like to have. For example, 10-year-old Layla says, "I'm kind of shy. I wish I could be more talkative like my friend Alexa."

Development of a positive self-concept is important to healthy development. Children with a positive self-concept tend to be more confident, do better in school, act more independently, and are more willing to try new activities (Maccoby, 1980; Ferrer & Fugate, 2003). Formation of a positive self-concept begins in Erikson's toddlerhood stage, when children establish autonomy and become confident in their abilities. Development of self-concept continues in elementary school, when children compare themselves to others. When the comparison is favorable, children feel a sense of competence and are motivated to work harder and accomplish more. Self-concept is re-evaluated in Erikson's adolescence stage, as teens form an identity. They internalize the messages they have received regarding their strengths and weaknesses, keeping some messages and rejecting others. Adolescents who have achieved identity formation are capable of contributing positively to society (Erikson, 1968).

> **DIG DEEPER**
>
> **Phenomenological Variant of Ecological Systems Theory (PVEST)**
>
> Kenneth and Mamie Clark were pioneering psychologists responsible for the first psychological study used in

a Supreme Court case. Their research with African American children and doll choices was used to highlight the harmful effects of segregation and provided support for the Browns and the NAACP in their lawsuit against the Board of Education. The finding that African American children were more likely to choose a white doll over a black doll, in both northern and southern states, led them to theorize that the children did not have a healthy concept of themselves (Clark & Clark, 1950).

The Clarks' research differed from that of Inez Beverly Prosser, who also studied African American children in segregated and integrated schools in Cincinnati. Parents could choose either environment for their children during the 1930s. She found, among other factors, that the self-concept of children at segregated schools was more positive versus those in integrated schools, partly due to teachers' low expectations. Prosser also noted that the child's personality should be considered when choosing a segregated school or an integrated school (Benjamin, Henry, & McMahon, 2005).

Later researchers suggested that African American children choosing a doll that did not look like them was not an indication of their self-esteem or their self-image. For instance, Rogers and Meltzoff (2017) found that gender identity was more important than race in their study of diverse children whose average age was about 10 years old. Thus, for children that young, the meaning of race is an evolving process, as opposed to adolescents' search for identity. The ethnic minority children in the study did view racial identity as important, compared to their white counterparts.

For teenagers who are members of ethnic minority groups, racial/ethnic/cultural identity can be paramount, depending on the family's processes. Racial socialization involves teaching them the positive aspects of their in-group, usually by caregivers. Most of the students in a study by Neblett, Smalls, Ford, Nguyen, and Sellers (2009) reported having received such messages but a few received no racial socialization messages. They found that these messages played a role in how they felt about their in-group.

Some theories have been developed to explain the behaviors of ethnic minority youth. One such theory is the Phenomenological Variant of Ecological Systems Theory (PVEST), put forth by Margaret Beale Spencer. It is a merging of phenomenology and Bronfenbrenner's ecological systems theory. A phenomenological approach is based on how a person makes meaning of their experiences. For example, young African American boys have different experiences in educational settings compared to African American girls. Consequently, the meaning they assign to those experiences differs. Bronfenbrenner's ecological systems theory suggests that development occurs based on interactions among environments such as school, family, and community (Bronfenbrenner, 1977).

The research that Spencer, Dupree, and Hartmann (1997) conducted with African American adolescent boys and girls was explained by PVEST. They found that negative learning attitudes were predicted by unpopularity with peers for girls and boys. Additionally, for boys, more stress predicted a less negative attitude toward learning, possibly due to focus on the school environment instead of on personal issues. This occurred along with perceiving that teachers had positive expectations of African American boys. The researchers surmised that PVEST accounted for how others' perceptions and their subsequent attitudes were related and worked both ways.

What can parents do to nurture a healthy self-concept? Diana Baumrind (1971, 1991) thinks parenting style may be a factor. The way we parent is an important factor in a child's socioemotional growth. Baumrind developed and refined a theory describing four parenting styles: authoritative, authoritarian, permissive, and uninvolved. With the **authoritative style**, the parent gives reasonable demands and consistent limits, expresses warmth and affection, and listens to the child's point of view. Parents set rules and explain the reasons behind them. They are also flexible and willing to make exceptions to the rules in certain cases—for example, temporarily relaxing bedtime rules to allow for a nighttime swim during a family vacation. Of the four parenting styles, the authoritative style is the one that is most encouraged in modern American society. American children raised by authoritative parents tend to have high self-esteem and social skills. However, effective parenting styles vary as a function of culture and, as Small (1999) points out, the authoritative style is not necessarily preferred or appropriate in all cultures.

In **authoritarian style**, the parent places high value on conformity and obedience. The parents are often strict, tightly monitor their children, and express little warmth. In contrast to the authoritative style, authoritarian parents probably would not relax bedtime rules during a vacation because they consider the rules to be set, and they expect obedience. This style can create anxious, withdrawn, and unhappy kids. However, it is important to point out that authoritarian parenting is as beneficial as the authoritative style in some ethnic groups (Russell, Crockett, & Chao, 2010). For instance, first-generation Chinese American children raised by authoritarian parents did just as well in school as their peers who were raised by authoritative parents (Russell et al., 2010).

For parents who employ the **permissive style** of parenting, the kids run the show and anything goes. Permissive parents make few demands and rarely use punishment. They tend to be very nurturing and loving, and may play the role of friend rather than parent. In terms of our example of vacation bedtimes, permissive parents might not have bedtime rules at all—instead they allow the child to choose his bedtime whether on vacation or not. Not surprisingly, children raised by permissive parents tend to lack self-discipline, and the permissive parenting style is negatively associated with grades (Dornbusch, Ritter, Leiderman, Roberts, & Fraleigh, 1987). The permissive style may also contribute to other risky behaviors such as alcohol abuse (Bahr & Hoffman, 2010), risky sexual behavior especially among female children (Donenberg, Wilson, Emerson, & Bryant, 2002), and increased display of disruptive behaviors by male children (Parent et al., 2011). However, there are some positive outcomes associated with children raised by permissive parents. They tend to have higher self-esteem, better social skills, and report lower levels of depression (Darling, 1999).

With the **uninvolved style** of parenting, the parents are indifferent, uninvolved, and sometimes referred to as neglectful. They don't respond to the child's needs and make relatively few demands. This could be because of severe depression or substance abuse, or other factors such as the parents' extreme focus on work. These parents may provide for the child's basic needs, but little else. The children raised in this parenting style are usually emotionally withdrawn, fearful, anxious, perform poorly in school, and are at an increased risk of substance abuse (Darling, 1999).

As you can see, parenting styles influence childhood adjustment, but could a child's temperament likewise influence parenting? **Temperament** refers to innate traits that influence how one thinks, behaves, and reacts with the environment. Children with easy temperaments demonstrate positive emotions, adapt well to change, and are capable of regulating their emotions. Conversely, children with difficult temperaments demonstrate negative emotions and have difficulty adapting to change and regulating their emotions. Difficult children are much more likely to challenge parents, teachers, and other caregivers (Thomas, 1984). Therefore, it's possible that easy children (i.e., social, adaptable, and easy to soothe) tend to elicit warm and responsive parenting, while demanding, irritable, withdrawn children evoke irritation in their parents or cause their parents to withdraw (Sanson & Rothbart, 1995).

EVERYDAY CONNECTION

The Importance of Play and Recess

According to the American Academy of Pediatrics (2007), unstructured play is an integral part of a child's development. It builds creativity, problem solving skills, and social relationships. Play also allows children to develop a theory-of-mind as they imaginatively take on the perspective of others.

Outdoor play allows children the opportunity to directly experience and sense the world around them. While doing so, they may collect objects that they come across and develop lifelong interests and hobbies. They also benefit from increased exercise, and engaging in outdoor play can actually increase how much they enjoy physical activity. This helps support the development of a healthy heart and brain. Unfortunately, research suggests that today's children are engaging in less and less outdoor play (Clements, 2004). Perhaps, it is no surprise to learn that lowered levels of physical activity in conjunction with easy access to calorie-dense foods with little nutritional value are contributing to alarming levels of childhood obesity (Karnik & Kanekar, 2012).

Despite the adverse consequences associated with reduced play, some children are over scheduled and have little free time to engage in unstructured play. In addition, some schools have taken away recess time for children in a push for students to do better on standardized tests, and many schools commonly use loss of recess as a form of punishment. Do you agree with these practices? Why or why not?

ADOLESCENCE

Adolescence is a socially constructed concept. In pre-industrial society, children were considered adults when they reached physical maturity, but today we have an extended time between childhood and adulthood called adolescence. **Adolescence** is the period of development that begins at puberty and ends at emerging adulthood, which is discussed later. In the United States, adolescence is seen as a time to develop independence from parents while remaining connected to them (Figure 9.15). The typical age range of adolescence is from 12 to 18 years, and this stage of development also has some predictable physical, cognitive, and psychosocial milestones.

Figure 9.15 Peers are a primary influence on our development in adolescence. (credit: "manseok_Pixabay"/Pixabay)

Physical Development

As noted above, adolescence begins with puberty. While the sequence of physical changes in puberty is predictable, the onset and pace of puberty vary widely. Several physical changes occur during puberty, such as **adrenarche** and **gonadarche**, the maturing of the adrenal glands and sex glands, respectively. Also during this time, primary and secondary sexual characteristics develop and mature. **Primary sexual characteristics** are organs specifically needed for reproduction, like the uterus and ovaries in females and testes in males. **Secondary sexual characteristics** are physical signs of sexual maturation that do not directly involve sex organs, such as development of breasts and hips in girls, and development of facial hair and a deepened voice in boys. Girls experience **menarche**, the beginning of menstrual periods, usually around 12–13 years old, and boys experience **spermarche**, the first ejaculation, around 13–14 years old.

During puberty, both sexes experience a rapid increase in height (i.e., growth spurt). For girls this begins between 8 and 13 years old, with adult height reached between 10 and 16 years old. Boys begin their growth spurt slightly later, usually between 10 and 16 years old, and reach their adult height between 13 and 17 years old. Both nature (i.e., genes) and nurture (e.g., nutrition, medications, and medical conditions) can influence height.

Because rates of physical development vary so widely among teenagers, puberty can be a source of pride or embarrassment. Early maturing boys tend to be stronger, taller, and more athletic than their later maturing peers. They are usually more popular, confident, and independent, but they are also at a greater risk for substance abuse and early sexual activity (Flannery, Rowe, & Gulley, 1993; Kaltiala-Heino, Rimpela, Rissanen, & Rantanen, 2001). Early maturing girls may be teased or overtly admired, which can cause them to feel self-conscious about their developing bodies. These girls are at a higher risk for depression, substance abuse, and eating disorders (Ge, Conger, & Elder, 2001; Graber, Lewinsohn, Seeley, & Brooks-Gunn, 1997; Striegel-Moore & Cachelin, 1999). Late blooming boys and girls (i.e., they develop more slowly than their peers) may feel self-conscious about their lack of physical development. Negative feelings are particularly a problem for late maturing boys, who are at a higher risk for depression and conflict with parents (Graber et al., 1997) and more likely to be bullied (Pollack & Shuster, 2000).

The adolescent brain also remains under development. Up until puberty, brain cells continue to bloom in the frontal region. Adolescents engage in increased risk-taking behaviors and emotional outbursts possibly because the frontal lobes of their brains are still developing (Figure 9.16). Recall that this area is responsible for judgment, impulse control, and planning, and it is still maturing into early adulthood (Casey, Tottenham, Liston, & Durston, 2005).

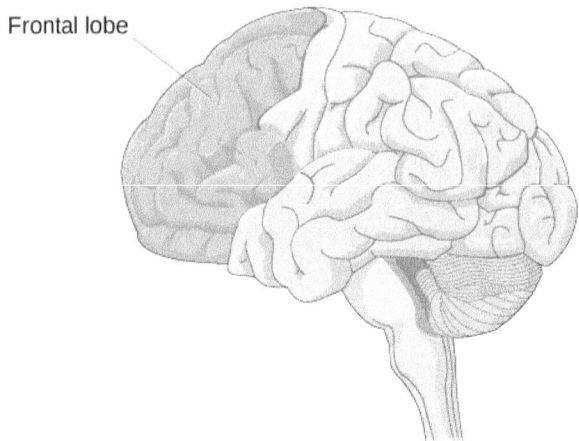

Figure 9.16 Brain growth continues into the early 20s. The development of the frontal lobe, in particular, is important during this stage.

LINK TO LEARNING

According to neuroscientist Jay Giedd in the Frontline video "Inside the Teenage Brain" (2013), "It's sort of unfair to expect [teens] to have adult levels of organizational skills or decision-making before their brains are finished being built." Watch this segment on "The Wiring of the Adolescent Brain" (http://openstax.org/l/wiringbrain) to find out more about the developing brain during adolescence.

Cognitive Development

More complex thinking abilities emerge during adolescence. Some researchers suggest this is due to increases in processing speed and efficiency rather than as the result of an increase in mental capacity—in other words, due to improvements in existing skills rather than development of new ones (Bjorkland, 1987; Case, 1985). During adolescence, teenagers move beyond concrete thinking and become capable of abstract thought. Recall that Piaget refers to this stage as formal operational thought. Teen thinking is also characterized by the ability to consider multiple points of view, imagine hypothetical situations, debate ideas and opinions (e.g., politics, religion, and justice), and form new ideas (Figure 9.17). In addition, it's not uncommon for adolescents to question authority or challenge established societal norms.

Cognitive empathy, also known as theory-of-mind (which we discussed earlier with regard to egocentrism), relates to the ability to take the perspective of others and feel concern for others (Shamay-Tsoory, Tomer, & Aharon-Peretz, 2005). Cognitive empathy begins to increase in adolescence and is an important component of social problem solving and conflict avoidance. According to one longitudinal study, levels of cognitive empathy begin rising in girls around 13 years old, and around 15 years old in boys (Van der Graaff et al., 2013). Teens who reported having supportive fathers with whom they could discuss their worries were found to be better able to take the perspective of others (Miklikowska, Duriez, & Soenens, 2011).

Figure 9.17 Teenage thinking is characterized by the ability to reason logically and solve hypothetical problems such as how to design, plan, and build a structure. (credit: U.S. Army RDECOM)

Psychosocial Development

Adolescents continue to refine their sense of self as they relate to others. Erikson referred to the task of the adolescent as one of identity versus role confusion. Thus, in Erikson's view, an adolescent's main questions are "Who am I?" and "Who do I want to be?" Some adolescents adopt the values and roles that their parents expect for them. Other teens develop identities that are in opposition to their parents but align with a peer group. This is common as peer relationships become a central focus in adolescents' lives.

As adolescents work to form their identities, they pull away from their parents, and the peer group becomes very important (Shanahan, McHale, Osgood, & Crouter, 2007). Despite spending less time with their parents, most teens report positive feelings toward them (Moore, Guzman, Hair, Lippman, & Garrett, 2004). Warm and healthy parent-child relationships have been associated with positive child outcomes, such as better grades and fewer school behavior problems, in the United States as well as in other countries (Hair et al., 2005).

It appears that most teens don't experience adolescent storm and stress to the degree once famously suggested by G. Stanley Hall, a pioneer in the study of adolescent development. Only small numbers of teens have major conflicts with their parents (Steinberg & Morris, 2001), and most disagreements are minor. For example, in a study of over 1,800 parents of adolescents from various cultural and ethnic groups, Barber (1994) found that conflicts occurred over day-to-day issues such as homework, money, curfews, clothing, chores, and friends. These types of arguments tend to decrease as teens develop (Galambos & Almeida, 1992). There is emerging research on the adolescent brain. Galvan, Hare, Voss, Glover and Casey (2007) examined its role in risk-taking behavior. They used fMRI to assess the readings' relationship to risk-taking, risk perception, and impulsivity. The researchers found that there was no correlation between brain activity in the neural reward center and impulsivity and risk perception. However, activity in that part of the brain was correlated to risk taking. In other words, risk-taking adolescents experienced brain activity in the reward center. The idea that adolescents, however, are more impulsive than other demographics was challenged in their research, which included children and adults.

Emerging Adulthood

The next stage of development is **emerging adulthood**. This is a relatively newly defined period of lifespan development spanning from 18 years old to the mid-20s, characterized as an in-between time where identity exploration is focused on work and love.

When does a person become an adult? There are many ways to answer this question. In the United States, you are legally considered an adult at 18 years old. But other definitions of adulthood vary widely; in sociology, for example, a person may be considered an adult when she becomes self-supporting, chooses a career, gets married, or starts a family. The ages at which we achieve these milestones vary from person to person as well as from culture to culture. For example, in the African country of Malawi, 15-year-old Njemile was married at 14 years old and had her first child at 15 years old. In her culture she is considered an adult. Children in Malawi take on adult responsibilities such as marriage and work (e.g., carrying water, tending babies, and working fields) as early as 10 years old. In stark contrast, independence in Western cultures is taking longer and longer, effectively delaying the onset of adult life.

Why is it taking twentysomethings so long to grow up? It seems that emerging adulthood is a product of both Western culture and our current times (Arnett, 2000). People in developed countries are living longer, allowing the freedom to take an extra decade to start a career and family. Changes in the workforce also play a role. For example, 50 years ago, a young adult with a high school diploma could immediately enter the work force and climb the corporate ladder. That is no longer the case. Bachelor's and even graduate degrees are required more and more often—even for entry-level jobs (Arnett, 2000). In addition, many students are taking longer (five or six years) to complete a college degree as a result of working and going to school at the same time. After graduation, many young adults return to the family home because they have difficulty finding a job. Changing cultural expectations may be the most important reason for the delay in entering adult roles. Young people are spending more time exploring their options, so they are delaying marriage and work as they change majors and jobs multiple times, putting them on a much later timetable than their parents (Arnett, 2000).

ADULTHOOD

Adulthood begins around 20 years old and has three distinct stages: early, middle, and late. Each stage brings its own set of rewards and challenges.

Physical Development

By the time we reach early adulthood (20 to early 40s), our physical maturation is complete, although our height and weight may increase slightly. In young adulthood, our physical abilities are at their peak, including muscle strength, reaction time, sensory abilities, and cardiac functioning. Most professional athletes are at the top of their game during this stage. Many women have children in the young adulthood years, so they may see additional weight gain and breast changes.

Middle adulthood extends from the 40s to the 60s (Figure 9.18). Physical decline is gradual. The skin loses some elasticity, and wrinkles are among the first signs of aging. Visual acuity decreases during this time. Women experience a gradual decline in fertility as they approach the onset of menopause, the end of the menstrual cycle, around 50 years old. Both men and women tend to gain weight: in the abdominal area for men and in the hips and thighs for women. Hair begins to thin and turn gray.

Figure 9.18 Physical declines of middle and late adulthood can be minimized with proper exercise, nutrition, and an active lifestyle. (credit: modification of work by Peter Stevens)

Late adulthood is considered to extend from the 60s on. This is the last stage of physical change. The skin continues to lose elasticity, reaction time slows further, and muscle strength diminishes. Smell, taste, hearing, and vision, so sharp in our twenties, decline significantly. The brain may also no longer function at optimal levels, leading to problems like memory loss, dementia, and Alzheimer's disease in later years.

> **LINK TO LEARNING**
>
> Aging doesn't mean a person can't explore new pursuits, learn new skills, and continue to grow. Watch this inspiring story about Neil Unger who is a newbie to the world of skateboarding at 60 years old (http://openstax.org/l/Unger) to learn more.

Cognitive Development

Because we spend so many years in adulthood (more than any other stage), cognitive changes are numerous. In fact, research suggests that adult cognitive development is a complex, ever changing process that may be even more active than cognitive development in infancy and early childhood (Fischer, Yan, & Stewart, 2003).

> **LINK TO LEARNING**
>
> There is good news for the middle age brain. View this brief video about the middle age brain (http://openstax.org/l/oldbrain) to find out what it is.

Unlike our physical abilities, which peak in our mid-20s and then begin a slow decline, our cognitive abilities remain steady throughout early and middle adulthood. Our crystallized intelligence (information, skills, and strategies we have gathered through a lifetime of experience) tends to hold steady as we age—it may even improve. For example, adults show relatively stable to increasing scores on intelligence tests until their mid-30s to mid-50s (Bayley & Oden, 1955). However, in late adulthood we begin to experience a decline in another area of our cognitive abilities—fluid intelligence (information processing abilities, reasoning, and memory). These processes become slower. How can we delay the onset of cognitive decline? Mental and physical activity seems to play a part (Figure 9.19). Research has found adults who engage in mentally and physically stimulating activities experience less cognitive decline and have a reduced incidence of mild cognitive impairment and dementia (Hertzog, Kramer, Wilson, & Lindenberger, 2009; Larson et al., 2006; Podewils et al., 2005).

Figure 9.19 Cognitive activities such as playing mahjong, chess, or other games, can keep you mentally fit. The same is true for solo pastimes like reading and completing crossword puzzles. (credit: Philippe Put)

Researchers have examined the aging brain by comparing it to brain functioning in younger people. Forstmann and colleagues (2011) compared elderly participants to younger participants, who in the study were asked to report the direction of movement of a set of dots. They were given feedback regarding speed and accuracy. The researchers found that older participants made more errors and were slower due to degeneration of corticostriatal connections. In other words, the decreased ability typically assigned to elderly people may be due to circumstances in the brain beyond their control. Interestingly, other researchers have found similarities in spatial representations when comparing children aged 6–7 to those over the age of 80. Ruggiero, D'Errico, and Iachini (2016) reported that this is due to neurodegeneration in older adults and immature neurology in young children.

Many elderly people experience dementia, changes in the brain that negatively affect cognition. Alzheimer's disease is one type of dementia, initially studied by medical researcher Solomon Carter Fuller. Alzheimer's disease has a genetic basis. Plaques in the brain are due to cell death, which then causes those affected with the disease severe forgetfulness. A person can forget how to walk, talk, and eventually eat. The disease can be mitigated by assessing environmental factors (exposure to lead, iron, and zinc increase risk) and nutritional factors (the Mediterranean diet lowers risk) (Arora, Mittal, & Kakkar, 2015). Although there is no cure, there is hope. Cognitive rehabilitation can offset mild cognitive impairment, as it can evolve into dementia. Garcia-Betances, Jimenez-Mixco, Arredondo, and Cabrera-Umpierrez (2015) examined the use of virtual reality as a possible cognitive rehabilitative method. They suggested that virtual reality technology should involve daily living activities, memory, and language, among other considerations.

Psychosocial Development

There are many theories about the social and emotional aspects of aging. Some aspects of healthy aging include activities, social connectedness, and the role of a person's culture. According to many theorists, including George Vaillant (2002), who studied and analyzed over 50 years of data, we need to have and continue to find meaning throughout our lives. For those in early and middle adulthood, meaning is found through work (Sterns & Huyck, 2001) and family life (Markus, Ryff, Curan, & Palmersheim, 2004). These areas relate to the tasks that Erikson referred to as generativity and intimacy. As mentioned previously, adults tend to define themselves by what they do—their careers. Earnings peak during this time, yet job satisfaction is more closely tied to work that involves contact with other people, is interesting, provides opportunities for advancement, and allows some independence (Mohr & Zoghi, 2006) than it is to salary (Iyengar, Wells, & Schwartz, 2006). How might being unemployed or being in a dead-end job challenge adult well-being?

Positive relationships with significant others in our adult years have been found to contribute to a state of well-being (Ryff & Singer, 2009). Most adults in the United States identify themselves through their relationships with family—particularly with spouses, children, and parents (Markus et al., 2004). While raising children can be stressful, especially when they are young, research suggests that parents reap the rewards down the road, as adult children tend to have a positive effect on parental well-being (Umberson, Pudrovska, & Reczek, 2010). Having a stable marriage has also been found to contribute to well-being throughout adulthood (Vaillant, 2002).

Another aspect of positive aging is believed to be social connectedness and social support. As we get older, **socioemotional selectivity theory** suggests that our social support and friendships dwindle in number, but remain as close, if not more close than in our earlier years (Carstensen, 1992) (**Figure 9.20**).

Figure 9.20 Social support is important as we age. (credit: Gabriel Rocha)

LINK TO LEARNING

Read the **poem "When I Am Old" by Jenny Joseph (http://openstax.org/l/wheniamold)** to see a humorous and heartfelt approach to aging.

LINK TO LEARNING

View this **video about aging in America (http://openstax.org/l/aginginusa)** to learn more.

9.4 Death and Dying

Learning Objectives

By the end of this section, you will be able to:
- Discuss hospice care
- Describe the five stages of grief
- Critique issues regarding living wills, Do Not Resuscitate (DNR) orders, and hospice care

Every story has an ending. Death marks the end of your life story (**Figure 9.21**). Our culture and individual backgrounds influence how we view death. In some cultures, death is accepted as a natural part of life and is embraced. In contrast, until about 50 years ago in the United States, a doctor might not inform someone that they were dying, and the majority of deaths occurred in hospitals. In 1967 that reality began to change with Cicely Saunders, who created the first modern **hospice** in England. The aim of hospice is to help provide a death with dignity and pain management in a humane and comfortable environment, which is usually outside of a hospital setting. In 1974, Florence Wald founded the first hospice in the United States. Today, hospice provides care for 1.65 million Americans and their families. Because of hospice care, many terminally ill people are able to spend their last days at home.

(a) (b) (c)

Figure 9.21 Different cultures, societies, and religions have varying practices surrounding death. For example, people's bodies may be (a) buried in a cemetery, (b) cremated and buried at sea as in this U.S. Navy ceremony, or (c) cremated such as in this Hindu ceremony in Bali. (credit a: modification of work by Christina Rutz; credit b: modification of work by Chief Journalist Alan J. Baribeau/Wikimedia; credit c: modification of work by "CazzJj_Flickr"/Flickr)

Research has indicated that hospice care is beneficial for the patient (Brumley, Enquidanos, & Cherin, 2003; Brumley et al., 2007; Godkin, Krant, & Doster, 1984) and for the patient's family (Rhodes, Mitchell, Miller, Connor, & Teno, 2008; Godkin et al., 1984). Hospice patients report high levels of satisfaction with hospice care because they are able to remain at home and are not completely dependent on strangers for care (Brumley et al., 2007). In addition, hospice patients tend to live longer than non-hospice patients (Connor, Pyenson, Fitch, Spence, & Iwasaki, 2007; Temel et al., 2010). Family members receive emotional support and are regularly informed of their loved one's treatment and condition. The family member's burden of care is also reduced (McMillan et al., 2006). Both the patient and the patient's family members report increased family support, increased social support, and improved coping while receiving hospice services (Godkin et al., 1984).

How do you think you might react if you were diagnosed with a terminal illness like cancer? Elizabeth Kübler-Ross (1969), who worked with the founders of hospice care, described the process of an individual accepting his own death. She proposed five stages of grief: denial, anger, bargaining, depression, and acceptance. Most individuals experience these stages, but the stages may occur in different orders, depending on the individual. In addition, not all people experience all of the stages. It is also important to note that some psychologists believe that the more a dying person fights death, the more likely he is to remain stuck in the denial phase. This could make it difficult for the dying person to face death with dignity. However, other psychologists believe that not facing death until the very end is an adaptive coping mechanism for some people.

Whether due to illness or old age, not everyone facing death or the loss of a loved one experiences the negative emotions outlined in the Kübler-Ross model (Nolen-Hoeksema & Larson, 1999). For example, research suggests that people with religious or spiritual beliefs are better able to cope with death because of their hope in an afterlife and because of social support from religious or spiritual associations (Hood, Spilka, Hunsberger, & Corsuch, 1996; McIntosh, Silver, & Wortman, 1993; Paloutzian, 1996; Samarel, 1991; Wortman & Park, 2008).

A prominent example of a person creating meaning through death is Randy Pausch, who was a well-loved and respected professor at Carnegie Mellon University. Diagnosed with terminal pancreatic cancer in his mid-40s and given only 3–6 months to live, Pausch focused on living in a fulfilling way in the time he had left. Instead of becoming angry and depressed, he presented his now famous last lecture called "Really Achieving Your Childhood Dreams." In his moving, yet humorous talk, he shares his insights on seeing the good in others, overcoming obstacles, and experiencing zero gravity, among many other things. Despite his terminal diagnosis, Pausch lived the final year of his life with joy and hope, showing us that our plans for the future still matter, even if we know that we are dying.

> **LINK TO LEARNING**
>
> Listen to **Randy Pausch's last lecture titled Really Achieving Your Childhood Dreams (http://openstax.org/l/lastlecture)** to learn more.

As individuals become more knowledgeable about medical procedures and practices, some people want to ensure that their wishes and desires are known in advance. This ensures that if the person ever becomes incapacitated or can no longer express herself, her loved ones will know what she wants. For this reason, a person might write a **living will** or **advance directive**, which is a written legal document that details specific interventions a person wants. For example, a person in the last stages of a terminal illness may not want to receive life-extending treatments. A person may also include a **Do Not Resuscitate (DNR) Order** and he would share this with his family and close friends. A DNR Order states that if a person stops breathing or his heart stops beating, medical personnel such as doctors and nurses are *not* to take steps to revive or resuscitate the patient. A living will can also include a **health care proxy**, which appoints a specific person to make medical decisions for you if you are unable to speak for yourself. People's desire for living wills and DNRs are often influenced by their religion, culture, and upbringing.

Key Terms

accommodation adjustment of a schema by changing a scheme to accommodate new information different from what was already known

adolescence period of development that begins at puberty and ends at early adulthood

adrenarche maturing of the adrenal glands

advance directive a written legal document that details specific interventions a person wants (see living will)

assimilation adjustment of a schema by adding information similar to what is already known

attachment long-standing connection or bond with others

authoritarian parenting style parents place a high value on conformity and obedience, are often rigid, and express little warmth to the child

authoritative parenting style parents give children reasonable demands and consistent limits, express warmth and affection, and listen to the child's point of view

avoidant attachment characterized by child's unresponsiveness to parent, does not use the parent as a secure base, and does not care if parent leaves

cognitive development domain of lifespan development that examines learning, attention, memory, language, thinking, reasoning, and creativity

cognitive empathy ability to take the perspective of others and to feel concern for others

conception when a sperm fertilizes an egg and forms a zygote

concrete operational stage third stage in Piaget's theory of cognitive development; from about 7 to 11 years old, children can think logically about real (concrete) events

conservation idea that even if you change the appearance of something, it is still equal in size, volume, or number as long as nothing is added or removed

continuous development view that development is a cumulative process: gradually improving on existing skills

critical (sensitive) period time during fetal growth when specific parts or organs develop

developmental milestone approximate ages at which children reach specific normative events

discontinuous development view that development takes place in unique stages, which happen at specific times or ages

disorganized attachment characterized by the child's odd behavior when faced with the parent; type of attachment seen most often with kids that are abused

do not resuscitate (DNR) a legal document stating that if a person stops breathing or his or her heart stops, medical personnel such as doctors and nurses are not to take steps to revive or resuscitate the patient

egocentrism preoperational child's difficulty in taking the perspective of others

embryo multi-cellular organism in its early stages of development

emerging adulthood newly defined period of lifespan development from 18 years old to the mid-20s; young people are taking longer to complete college, get a job, get married, and start a family

fine motor skills use of muscles in fingers, toes, and eyes to coordinate small actions

formal operational stage final stage in Piaget's theory of cognitive development; from age 11 and up, children are able to deal with abstract ideas and hypothetical situations

gonadarche maturing of the sex glands

gross motor skills use of large muscle groups to control arms and legs for large body movements

health care proxy a legal document that appoints a specific person to make medical decisions for a patient if he or she is unable to speak for him/herself

hospice service that provides a death with dignity; pain management in a humane and comfortable environment; usually outside of a hospital setting

living will a written legal document that details specific interventions a person wants; may include health care proxy

menarche beginning of menstrual period; around 12–13 years old

mitosis process of cell division

motor skills ability to move our body and manipulate objects

nature genes and biology

newborn reflexes inborn automatic response to a particular form of stimulation that all healthy babies are born with

normative approach study of development using norms, or average ages, when most children reach specific developmental milestones

nurture environment and culture

object permanence idea that even if something is out of sight, it still exists

permissive parenting style parents make few demands and rarely use punishment

physical development domain of lifespan development that examines growth and changes in the body and brain, the senses, motor skills, and health and wellness

placenta structure connected to the uterus that provides nourishment and oxygen to the developing baby

prenatal care medical care during pregnancy that monitors the health of both the mother and the fetus

preoperational stage second stage in Piaget's theory of cognitive development; from ages 2 to 7, children learn to use symbols and language but do not understand mental operations and often think illogically

primary sexual characteristics organs specifically needed for reproduction

psychosexual development process proposed by Freud in which pleasure-seeking urges focus on different erogenous zones of the body as humans move through five stages of life

psychosocial development domain of lifespan development that examines emotions, personality, and social relationships

psychosocial development process proposed by Erikson in which social tasks are mastered as humans move through eight stages of life from infancy to adulthood

resistant attachment characterized by the child's tendency to show clingy behavior and rejection of the parent when she attempts to interact with the child

reversibility principle that objects can be changed, but then returned back to their original form or condition

schema (plural = schemata) concept (mental model) that is used to help us categorize and interpret information

secondary sexual characteristics physical signs of sexual maturation that do not directly involve sex organs

secure attachment characterized by the child using the parent as a secure base from which to explore

secure base parental presence that gives the infant/toddler a sense of safety as he explores his surroundings

sensorimotor stage first stage in Piaget's theory of cognitive development; from birth through age 2, a child learns about the world through senses and motor behavior

socioemotional selectivity theory social support/friendships dwindle in number, but remain as close, if not more close than in earlier years

spermarche first male ejaculation

stage of moral reasoning process proposed by Kohlberg; humans move through three stages of moral development

temperament innate traits that influence how one thinks, behaves, and reacts with the environment

teratogen biological, chemical, or physical environmental agent that causes damage to the developing embryo or fetus

uninvolved parenting style parents are indifferent, uninvolved, and sometimes referred to as neglectful; they don't respond to the child's needs and make relatively few demands

zygote structure created when a sperm and egg merge at conception; begins as a single cell and rapidly divides to form the embryo and placenta

Summary

9.1 What Is Lifespan Development?

Lifespan development explores how we change and grow from conception to death. This field of psychology is studied by developmental psychologists. They view development as a lifelong process that can be studied scientifically across three developmental domains: physical, cognitive development, and psychosocial. There are several theories of development that focus on the following issues: whether development is continuous or discontinuous, whether development follows one course or many, and the relative influence of nature versus nurture on development.

9.2 Lifespan Theories

There are many theories regarding how babies and children grow and develop into happy, healthy adults. Sigmund Freud suggested that we pass through a series of psychosexual stages in which our energy is focused on certain erogenous zones on the body. Eric Erikson modified Freud's ideas and suggested a theory of psychosocial development. Erikson said that our social interactions and successful completion of social tasks shape our sense of self. Jean Piaget proposed a theory of cognitive development that explains how children think and reason as they move through various stages. Finally, Lawrence Kohlberg turned his attention to moral development. He said that we pass through three levels of moral thinking that build on our cognitive development.

9.3 Stages of Development

At conception the egg and sperm cell are united to form a zygote, which will begin to divide rapidly. This marks the beginning of the first stage of prenatal development (germinal stage), which lasts about two weeks. Then the zygote implants itself into the lining of the woman's uterus, marking the beginning of the second stage of prenatal development (embryonic stage), which lasts about six weeks. The embryo begins to develop body and organ structures, and the neural tube forms, which will later become the brain and spinal cord. The third phase of prenatal development (fetal stage) begins at 9 weeks and lasts until birth. The body, brain, and organs grow rapidly during this stage. During all stages of pregnancy it is important that the mother receive prenatal care to reduce health risks to herself and to her developing baby.

Newborn infants weigh about 7.5 pounds. Doctors assess a newborn's reflexes, such as the sucking, rooting, and Moro reflexes. Our physical, cognitive, and psychosocial skills grow and change as we move through developmental stages from infancy through late adulthood. Attachment in infancy is a critical component of healthy development. Parenting styles have been found to have an effect on childhood outcomes of well-being. The transition from adolescence to adulthood can be challenging due to the timing of puberty, and due to the extended amount of time spent in emerging adulthood. Although physical decline begins in middle adulthood, cognitive decline does not begin until later. Activities that keep the body and mind active can help maintain good physical and cognitive health as we age. Social supports through family and friends remain important as we age.

9.4 Death and Dying

Death marks the endpoint of our lifespan. There are many ways that we might react when facing death. Kübler-Ross developed a five-stage model of grief as a way to explain this process. Many people facing death choose hospice care, which allows their last days to be spent at home in a comfortable, supportive environment.

Review Questions

1. The view that development is a cumulative process, gradually adding to the same type of skills is known as _____.
   a. nature
   b. nurture
   c. continuous development
   d. discontinuous development

2. Developmental psychologists study human growth and development across three domains. Which of the following is *not* one of these domains?
   a. cognitive
   b. psychological
   c. physical
   d. psychosocial

3. How is lifespan development defined?
   a. The study of how we grow and change from conception to death.
   b. The study of how we grow and change in infancy and childhood.
   c. The study of physical, cognitive, and psychosocial growth in children.
   d. The study of emotions, personality, and social relationships.

4. The idea that even if something is out of sight, it still exists is called _____.
   a. egocentrism
   b. object permanence
   c. conservation
   d. reversibility

5. Which theorist proposed that moral thinking proceeds through a series of stages?
   a. Sigmund Freud
   b. Erik Erikson
   c. John Watson
   d. Lawrence Kohlberg

6. According to Erikson's theory of psychosocial development, what is the main task of the adolescent?
   a. developing autonomy
   b. feeling competent
   c. forming an identity
   d. forming intimate relationships

7. Which of the following is the correct order of prenatal development?
   a. zygote, fetus, embryo
   b. fetus, embryo zygote
   c. fetus, zygote, embryo
   d. zygote, embryo, fetus

8. The time during fetal growth when specific parts or organs develop is known as _____.
   a. critical period
   b. mitosis
   c. conception
   d. pregnancy

9. What begins as a single-cell structure that is created when a sperm and egg merge at conception?
   a. embryo
   b. fetus
   c. zygote
   d. infant

10. Using scissors to cut out paper shapes is an example of _____.
    a. gross motor skills
    b. fine motor skills
    c. large motor skills
    d. small motor skills

11. The child uses the parent as a base from which to explore her world in which attachment style?
    a. secure
    b. insecure avoidant
    c. insecure ambivalent-resistant
    d. disorganized

12. The frontal lobes become fully developed _____.
    a. at birth
    b. at the beginning of adolescence
    c. at the end of adolescence
    d. by 25 years old

13. Who created the very first modern hospice?
    a. Elizabeth Kübler-Ross
    b. Cicely Saunders
    c. Florence Wald
    d. Florence Nightingale

14. Which of the following is the order of stages in Kübler-Ross's five-stage model of grief?
    a. denial, bargaining, anger, depression, acceptance
    b. anger, depression, bargaining, acceptance, denial
    c. denial, anger, bargaining, depression, acceptance
    d. anger, acceptance, denial, depression, bargaining

Critical Thinking Questions

15. Describe the nature versus nurture controversy, and give an example of a trait and how it might be influenced by each?

16. Compare and contrast continuous and discontinuous development.

17. Why should developmental milestones only be used as a general guideline for normal child development?

18. What is the difference between assimilation and accommodation? Provide examples of each.

19. Why was Carol Gilligan critical of Kohlberg's theory of moral development?

20. What is egocentrism? Provide an original example.

21. What are some known teratogens, and what kind of damage can they do to the developing fetus?

22. What is prenatal care and why is it important?

23. Describe what happens in the embryonic stage of development. Describe what happens in the fetal stage of development.

24. What makes a personal quality part of someone's personality?

25. Describe some of the newborn reflexes. How might they promote survival?

26. Compare and contrast the four parenting styles and describe the kinds of childhood outcomes we can expect with each.

27. What is emerging adulthood and what are some factors that have contributed to this new stage of development?

28. Describe the five stages of grief and provide examples of how a person might react in each stage.

29. What is the purpose of hospice care?

Personal Application Questions

30. How are you different today from the person you were at 6 years old? What about at 16 years old? How are you the same as the person you were at those ages?

31. Your 3-year-old daughter is not yet potty trained. Based on what you know about the normative approach, should you be concerned? Why or why not?

32. Explain how you would use your understanding of one of the major developmental theories to deal with each of the difficulties listed below:
    a. Your infant daughter puts everything in her mouth, including the dog's food.
    b. Your eight-year-old son is failing math; all he cares about is baseball.
    c. Your two-year-old daughter refuses to wear the clothes you pick for her every morning, which makes getting dressed a twenty-minute battle.
    d. Your sixty-eight-year-old neighbor is chronically depressed and feels she has wasted her life.
    e. Your 18-year-old daughter has decided not to go to college. Instead she's moving to Colorado to become a ski instructor.
    f. Your 11-year-old son is the class bully.

33. Which parenting style describes how you were raised? Provide an example or two to support your answer.

34. Would you describe your experience of puberty as one of pride or embarrassment? Why?

35. Your best friend is a smoker who just found out she is pregnant. What would you tell her about smoking and pregnancy?

36. Imagine you are a nurse working at a clinic that provides prenatal care for pregnant women. Your patient, Anna, has heard that it's a good idea to play music for her unborn baby, and she wants to know when her baby's hearing will develop. What will you tell her?

37. Have you ever had to cope with the loss of a loved one? If so, what concepts described in this section provide context that may help you understand your experience and process of grieving?

38. If you were diagnosed with a terminal illness would you choose hospice care or a traditional death in a hospital? Why?

Chapter 10

Emotion and Motivation

Figure 10.1 Emotions can change in an instant, especially in response to an unexpected event. Surprise, fear, anger, and sadness are some immediate emotions that people experienced in the aftermath of the April 15, 2013 Boston Marathon bombing. What are emotions? What causes them? What motivated some bystanders to immediately help others, while other people ran for safety? (credit: modification of work by Aaron "tango" Tang)

Chapter Outline

10.1 Motivation
10.2 Hunger and Eating
10.3 Sexual Behavior
10.4 Emotion

Introduction

What makes us behave as we do? What drives us to eat? What drives us toward sex? Is there a biological basis to explain the feelings we experience? How universal are emotions?

In this chapter, we will explore issues relating to both motivation and emotion. We will begin with a discussion of several theories that have been proposed to explain motivation and why we engage in a given behavior. You will learn about the physiological needs that drive some human behaviors, as well as the importance of our social experiences in influencing our actions.

Next, we will consider both eating and having sex as examples of motivated behaviors. What are the physiological mechanisms of hunger and satiety? What understanding do scientists have of why obesity occurs, and what treatments exist for obesity and eating disorders? How has research into human sex and sexuality evolved over the past century? How do psychologists understand and study the human experience of sexual orientation and gender identity? These questions—and more—will be explored.

This chapter will close with a discussion of emotion. You will learn about several theories that have been proposed to explain how emotion occurs, the biological underpinnings of emotion, and the universality of emotions.

10.1 Motivation

Learning Objectives

By the end of this section, you will be able to:
- Define intrinsic and extrinsic motivation
- Understand that instincts, drive reduction, self-efficacy, and social motives have all been proposed as theories of motivation
- Explain the basic concepts associated with Maslow's hierarchy of needs

Why do we do the things we do? What motivations underlie our behaviors? **Motivation** describes the wants or needs that direct behavior toward a goal. In addition to biological motives, motivations can be **intrinsic** (arising from internal factors) or **extrinsic** (arising from external factors) (Figure 10.2). Intrinsically motivated behaviors are performed because of the sense of personal satisfaction that they bring, while extrinsically motivated behaviors are performed in order to receive something from others.

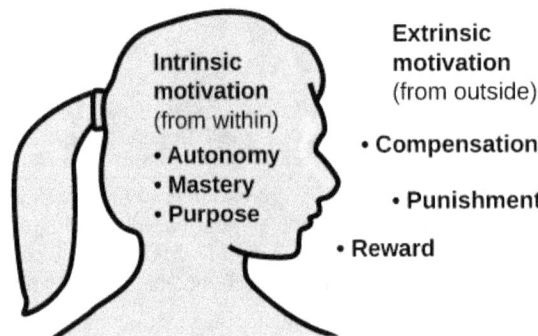

Figure 10.2 Intrinsic motivation comes from within the individual, while extrinsic motivation comes from outside the individual.

Think about why you are currently in college. Are you here because you enjoy learning and want to pursue an education to make yourself a more well-rounded individual? If so, then you are intrinsically motivated. However, if you are here because you want to get a college degree to make yourself more marketable for a high-paying career or to satisfy the demands of your parents, then your motivation is more extrinsic in nature.

In reality, our motivations are often a mix of both intrinsic and extrinsic factors, but the nature of the mix of these factors might change over time (often in ways that seem counter-intuitive). There is an old adage: "Choose a job that you love, and you will never have to work a day in your life," meaning that if you enjoy your occupation, work doesn't seem like . . . well, work. Some research suggests that this isn't necessarily the case (Daniel & Esser, 1980; Deci, 1972; Deci, Koestner, & Ryan, 1999). According to this research, receiving some sort of extrinsic reinforcement (i.e., getting paid) for engaging in behaviors that we enjoy leads to those behaviors being thought of as work no longer providing that same enjoyment. As a result, we might spend less time engaging in these reclassified behaviors in the absence of any extrinsic reinforcement. For example, Odessa loves baking, so in her free time, she bakes for fun. Oftentimes, after stocking shelves at her grocery store job, she often whips up pastries in the evenings because she enjoys baking. When a coworker in the store's bakery department leaves his job, Odessa applies for his position and gets transferred to the bakery department. Although she enjoys what she does in her new job, after a few months, she no longer has much desire to concoct tasty treats in her free time. Baking has become work in a way that changes her motivation to do it (Figure 10.3). What Odessa has experienced is called the overjustification effect—intrinsic motivation is diminished when extrinsic motivation is given. This can lead to extinguishing the intrinsic motivation and creating a dependence on extrinsic rewards for continued performance (Deci et al., 1999).

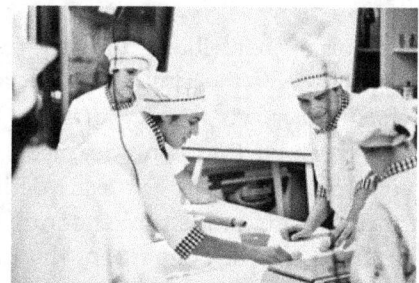

Figure 10.3 Research suggests that when something we love to do, like icing cakes, becomes our job, our intrinsic and extrinsic motivations to do it may change. (credit: Agustín Ruiz)

Other studies suggest that intrinsic motivation may not be so vulnerable to the effects of extrinsic reinforcements, and in fact, reinforcements such as verbal praise might actually increase intrinsic motivation (Arnold, 1976; Cameron & Pierce, 1994). In that case, Odessa's motivation to bake in her free time might remain high if, for example, customers regularly compliment her baking or cake decorating skills.

These apparent discrepancies in the researchers' findings may be understood by considering several factors. For one, physical reinforcement (such as money) and verbal reinforcement (such as praise) may affect an individual in very different ways. In fact, tangible rewards (i.e., money) tend to have more negative effects on intrinsic motivation than do intangible rewards (i.e., praise). Furthermore, the expectation of the extrinsic motivator by an individual is crucial: If the person expects to receive an extrinsic reward, then intrinsic motivation for the task tends to be reduced. If, however, there is no such expectation, and the extrinsic motivation is presented as a surprise, then intrinsic motivation for the task tends to persist (Deci et al., 1999).

In addition, culture may influence motivation. For example, in collectivistic cultures, it is common to do things for your family members because the emphasis is on the group and what is best for the entire group, rather than what is best for any one individual (Nisbett, Peng, Choi, & Norenzayan, 2001). This focus on others provides a broader perspective that takes into account both situational and cultural influences on behavior; thus, a more nuanced explanation of the causes of others' behavior becomes more likely. (You will learn more about collectivistic and individualistic cultures when you learn about social psychology.)

In educational settings, students are more likely to experience intrinsic motivation to learn when they feel a sense of belonging and respect in the classroom. This internalization can be enhanced if the evaluative aspects of the classroom are de-emphasized and if students feel that they exercise some control over the learning environment. Furthermore, providing students with activities that are challenging, yet doable, along with a rationale for engaging in various learning activities can enhance intrinsic motivation for those tasks (Niemiec & Ryan, 2009). Consider Hakim, a first-year law student with two courses this semester: Family Law and Criminal Law. The Family Law professor has a rather intimidating classroom: He likes to put students on the spot with tough questions, which often leaves students feeling belittled or embarrassed. Grades are based exclusively on quizzes and exams, and the instructor posts results of each test on the classroom door. In contrast, the Criminal Law professor facilitates classroom discussions and respectful debates in small groups. The majority of the course grade is not exam-based, but centers on a student-designed research project on a crime issue of the student's choice. Research suggests that Hakim will be less intrinsically motivated in his Family Law course, where students are intimidated in the classroom setting, and there is an emphasis on teacher-driven evaluations. Hakim is likely to experience a higher level of intrinsic motivation in his Criminal Law course, where the class setting encourages inclusive collaboration and a respect for ideas, and where students have more influence over their learning activities.

THEORIES ABOUT MOTIVATION

William James (1842–1910) was an important contributor to early research into motivation, and he is often referred to as the father of psychology in the United States. James theorized that behavior was driven by a number of instincts, which aid survival (**Figure 10.4**). From a biological perspective, an **instinct** is a species-specific pattern of behavior that is not learned. There was, however, considerable controversy among James and his contemporaries over the exact definition of instinct. James proposed several dozen special human instincts, but many of his contemporaries had their own lists that differed. A mother's protection of her baby, the urge to lick sugar, and hunting prey were among the human behaviors proposed as true instincts during James's era. This view—that human behavior is driven by instincts—received a fair amount of criticism because of the undeniable role of learning in shaping all sorts of human behavior. In fact, as early as the 1900s, some instinctive behaviors were experimentally demonstrated to result from associative learning (recall when you learned about Watson's conditioning of fear response in "Little Albert") (Faris, 1921).

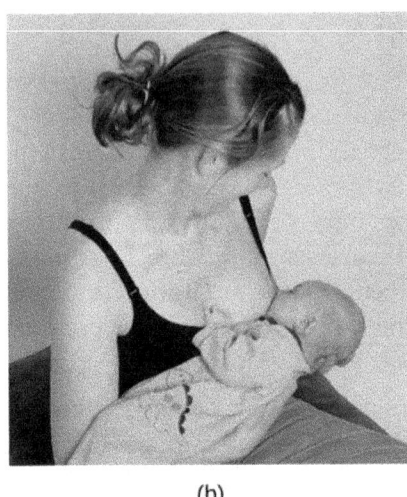

(a) (b)

Figure 10.4 (a) William James proposed the instinct theory of motivation, asserting that behavior is driven by instincts. (b) In humans, instincts may include behaviors such as an infant's rooting for a nipple and sucking. (credit b: modification of work by "Mothering Touch"/Flickr)

Another early theory of motivation proposed that the maintenance of homeostasis is particularly important in directing behavior. You may recall from your earlier reading that homeostasis is the tendency to maintain a balance, or optimal level, within a biological system. In a body system, a control center (which is often part of the brain) receives input from receptors (which are often complexes of neurons). The control center directs effectors (which may be other neurons) to correct any imbalance detected by the control center.

According to the **drive theory** of motivation, deviations from homeostasis create physiological needs. These needs result in psychological drive states that direct behavior to meet the need and, ultimately, bring the system back to homeostasis. For example, if it's been a while since you ate, your blood sugar levels will drop below normal. This low blood sugar will induce a physiological need and a corresponding drive state (i.e., hunger) that will direct you to seek out and consume food (**Figure 10.5**). Eating will eliminate the hunger, and, ultimately, your blood sugar levels will return to normal. Interestingly, drive theory also emphasizes the role that habits play in the type of behavioral response in which we engage. A **habit** is a pattern of behavior in which we regularly engage. Once we have engaged in a behavior that successfully reduces a drive, we are more likely to engage in that behavior whenever faced with that drive in the future (Graham & Weiner, 1996).

Figure 10.5 Hunger and subsequent eating are the result of complex physiological processes that maintain homeostasis. (credit "left": modification of work by "Gracie and Viv"/Flickr; credit "center": modification of work by Steven Depolo; credit "right": modification of work by Monica Renata)

Extensions of drive theory take into account levels of arousal as potential motivators. As you recall from your study of learning, these theories assert that there is an optimal level of arousal that we all try to maintain (Figure 10.6). If we are underaroused, we become bored and will seek out some sort of stimulation. On the other hand, if we are overaroused, we will engage in behaviors to reduce our arousal (Berlyne, 1960). Most students have experienced this need to maintain optimal levels of arousal over the course of their academic career. Think about how much stress students experience toward the end of spring semester. They feel overwhelmed with seemingly endless exams, papers, and major assignments that must be completed on time. They probably yearn for the rest and relaxation that awaits them over the extended summer break. However, once they finish the semester, it doesn't take too long before they begin to feel bored. Generally, by the time the next semester is beginning in the fall, many students are quite happy to return to school. This is an example of how arousal theory works.

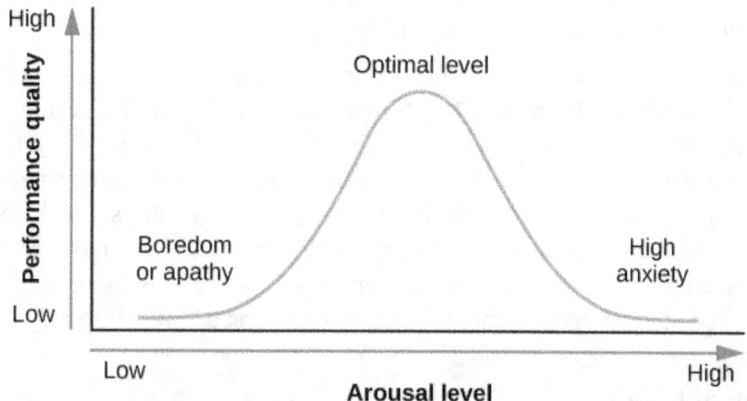

Figure 10.6 The concept of optimal arousal in relation to performance on a task is depicted here. Performance is maximized at the optimal level of arousal, and it tapers off during under- and overarousal.

So what is the optimal level of arousal? What level leads to the best performance? Research shows that moderate arousal is generally best; when arousal is very high or very low, performance tends to suffer (Yerkes & Dodson, 1908). Think of your arousal level regarding taking an exam for this class. If your level is very low, such as boredom and apathy, your performance will likely suffer. Similarly, a very high level, such as extreme anxiety, can be paralyzing and hinder performance. Consider the example of a softball team facing a tournament. They are favored to win their first game by a large margin, so they go into the game with a lower level of arousal and get beat by a less skilled team.

But optimal arousal level is more complex than a simple answer that the middle level is always best. Researchers Robert Yerkes (pronounced "Yerk-EES") and John Dodson discovered that the optimal arousal level depends on the complexity and difficulty of the task to be performed (Figure 10.7). This relationship is known as **Yerkes-Dodson law**, which holds that a simple task is performed best when arousal levels are relatively high and complex tasks are best performed when arousal levels are lower.

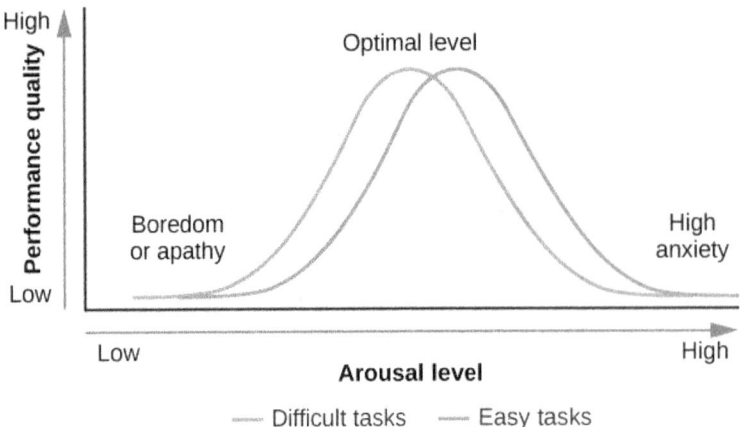

Figure 10.7 Task performance is best when arousal levels are in a middle range, with difficult tasks best performed under lower levels of arousal and simple tasks best performed under higher levels of arousal.

Self-efficacy and Social Motives

Self-efficacy is an individual's belief in her own capability to complete a task, which may include a previous successful completion of the exact task or a similar task. Albert Bandura (1994) theorized that an individual's sense of self-efficacy plays a pivotal role in motivating behavior. Bandura argues that motivation derives from expectations that we have about the consequences of our behaviors, and ultimately, it is the appreciation of our capacity to engage in a given behavior that will determine what we do and the future goals that we set for ourselves. For example, if you have a sincere belief in your ability to achieve at the highest level, you are more likely to take on challenging tasks and to not let setbacks dissuade you from seeing the task through to the end.

A number of theorists have focused their research on understanding social motives (McAdams & Constantian, 1983; McClelland & Liberman, 1949; Murray et al., 1938). Among the motives they describe are needs for achievement, affiliation, and intimacy. It is the need for achievement that drives accomplishment and performance. The need for affiliation encourages positive interactions with others, and the need for intimacy causes us to seek deep, meaningful relationships. Henry Murray et al. (1938) categorized these needs into domains. For example, the need for achievement and recognition falls under the domain of ambition. Dominance and aggression were recognized as needs under the domain of human power, and play was a recognized need in the domain of interpersonal affection.

Maslow's Hierarchy of Needs

While the theories of motivation described earlier relate to basic biological drives, individual characteristics, or social contexts, Abraham Maslow (1943) proposed a **hierarchy of needs** that spans the spectrum of motives ranging from the biological to the individual to the social. These needs are often depicted as a pyramid (Figure 10.8).

Figure 10.8 Maslow's hierarchy of needs is illustrated here. In some versions of the pyramid, cognitive and aesthetic needs are also included between esteem and self-actualization. Others include another tier at the top of the pyramid for self-transcendence.

At the base of the pyramid are all of the physiological needs that are necessary for survival. These are followed by basic needs for security and safety, the need to be loved and to have a sense of belonging, and the need to have self-worth and confidence. The top tier of the pyramid is self-actualization, which is a need that essentially equates to achieving one's full potential, and it can only be realized when needs lower on the pyramid have been met. To Maslow and humanistic theorists, self-actualization reflects the humanistic emphasis on positive aspects of human nature. Maslow suggested that this is an ongoing, life-long process and that only a small percentage of people actually achieve a self-actualized state (Francis & Kritsonis, 2006; Maslow, 1943).

According to Maslow (1943), one must satisfy lower-level needs before addressing those needs that occur higher in the pyramid. So, for example, if someone is struggling to find enough food to meet his nutritional requirements, it is quite unlikely that he would spend an inordinate amount of time thinking about whether others viewed him as a good person or not. Instead, all of his energies would be geared toward finding something to eat. However, it should be pointed out that Maslow's theory has been criticized for its subjective nature and its inability to account for phenomena that occur in the real world (Leonard, 1982). Other research has more recently addressed that late in life, Maslow proposed a self-transcendence level above self-actualization—to represent striving for meaning and purpose beyond the concerns of oneself (Koltko-Rivera, 2006). For example, people sometimes make self-sacrifices in order to make a political statement or in an attempt to improve the conditions of others. Mohandas K. Gandhi, a world-renowned advocate for independence through nonviolent protest, on several occasions went on hunger strikes to protest a particular situation. People may starve themselves or otherwise put themselves in danger displaying higher-level motives beyond their own needs.

> **LINK TO LEARNING**
>
> Check out this interactive exercise about Maslow's hierarchy of needs (http://openstax.org/l/hierneeds) to learn more.

10.2 Hunger and Eating

Learning Objectives

By the end of this section, you will be able to:
- Describe how hunger and eating are regulated
- Differentiate between levels of overweight and obesity and the associated health consequences
- Explain the health consequences resulting from anorexia and bulimia nervosa

Eating is essential for survival, and it is no surprise that a drive like hunger exists to ensure that we seek out sustenance. While this chapter will focus primarily on the physiological mechanisms that regulate hunger and eating, powerful social, cultural, and economic influences also play important roles. This section will explain the regulation of hunger, eating, and body weight, and we will discuss the adverse consequences of disordered eating.

PHYSIOLOGICAL MECHANISMS

There are a number of physiological mechanisms that serve as the basis for hunger. When our stomachs are empty, they contract. Typically, a person then experiences hunger pangs. Chemical messages travel to the brain, and serve as a signal to initiate feeding behavior. When our blood glucose levels drop, the pancreas and liver generate a number of chemical signals that induce hunger (Konturek et al., 2003; Novin, Robinson, Culbreth, & Tordoff, 1985) and thus initiate feeding behavior.

For most people, once they have eaten, they feel **satiation**, or fullness and satisfaction, and their eating behavior stops. Like the initiation of eating, satiation is also regulated by several physiological mechanisms. As blood glucose levels increase, the pancreas and liver send signals to shut off hunger and eating (Drazen & Woods, 2003; Druce, Small, & Bloom, 2004; Greary, 1990). The food's passage through the gastrointestinal tract also provides important satiety signals to the brain (Woods, 2004), and fat cells release **leptin**, a satiety hormone.

The various hunger and satiety signals that are involved in the regulation of eating are integrated in the brain. Research suggests that several areas of the hypothalamus and hindbrain are especially important sites where this integration occurs (Ahima & Antwi, 2008; Woods & D'Alessio, 2008). Ultimately, activity in the brain determines whether or not we engage in feeding behavior (Figure 10.9).

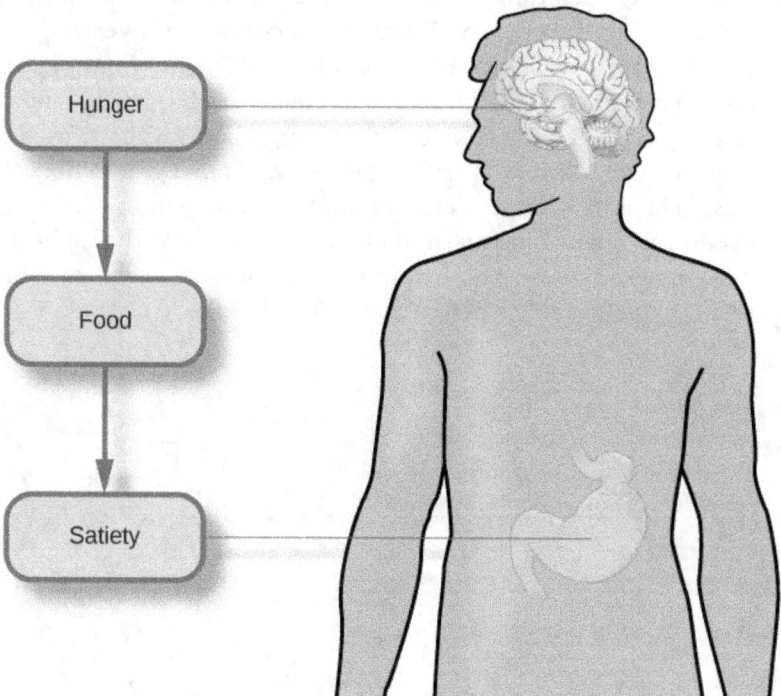

Figure 10.9 Hunger and eating are regulated by a complex interplay of hunger and satiety signals that are integrated in the brain.

METABOLISM AND BODY WEIGHT

Our body weight is affected by a number of factors, including gene-environment interactions, and the number of calories we consume versus the number of calories we burn in daily activity. If our caloric intake exceeds our caloric use, our bodies store excess energy in the form of fat. If we consume fewer calories than we burn off, then stored fat will be converted to energy. Our energy expenditure is obviously affected by our levels of activity, but our body's metabolic rate also comes into play. A person's **metabolic rate** is the amount of energy that is expended in a given period of time, and there is tremendous individual variability in our metabolic rates. People with high rates of metabolism are able to burn off calories more easily than those with lower rates of metabolism.

We all experience fluctuations in our weight from time to time, but generally, most people's weights fluctuate within a narrow margin, in the absence of extreme changes in diet and/or physical activity. This observation led some to propose a set-point theory of body weight regulation. The **set-point theory** asserts that each individual has an ideal body weight, or set point, which is resistant to change. This set-point is genetically predetermined and efforts to move our weight significantly from the set-point are resisted by compensatory changes in energy intake and/or expenditure (Speakman et al., 2011).

Some of the predictions generated from this particular theory have not received empirical support. For example, there are no changes in metabolic rate between individuals who had recently lost significant amounts of weight and a control group (Weinsier et al., 2000). In addition, the set-point theory fails to account for the influence of social and environmental factors in the regulation of body weight (Martin-Gronert & Ozanne, 2013; Speakman et al., 2011). Despite these limitations, set-point theory is still often used as a simple, intuitive explanation of how body weight is regulated. See **Psychological Disorders** for further discussion about eating disorders.

OBESITY

When someone weighs more than what is generally accepted as healthy for a given height, they are considered overweight or obese. According to the Centers for Disease Control and Prevention (CDC), an adult with a body mass index (BMI) between 25 and 29.9 is considered **overweight** (Figure 10.10). An adult with a BMI of 30 or higher is considered **obese** (Centers for Disease Control and Prevention [CDC], 2012). People who are so overweight that they are at risk for death are classified as morbidly obese. **Morbid obesity** is defined as having a BMI over 40. Note that although BMI has been used as a healthy weight indicator by the World Health Organization (WHO), the CDC, and other groups, its value as an assessment tool has been questioned. The BMI is most useful for studying populations, which is the work of these organizations. It is less useful in assessing an individual since height and weight measurements fail to account for important factors like fitness level. An athlete, for example, may have a high BMI because the tool doesn't distinguish between the body's percentage of fat and muscle in a person's weight.

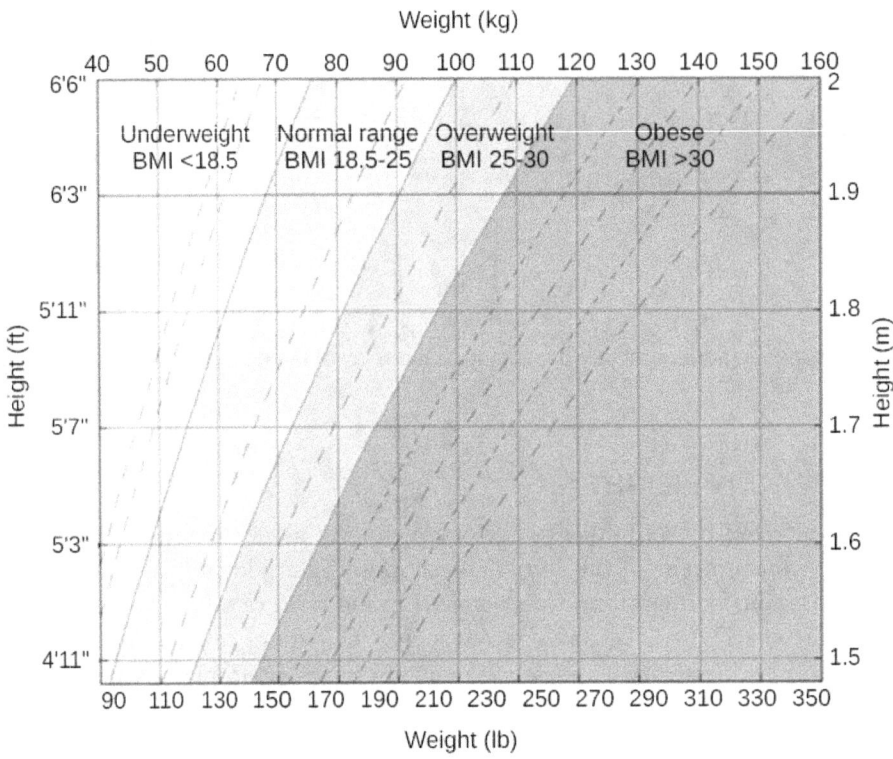

Figure 10.10 This chart shows how adult BMI is calculated. Individuals find their height on the y-axis and their weight on the x-axis to determine their BMI.

Being extremely overweight or obese is a risk factor for several negative health consequences. These include, but are not limited to, an increased risk for cardiovascular disease, stroke, Type 2 diabetes, liver disease, sleep apnea, colon cancer, breast cancer, infertility, and arthritis. Given that it is estimated that in the United States around one-third of the adult population is obese and that nearly two-thirds of adults and one in six children qualify as overweight (CDC, 2012), there is substantial interest in trying to understand how to combat this important public health concern.

What causes someone to be overweight or obese? You have already read that both genes and environment are important factors for determining body weight, and if more calories are consumed than expended, excess energy is stored as fat. However, socioeconomic status and the physical environment must also be considered as contributing factors (CDC, 2012). For example, an individual who lives in an impoverished neighborhood that is overrun with crime may never feel comfortable walking or biking to work or to the local market. This might limit the amount of physical activity in which he engages and result in an increased body weight. Similarly, some people may not be able to afford healthy food options from their market, or these options may be unavailable (especially in urban areas or poorer neighborhoods); therefore, some people rely primarily on available, inexpensive, high fat, and high calorie fast food as their primary source of nutrition.

Generally, overweight and obese individuals are encouraged to try to reduce their weights through a combination of both diet and exercise. While some people are very successful with these approaches, many struggle to lose excess weight. In cases in which a person has had no success with repeated attempts to reduce weight or is at risk for death because of obesity, bariatric surgery may be recommended. **Bariatric surgery** is a type of surgery specifically aimed at weight reduction, and it involves modifying the gastrointestinal system to reduce the amount of food that can be eaten and/or limiting how much of the digested food can be absorbed (Figure 10.11) (Mayo Clinic, 2013). A recent meta-analysis suggests that bariatric surgery is more effective than non-surgical treatment for obesity in the two-years immediately following the procedure, but to date, no long-term studies yet exist (Gloy et al., 2013).

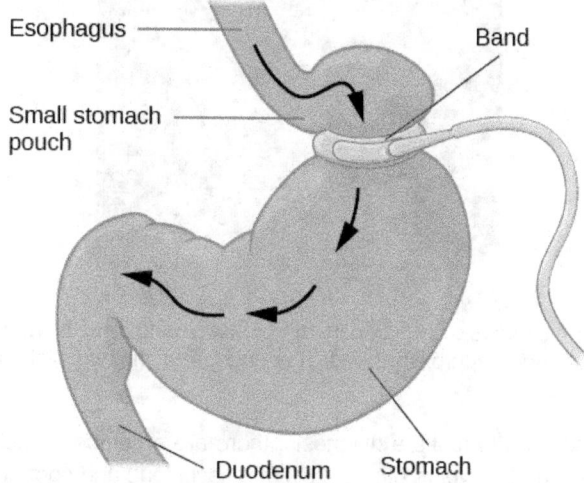

Figure 10.11 Gastric banding surgery creates a small pouch of stomach, reducing the size of the stomach that can be used for digestion.

LINK TO LEARNING

Watch this **video that describes two different types of bariatric surgeries** (http://openstax.org/l/barsurgery) to learn more.

DIG DEEPER

Prader-Willi Syndrome

Prader-Willi Syndrome (PWS) is a genetic disorder that results in persistent feelings of intense hunger and reduced rates of metabolism. Typically, affected children have to be supervised around the clock to ensure that they do not engage in excessive eating. Currently, PWS is the leading genetic cause of morbid obesity in children, and it is associated with a number of cognitive deficits and emotional problems (Figure 10.12).

Figure 10.12 Eugenia Martínez Vallejo, depicted in this 1680 painting, may have had Prader-Willi syndrome. At just eight years old, she weighed approximately 120 pounds, and she was nicknamed "La Monstrua" (the monster).

While genetic testing can be used to make a diagnosis, there are a number of behavioral diagnostic criteria associated with PWS. From birth to 2 years of age, lack of muscle tone and poor sucking behavior may serve as early signs of PWS. Developmental delays are seen between the ages of 6 and 12, and excessive eating and cognitive deficits associated with PWS usually onset a little later.

While the exact mechanisms of PWS are not fully understood, there is evidence that affected individuals have hypothalamic abnormalities. This is not surprising, given the hypothalamus's role in regulating hunger and eating. However, as you will learn in the next section of this chapter, the hypothalamus is also involved in the regulation of sexual behavior. Consequently, many individuals suffering from PWS fail to reach sexual maturity during adolescence.

There is no current treatment or cure for PWS. However, if weight can be controlled in these individuals, then their life expectancies are significantly increased (historically, sufferers of PWS often died in adolescence or early adulthood). Advances in the use of various psychoactive medications and growth hormones continue to enhance the quality of life for individuals with PWS (Cassidy & Driscoll, 2009; Prader-Willi Syndrome Association, 2012).

EATING DISORDERS

While nearly two out of three US adults struggle with issues related to being overweight, a smaller, but significant, portion of the population has eating disorders that typically result in being normal weight or underweight. Often, these individuals are fearful of gaining weight. Individuals who suffer from bulimia nervosa and anorexia nervosa face many adverse health consequences (Mayo Clinic, 2012a, 2012b).

People suffering from **bulimia nervosa** engage in binge eating behavior that is followed by an attempt to compensate for the large amount of food consumed. Purging the food by inducing vomiting or through the use of laxatives are two common compensatory behaviors. Some affected individuals engage in excessive amounts of exercise to compensate for their binges. Bulimia is associated with many adverse health consequences that can include kidney failure, heart failure, and tooth decay. In addition, these individuals often suffer from anxiety and depression, and they are at an increased risk for substance abuse (Mayo Clinic, 2012b). The lifetime prevalence rate for bulimia nervosa is estimated at around 1% for women and less than 0.5% for men (Smink, van Hoeken, & Hoek, 2012).

As of the 2013 release of the *Diagnostic and Statistical Manual, fifth edition*, **Binge eating disorder** is a disorder recognized by the American Psychiatric Association (APA). Unlike with bulimia, eating binges are not followed by inappropriate behavior, such as purging, but they are followed by distress, including feelings of guilt and embarrassment. The resulting psychological distress distinguishes binge eating disorder from overeating (American Psychiatric Association [APA], 2013).

Anorexia nervosa is an eating disorder characterized by the maintenance of a body weight well below average through starvation and/or excessive exercise. Individuals suffering from anorexia nervosa often have a **distorted body image**, referenced in literature as a type of body dysmorphia, meaning that they view themselves as overweight even though they are not. Like bulimia nervosa, anorexia nervosa is associated with a number of significant negative health outcomes: bone loss, heart failure, kidney failure, amenorrhea (cessation of the menstrual period), reduced function of the gonads, and in extreme cases, death. Furthermore, there is an increased risk for a number of psychological problems, which include anxiety disorders, mood disorders, and substance abuse (Mayo Clinic, 2012a). Estimates of the prevalence of anorexia nervosa vary from study to study but generally range from just under one percent to just over four percent in women. Generally, prevalence rates are considerably lower for men (Smink et al., 2012).

LINK TO LEARNING

Watch this news story about an Italian advertising campaign to raise public awareness of anorexia nervosa (http://openstax.org/l/anorexic) to learn more.

While both anorexia and bulimia nervosa occur in men and women of many different cultures, Caucasian females from Western societies tend to be the most at-risk population. Recent research indicates that females between the ages of 15 and 19 are most at risk, and it has long been suspected that these eating disorders are culturally-bound phenomena that are related to messages of a thin ideal often portrayed in popular media and the fashion world (**Figure 10.13**) (Smink et al., 2012). While social factors play an important role in the development of eating disorders, there is also evidence that genetic factors may predispose people to these disorders (Collier & Treasure, 2004).

Figure 10.13 Young women in our society are inundated with images of extremely thin models (sometimes accurately depicted and sometimes digitally altered to make them look even thinner). These images may contribute to eating disorders. (credit: Peter Duhon)

10.3 Sexual Behavior

Learning Objectives

By the end of this section, you will be able to:
- Understand basic biological mechanisms regulating sexual behavior and motivation
- Appreciate the importance of Alfred Kinsey's research on human sexuality
- Recognize the contributions that William Masters and Virginia Johnson's research made to our understanding of the sexual response cycle
- Define sexual orientation and gender identity

Like food, sex is an important part of our lives. From an evolutionary perspective, the reason is obvious—perpetuation of the species. Sexual behavior in humans, however, involves much more than reproduction. This section provides an overview of research that has been conducted on human sexual behavior and motivation. This section will close with a discussion of issues related to gender and sexual orientation.

PHYSIOLOGICAL MECHANISMS OF SEXUAL BEHAVIOR AND MOTIVATION

Much of what we know about the physiological mechanisms that underlie sexual behavior and motivation comes from animal research. As you've learned, the hypothalamus plays an important role in motivated behaviors, and sex is no exception. In fact, lesions to an area of the hypothalamus called the medial preoptic area completely disrupt a male rat's ability to engage in sexual behavior. Surprisingly, medial preoptic lesions do not change how hard a male rat is willing to work to gain access to a sexually receptive female (Figure 10.14). This suggests that the ability to engage in sexual behavior and the motivation to do so may be mediated by neural systems distinct from one another.

Figure 10.14 A male rat that cannot engage in sexual behavior still seeks receptive females, suggesting that the ability to engage in sexual behavior and the motivation to do so are mediated by different systems in the brain. (credit: Jason Snyder)

Animal research suggests that limbic system structures such as the amygdala and nucleus accumbens are especially important for sexual motivation. Damage to these areas results in a decreased motivation to engage in sexual behavior, while leaving the ability to do so intact (**Figure 10.15**) (Everett, 1990). Similar dissociations of sexual motivation and sexual ability have also been observed in the female rat (Becker, Rudick, & Jenkins, 2001; Jenkins & Becker, 2001).

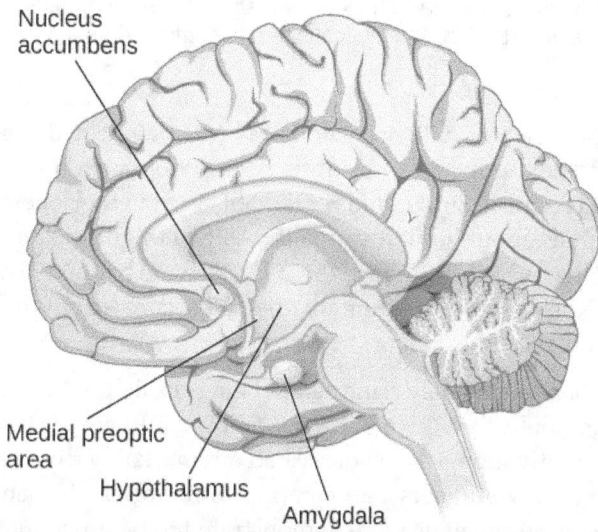

Figure 10.15 The medial preoptic area, an area of the hypothalamus, is involved in the ability to engage in sexual behavior, but it does not affect sexual motivation. In contrast, the amygdala and nucleus accumbens are involved in motivation for sexual behavior, but they do not affect the ability to engage in it.

Although human sexual behavior is much more complex than that seen in rats, some parallels between animals and humans can be drawn from this research. The worldwide popularity of drugs used to treat erectile dysfunction (Conrad, 2005) speaks to the fact that sexual motivation and the ability to engage in sexual behavior can also be dissociated in humans. Moreover, disorders that involve abnormal hypothalamic function are often associated with hypogonadism (reduced function of the gonads) and reduced sexual function (e.g., Prader-Willi syndrome). Given the hypothalamus's role in endocrine function, it is not surprising that hormones secreted by the endocrine system also play important roles in sexual motivation and behavior. For example, many animals show no sign of sexual motivation in the absence of the appropriate combination of sex hormones from their gonads. While this is not the case for humans, there is considerable evidence that sexual motivation for both men and women varies as a function of circulating testosterone levels (Bhasin, Enzlin, Coviello, & Basson, 2007; Carter, 1992; Sherwin, 1988).

KINSEY'S RESEARCH

Before the late 1940s, access to reliable, empirically-based information on sex was limited. Physicians were considered authorities on all issues related to sex, despite the fact that they had little to no training in these issues, and it is likely that most of what people knew about sex had been learned either through their own experiences or by talking with their peers. Convinced that people would benefit from a more open dialogue on issues related to human sexuality, Dr. Alfred Kinsey of Indiana University initiated large-scale survey research on the topic (Figure 10.16). The results of some of these efforts were published in two books—*Sexual Behavior in the Human Male* and *Sexual Behavior in the Human Female*—which were published in 1948 and 1953, respectively (Bullough, 1998).

Figure 10.16 In 1947, Alfred Kinsey established The Kinsey Institute for Research, Sex, Gender and Reproduction at Indiana University, shown here in 2011. The Kinsey Institute has continued as a research site of important psychological studies for decades.

At the time, the Kinsey reports were quite sensational. Never before had the American public seen its private sexual behavior become the focus of scientific scrutiny on such a large scale. The books, which were filled with statistics and scientific lingo, sold remarkably well to the general public, and people began to engage in open conversations about human sexuality. As you might imagine, not everyone was happy that this information was being published. In fact, these books were banned in some countries. Ultimately, the controversy resulted in Kinsey losing funding that he had secured from the Rockefeller Foundation to continue his research efforts (Bancroft, 2004).

Although Kinsey's research has been widely criticized as being riddled with sampling and statistical errors (Jenkins, 2010), there is little doubt that this research was very influential in shaping future research on human sexual behavior and motivation. Kinsey described a remarkably diverse range of sexual behaviors and experiences reported by the volunteers participating in his research. Behaviors that had once been considered exceedingly rare or problematic were demonstrated to be much more common and innocuous than previously imagined (Bancroft, 2004; Bullough, 1998).

LINK TO LEARNING

Watch this trailer for the 2004 film Kinsey that depicts Alfred Kinsey's life and research (http://openstax.org/l/Kinsey) to learn more.

Among the results of Kinsey's research were the findings that women are as interested and experienced in sex as their male counterparts, that both males and females masturbate without adverse health consequences, and that homosexual acts are fairly common (Bancroft, 2004). Kinsey also developed a continuum known as the Kinsey scale that is still commonly used today to categorize an individual's sexual orientation (Jenkins, 2010). According to that scale, **sexual orientation** is an individual's emotional and erotic attractions to same-sexed individuals (**homosexual**), opposite-sexed individuals (**heterosexual**), or both (**bisexual**).

MASTERS AND JOHNSON'S RESEARCH

In 1966, William Masters and Virginia Johnson published a book detailing the results of their observations of nearly 700 people who agreed to participate in their study of physiological responses during sexual behavior. Unlike Kinsey, who used personal interviews and surveys to collect data, Masters and Johnson observed people having intercourse in a variety of positions, and they observed people masturbating, manually or with the aid of a device. While this was occurring, researchers recorded measurements of physiological variables, such as blood pressure and respiration rate, as well as measurements of sexual arousal, such as vaginal lubrication and penile tumescence (swelling associated with an erection). In total, Masters and Johnson observed nearly 10,000 sexual acts as a part of their research (Hock, 2008).

Based on these observations, Masters and Johnson divided the **sexual response cycle** into four phases that are fairly similar in men and women: excitement, plateau, orgasm, and resolution (**Figure 10.17**). The **excitement** phase is the arousal phase of the sexual response cycle, and it is marked by erection of the penis or clitoris and lubrication and expansion of the vaginal canal. During **plateau**, women experience further swelling of the vagina and increased blood flow to the labia minora, and men experience full erection and often exhibit pre-ejaculatory fluid. Both men and women experience increases in muscle tone during this time. **Orgasm** is marked in women by rhythmic contractions of the pelvis and uterus along with increased muscle tension. In men, pelvic contractions are accompanied by a buildup of seminal fluid near the urethra that is ultimately forced out by contractions of genital muscles, (i.e., ejaculation). **Resolution** is the relatively rapid return to an unaroused state accompanied by a decrease in blood pressure and muscular relaxation. While many women can quickly repeat the sexual response cycle, men must pass through a longer refractory period as part of resolution. The **refractory period** is a period of time that follows an orgasm during which an individual is incapable of experiencing another orgasm. In men, the duration of the refractory period can vary dramatically from individual to individual with some refractory periods as short as several minutes and others as long as a day. As men age, their refractory periods tend to span longer periods of time.

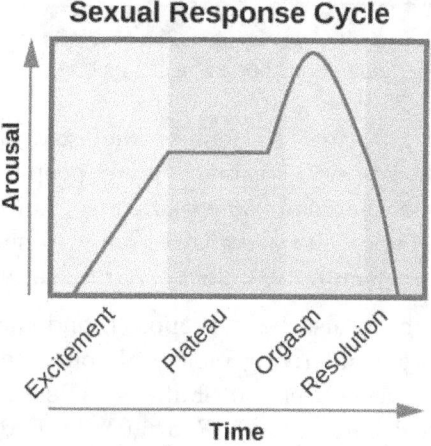

Figure 10.17 This graph illustrates the different phases of the sexual response cycle as described by Masters and Johnson.

In addition to the insights that their research provided with regards to the sexual response cycle and the multi-orgasmic potential of women, Masters and Johnson also collected important information about reproductive anatomy. Their research demonstrated the oft-cited statistic of the average size of a flaccid and an erect penis (3 and 6 inches, respectively) as well as dispelling long-held beliefs about relationships between the size of a man's erect penis and his ability to provide sexual pleasure to his female partner. Furthermore, they determined that the vagina is a very elastic structure that can conform to penises of various sizes (Hock, 2008).

SEXUAL ORIENTATION

As mentioned earlier, a person's sexual orientation is their emotional and erotic attraction toward another individual (Figure 10.18). While the majority of people identify as heterosexual, there is a sizable population of people within the United States who identify as homosexual, bisexual, pansexual, asexual, or other non-hetero sexualities. Research suggests that somewhere between 3% and 10% of the population identifies as homosexual (Kinsey, Pomeroy, & Martin, 1948; LeVay, 1996; Pillard & Bailey, 1995). (Bisexual people are attracted to people of their own gender and another gender; pansexual people experience attraction without regard to sex, gender identity or gender expression; asexual people do not experience sexual attraction or have little or no interest in sexual activity.)

Figure 10.18 Between 3% and 10% of the adult population identifies as homosexual. (credit: Till Krech)

Issues of sexual orientation have long fascinated scientists interested in determining what causes one individual to be straight while another is gay. For many years, people believed that these differences arose because of different socialization and familial experiences. However, research has consistently demonstrated that the family backgrounds and experiences are very similar among heterosexuals and homosexuals (Bell, Weinberg, & Hammersmith, 1981; Ross & Arrindell, 1988).

Genetic and biological mechanisms have also been proposed, and the balance of research evidence suggests that sexual orientation has an underlying biological component. For instance, over the past 25 years, research has demonstrated gene-level contributions to sexual orientation (Bailey & Pillard, 1991; Hamer, Hu, Magnuson, Hu, & Pattatucci, 1993; Rodriguez-Larralde & Paradisi, 2009), with some researchers estimating that genes account for at least half of the variability seen in human sexual orientation (Pillard & Bailey, 1998). Other studies report differences in brain structure and function between heterosexuals and homosexuals (Allen & Gorski, 1992; Byne et al., 2001; Hu et al., 2008; LeVay, 1991; Ponseti et al., 2006; Rahman & Wilson, 2003a; Swaab & Hofman, 1990), and even differences in basic body structure and function have been observed (Hall & Kimura, 1994; Lippa, 2003; Loehlin & McFadden, 2003; McFadden & Champlin, 2000; McFadden & Pasanen, 1998; Rahman & Wilson, 2003b). In aggregate, the data suggest that to a significant extent, sexual orientations are something with which we are born.

Misunderstandings About Sexual Orientation

Regardless of how sexual orientation is determined, research has made clear that sexual orientation is not a choice, but rather it is a relatively stable characteristic of a person that cannot be changed. Claims of successful gay conversion therapy have received wide criticism from the research community due to significant concerns with research design, recruitment of experimental participants, and interpretation of data. As such, there is no credible scientific evidence to suggest that individuals can change their sexual orientation (Jenkins, 2010).

Dr. Robert Spitzer, the author of one of the most widely-cited examples of successful conversion therapy, apologized to both the scientific community and the gay community for his mistakes, and he publically recanted his own paper in a public letter addressed to the editor of *Archives of Sexual Behavior* in the spring of 2012 (Carey, 2012). In this letter, Spitzer wrote,

> I was considering writing something that would acknowledge that I now judge the major critiques of the study as largely correct. . . . I believe I owe the gay community an apology for my study making unproven claims of the efficacy of reparative therapy. I also apologize to any gay person who wasted time or energy undergoing some form of reparative therapy because they believed that I had proven that reparative therapy works with some "highly motivated" individuals. (Becker, 2012, pars. 2, 5)

Citing research that suggests not only that gay conversion therapy is ineffective, but also potentially harmful, legislative efforts to make such therapy illegal have either been enacted (e.g., it is now illegal in California) or are underway across the United States, and many professional organizations have issued statements against this practice (Human Rights Campaign, n.d.).

LINK TO LEARNING

Read this **draft of Dr. Spitzer's letter (http://openstax.org/l/spitzer)** to learn more.

GENDER IDENTITY

Many people conflate sexual orientation with gender identity because of stereotypical attitudes that exist about gay and lesbian sexuality. In reality, these are two related, but different, issues. **Gender identity** refers to one's sense of being male or female. Generally, our gender identities correspond to our chromosomal and phenotypic sex, but this is not always the case. When individuals do not feel comfortable identifying with the gender associated with their biological sex, then they experience gender dysphoria. **Gender dysphoria** is a diagnostic category in the fifth edition of the *Diagnostic and Statistical Manual of Mental Disorders* (DSM-5) that describes individuals who do not identify as the gender that most people would assume they are. This dysphoria must persist for at least six months and result in significant distress or dysfunction to meet DSM-5 diagnostic criteria. In order for children to be assigned this diagnostic category, they must verbalize their desire to become the other gender.

Many people who are classified as gender dysphoric seek to live their lives in ways that are consistent with their own gender identity. This involves dressing in opposite-sex clothing and assuming an opposite-sex identity. These individuals may also undertake **transgender hormone therapy** in an attempt to make their bodies look more like the opposite sex, and in some cases, they elect to have surgeries to alter the appearance of their external genitalia to resemble that of their gender identity (Figure 10.19). While these may sound like drastic changes, gender dysphoric individuals take these steps because their bodies seem to them to be a mistake of nature, and they seek to correct this mistake.

Our scientific knowledge and general understanding about gender identity continue to evolve, and young people today have more opportunity to explore and openly express different ideas about what gender means than previous generations. Recent studies indicate that that majority of millennials (those ages 18–34) regard gender as a spectrum instead of a strict male/female binary, and that 12% identify as transgender or gender non-conforming. Additionally, over half of people ages 13–20 know people who use gender-neutral pronouns (such as they/them) (Kennedy, 2017). This change in language means that millennials and Generation Z people understand the experience of gender itself differently. As young people lead this change, other changes are emerging in a range of spheres, from public bathroom policies to retail organizations. For example, some retailers are starting to change traditional gender-based marketing of products, such as removing "pink and blue" clothing and toy aisles. Even with these changes, those who exist outside of traditional gender norms face difficult challenges. Even people who vary slightly from traditional norms can be the target of discrimination and sometimes even violence.

Figure 10.19 Actress Laverne Cox, who is openly transgender, is the first transgender actress to portray a transgender character on a regular television series. She is also an advocate for LGBTQ+ issues outside of her career, such as in this "Ain't I a Woman?" speaking tour. (credit: modification of work by "KOMUnews_Flickr"/Flickr)

LINK TO LEARNING

Hear firsthand about the transgender experience and the disconnect that occurs when one's self-identity is betrayed by one's body. Watch this brief interview with Carmen Carrera and Laverne Cox on Katie Couric's talk show (http://openstax.org/l/lcox) to learn more. This video about transgender immigrants' experiences (http://openstax.org/l/transimm) explains more struggles faced globally by those in the transgender community.

CULTURAL FACTORS IN SEXUAL ORIENTATION AND GENDER IDENTITY

Issues related to sexual orientation and gender identity are very much influenced by sociocultural factors. Even the ways in which we define sexual orientation and gender vary from one culture to the next. While in the United States heterosexuality has historically been viewed as the norm, there are societies that have different attitudes regarding gay behavior. In fact, in some instances, periods of exclusively homosexual behavior are socially prescribed as a part of normal development and maturation. For example, in parts of New Guinea, young boys are expected to engage in sexual behavior with other boys for a given period of time because it is believed that doing so is necessary for these boys to become men (Baldwin & Baldwin, 1989).

There has historically been a two-gendered culture in the United States. We have tended to classify an individual as either male or female. However, in some cultures there are additional gender variants resulting in more than two gender categories. For example, in Thailand, you can be male, female, or kathoey. A kathoey is an individual who would be described as intersexed or transgender in the United States (Tangmunkongvorakul, Banwell, Carmichael, Utomo, & Sleigh, 2010). Intersex is a broad term referring to people whose bodies are not strictly biologically male or female (Hughes, et al. 2006). Intersex conditions can present at any time during life (Creighton, 2001). Sometimes a child may be born with components of male and female genitals, and other times XY chromosomal differences are present (Creighton, 2001; Hughes, et al. 2006).

> ### DIG DEEPER
>
> **The Case of David Reimer**
>
> In August of 1965, Janet and Ronald Reimer of Winnipeg, Canada, welcomed the birth of their twin sons, Bruce and Brian. Within a few months, the twins were experiencing urinary problems; doctors recommended the problems could be alleviated by having the boys circumcised. A malfunction of the medical equipment used to perform the circumcision resulted in Bruce's penis being irreparably damaged. Distraught, Janet and Ronald looked to expert advice on what to do with their baby boy. By happenstance, the couple became aware of Dr. John Money at Johns Hopkins University and his theory of psychosexual neutrality (Colapinto, 2000).
>
> Dr. Money had spent a considerable amount of time researching transgender individuals and individuals born with ambiguous genitalia. As a result of this work, he developed a theory of psychosexual neutrality. His theory asserted that we are essentially neutral at birth with regard to our gender identity and that we don't assume a concrete gender identity until we begin to master language. Furthermore, Dr. Money believed that the way in which we are socialized in early life is ultimately much more important than our biology in determining our gender identity (Money, 1962).
>
> Dr. Money encouraged Janet and Ronald to bring the twins to Johns Hopkins University, and he convinced them that they should raise Bruce as a girl. Left with few other options at the time, Janet and Ronald agreed to have Bruce's testicles removed and to raise him as a girl. When they returned home to Canada, they brought with them Brian and his "sister," Brenda, along with specific instructions to never reveal to Brenda that she had been born a boy (Colapinto, 2000).
>
> Early on, Dr. Money shared with the scientific community the great success of this natural experiment that seemed to fully support his theory of psychosexual neutrality (Money, 1975). Indeed, in early interviews with the children it appeared that Brenda was a typical little girl who liked to play with "girly" toys and do "girly" things.
>
> However, Dr. Money was less than forthcoming with information that seemed to argue against the success of the case. In reality, Brenda's parents were constantly concerned that their little girl wasn't really behaving as most girls did, and by the time Brenda was nearing adolescence, it was painfully obvious to the family that she was really having a hard time identifying as a female. In addition, Brenda was becoming increasingly reluctant to continue her visits with Dr. Money to the point that she threatened suicide if her parents made her go back to see him again.
>
> At that point, Janet and Ronald disclosed the true nature of Brenda's early childhood to their daughter. While initially shocked, Brenda reported that things made sense to her now, and ultimately, by the time she was an adolescent, Brenda had decided to identify as a male. Thus, she became David Reimer.
>
> David was quite comfortable in his masculine role. He made new friends and began to think about his future. Although his castration had left him infertile, he still wanted to be a father. In 1990, David married a single mother and loved his new role as a husband and father. In 1997, David was made aware that Dr. Money was continuing to publicize his case as a success supporting his theory of psychosexual neutrality. This prompted David and his brother to go public with their experiences in attempt to discredit the doctor's publications. While this revelation created a firestorm in the scientific community for Dr. Money, it also triggered a series of unfortunate events that ultimately led to David committing suicide in 2004 (O'Connell, 2004).
>
> This sad story speaks to the complexities involved in gender identity. While the Reimer case had earlier been paraded as a hallmark of how socialization trumped biology in terms of gender identity, the truth of the story made the scientific and medical communities more cautious in dealing with cases that involve intersex children and how to deal with their unique circumstances. In fact, stories like this one have prompted measures to prevent unnecessary harm and suffering to children who might have issues with gender identity. For example,

in 2013, a law took effect in Germany allowing parents of intersex children to classify their children as indeterminate so that children can self-assign the appropriate gender once they have fully developed their own gender identities (Paramaguru, 2013).

LINK TO LEARNING

Watch this news story about the experiences of David Reimer and his family (http://openstax.org/l/reimer) to learn more.

10.4 Emotion

Learning Objectives

By the end of this section, you will be able to:
- Explain the major theories of emotion
- Describe the role that limbic structures play in emotional processing
- Understand the ubiquitous nature of producing and recognizing emotional expression

As we move through our daily lives, we experience a variety of emotions. An **emotion** is a subjective state of being that we often describe as our feelings. Emotions result from the combination of subjective experience, expression, cognitive appraisal, and physiological responses (Levenson, Carstensen, Friesen, & Ekman, 1991). However, as discussed later in the chapter, the exact order in which the components occur is not clear, and some parts may happen at the same time. An emotion often begins with a subjective (individual) experience, which is a stimulus. Often the stimulus is external, but it does not have to be from the outside world. For example, it might be that one thinks about war and becomes sad, even though he or she never experienced war. Emotional expression refers to the way one displays an emotion and includes nonverbal and verbal behaviors (Gross, 1999). One also performs a cognitive appraisal in which a person tries to determine the way he or she will be impacted by a situation (Roseman & Smith, 2001). In addition, emotions include physiological responses, such as possible changes in heart rate, sweating, etc. (Soussignan, 2002).

The words emotion and mood are sometimes used interchangeably, but psychologists use these words to refer to two different things. Typically, the word emotion indicates a subjective, affective state that is relatively intense and that occurs in response to something we experience (**Figure 10.20**). Emotions are often thought to be consciously experienced and intentional. Mood, on the other hand, refers to a prolonged, less intense, affective state that does not occur in response to something we experience. Mood states may not be consciously recognized and do not carry the intentionality that is associated with emotion (Beedie, Terry, Lane, & Devonport, 2011). Here we will focus on emotion, and you will learn more about mood in the chapter that covers psychological disorders.

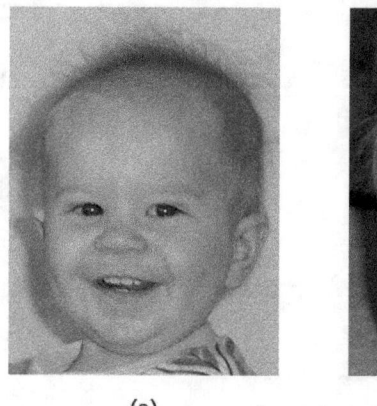 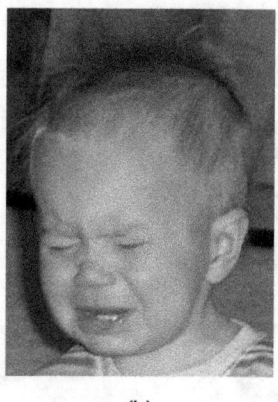

(a) (b)

Figure 10.20 Toddlers can cycle through emotions quickly, being (a) extremely happy one moment and (b) extremely sad the next. (credit a: modification of work by Kerry Ceszyk; credit b: modification of work by Kerry Ceszyk)

We can be at the heights of joy or in the depths of despair. We might feel angry when we are betrayed, fear when we are threatened, and surprised when something unexpected happens. This section will outline some of the most well-known theories explaining our emotional experience and provide insight into the biological bases of emotion. This section closes with a discussion of the ubiquitous nature of facial expressions of emotion and our abilities to recognize those expressions in others.

THEORIES OF EMOTION

Our emotional states are combinations of physiological arousal, psychological appraisal, and subjective experiences. Together, these are the **components of emotion**, and our experiences, backgrounds, and cultures inform our emotions. Therefore, different people may have different emotional experiences even when faced with similar circumstances. Over time, several different theories of emotion, shown in Figure 10.21, have been proposed to explain how the various components of emotion interact with one another.

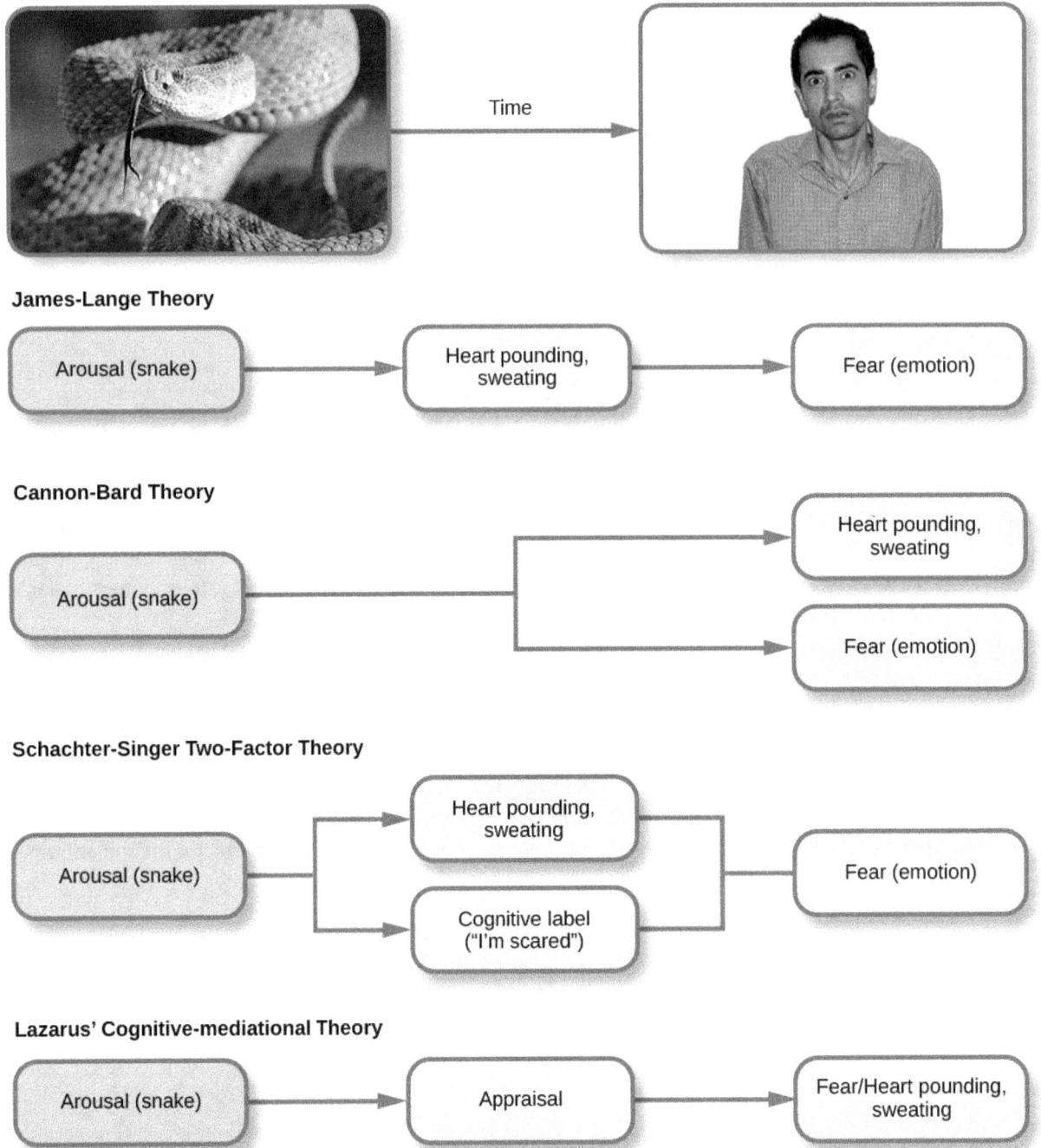

Figure 10.21 This figure illustrates the major assertions of the James-Lange, Cannon-Bard, and Schachter-Singer two-factor theories of emotion. (credit "snake": modification of work by "tableatny"/Flickr; credit "face": modification of work by Cory Zanker)

The **James-Lange theory** of emotion asserts that emotions arise from physiological arousal. Recall what you have learned about the sympathetic nervous system and our fight or flight response when threatened. If you were to encounter some threat in your environment, like a venomous snake in your backyard, your sympathetic nervous system would initiate significant physiological arousal, which would make your heart race and increase your respiration rate. According to the James-Lange theory of emotion, you would only experience a feeling of fear after this physiological arousal had taken place. Furthermore, different arousal patterns would be associated with different feelings.

Other theorists, however, doubted that the physiological arousal that occurs with different types of emotions is distinct enough to result in the wide variety of emotions that we experience. Thus, the **Cannon-Bard theory** of emotion was developed. According to this view, physiological arousal and emotional experience occur simultaneously, yet independently (Lang, 1994). So, when you see the venomous snake, you feel fear at exactly the same time that your body mounts its fight or flight response. This emotional reaction would be separate and independent of the physiological arousal, even though they co-occur.

Does smiling make you happy? Alternatively, does being happy make you smile? The facial feedback hypothesis proposes that your facial expression can actually affect your emotional experience (Adelman & Zajonc, 1989; Boiger & Mesquita, 2012; Buck, 1980; Capella, 1993; Soussignan, 2001; Strack, Martin, & Stepper, 1988). Research investigating the facial feedback hypothesis suggested that suppression of facial expression of emotion lowered the intensity of some emotions experienced by participants (Davis, Senghas, & Ochsner, 2009). Havas, Glenberg, Gutowski, Lucarelli, and Davidson (2010) used Botox injections to paralyze facial muscles and limit facial expressions, including frowning, and they found that depressed people reported less depression after their frowning muscles were paralyzed. Other research found that the intensities of facial expressions affected the emotional reactions (Soussignan, 2002; Strack, Martin, & Stepper, 1988). In other words, if something insignificant occurs and you smile as if you just won lottery, you will actually be happier about the little thing than you would be if you only had a tiny smile. Conversely, if you walk around frowning all the time, it might cause you to have less positive emotions than you would if you had smiled. Interestingly, Soussignan (2002) also reported physiological arousal differences associated with the intensities of one type of smile.

G. Marañon Posadillo was a Spanish physician who studied the psychological effects of adrenaline to create a model for the experience of emotion. Marañon's model preceded Schachter's two-factor or arousal-cognition theory of emotion (Cornelius, 1991). The **Schachter-Singer two-factor theory** of emotion is another variation on theories of emotions that takes into account both physiological arousal and the emotional experience. According to this theory, emotions are composed of two factors: physiological and cognitive. In other words, physiological arousal is interpreted in context to produce the emotional experience. In revisiting our example involving the venomous snake in your backyard, the two-factor theory maintains that the snake elicits sympathetic nervous system activation that is labeled as fear given the context, and our experience is that of fear. If you had labeled your sympathetic nervous system activation as joy, you would have experienced joy. The Schachter-Singer two-factor theory depends on labeling the physiological experience, which is a type of cognitive appraisal.

Magda Arnold was the first theorist to offer an exploration of the meaning of appraisal, and to present an outline of what the appraisal process might be and how it relates to emotion (Roseman & Smith, 2001). The key idea of appraisal theory is that you have thoughts (a cognitive appraisal) before you experience an emotion, and the emotion you experience depends on the thoughts you had (Frijda, 1988; Lazarus, 1991). If you think something is positive, you will have more positive emotions about it than if your appraisal was negative, and the opposite is true. Appraisal theory explains the way two people can have two completely different emotions regarding the same event. For example, suppose your psychology instructor selected you to lecture on emotion; you might see that as positive, because it represents an opportunity to be the center of attention, and you would experience happiness. However, if you dislike speaking in public, you could have a negative appraisal and experience discomfort.

Schachter and Singer believed that physiological arousal is very similar across the different types of emotions that we experience, and therefore, the cognitive appraisal of the situation is critical to the actual emotion experienced. In fact, it might be possible to misattribute arousal to an emotional experience if the circumstances were right (Schachter & Singer, 1962). They performed a clever experiment to test their idea. Male participants were randomly assigned to one of several groups. Some of the participants received injections of epinephrine that caused bodily changes that mimicked the fight-or-flight response of the sympathetic nervous system; however, only some of these men were told to expect these reactions as side effects of the injection. The other men that received injections of epinephrine were told either that the injection would have no side effects or that it would result in a side effect unrelated to a sympathetic response, such as itching feet or headache. After receiving these injections, participants waited in a room with someone else they thought was another subject in the research project. In reality, the other person was a confederate of the researcher. The confederate engaged in scripted displays of euphoric or angry behavior (Schachter & Singer, 1962).

When those participants who were told that they should expect to feel symptoms of physiological arousal were asked about any emotional changes that they had experienced related to either euphoria or anger (depending on the way the confederate behaved), they reported none. However, the men who weren't expecting physiological arousal as a function of the injection were more likely to report that they experienced euphoria or anger as a function of their assigned confederate's behavior. While everyone who received an injection of epinephrine experienced the same physiological arousal, only those who were not expecting the arousal used context to interpret the arousal as a change in emotional state (Schachter & Singer, 1962).

Strong emotional responses are associated with strong physiological arousal, which caused some theorists to suggest that the signs of physiological arousal, including increased heart rate, respiration rate, and sweating, might be used to determine whether someone is telling the truth or not. The assumption is that most of us would show signs of physiological arousal if we were being dishonest with someone. A **polygraph**, or lie detector test, measures the physiological arousal of an individual responding to a series of questions. Someone trained in reading these tests would look for answers to questions that are associated with increased levels of arousal as potential signs that the respondent may have been dishonest on those answers. While polygraphs are still commonly used, their validity and accuracy are highly questionable because there is no evidence that lying is associated with any particular pattern of physiological arousal (Saxe & Ben-Shakhar, 1999).

The relationship between our experiencing of emotions and our cognitive processing of them, and the order in which these occur, remains a topic of research and debate. Lazarus (1991) developed the **cognitive-mediational theory** that asserts our emotions are determined by our appraisal of the stimulus. This appraisal mediates between the stimulus and the emotional response, and it is immediate and often unconscious. In contrast to the Schachter-Singer model, the appraisal precedes a cognitive label. You will learn more about Lazarus's appraisal concept when you study stress, health, and lifestyle. However, there are other views of emotions that also emphasize the cognitive processes.

Return to the example of being asked to lecture by your professor. Even if you do not enjoy speaking in public, you probably could manage to do it. You would purposefully control your emotions, which would allow you to speak, but we constantly regulate our emotions, and much of our emotion regulation occurs without us actively thinking about it. Mauss and her colleagues studied automatic emotion regulation (AER), which refers to the non-deliberate control of emotions. It is simply not reacting with your emotions, and AER can affect all aspects of emotional processes. AER can influence the things you attend to, your appraisal, your choice to engage in an emotional experience, and your behaviors after an emotion is experienced (Mauss, Bunge, & Gross, 2007; Mauss, Levenson, McCarter, Wilhelm, & Gross, 2005). AER is similar to other automatic cognitive processes in which sensations activate knowledge structures that affect functioning. These knowledge structures can include concepts, schemas, or scripts.

The idea of AER is that people develop an automatic process that works like a script or schema, and the process does not require deliberate thought to regulate emotions. AER works like riding a bicycle. Once you develop the process, you just do it without thinking about it. AER can be adaptive or maladaptive and has important health implications (Hopp, Troy, & Mauss, 2011). Adaptive AER leads to better health outcomes than maladaptive AER, primarily due to experiencing or mitigating stressors better than people with maladaptive AERs (Hopp, Troy, & Mauss, 2011). Alternatively, maladaptive AERs may be critical for maintaining some psychological disorders (Hopp, Troy, & Mauss, 2011). Mauss and her colleagues found that strategies could reduce negative emotions, which in turn should increase psychological health (Mauss, Cook, Cheng, & Gross, 2007; Mauss, Cook, & Gross, 2007; Shallcross, Troy, Boland, & Mauss, 2010; Troy, Shallcross, & Mauss, 2013; Troy, Wilhelm, Shallcross, & Mauss, 2010). Mauss has also suggested there are problems with the way emotions are measured, but she believes most of the aspects of emotions that are typically measured are useful (Mauss, et al., 2005; Mauss & Robinson, 2009). However, another way of considering emotions challenges our entire understanding of emotions.

After about three decades of interdisciplinary research, Barrett argued that we do not understand emotions. She proposed that emotions were not built into your brain at birth, but rather they were constructed based on your experiences. Emotions in the constructivist theory are predictions that construct your experience of the world. In chapter 7 you learned that concepts are categories or groupings of linguistic information, images, ideas, or memories, such as life experiences. Barrett extended that to include emotions as concepts that are predictions (Barrett, 2017). Two identical physiological states can result in different emotional states depending on your predictions. For example, your brain predicting a churning stomach in a bakery could lead to you constructing hunger. However, your brain predicting a churning stomach while you were waiting for medical test results could lead your brain to construct worry. Thus, you can construct two different emotions from the same physiological sensations. Rather than emotions being something over which you have no control, you can control and influence your emotions.

LINK TO LEARNING

Watch this video in which Dr. Barrett explains constructed emotions (http://openstax.org/l/barrett) to learn more.

Two other prominent views arise from the work of Robert Zajonc and Joseph LeDoux. Zajonc asserted that some emotions occur separately from or prior to our cognitive interpretation of them, such as feeling fear in response to an unexpected loud sound (Zajonc, 1998). He also believed in what we might casually refer to as a gut feeling—that we can experience an instantaneous and unexplainable like or dislike for someone or something (Zajonc, 1980). LeDoux also views some emotions as requiring no cognition: some emotions completely bypass contextual interpretation. His research into the neuroscience of emotion has demonstrated the amygdala's primary role in fear (Cunha, Monfils, & LeDoux, 2010; LeDoux 1996, 2002). A fear stimulus is processed by the brain through one of two paths: from the thalamus (where it is perceived) directly to the amygdala or from the thalamus through the cortex and then to the amygdala. The first path is quick, while the second enables more processing about details of the stimulus. In the following section, we will look more closely at the neuroscience of emotional response.

THE BIOLOGY OF EMOTIONS

Earlier, you learned about the limbic system, which is the area of the brain involved in emotion and memory (Figure 10.22). The limbic system includes the hypothalamus, thalamus, amygdala, and the hippocampus. The hypothalamus plays a role in the activation of the sympathetic nervous system that is a part of any given emotional reaction. The thalamus serves as a sensory relay center whose neurons project to both the amygdala and the higher cortical regions for further processing. The amygdala plays a role in processing emotional information and sending that information on (Fossati, 2012).The hippocampus integrates emotional experience with cognition (Femenía, Gómez-Galán, Lindskog, & Magara, 2012).

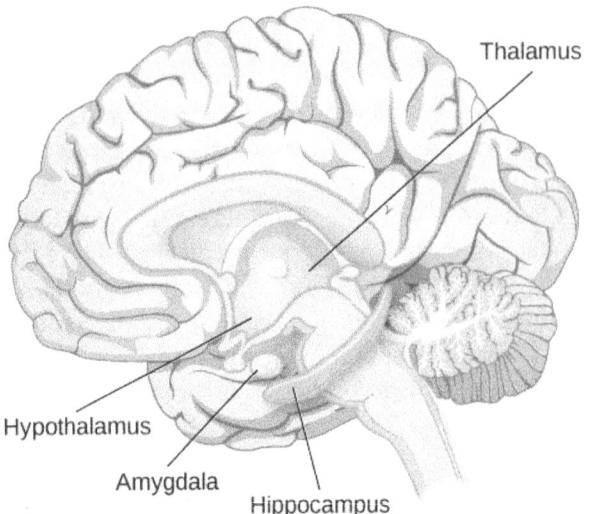

Figure 10.22 The limbic system, which includes the hypothalamus, thalamus, amygdala, and the hippocampus, is involved in mediating emotional response and memory.

LINK TO LEARNING

Work through this Open Colleges interactive 3D brain simulator (http://openstax.org/l/bparts1) for a refresher on the brain's parts and their functions. To begin, click the "Start Exploring" button. To access the limbic system, click the plus sign in the right-hand menu (set of three tabs).

Amygdala

The amygdala has received a great deal of attention from researchers interested in understanding the biological basis for emotions, especially fear and anxiety (Blackford & Pine, 2012; Goosens & Maren, 2002; Maren, Phan, & Liberzon, 2013). The amygdala is composed of various subnuclei, including the basolateral complex and the central nucleus (Figure 10.23). The **basolateral complex** has dense connections with a variety of sensory areas of the brain. It is critical for classical conditioning and for attaching emotional value to learning processes and memory. The **central nucleus** plays a role in attention, and it has connections with the hypothalamus and various brainstem areas to regulate the autonomic nervous and endocrine systems' activity (Pessoa, 2010).

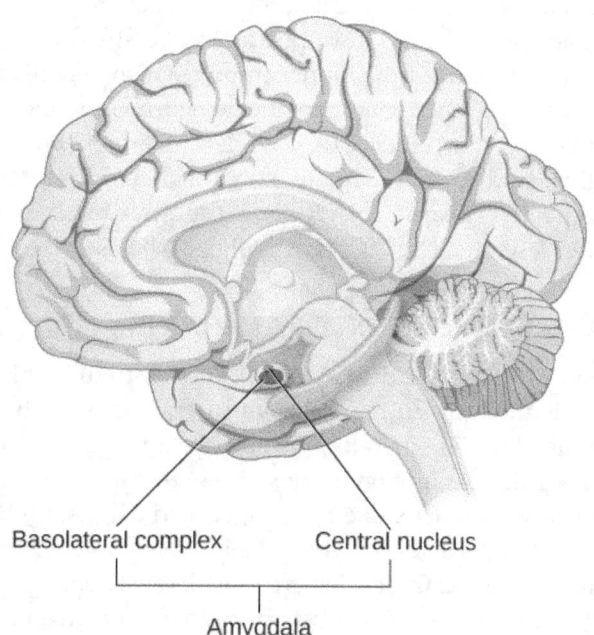

Figure 10.23 The anatomy of the basolateral complex and central nucleus of the amygdala are illustrated in this diagram.

Animal research has demonstrated that there is increased activation of the amygdala in rat pups that have odor cues paired with electrical shock when their mother is absent. This leads to an aversion to the odor cue that suggests the rats learned to fear the odor cue. Interestingly, when the mother was present, the rats actually showed a preference for the odor cue despite its association with an electrical shock. This preference was associated with no increases in amygdala activation. This suggests a differential effect on the amygdala by the *context* (the presence or absence of the mother) determined whether the pups learned to fear the odor or to be attracted to it (Moriceau & Sullivan, 2006).

Raineki, Cortés, Belnoue, and Sullivan (2012) demonstrated that, in rats, negative early life experiences could alter the function of the amygdala and result in adolescent patterns of behavior that mimic human mood disorders. In this study, rat pups received either abusive or normal treatment during postnatal days 8–12. There were two forms of abusive treatment. The first form of abusive treatment had an insufficient bedding condition. The mother rat had insufficient bedding material in her cage to build a proper nest that resulted in her spending more time away from her pups trying to construct a nest and less times nursing her pups. The second form of abusive treatment had an associative learning task that involved pairing odors and an electrical stimulus in the absence of the mother, as described above. The control group was in a cage with sufficient bedding and was left undisturbed with their mothers during the same time period. The rat pups that experienced abuse were much more likely to exhibit depressive-like symptoms during adolescence when compared to controls. These depressive-like behaviors were associated with increased activation of the amygdala.

Human research also suggests a relationship between the amygdala and psychological disorders of mood or anxiety. Changes in amygdala structure and function have been demonstrated in adolescents who are either at-risk or have been diagnosed with various mood and/or anxiety disorders (Miguel-Hidalgo, 2013; Qin et al., 2013). It has also been suggested that functional differences in the amygdala could serve as a biomarker to differentiate individuals suffering from bipolar disorder from those suffering from major depressive disorder (Fournier, Keener, Almeida, Kronhaus, & Phillips, 2013).

Hippocampus

As mentioned earlier, the hippocampus is also involved in emotional processing. Like the amygdala, research has demonstrated that hippocampal structure and function are linked to a variety of mood and anxiety disorders. Individuals suffering from posttraumatic stress disorder (PTSD) show marked reductions in the volume of several parts of the hippocampus, which may result from decreased levels of neurogenesis and dendritic branching (the generation of new neurons and the generation of new dendrites in existing neurons, respectively) (Wang et al., 2010). While it is impossible to make a causal claim with correlational research like this, studies have demonstrated behavioral improvements and hippocampal volume increases following either pharmacological or cognitive-behavioral therapy in individuals suffering from PTSD (Bremner & Vermetten, 2004; Levy-Gigi, Szabó, Kelemen, & Kéri, 2013).

FACIAL EXPRESSION AND RECOGNITION OF EMOTIONS

Culture can impact the way in which people display emotion. A **cultural display rule** is one of a collection of culturally specific standards that govern the types and frequencies of displays of emotions that are acceptable (Malatesta & Haviland, 1982). Therefore, people from varying cultural backgrounds can have very different cultural display rules of emotion. For example, research has shown that individuals from the United States express negative emotions like fear, anger, and disgust both alone and in the presence of others, while Japanese individuals only do so while alone (Matsumoto, 1990). Furthermore, individuals from cultures that tend to emphasize social cohesion are more likely to engage in suppression of emotional reaction so they can evaluate which response is most appropriate in a given context (Matsumoto, Yoo, & Nakagawa, 2008).

Other distinct cultural characteristics might be involved in emotionality. For instance, there may be gender differences involved in emotional processing. While research into gender differences in emotional display is equivocal, there is some evidence that men and women may differ in regulation of emotions (McRae, Ochsner, Mauss, Gabrieli, & Gross, 2008).

Paul Ekman (1972) researched a New Guinea man who was living in a preliterate culture using stone implements, and which was isolated and had never seen any outsiders before. Ekman asked the man to show what his facial expression would be if: (1) friends visited, (2) his child had just died, (3) he was about to fight, (4) he stepped on a smelly dead pig. After Ekman's return from New Guinea, he researched facial expressions for more than four decades. Despite different emotional display rules, our ability to recognize and produce facial expressions of emotion appears to be universal. In fact, even congenitally blind individuals produce the same facial expression of emotions, despite their never having the opportunity to observe these facial displays of emotion in other people. This would seem to suggest that the pattern of activity in facial muscles involved in generating emotional expressions is universal, and indeed, this idea was suggested in the late 19th century in Charles Darwin's book *The Expression of Emotions in Man and Animals* (1872). In fact, there is substantial evidence for seven universal emotions that are each associated with distinct facial expressions. These include: happiness, surprise, sadness, fright, disgust, contempt, and anger (**Figure 10.24**) (Ekman & Keltner, 1997).

Figure 10.24 The seven universal facial expressions of emotion are shown. (credit: modification of work by Cory Zanker)

Of course, emotion is not only displayed through facial expression. We also use the tone of our voices, various behaviors, and body language to communicate information about our emotional states. **Body language** is the expression of emotion in terms of body position or movement. Research suggests that we are quite sensitive to the emotional information communicated through body language, even if we're not consciously aware of it (de Gelder, 2006; Tamietto et al., 2009).

LINK TO LEARNING

Watch this short **CNN video about body language in the tense situation of a political debate (http://openstax.org/l/blanguage1)** to learn more. Watch this **Today Show interview with body language expert Janine Driver (http://openstax.org/l/todayshow)** to learn how to apply the same concepts to more everyday situations.

CONNECT THE CONCEPTS

Emotional Expression and Emotion Regulation

Autism spectrum disorder (ASD) is a set of neurodevelopmental disorders characterized by repetitive behaviors and communication and social problems. Children who have autism spectrum disorders have difficulty recognizing the emotional states of others, and research has shown that this may stem from an inability to distinguish various nonverbal expressions of emotion (i.e., facial expressions) from one another (Hobson, 1986). In addition, there is evidence to suggest that autistic individuals also have difficulty expressing emotion through tone of voice and by producing facial expressions (Macdonald et al., 1989). Difficulties with emotional recognition and expression may contribute to the impaired social interaction and communication that characterize autism; therefore, various therapeutic approaches have been explored to address these difficulties. Various educational curricula, cognitive-behavioral therapies, and pharmacological therapies have shown some promise in helping autistic individuals process emotionally relevant information (Bauminger, 2002; Golan & Baron-Cohen, 2006; Guastella et al., 2010).

Emotion regulation describes how people respond to situations and experiences by modifying their emotional experiences and expressions. Covert emotion regulation strategies are those that occur within the individual, while overt strategies involve others or actions (such as seeking advice or consuming alcohol). Aldao and Dixon (2014) studied the relationship between overt emotional regulation strategies and psychopathology. They researched how 218 undergraduate students reported their use of covert and overt strategies and their reported symptoms associated with selected mental disorders, and found that overt emotional regulation strategies were better predictors of psychopathology than covert strategies. Another study examined the relationship between pregaming (the act of drinking heavily before a social event) and two emotion regulation strategies to understand how these might contribute to alcohol-related problems; results suggested a relationship but a complicated one (Pederson, 2016). Further research is needed in these areas to better understand patterns of adaptive and maladaptive emotion regulation (Aldao & Dixon-Gordon, 2014).

Key Terms

anorexia nervosa eating disorder characterized by an individual maintaining body weight that is well below average through starvation and/or excessive exercise

bariatric surgery type of surgery that modifies the gastrointestinal system to reduce the amount of food that can be eaten and/or limiting how much of the digested food can be absorbed

basolateral complex part of the brain with dense connections with a variety of sensory areas of the brain; it is critical for classical conditioning and attaching emotional value to memory

binge eating disorder type of eating disorder characterized by binge eating and associated distress

bisexual emotional and erotic attractions to both same-sexed individuals and opposite-sexed individuals

body language emotional expression through body position or movement

bulimia nervosa type of eating disorder characterized by binge eating followed by purging

Cannon-Bard theory of emotion physiological arousal and emotional experience occur at the same time

central nucleus part of the brain involved in attention and has connections with the hypothalamus and various brainstem areas to regulate the autonomic nervous and endocrine systems' activity

cognitive-mediational theory our emotions are determined by our appraisal of the stimulus

components of emotion physiological arousal, psychological appraisal, and subjective experience

cultural display rule one of the culturally specific standards that govern the types and frequencies of emotions that are acceptable

distorted body image individuals view themselves as overweight even though they are not

drive theory deviations from homeostasis create physiological needs that result in psychological drive states that direct behavior to meet the need and ultimately bring the system back to homeostasis

emotion subjective state of being often described as feelings

excitement phase of the sexual response cycle that involves sexual arousal

extrinsic motivation motivation that arises from external factors or rewards

facial feedback hypothesis facial expressions are capable of influencing our emotions

gender dysphoria diagnostic category in DSM-5 for individuals who do not identify as the gender associated with their biological sex

gender identity individual's sense of being male or female

habit pattern of behavior in which we regularly engage

heterosexual emotional and erotic attractions to opposite-sexed individuals

hierarchy of needs spectrum of needs ranging from basic biological needs to social needs to self-actualization

homosexual emotional and erotic attractions to same-sexed individuals

instinct species-specific pattern of behavior that is unlearned

intrinsic motivation motivation based on internal feelings rather than external rewards

James-Lange theory of emotion emotions arise from physiological arousal

leptin satiety hormone

metabolic rate amount of energy that is expended in a given period of time

morbid obesity adult with a BMI over 40

motivation wants or needs that direct behavior toward some goal

obese adult with a BMI of 30 or higher

orgasm peak phase of the sexual response cycle associated with rhythmic muscle contractions (and ejaculation)

overweight adult with a BMI between 25 and 29.9

plateau phase of the sexual response cycle that falls between excitement and orgasm

polygraph lie detector test that measures physiological arousal of individuals as they answer a series of questions

refractory period time immediately following an orgasm during which an individual is incapable of experiencing another orgasm

resolution phase of the sexual response cycle following orgasm during which the body returns to its unaroused state

satiation fullness; satisfaction

Schachter-Singer two-factor theory of emotion emotions consist of two factors: physiological and cognitive

self-efficacy individual's belief in his own capabilities or capacities to complete a task

set point theory assertion that each individual has an ideal body weight, or set point, that is resistant to change

sexual orientation emotional and erotic attraction to same-sexed individuals, opposite-sexed individuals, or both

sexual response cycle divided into 4 phases including excitement, plateau, orgasm, and resolution

transgender hormone therapy use of hormones to make one's body look more like the opposite-sex

Yerkes-Dodson law simple tasks are performed best when arousal levels are relatively high, while complex tasks are best performed when arousal is lower

Summary

10.1 Motivation
Motivation to engage in a given behavior can come from internal and/or external factors. Multiple

theories have been put forward regarding motivation. More biologically oriented theories deal with the ways that instincts and the need to maintain bodily homeostasis motivate behavior. Bandura postulated that our sense of self-efficacy motivates behaviors, and there are a number of theories that focus on a variety of social motives. Abraham Maslow's hierarchy of needs is a model that shows the relationship among multiple motives that range from lower-level physiological needs to the very high level of self-actualization.

10.2 Hunger and Eating

Hunger and satiety are highly regulated processes that result in a person maintaining a fairly stable weight that is resistant to change. When more calories are consumed than expended, a person will store excess energy as fat. Being significantly overweight adds substantially to a person's health risks and problems, including cardiovascular disease, type 2 diabetes, certain cancers, and other medical issues. Sociocultural factors that emphasize thinness as a beauty ideal and a genetic predisposition contribute to the development of eating disorders in many young females, though eating disorders span ages and genders.

10.3 Sexual Behavior

The hypothalamus and structures of the limbic system are important in sexual behavior and motivation. There is evidence to suggest that our motivation to engage in sexual behavior and our ability to do so are related, but separate, processes. Alfred Kinsey conducted large-scale survey research that demonstrated the incredible diversity of human sexuality. William Masters and Virginia Johnson observed individuals engaging in sexual behavior in developing their concept of the sexual response cycle. While often confused, sexual orientation and gender identity are related, but distinct, concepts.

10.4 Emotion

Emotions are subjective experiences that consist of physiological arousal and cognitive appraisal. Various theories have been put forward to explain our emotional experiences. The James-Lange theory asserts that emotions arise as a function of physiological arousal. The Cannon-Bard theory maintains that emotional experience occurs simultaneous to and independent of physiological arousal. The Schachter-Singer two-factor theory suggests that physiological arousal receives cognitive labels as a function of the relevant context and that these two factors together result in an emotional experience.

The limbic system is the brain's emotional circuit, which includes the amygdala and the hippocampus. Both of these structures are implicated in playing a role in normal emotional processing as well as in psychological mood and anxiety disorders. Increased amygdala activity is associated with learning to fear, and it is seen in individuals who are at risk for or suffering from mood disorders. The volume of the hippocampus has been shown to be reduced in individuals suffering from posttraumatic stress disorder.

The ability to produce and recognize facial expressions of emotions seems to be universal regardless of cultural background. However, there are cultural display rules which influence how often and under what circumstances various emotions can be expressed. Tone of voice and body language also serve as a means by which we communicate information about our emotional states.

Review Questions

1. Need for _____ refers to maintaining positive relationships with others.
    a. achievement
    b. affiliation
    c. intimacy
    d. power

2. _____ proposed the hierarchy of needs.
    a. William James
    b. David McClelland
    c. Abraham Maslow
    d. Albert Bandura

3. _____ is an individual's belief in her capability to complete some task.
   a. physiological needs
   b. self-esteem
   c. self-actualization
   d. self-efficacy

4. Carl mows the yard of his elderly neighbor each week for $20. What type of motivation is this?
   a. extrinsic
   b. intrinsic
   c. drive
   d. biological

5. According to your reading, nearly _____ of the adult population in the United States can be classified as obese.
   a. one half
   b. one third
   c. one fourth
   d. one fifth

6. _____ is a chemical messenger secreted by fat cells that acts as an appetite suppressant.
   a. orexin
   b. angiotensin
   c. leptin
   d. ghrelin

7. _____ is characterized by episodes of binge eating followed by attempts to compensate for the excessive amount of food that was consumed.
   a. Prader-Willi syndrome
   b. morbid obesity
   c. anorexia nervosa
   d. bulimia nervosa

8. In order to be classified as morbidly obese, an adult must have a BMI of _____.
   a. less than 25
   b. 25–29.9
   c. 30–39.9
   d. 40 or more

9. Animal research suggests that in male rats the _____ is critical for the ability to engage in sexual behavior, but not for the motivation to do so.
   a. nucleus accumbens
   b. amygdala
   c. medial preoptic area of the hypothalamus
   d. hippocampus

10. During the _____ phase of the sexual response cycle, individuals experience rhythmic contractions of the pelvis that are accompanied by uterine contractions in women and ejaculation in men.
    a. excitement
    b. plateau
    c. orgasm
    d. resolution

11. Which of the following findings was not a result of the Kinsey study?
    a. Sexual desire and sexual ability can be separate functions.
    b. Females enjoy sex as much as males.
    c. Homosexual behavior is fairly common.
    d. Masturbation has no adverse consequences.

12. If someone is uncomfortable identifying with the gender normally associated with their biological sex, then he could be classified as experiencing _____.
    a. homosexuality
    b. bisexuality
    c. asexuality
    d. gender dysphoria

13. Individuals suffering from posttraumatic stress disorder have been shown to have reduced volumes of the _____.
    a. amygdala
    b. hippocampus
    c. hypothalamus
    d. thalamus

14. According to the _____ theory of emotion, emotional experiences arise from physiological arousal.
    a. James-Lange
    b. Cannon-Bard
    c. Schachter-Singer two-factor
    d. Darwinian

15. Which of the following is not one of the seven universal emotions described in this chapter?
    a. contempt
    b. disgust
    c. melancholy
    d. anger

16. Which of the following theories of emotion would suggest that polygraphs should be quite accurate at differentiating one emotion from another?
    a. Cannon-Bard theory
    b. James-Lange theory
    c. Schachter-Singer two-factor theory
    d. Darwinian theory

Critical Thinking Questions

17. How might someone espousing an arousal theory of motivation explain visiting an amusement park?

18. Schools often use concrete rewards to increase adaptive behaviors. How might this be a disadvantage for students intrinsically motivated to learn? What are educational implications of the potential for concrete rewards to diminish intrinsic motivation for a given task?

19. The index that is often used to classify people as being underweight, normal weight, overweight, obese, or morbidly obese is called BMI. Given that BMI is calculated solely on weight and height, how could it be misleading?

20. As indicated in this section, Caucasian women from industrialized, Western cultures tend to be at the highest risk for eating disorders like anorexia and bulimia nervosa. Why might this be?

21. While much research has been conducted on how an individual develops a given sexual orientation, many people question the validity of this research citing that the participants used may not be representative. Why do you think this might be a legitimate concern?

22. There is no reliable scientific evidence that gay conversion therapy actually works. What kinds of evidence would you need to see in order to be convinced by someone arguing that she had successfully converted her sexual orientation?

23. Imagine you find a venomous snake crawling up your leg just after taking a drug that prevented sympathetic nervous system activation. What would the James-Lange theory predict about your experience?

24. Why can we not make causal claims regarding the relationship between the volume of the hippocampus and PTSD?

Personal Application Questions

25. Can you think of recent examples of how Maslow's hierarchy of needs might have affected your behavior in some way?

26. Think about popular television programs on the air right now. What do the women in these programs look like? What do the men look like? What kinds of messages do you think the media is sending about men and women in our society?

27. Issues related to sexual orientation have been at the forefront of the current political landscape. What do you think about current debates on legalizing same-sex marriage?

28. Think about times in your life when you have been absolutely elated (e.g., perhaps your school's basketball team just won a closely contested ballgame for the national championship) and very fearful (e.g., you are about to give a speech in your public speaking class to a roomful of 100 strangers). How would you describe how your arousal manifested itself physically? Were there marked differences in physiological arousal associated with each emotional state?

Chapter 11

Personality

Figure 11.1 What makes two individuals have different personalities? (credit: modification of work by Nicolas Alejandro)

Chapter Outline

11.1 What Is Personality?
11.2 Freud and the Psychodynamic Perspective
11.3 Neo-Freudians: Adler, Erikson, Jung, and Horney
11.4 Learning Approaches
11.5 Humanistic Approaches
11.6 Biological Approaches
11.7 Trait Theorists
11.8 Cultural Understandings of Personality
11.9 Personality Assessment

Introduction

Three months before William Jefferson Blythe III was born, his father died in a car accident. He was raised by his mother, Virginia Dell, and grandparents, in Hope, Arkansas. When he turned 4, his mother married Roger Clinton, Jr., an alcoholic who was physically abusive to William's mother. Six years later, Virginia gave birth to another son, Roger. William, who later took the last name Clinton from his stepfather, became the 42nd president of the United States. While Bill Clinton was making his political ascendance, his half-brother, Roger Clinton, was arrested numerous times for drug charges, including possession, conspiracy to distribute cocaine, and driving under the influence, serving time in jail. Two brothers, raised by the same people, took radically different paths in their lives. Why did they make the choices they did? What internal forces shaped their decisions? Personality psychology can help us answer these questions and more.

11.1 What Is Personality?

Learning Objectives

By the end of this section, you will be able to:
- Define personality
- Describe early theories about personality development

Personality refers to the long-standing traits and patterns that propel individuals to consistently think, feel, and behave in specific ways. Our personality is what makes us unique individuals. Each person has an idiosyncratic pattern of enduring, long-term characteristics and a manner in which he or she interacts with other individuals and the world around them. Our personalities are thought to be long term, stable, and not easily changed. The word *personality* comes from the Latin word *persona*. In the ancient world, a persona was a mask worn by an actor. While we tend to think of a mask as being worn to conceal one's identity, the theatrical mask was originally used to either represent or project a specific personality trait of a character (Figure 11.2).

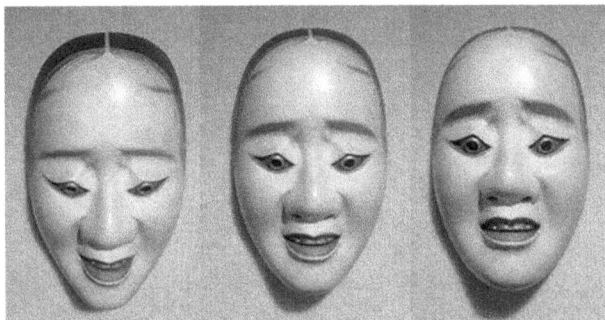

Figure 11.2 Happy, sad, impatient, shy, fearful, curious, helpful. What characteristics describe your personality?

HISTORICAL PERSPECTIVES

The concept of personality has been studied for at least 2,000 years, beginning with Hippocrates in 370 BCE (Fazeli, 2012). Hippocrates theorized that personality traits and human behaviors are based on four separate temperaments associated with four fluids ("humors") of the body: choleric temperament (yellow bile from the liver), melancholic temperament (black bile from the kidneys), sanguine temperament (red blood from the heart), and phlegmatic temperament (white phlegm from the lungs) (Clark & Watson, 2008; Eysenck & Eysenck, 1985; Lecci & Magnavita, 2013; Noga, 2007). Centuries later, the influential Greek physician and philosopher Galen built on Hippocrates's theory, suggesting that both diseases and personality differences could be explained by imbalances in the humors and that each person exhibits one of the four temperaments. For example, the choleric person is passionate, ambitious, and bold; the melancholic person is reserved, anxious, and unhappy; the sanguine person is joyful, eager, and optimistic; and the phlegmatic person is calm, reliable, and thoughtful (Clark & Watson, 2008; Stelmack & Stalikas, 1991). Galen's theory was prevalent for over 1,000 years and continued to be popular through the Middle Ages.

In 1780, Franz Gall, a German physician, proposed that the distances between bumps on the skull reveal a person's personality traits, character, and mental abilities (Figure 11.3). According to Gall, measuring these distances revealed the sizes of the brain areas underneath, providing information that could be used to determine whether a person was friendly, prideful, murderous, kind, good with languages, and so on. Initially, phrenology was very popular; however, it was soon discredited for lack of empirical support and has long been relegated to the status of pseudoscience (Fancher, 1979).

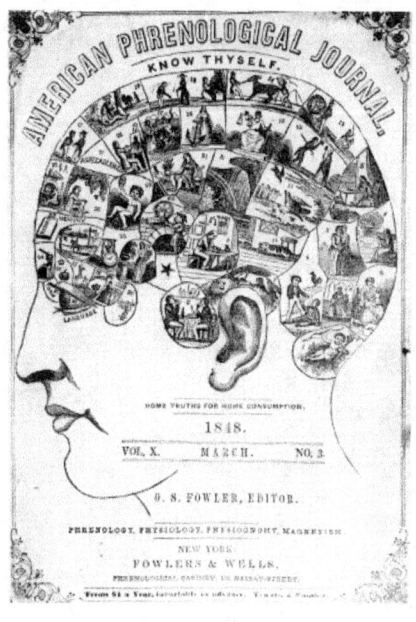 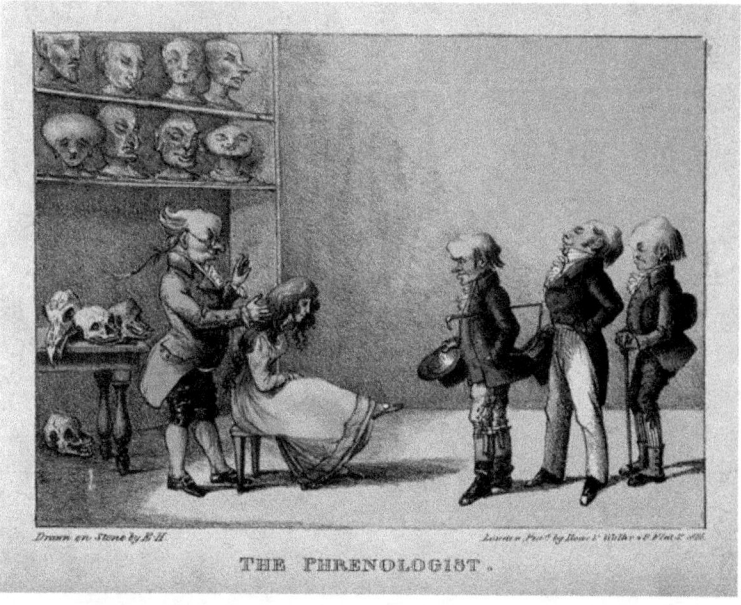

(a) (b)

Figure 11.3 The pseudoscience of measuring the areas of a person's skull is known as phrenology. (a) Gall developed a chart that depicted which areas of the skull corresponded to particular personality traits or characteristics (Hothersall, 1995). (b) An 1825 lithograph depicts Gall examining the skull of a young woman. (credit b: modification of work by Wellcome Library, London)

In the centuries after Galen, other researchers contributed to the development of his four primary temperament types, most prominently Immanuel Kant (in the 18th century) and psychologist Wilhelm Wundt (in the 19th century) (Eysenck, 2009; Stelmack & Stalikas, 1991; Wundt, 1874/1886) (Figure 11.4). Kant agreed with Galen that everyone could be sorted into one of the four temperaments and that there was no overlap between the four categories (Eysenck, 2009). He developed a list of traits that could be used to describe the personality of a person from each of the four temperaments. However, Wundt suggested that a better description of personality could be achieved using two major axes: emotional/nonemotional and changeable/unchangeable. The first axis separated strong from weak emotions (the melancholic and choleric temperaments from the phlegmatic and sanguine). The second axis divided the changeable temperaments (choleric and sanguine) from the unchangeable ones (melancholic and phlegmatic) (Eysenck, 2009).

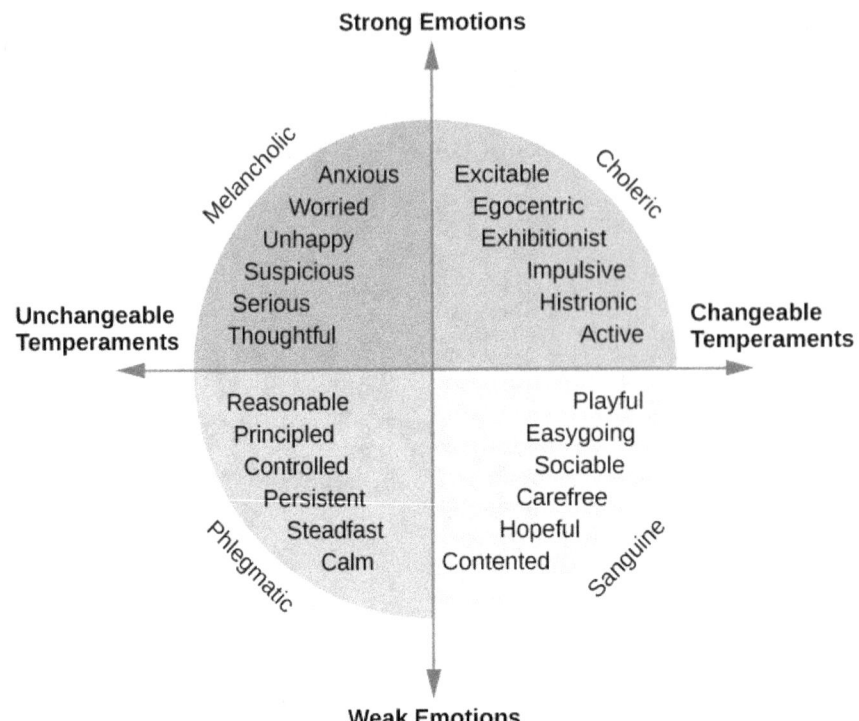

Figure 11.4 Developed from Galen's theory of the four temperaments, Kant proposed trait words to describe each temperament. Wundt later suggested the arrangement of the traits on two major axes.

Sigmund Freud's psychodynamic perspective of personality was the first comprehensive theory of personality, explaining a wide variety of both normal and abnormal behaviors. According to Freud, unconscious drives influenced by sex and aggression, along with childhood sexuality, are the forces that influence our personality. Freud attracted many followers who modified his ideas to create new theories about personality. These theorists, referred to as neo-Freudians, generally agreed with Freud that childhood experiences matter, but they reduced the emphasis on sex and focused more on the social environment and effects of culture on personality. The perspective of personality proposed by Freud and his followers was the dominant theory of personality for the first half of the 20th century.

Other major theories then emerged, including the learning, humanistic, biological, evolutionary, trait, and cultural perspectives. In this chapter, we will explore these various perspectives on personality in depth.

LINK TO LEARNING

View this **video of an overview of some of the psychological perspectives on personality (http://openstax.org/l/mandela)** to learn more.

11.2 Freud and the Psychodynamic Perspective

Learning Objectives

By the end of this section, you will be able to:
- Describe the assumptions of the psychodynamic perspective on personality development
- Define and describe the nature and function of the id, ego, and superego
- Define and describe the defense mechanisms
- Define and describe the psychosexual stages of personality development

Sigmund Freud (1856–1939) is probably the most controversial and misunderstood psychological theorist. When reading Freud's theories, it is important to remember that he was a medical doctor, not a psychologist. There was no such thing as a degree in psychology at the time that he received his education, which can help us understand some of the controversy over his theories today. However, Freud was the first to systematically study and theorize the workings of the unconscious mind in the manner that we associate with modern psychology.

In the early years of his career, Freud worked with Josef Breuer, a Viennese physician. During this time, Freud became intrigued by the story of one of Breuer's patients, Bertha Pappenheim, who was referred to by the pseudonym Anna O. (Launer, 2005). Anna O. had been caring for her dying father when she began to experience symptoms such as partial paralysis, headaches, blurred vision, amnesia, and hallucinations (Launer, 2005). In Freud's day, these symptoms were commonly referred to as hysteria. Anna O. turned to Breuer for help. He spent 2 years (1880–1882) treating Anna O. and discovered that allowing her to talk about her experiences seemed to bring some relief of her symptoms. Anna O. called his treatment the "talking cure" (Launer, 2005). Despite the fact the Freud never met Anna O., her story served as the basis for the 1895 book, *Studies on Hysteria*, which he co-authored with Breuer. Based on Breuer's description of Anna O.'s treatment, Freud concluded that hysteria was the result of sexual abuse in childhood and that these traumatic experiences had been hidden from consciousness. Breuer disagreed with Freud, which soon ended their work together. However, Freud continued to work to refine talk therapy and build his theory on personality.

LEVELS OF CONSCIOUSNESS

To explain the concept of conscious versus unconscious experience, Freud compared the mind to an iceberg (**Figure 11.5**). He said that only about one-tenth of our mind is **conscious**, and the rest of our mind is **unconscious**. Our unconscious refers to that mental activity of which we are unaware and are unable to access (Freud, 1923). According to Freud, unacceptable urges and desires are kept in our unconscious through a process called repression. For example, we sometimes say things that we don't intend to say by unintentionally substituting another word for the one we meant. You've probably heard of a Freudian slip, the term used to describe this. Freud suggested that slips of the tongue are actually sexual or aggressive urges, accidentally slipping out of our unconscious. Speech errors such as this are quite common. Seeing them as a reflection of unconscious desires, linguists today have found that slips of the tongue tend to occur when we are tired, nervous, or not at our optimal level of cognitive functioning (Motley, 2002).

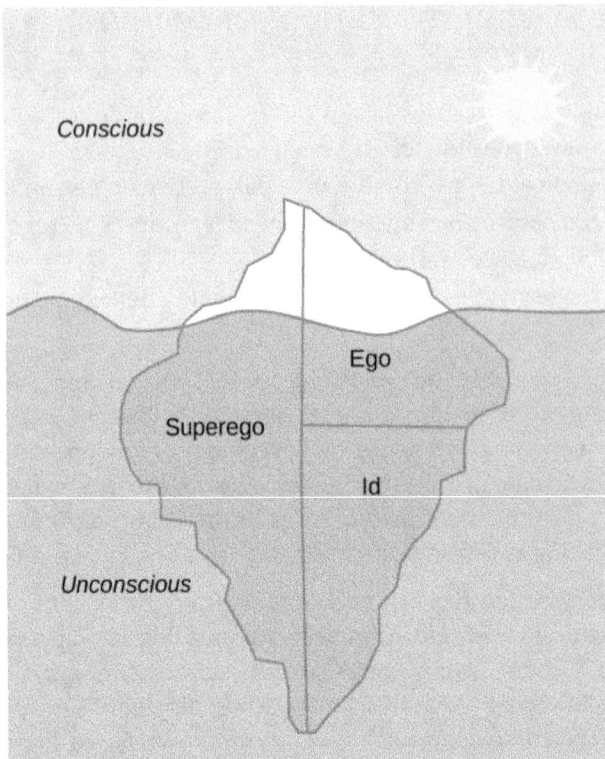

Figure 11.5 Freud believed that we are only aware of a small amount of our mind's activities and that most of it remains hidden from us in our unconscious. The information in our unconscious affects our behavior, although we are unaware of it.

According to Freud, our personality develops from a conflict between two forces: our biological aggressive and pleasure-seeking drives versus our internal (socialized) control over these drives. Our personality is the result of our efforts to balance these two competing forces. Freud suggested that we can understand this by imagining three interacting systems within our minds. He called them the id, ego, and superego (**Figure 11.6**).

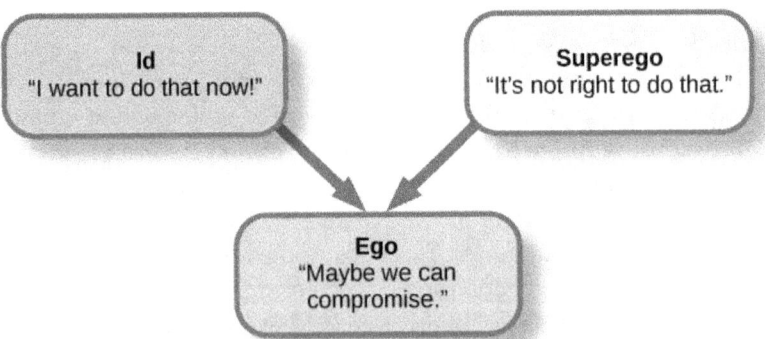

Figure 11.6 The job of the ego, or self, is to balance the aggressive/pleasure-seeking drives of the id with the moral control of the superego.

The unconscious **id** contains our most primitive drives or urges, and is present from birth. It directs impulses for hunger, thirst, and sex. Freud believed that the id operates on what he called the "pleasure principle," in which the id seeks immediate gratification. Through social interactions with parents and others in a child's environment, the ego and superego develop to help control the id. The **superego** develops as a child interacts with others, learning the social rules for right and wrong. The superego acts as our conscience; it is our moral compass that tells us how we should behave. It strives for perfection and judges our behavior, leading to feelings of pride or—when we fall short of the ideal—feelings of guilt. In contrast to the instinctual id and the rule-based superego, the **ego** is the rational part of our personality. It's what Freud considered to be the self, and it is the part of our personality that is seen by others. Its job is to balance the demands of the id and superego in the context of reality; thus, it operates on what Freud called the "reality principle." The ego helps the id satisfy its desires in a realistic way.

The id and superego are in constant conflict, because the id wants instant gratification regardless of the consequences, but the superego tells us that we must behave in socially acceptable ways. Thus, the ego's job is to find the middle ground. It helps satisfy the id's desires in a rational way that will not lead us to feelings of guilt. According to Freud, a person who has a strong ego, which can balance the demands of the id and the superego, has a healthy personality. Freud maintained that imbalances in the system can lead to **neurosis** (a tendency to experience negative emotions), anxiety disorders, or unhealthy behaviors. For example, a person who is dominated by their id might be narcissistic and impulsive. A person with a dominant superego might be controlled by feelings of guilt and deny themselves even socially acceptable pleasures; conversely, if the superego is weak or absent, a person might become a psychopath. An overly dominant superego might be seen in an over-controlled individual whose rational grasp on reality is so strong that they are unaware of their emotional needs, or, in a neurotic who is overly defensive (overusing ego defense mechanisms).

DEFENSE MECHANISMS

Freud believed that feelings of anxiety result from the ego's inability to mediate the conflict between the id and superego. When this happens, Freud believed that the ego seeks to restore balance through various protective measures known as defense mechanisms (**Figure 11.7**). When certain events, feelings, or yearnings cause an individual anxiety, the individual wishes to reduce that anxiety. To do that, the individual's unconscious mind uses ego **defense mechanisms**, unconscious protective behaviors that aim to reduce anxiety. The ego, usually conscious, resorts to unconscious strivings to protect the ego from being overwhelmed by anxiety. When we use defense mechanisms, we are unaware that we are using them. Further, they operate in various ways that distort reality. According to Freud, we all use ego defense mechanisms.

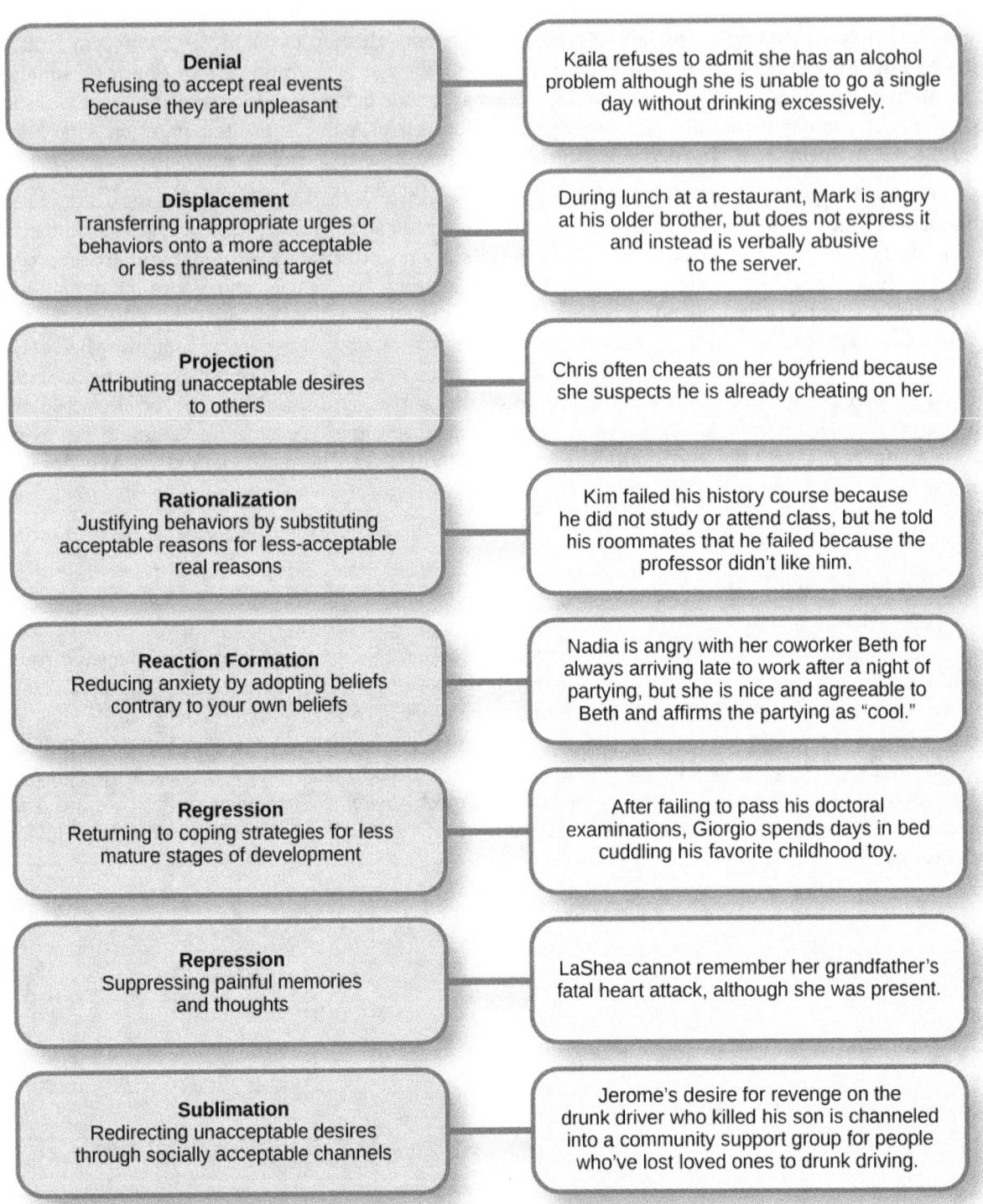

Figure 11.7 Defense mechanisms are unconscious protective behaviors that work to reduce anxiety.

While everyone uses defense mechanisms, Freud believed that overuse of them may be problematic. For example, let's say Joe is a high school football player. Deep down, Joe feels sexually attracted to males. His conscious belief is that being gay is immoral and that if he were gay, his family would disown him and he would be ostracized by his peers. Therefore, there is a conflict between his conscious beliefs (being gay is wrong and will result in being ostracized) and his unconscious urges (attraction to males). The idea that he might be gay causes Joe to have feelings of anxiety. How can he decrease his anxiety? Joe may find himself acting very "macho," making gay jokes, and picking on a school peer who is gay. This way, Joe's unconscious impulses are further submerged.

There are several different types of defense mechanisms. For instance, in repression, anxiety-causing memories from consciousness are blocked. As an analogy, let's say your car is making a strange noise, but because you do not have the money to get it fixed, you just turn up the radio so that you no longer hear the strange noise. Eventually you forget about it. Similarly, in the human psyche, if a memory is too overwhelming to deal with, it might be **repressed** and thus removed from conscious awareness (Freud, 1920). This repressed memory might cause symptoms in other areas.

Another defense mechanism is **reaction formation**, in which someone expresses feelings, thoughts, and behaviors opposite to their inclinations. In the above example, Joe made fun of a gay peer while himself being attracted to males. In **regression**, an individual acts much younger than their age. For example, a four-year-old child who resents the arrival of a newborn sibling may act like a baby and revert to drinking out of a bottle. In **projection**, a person refuses to acknowledge her own unconscious feelings and instead sees those feelings in someone else. Other defense mechanisms include **rationalization**, **displacement**, and **sublimation**.

LINK TO LEARNING

Watch this video of Freud's defense mechanisms (http://openstax.org/l/defmech) to review.

STAGES OF PSYCHOSEXUAL DEVELOPMENT

Freud believed that personality develops during early childhood: Childhood experiences shape our personalities as well as our behavior as adults. He asserted that we develop via a series of stages during childhood. Each of us must pass through these childhood stages, and if we do not have the proper nurturing and parenting during a stage, we will be stuck, or fixated, in that stage, even as adults.

In each **psychosexual stage of development**, the child's pleasure-seeking urges, coming from the id, are focused on a different area of the body, called an erogenous zone. The stages are oral, anal, phallic, latency, and genital (Table 11.1).

Freud's psychosexual development theory is quite controversial. To understand the origins of the theory, it is helpful to be familiar with the political, social, and cultural influences of Freud's day in Vienna at the turn of the 20th century. During this era, a climate of sexual repression, combined with limited understanding and education surrounding human sexuality, heavily influenced Freud's perspective. Given that sex was a taboo topic, Freud assumed that negative emotional states (neuroses) stemmed from suppression of unconscious sexual and aggressive urges. For Freud, his own recollections and interpretations of patients' experiences and dreams were sufficient proof that psychosexual stages were universal events in early childhood.

Freud's Stages of Psychosexual Development

Stage	Age (years)	Erogenous Zone	Major Conflict	Adult Fixation Example
Oral	0–1	Mouth	Weaning off breast or bottle	Smoking, overeating
Anal	1–3	Anus	Toilet training	Neatness, messiness

Freud's Stages of Psychosexual Development

Stage	Age (years)	Erogenous Zone	Major Conflict	Adult Fixation Example
Phallic	3–6	Genitals	Oedipus/Electra complex	Vanity, overambition
Latency	6–12	None	None	None
Genital	12+	Genitals	None	None

Table 11.1

Oral Stage

In the **oral stage** (birth to 1 year), pleasure is focused on the mouth. Eating and the pleasure derived from sucking (nipples, pacifiers, and thumbs) play a large part in a baby's first year of life. At around 1 year of age, babies are weaned from the bottle or breast, and this process can create conflict if not handled properly by caregivers. According to Freud, an adult who smokes, drinks, overeats, or bites her nails is fixated in the oral stage of her psychosexual development; she may have been weaned too early or too late, resulting in these fixation tendencies, all of which seek to ease anxiety.

Anal Stage

After passing through the oral stage, children enter what Freud termed the **anal stage** (1–3 years). In this stage, children experience pleasure in their bowel and bladder movements, so it makes sense that the conflict in this stage is over toilet training. During this stage of development, children work to master control of themselves. Freud suggested that success at the anal stage depended on how parents handled toilet training. Parents who offer praise and rewards encourage positive results and can help children feel competent. Parents who are harsh in toilet training can cause a child to become so fearful of soiling that they over-control and become fixated at the anal stage, leading to the development of an anal-retentive personality. The anal-retentive personality is stingy and stubborn, has a compulsive need for order and neatness, and might be considered a perfectionist. If parents are too lenient in toilet training, the child may fail to develop sufficient self-control, become fixated at this stage, and develop an anal-expulsive personality. The anal-expulsive personality is messy, careless, disorganized, and prone to emotional outbursts.

Phallic Stage

Freud's third stage of psychosexual development is the **phallic stage** (3–6 years), corresponding to the age when children become aware of their bodies and recognize the differences between boys and girls. The erogenous zone in this stage is the genitals. Conflict arises when the child feels a desire for the opposite-sex parent, and jealousy and hatred toward the same-sex parent. For boys, this is called the Oedipus complex, involving a boy's desire for his mother and his urge to replace his father who is seen as a rival for the mother's attention. At the same time, the boy is afraid his father will punish him for his feelings, so he experiences *castration anxiety*. The Oedipus complex is successfully resolved when the boy begins to identify with his father as an indirect way to have the mother. Failure to resolve the Oedipus complex may result in fixation and development of a personality that might be described as vain and overly ambitious.

Girls experience a comparable conflict in the phallic stage—the Electra complex. The Electra complex, while often attributed to Freud, was actually proposed by Freud's protégé, Carl Jung (Jung & Kerenyi, 1963). A girl desires the attention of her father and wishes to take her mother's place. Jung also said that girls are angry with the mother for not providing them with a penis—hence the term *penis envy*. While Freud initially embraced the Electra complex as a parallel to the Oedipus complex, he later rejected it, yet it remains as a cornerstone of Freudian theory, thanks in part to academics in the field (Freud, 1931/1968; Scott, 2005).

Latency Period

Following the phallic stage of psychosexual development is a period known as the **latency period** (6 years to puberty). This period is not considered a stage, because sexual feelings are dormant as children focus on other pursuits, such as school, friendships, hobbies, and sports. Children generally engage in activities with peers of the same sex, which serves to consolidate a child's gender-role identity.

Genital Stage

The final stage is the **genital stage** (from puberty on). In this stage, there is a sexual reawakening as the incestuous urges resurface. The young person redirects these urges to other, more socially acceptable partners (who often resemble the other-sex parent). People in this stage have mature sexual interests, which for Freud meant a strong desire for the opposite sex. Individuals who successfully completed the previous stages, reaching the genital stage with no fixations, are said to be well-balanced, healthy adults.

While most of Freud's ideas have not found support in modern research, we cannot discount the contributions that Freud has made to the field of psychology. It was Freud who pointed out that a large part of our mental life is influenced by the experiences of early childhood and takes place outside of our conscious awareness; his theories paved the way for others.

While Freud's focus on biological drives led him to emphasize the impact of sociocultural factors on personality development, his followers quickly realized that biology alone could not account for the diversity they encountered as the practice of psychoanalysis spread during the time of the Nazi Holocaust. The antisemitism which was prevalent during this period of time may have led mainstream psychoanalysts to focus primarily on the universality of the psychological structures of the mind.

11.3 Neo-Freudians: Adler, Erikson, Jung, and Horney

Learning Objectives

By the end of this section, you will be able to:
- Discuss the concept of the inferiority complex
- Discuss the core differences between Erikson's and Freud's views on personality
- Discuss Jung's ideas of the collective unconscious and archetypes
- Discuss the work of Karen Horney, including her revision of Freud's "penis envy"

Freud attracted many followers who modified his ideas to create new theories about personality. These theorists, referred to as neo-Freudians, generally agreed with Freud that childhood experiences matter, but deemphasized sex, focusing more on the social environment and effects of culture on personality. Four notable neo-Freudians include Alfred Adler, Erik Erikson, Carl Jung (pronounced "Yoong"), and Karen Horney (pronounced "HORN-eye").

ALFRED ADLER

Alfred Adler, a colleague of Freud's and the first president of the Vienna Psychoanalytical Society (Freud's inner circle of colleagues), was the first major theorist to break away from Freud (Figure 11.8). He subsequently founded a school of psychology called **individual psychology**, which focuses on our drive to compensate for feelings of inferiority. Adler (1937, 1956) proposed the concept of the **inferiority complex**. An inferiority complex refers to a person's feelings that they lack worth and don't measure up to the standards of others or of society. Adler's ideas about inferiority represent a major difference between his thinking and Freud's. Freud believed that we are motivated by sexual and aggressive urges, but Adler (1930, 1961) believed that feelings of inferiority in childhood are what drive people to attempt to gain superiority and that this striving is the force behind all of our thoughts, emotions, and behaviors.

Figure 11.8 Alfred Adler proposed the concept of the inferiority complex.

Adler also believed in the importance of social connections, seeing childhood development emerging through social development rather than the sexual stages Freud outlined. Adler noted the inter-relatedness of humanity and the need to work together for the betterment of all. He said, "The happiness of mankind lies in working together, in living as if each individual had set himself the task of contributing to the common welfare" (Adler, 1964, p. 255) with the main goal of psychology being "to recognize the equal rights and equality of others" (Adler, 1961, p. 691).

With these ideas, Adler identified three fundamental social tasks that all of us must experience: occupational tasks (careers), societal tasks (friendship), and love tasks (finding an intimate partner for a long-term relationship). Rather than focus on sexual or aggressive motives for behavior as Freud did, Adler focused on social motives. He also emphasized conscious rather than unconscious motivation, since he believed that the three fundamental social tasks are explicitly known and pursued. That is not to say that Adler did not also believe in unconscious processes—he did—but he felt that conscious processes were more important.

One of Adler's major contributions to personality psychology was the idea that our birth order shapes our personality. He proposed that older siblings, who start out as the focus of their parents' attention but must share that attention once a new child joins the family, compensate by becoming overachievers. The youngest children, according to Adler, may be spoiled, leaving the middle child with the opportunity to minimize the negative dynamics of the youngest and oldest children. Despite popular attention, research has not conclusively confirmed Adler's hypotheses about birth order.

LINK TO LEARNING

One of Adler's major contributions to personality psychology was the idea that our birth order shapes our personality. View this summary of birth order theory (http://openstax.org/l/best) to learn more.

ERIK ERIKSON

As an art school dropout with an uncertain future, young Erik Erikson met Freud's daughter, Anna Freud, while he was tutoring the children of an American couple undergoing psychoanalysis in Vienna. It was Anna Freud who encouraged Erikson to study psychoanalysis. Erikson received his diploma from the Vienna Psychoanalytic Institute in 1933, and as Nazism spread across Europe, he fled the country and immigrated to the United States that same year. As you learned when you studied lifespan development, Erikson later proposed a psychosocial theory of development, suggesting that an individual's personality develops throughout the lifespan—a departure from Freud's view that personality is fixed in early life. In his theory, Erikson emphasized the social relationships that are important at each stage of personality development, in contrast to Freud's emphasis on sex. Erikson identified eight stages, each of which represents a conflict or developmental task (Table 11.2). The development of a healthy personality and a sense of competence depend on the successful completion of each task.

Erikson's Psychosocial Stages of Development

Stage	Age (years)	Developmental Task	Description
1	0–1	Trust vs. mistrust	Trust (or mistrust) that basic needs, such as nourishment and affection, will be met
2	1–3	Autonomy vs. shame/doubt	Sense of independence in many tasks develops
3	3–6	Initiative vs. guilt	Take initiative on some activities, may develop guilt when success not met or boundaries overstepped
4	7–11	Industry vs. inferiority	Develop self-confidence in abilities when competent or sense of inferiority when not
5	12–18	Identity vs. confusion	Experiment with and develop identity and roles
6	19–29	Intimacy vs. isolation	Establish intimacy and relationships with others
7	30–64	Generativity vs. stagnation	Contribute to society and be part of a family
8	65–	Integrity vs. despair	Assess and make sense of life and meaning of contributions

Table 11.2

CARL JUNG

Carl Jung (Figure 11.9) was a Swiss psychiatrist and protégé of Freud, who later split off from Freud and developed his own theory, which he called **analytical psychology**. The focus of analytical psychology is on working to balance opposing forces of conscious and unconscious thought, and experience within one's personality. According to Jung, this work is a continuous learning process—mainly occurring in the second half of life—of becoming aware of unconscious elements and integrating them into consciousness.

Figure 11.9 Carl Jung was interested in exploring the collective unconscious.

Jung's split from Freud was based on two major disagreements. First, Jung, like Adler and Erikson, did not accept that sexual drive was the primary motivator in a person's mental life. Second, although Jung agreed with Freud's concept of a personal unconscious, he thought it to be incomplete. In addition to the personal unconscious, Jung focused on the collective unconscious.

The **collective unconscious** is a universal version of the personal unconscious, holding mental patterns, or memory traces, which are common to all of us (Jung, 1928). These ancestral memories, which Jung called **archetypes**, are represented by universal themes in various cultures, as expressed through literature, art, and dreams (Jung). Jung said that these themes reflect common experiences of people the world over, such as facing death, becoming independent, and striving for mastery. Jung (1964) believed that through biology, each person is handed down the same themes and that the same types of symbols—such as the hero, the maiden, the sage, and the trickster—are present in the folklore and fairy tales of every culture. In Jung's view, the task of integrating these unconscious archetypal aspects of the self is part of the self-realization process in the second half of life. With this orientation toward self-realization, Jung parted ways with Freud's belief that personality is determined solely by past events and anticipated the humanistic movement with its emphasis on self-actualization and orientation toward the future.

Jung also proposed two attitudes or approaches toward life: extroversion and introversion (Jung, 1923) (Table 11.3). These ideas are considered Jung's most important contributions to the field of personality psychology, as almost all models of personality now include these concepts. If you are an extrovert, then you are a person who is energized by being outgoing and socially oriented: You derive your energy from being around others. If you are an introvert, then you are a person who may be quiet and reserved, or you may be social, but your energy is derived from your inner psychic activity. Jung believed a balance between extroversion and introversion best served the goal of self-realization.

Introverts and Extroverts

Introvert	Extrovert
Energized by being alone	Energized by being with others
Avoids attention	Seeks attention

Introverts and Extroverts

Introvert	Extrovert
Speaks slowly and softly	Speaks quickly and loudly
Thinks before speaking	Thinks out loud
Stays on one topic	Jumps from topic to topic
Prefers written communication	Prefers verbal communication
Pays attention easily	Distractible
Cautious	Acts first, thinks later

Table 11.3

Another concept proposed by Jung was the persona, which he referred to as a mask that we adopt. According to Jung, we consciously create this persona; however, it is derived from both our conscious experiences and our collective unconscious. What is the purpose of the persona? Jung believed that it is a compromise between who we really are (our true self) and what society expects us to be. We hide those parts of ourselves that are not aligned with society's expectations.

LINK TO LEARNING

Jung's view of extroverted and introverted types serves as a basis of the Myers-Briggs Type Indicator (MBTI). This questionnaire describes a person's degree of introversion versus extroversion, thinking versus feeling, intuition versus sensation, and judging versus perceiving. Take this modified questionnaire based on the MBTI (http://openstax.org/l/myersbriggs) to learn more.

CONNECT THE CONCEPTS

Are Archetypes Genetically Based?

Jung proposed that human responses to archetypes are similar to instinctual responses in animals. One criticism of Jung is that there is no evidence that archetypes are biologically based or similar to animal instincts (Roesler, 2012). Jung formulated his ideas about 100 years ago, and great advances have been made in the field of genetics since that time. We've found that human babies are born with certain capacities, including the ability to acquire language. However, we've also found that symbolic information (such as archetypes) is not encoded on the genome and that babies cannot decode symbolism, refuting the idea of a biological basis to archetypes. Rather than being seen as purely biological, more recent research suggests that archetypes emerge directly from our experiences and are reflections of linguistic or cultural characteristics (Young-Eisendrath, 1995). Today, most Jungian scholars believe that the collective unconscious and archetypes are based on both innate and environmental influences, with the differences being in the role and degree of each (Sotirova-Kohli et al., 2013).

KAREN HORNEY

Karen Horney was one of the first women trained as a Freudian psychoanalyst. During the Great

Depression, Horney moved from Germany to the United States, and subsequently moved away from Freud's teachings. Like Jung, Horney believed that each individual has the potential for self-realization and that the goal of psychoanalysis should be moving toward a healthy self rather than exploring early childhood patterns of dysfunction. Horney also disagreed with the Freudian idea that girls have penis envy and are jealous of male biological features. According to Horney, any jealousy is most likely culturally based, due to the greater privileges that males often have, meaning that the differences between men's and women's personalities are culturally based, not biologically based. She further suggested that men have womb envy, because they cannot give birth.

Horney's theories focused on the role of unconscious anxiety. She suggested that normal growth can be blocked by basic anxiety stemming from needs not being met, such as childhood experiences of loneliness and/or isolation. How do children learn to handle this anxiety? Horney suggested three styles of coping (Table 11.4). The first coping style, *moving toward people*, relies on affiliation and dependence. These children become dependent on their parents and other caregivers in an effort to receive attention and affection, which provides relief from anxiety (Burger, 2008). When these children grow up, they tend to use this same coping strategy to deal with relationships, expressing an intense need for love and acceptance (Burger, 2008). The second coping style, *moving against people*, relies on aggression and assertiveness. Children with this coping style find that fighting is the best way to deal with an unhappy home situation, and they deal with their feelings of insecurity by bullying other children (Burger, 2008). As adults, people with this coping style tend to lash out with hurtful comments and exploit others (Burger, 2008). The third coping style, *moving away from people*, centers on detachment and isolation. These children handle their anxiety by withdrawing from the world. They need privacy and tend to be self-sufficient. When these children are adults, they continue to avoid such things as love and friendship, and they also tend to gravitate toward careers that require little interaction with others (Burger, 2008).

Horney's Coping Styles

Coping Style	Description	Example
Moving toward people	Affiliation and dependence	Child seeking positive attention and affection from parent; adult needing love
Moving against people	Aggression and manipulation	Child fighting or bullying other children; adult who is abrasive and verbally hurtful, or who exploits others
Moving away from people	Detachment and isolation	Child withdrawn from the world and isolated; adult loner

Table 11.4

Horney believed these three styles are ways in which people typically cope with day-to-day problems; however, the three coping styles can become neurotic strategies if they are used rigidly and compulsively, leading a person to become alienated from others.

11.4 Learning Approaches

Learning Objectives

By the end of this section, you will be able to:
- Describe the behaviorist perspective on personality
- Describe the cognitive perspective on personality
- Describe the social cognitive perspective on personality

In contrast to the psychodynamic approaches of Freud and the neo-Freudians, which relate personality to inner (and hidden) processes, the learning approaches focus only on observable behavior. This illustrates one significant advantage of the learning approaches over psychodynamics: Because learning approaches involve observable, measurable phenomena, they can be scientifically tested.

THE BEHAVIORAL PERSPECTIVE

Behaviorists do not believe in biological determinism: They do not see personality traits as inborn. Instead, they view personality as significantly shaped by the reinforcements and consequences outside of the organism. In other words, people behave in a consistent manner based on prior learning. B. F. Skinner, a strict behaviorist, believed that environment was solely responsible for all behavior, including the enduring, consistent behavior patterns studied by personality theorists.

As you may recall from your study on the psychology of learning, Skinner proposed that we demonstrate consistent behavior patterns because we have developed certain response tendencies (Skinner, 1953). In other words, we *learn* to behave in particular ways. We increase the behaviors that lead to positive consequences, and we decrease the behaviors that lead to negative consequences. Skinner disagreed with Freud's idea that personality is fixed in childhood. He argued that personality develops over our entire life, not only in the first few years. Our responses can change as we come across new situations; therefore, we can expect more variability over time in personality than Freud would anticipate. For example, consider a young woman, Greta, a risk taker. She drives fast and participates in dangerous sports such as hang gliding and kiteboarding. But after she gets married and has children, the system of reinforcements and punishments in her environment changes. Speeding and extreme sports are no longer reinforced, so she no longer engages in those behaviors. In fact, Greta now describes herself as a cautious person.

THE SOCIAL-COGNITIVE PERSPECTIVE

Albert Bandura agreed with Skinner that personality develops through learning. He disagreed, however, with Skinner's strict behaviorist approach to personality development, because he felt that thinking and reasoning are important components of learning. He presented a **social-cognitive theory** of personality that emphasizes both learning and cognition as sources of individual differences in personality. In social-cognitive theory, the concepts of reciprocal determinism, observational learning, and self-efficacy all play a part in personality development.

Reciprocal Determinism

In contrast to Skinner's idea that the environment alone determines behavior, Bandura (1990) proposed the concept of **reciprocal determinism**, in which cognitive processes, behavior, and context all interact, each factor influencing and being influenced by the others simultaneously (Figure 11.10). *Cognitive processes* refer to all characteristics previously learned, including beliefs, expectations, and personality characteristics. *Behavior* refers to anything that we do that may be rewarded or punished. Finally, the *context* in which the behavior occurs refers to the environment or situation, which includes rewarding/punishing stimuli.

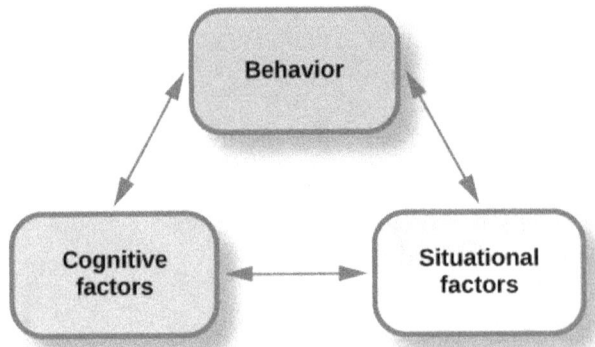

Figure 11.10 Bandura proposed the idea of reciprocal determinism: Our behavior, cognitive processes, and situational context all influence each other.

Consider, for example, that you're at a festival and one of the attractions is bungee jumping from a bridge. Do you do it? In this example, the behavior is bungee jumping. Cognitive factors that might influence this behavior include your beliefs and values, and your past experiences with similar behaviors. Finally, context refers to the reward structure for the behavior. According to reciprocal determinism, all of these factors are in play.

Observational Learning

Bandura's key contribution to learning theory was the idea that much learning is vicarious. We learn by observing someone else's behavior and its consequences, which Bandura called observational learning. He felt that this type of learning also plays a part in the development of our personality. Just as we learn individual behaviors, we learn new behavior patterns when we see them performed by other people or models. Drawing on the behaviorists' ideas about reinforcement, Bandura suggested that whether we choose to imitate a model's behavior depends on whether we see the model reinforced or punished. Through observational learning, we come to learn what behaviors are acceptable and rewarded in our culture, and we also learn to inhibit deviant or socially unacceptable behaviors by seeing what behaviors are punished.

We can see the principles of reciprocal determinism at work in observational learning. For example, personal factors determine which behaviors in the environment a person chooses to imitate, and those environmental events in turn are processed cognitively according to other personal factors. One person may experience receiving attention as reinforcing, and that person may be more inclined to imitate behaviors such as boasting when a model has been reinforced. For others, boasting may be viewed negatively, despite the attention that might result—or receiving heightened attention may be perceived as being scrutinized. In either case, the person may be less likely to imitate those behaviors even though the reasons for not doing so would be different.

Self-Efficacy

Bandura (1977, 1995) has studied a number of cognitive and personal factors that affect learning and personality development, and most recently has focused on the concept of self-efficacy. **Self-efficacy** is our level of confidence in our own abilities, developed through our social experiences. Self-efficacy affects how we approach challenges and reach goals. In observational learning, self-efficacy is a cognitive factor that affects which behaviors we choose to imitate as well as our success in performing those behaviors.

People who have high self-efficacy believe that their goals are within reach, have a positive view of challenges seeing them as tasks to be mastered, develop a deep interest in and strong commitment to the activities in which they are involved, and quickly recover from setbacks. Conversely, people with low self-efficacy avoid challenging tasks because they doubt their ability to be successful, tend to focus on failure and negative outcomes, and lose confidence in their abilities if they experience setbacks. Feelings of self-efficacy can be specific to certain situations. For instance, a student might feel confident in her ability in English class but much less so in math class.

JULIAN ROTTER AND LOCUS OF CONTROL

Julian Rotter (1966) proposed the concept of locus of control, another cognitive factor that affects learning and personality development. Distinct from self-efficacy, which involves our belief in our own abilities, **locus of control** refers to our beliefs about the power we have over our lives. In Rotter's view, people possess either an internal or an external locus of control (**Figure 11.11**). Those of us with an internal locus of control ("internals") tend to believe that most of our outcomes are the direct result of our efforts. Those of us with an external locus of control ("externals") tend to believe that our outcomes are outside of our control. Externals see their lives as being controlled by other people, luck, or chance. For example, say you didn't spend much time studying for your psychology test and went out to dinner with friends instead. When you receive your test score, you see that you earned a D. If you possess an internal locus of control, you would most likely admit that you failed because you didn't spend enough time studying and decide to study more for the next test. On the other hand, if you possess an external locus of control, you might conclude that the test was too hard and not bother studying for the next test, because you figure you will fail it anyway. Researchers have found that people with an internal locus of control perform better academically, achieve more in their careers, are more independent, are healthier, are better able to cope, and are less depressed than people who have an external locus of control (Benassi, Sweeney, & Durfour, 1988; Lefcourt, 1982; Maltby, Day, & Macaskill, 2007; Whyte, 1977, 1978, 1980).

Figure 11.11 Locus of control occurs on a continuum from internal to external.

LINK TO LEARNING

Take the Locus of Control questionnaire (http://openstax.org/l/locuscontrol) to learn more. Scores range from 0 to 13. A low score on this questionnaire indicates an internal locus of control, and a high score indicates an external locus of control.

WALTER MISCHEL AND THE PERSON-SITUATION DEBATE

Walter Mischel was a student of Julian Rotter and taught for years at Stanford, where he was a colleague of Albert Bandura. Mischel surveyed several decades of empirical psychological literature regarding trait prediction of behavior, and his conclusion shook the foundations of personality psychology. Mischel found that the data did not support the central principle of the field—that a person's personality traits are consistent across situations. His report triggered a decades-long period of self-examination, known as the person-situation debate, among personality psychologists.

Mischel suggested that perhaps we were looking for consistency in the wrong places. He found that although behavior was inconsistent across different situations, it was much more consistent within situations—so that a person's behavior in one situation would likely be repeated in a similar one. And as you will see next regarding his famous "marshmallow test," Mischel also found that behavior is consistent in equivalent situations across time.

One of Mischel's most notable contributions to personality psychology was his ideas on self-regulation. According to Lecci & Magnavita (2013), "Self-regulation is the process of identifying a goal or set of goals and, in pursuing these goals, using both internal (e.g., thoughts and affect) and external (e.g., responses of anything or anyone in the environment) feedback to maximize goal attainment" (p. 6.3). Self-regulation is also known as will power. When we talk about will power, we tend to think of it as the ability to delay gratification. For example, Bettina's teenage daughter made strawberry cupcakes, and they looked delicious. However, Bettina forfeited the pleasure of eating one, because she is training for a 5K race and wants to be fit and do well in the race. Would you be able to resist getting a small reward now in order to get a larger reward later? This is the question Mischel investigated in his now-classic marshmallow test.

Mischel designed a study to assess self-regulation in young children. In the marshmallow study, Mischel and his colleagues placed a preschool child in a room with one marshmallow on the table. The children were told they could either eat the marshmallow now, or wait until the researcher returned to the room, and then they could have two marshmallows (Mischel, Ebbesen & Raskoff, 1972). This was repeated with hundreds of preschoolers. What Mischel and his team found was that young children differ in their degree of self-control. Mischel and his colleagues continued to follow this group of preschoolers through high school, and what do you think they discovered? The children who had more self-control in preschool (the ones who waited for the bigger reward) were more successful in high school. They had higher SAT scores, had positive peer relationships, and were less likely to have substance abuse issues; as adults, they also had more stable marriages (Mischel, Shoda, & Rodriguez, 1989; Mischel et al., 2010). On the other hand, those children who had poor self-control in preschool (the ones who grabbed the one marshmallow) were not as successful in high school, and they were found to have academic and behavioral problems. A more recent study using a larger and more representative sample found associations between early delay of gratification (Watts, Duncan, & Quan, 2018) and measures of achievement in adolescence. However, researchers also found that the associations were not as strong as those reported during Mischel's initial experiment and were quite sensitive to situational factors such as early measures of cognitive capacity, family background, and home environment. This research suggests that consideration of situational factors is important to better understand behavior.

LINK TO LEARNING

Watch Joachim de Posada's TEDTalk about the marshmallow test (http://openstax.org/l/TEDPosada) to learn more and to see the test given to children in Columbia.

Today, the debate is mostly resolved, and most psychologists consider both the situation and personal factors in understanding behavior. For Mischel (1993), people are situation processors. The children in the marshmallow test each processed, or interpreted, the rewards structure of that situation in their own way. Mischel's approach to personality stresses the importance of both the situation and the way the person perceives the situation. Instead of behavior being determined by the situation, people use cognitive processes to interpret the situation and then behave in accordance with that interpretation.

11.5 Humanistic Approaches

Learning Objectives

By the end of this section, you will be able to:
- Discuss the contributions of Abraham Maslow and Carl Rogers to personality development

As the "third force" in psychology, humanism is touted as a reaction both to the pessimistic determinism of psychoanalysis, with its emphasis on psychological disturbance, and to the behaviorists' view of humans passively reacting to the environment, which has been criticized as making people out to be personality-less robots. It does not suggest that psychoanalytic, behaviorist, and other points of view are incorrect but argues that these perspectives do not recognize the depth and meaning of human experience, and fail to recognize the innate capacity for self-directed change and transforming personal experiences. This perspective focuses on how healthy people develop. One pioneering humanist, Abraham Maslow, studied people who he considered to be healthy, creative, and productive, including Albert Einstein, Eleanor Roosevelt, Thomas Jefferson, Abraham Lincoln, and others. Maslow (1950, 1970) found that such people share similar characteristics, such as being open, creative, loving, spontaneous, compassionate, concerned for others, and accepting of themselves. When you studied motivation, you learned about one of the best-known humanistic theories, Maslow's hierarchy of needs theory, in which Maslow proposes that human beings have certain needs in common and that these needs must be met in a certain order. The highest need is the need for self-actualization, which is the achievement of our fullest potential. Maslow differentiated between needs that motivate us to fulfill something that is missing and needs that inspire us to grow. He believed that many emotional and behavioral concerns arise as a result of failing to meet these hierarchical needs.

Another humanistic theorist was Carl Rogers. One of Rogers's main ideas about personality regards **self-concept**, our thoughts and feelings about ourselves. How would you respond to the question, "Who am I?" Your answer can show how you see yourself. If your response is primarily positive, then you tend to feel good about who you are, and you see the world as a safe and positive place. If your response is mainly negative, then you may feel unhappy with who you are. Rogers further divided the self into two categories: the ideal self and the real self. The **ideal self** is the person that you would like to be; the **real self** is the person you actually are. Rogers focused on the idea that we need to achieve consistency between these two selves. We experience **congruence** when our thoughts about our real self and ideal self are very similar—in other words, when our self-concept is accurate. High congruence leads to a greater sense of self-worth and a healthy, productive life. Parents can help their children achieve this by giving them unconditional positive regard, or unconditional love. According to Rogers (1980), "As persons are accepted and prized, they tend to develop a more caring attitude towards themselves" (p. 116). Conversely, when there is a great discrepancy between our ideal and actual selves, we experience a state Rogers called **incongruence**, which can lead to maladjustment. Both Rogers's and Maslow's theories focus on individual choices and do not believe that biology is deterministic.

11.6 Biological Approaches

Learning Objectives

By the end of this section, you will be able to:
- Discuss the findings of the Minnesota Study of Twins Reared Apart as they relate to personality and genetics
- Discuss temperament and describe the three infant temperaments identified by Thomas and Chess
- Discuss the evolutionary perspective on personality development

How much of our personality is in-born and biological, and how much is influenced by the environment and culture we are raised in? Psychologists who favor the biological approach believe that inherited predispositions as well as physiological processes can be used to explain differences in our personalities (Burger, 2008).

Evolutionary psychology relative to personality development looks at personality traits that are universal, as well as differences across individuals. In this view, adaptive differences have evolved and then provide a survival and reproductive advantage. Individual differences are important from an evolutionary viewpoint for several reasons. Certain individual differences, and the heritability of these characteristics, have been well documented. David Buss has identified several theories to explore this relationship between personality traits and evolution, such as life-history theory, which looks at how people expend their time and energy (such as on bodily growth and maintenance, reproduction, or parenting). Another example is costly signaling theory, which examines the honesty and deception in the signals people send one another about their quality as a mate or friend (Buss, 2009).

In the field of behavioral genetics, the Minnesota Study of Twins Reared Apart—a well-known study of the genetic basis for personality—conducted research with twins from 1979 to 1999. In studying 350 pairs of twins, including pairs of identical and fraternal twins reared together and apart, researchers found that identical twins, whether raised together or apart, have very similar personalities (Bouchard, 1994; Bouchard, Lykken, McGue, Segal, & Tellegen, 1990; Segal, 2012). These findings suggest the heritability of some personality traits. **Heritability** refers to the proportion of difference among people that is attributed to genetics. Some of the traits that the study reported as having more than a 0.50 heritability ratio include leadership, obedience to authority, a sense of well-being, alienation, resistance to stress, and fearfulness. The implication is that some aspects of our personalities are largely controlled by genetics; however, it's important to point out that traits are not determined by a single gene, but by a combination of many genes, as well as by epigenetic factors that control whether the genes are expressed.

Other research that has examined the link between personality and other factors has identified and studied Type A and Type B personalities, which you will learn more about in the chapter on Stress, Health, and Lifestyle.

> **LINK TO LEARNING**
>
> Watch this video about genetic makeup's influence on personality (http://openstax.org/l/persondna) to learn more.

TEMPERAMENT

Most contemporary psychologists believe temperament has a biological basis due to its appearance very early in our lives (Rothbart, 2011). As you learned when you studied lifespan development, Thomas and Chess (1977) found that babies could be categorized into one of three temperaments: easy, difficult, or slow to warm up. However, environmental factors (family interactions, for example) and maturation can affect the ways in which children's personalities are expressed (Carter et al., 2008).

Research suggests that there are two dimensions of our temperament that are important parts of our adult personality—reactivity and self-regulation (Rothbart, Ahadi, & Evans, 2000). Reactivity refers to how we respond to new or challenging environmental stimuli; self-regulation refers to our ability to control that response (Rothbart & Derryberry, 1981; Rothbart, Sheese, Rueda, & Posner, 2011). For example, one person may immediately respond to new stimuli with a high level of anxiety, while another barely notices it.

11.7 Trait Theorists

Learning Objectives

By the end of this section, you will be able to:
- Discuss early trait theories of Cattell and Eysenck
- Discuss the Big Five factors and describe someone who is high and low on each of the five factors

Trait theorists believe personality can be understood via the approach that all people have certain **traits**, or characteristic ways of behaving. Do you tend to be sociable or shy? Passive or aggressive? Optimistic or pessimistic? Moody or even-tempered? Early trait theorists tried to describe all human personality traits. For example, one trait theorist, Gordon Allport (Allport & Odbert, 1936), found 4,500 words in the English language that could describe people. He organized these personality traits into three categories: cardinal traits, central traits, and secondary traits. A cardinal trait is one that dominates your entire personality, and hence your life—such as Ebenezer Scrooge's greed and Mother Theresa's altruism. Cardinal traits are not very common: Few people have personalities dominated by a single trait. Instead, our personalities typically are composed of multiple traits. Central traits are those that make up our personalities (such as loyal, kind, agreeable, friendly, sneaky, wild, and grouchy). Secondary traits are those that are not quite as obvious or as consistent as central traits. They are present under specific circumstances and include preferences and attitudes. For example, one person gets angry when people try to tickle him; another can only sleep on the left side of the bed; and yet another always orders her salad dressing on the side. And you—although not normally an anxious person—feel nervous before making a speech in front of your English class.

In an effort to make the list of traits more manageable, Raymond Cattell (1946, 1957) narrowed down the list to about 171 traits. However, saying that a trait is either present or absent does not accurately reflect a person's uniqueness, because all of our personalities are actually made up of the same traits; we differ only in the degree to which each trait is expressed. Cattell (1957) identified 16 factors or dimensions of personality: warmth, reasoning, emotional stability, dominance, liveliness, rule-consciousness, social boldness, sensitivity, vigilance, abstractedness, privateness, apprehension, openness to change, self-reliance, perfectionism, and tension (**Table 11.5**). He developed a personality assessment based on these 16 factors, called the 16PF. Instead of a trait being present or absent, each dimension is scored over a continuum, from high to low. For example, your level of warmth describes how warm, caring, and nice to others you are. If you score low on this index, you tend to be more distant and cold. A high score on this index signifies you are supportive and comforting.

Personality Factors Measured by the 16PF Questionnaire

Factor	Low Score	High Score
Warmth	Reserved, detached	Outgoing, supportive
Intellect	Concrete thinker	Analytical
Emotional stability	Moody, irritable	Stable, calm
Aggressiveness	Docile, submissive	Controlling, dominant
Liveliness	Somber, prudent	Adventurous, spontaneous
Dutifulness	Unreliable	Conscientious
Social assertiveness	Shy, restrained	Uninhibited, bold
Sensitivity	Tough-minded	Sensitive, caring
Paranoia	Trusting	Suspicious
Abstractness	Conventional	Imaginative
Introversion	Open, straightforward	Private, shrewd
Anxiety	Confident	Apprehensive
Openmindedness	Closeminded, traditional	Curious, experimental
Independence	Outgoing, social	Self-sufficient
Perfectionism	Disorganized, casual	Organized, precise
Tension	Relaxed	Stressed

Table 11.5

LINK TO LEARNING

Take this **assessment based on Cattell's 16PF questionnaire** (http://openstax.org/l/cattell) to see which personality traits dominate your personality.

Psychologists Hans and Sybil Eysenck were personality theorists (Figure 11.12) who focused on **temperament**, the inborn, genetically based personality differences that you studied earlier in the chapter. They believed personality is largely governed by biology. The Eysencks (Eysenck, 1990, 1992; Eysenck & Eysenck, 1963) viewed people as having two specific personality dimensions: extroversion/introversion and neuroticism/stability.

Figure 11.12 Hans and Sybil Eysenck believed that our personality traits are influenced by our genetic inheritance. (credit: "Sirswindon"/Wikimedia Commons)

According to their theory, people high on the trait of extroversion are sociable and outgoing, and readily connect with others, whereas people high on the trait of introversion have a higher need to be alone, engage in solitary behaviors, and limit their interactions with others. In the neuroticism/stability dimension, people high on neuroticism tend to be anxious; they tend to have an overactive sympathetic nervous system and, even with low stress, their bodies and emotional state tend to go into a flight-or-fight reaction. In contrast, people high on stability tend to need more stimulation to activate their flight-or-fight reaction and are considered more emotionally stable. Based on these two dimensions, the Eysencks' theory divides people into four quadrants. These quadrants are sometimes compared with the four temperaments described by the Greeks: melancholic, choleric, phlegmatic, and sanguine (Figure 11.13).

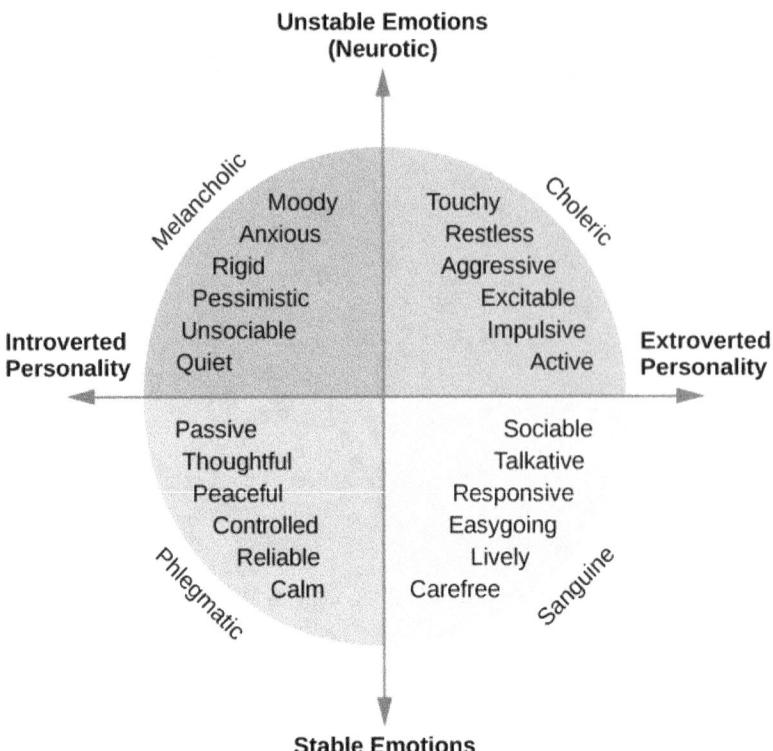

Figure 11.13 The Eysencks described two factors to account for variations in our personalities: extroversion/introversion and emotional stability/instability.

Later, the Eysencks added a third dimension: psychoticism versus superego control (Eysenck, Eysenck & Barrett, 1985). In this dimension, people who are high on psychoticism tend to be independent thinkers, cold, nonconformists, impulsive, antisocial, and hostile, whereas people who are high on superego control tend to have high impulse control—they are more altruistic, empathetic, cooperative, and conventional (Eysenck, Eysenck & Barrett, 1985).

While Cattell's 16 factors may be too broad, the Eysenck's two-factor system has been criticized for being too narrow. Another personality theory, called the **Five Factor Model**, effectively hits a middle ground, with its five factors referred to as the Big Five personality factors. It is the most popular theory in personality psychology today and the most accurate approximation of the basic personality dimensions (Funder, 2001). The five factors are openness to experience, conscientiousness, extroversion, agreeableness, and neuroticism (Figure 11.14). A helpful way to remember the factors is by using the mnemonic OCEAN.

In the Five Factor Model, each person has each factor, but they occur along a spectrum. Openness to experience is characterized by imagination, feelings, actions, and ideas. People who score high on this factor tend to be curious and have a wide range of interests. Conscientiousness is characterized by competence, self-discipline, thoughtfulness, and achievement-striving (goal-directed behavior). People who score high on this factor are hardworking and dependable. Numerous studies have found a positive correlation between conscientiousness and academic success (Akomolafe, 2013; Chamorro-Premuzic & Furnham, 2008; Conrad & Patry, 2012; Noftle & Robins, 2007; Wagerman & Funder, 2007). Extroversion is characterized by sociability, assertiveness, excitement-seeking, and emotional expression. People who score high on this factor are usually described as outgoing and warm. Not surprisingly, people who score high on both extroversion and openness are more likely to participate in adventure and risky sports due to their curious and excitement-seeking nature (Tok, 2011). The fourth factor is agreeableness, which is the tendency to be pleasant, cooperative, trustworthy, and good-natured. People who score low on agreeableness tend to be described as rude and uncooperative, yet one recent study reported that men who scored low on this factor actually earned more money than men who were considered more agreeable

(Judge, Livingston, & Hurst, 2012). The last of the Big Five factors is neuroticism, which is the tendency to experience negative emotions. People high on neuroticism tend to experience emotional instability and are characterized as angry, impulsive, and hostile. Watson and Clark (1984) found that people reporting high levels of neuroticism also tend to report feeling anxious and unhappy. In contrast, people who score low in neuroticism tend to be calm and even-tempered.

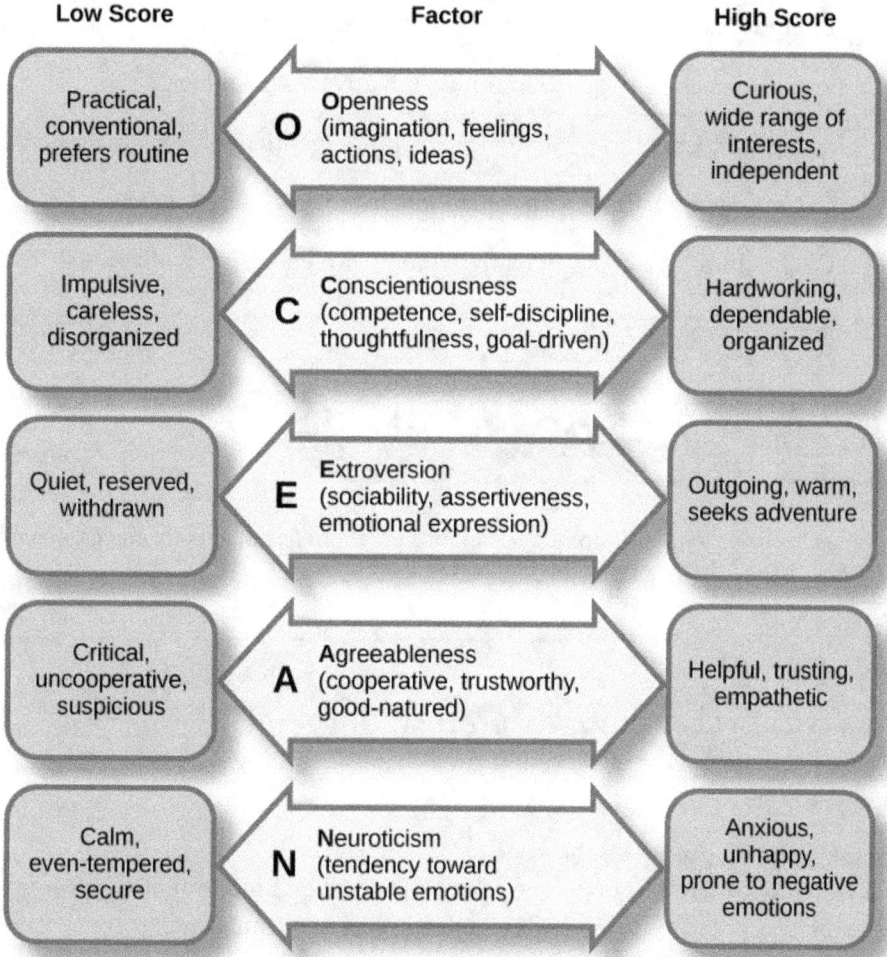

Figure 11.14 In the Five Factor Model, each person has five factors, each scored on a continuum from high to low. In the center column, notice that the first letter of each factor spells the mnemonic OCEAN.

The Big Five personality factors each represent a range between two extremes. In reality, most of us tend to lie somewhere midway along the continuum of each factor, rather than at polar ends. It's important to note that the Big Five factors are relatively stable over our lifespan, with some tendency for the factors to increase or decrease slightly. Researchers have found that conscientiousness increases through young adulthood into middle age, as we become better able to manage our personal relationships and careers (Donnellan & Lucas, 2008). Agreeableness also increases with age, peaking between 50 to 70 years (Terracciano, McCrae, Brant, & Costa, 2005). Neuroticism and extroversion tend to decline slightly with age (Donnellan & Lucas; Terracciano et al.). Additionally, The Big Five factors have been shown to exist across ethnicities, cultures, and ages, and may have substantial biological and genetic components (Jang, Livesley, & Vernon, 1996; Jang et al., 2006; McCrae & Costa, 1997; Schmitt et al., 2007).

Another model of personality traits is the HEXACO model. HEXACO is an acronym for six broad traits: honesty-humility, emotionality, extraversion, agreeableness, conscientiousness, and openness to experience (Anglim & O'Connor, 2018). Table 11.6 provides a brief overview of each trait.

The HEXACO Traits

Trait	Example Aspects of Trait
(H) Honesty-humility	Sincerity, modesty, faithfulness
(E) Emotionality	Sentimentality, anxiety, sensitivity
(X) Extraversion	Sociability, talkativeness, boldness
(A) Agreeableness	Patience, tolerance, gentleness
(C) Conscientiousness	Organization, thoroughness, precision
(O) Openness	Creativity, inquisitiveness, innovativeness

Table 11.6

LINK TO LEARNING

Take the Big Five Personality test (http://openstax.org/l/big5) to find out about your personality and where you fall on the Big Five factors.

11.8 Cultural Understandings of Personality

Learning Objectives

By the end of this section you should be able to:
- Discuss personality differences of people from collectivist and individualist cultures
- Discuss the three approaches to studying personality in a cultural context

As you have learned in this chapter, personality is shaped by both genetic and environmental factors. The culture in which you live is one of the most important environmental factors that shapes your personality (Triandis & Suh, 2002). The term **culture** refers to all of the beliefs, customs, art, and traditions of a particular society. Culture is transmitted to people through language as well as through the modeling of culturally acceptable and nonacceptable behaviors that are either rewarded or punished (Triandis & Suh, 2002). With these ideas in mind, personality psychologists have become interested in the role of culture in understanding personality. They ask whether personality traits are the same across cultures or if there are variations. It appears that there are both universal and culture-specific aspects that account for variation in people's personalities.

Why might it be important to consider cultural influences on personality? Western ideas about personality may not be applicable to other cultures (Benet-Martinez & Oishi, 2008). In fact, there is evidence that the strength of personality traits varies across cultures. Let's take a look at some of the Big Five factors (conscientiousness, neuroticism, openness, and extroversion) across cultures. As you will learn when you study social psychology, Asian cultures are more collectivist, and people in these cultures tend to be less extroverted. People in Central and South American cultures tend to score higher on openness to experience, whereas Europeans score higher on neuroticism (Benet-Martinez & Karakitapoglu-Aygun,

2003).

According to a study by Rentfrow and colleagues, there also seem to be regional personality differences within the United States (Figure 11.15). Researchers analyzed responses from over 1.5 million individuals in the United States and found that there are three distinct regional personality clusters: Cluster 1, which is in the Upper Midwest and Deep South, is dominated by people who fall into the "friendly and conventional" personality; Cluster 2, which includes the West, is dominated by people who are more relaxed, emotionally stable, calm, and creative; and Cluster 3, which includes the Northeast, has more people who are stressed, irritable, and depressed. People who live in Clusters 2 and 3 are also generally more open (Rentfrow et al., 2013).

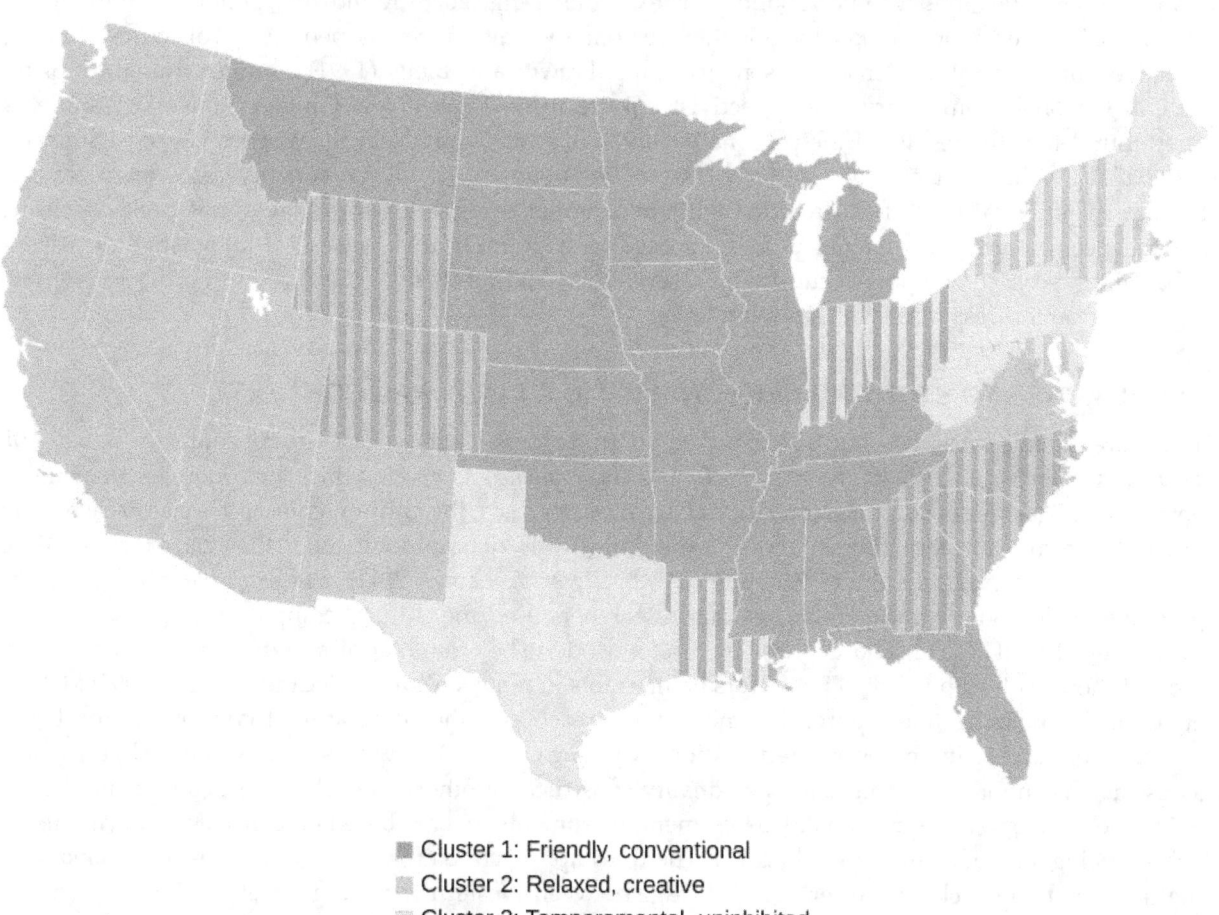

Figure 11.15 Researchers found three distinct regional personality clusters in the United States. People tend to be friendly and conventional in the Upper Midwest and Deep South; relaxed, emotionally stable, and creative in the West; and stressed, irritable, and depressed in the Northeast (Rentfrow et al., 2013).

One explanation for the regional differences is **selective migration** (Rentfrow et al., 2013). Selective migration is the concept that people choose to move to places that are compatible with their personalities and needs. For example, a person high on the agreeable scale would likely want to live near family and friends, and would choose to settle or remain in such an area. In contrast, someone high on openness would prefer to settle in a place that is recognized as diverse and innovative (such as California). Further, Rentfrow, Jost, Gosling, & Potter (2009) noted an overlap between geographical regions and personality characteristics that goes beyond the often-used explanations of religion, racial diversity, and education. Their research suggests that the psychological profile of a region is closely related to that of its residents. They found that levels of openness and conscientiousness in a state may predict voting patterns, indicating that there are correlations between geographic regions and personality differences between liberals and conservatives relating to political views, levels of economic vitality, and entrepreneurial rates.

PERSONALITY IN INDIVIDUALIST AND COLLECTIVIST CULTURES

Individualist cultures and collectivist cultures place emphasis on different basic values. People who live in individualist cultures tend to believe that independence, competition, and personal achievement are important. Individuals in Western nations such as the United States, England, and Australia score high on individualism (Oyserman, Coon, & Kemmelmier, 2002). People who live in collectivist cultures value social harmony, respectfulness, and group needs over individual needs. Individuals who live in countries in Asia, Africa, and South America score high on collectivism (Hofstede, 2001; Triandis, 1995). These values influence personality. For example, Yang (2006) found that people in individualist cultures displayed more personally oriented personality traits, whereas people in collectivist cultures displayed more socially oriented personality traits. Frewer and Bleus (1991) conducted a study of the Eysenk Personality Inventory in a collectivist culture using Papua New Guinean university students. They found that the results of the personality inventory were only relevant when analyzed within the context of a collectivist society. Similarly, Dana (1986) suggested that personality assessment services for Native Americans are often provided without a proper recognition of culture-specific responses and a tribe-specific frame of reference. Assessors need to have more than a general knowledge of history, tribal differences, contemporary culture on reservations, and levels of acculturation in order to interpret psychological test responses with a minimal bias.

APPROACHES TO STUDYING PERSONALITY IN A CULTURAL CONTEXT

There are three approaches that can be used to study personality in a cultural context, the *cultural-comparative approach*; the *indigenous approach*; and the *combined approach*, which incorporates elements of both views. Since ideas about personality have a Western basis, the cultural-comparative approach seeks to test Western ideas about personality in other cultures to determine whether they can be generalized and if they have cultural validity (Cheung van de Vijver, & Leong, 2011). For example, recall from the previous section on the trait perspective that researchers used the cultural-comparative approach to test the universality of McCrae and Costa's Five Factor Model. They found applicability in numerous cultures around the world, with the Big Five factors being stable in many cultures (McCrae & Costa, 1997; McCrae et al., 2005). The indigenous approach came about in reaction to the dominance of Western approaches to the study of personality in non-Western settings (Cheung et al., 2011). Because Western-based personality assessments cannot fully capture the personality constructs of other cultures, the indigenous model has led to the development of personality assessment instruments that are based on constructs relevant to the culture being studied (Cheung et al., 2011). The third approach to cross-cultural studies of personality is the combined approach, which serves as a bridge between Western and indigenous psychology as a way of understanding both universal and cultural variations in personality (Cheung et al., 2011).

11.9 Personality Assessment

Learning Objectives

By the end of this section, you will be able to:
- Discuss the Minnesota Multiphasic Personality Inventory
- Recognize and describe common projective tests used in personality assessment

Roberto, Mikhail, and Nat are college friends and all want to be police officers. Roberto is quiet and shy, lacks self-confidence, and usually follows others. He is a kind person, but lacks motivation. Mikhail is loud and boisterous, a leader. He works hard, but is impulsive and drinks too much on the weekends. Nat is thoughtful and well liked. She is trustworthy, but sometimes she has difficulty making quick decisions. Of these three, who would make the best police officer? What qualities and personality factors make someone a good police officer? What makes someone a bad or dangerous police officer?

A police officer's job is very high in stress, and law enforcement agencies want to make sure they hire the right people. Personality testing is often used for this purpose—to screen applicants for employment and job training. Personality tests are also used in criminal cases and custody battles, and to assess psychological disorders. This section explores the best known among the many different types of personality tests.

SELF-REPORT INVENTORIES

Self-report inventories are a kind of objective test used to assess personality. They typically use multiple-choice items or numbered scales, which represent a range from 1 (strongly disagree) to 5 (strongly agree). They often are called Likert scales after their developer, Rensis Likert (1932) (Figure 11.16). Self-report inventories are generally easy to administer and cost effective. There is also an increased likelihood of test takers being inclined to answer in ways that are intentionally or unintentionally more socially desirable, exaggerated, biased, or misleading. For example, someone applying for a job will likely try to present themselves in a positive light, perhaps as an even better candidate than they actually are.

	Strongly Disagree	Somewhat Disagree	No Opinion	Somewhat Agree	Strongly Agree
I am easygoing.	O	O	O	O	O
I have high standards.	O	O	O	O	O
I enjoy time alone.	O	O	O	O	O
I work well with others.	O	O	O	O	O
I dislike confrontation.	O	O	O	O	O
I prefer crowds over intimacy.	O	O	O	O	O

Figure 11.16 If you've ever taken a survey, you are probably familiar with Likert-type scale questions. Most personality inventories employ these types of response scales.

One of the most widely used personality inventories is the **Minnesota Multiphasic Personality Inventory (MMPI)**, first published in 1943, with 504 true/false questions, and updated to the MMPI-2 in 1989, with 567 questions. The original MMPI was based on a small, limited sample, composed mostly of Minnesota farmers and psychiatric patients; the revised inventory was based on a more representative, national sample to allow for better standardization. The MMPI-2 takes 1–2 hours to complete. Responses are scored to produce a clinical profile composed of 10 scales: hypochondriasis, depression, hysteria, psychopathic deviance (social deviance), masculinity versus femininity, paranoia, psychasthenia (obsessive/compulsive qualities), schizophrenia, hypomania, and social introversion. There is also a scale to ascertain risk factors for alcohol abuse. In 2008, the test was again revised, using more advanced methods, to the MMPI-2-RF. This version takes about one-half the time to complete and has only 338 questions (Figure 11.17). Despite the new test's advantages, the MMPI-2 is more established and is still more widely used. Typically, the tests are administered by computer. Although the MMPI was originally developed to assist in the clinical diagnosis of psychological disorders, it is now also used for occupational screening, such as in law enforcement, and in college, career, and marital counseling (Ben-Porath & Tellegen, 2008).

	True	False
1. I like gardening magazines.	O	O
2. I am unhappy with my sex life.	O	O
3. I feel like no one understands me.	O	O
4. I think I would enjoy the work of a teacher.	O	O
5. I am not easily awakened by noise.	O	O

Figure 11.17 These true/false questions resemble the kinds of questions you would find on the MMPI.

In addition to clinical scales, the tests also have validity and reliability scales. (Recall the concepts of reliability and validity from your study of psychological research.) One of the validity scales, the Lie Scale (or "L" Scale), consists of 15 items and is used to ascertain whether the respondent is "faking good" (underreporting psychological problems to appear healthier). For example, if someone responds "yes" to a number of unrealistically positive items such as "I have never told a lie," they may be trying to "fake good" or appear better than they actually are.

Reliability scales test an instrument's consistency over time, assuring that if you take the MMPI-2-RF today and then again 5 years later, your two scores will be similar. Beutler, Nussbaum, and Meredith (1988) gave the MMPI to newly recruited police officers and then to the same police officers 2 years later. After 2 years on the job, police officers' responses indicated an increased vulnerability to alcoholism, somatic symptoms (vague, unexplained physical complaints), and anxiety. When the test was given an additional 2 years later (4 years after starting on the job), the results suggested high risk for alcohol-related difficulties.

PROJECTIVE TESTS

Another method for assessment of personality is **projective testing**. This kind of test relies on one of the defense mechanisms proposed by Freud—projection—as a way to assess unconscious processes. During this type of testing, a series of ambiguous cards is shown to the person being tested, who then is encouraged to project his feelings, impulses, and desires onto the cards—by telling a story, interpreting an image, or completing a sentence. Many projective tests have undergone standardization procedures (for example, Exner, 2002) and can be used to access whether someone has unusual thoughts or a high level of anxiety, or is likely to become volatile. Some examples of projective tests are the Rorschach Inkblot Test, the Thematic Apperception Test (TAT), the Contemporized-Themes Concerning Blacks test, the TEMAS (Tell-Me-A-Story), and the Rotter Incomplete Sentence Blank (RISB). Projective tests are less subject to intentional distortion; it is hard to fake "good" because it is not obvious what a "good" answer is. Projective tests are more time consuming for the evaluator than self-report inventories. If an evaluator scores the Rorschach using the Exner scoring system, the test is considered a valid and reliable measure. However, the validity of the other projective tests is questionable, and the results are often not usable for court cases (Goldstein, n.d.).

The **Rorschach Inkblot Test** was developed in 1921 by a Swiss psychologist named Hermann Rorschach (pronounced "ROAR-shock"). It is a series of symmetrical inkblot cards that are presented to a client by a psychologist. Upon presentation of each card, the psychologist asks the client, "What might this be?" What the test-taker sees reveals unconscious feelings and struggles (Piotrowski, 1987; Weiner, 2003). The Rorschach has been standardized using the Exner system and is effective in measuring depression, psychosis, and anxiety.

A second projective test is the **Thematic Apperception Test (TAT)**, created in the 1930s by Henry Murray, an American psychologist, and a psychoanalyst named Christiana Morgan. A person taking the TAT is shown 8–12 ambiguous pictures and is asked to tell a story about each picture (Figure 11.18). The stories give insight into their social world, revealing hopes, fears, interests, and goals. The storytelling format helps to lower a person's resistance divulging unconscious personal details (Cramer, 2004). The TAT has been used in clinical settings to evaluate psychological disorders; more recently, it has been used in counseling settings to help clients gain a better understanding of themselves and achieve personal growth. Standardization of test administration is virtually nonexistent among clinicians, and the test tends to be modest to low on validity and reliability (Aronow, Weiss, & Rezinkoff, 2001; Lilienfeld, Wood, & Garb, 2000). Despite these shortcomings, the TAT has been one of the most widely used projective tests.

Figure 11.18 This image from the Thematic Apperception Tests (TAT) can be used in counseling settings.

A third projective test is the **Rotter Incomplete Sentence Blank (RISB)** developed by Julian Rotter in 1950 (recall his theory of locus of control, covered earlier in this chapter). There are three forms of this test for use with different age groups: the school form, the college form, and the adult form. The tests include 40 incomplete sentences that people are asked to complete as quickly as possible (Figure 11.19). The average time for completing the test is approximately 20 minutes, as responses are only 1–2 words in length. This test is similar to a word association test, and like other types of projective tests, it is presumed that responses will reveal desires, fears, and struggles. The RISB is used in screening college students for adjustment problems and in career counseling (Holaday, Smith, & Sherry, 2010; Rotter & Rafferty 1950).

1. I feel...	
2. I regret...	
3. At home...	
4. My mother...	
5. My greatest worry...	

Figure 11.19 These incomplete sentences resemble the types of questions on the RISB. How would you complete these sentences?

For many decades, these traditional projective tests have been used in cross-cultural personality assessments. However, it was found that test bias limited their usefulness (Hoy-Watkins & Jenkins-Moore, 2008). It is difficult to assess the personalities and lifestyles of members of widely divergent ethnic/cultural groups using personality instruments based on data from a single culture or race (Hoy-Watkins

& Jenkins-Moore, 2008). For example, when the TAT was used with African-American test takers, the result was often shorter story length and low levels of cultural identification (Duzant, 2005). Therefore, it was vital to develop other personality assessments that explored factors such as race, language, and level of acculturation (Hoy-Watkins & Jenkins-Moore, 2008). To address this need, Robert Williams developed the first culturally specific projective test designed to reflect the everyday life experiences of African Americans (Hoy-Watkins & Jenkins-Moore, 2008). The updated version of the instrument is the **Contemporized-Themes Concerning Blacks Test (C-TCB)** (Williams, 1972). The C-TCB contains 20 color images that show scenes of African-American lifestyles. When the C-TCB was compared with the TAT for African Americans, it was found that use of the C-TCB led to increased story length, higher degrees of positive feelings, and stronger identification with the C-TCB (Hoy, 1997; Hoy-Watkins & Jenkins-Moore, 2008).

The **TEMAS Multicultural Thematic Apperception Test** is another tool designed to be culturally relevant to minority groups, especially Hispanic youths. TEMAS—standing for "Tell Me a Story" but also a play on the Spanish word *temas* (themes)—uses images and storytelling cues that relate to minority culture (Constantino, 1982).

Key Terms

anal stage psychosexual stage in which children experience pleasure in their bowel and bladder movements

analytical psychology Jung's theory focusing on the balance of opposing forces within one's personality and the significance of the collective unconscious

archetype pattern that exists in our collective unconscious across cultures and societies

collective unconscious common psychological tendencies that have been passed down from one generation to the next

congruence state of being in which our thoughts about our real and ideal selves are very similar

conscious mental activity (thoughts, feelings, and memories) that we can access at any time

Contemporized-Themes Concerning Blacks Test (C-TCB) projective test designed to be culturally relevant to African Americans, using images that relate to African-American culture

culture all of the beliefs, customs, art, and traditions of a particular society

defense mechanism unconscious protective behaviors designed to reduce ego anxiety

displacement ego defense mechanism in which a person transfers inappropriate urges or behaviors toward a more acceptable or less threatening target

ego aspect of personality that represents the self, or the part of one's personality that is visible to others

Five Factor Model theory that personality is composed of five factors, including openness, conscientiousness, extroversion, agreeableness, and neuroticism

genital stage psychosexual stage in which the focus is on mature sexual interests

heritability proportion of difference among people that is attributed to genetics

id aspect of personality that consists of our most primitive drives or urges, including impulses for hunger, thirst, and sex

ideal self person we would like to be

incongruence state of being in which there is a great discrepancy between our real and ideal selves

individual psychology school of psychology proposed by Adler that focuses on our drive to compensate for feelings of inferiority

inferiority complex refers to a person's feelings that they lack worth and don't measure up to others' or to society's standards

latency period psychosexual stage in which sexual feelings are dormant

locus of control beliefs about the power we have over our lives; an external locus of control is the belief that our outcomes are outside of our control; an internal locus of control is the belief that we control our own outcomes

Minnesota Multiphasic Personality Inventory (MMPI) personality test composed of a series of true/false questions in order to establish a clinical profile of an individual

neurosis tendency to experience negative emotions

oral stage psychosexual stage in which an infant's pleasure is focused on the mouth

personality long-standing traits and patterns that propel individuals to consistently think, feel, and behave in specific ways

phallic stage psychosexual stage in which the focus is on the genitals

projection ego defense mechanism in which a person confronted with anxiety disguises their unacceptable urges or behaviors by attributing them to other people

Projective test personality assessment in which a person responds to ambiguous stimuli, revealing hidden feelings, impulses, and desires

psychosexual stages of development stages of child development in which a child's pleasure-seeking urges are focused on specific areas of the body called erogenous zones

rationalization ego defense mechanism in which a person confronted with anxiety makes excuses to justify behavior

reaction formation ego defense mechanism in which a person confronted with anxiety swaps unacceptable urges or behaviors for their opposites

real self person who we actually are

reciprocal determinism belief that one's environment can determine behavior, but at the same time, people can influence the environment with both their thoughts and behaviors

regression ego defense mechanism in which a person confronted with anxiety returns to a more immature behavioral state

repression ego defense mechanism in which anxiety-related thoughts and memories are kept in the unconscious

Rorschach Inkblot Test projective test that employs a series of symmetrical inkblot cards that are presented to a client by a psychologist in an effort to reveal the person's unconscious desires, fears, and struggles

Rotter Incomplete Sentence Blank (RISB) projective test that is similar to a word association test in which a person completes sentences in order to reveal their unconscious desires, fears, and struggles

selective migration concept that people choose to move to places that are compatible with their personalities and needs

self-concept our thoughts and feelings about ourselves

self-efficacy someone's level of confidence in their own abilities

social-cognitive theory Bandura's theory of personality that emphasizes both cognition and learning as sources of individual differences in personality

sublimation ego defense mechanism in which unacceptable urges are channeled into more appropriate activities

superego aspect of the personality that serves as one's moral compass, or conscience

TEMAS Multicultural Thematic Apperception Test projective test designed to be culturally relevant to minority groups, especially Hispanic youths, using images and storytelling that relate to minority culture

temperament how a person reacts to the world, including their activity level, starting when they are very young

Thematic Apperception Test (TAT) projective test in which people are presented with ambiguous images, and they then make up stories to go with the images in an effort to uncover their unconscious desires, fears, and struggles

traits characteristic ways of behaving

unconscious mental activity of which we are unaware and unable to access

Summary

11.1 What Is Personality?
Personality has been studied for over 2,000 years, beginning with Hippocrates. More recent theories of personality have been proposed, including Freud's psychodynamic perspective, which holds that personality is formed through early childhood experiences. Other perspectives then emerged in reaction to the psychodynamic perspective, including the learning, humanistic, biological, trait, and cultural perspectives.

11.2 Freud and the Psychodynamic Perspective
Sigmund Freud presented the first comprehensive theory of personality. He was also the first to recognize that much of our mental life takes place outside of our conscious awareness. Freud also proposed three components to our personality: the id, ego, and superego. The job of the ego is to balance the sexual and aggressive drives of the id with the moral ideal of the superego. Freud also said that personality develops through a series of psychosexual stages. In each stage, pleasure focuses on a specific erogenous zone. Failure to resolve a stage can lead one to become fixated in that stage, leading to unhealthy personality traits. Successful resolution of the stages leads to a healthy adult.

11.3 Neo-Freudians: Adler, Erikson, Jung, and Horney
The neo-Freudians were psychologists whose work followed from Freud's. They generally agreed with Freud that childhood experiences matter, but they decreased the emphasis on sex and focused more on the social environment and effects of culture on personality. Some of the notable neo-Freudians are Alfred Adler, Carl Jung, Erik Erikson, and Karen Horney. The neo-Freudian approaches have been criticized, because they tend to be philosophical rather than based on sound scientific research. For example, Jung's conclusions about the existence of the collective unconscious are based on myths, legends, dreams, and art. In addition, as with Freud's psychoanalytic theory, the neo-Freudians based much of their theories of personality on information from their patients.

11.4 Learning Approaches
Behavioral theorists view personality as significantly shaped and impacted by the reinforcements and consequences outside of the organism. People behave in a consistent manner based on prior learning. B. F. Skinner, a prominent behaviorist, said that we demonstrate consistent behavior patterns, because we have developed certain response tendencies. Mischel focused on how personal goals play a role in the self-regulation process. Albert Bandura said that one's environment can determine behavior, but at the same time, people can influence the environment with both their thoughts and behaviors, which is known as reciprocal determinism. Bandura also emphasized how we learn from watching others. He felt that this type of learning also plays a part in the development of our personality. Bandura discussed the concept of self-efficacy, which is our level of confidence in our own abilities. Finally, Rotter proposed the concept of locus of control, which refers to our beliefs about the power we have over our lives. He said that people

fall along a continuum between a purely internal and a purely external locus of control.

11.5 Humanistic Approaches
Humanistic psychologists Abraham Maslow and Carl Rogers focused on the growth potential of healthy individuals. They believed that people strive to become self-actualized. Both Rogers's and Maslow's theories greatly contributed to our understanding of the self. They emphasized free will and self-determination, with each individual desiring to become the best person they can become.

11.6 Biological Approaches
Some aspects of our personalities are largely controlled by genetics; however, environmental factors (such as family interactions) and maturation can affect the ways in which children's personalities are expressed.

11.7 Trait Theorists
Trait theorists attempt to explain our personality by identifying our stable characteristics and ways of behaving. They have identified important dimensions of personality. The Five Factor Model is the most widely accepted theory today. The five factors are openness, conscientiousness, extroversion, agreeableness, and neuroticism. These factors occur along a continuum.

11.8 Cultural Understandings of Personality
The culture in which you live is one of the most important environmental factors that shapes your personality. Western ideas about personality may not be applicable to other cultures. In fact, there is evidence that the strength of personality traits varies across cultures. Individualist cultures and collectivist cultures place emphasis on different basic values. People who live in individualist cultures tend to believe that independence, competition, and personal achievement are important. People who live in collectivist cultures value social harmony, respectfulness, and group needs over individual needs. There are three approaches that can be used to study personality in a cultural context: the cultural-comparative approach, the indigenous approach, and the combined approach, which incorporates both elements of both views.

11.9 Personality Assessment
Personality tests are techniques designed to measure one's personality. They are used to diagnose psychological problems as well as to screen candidates for college and employment. There are two types of personality tests: self-report inventories and projective tests. The MMPI is one of the most common self-report inventories. It asks a series of true/false questions that are designed to provide a clinical profile of an individual. Projective tests use ambiguous images or other ambiguous stimuli to assess an individual's unconscious fears, desires, and challenges. The Rorschach Inkblot Test, the TAT, the RISB, and the C-TCB are all forms of projective tests.

Review Questions

1. Personality is thought to be _____.
    a. short term and easily changed
    b. a pattern of short-term characteristics
    c. unstable and short term
    d. long term, stable and not easily changed

2. The long-standing traits and patterns that propel individuals to consistently think, feel, and behave in specific ways are known as _____.
    a. psychodynamic
    b. temperament
    c. humors
    d. personality

3. _____ is credited with the first comprehensive theory of personality.
    a. Hippocrates
    b. Gall
    c. Wundt
    d. Freud

4. An early science that tried to correlate personality with measurements of parts of a person's skull is known as _____.
    a. phrenology
    b. psychology
    c. physiology
    d. personality psychology

5. The id operates on the _____ principle.
   a. reality
   b. pleasure
   c. instant gratification
   d. guilt

6. The ego defense mechanism in which a person who is confronted with anxiety returns to a more immature behavioral stage is called _____.
   a. repression
   b. regression
   c. reaction formation
   d. rationalization

7. The Oedipus complex occurs in the _____ stage of psychosexual development.
   a. oral
   b. anal
   c. phallic
   d. latency

8. The universal bank of ideas, images, and concepts that have been passed down through the generations from our ancestors refers to _____.
   a. archetypes
   b. intuition
   c. collective unconscious
   d. personality types

9. Self-regulation is also known as _____.
   a. self-efficacy
   b. will power
   c. internal locus of control
   d. external locus of control

10. Your level of confidence in your own abilities is known as _____.
    a. self-efficacy
    b. self-concept
    c. self-control
    d. self-esteem

11. Jane believes that she got a bad grade on her psychology paper because her professor doesn't like her. Jane most likely has an _____ locus of control.
    a. internal
    b. external
    c. intrinsic
    d. extrinsic

12. Self-concept refers to _____.
    a. our level of confidence in our own abilities
    b. all of our thoughts and feelings about ourselves
    c. the belief that we control our own outcomes
    d. the belief that our outcomes are outside of our control

13. The idea that people's ideas about themselves should match their actions is called _____.
    a. confluence
    b. conscious
    c. conscientiousness
    d. congruence

14. The way a person reacts to the world, starting when they are very young, including the person's activity level is known as _____.
    a. traits
    b. temperament
    c. heritability
    d. personality

15. Brianna is 18 months old. She cries frequently, is hard to soothe, and wakes frequently during the night. According to Thomas and Chess, she would be considered _____.
    a. an easy baby
    b. a difficult baby
    c. a slow to warm up baby
    d. a colicky baby

16. According to the findings of the Minnesota Study of Twins Reared Apart, identical twins, whether raised together or apart have _____ personalities.
    a. slightly different
    b. very different
    c. slightly similar
    d. very similar

17. Temperament refers to _____.
    a. inborn, genetically based personality differences
    b. characteristic ways of behaving
    c. conscientiousness, agreeableness, neuroticism, openness, and extroversion
    d. degree of introversion-extroversion

18. According to the Eysencks' theory, people who score high on neuroticism tend to be _____.
    a. calm
    b. stable
    c. outgoing
    d. anxious

19. The United States is considered a _____ culture.
    a. collectivistic
    b. individualist
    c. traditional
    d. nontraditional

20. The concept that people choose to move to places that are compatible with their personalities and needs is known as _____.
    a. selective migration
    b. personal oriented personality
    c. socially oriented personality
    d. individualism

21. Which of the following is NOT a projective test?
    a. Minnesota Multiphasic Personality Inventory (MMPI)
    b. Rorschach Inkblot Test
    c. Thematic Apperception Test (TAT)
    d. Rotter Incomplete Sentence Blank (RISB)

22. A personality assessment in which a person responds to ambiguous stimuli, revealing unconscious feelings, impulses, and desires _____.
    a. self-report inventory
    b. projective test
    c. Minnesota Multiphasic Personality Inventory (MMPI)
    d. Myers-Briggs Type Indicator (MBTI)

23. Which personality assessment employs a series of true/false questions?
    a. Minnesota Multiphasic Personality Inventory (MMPI)
    b. Thematic Apperception Test (TAT)
    c. Rotter Incomplete Sentence Blank (RISB)
    d. Myers-Briggs Type Indicator (MBTI)

Critical Thinking Questions

24. What makes a personal quality part of someone's personality?

25. How might the common expression "daddy's girl" be rooted in the idea of the Electra complex?

26. Describe the personality of someone who is fixated at the anal stage.

27. Describe the difference between extroverts and introverts in terms of what is energizing to each.

28. Discuss Horney's perspective on Freud's concept of penis envy.

29. Compare the personalities of someone who has high self-efficacy to someone who has low self-efficacy.

30. Compare and contrast Skinner's perspective on personality development to Freud's.

31. How might a temperament mix between parent and child affect family life?

32. How stable are the Big Five factors over one's lifespan?

33. Compare the personality of someone who scores high on agreeableness to someone who scores low on agreeableness.

34. Why might it be important to consider cultural influences on personality?

35. Why might a prospective employer screen applicants using personality assessments?

36. Why would a clinician give someone a projective test?

Personal Application Questions

37. How would you describe your own personality? Do you think that friends and family would describe you in much the same way? Why or why not?

38. How would you describe your personality in an online dating profile?

39. What are some of your positive and negative personality qualities? How do you think these qualities will affect your choice of career?

40. What are some examples of defense mechanisms that you have used yourself or have witnessed others using?

41. What is your birth order? Do you agree or disagree with Adler's description of your personality based on his birth order theory, as described in the Link to Learning? Provide examples for support.

42. Would you describe yourself as an extrovert or an introvert? Does this vary based on the situation? Provide examples to support your points.

43. Select an epic story that is popular in contemporary society (such as *Harry Potter* or *Star Wars*) and explain it terms of Jung's concept of archetypes.

44. Do you have an internal or an external locus of control? Provide examples to support your answer.

45. Respond to the question, "Who am I?" Based on your response, do you have a negative or a positive self-concept? What are some experiences that led you to develop this particular self-concept?

46. Research suggests that many of our personality characteristics have a genetic component. What traits do you think you inherited from your parents? Provide examples. How might modeling (environment) influenced your characteristics as well?

47. Review the Big Five personality factors shown in **Figure 11.14**. On which areas would you expect you'd score high? In which areas does the low score more accurately describe you?

48. According to the work of Rentfrow and colleagues, personalities are not randomly distributed. Instead they fit into distinct geographic clusters. Based on where you live, do you agree or disagree with the traits associated with yourself and the residents of your area of the country? Why or why not?

49. How objective do you think you can be about yourself in answering questions on self-report personality assessment measures? What implications might this have for the validity of the personality test?

Chapter 12

Social Psychology

Figure 12.1 Trayvon Martin, 17, was shot to death at the hands of George Zimmerman, a volunteer neighborhood watchman, in 2012. Was his death the result of self-defense or racial bias? That question drew hundreds of people to rally on each side of this heated debate. (credit "signs": modification of work by David Shankbone; credit "walk": modification of work by "Fibonacci Blue"/Flickr)

Chapter Outline

12.1 What Is Social Psychology?
12.2 Self-presentation
12.3 Attitudes and Persuasion
12.4 Conformity, Compliance, and Obedience
12.5 Prejudice and Discrimination
12.6 Aggression
12.7 Prosocial Behavior

Introduction

On the night of February 26, 2012, Trayvon Martin, a 17-year-old African American high school student, was shot by a neighborhood watch volunteer, George Zimmerman, in a predominantly White neighborhood. Zimmerman grew suspicious of the boy dressed in a hoodie and pursued Martin. A physical altercation ended with Zimmerman fatally shooting Martin. Zimmerman claimed that he acted in self-defense. Martin was unarmed, and after his death, there was a nationwide outcry. A Florida jury found Zimmerman not guilty of second degree murder nor of manslaughter. George Zimmerman was a resident in the housing complex, not on the job, when the shooting occurred.

There have also been tragic situations with deadly consequences in which police officers have shot innocent civilians. In 2019, Atatiana Jefferson's neighbor used a non-emergency line to call the police because Jefferson's front door was open in the late hours of the night. The police arrived and an officer went to the back of the yard. Jefferson, not knowing that the police had been called, reached into her purse and got out her legally owned gun. The officer perceived a threat and fired upon Jefferson, killing her. Her 8-year-old nephew witnessed the incident, as he was playing video games with his aunt. Why did each of these nights end so tragically for those involved? What dynamics contributed to the outcomes? How can these deaths be prevented?

Social psychologists examine how the presence of others impacts how a person behaves and reacts, whether that person is an athlete playing a game, a police officer on the job, or a worshiper attending a religious service. Social psychologists believe that a person's behavior is influenced by who else is present in a given situation and the composition of social groups.

12.1 What Is Social Psychology?

Learning Objectives

By the end of this section, you will be able to:
- Define social psychology
- Describe situational versus dispositional influences on behavior
- Describe the fundamental attribution error
- Explain actor-observer bias
- Describe self-serving bias
- Explain the just-world hypothesis

Social psychology examines how people affect one another, and it looks at the power of the situation. According to the American Psychological Association (n.d.), social psychologists "are interested in all aspects of personality and social interaction, exploring the influence of interpersonal and group relationships on human behavior." Throughout this chapter, we will examine how the presence of other individuals and groups of people impacts a person's behaviors, thoughts, and feelings. Essentially, people will change their behavior to align with the social situation at hand. If we are in a new situation or are unsure how to behave, we will take our cues from other individuals.

The field of social psychology studies topics at both the intra- and interpersonal levels. Intrapersonal topics (those that pertain to the individual) include emotions and attitudes, the self, and social cognition (the ways in which we think about ourselves and others). Interpersonal topics (those that pertain to dyads and groups) include helping behavior (**Figure 12.2**), aggression, prejudice and discrimination, attraction and close relationships, and group processes and intergroup relationships.

Figure 12.2 Social psychology deals with all kinds of interactions between people, spanning a wide range of how we connect: from moments of confrontation to moments of working together and helping others, as shown here. (credit: Sgt. Derec Pierson, U.S. Army)

Social psychologists focus on how people conceptualize and interpret situations and how these interpretations influence their thoughts, feelings, and behaviors (Ross & Nisbett, 1991). Thus, social psychology studies individuals in a social context and how situational variables interact to influence behavior. In this chapter, we discuss the intrapersonal processes of self-presentation, cognitive dissonance and attitude change, and the interpersonal processes of conformity and obedience, aggression and altruism, and, finally, love and attraction.

SITUATIONAL AND DISPOSITIONAL INFLUENCES ON BEHAVIOR

Behavior is a product of both the situation (e.g., cultural influences, social roles, and the presence of bystanders) and of the person (e.g., personality characteristics). Subfields of psychology tend to focus on one influence or behavior over others. **Situationism** is the view that our behavior and actions are determined by our immediate environment and surroundings. In contrast, **dispositionism** holds that our behavior is determined by internal factors (Heider, 1958). An **internal factor** is an attribute of a person and includes personality traits and temperament. Social psychologists have tended to take the situationist perspective, whereas personality psychologists have promoted the dispositionist perspective. Modern approaches to social psychology, however, take both the situation and the individual into account when studying human behavior (Fiske, Gilbert, & Lindzey, 2010). In fact, the field of social-personality psychology has emerged to study the complex interaction of internal and situational factors that affect human behavior (Mischel, 1977; Richard, Bond, & Stokes-Zoota, 2003).

FUNDAMENTAL ATTRIBUTION ERROR

In the United States, the predominant culture tends to favor a dispositional approach in explaining human behavior. Why do you think this is? We tend to think that people are in control of their own behaviors, and, therefore, any behavior change must be due to something internal, such as their personality, habits, or temperament. According to some social psychologists, people tend to overemphasize internal factors as explanations—or attributions—for the behavior of other people. They tend to assume that the behavior of another person is a *trait* of that person, and to underestimate the power of the situation on the behavior of others. They tend to fail to recognize when the behavior of another is due to situational variables, and thus to the person's *state*. This erroneous assumption is called the **fundamental attribution error** (Ross, 1977; Riggio & Garcia, 2009). To better understand, imagine this scenario: Jamie returns home from work, and opens the front door to a happy greeting from spouse Morgan who inquires how the day has been. Instead of returning the spouse's kind greeting, Jamie yells, "Leave me alone!" Why did Jamie yell? How would someone committing the fundamental attribution error explain Jamie's behavior? The most common response is that Jamie is a mean, angry, or unfriendly person (traits). This is an internal or dispositional explanation. However, imagine that Jamie was just laid off from work due to company downsizing. Would your explanation for Jamie's behavior change? Your revised explanation might be that Jamie was frustrated and disappointed about being laid off and was therefore in a bad mood (state). This is now an external or situational explanation for Jamie's behavior.

The fundamental attribution error is so powerful that people often overlook obvious situational influences on behavior. A classic example was demonstrated in a series of experiments known as the quizmaster study (Ross, Amabile, & Steinmetz, 1977). Student participants were randomly assigned to play the role of a questioner (the quizmaster) or a contestant in a quiz game. Questioners developed difficult questions to which they knew the answers, and they presented these questions to the contestants. The contestants answered the questions correctly only 4 out of 10 times (**Figure 12.3**). After the task, the questioners and contestants were asked to rate their own general knowledge compared to the average student. Questioners did not rate their general knowledge higher than the contestants, but the contestants rated the questioners' intelligence higher than their own. In a second study, observers of the interaction also rated the questioner as having more general knowledge than the contestant. The obvious influence on performance is the situation. The questioners wrote the questions, so of course they had an advantage. Both the contestants and observers made an internal attribution for the performance. They concluded that the questioners must be more intelligent than the contestants.

Figure 12.3 In the quizmaster study, people tended to disregard the influence of the situation and wrongly concluded that a questioner's knowledge was greater than their own. (credit: Steve Jurvetson)

The halo effect refers to the tendency to let the overall impression of an individual color the way in which we feel about their character. For instance, we might assume that people who are physically attractive are more likely to be good people than less attractive individuals. Another example of how the halo effect might manifest would involve assuming that someone whom we perceive to be outgoing or friendly has a better moral character than someone who is not.

As demonstrated in the examples above, the fundamental attribution error is considered a powerful influence in how we explain the behaviors of others. However, it should be noted that some researchers have suggested that the fundamental attribution error may not be as powerful as it is often portrayed. In fact, a recent review of more than 173 published studies suggests that several factors (e.g., high levels of idiosyncrasy of the character and how well hypothetical events are explained) play a role in determining just how influential the fundamental attribution error is (Malle, 2006).

IS THE FUNDAMENTAL ATTRIBUTION ERROR A UNIVERSAL PHENOMENON?

You may be able to think of examples of the fundamental attribution error in your life. Do people in all cultures commit the fundamental attribution error? Research suggests that they do not. People from an **individualistic culture**, that is, a culture that focuses on individual achievement and autonomy, have the greatest tendency to commit the fundamental attribution error. Individualistic cultures, which tend to be found in western countries such as the United States, Canada, and the United Kingdom, promote a focus on the individual. Therefore, a person's disposition is thought to be the primary explanation for her behavior. In contrast, people from a **collectivistic culture**, that is, a culture that focuses on communal relationships with others, such as family, friends, and community (Figure 12.4), are less likely to commit the fundamental attribution error (Markus & Kitayama, 1991; Triandis, 2001).

(a)   (b)   (c)

Figure 12.4 People from collectivistic cultures, such as some Asian cultures, are more likely to emphasize relationships with others than to focus primarily on the individual. Activities such as (a) preparing a meal, (b) hanging out, and (c) playing a game engage people in a group. (credit a: modification of work by Arian Zwegers; credit b: modification of work by "conbon33"/Flickr; credit c: modification of work by Anja Disseldorp)

Why do you think this is the case? Collectivistic cultures, which tend to be found in east Asian countries and in Latin American and African countries, focus on the group more than on the individual (Nisbett, Peng, Choi, & Norenzayan, 2001). This focus on others provides a broader perspective that takes into account both situational and cultural influences on behavior; thus, a more nuanced explanation of the causes of others' behavior becomes more likely. Table 12.1 summarizes compares individualistic and collectivist cultures.

Characteristics of Individualistic and Collectivistic Cultures

Individualistic Culture	Collectivistic Culture
Achievement oriented	Relationship oriented
Focus on autonomy	Focus on group harmony
Dispositional perspective	Situational perspective
Independent	Interdependent
Analytic thinking style	Holistic thinking style

Table 12.1

Masuda and Nisbett (2001) demonstrated that the kinds of information that people attend to when viewing visual stimuli (e.g., an aquarium scene) can differ significantly depending on whether the observer comes from a collectivistic versus an individualistic culture. Japanese participants were much more likely to recognize objects that were presented when they occurred in the same context in which they were originally viewed. Manipulating the context in which object recall occurred had no such impact on American participants. Other researchers have shown similar differences across cultures. For example, Zhang, Fung, Stanley, Isaacowitz, and Zhang (2014) demonstrated differences in the ways that holistic thinking might develop between Chinese and American participants, and Ramesh and Gelfand (2010) demonstrated that job turnover rates are more related to the fit between a person and the organization in which they work in an Indian sample, but the fit between the person and their specific job was more predictive of turnover in an American sample.

ACTOR-OBSERVER BIAS

Returning to our earlier example, Jamie was laid off, but an observer would not know. So a naïve observer would tend to attribute Jamie's hostile behavior to Jamie's disposition rather than to the true, situational cause. Why do you think we underestimate the influence of the situation on the behaviors of others? One reason is that we often don't have all the information we need to make a situational explanation for another person's behavior. The only information we might have is what is observable. Due to this lack of information we have a tendency to assume the behavior is due to a dispositional, or internal, factor. When it comes to explaining our own behaviors, however, we have much more information available to us. If you came home from school or work angry and yelled at your dog or a loved one, what would your explanation be? You might say you were very tired or feeling unwell and needed quiet time—a situational explanation. The **actor-observer bias** is the phenomenon of attributing other people's behavior to internal factors (fundamental attribution error) while attributing our own behavior to situational forces (Jones & Nisbett, 1971; Nisbett, Caputo, Legant, & Marecek, 1973; Choi & Nisbett, 1998). As actors of behavior, we have more information available to explain our own behavior. However as observers, we have less information available; therefore, we tend to default to a dispositionist perspective.

One study on the actor-observer bias investigated reasons male participants gave for why they liked their girlfriend (Nisbett et al., 1973). When asked why participants liked their own girlfriend, participants focused on internal, dispositional qualities of their girlfriends (for example, her pleasant personality). The participants' explanations rarely included causes internal to themselves, such as dispositional traits (for example, "I need companionship."). In contrast, when speculating why a male friend likes his girlfriend, participants were equally likely to give dispositional and external explanations. This supports the idea that actors tend to provide few internal explanations but many situational explanations for their own behavior. In contrast, observers tend to provide more dispositional explanations for a friend's behavior (Figure 12.5).

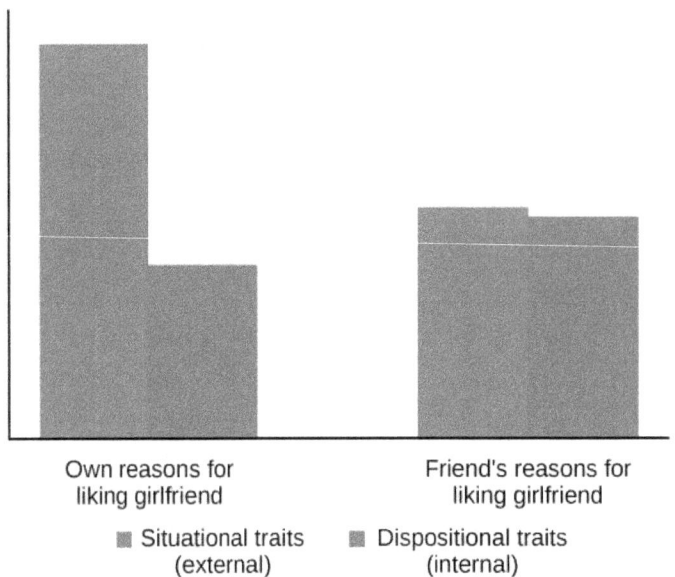

Figure 12.5 Actor-observer bias is evident when subjects explain their own reasons for liking a girlfriend versus their impressions of others' reasons for liking a girlfriend.

SELF-SERVING BIAS

We can understand self-serving bias by digging more deeply into **attribution**, a belief about the cause of a result. One model of attribution proposes three main dimensions: locus of control (internal versus external), stability (stable versus unstable), and controllability (controllable versus uncontrollable). In this context, stability refers the extent to which the circumstances that result in a given outcome are changeable. The circumstances are considered stable if they are unlikely to change. Controllability refers to the extent to which the circumstances that are associated with a given outcome can be controlled. Obviously, those things that we have the power to control would be labeled controllable (Weiner, 1979).

Following an outcome, self-serving biases are those attributions that enable us to see ourselves in a favorable light (for example, making internal attributions for success and external attributions for failures). When you do well at a task, for example acing an exam, it is in your best interest to make a dispositional attribution for your behavior ("I'm smart,") instead of a situational one ("The exam was easy,"). The tendency of an individual to take credit by making dispositional or internal attributions for positive outcomes (Miller & Ross, 1975). **Self-serving bias** is the tendency to explain our successes as due to dispositional (internal) characteristics, but to explain our failures as due to situational (external) factors. Again, this is culture dependent. This bias serves to protect self-esteem. You can imagine that if people always made situational attributions for their behavior, they would never be able to take credit and feel good about their accomplishments.

Consider the example of how we explain our favorite sports team's wins. Research shows that we make internal, stable, and controllable attributions for our team's victory (Figure 12.6) (Grove, Hanrahan, & McInman, 1991). For example, we might tell ourselves that our team is talented (internal), consistently works hard (stable), and uses effective strategies (controllable). In contrast, we are more likely to make external, unstable, and uncontrollable attributions when our favorite team loses. For example, we might tell ourselves that the other team has more experienced players or that the referees were unfair (external), the other team played at home (unstable), and the cold weather affected our team's performance (uncontrollable).

Figure 12.6 We tend to believe that our team wins because it's better, but loses for reasons it cannot control (Roesch & Amirkham, 1997). (credit: "TheAHL"/Flickr)

JUST-WORLD HYPOTHESIS

One consequence of westerners' tendency to provide dispositional explanations for behavior is victim blame (Jost & Major, 2001). When people experience bad fortune, others tend to assume that they somehow are responsible for their own fate. A common ideology, or worldview, in the United States is the just-world hypothesis. The **just-world hypothesis** is the belief that people get the outcomes they deserve (Lerner & Miller, 1978). In order to maintain the belief that the world is a fair place, people tend to think that good people experience positive outcomes, and bad people experience negative outcomes (Jost, Banaji, & Nosek, 2004; Jost & Major, 2001). The ability to think of the world as a fair place, where people get what they deserve, allows us to feel that the world is predictable and that we have some control over our life outcomes (Jost et al., 2004; Jost & Major, 2001). For example, if you want to experience positive outcomes, you just need to work hard to get ahead in life.

Can you think of a negative consequence of the just-world hypothesis? One negative consequence is people's tendency to blame poor individuals for their plight. What common explanations are given for why people live in poverty? Have you heard statements such as, "The poor are lazy and just don't want to work" or "Poor people just want to live off the government"? What types of explanations are these, dispositional or situational? These dispositional explanations are clear examples of the fundamental attribution error. Blaming poor people for their poverty ignores situational factors that impact them, such as high unemployment rates, recession, poor educational opportunities, and the familial cycle of poverty (**Figure 12.7**). Other research shows that people who hold just-world beliefs have negative attitudes toward people who are unemployed and people living with AIDS (Sutton & Douglas, 2005). In the United States and other countries, victims of sexual assault may find themselves blamed for their abuse. Victim advocacy groups, such as Domestic Violence Ended (DOVE), attend court in support of victims to ensure that blame is directed at the perpetrators of sexual violence, not the victims.

Figure 12.7 People who hold just-world beliefs tend to blame the people in poverty for their circumstances, ignoring situational and cultural causes of poverty. (credit: Adrian Miles)

12.2 Self-presentation

Learning Objectives

By the end of this section, you will be able to:
- Describe social roles and how they influence behavior
- Explain what social norms are and how they influence behavior
- Define script
- Describe the findings of Zimbardo's Stanford prison experiment

As you've learned, social psychology is the study of how people affect one another's thoughts, feelings, and behaviors. We have discussed situational perspectives and social psychology's emphasis on the ways in which a person's environment, including culture and other social influences, affect behavior. In this section, we examine situational forces that have a strong influence on human behavior including social roles, social norms, and scripts. We discuss how humans use the social environment as a source of information, or cues, on how to behave. Situational influences on our behavior have important consequences, such as whether we will help a stranger in an emergency or how we would behave in an unfamiliar environment.

SOCIAL ROLES

One major social determinant of human behavior is our social roles. A **social role** is a pattern of behavior that is expected of a person in a given setting or group (Hare, 2003). Each one of us has several social roles. You may be, at the same time, a student, a parent, an aspiring teacher, a son or daughter, a spouse, and a lifeguard. How do these social roles influence your behavior? Social roles are defined by culturally shared knowledge. That is, nearly everyone in a given culture knows what behavior is expected of a person in a given role. For example, what is the social role for a student? If you look around a college classroom you will likely see students engaging in studious behavior, taking notes, listening to the professor, reading the textbook, and sitting quietly at their desks (Figure 12.8). Of course you may see students deviating from the expected studious behavior such as texting on their phones or using Facebook on their laptops, but in all cases, the students that you observe are attending class—a part of the social role of students.

Figure 12.8 Being a student is just one of the many social roles you have. (credit: modification of work by "Rural Institute"/Flickr)

Social roles, and our related behavior, can vary across different settings. How do you behave when you are engaging in the role of a child attending a family function? Now imagine how you behave when you are engaged in the role of employee at your workplace. It is very likely that your behavior will be different. Perhaps you are more relaxed and outgoing with your family, making jokes and doing silly things. But at your workplace you might speak more professionally, and although you may be friendly, you are also serious and focused on getting the work completed. These are examples of how our social roles influence and often dictate our behavior to the extent that identity and personality can vary with context (that is, in different social groups) (Malloy, Albright, Kenny, Agatstein & Winquist, 1997).

SOCIAL NORMS

As discussed previously, social roles are defined by a culture's shared knowledge of what is expected behavior of an individual in a specific role. This shared knowledge comes from social norms. A **social norm** is a group's expectation of what is appropriate and acceptable behavior for its members—how they are supposed to behave and think (Deutsch & Gerard, 1955; Berkowitz, 2004). How are we expected to act? What are we expected to talk about? What are we expected to wear? In our discussion of social roles we noted that colleges have social norms for students' behavior in the role of student and workplaces have social norms for employees' behaviors in the role of employee. Social norms are everywhere including in families, gangs, and on social media outlets. What are some social norms on Facebook?

CONNECT THE CONCEPTS

Tweens, Teens, and Social Norms

My 11-year-old daughter, Janelle, recently told me she needed shorts and shirts for the summer, and that she wanted me to take her to a store at the mall that is popular with preteens and teens to buy them. I have noticed that many girls have clothes from that store, so I tried teasing her. I said, "All the shirts say 'Aero' on the front. If you are wearing a shirt like that and you have a substitute teacher, and the other girls are all wearing that type of shirt, won't the substitute teacher think you are all named 'Aero'?"

My daughter replied, in typical 11-year-old fashion, "Mom, you are not funny. Can we please go shopping?"

I tried a different tactic. I asked Janelle if having clothing from that particular store will make her popular. She replied, "No, it will not make me popular. It is what the popular kids wear. It will make me feel happier." How can a label or name brand make someone feel happier? Think back to what you've learned about lifespan development. What is it about pre-teens and young teens that make them want to fit in (Figure 12.9)? Does this change over time? Think back to your high school experience, or look around your college campus. What is the main name brand clothing you see? What messages do we get from the media about how to fit in?

Figure 12.9 Young people struggle to become independent at the same time they are desperately trying to fit in with their peers. (credit: Monica Arellano-Ongpin)

SCRIPTS

Because of social roles, people tend to know what behavior is expected of them in specific, familiar settings. A **script** is a person's knowledge about the sequence of events expected in a specific setting (Schank & Abelson, 1977). How do you act on the first day of school, when you walk into an elevator, or are at a restaurant? For example, at a restaurant in the United States, if we want the server's attention, we try to make eye contact. In Brazil, you would make the sound "psst" to get the server's attention. You can see the cultural differences in scripts. To an American, saying "psst" to a server might seem rude, yet to a Brazilian, trying to make eye contact might not seem an effective strategy. Scripts are important sources of information to guide behavior in given situations. Can you imagine being in an unfamiliar situation and not having a script for how to behave? This could be uncomfortable and confusing. How could you find out about social norms in an unfamiliar culture?

ZIMBARDO'S STANFORD PRISON EXPERIMENT

The famous **Stanford prison experiment**, conducted by social psychologist Philip Zimbardo and his colleagues at Stanford University, demonstrated the power of social roles, social norms, and scripts. In the summer of 1971, an advertisement was placed in a California newspaper asking for male volunteers to participate in a study about the psychological effects of prison life. More than 70 men volunteered, and these volunteers then underwent psychological testing to eliminate candidates who had underlying psychiatric issues, medical issues, or a history of crime or drug abuse. The pool of volunteers was whittled down to 24 healthy male college students. Each student was paid $15 per day (equivalent to about $80 today) and was randomly assigned to play the role of either a prisoner or a guard in the study. Based on what you have learned about research methods, why is it important that participants were randomly assigned?

A mock prison was constructed in the basement of the psychology building at Stanford. Participants assigned to play the role of prisoners were "arrested" at their homes by Palo Alto police officers, booked at a police station, and subsequently taken to the mock prison. The experiment was scheduled to run for several weeks. To the surprise of the researchers, both the "prisoners" and "guards" assumed their roles with zeal. On the second day of the experiment, the guards forced the prisoners to strip, took their beds, and isolated the ringleaders using solitary confinement. In a relatively short time, the guards came to harass the prisoners in an increasingly sadistic manner, through a complete lack of privacy, lack of basic comforts such as mattresses to sleep on, and through degrading chores and late-night counts.

The prisoners, in turn, began to show signs of severe anxiety and hopelessness—they began tolerating the guards' abuse. Even the Stanford professor who designed the study and was the head researcher, Philip Zimbardo, found himself acting as if the prison was real and his role, as prison supervisor, was real as well. After only six days, the experiment had to be ended due to the participants' deteriorating behavior. Zimbardo explained,

At this point it became clear that we had to end the study. We had created an overwhelmingly powerful situation—a situation in which prisoners were withdrawing and behaving in pathological ways, and in which some of the guards were behaving sadistically. Even the "good" guards felt helpless to intervene, and none of the guards quit while the study was in progress. Indeed, it should be noted that no guard ever came late for his shift, called in sick, left early, or demanded extra pay for overtime work. (Zimbardo, 2013)

The Stanford prison experiment demonstrated the power of social roles, norms, and scripts in affecting human behavior. The guards and prisoners enacted their social roles by engaging in behaviors appropriate to the roles: The guards gave orders and the prisoners followed orders. Social norms require guards to be authoritarian and prisoners to be submissive. When prisoners rebelled, they violated these social norms, which led to upheaval. The specific acts engaged by the guards and the prisoners derived from scripts. For example, guards degraded the prisoners by forcing them do push-ups and by removing all privacy. Prisoners rebelled by throwing pillows and trashing their cells. Some prisoners became so immersed in their roles that they exhibited symptoms of mental breakdown; however, according to Zimbardo, none of the participants suffered long term harm (Alexander, 2001).

The Stanford Prison Experiment has some parallels with the abuse of prisoners of war by U.S. Army troops and CIA personnel at the Abu Ghraib prison in 2003 and 2004 during the Iraq War. The offenses at Abu Ghraib were documented by photographs of the abuse, some taken by the abusers themselves (**Figure 12.10**).

Figure 12.10 Iraqi prisoners of war were abused by their American captors in Abu Ghraib prison, during the second Iraq war. (credit: United States Department of Defense)

LINK TO LEARNING

Listen to this **NPR interview with Philip Zimbardo where he discusses the parallels between the Stanford prison experiment and the Abu Ghraib prison in Iraq** (http://openstax.org/l/Stanford_psych) to learn more.

12.3 Attitudes and Persuasion

Learning Objectives

By the end of this section, you will be able to:
- Define attitude
- Describe how people's attitudes are internally changed through cognitive dissonance
- Explain how people's attitudes are externally changed through persuasion
- Describe the peripheral and central routes to persuasion

Social psychologists have documented how the power of the situation can influence our behaviors. Now we turn to how the power of the situation can influence our attitudes and beliefs. **Attitude** is our evaluation of a person, an idea, or an object. We have attitudes for many things ranging from products that we might pick up in the supermarket to people around the world to political policies. Typically, attitudes are favorable or unfavorable: positive or negative (Eagly & Chaiken, 1993). And, they have three components: an affective component (feelings), a behavioral component (the effect of the attitude on behavior), and a cognitive component (belief and knowledge) (Rosenberg & Hovland, 1960).

For example, you may hold a positive attitude toward recycling. This attitude should result in positive feelings toward recycling (such as "It makes me feel good to recycle" or "I enjoy knowing that I make a small difference in reducing the amount of waste that ends up in landfills"). Certainly, this attitude should be reflected in our behavior: You actually recycle as often as you can. Finally, this attitude will be reflected in favorable thoughts (for example, "Recycling is good for the environment" or "Recycling is the responsible thing to do").

Our attitudes and beliefs are not only influenced by external forces, but also by internal influences that we control. Like our behavior, our attitudes and thoughts are not always changed by situational pressures, but they can be consciously changed by our own free will. In this section we discuss the conditions under which we would want to change our own attitudes and beliefs.

WHAT IS COGNITIVE DISSONANCE?

Social psychologists have documented that feeling good about ourselves and maintaining positive self-esteem is a powerful motivator of human behavior (Tavris & Aronson, 2008). In the United States, members of the predominant culture typically think very highly of themselves and view themselves as good people who are above average on many desirable traits (Ehrlinger, Gilovich, & Ross, 2005). Often, our behavior, attitudes, and beliefs are affected when we experience a threat to our self-esteem or positive self-image. Psychologist Leon Festinger (1957) defined **cognitive dissonance** as psychological discomfort arising from holding two or more inconsistent attitudes, behaviors, or cognitions (thoughts, beliefs, or opinions). Festinger's theory of cognitive dissonance states that when we experience a conflict in our behaviors, attitudes, or beliefs that runs counter to our positive self-perceptions, we experience psychological discomfort (dissonance). For example, if you believe smoking is bad for your health but you continue to smoke, you experience conflict between your belief and behavior (Figure 12.11).

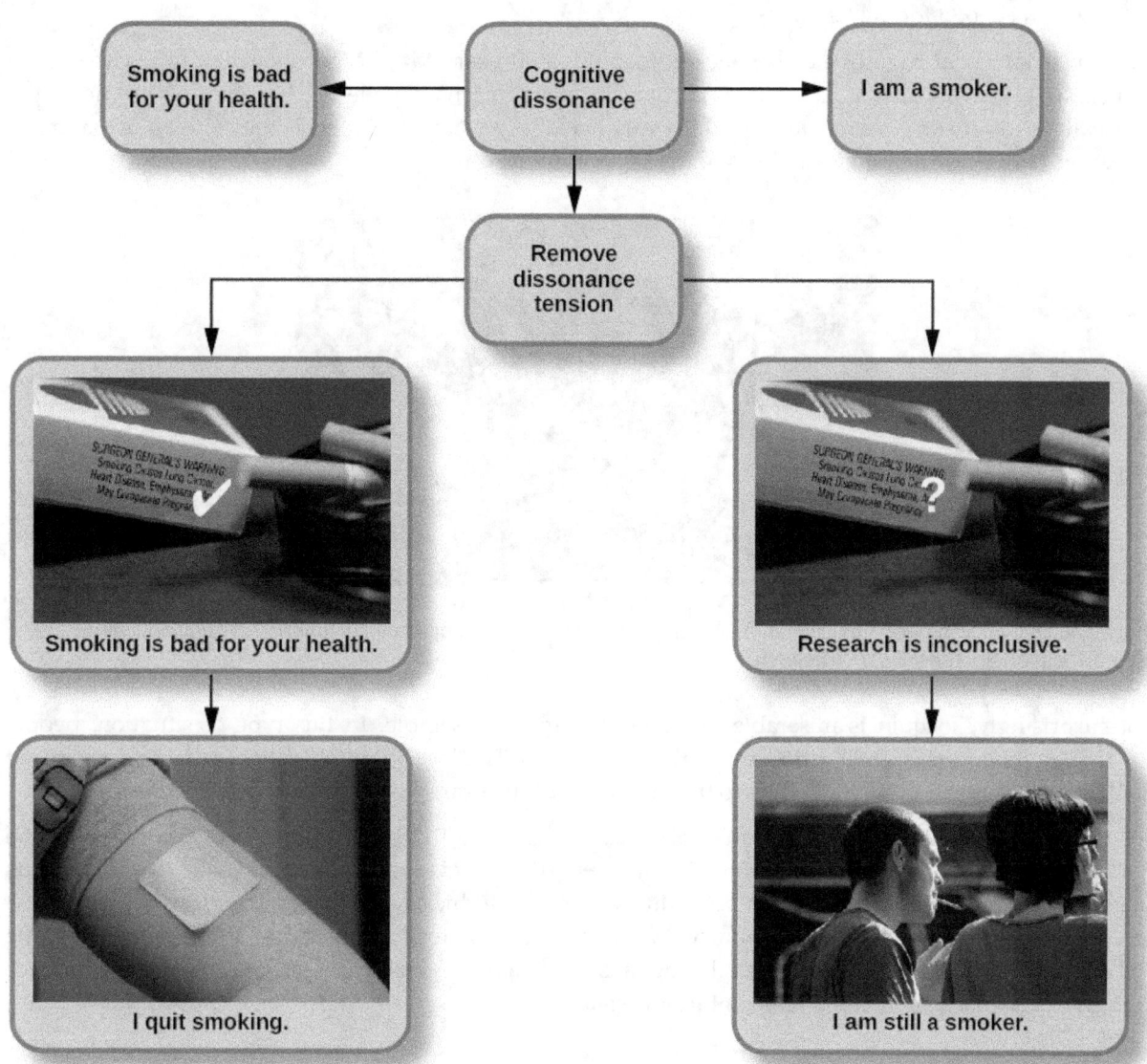

Figure 12.11 Cognitive dissonance is aroused by inconsistent beliefs and behaviors. Believing cigarettes are bad for your health, but smoking cigarettes anyway, can cause cognitive dissonance. To reduce cognitive dissonance, individuals can change their behavior, as in quitting smoking, or change their belief, such as discounting the evidence that smoking is harmful. (credit "cigarettes": modification of work by CDC/Debora Cartagena; "patch": modification of "RegBarc"/Wikimedia Commons; "smoking": modification of work by Tim Parkinson)

Later research documented that only conflicting cognitions that threaten individuals' positive self-image cause dissonance (Greenwald & Ronis, 1978). Additional research found that dissonance is not only psychologically uncomfortable but also can cause physiological arousal (Croyle & Cooper, 1983) and activate regions of the brain important in emotions and cognitive functioning (van Veen, Krug, Schooler, & Carter, 2009). When we experience cognitive dissonance, we are motivated to decrease it because it is psychologically, physically, and mentally uncomfortable. We can reduce cognitive dissonance by bringing our cognitions, attitudes, and behaviors in line—that is, making them harmonious. This can be done in different ways, such as:

- changing our discrepant behavior (e.g., stop smoking),
- changing our cognitions through rationalization or denial (e.g., telling ourselves that health risks can be reduced by smoking filtered cigarettes),
- adding a new cognition (e.g., "Smoking suppresses my appetite so I don't become overweight,

which is good for my health.").

A classic example of cognitive dissonance is Joaquin, a 20-year-old who enlists in the military. During boot camp he is awakened at 5:00 a.m., is chronically sleep deprived, yelled at, covered in sand flea bites, physically bruised and battered, and mentally exhausted (Figure 12.12). It gets worse. Recruits that make it to week 11 of boot camp have to do 54 hours of continuous training.

Figure 12.12 A person who has chosen a difficult path must deal with cognitive dissonance in addition to many other discomforts. (credit: Tyler J. Bolken)

Not surprisingly, Joaquin is miserable. No one likes to be miserable. In this type of situation, people can change their beliefs, their attitudes, or their behaviors. The last option, a change of behaviors, is not available to Joaquin. He has signed on to the military for four years, and he cannot legally leave.

If Joaquin keeps thinking about how miserable he is, it is going to be a very long four years. He will be in a constant state of cognitive dissonance. As an alternative to this misery, Joaquin can change his beliefs or attitudes. He can tell himself, "I am becoming stronger, healthier, and sharper. I am learning discipline and how to defend myself and my country. What I am doing is really important." If this is his belief, he will realize that he is becoming stronger through his challenges. He then will feel better and not experience cognitive dissonance, which is an uncomfortable state.

The Effect of Initiation

The military example demonstrates the observation that a difficult initiation into a group influences us to like the group more. Another social psychology concept, **justification of effort**, suggests that we value goals and achievements that we put a lot of effort into. According to this theory, if something is difficult for us to achieve, we believe it is more worthwhile. For example, if you move to an apartment and spend hours assembling a dresser you bought from Ikea, you will value that more than a fancier dresser your parents bought you. We do not want to have wasted time and effort to join a group that we eventually leave. A classic experiment by Aronson and Mills (1959) demonstrated this justification of effort effect. College students volunteered to join a campus group that would meet regularly to discuss the psychology of sex. Participants were randomly assigned to one of three conditions: no initiation, an easy initiation, and a difficult initiation into the group. After participating in the first discussion, which was deliberately made very boring, participants rated how much they liked the group. Participants who underwent a difficult initiation process to join the group rated the group more favorably than did participants with an easy initiation or no initiation (Figure 12.13).

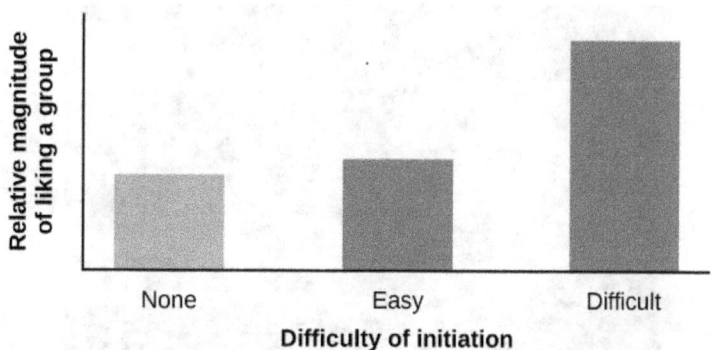

Figure 12.13 Justification of effort has a distinct effect on a person liking a group. Students in the difficult initiation condition liked the group more than students in other conditions due to the justification of effort.

Similar effects can be seen in a more recent study of how student effort affects course evaluations. Heckert, Latier, Ringwald-Burton, and Drazen (2006) surveyed 463 undergraduates enrolled in courses at a midwestern university about the amount of effort that their courses required of them. In addition, the students were also asked to evaluate various aspects of the course. Given what you've just read, it will come as no surprise that those courses that were associated with the highest level of effort were evaluated as being more valuable than those that did not. Furthermore, students indicated that they learned more in courses that required more effort, regardless of the grades that they received in those courses (Heckert et al., 2006).

Besides the classic military example and group initiation, can you think of other examples of cognitive dissonance? Here is one: Maria and Marco live in Fairfield County, Connecticut, which is one of the wealthiest areas in the United States and has a very high cost of living. Maria telecommutes from home and Marco does not work outside of the home. They rent a very small house for more than $3000 a month. Marco shops at consignment stores for clothes and economizes when possible. They complain that they never have any money and that they cannot buy anything new. When asked why they do not move to a less expensive location, since Maria telecommutes, they respond that Fairfield County is beautiful, they love the beaches, and they feel comfortable there. How does the theory of cognitive dissonance apply to Maria and Marco's choices?

PERSUASION

In the previous section we discussed that the motivation to reduce cognitive dissonance leads us to change our attitudes, behaviors, and/or cognitions to make them consonant. **Persuasion** is the process of changing our attitude toward something based on some kind of communication. Much of the persuasion we experience comes from outside forces. How do people convince others to change their attitudes, beliefs, and behaviors (Figure 12.14)? What communications do you receive that attempt to persuade you to change your attitudes, beliefs, and behaviors?

Figure 12.14 We encounter attempts at persuasion attempts everywhere. Persuasion is not limited to formal advertising; we are confronted with it throughout our everyday world. (credit: Robert Couse-Baker)

A subfield of social psychology studies persuasion and social influence, providing us with a plethora of information on how humans can be persuaded by others.

Yale Attitude Change Approach

The topic of persuasion has been one of the most extensively researched areas in social psychology (Fiske et al., 2010). During the Second World War, Carl Hovland extensively researched persuasion for the U.S. Army. After the war, Hovland continued his exploration of persuasion at Yale University. Out of this work came a model called the Yale attitude change approach, which describes the conditions under which people tend to change their attitudes. Hovland demonstrated that certain features of the source of a persuasive message, the content of the message, and the characteristics of the audience will influence the persuasiveness of a message (Hovland, Janis, & Kelley, 1953).

Features of the source of the persuasive message include the credibility of the speaker (Hovland & Weiss, 1951) and the physical attractiveness of the speaker (Eagly & Chaiken, 1975; Petty, Wegener, & Fabrigar, 1997). Thus, speakers who are credible, or have expertise on the topic, and who are deemed as trustworthy are more persuasive than less credible speakers. Similarly, more attractive speakers are more persuasive than less attractive speakers. The use of famous actors and athletes to advertise products on television and in print relies on this principle. The immediate and long term impact of the persuasion also depends, however, on the credibility of the messenger (Kumkale & Albarracín, 2004).

Features of the message itself that affect persuasion include subtlety (the quality of being important, but not obvious) (Petty & Cacioppo, 1986; Walster & Festinger, 1962); sidedness (that is, having more than one side) (Crowley & Hoyer, 1994; Igou & Bless, 2003; Lumsdaine & Janis, 1953); timing (Haugtvedt & Wegener, 1994; Miller & Campbell, 1959), and whether both sides are presented. Messages that are more subtle are more persuasive than direct messages. Arguments that occur first, such as in a debate, are more influential if messages are given back-to-back. However, if there is a delay after the first message, and before the audience needs to make a decision, the last message presented will tend to be more persuasive (Miller & Campbell, 1959).

Features of the audience that affect persuasion are attention (Albarracín & Wyer, 2001; Festinger & Maccoby, 1964), intelligence, self-esteem (Rhodes & Wood, 1992), and age (Krosnick & Alwin, 1989). In order to be persuaded, audience members must be paying attention. People with lower intelligence are more easily persuaded than people with higher intelligence; whereas people with moderate self-esteem are more easily persuaded than people with higher or lower self-esteem (Rhodes & Wood, 1992). Finally, younger adults aged 18–25 are more persuadable than older adults.

Elaboration Likelihood Model

An especially popular model that describes the dynamics of persuasion is the elaboration likelihood model of persuasion (Petty & Cacioppo, 1986). The elaboration likelihood model considers the variables of the attitude change approach—that is, features of the source of the persuasive message, contents of the message, and characteristics of the audience are used to determine when attitude change will occur. According to the elaboration likelihood model of persuasion, there are two main routes that play a role in delivering a persuasive message: central and peripheral (**Figure 12.15**).

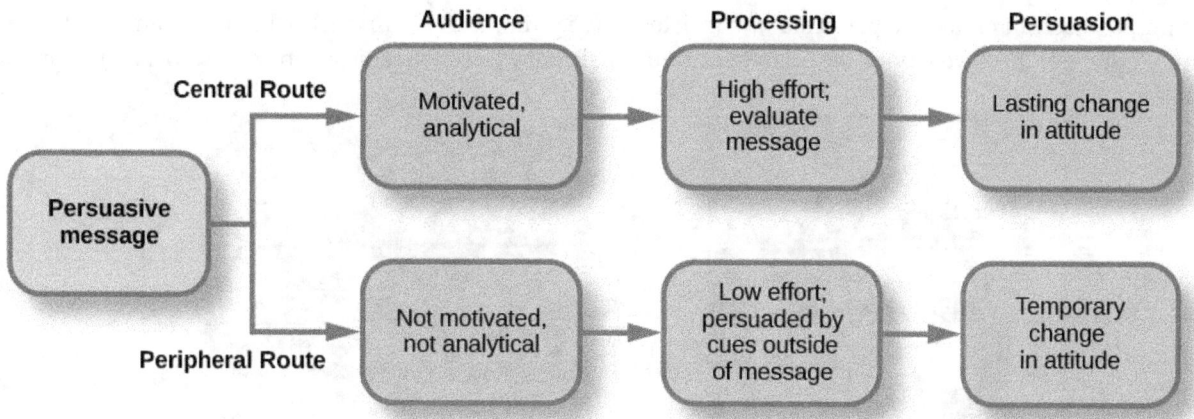

Figure 12.15 Persuasion can take one of two paths, and the durability of the end result depends on the path.

The **central route** is logic driven and uses data and facts to convince people of an argument's worthiness. For example, a car company seeking to persuade you to purchase their model will emphasize the car's safety features and fuel economy. This is a direct route to persuasion that focuses on the quality of the information. In order for the central route of persuasion to be effective in changing attitudes, thoughts, and behaviors, the argument must be strong and, if successful, will result in lasting attitude change.

The central route to persuasion works best when the target of persuasion, or the audience, is analytical and willing to engage in processing of the information. From an advertiser's perspective, what products would be best sold using the central route to persuasion? What audience would most likely be influenced to buy the product? One example is buying a computer. It is likely, for example, that small business owners might be especially influenced by the focus on the computer's quality and features such as processing speed and memory capacity.

The **peripheral route** is an indirect route that uses peripheral cues to associate positivity with the message (Petty & Cacioppo, 1986). Instead of focusing on the facts and a product's quality, the peripheral route relies on association with positive characteristics such as positive emotions and celebrity endorsement. For example, having a popular athlete advertise athletic shoes is a common method used to encourage young adults to purchase the shoes. This route to attitude change does not require much effort or information processing. This method of persuasion may promote positivity toward the message or product, but it typically results in less permanent attitude or behavior change. The audience does not need to be analytical or motivated to process the message. In fact, a peripheral route to persuasion may not even be noticed by the audience, for example in the strategy of product placement. Product placement refers to putting a product with a clear brand name or brand identity in a TV show or movie to promote the product (Gupta & Lord, 1998). For example, one season of the reality series *American Idol* prominently showed the panel of judges drinking out of cups that displayed the Coca-Cola logo. What other products would be best sold using the peripheral route to persuasion? Another example is clothing: A retailer may focus on celebrities that are wearing the same style of clothing.

Foot-in-the-door Technique

Researchers have tested many persuasion strategies that are effective in selling products and changing people's attitude, ideas, and behaviors. One effective strategy is the foot-in-the-door technique (Cialdini, 2001; Pliner, Hart, Kohl, & Saari, 1974). Using the **foot-in-the-door technique**, the persuader gets a person to agree to bestow a small favor or to buy a small item, only to later request a larger favor or purchase of a bigger item. The foot-in-the-door technique was demonstrated in a study by Freedman and Fraser (1966) in which participants who agreed to post small sign in their yard or sign a petition were more likely to agree to put a large sign in their yard than people who declined the first request (Figure 12.16). Research on this technique also illustrates the principle of consistency (Cialdini, 2001): Our past behavior often directs our future behavior, and we have a desire to maintain consistency once we have a committed to a behavior.

(a)　　　　　　　　　　　　(b)

Figure 12.16 With the foot-in-the-door technique, getting someone to agree to a small request such as (a) wearing a campaign button can make them more likely to agree to a larger request, such as (b) putting campaigns signs in your yard. (credit a: modification of work by Joe Crawford; credit b: modification of work by "shutterblog"/Flickr)

A common application of foot-in-the-door is when teens ask their parents for a small permission (for example, extending curfew by a half hour) and then asking them for something larger. Having granted the smaller request increases the likelihood that parents will acquiesce with the later, larger request.

How would a store owner use the foot-in-the-door technique to sell you an expensive product? For example, say that you are buying the latest model smartphone, and the salesperson suggests you purchase the best data plan. You agree to this. The salesperson then suggests a bigger purchase—the three-year extended warranty. After agreeing to the smaller request, you are more likely to also agree to the larger request. You may have encountered this if you have bought a car. When salespeople realize that a buyer intends to purchase a certain model, they might try to get the customer to pay for many or most available options on the car. Another example of the foot-in-the-door technique would be applied to an individual in the market for a used car who decides to buy a fully loaded new car. Why? Because the salesperson convinced the buyer that they need a car that has all of the safety features that were not available in the used car.

12.4 Conformity, Compliance, and Obedience

Learning Objectives

By the end of this section, you will be able to:
- Explain the Asch effect
- Define conformity and types of social influence
- Describe Stanley Milgram's experiment and its implications
- Define groupthink, social facilitation, and social loafing

In this section, we discuss additional ways in which people influence others. The topics of conformity, social influence, obedience, and group processes demonstrate the power of the social situation to change our thoughts, feelings, and behaviors. We begin this section with a discussion of a famous social psychology experiment that demonstrated how susceptible humans are to outside social pressures.

CONFORMITY

Solomon Asch conducted several experiments in the 1950s to determine how people are affected by the thoughts and behaviors of other people. In one study, a group of participants was shown a series of printed line segments of different lengths: a, b, and c (**Figure 12.17**). Participants were then shown a fourth line segment: x. They were asked to identify which line segment from the first group (a, b, or c) most closely resembled the fourth line segment in length.

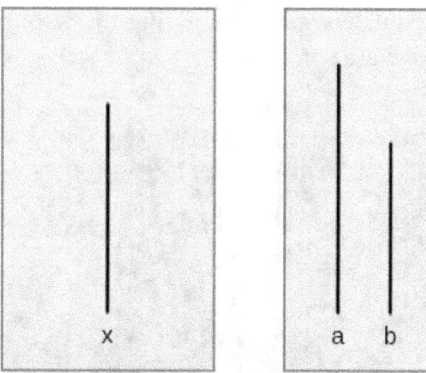

Figure 12.17 These line segments illustrate the judgment task in Asch's conformity study. Which line on the right—a, b, or c—is the same length as line x on the left?

Each group of participants had only one true, naïve subject. The remaining members of the group were confederates of the researcher. A **confederate** is a person who is aware of the experiment and works for the researcher. Confederates are used to manipulate social situations as part of the research design, and the true, naïve participants believe that confederates are, like them, uninformed participants in the experiment. In Asch's study, the confederates identified a line segment that was obviously shorter than the target line—a wrong answer. The naïve participant then had to identify aloud the line segment that best matched the target line segment.

How often do you think the true participant aligned with the confederates' response? That is, how often do you think the group influenced the participant, and the participant gave the wrong answer? Asch (1955) found that 76% of participants conformed to group pressure at least once by indicating the incorrect line. **Conformity** is the change in a person's behavior to go along with the group, even if he does not agree with the group. Why would people give the wrong answer? What factors would increase or decrease someone giving in or conforming to group pressure?

The **Asch effect** is the influence of the group majority on an individual's judgment.

What factors make a person more likely to yield to group pressure? Research shows that the size of the majority, the presence of another dissenter, and the public or relatively private nature of responses are key influences on conformity.

- The size of the majority: The greater the number of people in the majority, the more likely an individual will conform. There is, however, an upper limit: a point where adding more members does not increase conformity. In Asch's study, conformity increased with the number of people in the majority—up to seven individuals. At numbers beyond seven, conformity leveled off and decreased slightly (Asch, 1955).

- The presence of another dissenter: If there is at least one dissenter, conformity rates drop to near zero (Asch, 1955).

- The public or private nature of the responses: When responses are made publicly (in front of others), conformity is more likely; however, when responses are made privately (e.g., writing down the response), conformity is less likely (Deutsch & Gerard, 1955).

The finding that conformity is more likely to occur when responses are public than when they are private is the reason government elections require voting in secret, so we are not coerced by others (**Figure 12.18**). The Asch effect can be easily seen in children when they have to publicly vote for something. For example, if the teacher asks whether the children would rather have extra recess, no homework, or candy, once a few children vote, the rest will comply and go with the majority. In a different classroom, the majority might vote differently, and most of the children would comply with that majority. When someone's vote changes if it is made in public versus private, this is known as compliance. Compliance can be a form of conformity. Compliance is going along with a request or demand, even if you do not agree with the request. In Asch's studies, the participants complied by giving the wrong answers, but privately did not accept that the obvious wrong answers were correct.

Figure 12.18 Voting for government officials in the United States is private to reduce the pressure of conformity. (credit: Nicole Klauss)

Now that you have learned about the Asch line experiments, why do you think the participants conformed? The correct answer to the line segment question was obvious, and it was an easy task. Researchers have categorized the motivation to conform into two types: normative social influence and informational social influence (Deutsch & Gerard, 1955).

In **normative social influence**, people conform to the group norm to fit in, to feel good, and to be accepted by the group. However, with **informational social influence**, people conform because they believe the group is competent and has the correct information, particularly when the task or situation is ambiguous. What type of social influence was operating in the Asch conformity studies? Since the line judgment task was unambiguous, participants did not need to rely on the group for information. Instead, participants complied to fit in and avoid ridicule, an instance of normative social influence.

An example of informational social influence may be what to do in an emergency situation. Imagine that you are in a movie theater watching a film and what seems to be smoke comes in the theater from under the emergency exit door. You are not certain that it is smoke—it might be a special effect for the movie, such as a fog machine. When you are uncertain you will tend to look at the behavior of others in the theater. If other people show concern and get up to leave, you are likely to do the same. However, if others seem unconcerned, you are likely to stay put and continue watching the movie (**Figure 12.19**).

Figure 12.19 People in crowds tend to take cues from others and act accordingly. (a) An audience is listening to a lecture and people are relatively quiet, still, and attentive to the speaker on the stage. (b) An audience is at a rock concert where people are dancing, singing, and possibly engaging in activities like crowd surfing. (credit a: modification of work by Matt Brown; credit b: modification of work by Christian Holmér)

How would you have behaved if you were a participant in Asch's study? Many students say they would not conform, that the study is outdated, and that people nowadays are more independent. To some extent this may be true. Research suggests that overall rates of conformity may have reduced since the time of Asch's research. Furthermore, efforts to replicate Asch's study have made it clear that many factors determine how likely it is that someone will demonstrate conformity to the group. These factors include the participant's age, gender, and socio-cultural background (Bond & Smith, 1996; Larsen, 1990; Walker & Andrade, 1996).

LINK TO LEARNING

Watch this **video of a replication of the Asch experiment (http://openstax.org/l/Asch2)** to learn more.

STANLEY MILGRAM'S EXPERIMENT

Conformity is one effect of the influence of others on our thoughts, feelings, and behaviors. Another form of social influence is obedience to authority. **Obedience** is the change of an individual's behavior to comply with a demand by an authority figure. People often comply with the request because they are concerned about a consequence if they do not comply. To demonstrate this phenomenon, we review another classic social psychology experiment.

Stanley Milgram was a social psychology professor at Yale who was influenced by the trial of Adolf Eichmann, a Nazi war criminal. Eichmann's defense for the atrocities he committed was that he was "just following orders." Milgram (1963) wanted to test the validity of this defense, so he designed an experiment and initially recruited 40 men for his experiment. The volunteer participants were led to believe that they were participating in a study to improve learning and memory. The participants were told that they were to teach other students (learners) correct answers to a series of test items. The participants were shown how to use a device that they were told delivered electric shocks of different intensities to the learners. The participants were told to shock the learners if they gave a wrong answer to a test item—that the shock would help them to learn. The participants believed they gave the learners shocks, which increased in 15-volt increments, all the way up to 450 volts. The participants did not know that the learners were confederates and that the confederates did not actually receive shocks.

In response to a string of incorrect answers from the learners, the participants obediently and repeatedly shocked them. The confederate learners cried out for help, begged the participant teachers to stop, and even complained of heart trouble. Yet, when the researcher told the participant-teachers to continue the shock, 65% of the participants continued the shock to the maximum voltage and to the point that the learner became unresponsive (Figure 12.20). What makes someone obey authority to the point of potentially causing serious harm to another person?

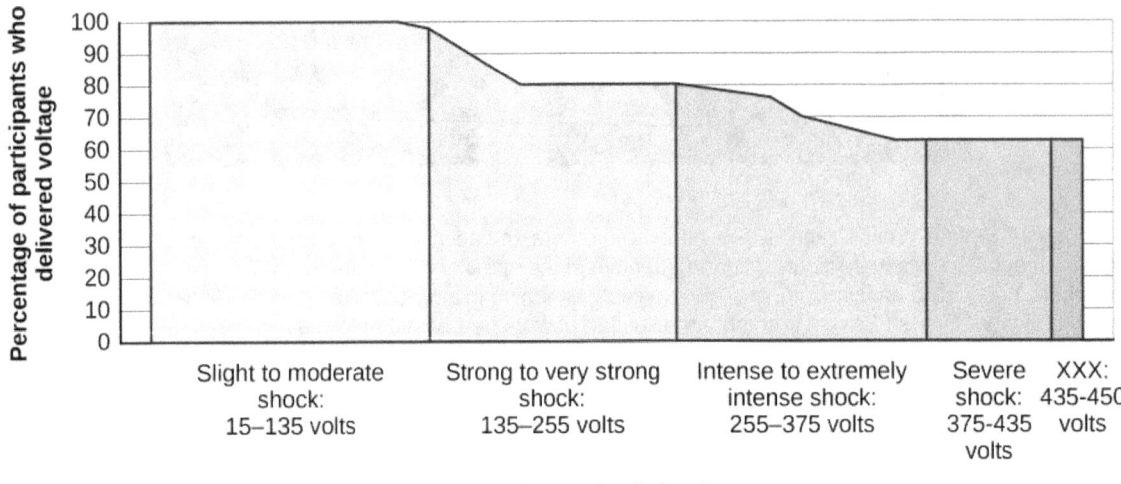

Figure 12.20 The Milgram experiment showed the surprising degree to which people obey authority. Two out of three (65%) participants continued to administer shocks to an unresponsive learner.

Several variations of the original Milgram experiment were conducted to test the boundaries of obedience. When certain features of the situation were changed, participants were less likely to continue to deliver shocks (Milgram, 1965). For example, when the setting of the experiment was moved to an off-campus office building, the percentage of participants who delivered the highest shock dropped to 48%. When the learner was in the same room as the teacher, the highest shock rate dropped to 40%. When the teachers' and learners' hands were touching, the highest shock rate dropped to 30%. When the researcher gave the orders by phone, the rate dropped to 23%. These variations show that when the humanity of the person being shocked was increased, obedience decreased. Similarly, when the authority of the experimenter decreased, so did obedience.

This case is still very applicable today. What does a person do if an authority figure orders something done? What if the person believes it is incorrect, or worse, unethical? In a study by Martin and Bull (2008), midwives privately filled out a questionnaire regarding best practices and expectations in delivering a baby. Then, a more senior midwife and supervisor asked the junior midwives to do something they had previously stated they were opposed to. Most of the junior midwives were obedient to authority, going against their own beliefs. Burger (2009) partially replicated this study. He found among a multicultural sample of women and men that their levels of obedience matched Milgram's research. Doliński et al. (2017) performed a replication of Burger's work in Poland and controlled for the gender of both participants and learners, and once again, results that were consistent with Milgram's original work were observed.

GROUPTHINK

When in group settings, we are often influenced by the thoughts, feelings, and behaviors of people around us. Whether it is due to normative or informational social influence, groups have power to influence individuals. Another phenomenon of group conformity is groupthink. **Groupthink** is the modification of the opinions of members of a group to align with what they believe is the group consensus (Janis, 1972). In group situations, the group often takes action that individuals would not perform outside the group setting because groups make more extreme decisions than individuals do. Moreover, groupthink can hinder opposing trains of thought. This elimination of diverse opinions contributes to faulty decision by the group.

> ### DIG DEEPER
>
> **Groupthink in the U.S. Government**
>
> There have been several instances of groupthink in the U.S. government. One example occurred when the United States led a small coalition of nations to invade Iraq in March 2003. This invasion occurred because a small group of advisors and former President George W. Bush were convinced that Iraq represented a significant terrorism threat with a large stockpile of weapons of mass destruction at its disposal. Although some of these individuals may have had some doubts about the credibility of the information available to them at the time, in the end, the group arrived at a consensus that Iraq had weapons of mass destruction and represented a significant threat to national security. It later came to light that Iraq did not have weapons of mass destruction, but not until the invasion was well underway. As a result, 6000 American soldiers were killed and many more civilians died. How did the Bush administration arrive at their conclusions? View this **video of Colin Powell, 10 years after his famous United Nations speech, discussing the information he had at the time (https://www.openstax.org/l/GroupThink)** that his decisions were based on. ("CNN Official Interview: Colin Powell now regrets UN speech about WMDs," 2010).
>
> Do you see evidence of groupthink?

Why does groupthink occur? There are several causes of groupthink, which makes it preventable. When the group is highly cohesive, or has a strong sense of connection, maintaining group harmony may become more important to the group than making sound decisions. If the group leader is directive and makes his opinions known, this may discourage group members from disagreeing with the leader. If the group is isolated from hearing alternative or new viewpoints, groupthink may be more likely. How do you know when groupthink is occurring?

There are several symptoms of groupthink including the following:

- perceiving the group as invulnerable or invincible—believing it can do no wrong
- believing the group is morally correct
- self-censorship by group members, such as withholding information to avoid disrupting the group consensus
- the quashing of dissenting group members' opinions
- the shielding of the group leader from dissenting views
- perceiving an illusion of unanimity among group members
- holding stereotypes or negative attitudes toward the out-group or others' with differing viewpoints (Janis, 1972)

Given the causes and symptoms of groupthink, how can it be avoided? There are several strategies that can improve group decision making including seeking outside opinions, voting in private, having the leader withhold position statements until all group members have voiced their views, conducting research on all viewpoints, weighing the costs and benefits of all options, and developing a contingency plan (Janis, 1972; Mitchell & Eckstein, 2009).

GROUP POLARIZATION

Another phenomenon that occurs within group settings is group polarization. **Group polarization** (Teger & Pruitt, 1967) is the strengthening of an original group attitude after the discussion of views within a group. That is, if a group initially favors a viewpoint, after discussion the group consensus is likely a stronger endorsement of the viewpoint. Conversely, if the group was initially opposed to a viewpoint, group discussion would likely lead to stronger opposition. Group polarization explains many actions taken by groups that would not be undertaken by individuals. Group polarization can be observed at political conventions, when platforms of the party are supported by individuals who, when not in a group, would decline to support them. Recently, some theorists have argued that group polarization may be partly responsible for the extreme political partisanship that seems ubiquitous in modern society. Given that people can self-select media outlets that are most consistent with their own political views, they are less likely to encounter opposing viewpoints. Over time, this leads to a strengthening of their own perspective and of hostile attitudes and behaviors towards those with different political ideals. Remarkably, political polarization leads to open levels of discrimination that are on par with, or perhaps exceed, racial discrimination (Iyengar & Westwood, 2015). A more everyday example is a group's discussion of how attractive someone is. Does your opinion change if you find someone attractive, but your friends do not agree? If your friends vociferously agree, might you then find this person even more attractive?

Social traps refer to situations that arise when individuals or groups of individuals behave in ways that are not in their best interest and that may have negative, long-term consequences. However, once established, a social trap is very difficult to escape. For example, following World War II, the United States and the former Soviet Union engaged in a nuclear arms race. While the presence of nuclear weapons is not in either party's best interest, once the arms race began, each country felt the need to continue producing nuclear weapons to protect itself from the other.

Social Loafing

Imagine you were just assigned a group project with other students whom you barely know. Everyone in your group will get the same grade. Are you the type who will do most of the work, even though the final grade will be shared? Or are you more likely to do less work because you know others will pick up the slack? **Social loafing** involves a reduction in individual output on tasks where contributions are pooled. Because each individual's efforts are not evaluated, individuals can become less motivated to perform well. Karau and Williams (1993) and Simms and Nichols (2014) reviewed the research on social loafing and discerned when it was least likely to happen. The researchers noted that social loafing could be alleviated if, among other situations, individuals knew their work would be assessed by a manager (in a workplace setting) or instructor (in a classroom setting), or if a manager or instructor required group members to complete self-evaluations.

The likelihood of social loafing in student work groups increases as the size of the group increases (Shepperd & Taylor, 1999). According to Kamau and Williams (1993), college students were the population most likely to engage in social loafing. Their study also found that women and participants from collectivistic cultures were less likely to engage in social loafing, explaining that their group orientation may account for this.

College students could work around social loafing or "free-riding" by suggesting to their professors use of a flocking method to form groups. Harding (2018) compared groups of students who had self-selected into groups for class to those who had been formed by flocking, which involves assigning students to groups who have similar schedules and motivations. Not only did she find that students reported less "free riding," but that they also did better in the group assignments compared to those whose groups were self-selected.

Interestingly, the opposite of social loafing occurs when the task is complex and difficult (Bond & Titus, 1983; Geen, 1989). In a group setting, such as the student work group, if your individual performance cannot be evaluated, there is less pressure for you to do well, and thus less anxiety or physiological arousal (Latané, Williams, & Harkens, 1979). This puts you in a relaxed state in which you can perform your best, if you choose (Zajonc, 1965). If the task is a difficult one, many people feel motivated and believe that their group needs their input to do well on a challenging project (Jackson & Williams, 1985).

Deindividuation

Another way that being part of a group can affect behavior is exhibited in instances in which deindividuation occurs. Deindividuation refers to situations in which a person may feel a sense of anonymity and therefore a reduction in accountability and sense of self when among others. Deindividuation is often pointed to in cases in which mob or riot-like behaviors occur (Zimbardo, 1969), but research on the subject and the role that deindividuation plays in such behaviors has resulted in inconsistent results (as discussed in Granström, Guvå, Hylander, & Rosander, 2009).

Table 12.2 summarizes the types of social influence you have learned about in this chapter.

Types of Social Influence

Type of Social Influence	Description
Conformity	Changing your behavior to go along with the group even if you do not agree with the group
Compliance	Going along with a request or demand
Normative social influence	Conformity to a group norm to fit in, feel good, and be accepted by the group
Informational social influence	Conformity to a group norm prompted by the belief that the group is competent and has the correct information
Obedience	Changing your behavior to please an authority figure or to avoid aversive consequences
Groupthink	Tendency to prioritize group cohesion over critical thinking that might lead to poor decision making; more likely to occur when there is perceived unanimity among the group
Group polarization	Strengthening of the original group attitude after discussing views within a group
Social facilitation	Improved performance when an audience is watching versus when the individual performs the behavior alone
Social loafing	Exertion of less effort by a person working in a group because individual performance cannot be evaluated separately from the group, thus causing performance decline on easy tasks
Deindividuation	Group situation in which a person may feel a sense of anonymity and a resulting reduction in accountability and sense of self

Table 12.2

12.5 Prejudice and Discrimination

Learning Objectives

By the end of this section, you will be able to:
- Define and distinguish among prejudice, stereotypes, and discrimination
- Provide examples of prejudice, stereotypes, and discrimination
- Explain why prejudice and discrimination exist

Human conflict can result in crime, war, and mass murder, such as genocide. Prejudice and discrimination often are root causes of human conflict, which explains how strangers come to hate one another to the extreme of causing others harm. Prejudice and discrimination affect everyone. In this section we will examine the definitions of prejudice and discrimination, examples of these concepts, and causes of these biases.

(a) (b) (c)

Figure 12.21 Prejudice and discrimination occur across the globe. (a) A 1939 sign in German-occupied Poland warns "No Entrance for Poles!" (b) An African-American male drinks from a designated "colored" water fountain in Oklahoma in 1939 during the era of racial segregation as a practice of discrimination. (c) Members of the Westboro Baptist Church, widely identified as a hate group, engage in discrimination based on religion and sexual orientation. (credit b: modification of work by United States Farm Security Administration; credit c: modification of work by "JCWilmore"/Wikimedia Commons)

UNDERSTANDING PREJUDICE AND DISCRIMINATION

As we discussed in the opening story of Trayvon Martin, humans are very diverse and although we share many similarities, we also have many differences. The social groups we belong to help form our identities (Tajfel, 1974). These differences may be difficult for some people to reconcile, which may lead to prejudice toward people who are different. **Prejudice** is a negative attitude and feeling toward an individual based solely on one's membership in a particular social group (Allport, 1954; Brown, 2010). Prejudice is common against people who are members of an unfamiliar cultural group. Thus, certain types of education, contact, interactions, and building relationships with members of different cultural groups can reduce the tendency toward prejudice. In fact, simply imagining interacting with members of different cultural groups might affect prejudice. Indeed, when experimental participants were asked to imagine themselves positively interacting with someone from a different group, this led to an increased positive attitude toward the other group and an increase in positive traits associated with the other group. Furthermore, imagined social interaction can reduce anxiety associated with inter-group interactions (Crisp & Turner, 2009). What are some examples of social groups that you belong to that contribute to your identity? Social groups can include gender, race, ethnicity, nationality, social class, religion, sexual orientation, profession, and many more. And, as is true for social roles, you can simultaneously be a member of more than one social group. An example of prejudice is having a negative attitude toward people who are not born in the United States. Although people holding this prejudiced attitude do not know all people who were not born in the United States, they dislike them due to their status as foreigners.

Can you think of a prejudiced attitude you have held toward a group of people? How did your prejudice develop? Prejudice often begins in the form of a **stereotype**—that is, a specific belief or assumption about individuals based solely on their membership in a group, regardless of their individual characteristics. Stereotypes become overgeneralized and applied to all members of a group. For example, someone holding prejudiced attitudes toward older adults, may believe that older adults are slow and incompetent (Cuddy, Norton, & Fiske, 2005; Nelson, 2004). We cannot possibly know each individual person of advanced age to know that all older adults are slow and incompetent. Therefore, this negative belief is overgeneralized to all members of the group, even though many of the individual group members may in fact be spry and intelligent.

Another example of a well-known stereotype involves beliefs about racial differences among athletes. As Hodge, Burden, Robinson, and Bennett (2008) point out, Black male athletes are often believed to be more athletic, yet less intelligent, than their White male counterparts. These beliefs persist despite a number of high profile examples to the contrary. Sadly, such beliefs often influence how these athletes are treated by others and how they view themselves and their own capabilities. Whether or not you agree with a stereotype, stereotypes are generally well-known within in a given culture (Devine, 1989).

Sometimes people will act on their prejudiced attitudes toward a group of people, and this behavior is known as discrimination. **Discrimination** is negative action toward an individual as a result of one's membership in a particular group (Allport, 1954; Dovidio & Gaertner, 2004). As a result of holding negative beliefs (stereotypes) and negative attitudes (prejudice) about a particular group, people often treat the target of prejudice poorly, such as excluding older adults from their circle of friends. An example of a psychologist experiencing gender discrimination is found in the life and studies of Mary Whiton Calkins. Calkins was given special permission to attend graduate seminars at Harvard (at that time in the late 1880s, Harvard did not accept women) and at one point was the sole student of the famous psychologist William James. She passed all the requirements needed for a PhD and was described by psychologist Hugo Münsterberg as "one of the strongest professors of psychology in this country." However, Harvard refused to grant Calkins a PhD because she was a woman (Harvard University, 2019). **Table 12.3** summarizes the characteristics of stereotypes, prejudice, and discrimination. Have you ever been the target of discrimination? If so, how did this negative treatment make you feel?

Connecting Stereotypes, Prejudice, and Discrimination

Item	Function	Connection	Example
Stereotype	Cognitive; thoughts about people	Overgeneralized beliefs about people may lead to prejudice.	"Yankees fans are arrogant and obnoxious."
Prejudice	Affective; feelings about people, both positive and negative	Feelings may influence treatment of others, leading to discrimination.	"I hate Yankees fans; they make me angry."
Discrimination	Behavior; positive or negative treatment of others	Holding stereotypes and harboring prejudice may lead to excluding, avoiding, and biased treatment of group members.	"I would never hire nor become friends with a person if I knew he or she were a Yankees fan."

Table 12.3

So far, we've discussed stereotypes, prejudice, and discrimination as negative thoughts, feelings, and behaviors because these are typically the most problematic. However, it is important to also point out that people can hold positive thoughts, feelings, and behaviors toward individuals based on group membership; for example, they would show preferential treatment for people who are like themselves—that is, who share the same gender, race, or favorite sports team.

> ### LINK TO LEARNING
>
> Watch this video of a social experiment conducted in a park (http://openstax.org/l/racismexp) that demonstrates the concepts of prejudice, stereotypes, and discrimination. In the video, three people try to steal a bike out in the open. The race and gender of the thief is varied: a White male teenager, a Black male teenager, and a White female. Does anyone try to stop them? The treatment of the teenagers in the video demonstrates the concept of racism.

TYPES OF PREJUDICE AND DISCRIMINATION

When we meet strangers we automatically process three pieces of information about them: their race, gender, and age (Ito & Urland, 2003). Why are these aspects of an unfamiliar person so important? Why don't we instead notice whether their eyes are friendly, whether they are smiling, their height, the type of clothes they are wearing? Although these secondary characteristics are important in forming a first impression of a stranger, the social categories of race, gender, and age provide a wealth of information about an individual. This information, however, often is based on stereotypes. We may have different expectations of strangers depending on their race, gender, and age. What stereotypes and prejudices do you hold about people who are from a race, gender, and age group different from your own?

Racism

Racism is prejudice and discrimination against an individual based solely on one's membership in a specific racial group (such as toward African Americans, Asian Americans, Latinos, Native Americans, European Americans). What are some stereotypes of various racial or ethnic groups? Research suggests cultural stereotypes for Asian Americans include cold, sly, and intelligent; for Latinos, cold and unintelligent; for European Americans, cold and intelligent; and for African Americans, aggressive, athletic, and more likely to be law breakers (Devine & Elliot, 1995; Fiske, Cuddy, Glick, & Xu, 2002; Sommers & Ellsworth, 2000; Dixon & Linz, 2000).

Racism exists for many racial and ethnic groups. For example, Blacks are significantly more likely to have their vehicles searched during traffic stops than Whites, particularly when Blacks are driving in predominately White neighborhoods, a phenomenon often termed "DWB" or "driving while Black" (Rojek, Rosenfeld, & Decker, 2012).

Mexican Americans and other Latino groups also are targets of racism from the police and other members of the community. For example, when purchasing items with a personal check, Latino shoppers are more likely than White shoppers to be asked to show formal identification (Dovidio et al., 2010).

In one case of alleged harassment by the police, several East Haven, Connecticut, police officers were arrested on federal charges due to reportedly continued harassment and brutalization of Latinos. When the accusations came out, the mayor of East Haven was asked, "What are you doing for the Latino community today?" The Mayor responded, "I might have tacos when I go home, I'm not quite sure yet" ("East Haven Mayor," 2012). This statement undermines the important issue of racial profiling and police harassment of Latinos, while belittling Latino culture by emphasizing an interest in a food product stereotypically associated with Latinos.

Racism is prevalent toward many other groups in the United States including Native Americans, Arab

Americans, Jewish Americans, and Asian Americans. Have you experienced or witnessed racism toward any of these racial or ethnic groups? Are you aware of racism in your community?

One reason modern forms of racism, and prejudice in general, are hard to detect is related to the dual attitudes model (Wilson, Lindsey, & Schooler, 2000). Humans have two forms of attitudes: explicit attitudes, which are conscious and controllable, and implicit attitudes, which are unconscious and uncontrollable (Devine, 1989; Olson & Fazio, 2003). Because holding egalitarian views is socially desirable (Plant & Devine, 1998), most people do not show extreme racial bias or other prejudices on measures of their explicit attitudes. However, measures of implicit attitudes often show evidence of mild to strong racial bias or other prejudices (Greenwald, McGee, & Schwartz, 1998; Olson & Fazio, 2003).

Sexism

Sexism is prejudice and discrimination toward individuals based on their sex. Typically, sexism takes the form of men holding biases against women, but either sex can show sexism toward their own or their opposite sex. Like racism, sexism may be subtle and difficult to detect. Common forms of sexism in modern society include gender role expectations, such as expecting women to be the caretakers of the household. Sexism also includes people's expectations for how members of a gender group should behave. For example, women are expected to be friendly, passive, and nurturing, and when women behave in an unfriendly, assertive, or neglectful manner they often are disliked for violating their gender role (Rudman, 1998). Research by Laurie Rudman (1998) finds that when female job applicants self-promote, they are likely to be viewed as competent, but they may be disliked and are less likely to be hired because they violated gender expectations for modesty. Sexism can exist on a societal level such as in hiring, employment opportunities, and education. Women are less likely to be hired or promoted in male-dominated professions such as engineering, aviation, and construction (**Figure 12.22**) (Blau, Ferber, & Winkler, 2010; Ceci & Williams, 2011). Have you ever experienced or witnessed sexism? Think about your family members' jobs or careers. Why do you think there are differences in the jobs women and men have, such as more women nurses but more male surgeons (Betz, 2008)?

Figure 12.22 Women now have many jobs previously closed to them, though they still face challenges in male-dominated occupations. (credit: "The National Guard"/Flickr)

Ageism

People often form judgments and hold expectations about people based on their age. These judgments and expectations can lead to **ageism**, or prejudice and discrimination toward individuals based solely on their age. Think of expectations you hold for older adults. How could someone's expectations influence the feelings they hold toward individuals from older age groups? Ageism is widespread in U.S. culture (Nosek, 2005), and a common ageist attitude toward older adults is that they are incompetent, physically weak, and slow (Greenberg, Schimel, & Martens, 2002) and some people consider older adults less attractive. Chang, Kannoth, Levy, Wang, Lee, and Levy (2020) reported on relationships between ageism and health outcomes over a 40-year-plus period from countries around the world. Across 11 health domains, people over 50 were likely to experience ageism most often in the form of being denied access to health services and work opportunities. Some cultures, however, including some Asian, Latino, and African American cultures, both outside and within the United States afford older adults respect and honor.

Typically, ageism occurs against older adults, but ageism also can occur toward younger adults. What expectations do you hold toward younger people? Does society expect younger adults to be immature and irresponsible? Raymer, Reed, Spiegel, and Purvanova (2017) examined ageism against younger workers. They found that older workers endorsed negative stereotypes of younger workers, believing that they had more work deficit characteristics (including perceptions of incompetence). How might these forms of ageism affect a younger and older adult who are applying for a sales clerk position?

Homophobia

Another form of prejudice is **homophobia**: prejudice and discrimination of individuals based solely on their sexual orientation. Like ageism, homophobia is a widespread prejudice in U.S. society that is tolerated by many people (Herek & McLemore, 2013; Nosek, 2005). Negative feelings often result in discrimination, such as the exclusion of lesbian, gay, bisexual, transgender, and queer (LBGTQ+) people from social groups and the avoidance of LGBTQ+ neighbors and co-workers. This discrimination also extends to employers deliberately declining to hire qualified LGBTQ+ job applicants. Have you experienced or witnessed homophobia? If so, what stereotypes, prejudiced attitudes, and discrimination were evident?

> **DIG DEEPER**
>
> **Research into Homophobia**
>
> Some people are quite passionate in their hatred for nonheterosexuals in our society. In some cases, people have been tortured and/or murdered simply because they were not straight. This passionate response has led some researchers to question what motives might exist for homophobic people. Adams, Wright, & Lohr (1996) conducted a study investigating this issue and their results were quite an eye-opener.
>
> In this experiment, male college students were given a scale that assessed how homophobic they were; those with extreme scores were recruited to participate in the experiment. In the end, 64 men agreed to participate and were split into 2 groups: homophobic men and nonhomophobic men. Both groups of men were fitted with a penile plethysmograph, an instrument that measures changes in blood flow to the penis and serves as an objective measurement of sexual arousal.
>
> All men were shown segments of sexually explicit videos. One of these videos involved a sexual interaction between a man and a woman (straight clip). One video displayed two females engaged in a sexual interaction (lesbian clip), and the final video displayed two men engaged in a sexual interaction (gay clip). Changes in penile tumescence (a measure of physiological genital arousal) were recorded during all three clips, and a subjective measurement of sexual arousal was also obtained. While both groups of men became sexually aroused to the straight and lesbian video clips, only those men who were identified as homophobic showed sexual arousal to the gay male video clip. While all men reported that their erections indicated arousal for the straight and lesbian clips, the homophobic men indicated that they were not sexually aroused (despite their erections) to the gay clips. Adams et al. (1996) suggest that these findings may indicate that homophobia is related to gay arousal that the homophobic individuals either deny or are unaware.

WHY DO PREJUDICE AND DISCRIMINATION EXIST?

Prejudice and discrimination persist in society due to social learning and conformity to social norms. Children learn prejudiced attitudes and beliefs from society: their parents, teachers, friends, the media, and other sources of socialization, such as Facebook (O'Keeffe & Clarke-Pearson, 2011). If certain types of prejudice and discrimination are acceptable in a society, there may be normative pressures to conform and share those prejudiced beliefs, attitudes, and behaviors. For example, public and private schools are still somewhat segregated by social class. Historically, only children from wealthy families could afford to attend private schools, whereas children from middle- and low-income families typically attended public schools. If a child from a low-income family received a merit scholarship to attend a private school, how might the child be treated by classmates? Can you recall a time when you held prejudiced attitudes or beliefs or acted in a discriminatory manner because your group of friends expected you to?

STEREOTYPES AND SELF-FULFILLING PROPHECY

When we hold a stereotype about a person, we have expectations that he or she will fulfill that stereotype. A **self-fulfilling prophecy** is an expectation held by a person that alters his or her behavior in a way that tends to make it true. When we hold stereotypes about a person, we tend to treat the person according to our expectations. This treatment can influence the person to act according to our stereotypic expectations, thus confirming our stereotypic beliefs. Research by Rosenthal and Jacobson (1968) found that disadvantaged students whose teachers expected them to perform well had higher grades than disadvantaged students whose teachers expected them to do poorly.

Consider this example of cause and effect in a self-fulfilling prophecy: If an employer expects an openly gay male job applicant to be incompetent, the potential employer might treat the applicant negatively during the interview by engaging in less conversation, making little eye contact, and generally behaving coldly toward the applicant (Hebl, Foster, Mannix, & Dovidio, 2002). In turn, the job applicant will perceive that the potential employer dislikes him, and he will respond by giving shorter responses to interview questions, making less eye contact, and generally disengaging from the interview. After the interview, the employer will reflect on the applicant's behavior, which seemed cold and distant, and the employer will conclude, based on the applicant's poor performance during the interview, that the applicant was in fact incompetent. Thus, the employer's stereotype—gay men are incompetent and do not make good employees—is reinforced. Do you think this job applicant is likely to be hired? Treating individuals according to stereotypic beliefs can lead to prejudice and discrimination.

Another dynamic that can reinforce stereotypes is confirmation bias. When interacting with the target of our prejudice, we tend to pay attention to information that is consistent with our stereotypic expectations and ignore information that is inconsistent with our expectations. In this process, known as **confirmation bias**, we seek out information that supports our stereotypes and ignore information that is inconsistent with our stereotypes (Wason & Johnson-Laird, 1972). In the job interview example, the employer may not have noticed that the job applicant was friendly and engaging, and that he provided competent responses to the interview questions in the beginning of the interview. Instead, the employer focused on the job applicant's performance in the later part of the interview, after the applicant changed his demeanor and behavior to match the interviewer's negative treatment. Have you ever fallen prey to the self-fulfilling prophecy or confirmation bias, either as the source or target of such bias? How might we stop the cycle of the self-fulfilling prophecy?

IN-GROUPS AND OUT-GROUPS

As discussed previously in this section, we all belong to a gender, race, age, and social economic group. These groups provide a powerful source of our identity and self-esteem (Tajfel & Turner, 1979). These groups serve as our in-groups. An **in-group** is a group that we identify with or see ourselves as belonging to. A group that we don't belong to, or an **out-group**, is a group that we view as fundamentally different from us. For example, if you are female, your gender in-group includes all females, and your gender out-group includes all males (Figure 12.23). People often view gender groups as being fundamentally different from each other in personality traits, characteristics, social roles, and interests. Because we often feel a strong sense of belonging and emotional connection to our in-groups, we develop in-group bias: a preference for our own group over other groups. This **in-group bias** can result in prejudice and discrimination because the out-group is perceived as different and is less preferred than our in-group.

Figure 12.23 These children are very young, but they are already aware of their gender in-group and out-group. (credit: modification of work by "Reiner Kraft"/Flickr)

Despite the group dynamics that seem only to push groups toward conflict, there are forces that promote reconciliation between groups: the expression of empathy, of acknowledgment of past suffering on both sides, and the halt of destructive behaviors.

One function of prejudice is to help us feel good about ourselves and maintain a positive self-concept. This need to feel good about ourselves extends to our in-groups: We want to feel good and protect our in-groups. We seek to resolve threats individually and at the in-group level. This often happens by blaming an out-group for the problem. **Scapegoating** is the act of blaming an out-group when the in-group experiences frustration or is blocked from obtaining a goal (Allport, 1954).

12.6 Aggression

Learning Objectives

By the end of this section, you will be able to:
- Define aggression
- Define cyberbullying
- Describe the bystander effect

Throughout this chapter we have discussed how people interact and influence one another's thoughts, feelings, and behaviors in both positive and negative ways. People can work together to achieve great things, such as helping each other in emergencies: recall the heroism displayed during the 9/11 terrorist attacks. People also can do great harm to one another, such as conforming to group norms that are immoral and obeying authority to the point of murder: consider the mass conformity of Nazis during WWII. In this section we will discuss a negative side of human behavior—aggression.

A number of researchers have explored ways to reduce prejudice. One of the earliest was a study by Sherif et al. (1961) known as the Robbers Cave experiment. They found that when two opposing groups at a camp worked together toward a common goal, prejudicial attitudes between the groups decreased (Gaertner, Dovidio, Banker, Houlette, Johnson, & McGlynn, 2000). Focusing on superordinate goals was the key to attitude change in the research. Another study examined the jigsaw classroom, a technique designed by Aronson and Bridgeman in an effort to increase success in desegregated classrooms. In this technique, students work on an assignment in groups inclusive of various races and abilities. They are assigned tasks within their group, then collaborate with peers from other groups who were assigned the same task, and then report back to their original group. Walker and Crogan (1998) noted that the jigsaw classroom reduced potential for prejudice in Australia, as diverse students worked together on projects needing all of the pieces to succeed. This research suggests that anything that can allow individuals to work together toward common goals can decrease prejudicial attitudes. Obviously, the application of such strategies in real-world settings would enhance opportunities for conflict resolution.

AGGRESSION

Humans engage in **aggression** when they seek to cause harm or pain to another person. Aggression takes two forms depending on one's motives: hostile or instrumental. **Hostile aggression** is motivated by feelings of anger with intent to cause pain; a fight in a bar with a stranger is an example of hostile aggression. In contrast, **instrumental aggression** is motivated by achieving a goal and does not necessarily involve intent to cause pain (Berkowitz, 1993); a contract killer who murders for hire displays instrumental aggression.

There are many different theories as to why aggression exists. Some researchers argue that aggression serves an evolutionary function (Buss, 2004). Men are more likely than women to show aggression (Wilson & Daly, 1985). From the perspective of evolutionary psychology, human male aggression, like that in nonhuman primates, likely serves to display dominance over other males, both to protect a mate and to perpetuate the male's genes (Figure 12.24). Sexual jealousy is part of male aggression; males endeavor to make sure their mates are not copulating with other males, thus ensuring their own paternity of the female's offspring. Although aggression provides an obvious evolutionary advantage for men, women also engage in aggression. Women typically display more indirect forms of aggression, with their aggression serving as a means to an end (Dodge & Schwartz, 1997). For example, women may express their aggression covertly by communication that impairs the social standing of another person. Another theory that explains one of the functions of human aggression is frustration aggression theory (Dollard, Doob, Miller, Mowrer, & Sears, 1939). This theory states that when humans are prevented from achieving an important goal, they become frustrated and aggressive.

Figure 12.24 Human males and nonhuman male primates endeavor to gain and display dominance over other males, as demonstrated in the behavior of these monkeys. (credit: "Arcadiuš"/Flickr)

Bullying

Another form of aggression is bullying. As you learn in your study of child development, socializing and playing with other children is beneficial for children's psychological development. However, as you may have experienced as a child, not all play behavior has positive outcomes. Some children are aggressive and want to play roughly. Other children are selfish and do not want to share toys. One form of negative social interactions among children that has become a national concern is bullying. **Bullying** is repeated negative treatment of another person, often an adolescent, over time (Olweus, 1993). A one-time incident in which one child hits another child on the playground would not be considered bullying: Bullying is repeated behavior. The negative treatment typical in bullying is the attempt to inflict harm, injury, or humiliation, and bullying can include physical or verbal attacks. However, bullying doesn't have to be physical or verbal, it can be psychological. Research finds gender differences in how girls and boys bully others (American Psychological Association, 2010; Olweus, 1993). Boys tend to engage in direct, physical aggression such as physically harming others. Girls tend to engage in indirect, social forms of aggression such as spreading rumors, ignoring, or socially isolating others. Based on what you have learned about child development and social roles, why do you think boys and girls display different types of bullying behavior?

Bullying involves three parties: the bully, the victim, and witnesses or bystanders. The act of bullying involves an imbalance of power with the bully holding more power—physically, emotionally, and/or socially over the victim. The experience of bullying can be positive for the bully, who may enjoy a boost to self-esteem. However, there are several negative consequences of bullying for the victim, and also for the bystanders. How do you think bullying negatively impacts adolescents? Being the victim of bullying is associated with decreased mental health, including experiencing anxiety and depression (APA, 2010). Victims of bullying may underperform in schoolwork (Bowen, 2011). Bullying also can result in the victim committing suicide (APA, 2010). How might bullying negatively affect witnesses?

Although there is not one single personality profile for who becomes a bully and who becomes a victim of bullying (APA, 2010), researchers have identified some patterns in children who are at a greater risk of being bullied (Olweus, 1993):

- Children who are emotionally reactive are at a greater risk for being bullied. Bullies may be attracted to children who get upset easily because the bully can quickly get an emotional reaction from them.
- Children who are different from others are likely to be targeted for bullying. Children who are overweight, cognitively impaired, or racially or ethnically different from their peer group may be at higher risk.
- Gay, lesbian, bisexual, and transgender teens are at very high risk of being bullied and hurt due to their sexual orientation.

Cyberbullying

With the rapid growth of technology, and widely available mobile technology and social networking media, a new form of bullying has emerged: cyberbullying (Hoff & Mitchell, 2009). **Cyberbullying**, like bullying, is repeated behavior that is intended to cause psychological or emotional harm to another person. What is unique about cyberbullying is that it is typically covert, concealed, done in private, and the bully can remain anonymous. This anonymity gives the bully power, and the victim may feel helpless, unable to escape the harassment, and unable to retaliate (Spears, Slee, Owens, & Johnson, 2009).

Cyberbullying can take many forms, including harassing a victim by spreading rumors, creating a website defaming the victim, and ignoring, insulting, laughing at, or teasing the victim (Spears et al., 2009). In cyberbullying, it is more common for girls to be the bullies and victims because cyberbullying is nonphysical and is a less direct form of bullying (**Figure 12.25**) (Hoff & Mitchell, 2009). Interestingly, girls who become cyberbullies often have been the victims of cyberbullying at one time (Vandebosch & Van Cleemput, 2009). The effects of cyberbullying are just as harmful as traditional bullying and include the victim feeling frustration, anger, sadness, helplessness, powerlessness, and fear. Victims will also experience lower self-esteem (Hoff & Mitchell, 2009; Spears et al., 2009). Furthermore, recent research suggests that both cyberbullying victims and perpetrators are more likely to experience suicidal ideation, and they are more likely to attempt suicide than individuals who have no experience with cyberbullying (Hinduja & Patchin, 2010). What features of technology make cyberbullying easier and perhaps more accessible to young adults? What can parents, teachers, and social networking websites, like Facebook, do to prevent cyberbullying?

Figure 12.25 Because cyberbullying is not physical in nature, cyberbullies and their victims are most often female; however, there is much evidence that gay men are frequently victims of cyberbullying as well (Hinduja & Patchin, 2011). (credit: Steven Depolo)

THE BYSTANDER EFFECT

The discussion of bullying highlights the problem of witnesses not intervening to help a victim. Researchers Latané and Darley (1968) described a phenomenon called the bystander effect. The **bystander effect** is a phenomenon in which a witness or bystander does not volunteer to help a victim or person in distress. Instead, they just watch what is happening. Social psychologists hold that we make these decisions based on the social situation, not our own personality variables. The impetus behind the bystander effect was the murder of a young woman named Kitty Genovese in 1964. The story of her tragic death took on a life of its own when it was reported that none of her neighbors helped her or called the police when she was being attacked. However, Kassin (2017) noted that her killer was apprehended due to neighbors who called the police when they saw him committing a burglary days later. Not only did bystanders indeed intervene in her murder (one man who shouted at the killer, a woman who said she called the police, and a friend who comforted her in her last moments), but other bystanders intervened in the capture of the murderer. Social psychologists claim that diffusion of responsibility is the likely explanation. **Diffusion of responsibility** is the tendency for no one in a group to help because the responsibility to help is spread throughout the group (Bandura, 1999). Because there were many witnesses to the attack on Genovese, as evidenced by the number of lit apartment windows in the building, individuals assumed someone else must have already called the police. The responsibility to call the police was diffused across the number of witnesses to the crime. Have you ever passed an accident on the freeway and assumed that a victim or certainly another motorist has already reported the accident? In general, the greater the number of bystanders, the less likely any one person will help.

12.7 Prosocial Behavior

Learning Objectives

By the end of this section, you will be able to:
- Describe altruism
- Describe conditions that influence the formation of relationships
- Identify what attracts people to each other
- Describe the triangular theory of love
- Explain social exchange theory in relationships

You've learned about many of the negative behaviors of social psychology, but the field also studies many positive social interactions and behaviors. What makes people like each other? With whom are we friends? Whom do we date? Researchers have documented several features of the situation that influence whether we form relationships with others. There are also universal traits that humans find attractive in others. In this section we discuss conditions that make forming relationships more likely, what we look for in friendships and romantic relationships, the different types of love, and a theory explaining how our relationships are formed, maintained, and terminated.

PROSOCIAL BEHAVIOR AND ALTRUISM

Do you voluntarily help others? Voluntary behavior with the intent to help other people is called **prosocial behavior**. Why do people help other people? Is personal benefit such as feeling good about oneself the only reason people help one another? Research suggests there are many other reasons. **Altruism** is people's desire to help others even if the costs outweigh the benefits of helping. In fact, people acting in altruistic ways may disregard the personal costs associated with helping (Figure 12.26). For example, news accounts of the 9/11 terrorist attacks on the World Trade Center in New York reported an employee in the first tower helped his co-workers make it to the exit stairwell. After helping a co-worker to safety he went back in the burning building to help additional co-workers. In this case the costs of helping were great, and the hero lost his life in the destruction (Stewart, 2002).

Figure 12.26 The events of 9/11 unleashed an enormous show of altruism and heroism on the parts of first responders and many ordinary people. (credit: Don Halasy)

Some researchers suggest that altruism operates on empathy. **Empathy** is the capacity to understand another person's perspective, to feel what he or she feels. An empathetic person makes an emotional connection with others and feels compelled to help (Batson, 1991). Other researchers argue that altruism is a form of selfless helping that is not motivated by benefits or feeling good about oneself. Certainly, after helping, people feel good about themselves, but some researchers argue that this is a consequence of altruism, not a cause. Other researchers argue that helping is always self-serving because our egos are involved, and we receive benefits from helping (Cialdini, Brown, Lewis, Luce, & Neuberg 1997). It is challenging to determine experimentally the true motivation for helping, whether is it largely self-serving (egoism) or selfless (altruism). Thus, a debate on whether pure altruism exists continues.

LINK TO LEARNING

See this excerpt from the popular TV series Friends in which egoism versus altruism is debated (http://openstax.org/l/friendsclip) to learn more.

FORMING RELATIONSHIPS

What do you think is the single most influential factor in determining with whom you become friends and whom you form romantic relationships? You might be surprised to learn that the answer is simple: the people with whom you have the most contact. This most important factor is proximity. You are more likely to be friends with people you have regular contact with. For example, there are decades of research that shows that you are more likely to become friends with people who live in your dorm, your apartment building, or your immediate neighborhood than with people who live farther away (Festinger, Schachler, & Back, 1950). It is simply easier to form relationships with people you see often because you have the opportunity to get to know them.

Similarity is another factor that influences who we form relationships with. We are more likely to become friends or lovers with someone who is similar to us in background, attitudes, and lifestyle. In fact, there is no evidence that opposites attract. Rather, we are attracted to people who are most like us (**Figure 12.27**) (McPherson, Smith-Lovin, & Cook, 2001). Why do you think we are attracted to people who are similar to us? Sharing things in common will certainly make it easy to get along with others and form connections. When you and another person share similar music taste, hobbies, food preferences, and so on, deciding what to do with your time together might be easy. **Homophily** is the tendency for people to form social networks, including friendships, marriage, business relationships, and many other types of relationships, with others who are similar (McPherson et al., 2001).

Figure 12.27 People tend to be attracted to similar people. Many couples share a cultural background. This can be quite obvious in a ceremony such as a wedding, and more subtle (but no less significant) in the day-to-day workings of a relationship. (credit: modification of work by Shiraz Chanawala)

But, homophily limits our exposure to diversity (McPherson et al., 2001). By forming relationships only with people who are similar to us, we will have homogenous groups and will not be exposed to different points of view. In other words, because we are likely to spend time with those who are most like ourselves, we will have limited exposure to those who are different than ourselves, including people of different races, ethnicities, social-economic status, and life situations.

Once we form relationships with people, we desire reciprocity. **Reciprocity** is the give and take in relationships. We contribute to relationships, but we expect to receive benefits as well. That is, we want our relationships to be a two way street. We are more likely to like and engage with people who like us back. Self-disclosure is part of the two way street. **Self-disclosure** is the sharing of personal information (Laurenceau, Barrett, & Pietromonaco, 1998). We form more intimate connections with people with whom we disclose important information about ourselves. Indeed, self-disclosure is a characteristic of healthy intimate relationships, as long as the information disclosed is consistent with our own views (Cozby, 1973).

ATTRACTION

We have discussed how proximity and similarity lead to the formation of relationships, and that reciprocity and self-disclosure are important for relationship maintenance. But, what features of a person do we find attractive? We don't form relationships with everyone that lives or works near us, so how is it that we decide which specific individuals we will select as friends and lovers?

Researchers have documented several characteristics that humans find attractive. First we look for friends and lovers who are physically attractive. People differ in what they consider attractive, and attractiveness is culturally influenced. Research, however, suggests that some universally attractive features in women include large eyes, high cheekbones, a narrow jaw line, a slender build (Buss, 1989), and a lower waist-to-hip ratio (Singh, 1993). For men, attractive traits include being tall, having broad shoulders, and a narrow waist (Buss, 1989). Both men and women with high levels of facial and body symmetry are generally considered more attractive than asymmetric individuals (Fink, Neave, Manning, & Grammer, 2006; Penton-Voak et al., 2001; Rikowski & Grammer, 1999). Social traits that people find attractive in potential female mates include warmth, affection, and social skills; in males, the attractive traits include achievement, leadership qualities, and job skills (Regan & Berscheid, 1997). Although humans want mates who are physically attractive, this does not mean that we look for the most attractive person possible. In fact, this observation has led some to propose what is known as the matching hypothesis which asserts that people tend to pick someone they view as their equal in physical attractiveness and social desirability (Taylor, Fiore, Mendelsohn, & Cheshire, 2011). For example, you and most people you know likely would say that a very attractive movie star is out of your league. So, even if you had proximity to that person, you likely would not ask them out on a date because you believe you likely would be rejected. People weigh a potential partner's attractiveness against the likelihood of success with that person. If you think you are particularly unattractive (even if you are not), you likely will seek partners that are fairly unattractive (that is, unattractive in physical appearance or in behavior).

STERNBERG'S TRIANGULAR THEORY OF LOVE

We typically love the people with whom we form relationships, but the type of love we have for our family, friends, and lovers differs. Robert Sternberg (1986) proposed that there are three components of love: intimacy, passion, and commitment. These three components form a triangle that defines multiple types of love: this is known as Sternberg's **triangular theory of love** (Figure 12.28). Intimacy is the sharing of details and intimate thoughts and emotions. Passion is the physical attraction—the flame in the fire. Commitment is standing by the person—the "in sickness and health" part of the relationship.

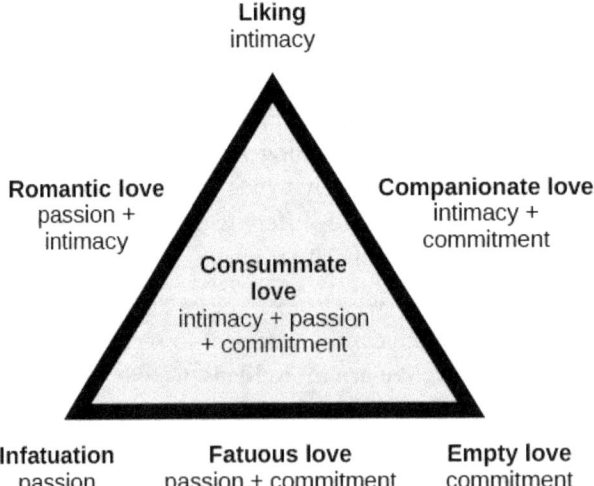

Figure 12.28 According to Sternberg's triangular theory of love, seven types of love can be described from combinations of three components: intimacy, passion, and commitment. (credit: modification of work by "Lnesa"/Wikimedia Commons)

Sternberg (1986) states that a healthy relationship will have all three components of love—intimacy, passion, and commitment—which is described as **consummate love** (Figure 12.29). However, different aspects of love might be more prevalent at different life stages. Other forms of love include liking, which is defined as having intimacy but no passion or commitment. Infatuation is the presence of passion without intimacy or commitment. Empty love is having commitment without intimacy or passion. **Companionate love**, which is characteristic of close friendships and family relationships, consists of intimacy and commitment but no passion. **Romantic love** is defined by having passion and intimacy, but no commitment. Finally, fatuous love is defined by having passion and commitment, but no intimacy, such as a long term sexual love affair. Can you describe other examples of relationships that fit these different types of love?

Figure 12.29 According to Sternberg, consummate love describes a healthy relationship containing intimacy, passion, and commitment. (credit: Carloxito/Wikimedia)

SOCIAL EXCHANGE THEORY

We have discussed why we form relationships, what attracts us to others, and different types of love. But what determines whether we are satisfied with and stay in a relationship? One theory that provides an explanation is social exchange theory. According to **social exchange theory**, we act as naïve economists in keeping a tally of the ratio of costs and benefits of forming and maintaining a relationship with others (Figure 12.30) (Rusbult & Van Lange, 2003).

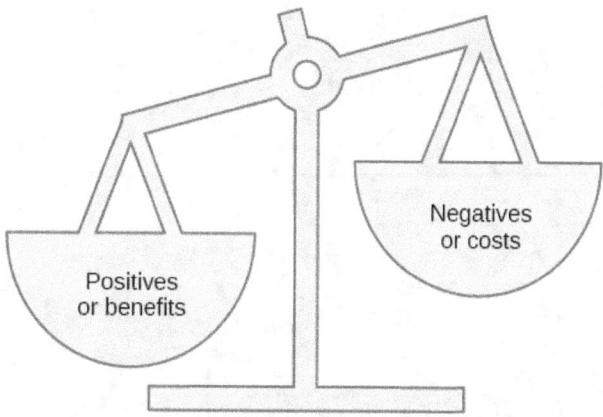

Figure 12.30 Acting like naïve economists, people may keep track of the costs and benefits of maintaining a relationship. Typically, only those relationships in which the benefits outweigh the costs will be maintained.

People are motivated to maximize the benefits of social exchanges, or relationships, and minimize the costs. People prefer to have more benefits than costs, or to have nearly equal costs and benefits, but most people are dissatisfied if their social exchanges create more costs than benefits. Let's discuss an example. If you have ever decided to commit to a romantic relationship, you probably considered the advantages and disadvantages of your decision. What are the benefits of being in a committed romantic relationship? You may have considered having companionship, intimacy, and passion, but also being comfortable with a person you know well. What are the costs of being in a committed romantic relationship? You may think that over time boredom from being with only one person may set in; moreover, it may be expensive to share activities such as attending movies and going to dinner. However, the benefits of dating your romantic partner presumably outweigh the costs, or you wouldn't continue the relationship.

Key Terms

actor-observer bias phenomenon of explaining other people's behaviors are due to internal factors and our own behaviors are due to situational forces

ageism prejudice and discrimination toward individuals based solely on their age

aggression seeking to cause harm or pain to another person

altruism humans' desire to help others even if the costs outweigh the benefits of helping

Asch effect group majority influences an individual's judgment, even when that judgment is inaccurate

attitude evaluations of or feelings toward a person, idea, or object that are typically positive or negative

attribution explanation for the behavior of other people

bullying a person, often an adolescent, being treated negatively repeatedly and over time

bystander effect situation in which a witness or bystander does not volunteer to help a victim or person in distress

central route persuasion logic-driven arguments using data and facts to convince people of an argument's worthiness

cognitive dissonance psychological discomfort that arises from a conflict in a person's behaviors, attitudes, or beliefs that runs counter to one's positive self-perception

collectivist culture culture that focuses on communal relationships with others such as family, friends, and community

companionate love type of love consisting of intimacy and commitment, but not passion; associated with close friendships and family relationships

confederate person who works for a researcher and is aware of the experiment, but who acts as a participant; used to manipulate social situations as part of the research design

confirmation bias seeking out information that supports our stereotypes while ignoring information that is inconsistent with our stereotypes

conformity when individuals change their behavior to go along with the group even if they do not agree with the group

consummate love type of love occurring when intimacy, passion, and commitment are all present

cyberbullying repeated behavior that is intended to cause psychological or emotional harm to another person and that takes place online

diffusion of responsibility tendency for no one in a group to help because the responsibility to help is spread throughout the group

discrimination negative actions toward individuals as a result of their membership in a particular group

dispositionism describes a perspective common to personality psychologists, which asserts that our behavior is determined by internal factors, such as personality traits and temperament

empathy capacity to understand another person's perspective—to feel what he or she feels

foot-in-the-door technique persuasion of one person by another person, encouraging a person to agree to a small favor, or to buy a small item, only to later request a larger favor or purchase of a larger item

fundamental attribution error tendency to overemphasize internal factors as attributions for behavior and underestimate the power of the situation

group polarization strengthening of the original group attitude after discussing views within the group

groupthink group members modify their opinions to match what they believe is the group consensus

homophily tendency for people to form social networks, including friendships, marriage, business relationships, and many other types of relationships, with others who are similar

homophobia prejudice and discrimination against individuals based solely on their sexual orientation

hostile aggression aggression motivated by feelings of anger with intent to cause pain

in-group group that we identify with or see ourselves as belonging to

in-group bias preference for our own group over other groups

individualistic culture culture that focuses on individual achievement and autonomy

informational social influence conformity to a group norm prompted by the belief that the group is competent and has the correct information

instrumental aggression aggression motivated by achieving a goal and does not necessarily involve intent to cause pain

internal factor internal attribute of a person, such as personality traits or temperament

just-world hypothesis ideology common in the United States that people get the outcomes they deserve

justification of effort theory that people value goals and achievements more when they have put more effort into them

normative social influence conformity to a group norm to fit in, feel good, and be accepted by the group

obedience change of behavior to please an authority figure or to avoid aversive consequences

out-group group that we don't belong to—one that we view as fundamentally different from us

peripheral route persuasion one person persuades another person; an indirect route that relies on association of peripheral cues (such as positive emotions and celebrity endorsement) to associate positivity with a message

persuasion process of changing our attitude toward something based on some form of communication

prejudice negative attitudes and feelings toward individuals based solely on their membership in a particular group

prosocial behavior voluntary behavior with the intent to help other people

racism prejudice and discrimination toward individuals based solely on their race

reciprocity give and take in relationships

romantic love type of love consisting of intimacy and passion, but no commitment

scapegoating act of blaming an out-group when the in-group experiences frustration or is blocked from obtaining a goal

script person's knowledge about the sequence of events in a specific setting

self-disclosure sharing personal information in relationships

self-fulfilling prophecy treating stereotyped group members according to our biased expectations only to have this treatment influence the individual to act according to our stereotypic expectations, thus confirming our stereotypic beliefs

self-serving bias tendency for individuals to take credit by making dispositional or internal attributions for positive outcomes and situational or external attributions for negative outcomes

sexism prejudice and discrimination toward individuals based on their sex

situationism describes a perspective that behavior and actions are determined by the immediate environment and surroundings; a view promoted by social psychologists

social exchange theory humans act as naïve economists in keeping a tally of the ratio of costs and benefits of forming and maintain a relationship, with the goal to maximize benefits and minimize costs

social facilitation improved performance when an audience is watching versus when the individual performs the behavior alone

social loafing exertion of less effort by a person working in a group because individual performance cannot be evaluated separately from the group, thus causing performance decline on easy tasks

social norm group's expectations regarding what is appropriate and acceptable for the thoughts and behavior of its members

social psychology field of psychology that examines how people impact or affect each other, with particular focus on the power of the situation

social role socially defined pattern of behavior that is expected of a person in a given setting or group

stanford prison experiment Stanford University conducted an experiment in a mock prison that demonstrated the power of social roles, social norms, and scripts

stereotype specific beliefs or assumptions about individuals based solely on their membership in a group, regardless of their individual characteristics

triangular theory of love model of love based on three components: intimacy, passion, and commitment; several types of love exist, depending on the presence or absence of each of these components

Summary

12.1 What Is Social Psychology?
Social psychology is the subfield of psychology that studies the power of the situation to influence individuals' thoughts, feelings, and behaviors. Psychologists categorize the causes of human behavior as those due to internal factors, such as personality, or those due to external factors, such as cultural and other social influences. Behavior is better explained, however, by using both approaches. Lay people tend to over-rely on dispositional explanations for behavior and ignore the power of situational influences, a perspective called the fundamental attribution error. People from individualistic cultures are more likely to display this bias versus people from collectivistic cultures. Our explanations for our own and others

behaviors can be biased due to not having enough information about others' motivations for behaviors and by providing explanations that bolster our self-esteem.

12.2 Self-presentation

Human behavior is largely influenced by our social roles, norms, and scripts. In order to know how to act in a given situation, we have shared cultural knowledge of how to behave depending on our role in society. Social norms dictate the behavior that is appropriate or inappropriate for each role. Each social role has scripts that help humans learn the sequence of appropriate behaviors in a given setting. The famous Stanford prison experiment is an example of how the power of the situation can dictate the social roles, norms, and scripts we follow in a given situation, even if this behavior is contrary to our typical behavior.

12.3 Attitudes and Persuasion

Attitudes are our evaluations or feelings toward a person, idea, or object and typically are positive or negative. Our attitudes and beliefs are influenced not only by external forces, but also by internal influences that we control. An internal form of attitude change is cognitive dissonance or the tension we experience when our thoughts, feelings, and behaviors are in conflict. In order to reduce dissonance, individuals can change their behavior, attitudes, or cognitions, or add a new cognition. External forces of persuasion include advertising; the features of advertising that influence our behaviors include the source, message, and audience. There are two primary routes to persuasion. The central route to persuasion uses facts and information to persuade potential consumers. The peripheral route uses positive association with cues such as beauty, fame, and positive emotions.

12.4 Conformity, Compliance, and Obedience

The power of the situation can lead people to conform, or go along with the group, even in the face of inaccurate information. Conformity to group norms is driven by two motivations, the desire to fit in and be liked and the desire to be accurate and gain information from the group. Authority figures also have influence over our behaviors, and many people become obedient and follow orders even if the orders are contrary to their personal values. Conformity to group pressures can also result in groupthink, or the faulty decision-making process that results from cohesive group members trying to maintain group harmony. Group situations can improve human behavior through facilitating performance on easy tasks, but inhibiting performance on difficult tasks. The presence of others can also lead to social loafing when individual efforts cannot be evaluated.

12.5 Prejudice and Discrimination

As diverse individuals, humans can experience conflict when interacting with people who are different from each other. Prejudice, or negative feelings and evaluations, is common when people are from a different social group (i.e., out-group). Negative attitudes toward out-groups can lead to discrimination. Prejudice and discrimination against others can be based on gender, race, ethnicity, social class, sexual orientation, or a variety of other social identities. In-group's who feel threatened may blame the out-groups for their plight, thus using the out-group as a scapegoat for their frustration.

12.6 Aggression

Aggression is seeking to cause another person harm or pain. Hostile aggression is motivated by feelings of anger with intent to cause pain, and instrumental aggression is motivated by achieving a goal and does not necessarily involve intent to cause pain Bullying is an international public health concern that largely affects the adolescent population. Bullying is repeated behaviors that are intended to inflict harm on the victim and can take the form of physical, psychological, emotional, or social abuse. Bullying has negative mental health consequences for youth including suicide. Cyberbullying is a newer form of bullying that takes place in an online environment where bullies can remain anonymous and victims are helpless to address the harassment. Despite the social norm of helping others in need, when there are many bystanders witnessing an emergency, diffusion of responsibility will lead to a lower likelihood of any one person helping.

12.7 Prosocial Behavior

Altruism is a pure form of helping others out of empathy, which can be contrasted with egoistic motivations for helping. Forming relationships with others is a necessity for social beings. We typically form relationships with people who are close to us in proximity and people with whom we share similarities. We expect reciprocity and self-disclosure in our relationships. We also want to form relationships with people who are physically attractive, though standards for attractiveness vary by culture and gender. There are many types of love that are determined by various combinations of intimacy, passion, and commitment; consummate love, which is the ideal form of love, contains all three components. When determining satisfaction and whether to maintain a relationship, individuals often use a social exchange approach and weigh the costs and benefits of forming and maintaining a relationship.

Review Questions

1. As a field, social psychology focuses on _____ in predicting human behavior.
   a. personality traits
   b. genetic predispositions
   c. biological forces
   d. situational factors

2. Making internal attributions for your successes and making external attributions for your failures is an example of _____.
   a. actor-observer bias
   b. fundamental attribution error
   c. self-serving bias
   d. just-world hypothesis

3. Collectivistic cultures are to _____ as individualistic cultures are to _____.
   a. dispositional; situational
   b. situational; dispositional
   c. autonomy; group harmony
   d. just-world hypothesis; self-serving bias

4. According to the actor-observer bias, we have more information about _____.
   a. situational influences on behavior
   b. influences on our own behavior
   c. influences on others' behavior
   d. dispositional influences on behavior

5. A(n) _____ is a set of group expectations for appropriate thoughts and behaviors of its members.
   a. social role
   b. social norm
   c. script
   d. attribution

6. On his first day of soccer practice, Jose suits up in a t-shirt, shorts, and cleats and runs out to the field to join his teammates. Jose's behavior is reflective of _____.
   a. a script
   b. social influence
   c. good athletic behavior
   d. normative behavior

7. When it comes to buying clothes, teenagers often follow social norms; this is likely motivated by _____.
   a. following parents' rules
   b. saving money
   c. fitting in
   d. looking good

8. In the Stanford prison experiment, even the lead researcher succumbed to his role as a prison supervisor. This is an example of the power of _____ influencing behavior.
   a. scripts
   b. social norms
   c. conformity
   d. social roles

9. Attitudes describe our _____ of people, objects, and ideas.
   a. treatment
   b. evaluations
   c. cognitions
   d. knowledge

10. Cognitive dissonance causes discomfort because it disrupts our sense of _____.
   a. dependency
   b. unpredictability
   c. consistency
   d. power

11. In order for the central route to persuasion to be effective, the audience must be _____ and _____.
   a. analytical; motivated
   b. attentive; happy
   c. intelligent; unemotional
   d. gullible; distracted

12. Examples of cues used in peripheral route persuasion include all of the following except _____.
   a. celebrity endorsement
   b. positive emotions
   c. attractive models
   d. factual information

13. In the Asch experiment, participants conformed due to _____ social influence.
   a. informational
   b. normative
   c. inspirational
   d. persuasive

14. Under what conditions will informational social influence be more likely?
   a. when individuals want to fit in
   b. when the answer is unclear
   c. when the group has expertise
   d. both b and c

15. Social loafing occurs when _____.
   a. individual performance cannot be evaluated
   b. the task is easy
   c. both a and b
   d. none of the above

16. If group members modify their opinions to align with a perceived group consensus, then _____ has occurred.
   a. group cohesion
   b. social facilitation
   c. groupthink
   d. social loafing

17. Prejudice is to _____ as discrimination is to _____.
   a. feelings; behavior
   b. thoughts; feelings
   c. feelings; thoughts
   d. behavior; feelings

18. Which of the following is *not* a type of prejudice?
   a. homophobia
   b. racism
   c. sexism
   d. individualism

19. _____ occurs when the out-group is blamed for the in-group's frustration.
   a. stereotyping
   b. in-group bias
   c. scapegoating
   d. ageism

20. When we seek out information that supports our stereotypes we are engaged in _____.
   a. scapegoating
   b. confirmation bias
   c. self-fulfilling prophecy
   d. in-group bias

21. Typically, bullying from boys is to _____ as bullying from girls is to _____.
   a. emotional harm; physical harm
   b. physical harm; emotional harm
   c. psychological harm; physical harm
   d. social exclusion; verbal taunting

22. Which of the following adolescents is least likely to be targeted for bullying?
   a. a child with a physical disability
   b. a transgender adolescent
   c. an emotionally sensitive boy
   d. the captain of the football team

23. The bystander effect likely occurs due to _____.
   a. desensitization to violence
   b. people not noticing the emergency
   c. diffusion of responsibility
   d. emotional insensitivity

24. Altruism is a form of prosocial behavior that is motivated by _____.
    a. feeling good about oneself
    b. selfless helping of others
    c. earning a reward
    d. showing bravery to bystanders

25. After moving to a new apartment building, research suggests that Sam will be most likely to become friends with _____.
    a. his next door neighbor
    b. someone who lives three floors up in the apartment building
    c. someone from across the street
    d. his new postal delivery person

26. What trait do both men and women tend to look for in a romantic partner?
    a. sense of humor
    b. social skills
    c. leadership potential
    d. physical attractiveness

27. According to the triangular theory of love, what type of love is defined by passion and intimacy but no commitment?
    a. consummate love
    b. empty love
    c. romantic love
    d. liking

28. According to social exchange theory, humans want to maximize the _____ and minimize the _____ in relationships.
    a. intimacy; commitment
    b. benefits; costs
    c. costs; benefits
    d. passion; intimacy

Critical Thinking Questions

29. Compare and contrast situational influences and dispositional influences and give an example of each. Explain how situational influences and dispositional influences might explain inappropriate behavior.

30. Provide an example of how people from individualistic and collectivistic cultures would differ in explaining why they won an important sporting event.

31. Why didn't the "good" guards in the Stanford prison experiment object to other guards' abusive behavior? Were the student prisoners simply weak people? Why didn't they object to being abused?

32. Describe how social roles, social norms, and scripts were evident in the Stanford prison experiment. How can this experiment be applied to everyday life? Are there any more recent examples where people started fulfilling a role and became abusive?

33. Give an example (one *not* used in class or your text) of cognitive dissonance and how an individual might resolve this.

34. Imagine that you work for an advertising agency, and you've been tasked with developing an advertising campaign to increase sales of Bliss Soda. How would you develop an advertisement for this product that uses a central route of persuasion? How would you develop an ad using a peripheral route of persuasion?

35. Describe how seeking outside opinions can prevent groupthink.

36. Compare and contrast social loafing and social facilitation.

37. Some people seem more willing to openly display prejudice regarding sexual orientation than prejudice regarding race and gender. Speculate on why this might be.

38. When people blame a scapegoat, how do you think they choose evidence to support the blame?

39. Compare and contrast hostile and instrumental aggression.

40. What evidence discussed in the previous section suggests that cyberbullying is difficult to detect and prevent?

41. Describe what influences whether relationships will be formed.

42. The evolutionary theory argues that humans are motivated to perpetuate their genes and reproduce. Using an evolutionary perspective, describe traits in men and women that humans find attractive.

Personal Application Questions

43. Provide a personal example of an experience in which your behavior was influenced by the power of the situation.

44. Think of an example in the media of a sports figure—player or coach—who gives a self-serving attribution for winning or losing. Examples might include accusing the referee of incorrect calls, in the case of losing, or citing their own hard work and talent, in the case of winning.

45. Try attending a religious service very different from your own and see how you feel and behave without knowing the appropriate script. Or, try attending an important, personal event that you have never attended before, such as a bar mitzvah (a coming-of-age ritual in Jewish culture), a quinceañera (in some Latin American cultures a party is given to a girl who is turning 15 years old), a wedding, a funeral, or a sporting event new to you, such as horse racing or bull riding. Observe and record your feelings and behaviors in this unfamiliar setting for which you lack the appropriate script. Do you silently observe the action, or do you ask another person for help interpreting the behaviors of people at the event? Describe in what ways your behavior would change if you were to attend a similar event in the future?

46. Name and describe at least three social roles you have adopted for yourself. Why did you adopt these roles? What are some roles that are expected of you, but that you try to resist?

47. Cognitive dissonance often arises after making an important decision, called post-decision dissonance (or in popular terms, buyer's remorse). Describe a recent decision you made that caused dissonance and describe how you resolved it.

48. Describe a time when you or someone you know used the foot-in-the-door technique to gain someone's compliance.

49. Conduct a conformity study the next time you are in an elevator. After you enter the elevator, stand with your back toward the door. See if others conform to your behavior. Watch this video (https://www.youtube.com/watch?v=dDAbdMv14Is) for a candid camera demonstration of this phenomenon. Did your results turn out as expected?

50. Most students adamantly state that they would never have turned up the voltage in the Milligram experiment. Do you think you would have refused to shock the learner? Looking at your own past behavior, what evidence suggests that you would go along with the order to increase the voltage?

51. Give an example when you felt that someone was prejudiced against you. What do you think caused this attitude? Did this person display any discrimination behaviors and, if so, how?

52. Give an example when you felt prejudiced against someone else. How did you discriminate against them? Why do you think you did this?

53. Have you ever experienced or witnessed bullying or cyberbullying? How did it make you feel? What did you do about it? After reading this section would you have done anything differently?

54. The next time you see someone needing help, observe your surroundings. Look to see if the bystander effect is in action and take measures to make sure the person gets help. If you aren't able to help, notify an adult or authority figure that can.

55. Think about your recent friendships and romantic relationship(s). What factors do you think influenced the development of these relationships? What attracted you to becoming friends or romantic partners?

56. Have you ever used a social exchange theory approach to determine how satisfied you were in a relationship, either a friendship or romantic relationship? Have you ever had the costs outweigh the benefits of a relationship? If so, how did you address this imbalance?

Chapter 13

Industrial-Organizational Psychology

Figure 13.1 What does an office look like? For people who telecommute, their workspace may be adapted to fit their lifestyle. (credit: "left": modification of work by Cory Zanker; credit "center": modification of work by "@Saigon"/Flickr; credit "right": modification of work by Daniel Lobo)

Chapter Outline

13.1 What Is Industrial and Organizational Psychology?
13.2 Industrial Psychology: Selecting and Evaluating Employees
13.3 Organizational Psychology: The Social Dimension of Work
13.4 Human Factors Psychology and Workplace Design

Introduction

In October 2019, Social Security Administration Commissioner Andrew Saul announced that the Social Security Administration would end a telework program it began 6 years previous serving approximately 12,000 of its employees. Then-Deputy Commissioner Grace Kim wrote a letter to Social Security employees explaining the reasons the program was ending and cited an increased workload and a backlog of cases as reasons for ending the pilot program. This change in the telework policy came on the heels of a negotiation between the American Federal Government Employee Union and the Social Security Administration, a negotiation that had to be brokered by the Federal Services Impasse Panel (a third-party federal organization developed specifically to arbitrate in situations where negotiations between union officials and federal organizations break down and progress halts between the organization and the union representatives) (Wagner, 2019a).

The May 2019 decision by the panel gave Social Security Agency managers the ability to limit or restrict telework for employees using their discretion to ensure that all tasks were being completed and wait times were normal. One of the biggest reasons cited for this was that the organization was able to provide evidence that after the implementation of a telework program, the average wait time for individuals temporarily increased, causing a backlog of work to be completed at a later date. Although the Social Security Administration pushed the official end date for all telework in the agency to March of 2020, the program was officially ended. In the wake of the COVID-19 pandemic, Congress requested a review of the telework policy and raised questions about whether it should be revived to serve as a preventative measure for reducing and slowing the spread of the virus (Wagner, 2019b). Could this allow employees to continue working while not coming to the workplace in order to help prevent the spread of illness? What were the benefits versus the costs of implementing a telework policy again for employees as the spread of the virus continued? What did previous research show related to the positive and negative benefits to the organization and the employees with respect to telework?

13.1 What Is Industrial and Organizational Psychology?

Learning Objectives

By the end of this section, you will be able to:
- Understand the scope of study in the field of industrial and organizational psychology
- Describe the history of industrial and organizational psychology

In 2019, people who worked in the United States spent an average of about 42–54 hours per week working (Bureau of Labor Statistics—U.S. Department of Labor, 2019). Sleeping was the only other activity they spent more time on with an average of about 43–62 hours per week. The workday is a significant portion of workers' time and energy. It impacts their lives and their family's lives in positive and negative physical and psychological ways. **Industrial and organizational (I-O) psychology** is a branch of psychology that studies how human behavior and psychology affect work and how they are affected by work.

Industrial and organizational psychologists work in four main contexts: academia, government, consulting firms, and business. Most I-O psychologists have a master's or doctorate degree. The field of I-O psychology can be divided into three broad areas (Figure 13.2 and Figure 13.3): industrial, organizational, and human factors. **Industrial psychology** is concerned with describing job requirements and assessing individuals for their ability to meet those requirements. In addition, once employees are hired, industrial psychology studies and develops ways to train, evaluate, and respond to those evaluations. As a consequence of its concern for candidate characteristics, industrial psychology must also consider issues of legality regarding discrimination in hiring. **Organizational psychology** is a discipline interested in how the relationships among employees affect those employees and the performance of a business. This includes studying worker satisfaction, motivation, and commitment. This field also studies management, leadership, and organizational culture, as well as how an organization's structures, management and leadership styles, social norms, and role expectations affect individual behavior. As a result of its interest in worker wellbeing and relationships, organizational psychology also considers the subjects of harassment, including sexual harassment, and workplace violence. **Human factors psychology** is the study of how workers interact with the tools of work and how to design those tools to optimize workers' productivity, safety, and health. These studies can involve interactions as straightforward as the fit of a desk, chair, and computer to a human having to sit on the chair at the desk using the computer for several hours each day. They can also include the examination of how humans interact with complex displays and their ability to interpret them accurately and quickly. In Europe, this field is referred to as ergonomics.

Figure 13.2 (a) Industrial psychology focuses on hiring and maintaining employees. (b) Organizational psychology is interested in employee relationships and organizational culture. (credit a: modification of work by Cory Zanker; credit b: modification of work by Vitor Lima)

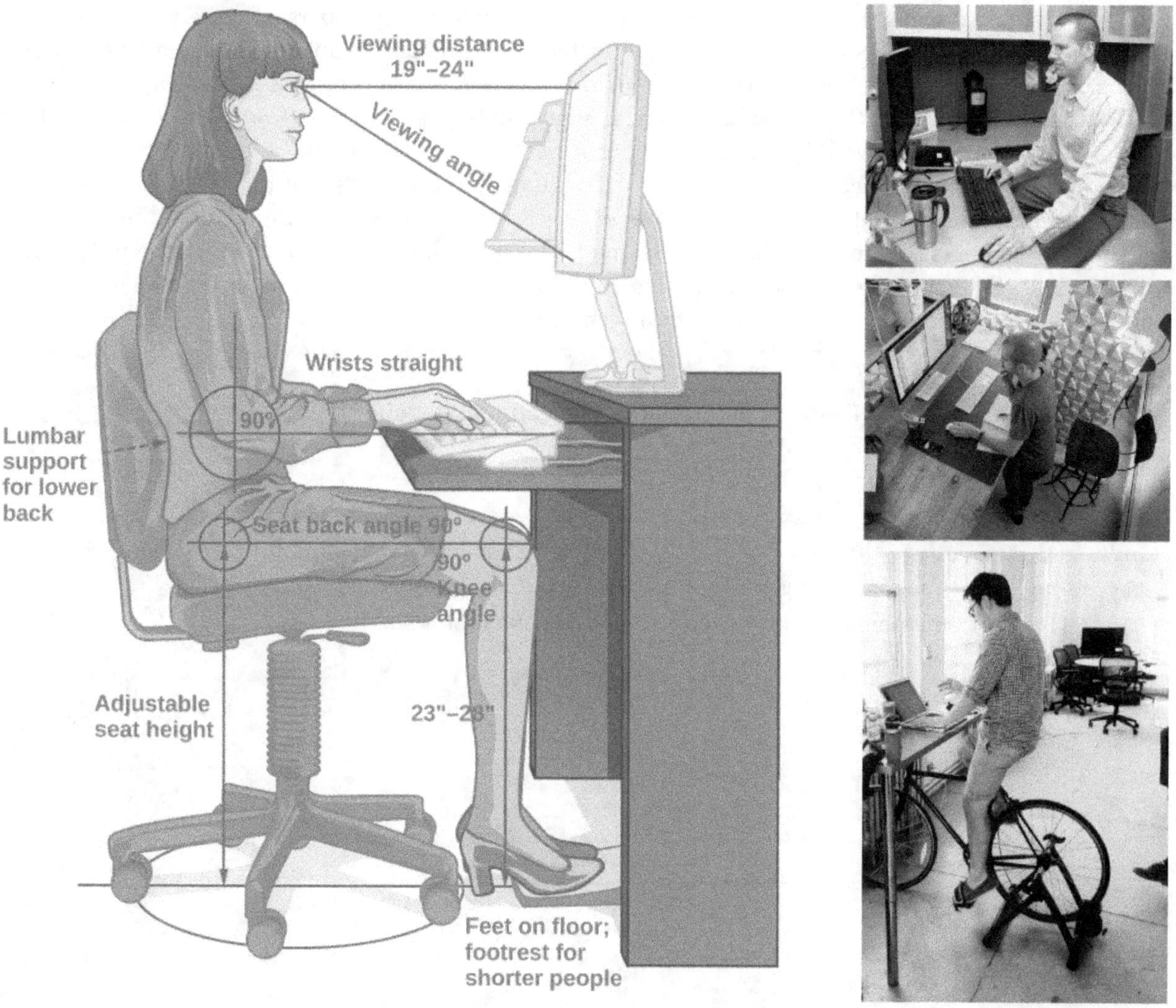

Figure 13.3 Human factors psychology is the study of interactions between humans, tools, and work systems. (a) At a traditional desk, certain positioning is ideal for ergonomics and health. (b) Recent developments in workspaces include desks where people might sit on a ball, stand, or even cycle while working. (credit "ball chair": modification of work by Chris Rosario; credit "standing desk": modification of work by "juhansonin_Flickr"/Flickr; credit "cycle desk": modification of work by "Benny Wong_Flickr"/Flickr)

Occupational health psychology (OHP) deals with the stress, diseases, and disorders that can affect employees as a result of the workplace. As such, the field is informed by research from the medical, biological, psychological, organizational, human factors, human resources, and industrial fields. Individuals in this field seek to examine the ways in which the organization affects the quality of work life for an employee and the responses that employees have towards their organization or as a result of their organization's influence on them. The responses for employees are not limited to the workplace as there may be some spillover into their personal lives outside of work, especially if there is not good work-life balance. The ultimate goal of an occupational health psychologist is to improve the overall health and well-being of an individual, and, as a result, increase the overall health of the organization (Society for Occupational Health Psychology, 2020).

In 2009, the field of humanitarian work psychology (HWP) was developed as the brainchild of a small group of I-O psychologists who met at a conference. Realizing they had a shared set of goals involving helping those who are underserved and underprivileged, the I-O psychologists formally formed the group in 2012 and have approximately 300 members worldwide. Although this is a small number, the group continues to expand. The group seeks to help marginalized members of society, such as low-income individuals, find work. In addition, they help to determine ways to deliver humanitarian aid during major catastrophes. The Humanitarian Work Psychology group can also reach out to those in the local community who do not have the knowledge, skills, and abilities (KSAs) to be able to find gainful employment that would enable them to not need to receive aid. In both cases, humanitarian work psychologists try to help the underserved individuals develop KSAs that they can use to improve their lives and their current situations. When ensuring these underserved individuals receive training or education, the focus is on skills that, once learned, will never be forgotten and can serve individuals throughout their lifetimes as they seek employment (APA, 2016). Table 13.1 summarizes the main fields in I-O psychology, their focuses, and jobs within each field.

Fields of Industrial Organizational Psychology

Field of I-O Psychology	Description	Types of Jobs
Industrial Psychology	Specializes and focuses on the retention of employees and hiring practices to ensure the least number of firings and the greatest number of hirings relative to the organization's size.	Personnel Analyst Instructional Designer Professor Research Analyst

Fields of Industrial Organizational Psychology

Field of I-O Psychology	Description	Types of Jobs
Organizational Psychology	Works with the relationships that employees develop with their organizations and conversely that their organization develops with them. In addition, studies the relationships that develop between co-workers and how that is influenced by organizational norms.	HR Research Specialist Professor Project Consultant Personnel Psychologist Test Developer Training Developer Leadership Developer Talent Developer
Human Factors and Engineering	Researches advances and changes in technology in an effort to improve the way technology is used by consumers, whether with consumer products, technologies, transportation, work environments, or communications. Seeks to be better able to predict the ways in which people can and will utilize technology and products in an effort to provide improved safety and reliability.	Professor Ergonomist Safety Scientist Project Consultant Inspector Research Scientist Marketer Product Development

Fields of Industrial Organizational Psychology

Field of I-O Psychology	Description	Types of Jobs
Humanitarian Work Psychology	Works to improve the conditions of individuals who have faced serious disaster or who are part of an underserved population. Focuses on labor relations, enhancing public health services, effects on populations due to climate change, recession, and diseases.	Professor; Instructional Designer; Research Scientist; Counselor; Consultant; Program Manager; Senior Response Officer
Occupational Health Psychology	Concerned with the overall well-being of both employees and organizations.	Occupational Therapist; Research Scientist; Consultant; Human Resources (HR) Specialist; Professor

Table 13.1

LINK TO LEARNING

Find out what I-O psychologists do on the Society for Industrial and Organizational Psychology (SIOP) (http://openstax.org/l/siop) website—a professional organization for people working in the discipline. This site also offers several I-O psychologist profiles.

THE HISTORICAL DEVELOPMENT OF INDUSTRIAL AND ORGANIZATIONAL PSYCHOLOGY

Industrial and organizational psychology had its origins in the early 20th century. Several influential early psychologists studied issues that today would be categorized as industrial psychology: James Cattell (1860–1944), Hugo Münsterberg (1863–1916), Walter Dill Scott (1869–1955), Robert Yerkes (1876–1956),

Walter Bingham (1880–1952), and Lillian Gilbreth (1878–1972). Cattell, Münsterberg, and Scott had been students of Wilhelm Wundt, the father of experimental psychology. Some of these researchers had been involved in work in the area of industrial psychology before World War I. Cattell's contribution to industrial psychology is largely reflected in his founding of a psychological consulting company, which is still operating today called the Psychological Corporation, and in the accomplishments of students at Columbia in the area of industrial psychology. In 1913, Münsterberg published *Psychology and Industrial Efficiency*, which covered topics such as employee selection, employee training, and effective advertising.

Scott was one of the first psychologists to apply psychology to advertising, management, and personnel selection. In 1903, Scott published two books: *The Theory of Advertising* and *Psychology of Advertising*. They are the first books to describe the use of psychology in the business world. By 1911 he published two more books, *Influencing Men in Business* and *Increasing Human Efficiency in Business*. In 1916 a newly formed division in the Carnegie Institute of Technology hired Scott to conduct applied research on employee selection (Katzell & Austin, 1992).

The focus of all this research was in what we now know as industrial psychology; it was only later in the century that the field of organizational psychology developed as an experimental science (Katzell & Austin, 1992). In addition to their academic positions, these researchers also worked directly for businesses as consultants.

When the United States entered World War I in April 1917, the work of psychologists working in this discipline expanded to include their contributions to military efforts. At that time Yerkes was the president of the 25-year-old American Psychological Association (APA). The APA is a professional association in the United States for clinical and research psychologists. Today the APA performs a number of functions including holding conferences, accrediting university degree programs, and publishing scientific journals. Yerkes organized a group under the Surgeon General's Office (SGO) that developed methods for screening and selecting enlisted men. They developed the Army Alpha test to measure mental abilities. The Army Beta test was a non-verbal form of the test that was administered to illiterate and non-English-speaking draftees. Scott and Bingham organized a group under the Adjutant General's Office (AGO) with the goal to develop selection methods for officers. They created a catalogue of occupational needs for the Army, essentially a job-description system and a system of performance ratings and occupational skill tests for officers (Katzell & Austin, 1992). After the war, work on personnel selection continued. For example, Millicent Pond researched the selection of factory workers, comparing the results of pre-employment tests with various indicators of job performance (Vinchur & Koppes, 2014).

From 1929 to 1932 Elton Mayo (1880–1949) and his colleagues began a series of studies at a plant near Chicago, Western Electric's Hawthorne Works (Figure 13.4). This long-term project took industrial psychology beyond just employee selection and placement to a study of more complex problems of interpersonal relations, motivation, and organizational dynamics. These studies mark the origin of organizational psychology. They began as research into the effects of the physical work environment (e.g., level of lighting in a factory), but the researchers found that the psychological and social factors in the factory were of more interest than the physical factors. These studies also examined how human interaction factors, such as supervisorial style, increased or decreased productivity.

Figure 13.4 Hawthorne Works provided the setting for several early I-O studies.

Analysis of the findings by later researchers led to the term the **Hawthorne effect**, which describes the increase in performance of individuals who are aware they are being observed by researchers or supervisors (Figure 13.5). What the original researchers found was that any change in a variable, such as lighting levels, led to an improvement in productivity; this was true even when the change was negative, such as a return to poor lighting. The effect faded when the attention faded (Roethlisberg & Dickson, 1939). The Hawthorne-effect concept endures today as an important experimental consideration in many fields and a factor that has to be controlled for in an experiment. In other words, an experimental treatment of some kind may produce an effect simply because it involves greater attention of the researchers on the participants (McCarney et al., 2007).

Figure 13.5 Researchers discovered that employees performed better when researchers or supervisors observed and interacted with them, a dynamic termed the Hawthorne effect.

> ### LINK TO LEARNING
>
> Watch this **video of first-hand accounts of the original Hawthorne studies (http://openstax.org/l/ATT)** to learn more.

In the 1930s, researchers began to study employees' feelings about their jobs. Kurt Lewin also conducted research on the effects of various leadership styles, team structure, and team dynamics (Katzell & Austin, 1992). Lewin is considered the founder of social psychology and much of his work and that of his students produced results that had important influences in organizational psychology. Lewin and his students' research included an important early study that used children to study the effect of leadership style on aggression, group dynamics, and satisfaction (Lewin, Lippitt, & White, 1939). Lewin was also responsible for coining the term *group dynamics*, and he was involved in studies of group interactions, cooperation, competition, and communication that bear on organizational psychology.

Parallel to these studies in industrial and organizational psychology, the field of human factors psychology was also developing. Frederick Taylor was an engineer who saw that if one could redesign the workplace there would be an increase in both output for the company and wages for the workers. In 1911 he put forward his theory in a book titled, *The Principles of Scientific Management* (**Figure 13.6**). His book examines management theories, personnel selection and training, as well as the work itself, using time and motion studies. Taylor argued that the principle goal of management should be to make the most money for the employer, along with the best outcome for the employee. He believed that the best outcome for the employee and management would be achieved through training and development so that each employee could provide the best work. He believed that by conducting time and motion studies for both the organization and the employee, the best interests of both were addressed. Time-motion studies were methods aimed to improve work by dividing different types of operations into sections that could be measured. These analyses were used to standardize work and to check the efficiency of people and equipment.

Personnel selection is a process used by recruiting personnel within the company to recruit and select the best candidates for the job. Training may need to be conducted depending on what skills the hired candidate has. Often companies will hire someone with the personality that fits in with others but who may be lacking in skills. Skills can be taught, but personality cannot be easily changed.

(a)
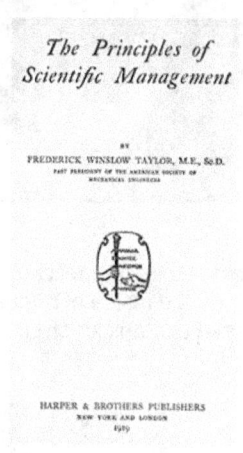
(b)

(c)

Figure 13.6 (a) Frederick Taylor (1911) strived to engineer workplaces to increase productivity, based on the ideas he set forth in (b) his book, *The Principles of Scientific Management*. (c) Taylor designed this steam hammer at the Midvale Steel Company. (credit c: modification of work by "Kheel Center, Cornell University"/Flickr)

One of the examples of Taylor's theory in action involved workers handling heavy iron ingots. Taylor showed that the workers could be more productive by taking work rests. This method of rest increased worker productivity from 12.5 to 47.0 tons moved per day with less reported fatigue as well as increased wages for the workers who were paid by the ton. At the same time, the company's cost was reduced from 9.2 cents to 3.9 cents per ton. Despite these increases in productivity, Taylor's theory received a great deal of criticism at the time because it was believed that it would exploit workers and reduce the number of workers needed. Also controversial was the underlying concept that only a manager could determine the most efficient method of working, and that while at work, a worker was incapable of this. Taylor's theory was underpinned by the notion that a worker was fundamentally lazy and the goal of Taylor's scientific management approach was to maximize productivity without much concern for worker well-being. His approach was criticized by unions and those sympathetic to workers (Van De Water, 1997).

Gilbreth was another influential I-O psychologist who strove to find ways to increase productivity (**Figure 13.7**). Using time and motion studies, Gilbreth and her husband, Frank, worked to make workers more efficient by reducing the number of motions required to perform a task. She not only applied these methods to industry but also to the home, office, shops, and other areas. She investigated employee fatigue and time management stress and found many employees were motivated by money and job satisfaction. In 1914, Gilbreth wrote the book title, *The Psychology of Management: The Function of the Mind in Determining, Teaching, and Installing Methods of Least Waste*, and she is known as the mother of modern management. Some of Gilbreth's contributions are still in use today: you can thank her for the idea to put shelves inside on refrigerator doors, and she also came up with the concept of using a foot pedal to operate the lid of trash can (Gilbreth, 1914, 1998; Koppes, 1997; Lancaster, 2004). Gilbreth was the first woman to join the American Society of Mechanical Engineers in 1926, and in 1966 she was awarded the Hoover Medal of the American Society of Civil Engineers.

Taylor and Gilbreth's work improved productivity, but these innovations also improved the fit between technology and the human using it. The study of machine–human fit is known as ergonomics or human factors psychology.

(a) (b) (c)

Figure 13.7 (a) Lillian Gilbreth studied efficiency improvements that were applicable in the workplace, home, and other areas. She is credited with the idea of (b) putting shelves on the inside of refrigerator doors and (c) foot-pedal-operated garbage cans. (credit b: modification of work by "Goedeker's"/Flickr; credit c: modification of work by Kerry Ceszyk)

FROM WORLD WAR II TO TODAY

World War II also drove the expansion of industrial psychology. Bingham was hired as the chief psychologist for the War Department (now the Department of Defense) and developed new systems for job selection, classification, training, ad performance review, plus methods for team development, morale change, and attitude change (Katzell & Austin, 1992). Other countries, such as Canada and the United Kingdom, likewise saw growth in I-O psychology during World War II (McMillan, Stevens, & Kelloway, 2009). In the years after the war, both industrial psychology and organizational psychology became areas of significant research effort. Concerns about the fairness of employment tests arose, and the ethnic and gender biases in various tests were evaluated with mixed results. In addition, a great deal of research went into studying job satisfaction and employee motivation (Katzell & Austin, 1992).

The research and work of I-O psychologists in the areas of employee selection, placement, and performance appraisal became increasingly important in the 1960s. When Congress passed the 1964 Civil Rights Act, Title VII covered what is known as equal employment opportunity. This law protects employees against discrimination based on race, color, religion, sex, or national origin, as well as discrimination against an employee for associating with an individual in one of these categories. Organizations had to adjust to the social, political, and legal climate of the Civil Rights movement, and these issues needed to be addressed by members of I/O in research and practice.

There are many reasons for organizations to be interested in I/O so that they can better understand the psychology of their workers, which in turn helps them understand how their organizations can become more productive and competitive. For example, most large organizations are now competing on a global level, and they need to understand how to motivate workers in order to achieve high productivity and efficiency. Most companies also have a diverse workforce and need to understand the psychological complexity of the people in these diverse backgrounds.

Today, I-O psychology is a diverse and deep field of research and practice, as you will learn about in the rest of this chapter. The Society for Industrial and Organizational Psychology (SIOP), a division of the APA, lists 8,000 members (SIOP, 2014) and the Bureau of Labor Statistics—U.S. Department of Labor (2013) has projected this profession will have the greatest growth of all job classifications in the 20 years following 2012. On average, a person with a master's degree in industrial-organizational psychology will earn over $80,000 a year, while someone with a doctorate will earn over $110,000 a year (Khanna, Medsker, & Ginter, 2012).

13.2 Industrial Psychology: Selecting and Evaluating Employees

Learning Objectives

By the end of this section, you will be able to:
- Explain the aspects of employee selection
- Describe the kinds of job training
- Describe the approaches to and issues surrounding performance assessment

The branch of I-O psychology known as industrial psychology focuses on identifying and matching persons to tasks within an organization. This involves **job analysis**, which means accurately describing the task or job. Then, organizations must identify the characteristics of applicants for a match to the job analysis. It also involves training employees from their first day on the job throughout their tenure within the organization, and appraising their performance along the way.

SELECTING EMPLOYEES

When you read job advertisements, do you ever wonder how the company comes up with the job description? Often, this is done with the help of I-O psychologists. There are two related but different approaches to job analysis—you may be familiar with the results of each as they often appear on the same job advertisement. The first approach is task-oriented and lists in detail the tasks that will be performed for the job. Each task is typically rated on scales for how frequently it is performed, how difficult it is, and how important it is to the job. The second approach is worker-oriented. This approach describes the characteristics required of the worker to successfully perform the job. This second approach has been called job specification (Dierdorff & Wilson, 2003). For job specification, the knowledge, skills, and abilities (KSAs) that the job requires are identified.

Observation, surveys, and interviews are used to obtain the information required for both types of job analysis. It is possible to observe someone who is proficient in a position and analyze what skills are apparent. Another approach used is to interview people presently holding that position, their peers, and their supervisors to get a consensus of what they believe are the requirements of the job.

How accurate and reliable is a job analysis? Research suggests that it can depend on the nature of the descriptions and the source for the job analysis. For example, Dierdorff & Wilson (2003) found that job analyses developed from descriptions provided by people holding the job themselves were the least reliable; however, they did not study or speculate why this was the case.

The United States Department of Labor maintains a database of previously compiled job analyses for different jobs and occupations. This allows the I-O psychologist to access previous analyses for nearly any type of occupation. This system is called O*Net (accessible at www.onetonline.org). The site is open and you can see the KSAs that are listed for your own position or one you might be curious about (**Figure 13.8**). Each occupation lists the tasks, knowledge, skills, abilities, work context, work activities, education requirements, interests, personality requirements, and work styles that are deemed necessary for success in that position. You can also see data on average earnings and projected job growth in that industry.

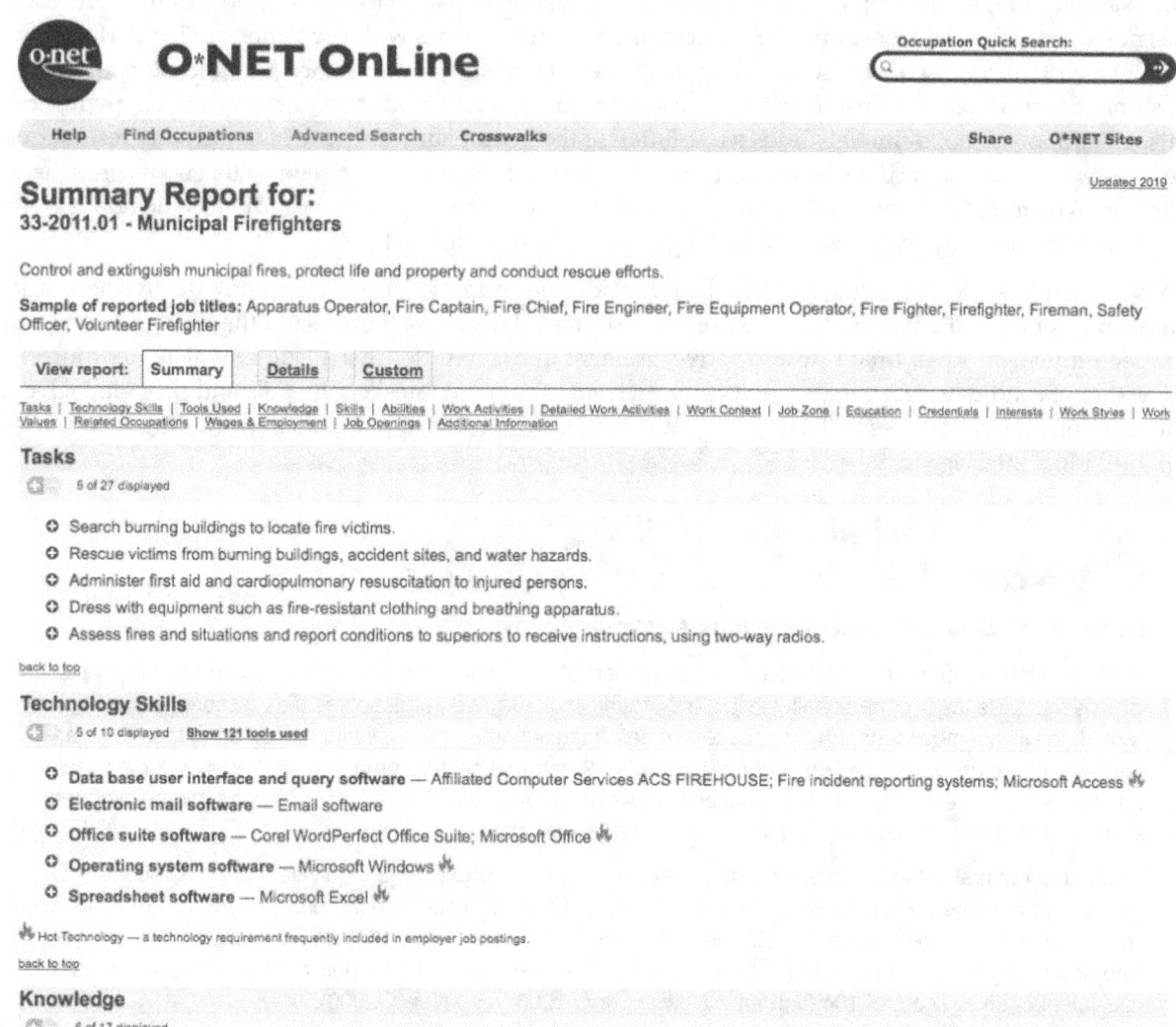

Figure 13.8 The O*Net database from the United States Department of Labor provides information about a variety of occupations, including the knowledge, skills, and abilities desired for the position. In this example, the search shows information related to the job of being a municipal firefighter.

LINK TO LEARNING

The O*Net database describes the skills, knowledge, and education required for occupations, as well as what personality types and work styles are best suited to the role. See what it has to say about being a food server in a restaurant (http://openstax.org/l/sumreport1) or an elementary school teacher (http://openstax.org/l/sumreport2) or an industrial-organizational psychologist (http://openstax.org/l/sumreport3) to learn more about these career paths.

Candidate Analysis and Testing

Once a company identifies potential candidates for a position, the candidates' knowledge, skills, and other abilities must be evaluated and compared with the job description. These evaluations can involve testing, an interview, and work samples or exercises. You learned about personality tests in the chapter on personality; in the I-O context, they are used to identify the personality characteristics of the candidate in an effort to match those to personality characteristics that would ensure good performance on the job.

For example, a high rating of agreeableness might be desirable in a customer support position. However, it is not always clear how best to correlate personality characteristics with predictions of job performance. It might be that too high of a score on agreeableness is actually a hindrance in the customer support position. For example, if a customer has a misperception about a product or service, agreeing with their misperception will not ultimately lead to resolution of their complaint. Any use of personality tests should be accompanied by a verified assessment of what scores on the test correlate with good performance (Arthur, Woehr, & Graziano, 2001). Other types of tests that may be given to candidates include IQ tests, integrity tests, and physical tests, such as drug tests or physical fitness tests.

To better understand the hiring process, let's consider an example case. A company determined it had an open position and advertised it. The human resources (HR) manager directed the hiring team to start the recruitment process. Imani saw the advertisement and submitted her résumé, which went into the collection of candidate résumés. The HR team reviewed the candidates' credentials and provided a list of the best potential candidates to the department manager, who reached out to them (including Imani) to set up individual interviews.

WHAT DO YOU THINK?

Using Cutoff Scores to Determine Job Selection

Many positions require applicants to take tests as part of the selection process. These can include IQ tests, job-specific skills tests, or personality tests. The organization may set cutoff scores (i.e., a score below which a candidate will not move forward) for each test to determine whether the applicant moves on to the next stage. For example, there was a case of Robert Jordan, a 49-year-old college graduate who applied for a position with the police force in New London, Connecticut. As part of the selection process, Jordan took the Wonderlic Personnel Test (WPT), a test designed to measure cognitive ability.

Jordan did not make it to the interview stage because his WPT score of 33, equivalent to an IQ score of 125 (100 is the average IQ score), was too high. The New London Police department policy is to not interview anyone who has a WPT score over 27 (equivalent to an IQ score over 104) because they believe anyone who scores higher would be bored with police work. The average score for police officers nationwide is the equivalent of an IQ score of 104 (*Jordan v. New London*, 2000; ABC News, 2000).

Jordan sued the police department alleging that his rejection was discrimination and his civil rights were violated because he was denied equal protection under the law. The 2nd U.S. Circuit Court of Appeals upheld a lower court's decision that the city of New London did not discriminate against him because the same standards were applied to everyone who took the exam (The New York Times, 1999).

What do you think? When might universal cutoff points make sense in a hiring decision, and when might they eliminate otherwise potentially strong employees?

Interviews

Most jobs for mid-size to large-size businesses in the United States require a personal interview as a step in the selection process. Because interviews are commonly used, they have been the subject of considerable research by industrial psychologists. Information derived from job analysis usually forms the basis for the types of questions asked. Interviews can provide a more dynamic source of information about the candidate than standard testing measures. Importantly, social factors and body language can influence the outcome of the interview. These include influences, such as the degree of similarity of the applicant to the interviewer and nonverbal behaviors, such as hand gestures, head nodding, and smiling (Bye, Horverak, Sandal, Sam, & Vivjer, 2014; Rakić, Steffens, & Mummendey, 2011).

There are two types of interviews: unstructured and structured. In an unstructured interview, the interviewer may ask different questions of each different candidate. One candidate might be asked about her career goals, and another might be asked about his previous work experience. In an unstructured interview, the questions are often, though not always, unspecified beforehand. And in an unstructured interview the responses to questions asked are generally not scored using a standard system. In a structured interview, the interviewer asks the same questions of every candidate, the questions are prepared in advance, and the interviewer uses a standardized rating system for each response. With this approach, the interviewer can accurately compare two candidates' interviews. In a meta-analysis of studies examining the effectiveness of various types of job interviews, McDaniel, Whetzel, Schmidt & Maurer (1994) found that structured interviews were more effective at predicting subsequent job performance of the job candidate.

Let's return to our example case. For her first interview, Imani was interviewed by a team of employees at the company. She was one of five candidates interviewed that day for the position. Each interviewee was asked the same list of questions, by the same people, so the interview experience was as consistent as possible across applicants. At the end of the interviews, the HR team met and reviewed the answers given by Imani and the other candidates. The HR team then identified a few new qualified candidates and conducted a new round of initial interviews, while the first group of potential hires waited to hear back from the company.

EVERYDAY CONNECTION

Preparing for the Job Interview

You might be wondering if psychology research can tell you how to succeed in a job interview. As you can imagine, most research is concerned with the employer's interest in choosing the most appropriate candidate for the job, a goal that makes sense for the candidate too. But suppose you are not the only qualified candidate for the job; is there a way to increase your chances of being hired? A limited amount of research has addressed this question.

As you might expect, nonverbal cues are important in an interview. Liden, Martin, & Parsons (1993) found that lack of eye contact and smiling on the part of the applicant led to lower applicant ratings. Studies of impression management on the part of an applicant have shown that self-promotion behaviors generally have a positive impact on interviewers (Gilmore & Ferris, 1989). Different personality types use different forms of impression management, for example extroverts use verbal self-promotion, and applicants high in agreeableness use non-verbal methods such as smiling and eye contact. Self-promotion was most consistently related with a positive outcome for the interview, particularly if it was related to the candidate's person–job fit. However, it is possible to overdo self-promotion with experienced interviewers (Howard & Ferris, 1996). Barrick, Swider & Stewart (2010) examined the effect of first impressions during the rapport building that typically occurs before an interview begins. They found that initial judgments by interviewers during this period were related to job offers and that the judgments were about the candidate's competence and not just likability. Levine and Feldman (2002) looked at the influence of several nonverbal behaviors in mock interviews on candidates' likability and projections of competence. Likability was affected positively by greater smiling behavior. Interestingly, other behaviors affected likability differently depending on the gender of the applicant. Men who displayed higher eye contact were less likable; women were more likable when they made greater eye contact. However, for this study male applicants were interviewed by men and female applicants were interviewed by women. In a study carried out in a real setting, DeGroot & Gooty (2009) found that nonverbal cues affected interviewers' assessments about candidates. They looked at visual cues, which can often be modified by the candidate and vocal (nonverbal) cues, which are more difficult to modify. They found that interviewer judgment was positively affected by visual and vocal cues of conscientiousness, visual and vocal cues of openness to experience, and vocal cues of extroversion.

What is the take home message from the limited research that has been done? Learn to be aware of your behavior during an interview. You can do this by practicing and soliciting feedback from mock interviews. Pay attention to any nonverbal cues you are projecting and work at presenting nonverbal cures that project confidence and positive personality traits. And finally, pay attention to the first impression you are making as it may also have an impact in the interview.

Training

Training is an important element of success and performance in many jobs. Most jobs begin with an orientation period during which the new employee is provided information regarding the company history, policies, and administrative protocols such as time tracking, benefits, and reporting requirements. An important goal of orientation training is to educate the new employee about the organizational culture, the values, visions, hierarchies, norms and ways the company's employees interact—essentially how the organization is run, how it operates, and how it makes decisions. There will also be training that is specific to the job the individual was hired to do, or training during the individual's period of employment that teaches aspects of new duties, or how to use new physical or software tools. Much of these kinds of training will be formalized for the employee; for example, orientation training is often accomplished using software presentations, group presentations by members of the human resources department or with people in the new hire's department (Figure 13.9).

Figure 13.9 Training usually begins with an orientation period during which a new employee learns about company policies, practices, and culture. (credit: Cory Zanker)

Mentoring is a form of informal training in which an experienced employee guides the work of a new employee. In some situations, mentors will be formally assigned to a new employee, while in others a mentoring relationship may develop informally.

Mentoring effects on the mentor and the employee being mentored, the protégé, have been studied in recent years. In a review of mentoring studies, Eby, Allen, Evans, Ng, & DuBois (2008) found significant but small effects of mentoring on performance (i.e., behavioral outcomes), motivation and satisfaction, and actual career outcomes. In a more detailed review, Allen, Eby, Poteet, Lentz, & Lima (2004) found that mentoring positively affected a protégé's compensation and number of promotions compared with non-mentored employees. In addition, protégés were more satisfied with their careers and had greater job satisfaction. All of the effects were small but significant. Eby, Durley, Evans, & Ragins (2006) examined mentoring effects on the mentor and found that mentoring was associated with greater job satisfaction and organizational commitment. Gentry, Weber, & Sadri (2008) found that mentoring was positively related with performance ratings by supervisors. Allen, Lentz, & Day (2006) found in a comparison of mentors and non-mentors that mentoring led to greater reported salaries and promotions.

Mentoring is recognized to be particularly important to the career success of women (McKeen & Bujaki, 2007) by creating connections to informal networks, adopting a style of interaction that male managers are comfortable with, and with overcoming discrimination in job promotions.

Gender combinations in mentoring relationships are also an area of active study. Ragins & Cotton (1999) studied the effects of gender on the outcomes of mentoring relationships and found that protégés with a history of male mentors had significantly higher compensation especially for male protégés. The study found that female mentor–male protégé relationships were considerably rarer than the other gender combinations.

A 2003 study by Arthur, Bennett, Edens, and Bell examined multiple other studies to determine how effective organizational training is. Their results showed that training was effective, based on four types of measurement: (1) the immediate response of the employee to the training effort, (2) testing at the end of training to demonstrate that learning outcomes were met, (3) behavioral measurements of job activities by supervisors, and (4) results such as productivity and profits. The examined studies represented diverse forms of training including self-instruction, lecture and discussion, and computer assisted training.

EVALUATING EMPLOYEES

Industrial and organizational psychologists are typically involved in designing performance-appraisal systems for organizations. These systems are designed to evaluate whether each employee is performing her job satisfactorily. Industrial and organizational psychologists study, research, and implement ways to make work evaluations as fair and positive as possible; they also work to decrease the subjectivity involved with performance ratings. Fairly evaluated work helps employees do their jobs better, improves the likelihood of people being in the right jobs for their talents, maintains fairness, and identifies company and individual training needs. In our example case, Imani was offered the position and was hired with a 90-day probation period. During that time, she met with her supervisor to discuss her performance and the expectations of the position and her growth. At the end of the 90 days, it was determined that Imani was meeting the expectations of her employer and had passed her probationary period. Imani was excited to now have a permanent job.

Performance appraisals are typically documented several times a year, often with a formal process and an annual face-to-face brief meeting between an employee and his supervisor. It is important that the original job analysis play a role in performance appraisal as well as any goals that have been set by the employee or by the employee and supervisor. The meeting is often used for the supervisor to communicate specific concerns about the employee's performance and to positively reinforce elements of good performance. It may also be used to discuss specific performance rewards, such as a pay increase, or consequences of poor performance, such as a probationary period. Part of the function of performance appraisals for the organization is to document poor performance to bolster decisions to terminate an employee.

Performance appraisals are becoming more complex processes within organizations and are often used to motivate employees to improve performance and expand their areas of competence, in addition to assessing their job performance. In this capacity, performance appraisals can be used to identify opportunities for training or whether a particular training program has been successful. One approach to performance appraisal is called 360-degree feedback appraisal (**Figure 13.10**). In this system, the employee's appraisal derives from a combination of ratings by supervisors, peers, employees supervised by the employee, and from the employee herself. Occasionally, outside observers may be used as well, such as customers. The purpose of 360-degree system is to give the employee (who may be a manager) and supervisor different perspectives of the employee's job performance; the system should help employees make improvements through their own efforts or through training. The system is also used in a traditional performance-appraisal context, providing the supervisor with more information with which to make decisions about the employee's position and compensation (Tornow, 1993a).

Figure 13.10 In a 360-degree performance appraisal, supervisors, customers, direct reports, peers, and the employee himself rate an employee's performance.

Few studies have assessed the effectiveness of 360-degree methods, but Atkins and Wood (2002) found that the self and peer ratings were unreliable as an assessment of an employee's performance and that even supervisors tended to underrate employees that gave themselves modest feedback ratings. However, a different perspective sees this variability in ratings as a positive in that it provides for greater learning on the part of the employees as they and their supervisor discuss the reasons for the discrepancies (Tornow, 1993b).

In theory, performance appraisals should be an asset for an organization wishing to achieve its goals, and most employees will actually solicit feedback regarding their jobs if it is not offered (DeNisi & Kluger, 2000). However, in practice, many performance evaluations are disliked by organizations, employees, or both (Fletcher, 2001), and few of them have been adequately tested to see if they do in fact improve performance or motivate employees (DeNisi & Kluger, 2000). One of the reasons evaluations fail to accomplish their purpose in an organization is that performance appraisal systems are often used incorrectly or are of an inappropriate type for an organization's particular culture (Schraeder, Becton, & Portis, 2007). An organization's culture is how the organization is run, how it operates, and how it makes decisions. It is based on the collective values, hierarchies, and how individuals within the organization interact. Examining the effectiveness of performance appraisal systems in particular organizations and the effectiveness of training for the implementation of the performance appraisal system is an active area of research in industrial psychology (Fletcher, 2001).

BIAS AND PROTECTIONS IN HIRING

In an ideal hiring process, an organization would generate a job analysis that accurately reflects the requirements of the position, and it would accurately assess candidates' KSAs to determine who the best individual is to carry out the job's requirements. For many reasons, hiring decisions in the real world are often made based on factors other than matching a job analysis to KSAs. As mentioned earlier, interview rankings can be influenced by other factors: similarity to the interviewer (Bye, Horverak, Sandal, Sam, & Vijver, 2014) and the regional accent of the interviewee (Rakić, Steffens, & Mummendey 2011). A study by Agerström & Rooth (2011) examined hiring managers' decisions to invite equally qualified normal-weight and obese job applicants to an interview. The decisions of the hiring managers were based on photographs of the two applicants. The study found that hiring managers that scored high on a test of negative associations with overweight people displayed a bias in favor of inviting the equally qualified normal-weight applicant but not inviting the obese applicant. The association test measures automatic or subconscious associations between an individual's negative or positive values and, in this case, the body-weight attribute. A meta-analysis of experimental studies found that physical attractiveness benefited individuals in various job-related outcomes such as hiring, promotion, and performance review (Hosoda, Stone-Romero, & Coats, 2003). They also found that the strength of the benefit appeared to be decreasing with time between the late 1970s and the late 1990s.

Some hiring criteria may be related to a particular group an applicant belongs to and not individual abilities. Unless membership in that group directly affects potential job performance, a decision based on group membership is discriminatory (Figure 13.11). To combat hiring discrimination, in the United States there are numerous city, state, and federal laws that prevent hiring based on various group-membership criteria. For example, did you know it is illegal for a potential employer to ask your age in an interview? Did you know that an employer cannot ask you whether you are married, a U.S. citizen, have disabilities, or what your race or religion is? They cannot even ask questions that might shed some light on these attributes, such as where you were born or who you live with. These are only a few of the restrictions that are in place to prevent discrimination in hiring. In the United States, federal anti-discrimination laws are administered by the U.S. Equal Employment Opportunity Commission (EEOC).

Figure 13.11 (a) Pregnancy, (b) religion, and (c) age are some of the criteria on which hiring decisions cannot legally be made. (credit a: modification of work by Sean McGrath; credit b: modification of work by Ze'ev Barkan; credit c: modification of work by David Hodgson)

THE U.S. EQUAL EMPLOYMENT OPPORTUNITY COMMISSION (EEOC)

The **U.S. Equal Employment Opportunity Commission (EEOC)** is responsible for enforcing federal laws that make it illegal to discriminate against a job applicant or an employee because of the person's race, color, religion, sex (including pregnancy), national origin, age (40 or older), disability, or genetic information. Figure 13.12 provides some of the legal language from laws that have been passed to prevent discrimination.

Selected Text from Legislation Prohibiting Employment Discrimination

Title VII of the Civil Rights Act of 1964
It shall be an unlawful employment practice for an employer (1) to fail or refuse to hire or to discharge any individual, or otherwise to discriminate against any individual with respect to his compensation, terms, conditions, or privileges of employment, because of such individual's race, color, religion, sex, or national origin; or (2) to limit, segregate, or classify his employees or applicants for employment in any way which would deprive or tend to deprive any individual of employment opportunities or otherwise adversely affect his status as an employee, because of such individual's race, color, religion, sex, or national origin.

The Age Discrimination in Employment Act of 1967
It shall be unlawful for an employer (1) to fail or refuse to hire or to discharge any individual or otherwise discriminate against any individual with respect to his compensation, terms, conditions, or privileges of employment, because of such individual's age.

Titles I and V of the Americans with Disabilities Act of 1990 (ADA)
No covered entity shall discriminate against a qualified individual on the basis of disability in regard to job application procedures, the hiring, advancement, or discharge of employees, employee compensation, job training, and other terms, conditions, and privileges of employment. . . .
The term "discriminate against a qualified individual on the basis of disability" includes . . . not making reasonable accommodations to the known physical or mental limitations of an otherwise qualified individual with a disability who is an applicant or employee, unless such covered entity can demonstrate that the accommodation would impose an undue hardship on the operation of the business of such covered entity.

Figure 13.12 The laws shown here protect employees in the U.S. from discriminatory practices.

The United States has several specific laws regarding fairness and avoidance of discrimination. The Equal Pay Act requires that equal pay for men and women in the same workplace who are performing equal work. Despite the law, persistent inequities in earnings between men and women exist. Corbett & Hill (2012) studied one facet of the gender gap by looking at earnings in the first year after college in the United States. Just comparing the earnings of women to men, women earn about 82 cents for every dollar a man earns in their first year out of college. However, some of this difference can be explained by education, career, and life choices, such as choosing majors with lower earning potential or specific jobs within a field that have less responsibility. When these factors were corrected the study found an unexplained seven-cents-on-the-dollar gap in the first year after college that can be attributed to gender discrimination in pay. This approach to analysis of the gender pay gap, called the human capital model, has been criticized. Lips (2013) argues that the education, career, and life choices can, in fact, be constrained by necessities imposed by gender discrimination. This suggests that removing these factors entirely from the gender gap equation leads to an estimate of the size of the pay gap that is too small.

Title VII of the Civil Rights Act of 1964 makes it illegal to treat individuals unfavorably because of their race or color of their skin: An employer cannot discriminate based on skin color, hair texture, or other **immutable characteristics**, which are traits of an individual that are fundamental to her identity, in hiring, benefits, promotions, or termination of employees. The Pregnancy Discrimination Act of 1978 amends the Civil Rights Act; it prohibits job (e.g., employment, pay, and termination) discrimination of a woman because she is pregnant as long as she can perform the work required.

The Supreme Court ruling in *Griggs v. Duke Power Co.* made it illegal under Title VII of the Civil Rights Act to include educational requirements in a job description (e.g., high school diploma) that negatively impacts one race over another if the requirement cannot be shown to be directly related to job performance. The EEOC (2014) received more than 94,000 charges of various kinds of employment discrimination in 2013. Many of the filings are for multiple forms of discrimination and include charges of retaliation for making a claim, which itself is illegal. Only a small fraction of these claims become suits filed in a federal court, although the suits may represent the claims of more than one person. In 2013, there were 148 suits filed in federal courts.

LINK TO LEARNING

In 2011, the U.S. Supreme Court decided a case in which women plaintiffs were attempting to group together in a class-action suit against Walmart for gender discrimination in promotion and pay. The case was important because it was the only practical way for individual women who felt they had been discriminated against to sustain a court battle for redress of their claims. The Court ultimately decided against the plaintiffs, and the right to a class-action suit was denied. However, the case itself effectively publicized the issue of gender discrimination in employment. Watch this video about the case history and issues (http://openstax.org/l/SCOTUS1) and this PBS NewsHour video about the arguments (http://openstax.org/l/SCOTUS2) to learn more.

Federal legislation does not protect employees in the private sector from discrimination related to sexual orientation and gender identity. These groups include lesbian, gay, bisexual, and transgender individuals. There is evidence of discrimination derived from surveys of workers, studies of complaint filings, wage comparison studies, and controlled job-interview studies (Badgett, Sears, Lau, & Ho, 2009). Federal legislation protects federal employees from such discrimination; the District of Columbia and 20 states have laws protecting public and private employees from discrimination for sexual orientation (American Civil Liberties Union, n.d). Most of the states with these laws also protect against discrimination based on gender identity. Gender identity, as discussed when you learned about sexual behavior, refers to one's sense of being male or female.

Many cities and counties have adopted local legislation preventing discrimination based on sexual orientation or gender identity (Human Rights Campaign, 2013a), and some companies have recognized a benefit to explicitly stating that their hiring must not discriminate on these bases (Human Rights Campaign, 2013b).

AMERICANS WITH DISABILITIES ACT (ADA)

The **Americans with Disabilities Act (ADA)** of 1990 states people may not be discriminated against due to the nature of their disability. A disability is defined as a physical or mental impairment that limits one or more major life activities such as hearing, walking, and breathing. An employer must make reasonable accommodations for the performance of the job of an employee with disabilities. This might include making the work facility accessible with ramps, providing readers for blind personnel, or allowing for more frequent breaks. The ADA has now been expanded to include individuals with alcoholism, former drug use, obesity, or psychiatric disabilities. The premise of the law is that individuals with disabilities can contribute to an organization and they cannot be discriminated against because of their disabilities (O'Keefe & Bruyere, 1994).

The Civil Rights Act and the Age Discrimination in Employment Act make provisions for **bona fide occupational qualifications (BFOQs)**, which are requirements of certain occupations for which denying an individual employment would otherwise violate the law. For example, there may be cases in which religion, national origin, age, and sex are bona fide occupational qualifications. There are no BFOQ exceptions that apply to race, although the first amendment protects artistic expressions, such as films, in making race a requirement of a role. Clearcut examples of BFOQs would be hiring someone of a specific religion for a leadership position in a worship facility, or for an executive position in religiously affiliated institutions, such as the president of a university with religious ties. Age has been determined to be a BFOQ for airline pilots; hence, there are mandatory retirement ages for safety reasons. Sex has been determined as a BFOQ for guards in male prisons.

Sex (gender) is the most common reason for invoking a BFOQ as a defense against accusing an employer of discrimination (Manley, 2009). Courts have established a three-part test for sex-related BFOQs that are often used in other types of legal cases for determining whether a BFOQ exists. The first of these is whether all or substantially all women would be unable to perform a job. This is the reason most physical limitations, such as "able to lift 30 pounds," fail as reasons to discriminate because most women are able to lift this weight. The second test is the "essence of the business" test, in which having to choose the other gender would undermine the essence of the business operation. This test was the reason the now defunct Pan American World Airways (i.e., Pan Am) was told it could not hire only female flight attendants. Hiring men would not have undermined the essense of this business. On a deeper level, this means that hiring cannot be made purely on customers' or others' preferences. The third and final test is whether the employer cannot make reasonable alternative accomodations, such as reassigning staff so that a woman does not have to work in a male-only part of a jail or other gender-specific facility. Privacy concerns are a major reason why discrimination based on gender is upheld by the courts, for example in situations such as hires for nursing or custodial staff (Manley, 2009). Most cases of BFOQs are decided on a case-by-case basis and these court decisions inform policy and future case decisions.

WHAT DO YOU THINK?

Hooters and BFOQ Laws

Figure 13.13 Hooters restaurants only hire female wait staff. (credit: "BemLoira BemDavassa"/Flickr)

The restaurant chain Hooters, which hires only female wait staff and has them dress in a sexually provocative manner, is commonly cited as a discriminatory employer. The chain would argue that the female employees are an essential part of their business in that they market through sex appeal and the wait staff attract customers. Men have filed discrimination charges against Hooters in the past for not hiring them as wait staff simply

> because they are men. The chain has avoided a court decision on their hiring practices by settling out of court with the plaintiffs in each case. Do you think their practices violate the Civil Rights Act? See if you can apply the three court tests to this case and make a decision about whether a case that went to trial would find in favor of the plaintiff or the chain.

13.3 Organizational Psychology: The Social Dimension of Work

Learning Objectives

By the end of this section, you will be able to:
- Define organizational psychology
- Explain the measurement and determinants of job satisfaction
- Describe key elements of management and leadership
- Explain the significance of organizational culture

Organizational psychology is the second major branch of study and practice within the discipline of industrial and organizational psychology. In organizational psychology, the focus is on social interactions and their effect on the individual and on the functioning of the organization. In this section, you will learn about the work organizational psychologists have done to understand job satisfaction, different styles of management, different styles of leadership, organizational culture, and teamwork.

JOB SATISFACTION

Some people love their jobs, some people tolerate their jobs, and some people cannot stand their jobs. **Job satisfaction** describes the degree to which individuals enjoy their job. It was described by Edwin Locke (1976) as the state of feeling resulting from appraising one's job experiences. While job satisfaction results from both how we think about our work (our cognition) and how we feel about our work (our affect) (Saari & Judge, 2004), it is described in terms of affect. Job satisfaction is impacted by the work itself, our personality, and the culture we come from and live in (Saari & Judge, 2004).

Job satisfaction is typically measured after a change in an organization, such as a shift in the management model, to assess how the change affects employees. It may also be routinely measured by an organization to assess one of many factors expected to affect the organization's performance. In addition, polling companies like Gallup regularly measure job satisfaction on a national scale to gather broad information on the state of the economy and the workforce (Saad, 2012).

Job satisfaction is measured using questionnaires that employees complete. Sometimes a single question might be asked in a very straightforward way to which employees respond using a rating scale, such as a Likert scale, which was discussed in the chapter on personality. A Likert scale (typically) provides five possible answers to a statement or question that allows respondents to indicate their positive-to-negative strength of agreement or strength of feeling regarding the question or statement. Thus the possible responses to a question such as "How satisfied are you with your job today?" might be "Very satisfied," "Somewhat satisfied," "Neither satisfied, nor dissatisfied," "Somewhat dissatisfied," and "Very dissatisfied." More commonly the survey will ask a number of questions about the employee's satisfaction to determine more precisely why he is satisfied or dissatisfied. Sometimes these surveys are created for specific jobs; at other times, they are designed to apply to any job. Job satisfaction can be measured at a global level, meaning how satisfied in general the employee is with work, or at the level of specific factors intended to measure which aspects of the job lead to satisfaction (Table 13.2).

Factors Involved in Job Satisfaction and Dissatisfaction

Factor	Description
Autonomy	Individual responsibility, control over decisions
Work content	Variety, challenge, role clarity
Communication	Feedback
Financial rewards	Salary and benefits
Growth and development	Personal growth, training, education
Promotion	Career advancement opportunity
Coworkers	Professional relations or adequacy
Supervision and feedback	Support, recognition, fairness
Workload	Time pressure, tedium
Work demands	Extra work requirements, insecurity of position

Table 13.2

Research has suggested that the work-content factor, which includes variety, difficulty level, and role clarity of the job, is the most strongly predictive factor of overall job satisfaction (Saari & Judge, 2004). In contrast, there is only a weak correlation between pay level and job satisfaction (Judge, Piccolo, Podsakoff, Shaw, & Rich, 2010). Judge et al. (2010) suggest that individuals adjust or adapt to higher pay levels: Higher pay no longer provides the satisfaction the individual may have initially felt when her salary increased.

Why should we care about job satisfaction? Or more specifically, why should an employer care about job satisfaction? Measures of job satisfaction are somewhat correlated with job performance; in particular, they appear to relate to organizational citizenship or discretionary behaviors on the part of an employee that further the goals of the organization (Judge & Kammeyer-Mueller, 2012). Job satisfaction is related to general life satisfaction, although there has been limited research on how the two influence each other or whether personality and cultural factors affect both job and general life satisfaction. One carefully controlled study suggested that the relationship is reciprocal: Job satisfaction affects life satisfaction positively, and vice versa (Judge & Watanabe, 1993). Of course, organizations cannot control life satisfaction's influence on job satisfaction. Job satisfaction, specifically low job satisfaction, is also related to withdrawal behaviors, such as leaving a job or absenteeism (Judge & Kammeyer-Mueller, 2012). The relationship with turnover itself, however, is weak (Judge & Kammeyer-Mueller, 2012). Finally, it appears that job satisfaction is related to organizational performance, which suggests that implementing organizational changes to improve employee job satisfaction will improve organizational performance (Judge & Kammeyer-Mueller, 2012).

There is opportunity for more research in the area of job satisfaction. For example, Weiss (2002) suggests that the concept of job satisfaction measurements have combined both emotional and cognitive concepts, and measurements would be more reliable and show better relationships with outcomes like performance if the measurement of job satisfaction separated these two possible elements of job satisfaction.

> ### DIG DEEPER
>
> **Job Satisfaction in Federal Government Agencies**
>
> A 2013 study of job satisfaction in the U.S. federal government found indexes of job satisfaction plummeting compared to the private sector. The largest factor in the decline was satisfaction with pay, followed by training and development opportunities. The Partnership for Public Service, a nonprofit, nonpartisan organization, has conducted research on federal employee job satisfaction since 2003. Its primary goal is to improve the federal government's management. However, the results also provide information to those interested in obtaining employment with the federal government.
>
> Among large agencies, the highest job satisfaction ranking went to NASA, followed by the Department of Commerce and the intelligence community. The lowest scores went to the Department of Homeland Security.
>
> The data used to derive the job satisfaction score come from three questions on the Federal Employee Viewpoint Survey. The questions are:
>
> 1. I recommend my organization as a good place to work.
> 2. Considering everything, how satisfied are you with your job?
> 3. Considering everything, how satisfied are you with your organization?
>
> The questions have a range of six possible answers, spanning a range of strong agreement or satisfaction to strong disagreement or dissatisfaction. How would you answer these questions with regard to your own job? Would these questions adequately assess your job satisfaction?
>
> You can explore the Best Places To Work In The Federal Government study at their Web site: www.bestplacestowork.org. The Office of Personnel Management also produces a report based on their survey: www.fedview.opm.gov.

Job stress affects job satisfaction. Job stress, or job strain, is caused by specific stressors in an occupation. Stress can be an ambigious term as it is used in common language. Stress is the perception and response of an individual to events judged as ovewhelming or threatening to the individual's well-being (Gyllensten & Palmer, 2005). The events themselves are the stressors. Stress is a result of an employee's perception that the demands placed on them exceed their ability to meet them (Gyllensten & Palmer, 2005), such as having to fill multiple roles in a job or life in general, workplace role ambiguity, lack of career progress, lack of job security, lack of control over work outcomes, isolation, work overload, discrimination, harrassment, and bullying (Colligan & Higgins, 2005). The stressors are different for women than men and these differences are a significant area of research (Gyllensten & Palmer, 2005). Job stress leads to poor employee health, job performance, and family life (Colligan & Higgins, 2005).

As already mentioned, job insecurity contributes significantly to job stress. Two increasing threats to job security are downsizing events and corporate mergers. Businesses typically involve I-O psychologists in planning for, implementing, and managing these types of organizational change.

Downsizing is an increasingly common response to a business's pronounced failure to achieve profit goals, and it involves laying off a significant percentage of the company's employees. Industrial-organizational psychologists may be involved in all aspects of downsizing: how the news is delivered to employees (both those being let go and those staying), how laid-off employees are supported (e.g., separation packages), and how retained employees are supported. The latter is important for the organization because downsizing events affect the retained employee's intent to quit, organizational commitment, and job insecurity (Ugboro, 2006).

In addition to downsizing as a way of responding to outside strains on a business, corporations often grow larger by combining with other businesses. This can be accomplished through a merger (i.e., the joining of two organizations of equal power and status) or an acquisition (i.e., one organization purchases the other). In an acquisition, the purchasing organization is usually the more powerful or dominant partner. In both cases, there is usually a duplication of services between the two companies, such as two accounting departments and two sales forces. Both departments must be merged, which commonly involves a reduction of staff (Figure 13.14). This leads to organizational processes and stresses similar to those that occur in downsizing events. Mergers require determining how the organizational culture will change, to which employees also must adjust (van Knippenberg, van Knippenberg, Monden, & de Lima, 2002). There can be additional stress on workers as they lose their connection to the old organization and try to make connections with the new combined group (Amiot, Terry, Jimmieson, & Callan, 2006). Research in this area focuses on understanding employee reactions and making practical recommendations for managing these organizational changes.

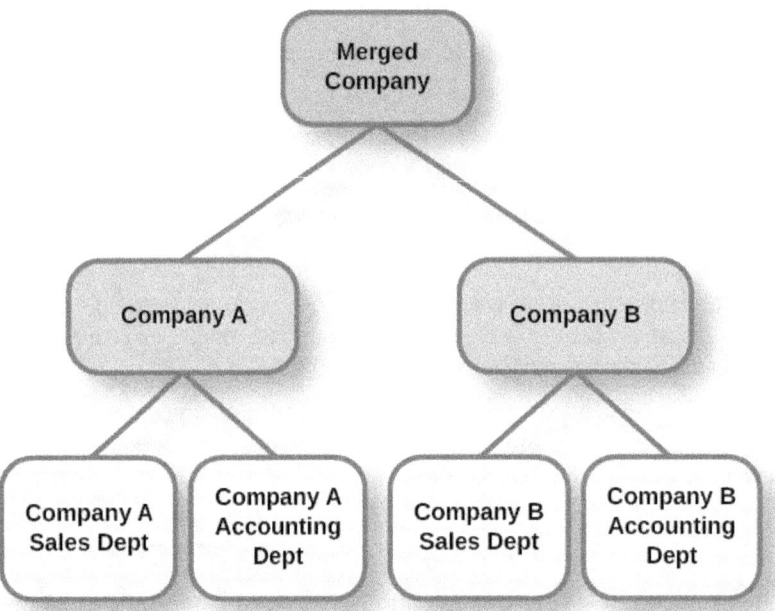

Figure 13.14 When companies are combined through a merger (or acquisition), there are often cuts due to duplication of core functions, like sales and accounting, at each company.

WORK–FAMILY BALANCE

Many people juggle the demands of work life with the demands of their home life, whether it be caring for children or taking care of an elderly parent; this is known as **work-family balance**. We might commonly think about work interfering with family, but it is also the case that family responsibilities may conflict with work obligations (Carlson, Kacmar, & Williams, 2000). Greenhaus and Beutell (1985) first identified three sources of work–family conflicts:

- time devoted to work makes it difficult to fulfill requirements of family, or vice versa,
- strain from participation in work makes it difficult to fulfill requirements of family, or vice versa, and
- specific behaviors required by work make it difficult to fulfill the requirements of family, or vice versa.

Women often have greater responsibility for family demands, including home care, child care, and caring for aging parents, yet men in the United States are increasingly assuming a greater share of domestic responsibilities. However, research has documented that women report greater levels of stress from work–family conflict (Gyllensten & Palmer, 2005).

There are many ways to decrease work–family conflict and improve people's job satisfaction (Posig & Kickul, 2004). These include support in the home, which can take various forms: emotional (listening), practical (help with chores). Workplace support can include understanding supervisors, flextime, leave with pay, and telecommuting. Flextime usually involves a requirement of core hours spent in the workplace around which the employee may schedule his arrival and departure from work to meet family demands. **Telecommuting** involves employees working at home and setting their own hours, which allows them to work during different parts of the day, and to spend part of the day with their family; this may also be known as ecommuting, working remotely, flexible workspace, or simply working from home. Recall that Yahoo! had a policy of allowing employees to telecommute and then rescinded the policy. There are also organizations that have onsite daycare centers, and some companies even have onsite fitness centers and health clinics. In a study of the effectiveness of different coping methods, Lapierre & Allen (2006) found practical support from home more important than emotional support. They also found that immediate-supervisor support for a worker significantly reduced work–family conflict through such mechanisms as allowing an employee the flexibility needed to fulfill family obligations. In contrast, flextime did not help with coping and telecommuting actually made things worse, perhaps reflecting the fact that being at home intensifies the conflict between work and family because with the employee in the home, the demands of family are more evident.

Posig & Kickul (2004) identify exemplar corporations with policies designed to reduce work–family conflict. Examples include IBM's policy of three years of job-guaranteed leave after the birth of a child, Lucent Technologies offer of one year's childbirth leave at half pay, and SC Johnson's program of concierge services for daytime errands.

LINK TO LEARNING

The Glassdoor website (http://openstax.org/l/glassdoor) posts job satisfaction reviews for different careers and organizations. Use this site to research possible careers and/or organizations that interest you.

MANAGEMENT AND ORGANIZATIONAL STRUCTURE

A significant portion of I-O research focuses on management and human relations. Douglas McGregor (1960) combined **scientific management** (a theory of management that analyzes and synthesizes workflows with the main objective of improving economic efficiency, especially labor productivity) and human relations into the notion of leadership behavior. His theory lays out two different styles called Theory X and Theory Y. In the **Theory X** approach to management, managers assume that most people dislike work and are not innately self-directed. Theory X managers perceive employees as people who prefer to be led and told which tasks to perform and when. Their employees have to be watched carefully to be sure that they work hard enough to fulfill the organization's goals. Theory X workplaces will often have employees punch a clock when arriving and leaving the workplace: Tardiness is punished. Supervisors, not employees, determine whether an employee needs to stay late, and even this decision would require someone higher up in the command chain to approve the extra hours. Theory X supervisors will ignore employees' suggestions for improved efficiency and reprimand employees for speaking out of order. These supervisors blame efficiency failures on individual employees rather than the systems or policies in place. Managerial goals are achieved through a system of punishments and threats rather than enticements and rewards. Managers are suspicious of employees' motivations and always suspect selfish motivations for their behavior at work (e.g., being paid is their sole motivation for working).

In the **Theory Y** approach, on the other hand, managers assume that most people seek inner satisfaction and fulfillment from their work. Employees function better under leadership that allows them to participate in, and provide input about, setting their personal and work goals. In Theory Y workplaces, employees participate in decisions about prioritizing tasks; they may belong to teams that, once given a goal, decide themselves how it will be accomplished. In such a workplace, employees are able to provide input on matters of efficiency and safety. One example of Theory Y in action is the policy of Toyota production lines that allows any employee to stop the entire line if a defect or other issue appears, so that the defect can be fixed and its cause remedied (Toyota Motor Manufacturing, 2013). A Theory Y workplace will also meaningfully consult employees on any changes to the work process or management system. In addition, the organization will encourage employees to contribute their own ideas. McGregor (1960) characterized Theory X as the traditional method of management used in the United States. He agued that a Theory Y approach was needed to improve organizational output and the wellbeing of individuals. Table 13.3 summarizes how these two management approaches differ.

Theory X and Theory Y Management Styles

Theory X	Theory Y
People dislike work and avoid it.	People enjoy work and find it natural.
People avoid responsibility.	People are more satisified when given responsibility.
People want to be told what to do.	People want to take part in setting their own work goals.
Goals are achieved through rules and punishments.	Goals are achieved through enticements and rewards.

Table 13.3

Another management style was described by Donald Clifton, who focused his research on how an organization can best use an individual's strengths, an approach he called strengths-based management. He and his colleagues interviewed 8,000 managers and concluded that it is important to focus on a person's strengths, not their weaknesses. A strength is a particular enduring talent possessed by an individual that allows her to provide consistent, near-perfect performance in tasks involving that talent. Clifton argued that our strengths provide the greatest opportunity for growth (Buckingham & Clifton, 2001). An example of a strength is public speaking or the ability to plan a successful event. The strengths-based approach is very popular although its effect on organization performance is not well-studied. However, Kaiser & Overfield (2011) found that managers often neglected improving their weaknesses and overused their strengths, both of which interfered with performance.

Leadership is an important element of management. Leadership styles have been of major interest within I-O research, and researchers have proposed numerous theories of leadership. Bass (1985) popularized and developed the concepts of transactional leadership versus transformational leadership styles. In **transactional leadership**, the focus is on supervision and organizational goals, which are achieved through a system of rewards and punishments (i.e., transactions). Transactional leaders maintain the status quo: They are managers. This is in contrast to the transformational leader. People who have **transformational leadership** possess four attributes to varying degrees: They are charismatic (highly liked role models), inspirational (optimistic about goal attainment), intellectually stimulating (encourage critical thinking and problem solving), and considerate (Bass, Avolio, & Atwater, 1996).

As women increasingly take on leadership roles in corporations, questions have arisen as to whether there are differences in leadership styles between men and women (Eagly, Johannesen-Schmidt, & van Engen, 2003). Eagly & Johnson (1990) conducted a meta-analysis to examine gender and leadership style. They found, to a slight but significant degree, that women tend to practice an interpersonal style of leadership (i.e., she focuses on the morale and welfare of the employees) and men practice a task-oriented style (i.e., he focuses on accomplishing tasks). However, the differences were less pronounced when one looked only at organizational studies and excluded laboratory experiments or surveys that did not involve actual organizational leaders. Larger sex-related differences were observed when leadership style was categorized as democratic or autocratic, and these differences were consistent across all types of studies. The authors suggest that similarities between the sexes in leadership styles are attributable to both sexes needing to conform the organization's culture; additionally, they propose that sex-related differences reflect inherent differences in the strengths each sex brings to bear on leadership practice. In another meta-analysis of leadership style, Eagly, Johannesen-Schmidt, & van Engen (2003) found that women tended to exhibit the characteristics of transformational leaders, while men were more likely to be transactional leaders. However, the differences are not absolute; for example, women were found to use methods of reward for performance more often than men, which is a component of transactional leadership. The differences they found were relatively small. As Eagly, Johannesen-Schmidt, & van Engen (2003) point out, research shows that transformational leadership approaches are more effective than transactional approaches, although individual leaders typically exhibit elements of both approaches.

A new and emerging area of research within psychology focuses on leadership and the relationship with leaders from the perspective of a follower. This "followership" research suggests that studies need to examine the leader-follower relationship in both directions—instead of focusing only on leadership—to better understand the dynamics of the relationship. Put differently, people are individuals, and because they are different, there probably is no single best leadership-follower dynamic between leaders and followers. For instance, think about the differences between yourself and someone you know well. Do you respond the same way to criticism? Maybe one of you likes a lot of structure and other seems to work best with less structure. Perhaps, one of you is ready to try a new restaurant at any time and the other prefers to go to the tried-and-true place that you've visited so many times the servers know your order before you place it.

Some early research has discovered that the characteristics of individual followers will result in different types of relationships with a leader depending on the leadership style. It appears that not all leadership styles work well with all follower types. One characteristic of followers, for example, is their degree of extroversion. Previous research suggests that individuals with a high degree of extroversion would need a larger amount of interaction with their leaders in order to function well; however, other research suggests this may not necessarily be the case and instead other factors may be at work (Phillips & Bedeian; Bauer et al, 2006).

Another characteristic of followers is their individual need for growth. For followers who have a strong desire to learn and grow within their organization, a leader who provides developmental opportunities might be better received than one who does not. In addition, for those followers who are low on growth and need strength, leaders who push them to grow may make them less satisfied followers as they feel forced into further development and training, possibly signaling a lower level of achievement from their supervisor. Training for leaders in both helping employees who have a strong drive for growth and those who do not appears to be helpful in improving the relationship between both types of followers and their leaders (Schyns, Kroon, & Moors, 2008).

Finally, an employee's need for leadership is an important component of the leader-follower relationship. Some individuals are significantly more autonomous than others and as a result do not respond as well to leaders who provide a lot of structure and rigidity of processes, in turn reducing the quality of their relationship with their leader. Other employees who are high in need for leadership have a better relationship with their leader if they are provided with a well-structured environment with clear responsibilities and little ambiguity in their work. These followers work best in situations where they feel they can comfortably perform the work with little requirement to think outside of the guidelines that have been provided. For these individuals, having a leader who is able to set a clear path forward for the employee with little need for deviation promotes a strong positive leader-follower relationship (Felfe & Schyns, 2006).

GOALS, TEAMWORK AND WORK TEAMS

The workplace today is rapidly changing due to a variety of factors, such as shifts in technology, economics, foreign competition, globalization, and workplace demographics. Organizations need to respond quickly to changes in these factors. Many companies are responding to these changes by structuring their organizations so that work can be delegated to **work teams**, which bring together diverse skills, experience, and expertise. This is in contrast to organizational structures that have individuals at their base (Naquin & Tynan, 2003). In the team-based approach, teams are brought together and given a specific task or goal to accomplish. Despite their burgeoning popularity, team structures do not always deliver greater productivity—the work of teams is an active area of research (Naquin & Tynan, 2003).

Why do some teams work well while others do not? There are many contributing factors. For example, teams can mask team members that are not working (i.e., social loafing). Teams can be inefficient due to poor communication; they can have poor decision-making skills due to conformity effects; and, they can have conflict within the group. The popularity of teams may in part result from the team halo effect: Teams are given credit for their successes. but individuals within a team are blamed for team failures (Naquin & Tynan, 2003). One aspect of team diversity is their gender mix. Researchers have explored whether gender mix has an effect on team performance. On the one hand, diversity can introduce communication and interpersonal-relationship problems that hinder performance, but on the other hand diversity can also increase the team's skill set, which may include skills that can actually improve team member interactions. Hoogendoorn, Oosterbeek, & van Praag (2013) studied project teams in a university business school in which the gender mix of the teams was manipulated. They found that gender-balanced teams (i.e., nearly equal numbers of men and women) performed better, as measured by sales and profits, than predominantly male teams. The study did not have enough data to determine the relative performance of female dominated teams. The study was unsuccessful in identifying which mechanism (interpersonal relationships, learning, or skills mixes) accounted for performance improvement.

There are three basic types of teams: problem resolution teams, creative teams, and tactical teams. Problem resolution teams are created for the purpose of solving a particular problem or issue; for example, the diagnostic teams at the Centers for Disease Control. Creative teams are used to develop innovative possibilities or solutions; for example, design teams for car manufacturers create new vehicle models. Tactical teams are used to execute a well-defined plan or objective, such as a police or FBI SWAT team handling a hostage situation (Larson & LaFasto, 1989). One area of active research involves a fourth kind of team—the virtual team; these studies examine how groups of geographically disparate people brought together using digital communications technology function (Powell, Piccoli, & Ives, 2004). Virtual teams are more common due to the growing globalization of organizations and the use of consulting and partnerships facilitated by digital communication.

ORGANIZATIONAL CULTURE

Each company and organization has an organizational culture. **Organizational culture** encompasses the values, visions, hierarchies, norms, and interactions among its employees. It is how an organization is run, how it operates, and how it makes decisions—the industry in which the organization participates may have an influence. Different departments within one company can develop their own subculture within the organization's culture. Ostroff, Kinicki, and Tamkins (2003) identify three layers in organizational culture: observable artifacts, espoused values, and basic assumptions. Observable artifacts are the symbols, language (jargon, slang, and humor), narratives (stories and legends), and practices (rituals) that represent the underlying cultural assumptions. Espoused values are concepts or beliefs that the management or the entire organization endorses. They are the rules that allow employees to know which actions they should take in different situations and which information they should adhere to. These basic assumptions generally are unobservable and unquestioned. Researchers have developed survey instruments to measure organizational culture.

With the workforce being a global marketplace, your company may have a supplier in Korea and another in Honduras and have employees in the United States, China, and South Africa. You may have coworkers of different religious, ethnic, or racial backgrounds than yourself. Your coworkers may be from different places around the globe. Many workplaces offer diversity training to help everyone involved bridge and understand cultural differences. **Diversity training** educates participants about cultural differences with the goal of improving teamwork. There is always the potential for prejudice between members of two groups, but the evidence suggests that simply working together, particularly if the conditions of work are set carefully that such prejudice can be reduced or eliminated. Pettigrew and Tropp (2006) conducted a meta-analysis to examine the question of whether contact between groups reduced prejudice between those groups. They found that there was a moderate but significant effect. They also found that, as previously theorized, the effect was enhanced when the two groups met under conditions in which they have equal standing, common goals, cooperation between the groups, and especially support on the part of the institution or authorities for the contact.

DIG DEEPER

Managing Generational Differences

An important consideration in managing employees is age. Workers' expectations and attitudes are developed in part by experience in particular cultural time periods. Generational constructs are somewhat arbitrary, yet they may be helpful in setting broad directions to organizational management as one generation leaves the workforce and another enters it. The baby boomer generation (born between 1946 and 1964) is in the process of leaving the workforce and will continue to depart it for a decade or more. Generation X (born between the early 1960s and the 1980s) are now in the middle of their careers. Millennials (born from 1979 to the early 1994) began to come of age at the turn of the century, and are early in their careers.

Today, as these three different generations work side by side in the workplace, employers and managers need to be able to identify their unique characteristics. Each generation has distinctive expectations, habits, attitudes, and motivations (Elmore, 2010). One of the major differences among these generations is knowledge of the use of technology in the workplace. Millennials are technologically sophisticated and believe their use of technology sets them apart from other generations. They have also been characterized as self-centered and overly self-confident. Their attitudinal differences have raised concerns for managers about maintaining their motivation as employees and their ability to integrate into organizational culture created by baby boomers (Myers & Sadaghiani, 2010). For example, millennials may expect to hear that they need to pay their dues in their jobs from baby boomers who believe they paid their dues in their time. Yet millennials may resist doing so because they value life outside of work to a greater degree (Myers & Sadaghiani, 2010). Meister & Willyerd (2010) suggest alternative approaches to training and mentoring that will engage millennials and adapt to their need for feedback from supervisors: reverse mentoring, in which a younger employee educates a senior employee in social media or other digital resources. The senior employee then has the opportunity to provide useful guidance within a less demanding role.

Recruiting and retaining millennials and Generation X employees poses challenges that did not exist in previous generations. The concept of building a career with the company is not relatable to most Generation X employees, who do not expect to stay with one employer for their career. This expectation arises from of a reduced sense of loyalty because they do not expect their employer to be loyal to them (Gibson, Greenwood, & Murphy, 2009). Retaining Generation X workers thus relies on motivating them by making their work meaningful (Gibson, Greenwood, & Murphy, 2009). Since millennials lack an inherent loyalty to the company, retaining them also requires effort in the form of nurturing through frequent rewards, praise, and feedback.

Millennials are also interested in having many choices, including options in work scheduling, choice of job duties, and so on. They also expect more training and education from their employers. Companies that offer the best benefit package and brand attract millennials (Myers & Sadaghiani, 2010).

One well-recognized negative aspect of organizational culture is a culture of harassment, including sexual harassment. Most organizations of any size have developed sexual harassment policies that define sexual harassment (or harassment in general) and the procedures the organization has set in place to prevent and address it when it does occur. Thus, in most jobs you have held, you were probably made aware of the company's sexual harassment policy and procedures, and may have received training related to the policy. The U.S. Equal Employment Opportunity Commission (n.d.) provides the following description of **sexual harassment**:

> Unwelcome sexual advances, requests for sexual favors, and other verbal or physical conduct of a sexual nature constitute sexual harassment when this conduct explicitly or implicitly affects an individual's employment, unreasonably interferes with an individual's work performance, or creates an intimidating, hostile, or offensive work environment. (par. 2)

One form of sexual harassment is called quid pro quo. Quid pro quo means you give something to get something, and it refers to a situation in which organizational rewards are offered in exchange for sexual favors. Quid pro quo harassment is often between an employee and a person with greater power in the organization. For example, a supervisor might request an action, such as a kiss or a touch, in exchange for a promotion, a positive performance review, or a pay raise. Another form of sexual harassment is the threat of withholding a reward if a sexual request is refused. Hostile environment sexual harassment is another type of workplace harassment. In this situation, an employee experiences conditions in the workplace that are considered hostile or intimidating. For example, a work environment that allows offensive language or jokes or displays sexually explicit images. Isolated occurrences of these events do not constitute harassment, but a pattern of repeated occurrences does. In addition to violating organizational policies against sexual harassment, these forms of harassment are illegal.

Harassment does not have to be sexual; it may be related to any of the protected classes in the statutes regulated by the EEOC: race, national origin, religion, or age.

VIOLENCE IN THE WORKPLACE

In the summer of August 1986, a part-time postal worker with a troubled work history walked into the Edmond, Oklahoma, post office and shot and killed 15 people, including himself. From his action, the term "going postal" was coined, describing a troubled employee who engages in extreme violence.

Workplace violence is one aspect of workplace safety that I-O psychologists study. **Workplace violence** is any act or threat of physical violence, harassment, intimidation, or other threatening, disruptive behavior that occurs at the workplace. It ranges from threats and verbal abuse to physical assaults and even homicide (Occupational Safety & Health Administration, 2014).

There are different targets of workplace violence: a person could commit violence against coworkers, supervisors, or property. Warning signs often precede such actions: intimidating behavior, threats, sabotaging equipment, or radical changes in a coworker's behavior. Often there is intimidation and then escalation that leads to even further escalation. It is important for employees to involve their immediate supervisor if they ever feel intimidated or unsafe.

Murder is the second leading cause of death in the workplace. It is also the primary cause of death for women in the workplace. Every year there are nearly two million workers who are physically assaulted or threatened with assault. Many are murdered in domestic violence situations by boyfriends or husbands who chose the woman's workplace to commit their crimes.

There are many triggers for workplace violence. A significant trigger is the feeling of being treated unfairly, unjustly, or disrespectfully. In a research experiment, Greenberg (1993) examined the reactions of students who were given pay for a task. In one group, the students were given extensive explanations for the pay rate. In the second group, the students were given a curt uninformative explanation. The students were made to believe the supervisor would not know how much money the student withdrew for payment. The rate of stealing (taking more pay than they were told they deserved) was higher in the group who had been given the limited explanation. This is a demonstration of the importance of procedural justice in organizations. **Procedural justice** refers to the fairness of the processes by which outcomes are determined in conflicts with or among employees.

In another study by Greenberg & Barling (1999), they found a history of aggression and amount of alcohol consumed to be accurate predictors of workplace violence against a coworker. Aggression against a supervisor was predicted if a worker felt unfairly treated or untrusted. Job security and alcohol consumption predicted aggression against a subordinate. To understand and predict workplace violence, Greenberg & Barling (1999) emphasize the importance of considering the employee target of aggression or violence and characteristics of both the workplace characteristics and the aggressive or violent person.

13.4 Human Factors Psychology and Workplace Design

Learning Objectives

By the end of this section, you will be able to:
- Describe the field of human factors psychology
- Explain the role of human factors psychology in safety, productivity, and job satisfaction

Human factors psychology (or ergonomics, a term that is favored in Europe) is the third subject area within industrial and organizational psychology. This field is concerned with the integration of the human-machine interface in the workplace, through design, and specifically with researching and designing machines that fit human requirements. The integration may be physical or cognitive, or a combination of both. Anyone who needs to be convinced that the field is necessary need only try to operate an unfamiliar television remote control or use a new piece of software for the first time. Whereas the two other areas of I-O psychology focus on the interface between the worker and team, group, or organization, human factors psychology focuses on the individual worker's interaction with a machine, work station, information displays, and the local environment, such as lighting. In the United States, human factors psychology has origins in both psychology and engineering; this is reflected in the early contributions of Lillian Gilbreth (psychologist and engineer) and her husband Frank Gilbreth (engineer).

Human factor professionals are involved in design from the beginning of a project, as is more common in software design projects, or toward the end in testing and evaluation, as is more common in traditional industries (Howell, 2003). Another important role of human factor professionals is in the development of regulations and principles of best design. These regulations and principles are often related to work safety. For example, the Three Mile Island nuclear accident lead to Nuclear Regulatory Commission (NRC) requirements for additional instrumentation in nuclear facilities to provide operators with more critical information and increased operator training (United States Nuclear Regulatory Commission, 2013). The American National Standards Institute (ANSI, 2000), an independent developer of industrial standards, develops many standards related to ergonomic design, such as the design of control-center workstations that are used for transportation control or industrial process control.

Many of the concerns of human factors psychology are related to workplace safety. These concerns can be studied to help prevent work-related injuries of individual workers or those around them. Safety protocols may also be related to activities, such as commercial driving or flying, medical procedures, and law enforcement, that have the potential to impact the public.

One of the methods used to reduce accidents in the workplace is a **checklist**. The airline industry is one industry that uses checklists. Pilots are required to go through a detailed checklist of the different parts of the aircraft before takeoff to ensure that all essential equipment is working correctly. Astronauts also go through checklists before takeoff. The surgical safety checklist shown in **Figure 13.15** was developed by the World Health Organization (WHO) and serves as the basis for many checklists at medical facilities.

> **Sign in**
>
> Before induction of anesthesia, members of the team (at least the nurse and an anesthesia professional) orally confirm that:
>
> - The patient has verified his or her identity, the surgical site and procedure, and consent. The surgical site is marked or site marking is not applicable. The pulse oximeter is on the patient and functioning
> - All members of the team are aware of whether the patient has a known allergy
> - The patient's airway and risk of aspiration have been evaluated and appropriate equipment and assistance are available
> - If there is a risk of blood loss of at least 500 ml (or 7 ml/kg of body weight, in children), appropriate access and fluids are available
>
> **Time out**
>
> Before skin incision, the entire team (nurses, surgeons, anesthesia professionals, and any others participating in the care of the patient) orally:
>
> - Confirms that all team members have been introduced by name and role. Confirms the patient's identity, surgical site, and procedure. Reviews the anticipated critical events:
>   - Surgeon reviews critical and unexpected steps, operative duration, and anticipated blood loss
>   - Anesthesia staff review concerns specific to the patient
>   - Nursing staff review confirmation of sterility, equipment availability, and other concerns
> - Confirms that prophylactic antibiotics have been administered = 60 min before incision is made or that antibiotics are not indicated
> - Confirms that all essential imaging results for the correct patient are displayed in the operating room
>
> **Sign out**
>
> Before the patient leaves the operating room:
>
> - Nurse reviews items aloud with the team:
>   - Name of the procedure as recorded
>   - That the needle, sponge, and instrument counts are complete (or not applicable)
>   - That the specimen (if any) is correctly labeled, including with the patient's name
>   - Whether there are any issues with equipment to be addressed
> - The surgeon, nurse, and anesthesia professional review aloud the key concerns for the recovery and care of the patient

Figure 13.15 Checklists, such as the WHO surgical checklist shown here, help reduce workplace accidents.

Safety concerns also lead to limits to how long an operator, such as a pilot or truck driver, is allowed to operate the equipment. Recently the Federal Aviation Administration (FAA) introduced limits for how long a pilot is allowed to fly without an overnight break.

Howell (2003) outlines some important areas of research and practice in the field of human factors. These are summarized in Table 13.4.

Areas of Study in Human Factors Psychology

Area	Description	I-O Questions
Attention	Includes vigilance and monitoring, recognizing signals in noise, mental resources, and divided attention	How is attention maintained? What about tasks maintains attention? How to design systems to support attention?
Cognitive engineering	Includes human software interactions in complex automated systems, especially the decision-making processes of workers as they are supported by the software system	How do workers use and obtain information provided by software?
Task analysis	Breaking down the elements of a task	How can a task be performed more efficiently? How can a task be performed more safely?
Cognitive task analysis	Breaking down the elements of a cognitive task	How are decisions made?

Table 13.4

As an example of research in human factors psychology Bruno & Abrahão (2012) examined the impact of the volume of operator decisions on the accuracy of decisions made within an information security center at a banking institution in Brazil. The study examined a total of about 45,000 decisions made by 35 operators and 4 managers over a period of 60 days. Their study found that as the number of decisions made per day by the operators climbed, that is, as their cognitive effort increased, the operators made more mistakes in falsely identifying incidents as real security breaches (when, in reality, they were not). Interestingly, the opposite mistake of identifying real intrusions as false alarms did not increase with increased cognitive demand. This appears to be good news for the bank, since false alarms are not as costly as incorrectly rejecting a genuine threat. These kinds of studies combine research on attention, perception, teamwork, and human–computer interactions in a field of considerable societal and business significance. This is exactly the context of the events that led to the massive data breach for Target in the fall of 2013. Indications are that security personnel received signals of a security breach but did not interpret them correctly, thus allowing the breach to continue for two weeks until an outside agency, the FBI, informed the company (Riley, Elgin, Lawrence, & Matlack, 2014).

Key Terms

Americans with Disabilities Act employers cannot discriminate against any individual based on a disability

bona fide occupational qualification (BFOQ) requirement of certain occupations for which denying an individual employment would otherwise violate the law, such as requirements concerning religion or sex

checklist method used to reduce workplace accidents

diversity training training employees about cultural differences with the goal of improving teamwork

downsizing process in which an organization tries to achieve greater overall efficiency by reducing the number of employees

Hawthorne effect increase in performance of individuals who are noticed, watched, and paid attention to by researchers or supervisors

human factors psychology branch of psychology that studies how workers interact with the tools of work and how to design those tools to optimize workers' productivity, safety, and health

immutable characteristic traits that employers cannot use to discriminate in hiring, benefits, promotions, or termination; these traits are fundamental to one's personal identity (e.g. skin color and hair texture)

industrial and organizational (I-O) psychology field in psychology that applies scientific principles to the study of work and the workplace

industrial psychology branch of psychology that studies job characteristics, applicant characteristics, and how to match them; also studies employee training and performance appraisal

job analysis determining and listing tasks associated with a particular job

job satisfaction degree of pleasure that employees derive from their job

organizational culture values, visions, hierarchies, norms and interactions between its employees; how an organization is run, how it operates, and how it makes decisions

organizational psychology branch of psychology that studies the interactions between people working in organizations and the effects of those interactions on productivity

performance appraisal evaluation of an employee's success or lack of success at performing the duties of the job

procedural justice fairness by which means are used to achieve results in an organization

scientific management theory of management that analyzed and synthesized workflows with the main objective of improving economic efficiency, especially labor productivity

sexual harassment sexually-based behavior that is knowingly unwanted and has an adverse effect of a person's employment status, interferes with a person's job performance, or creates a hostile or intimidating work environment

telecommuting employees' ability to set their own hours allowing them to work from home at different parts of the day

Theory X assumes workers are inherently lazy and unproductive; managers must have control and use punishments

Theory Y assumes workers are people who seek to work hard and productively; managers and workers can find creative solutions to problems; workers do not need to be controlled and punished

transactional leadership style characteristic of leaders who focus on supervision and organizational goals achieved through a system of rewards and punishments; maintenance of the organizational status quo

transformational leadership style characteristic of leaders who are charismatic role models, inspirational, intellectually stimulating, and individually considerate and who seek to change the organization

U.S. Equal Employment Opportunity Commission (EEOC) responsible for enforcing federal laws that make it illegal to discriminate against a job applicant or an employee because of the person's race, color, religion, sex (including pregnancy), national origin, age (40 or older), disability, or genetic information

work team group of people within an organization or company given a specific task to achieve together

workplace violence violence or the threat of violence against workers; can occur inside or outside the workplace

work–family balance occurs when people juggle the demands of work life with the demands of family life

Summary

13.1 What Is Industrial and Organizational Psychology?
The field of I-O psychology had its birth in industrial psychology and the use of psychological concepts to aid in personnel selection. However, with research such as the Hawthorne study, it was found that productivity was affected more by human interaction and not physical factors; the field of industrial psychology expanded to include organizational psychology. Both WWI and WWII had a strong influence on the development of an expansion of industrial psychology in the United States and elsewhere: The tasks the psychologists were assigned led to development of tests and research in how the psychological concepts could assist industry and other areas. This movement aided in expanding industrial psychology to include organizational psychology.

13.2 Industrial Psychology: Selecting and Evaluating Employees
Industrial psychology studies the attributes of jobs, applicants of those jobs, and methods for assessing fit to a job. These procedures include job analysis, applicant testing, and interviews. It also studies and puts into place procedures for the orientation of new employees and ongoing training of employees. The process of hiring employees can be vulnerable to bias, which is illegal, and industrial psychologists must develop methods for adhering to the law in hiring. Performance appraisal systems are an active area of research and practice in industrial psychology.

13.3 Organizational Psychology: The Social Dimension of Work
Organizational psychology is concerned with the effects of interactions among people in the workplace on the employees themselves and on organizational productivity. Job satisfaction and its determinants and outcomes are a major focus of organizational psychology research and practice. Organizational psychologists have also studied the effects of management styles and leadership styles on productivity. In addition to the employees and management, organizational psychology also looks at the organizational culture and how that might affect productivity. One aspect of organization culture is the prevention and addressing of sexual and other forms of harassment in the workplace. Sexual harassment includes language, behavior, or displays that create a hostile environment; it also includes sexual favors requested in exchange for workplace rewards (i.e., quid pro quo). Industrial-organizational psychology has

conducted extensive research on the triggers and causes of workplace violence and safety. This enables the organization to establish procedures that can identify these triggers before they become a problem.

13.4 Human Factors Psychology and Workplace Design

Human factors psychology, or ergonomics, studies the interface between workers and their machines and physical environments. Human factors psychologists specifically seek to design machines to better support the workers using them. Psychologists may be involved in design of work tools such as software, displays, or machines from the beginning of the design process or during the testing an already developed product. Human factor psychologists are also involved in the development of best design recommendations and regulations. One important aspect of human factors psychology is enhancing worker safety. Human factors research involves efforts to understand and improve interactions between technology systems and their human operators. Human–software interactions are a large sector of this research.

Review Questions

1. Who was the first psychologist to use psychology in advertising?
    a. Hugo Münsterberg
    b. Elton Mayo
    c. Walter Dill Scott
    d. Walter Bingham

2. Which test designed for the Army was used for recruits who were not fluent in English?
    a. Army Personality
    b. Army Alpha
    c. Army Beta
    d. Army Intelligence

3. Which area of I-O psychology measures job satisfaction?
    a. industrial psychology
    b. organizational psychology
    c. human factors psychology
    d. advertising psychology

4. Which statement best describes the Hawthorne effect?
    a. Giving workers rest periods seems like it should decrease productivity, but it actually increases productivity.
    b. Social relations among workers have a greater effect on productivity than physical environment.
    c. Changes in light levels improve working conditions and therefore increase productivity.
    d. The attention of researchers on subjects causes the effect the experimenter is looking for.

5. Which of the following questions is illegal to ask in a job interview in the United States?
    a. Which university did you attend?
    b. Which state were you born in?
    c. Do you have a commercial driver's license?
    d. What salary would you expect for this position?

6. Which of the following items is *not* a part of KSAs?
    a. aspiration
    b. knowledge
    c. skill
    d. other abilities

7. Who is responsible for enforcing federal laws that make it illegal to discriminate against a job applicant?
    a. Americans with Disabilities Act
    b. Supreme Court of the United States
    c. U.S. Equal Employment Opportunity Commission
    d. Society for Industrial and Organizational Psychology

8. A _____ is an example of a tactical team.
    a. surgical team
    b. car design team
    c. budget committee
    d. sports team

9. Which practice is an example of Theory X management?
   a. telecommuting
   b. flextime
   c. keystroke monitoring
   d. team meetings

10. Which is one effect of the team halo effect?
    a. teams appear to work better than they do
    b. teams never fail
    c. teams lead to greater job satisfaction
    d. teams boost productivity

11. Which of the following is the most strongly predictive factor of overall job satisfaction?
    a. financial rewards
    b. personality
    c. autonomy
    d. work content

12. What is the name for what occurs when a supervisor offers a work-related reward in exchange for a sexual favor?
    a. hiring bias
    b. quid pro quo
    c. hostile work environment
    d. immutable characteristics

13. What aspect of an office workstation would a human factors psychologist be concerned about?
    a. height of the chair
    b. closeness to the supervisor
    c. frequency of coworker visits
    d. presence of an offensive sign

14. A human factors psychologist who studied how a worker interacted with a search engine would be researching in the area of _____.
    a. attention
    b. cognitive engineering
    c. job satisfaction
    d. management

Critical Thinking Questions

15. What societal and management attitudes might have caused organizational psychology to develop later than industrial psychology?

16. Many of the examples of I-O psychology are applications to businesses. Name four different non-business contexts that I-O psychology could impact?

17. Construct a good interview question for a position of your choosing. The question should relate to a specific skill requirement for the position and you will need to include the criteria for rating the applicants answer.

18. What might be useful mechanisms for avoiding bias during employment interviews?

19. If you designed an assessment of job satisfaction, what elements would it include?

20. Downsizing has commonly shown to result in a period of lowered productivity for the organizations experiencing it. What might be some of the reasons for this observation?

21. What role could a flight simulator play in the design of a new aircraft?

Personal Application Questions

22. Which of the broad areas of I-O psychology interests you the most and why?

23. What are some of the KSAs (knowledge, skills, and abilities) that are required for your current position or a position you wish to have in the future?

24. How would you handle the situation if you were being sexually harassed? What would you consider sexual harassment?

25. Describe an example of a technology or team and technology interaction that you have had in the context of school or work that could have benefited from better design. What were the effects of the poor design? Make one suggestion for its improvement.

Chapter 14

Stress, Lifestyle, and Health

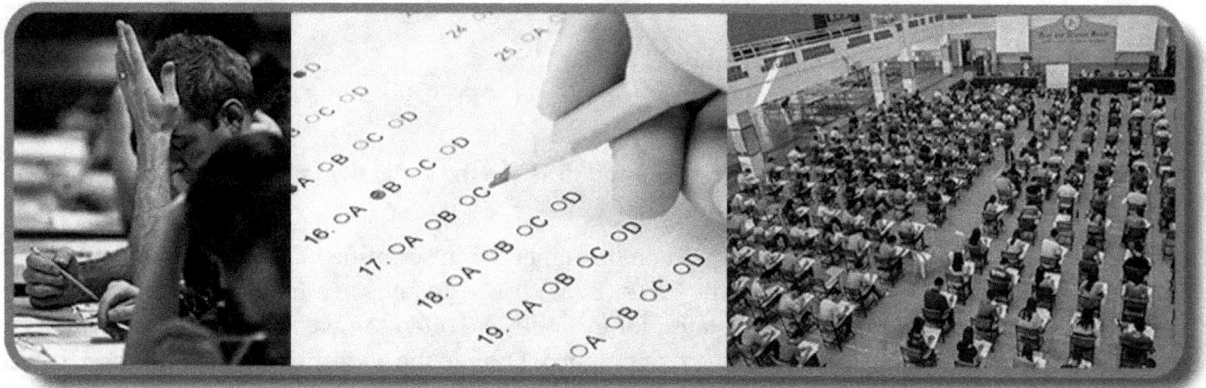

Figure 14.1 Exams are a stressful, but unavoidable, element of college life. (credit "left": modification of work by Travis K. Mendoza; credit "center": modification of work by "albertogp123"/Flickr; credit "right": modification of work by Jeffrey Pioquinto, SJ)

Chapter Outline

14.1 What Is Stress?
14.2 Stressors
14.3 Stress and Illness
14.4 Regulation of Stress
14.5 The Pursuit of Happiness

Introduction

Few would deny that today's college students are under a lot of pressure. In addition to many usual stresses and strains incidental to the college experience (e.g., exams and term papers), students today are faced with increased college tuitions, burdensome debt, and difficulty finding employment after graduation. A significant population of non-traditional college students may face additional stressors, such as raising children or holding down a full-time job while working toward a degree.

Of course, life is filled with many additional challenges beyond those incurred in college or the workplace. We might have concerns with financial security, difficulties with friends or neighbors, family responsibilities, and we may not have enough time to do the things we want to do. Even minor hassles—losing things, traffic jams, and loss of internet service—all involve pressure and demands that can make life seem like a struggle and that can compromise our sense of well-being. That is, all can be stressful in some way.

Scientific interest in stress, including how we adapt and cope, has been longstanding in psychology; indeed, after nearly a century of research on the topic, much has been learned and many insights have been developed. This chapter examines stress and highlights our current understanding of the phenomenon, including its psychological and physiological natures, its causes and consequences, and the steps we can take to master stress rather than become its victim.

14.1 What Is Stress?

Learning Objectives

By the end of this section, you will be able to:
- Differentiate between stimulus-based and response-based definitions of stress
- Define stress as a process
- Differentiate between good stress and bad stress
- Describe the early contributions of Walter Cannon and Hans Selye to the stress research field
- Understand the physiological basis of stress and describe the general adaptation syndrome

The term stress as it relates to the human condition first emerged in scientific literature in the 1930s, but it did not enter the popular vernacular until the 1970s (Lyon, 2012). Today, we often use the term loosely in describing a variety of unpleasant feeling states; for example, we often say we are stressed out when we feel frustrated, angry, conflicted, overwhelmed, or fatigued. Despite the widespread use of the term, stress is a fairly vague concept that is difficult to define with precision.

Researchers have had a difficult time agreeing on an acceptable definition of stress. Some have conceptualized stress as a demanding or threatening event or situation (e.g., a high-stress job, overcrowding, and long commutes to work). Such conceptualizations are known as stimulus-based definitions because they characterize stress as a stimulus that causes certain reactions. Stimulus-based definitions of stress are problematic, however, because they fail to recognize that people differ in how they view and react to challenging life events and situations. For example, a conscientious student who has studied diligently all semester would likely experience less stress during final exams week than would a less responsible, unprepared student.

Others have conceptualized stress in ways that emphasize the physiological responses that occur when faced with demanding or threatening situations (e.g., increased arousal). These conceptualizations are referred to as response-based definitions because they describe stress as a response to environmental conditions. For example, the endocrinologist Hans Selye, a famous stress researcher, once defined stress as the "response of the body to any demand, whether it is caused by, or results in, pleasant or unpleasant conditions" (Selye, 1976, p. 74). Selye's definition of stress is response-based in that it conceptualizes stress chiefly in terms of the body's physiological reaction to any demand that is placed on it. Neither stimulus-based nor response-based definitions provide a complete definition of stress. Many of the physiological reactions that occur when faced with demanding situations (e.g., accelerated heart rate) can also occur in response to things that most people would not consider to be genuinely stressful, such as receiving unanticipated good news: an unexpected promotion or raise.

A useful way to conceptualize **stress** is to view it as a process whereby an individual perceives and responds to events that he appraises as overwhelming or threatening to his well-being (Lazarus & Folkman, 1984). A critical element of this definition is that it emphasizes the importance of how we appraise—that is, judge—demanding or threatening events (often referred to as **stressors**); these appraisals, in turn, influence our reactions to such events. Two kinds of appraisals of a stressor are especially important in this regard: primary and secondary appraisals. A **primary appraisal** involves judgment about the degree of potential harm or threat to well-being that a stressor might entail. A stressor would likely be appraised as a threat if one anticipates that it could lead to some kind of harm, loss, or other negative consequence; conversely, a stressor would likely be appraised as a challenge if one believes that it carries the potential for gain or personal growth. For example, an employee who is promoted to a leadership position would likely perceive the promotion as a much greater threat if she believed the promotion would lead to excessive work demands than if she viewed it as an opportunity to gain new skills and grow professionally. Similarly, a college student on the cusp of graduation may face the change as a threat or a challenge (Figure 14.2).

Figure 14.2 Graduating from college and entering the workforce can be viewed as either a threat (loss of financial support) or a challenge (opportunity for independence and growth). (credit: Timothy Zanker)

The perception of a threat triggers a **secondary appraisal**: judgment of the options available to cope with a stressor, as well as perceptions of how effective such options will be (Lyon, 2012) (Figure 14.3). As you may recall from what you learned about self-efficacy, an individual's belief in his ability to complete a task is important (Bandura, 1994). A threat tends to be viewed as less catastrophic if one believes something can be done about it (Lazarus & Folkman, 1984). Imagine that two middle-aged people Robin and Madhuri, perform breast self-examinations one morning and each notices a lump on the lower region of their left breast. Although both view the breast lump as a potential threat (primary appraisal), their secondary appraisals differ considerably. In considering the breast lump, some of the thoughts racing through Robin's mind are, "Oh my God, I could have breast cancer! What if the cancer has spread to the rest of my body and I cannot recover? What if I have to go through chemotherapy? I've heard that experience is awful! What if I have to quit my job? My partner and I won't have enough money to pay the mortgage. Oh, this is just horrible...I can't deal with it!" On the other hand, Madhuri thinks, "Hmm, this may not be good. Although most times these things turn out to be benign, I need to have it checked out. If it turns out to be breast cancer, there are doctors who can take care of it because the medical technology today is quite advanced. I'll have a lot of different options, and I'll be just fine." Clearly, Robin and Madhuri have different outlooks on what might turn out to be a very serious situation: Robin seems to think that little could be done about it, whereas Madhuri believes that, worst case scenario, a number of options that are likely to be effective would be available. As such, Robin would clearly experience greater stress than would Madhuri.

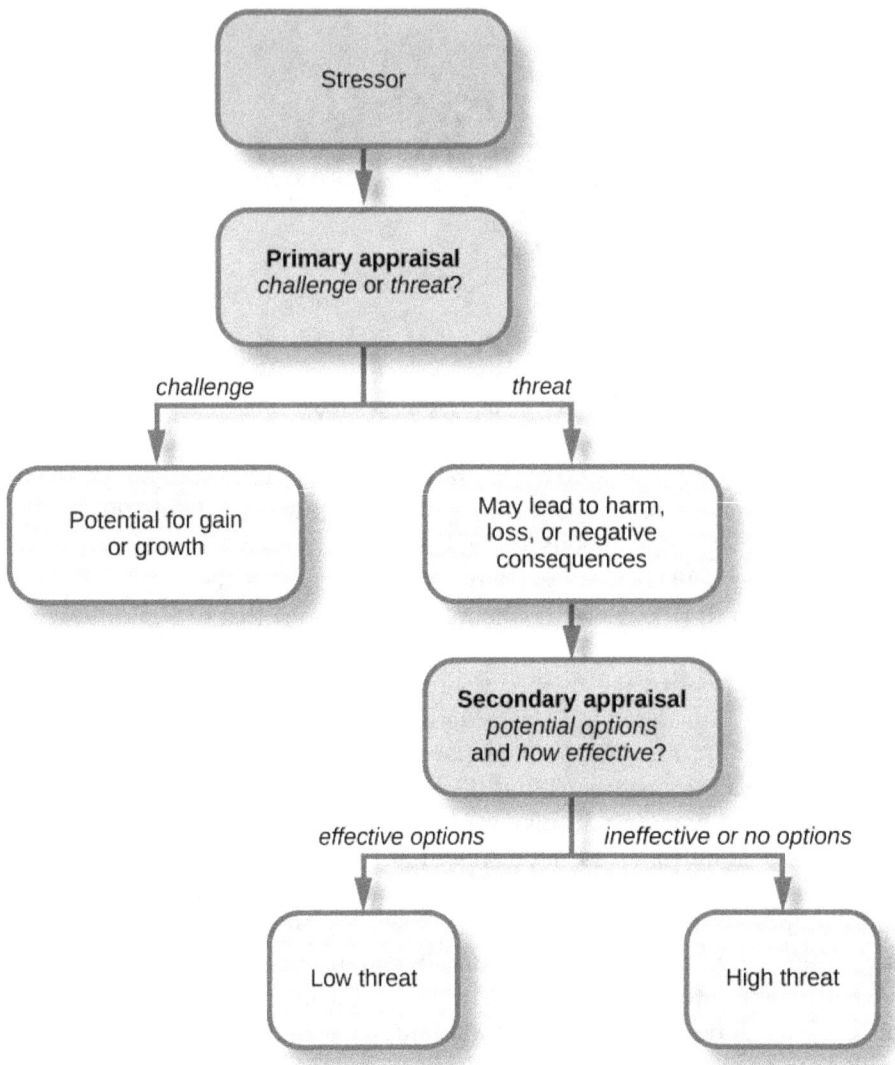

Figure 14.3 When encountering a stressor, a person judges its potential threat (primary appraisal) and then determines if effective options are available to manage the situation. Stress is likely to result if a stressor is perceived as extremely threatening or threatening with few or no effective coping options available.

To be sure, some stressors are inherently more stressful than others in that they are more threatening and leave less potential for variation in cognitive appraisals (e.g., objective threats to one's health or safety). Nevertheless, appraisal will still play a role in augmenting or diminishing our reactions to such events (Everly & Lating, 2002).

If a person appraises an event as harmful and believes that the demands imposed by the event exceed the available resources to manage or adapt to it, the person will subjectively experience a state of stress. In contrast, if one does not appraise the same event as harmful or threatening, she is unlikely to experience stress. According to this definition, environmental events trigger stress reactions by the way they are interpreted and the meanings they are assigned. In short, stress is largely in the eye of the beholder: it's not so much what happens to you as it is how you respond (Selye, 1976).

GOOD STRESS?

Although stress carries a negative connotation, at times it may be of some benefit. Stress can motivate us to do things in our best interests, such as study for exams, visit the doctor regularly, exercise, and perform to the best of our ability at work. Indeed, Selye (1974) pointed out that not all stress is harmful.

He argued that stress can sometimes be a positive, motivating force that can improve the quality of our lives. This kind of stress, which Selye called **eustress** (from the Greek *eu* = "good"), is a good kind of stress associated with positive feelings, optimal health, and performance. A moderate amount of stress can be beneficial in challenging situations. For example, athletes may be motivated and energized by pregame stress, and students may experience similar beneficial stress before a major exam. Indeed, research shows that moderate stress can enhance both immediate and delayed recall of educational material. Male participants in one study who memorized a scientific text passage showed improved memory of the passage immediately after exposure to a mild stressor as well as one day following exposure to the stressor (Hupbach & Fieman, 2012).

Increasing one's level of stress will cause performance to change in a predictable way. As shown in **Figure 14.4**, as stress increases, so do performance and general well-being (eustress); when stress levels reach an optimal level (the highest point of the curve), performance reaches its peak. A person at this stress level is colloquially at the top of his game, meaning he feels fully energized, focused, and can work with minimal effort and maximum efficiency. But when stress exceeds this optimal level, it is no longer a positive force—it becomes excessive and debilitating, or what Selye termed **distress** (from the Latin *dis* = "bad"). People who reach this level of stress feel burned out; they are fatigued, exhausted, and their performance begins to decline. If the stress remains excessive, health may begin to erode as well (Everly & Lating, 2002). A good example of distress is severe test anxiety. When students are feeling very stressed about a test, negative emotions combined with physical symptoms may make concentration difficult, thereby negatively affecting test scores.

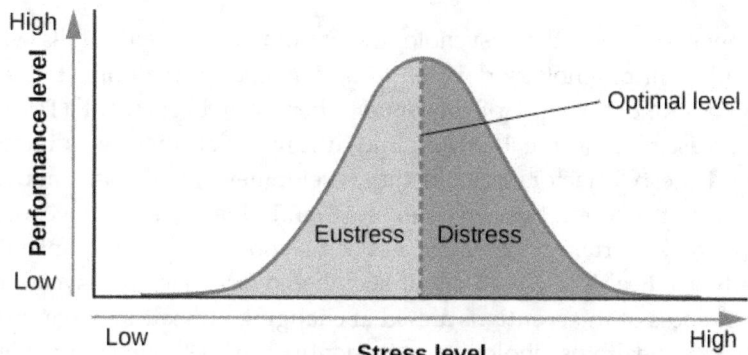

Figure 14.4 As the stress level increases from low to moderate, so does performance (eustress). At the optimal level (the peak of the curve), performance has reached its peak. If stress exceeds the optimal level, it will reach the distress region, where it will become excessive and debilitating, and performance will decline (Everly & Lating, 2002).

THE PREVALENCE OF STRESS

Stress is everywhere and, as shown in **Figure 14.5**, it has been on the rise over the last several years. Each of us is acquainted with stress—some are more familiar than others. In many ways, stress feels like a load you just can't carry—a feeling you experience when, for example, you have to drive somewhere in a blizzard, when you wake up late the morning of an important job interview, when you run out of money before the next pay period, and before taking an important exam for which you realize you are not fully prepared.

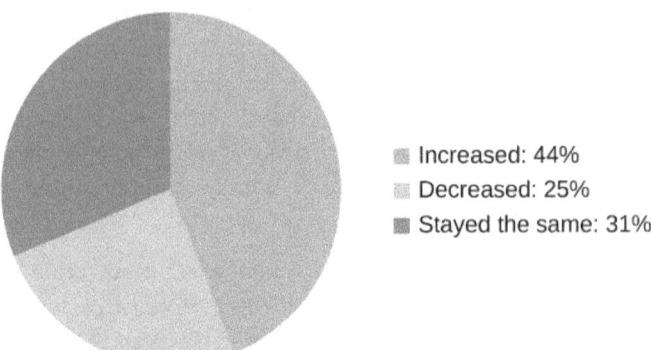

Figure 14.5 Nearly half of U.S. adults indicated that their stress levels have increased over the last five years (Neelakantan, 2013).

Stress is an experience that evokes a variety of responses, including those that are physiological (e.g., accelerated heart rate, headaches, or gastrointestinal problems), cognitive (e.g., difficulty concentrating or making decisions), and behavioral (e.g., drinking alcohol, smoking, or taking actions directed at eliminating the cause of the stress). Although stress can be positive at times, it can have deleterious health implications, contributing to the onset and progression of a variety of physical illnesses and diseases (Cohen & Herbert, 1996).

The scientific study of how stress and other psychological factors impact health falls within the realm of **health psychology**, a subfield of psychology devoted to understanding the importance of psychological influences on health, illness, and how people respond when they become ill (Taylor, 1999). Health psychology emerged as a discipline in the 1970s, a time during which there was increasing awareness of the role behavioral and lifestyle factors play in the development of illnesses and diseases (Straub, 2007). In addition to studying the connection between stress and illness, health psychologists investigate issues such as why people make certain lifestyle choices (e.g., smoking or eating unhealthy food despite knowing the potential adverse health implications of such behaviors). Health psychologists also design and investigate the effectiveness of interventions aimed at changing unhealthy behaviors. Perhaps one of the more fundamental tasks of health psychologists is to identify which groups of people are especially at risk for negative health outcomes, based on psychological or behavioral factors. For example, measuring differences in stress levels among demographic groups and how these levels change over time can help identify populations who may have an increased risk for illness or disease.

Figure 14.6 depicts the results of three national surveys in which several thousand individuals from different demographic groups completed a brief stress questionnaire; the surveys were administered in 1983, 2006, and 2009 (Cohen & Janicki-Deverts, 2012). All three surveys demonstrated higher stress in women than in men. Unemployed individuals reported high levels of stress in all three surveys, as did those with less education and income; retired persons reported the lowest stress levels. However, from 2006 to 2009 the greatest increase in stress levels occurred among men, Hispanics people aged 45–64, college graduates, and those with full-time employment. One interpretation of these findings is that concerns surrounding the 2008–2009 economic downturn (e.g., threat of or actual job loss and substantial loss of retirement savings) may have been especially stressful to college-educated employed men with limited time remaining in their working careers.

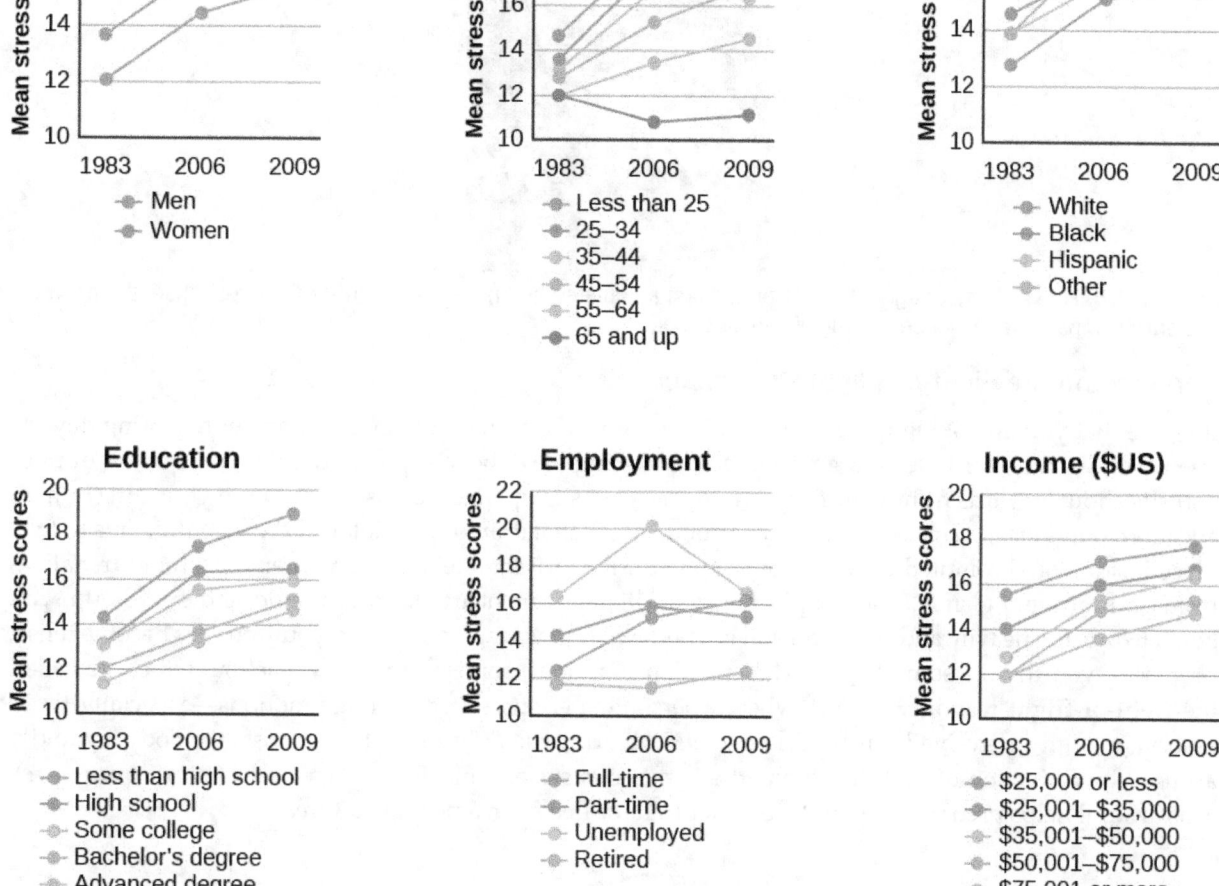

Figure 14.6 The charts above, adapted from Cohen & Janicki-Deverts (2012), depict the mean stress level scores among different demographic groups during the years 1983, 2006, and 2009. Across categories of sex, age, race, education level, employment status, and income, stress levels generally show a marked increase over this quarter-century time span.

EARLY CONTRIBUTIONS TO THE STUDY OF STRESS

As previously stated, scientific interest in stress goes back nearly a century. One of the early pioneers in the study of stress was Walter Cannon, an eminent American physiologist at Harvard Medical School (**Figure 14.7**). In the early part of the 20th century, Cannon was the first to identify the body's physiological reactions to stress.

Figure 14.7 Harvard physiologist Walter Cannon first articulated and named the fight-or-flight response, the nervous system's sympathetic response to a significant stressor.

Cannon and the Fight-or-Flight Response

Imagine that you are hiking in the beautiful mountains of Colorado on a warm and sunny spring day. At one point during your hike, a large, frightening-looking black bear appears from behind a stand of trees and sits about 50 yards from you. The bear notices you, sits up, and begins to lumber in your direction. In addition to thinking, "This is definitely not good," a constellation of physiological reactions begins to take place inside you. Prompted by a deluge of epinephrine (adrenaline) and norepinephrine (noradrenaline) from your adrenal glands, your pupils begin to dilate. Your heart starts to pound and speeds up, you begin to breathe heavily and perspire, you get butterflies in your stomach, and your muscles become tense, preparing you to take some kind of direct action. Cannon proposed that this reaction, which he called the **fight-or-flight response**, occurs when a person experiences very strong emotions—especially those associated with a perceived threat (Cannon, 1932). During the fight-or-flight response, the body is rapidly aroused by activation of both the sympathetic nervous system and the endocrine system (Figure 14.8). This arousal helps prepare the person to either fight or flee from a perceived threat.

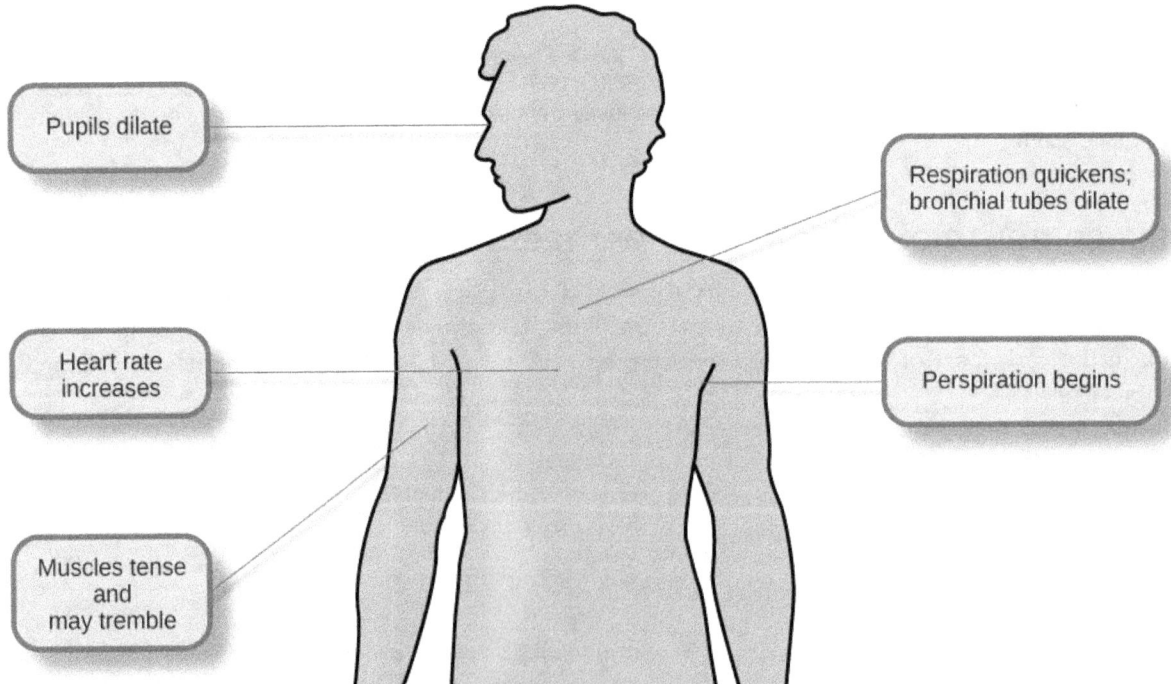

Figure 14.8 Fight or flight is a physiological response to a stressor.

According to Cannon, the fight-or-flight response is a built-in mechanism that assists in maintaining homeostasis—an internal environment in which physiological variables such as blood pressure, respiration, digestion, and temperature are stabilized at levels optimal for survival. Thus, Cannon viewed the fight-or-flight response as adaptive because it enables people to adjust internally and externally to threats in their environment, allowing them to continue to be alive and overcome the threat.

Selye and the General Adaptation Syndrome

Another important early contributor to the stress field was Hans Selye, mentioned earlier. He would eventually become one of the world's foremost experts in the study of stress (Figure 14.9). As a young assistant in the biochemistry department at McGill University in the 1930s, Selye was engaged in research involving sex hormones in rats. Although he was unable to find an answer for what he was initially researching, he incidentally discovered that when exposed to prolonged negative stimulation (stressors)—such as extreme cold, surgical injury, excessive muscular exercise, and shock—the rats showed signs of adrenal enlargement, thymus and lymph node shrinkage, and stomach ulceration. Selye realized that these responses were triggered by a coordinated series of physiological reactions that unfold over time during continued exposure to a stressor. These physiological reactions were nonspecific, which means that regardless of the type of stressor, the same pattern of reactions would occur. What Selye discovered was the **general adaptation syndrome**, the body's nonspecific physiological response to stress.

Figure 14.9 Hans Selye specialized in research about stress. In 2009, his native Hungary honored his work with this stamp, released in conjunction with the 2nd annual World Conference on Stress.

The general adaptation syndrome, shown in Figure 14.10, consists of three stages: (1) alarm reaction, (2) stage of resistance, and (3) stage of exhaustion (Selye, 1936; 1976). **Alarm reaction** describes the body's immediate reaction upon facing a threatening situation or emergency, and it is roughly analogous to the fight-or-flight response described by Cannon. During an alarm reaction, you are alerted to a stressor, and your body alarms you with a cascade of physiological reactions that provide you with the energy to manage the situation. A person who wakes up in the middle of the night to discover her house is on fire, for example, is experiencing an alarm reaction.

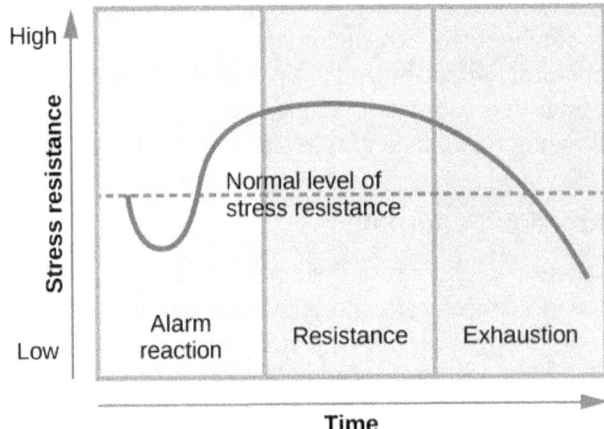

Figure 14.10 The three stages of Selye's general adaptation syndrome are shown in this graph. Prolonged stress ultimately results in exhaustion.

If exposure to a stressor is prolonged, the organism will enter the **stage of resistance**. During this stage, the initial shock of alarm reaction has worn off and the body has adapted to the stressor. Nevertheless, the body also remains on alert and is prepared to respond as it did during the alarm reaction, although with less intensity. For example, suppose a child who went missing is still missing 72 hours later. Although the parents would obviously remain extremely disturbed, the magnitude of physiological reactions would likely have diminished over the 72 intervening hours due to some adaptation to this event.

If exposure to a stressor continues over a longer period of time, the **stage of exhaustion** ensues. At this stage, the person is no longer able to adapt to the stressor: the body's ability to resist becomes depleted as physical wear takes its toll on the body's tissues and organs. As a result, illness, disease, and other permanent damage to the body—even death—may occur. If a missing child still remained missing after three months, the long-term stress associated with this situation may cause a parent to literally faint with exhaustion at some point or even to develop a serious and irreversible illness.

In short, Selye's general adaptation syndrome suggests that stressors tax the body via a three-phase process—an initial jolt, subsequent readjustment, and a later depletion of all physical resources—that ultimately lays the groundwork for serious health problems and even death. It should be pointed out, however, that this model is a response-based conceptualization of stress, focusing exclusively on the body's physical responses while largely ignoring psychological factors such as appraisal and interpretation of threats. Nevertheless, Selye's model has had an enormous impact on the field of stress because it offers a general explanation for how stress can lead to physical damage and, thus, disease. As we shall discuss later, prolonged or repeated stress has been implicated in development of a number of disorders such as hypertension and coronary artery disease.

THE PHYSIOLOGICAL BASIS OF STRESS

What goes on inside our bodies when we experience stress? The physiological mechanisms of stress are extremely complex, but they generally involve the work of two systems—the sympathetic nervous system and the **hypothalamic-pituitary-adrenal (HPA) axis**. When a person first perceives something as stressful (Selye's alarm reaction), the sympathetic nervous system triggers arousal via the release of adrenaline from the adrenal glands. Release of these hormones activates the fight-or-flight responses to stress, such as accelerated heart rate and respiration. At the same time, the HPA axis, which is primarily endocrine in nature, becomes especially active, although it works much more slowly than the sympathetic nervous system. In response to stress, the hypothalamus (one of the limbic structures in the brain) releases corticotrophin-releasing factor, a hormone that causes the pituitary gland to release adrenocorticotropic hormone (ACTH) (**Figure 14.11**). The ACTH then activates the adrenal glands to secrete a number of hormones into the bloodstream; an important one is cortisol, which can affect virtually every organ within the body. **Cortisol** is commonly known as a stress hormone and helps provide that boost of energy when we first encounter a stressor, preparing us to run away or fight. However, sustained elevated levels of cortisol weaken the immune system.

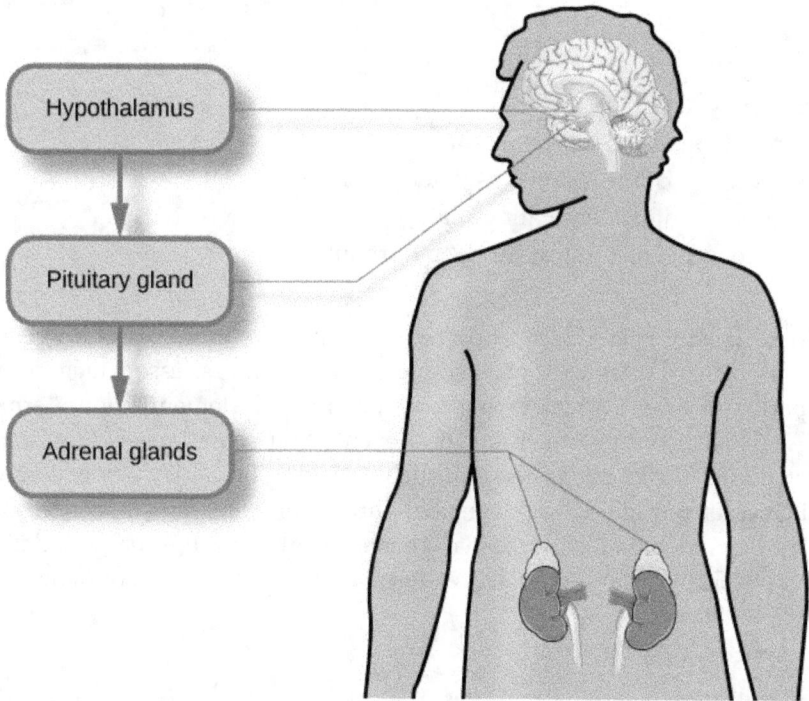

Figure 14.11 This diagram shows the functioning of the hypothalamic-pituitary-adrenal (HPA) axis. The hypothalamus activates the pituitary gland, which in turn activates the adrenal glands, increasing their secretion of cortisol.

In short bursts, this process can have some favorable effects, such as providing extra energy, improving immune system functioning temporarily, and decreasing pain sensitivity. However, extended release of cortisol—as would happen with prolonged or chronic stress—often comes at a high price. High levels of cortisol have been shown to produce a number of harmful effects. For example, increases in cortisol can significantly weaken our immune system (Glaser & Kiecolt-Glaser, 2005), and high levels are frequently observed among depressed individuals (Geoffroy, Hertzman, Li, & Power, 2013). In summary, a stressful event causes a variety of physiological reactions that activate the adrenal glands, which in turn release epinephrine, norepinephrine, and cortisol. These hormones affect a number of bodily processes in ways that prepare the stressed person to take direct action, but also in ways that may heighten the potential for illness.

When stress is extreme or chronic, it can have profoundly negative consequences. For example, stress often contributes to the development of certain psychological disorders, including post-traumatic stress disorder, major depressive disorder, and other serious psychiatric conditions. Additionally, we noted earlier that stress is linked to the development and progression of a variety of physical illnesses and diseases. For example, researchers in one study found that people injured during the September 11, 2001, World Trade Center disaster or who developed post-traumatic stress symptoms afterward later suffered significantly elevated rates of heart disease (Jordan, Miller-Archie, Cone, Morabia, & Stellman, 2011). Another investigation yielded that self-reported stress symptoms among aging and retired Finnish food industry workers were associated with morbidity 11 years later. This study also predicted the onset of musculoskeletal, nervous system, and endocrine and metabolic disorders (Salonen, Arola, Nygård, & Huhtala, 2008). Another study reported that male South Korean manufacturing employees who reported high levels of work-related stress were more likely to catch the common cold over the next several months than were those employees who reported lower work-related stress levels (Park et al., 2011). Later, you will explore the mechanisms through which stress can produce physical illness and disease.

14.2 Stressors

Learning Objectives

By the end of this section, you will be able to:
- Describe different types of possible stressors
- Explain the importance of life changes as potential stressors
- Describe the Social Readjustment Rating Scale
- Understand the concepts of job strain and job burnout

For an individual to experience stress, he must first encounter a potential stressor. In general, stressors can be placed into one of two broad categories: chronic and acute. Chronic stressors include events that persist over an extended period of time, such as caring for a parent with dementia, long-term unemployment, or imprisonment. Acute stressors involve brief focal events that sometimes continue to be experienced as overwhelming well after the event has ended, such as falling on an icy sidewalk and breaking your leg (Cohen, Janicki-Deverts, & Miller, 2007). Whether chronic or acute, potential stressors come in many shapes and sizes. They can include major traumatic events, significant life changes, daily hassles, as well as other situations in which a person is regularly exposed to threat, challenge, or danger.

TRAUMATIC EVENTS

Some stressors involve traumatic events or situations in which a person is exposed to actual or threatened death or serious injury. Stressors in this category include exposure to military combat, threatened or actual physical assaults (e.g., physical attacks, sexual assault, robbery, childhood abuse), terrorist attacks, natural disasters (e.g., earthquakes, floods, hurricanes), and automobile accidents. Men, non-Whites, and individuals in lower socioeconomic status (SES) groups report experiencing a greater number of traumatic events than do women, Whites, and individuals in higher SES groups (Hatch & Dohrenwend, 2007). Some individuals who are exposed to stressors of extreme magnitude develop post-traumatic stress disorder (PTSD): a chronic stress reaction characterized by experiences and behaviors that may include intrusive and painful memories of the stressor event, jumpiness, persistent negative emotional states, detachment from others, angry outbursts, and avoidance of reminders of the event (American Psychiatric Association [APA], 2013).

LIFE CHANGES

Most stressors that we encounter are not nearly as intense as the ones described above. Many potential stressors we face involve events or situations that require us to make changes in our ongoing lives and require time as we adjust to those changes. Examples include death of a close family member, marriage, divorce, and moving (Figure 14.12).

Figure 14.12 Some fairly typical life events, such as moving, can be significant stressors. Even when the move is intentional and positive, the amount of resulting change in daily life can cause stress. (credit: "Jellaluna"/Flickr)

In the 1960s, psychiatrists Thomas Holmes and Richard Rahe wanted to examine the link between life stressors and physical illness, based on the hypothesis that life events requiring significant changes in a person's normal life routines are stressful, whether these events are desirable or undesirable. They developed the **Social Readjustment Rating Scale (SRRS)**, consisting of 43 life events that require varying degrees of personal readjustment (Holmes & Rahe, 1967). Many life events that most people would consider pleasant (e.g., holidays, retirement, marriage) are among those listed on the SRRS; these are examples of eustress. Holmes and Rahe also proposed that life events can add up over time, and that experiencing a cluster of stressful events increases one's risk of developing physical illnesses.

In developing their scale, Holmes and Rahe asked 394 participants to provide a numerical estimate for each of the 43 items; each estimate corresponded to how much readjustment participants felt each event would require. These estimates resulted in mean value scores for each event—often called life change units (LCUs) (Rahe, McKeen, & Arthur, 1967). The numerical scores ranged from 11 to 100, representing the perceived magnitude of life change each event entails. Death of a spouse ranked highest on the scale with 100 LCUs, and divorce ranked second highest with 73 LCUs. In addition, personal injury or illness, marriage, and job termination also ranked highly on the scale with 53, 50, and 47 LCUs, respectively. Conversely, change in residence (20 LCUs), change in eating habits (15 LCUs), and vacation (13 LCUs) ranked low on the scale (Table 14.1). Minor violations of the law ranked the lowest with 11 LCUs. To complete the scale, participants checked yes for events experienced within the last 12 months. LCUs for each checked item are totaled for a score quantifying the amount of life change. Agreement on the amount of adjustment required by the various life events on the SRRS is highly consistent, even cross-culturally (Holmes & Masuda, 1974).

Some Stressors on the Social Readjustment Rating Scale (Holmes & Rahe, 1967)

Life event	Life change units
Death of a close family member	63
Personal injury or illness	53
Dismissal from work	47
Change in financial state	38
Change to different line of work	36

Some Stressors on the Social Readjustment Rating Scale (Holmes & Rahe, 1967)

Life event	Life change units
Outstanding personal achievement	28
Beginning or ending school	26
Change in living conditions	25
Change in working hours or conditions	20
Change in residence	20
Change in schools	20
Change in social activities	18
Change in sleeping habits	16
Change in eating habits	15
Minor violation of the law	11

Table 14.1

Extensive research has demonstrated that accumulating a high number of life change units within a brief period of time (one or two years) is related to a wide range of physical illnesses (even accidents and athletic injuries) and mental health problems (Monat & Lazarus, 1991; Scully, Tosi, & Banning, 2000). In an early demonstration, researchers obtained LCU scores for U.S. and Norwegian Navy personnel who were about to embark on a six-month voyage. A later examination of medical records revealed positive (but small) correlations between LCU scores prior to the voyage and subsequent illness symptoms during the ensuing six-month journey (Rahe, 1974). In addition, people tend to experience more physical symptoms, such as backache, upset stomach, diarrhea, and acne, on specific days in which self-reported LCU values are considerably higher than normal, such as the day of a family member's wedding (Holmes & Holmes, 1970).

The Social Readjustment Rating Scale (SRRS) provides researchers a simple, easy-to-administer way of assessing the amount of stress in people's lives, and it has been used in hundreds of studies (Thoits, 2010). Despite its widespread use, the scale has been subject to criticism. First, many of the items on the SRRS are vague; for example, death of a close friend could involve the death of a long-absent childhood friend that requires little social readjustment (Dohrenwend, 2006). In addition, some have challenged its assumption that undesirable life events are no more stressful than desirable ones (Derogatis & Coons, 1993). However, most of the available evidence suggests that, at least as far as mental health is concerned, undesirable or negative events are more strongly associated with poor outcomes (such as depression) than are desirable, positive events (Hatch & Dohrenwend, 2007). Perhaps the most serious criticism is that the scale does not take into consideration respondents' appraisals of the life events it contains. As you recall, appraisal of a stressor is a key element in the conceptualization and overall experience of stress. Being fired from work may be devastating to some but a welcome opportunity to obtain a better job for others. The SRRS remains one of the most well-known instruments in the study of stress, and it is a useful tool for identifying potential stress-related health outcomes (Scully et al., 2000).

LINK TO LEARNING

Go to this **site and complete the SRRS scale (http://openstax.org/l/SRRS)** to determine the total number of LCUs you have experienced over the last year.

CONNECT THE CONCEPTS

Correlational Research

The Holmes and Rahe Social Readjustment Rating Scale (SRRS) uses the correlational research method to identify the connection between stress and health. That is, respondents' LCU scores are correlated with the number or frequency of self-reported symptoms indicating health problems. These correlations are typically positive—as LCU scores increase, the number of symptoms increase. Consider all the thousands of studies that have used this scale to correlate stress and illness symptoms: If you were to assign an average correlation coefficient to this body of research, what would be your best guess? How strong do you think the correlation coefficient would be? Why can't the SRRS show a causal relationship between stress and illness? If it were possible to show causation, do you think stress causes illness or illness causes stress?

HASSLES

Potential stressors do not always involve major life events. **Daily hassles**—the minor irritations and annoyances that are part of our everyday lives (e.g., rush hour traffic, lost keys, obnoxious coworkers, inclement weather, arguments with friends or family)—can build on one another and leave us just as stressed as life change events (**Figure 14.13**) (Kanner, Coyne, Schaefer, & Lazarus, 1981).

(a) (b)

Figure 14.13 Daily commutes, whether (a) on the road or (b) via public transportation, can be hassles that contribute to our feelings of everyday stress. (credit a: modification of work by Jeff Turner; credit b: modification of work by "epSos.de"/Flickr)

Researchers have demonstrated that the frequency of daily hassles is actually a better predictor of both physical and psychological health than are life change units. In a well-known study of San Francisco residents, the frequency of daily hassles was found to be more strongly associated with physical health problems than were life change events (DeLongis, Coyne, Dakof, Folkman, & Lazarus, 1982). In addition, daily minor hassles, especially interpersonal conflicts, often lead to negative and distressed mood states (Bolger, DeLongis, Kessler, & Schilling, 1989). Cyber hassles that occur on social media may represent a modern and evolving source of stress. In one investigation, social media stress was tied to loss of sleep in adolescents, presumably because ruminating about social media caused a physiological stress response that increased arousal (van der Schuur, Baumgartner, & Sumter, 2018). Clearly, daily hassles can add up and take a toll on us both emotionally and physically.

OCCUPATION-RELATED STRESSORS

Stressors can include situations in which one is frequently exposed to challenging and unpleasant events, such as difficult, demanding, or unsafe working conditions. Although most jobs and occupations can at times be demanding, some are clearly more stressful than others (Figure 14.14). For example, most people would likely agree that a firefighter's work is inherently more stressful than that of a florist. Equally likely, most would agree that jobs containing various unpleasant elements, such as those requiring exposure to loud noise (heavy equipment operator), constant harassment and threats of physical violence (prison guard), perpetual frustration (bus driver in a major city), or those mandating that an employee work alternating day and night shifts (hotel desk clerk), are much more demanding—and thus, more stressful—than those that do not contain such elements. Table 14.2 lists several occupations and some of the specific stressors associated with those occupations (Sulsky & Smith, 2005).

(a) (b)

Figure 14.14 (a) Police officers and (b) firefighters hold high stress occupations. (credit a: modification of work by Australian Civil-Military Centre; credit b: modification of work by Andrew Magill)

Occupations and Their Related Stressors

Occupation	Stressors Specific to Occupation
Police officer	physical dangers, excessive paperwork, dealing with court system, tense interactions, life-and-death decision making
Firefighter	uncertainty over whether a serious fire or hazard awaits after an alarm, potential for extreme physical danger
Social worker	little positive feedback from jobs or from the public, unsafe work environments, frustration in dealing with bureaucracy, excessive paperwork, sense of personal responsibility for clients, work overload
Teacher	Excessive paperwork, lack of adequate supplies or facilities, work overload, lack of positive feedback, threat of physical violence, lack of support from parents and administrators
Nurse	Work overload, heavy physical work, patient concerns (dealing with death and medical concerns), interpersonal problems with other medical staff (especially physicians)
Emergency medical worker	Unpredictable and extreme nature of the job, inexperience

Occupations and Their Related Stressors

Occupation	Stressors Specific to Occupation
Clerical and secretarial work	Few opportunities for advancement, unsupportive supervisors, work overload, lack of perceived control
Managerial work	Work overload, conflict and ambiguity in defining the managerial role, difficult work relationships

Table 14.2

Although the specific stressors for these occupations are diverse, they seem to share some common denominators such as heavy workload and uncertainty about and lack of control over certain aspects of a job. Chronic occupational stress contributes to **job strain**, a work situation that combines excessive job demands and workload with little discretion in decision making or job control (Karasek & Theorell, 1990). Clearly, many occupations other than the ones listed in Table 14.2 involve at least a moderate amount of job strain in that they often involve heavy workloads and little job control (e.g., inability to decide when to take breaks). Such jobs are often low-status and include those of factory workers, postal clerks, supermarket cashiers, taxi drivers, and short-order cooks. Job strain can have adverse consequences on both physical and mental health; it has been shown to be associated with increased risk of hypertension (Schnall & Landsbergis, 1994), heart attacks (Theorell et al., 1998), recurrence of heart disease after a first heart attack (Aboa-Éboulé et al., 2007), significant weight loss or gain (Kivimäki et al., 2006), and major depressive disorder (Stansfeld, Shipley, Head, & Fuhrer, 2012). A longitudinal study of over 10,000 British civil servants reported that workers under 50 years old who earlier had reported high job strain were 68% more likely to later develop heart disease than were those workers under 50 years old who reported little job strain (Chandola et al., 2008).

Some people who are exposed to chronically stressful work conditions can experience **job burnout**, which is a general sense of emotional exhaustion and cynicism in relation to one's job (Maslach & Jackson, 1981). Job burnout occurs frequently among those in human service jobs (e.g., social workers, teachers, therapists, and police officers). Job burnout consists of three dimensions. The first dimension is exhaustion—a sense that one's emotional resources are drained or that one is at the end of her rope and has nothing more to give at a psychological level. Second, job burnout is characterized by depersonalization: a sense of emotional detachment between the worker and the recipients of his services, often resulting in callous, cynical, or indifferent attitudes toward these individuals. Third, job burnout is characterized by diminished personal accomplishment, which is the tendency to evaluate one's work negatively by, for example, experiencing dissatisfaction with one's job-related accomplishments or feeling as though one has categorically failed to influence others' lives through one's work.

Job strain appears to be one of the greatest risk factors leading to job burnout, which is most commonly observed in workers who are older (ages 55–64), unmarried, and whose jobs involve manual labor. Heavy alcohol consumption, physical inactivity, being overweight, and having a physical or lifetime mental disorder are also associated with job burnout (Ahola, et al., 2006). In addition, depression often co-occurs with job burnout. One large-scale study of over 3,000 Finnish employees reported that half of the participants with severe job burnout had some form of depressive disorder (Ahola et al., 2005). Job burnout is often precipitated by feelings of having invested considerable energy, effort, and time into one's work while receiving little in return (e.g., little respect or support from others or low pay) (Tatris, Peeters, Le Blanc, Schreurs, & Schaufeli, 2001).

As an illustration, consider Tyre, a nursing assistant who worked in a nursing home. Tyre worked long hours for little pay in a difficult facility. Tyre's supervisor was domineering, unpleasant, and unsupportive, as well as disrespectful of Tyre's personal time, frequently informing them at the last minute they must work several additional hours after their shift ended or report to work on weekends. Tyre had very little autonomy at work. They had little input in day-to-day duties and how to perform them, and was not permitted to take breaks unless explicitly told by their supervisor. Tyre did not feel as though their hard work was appreciated, either by supervisory staff or by the residents of the home. Tyre was very unhappy over the low pay, and felt that many of the residents treated them disrespectfully.

After several years, Tyre began to hate their job. Tyre dreaded going to work in the morning, and gradually developed a callous, hostile attitude toward many of the residents. Eventually, they began to feel they could no longer help the nursing home residents. Tyre's absenteeism from work increased, and one day they decided that they had had enough and quit. Tyre now has a job in sales, vowing never to work in nursing again.

LINK TO LEARNING

Watch this **clip from the 1999 comedy Office Space for a humorous illustration of lack of supervisory support (http://openstax.org/l/officespace)** in which a sympathetic character's insufferable boss makes a last-minute demand that he "go ahead and come in" to the office on both Saturday and Sunday.

Finally, our close relationships with friends and family—particularly the negative aspects of these relationships—can be a potent source of stress. Negative aspects of close relationships can include conflicts such as disagreements or arguments, lack of emotional support or confiding, and lack of reciprocity. All of these can be overwhelming, threatening to the relationship, and thus stressful. Such stressors can take a toll both emotionally and physically. A longitudinal investigation of over 9,000 British civil servants found that those who at one point had reported the highest levels of negative interactions in their closest relationship were 34% more likely to experience serious heart problems (fatal or nonfatal heart attacks) over a 13–15 year period, compared to those who experienced the lowest levels of negative interaction (De Vogli, Chandola & Marmot, 2007).

14.3 Stress and Illness

Learning Objectives

By the end of this section, you will be able to:
- Explain the nature of psychophysiological disorders
- Describe the immune system and how stress impacts its functioning
- Describe how stress and emotional factors can lead to the development and exacerbation of cardiovascular disorders, asthma, and tension headaches

In this section, we will discuss stress and illness. As stress researcher Robert Sapolsky (1998) describes,

> stress-related disease emerges, predominantly, out of the fact that we so often activate a physiological system that has evolved for responding to acute physical emergencies, but we turn it on for months on end, worrying about mortgages, relationships, and promotions. (p. 6)

The stress response, as noted earlier, consists of a coordinated but complex system of physiological reactions that are called upon as needed. These reactions are beneficial at times because they prepare us to deal with potentially dangerous or threatening situations (for example, recall our old friend, the fearsome bear on the trail). However, health is affected when physiological reactions are sustained, as can happen in response to ongoing stress.

PSYCHOPHYSIOLOGICAL DISORDERS

If the reactions that compose the stress response are chronic or if they frequently exceed normal ranges, they can lead to cumulative wear and tear on the body, in much the same way that running your air conditioner on full blast all summer will eventually cause wear and tear on it. For example, the high blood pressure that a person under considerable job strain experiences might eventually take a toll on his heart and set the stage for a heart attack or heart failure. Also, someone exposed to high levels of the stress hormone cortisol might become vulnerable to infection or disease because of weakened immune system functioning (McEwen, 1998).

LINK TO LEARNING

Neuroscientists Robert Sapolsky and Carol Shively have conducted extensive research on stress in non-human primates for over 30 years. Both have shown that position in the social hierarchy predicts stress, mental health status, and disease. Their research sheds light on how stress may lead to negative health outcomes for stigmatized or ostracized people. Here are two videos featuring Dr. Sapolsky: one is regarding killer stress (http://openstax.org/l/sapolsky1) and the other is an excellent in-depth documentary (http://openstax.org/l/sapolsky2) from *National Geographic*.

Physical disorders or diseases whose symptoms are brought about or worsened by stress and emotional factors are called **psychophysiological disorders**. The physical symptoms of psychophysiological disorders are real and they can be produced or exacerbated by psychological factors (hence the *psycho* and *physiological* in psychophysiological). A list of frequently encountered psychophysiological disorders is provided in Table 14.3.

Types of Psychophysiological Disorders (adapted from Everly & Lating, 2002)

Type of Psychophysiological Disorder	Examples
Cardiovascular	hypertension, coronary heart disease
Gastrointestinal	irritable bowel syndrome
Respiratory	asthma, allergy
Musculoskeletal	low back pain, tension headaches
Skin	acne, eczema, psoriasis

Table 14.3

Friedman and Booth-Kewley (1987) statistically reviewed 101 studies to examine the link between personality and illness. They proposed the existence of disease-prone personality characteristics, including depression, anger/hostility, and anxiety. Indeed, a study of over 61,000 Norwegians identified depression as a risk factor for all major disease-related causes of death (Mykletun et al., 2007). In addition, neuroticism—a personality trait that reflects how anxious, moody, and sad one is—has been identified as a risk factor for chronic health problems and mortality (Ploubidis & Grundy, 2009).

Below, we discuss two kinds of psychophysiological disorders about which a great deal is known: cardiovascular disorders and asthma. First, however, it is necessary to turn our attention to a discussion of the immune system—one of the major pathways through which stress and emotional factors can lead to illness and disease.

> **EVERYDAY CONNECTION**
>
> **Social Status, Stress, and Health Care**
>
> Psychologists have long been aware that social status (e.g., wealth, privilege) is intimately tied to stress, health, and well-being. Some factors that contribute to high stress and poor health among people with lower social status include lack of control and predictability (e.g., greater unemployment) and resource inequality (e.g., less access to health care and other community resources) (Marmot & Sapolsky, 2014).
>
> In the United States, resource inequalities tied to social status often create race and gender differences in health care. For example, African American women have the highest rates of emergency room visits and unmet health care needs compared to any other group, and this disparity increased significantly from 2006 to 2014 (Manuel, 2018). Lesbian, gay, bisexual, and transgender youth often experience poor quality of care as a result of stigma, lack of understanding, and insensitivity among health care professionals (Hafeez, Zeshan, Tahir, Jahan, & Naveed, 2017). One goal of the U.S. government's Healthy People 2020 initiative is to eliminate gender and race disparities in health care. Their interactive dataset provides an updated snapshot of health disparities: https://www.healthypeople.gov/2020/data-search/health-disparities-data.

STRESS AND THE IMMUNE SYSTEM

In a sense, the **immune system** is the body's surveillance system. It consists of a variety of structures, cells, and mechanisms that serve to protect the body from invading microorganisms that can harm or damage the body's tissues and organs. When the immune system is working as it should, it keeps us healthy and disease free by eliminating harmful bacteria, viruses, and other foreign substances that have entered the body (Everly & Lating, 2002).

Immune System Errors

Sometimes, the immune system will function erroneously. For example, sometimes it can go awry by mistaking your body's own healthy cells for invaders and repeatedly attacking them. When this happens, the person is said to have an autoimmune disease, which can affect almost any part of the body. How an autoimmune disease affects a person depends on what part of the body is targeted. For instance, rheumatoid arthritis, an autoimmune disease that affects the joints, results in joint pain, stiffness, and loss of function. Systemic lupus erythematosus, an autoimmune disease that affects the skin, can result in rashes and swelling of the skin. Grave's disease, an autoimmune disease that affects the thyroid gland, can result in fatigue, weight gain, and muscle aches (National Institute of Arthritis and Musculoskeletal and Skin Diseases [NIAMS], 2012).

In addition, the immune system may sometimes break down and be unable to do its job. This situation is referred to as **immunosuppression**, the decreased effectiveness of the immune system. When people experience immunosuppression, they become susceptible to any number of infections, illness, and diseases. For example, acquired immune deficiency syndrome (AIDS) is a serious and lethal disease that is caused by human immunodeficiency virus (HIV), which greatly weakens the immune system by infecting and destroying antibody-producing cells, thus rendering an untreated person vulnerable to any of a number of opportunistic infections (Powell, 1996).

Stressors and Immune Function

The question of whether stress and negative emotional states can influence immune function has captivated researchers for over three decades, and discoveries made over that time have dramatically changed the face of health psychology (Kiecolt-Glaser, 2009). **Psychoneuroimmunology** is the field that studies how psychological factors such as stress influence the immune system and immune functioning. The term psychoneuroimmunology was first coined in 1981, when it appeared as the title of a book that reviewed available evidence for associations between the brain, endocrine system, and immune system (Zacharie, 2009). To a large extent, this field evolved from the discovery that there is a connection between the central nervous system and the immune system.

Some of the most compelling evidence for a connection between the brain and the immune system comes from studies in which researchers demonstrated that immune responses in animals could be classically conditioned (Everly & Lating, 2002). For example, Ader and Cohen (1975) paired flavored water (the conditioned stimulus) with the presentation of an immunosuppressive drug (the unconditioned stimulus), causing sickness (an unconditioned response). Not surprisingly, rats exposed to this pairing developed a conditioned aversion to the flavored water. However, the taste of the water itself later produced immunosuppression (a conditioned response), indicating that the immune system itself had been conditioned. Many subsequent studies over the years have further demonstrated that immune responses can be classically conditioned in both animals and humans (Ader & Cohen, 2001). Thus, if classical conditioning can alter immunity, other psychological factors should be capable of altering it as well.

Hundreds of studies involving tens of thousands of participants have tested many kinds of brief and chronic stressors and their effects on the immune system (e.g., public speaking, medical school examinations, unemployment, marital discord, divorce, death of spouse, burnout and job strain, caring for a relative with Alzheimer's disease, and exposure to the harsh climate of Antarctica). It has been repeatedly demonstrated that many kinds of stressors are associated with poor or weakened immune functioning (Glaser & Kiecolt-Glaser, 2005; Kiecolt-Glaser, McGuire, Robles, & Glaser, 2002; Segerstrom & Miller, 2004).

When evaluating these findings, it is important to remember that there is a tangible physiological connection between the brain and the immune system. For example, the sympathetic nervous system innervates immune organs such as the thymus, bone marrow, spleen, and even lymph nodes (Maier, Watkins, & Fleshner, 1994). Also, we noted earlier that stress hormones released during hypothalamic-pituitary-adrenal (HPA) axis activation can adversely impact immune function. One way they do this is by inhibiting the production of **lymphocytes**, white blood cells that circulate in the body's fluids that are important in the immune response (Everly & Lating, 2002).

Some of the more dramatic examples demonstrating the link between stress and impaired immune function involve studies in which volunteers were exposed to viruses. The rationale behind this research is that because stress weakens the immune system, people with high stress levels should be more likely to develop an illness compared to those under little stress. In one memorable experiment using this method, researchers interviewed 276 healthy volunteers about recent stressful experiences (Cohen et al., 1998). Following the interview, these participants were given nasal drops containing the cold virus (in case you are wondering why anybody would ever want to participate in a study in which they are subjected to such treatment, the participants were paid $800 for their trouble). When examined later, participants who reported experiencing chronic stressors for more than one month—especially enduring difficulties involving work or relationships—were considerably more likely to have developed colds than were participants who reported no chronic stressors (Figure 14.15).

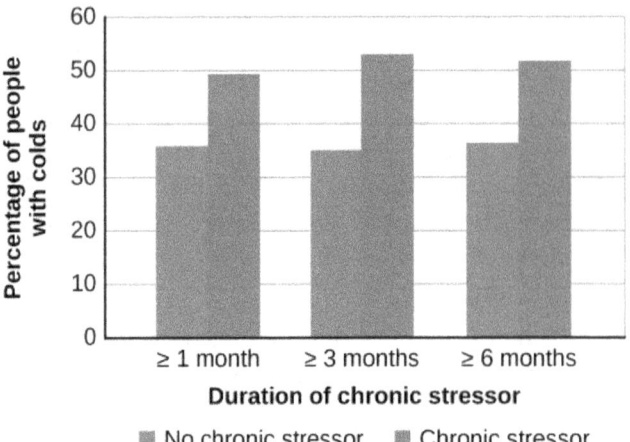

Figure 14.15 This graph shows the percentages of participants who developed colds (after receiving the cold virus) after reporting having experienced chronic stressors lasting at least one month, three months, and six months (adapted from Cohen et al., 1998).

In another study, older volunteers were given an influenza virus vaccination. Compared to controls, those who were caring for a spouse with Alzheimer's disease (and thus were under chronic stress) showed poorer antibody response following the vaccination (Kiecolt-Glaser, Glaser, Gravenstein, Malarkey, & Sheridan, 1996).

Other studies have demonstrated that stress slows down wound healing by impairing immune responses important to wound repair (Glaser & Kiecolt-Glaser, 2005). In one study, for example, skin blisters were induced on the forearm. Subjects who reported higher levels of stress produced lower levels of immune proteins necessary for wound healing (Glaser et al., 1999). Stress, then, is not so much the sword that kills the knight, so to speak; rather, it's the sword that breaks the knight's shield, and your immune system is that shield.

DIG DEEPER

Stress and Aging: A Tale of Telomeres

Have you ever wondered why people who are stressed often seem to have a haggard look about them? A pioneering study from 2004 suggests that the reason is because stress can actually accelerate the cell biology of aging.

Stress, it seems, can shorten telomeres, which are segments of DNA that protect the ends of chromosomes. Shortened telomeres can inhibit or block cell division, which includes growth and proliferation of new cells, thereby leading to more rapid aging (Sapolsky, 2004). In the study, researchers compared telomere lengths in the white blood cells in mothers of chronically ill children to those of mothers of healthy children (Epel et al., 2004). Mothers of chronically ill children would be expected to experience more stress than would mothers of healthy children. The longer a mother had spent caring for her ill child, the shorter her telomeres (the correlation between years of caregiving and telomere length was $r = -.40$). In addition, higher levels of perceived stress were negatively correlated with telomere size ($r = -.31$). These researchers also found that the average telomere length of the most stressed mothers, compared to the least stressed, was similar to what you would find in people who were 9–17 years older than they were on average.

Numerous other studies since have continued to find associations between stress and eroded telomeres (Blackburn & Epel, 2012). Some studies have even demonstrated that stress can begin to erode telomeres in childhood and perhaps even before children are born. For example, childhood exposure to violence (e.g., maternal domestic violence, bullying victimization, and physical maltreatment) was found in one study to accelerate telomere erosion from ages 5 to 10 (Shalev et al., 2013). Another study reported that young adults whose mothers had experienced severe stress during their pregnancy had shorter telomeres than did those whose mothers had stress-free and uneventful pregnancies (Entringer et al., 2011). Further, the corrosive effects of childhood stress on telomeres can extend into young adulthood. In an investigation of over 4,000 U.K. women ages 41–80, adverse experiences during childhood (e.g., physical abuse, being sent away from home, and parent divorce) were associated with shortened telomere length (Surtees et al., 2010), and telomere size decreased as the amount of experienced adversity increased (Figure 14.16).

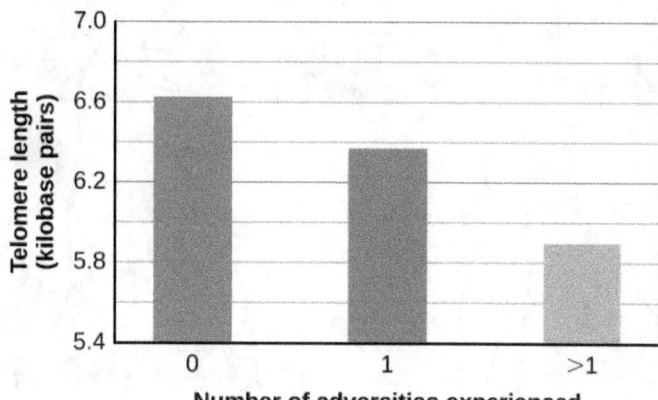

Figure 14.16 Telomeres are shorter in adults who experienced more trauma as children (adapted from Blackburn & Epel, 2012).

Efforts to dissect the precise cellular and physiological mechanisms linking short telomeres to stress and disease are currently underway. For the time being, telomeres provide us with yet another reminder that stress, especially during early life, can be just as harmful to our health as smoking or fast food (Blackburn & Epel, 2012).

CARDIOVASCULAR DISORDERS

The cardiovascular system is composed of the heart and blood circulation system. For many years, disorders that involve the cardiovascular system—known as **cardiovascular disorders**—have been a major focal point in the study of psychophysiological disorders because of the cardiovascular system's centrality in the stress response (Everly & Lating, 2002). **Heart disease** is one such condition. Each year, heart disease causes approximately one in three deaths in the United States, and it is the leading cause of death in the developed world (Centers for Disease Control and Prevention [CDC], 2011; Shapiro, 2005).

The symptoms of heart disease vary somewhat depending on the specific kind of heart disease one has, but they generally involve angina—chest pains or discomfort that occur when the heart does not receive enough blood (Office on Women's Health, 2009). The pain often feels like the chest is being pressed or squeezed; burning sensations in the chest and shortness of breath are also commonly reported. Such pain and discomfort can spread to the arms, neck, jaws, stomach (as nausea), and back (American Heart Association [AHA], 2012a) (Figure 14.17).

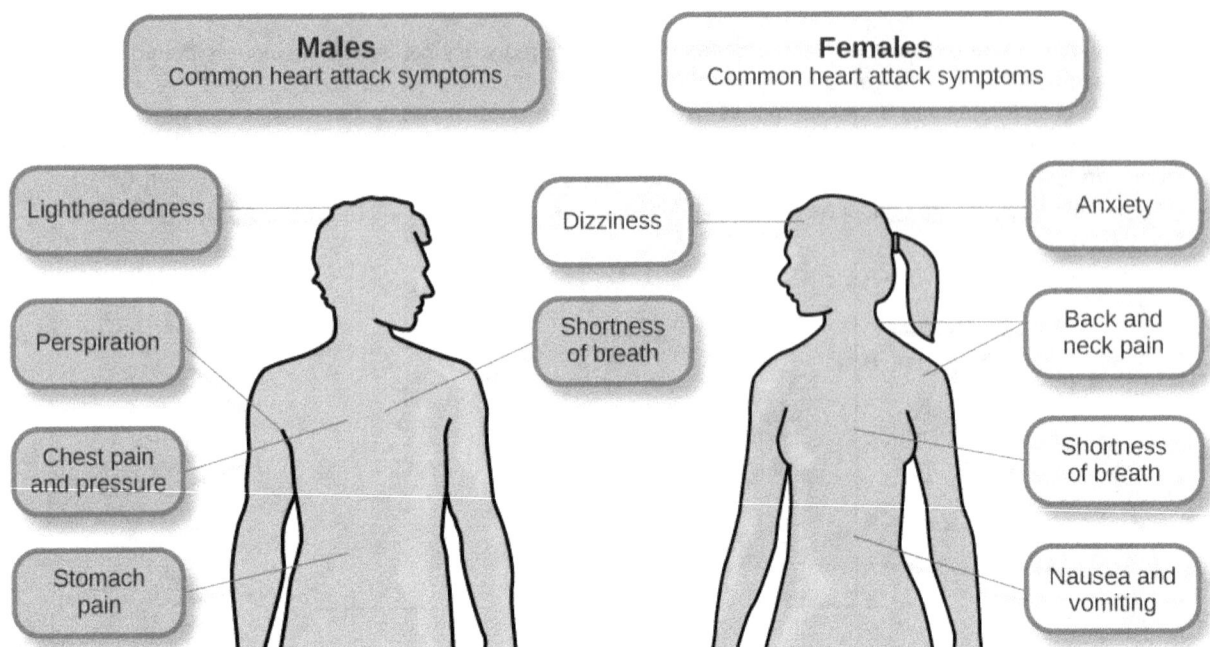

Figure 14.17 Males and females often experience different symptoms of a heart attack.

A major risk factor for heart disease is **hypertension**, which is high blood pressure. Hypertension forces a person's heart to pump harder, thus putting more physical strain on the heart. If left unchecked, hypertension can lead to a heart attack, stroke, or heart failure; it can also lead to kidney failure and blindness. Hypertension is a serious cardiovascular disorder, and it is sometimes called the silent killer because it has no symptoms—one who has high blood pressure may not even be aware of it (AHA, 2012b).

Many risk factors contributing to cardiovascular disorders have been identified. These risk factors include social determinants such as aging, income, education, and employment status, as well as behavioral risk factors that include unhealthy diet, tobacco use, physical inactivity, and excessive alcohol consumption; obesity and diabetes are additional risk factors (World Health Organization [WHO], 2013).

Over the past few decades, there has been much greater recognition and awareness of the importance of stress and other psychological factors in cardiovascular health (Nusair, Al-dadah, & Kumar, 2012). Indeed, exposure to stressors of many kinds has also been linked to cardiovascular problems; in the case of hypertension, some of these stressors include job strain (Trudel, Brisson, & Milot, 2010), natural disasters (Saito, Kim, Maekawa, Ikeda, & Yokoyama, 1997), marital conflict (Nealey-Moore, Smith, Uchino, Hawkins, & Olson-Cerny, 2007), and exposure to high traffic noise levels at one's home (de Kluizenaar, Gansevoort, Miedema, & de Jong, 2007). Perceived discrimination appears to be associated with hypertension among African Americans (Sims et al., 2012). In addition, laboratory-based stress tasks, such as performing mental arithmetic under time pressure, immersing one's hand into ice water (known as the cold pressor test), mirror tracing, and public speaking have all been shown to elevate blood pressure (Phillips, 2011).

ARE YOU TYPE A OR TYPE B?

Sometimes research ideas and theories emerge from seemingly trivial observations. In the 1950s, cardiologist Meyer Friedman was looking over his waiting room furniture, which consisted of upholstered chairs with armrests. Friedman decided to have these chairs reupholstered. When the man doing the reupholstering came to the office to do the work, he commented on how the chairs were worn in a unique manner—the front edges of the cushions were worn down, as were the front tips of the arm rests. It seemed like the cardiology patients were tapping or squeezing the front of the armrests, as well as literally sitting on the edge of their seats (Friedman & Rosenman, 1974). Were cardiology patients somehow different than other types of patients? If so, how?

After researching this matter, Friedman and his colleague, Ray Rosenman, came to understand that people who are prone to heart disease tend to think, feel, and act differently than those who are not. These individuals tend to be intensively driven workaholics who are preoccupied with deadlines and always seem to be in a rush. According to Friedman and Rosenman, these individuals exhibit **Type A** behavior pattern; those who are more relaxed and laid-back were characterized as **Type B** (Figure 14.18). In a sample of Type As and Type Bs, Friedman and Rosenman were startled to discover that heart disease was over seven times more frequent among the Type As than the Type Bs (Friedman & Rosenman, 1959).

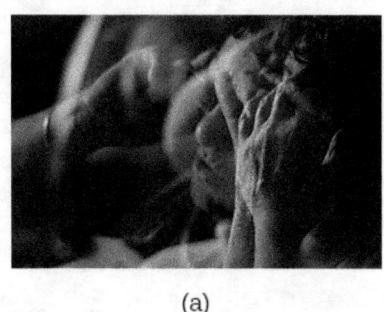
(a)

(b)

Figure 14.18 (a) Type A individuals are characterized as intensely driven, (b) while Type B people are characterized as laid-back and relaxed. (credit a: modification of work by Greg Hernandez; credit b: modification of work by Elvert Barnes)

The major components of the Type A pattern include an aggressive and chronic struggle to achieve more and more in less and less time (Friedman & Rosenman, 1974). Specific characteristics of the Type A pattern include an excessive competitive drive, chronic sense of time urgency, impatience, and hostility toward others (particularly those who get in the person's way).

An example of a person who exhibits Type A behavior pattern is Jeffrey. Even as a child, Jeffrey was intense and driven. He excelled at school, was captain of the swim team, and graduated with honors from an Ivy League college. Jeffrey never seems able to relax; he is always working on something, even on the weekends. However, Jeffrey always seems to feel as though there are not enough hours in the day to accomplish all he feels he should. He volunteers to take on extra tasks at work and often brings his work home with him; he often goes to bed frustrated late at night because he feels that he has not done enough. Jeffrey is quick tempered with his coworkers; he often becomes noticeably agitated when dealing with those coworkers he feels work too slowly or whose work does not meet his standards. He typically reacts with hostility when interrupted at work. He has experienced problems in his marriage over his lack of time spent with family. When caught in traffic during his commute to and from work, Jeffrey incessantly pounds on his horn and swears loudly at other drivers. When Jeffrey was 52, he suffered his first heart attack.

By the 1970s, a majority of practicing cardiologists believed that Type A behavior pattern was a significant risk factor for heart disease (Friedman, 1977). Indeed, a number of early longitudinal investigations demonstrated a link between Type A behavior pattern and later development of heart disease (Rosenman et al., 1975; Haynes, Feinleib, & Kannel, 1980).

Subsequent research examining the association between Type A and heart disease, however, failed to replicate these earlier findings (Glassman, 2007; Myrtek, 2001). Because Type A theory did not pan out as well as they had hoped, researchers shifted their attention toward determining if any of the specific elements of Type A predict heart disease.

Extensive research clearly suggests that the anger/hostility dimension of Type A behavior pattern may be one of the most important factors in the development of heart disease. This relationship was initially described in the Haynes et al. (1980) study mentioned above: Suppressed hostility was found to substantially elevate the risk of heart disease for both men and women. Also, one investigation followed over 1,000 male medical students from 32 to 48 years. At the beginning of the study, these men completed a questionnaire assessing how they react to pressure; some indicated that they respond with high levels of anger, whereas others indicated that they respond with less anger. Decades later, researchers found that those who earlier had indicated the highest levels of anger were over 6 times more likely than those who indicated less anger to have had a heart attack by age 55, and they were 3.5 times more likely to have experienced heart disease by the same age (Chang, Ford, Meoni, Wang, & Klag, 2002). From a health standpoint, it clearly does not pay to be an angry person.

After reviewing and statistically summarizing 35 studies from 1983 to 2006, Chida and Steptoe (2009) concluded that the bulk of the evidence suggests that anger and hostility constitute serious long-term risk factors for adverse cardiovascular outcomes among both healthy individuals and those already suffering from heart disease. One reason angry and hostile moods might contribute to cardiovascular diseases is that such moods can create social strain, mainly in the form of antagonistic social encounters with others. This strain could then lay the foundation for disease-promoting cardiovascular responses among hostile individuals (Vella, Kamarck, Flory, & Manuck, 2012). In this transactional model, hostility and social strain form a cycle (Figure 14.19).

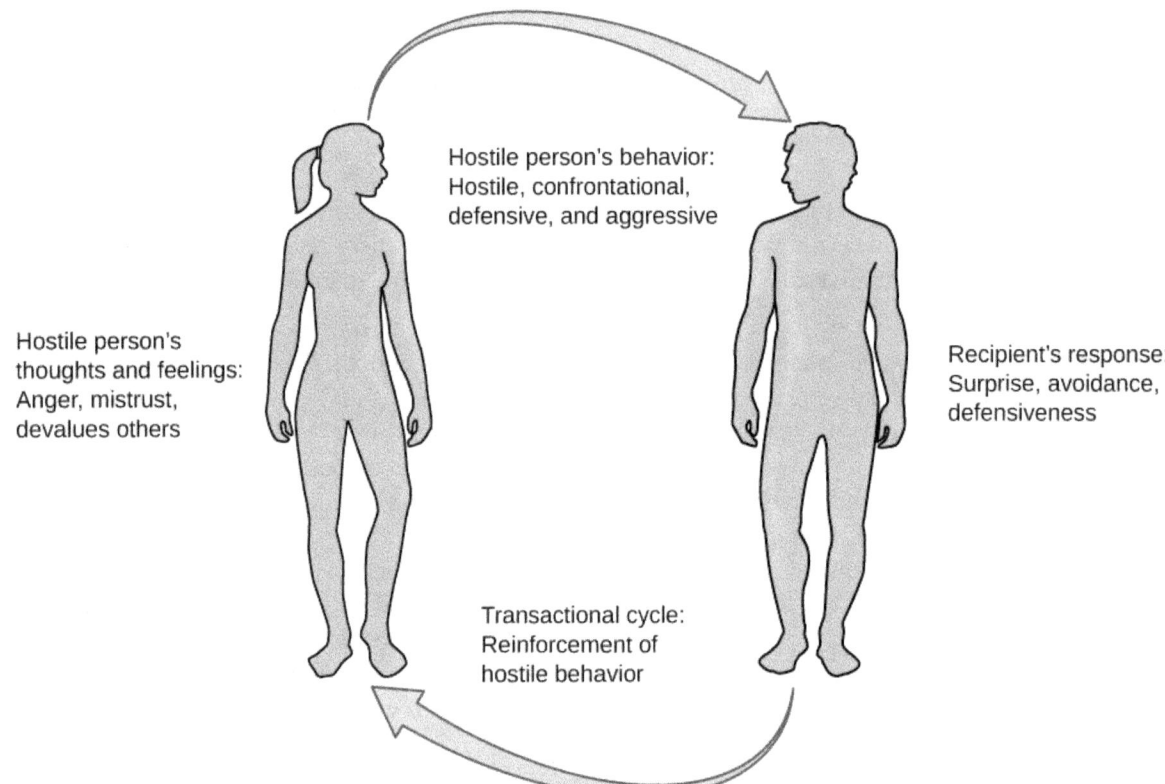

Figure 14.19 According to the transactional model of hostility for predicting social interactions (Vella et al., 2012), the thoughts and feelings of a hostile person promote antagonistic behavior toward others, which in turn reinforces complimentary reactions from others, thereby intensifying ones' hostile disposition and intensifying the cyclical nature of this relationship.

For example, suppose Kaitlin has a hostile disposition; she has a cynical, distrustful attitude toward others and often thinks that other people are out to get her. She is very defensive around people, even those she has known for years, and she is always looking for signs that others are either disrespecting or belittling her. In the shower each morning before work, she often mentally rehearses what she would say to someone who said or did something that angered her, such as making a political statement that was counter to her own ideology. As Kaitlin goes through these mental rehearsals, she often grins and thinks about the retaliation on anyone who will irk her that day.

Socially, she is confrontational and tends to use a harsh tone with people, which often leads to very disagreeable and sometimes argumentative social interactions. As you might imagine, Kaitlin is not especially popular with others, including coworkers, neighbors, and even members of her own family. They either avoid her at all costs or snap back at her, which causes Kaitlin to become even more cynical and distrustful of others, making her disposition even more hostile. Kaitlin's hostility—through her own doing—has created an antagonistic environment that cyclically causes her to become even more hostile and angry, thereby potentially setting the stage for cardiovascular problems.

In addition to anger and hostility, a number of other negative emotional states have been linked with heart disease, including negative affectivity and depression (Suls & Bunde, 2005). **Negative affectivity** is a tendency to experience distressed emotional states involving anger, contempt, disgust, guilt, fear, and nervousness (Watson, Clark, & Tellegen, 1988). It has been linked with the development of both hypertension and heart disease. For example, over 3,000 initially healthy participants in one study were tracked longitudinally, up to 22 years. Those with higher levels of negative affectivity at the time the study began were substantially more likely to develop and be treated for hypertension during the ensuing years than were those with lower levels of negative affectivity (Jonas & Lando, 2000). In addition, a study of over 10,000 middle-aged London-based civil servants who were followed an average of 12.5 years revealed that those who earlier had scored in the upper third on a test of negative affectivity were 32% more likely to have experienced heart disease, heart attack, or angina over a period of years than were those who scored in the lowest third (Nabi, Kivimaki, De Vogli, Marmot, & Singh-Manoux, 2008). Hence, negative affectivity appears to be a potentially vital risk factor for the development of cardiovascular disorders.

DEPRESSION AND THE HEART

For centuries, poets and folklore have asserted that there is a connection between moods and the heart (Glassman & Shapiro, 1998). You are no doubt familiar with the notion of a broken heart following a disappointing or depressing event and have encountered that notion in songs, films, and literature.

Perhaps the first to recognize the link between depression and heart disease was Benjamin Malzberg (1937), who found that the death rate among institutionalized patients with melancholia (an archaic term for depression) was six times higher than that of the population. A classic study in the late 1970s looked at over 8,000 people diagnosed with manic-depressive disorder (now classified as bipolar disorder) in Denmark, finding a nearly 50% increase in deaths from heart disease among these patients compared with the general Danish population (Weeke, 1979). By the early 1990s, evidence began to accumulate showing that depressed individuals who were followed for long periods of time were at increased risk for heart disease and cardiac death (Glassman, 2007). In one investigation of over 700 Denmark residents, those with the highest depression scores were 71% more likely to have experienced a heart attack than were those with lower depression scores (Barefoot & Schroll, 1996). **Figure 14.20** illustrates the gradation in risk of heart attacks for both men and women.

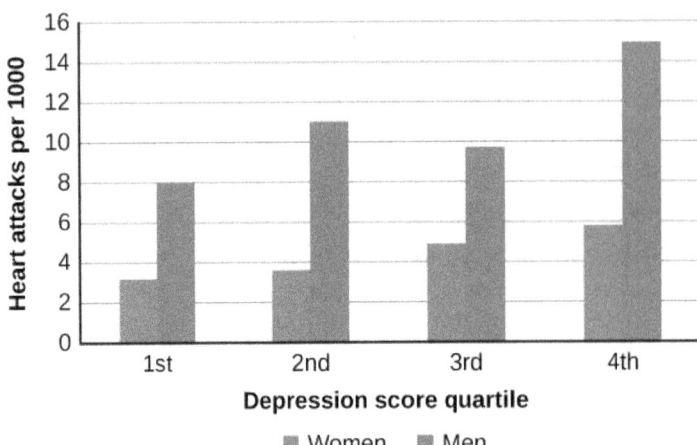

Figure 14.20 This graph shows the incidence of heart attacks among men and women by depression score quartile (adapted from Barefoot & Schroll, 1996).

After more than two decades of research, it is now clear that a relationship exists: Patients with heart disease have more depression than the general population, and people with depression are more likely to eventually develop heart disease and experience higher mortality than those who do not have depression (Hare, Toukhsati, Johansson, & Jaarsma, 2013); the more severe the depression, the higher the risk (Glassman, 2007). Consider the following:

- In one study, death rates from cardiovascular problems was substantially higher in depressed people; depressed men were 50% more likely to have died from cardiovascular problems, and depressed women were 70% more likely (Ösby, Brandt, Correia, Ekbom, & Sparén, 2001).

- A statistical review of 10 longitudinal studies involving initially healthy individuals revealed that those with elevated depressive symptoms have, on average, a 64% greater risk of developing heart disease than do those with fewer symptoms (Wulsin & Singal, 2003).

- A study of over 63,000 registered nurses found that those with more depressed symptoms when the study began were 49% more likely to experience fatal heart disease over a 12-year period (Whang et al., 2009).

The American Heart Association, fully aware of the established importance of depression in cardiovascular diseases, several years ago recommended routine depression screening for all heart disease patients (Lichtman et al., 2008). Recently, they have recommended including depression as a risk factor for heart disease patients (AHA, 2014).

Although the exact mechanisms through which depression might produce heart problems have not been fully clarified, a recent investigation examining this connection in early life has shed some light. In an ongoing study of childhood depression, adolescents who had been diagnosed with depression as children were more likely to be obese, smoke, and be physically inactive than were those who had not received this diagnosis (Rottenberg et al., 2014). One implication of this study is that depression, especially if it occurs early in life, may increase the likelihood of living an unhealthy lifestyle, thereby predisposing people to an unfavorable cardiovascular disease risk profile.

It is important to point out that depression may be just one piece of the emotional puzzle in elevating the risk for heart disease, and that chronically experiencing several negative emotional states may be especially important. A longitudinal investigation of Vietnam War veterans found that depression, anxiety, hostility, and trait anger each independently predicted the onset of heart disease (Boyle, Michalek, & Suarez, 2006). However, when each of these negative psychological attributes was combined into a single variable, this new variable (which researchers called psychological risk factor) predicted heart disease more strongly than any of the individual variables. Thus, rather than examining the predictive power of isolated psychological risk factors, it seems crucial for future researchers to examine the effects of combined and more general negative emotional and psychological traits in the development of cardiovascular illnesses.

ASTHMA

Asthma is a chronic and serious disease in which the airways of the respiratory system become obstructed, leading to great difficulty expelling air from the lungs. The airway obstruction is caused by inflammation of the airways (leading to thickening of the airway walls) and a tightening of the muscles around them, resulting in a narrowing of the airways (**Figure 14.21**) (American Lung Association, 2010). Because airways become obstructed, a person with asthma will sometimes have great difficulty breathing and will experience repeated episodes of wheezing, chest tightness, shortness of breath, and coughing, the latter occurring mostly during the morning and night (CDC, 2006).

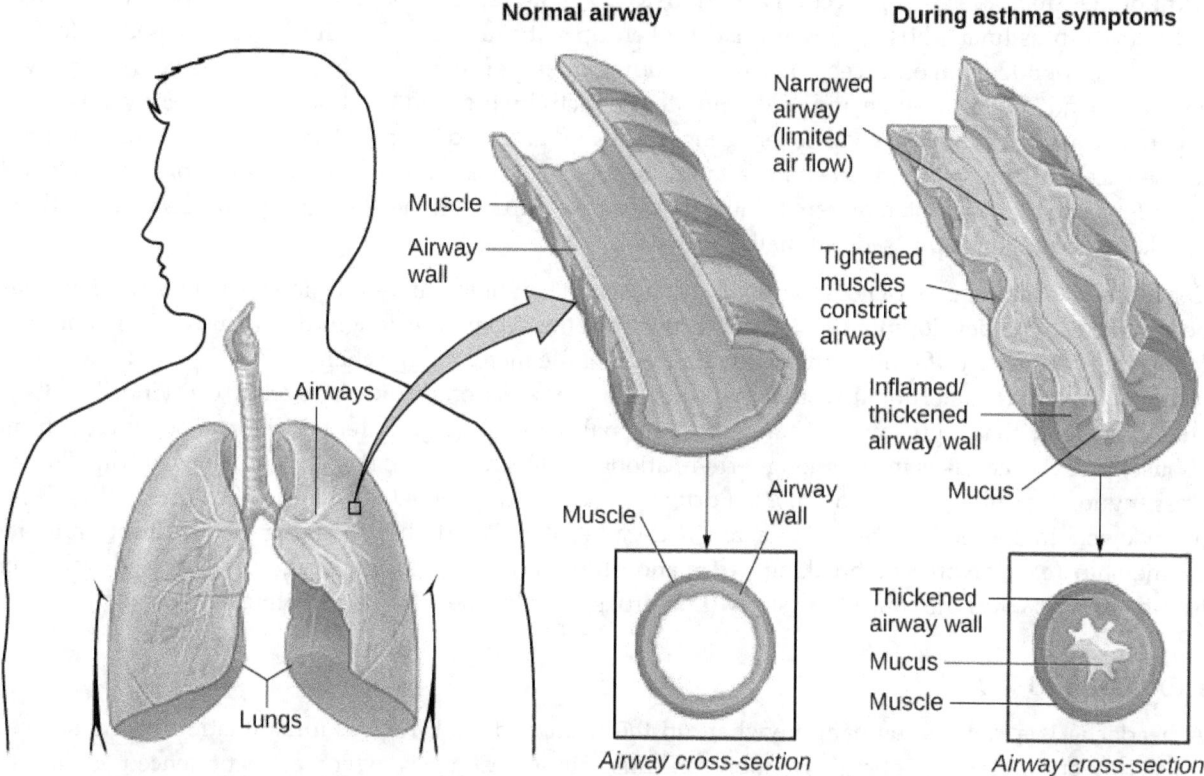

Figure 14.21 In asthma, the airways become inflamed and narrowed.

According to the Centers for Disease Control and Prevention (CDC), around 4,000 people die each year from asthma-related causes, and asthma is a contributing factor to another 7,000 deaths each year (CDC, 2013a). The CDC has revealed that asthma affects 18.7 million U.S. adults and is more common among people with lower education and income levels (CDC, 2013b). Especially concerning is that asthma is on the rise, with rates of asthma increasing 157% between 2000 and 2010 (CDC, 2013b).

Asthma attacks are acute episodes in which an asthma sufferer experiences the full range of symptoms. Asthma exacerbation is often triggered by environmental factors, such as air pollution, allergens (e.g., pollen, mold, and pet hairs), cigarette smoke, airway infections, cold air or a sudden change in temperature, and exercise (CDC, 2013b).

Psychological factors appear to play an important role in asthma (Wright, Rodriguez, & Cohen, 1998), although some believe that psychological factors serve as potential triggers in only a subset of asthma patients (Ritz, Steptoe, Bobb, Harris, & Edwards, 2006). Many studies over the years have demonstrated that some people with asthma will experience asthma-like symptoms if they expect to experience such symptoms, such as when breathing an inert substance that they (falsely) believe will lead to airway obstruction (Sodergren & Hyland, 1999). As stress and emotions directly affect immune and respiratory functions, psychological factors likely serve as one of the most common triggers of asthma exacerbation (Trueba & Ritz, 2013).

People with asthma tend to report and display a high level of negative emotions such as anxiety, and asthma attacks have been linked to periods of high emotionality (Lehrer, Isenberg, & Hochron, 1993). In addition, high levels of emotional distress during both laboratory tasks and daily life have been found to negatively affect airway function and can produce asthma-like symptoms in people with asthma (von Leupoldt, Ehnes, & Dahme, 2006). In one investigation, 20 adults with asthma wore preprogrammed wristwatches that signaled them to breathe into a portable device that measures airway function. Results showed that higher levels of negative emotions and stress were associated with increased airway obstruction and self-reported asthma symptoms (Smyth, Soefer, Hurewitz, Kliment, & Stone, 1999). In addition, D'Amato, Liccardi, Cecchi, Pellegrino, & D'Amato (2010) described a case study of an 18-year-old man with asthma whose girlfriend had broken up with him, leaving him in a depressed state. She had also unfriended him on Facebook, while friending other young males. Eventually, the young man was able to "friend" her once again and could monitor her activity through Facebook. Subsequently, he would experience asthma symptoms whenever he logged on and accessed her profile. When he later resigned not to use Facebook any longer, the asthma attacks stopped. This case suggests that the use of Facebook and other forms of social media may represent a new source of stress—it may be a triggering factor for asthma attacks, especially in depressed asthmatic individuals.

Exposure to stressful experiences, particularly those that involve parental or interpersonal conflicts, has been linked to the development of asthma throughout the lifespan. A longitudinal study of 145 children found that parenting difficulties during the first year of life increased the chances that the child developed asthma by 107% (Klinnert et al., 2001). In addition, a cross-sectional study of over 10,000 Finnish college students found that high rates of parent or personal conflicts (e.g., parental divorce, separation from spouse, or severe conflicts in other long-term relationships) increased the risk of asthma onset (Kilpeläinen, Koskenvuo, Helenius, & Terho, 2002). Further, a study of over 4,000 middle-aged men who were interviewed in the early 1990s and again a decade later found that breaking off an important life partnership (e.g., divorce or breaking off relationship from parents) increased the risk of developing asthma by 124% over the time of the study (Loerbroks, Apfelbacher, Thayer, Debling, & Stürmer, 2009).

HEADACHES

A headache is a continuous pain anywhere in the head and neck region. Inflammation of the sinuses caused by an infection or allergic reaction can cause sinus headaches, which are experienced as pain in the cheeks and forehead. Migraine headaches are a type of headache thought to be caused by blood vessel swelling and increased blood flow (McIntosh, 2013). Migraines are characterized by severe pain on one or both sides of the head, an upset stomach, and disturbed vision. They are more frequently experienced by women than by men (American Academy of Neurology, 2014). Tension headaches are triggered by tightening/tensing of facial and neck muscles; they are the most commonly experienced kind of headache, accounting for about 42% of all headaches worldwide (Stovner et al., 2007). In the United States, well over one-third of the population experiences tension headaches each year, and 2–3% of the population suffers from chronic tension headaches (Schwartz, Stewart, Simon, & Lipton, 1998).

A number of factors can contribute to tension headaches, including sleep deprivation, skipping meals, eye strain, overexertion, muscular tension caused by poor posture, and stress (MedicineNet, 2013). Although there is uncertainty regarding the exact mechanisms through which stress can produce tension headaches, stress has been demonstrated to increase sensitivity to pain (Caceres & Burns, 1997; Logan et al., 2001). In general, tension headache sufferers, compared to non-sufferers, have a lower threshold for and greater sensitivity to pain (Ukestad & Wittrock, 1996), and they report greater levels of subjective stress when faced with a stressor (Myers, Wittrock, & Foreman, 1998). Thus, stress may contribute to tension headaches by increasing pain sensitivity in already-sensitive pain pathways in tension headache sufferers (Cathcart,

Petkov, & Pritchard, 2008).

14.4 Regulation of Stress

Learning Objectives

By the end of this section, you will be able to:
- Define coping and differentiate between problem-focused and emotion-focused coping
- Describe the importance of perceived control in our reactions to stress
- Explain how social support is vital in health and longevity

As we learned in the previous section, stress—especially if it is chronic—takes a toll on our bodies and can have enormously negative health implications. When we experience events in our lives that we appraise as stressful, it is essential that we use effective coping strategies to manage our stress. **Coping** refers to mental and behavioral efforts that we use to deal with problems relating to stress.

COPING STYLES

Lazarus and Folkman (1984) distinguished two fundamental kinds of coping: problem-focused coping and emotion-focused coping. In problem-focused coping, one attempts to manage or alter the problem that is causing one to experience stress (i.e., the stressor). Problem-focused coping strategies are similar to strategies used in everyday problem-solving: they typically involve identifying the problem, considering possible solutions, weighing the costs and benefits of these solutions, and then selecting an alternative (Lazarus & Folkman, 1984). As an example, suppose Bradford receives a midterm notice that he is failing statistics class. If Bradford adopts a problem-focused coping approach to managing his stress, he would be proactive in trying to alleviate the source of the stress. He might contact his professor to discuss what must be done to raise his grade, he might also decide to set aside two hours daily to study statistics assignments, and he may seek tutoring assistance. A problem-focused approach to managing stress means we actively try to do things to address the problem.

Emotion-focused coping, in contrast, consists of efforts to change or reduce the negative emotions associated with stress. These efforts may include avoiding, minimizing, or distancing oneself from the problem, or positive comparisons with others ("I'm not as bad off as she is"), or seeking something positive in a negative event ("Now that I've been fired, I can sleep in for a few days"). In some cases, emotion-focused coping strategies involve reappraisal, whereby the stressor is construed differently (and somewhat self-deceptively) without changing its objective level of threat (Lazarus & Folkman, 1984). For example, a person sentenced to federal prison who thinks, "This will give me a great chance to network with others," is using reappraisal. If Bradford adopted an emotion-focused approach to managing his midterm deficiency stress, he might watch a comedy movie, play video games, or spend hours on social media to take his mind off the situation. In a certain sense, emotion-focused coping can be thought of as treating the symptoms rather than the actual cause.

While many stressors elicit both kinds of coping strategies, problem-focused coping is more likely to occur when encountering stressors we perceive as controllable, while emotion-focused coping is more likely to predominate when faced with stressors that we believe we are powerless to change (Folkman & Lazarus, 1980). Clearly, emotion-focused coping is more effective in dealing with uncontrollable stressors. For example, the stress you experience when a loved one dies can be overwhelming. You are simply powerless to change the situation as there is nothing you can do to bring this person back. The most helpful coping response is emotion-focused coping aimed at minimizing the pain of the grieving period.

Fortunately, most stressors we encounter can be modified and are, to varying degrees, controllable. A person who cannot stand her job can quit and look for work elsewhere; a middle-aged divorcee can find another potential partner; the freshman who fails an exam can study harder next time, and a breast lump does not necessarily mean that one is fated to die of breast cancer.

CONTROL AND STRESS

The desire and ability to predict events, make decisions, and affect outcomes—that is, to enact control in our lives—is a basic tenet of human behavior (Everly & Lating, 2002). Albert Bandura (1997) stated that "the intensity and chronicity of human stress is governed largely by perceived control over the demands of one's life" (p. 262). As cogently described in his statement, our reaction to potential stressors depends to a large extent on how much control we feel we have over such things. **Perceived control** is our beliefs about our personal capacity to exert influence over and shape outcomes, and it has major implications for our health and happiness (Infurna & Gerstorf, 2014). Extensive research has demonstrated that perceptions of personal control are associated with a variety of favorable outcomes, such as better physical and mental health and greater psychological well-being (Diehl & Hay, 2010). Greater personal control is also associated with lower reactivity to stressors in daily life. For example, researchers in one investigation found that higher levels of perceived control at one point in time were later associated with lower emotional and physical reactivity to interpersonal stressors (Neupert, Almeida, & Charles, 2007). Further, a daily diary study with 34 older widows found that their stress and anxiety levels were significantly reduced on days during which the widows felt greater perceived control (Ong, Bergeman, & Bisconti, 2005).

DIG DEEPER

Learned Helplessness

When we lack a sense of control over the events in our lives, particularly when those events are threatening, harmful, or noxious, the psychological consequences can be profound. In one of the better illustrations of this concept, psychologist Martin Seligman conducted a series of classic experiments in the 1960s (Seligman & Maier, 1967) in which dogs were placed in a chamber where they received electric shocks from which they could not escape. Later, when these dogs were given the opportunity to escape the shocks by jumping across a partition, most failed to even try; they seemed to just give up and passively accept any shocks the experimenters chose to administer. In comparison, dogs who were previously allowed to escape the shocks tended to jump the partition and escape the pain (Figure 14.22).

Figure 14.22 Seligman's learned helplessness experiments with dogs used an apparatus that measured when the animals would move from a floor delivering shocks to one without.

Seligman believed that the dogs who failed to try to escape the later shocks were demonstrating learned helplessness: They had acquired a belief that they were powerless to do anything about the stimulation they were receiving. Seligman also believed that the passivity and lack of initiative these dogs demonstrated was similar to that observed in human depression. Therefore, Seligman speculated that learned helplessness might be an important cause of depression in humans: Humans who experience negative life events that they believe they are unable to control may become helpless. As a result, they give up trying to change the situation and some may become depressed and show lack of initiative in future situations in which they can control the outcomes (Seligman, Maier, & Geer, 1968). Sadly, learned helplessness was later used to justify the torture of prisoners by U.S. military personnel following the 2001 attacks on the World Trade Center. The hypothesis was that detainees who were subjected to uncontrollable afflictions would eventually become passive and compliant, making them more likely to reveal information to their interrogators. There is little evidence that the program achieved worthwhile results. It is now widely regarded as unethical and unjustified. This example emphasizes the need to consistently consider the ethics of research studies and their applications (Konnikova, 2015).

Seligman and colleagues later reformulated the original learned helplessness model of depression (Abramson, Seligman, & Teasdale, 1978). In their reformulation, they emphasized attributions (i.e., a mental explanation for why something occurred) that fostered a sense of learned helplessness. For example, suppose a coworker shows up late to work; your belief as to what caused the coworker's tardiness would be an attribution (e.g., too much traffic, slept too late, or just doesn't care about being on time).

The reformulated version of Seligman's study holds that the attributions made for negative life events contribute to depression. Consider the example of a student who performs poorly on a midterm exam. This model suggests that the student will make three kinds of attributions for this outcome: internal vs. external (believing the outcome was caused by his own personal inadequacies or by environmental factors), stable vs. unstable (believing the cause can be changed or is permanent), and global vs. specific (believing the outcome is a sign of inadequacy in most everything versus just this area). Assume that the student makes an internal ("I'm just not smart"), stable ("Nothing can be done to change the fact that I'm not smart") and global ("This is another example of how lousy I am at everything") attribution for the poor performance. The reformulated theory predicts that the student would perceive a lack of control over this stressful event and thus be especially prone to developing depression. Indeed, research has demonstrated that people who have a tendency to make internal, global, and stable attributions for bad outcomes tend to develop symptoms of depression when faced with negative life experiences (Peterson & Seligman, 1984). Fortunately, attribution habits can be changed through practice. Training in healthy attribution habits has been shown to make people less vulnerable to depression (Konnikova, 2015).

Seligman's learned helplessness model has emerged over the years as a leading theoretical explanation for the onset of major depressive disorder. When you study psychological disorders, you will learn more about the latest reformulation of this model—now called hopelessness theory.

People who report higher levels of perceived control view their health as controllable, thereby making it more likely that they will better manage their health and engage in behaviors conducive to good health (Bandura, 2004). Not surprisingly, greater perceived control has been linked to lower risk of physical health problems, including declines in physical functioning (Infurna, Gerstorf, Ram, Schupp, & Wagner, 2011), heart attacks (Rosengren et al., 2004), and both cardiovascular disease incidence (Stürmer, Hasselbach, & Amelang, 2006) and mortality from cardiac disease (Surtees et al., 2010). In addition, longitudinal studies of British civil servants have found that those in low-status jobs (e.g., clerical and office support staff) in which the degree of control over the job is minimal are considerably more likely to develop heart disease than those with high-status jobs or considerable control over their jobs (Marmot, Bosma, Hemingway, & Stansfeld, 1997).

The link between perceived control and health may provide an explanation for the frequently observed relationship between social class and health outcomes (Kraus, Piff, Mendoza-Denton, Rheinschmidt, & Keltner, 2012). In general, research has found that more affluent individuals experience better health partly because they tend to believe that they can personally control and manage their reactions to life's stressors (Johnson & Krueger, 2006). Perhaps buoyed by the perceived level of control, individuals of higher social class may be prone to overestimating the degree of influence they have over particular outcomes. For example, those of higher social class tend to believe that their votes have greater sway on election outcomes than do those of lower social class, which may explain higher rates of voting in more affluent communities (Krosnick, 1990). Other research has found that a sense of perceived control can protect less affluent individuals from poorer health, depression, and reduced life-satisfaction—all of which tend to accompany lower social standing (Lachman & Weaver, 1998).

Taken together, findings from these and many other studies clearly suggest that perceptions of control and coping abilities are important in managing and coping with the stressors we encounter throughout life.

SOCIAL SUPPORT

The need to form and maintain strong, stable relationships with others is a powerful, pervasive, and fundamental human motive (Baumeister & Leary, 1995). Building strong interpersonal relationships with others helps us establish a network of close, caring individuals who can provide social support in times of distress, sorrow, and fear. **Social support** can be thought of as the soothing impact of friends, family, and acquaintances (Baron & Kerr, 2003). Social support can take many forms, including advice, guidance, encouragement, acceptance, emotional comfort, and tangible assistance (such as financial help). Thus, other people can be very comforting to us when we are faced with a wide range of life stressors, and they can be extremely helpful in our efforts to manage these challenges. Even in nonhuman animals, species mates can offer social support during times of stress. For example, elephants seem to be able to sense when other elephants are stressed and will often comfort them with physical contact—such as a trunk touch—or an empathetic vocal response (Krumboltz, 2014).

Scientific interest in the importance of social support first emerged in the 1970s when health researchers developed an interest in the health consequences of being socially integrated (Stroebe & Stroebe, 1996). Interest was further fueled by longitudinal studies showing that social connectedness reduced mortality. In one classic study, nearly 7,000 Alameda County, California, residents were followed over 9 years. Those who had previously indicated that they lacked social and community ties were more likely to die during the follow-up period than those with more extensive social networks. Compared to those with the most social contacts, isolated men and women were, respectively, 2.3 and 2.8 times more likely to die. These trends persisted even after controlling for a variety of health-related variables, such as smoking, alcohol consumption, self-reported health at the beginning of the study, and physical activity (Berkman & Syme, 1979).

Since the time of that study, social support has emerged as one of the well-documented psychosocial factors affecting health outcomes (Uchino, 2009). A statistical review of 148 studies conducted between 1982 and 2007 involving over 300,000 participants concluded that individuals with stronger social relationships have a 50% greater likelihood of survival compared to those with weak or insufficient social relationships (Holt-Lunstad, Smith, & Layton, 2010). According to the researchers, the magnitude of the effect of social support observed in this study is comparable with quitting smoking and exceeded many well-known risk factors for mortality, such as obesity and physical inactivity (Figure 14.23).

(a)   (b)

Figure 14.23 Close relationships with others, whether (a) a group of friends or (b) a family circle, provide more than happiness and fulfillment—they can help foster good health. (credit a: modification of work by "Damian Gadal_Flickr"/Flickr; credit b: modification of work by Christian Haugen)

A number of large-scale studies have found that individuals with low levels of social support are at greater risk of mortality, especially from cardiovascular disorders (Brummett et al., 2001). Further, higher levels of social supported have been linked to better survival rates following breast cancer (Falagas et al., 2007) and infectious diseases, especially HIV infection (Lee & Rotheram-Borus, 2001). In fact, a person with high levels of social support is less likely to contract a common cold. In one study, 334 participants completed questionnaires assessing their sociability; these individuals were subsequently exposed to a virus that causes a common cold and monitored for several weeks to see who became ill. Results showed that increased sociability was linearly associated with a decreased probability of developing a cold (Cohen, Doyle, Turner, Alper, & Skoner, 2003).

For many of us, friends are a vital source of social support. But what if you find yourself in a situation in which you have few friends and companions? Many students who leave home to attend and live at college experience drastic reductions in their social support, which makes them vulnerable to anxiety, depression, and loneliness. Social media can sometimes be useful in navigating these transitions (Raney & Troop Gordon, 2012) but might also cause increases in loneliness (Hunt, Marx, Lipson, & Young, 2018). For this reason, many colleges have designed first-year programs, such as peer mentoring (Raymond & Shepard, 2018), that can help students build new social networks. For some people, our families—especially our parents—are a major source of social support.

Social support appears to work by boosting the immune system, especially among people who are experiencing stress (Uchino, Vaughn, Carlisle, & Birmingham, 2012). In a pioneering study, spouses of cancer patients who reported high levels of social support showed indications of better immune functioning on two out of three immune functioning measures, compared to spouses who were below the median on reported social support (Baron, Cutrona, Hicklin, Russell, & Lubaroff, 1990). Studies of other populations have produced similar results, including those of spousal caregivers of dementia sufferers, medical students, elderly adults, and cancer patients (Cohen & Herbert, 1996; Kiecolt-Glaser, McGuire,

Robles, & Glaser, 2002).

In addition, social support has been shown to reduce blood pressure for people performing stressful tasks, such as giving a speech or performing mental arithmetic (Lepore, 1998). In these kinds of studies, participants are usually asked to perform a stressful task either alone, with a stranger present (who may be either supportive or unsupportive), or with a friend present. Those tested with a friend present generally exhibit lower blood pressure than those tested alone or with a stranger (Fontana, Diegnan, Villeneuve, & Lepore, 1999). In one study, 112 female participants who performed stressful mental arithmetic exhibited lower blood pressure when they received support from a friend rather than a stranger, but only if the friend was a male (Phillips, Gallagher, & Carroll, 2009). Although these findings are somewhat difficult to interpret, the authors mention that it is possible that females feel less supported and more evaluated by other females, particularly females whose opinions they value.

Taken together, the findings above suggest one of the reasons social support is connected to favorable health outcomes is because it has several beneficial physiological effects in stressful situations. However, it is also important to consider the possibility that social support may lead to better health behaviors, such as a healthy diet, exercising, smoking cessation, and cooperation with medical regimens (Uchino, 2009).

DIG DEEPER

Stress and Discrimination

Being the recipient of prejudice and discrimination is associated with a number of negative outcomes. Many studies have shown how perceived discrimination is a significant stressor for marginalized groups (Pascoe & Smart Richman, 2009). Discrimination negatively impacts both physical and mental health for individuals in stigmatized groups. As you'll learn when you study social psychology, various social identities (such as gender, age, religion, sexuality, ethnicity) often lead people to simultaneously be exposed to multiple forms of discrimination, which can have even stronger negative effects on mental and physical health (Vines, Ward, Cordoba, & Black, 2017). For example, the amplified levels of discrimination faced by Latinx transgender women may have related effects, leading to high stress levels and poor mental and physical health outcomes.

Perceived control and the general adaptation syndrome help explain the process by which discrimination affects mental and physical health. Discrimination can be conceptualized as an uncontrollable, persistent, and unpredictable stressor. When a discriminatory event occurs, the target of the event initially experiences an acute stress response (alarm stage). This acute reaction alone does not typically have a great impact on health. However, discrimination tends to be a chronic stressor. As people in marginalized groups experience repeated discrimination, they develop a heightened reactivity as their bodies prepare to act quickly (resistance stage). This long-term accumulation of stress responses can eventually lead to increases in negative emotion and wear on physical health (exhaustion stage). This explains why a history of perceived discrimination is associated with a host of mental and physical health problems including depression, cardiovascular disease, and cancer (Pascoe & Smart Richman, 2009).

Protecting stigmatized groups from the negative impact of discrimination-induced stress may involve reducing the incidence of discriminatory behaviors in conjunction with protective strategies that reduce the impact of discriminatory events when they occur. Civil rights legislation has protected some stigmatized groups by making discrimination a prosecutable offense in many social contexts. However, some groups (e.g., transgender people) often lack important legal recourse when discrimination occurs. Moreover, most modern discrimination comes in subtle forms that fall below the radar of the law. For example, discrimination may be experienced as selective inhospitality that the target perceives as race-based discrimination, but little is done in response since it would be easy to attribute the behavior to other causes. Although some cultural changes are increasingly helping people to recognize and control subtle discrimination, such shifts may take a long time.

Similar to other stressors, buffers like social support and healthy coping strategies appear to be effective in lowering the impact of perceived discrimination. For example, one study (Ajrouch, Reisine, Lim, Sohn, & Ismail, 2010) showed that discrimination predicted high psychological distress among African American mothers living in Detroit. However, the women who had readily available emotional support from friends and family experienced less distress than those with fewer social resources. While coping strategies and social support may buffer the effects of discrimination, they fail to erase all of the negative impacts. Vigilant antidiscrimination efforts, including the development of legal protections for vulnerable groups, are needed to reduce discrimination, stress, and the resulting physical and mental health effects.

STRESS REDUCTION TECHNIQUES

Beyond having a sense of control and establishing social support networks, there are numerous other means by which we can manage stress (Figure 14.24). A common technique people use to combat stress is exercise (Salmon, 2001). It is well-established that exercise, both of long (aerobic) and short (anaerobic) duration, is beneficial for both physical and mental health (Everly & Lating, 2002). There is considerable evidence that physically fit individuals are more resistant to the adverse effects of stress and recover more quickly from stress than less physically fit individuals (Cotton, 1990). In a study of more than 500 Swiss police officers and emergency service personnel, increased physical fitness was associated with reduced stress, and regular exercise was reported to protect against stress-related health problems (Gerber, Kellman, Hartman, & Pühse, 2010).

(a)

(b)
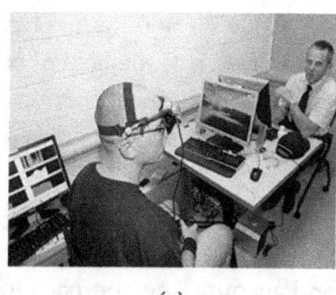
(c)

Figure 14.24 Stress reduction techniques may include (a) exercise, (b) meditation and relaxation, or (c) biofeedback. (credit a: modification of work by "UNE Photos"/Flickr; credit b: modification of work by Caleb Roenigk; credit c: modification of work by Dr. Carmen Russoniello)

One reason exercise may be beneficial is because it might buffer some of the deleterious physiological mechanisms of stress. One study found rats that exercised for six weeks showed a decrease in hypothalamic-pituitary-adrenal responsiveness to mild stressors (Campeau et al., 2010). In high-stress humans, exercise has been shown to prevent telomere shortening, which may explain the common observation of a youthful appearance among those who exercise regularly (Puterman et al., 2010). Further, exercise in later adulthood appears to minimize the detrimental effects of stress on the hippocampus and memory (Head, Singh, & Bugg, 2012). Among cancer survivors, exercise has been shown to reduce anxiety (Speck, Courneya, Masse, Duval, & Schmitz, 2010) and depressive symptoms (Craft, VanIterson, Helenowski, Rademaker, & Courneya, 2012). Clearly, exercise is a highly effective tool for regulating stress.

In the 1970s, Herbert Benson, a cardiologist, developed a stress reduction method called the **relaxation response technique** (Greenberg, 2006). The relaxation response technique combines relaxation with transcendental meditation, and consists of four components (Stein, 2001):

1. sitting upright on a comfortable chair with feet on the ground and body in a relaxed position,
2. being in a quiet environment with eyes closed,
3. repeating a word or a phrase—a mantra—to oneself, such as "alert mind, calm body,"
4. passively allowing the mind to focus on pleasant thoughts, such as nature or the warmth of your

blood nourishing your body.

The relaxation response approach is conceptualized as a general approach to stress reduction that reduces sympathetic arousal, and it has been used effectively to treat people with high blood pressure (Benson & Proctor, 1994).

Another technique to combat stress, **biofeedback**, was developed by Gary Schwartz at Harvard University in the early 1970s. Biofeedback is a technique that uses electronic equipment to accurately measure a person's neuromuscular and autonomic activity—feedback is provided in the form of visual or auditory signals. The main assumption of this approach is that providing somebody biofeedback will enable the individual to develop strategies that help gain some level of voluntary control over what are normally involuntary bodily processes (Schwartz & Schwartz, 1995). A number of different bodily measures have been used in biofeedback research, including facial muscle movement, brain activity, and skin temperature, and it has been applied successfully with individuals experiencing tension headaches, high blood pressure, asthma, and phobias (Stein, 2001).

14.5 The Pursuit of Happiness

Learning Objectives

By the end of this section, you will be able to:
- Define and discuss happiness, including its determinants
- Describe the field of positive psychology and identify the kinds of problems it addresses
- Explain the meaning of positive affect and discuss its importance in health outcomes
- Describe the concept of flow and its relationship to happiness and fulfillment

Although the study of stress and how it affects us physically and psychologically is fascinating, it is—admittedly—somewhat of a grim topic. Psychology is also interested in the study of a more upbeat and encouraging approach to human affairs—the quest for happiness.

HAPPINESS

America's founders declared that its citizens have an unalienable right to pursue happiness. But what is happiness? When asked to define the term, people emphasize different aspects of this elusive state. Indeed, happiness is somewhat ambiguous and can be defined from different perspectives (Martin, 2012). Some people, especially those who are highly committed to their religious faith, view happiness in ways that emphasize virtuosity, reverence, and enlightened spirituality. Others see happiness as primarily contentment—the inner peace and joy that come from deep satisfaction with one's surroundings, relationships with others, accomplishments, and oneself. Still others view happiness mainly as pleasurable engagement with their personal environment—having a career and hobbies that are engaging, meaningful, rewarding, and exciting. These differences, of course, are merely differences in emphasis. Most people would probably agree that each of these views, in some respects, captures the essence of happiness.

Elements of Happiness

Some psychologists have suggested that happiness consists of three distinct elements: the pleasant life, the good life, and the meaningful life, as shown in Figure 14.25 (Seligman, 2002; Seligman, Steen, Park, & Peterson, 2005). The pleasant life is realized through the attainment of day-to-day pleasures that add fun, joy, and excitement to our lives. For example, evening walks along the beach and a fulfilling sex life can enhance our daily pleasure and contribute to the pleasant life. The good life is achieved through identifying our unique skills and abilities and engaging these talents to enrich our lives; those who achieve the good life often find themselves absorbed in their work or their recreational pursuits. The meaningful life involves a deep sense of fulfillment that comes from using our talents in the service of the greater good: in ways that benefit the lives of others or that make the world a better place. In general, the happiest people tend to be those who pursue the full life—they orient their pursuits toward all three elements (Seligman et al., 2005).

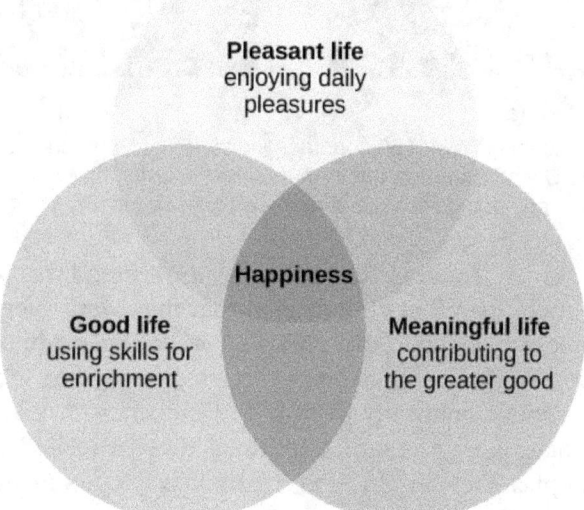

Figure 14.25 Happiness is an enduring state of well-being involving satisfaction in the pleasant, good, and meaningful aspects of life.

For practical purposes, a precise definition of **happiness** might incorporate each of these elements: an enduring state of mind consisting of joy, contentment, and other positive emotions, plus the sense that one's life has meaning and value (Lyubomirsky, 2001). The definition implies that happiness is a long-term state—what is often characterized as subjective well-being—rather than merely a transient positive mood we all experience from time to time. It is this enduring happiness that has captured the interests of psychologists and other social scientists.

The study of happiness has grown dramatically in the last three decades (Diener, 2013). One of the most basic questions that happiness investigators routinely examine is this: How happy are people in general? The average person in the world tends to be relatively happy and tends to indicate experiencing more positive feelings than negative feelings (Diener, Ng, Harter, & Arora, 2010). When asked to evaluate their current lives on a scale ranging from 0 to 10 (with 0 representing "worst possible life" and 10 representing "best possible life"), people in more than 150 countries surveyed from 2010–2012 reported an average score of 5.2. People who live in North America, Australia, and New Zealand reported the highest average score at 7.1, whereas those living Sub-Saharan Africa reported the lowest average score at 4.6 (Helliwell, Layard, & Sachs, 2013). Worldwide, the five happiest countries are Denmark, Norway, Switzerland, the Netherlands, and Sweden; the United States is ranked 17th happiest (**Figure 14.26**) (Helliwell et al., 2013).

Figure 14.26 (a) Surveys of residents in over 150 countries indicate that Denmark has the happiest citizens in the world. (b) Americans ranked the United States as the 17th happiest country in which to live. (credit a: modification of work by "JamesZ_Flickr"/Flickr; credit b: modification of work by Ryan Swindell)

Several years ago, a Gallup survey of more than 1,000 U.S. adults found that 52% reported that they were "very happy." In addition, more than 8 in 10 indicated that they were "very satisfied" with their lives (Carroll, 2007). However, a recent poll found that only 42% of American adults report being "very happy." The groups that show the greatest declines in happiness are people of color, those who have not completed a college education, and those who politically identify as Democrats or independents (McCarthy, 2020). These results suggest that challenging economic conditions may be related to declines in happiness. Of course, this interpretation implies that happiness is closely tied to one's finances. But, is it? What factors influence happiness?

Factors Connected to Happiness

What really makes people happy? What factors contribute to sustained joy and contentment? Is it money, attractiveness, material possessions, a rewarding occupation, a satisfying relationship? Extensive research over the years has examined this question. One finding is that age is related to happiness: Life satisfaction usually increases the older people get, but there do not appear to be gender differences in happiness (Diener, Suh, Lucas, & Smith, 1999). Although it is important to point out that much of this work has been correlational, many of the key findings (some of which may surprise you) are summarized below.

Family and other social relationships appear to be key factors correlated with happiness. Studies show that married people report being happier than those who are single, divorced, or widowed (Diener et al., 1999). Happy individuals also report that their marriages are fulfilling (Lyubomirsky, King, & Diener, 2005). In fact, some have suggested that satisfaction with marriage and family life is the strongest predictor of happiness (Myers, 2000). Happy people tend to have more friends, more high-quality social relationships, and stronger social support networks than less happy people (Lyubomirsky et al., 2005). Happy people also have a high frequency of contact with friends (Pinquart & Sörensen, 2000).

Can money buy happiness? In general, extensive research suggests that the answer is yes, but with several caveats. While a nation's per capita gross domestic product (GDP) is associated with happiness levels (Helliwell et al., 2013), changes in GDP (which is a less certain index of household income) bear little relationship to changes in happiness (Diener, Tay, & Oishi, 2013). On the whole, residents of affluent countries tend to be happier than residents of poor countries; within countries, wealthy individuals are happier than poor individuals, but the association is much weaker (Diener & Biswas-Diener, 2002). To the extent that it leads to increases in purchasing power, increases in income are associated with increases in happiness (Diener, Oishi, & Ryan, 2013). However, income within societies appears to correlate with happiness only up to a point. In a study of over 450,000 U.S. residents surveyed by the Gallup Organization, Kahneman and Deaton (2010) found that well-being rises with annual income, but only up to $75,000. The average increase in reported well-being for people with incomes greater than $75,000 was null. As implausible as these findings might seem—after all, higher incomes would enable people to indulge in Hawaiian vacations, prime seats as sporting events, expensive automobiles, and expansive new homes—higher incomes may impair people's ability to savor and enjoy the small pleasures of life (Kahneman, 2011). Indeed, researchers in one study found that participants exposed to a subliminal reminder of wealth spent less time savoring a chocolate candy bar and exhibited less enjoyment of this experience than did participants who were not reminded of wealth (Quoidbach, Dunn, Petrides, & Mikolajczak, 2010).

What about education and employment? Happy people, compared to those who are less happy, are more likely to graduate from college and secure more meaningful and engaging jobs. Once they obtain a job, they are also more likely to succeed (Lyubomirsky et al., 2005). While education shows a positive (but weak) correlation with happiness, intelligence is not appreciably related to happiness (Diener et al., 1999).

Does religiosity correlate with happiness? In general, the answer is yes (Hackney & Sanders, 2003). However, the relationship between religiosity and happiness depends on societal circumstances. Nations and states with more difficult living conditions (e.g., widespread hunger and low life expectancy) tend to be more highly religious than societies with more favorable living conditions. Among those who live in nations with difficult living conditions, religiosity is associated with greater well-being; in nations with more favorable living conditions, religious and nonreligious individuals report similar levels of well-being (Diener, Tay, & Myers, 2011).

Clearly the living conditions of one's nation can influence factors related to happiness. What about the influence of one's culture? To the extent that people possess characteristics that are highly valued by their culture, they tend to be happier (Diener, 2012). For example, self-esteem is a stronger predictor of life satisfaction in individualistic cultures than in collectivistic cultures (Diener, Diener, & Diener, 1995), and extraverted people tend to be happier in extraverted cultures than in introverted cultures (Fulmer et al., 2010).

So we've identified many factors that exhibit some correlation to happiness. What factors don't show a correlation? Researchers have studied both parenthood and physical attractiveness as potential contributors to happiness, but no link has been identified. Although people tend to believe that parenthood is central to a meaningful and fulfilling life, aggregate findings from a range of countries indicate that people who do not have children are generally happier than those who do (Hansen, 2012). And although one's perceived level of attractiveness seems to predict happiness, a person's objective physical attractiveness is only weakly correlated with her happiness (Diener, Wolsic, & Fujita, 1995).

Life Events and Happiness

An important point should be considered regarding happiness. People are often poor at affective forecasting: predicting the intensity and duration of their future emotions (Wilson & Gilbert, 2003). In one study, nearly all newlywed spouses predicted their marital satisfaction would remain stable or improve over the following four years; despite this high level of initial optimism, their marital satisfaction actually declined during this period (Lavner, Karner, & Bradbury, 2013). In addition, we are often incorrect when estimating how our long-term happiness would change for the better or worse in response to certain life events. For example, it is easy for many of us to imagine how euphoric we would feel if we won the lottery, were asked on a date by an attractive celebrity, or were offered our dream job. It is also easy to understand how long-suffering fans of the Chicago Cubs baseball team, which had not won a World Series championship since 1908, thought they would feel permanently elated when their team finally won another World Series in 2016. Likewise, it is easy to predict that we would feel permanently miserable if we suffered a disabling accident or if a romantic relationship ended.

However, something similar to sensory adaptation often occurs when people experience emotional reactions to life events. In much the same way our senses adapt to changes in stimulation (e.g., our eyes adapting to bright light after walking out of the darkness of a movie theater into the bright afternoon sun), we eventually adapt to changing emotional circumstances in our lives (Brickman & Campbell, 1971; Helson, 1964). When an event that provokes positive or negative emotions occurs, at first we tend to experience its emotional impact at full intensity. We feel a burst of pleasure following such things as a marriage proposal, birth of a child, acceptance to law school, an inheritance, and the like; as you might imagine, lottery winners experience a surge of happiness after hitting the jackpot (Lutter, 2007). Likewise, we experience a surge of misery following widowhood, a divorce, or a layoff from work. In the long run, however, we eventually adjust to the emotional new normal; the emotional impact of the event tends to erode, and we eventually revert to our original baseline happiness levels. Thus, what was at first a thrilling lottery windfall or World Series championship eventually loses its luster and becomes the status quo (Figure 14.27). Indeed, dramatic life events have much less long-lasting impact on happiness than might be expected (Brickman, Coats, & Janoff-Bulman, 1978).

(a)

(b)

Figure 14.27 (a) Long-suffering Chicago Cub fans felt elated in 2016 when their team won a World Series championship, a feat that had not been accomplished by that franchise in over a century. (b) In ways that are similar, those who play the lottery rightfully think that choosing the correct numbers and winning millions would lead to a surge in happiness. However, the initial burst of elation following such elusive events would most likely erode with time. (credit a: modification of work by Phil Roeder; credit b: modification of work by Robert S. Donovan)

Recently, some have raised questions concerning the extent to which important life events can permanently alter people's happiness set points (Diener, Lucas, & Scollon, 2006). Evidence from a number of investigations suggests that, in some circumstances, happiness levels do not revert to their original positions. For example, although people generally tend to adapt to marriage so that it no longer makes them happier or unhappier than before, they often do not fully adapt to unemployment or severe disabilities (Diener, 2012). Figure 14.28, which is based on longitudinal data from a sample of over 3,000 German respondents, shows life satisfaction scores several years before, during, and after various life events, and it illustrates how people adapt (or fail to adapt) to these events. German respondents did not get lasting emotional boosts from marriage; instead, they reported brief increases in happiness, followed by quick adaptation. In contrast, widows and those who had been laid off experienced sizeable decreases in happiness that appeared to result in long-term changes in life satisfaction (Diener et al., 2006). Further, longitudinal data from the same sample showed that happiness levels changed significantly over time for nearly a quarter of respondents, with 9% showing major changes (Fujita & Diener, 2005). Thus, long-term happiness levels can and do change for some people.

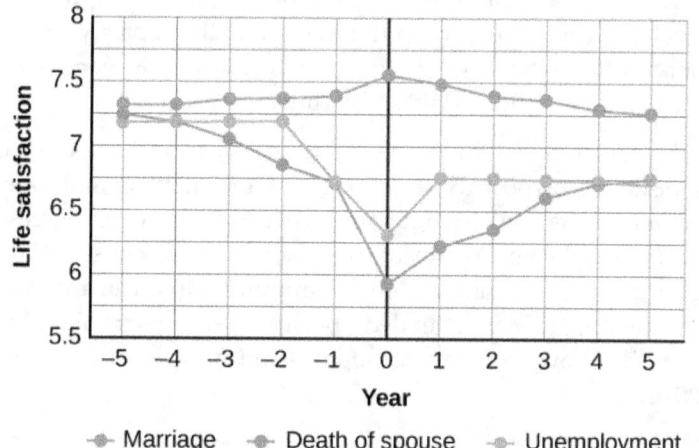

Figure 14.28 This graphs shows life satisfaction scores several years before and after three significant life events (0 represents the year the event happened) (Diener et al., 2006).

Increasing Happiness

Some recent findings about happiness provide an optimistic picture, suggesting that real changes in happiness are possible. For example, thoughtfully developed well-being interventions designed to augment people's baseline levels of happiness may increase happiness in ways that are permanent and long-lasting, not just temporary. These changes in happiness may be targeted at individual, organizational, and societal levels (Diener et al., 2006). Researchers in one study found that a series of happiness interventions involving such exercises as writing down three good things that occurred each day led to increases in happiness that lasted over six months (Seligman et al., 2005).

Measuring happiness and well-being at the societal level over time may assist policy makers in determining if people are generally happy or miserable, as well as when and why they might feel the way they do. Studies show that average national happiness scores (over time and across countries) relate strongly to six key variables: per capita gross domestic product (GDP, which reflects a nation's economic standard of living), social support, freedom to make important life choices, healthy life expectancy, freedom from perceived corruption in government and business, and generosity (Helliwell et al., 2013). Investigating why people are happy or unhappy might help policymakers develop programs that increase happiness and well-being within a society (Diener et al., 2006). Resolutions about contemporary political and social issues that are frequent topics of debate—such as poverty, taxation, affordable health care and housing, clean air and water, and income inequality—might be best considered with people's happiness in mind.

POSITIVE PSYCHOLOGY

In 1998, Seligman (the same person who conducted the learned helplessness experiments mentioned earlier), who was then president of the American Psychological Association, urged psychologists to focus more on understanding how to build human strength and psychological well-being. In deliberately setting out to create a new direction and new orientation for psychology, Seligman helped establish a growing movement and field of research called positive psychology (Compton, 2005). In a very general sense, **positive psychology** can be thought of as the science of happiness; it is an area of study that seeks to identify and promote those qualities that lead to greater fulfillment in our lives. This field looks at people's strengths and what helps individuals to lead happy, contented lives, and it moves away from focusing on people's pathology, faults, and problems. According to Seligman and Csikszentmihalyi (2000), positive psychology,

at the subjective level is about valued subjective experiences: well-being, contentment, and satisfaction (in the past); hope and optimism (for the future); and… happiness (in the present). At the individual level, it is about positive individual traits: the capacity for love and vocation, courage, interpersonal skill, aesthetic sensibility, perseverance, forgiveness, originality, future mindedness, spirituality, high talent, and wisdom. (p. 5)

Some of the topics studied by positive psychologists include altruism and empathy, creativity, forgiveness and compassion, the importance of positive emotions, enhancement of immune system functioning, savoring the fleeting moments of life, and strengthening virtues as a way to increase authentic happiness (Compton, 2005). Recent efforts in the field of positive psychology have focused on extending its principles toward peace and well-being at the level of the global community. In a war-torn world in which conflict, hatred, and distrust are common, such an extended "positive peace psychology" could have important implications for understanding how to overcome oppression and work toward global peace (Cohrs, Christie, White, & Das, 2013).

DIG DEEPER

The Center for Investigating Healthy Minds

On the campus of the University of Wisconsin–Madison, the Center for Investigating Healthy Minds at the Waisman Center conducts rigorous scientific research on healthy aspects of the mind, such as kindness, forgiveness, compassion, and mindfulness. Established in 2008 and led by renowned neuroscientist Dr. Richard J. Davidson, the Center examines a wide range of ideas, including such things as a kindness curriculum in schools, neural correlates of prosocial behavior, psychological effects of Tai Chi training, digital games to foster prosocial behavior in children, and the effectiveness of yoga and breathing exercises in reducing symptoms of post-traumatic stress disorder.

According to its website, the Center was founded after Dr. Davidson was challenged by His Holiness, the 14th Dalai Lama, "to apply the rigors of science to study positive qualities of mind" (Center for Investigating Health Minds, 2013). The Center continues to conduct scientific research with the aim of developing mental health training approaches that help people to live happier, healthier lives.

Positive Affect and Optimism

Taking a cue from positive psychology, extensive research over the last 10-15 years has examined the importance of positive psychological attributes in physical well-being. Qualities that help promote psychological well-being (e.g., having meaning and purpose in life, a sense of autonomy, positive emotions, and satisfaction with life) are linked with a range of favorable health outcomes (especially improved cardiovascular health) mainly through their relationships with biological functions and health behaviors (such as diet, physical activity, and sleep quality) (Boehm & Kubzansky, 2012). The quality that has received attention is **positive affect**, which refers to pleasurable engagement with the environment, such as happiness, joy, enthusiasm, alertness, and excitement (Watson, Clark, & Tellegen, 1988). The characteristics of positive affect, as with negative affect (discussed earlier), can be brief, long-lasting, or trait-like (Pressman & Cohen, 2005). Independent of age, gender, and income, positive affect is associated with greater social connectedness, emotional and practical support, adaptive coping efforts, and lower depression; it is also associated with longevity and favorable physiological functioning (Steptoe, O'Donnell, Marmot, & Wardle, 2008).

Positive affect also serves as a protective factor against heart disease. In a 10-year study of Nova Scotians, the rate of heart disease was 22% lower for each one-point increase on the measure of positive affect, from 1 (no positive affect expressed) to 5 (extreme positive affect) (Davidson, Mostofsky, & Whang, 2010). In terms of our health, the expression, "don't worry, be happy" is helpful advice indeed. There has also been much work suggesting that **optimism**—the general tendency to look on the bright side of things—is also a significant predictor of positive health outcomes.

Although positive affect and optimism are related in some ways, they are not the same (Pressman & Cohen, 2005). Whereas positive affect is mostly concerned with positive feeling states, optimism has been regarded as a generalized tendency to expect that good things will happen (Chang, 2001). It has also been conceptualized as a tendency to view life's stressors and difficulties as temporary and external to oneself (Peterson & Steen, 2002). Numerous studies over the years have consistently shown that optimism is linked to longevity, healthier behaviors, fewer postsurgical complications, better immune functioning among men with prostate cancer, and better treatment adherence (Rasmussen & Wallio, 2008). Further, optimistic people report fewer physical symptoms, less pain, better physical functioning, and are less likely to be rehospitalized following heart surgery (Rasmussen, Scheier, & Greenhouse, 2009).

FLOW

Another factor that seems to be important in fostering a deep sense of well-being is the ability to derive flow from the things we do in life. **Flow** is described as a particular experience that is so engaging and engrossing that it becomes worth doing for its own sake (Csikszentmihalyi, 1997). It is usually related to creative endeavors and leisure activities, but it can also be experienced by workers who like their jobs or students who love studying (Csikszentmihalyi, 1999). Many of us instantly recognize the notion of flow. In fact, the term derived from respondents' spontaneous use of the term when asked to describe how it felt when what they were doing was going well. When people experience flow, they become involved in an activity to the point where they feel they lose themselves in the activity. They effortlessly maintain their concentration and focus, they feel as though they have complete control of their actions, and time seems to pass more quickly than usual (Csikszentmihalyi, 1997). Flow is considered a pleasurable experience, and it typically occurs when people are engaged in challenging activities that require skills and knowledge they know they possess. For example, people would be more likely report flow experiences in relation to their work or hobbies than in relation to eating. When asked the question, "Do you ever get involved in something so deeply that nothing else seems to matter, and you lose track of time?" about 20% of Americans and Europeans report having these flow-like experiences regularly (Csikszentmihalyi, 1997).

Although wealth and material possessions are nice to have, the notion of flow suggests that neither are prerequisites for a happy and fulfilling life. Finding an activity that you are truly enthusiastic about, something so absorbing that doing it is reward itself (whether it be playing tennis, studying Arabic, writing children's novels, or cooking lavish meals) is perhaps the real key. According to Csikszentmihalyi (1999), creating conditions that make flow experiences possible should be a top social and political priority. How might this goal be achieved? How might flow be promoted in school systems? In the workplace? What potential benefits might be accrued from such efforts?

In an ideal world, scientific research endeavors should inform us on how to bring about a better world for all people. The field of positive psychology promises to be instrumental in helping us understand what truly builds hope, optimism, happiness, healthy relationships, flow, and genuine personal fulfillment.

Key Terms

alarm reaction first stage of the general adaptation syndrome; characterized as the body's immediate physiological reaction to a threatening situation or some other emergency; analogous to the fight-or-flight response

asthma psychophysiological disorder in which the airways of the respiratory system become obstructed, leading to great difficulty expelling air from the lungs

biofeedback stress-reduction technique using electronic equipment to measure a person's involuntary (neuromuscular and autonomic) activity and provide feedback to help the person gain a level of voluntary control over these processes

cardiovascular disorders disorders that involve the heart and blood circulation system

coping mental or behavioral efforts used to manage problems relating to stress, including its cause and the unpleasant feelings and emotions it produces

cortisol stress hormone released by the adrenal glands when encountering a stressor; helps to provide a boost of energy, thereby preparing the individual to take action

daily hassles minor irritations and annoyances that are part of our everyday lives and are capable of producing stress

distress bad form of stress; usually high in intensity; often leads to exhaustion, fatigue, feeling burned out; associated with erosions in performance and health

eustress good form of stress; low to moderate in intensity; associated with positive feelings, as well as optimal health and performance

fight-or-flight response set of physiological reactions (increases in blood pressure, heart rate, respiration rate, and sweat) that occur when an individual encounters a perceived threat; these reactions are produced by activation of the sympathetic nervous system and the endocrine system

flow state involving intense engagement in an activity; usually is experienced when participating in creative, work, and leisure endeavors

general adaptation syndrome Hans Selye's three-stage model of the body's physiological reactions to stress and the process of stress adaptation: alarm reaction, stage of resistance, and stage of exhaustion

happiness enduring state of mind consisting of joy, contentment, and other positive emotions; the sense that one's life has meaning and value

health psychology subfield of psychology devoted to studying psychological influences on health, illness, and how people respond when they become ill

heart disease several types of adverse heart conditions, including those that involve the heart's arteries or valves or those involving the inability of the heart to pump enough blood to meet the body's needs; can include heart attack and stroke

hypertension high blood pressure

hypothalamic-pituitary-adrenal (HPA) axis set of structures found in both the limbic system (hypothalamus) and the endocrine system (pituitary gland and adrenal glands) that regulate many of the body's physiological reactions to stress through the release of hormones

immune system various structures, cells, and mechanisms that protect the body from foreign substances that can damage the body's tissues and organs

immunosuppression decreased effectiveness of the immune system

job burnout general sense of emotional exhaustion and cynicism in relation to one's job; consists of three dimensions: exhaustion, depersonalization, and sense of diminished personal accomplishment

job strain work situation involving the combination of excessive job demands and workload with little decision making latitude or job control

lymphocytes white blood cells that circulate in the body's fluids and are especially important in the body's immune response

negative affectivity tendency to experience distressed emotional states involving anger, contempt, disgust, guilt, fear, and nervousness

optimism tendency toward a positive outlook and positive expectations

perceived control peoples' beliefs concerning their capacity to influence and shape outcomes in their lives

positive affect state or a trait that involves pleasurable engagement with the environment, the dimensions of which include happiness, joy, enthusiasm, alertness, and excitement

positive psychology scientific area of study seeking to identify and promote those qualities that lead to happy, fulfilled, and contented lives

primary appraisal judgment about the degree of potential harm or threat to well-being that a stressor might entail

psychoneuroimmunology field that studies how psychological factors (such as stress) influence the immune system and immune functioning

psychophysiological disorders physical disorders or diseases in which symptoms are brought about or worsened by stress and emotional factors

relaxation response technique stress reduction technique combining elements of relaxation and meditation

secondary appraisal judgment of options available to cope with a stressor and their potential effectiveness

Social Readjustment Rating Scale (SRRS) popular scale designed to measure stress; consists of 43 potentially stressful events, each of which has a numerical value quantifying how much readjustment is associated with the event

social support soothing and often beneficial support of others; can take different forms, such as advice, guidance, encouragement, acceptance, emotional comfort, and tangible assistance

stage of exhaustion third stage of the general adaptation syndrome; the body's ability to resist stress becomes depleted; illness, disease, and even death may occur

stage of resistance second stage of the general adaptation syndrome; the body adapts to a stressor for a period of time

stress process whereby an individual perceives and responds to events that one appraises as overwhelming or threatening to one's well-being

stressors environmental events that may be judged as threatening or demanding; stimuli that initiate the stress process

Type A psychological and behavior pattern exhibited by individuals who tend to be extremely competitive, impatient, rushed, and hostile toward others

Type B psychological and behavior pattern exhibited by a person who is relaxed and laid back

Summary

14.1 What Is Stress?
Stress is a process whereby an individual perceives and responds to events appraised as overwhelming or threatening to one's well-being. The scientific study of how stress and emotional factors impact health and well-being is called health psychology, a field devoted to studying the general impact of psychological factors on health. The body's primary physiological response during stress, the fight-or-flight response, was first identified in the early 20th century by Walter Cannon. The fight-or-flight response involves the coordinated activity of both the sympathetic nervous system and the hypothalamic-pituitary-adrenal (HPA) axis. Hans Selye, a noted endocrinologist, referred to these physiological reactions to stress as part of general adaptation syndrome, which occurs in three stages: alarm reaction (fight-or-flight reactions begin), resistance (the body begins to adapt to continuing stress), and exhaustion (adaptive energy is depleted, and stress begins to take a physical toll).

14.2 Stressors
Stressors can be chronic (long term) or acute (short term), and can include traumatic events, significant life changes, daily hassles, and situations in which people are frequently exposed to challenging and unpleasant events. Many potential stressors include events or situations that require us to make changes in our lives, such as a divorce or moving to a new residence. Thomas Holmes and Richard Rahe developed the Social Readjustment Rating Scale (SRRS) to measure stress by assigning a number of life change units to life events that typically require some adjustment, including positive events. Although the SRRS has been criticized on a number of grounds, extensive research has shown that the accumulation of many LCUs is associated with increased risk of illness. Many potential stressors also include daily hassles, which are minor irritations and annoyances that can build up over time. In addition, jobs that are especially demanding, offer little control over one's working environment, or involve unfavorable working conditions can lead to job strain, thereby setting the stage for job burnout.

14.3 Stress and Illness
Psychophysiological disorders are physical diseases that are either brought about or worsened by stress and other emotional factors. One of the mechanisms through which stress and emotional factors can influence the development of these diseases is by adversely affecting the body's immune system. A number of studies have demonstrated that stress weakens the functioning of the immune system. Cardiovascular disorders are serious medical conditions that have been consistently shown to be influenced by stress and negative emotions, such as anger, negative affectivity, and depression. Other psychophysiological disorders that are known to be influenced by stress and emotional factors include asthma and tension headaches.

14.4 Regulation of Stress
When faced with stress, people must attempt to manage or cope with it. In general, there are two basic forms of coping: problem-focused coping and emotion-focused coping. Those who use problem-focused coping strategies tend to cope better with stress because these strategies address the source of stress rather than the resulting symptoms. To a large extent, perceived control greatly impacts reaction to stressors and is associated with greater physical and mental well-being. Social support has been demonstrated to

be a highly effective buffer against the adverse effects of stress. Extensive research has shown that social support has beneficial physiological effects for people, and it seems to influence immune functioning. However, the beneficial effects of social support may be related to its influence on promoting healthy behaviors.

14.5 The Pursuit of Happiness

Happiness is conceptualized as an enduring state of mind that consists of the capacity to experience pleasure in daily life, as well as the ability to engage one's skills and talents to enrich one's life and the lives of others. Although people around the world generally report that they are happy, there are differences in average happiness levels across nations. Although people have a tendency to overestimate the extent to which their happiness set points would change for the better or for the worse following certain life events, researchers have identified a number of factors that are consistently related to happiness. In recent years, positive psychology has emerged as an area of study seeking to identify and promote qualities that lead to greater happiness and fulfillment in our lives. These components include positive affect, optimism, and flow.

Review Questions

1. Negative effects of stress are most likely to be experienced when an event is perceived as _____.
    a. negative, but it is likely to affect one's friends rather than oneself
    b. challenging
    c. confusing
    d. threatening, and no clear options for dealing with it are apparent

2. Between 2006 and 2009, the greatest increases in stress levels were found to occur among _____.
    a. Blacks
    b. those aged 45–64
    c. the unemployed
    d. those without college degrees

3. At which stage of Selye's general adaptation syndrome is a person especially vulnerable to illness?
    a. exhaustion
    b. alarm reaction
    c. fight-or-flight
    d. resistance

4. During an encounter judged as stressful, cortisol is released by the _____.
    a. sympathetic nervous system
    b. hypothalamus
    c. pituitary gland
    d. adrenal glands

5. According to the Holmes and Rahe scale, which life event requires the greatest amount of readjustment?
    a. marriage
    b. personal illness
    c. divorce
    d. death of spouse

6. While waiting to pay for his weekly groceries at the supermarket, Paul had to wait about 20 minutes in a long line at the checkout because only one cashier was on duty. When he was finally ready to pay, his debit card was declined because he did not have enough money left in his checking account. Because he had left his credit cards at home, he had to place the groceries back into the cart and head home to retrieve a credit card. While driving back to his home, traffic was backed up two miles due to an accident. These events that Paul had to endure are best characterized as _____.
    a. chronic stressors
    b. acute stressors
    c. daily hassles
    d. readjustment occurrences

7. What is one of the major criticisms of the Social Readjustment Rating Scale?
    a. It has too few items.
    b. It was developed using only people from the New England region of the United States.
    c. It does not take into consideration how a person appraises an event.
    d. None of the items included are positive.

8. Which of the following is not a dimension of job burnout?
    a. depersonalization
    b. hostility
    c. exhaustion
    d. diminished personal accomplishment

9. The white blood cells that attack foreign invaders to the body are called _____.
    a. antibodies
    b. telomeres
    c. lymphocytes
    d. immune cells

10. The risk of heart disease is especially high among individuals with _____.
    a. depression
    b. asthma
    c. telomeres
    d. lymphocytes

11. The most lethal dimension of Type A behavior pattern seems to be _____.
    a. hostility
    b. impatience
    c. time urgency
    d. competitive drive

12. Which of the following statements pertaining to asthma is *false*?
    a. Parental and interpersonal conflicts have been tied to the development of asthma.
    b. Asthma sufferers can experience asthma-like symptoms simply by believing that an inert substance they breathe will lead to airway obstruction.
    c. Asthma has been shown to be linked to periods of depression.
    d. Rates of asthma have decreased considerably since 2000.

13. Emotion-focused coping would likely be a better method than problem-focused coping for dealing with which of the following stressors?
    a. terminal cancer
    b. poor grades in school
    c. unemployment
    d. divorce

14. Studies of British civil servants have found that those in the lowest status jobs are much more likely to develop heart disease than those who have high status jobs. These findings attest to the importance of _____ in dealing with stress.
    a. biofeedback
    b. social support
    c. perceived control
    d. emotion-focused coping

15. Relative to those with low levels of social support, individuals with high levels of social support _____.
    a. are more likely to develop asthma
    b. tend to have less perceived control
    c. are more likely to develop cardiovascular disorders
    d. tend to tolerate stress well

16. The concept of learned helplessness was formulated by Seligman to explain the _____.
    a. inability of dogs to attempt to escape avoidable shocks after having received inescapable shocks
    b. failure of dogs to learn to from prior mistakes
    c. ability of dogs to learn to help other dogs escape situations in which they are receiving uncontrollable shocks
    d. inability of dogs to learn to help other dogs escape situations in which they are receiving uncontrollable electric shocks

17. Which of the following is *not* one of the presumed components of happiness?
    a. using our talents to help improve the lives of others
    b. learning new skills
    c. regular pleasurable experiences
    d. identifying and using our talents to enrich our lives

18. Researchers have identified a number of factors that are related to happiness. Which of the following is *not* one of them?
    a. age
    b. annual income up to $75,000
    c. physical attractiveness
    d. marriage

19. How does positive affect differ from optimism?
    a. Optimism is more scientific than positive affect.
    b. Positive affect is more scientific than optimism.
    c. Positive affect involves feeling states, whereas optimism involves expectations.
    d. Optimism involves feeling states, whereas positive affect involves expectations.

20. Carson enjoys writing mystery novels, and has even managed to publish some of his work. When he's writing, Carson becomes extremely focused on his work; in fact, he becomes so absorbed that that he often loses track of time, often staying up well past 3 a.m. Carson's experience best illustrates the concept of _____.
    a. happiness set point
    b. adaptation
    c. positive affect
    d. flow

Critical Thinking Questions

21. Provide an example (other than the one described earlier) of a situation or event that could be appraised as either threatening or challenging.

22. Provide an example of a stressful situation that may cause a person to become seriously ill. How would Selye's general adaptation syndrome explain this occurrence?

23. Review the items on the Social Readjustment Rating Scale. Select one of the items and discuss how it might bring about distress and eustress.

24. Job burnout tends to be high in people who work in human service jobs. Considering the three dimensions of job burnout, explain how various job aspects unique to being a police officer might lead to job burnout in that line of work.

25. Discuss the concept of Type A behavior pattern, its history, and what we now know concerning its role in heart disease.

26. Consider the study in which volunteers were given nasal drops containing the cold virus to examine the relationship between stress and immune function (Cohen et al., 1998). How might this finding explain how people seem to become sick during stressful times in their lives (e.g., final exam week)?

27. Although problem-focused coping seems to be a more effective strategy when dealing with stressors, do you think there are any kinds of stressful situations in which emotion-focused coping might be a better strategy?

28. Describe how social support can affect health both directly and indirectly.

29. In considering the three dimensions of happiness discussed in this section (the pleasant life, the good life, and the meaningful life), what are some steps you could take to improve your personal level of happiness?

30. The day before the drawing of a $300 million Powerball lottery, you notice that a line of people waiting to buy their Powerball tickets is stretched outside the door of a nearby convenience store. Based on what you've learned, provide some perspective on why these people are doing this, and what would likely happen if one of these individuals happened to pick the right numbers.

Personal Application Questions

31. Think of a time in which you and others you know (family members, friends, and classmates) experienced an event that some viewed as threatening and others viewed as challenging. What were some of the differences in the reactions of those who experienced the event as threatening compared to those who viewed the event as challenging? Why do you think there were differences in how these individuals judged the same event?

32. Suppose you want to design a study to examine the relationship between stress and illness, but you cannot use the Social Readjustment Rating Scale. How would you go about measuring stress? How would you measure illness? What would you need to do in order to tell if there is a cause-effect relationship between stress and illness?

33. If a family member or friend of yours has asthma, talk to that person (if he or she is willing) about their symptom triggers. Does this person mention stress or emotional states? If so, are there any commonalities in these asthma triggers?

34. Try to think of an example in which you coped with a particular stressor by using problem-focused coping. What was the stressor? What did your problem-focused efforts involve? Were they effective?

35. Think of an activity you participate in that you find engaging and absorbing. For example, this might be something like playing video games, reading, or a hobby. What are your experiences typically like while engaging in this activity? Do your experiences conform to the notion of flow? If so, how? Do you think these experiences have enriched your life? Why or why not?

Chapter 15
Psychological Disorders

Figure 15.1 A wreath is laid in memoriam to victims of the Washington Navy Yard shooting. (credit: modification of work by D. Myles Cullen, US Department of Defense)

Chapter Outline

15.1 What Are Psychological Disorders?
15.2 Diagnosing and Classifying Psychological Disorders
15.3 Perspectives on Psychological Disorders
15.4 Anxiety Disorders
15.5 Obsessive-Compulsive and Related Disorders
15.6 Posttraumatic Stress Disorder
15.7 Mood Disorders
15.8 Schizophrenia
15.9 Dissociative Disorders
15.10 Disorders in Childhood
15.11 Personality Disorders

Introduction

On Monday, September 16, 2013, a gunman killed 12 people as the workday began at the Washington Navy Yard in Washington, DC. Aaron Alexis, 34, had a troubled history: he thought that he was being controlled by radio waves. He called the police to complain about voices in his head and being under surveillance by "shadowy forces" (Thomas, Levine, Date, & Cloherty, 2013). While Alexis's actions cannot be excused, it is clear that he had some form of mental illness. Mental illness is not necessarily a cause of violence; it is far more likely that the mentally ill will be victims rather than perpetrators of violence (Stuart, 2003). If, however, Alexis had received the help he needed, this tragedy might have been averted.

15.1 What Are Psychological Disorders?

Learning Objectives

By the end of this section, you will be able to:
- Understand the problems inherent in defining the concept of psychological disorder
- Describe what is meant by harmful dysfunction
- Identify the formal criteria that thoughts, feelings, and behaviors must meet to be considered abnormal and, thus, symptomatic of a psychological disorder

A **psychological disorder** is a condition characterized by abnormal thoughts, feelings, and behaviors. **Psychopathology** is the study of psychological disorders, including their symptoms, **etiology** (i.e., their causes), and treatment. The term *psychopathology* can also refer to the manifestation of a psychological disorder. Although consensus can be difficult, it is extremely important for mental health professionals to agree on what kinds of thoughts, feelings, and behaviors are truly abnormal in the sense that they genuinely indicate the presence of psychopathology. Certain patterns of behavior and inner experience can easily be labeled as abnormal and clearly signify some kind of psychological disturbance. The person who washes his hands 40 times per day and the person who claims to hear the voices of demons exhibit behaviors and inner experiences that most would regard as abnormal: beliefs and behaviors that suggest the existence of a psychological disorder. But, consider the nervousness a young man feels when talking to an attractive person or the loneliness and longing for home a first-year student experiences during her first semester of college—these feelings may not be regularly present, but they fall in the range of normal. So, what kinds of thoughts, feelings, and behaviors represent a true psychological disorder? Psychologists work to distinguish psychological disorders from inner experiences and behaviors that are merely situational, idiosyncratic, or unconventional.

DEFINITION OF A PSYCHOLOGICAL DISORDER

Perhaps the simplest approach to conceptualizing psychological disorders is to label behaviors, thoughts, and inner experiences that are atypical, distressful, dysfunctional, and sometimes even dangerous, as signs of a disorder. For example, if you ask a classmate for a date and you are rejected, you probably would feel a little dejected. Such feelings would be normal. If you felt extremely depressed—so much so that you lost interest in activities, had difficulty eating or sleeping, felt utterly worthless, and contemplated suicide—your feelings would be **atypical**, would deviate from the norm, and could signify the presence of a psychological disorder. Just because something is atypical, however, does not necessarily mean it is disordered.

For example, only about 4% of people in the United States have red hair, so red hair is considered an atypical characteristic (Figure 15.2), but it is not considered disordered, it's just unusual. And it is less unusual in Scotland, where approximately 13% of the population has red hair ("DNA Project Aims," 2012). As you will learn, some disorders, although not exactly typical, are far from atypical, and the rates in which they appear in the population are surprisingly high.

Figure 15.2 Red hair is considered unusual, but not abnormal. (a) Isla Fischer, (b) Prince Harry, and (c) Marcia Cross are three natural redheads. (credit a: modification of work by Richard Goldschmidt; credit b: modification of work by Glyn Lowe; credit c: modification of work by Kirk Weaver)

If we can agree that merely being atypical is an insufficient criterion for a having a psychological disorder, is it reasonable to consider behavior or inner experiences that differ from widely expected cultural values or expectations as disordered? Using this criterion, a person who walks around a subway platform wearing a heavy winter coat in July while screaming obscenities at strangers may be considered as exhibiting symptoms of a psychological disorder. Their actions and clothes violate socially accepted rules governing appropriate dress and behavior; these characteristics are atypical.

CULTURAL EXPECTATIONS

Violating cultural expectations is not, in and of itself, a satisfactory means of identifying the presence of a psychological disorder. Since behavior varies from one culture to another, what may be expected and considered appropriate in one culture may not be viewed as such in other cultures. For example, returning a stranger's smile is expected in the United States because a pervasive social norm dictates that we reciprocate friendly gestures. A person who refuses to acknowledge such gestures might be considered socially awkward—perhaps even disordered—for violating this expectation. However, such expectations are not universally shared. Cultural expectations in Japan involve showing reserve, restraint, and a concern for maintaining privacy around strangers. Japanese people are generally unresponsive to smiles from strangers (Patterson et al., 2007). Eye contact provides another example. In the United States and Europe, eye contact with others typically signifies honesty and attention. However, most Latin-American, Asian, and African cultures interpret direct eye contact as rude, confrontational, and aggressive (Pazain, 2010). Thus, someone who makes eye contact with you could be considered appropriate and respectful or brazen and offensive, depending on your culture (Figure 15.3).

Figure 15.3 Eye contact is one of many social gestures that vary from culture to culture. (credit: Joi Ito)

Hallucinations (seeing or hearing things that are not physically present) in Western societies is a violation of cultural expectations, and a person who reports such inner experiences is readily labeled as psychologically disordered. In other cultures, visions that, for example, pertain to future events may be regarded as normal experiences that are positively valued (Bourguignon, 1970). Finally, it is important to recognize that cultural norms change over time: what might be considered typical in a society at one time may no longer be viewed this way later, similar to how fashion trends from one era may elicit quizzical looks decades later—imagine how a headband, legwarmers, and the big hair of the 1980s would go over on your campus today.

DIG DEEPER

The Myth of Mental Illness

In the 1950s and 1960s, the concept of mental illness was widely criticized. One of the major criticisms focused on the notion that mental illness was a "myth that justifies psychiatric intervention in socially disapproved behavior" (Wakefield, 1992). Thomas Szasz (1960), a noted psychiatrist, was perhaps the biggest proponent of this view. Szasz argued that the notion of mental illness was invented by society (and the mental health establishment) to stigmatize and subjugate people whose behavior violates accepted social and legal norms. Indeed, Szasz suggested that what appear to be symptoms of mental illness are more appropriately characterized as "problems in living" (Szasz, 1960).

In his 1961 book, *The Myth of Mental Illness: Foundations of a Theory of Personal Conduct*, Szasz expressed his disdain for the concept of mental illness and for the field of psychiatry in general (Oliver, 2006). The basis for Szasz's attack was his contention that detectable abnormalities in bodily structures and functions (e.g., infections and organ damage or dysfunction) represent the defining features of genuine illness or disease, and because symptoms of purported mental illness are not accompanied by such detectable abnormalities, so-called psychological disorders are not disorders at all. Szasz (1961/2010) proclaimed that "disease or illness can only affect the body; hence, there can be no mental illness" (p. 267).

Today, we recognize the extreme level of psychological suffering experienced by people with psychological disorders: the painful thoughts and feelings they experience, the disordered behavior they demonstrate, and the levels of distress and impairment they exhibit. This makes it very difficult to deny the reality of mental illness.

However controversial Szasz's views and those of his supporters might have been, they have influenced the mental health community and society in several ways. First, lay people, politicians, and professionals now often refer to mental illness as mental health "problems," implicitly acknowledging the "problems in living" perspective Szasz described (Buchanan-Barker & Barker, 2009). Also influential was Szasz's view of homosexuality. Szasz was perhaps the first psychiatrist to openly challenge the idea that homosexuality represented a form of mental illness or disease (Szasz, 1965). By challenging the idea that homosexuality represented a form a mental illness, Szasz helped pave the way for the social and civil rights that gay and lesbian people now have (Barker, 2010). His work also inspired legal changes that protect the rights of people in psychiatric institutions and allow such individuals a greater degree of influence and responsibility over their lives (Buchanan-Barker & Barker, 2009).

HARMFUL DYSFUNCTION

If none of the criterion discussed so far is adequate by itself to define the presence of a psychological disorder, how can a disorder be conceptualized? Many efforts have been made to identify the specific dimensions of psychological disorders, yet none is entirely satisfactory. No universal definition of psychological disorder exists that can apply to all situations in which a disorder is thought to be present (Zachar & Kendler, 2007). However, one of the more influential conceptualizations was proposed by Wakefield (1992), who defined psychological disorder as a **harmful dysfunction**. Wakefield argued that natural internal mechanisms—that is, psychological processes honed by evolution, such as cognition, perception, and learning—have important functions, such as enabling us to experience the world the way others do and to engage in rational thought, problem solving, and communication. For example, learning allows us to associate a fear with a potential danger in such a way that the intensity of fear is roughly equal to the degree of actual danger. Dysfunction occurs when an internal mechanism breaks down and can no longer perform its normal function. But, the presence of a dysfunction by itself does not determine a disorder. The dysfunction must be harmful in that it leads to negative consequences for the individual or for others, as judged by the standards of the individual's culture. The harm may include significant internal anguish (e.g., high levels of anxiety or depression) or problems in day-to-day living (e.g., in one's social or work life).

To illustrate, Janet has an extreme fear of spiders. Janet's fear might be considered a dysfunction in that it signals that the internal mechanism of learning is not working correctly (i.e., a faulty process prevents Janet from appropriately associating the magnitude of fear with the actual threat posed by spiders). Janet's fear of spiders has a significant negative influence on daily life: she avoids all situations in which she suspects spiders to be present (e.g., the basement or a friend's home), and she quit her job last month because she saw a spider in the restroom at work and is now unemployed. According to the harmful dysfunction model, Janet's condition would signify a disorder because (a) there is a dysfunction in an internal mechanism, and (b) the dysfunction has resulted in harmful consequences. Similar to how the symptoms of physical illness reflect dysfunctions in biological processes, the symptoms of psychological disorders presumably reflect dysfunctions in mental processes. The internal mechanism component of this model is especially appealing because it implies that disorders may occur through a breakdown of biological functions that govern various psychological processes, thus supporting contemporary neurobiological models of psychological disorders (Fabrega, 2007).

THE AMERICAN PSYCHIATRIC ASSOCIATION (APA) DEFINITION

Many of the features of the harmful dysfunction model are incorporated in a formal definition of psychological disorder developed by the American Psychiatric Association (APA). According to the APA (2013), a psychological disorder is a condition that is said to consist of the following:

- **There are significant disturbances in thoughts, feelings, and behaviors.** A person must experience inner states (e.g., thoughts and/or feelings) and exhibit behaviors that are clearly disturbed—that is, unusual, but in a negative, self-defeating way. Often, such disturbances are troubling to those around the individual who experiences them. For example, an individual who is uncontrollably preoccupied by thoughts of germs spends hours each day bathing, has inner experiences, and displays behaviors that most would consider atypical and negative (disturbed) and that would likely be troubling to family members.

- **The disturbances reflect some kind of biological, psychological, or developmental dysfunction.** Disturbed patterns of inner experiences and behaviors should reflect some flaw (dysfunction) in the internal biological, psychological, and developmental mechanisms that lead to normal, healthy psychological functioning. For example, the hallucinations observed in schizophrenia could be a sign of brain abnormalities.

- **The disturbances lead to significant distress or disability in one's life.** A person's inner experiences and behaviors are considered to reflect a psychological disorder if they cause the person considerable distress, or greatly impair his ability to function as a normal individual (often referred to as functional impairment, or occupational and social impairment). As an illustration, a person's fear of social situations might be so distressing that it causes the person to avoid all social situations (e.g., preventing that person from being able to attend class or apply for a job).

- **The disturbances do not reflect expected or culturally approved responses to certain events.** Disturbances in thoughts, feelings, and behaviors must be socially unacceptable responses to certain events that often happen in life. For example, it is perfectly natural (and expected) that a person would experience great sadness and might wish to be left alone following the death of a close family member. Because such reactions are in some ways culturally expected, the individual would not be assumed to signify a mental disorder.

Some believe that there is no essential criterion or set of criteria that can definitively distinguish all cases of disorder from nondisorder (Lilienfeld & Marino, 1999). In truth, no single approach to defining a psychological disorder is adequate by itself, nor is there universal agreement on where the boundary is between disordered and not disordered. From time to time we all experience anxiety, unwanted thoughts, and moments of sadness; our behavior at other times may not make much sense to ourselves or to others. These inner experiences and behaviors can vary in their intensity, but are only considered disordered when they are highly disturbing to us and/or others, suggest a dysfunction in normal mental functioning, and are associated with significant distress or disability in social or occupational activities.

15.2 Diagnosing and Classifying Psychological Disorders

Learning Objectives

By the end of this section, you will be able to:
- Explain why classification systems are necessary in the study of psychopathology
- Describe the basic features of the Diagnostic and Statistical Manual of Mental Disorders, Fifth Edition (DSM-5)
- Discuss changes in the DSM over time, including criticisms of the current edition
- Identify which disorders are generally the most common

A first step in the study of psychological disorders is carefully and systematically discerning significant signs and symptoms. How do mental health professionals ascertain whether or not a person's inner states and behaviors truly represent a psychological disorder? Arriving at a proper **diagnosis**—that is, appropriately identifying and labeling a set of defined symptoms—is absolutely crucial. This process enables professionals to use a common language with others in the field and aids in communication about the disorder with the patient, colleagues and the public. A proper diagnosis is an essential element to guide proper and successful treatment. For these reasons, classification systems that organize psychological disorders systematically are necessary.

THE DIAGNOSTIC AND STATISTICAL MANUAL OF MENTAL DISORDERS (DSM)

Although a number of classification systems have been developed over time, the one that is used by most mental health professionals in the United States is the ***Diagnostic and Statistical Manual of Mental Disorders* (DSM-5)**, published by the American Psychiatric Association (2013). (Note that the American Psychiatric Association differs from the American Psychological Association; both are abbreviated APA.) The first edition of the DSM, published in 1952, classified psychological disorders according to a format developed by the U.S. Army during World War II (Clegg, 2012). In the years since, the DSM has undergone numerous revisions and editions. The most recent edition, published in 2013, is the DSM-5 (APA, 2013). The DSM-5 includes many categories of disorders (e.g., anxiety disorders, depressive disorders, and dissociative disorders). Each disorder is described in detail, including an overview of the disorder (diagnostic features), specific symptoms required for diagnosis (diagnostic criteria), prevalence information (what percent of the population is thought to be afflicted with the disorder), and risk factors associated with the disorder. Figure 15.4 shows lifetime prevalence rates—the percentage of people in a population who develop a disorder in their lifetime—of various psychological disorders among U.S. adults. These data were based on a national sample of 9,282 U.S. residents (National Comorbidity Survey, 2007).

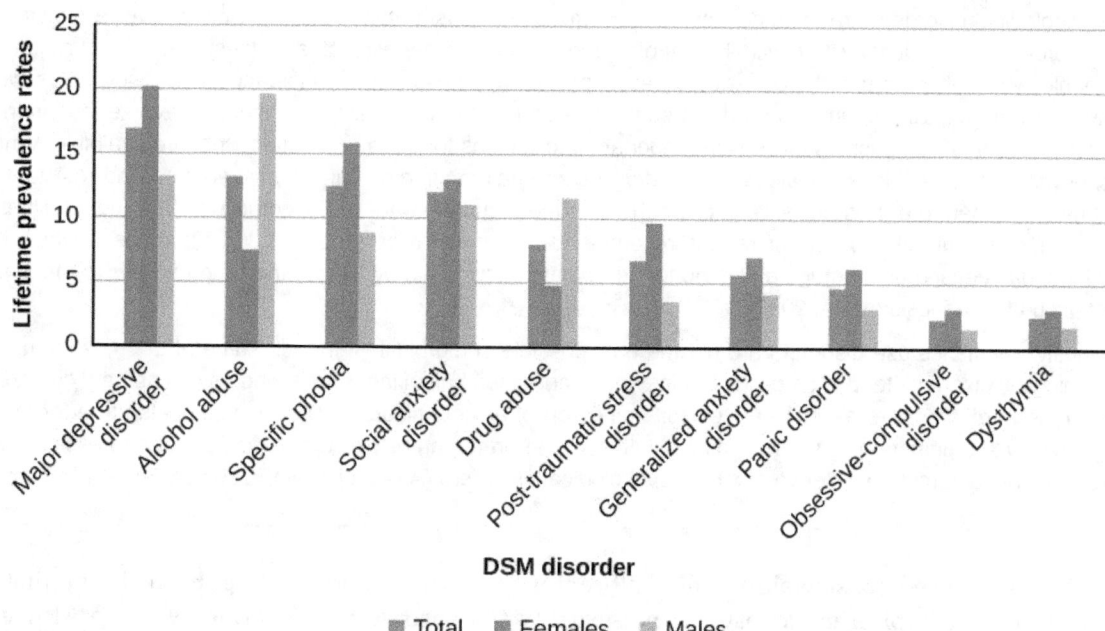

Figure 15.4 The graph shows the breakdown of psychological disorders, comparing the percentage prevalence among adult males and adult females in the United States. Because the data is from 2007, the categories shown here are from the DSM-IV, which has been supplanted by the DSM-5. Most categories remain the same; however, alcohol abuse now falls under a broader Alcohol Use Disorder category.

The DSM-5 also provides information about **comorbidity**; the co-occurrence of two disorders. For example, the DSM-5 mentions that 41% of people with obsessive-compulsive disorder (OCD) also meet the diagnostic criteria for major depressive disorder (**Figure 15.5**). Drug use is highly comorbid with other mental illnesses; 6 out of 10 people who have a substance use disorder also suffer from another form of mental illness (National Institute on Drug Abuse [NIDA], 2007).

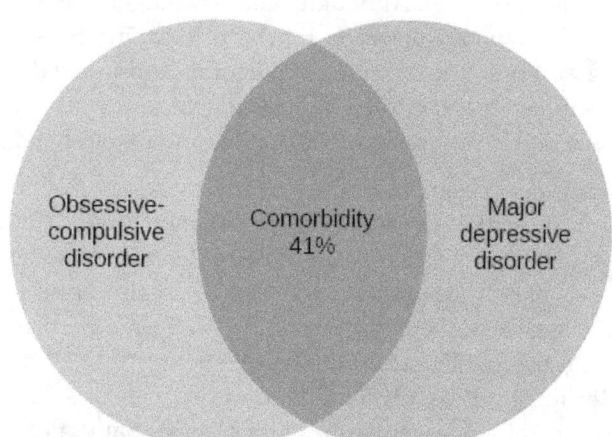

Figure 15.5 Obsessive-compulsive disorder and major depressive disorder frequently occur in the same person.

CONNECT THE CONCEPTS

Comorbidity

As you've learned in the text, comorbidity refers to situations in which an individual suffers from more than one disorder, and often the symptoms of each can interact in negative ways. Co-occurrence and comorbidity of psychological disorders are quite common, and some of the most pervasive comorbidities involve substance use disorders that co-occur with psychological disorders. Indeed, some estimates suggest that around a quarter of people who suffer from the most severe cases of mental illness exhibit substance use disorder as well. Conversely, around 10 percent of individuals seeking treatment for substance use disorder have serious mental illnesses. Observations such as these have important implications for treatment options that are available. When people with a mental illness are also habitual drug users, their symptoms can be exacerbated and resistant to treatment. Furthermore, it is not always clear whether the symptoms are due to drug use, the mental illness, or a combination of the two. Therefore, it is recommended that behavior is observed in situations in which the individual has ceased using drugs and is no longer experiencing withdrawal from the drug in order to make the most accurate diagnosis (NIDA, 2018).

Obviously, substance use disorders are not the only possible comorbidities. In fact, some of the most common psychological disorders tend to co-occur. For instance, more than half of individuals who have a primary diagnosis of depressive disorder are estimated to exhibit some sort of anxiety disorder. The reverse is also true for those diagnosed with a primary diagnosis of an anxiety disorder. Further, anxiety disorders and major depression have a high rate of comorbidity with several other psychological disorders (Al-Asadi, Klein, & Meyer, 2015).

The DSM has changed considerably in the half-century since it was originally published. The first two editions of the DSM, for example, listed homosexuality as a disorder; however, in 1973, the APA voted to remove it from the manual (Silverstein, 2009). While the DSM-III did not list homosexuality as a disorder, it introduced a new diagnosis, ego-dystonic homosexuality, which emphasized homosexual arousal that the patient viewed as interfering with desired heterosexual relationships and causing distress for the individual. This new diagnosis was considered by many as a compromise to appease those who viewed homosexuality as a mental illness. Other professionals questioned how appropriate it was to have a separate diagnosis that described the content of an individual's distress. In 1986, the diagnosis was removed from the DSM-III-R (Herek, 2012). Additionally, beginning with the DSM-III in 1980, mental disorders have been described in much greater detail, and the number of diagnosable conditions has grown steadily, as has the size of the manual itself. DSM-I included 106 diagnoses and was 130 total pages, whereas DSM-III included more than 2 times as many diagnoses (265) and was nearly seven times its size (886 total pages) (Mayes & Horowitz, 2005). Although DSM-5 is longer than DSM-IV, the volume includes only 237 disorders, a decrease from the 297 disorders that were listed in DSM-IV. The latest edition, DSM-5, includes revisions in the organization and naming of categories and in the diagnostic criteria for various disorders (Regier, Kuhl, & Kupfer, 2012), while emphasizing careful consideration of the importance of gender and cultural difference in the expression of various symptoms (Fisher, 2010).

Some believe that establishing new diagnoses might overpathologize the human condition by turning common human problems into mental illnesses (The Associated Press, 2013). Indeed, the finding that nearly half of all Americans will meet the criteria for a DSM disorder at some point in their life (Kessler et al., 2005) likely fuels much of this skepticism. The DSM-5 is also criticized on the grounds that its diagnostic criteria have been loosened, thereby threatening to "turn our current diagnostic inflation into diagnostic hyperinflation" (Frances, 2012, para. 22). For example, DSM-IV specified that the symptoms of major depressive disorder must not be attributable to normal bereavement (loss of a loved one). The DSM-5, however, has removed this bereavement exclusion, essentially meaning that grief and sadness after a loved one's death can constitute major depressive disorder.

THE INTERNATIONAL CLASSIFICATION OF DISEASES

A second classification system, the *International Classification of Diseases* (ICD), is also widely recognized. Published by the World Health Organization (WHO), the ICD was developed in Europe shortly after World War II and, like the DSM, has been revised several times. The categories of psychological disorders in both the DSM and ICD are similar, as are the criteria for specific disorders; however, some differences exist. Although the ICD is used for clinical purposes, this tool is also used to examine the general health of populations and to monitor the prevalence of diseases and other health problems internationally (WHO, 2013). The ICD is in its 10th edition (ICD-10); however, efforts are now underway to develop a new edition (ICD-11) that, in conjunction with the changes in DSM-5, will help harmonize the two classification systems as much as possible (APA, 2013).

A study that compared the use of the two classification systems found that worldwide the ICD is more frequently used for clinical diagnosis, whereas the DSM is more valued for research (Mezzich, 2002). Most research findings concerning the etiology and treatment of psychological disorders are based on criteria set forth in the DSM (Oltmanns & Castonguay, 2013). The DSM also includes more explicit disorder criteria, along with an extensive and helpful explanatory text (Regier et al., 2012). The DSM is the classification system of choice among U.S. mental health professionals, and this chapter is based on the DSM paradigm.

THE COMPASSIONATE VIEW OF PSYCHOLOGICAL DISORDERS

As these disorders are outlined, please bear two things in mind. First, remember that psychological disorders represent *extremes* of inner experience and behavior. If, while reading about these disorders, you feel that these descriptions begin to personally characterize you, do not worry—this moment of enlightenment probably means nothing more than you are normal. Each of us experiences episodes of sadness, anxiety, and preoccupation with certain thoughts—times when we do not quite feel ourselves. These episodes should not be considered problematic unless the accompanying thoughts and behaviors become extreme and have a disruptive effect on one's life. Second, understand that people with psychological disorders are far more than just embodiments of their disorders. We do not use terms such as schizophrenics, depressives, or phobics because they are labels that objectify people who suffer from these conditions, thus promoting biased and disparaging assumptions about them. It is important to remember that a psychological disorder is not what a person *is*; it is something that a person *has*—through no fault of his or her own. As is the case with cancer or diabetes, those with psychological disorders suffer debilitating, often painful conditions that are not of their own choosing. These individuals deserve to be viewed and treated with compassion, understanding, and dignity.

15.3 Perspectives on Psychological Disorders

Learning Objectives

By the end of this section, you will be able to:
- Discuss supernatural perspectives on the origin of psychological disorders, in their historical context
- Describe modern biological and psychological perspectives on the origin of psychological disorders
- Identify which disorders generally show the highest degree of heritability
- Describe the diathesis-stress model and its importance to the study of psychopathology

Scientists, mental health professionals, and cultural healers may adopt different perspectives in attempting to understand or explain the underlying mechanisms that contribute to the development of a psychological disorder. The specific perspective used in explaining a psychological disorder is extremely important. Each perspective explains psychological disorders, their causes or etiology, and effective treatments from a different viewpoint. Different perspectives provide alternate ways for how to think about the nature of psychopathology.

SUPERNATURAL PERSPECTIVES OF PSYCHOLOGICAL DISORDERS

For centuries, psychological disorders were viewed from a **supernatural** perspective: attributed to a force beyond scientific understanding. Those afflicted were thought to be practitioners of black magic or possessed by spirits (Figure 15.6) (Maher & Maher, 1985). For example, convents throughout Europe in the 16th and 17th centuries reported hundreds of nuns falling into a state of frenzy in which the afflicted foamed at the mouth, screamed and convulsed, sexually propositioned priests, and confessed to having carnal relations with devils or Christ. Although, today, these cases would suggest serious mental illness; at the time, these events were routinely explained as possession by devilish forces (Waller, 2009a). Similarly, grievous fits by young girls are believed to have precipitated the witch panic in New England late in the 17th century (Demos, 1983). Such beliefs in supernatural causes of mental illness are still held in some societies today; for example, beliefs that supernatural forces cause mental illness are common in some cultures in modern-day Nigeria (Aghukwa, 2012).

Figure 15.6 In *The Extraction of the Stone of Madness*, a 15th century painting by Hieronymus Bosch, a practitioner is using a tool to extract an object (the supposed "stone of madness") from the head of an afflicted person.

DIG DEEPER

Dancing Mania

Between the 11th and 17th centuries, a curious epidemic swept across Western Europe. Groups of people would suddenly begin to dance with wild abandon. This compulsion to dance—referred to as dancing mania—sometimes gripped thousands of people at a time (Figure 15.7). Historical accounts indicate that those afflicted would sometimes dance with bruised and bloody feet for days or weeks, screaming of terrible visions and begging priests and monks to save their souls (Waller, 2009b). What caused dancing mania is not known, but several explanations have been proposed, including spider venom and ergot poisoning ("Dancing Mania," 2011).

Figure 15.7 Although the cause of dancing mania, depicted in this painting, was unclear, the behavior was attributed to supernatural forces.

Historian John Waller (2009a, 2009b) has provided a comprehensive and convincing explanation of dancing mania that suggests the phenomenon was attributable to a combination of three factors: psychological distress, social contagion, and belief in supernatural forces. Waller argued that various disasters of the time (such as famine, plagues, and floods) produced high levels of psychological distress that could increase the likelihood of succumbing to an involuntary trance state. Waller indicated that anthropological studies and accounts of possession rituals show that people are more likely to enter a trance state if they expect it to happen, and that entranced individuals behave in a ritualistic manner, their thoughts and behavior shaped by the spiritual beliefs of their culture. Thus, during periods of extreme physical and mental distress, all it took were a few people—believing themselves to have been afflicted with a dancing curse—to slip into a spontaneous trance and then act out the part of one who is cursed by dancing for days on end.

BIOLOGICAL PERSPECTIVES OF PSYCHOLOGICAL DISORDERS

The biological perspective views psychological disorders as linked to biological phenomena, such as genetic factors, chemical imbalances, and brain abnormalities; it has gained considerable attention and acceptance in recent decades (Wyatt & Midkiff, 2006). Evidence from many sources indicates that most psychological disorders have a genetic component; in fact, there is little dispute that some disorders are largely due to genetic factors. The graph in **Figure 15.8** shows heritability estimates for schizophrenia.

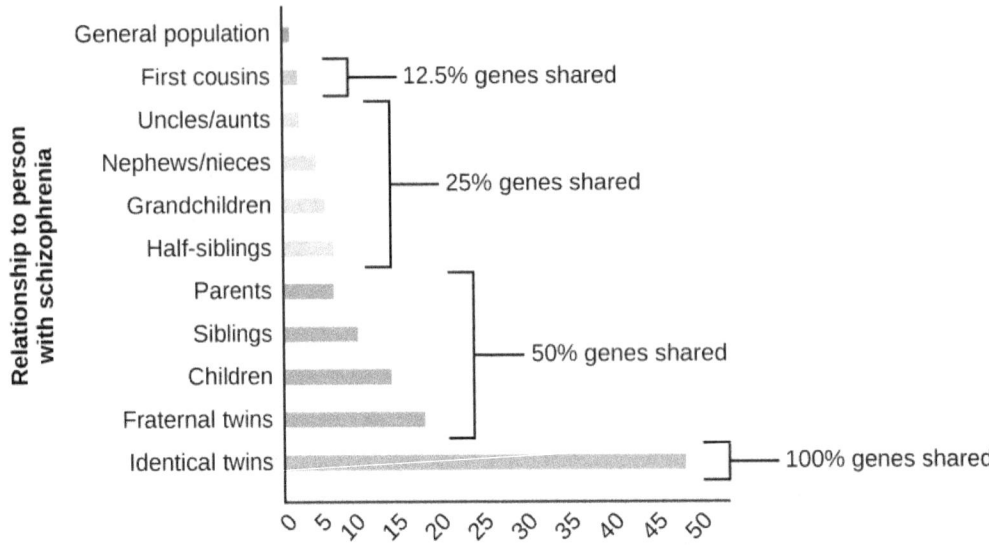

Figure 15.8 A person's risk of developing schizophrenia increases if a relative has schizophrenia. The closer the genetic relationship, the higher the risk.

Findings such as these have led many of today's researchers to search for specific genes and genetic mutations that contribute to mental disorders. Also, sophisticated neural imaging technology in recent decades has revealed how abnormalities in brain structure and function might be directly involved in many disorders, and advances in our understanding of neurotransmitters and hormones have yielded insights into their possible connections. The biological perspective is currently thriving in the study of psychological disorders.

THE DIATHESIS-STRESS MODEL OF PSYCHOLOGICAL DISORDERS

Despite advances in understanding the biological basis of psychological disorders, the psychosocial perspective is still very important. This perspective emphasizes the importance of learning, stress, faulty and self-defeating thinking patterns, and environmental factors. Perhaps the best way to think about psychological disorders, then, is to view them as originating from a combination of biological and psychological processes. Many develop not from a single cause, but from a delicate fusion between partly biological and partly psychosocial factors.

The **diathesis-stress model** (Zuckerman, 1999) integrates biological and psychosocial factors to predict the likelihood of a disorder. This diathesis-stress model suggests that people with an underlying predisposition for a disorder (i.e., a diathesis) are more likely than others to develop a disorder when faced with adverse environmental or psychological events (i.e., stress), such as childhood maltreatment, negative life events, trauma, and so on. A diathesis is not always a biological vulnerability to an illness; some diatheses may be psychological (e.g., a tendency to think about life events in a pessimistic, self-defeating way).

The key assumption of the diathesis-stress model is that both factors, diathesis and stress, are necessary in the development of a disorder. Different models explore the relationship between the two factors: the level of stress needed to produce the disorder is inversely proportional to the level of diathesis.

15.4 Anxiety Disorders

Learning Objectives

By the end of this section, you will be able to:
- Distinguish normal anxiety from pathological anxiety
- List and describe the major anxiety disorders, including their main features and prevalence
- Describe basic psychological and biological factors that are suspected to be important in the etiology of anxiety disorder

Everybody experiences anxiety from time to time. Although anxiety is closely related to fear, the two states possess important differences. Fear involves an instantaneous reaction to an imminent threat, whereas anxiety involves apprehension, avoidance, and cautiousness regarding a potential threat, danger, or other negative event (Craske, 1999). While anxiety is unpleasant to most people, it is important to our health, safety, and well-being. Anxiety motivates us to take actions—such as preparing for exams, watching our weight, showing up to work on time—that enable us to avert potential future problems. Anxiety also motivates us to avoid certain things—such as running up debts and engaging in illegal activities—that could lead to future trouble. Most individuals' level and duration of anxiety approximates the magnitude of the potential threat they face. For example, suppose a student who came to the U.S. as a "Dreamer" (someone whose parents didn't lawfully immigrate) is concerned about the possibility of being unable to continue in the university program or of losing access to academic financial aid, due to changes and litigation around the Deferred Action for Childhood Arrivals (DACA) program. This person likely would experience anxiety of greater intensity and duration than would a 21-year-old junior who entered college as a birthright citizen. Some people experience anxiety that is excessive, persistent, and greatly out of proportion to the actual threat; if one's anxiety has a disruptive influence on one's life, this is a strong indicator that the individual is experiencing an anxiety disorder.

Anxiety disorders are characterized by excessive and persistent fear and anxiety, and by related disturbances in behavior (APA, 2013). Although anxiety is universally experienced, anxiety disorders cause considerable distress. As a group, anxiety disorders are common: approximately 25%–30% of the U.S. population meets the criteria for at least one anxiety disorder during their lifetime (Kessler et al., 2005). Also, these disorders appear to be much more common in women than they are in men; within a 12-month period, around 23% of women and 14% of men will experience at least one anxiety disorder (National Comorbidity Survey, 2007). Anxiety disorders are the most frequently occurring class of mental disorders and are often comorbid with each other and with other mental disorders (Kessler, Ruscio, Shear, & Wittchen, 2009).

SPECIFIC PHOBIA

Phobia is a Greek word that means fear. A person diagnosed with a **specific phobia** (formerly known as simple phobia) experiences excessive, distressing, and persistent fear or anxiety about a specific object or situation (such as animals, enclosed spaces, elevators, or flying) (APA, 2013). Even though people realize their level of fear and anxiety in relation to the phobic stimulus is irrational, some people with a specific phobia may go to great lengths to avoid the phobic stimulus (the object or situation that triggers the fear and anxiety). Typically, the fear and anxiety a phobic stimulus elicits is disruptive to the person's life. For example, a man with a phobia of flying might refuse to accept a job that requires frequent air travel, thus negatively affecting his career. Clinicians who have worked with people who have specific phobias have encountered many kinds of phobias, some of which are shown in Table 15.1.

Specific Phobias

Phobia	Feared Object or Situation
Acrophobia	heights
Aerophobia	flying
Arachnophobia	spiders
Claustrophobia	enclosed spaces
Cynophobia	dogs
Hematophobia	blood
Ophidiophobia	snakes
Taphophobia	being buried alive
Trypanophobia	injections
Xenophobia	strangers

Table 15.1

Specific phobias are common; in the United States, around 12.5% of the population will meet the criteria for a specific phobia at some point in their lifetime (Kessler et al., 2005). One type of phobia, **agoraphobia**, is listed in the DSM-5 as a separate anxiety disorder. Agoraphobia, which literally means "fear of the marketplace," is characterized by intense fear, anxiety, and avoidance of situations in which it might be difficult to escape or receive help if one experiences symptoms of a panic attack (a state of extreme anxiety that we will discuss shortly). These situations include public transportation, open spaces (parking lots), enclosed spaces (stores), crowds, or being outside the home alone (APA, 2013). About 1.4% of Americans experience agoraphobia during their lifetime (Kessler et al., 2005).

ACQUISITION OF PHOBIAS THROUGH LEARNING

Many theories suggest that phobias develop through learning. Rachman (1977) proposed that phobias can be acquired through three major learning pathways. The first pathway is through classical conditioning. As you may recall, classical conditioning is a form of learning in which a previously neutral stimulus is paired with an unconditioned stimulus (UCS) that reflexively elicits an unconditioned response (UCR), eliciting the same response through its association with the unconditioned stimulus. The response is called a conditioned response (CR). For example, a child who has been bitten by a dog may come to fear dogs because of a past association with pain. In this case, the dog bite is the UCS and the fear it elicits is the UCR. Because a dog was associated with the bite, any dog may come to serve as a conditioned stimulus, thereby eliciting fear; the fear the child experiences around dogs, then, becomes a CR.

The second pathway of phobia acquisition is through vicarious learning, such as modeling. For example, a child who observes his cousin react fearfully to spiders may later express the same fears, even though spiders have never presented any danger to him. This phenomenon has been observed in both humans and nonhuman primates (Olsson & Phelps, 2007). A study of laboratory-reared monkeys readily acquired a fear of snakes after observing wild-reared monkeys react fearfully to snakes (Mineka & Cook, 1993).

The third pathway is through verbal transmission or information. For example, a child whose parents, siblings, friends, and classmates constantly tell her how disgusting and dangerous snakes are may come to acquire a fear of snakes.

Interestingly, people are more likely to develop phobias of things that do not represent much actual danger to themselves, such as animals and heights, and are less likely to develop phobias toward things that present legitimate danger in contemporary society, such as motorcycles and weapons (Öhman & Mineka, 2001). Why might this be so? One theory suggests that the human brain is evolutionarily predisposed to more readily associate certain objects or situations with fear (Seligman, 1971). This theory argues that throughout our evolutionary history, our ancestors associated certain stimuli (e.g., snakes, spiders, heights, and thunder) with potential danger. As time progressed, the mind has become adapted to more readily develop fears of these things than of others. Experimental evidence has consistently demonstrated that conditioned fears develop more readily to fear-relevant stimuli (images of snakes and spiders) than to fear-irrelevant stimuli (images of flowers and berries) (Öhman & Mineka, 2001). Such prepared learning has also been shown to occur in monkeys. In one study (Cook & Mineka, 1989), monkeys watched videotapes of model monkeys reacting fearfully to either fear-relevant stimuli (toy snakes or a toy crocodile) or fear-irrelevant stimuli (flowers or a toy rabbit). The observer monkeys developed fears of the fear-relevant stimuli but not the fear-irrelevant stimuli.

SOCIAL ANXIETY DISORDER

Social anxiety disorder (formerly called social phobia) is characterized by extreme and persistent fear or anxiety and avoidance of social situations in which the person could potentially be evaluated negatively by others (APA, 2013). As with specific phobias, social anxiety disorder is common in the United States; a little over 12% of all Americans experience social anxiety disorder during their lifetime (Kessler et al., 2005).

The heart of the fear and anxiety in social anxiety disorder is the person's concern that he may act in a humiliating or embarrassing way, such as appearing foolish, showing symptoms of anxiety (blushing), or doing or saying something that might lead to rejection (such as offending others). The kinds of social situations in which individuals with social anxiety disorder usually have problems include public speaking, having a conversation, meeting strangers, eating in restaurants, and, in some cases, using public restrooms. Although many people become anxious in social situations like public speaking, the fear, anxiety, and avoidance experienced in social anxiety disorder are highly distressing and lead to serious impairments in life. Adults with this disorder are more likely to experience lower educational attainment and lower earnings (Katzelnick et al., 2001), perform more poorly at work and are more likely to be unemployed (Moitra, Beard, Weisberg, & Keller, 2011), and report greater dissatisfaction with their family lives, friends, leisure activities, and income (Stein & Kean, 2000).

When people with social anxiety disorder are unable to avoid situations that provoke anxiety, they typically perform **safety behaviors**: mental or behavioral acts that reduce anxiety in social situations by reducing the chance of negative social outcomes. Safety behaviors include avoiding eye contact, rehearsing sentences before speaking, talking only briefly, and not talking about oneself (Alden & Bieling, 1998). Other examples of safety behaviors include the following (Marker, 2013):

- assuming roles in social situations that minimize interaction with others (e.g., taking pictures, setting up equipment, or helping prepare food)
- asking people many questions to keep the focus off of oneself
- selecting a position to avoid scrutiny or contact with others (sitting in the back of the room)
- wearing bland, neutral clothes to avoid drawing attention to oneself
- avoiding substances or activities that might cause anxiety symptoms (such as caffeine, warm clothing, and physical exercise)

Although these behaviors are intended to prevent the person with social anxiety disorder from doing something awkward that might draw criticism, these actions usually exacerbate the problem because they do not allow the individual to disconfirm his negative beliefs, often eliciting rejection and other negative reactions from others (Alden & Bieling, 1998).

People with social anxiety disorder may resort to self-medication, such as drinking alcohol, as a means to avert the anxiety symptoms they experience in social situations (Battista & Kocovski, 2010). The use of alcohol when faced with such situations may become negatively reinforcing: encouraging individuals with social anxiety disorder to turn to the substance whenever they experience anxiety symptoms. The tendency to use alcohol as a coping mechanism for social anxiety, however, can come with a hefty price tag: a number of large scale studies have reported a high rate of comorbidity between social anxiety disorder and alcohol use disorder (Morris, Stewart, & Ham, 2005).

As with specific phobias, it is highly probable that the fears inherent to social anxiety disorder can develop through conditioning experiences. For example, a child who is subjected to early unpleasant social experiences (e.g., bullying at school) may develop negative social images of herself that become activated later in anxiety-provoking situations (Hackmann, Clark, & McManus, 2000). Indeed, one study reported that 92% of a sample of adults with social anxiety disorder reported a history of severe teasing in childhood, compared to only 35% of a sample of adults with panic disorder (McCabe, Antony, Summerfeldt, Liss, & Swinson, 2003).

One of the most well-established risk factors for developing social anxiety disorder is behavioral inhibition (Clauss & Blackford, 2012). Behavioral inhibition is thought to be an inherited trait, and it is characterized by a consistent tendency to show fear and restraint when presented with unfamiliar people or situations (Kagan, Reznick, & Snidman, 1988). Behavioral inhibition is displayed very early in life; behaviorally inhibited toddlers and children respond with great caution and restraint in unfamiliar situations, and they are often timid, fearful, and shy around unfamiliar people (Fox, Henderson, Marshall, Nichols, & Ghera, 2005). A recent statistical review of studies demonstrated that behavioral inhibition was associated with more than a sevenfold increase in the risk of development of social anxiety disorder, demonstrating that behavioral inhibition is a major risk factor for the disorder (Clauss & Blackford, 2012).

PANIC DISORDER

Imagine that you are at the mall one day with your friends and—suddenly and inexplicably—you begin sweating and trembling, your heart starts pounding, you have trouble breathing, and you start to feel dizzy and nauseous. This episode lasts for 10 minutes and is terrifying because you start to think that you are going to die. When you visit your doctor the following morning and describe what happened, she tells you that you have experienced a panic attack (Figure 15.9). If you experience another one of these episodes two weeks later and worry for a month or more that similar episodes will occur in the future, it is likely that you have developed panic disorder.

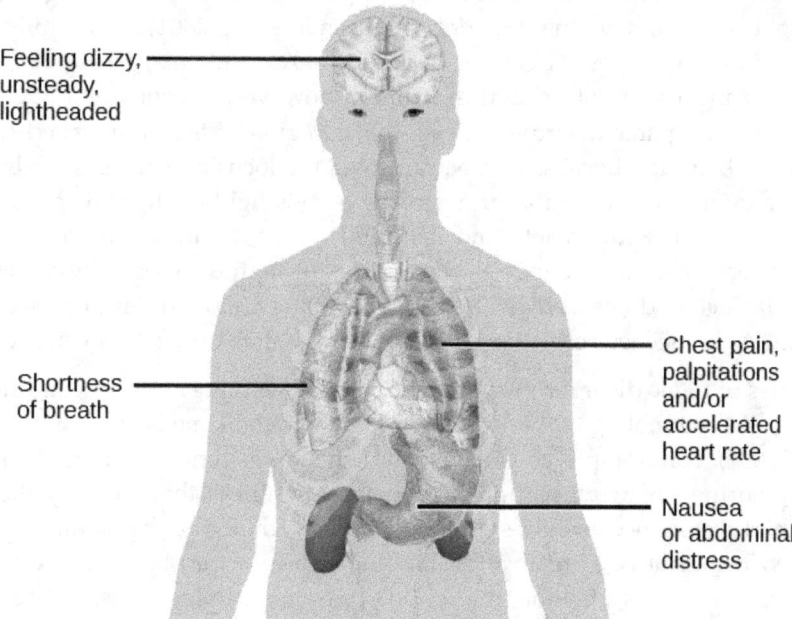

Figure 15.9 Some of the physical manifestations of a panic attack are shown. People may also experience sweating, trembling, feelings of faintness, or a fear of losing control, among other symptoms.

People with **panic disorder** experience recurrent (more than one) and unexpected panic attacks, along with at least one month of persistent concern about additional panic attacks, worry over the consequences of the attacks, or self-defeating changes in behavior related to the attacks (e.g., avoidance of exercise or unfamiliar situations) (APA, 2013). As is the case with other anxiety disorders, the panic attacks cannot result from the physiological effects of drugs and other substances, a medical condition, or another mental disorder. A **panic attack** is defined as a period of extreme fear or discomfort that develops abruptly and reaches a peak within 10 minutes. Its symptoms include accelerated heart rate, sweating, trembling, choking sensations, hot flashes or chills, dizziness or lightheadedness, fears of losing control or going crazy, and fears of dying (APA, 2013). Sometimes panic attacks are expected, occurring in response to specific environmental triggers (such as being in a tunnel); other times, these episodes are unexpected and emerge randomly (such as when relaxing). According to the DSM-5, the person must experience unexpected panic attacks to qualify for a diagnosis of panic disorder.

Experiencing a panic attack is often terrifying. Rather than recognizing the symptoms of a panic attack merely as signs of intense anxiety, individuals with panic disorder often misinterpret them as a sign that something is intensely wrong internally (thinking, for example, that the pounding heart represents an impending heart attack). Panic attacks can occasionally precipitate trips to the emergency room because several symptoms of panic attacks are, in fact, similar to those associated with heart problems (e.g., palpitations, racing pulse, and a pounding sensation in the chest) (Root, 2000). Unsurprisingly, those with panic disorder fear future attacks and may become preoccupied with modifying their behavior in an effort to avoid future panic attacks. For this reason, panic disorder is often characterized as fear of fear (Goldstein & Chambless, 1978).

Panic attacks themselves are not mental disorders. Indeed, around 23% of Americans experience isolated panic attacks in their lives without meeting the criteria for panic disorder (Kessler et al., 2006), indicating that panic attacks are fairly common. Panic disorder is, of course, much less common, afflicting 4.7% of Americans during their lifetime (Kessler et al., 2005). Many people with panic disorder develop agoraphobia, which is marked by fear and avoidance of situations in which escape might be difficult or help might not be available if one were to develop symptoms of a panic attack. People with panic disorder often experience a comorbid disorder, such as other anxiety disorders or major depressive disorder (APA, 2013).

Researchers are not entirely sure what causes panic disorder. Children are at a higher risk of developing panic disorder if their parents have the disorder (Biederman et al., 2001), and family and twins studies indicate that the heritability of panic disorder is around 43% (Hettema, Neale, & Kendler, 2001). The exact genes and gene functions involved in this disorder, however, are not well-understood (APA, 2013). Neurobiological theories of panic disorder suggest that a region of the brain called the **locus coeruleus** may play a role in this disorder. Located in the brainstem, the locus coeruleus is the brain's major source of norepinephrine, a neurotransmitter that triggers the body's fight-or-flight response. Activation of the locus coeruleus is associated with anxiety and fear, and research with nonhuman primates has shown that stimulating the locus coeruleus either electrically or through drugs produces panic-like symptoms (Charney et al., 1990). Such findings have led to the theory that panic disorder may be caused by abnormal norepinephrine activity in the locus coeruleus (Bremner, Krystal, Southwick, & Charney, 1996).

Conditioning theories of panic disorder propose that panic attacks are classical conditioning responses to subtle bodily sensations resembling those normally occurring when one is anxious or frightened (Bouton, Mineka, & Barlow, 2001). For example, consider a child who has asthma. An acute asthma attack produces sensations, such as shortness of breath, coughing, and chest tightness, that typically elicit fear and anxiety. Later, when the child experiences subtle symptoms that resemble the frightening symptoms of earlier asthma attacks (such as shortness of breath after climbing stairs), he may become anxious, fearful, and then experience a panic attack. In this situation, the subtle symptoms would represent a conditioned stimulus, and the panic attack would be a conditioned response. The finding that panic disorder is nearly three times as frequent among people with asthma as it is among people without asthma (Weiser, 2007) supports the possibility that panic disorder has the potential to develop through classical conditioning.

Cognitive factors may play an integral part in panic disorder. Generally, cognitive theories (Clark, 1996) argue that those with panic disorder are prone to interpret ordinary bodily sensations catastrophically, and these fearful interpretations set the stage for panic attacks. For example, a person might detect bodily changes that are routinely triggered by innocuous events such getting up from a seated position (dizziness), exercising (increased heart rate, shortness of breath), or drinking a large cup of coffee (increased heart rate, trembling). The individual interprets these subtle bodily changes catastrophically ("Maybe I'm having a heart attack!"). Such interpretations create fear and anxiety, which trigger additional physical symptoms; subsequently, the person experiences a panic attack. Support of this contention rests with findings that people with more severe catastrophic thoughts about sensations have more frequent and severe panic attacks, and among those with panic disorder, reducing catastrophic cognitions about their sensations is as effective as medication in reducing panic attacks (Good & Hinton, 2009).

GENERALIZED ANXIETY DISORDER

Alex was always worried about many things. He worried that his children would drown when they played at the beach. Each time he left the house, he worried that an electrical short circuit would start a fire in his home. He worried that his husband would lose his job at the prestigious law firm. He worried that his daughter's minor staph infection could turn into a massive life-threatening condition. These and other worries constantly weighed heavily on Alex's mind, so much so that they made it difficult for him to make decisions and often left him feeling tense, irritable, and worn out. One night, Alex's husband was to drive their son home from a soccer game. However, his husband stayed after the game and talked with some of the other parents, resulting in her arriving home 45 minutes late. Alex had tried to call his cell phone three or four times, but he could not get through because the soccer field did not have a signal. Extremely worried, Alex eventually called the police, convinced that his husband and son had not arrived home because they had been in a terrible car accident.

Alex suffers from **generalized anxiety disorder**: a relatively continuous state of excessive, uncontrollable, and pointless worry and apprehension. People with generalized anxiety disorder often worry about routine, everyday things, even though their concerns are unjustified (**Figure 15.10**). For example, an individual may worry about her health and finances, the health of family members, the safety of her children, or minor matters (e.g., being late for an appointment) without having any legitimate reason for doing so (APA, 2013). A diagnosis of generalized anxiety disorder requires that the diffuse worrying and apprehension characteristic of this disorder—what Sigmund Freud referred to as free-floating anxiety—is not part of another disorder, occurs more days than not for at least six months, and is accompanied by any three of the following symptoms: restlessness, difficulty concentrating, being easily fatigued, muscle tension, irritability, and sleep difficulties.

Figure 15.10 Worry is a defining feature of generalized anxiety disorder. (credit: Freddie Peña)

About 5.7% of the U.S. population will develop symptoms of generalized anxiety disorder during their lifetime (Kessler et al., 2005), and females are 2 times as likely as males to experience the disorder (APA, 2013). Generalized anxiety disorder is highly comorbid with mood disorders and other anxiety disorders (Noyes, 2001), and it tends to be chronic. Also, generalized anxiety disorder appears to increase the risk for heart attacks and strokes, especially in people with preexisting heart conditions (Martens et al., 2010).

Although there have been few investigations aimed at determining the heritability of generalized anxiety disorder, a summary of available family and twin studies suggests that genetic factors play a modest role in the disorder (Hettema et al., 2001). Cognitive theories of generalized anxiety disorder suggest that worry represents a mental strategy to avoid more powerful negative emotions (Aikins & Craske, 2001), perhaps stemming from earlier unpleasant or traumatic experiences. Indeed, one longitudinal study found that childhood maltreatment was strongly related to the development of this disorder during adulthood (Moffitt et al., 2007); worrying might distract people from remembering painful childhood experiences.

15.5 Obsessive-Compulsive and Related Disorders

Learning Objectives

By the end of this section, you will be able to:
- Describe the main features and prevalence of obsessive-compulsive disorder, body dysmorphic disorder, and hoarding disorder
- Understand some of the factors in the development of obsessive-compulsive disorder

Obsessive-compulsive and related disorders are a group of overlapping disorders that generally involve intrusive, unpleasant thoughts and repetitive behaviors. Many of us experience unwanted thoughts from time to time (e.g., craving double cheeseburgers when dieting), and many of us engage in repetitive behaviors on occasion (e.g., pacing when nervous). However, obsessive-compulsive and related disorders elevate the unwanted thoughts and repetitive behaviors to a status so intense that these cognitions and activities disrupt daily life. Included in this category are obsessive-compulsive disorder (OCD), body dysmorphic disorder, and hoarding disorder.

OBSESSIVE-COMPULSIVE DISORDER

People with **obsessive-compulsive disorder (OCD)** experience thoughts and urges that are intrusive and unwanted (obsessions) and/or the need to engage in repetitive behaviors or mental acts (compulsions).

A person with this disorder might, for example, spend hours each day washing his hands or constantly checking and rechecking to make sure that a stove, faucet, or light has been turned off.

Obsessions are more than just unwanted thoughts that seem to randomly jump into our head from time to time, such as recalling an insensitive remark a coworker made recently, and they are more significant than day-to-day worries we might have, such as justifiable concerns about being laid off from a job. Rather, obsessions are characterized as persistent, unintentional, and unwanted thoughts and urges that are highly intrusive, unpleasant, and distressing (APA, 2013). Common obsessions include concerns about germs and contamination, doubts ("Did I turn the water off?"), order and symmetry ("I need all the spoons in the tray to be arranged a certain way"), and urges that are aggressive or lustful. Usually, the person knows that such thoughts and urges are irrational and thus tries to suppress or ignore them, but has an extremely difficult time doing so. These obsessive symptoms sometimes overlap, such that someone might have both contamination and aggressive obsessions (Abramowitz & Siqueland, 2013).

Compulsions are repetitive and ritualistic acts that are typically carried out primarily as a means to minimize the distress that obsessions trigger or to reduce the likelihood of a feared event (APA, 2013). Compulsions often include such behaviors as repeated and extensive hand washing, cleaning, checking (e.g., that a door is locked), and ordering (e.g., lining up all the pencils in a particular way), and they also include such mental acts as counting, praying, or reciting something to oneself (**Figure 15.11**). Compulsions characteristic of OCD are not performed out of pleasure, nor are they connected in a realistic way to the source of the distress or feared event. Approximately 2.3% of the U.S. population will experience OCD in their lifetime (Ruscio, Stein, Chiu, & Kessler, 2010) and, if left untreated, OCD tends to be a chronic condition creating lifelong interpersonal and psychological problems (Norberg, Calamari, Cohen, & Riemann, 2008).

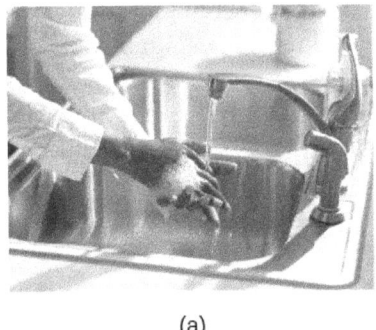

(a)   (b)

Figure 15.11 (a) Repetitive hand washing and (b) checking (e.g., that a door is locked) are common compulsions among those with obsessive-compulsive disorder. (credit a: modification of work by the USDA; credit b: modification of work by Bradley Gordon)

BODY DYSMORPHIC DISORDER

An individual with **body dysmorphic disorder** is preoccupied with a perceived flaw in physical appearance that is either nonexistent or barely noticeable to other people (APA, 2013). These perceived physical defects cause people to think they are unattractive, ugly, hideous, or deformed. These preoccupations can focus on any bodily area, but they typically involve the skin, face, or hair. The preoccupation with imagined physical flaws drives the person to engage in repetitive and ritualistic behavioral and mental acts, such as constantly looking in the mirror, trying to hide the offending body part, comparisons with others, and, in some extreme cases, cosmetic surgery (Phillips, 2005). An estimated 2.4% of the adults in the United States meet the criteria for body dysmorphic disorder, with slightly higher rates in women than in men (APA, 2013).

HOARDING DISORDER

Although hoarding was traditionally considered to be a symptom of OCD, considerable evidence suggests that hoarding represents an entirely different disorder (Mataix-Cols et al., 2010). People with **hoarding disorder** cannot bear to part with personal possessions, regardless of how valueless or useless these possessions are. As a result, these individuals accumulate excessive amounts of usually worthless items that clutter their living areas (**Figure 15.12**). Often, the quantity of cluttered items is so excessive that the person is unable use his kitchen, or sleep in his bed. People who suffer from this disorder have great difficulty parting with items because they believe the items might be of some later use, or because they form a sentimental attachment to the items (APA, 2013). Importantly, a diagnosis of hoarding disorder is made only if the hoarding is not caused by another medical condition and if the hoarding is not a symptom of another disorder (e.g., schizophrenia) (APA, 2013).

Figure 15.12 Those who suffer from hoarding disorder have great difficulty in discarding possessions, usually resulting in an accumulation of items that clutter living or work areas. (credit: "puuikibeach"/Flickr)

CAUSES OF OCD

The results of family and twin studies suggest that OCD has a moderate genetic component. The disorder is five times more frequent in the first-degree relatives of people with OCD than in people without the disorder (Nestadt et al., 2000). Additionally, the concordance rate of OCD among identical twins is around 57%; however, the concordance rate for fraternal twins is 22% (Bolton, Rijsdijk, O'Connor, Perrin, & Eley, 2007). Studies have implicated about two dozen potential genes that may be involved in OCD; these genes regulate the function of three neurotransmitters: serotonin, dopamine, and glutamate (Pauls, 2010). Many of these studies included small sample sizes and have yet to be replicated. Thus, additional research needs to be done in this area.

A brain region that is believed to play a critical role in OCD is the **orbitofrontal cortex** (Kopell & Greenberg, 2008), an area of the frontal lobe involved in learning and decision-making (Rushworth, Noonan, Boorman, Walton, & Behrens, 2011) (**Figure 15.13**). In people with OCD, the orbitofrontal cortex becomes especially hyperactive when they are provoked with tasks in which, for example, they are asked to look at a photo of a toilet or of pictures hanging crookedly on a wall (Simon, Kaufmann, Müsch, Kischkel, & Kathmann, 2010). The orbitofrontal cortex is part of a series of brain regions that, collectively, is called the OCD circuit; this circuit consists of several interconnected regions that influence the perceived emotional value of stimuli and the selection of both behavioral and cognitive responses (Graybiel & Rauch, 2000). As with the orbitofrontal cortex, other regions of the OCD circuit show heightened activity during symptom provocation (Rotge et al., 2008), which suggests that abnormalities in these regions may produce the symptoms of OCD (Saxena, Bota, & Brody, 2001). Consistent with this explanation, people with OCD show a substantially higher degree of connectivity of the orbitofrontal cortex and other regions of the OCD circuit than do those without OCD (Beucke et al., 2013).

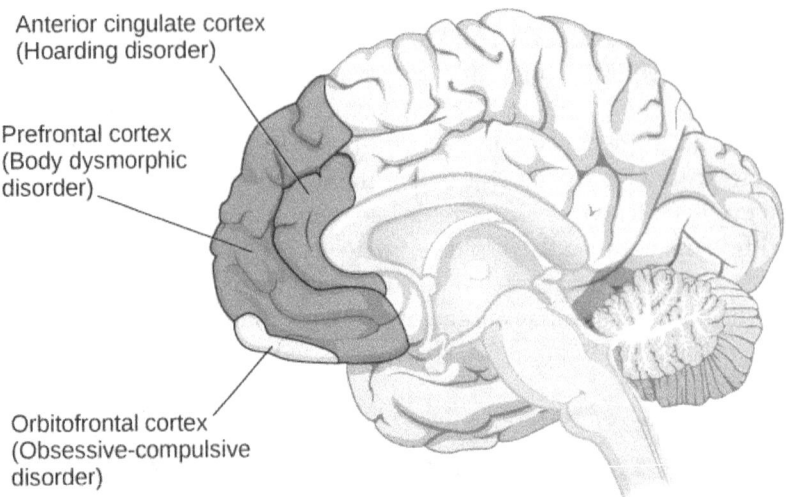

Figure 15.13 Different regions of the brain may be associated with different psychological disorders.

The findings discussed above were based on imaging studies, and they highlight the potential importance of brain dysfunction in OCD. However, one important limitation of these findings is the inability to explain differences in obsessions and compulsions. Another limitation is that the correlational relationship between neurological abnormalities and OCD symptoms cannot imply causation (Abramowitz & Siqueland, 2013).

CONNECT THE CONCEPTS

Conditioning and OCD

The symptoms of OCD have been theorized to be learned responses, acquired and sustained as the result of a combination of two forms of learning: classical conditioning and operant conditioning (Mowrer, 1960; Steinmetz, Tracy, & Green, 2001). Specifically, the acquisition of OCD may occur first as the result of classical conditioning, whereby a neutral stimulus becomes associated with an unconditioned stimulus that provokes anxiety or distress. When an individual has acquired this association, subsequent encounters with the neutral stimulus trigger anxiety, including obsessive thoughts; the anxiety and obsessive thoughts (which are now a conditioned response) may persist until she identifies some strategy to relieve it. Relief may take the form of a ritualistic behavior or mental activity that, when enacted repeatedly, reduces the anxiety. Such efforts to relieve anxiety constitute an example of negative reinforcement (a form of operant conditioning). Recall from the chapter on learning that negative reinforcement involves the strengthening of behavior through its ability to remove something unpleasant or aversive. Hence, compulsive acts observed in OCD may be sustained because they are negatively reinforcing, in the sense that they reduce anxiety triggered by a conditioned stimulus.

Suppose an individual with OCD experiences obsessive thoughts about germs, contamination, and disease whenever she encounters a doorknob. What might have constituted a viable unconditioned stimulus? Also, what would constitute the conditioned stimulus, unconditioned response, and conditioned response? What kinds of compulsive behaviors might we expect, and how do they reinforce themselves? What is decreased? Additionally, and from the standpoint of learning theory, how might the symptoms of OCD be treated successfully?

15.6 Posttraumatic Stress Disorder

Learning Objectives

By the end of this section, you will be able to:
- Describe the nature and symptoms of posttraumatic stress disorder
- Identify the risk factors associated with this disorder
- Understand the role of learning and cognitive factors in its development

Extremely stressful or traumatic events, such as combat, natural disasters, and terrorist attacks, place the people who experience them at an increased risk for developing psychological disorders such as **posttraumatic stress disorder (PTSD)**. Throughout much of the 20th century, this disorder was called *shell shock* and *combat neurosis* because its symptoms were observed in soldiers who had engaged in wartime combat. By the late 1970s it had become clear that women who had experienced sexual traumas (e.g., rape, domestic battery, and incest) often experienced the same set of symptoms as did soldiers (Herman, 1997). The term *posttraumatic stress disorder* was developed given that these symptoms could happen to anyone who experienced psychological trauma.

A BROADER DEFINITION OF PTSD

PTSD was listed among the anxiety disorders in previous DSM editions. In DSM-5, it is now listed among a group called Trauma-and-Stressor-Related Disorders. For a person to be diagnosed with PTSD, she must be exposed to, witness, or experience the details of a traumatic experience (e.g., a first responder), one that involves "actual or threatened death, serious injury, or sexual violence" (APA, 2013, p. 271). These experiences can include such events as combat, threatened or actual physical attack, sexual assault, natural disasters, terrorist attacks, and automobile accidents. This criterion makes PTSD the only disorder listed in the DSM in which a cause (extreme trauma) is explicitly specified.

Symptoms of PTSD include intrusive and distressing memories of the event, **flashbacks** (states that can last from a few seconds to several days, during which the individual relives the event and behaves as if the event were occurring at that moment [APA, 2013]), avoidance of stimuli connected to the event, persistently negative emotional states (e.g., fear, anger, guilt, and shame), feelings of detachment from others, irritability, proneness toward outbursts, and an exaggerated startle response (jumpiness). For PTSD to be diagnosed, these symptoms must occur for at least one month.

Roughly 7% of adults in the United States, including 9.7% of women and 3.6% of men, experience PTSD in their lifetime (National Comorbidity Survey, 2007), with higher rates among people exposed to mass trauma and people whose jobs involve duty-related trauma exposure (e.g., police officers, firefighters, and emergency medical personnel) (APA, 2013). Nearly 21% of residents of areas affected by Hurricane Katrina suffered from PTSD one year following the hurricane (Kessler et al., 2008), and 12.6% of Manhattan residents were observed as having PTSD 2–3 years after the 9/11 terrorist attacks (DiGrande et al., 2008).

RISK FACTORS FOR PTSD

Of course, not everyone who experiences a traumatic event will go on to develop PTSD; several factors strongly predict the development of PTSD: trauma experience, greater trauma severity, lack of immediate social support, and more subsequent life stress (Brewin, Andrews, & Valentine, 2000). Traumatic events that involve harm by others (e.g., combat, rape, and sexual molestation) carry greater risk than do other traumas (e.g., natural disasters) (Kessler, Sonnega, Bromet, Hughes, & Nelson, 1995). Women are more likely to have been traumatized because of sexual trauma, childhood neglect, and childhood physical abuse. Men are more likely to have been traumatized by natural disaster, life-threatening accident, and physical violence, either witnessed or directed at them. Adolescent boys are more likely to experience accident, physical assault, and witness death/injury; adolescent girls are more likely to experience rape/

sexual assault, intimate partner violence, or unexpected death or injury of a loved one. Assaultive violence and witnessing trauma to others is more prevalent among non-whites when compared to whites. African American males are more likely to be exposed to and victims of violence than males of other races (Kilpatrick, Badour, & Resnick, 2017). A 2012 study found that 27% of corrections officers reported experiencing symptoms of PTSD in the past 30 days. Rates were higher for males (31%) than females (22%) (Spinaris, Denhof, & Kellaway, 2012). A study conducted by Jaegers et al (2019) found that 53.4% of jail correctional officers screened positively for PTSD. PTSD is more prevalent in prison populations than in the general public, with prevalence estimates of 6% in male prisoners and 21% in female prisoners (Facer-Irwin et al, 2019). Factors that increase the risk of PTSD include female gender, low socioeconomic status, low intelligence, personal history of mental disorders, history of childhood adversity (abuse or other trauma during childhood), and family history of mental disorders (Brewin et al., 2000). Personality characteristics such as neuroticism and somatization (the tendency to experience physical symptoms when one encounters stress) have been shown to elevate the risk of PTSD (Bramsen, Dirkzwager, & van der Ploeg, 2000). People who experience childhood adversity and/or traumatic experiences during adulthood are at significantly higher risk of developing PTSD if they possess one or two short versions of a gene that regulates the neurotransmitter serotonin (Xie et al., 2009). This suggests a possible diathesis-stress interpretation of PTSD: its development is influenced by the interaction of psychosocial and biological factors.

SUPPORT FOR SUFFERERS OF PTSD

Research has shown that social support following a traumatic event can reduce the likelihood of PTSD (Ozer, Best, Lipsey, & Weiss, 2003). Social support is often defined as the comfort, advice, and assistance received from relatives, friends, and neighbors. Social support can help individuals cope during difficult times by allowing them to discuss feelings and experiences and providing a sense of being loved and appreciated. A 14-year study of 1,377 American Legionnaires who had served in the Vietnam War found that those who perceived less social support when they came home were more likely to develop PTSD than were those who perceived greater support (Figure 15.14). In addition, those who became involved in the community were less likely to develop PTSD, and they were more likely to experience a remission of PTSD than were those who were less involved (Koenen, Stellman, Stellman, & Sommer, 2003).

Figure 15.14 PTSD was first recognized in soldiers who had engaged in combat. Research has shown that strong social support decreases the risk of PTSD. This person stands at the Vietnam Traveling Memorial Wall. (credit: Kevin Stanchfield)

LEARNING AND THE DEVELOPMENT OF PTSD

PTSD learning models suggest that some symptoms are developed and maintained through classical conditioning. The traumatic event may act as an unconditioned stimulus that elicits an unconditioned response characterized by extreme fear and anxiety. Cognitive, emotional, physiological, and environmental cues accompanying or related to the event are conditioned stimuli. These traumatic reminders evoke conditioned responses (extreme fear and anxiety) similar to those caused by the event itself (Nader, 2001). A person who was in the vicinity of the Twin Towers during the 9/11 terrorist attacks and who developed PTSD may display excessive hypervigilance and distress when planes fly overhead; this behavior constitutes a conditioned response to the traumatic reminder (conditioned stimulus of the sight and sound of an airplane). Differences in how conditionable individuals are help to explain differences in the development and maintenance of PTSD symptoms (Pittman, 1988). Conditioning studies demonstrate facilitated acquisition of conditioned responses and delayed extinction of conditioned responses in people with PTSD (Orr et al., 2000).

Cognitive factors are important in the development and maintenance of PTSD. One model suggests that two key processes are crucial: disturbances in memory for the event, and negative appraisals of the trauma and its aftermath (Ehlers & Clark, 2000). According to this theory, some people who experience traumas do not form coherent memories of the trauma; memories of the traumatic event are poorly encoded and, thus, are fragmented, disorganized, and lacking in detail. Therefore, these individuals are unable remember the event in a way that gives it meaning and context. A rape victim who cannot coherently remember the event may remember only bits and pieces (e.g., the attacker repeatedly telling her she is stupid); because she was unable to develop a fully integrated memory, the fragmentary memory tends to stand out. Although unable to retrieve a complete memory of the event, she may be haunted by intrusive fragments involuntarily triggered by stimuli associated with the event (e.g., memories of the attacker's comments when encountering a person who resembles the attacker). This interpretation fits previously discussed material concerning PTSD and conditioning. The model also proposes that negative appraisals of the event ("I deserved to be raped because I'm stupid") may lead to dysfunctional behavioral strategies (e.g., avoiding social activities where men are likely to be present) that maintain PTSD symptoms by preventing both a change in the nature of the memory and a change in the problematic appraisals.

15.7 Mood Disorders

Learning Objectives

By the end of this section, you will be able to:
- Distinguish normal states of sadness and euphoria from states of depression and mania
- Describe the symptoms of major depressive disorder and bipolar disorder
- Understand the differences between major depressive disorder and persistent depressive disorder, and identify two subtypes of depression
- Define the criteria for a manic episode
- Understand genetic, biological, and psychological explanations of major depressive disorder
- Discuss the relationship between mood disorders and suicidal ideation, as well as factors associated with suicide

Blake cries all day and feeling that he is worthless and his life is hopeless, he cannot get out of bed. Crystal stays up all night, talks very rapidly, and went on a shopping spree in which she spent $3,000 on furniture, although she cannot afford it. Maria recently had a baby, and she feels overwhelmed, teary, anxious, and panicked, and believes she is a terrible mother—practically every day since the baby was born. All these individuals demonstrate symptoms of a potential mood disorder.

Mood disorders (Figure 15.15) are characterized by severe disturbances in mood and emotions—most often depression, but also mania and elation (Rothschild, 1999). All of us experience fluctuations in our moods and emotional states, and often these fluctuations are caused by events in our lives. We become elated if our favorite team wins the World Series and dejected if a romantic relationship ends or if we lose our job. At times, we feel fantastic or miserable for no clear reason. People with mood disorders also experience mood fluctuations, but their fluctuations are extreme, distort their outlook on life, and impair their ability to function.

Figure 15.15 Mood disorders are characterized by massive disruptions in mood. Symptoms can range from the extreme sadness and hopelessness of depression to the extreme elation and irritability of mania. (credit: Kiran Foster)

The DSM-5 lists two general categories of mood disorders. **Depressive disorders** are a group of disorders in which depression is the main feature. Depression is a vague term that, in everyday language, refers to an intense and persistent sadness. Depression is a heterogeneous mood state—it consists of a broad spectrum of symptoms that range in severity. Depressed people feel sad, discouraged, and hopeless. These individuals lose interest in activities once enjoyed, often experience a decrease in drives such as hunger and sex, and frequently doubt personal worth. Depressive disorders vary by degree, but this chapter highlights the most well-known: major depressive disorder (sometimes called unipolar depression).

Bipolar and related disorders are a group of disorders in which mania is the defining feature. **Mania** is a state of extreme elation and agitation. When people experience mania, they may become extremely talkative, behave recklessly, or attempt to take on many tasks simultaneously. The most recognized of these disorders is bipolar disorder.

MAJOR DEPRESSIVE DISORDER

According to the DSM-5, the defining symptoms of **major depressive disorder** include "depressed mood most of the day, nearly every day" (feeling sad, empty, hopeless, or appearing tearful to others), and loss of interest and pleasure in usual activities (APA, 2013). In addition to feeling overwhelmingly sad most of each day, people with depression will no longer show interest or enjoyment in activities that previously were gratifying, such as hobbies, sports, sex, social events, time spent with family, and so on. Friends and family members may notice that the person has completely abandoned previously enjoyed hobbies; for example, an avid tennis player who develops major depressive disorder no longer plays tennis (Rothschild, 1999).

To receive a diagnosis of major depressive disorder, one must experience a total of five symptoms for at least a two-week period; these symptoms must cause significant distress or impair normal functioning, and they must not be caused by substances or a medical condition. At least one of the two symptoms mentioned above must be present, plus any combination of the following symptoms (APA, 2013):

- significant weight loss (when not dieting) or weight gain and/or significant decrease or increase in appetite;
- difficulty falling asleep or sleeping too much;

- psychomotor agitation (the person is noticeably fidgety and jittery, demonstrated by behaviors like the inability to sit, pacing, hand-wringing, pulling or rubbing of the skin, clothing, or other objects) or psychomotor retardation (the person talks and moves slowly, for example, talking softly, very little, or in a monotone);
- fatigue or loss of energy;
- feelings of worthlessness or guilt;
- difficulty concentrating and indecisiveness; and
- **suicidal ideation**: thoughts of death (not just fear of dying), thinking about or planning suicide, or making an actual suicide attempt.

Major depressive disorder is considered episodic: its symptoms are typically present at their full magnitude for a certain period of time and then gradually abate. Approximately 50%–60% of people who experience an episode of major depressive disorder will have a second episode at some point in the future; those who have had two episodes have a 70% chance of having a third episode, and those who have had three episodes have a 90% chance of having a fourth episode (Rothschild, 1999). Although the episodes can last for months, a majority a people diagnosed with this condition (around 70%) recover within a year. However, a substantial number do not recover; around 12% show serious signs of impairment associated with major depressive disorder after 5 years (Boland & Keller, 2009). In the long-term, many who do recover will still show minor symptoms that fluctuate in their severity (Judd, 2012).

Results of Major Depressive Disorder

Major depressive disorder is a serious and incapacitating condition that can have a devastating effect on the quality of one's life. The person suffering from this disorder lives a profoundly miserable existence that often results in unavailability for work or education, abandonment of promising careers, and lost wages; occasionally, the condition requires hospitalization. The majority of those with major depressive disorder report having faced some kind of discrimination, and many report that having received such treatment has stopped them from initiating close relationships, applying for jobs for which they are qualified, and applying for education or training (Lasalvia et al., 2013). Major depressive disorder also takes a toll on health. Depression is a risk factor for the development of heart disease in healthy patients, as well as adverse cardiovascular outcomes in patients with preexisting heart disease (Whooley, 2006).

Risk Factors for Major Depressive Disorder

Major depressive disorder is often referred to as the common cold of psychiatric disorders. Around 6.6% of the U.S. population experiences major depressive disorder each year; 16.9% will experience the disorder during their lifetime (Kessler & Wang, 2009). It is more common among women than among men, affecting approximately 20% of women and 13% of men at some point in their life (National Comorbidity Survey, 2007). The greater risk among women is not accounted for by a tendency to report symptoms or to seek help more readily, suggesting that gender differences in the rates of major depressive disorder may reflect biological and gender-related environmental experiences (Kessler, 2003).

Lifetime rates of major depressive disorder tend to be highest in North and South America, Europe, and Australia; they are considerably lower in Asian countries (Hasin, Fenton, & Weissman, 2011). The rates of major depressive disorder are higher among younger age cohorts than among older cohorts, perhaps because people in younger age cohorts are more willing to admit depression (Kessler & Wang, 2009).

A number of risk factors are associated with major depressive disorder: unemployment (including homemakers); earning less than $20,000 per year; living in urban areas; or being separated, divorced, or widowed (Hasin et al., 2011). Comorbid disorders include anxiety disorders and substance abuse disorders (Kessler & Wang, 2009).

SUBTYPES OF DEPRESSION

The DSM-5 lists several different subtypes of depression. These subtypes—what the DSM-5 refer to as specifiers—are not specific disorders; rather, they are labels used to indicate specific patterns of symptoms or to specify certain periods of time in which the symptoms may be present. One subtype, **seasonal pattern**, applies to situations in which a person experiences the symptoms of major depressive disorder only during a particular time of year (e.g., fall or winter). In everyday language, people often refer to this subtype as the winter blues.

Another subtype, **peripartum onset** (commonly referred to as postpartum depression), applies to women who experience major depression during pregnancy or in the four weeks following the birth of their child (APA, 2013). These women often feel very anxious and may even have panic attacks. They may feel guilty, agitated, and be weepy. They may not want to hold or care for their newborn, even in cases in which the pregnancy was desired and intended. In extreme cases, the mother may have feelings of wanting to harm her child or herself. In a horrific illustration, a woman named Andrea Yates, who suffered from extreme peripartum-onset depression (as well as other mental illnesses), drowned her five children in a bathtub (Roche, 2002). Most women with peripartum-onset depression do not physically harm their children, but most do have difficulty being adequate caregivers (Fields, 2010). A surprisingly high number of women experience symptoms of peripartum-onset depression. A study of 10,000 women who had recently given birth found that 14% screened positive for peripartum-onset depression, and that nearly 20% reported having thoughts of wanting to harm themselves (Wisner et al., 2013).

People with **persistent depressive disorder** (previously known as dysthymia) experience depressed moods most of the day nearly every day for at least two years, as well as at least two of the other symptoms of major depressive disorder. People with persistent depressive disorder are chronically sad and melancholy, but do not meet all the criteria for major depression. However, episodes of full-blown major depressive disorder can occur during persistent depressive disorder (APA, 2013).

BIPOLAR DISORDER

A person with **bipolar disorder** (commonly known as manic depression) often experiences mood states that vacillate between depression and mania; that is, the person's mood is said to alternate from one emotional extreme to the other (in contrast to unipolar, which indicates a persistently sad mood).

To be diagnosed with bipolar disorder, a person must have experienced a manic episode at least once in his life; although major depressive episodes are common in bipolar disorder, they are not required for a diagnosis (APA, 2013). According to the DSM-5, a **manic episode** is characterized as a "distinct period of abnormally and persistently elevated, expansive, or irritable mood and abnormally and persistently increased activity or energy lasting at least one week," that lasts most of the time each day (APA, 2013, p. 124). During a manic episode, some experience a mood that is almost euphoric and become excessively talkative, sometimes spontaneously starting conversations with strangers; others become excessively irritable and complain or make hostile comments. The person may talk loudly and rapidly, exhibiting **flight of ideas**, abruptly switching from one topic to another. These individuals are easily distracted, which can make a conversation very difficult. They may exhibit grandiosity, in which they experience inflated but unjustified self-esteem and self-confidence. For example, they might quit a job in order to "strike it rich" in the stock market, despite lacking the knowledge, experience, and capital for such an endeavor. They may take on several tasks at the same time (e.g., several time-consuming projects at work) and yet show little, if any, need for sleep; some may go for days without sleep. Patients may also recklessly engage in pleasurable activities that could have harmful consequences, including spending sprees, reckless driving, making foolish investments, excessive gambling, or engaging in sexual encounters with strangers (APA, 2013).

During a manic episode, individuals usually feel as though they are not ill and do not need treatment. However, the reckless behaviors that often accompany these episodes—which can be antisocial, illegal, or physically threatening to others—may require involuntary hospitalization (APA, 2013). Some patients with bipolar disorder will experience a rapid-cycling subtype, which is characterized by at least four manic episodes (or some combination of at least four manic and major depressive episodes) within one year.

LINK TO LEARNING

In the 1997 independent film *Sweetheart*, actress Janeane Garofalo plays the part of Jasmine, a young woman with bipolar disorder. Watch this firsthand account from a person living with bipolar disorder (http://openstax.org/l/sweetheart) to learn more.

Risk Factors for Bipolar Disorder

Bipolar disorder is considerably less frequent than major depressive disorder. In the United States, 1 out of every 167 people meets the criteria for bipolar disorder each year, and 1 out of 100 meet the criteria within their lifetime (Merikangas et al., 2011). The rates are higher in men than in women, and about half of those with this disorder report onset before the age of 25 (Merikangas et al., 2011). Around 90% of those with bipolar disorder have a comorbid disorder, most often an anxiety disorder or a substance abuse problem. Unfortunately, close to half of the people suffering from bipolar disorder do not receive treatment (Merikangas & Tohen, 2011). Suicide rates are extremely high among those with bipolar disorder: around 36% of individuals with this disorder attempt suicide at least once in their lifetime (Novick, Swartz, & Frank, 2010), and between 15%–19% complete suicide (Newman, 2004).

THE BIOLOGICAL BASIS OF MOOD DISORDERS

Mood disorders have been shown to have a strong genetic and biological basis. Relatives of those with major depressive disorder have double the risk of developing major depressive disorder, whereas relatives of patients with bipolar disorder have over nine times the risk (Merikangas et al., 2011). The rate of concordance for major depressive disorder is higher among identical twins than fraternal twins (50% vs. 38%, respectively), as is that of bipolar disorder (67% vs. 16%, respectively), suggesting that genetic factors play a stronger role in bipolar disorder than in major depressive disorder (Merikangas et al. 2011).

People with mood disorders often have imbalances in certain neurotransmitters, particularly norepinephrine and serotonin (Thase, 2009). These neurotransmitters are important regulators of the bodily functions that are disrupted in mood disorders, including appetite, sex drive, sleep, arousal, and mood. Medications that are used to treat major depressive disorder typically boost serotonin and norepinephrine activity, whereas lithium—used in the treatment of bipolar disorder—blocks norepinephrine activity at the synapses (Figure 15.16).

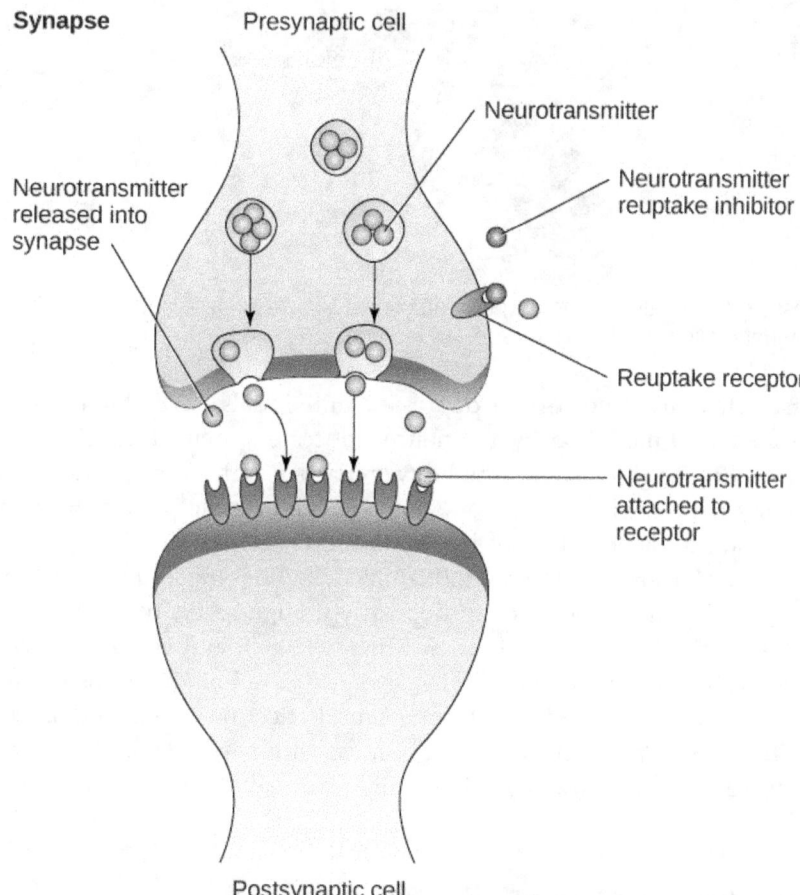

Figure 15.16 Many medications designed to treat mood disorders work by altering neurotransmitter activity in the neural synapse.

Depression is linked to abnormal activity in several regions of the brain (Fitzgerald, Laird, Maller, & Daskalakis, 2008) including those important in assessing the emotional significance of stimuli and experiencing emotions (amygdala), and in regulating and controlling emotions (like the prefrontal cortex, or PFC) (LeMoult, Castonguay, Joormann, & McAleavey, 2013). Depressed individuals show elevated amygdala activity (Drevets, Bogers, & Raichle, 2002), especially when presented with negative emotional stimuli, such as photos of sad faces (**Figure 15.17**) (Surguladze et al., 2005). Interestingly, heightened amygdala activation to negative emotional stimuli among depressed persons occurs even when stimuli are presented outside of conscious awareness (Victor, Furey, Fromm, Öhman, & Drevets, 2010), and it persists even after the negative emotional stimuli are no longer present (Siegle, Thompson, Carter, Steinhauer, & Thase, 2007). Additionally, depressed individuals exhibit less activation in the prefrontal, particularly on the left side (Davidson, Pizzagalli, & Nitschke, 2009). Because the PFC can dampen amygdala activation, thereby enabling one to suppress negative emotions (Phan et al., 2005), decreased activation in certain regions of the PFC may inhibit its ability to override negative emotions that might then lead to more negative mood states (Davidson et al., 2009). These findings suggest that depressed persons are more prone to react to emotionally negative stimuli, yet have greater difficulty controlling these reactions.

Figure 15.17 Depressed individuals react to negative emotional stimuli, such as sad faces, with greater amygdala activation than do non-depressed individuals. (credit: Ian Munroe)

Since the 1950s, researchers have noted that depressed individuals have abnormal levels of cortisol, a stress hormone released into the blood by the neuroendocrine system during times of stress (Mackin & Young, 2004). When cortisol is released, the body initiates a fight-or-flight response in reaction to a threat or danger. Many people with depression show elevated cortisol levels (Holsboer & Ising, 2010), especially those reporting a history of early life trauma such as the loss of a parent or abuse during childhood (Baes, Tofoli, Martins, & Juruena, 2012). Such findings raise the question of whether high cortisol levels are a cause or a consequence of depression. High levels of cortisol are a risk factor for future depression (Halligan, Herbert, Goodyer, & Murray, 2007), and cortisol activates activity in the amygdala while deactivating activity in the PFC (McEwen, 2005)—both brain disturbances are connected to depression. Thus, high cortisol levels may have a causal effect on depression, as well as on its brain function abnormalities (van Praag, 2005). Also, because stress results in increased cortisol release (Michaud, Matheson, Kelly, Anisman, 2008), it is equally reasonable to assume that stress may precipitate depression.

A Diathesis-Stress Model and Major Depressive Disorders

Indeed, it has long been believed that stressful life events can trigger depression, and research has consistently supported this conclusion (Mazure, 1998). Stressful life events include significant losses, such as death of a loved one, divorce or separation, and serious health and money problems; life events such as these often precede the onset of depressive episodes (Brown & Harris, 1989). In particular, exit events—instances in which an important person departs (e.g., a death, divorce or separation, or a family member leaving home)—often occur prior to an episode (Paykel, 2003). Exit events are especially likely to trigger depression if these happenings occur in a way that humiliates or devalues the individual. For example, people who experience the breakup of a relationship initiated by the other person develop major depressive disorder at a rate more than 2 times that of people who experience the death of a loved one (Kendler, Hettema, Butera, Gardner, & Prescott, 2003).

Likewise, individuals who are exposed to traumatic stress during childhood—such as separation from a parent, family turmoil, and maltreatment (physical or sexual abuse)—are at a heightened risk of developing depression at any point in their lives (Kessler, 1997). A recent review of 16 studies involving over 23,000 subjects concluded that those who experience childhood maltreatment are more than 2 times as likely to develop recurring and persistent depression (Nanni, Uher, & Danese, 2012).

Of course, not everyone who experiences stressful life events or childhood adversities succumbs to depression—indeed, most do not. Clearly, a diathesis-stress interpretation of major depressive disorder, in which certain predispositions or vulnerability factors influence one's reaction to stress, would seem logical. If so, what might such predispositions be? A study by Caspi and others (2003) suggests that an alteration in a specific gene that regulates serotonin (the 5-HTTLPR gene) might be one culprit. These investigators found that people who experienced several stressful life events were significantly more likely to experience episodes of major depression if they carried one or two short versions of this gene than if they carried two long versions. Those who carried one or two short versions of the 5-HTTLPR gene were unlikely to experience an episode, however, if they had experienced few or no stressful life events. Numerous studies have replicated these findings, including studies of people who experienced maltreatment during childhood (Goodman & Brand, 2009). In a recent investigation conducted in the United Kingdom (Brown & Harris, 2013), researchers found that childhood maltreatment before age 9 elevated the risk of chronic adult depression (a depression episode lasting for at least 12 months) among those individuals having one (LS) or two (SS) short versions of the 5-HTTLPR gene (Figure 15.18). Childhood maltreatment did not increase the risk for chronic depression for those have two long (LL) versions of this gene. Thus, genetic vulnerability may be one mechanism through which stress potentially leads to depression.

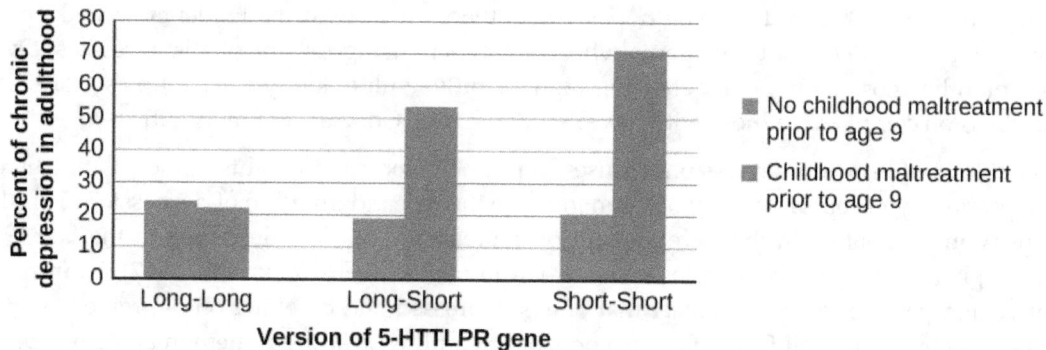

Figure 15.18 A study on gene-environment interaction in people experiencing chronic depression in adulthood suggests a much higher incidence in individuals with a short version of the gene in combination with childhood maltreatment (Brown & Harris, 2013).

Cognitive Theories of Depression

Cognitive theories of depression take the view that depression is triggered by negative thoughts, interpretations, self-evaluations, and expectations (Joormann, 2009). These diathesis-stress models propose that depression is triggered by a "cognitive vulnerability" (negative and maladaptive thinking) and by precipitating stressful life events (Gotlib & Joormann, 2010). Perhaps the most well-known cognitive theory of depression was developed in the 1960s by psychiatrist Aaron Beck, based on clinical observations and supported by research (Beck, 2008). Beck theorized that depression-prone people possess depressive schemas, or mental predispositions to think about most things in a negative way (Beck, 1976). Depressive schemas contain themes of loss, failure, rejection, worthlessness, and inadequacy, and may develop early in childhood in response to adverse experiences, then remain dormant until they are activated by stressful or negative life events. Depressive schemas prompt dysfunctional and pessimistic thoughts about the self, the world, and the future. Beck believed that this dysfunctional style of thinking is maintained by cognitive biases, or errors in how we process information about ourselves, which lead us to focus on negative aspects of experiences, interpret things negatively, and block positive memories (Beck, 2008). A person whose depressive schema consists of a theme of rejection might be overly attentive to social cues of rejection (more likely to notice another's frown), and he might interpret this cue as a sign of rejection and automatically remember past incidents of rejection. Longitudinal studies have supported Beck's theory, in showing that a preexisting tendency to engage in this negative, self-defeating style of thinking—when combined with life stress—over time predicts the onset of depression (Dozois & Beck, 2008). Cognitive therapies for depression, aimed at changing a depressed person's negative thinking, were developed as an expansion of this theory (Beck, 1976).

Another cognitive theory of depression, **hopelessness theory**, postulates that a particular style of negative thinking leads to a sense of hopelessness, which then leads to depression (Abramson, Metalsky, & Alloy, 1989). According to this theory, hopelessness is an expectation that unpleasant outcomes will occur or that desired outcomes will not occur, and there is nothing one can do to prevent such outcomes. A key assumption of this theory is that hopelessness stems from a tendency to perceive negative life events as having stable ("It's never going to change") and global ("It's going to affect my whole life") causes, in contrast to unstable ("It's fixable") and specific ("It applies only to this particular situation") causes, especially if these negative life events occur in important life realms, such as relationships, academic achievement, and the like. Suppose a student who wishes to go to law school does poorly on an admissions test. If the student infers negative life events as having stable and global causes, she may believe that her poor performance has a stable and global cause ("I lack intelligence, and it's going to prevent me from ever finding a meaningful career"), as opposed to an unstable and specific cause ("I was sick the day of the exam, so my low score was a fluke"). Hopelessness theory predicts that people who exhibit this cognitive style in response to undesirable life events will view such events as having negative implications for their future and self-worth, thereby increasing the likelihood of hopelessness—the primary cause of depression (Abramson et al., 1989). One study testing hopelessness theory measured the tendency to make negative inferences for bad life effects in participants who were experiencing uncontrollable stressors. Over the ensuing six months, those with scores reflecting high cognitive vulnerability were 7 times more likely to develop depression compared to those with lower scores (Kleim, Gonzalo, & Ehlers, 2011).

A third cognitive theory of depression focuses on how people's thoughts about their distressed moods—depressed symptoms in particular—can increase the risk and duration of depression. This theory, which focuses on rumination in the development of depression, was first described in the late 1980s to explain the higher rates of depression in women than in men (Nolen-Hoeksema, 1987). **Rumination** is the repetitive and passive focus on the fact that one is depressed and dwelling on depressed symptoms, rather that distracting one's self from the symptoms or attempting to address them in an active, problem-solving manner (Nolen-Hoeksema, 1991). When people ruminate, they have thoughts such as "Why am I so unmotivated? I just can't get going. I'm never going to get my work done feeling this way" (Nolen-Hoeksema & Hilt, 2009, p. 393). Women are more likely than men to ruminate when they are sad or depressed (Butler & Nolen-Hoeksema, 1994), and the tendency to ruminate is associated with increases in depression symptoms (Nolen-Hoeksema, Larson, & Grayson, 1999), heightened risk of major depressive episodes (Abela & Hankin, 2011), and chronicity of such episodes (Robinson & Alloy, 2003)

SUICIDE

For some people with mood disorders, the extreme emotional pain they experience becomes unendurable. Overwhelmed by hopelessness, devastated by incapacitating feelings of worthlessness, and burdened with the inability to adequately cope with such feelings, they may consider suicide to be a reasonable way out. **Suicide**, defined by the CDC as "death caused by self-directed injurious behavior with any intent to die as the result of the behavior" (CDC, 2013a), in a sense represents an outcome of several things going wrong all at the same time (Crosby, Ortega, & Melanson, 2011). Not only must the person be biologically or psychologically vulnerable, but he must also have the means to perform the suicidal act, and he must lack the necessary protective factors (e.g., social support from friends and family, religion, coping skills, and problem-solving skills) that provide comfort and enable one to cope during times of crisis or great psychological pain (Berman, 2009).

Suicide is not listed as a disorder in the DSM-5; however, suffering from a mental disorder—especially a mood disorder—poses the greatest risk for suicide. Around 90% of those who complete suicides have a diagnosis of at least one mental disorder, with mood disorders being the most frequent (Fleischman, Bertolote, Belfer, & Beautrais, 2005). In fact, the association between major depressive disorder and suicide is so strong that one of the criteria for the disorder is thoughts of suicide, as discussed above (APA, 2013).

Suicide rates can be difficult to interpret because some deaths that appear to be accidental may in fact be acts of suicide (e.g., automobile crash). Nevertheless, investigations into U.S. suicide rates have uncovered these facts:

- Suicide was the 10th leading cause of death for all ages in 2010 (Centers for Disease Control and Prevention [CDC], 2012).

- There were 38,364 suicides in 2010 in the United States—an average of 105 each day (CDC, 2012).

- Suicide among males is 4 times higher than among females and accounts for 79% of all suicides; firearms are the most commonly used method of suicide for males, whereas poisoning is the most commonly used method for females (CDC, 2012).

- From 1991 to 2003, suicide rates were consistently higher among those 65 years and older. Since 2001, however, suicide rates among those ages 25–64 have risen consistently, and, since 2006, suicide rates have been greater for those ages 65 and older (CDC, 2013b). This increase in suicide rates among middle-aged Americans has prompted concern in some quarters that baby boomers (individuals born between 1946–1964) who face economic worry and easy access to prescription medication may be particularly vulnerable to suicide (Parker-Pope, 2013).

- The highest rates of suicide within the United States are among American Indians/Alaskan natives and Non-Hispanic Whites (CDC, 2013b).

- Suicide rates vary across the United States, with the highest rates consistently found in the mountain states of the west (Alaska, Montana, Nevada, Wyoming, Colorado, and Idaho) (Berman, 2009).

Contrary to popular belief, suicide rates peak during the springtime (April and May), not during the holiday season or winter. In fact, suicide rates are generally lowest during the winter months (Postolache et al., 2010).

RISK FACTORS FOR SUICIDE

Suicidal risk is especially high among people with substance abuse problems. Individuals with alcohol dependence are at 10 times greater risk for suicide than the general population (Wilcox, Conner, & Caine, 2004). The risk of suicidal behavior is especially high among those who have made a prior suicide attempt. Among those who attempt suicide, 16% make another attempt within a year and over 21% make another attempt within four years (Owens, Horrocks, & House, 2002). Suicidal individuals may be at high risk for terminating their life if they have a lethal means in which to act, such as a firearm in the home (Brent & Bridge, 2003). Withdrawal from social relationships, feeling as though one is a burden to others, and engaging in reckless and risk-taking behaviors may be precursors to suicidal behavior (Berman, 2009). A sense of entrapment or feeling unable to escape one's miserable feelings or external circumstances (e.g., an abusive relationship with no perceived way out) predicts suicidal behavior (O'Connor, Smyth, Ferguson, Ryan, & Williams, 2013). Tragically, reports of suicides among adolescents following instances of cyberbullying have emerged in recent years. In one widely-publicized case a few years ago, Phoebe Prince, a 15-year-old Massachusetts high school student, committed suicide following incessant harassment and taunting from her classmates via texting and Facebook (McCabe, 2010).

Suicides can have a contagious effect on people. For example, another's suicide, especially that of a family member, heightens one's risk of suicide (Agerbo, Nordentoft, & Mortensen, 2002). Additionally, widely-publicized suicides tend to trigger copycat suicides in some individuals. One study examining suicide statistics in the United States from 1947–1967 found that the rates of suicide skyrocketed for the first month after a suicide story was printed on the front page of the *New York Times* (Phillips, 1974). Austrian researchers found a significant increase in the number of suicides by firearms in the three weeks following extensive reports in Austria's largest newspaper of a celebrity suicide by gun (Etzersdorfer, Voracek, & Sonneck, 2004). A review of 42 studies concluded that media coverage of celebrity suicides is more than 14 times more likely to trigger copycat suicides than is coverage of non-celebrity suicides (Stack, 2000). This review also demonstrated that the medium of coverage is important: televised stories are considerably less likely to prompt a surge in suicides than are newspaper stories. Research suggests that a trend appears to be emerging whereby people use online social media to leave suicide notes, although it is not clear to what extent suicide notes on such media might induce copycat suicides (Ruder, Hatch, Ampanozi, Thali, & Fischer, 2011). Nevertheless, it is reasonable to conjecture that suicide notes left by individuals on social media may influence the decisions of other vulnerable people who encounter them (Luxton, June, & Fairall, 2012).

One possible contributing factor in suicide is brain chemistry. Contemporary neurological research shows that disturbances in the functioning of serotonin are linked to suicidal behavior (Pompili et al., 2010).

Low levels of serotonin predict future suicide attempts and suicide completions, and low levels have been observed post-mortem among suicide victims (Mann, 2003). Serotonin dysfunction, as noted earlier, is also known to play an important role in depression; low levels of serotonin have also been linked to aggression and impulsivity (Stanley et al., 2000). The combination of these three characteristics constitutes a potential formula for suicide—especially violent suicide. A classic study conducted during the 1970s found that patients with major depressive disorder who had very low levels of serotonin attempted suicide more frequently and more violently than did patients with higher levels (Asberg, Thorén, Träskman, Bertilsson, & Ringberger, 1976; Mann, 2003).

Suicidal thoughts, plans, and even off-hand remarks ("I might kill myself this afternoon") should always be taken extremely seriously. People who contemplate terminating their life need immediate help. Below are links to two excellent websites that contain resources (including hotlines) for people who are struggling with suicidal ideation, have loved ones who may be suicidal, or who have lost loved ones to suicide: http://www.afsp.org and http://suicidology.org.

15.8 Schizophrenia

Learning Objectives

By the end of this section, you will be able to:
- Recognize the essential nature of schizophrenia, avoiding the misconception that it involves a split personality
- Categorize and describe the major symptoms of schizophrenia
- Understand the interplay between genetic, biological, and environmental factors that are associated with the development of schizophrenia
- Discuss the importance of research examining prodromal symptoms of schizophrenia

Schizophrenia is a devastating psychological disorder that is characterized by major disturbances in thought, perception, emotion, and behavior. About 1% of the population experiences schizophrenia in their lifetime, and usually the disorder is first diagnosed during early adulthood (early to mid-20s). Most people with schizophrenia experience significant difficulties in many day-to-day activities, such as holding a job, paying bills, caring for oneself (grooming and hygiene), and maintaining relationships with others. Frequent hospitalizations are more often the rule rather than the exception with schizophrenia. Even when they receive the best treatments available, many with schizophrenia will continue to experience serious social and occupational impairment throughout their lives.

What is schizophrenia? First, schizophrenia is *not* a condition involving a split personality; that is, schizophrenia is not the same thing as dissociative identity disorder (better known as multiple personality disorder). These disorders are sometimes confused because the word *schizophrenia* first coined by the Swiss psychiatrist Eugen Bleuler in 1911, derives from Greek words that refer to a "splitting" (schizo) of psychic functions (phrene) (Green, 2001).

Schizophrenia is considered a psychotic disorder, or one in which the person's thoughts, perceptions, and behaviors are impaired to the point where she is not able to function normally in life. In informal terms, one who suffers from a psychotic disorder (that is, has a psychosis) is disconnected from the world in which most of us live.

SYMPTOMS OF SCHIZOPHRENIA

The main symptoms of schizophrenia include hallucinations, delusions, disorganized thinking, disorganized or abnormal motor behavior, and negative symptoms (APA, 2013). A **hallucination** is a perceptual experience that occurs in the absence of external stimulation. Auditory hallucinations (hearing voices) occur in roughly two-thirds of patients with schizophrenia and are by far the most common form of hallucination (Andreasen, 1987). The voices may be familiar or unfamiliar, they may have a conversation or argue, or the voices may provide a running commentary on the person's behavior (Tsuang, Farone, & Green, 1999).

Less common are visual hallucinations (seeing things that are not there) and olfactory hallucinations (smelling odors that are not actually present).

Delusions are beliefs that are contrary to reality and are firmly held even in the face of contradictory evidence. Many of us hold beliefs that some would consider odd, but a delusion is easily identified because it is clearly absurd. A person with schizophrenia may believe that his mother is plotting with the FBI to poison his coffee, or that his neighbor is an enemy spy who wants to kill him. These kinds of delusions are known as **paranoid delusions**, which involve the (false) belief that other people or agencies are plotting to harm the person. People with schizophrenia also may hold **grandiose delusions**, beliefs that one holds special power, unique knowledge, or is extremely important. For example, the person who claims to be Jesus Christ, or who claims to have knowledge going back 5,000 years, or who claims to be a great philosopher is experiencing grandiose delusions. Other delusions include the belief that one's thoughts are being removed (thought withdrawal) or thoughts have been placed inside one's head (thought insertion). Another type of delusion is **somatic delusion**, which is the belief that something highly abnormal is happening to one's body (e.g., that one's kidneys are being eaten by cockroaches).

Disorganized thinking refers to disjointed and incoherent thought processes—usually detected by what a person says. The person might ramble, exhibit loose associations (jump from topic to topic), or talk in a way that is so disorganized and incomprehensible that it seems as though the person is randomly combining words. Disorganized thinking is also exhibited by blatantly illogical remarks (e.g., "Fenway Park is in Boston. I live in Boston. Therefore, I live at Fenway Park.") and by tangentiality: responding to others' statements or questions by remarks that are either barely related or unrelated to what was said or asked. For example, if a person diagnosed with schizophrenia is asked if she is interested in receiving special job training, she might state that she once rode on a train somewhere. To a person with schizophrenia, the tangential (slightly related) connection between job *training* and riding a *train* are sufficient enough to cause such a response.

Disorganized or abnormal motor behavior refers to unusual behaviors and movements: becoming unusually active, exhibiting silly child-like behaviors (giggling and self-absorbed smiling), engaging in repeated and purposeless movements, or displaying odd facial expressions and gestures. In some cases, the person will exhibit **catatonic behaviors**, which show decreased reactivity to the environment, such as posturing, in which the person maintains a rigid and bizarre posture for long periods of time, or catatonic stupor, a complete lack of movement and verbal behavior.

Negative symptoms are those that reflect noticeable decreases and absences in certain behaviors, emotions, or drives (Green, 2001). A person who exhibits diminished emotional expression shows no emotion in his facial expressions, speech, or movements, even when such expressions are normal or expected. Avolition is characterized by a lack of motivation to engage in self-initiated and meaningful activity, including the most basic of tasks, such as bathing and grooming. Alogia refers to reduced speech output; in simple terms, patients do not say much. Another negative symptom is asociality, or social withdrawal and lack of interest in engaging in social interactions with others. A final negative symptom, anhedonia, refers to an inability to experience pleasure. One who exhibits anhedonia expresses little interest in what most people consider to be pleasurable activities, such as hobbies, recreation, or sexual activity.

> **LINK TO LEARNING**
>
> Watch this video of schizophrenia case studies (http://openstax.org/l/Schizo1) and try to identify which classic symptoms of schizophrenia are shown.

CAUSES OF SCHIZOPHRENIA

There is considerable evidence suggesting that schizophrenia has a genetic basis. The risk of developing schizophrenia is nearly 6 times greater if one has a parent with schizophrenia than if one does not (Goldstein, Buka, Seidman, & Tsuang, 2010). Additionally, one's risk of developing schizophrenia increases as genetic relatedness to family members diagnosed with schizophrenia increases (Gottesman, 2001).

Genes

When considering the role of genetics in schizophrenia, as in any disorder, conclusions based on family and twin studies are subject to criticism. This is because family members who are closely related (such as siblings) are more likely to share similar environments than are family members who are less closely related (such as cousins); further, identical twins may be more likely to be treated similarly by others than might fraternal twins. Thus, family and twin studies cannot completely rule out the possible effects of shared environments and experiences. Such problems can be corrected by using adoption studies, in which children are separated from their parents at an early age. One of the first adoption studies of schizophrenia conducted by Heston (1966) followed 97 adoptees, including 47 who were born to mothers with schizophrenia, over a 36-year period. Five of the 47 adoptees (11%) whose mothers had schizophrenia were later diagnosed with schizophrenia, compared to none of the 50 control adoptees. Other adoption studies have consistently reported that for adoptees who are later diagnosed with schizophrenia, their biological relatives have a higher risk of schizophrenia than do adoptive relatives (Shih, Belmonte, & Zandi, 2004).

Although adoption studies have supported the hypothesis that genetic factors contribute to schizophrenia, they have also demonstrated that the disorder most likely arises from a combination of genetic and environmental factors, rather than just genes themselves. For example, investigators in one study examined the rates of schizophrenia among 303 adoptees (Tienari et al., 2004). A total of 145 of the adoptees had biological mothers with schizophrenia; these adoptees constituted the high genetic risk group. The other 158 adoptees had mothers with no psychiatric history; these adoptees composed the low genetic risk group. The researchers managed to determine whether the adoptees' families were either healthy or disturbed. For example, the adoptees were considered to be raised in a disturbed family environment if the family exhibited a lot of criticism, conflict, and a lack of problem-solving skills. The findings revealed that adoptees whose mothers had schizophrenia (high genetic risk) *and* who had been raised in a disturbed family environment were much more likely to develop schizophrenia or another psychotic disorder (36.8%) than were adoptees whose biological mothers had schizophrenia but who had been raised in a healthy environment (5.8%), or than adoptees with a low genetic risk who were raised in either a disturbed (5.3%) or healthy (4.8%) environment. Because the adoptees who were at high genetic risk were likely to develop schizophrenia *only* if they were raised in a disturbed home environment, this study supports a diathesis-stress interpretation of schizophrenia—both genetic vulnerability and environmental stress are necessary for schizophrenia to develop, genes alone do not show the complete picture.

Neurotransmitters

If we accept that schizophrenia is at least partly genetic in origin, as it seems to be, it makes sense that the next step should be to identify biological abnormalities commonly found in people with the disorder. Perhaps not surprisingly, a number of neurobiological factors have indeed been found to be related to schizophrenia. One such factor that has received considerable attention for many years is the neurotransmitter dopamine. Interest in the role of dopamine in schizophrenia was stimulated by two sets of findings: drugs that increase dopamine levels can produce schizophrenia-like symptoms, and medications that block dopamine activity reduce the symptoms (Howes & Kapur, 2009). The **dopamine hypothesis** of schizophrenia proposed that an overabundance of dopamine or too many dopamine receptors are responsible for the onset and maintenance of schizophrenia (Snyder, 1976). More recent work in this area suggests that abnormalities in dopamine vary by brain region and thus contribute to symptoms in unique ways. In general, this research has suggested that an overabundance of dopamine in the limbic system may be responsible for some symptoms, such as hallucinations and delusions, whereas low levels of dopamine in the prefrontal cortex might be responsible primarily for the negative symptoms (avolition, alogia, asociality, and anhedonia) (Davis, Kahn, Ko, & Davidson, 1991). In recent years, serotonin has received attention, and newer antipsychotic medications used to treat the disorder work by blocking serotonin receptors (Baumeister & Hawkins, 2004).

Brain Anatomy

Brain imaging studies reveal that people with schizophrenia have enlarged **ventricles**, the cavities within the brain that contain cerebral spinal fluid (Green, 2001). This finding is important because larger than normal ventricles suggests that various brain regions are reduced in size, thus implying that schizophrenia is associated with a loss of brain tissue. In addition, many people with schizophrenia display a reduction in gray matter (cell bodies of neurons) in the frontal lobes (Lawrie & Abukmeil, 1998), and many show less frontal lobe activity when performing cognitive tasks (Buchsbaum et al., 1990). The frontal lobes are important in a variety of complex cognitive functions, such as planning and executing behavior, attention, speech, movement, and problem solving. Hence, abnormalities in this region provide merit in explaining why people with schizophrenia experience deficits in these of areas.

Events During Pregnancy

Why do people with schizophrenia have these brain abnormalities? A number of environmental factors that could impact normal brain development might be at fault. High rates of obstetric complications in the births of children who later developed schizophrenia have been reported (Cannon, Jones, & Murray, 2002). In addition, people are at an increased risk for developing schizophrenia if their mother was exposed to influenza during the first trimester of pregnancy (Brown et al., 2004). Research has also suggested that a mother's emotional stress during pregnancy may increase the risk of schizophrenia in offspring. One study reported that the risk of schizophrenia is elevated substantially in offspring whose mothers experienced the death of a relative during the first trimester of pregnancy (Khashan et al., 2008).

Marijuana

Another variable that is linked to schizophrenia is marijuana use. Although a number of reports have shown that individuals with schizophrenia are more likely to use marijuana than are individuals without schizophrenia (Thornicroft, 1990), such investigations cannot determine if marijuana use leads to schizophrenia, or vice versa. However, a number of longitudinal studies have suggested that marijuana use is, in fact, a risk factor for schizophrenia. A classic investigation of over 45,000 Swedish conscripts who were followed up after 15 years found that those individuals who had reported using marijuana at least once by the time of conscription were more than 2 times as likely to develop schizophrenia during the ensuing 15 years than were those who reported never using marijuana; those who had indicated using marijuana 50 or more times were 6 times as likely to develop schizophrenia (Andréasson, Allbeck, Engström, & Rydberg, 1987). More recently, a review of 35 longitudinal studies found a substantially increased risk of schizophrenia and other psychotic disorders in people who had used marijuana, with the greatest risk in the most frequent users (Moore et al., 2007). Other work has found that marijuana use is associated with an onset of psychotic disorders at an earlier age (Large, Sharma, Compton, Slade, & Nielssen, 2011). Overall, the available evidence seems to indicate that marijuana use plays a causal role in the development of schizophrenia, although it is important to point out that marijuana use is not an essential or sufficient risk factor as not all people with schizophrenia have used marijuana and the majority of marijuana users do not develop schizophrenia (Casadio, Fernandes, Murray, & Di Forti, 2011). One plausible interpretation of the data is that early marijuana use may disrupt normal brain development during important early maturation periods in adolescence (Trezza, Cuomo, & Vanderschuren, 2008). Thus, early marijuana use may set the stage for the development of schizophrenia and other psychotic disorders, especially among individuals with an established vulnerability (Casadio et al., 2011).

SCHIZOPHRENIA: EARLY WARNING SIGNS

Early detection and treatment of conditions such as heart disease and cancer have improved survival rates and quality of life for people who suffer from these conditions. A new approach involves identifying people who show minor symptoms of psychosis, such as unusual thought content, paranoia, odd communication, delusions, problems at school or work, and a decline in social functioning—which are coined **prodromal symptoms**—and following these individuals over time to determine which of them develop a psychotic disorder and which factors best predict such a disorder. A number of factors have been identified that predict a greater likelihood that prodromal individuals will develop a psychotic disorder: genetic risk (a family history of psychosis), recent deterioration in functioning, high levels of unusual thought content, high levels of suspicion or paranoia, poor social functioning, and a history of substance abuse (Fusar-Poli et al., 2013). Further research will enable a more accurate prediction of those at greatest risk for developing schizophrenia, and thus to whom early intervention efforts should be directed.

DIG DEEPER

Forensic Psychology

In August 2013, 17-year-old Cody Metzker-Madsen attacked 5-year-old Dominic Elkins on his foster parents' property. Believing that he was fighting goblins and that Dominic was the goblin commander, Metzker-Madsen beat Dominic with a brick and then held him face down in a creek. Dr. Alan Goldstein, a clinical and forensic psychologist, testified that Metzker-Madsen believed that the goblins he saw were real and was not aware that it was Dominic at the time. He was found not guilty by reason of insanity and was not held legally responsible for Dominic's death (Nelson, 2014). Cody was also found to be a danger to himself or others. He will be held in a psychiatric facility until he is judged to be no longer dangerous. This does not mean that he "got away with" anything. In fact, according to the American Psychiatric Association, individuals who are found not guilty by reason of insanity are often confined to psychiatric hospitals for as long or longer than they would have spent in prison for a conviction.

Most people with mental illness are not violent. Only 3–5% of violent acts are committed by individuals diagnosed with severe mental illness, whereas individuals with severe mental illnesses are more than ten times as likely to be victims of crime (MentalHealth.gov, 2017). The psychologists who work with individuals such as Metzker-Madsen are part of the subdiscipline of forensic psychology. Forensic psychologists are involved in psychological assessment and treatment of individuals involved with the legal system. They use their knowledge of human behavior and mental illness to assist the judicial and legal system in making decisions in cases involving such issues as personal injury suits, workers' compensation, competency to stand trial, and pleas of not guilty by reason of insanity.

15.9 Dissociative Disorders

Learning Objectives

By the end of this section, you will be able to:
- Describe the essential nature of dissociative disorders
- Identify and differentiate the symptoms of dissociative amnesia, depersonalization/derealization disorder, and dissociative identity disorder
- Discuss the potential role of both social and psychological factors in dissociative identity disorder

Dissociative disorders are characterized by an individual becoming split off, or dissociated, from her core sense of self. Memory and identity become disturbed; these disturbances have a psychological rather than physical cause. Dissociative disorders listed in the DSM-5 include dissociative amnesia, depersonalization/derealization disorder, and dissociative identity disorder.

DISSOCIATIVE AMNESIA

Amnesia refers to the partial or total forgetting of some experience or event. An individual with **dissociative amnesia** is unable to recall important personal information, usually following an extremely stressful or traumatic experience such as combat, natural disasters, or being the victim of violence. The memory impairments are not caused by ordinary forgetting. Some individuals with dissociative amnesia will also experience **dissociative fugue** (from the word "to flee" in French), whereby they suddenly wander away from their home, experience confusion about their identity, and sometimes even adopt a new identity (Cardeña & Gleaves, 2006). Most fugue episodes last only a few hours or days, but some can last longer. One study of residents in communities in upstate New York reported that about 1.8% experienced dissociative amnesia in the previous year (Johnson, Cohen, Kasen, & Brook, 2006).

Some have questioned the validity of dissociative amnesia (Pope, Hudson, Bodkin, & Oliva, 1998); it has even been characterized as a "piece of psychiatric folklore devoid of convincing empirical support" (McNally, 2003, p. 275). Notably, scientific publications regarding dissociative amnesia rose during the 1980s and reached a peak in the mid-1990s, followed by an equally sharp decline by 2003; in fact, only 13 cases of individuals with dissociative amnesia worldwide could be found in the literature that same year (Pope, Barry, Bodkin, & Hudson, 2006). Further, no description of individuals showing dissociative amnesia following a trauma exists in any fictional or nonfictional work prior to 1800 (Pope, Poliakoff, Parker, Boynes, & Hudson, 2006). However, a study of 82 individuals who enrolled for treatment at a psychiatric outpatient hospital found that nearly 10% met the criteria for dissociative amnesia, perhaps suggesting that the condition is underdiagnosed, especially in psychiatric populations (Foote, Smolin, Kaplan, Legatt, & Lipschitz, 2006).

DEPERSONALIZATION/DEREALIZATION DISORDER

Depersonalization/derealization disorder is characterized by recurring episodes of depersonalization, derealization, or both. Depersonalization is defined as feelings of "unreality or detachment from, or unfamiliarity with, one's whole self or from aspects of the self" (APA, 2013, p. 302). Individuals who experience depersonalization might believe their thoughts and feelings are not their own; they may feel robotic as though they lack control over their movements and speech; they may experience a distorted sense of time and, in extreme cases, they may sense an "out-of-body" experience in which they see themselves from the vantage point of another person. Derealization is conceptualized as a sense of "unreality or detachment from, or unfamiliarity with, the world, be it individuals, inanimate objects, or all surroundings" (APA, 2013, p. 303). A person who experiences derealization might feel as though he is in a fog or a dream, or that the surrounding world is somehow artificial and unreal. Individuals with depersonalization/derealization disorder often have difficulty describing their symptoms and may think they are going crazy (APA, 2013).

DISSOCIATIVE IDENTITY DISORDER

By far, the most well-known dissociative disorder is **dissociative identity disorder** (formerly called multiple personality disorder). People with dissociative identity disorder exhibit two or more separate personalities or identities, each well-defined and distinct from one another. They also experience memory gaps for the time during which another identity is in charge (e.g., one might find unfamiliar items in her shopping bags or among her possessions), and in some cases may report hearing voices, such as a child's voice or the sound of somebody crying (APA, 2013). The study of upstate New York residents mentioned above (Johnson et al., 2006) reported that 1.5% of their sample experienced symptoms consistent with dissociative identity disorder in the previous year.

Dissociative identity disorder (DID) is highly controversial. Some believe that people fake symptoms to avoid the consequences of illegal actions (e.g., "I am not responsible for shoplifting because it was my other personality"). In fact, it has been demonstrated that people are generally skilled at adopting the role of a person with different personalities when they believe it might be advantageous to do so. As an example, Kenneth Bianchi was an infamous serial killer who, along with his cousin, murdered over a dozen females around Los Angeles in the late 1970s. Eventually, he and his cousin were apprehended. At Bianchi's trial, he pled not guilty by reason of insanity, presenting himself as though he had DID and claiming that a different personality ("Steve Walker") committed the murders. When these claims were scrutinized, he admitted faking the symptoms and was found guilty (Schwartz, 1981).

A second reason DID is controversial is because rates of the disorder suddenly skyrocketed in the 1980s. More cases of DID were identified during the five years prior to 1986 than in the preceding two centuries (Putnam, Guroff, Silberman, Barban, & Post, 1986). Although this increase may be due to the development of more sophisticated diagnostic techniques, it is also possible that the popularization of DID—helped in part by *Sybil*, a popular 1970s book (and later film) about a woman with 16 different personalities—may have prompted clinicians to overdiagnose the disorder (Piper & Merskey, 2004). Casting further scrutiny on the existence of multiple personalities or identities is the recent suggestion that the story of Sybil was largely fabricated, and the idea for the book might have been exaggerated (Nathan, 2011).

Despite its controversial nature, DID is clearly a legitimate and serious disorder, and although some people may fake symptoms, others suffer their entire lives with it. People with this disorder tend to report a history of childhood trauma, some cases having been corroborated through medical or legal records (Cardeña & Gleaves, 2006). Research by Ross et al. (1990) suggests that in one study about 95% of people with DID were physically and/or sexually abused as children. Of course, not all reports of childhood abuse can be expected to be valid or accurate. However, there is strong evidence that traumatic experiences can cause people to experience states of dissociation, suggesting that dissociative states—including the adoption of multiple personalities—may serve as a psychologically important coping mechanism for threat and danger (Dalenberg et al., 2012).

15.10 Disorders in Childhood

Learning Objectives

By the end of this section, you will be able to:
- Describe the nature and symptoms of attention deficit/hyperactivity disorder and autism spectrum disorder
- Discuss the prevalence and factors that contribute to the development of these disorders

Most of the disorders we have discussed so far are typically diagnosed in adulthood, although they can and sometimes do occur during childhood. However, there are a group of conditions that, when present, are diagnosed early in childhood, often before the time a child enters school. These conditions are listed in the DSM-5 as **neurodevelopmental disorders**, and they involve developmental problems in personal, social, academic, and intellectual functioning (APA, 2013). In this section, we will discuss two such disorders: attention deficit/ hyperactivity disorder and autism.

ATTENTION DEFICIT/HYPERACTIVITY DISORDER

Diego is always active, from the time he wakes up in the morning until the time he goes to bed at night. His mother reports that he came out the womb kicking and screaming, and he has not stopped moving since. He has a sweet disposition, but always seems to be in trouble with his teachers, parents, and after-school program counselors. He seems to accidently break things; he lost his jacket three times last winter, and he never seems to sit still. His teachers believe he is a smart child, but he never finishes anything he starts and is so impulsive that he does not seem to learn much in school.

Diego likely has **attention deficit/hyperactivity disorder (ADHD)**. The symptoms of this disorder were first described by Hans Hoffman in the 1920s. While taking care of his son while his wife was in the hospital giving birth to a second child, Hoffman noticed that the boy had trouble concentrating on his homework, had a short attention span, and had to repeatedly go over easy homework to learn the material (Jellinek & Herzog, 1999). Later, it was discovered that many hyperactive children—those who are fidgety, restless, socially disruptive, and have trouble with impulse control—also display short attention spans, problems with concentration, and distractibility. By the 1970s, it had become clear that many children who display attention problems often also exhibit signs of hyperactivity. In recognition of such findings, the DSM-III (published in 1980) included a new disorder: attention deficit disorder with and without hyperactivity, now known as attention deficit/hyperactivity disorder (ADHD).

A child with ADHD shows a constant pattern of inattention and/or hyperactive and impulsive behavior that interferes with normal functioning (APA, 2013). Some of the signs of inattention include great difficulty with and avoidance of tasks that require sustained attention (such as conversations or reading), failure to follow instructions (often resulting in failure to complete school work and other duties), disorganization (difficulty keeping things in order, poor time management, sloppy and messy work), lack of attention to detail, becoming easily distracted, and forgetfulness. Hyperactivity is characterized by excessive movement, and includes fidgeting or squirming, leaving one's seat in situations when remaining seated is expected, having trouble sitting still (e.g., in a restaurant), running about and climbing on things, blurting out responses before another person's question or statement has been completed, difficulty waiting one's turn for something, and interrupting and intruding on others. Frequently, the hyperactive child comes across as noisy and boisterous. The child's behavior is hasty, impulsive, and seems to occur without much forethought; these characteristics may explain why adolescents and young adults diagnosed with ADHD receive more traffic tickets and have more automobile accidents than do others (Thompson, Molina, Pelham, & Gnagy, 2007).

ADHD occurs in about 5% of children (APA, 2013). On the average, boys are 3 times more likely to have ADHD than are girls; however, such findings might reflect the greater propensity of boys to engage in aggressive and antisocial behavior and thus incur a greater likelihood of being referred to psychological clinics (Barkley, 2006). Children with ADHD face severe academic and social challenges. Compared to their non-ADHD counterparts, children with ADHD have lower grades and standardized test scores and higher rates of expulsion, grade retention, and dropping out (Loe & Feldman, 2007). they also are less well-liked and more often rejected by their peers (Hoza et al., 2005).

Previously, ADHD was thought to fade away by adolescence. However, longitudinal studies have suggested that ADHD is a chronic problem, one that can persist into adolescence and adulthood (Barkley, Fischer, Smallish, & Fletcher, 2002). A recent study found that 29.3% of adults who had been diagnosed with ADHD decades earlier still showed symptoms (Barbaresi et al., 2013). Somewhat troubling, this study also reported that nearly 81% of those whose ADHD persisted into adulthood had experienced at least one other comorbid disorder, compared to 47% of those whose ADHD did not persist.

Life Problems from ADHD

Children diagnosed with ADHD face considerably worse long-term outcomes than do those children who do not receive such a diagnosis. In one investigation, 135 adults who had been identified as having ADHD symptoms in the 1970s were contacted decades later and interviewed (Klein et al., 2012). Compared to a control sample of 136 participants who had never been diagnosed with ADHD, those who were diagnosed as children:

- had worse educational attainment (more likely to have dropped out of high school and less likely to have earned a bachelor's degree);
- had lower socioeconomic status;
- held less prestigious occupational positions;
- were more likely to be unemployed;
- made considerably less in salary;
- scored worse on a measure of occupational functioning (indicating, for example, lower job satisfaction, poorer work relationships, and more firings);
- scored worse on a measure of social functioning (indicating, for example, fewer friendships and less involvement in social activities);
- were more likely to be divorced; and
- were more likely to have non-alcohol-related substance abuse problems. (Klein et al., 2012)

Longitudinal studies also show that children diagnosed with ADHD are at higher risk for substance abuse problems. One study reported that childhood ADHD predicted later drinking problems, daily smoking, and use of marijuana and other illicit drugs (Molina & Pelham, 2003). The risk of substance abuse problems appears to be even greater for those with ADHD who also exhibit antisocial tendencies (Marshal & Molina, 2006).

Causes of ADHD

Family and twin studies indicate that genetics play a significant role in the development of ADHD. Burt (2009), in a review of 26 studies, reported that the median rate of concordance for identical twins was .66 (one study reported a rate of .90), whereas the median concordance rate for fraternal twins was .20. This study also found that the median concordance rate for unrelated (adoptive) siblings was .09; although this number is small, it is greater than 0, thus suggesting that the environment may have at least some influence. Another review of studies concluded that the heritability of inattention and hyperactivity were 71% and 73%, respectively (Nikolas & Burt, 2010).

The specific genes involved in ADHD are thought to include at least two that are important in the regulation of the neurotransmitter dopamine (Gizer, Ficks, & Waldman, 2009), suggesting that dopamine may be important in ADHD. Indeed, medications used in the treatment of ADHD, such as methylphenidate (Ritalin) and amphetamine with dextroamphetamine (Adderall), have stimulant qualities and elevate dopamine activity. People with ADHD show less dopamine activity in key regions of the brain, especially those associated with motivation and reward (Volkow et al., 2009), which provides support to the theory that dopamine deficits may be a vital factor in the development this disorder (Swanson et al., 2007).

Brain imaging studies have shown that children with ADHD exhibit abnormalities in their frontal lobes, an area in which dopamine is in abundance. Compared to children without ADHD, those with ADHD appear to have smaller frontal lobe volume, and they show less frontal lobe activation when performing mental tasks. Recall that one of the functions of the frontal lobes is to inhibit our behavior. Thus, abnormalities in this region may go a long way toward explaining the hyperactive, uncontrolled behavior of ADHD.

By the 1970s, many had become aware of the connection between nutritional factors and childhood behavior. At the time, much of the public believed that hyperactivity was caused by sugar and food additives, such as artificial coloring and flavoring. Undoubtedly, part of the appeal of this hypothesis was that it provided a simple explanation of (and treatment for) behavioral problems in children. A statistical review of 16 studies, however, concluded that sugar consumption has no effect at all on the behavioral and cognitive performance of children (Wolraich, Wilson, & White, 1995). Additionally, although food additives have been shown to increase hyperactivity in non-ADHD children, the effect is rather small (McCann et al., 2007). Numerous studies, however, have shown a significant relationship between exposure to nicotine in cigarette smoke during the prenatal period and ADHD (Linnet et al., 2003). Maternal smoking during pregnancy is associated with the development of more severe symptoms of the disorder (Thakur et al., 2013).

Is ADHD caused by poor parenting? Not likely. Remember, the genetics studies discussed above suggested that the family environment does not seem to play much of a role in the development of this disorder; if it did, we would expect the concordance rates to be higher for fraternal twins and adoptive siblings than has been demonstrated. All things considered, the evidence seems to point to the conclusion that ADHD is triggered more by genetic and neurological factors and less by social or environmental ones.

DIG DEEPER

Why Is the Prevalence Rate of ADHD Increasing?

Many people believe that the rates of ADHD have increased in recent years, and there is evidence to support this contention. In a recent study, investigators found that the parent-reported prevalence of ADHD among children (4–17 years old) in the United States increased by 22% during a 4-year period, from 7.8% in 2003 to 9.5% in 2007 (CDC, 2010). Over time this increase in parent-reported ADHD was observed in all sociodemographic groups and was reflected by substantial increases in 12 states (Indiana, North Carolina, and Colorado were the top three). The increases were greatest for older teens (ages 15–17), multiracial and Hispanic children, and children with a primary language other than English. Another investigation found that from 1998–2000 through 2007–2009 the parent-reported prevalence of ADHD increased among U.S. children between the ages of 5–17 years old, from 6.9% to 9.0% (Akinbami, Liu, Pastor, & Reuben, 2011).

A major weakness of both studies was that children were not actually given a formal diagnosis. Instead, parents were simply asked whether or not a doctor or other health-care provider had ever told them their child had ADHD; the reported prevalence rates thus may have been affected by the accuracy of parental memory. Nevertheless, the findings from these studies raise important questions concerning what appears to be a demonstrable rise in the prevalence of ADHD. Although the reasons underlying this apparent increase in the rates of ADHD over time are poorly understood and, at best, speculative, several explanations are viable:

- ADHD may be over-diagnosed by doctors who are too quick to medicate children as a behavior treatment.

- There is greater awareness of ADHD now than in the past. Nearly everyone has heard of ADHD, and most parents and teachers are aware of its key symptoms. Thus, parents may be quick to take their children to a doctor if they believe their child possesses these symptoms, or teachers may be more likely now than in the past to notice the symptoms and refer the child for evaluation.

- The use of computers, video games, iPhones, and other electronic devices has become pervasive among children in the early 21st century, and these devices could potentially shorten children's attentions spans. Thus, what might seem like inattention to some parents and teachers could simply reflect exposure to too much technology.

- ADHD diagnostic criteria have changed over time.

AUTISM SPECTRUM DISORDER

A seminal paper published in 1943 by psychiatrist Leo Kanner described an unusual neurodevelopmental condition he observed in a group of children. He called this condition early infantile autism, and it was characterized mainly by an inability to form close emotional ties with others, speech and language abnormalities, repetitive behaviors, and an intolerance of minor changes in the environment and in normal routines (Bregman, 2005). What the DSM-5 refers to as **autism spectrum disorder** today, is a direct extension of Kanner's work.

Autism spectrum disorder is probably the most misunderstood and puzzling of the neurodevelopmental disorders. Children with this disorder show signs of significant disturbances in three main areas: (a) deficits in social interaction, (b) deficits in communication, and (c) repetitive patterns of behavior or interests. These disturbances appear early in life and cause serious impairments in functioning (APA, 2013). The child with autism spectrum disorder might exhibit deficits in social interaction by not initiating conversations with other children or turning their head away when spoken to. Typically, these children do not make eye contact with others and seem to prefer playing alone rather than with others. In a certain sense, it is almost as though these individuals live in a personal and isolated social world others are simply not privy to or able to penetrate. Communication deficits can range from a complete lack of speech, to one word responses (e.g., saying "Yes" or "No" when replying to questions or statements that require additional elaboration), to echoed speech (e.g., parroting what another person says, either immediately or several hours or even days later), to difficulty maintaining a conversation because of an inability to reciprocate others' comments. These deficits can also include problems in using and understanding nonverbal cues (e.g., facial expressions, gestures, and postures) that facilitate normal communication.

Repetitive patterns of behavior or interests can be exhibited a number of ways. The child might engage in stereotyped, repetitive movements (rocking, head-banging, or repeatedly dropping an object and then picking it up), or she might show great distress at small changes in routine or the environment. For example, the child might throw a temper tantrum if an object is not in its proper place or if a regularly-scheduled activity is rescheduled. In some cases, the person with autism spectrum disorder might show highly restricted and fixated interests that appear to be abnormal in their intensity. For instance, the person might learn and memorize every detail about something even though doing so serves no apparent purpose. Importantly, autism spectrum disorder is not the same thing as intellectual disability, although these two conditions are often comorbid. The DSM-5 specifies that the symptoms of autism spectrum disorder are not caused or explained by intellectual disability.

Life Problems From Autism Spectrum Disorder

Autism spectrum disorder is referred to in everyday language as autism; in fact, the disorder was termed "autistic disorder" in earlier editions of the DSM, and its diagnostic criteria were much narrower than those of autism spectrum disorder. The qualifier "spectrum" in autism spectrum disorder is used to indicate that individuals with the disorder can show a range, or spectrum, of symptoms that vary in their magnitude and severity: some severe, others less severe. The previous edition of the DSM included a diagnosis of Asperger's disorder, generally recognized as a less severe form of autistic disorder; individuals diagnosed with Asperger's disorder were described as having average or high intelligence and a strong vocabulary, but exhibiting impairments in social interaction and social communication, such as talking only about their special interests (Wing, Gould, & Gillberg, 2011). However, because research has failed to demonstrate that Asperger's disorder differs qualitatively from autistic disorder, the DSM-5 does not include it, which is prompting concerns among some parents that their children may no longer be eligible for special services ("Asperger's Syndrome Dropped," 2012). Some individuals with autism spectrum disorder, particularly those with better language and intellectual skills, can live and work independently as adults. However, most do not because the symptoms remain sufficient to cause serious impairment in many realms of life (APA, 2013).

> **LINK TO LEARNING**
>
> Watch this video about early signs of autism (http://openstax.org/l/sevautism) to learn more.

Current estimates from the Center for Disease Control and Prevention's Autism and Developmental Disabilities Monitoring Network indicate that 1 in 59 children in the United States has autism spectrum disorder; the disorder is 4 times more common among boys (1 in 38) than in girls (1 in 152) (Baio et al, 2018). Rates of autistic spectrum disorder have increased dramatically since the 1980s. For example, California saw an increase of 273% in reported cases from 1987 through 1998 (Byrd, 2002); between 2000 and 2008, the rate of autism diagnoses in the United States increased 78% (CDC, 2012). Although it is difficult to interpret this increase, it is possible that the rise in prevalence is the result of the broadening of the diagnosis, increased efforts to identify cases in the community, and greater awareness and acceptance of the diagnosis. In addition, mental health professionals are now more knowledgeable about autism spectrum disorder and are better equipped to make the diagnosis, even in subtle cases (Novella, 2008).

Causes of Autism Spectrum Disorder

Early theories of autism placed the blame squarely on the shoulders of the child's parents, particularly the mother. Bruno Bettelheim (an Austrian-born American child psychologist who was heavily influenced by Sigmund Freud's ideas) suggested that a mother's ambivalent attitudes and her frozen and rigid emotions toward her child were the main causal factors in childhood autism. In what must certainly stand as one of the more controversial assertions in psychology over the last 50 years, he wrote, "I state my belief that the precipitating factor in infantile autism is the parent's wish that his child should not exist" (Bettelheim, 1967, p. 125). As you might imagine, Bettelheim did not endear himself to a lot of people with this position; incidentally, no scientific evidence exists supporting his claims.

The exact causes of autism spectrum disorder remain unknown despite massive research efforts over the last two decades (Meek, Lemery-Chalfant, Jahromi, & Valiente, 2013). Autism appears to be strongly influenced by genetics, as identical twins show concordance rates of 60%–90%, whereas concordance rates for fraternal twins and siblings are 5%–10% (Autism Genome Project Consortium, 2007). Many different genes and gene mutations have been implicated in autism (Meek et al., 2013). Among the genes involved are those important in the formation of synaptic circuits that facilitate communication between different areas of the brain (Gauthier et al., 2011). A number of environmental factors are also thought to be associated with increased risk for autism spectrum disorder, at least in part, because they contribute to new mutations. These factors include exposure to pollutants, such as plant emissions and mercury, urban versus rural residence, and vitamin D deficiency (Kinney, Barch, Chayka, Napoleon, & Munir, 2009).

Child Vaccinations and Autism Spectrum Disorder

In the late 1990s, a prestigious medical journal published an article purportedly showing that autism is triggered by the MMR (measles, mumps, and rubella) vaccine. These findings were very controversial and drew a great deal of attention, sparking an international forum on whether children should be vaccinated. In a shocking turn of events, some years later the article was retracted by the journal that had published it after accusations of fraud on the part of the lead researcher. Despite the retraction, the reporting in popular media led to concerns about a possible link between vaccines and autism persisting. A recent survey of parents, for example, found that roughly a third of respondents expressed such a concern (Kennedy, LaVail, Nowak, Basket, & Landry, 2011); and perhaps fearing that their children would develop autism, more than 10% of parents of young children refuse or delay vaccinations (Dempsey et al., 2011). Some parents of children with autism mounted a campaign against scientists who refuted the vaccine-autism link. Even politicians and several well-known celebrities weighed in; for example, actress Jenny McCarthy (who believed that a vaccination caused her son's autism) co-authored a book on the matter. However, there is no scientific evidence that a link exists between autism and vaccinations (Hughes, 2007). Indeed, a recent study compared the vaccination histories of 256 children with autism spectrum disorder with that of 752 control children across three time periods during their first two years of life (birth to 3 months, birth to 7 months, and birth to 2 years) (DeStefano, Price, & Weintraub, 2013). At the time of the study, the children were between 6 and 13 years old, and their prior vaccination records were obtained. Because vaccines contain immunogens (substances that fight infections), the investigators examined medical records to see how many immunogens children received to determine if those children who received more immunogens were at greater risk for developing autism spectrum disorder. The results of this study, a portion of which are shown in Figure 15.19, clearly demonstrate that the quantity of immunogens from vaccines received during the first two years of life were not at all related to the development of autism spectrum disorder. There is not a relationship between vaccinations and autism spectrum disorders.

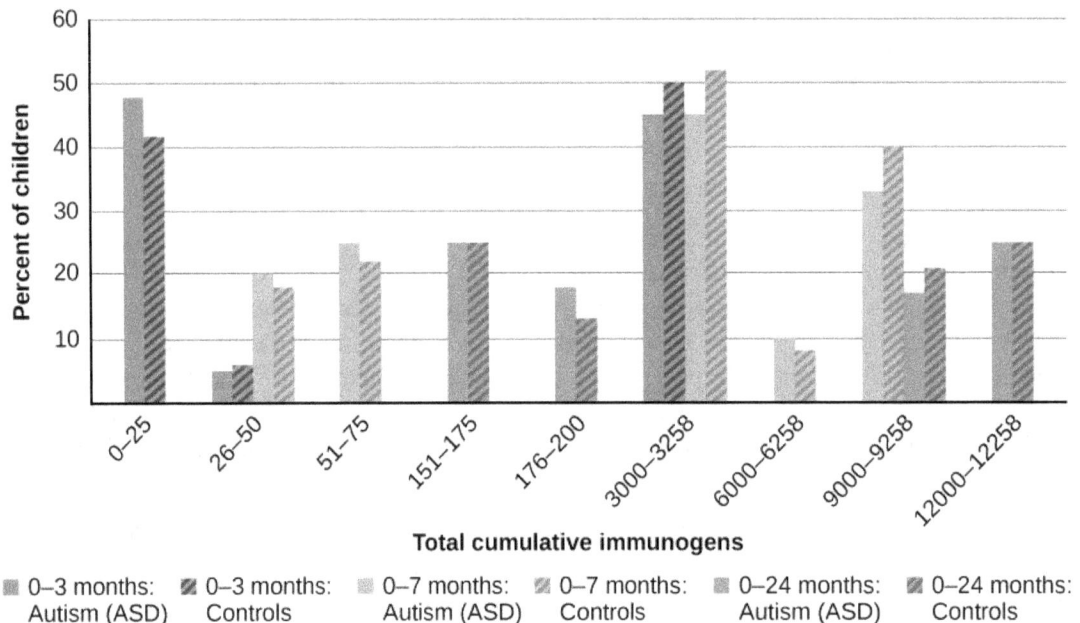

Figure 15.19 In terms of their exposure to immunogens in vaccines, overall, there is not a significant difference between children with autism spectrum disorder and their age-matched controls without the disorder (DeStefano et al., 2013).

Why does concern over vaccines and autism spectrum disorder persist? Since the proliferation of the Internet in the 1990s, parents have been constantly bombarded with online information that can become magnified and take on a life of its own. The enormous volume of electronic information pertaining to autism spectrum disorder, combined with how difficult it can be to grasp complex scientific concepts, can make separating good research from bad challenging (Downs, 2008). Notably, the study that fueled the controversy reported that 8 out of 12 children—according to their parents—developed symptoms consistent with autism spectrum disorder shortly after receiving a vaccination. To conclude that vaccines cause autism spectrum disorder on this basis, as many did, is clearly incorrect for a number of reasons, not the least of which is because correlation does not imply causation, as you've learned.

Additionally, as was the case with diet and ADHD in the 1970s, the notion that autism spectrum disorder is caused by vaccinations is appealing to some because it provides a simple explanation for this condition. Like all disorders, however, there are no simple explanations for autism spectrum disorder. Although the research discussed above has shed some light on its causes, science is still a long way from complete understanding of the disorder.

15.11 Personality Disorders

Learning Objectives

By the end of this section, you will be able to:
- Describe the nature of personality disorders and how they differ from other disorders
- List and distinguish between the three clusters of personality disorders
- Identify the basic features of borderline personality disorder and antisocial personality disorder, and the factors that are important in the etiology of both

The term *personality* refers loosely to one's stable, consistent, and distinctive way of thinking about, feeling, acting, and relating to the world. People with **personality disorders** exhibit a personality style that differs markedly from the expectations of their culture, is pervasive and inflexible, begins in adolescence or early adulthood, and causes distress or impairment (APA, 2013). Generally, individuals with these disorders exhibit enduring personality styles that are extremely troubling and often create problems for them and those with whom they come into contact. Their maladaptive personality styles frequently bring them into conflict with others, disrupt their ability to develop and maintain social relationships, and prevent them from accomplishing realistic life goals.

The DSM-5 recognizes 10 personality disorders, organized into 3 different clusters. Cluster A disorders include paranoid personality disorder, schizoid personality disorder, and schizotypal personality disorder. People with these disorders display a personality style that is odd or eccentric. Cluster B disorders include antisocial personality disorder, histrionic personality disorder, narcissistic personality disorder, and borderline personality disorder. People with these disorders usually are impulsive, overly dramatic, highly emotional, and erratic. Cluster C disorders include avoidant personality disorder, dependent personality disorder, and obsessive-compulsive personality disorder (which is not the same thing as obsessive-compulsive disorder). People with these disorders often appear to be nervous and fearful. **Table 15.2** provides a description of each of the DSM-5 personality disorders:

DSM-5 Personality Disorders

DSM-5 Personality Disorder	Description	Cluster
Paranoid	harbors a pervasive and unjustifiable suspiciousness and mistrust of others; reluctant to confide in or become close to others; reads hidden demeaning or threatening meaning into benign remarks or events; takes offense easily and bears grudges; not due to schizophrenia or other psychotic disorders	A
Schizoid	lacks interest and desire to form relationships with others; aloof and shows emotional coldness and detachment; indifferent to approval or criticism of others; lacks close friends or confidants; not due to schizophrenia or other psychotic disorders, not an autism spectrum disorder	A

DSM-5 Personality Disorders

DSM-5 Personality Disorder	Description	Cluster
Schizotypal	exhibits eccentricities in thought, perception, emotion, speech, and behavior; shows suspiciousness or paranoia; has unusual perceptual experiences; speech is often idiosyncratic; displays inappropriate emotions; lacks friends or confidants; not due to schizophrenia or other psychotic disorder, or to autism spectrum disorder	A
Antisocial	continuously violates the rights of others; history of antisocial tendencies prior to age 15; often lies, fights, and has problems with the law; impulsive and fails to think ahead; can be deceitful and manipulative in order to gain profit or pleasure; irresponsible and often fails to hold down a job or pay financial debts; lacks feelings for others and remorse over misdeeds	B
Histrionic	excessively overdramatic, emotional, and theatrical; feels uncomfortable when not the center of others' attention; behavior is often inappropriately seductive or provocative; speech is highly emotional but often vague and diffuse; emotions are shallow and often shift rapidly; may alienate friends with demands for constant attention	B
Narcissistic	overinflated and unjustified sense of self-importance and preoccupied with fantasies of success; believes he is entitled to special treatment from others; shows arrogant attitudes and behaviors; takes advantage of others; lacks empathy	B
Borderline	unstable in self-image, mood, and behavior; cannot tolerate being alone and experiences chronic feelings of emptiness; unstable and intense relationships with others; behavior is impulsive, unpredictable, and sometimes self-damaging; shows inappropriate and intense anger; makes suicidal gestures	B
Avoidant	socially inhibited and oversensitive to negative evaluation; avoids occupations that involve interpersonal contact because of fears of criticism or rejection; avoids relationships with others unless guaranteed to be accepted unconditionally; feels inadequate and views self as socially inept and unappealing; unwilling to take risks or engage in new activities if they may prove embarrassing	C
Dependent	allows others to take over and run her life; is submissive, clingy, and fears separation; cannot make decisions without advice and reassurance from others; lacks self-confidence; cannot do things on her own; feels uncomfortable or helpless when alone	C

DSM-5 Personality Disorders

DSM-5 Personality Disorder	Description	Cluster
Obsessive-Compulsive	pervasive need for perfectionism that interferes with the ability to complete tasks; preoccupied with details, rules, order, and schedules; excessively devoted to work at the expense of leisure and friendships; rigid, inflexible, and stubborn; insists things be done his way; miserly with money	C

Table 15.2

Slightly over 9% of the U.S. population suffers from a personality disorder, with avoidant and schizoid personality disorders the most frequent (Lezenweger, Lane, Loranger, & Kessler, 2007). Two of these personality disorders, borderline personality disorder and antisocial personality disorder, are regarded by many as especially problematic.

BORDERLINE PERSONALITY DISORDER

The "borderline" in borderline personality disorder was originally coined in the late 1930s in an effort to describe patients who appeared anxious, but were prone to brief psychotic experiences—that is, patients who were thought to be literally on the borderline between anxiety and psychosis (Freeman, Stone, Martin, & Reinecke, 2005). Today, **borderline personality disorder** has a completely different meaning. Borderline personality disorder is characterized chiefly by instability in interpersonal relationships, self-image, and mood, as well as marked impulsivity (APA, 2013). People with borderline personality disorder cannot tolerate the thought of being alone and will make frantic efforts (including making suicidal gestures and engaging in self-mutilation) to avoid abandonment or separation (whether real or imagined). Their relationships are intense and unstable; for example, a lover may be idealized early in a relationship, but then later vilified at the slightest sign she appears to no longer show interest. These individuals have an unstable view of self and, thus, might suddenly display a shift in personal attitudes, interests, career plans, and choice of friends. For example, a law school student may, despite having invested tens of thousands of dollars toward earning a law degree and despite having performed well in the program, consider dropping out and pursuing a career in another field. People with borderline personality disorder may be highly impulsive and may engage in reckless and self-destructive behaviors such as excessive gambling, spending money irresponsibly, substance abuse, engaging in unsafe sex, and reckless driving. They sometimes show intense and inappropriate anger that they have difficulty controlling, and they can be moody, sarcastic, bitter, and verbally abusive.

The prevalence of borderline personality disorder in the U.S. population is estimated to be around 1.4% (Lezenweger et al., 2007), but the rates are higher among those who use mental health services; approximately 10% of mental health outpatients and 20% of psychiatric inpatients meet the criteria for diagnosis (APA, 2013). Additionally, borderline personality disorder is comorbid with anxiety, mood, and substance use disorders (Lezenweger et al., 2007).

Biological Basis for Borderline Personality Disorder

Genetic factors appear to be important in the development of borderline personality disorder. For example, core personality traits that characterize this disorder, such as impulsivity and emotional instability, show a high degree of heritability (Livesley, 2008). Also, the rates of borderline personality disorder among relatives of people with this disorder have been found to be as high as 24.9% (White, Gunderson, Zanarani,

& Hudson, 2003). Individuals with borderline personality disorder report experiencing childhood physical, sexual, and/or emotional abuse at rates far greater than those observed in the general population (Afifi et al., 2010), indicating that environmental factors are also crucial. These findings would suggest that borderline personality disorder may be determined by an interaction between genetic factors and adverse environmental experiences. Consistent with this hypothesis, one study found that the highest rates of borderline personality disorder were among individuals with a borderline temperament (characterized by high novelty seeking and high harm-avoidance) and those who experienced childhood abuse and/or neglect (Joyce et al., 2003).

ANTISOCIAL PERSONALITY DISORDER

Most human beings live in accordance with a moral compass, a sense of right and wrong. Most individuals learn at a very young age that there are certain things that should not be done. We learn that we should not lie or cheat. We are taught that it is wrong to take things that do not belong to us, and that it is wrong to exploit others for personal gain. We also learn the importance of living up to our responsibilities, of doing what we say we will do. People with antisocial personality disorder, however, do not seem to have a moral compass. These individuals act as though they neither have a sense of nor care about right or wrong. Not surprisingly, these people represent a serious problem for others and for society in general.

According to the DSM-5, the individual with **antisocial personality disorder** shows no regard at all for other people's rights or feelings. This lack of regard is exhibited a number of ways and can include repeatedly performing illegal acts, lying to or conning others, impulsivity and recklessness, irritability and aggressiveness toward others, and failure to act in a responsible way (e.g., leaving debts unpaid) (APA, 2013). The worst part about antisocial personality disorder, however, is that people with this disorder have no remorse over their misdeeds; these people will hurt, manipulate, exploit, and abuse others and not feel any guilt. Signs of this disorder can emerge early in life; however, a person must be at least 18 years old to be diagnosed with antisocial personality disorder.

People with antisocial personality disorder seem to view the world as self-serving and unkind. They seem to think that they should use whatever means necessary to get by in life. They tend to view others not as living, thinking, feeling beings, but rather as pawns to be used or abused for a specific purpose. They often have an over-inflated sense of themselves and can appear extremely arrogant. They frequently display superficial charm; for example, without really meaning it they might say exactly what they think another person wants to hear. They lack empathy: they are incapable of understanding the emotional point-of-view of others. People with this disorder may become involved in illegal enterprises, show cruelty toward others, leave their jobs with no plans to obtain another job, have multiple sexual partners, repeatedly get into fights with others, and show reckless disregard for themselves and others (e.g., repeated arrests for driving while intoxicated) (APA, 2013).

The DSM-5 has included an alternative model for conceptualizing personality disorders based on the traits identified in the Five Factor Model of personality. This model addresses the level of personality functioning such as impairments in self (identity or self-direction) and interpersonal (empathy or intimacy) functioning. In the case of antisocial personality disorder, the DSM-5 identifies the predominant traits of antagonism (such as disregard for others' needs, manipulative or deceitful behavior) and disinhibition (characterized by impulsivity, irresponsibility, and risk-taking) (Harwood, Schade, Krueger, Wright, & Markon, 2012). A psychopathology specifier is also included that emphasizes traits such as attention seeking and low anxiousness (lack of concern about negative consequences for risky or harmful behavior) (Crego & Widiger, 2014).

Risk Factors for Antisocial Personality Disorder

Antisocial personality disorder is observed in about 3.6% of the population; the disorder is much more common among males, with a 3 to 1 ratio of men to women, and it is more likely to occur in men who are younger, widowed, separated, divorced, of lower socioeconomic status, who live in urban areas, and who live in the western United States (Compton, Conway, Stinson, Colliver, & Grant, 2005). Compared to men with antisocial personality disorder, women with the disorder are more likely to have experienced emotional neglect and sexual abuse during childhood, and they are more likely to have had parents who abused substances and who engaged in antisocial behaviors themselves (Alegria et al., 2013).

Table 15.3 shows some of the differences in the specific types of antisocial behaviors that men and women with antisocial personality disorder exhibit (Alegria et al., 2013).

Gender Differences in Antisocial Personality Disorder

Men with antisocial personality disorder are more likely than women with antisocial personality disorder to	Women with antisocial personality disorder are more likely than men with antisocial personality to
• do things that could easily hurt themselves or others • receive three or more traffic tickets for reckless driving • have their driver's license suspended • destroy others' property • start a fire on purpose • make money illegally • do anything that could lead to arrest • hit someone hard enough to injure them • hurt an animal on purpose	• run away from home overnight • frequently miss school or work • lie frequently • forge someone's signature • get into a fight that comes to blows with an intimate partner • live with others besides the family for at least one month • harass, threaten, or blackmail someone

Table 15.3

Family, twin, and adoption studies suggest that both genetic and environmental factors influence the development of antisocial personality disorder, as well as general antisocial behavior (criminality, violence, aggressiveness) (Baker, Bezdjian, & Raine, 2006). Personality and temperament dimensions that are related to this disorder, including fearlessness, impulsive antisociality, and callousness, have a substantial genetic influence (Livesley & Jang, 2008). Adoption studies clearly demonstrate that the development of antisocial behavior is determined by the interaction of genetic factors and adverse environmental circumstances (Rhee & Waldman, 2002). For example, one investigation found that adoptees of biological parents with antisocial personality disorder were more likely to exhibit adolescent and adult antisocial behaviors if they were raised in adverse adoptive family environments (e.g., adoptive parents had marital problems, were divorced, used drugs, and had legal problems) than if they were raised in a more normal adoptive environment (Cadoret, Yates, Ed, Woodworth, & Stewart, 1995).

Researchers who are interested in the importance of environment in the development of antisocial personality disorder have directed their attention to such factors as the community, the structure and functioning of the family, and peer groups. Each of these factors influences the likelihood of antisocial behavior. One longitudinal investigation of more than 800 Seattle-area youth measured risk factors for violence at 10, 14, 16, and 18 years of age (Herrenkohl et al., 2000). The risk factors examined included those involving the family, peers, and community. A portion of the findings from this study are provided in **Figure 15.20**.

Risk Factors During Adolescence That Predict Later Violence			
Risk factor	Age 10 predictor (elementary school)	Age 14 predictor (middle school)	Age 16 predictor (high school)
Family			
Parental violence		X	
Parental criminality		X	X
Poof family management		X	X
Family conflict		X	X
Parental attitudes favorable to violence	X		
Frequent moves			X
Peer			
Peer delinquency	X	X	X
Gang membership		X	X
Community			
Economic deprivation	X		X
Community disorganization		X	X
Availability of drugs	X	X	X
Neighborhood adults involved in crime		X	X

Figure 15.20 Longitudinal studies have helped to identify risk factors for predicting violent behavior.

Those with antisocial tendencies do not seem to experience emotions the way most other people do. These individuals fail to show fear in response to environment cues that signal punishment, pain, or noxious stimulation. For instance, they show less skin conductance (sweatiness on hands) in anticipation of electric shock than do people without antisocial tendencies (Hare, 1965). Skin conductance is controlled by the sympathetic nervous system and is used to assess autonomic nervous system functioning. When the sympathetic nervous system is active, people become aroused and anxious, and sweat gland activity increases. Thus, increased sweat gland activity, as assessed through skin conductance, is taken as a sign of arousal or anxiety. For those with antisocial personality disorder, a lack of skin conductance may indicate the presence of characteristics such as emotional deficits and impulsivity that underlie the propensity for antisocial behavior and negative social relationships (Fung et al., 2005).

Another example showing that those with antisocial personality disorder fail to respond to environmental cues comes from a recent study by Stuppy-Sullivan and Baskin-Sommers (2019). The researchers studied cognitive and reward factors associated with antisocial personality disorder dysfunction in 119 incarcerated males. Each subject was administered three tasks targeting different aspects of cognition and reward. High-magnitude rewards tended to impair perception in those with antisocial personality disorder, worsened executive function when they were consciously aware of the high rewards, and worsened inhibition when the tasks placed high demand on working memory.

Key Terms

agoraphobia anxiety disorder characterized by intense fear, anxiety, and avoidance of situations in which it might be difficult to escape if one experiences symptoms of a panic attack

antisocial personality disorder characterized by a lack of regard for others' rights, impulsivity, deceitfulness, irresponsibility, and lack of remorse over misdeeds

anxiety disorder characterized by excessive and persistent fear and anxiety, and by related disturbances in behavior

attention deficit/hyperactivity disorder childhood disorder characterized by inattentiveness and/or hyperactive, impulsive behavior

atypical describes behaviors or feelings that deviate from the norm

autism spectrum disorder childhood disorder characterized by deficits in social interaction and communication, and repetitive patterns of behavior or interests

bipolar and related disorders group of mood disorders in which mania is the defining feature

bipolar disorder mood disorder characterized by mood states that vacillate between depression and mania

body dysmorphic disorder involves excessive preoccupation with an imagined defect in physical appearance

borderline personality disorder instability in interpersonal relationships, self-image, and mood, as well as impulsivity; key features include intolerance of being alone and fear of abandonment, unstable relationships, unpredictable behavior and moods, and intense and inappropriate anger

catatonic behavior decreased reactivity to the environment; includes posturing and catatonic stupor

comorbidity co-occurrence of two disorders in the same individual

delusion belief that is contrary to reality and is firmly held, despite contradictory evidence

depersonalization/derealization disorder dissociative disorder in which people feel detached from the self (depersonalization), and the world feels artificial and unreal (derealization)

depressive disorder one of a group of mood disorders in which depression is the defining feature

diagnosis determination of which disorder a set of symptoms represents

Diagnostic and Statistical Manual of Mental Disorders, Fifth Edition **(DSM-5)** authoritative index of mental disorders and the criteria for their diagnosis; published by the American Psychiatric Association (APA)

diathesis-stress model suggests that people with a predisposition for a disorder (a diathesis) are more likely to develop the disorder when faced with stress; model of psychopathology

disorganized thinking disjointed and incoherent thought processes, usually detected by what a person says

disorganized/abnormal motor behavior highly unusual behaviors and movements (such as child-like behaviors), repeated and purposeless movements, and displaying odd facial expressions and gestures

dissociative amnesia dissociative disorder characterized by an inability to recall important personal information, usually following an extremely stressful or traumatic experience

dissociative disorders group of DSM-5 disorders in which the primary feature is that a person becomes dissociated, or split off, from his or her core sense of self, resulting in disturbances in identity and memory

dissociative fugue symptom of dissociative amnesia in which a person suddenly wanders away from one's home and experiences confusion about his or her identity

dissociative identity disorder dissociative disorder (formerly known as multiple personality disorder) in which a person exhibits two or more distinct, well-defined personalities or identities and experiences memory gaps for the time during which another identity emerged

dopamine hypothesis theory of schizophrenia that proposes that an overabundance of dopamine or dopamine receptors is responsible for the onset and maintenance of schizophrenia

etiology cause or causes of a psychological disorder

flashback psychological state lasting from a few seconds to several days, during which one relives a traumatic event and behaves as though the event were occurring at that moment

flight of ideas symptom of mania that involves an abruptly switching in conversation from one topic to another

generalized anxiety disorder characterized by a continuous state of excessive, uncontrollable, and pointless worry and apprehension

grandiose delusion characterized by beliefs that one holds special power, unique knowledge, or is extremely important

hallucination perceptual experience that occurs in the absence of external stimulation, such as the auditory hallucinations (hearing voices) common to schizophrenia

harmful dysfunction model of psychological disorders resulting from the inability of an internal mechanism to perform its natural function

hoarding disorder characterized by persistent difficulty in parting with possessions, regardless of their actual value or usefulness

hopelessness theory cognitive theory of depression proposing that a style of thinking that perceives negative life events as having stable and global causes leads to a sense of hopelessness and then to depression

International Classification of Diseases **(ICD)** authoritative index of mental and physical diseases, including infectious diseases, and the criteria for their diagnosis; published by the World Health Organization (WHO)

locus coeruleus area of the brainstem that contains norepinephrine, a neurotransmitter that triggers the body's fight-or-flight response; has been implicated in panic disorder

major depressive disorder commonly referred to as "depression" or "major depression," characterized by sadness or loss of pleasure in usual activities, as well other symptoms

mania state of extreme elation and agitation

manic episode period in which an individual experiences mania, characterized by extremely cheerful and euphoric mood, excessive talkativeness, irritability, increased activity levels, and other symptoms

mood disorder one of a group of disorders characterized by severe disturbances in mood and emotions; the categories of mood disorders listed in the DSM-5 are bipolar and related disorders and depressive disorders

negative symptom characterized by decreases and absences in certain normal behaviors, emotions, or drives, such as an expressionless face, lack of motivation to engage in activities, reduced speech, lack of social engagement, and inability to experience pleasure

neurodevelopmental disorder one of the disorders that are first diagnosed in childhood and involve developmental problems in academic, intellectual, social functioning

obsessive-compulsive and related disorders group of overlapping disorders listed in the DSM-5 that involves intrusive, unpleasant thoughts and/or repetitive behaviors

obsessive-compulsive disorder characterized by the tendency to experience intrusive and unwanted thoughts and urges (obsession) and/or the need to engage in repetitive behaviors or mental acts (compulsions) in response to the unwanted thoughts and urges

orbitofrontal cortex area of the frontal lobe involved in learning and decision-making

panic attack period of extreme fear or discomfort that develops abruptly; symptoms of panic attacks are both physiological and psychological

panic disorder anxiety disorder characterized by unexpected panic attacks, along with at least one month of worry about panic attacks or self-defeating behavior related to the attacks

paranoid delusion characterized by beliefs that others are out to harm them

peripartum onset subtype of depression that applies to women who experience an episode of major depression either during pregnancy or in the four weeks following childbirth

persistent depressive disorder depressive disorder characterized by a chronically sad and melancholy mood

personality disorder group of DSM-5 disorders characterized by an inflexible and pervasive personality style that differs markedly from the expectations of one's culture and causes distress and impairment; people with these disorders have a personality style that frequently brings them into conflict with others and disrupts their ability to develop and maintain social relationships

posttraumatic stress disorder (PTSD) experiencing a profoundly traumatic event leads to a constellation of symptoms that include intrusive and distressing memories of the event, avoidance of stimuli connected to the event, negative emotional states, feelings of detachment from others, irritability, proneness toward outbursts, hypervigilance, and a tendency to startle easily; these symptoms must occur for at least one month

prodromal symptom in schizophrenia, one of the early minor symptoms of psychosis

psychological disorder condition characterized by abnormal thoughts, feelings, and behaviors

psychopathology study of psychological disorders, including their symptoms, causes, and treatment; manifestation of a psychological disorder

rumination in depression, tendency to repetitively and passively dwell on one's depressed symptoms, their meanings, and their consequences

safety behavior mental and behavior acts designed to reduce anxiety in social situations by reducing the chance of negative social outcomes; common in social anxiety disorder

schizophrenia severe disorder characterized by major disturbances in thought, perception, emotion, and behavior with symptoms that include hallucinations, delusions, disorganized thinking and behavior, and negative symptoms

seasonal pattern subtype of depression in which a person experiences the symptoms of major depressive disorder only during a particular time of year

social anxiety disorder characterized by extreme and persistent fear or anxiety and avoidance of social situations in which one could potentially be evaluated negatively by others

somatic delusion belief that something highly unusual is happening to one's body or internal organs

specific phobia anxiety disorder characterized by excessive, distressing, and persistent fear or anxiety about a specific object or situation

suicidal ideation thoughts of death by suicide, thinking about or planning suicide, or making a suicide attempt

suicide death caused by intentional, self-directed injurious behavior

supernatural describes a force beyond scientific understanding

ventricle one of the fluid-filled cavities within the brain

Summary

15.1 What Are Psychological Disorders?
Psychological disorders are conditions characterized by abnormal thoughts, feelings, and behaviors. Although challenging, it is essential for psychologists and mental health professionals to agree on what kinds of inner experiences and behaviors constitute the presence of a psychological disorder. Inner experiences and behaviors that are atypical or violate social norms could signify the presence of a disorder; however, each of these criteria alone is inadequate. Harmful dysfunction describes the view that psychological disorders result from the inability of an internal mechanism to perform its natural function. Many of the features of harmful dysfunction conceptualization have been incorporated in the APA's formal definition of psychological disorders. According to this definition, the presence of a psychological disorder is signaled by significant disturbances in thoughts, feelings, and behaviors; these disturbances must reflect some kind of dysfunction (biological, psychological, or developmental), must cause significant impairment in one's life, and must not reflect culturally expected reactions to certain life events.

15.2 Diagnosing and Classifying Psychological Disorders
The diagnosis and classification of psychological disorders is essential in studying and treating psychopathology. The classification system used by most U.S. professionals is the DSM-5. The first edition of the DSM was published in 1952, and has undergone numerous revisions. The 5th and most recent edition, the DSM-5, was published in 2013. The diagnostic manual includes a total of 237 specific diagnosable disorders, each described in detail, including its symptoms, prevalence, risk factors, and comorbidity. Over time, the number of diagnosable conditions listed in the DSM has grown steadily, prompting criticism from some. Nevertheless, the diagnostic criteria in the DSM are more explicit than that of any other system, which makes the DSM system highly desirable for both clinical diagnosis and research.

15.3 Perspectives on Psychological Disorders

Psychopathology is very complex, involving a plethora of etiological theories and perspectives. For centuries, psychological disorders were viewed primarily from a supernatural perspective and thought to arise from divine forces or possession from spirits. Some cultures continue to hold this supernatural belief. Today, many who study psychopathology view mental illness from a biological perspective, whereby psychological disorders are thought to result largely from faulty biological processes. Indeed, scientific advances over the last several decades have provided a better understanding of the genetic, neurological, hormonal, and biochemical bases of psychopathology. The psychological perspective, in contrast, emphasizes the importance of psychological factors (e.g., stress and thoughts) and environmental factors in the development of psychological disorders. A contemporary, promising approach is to view disorders as originating from an integration of biological and psychosocial factors. The diathesis-stress model suggests that people with an underlying diathesis, or vulnerability, for a psychological disorder are more likely than those without the diathesis to develop the disorder when faced with stressful events.

15.4 Anxiety Disorders

Anxiety disorders are a group of disorders in which a person experiences excessive, persistent, and distressing fear and anxiety that interferes with normal functioning. Anxiety disorders include specific phobia: a specific unrealistic fear; social anxiety disorder: extreme fear and avoidance of social situations; panic disorder: suddenly overwhelmed by panic even though there is no apparent reason to be frightened; agoraphobia: an intense fear and avoidance of situations in which it might be difficult to escape; and generalized anxiety disorder: a relatively continuous state of tension, apprehension, and dread.

15.5 Obsessive-Compulsive and Related Disorders

Obsessive-compulsive and related disorders are a group of DSM-5 disorders that overlap somewhat in that they each involve intrusive thoughts and/or repetitive behaviors. Perhaps the most recognized of these disorders is obsessive-compulsive disorder, in which a person is obsessed with unwanted, unpleasant thoughts and/or compulsively engages in repetitive behaviors or mental acts, perhaps as a way of coping with the obsessions. Body dysmorphic disorder is characterized by the individual becoming excessively preoccupied with one or more perceived flaws in his physical appearance that are either nonexistent or unnoticeable to others. Preoccupation with the perceived physical defects causes the person to experience significant anxiety regarding how he appears to others. Hoarding disorder is characterized by persistent difficulty in discarding or parting with objects, regardless of their actual value, often resulting in the accumulation of items that clutter and congest her living area.

15.6 Posttraumatic Stress Disorder

Posttraumatic stress disorder (PTSD) was described through much of the 20th century and was referred to as shell shock and combat neurosis in the belief that its symptoms were thought to emerge from the stress of active combat. Today, PTSD is defined as a disorder in which the experience of a traumatic or profoundly stressful event, such as combat, sexual assault, or natural disaster, produces a constellation of symptoms that must last for one month or more. These symptoms include intrusive and distressing memories of the event, flashbacks, avoidance of stimuli or situations that are connected to the event, persistently negative emotional states, feeling detached from others, irritability, proneness toward outbursts, and a tendency to be easily startled. Not everyone who experiences a traumatic event will develop PTSD; a variety of risk factors associated with its development have been identified.

15.7 Mood Disorders

Mood disorders are those in which the person experiences severe disturbances in mood and emotion. They include depressive disorders and bipolar and related disorders. Depressive disorders include major depressive disorder, which is characterized by episodes of profound sadness and loss of interest or pleasure in usual activities and other associated features, and persistent depressive disorder, which marked by a chronic state of sadness. Bipolar disorder is characterized by mood states that vacillate between sadness and euphoria; a diagnosis of bipolar disorder requires experiencing at least one manic episode, which is defined as a period of extreme euphoria, irritability, and increased activity. Mood disorders appear to have a genetic component, with genetic factors playing a more prominent role in bipolar disorder than in depression. Both biological and psychological factors are important in the development of depression. People who suffer from mental health problems, especially mood disorders, are at heightened risk for suicide.

15.8 Schizophrenia

Schizophrenia is a severe disorder characterized by a complete breakdown in one's ability to function in life; it often requires hospitalization. People with schizophrenia experience hallucinations and delusions, and they have extreme difficulty regulating their emotions and behavior. Thinking is incoherent and disorganized, behavior is extremely bizarre, emotions are flat, and motivation to engage in most basic life activities is lacking. Considerable evidence shows that genetic factors play a central role in schizophrenia; however, adoption studies have highlighted the additional importance of environmental factors. Neurotransmitter and brain abnormalities, which may be linked to environmental factors such as obstetric complications or exposure to influenza during the gestational period, have also been implicated. A promising new area of schizophrenia research involves identifying individuals who show prodromal symptoms and following them over time to determine which factors best predict the development of schizophrenia. Future research may enable us to pinpoint those especially at risk for developing schizophrenia and who may benefit from early intervention.

15.9 Dissociative Disorders

The main characteristic of dissociative disorders is that people become dissociated from their sense of self, resulting in memory and identity disturbances. Dissociative disorders listed in the DSM-5 include dissociative amnesia, depersonalization/derealization disorder, and dissociative identity disorder. A person with dissociative amnesia is unable to recall important personal information, often after a stressful or traumatic experience.

Depersonalization/derealization disorder is characterized by recurring episodes of depersonalization (i.e., detachment from or unfamiliarity with the self) and/or derealization (i.e., detachment from or unfamiliarity with the world). A person with dissociative identity disorder exhibits two or more well-defined and distinct personalities or identities, as well as memory gaps for the time during which another identity was present.

Dissociative identity disorder has generated controversy, mainly because some believe its symptoms can be faked by patients if presenting its symptoms somehow benefits the patient in avoiding negative consequences or taking responsibility for one's actions. The diagnostic rates of this disorder have increased dramatically following its portrayal in popular culture. However, many people legitimately suffer over the course of a lifetime with this disorder.

15.10 Disorders in Childhood

Neurodevelopmental disorders are a group of disorders that are typically diagnosed during childhood and are characterized by developmental deficits in personal, social, academic, and intellectual realms; these disorders include attention deficit/hyperactivity disorder (ADHD) and autism spectrum disorder. ADHD is characterized by a pervasive pattern of inattention and/or hyperactive and impulsive behavior that interferes with normal functioning. Genetic and neurobiological factors contribute to the development of ADHD, which can persist well into adulthood and is often associated with poor long-term outcomes. The major features of autism spectrum disorder include deficits in social interaction and communication and repetitive movements or interests. As with ADHD, genetic factors appear to play a prominent role in the development of autism spectrum disorder; exposure to environmental pollutants such as mercury have also been linked to the development of this disorder. Although it is believed by some that autism is triggered by the MMR vaccination, evidence does not support this claim.

15.11 Personality Disorders

Individuals with personality disorders exhibit a personality style that is inflexible, causes distress and impairment, and creates problems for themselves and others. The DSM-5 recognizes 10 personality disorders, organized into three clusters. The disorders in Cluster A include those characterized by a personality style that is odd and eccentric. Cluster B includes personality disorders characterized chiefly by a personality style that is impulsive, dramatic, highly emotional, and erratic, and those in Cluster C are characterized by a nervous and fearful personality style. Two Cluster B personality disorders, borderline personality disorder and antisocial personality disorder, are especially problematic. People with borderline personality disorder show marked instability in mood, behavior, and self-image, as well as impulsivity. They cannot stand to be alone, are unpredictable, have a history of stormy relationships, and frequently display intense and inappropriate anger. Genetic factors and adverse childhood experiences (e.g., sexual abuse) appear to be important in its development. People with antisocial personality display a lack of regard for the rights of others; they are impulsive, deceitful, irresponsible, and unburdened by any sense of guilt. Genetic factors and socialization both appear to be important in the origin of antisocial personality disorder. Research has also shown that those with this disorder do not experience emotions the way most other people do.

Review Questions

1. In the harmful dysfunction definition of psychological disorders, dysfunction involves _____.
    a. the inability of an psychological mechanism to perform its function
    b. the breakdown of social order in one's community
    c. communication problems in one's immediate family
    d. all the above

2. Patterns of inner experience and behavior are thought to reflect the presence of a psychological disorder if they _____.
    a. are highly atypical
    b. lead to significant distress and impairment in one's life
    c. embarrass one's friends and/or family
    d. violate the norms of one's culture

3. The letters in the abbreviation DSM-5 stand for _____.
    a. Diseases and Statistics Manual of Medicine
    b. Diagnosable Standards Manual of Mental Disorders
    c. Diseases and Symptoms Manual of Mental Disorders
    d. Diagnostic and Statistical Manual of Mental Disorders

4. A study based on over 9,000 U. S. residents found that the most prevalent disorder was _____.
    a. major depressive disorder
    b. social anxiety disorder
    c. obsessive-compulsive disorder
    d. specific phobia

5. The diathesis-stress model presumes that psychopathology results from _____.
    a. vulnerability and adverse experiences
    b. biochemical factors
    c. chemical imbalances and structural abnormalities in the brain
    d. adverse childhood experiences

6. Dr. Anastasia believes that major depressive disorder is caused by an over-secretion of cortisol. His view on the cause of major depressive disorder reflects a _____ perspective.
    a. psychological
    b. supernatural
    c. biological
    d. diathesis-stress

7. In which of the following anxiety disorders is the person in a continuous state of excessive, pointless worry and apprehension?
    a. panic disorder
    b. generalized anxiety disorder
    c. agoraphobia
    d. social anxiety disorder

8. Which of the following would constitute a safety behavior?
   a. encountering a phobic stimulus in the company of other people
   b. avoiding a field where snakes are likely to be present
   c. avoiding eye contact
   d. worrying as a distraction from painful memories

9. Which of the following best illustrates a compulsion?
   a. mentally counting backward from 1,000
   b. persistent fear of germs
   c. thoughts of harming a neighbor
   d. falsely believing that a spouse has been cheating

10. Research indicates that the symptoms of OCD _____.
    a. are similar to the symptoms of panic disorder
    b. are triggered by low levels of stress hormones
    c. are related to hyperactivity in the orbitofrontal cortex
    d. are reduced if people are asked to view photos of stimuli that trigger the symptoms

11. Symptoms of PTSD include all of the following except _____.
    a. intrusive thoughts or memories of a traumatic event
    b. avoidance of things that remind one of a traumatic event
    c. jumpiness
    d. physical complaints that cannot be explained medically

12. Which of the following elevates the risk for developing PTSD?
    a. severity of the trauma
    b. frequency of the trauma
    c. high levels of intelligence
    d. social support

13. Common symptoms of major depressive disorder include all of the following except _____.
    a. periods of extreme elation and euphoria
    b. difficulty concentrating and making decisions
    c. loss of interest or pleasure in usual activities
    d. psychomotor agitation and retardation

14. Suicide rates are _____ among men than among women, and they are _____ during the winter holiday season than during the spring months.
    a. higher; higher
    b. lower; lower
    c. higher; lower
    d. lower; higher

15. Clifford falsely believes that the police have planted secret cameras in his home to monitor his every movement. Clifford's belief is an example of _____.
    a. a delusion
    b. a hallucination
    c. tangentiality
    d. a negative symptom

16. A study of adoptees whose biological mothers had schizophrenia found that the adoptees were most likely to develop schizophrenia _____.
    a. if their childhood friends later developed schizophrenia
    b. if they abused drugs during adolescence
    c. if they were raised in a disturbed adoptive home environment
    d. regardless of whether they were raised in a healthy or disturbed home environment

17. Dissociative amnesia involves _____.
    a. memory loss following head trauma
    b. memory loss following stress
    c. feeling detached from the self
    d. feeling detached from the world

18. Dissociative identity disorder mainly involves _____.
    a. depersonalization
    b. derealization
    c. schizophrenia
    d. different personalities

19. Which of the following is *not* a primary characteristic of ADHD?
    a. short attention span
    b. difficulty concentrating and distractibility
    c. restricted and fixated interest
    d. excessive fidgeting and squirming

20. One of the primary characteristics of autism spectrum disorder is _____.
    a. bed-wetting
    b. difficulty relating to others
    c. short attention span
    d. intense and inappropriate interest in others

21. People with borderline personality disorder often _____.
    a. try to be the center of attention
    b. are shy and withdrawn
    c. are impulsive and unpredictable
    d. tend to accomplish goals through cruelty

22. Antisocial personality disorder is associated with _____.
    a. emotional deficits
    b. memory deficits
    c. parental overprotection
    d. increased empathy

Critical Thinking Questions

23. Discuss why thoughts, feelings, or behaviors that are merely atypical or unusual would not necessarily signify the presence of a psychological disorder. Provide an example.

24. Describe the DSM-5. What is it, what kind of information does it contain, and why is it important to the study and treatment of psychological disorders?

25. The International Classification of Diseases (ICD) and the DSM differ in various ways. What are some of the differences in these two classification systems?

26. Why is the perspective one uses in explaining a psychological disorder important?

27. Describe how cognitive theories of the etiology of anxiety disorders differ from learning theories.

28. Discuss the common elements of each of the three disorders covered in this section: obsessive-compulsive disorder, body dysmorphic disorder, and hoarding disorder.

29. List some of the risk factors associated with the development of PTSD following a traumatic event.

30. Describe several of the factors associated with suicide.

31. Why is research following individuals who show prodromal symptoms of schizophrenia so important?

32. The prevalence of most psychological disorders has increased since the 1980s. However, as discussed in this section, scientific publications regarding dissociative amnesia peaked in the mid-1990s but then declined steeply through 2003. In addition, no fictional or nonfictional description of individuals showing dissociative amnesia following a trauma exists prior to 1800. How would you explain this phenomenon?

33. Compare the factors that are important in the development of ADHD with those that are important in the development of autism spectrum disorder.

34. Imagine that a child has a genetic vulnerability to antisocial personality disorder. How might this child's environment shape the likelihood of developing this personality disorder?

Personal Application Questions

35. Identify a behavior that is considered unusual or abnormal in your own culture; however, it would be considered normal and expected in another culture.

36. Even today, some believe that certain occurrences have supernatural causes. Think of an event, recent or historical, for which others have provided supernatural explanation.

37. Think of someone you know who seems to have a tendency to make negative, self-defeating explanations for negative life events. How might this tendency lead to future problems? What steps do you think could be taken to change this thinking style?

38. Try to find an example (via a search engine) of a past instance in which a person committed a horrible crime, was apprehended, and later claimed to have dissociative identity disorder during the trial. What was the outcome? Was the person revealed to be faking? If so, how was this determined?

39. Discuss the characteristics of autism spectrum disorder with a few of your friends or members of your family (choose friends or family members who know little about the disorder) and ask them if they think the cause is due to bad parenting or vaccinations. If they indicate that they believe either to be true, why do you think this might be the case? What would be your response?

Chapter 16

Therapy and Treatment

Figure 16.1 Many forms of therapy have been developed to treat a wide array of problems. These marines who served in Iraq and Afghanistan, together with community mental health volunteers, are part of the Ocean Therapy program at Camp Pendleton, a program in which learning to surf is combined with group discussions. The program helps vets recover, especially vets who suffer from post-traumatic stress disorder (PTSD).

Chapter Outline

16.1 Mental Health Treatment: Past and Present
16.2 Types of Treatment
16.3 Treatment Modalities
16.4 Substance-Related and Addictive Disorders: A Special Case
16.5 The Sociocultural Model and Therapy Utilization

Introduction

What comes to mind when you think about therapy for psychological problems? You might picture someone lying on a couch talking about his childhood while the therapist sits and takes notes, à la Sigmund Freud. But can you envision a therapy session in which someone is wearing virtual reality headgear to conquer a fear of snakes?

In this chapter, you will see that approaches to therapy include both psychological and biological interventions, all with the goal of alleviating distress. Because psychological problems can originate from various sources—biology, genetics, childhood experiences, conditioning, and sociocultural influences—psychologists have developed many different therapeutic techniques and approaches. The Ocean Therapy program shown in Figure 16.1 uses multiple approaches to support the mental health of veterans in the group.

16.1 Mental Health Treatment: Past and Present

Learning Objectives

By the end of this section, you will be able to:
- Explain how people with psychological disorders have been treated throughout the ages
- Discuss deinstitutionalization
- Discuss the ways in which mental health services are delivered today
- Distinguish between voluntary and involuntary treatment

Before we explore the various approaches to therapy used today, let's begin our study of therapy by looking at how many people experience mental illness and how many receive treatment. According to the U.S. Department of Health and Human Services (2017), 18.9% of U.S. adults experienced mental illness in 2017. For teens (ages 13–18), the rate is similar to that of adults, and for children ages 8–15, current estimates suggest that approximately 13% experience mental illness in a given year (National Institute of Mental Health [NIMH], 2017).

With many different treatment options available, approximately how many people receive mental health treatment per year? According to the Substance Abuse and Mental Health Services Administration (SAMHSA), in 2017, 14.8% of adults received treatment for a mental health issue (NIMH, 2017). These percentages, shown in **Figure 16.2**, reflect the number of adults who received care in inpatient and outpatient settings and/or used prescription medication for psychological disorders.

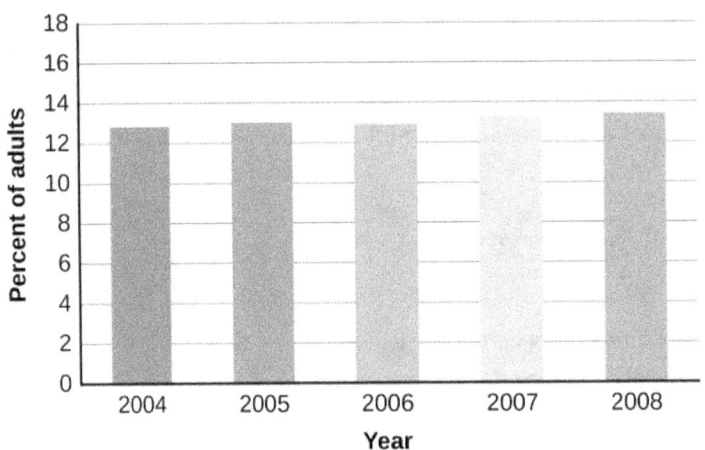

Figure 16.2 The percentage of adults who received mental health treatment in 2004–2008 is shown. Adults seeking treatment increased slightly from 2004 to 2008.

Children and adolescents also receive mental health services. The Centers for Disease Control and Prevention's National Health and Nutrition Examination Survey (NHANES) found that approximately half (50.6%) of children with mental disorders had received treatment for their disorder within the past year (NIMH, n.d.). However, there were some differences between treatment rates by category of disorder (**Figure 16.3**). For example, children with anxiety disorders were least likely to have received treatment in the past year, while children with ADHD or a conduct disorder were more likely to receive treatment. Can you think of some possible reasons for these differences in receiving treatment?

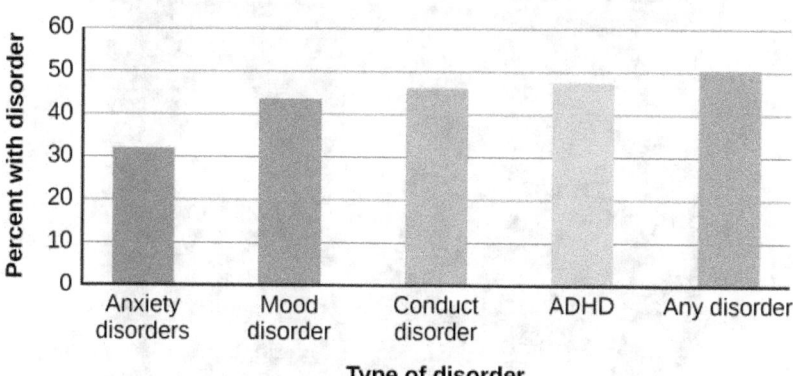

Figure 16.3 About one-third to one-half of U.S. adolescents (ages 8–15) with mental disorders receive treatment, with behavior-related disorders more likely to be treated.

Considering the many forms of treatment for mental health disorders available today, how did these forms of treatment emerge? Let's take a look at the history of mental health treatment from the past (with some questionable approaches in light of modern understanding of mental illness) to where we are today.

TREATMENT IN THE PAST

For much of history, the mentally ill have been treated very poorly. It was believed that mental illness was caused by demonic possession, witchcraft, or an angry god (Szasz, 1960). For example, in medieval times, abnormal behaviors were viewed as a sign that a person was possessed by demons. If someone was considered to be possessed, there were several forms of treatment to release spirits from the individual. The most common treatment was exorcism, often conducted by priests or other religious figures: Incantations and prayers were said over the person's body, and she may have been given some medicinal drinks. Another form of treatment for extreme cases of mental illness was trephining: A small hole was made in the afflicted individual's skull to release spirits from the body. Most people treated in this manner died. In addition to exorcism and trephining, other practices involved execution or imprisonment of people with psychological disorders. Still others were left to be homeless beggars. Generally speaking, most people who exhibited strange behaviors were greatly misunderstood and treated cruelly. The prevailing theory of psychopathology in earlier history was the idea that mental illness was the result of demonic possession by either an evil spirit or an evil god because early beliefs incorrectly attributed all unexplainable phenomena to deities deemed either good or evil.

From the late 1400s to the late 1600s, a common belief perpetuated by some religious organizations was that some people made pacts with the devil and committed horrible acts, such as eating babies (Blumberg, 2007). These people were considered to be witches and were tried and condemned by courts—they were often burned at the stake. Worldwide, it is estimated that tens of thousands of mentally ill people were killed after being accused of being witches or under the influence of witchcraft (Hemphill, 1966)

By the 18th century, people who were considered odd and unusual were placed in asylums (**Figure 16.4**). **Asylums** were the first institutions created for the specific purpose of housing people with psychological disorders, but the focus was ostracizing them from society rather than treating their disorders. Often these people were kept in windowless dungeons, beaten, chained to their beds, and had little to no contact with caregivers.

Figure 16.4 This painting by Francisco Goya, called *The Madhouse*, depicts a mental asylum and its inhabitants in the early 1800s. It portrays those with psychological disorders as victims.

In the late 1700s, a French physician, Philippe Pinel, argued for more humane treatment of the mentally ill. He suggested that they be unchained and talked to, and that's just what he did for patients at La Salpêtrière in Paris in 1795 (Figure 16.5). Patients benefited from this more humane treatment, and many were able to leave the hospital.

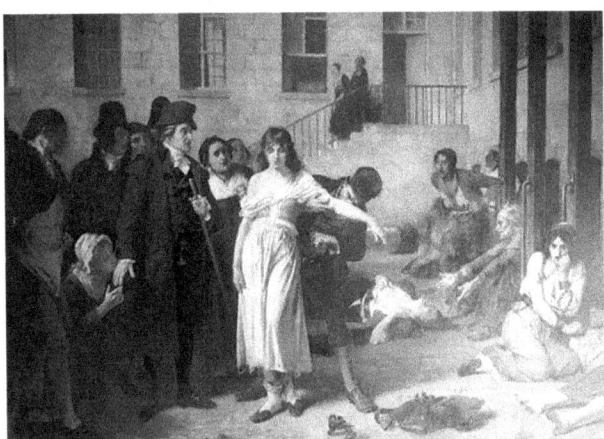

Figure 16.5 This painting by Tony Robert-Fleury depicts Dr. Philippe Pinel ordering the removal of chains from patients at the Salpêtrière asylum in Paris.

In the 19th century, Dorothea Dix led reform efforts for mental health care in the United States (Figure 16.6). She investigated how those who are mentally ill and poor were cared for, and she discovered an underfunded and unregulated system that perpetuated abuse of this population (Tiffany, 1891). Horrified by her findings, Dix began lobbying various state legislatures and the U.S. Congress for change (Tiffany, 1891). Her efforts led to the creation of the first mental asylums in the United States.

Figure 16.6 Dorothea Dix was a social reformer who became an advocate for the indigent insane and was instrumental in creating the first American mental asylum. She did this by relentlessly lobbying state legislatures and Congress to set up and fund such institutions.

Despite reformers' efforts, however, a typical asylum was filthy, offered very little treatment, and often kept people for decades. At Willard Psychiatric Center in upstate New York, for example, one treatment was to submerge patients in cold baths for long periods of time. Electroshock treatment was also used, and the way the treatment was administered often broke patients' backs; in 1943, doctors at Willard administered 1,443 shock treatments (Willard Psychiatric Center, 2009). (Electroshock is now called electroconvulsive treatment, and the therapy is still used, but with safeguards and under anesthesia. A brief application of electric stimulus is used to produce a generalized seizure. Controversy continues over its effectiveness versus the side effects.) Many of the wards and rooms were so cold that a glass of water would be frozen by morning (Willard Psychiatric Center, 2009). Willard's doors were not closed until 1995. Conditions like these remained commonplace until well into the 20th century.

Starting in 1954 and gaining popularity in the 1960s, antipsychotic medications were introduced. These proved a tremendous help in controlling the symptoms of certain psychological disorders, such as psychosis. Psychosis was a common diagnosis of individuals in mental hospitals, and it was often evidenced by symptoms like hallucinations and delusions, indicating a loss of contact with reality. Then in 1963, Congress passed and John F. Kennedy signed the Mental Retardation Facilities and Community Mental Health Centers Construction Act, which provided federal support and funding for community mental health centers (National Institutes of Health, 2013). This legislation changed how mental health services were delivered in the United States. It started the process of **deinstitutionalization**, the closing of large asylums, by providing for people to stay in their communities and be treated locally. In 1955, there were 558,239 severely mentally ill patients institutionalized at public hospitals (Torrey, 1997). By 1994, by percentage of the population, there were 92% fewer hospitalized individuals (Torrey, 1997).

MENTAL HEALTH TREATMENT TODAY

Today, there are community mental health centers across the nation. They are located in neighborhoods near the homes of clients, and they provide large numbers of people with mental health services of various kinds and for many kinds of problems. Unfortunately, part of what occurred with deinstitutionalization was that those released from institutions were supposed to go to newly created centers, but the system was not set up effectively. Centers were underfunded, staff was not trained to handle severe illnesses such as schizophrenia, there was high staff burnout, and no provision was made for the other services people needed, such as housing, food, and job training. Without these supports, those people released under deinstitutionalization often ended up homeless. Even today, a large portion of the homeless population is considered to be mentally ill (**Figure 16.7**). Statistics show that 26% of homeless adults living in shelters experience mental illness (U.S. Department of Housing and Urban Development [HUD], 2011).

Figure 16.7 (a) Of the homeless individuals in U.S. shelters, about one-quarter have a severe mental illness (HUD, 2011). (b) Correctional institutions also report a high number of individuals living with mental illness. (credit a: modification of work by "Carl Campbell"/Flickr; credit b: modification of work by Bart Everson)

Another group of the mentally ill population is involved in the corrections system. According to a 2006 special report by the Bureau of Justice Statistics (BJS), approximately 705,600 mentally ill adults were incarcerated in the state prison system, and another 78,800 were incarcerated in the federal prison system. A further 479,000 were in local jails. According to the study, "people with mental illnesses are overrepresented in probation and parole populations at estimated rates ranging from two to four times the general population" (Prins & Draper, 2009, p. 23). The Treatment Advocacy Center reported that the growing number of mentally ill inmates has placed a burden on the correctional system (Torrey et al., 2014).

Today, instead of asylums, there are psychiatric hospitals run by state governments and local community hospitals focused on short-term care. In all types of hospitals, the emphasis is on short-term stays, with the average length of stay being less than two weeks and often only several days. This is partly due to the very high cost of psychiatric hospitalization, which can be about $800 to $1000 per night (Stensland, Watson, & Grazier, 2012). Therefore, insurance coverage often limits the length of time a person can be hospitalized for treatment. Usually individuals are hospitalized only if they are an imminent threat to themselves or others.

LINK TO LEARNING

View this timeline that shows the history of mental institutions in the United States (http://openstax.org/l/timeline) to learn more.

Most people suffering from mental illnesses are not hospitalized. If someone is feeling very depressed, complains of hearing voices, or feels anxious all the time, he or she might seek psychological treatment. A friend, spouse, or parent might refer someone for treatment. The individual might go see his primary care physician first and then be referred to a mental health practitioner.

Some people seek treatment because they are involved with the state's child protective services—that is, their children have been removed from their care due to abuse or neglect. The parents might be referred to psychiatric or substance abuse facilities and the children would likely receive treatment for trauma. If the parents are interested in and capable of becoming better parents, the goal of treatment might be family reunification. For other children whose parents are unable to change—for example, the parent or parents who are heavily addicted to drugs and refuse to enter treatment—the goal of therapy might be to help the children adjust to foster care and/or adoption (**Figure 16.8**).

Figure 16.8 Therapy with children may involve play. (credit: modification of work by UNHCR Ukraine/Flickr)

Some people seek therapy because the criminal justice system referred them or required them to go. For some individuals, for example, attending weekly counseling sessions might be a condition of parole. If an individual is mandated to attend therapy, she is seeking services involuntarily. **Involuntary treatment** refers to therapy that is not the individual's choice. Other individuals might voluntarily seek treatment. **Voluntary treatment** means the person chooses to attend therapy to obtain relief from symptoms.

Psychological treatment can occur in a variety of places. An individual might go to a community mental health center or a practitioner in private or community practice. A child might see a school counselor, school psychologist, or school social worker. An incarcerated person might receive group therapy in prison. There are many different types of treatment providers, and licensing requirements vary from state to state. Besides psychologists and psychiatrists, there are clinical social workers, marriage and family therapists, and trained religious personnel who also perform counseling and therapy.

A range of funding sources pay for mental health treatment: health insurance, government, and private pay. In the past, even when people had health insurance, the coverage would not always pay for mental health services. This changed with the Mental Health Parity and Addiction Equity Act of 2008, which requires group health plans and insurers to make sure there is parity of mental health services (U.S. Department of Labor, n.d.). This means that co-pays, total number of visits, and deductibles for mental health and substance abuse treatment need to be equal to and cannot be more restrictive or harsher than those for physical illnesses and medical/surgical problems.

Finding treatment sources is also not always easy: there may be limited options, especially in rural areas and low-income urban areas; waiting lists; poor quality of care available for indigent patients; and financial obstacles such as co-pays, deductibles, and time off from work. Over 85% of the 1,669 federally designated mental health professional shortage areas are rural; often primary care physicians and law enforcement are the first-line mental health providers (Ivey, Scheffler, & Zazzali, 1998), although they do not have the specialized training of a mental health professional, who often would be better equipped to provide care. Availability, accessibility, and acceptability (the stigma attached to mental illness) are all problems in rural areas. Approximately two-thirds of those with symptoms receive no care at all (U.S. Department of Health and Human Services, 2005; Wagenfeld, Murray, Mohatt, & DeBruiynb, 1994). At the end of 2013, the U.S. Department of Agriculture announced an investment of $50 million to help improve access and treatment for mental health problems as part of the Obama administration's effort to strengthen rural communities.

16.2 Types of Treatment

Learning Objectives

By the end of this section, you will be able to:
- Distinguish between psychotherapy and biomedical therapy
- Recognize various orientations to psychotherapy
- Discuss psychotropic medications and recognize which medications are used to treat specific psychological disorders

One of the goals of therapy is to help a person stop repeating and reenacting destructive patterns and to start looking for better solutions to difficult situations. This goal is reflected in the following poem:

Autobiography in Five Short Chapters by Portia Nelson (1993)

Chapter One
I walk down the street.
There is a deep hole in the sidewalk.
I fall in.
I am lost. . . . I am helpless.
It isn't my fault.
It takes forever to find a way out.

Chapter Two
I walk down the same street.
There is a deep hole in the sidewalk.
I pretend I don't see it.
I fall in again.
I can't believe I am in this same place.
But, it isn't my fault.
It still takes a long time to get out.

Chapter Three
I walk down the same street.
There is a deep hole in the sidewalk.
I *see* it is there.
I still fall in . . . it's a habit . . . but,
my eyes are open.
I know where I am.
It is *my* fault.
I get out immediately.

Chapter Four
I walk down the same street.
There is a deep hole in the sidewalk.
I walk around it.

Chapter Five
I walk down another street.

Two types of therapy are psychotherapy and biomedical therapy. Both types of treatment help people with psychological disorders, such as depression, anxiety, and schizophrenia. **Psychotherapy** is a psychological treatment that employs various methods to help someone overcome personal problems, or to attain personal growth. In modern practice, it has evolved ino what is known as psychodynamic therapy, which will be discussed later. **Biomedical therapy** involves medication and/or medical procedures to treat psychological disorders. First, we will explore the various psychotherapeutic orientations outlined in **Table 16.1** (many of these orientations were discussed in the Introduction chapter).

Various Psychotherapy Techniques

Type	Description	Example
Psychodynamic psychotherapy	Talk therapy based on belief that the unconscious and childhood conflicts impact behavior	Patient talks about his past
Play therapy	Psychoanalytical therapy wherein interaction with toys is used instead of talk; used in child therapy	Patient (child) acts out family scenes with dolls
Behavior therapy	Principles of learning applied to change undesirable behaviors	Patient learns to overcome fear of elevators through several stages of relaxation techniques
Cognitive therapy	Awareness of cognitive process helps patients eliminate thought patterns that lead to distress	Patient learns not to overgeneralize failure based on single failure
Cognitive-behavioral therapy	Work to change cognitive distortions and self-defeating behaviors	Patient learns to identify self-defeating behaviors to overcome an eating disorder
Humanistic therapy	Increase self-awareness and acceptance through focus on conscious thoughts	Patient learns to articulate thoughts that keep her from achieving her goals

Table 16.1

PSYCHOTHERAPY TECHNIQUES: PSYCHOANALYSIS

Psychoanalysis was developed by Sigmund Freud and was the first form of psychotherapy. It was the dominant therapeutic technique in the early 20th century, but it has since waned significantly in popularity. Freud believed most of our psychological problems are the result of repressed impulses and trauma experienced in childhood, and he believed psychoanalysis would help uncover long-buried feelings. In a psychoanalyst's office, you might see a patient lying on a couch speaking of dreams or childhood memories, and the therapist using various Freudian methods such as free association and dream analysis (**Figure 16.9**). In **free association**, the patient relaxes and then says whatever comes to mind at the moment. However, Freud felt that the ego would at times try to block, or repress, unacceptable urges or painful conflicts during free association. Consequently, a patient would demonstrate resistance to recalling these thoughts or situations. In **dream analysis**, a therapist interprets the underlying meaning of dreams.

Psychoanalysis is a therapy approach that typically takes years. Over the course of time, the patient reveals a great deal about himself to the therapist. Freud suggested that during this patient-therapist relationship, the patient comes to develop strong feelings for the therapist—maybe positive feelings, maybe negative feelings. Freud called this **transference**: the patient transfers all the positive or negative emotions associated with the patient's other relationships to the psychoanalyst. For example, Crystal is seeing a psychoanalyst. During the years of therapy, she comes to see her therapist as a father figure. She transfers her feelings about her father onto her therapist, perhaps in an effort to gain the love and attention she did not receive from her own father.

Figure 16.9 This is the famous couch in Freud's consulting room. Patients were instructed to lie comfortably on the couch and to face away from Freud in order to feel less inhibited and to help them focus. Today, psychotherapy patients are not likely to lie on a couch; instead they are more likely to sit facing the therapist (Prochaska & Norcross, 2010). (credit: Robert Huffstutter)

Today, Freud's psychoanalytical perspective has been expanded upon by the developments of subsequent theories and methodologies: the psychodynamic perspective. This approach to therapy remains centered on the role of people's internal drives and forces, but treatment is less intensive than Freud's original model.

LINK TO LEARNING

View a brief video overview of psychoanalysis theory, research, and practice (http://openstax.org/l/psycanalysis) to learn more.

PSYCHOTHERAPY: PLAY THERAPY

Play therapy is often used with children since they are not likely to sit on a couch and recall their dreams or engage in traditional talk therapy. This technique uses a therapeutic process of play to "help clients prevent or resolve psychosocial difficulties and achieve optimal growth" (O'Connor, 2000, p. 7). The idea is that children play out their hopes, fantasies, and traumas while using dolls, stuffed animals, and sandbox figurines (Figure 16.10). Play therapy can also be used to help a therapist make a diagnosis. The therapist observes how the child interacts with toys (e.g., dolls, animals, and home settings) in an effort to understand the roots of the child's disturbed behavior. Play therapy can be nondirective or directive. In nondirective play therapy, children are encouraged to work through their problems by playing freely while the therapist observes (LeBlanc & Ritchie, 2001). In directive play therapy, the therapist provides more structure and guidance in the play session by suggesting topics, asking questions, and even playing with the child (Harter, 1977).

Figure 16.10 This type of play therapy is known as sandplay or sandtray therapy. Children can set up a three-dimensional world using various figures and objects that correspond to their inner state (Kalff, 1991). (credit: Kristina Walter)

PSYCHOTHERAPY: BEHAVIOR THERAPY

In **psychoanalysis**, therapists help their patients look into their past to uncover repressed feelings. In **behavior therapy**, a therapist employs principles of learning to help clients change undesirable behaviors—rather than digging deeply into one's unconscious. Therapists with this orientation believe that dysfunctional behaviors, like phobias and bedwetting, can be changed by teaching clients new, more constructive behaviors. Behavior therapy employs both classical and operant conditioning techniques to change behavior.

One type of behavior therapy utilizes classical conditioning techniques. Therapists using these techniques believe that dysfunctional behaviors are conditioned responses. Applying the conditioning principles developed by Ivan Pavlov, these therapists seek to recondition their clients and thus change their behavior. Emmie is eight years old, and frequently wets her bed at night. She's been invited to several sleepovers, but she won't go because of her problem. Using a type of conditioning therapy, Emmie begins to sleep on a liquid-sensitive bed pad that is hooked to an alarm. When moisture touches the pad, it sets off the alarm, waking up Emmie. When this process is repeated enough times, Emmie develops an association between urinary relaxation and waking up, and this stops the bedwetting. Emmie has now gone three weeks without wetting her bed and is looking forward to her first sleepover this weekend.

One commonly used classical conditioning therapeutic technique is **counterconditioning**: a client learns a new response to a stimulus that has previously elicited an undesirable behavior. Two counterconditioning techniques are aversive conditioning and exposure therapy. **Aversive conditioning** uses an unpleasant stimulus to stop an undesirable behavior. Therapists apply this technique to eliminate addictive behaviors, such as smoking, nail biting, and drinking. In aversion therapy, clients will typically engage in a specific behavior (such as nail biting) and at the same time are exposed to something unpleasant, such as a mild electric shock or a bad taste. After repeated associations between the unpleasant stimulus and the behavior, the client can learn to stop the unwanted behavior.

Aversion therapy has been used effectively for years in the treatment of alcoholism (Davidson, 1974; Elkins, 1991; Streeton & Whelan, 2001). One common way this occurs is through a chemically based substance known as Antabuse. When a person takes Antabuse and then consumes alcohol, uncomfortable side effects result including nausea, vomiting, increased heart rate, heart palpitations, severe headache, and shortness of breath. Antabuse is repeatedly paired with alcohol until the client associates alcohol with unpleasant feelings, which decreases the client's desire to consume alcohol. Antabuse creates a conditioned aversion to alcohol because it replaces the original pleasure response with an unpleasant one.

In **exposure therapy**, a therapist seeks to treat clients' fears or anxiety by presenting them with the object or situation that causes their problem, with the idea that they will eventually get used to it. This can be done via reality, imagination, or virtual reality. Exposure therapy was first reported in 1924 by Mary Cover Jones, who is considered the mother of behavior therapy. Jones worked with a boy named Peter who was afraid of rabbits. Her goal was to replace Peter's fear of rabbits with a conditioned response of relaxation, which is a response that is incompatible with fear (Figure 16.11). How did she do it? Jones began by placing a caged rabbit on the other side of a room with Peter while he ate his afternoon snack. Over the course of several days, Jones moved the rabbit closer and closer to where Peter was seated with his snack. After two months of being exposed to the rabbit while relaxing with his snack, Peter was able to hold the rabbit and pet it while eating (Jones, 1924).

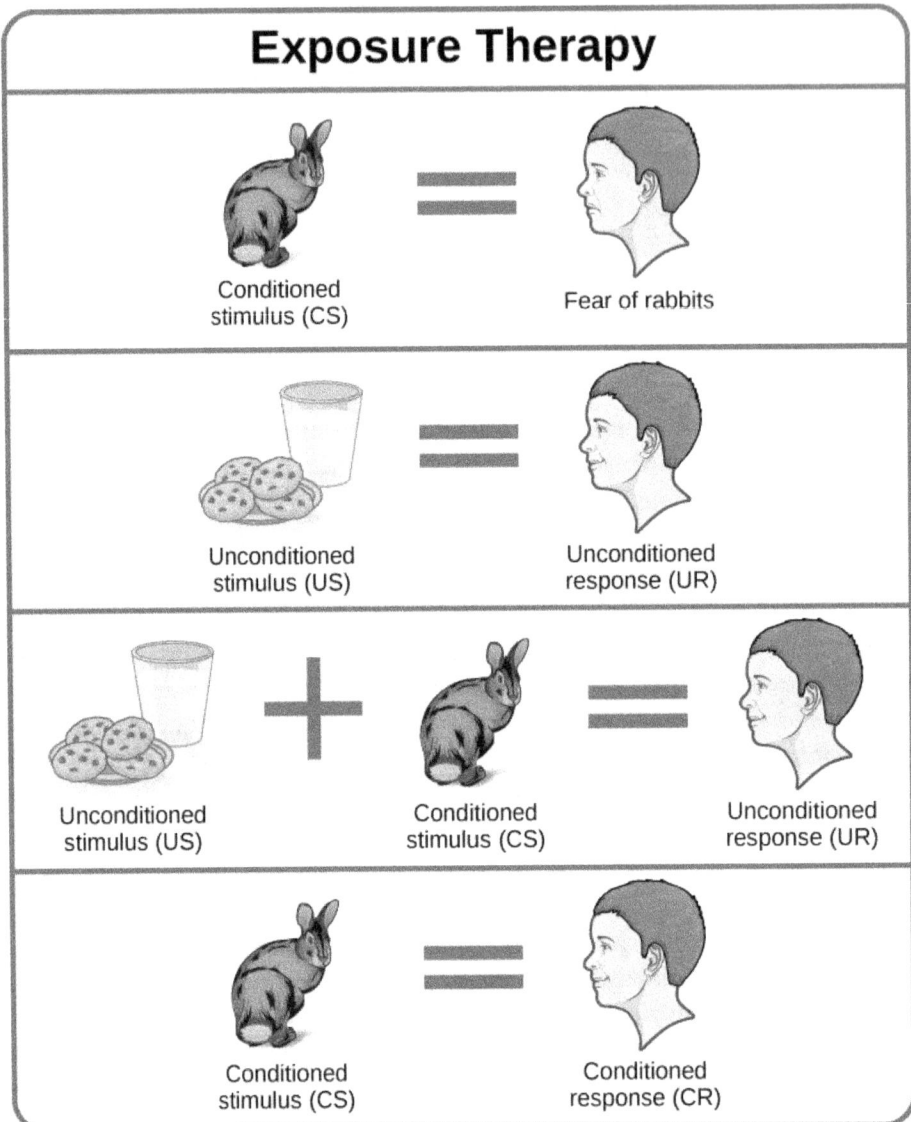

Figure 16.11 Exposure therapy seeks to change the response to a conditioned stimulus (CS). An unconditioned stimulus is presented over and over just after the presentation of the conditioned stimulus. This figure shows conditioning as conducted in Mary Cover Jones' 1924 study.

Thirty years later, Joseph Wolpe (1958) refined Jones's techniques, giving us the behavior therapy technique of exposure therapy that is used today. A popular form of exposure therapy is **systematic desensitization**, wherein a calm and pleasant state is gradually associated with increasing levels of anxiety-inducing stimuli. The idea is that you can't be nervous and relaxed at the same time. Therefore, if you can learn to relax when you are facing environmental stimuli that make you nervous or fearful, you can eventually eliminate your unwanted fear response (Wolpe, 1958) (Figure 16.12).

Figure 16.12 This person suffers from arachnophobia (fear of spiders). Through exposure therapy he is learning how to face his fear in a controlled, therapeutic setting. (credit: "GollyGforce – Living My Worst Nightmare"/Flickr)

How does exposure therapy work? Jayden is terrified of elevators. Nothing bad has ever happened to him on an elevator, but he's so afraid of elevators that he will always take the stairs. That wasn't a problem when Jayden worked on the second floor of an office building, but now he has a new job—on the 29th floor of a skyscraper in downtown Los Angeles. Jayden knows he can't climb 29 flights of stairs in order to get to work each day, so he decided to see a behavior therapist for help. The therapist asks Jayden to first construct a hierarchy of elevator-related situations that elicit fear and anxiety. They range from situations of mild anxiety such as being nervous around the other people in the elevator, to the fear of getting an arm caught in the door, to panic-provoking situations such as getting trapped or the cable snapping. Next, the therapist uses progressive relaxation. She teaches Jayden how to relax each of his muscle groups so that he achieves a drowsy, relaxed, and comfortable state of mind. Once he's in this state, she asks Jayden to imagine a mildly anxiety-provoking situation. Jayden is standing in front of the elevator thinking about pressing the call button.

If this scenario causes Jayden anxiety, he lifts his finger. The therapist would then tell Jayden to forget the scene and return to his relaxed state. She repeats this scenario over and over until Jayden can imagine himself pressing the call button without anxiety. Over time the therapist and Jayden use progressive relaxation and imagination to proceed through all of the situations on Jayden's hierarchy until he becomes desensitized to each one. After this, Jayden and the therapist begin to practice what he only previously envisioned in therapy, gradually going from pressing the button to actually riding an elevator. The goal is that Jayden will soon be able to take the elevator all the way up to the 29th floor of his office without feeling any anxiety.

Sometimes, it's too impractical, expensive, or embarrassing to re-create anxiety-producing situations, so a therapist might employ **virtual reality exposure therapy** by using a simulation to help conquer fears. Virtual reality exposure therapy has been used effectively to treat numerous anxiety disorders such as the fear of public speaking, claustrophobia (fear of enclosed spaces), aviophobia (fear of flying), and post-traumatic stress disorder (PTSD), a trauma and stressor-related disorder (Gerardi, Cukor, Difede, Rizzo, & Rothbaum, 2010).

LINK TO LEARNING

A new virtual reality exposure therapy is being used to treat PTSD in soldiers. Virtual Iraq is a simulation that mimics Middle Eastern cities and desert roads with situations similar to those soldiers experienced while deployed in Iraq. This method of virtual reality exposure therapy has been effective in treating PTSD for combat veterans. Approximately 80% of participants who completed treatment saw clinically significant reduction in their symptoms of PTSD, anxiety, and depression (Rizzo et al., 2010). Watch this Virtual Iraq video that shows soldiers being treated via simulation (http://openstax.org/l/virIraq) to learn more.

Some behavior therapies employ operant conditioning. Recall what you learned about operant conditioning: We have a tendency to repeat behaviors that are reinforced. What happens to behaviors that are not reinforced? They become extinguished. These principles, defined by Skinner as operant conditioning, can be applied to help people with a wide range of psychological problems. For instance, operant conditioning techniques designed to reinforce desirable behaviors and punish unwanted behaviors are effective behavior modification tools to help children with autism (Lovaas, 1987, 2003; Sallows & Graupner, 2005; Wolf & Risley, 1967). This technique is called Applied Behavior Analysis (ABA). In this treatment, a child's behavior is charted and analyzed. The ABA therapist, along with the caregivers, determines what reinforces the child, what sustains a behavior to continue, and how best to manage a behavior. For example, Nur may become overwhelmed and run out of the room when the classroom is too noisy. Whenever Nur runs out of the classroom, the teacher's aide chases him and places him in a special room where he can relax. Going into the special room and getting the aide's attention are reinforcing for Nur. In order to change Nur's behavior, he must be presented with other options before he becomes overwhelmed, and he cannot receive reinforcement for displaying maladaptive behaviors.

One popular operant conditioning intervention is called the **token economy**. This involves a controlled setting where individuals are reinforced for desirable behaviors with tokens, such as a poker chip, that can be exchanged for items or privileges. Token economies are often used in psychiatric hospitals to increase patient cooperation and activity levels. Patients are rewarded with tokens when they engage in positive behaviors (e.g., making their beds, brushing their teeth, coming to the cafeteria on time, and socializing with other patients). They can later exchange the tokens for extra TV time, private rooms, visits to the canteen, and so on (Dickerson, Tenhula, & Green-Paden, 2005).

PSYCHOTHERAPY: COGNITIVE THERAPY

Cognitive therapy is a form of psychotherapy that focuses on how a person's thoughts lead to feelings of distress. The idea behind cognitive therapy is that how you think determines how you feel and act. Cognitive therapists help their clients change dysfunctional thoughts in order to relieve distress. They help a client see how they misinterpret a situation (cognitive distortion). For example, a client may overgeneralize. Because Ray failed one test in Psychology 101, he feels he is stupid and worthless. These thoughts then cause his mood to worsen. Therapists also help clients recognize when they blow things out of proportion. Because Ray failed his Psychology 101 test, he has concluded that he's going to fail the entire course and probably flunk out of college altogether. These errors in thinking have contributed to Ray's feelings of distress. His therapist will help him challenge these irrational beliefs, focus on their illogical basis, and correct them with more logical and rational thoughts and beliefs.

Cognitive therapy was developed by psychiatrist Aaron Beck in the 1960s. His initial focus was on depression and how a client's self-defeating attitude served to maintain a depression despite positive factors in her life (Beck, Rush, Shaw, & Emery, 1979) (Figure 16.13). Through questioning, a cognitive therapist can help a client recognize dysfunctional ideas, challenge catastrophizing thoughts about themselves and their situations, and find a more positive way to view things (Beck, 2011).

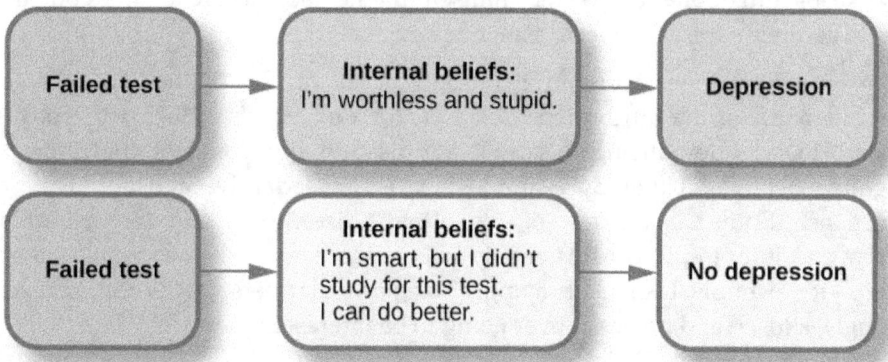

Figure 16.13 Your emotional reactions are the result of your thoughts about the situation rather than the situation itself. For instance, if you consistently interpret events and emotions around the themes of loss and defeat, then you are likely to be depressed. Through therapy, you can learn more logical ways to interpret situations.

LINK TO LEARNING

View a brief video in which **Judith Beck talks about cognitive therapy** (http://openstax.org/l/JBeck) and conducts a session with a client.

PSYCHOTHERAPY: COGNITIVE-BEHAVIORAL THERAPY

Cognitive-behavioral therapists focus much more on present issues than on a patient's childhood or past, as in other forms of psychotherapy. One of the first forms of cognitive-behavioral therapy was **rational emotive therapy (RET)**, which was founded by Albert Ellis and grew out of his dislike of Freudian psychoanalysis (Daniel, n.d.). Behaviorists such as Joseph Wolpe also influenced Ellis's therapeutic approach (National Association of Cognitive-Behavioral Therapists, 2009).

Cognitive-behavioral therapy (CBT) helps clients examine how their thoughts affect their behavior. It aims to change cognitive distortions and self-defeating behaviors. In essence, this approach is designed to change the way people think as well as how they act. It is similar to cognitive therapy in that CBT attempts to make individuals aware of their irrational and negative thoughts and helps people replace them with new, more positive ways of thinking. It is also similar to behavior therapies in that CBT teaches people how to practice and engage in more positive and healthy approaches to daily situations. In total, hundreds of studies have shown the effectiveness of cognitive-behavioral therapy in the treatment of numerous psychological disorders such as depression, PTSD, anxiety disorders, eating disorders, bipolar disorder, and substance abuse (Beck Institute for Cognitive Behavior Therapy, n.d.). For example, CBT has been found to be effective in decreasing levels of hopelessness and suicidal thoughts in previously suicidal teenagers (Alavi, Sharifi, Ghanizadeh, & Dehbozorgi, 2013). Cognitive-behavioral therapy has also been effective in reducing PTSD in specific populations, such as transit workers (Lowinger & Rombom, 2012).

Cognitive-behavioral therapy aims to change cognitive distortions and self-defeating behaviors using techniques like the ABC model. With this model, there is an **A**ction (sometimes called an activating event), the **B**elief about the event, and the **C**onsequences of this belief. Let's say Jon and Joe both go to a party. Jon and Joe each have met an interesting person at the party and spend a few hours chatting with them. At the end of the party, Jon and Joe ask to exchange phone numbers with the person they've been talking to, and the request is refused. Both Jon and Joe are surprised, as they thought things were going well. What can Jon and Joe tell themselves about why the person was not interested? Let's say Jon tells himself he is a loser, or is ugly, or "has no game." Jon then gets depressed and decides not to go to another party, which starts a cycle that keeps him depressed. Joe tells himself that he had bad breath, goes out and buys a new toothbrush, goes to another party, and meets someone new.

Jon's belief about what happened results in a consequence of further depression, whereas Joe's belief does not. Jon is internalizing the attribution or reason for the rebuffs, which triggers his depression. On the other hand, Joe is externalizing the cause, so his thinking does not contribute to feelings of depression. Cognitive-behavioral therapy examines specific maladaptive and automatic thoughts and cognitive distortions. Some examples of cognitive distortions are all-or-nothing thinking, overgeneralization, and jumping to conclusions. In overgeneralization, someone takes a small situation and makes it huge—for example, instead of saying, "This particular person was not interested in me," the man says, "I am ugly, a loser, and no one is ever going to be interested in me."

All or nothing thinking, which is a common type of cognitive distortion for people suffering from depression, reflects extremes. In other words, everything is black or white. After being turned down for a date, Jon begins to think, "No woman will ever go out with me. I'm going to be alone forever." He begins to feel anxious and sad as he contemplates his future.

The third kind of distortion involves jumping to conclusions—assuming that people are thinking negatively about you or reacting negatively to you, even though there is no evidence. Consider the example of Savannah and Hillaire, who recently met at a party. They have a lot in common, and Savannah thinks they could become friends. She calls Hillaire to invite her for coffee. Since Hillaire doesn't answer, Savannah leaves her a message. Several days go by and Savannah never hears back from her potential new friend. Maybe Hillaire never received the message because she lost her phone or she is too busy to return the phone call. But if Savannah believes that Hillaire didn't like Savannah or didn't want to be her friend, she is demonstrating the cognitive distortion of jumping to conclusions.

How effective is CBT? One client said this about his cognitive-behavioral therapy:

> I have had many painful episodes of depression in my life, and this has had a negative effect on my career and has put considerable strain on my friends and family. The treatments I have received, such as taking antidepressants and psychodynamic counseling, have helped [me] to cope with the symptoms and to get some insights into the roots of my problems. CBT has been by far the most useful approach I have found in tackling these mood problems. It has raised my awareness of how my thoughts impact on my moods. How the way I think about myself, about others and about the world can lead me into depression. It is a practical approach, which does not dwell so much on childhood experiences, whilst acknowledging that it was then that these patterns were learned. It looks at what is happening now, and gives tools to manage these moods on a daily basis. (Martin, 2007, n.p.)

PSYCHOTHERAPY: HUMANISTIC THERAPY

Humanistic psychology focuses on helping people achieve their potential. So it makes sense that the goal of **humanistic therapy** is to help people become more self-aware and accepting of themselves. In contrast to psychoanalysis, humanistic therapists focus on conscious rather than unconscious thoughts. They also emphasize the patient's present and future, as opposed to exploring the patient's past.

Psychologist Carl Rogers developed a therapeutic orientation known as **Rogerian**, or **client-centered therapy**. Note the change from *patients* to *clients*. Rogers (1951) felt that the term patient suggested the person seeking help was sick and looking for a cure. Since this is a form of **nondirective therapy**, a therapeutic approach in which the therapist does not give advice or provide interpretations but helps the person to identify conflicts and understand feelings, Rogers (1951) emphasized the importance of the person taking control of his own life to overcome life's challenges.

In client-centered therapy, the therapist uses the technique of active listening. In active listening, the therapist acknowledges, restates, and clarifies what the client expresses. Therapists also practice what Rogers called **unconditional positive regard**, which involves not judging clients and simply accepting them for who they are. Rogers (1951) also felt that therapists should demonstrate genuineness, empathy, and acceptance toward their clients because this helps people become more accepting of themselves, which results in personal growth.

EVALUATING VARIOUS FORMS OF PSYCHOTHERAPY

How can we assess the effectiveness of psychotherapy? Is one technique more effective than another? For anyone considering therapy, these are important questions. According to the American Psychological Association, three factors work together to produce successful treatment. The first is the use of evidence-based treatment that is deemed appropriate for your particular issue. The second important factor is the clinical expertise of the psychologist or therapist. The third factor is your own characteristics, values, preferences, and culture. Many people begin psychotherapy feeling like their problem will never be resolved; however, psychotherapy helps people see that they can do things to make their situation better. Psychotherapy can help reduce a person's anxiety, depression, and maladaptive behaviors. Through psychotherapy, individuals can learn to engage in healthy behaviors designed to help them better express emotions, improve relationships, think more positively, and perform more effectively at work or school.

Many studies have explored the effectiveness of psychotherapy. For example, one large-scale study that examined 16 meta-analyses of CBT reported that it was equally effective or more effective than other therapies in treating PTSD, generalized anxiety disorder, depression, and social phobia (Butlera, Chapmanb, Formanc, & Becka, 2006). Another study found that CBT was as effective at treating depression (43% success rate) as prescription medication (50% success rate) compared to the placebo rate of 25% (DeRubeis et al., 2005). Another meta-analysis found that psychodynamic therapy was also as effective at treating these types of psychological issues as CBT (Shedler, 2010). However, no studies have found one psychotherapeutic approach more effective than another (Abbass, Kisely, & Kroenke, 2006; Chorpita et al., 2011), nor have they shown any relationship between a client's treatment outcome and the level of the clinician's training or experience (Wampold, 2007). Regardless of which type of psychotherapy an individual chooses, one critical factor that determines the success of treatment is the person's relationship with the psychologist or therapist.

BIOMEDICAL THERAPIES

Individuals can be prescribed biologically based treatments or psychotropic medications that are used to treat mental disorders. While these are often used in combination with psychotherapy, they also are taken by individuals not in therapy. This is known as **biomedical therapy**. Medications used to treat psychological disorders are called psychotropic medications and are prescribed by medical doctors, including psychiatrists. In Louisiana and New Mexico, psychologists are able to prescribe some types of these medications (American Psychological Association, 2014).

Different types and classes of medications are prescribed for different disorders. An individual with depression might be given an antidepressant, an individual with bipolar disorder might be given a mood stabilizer, and an individual with schizophrenia might be given an antipsychotic. These medications treat the symptoms of a psychological disorder by altering the levels or effects of neurotransmitters. For example, each type of antidepressant affects a different neurotransmitter, such as SSRI (selective serotonin reuptake inhibitor) antidepressants that increase the level of the neurotransmitter serotonin, and SNRI (serotonin-norepinephrine reuptake inhibitor) antidepressants that increase the levels of both serotonin and norepinephrine. They can help people feel better so that they can function on a daily basis, but they do not cure the disorder. Some people may only need to take a psychotropic medication for a short period of time. Others with severe disorders like bipolar disorder or schizophrenia may need to take psychotropic medication for a long time.

Psychotropic medications are a popular treatment option for many types of disorders, and research suggests that they are most effective when combined with psychotherapy. This is especially true for the most common mental disorders, such as depressive and anxiety disorders (Cuijpers et al, 2014). When considering adding medication as a treatment option, individuals should know that some psychotropic medications have very concerning side effects. Table 16.2 shows the commonly prescribed types of medications, how they are used, and *some* of the potential side effects that may occur.

Some Commonly Prescribed Psychotropic Medications

Type of Medication	Used to Treat	Brand Names of Commonly Prescribed Medications	How They Work	Side Effects
Antipsychotics (developed in the 1950s)	Schizophrenia and other types of severe thought disorders	Haldol, Mellaril, Prolixin, Thorazine	Treat positive psychotic symptoms such as auditory and visual hallucinations, delusions, and paranoia by blocking the neurotransmitter dopamine	Long-term use can lead to tardive dyskinesia, involuntary movements of the arms, legs, tongue and facial muscles, resulting in Parkinson's-like tremors
Atypical Antipsychotics (developed in the late 1980s)	Schizophrenia and other types of severe thought disorders	Abilify, Risperdal, Clozaril	Treat the negative symptoms of schizophrenia, such as withdrawal and apathy, by targeting both dopamine and serotonin receptors; newer medications may treat both positive and negative symptoms	Can increase the risk of obesity and diabetes as well as elevate cholesterol levels; constipation, dry mouth, blurred vision, drowsiness, and dizziness

Some Commonly Prescribed Psychotropic Medications

Type of Medication	Used to Treat	Brand Names of Commonly Prescribed Medications	How They Work	Side Effects
Anti-depressants	Depression and increasingly for anxiety	Paxil, Prozac, Zoloft (selective serotonin reuptake inhibitors, [SSRIs]); Tofranil and Elavil (tricyclics)	Alter levels of neurotransmitters such as serotonin and norepinephrine	SSRIs: headache, nausea, weight gain, drowsiness, reduced sex drive. Tricyclics: dry mouth, constipation, blurred vision, drowsiness, reduced sex drive, increased risk of suicide
Anti-anxiety agents	Anxiety and agitation that occur in OCD, PTSD, panic disorder, and social phobia	Xanax, Valium, Ativan (Benzodiazepines) Buspar (non-Benzodiazepine)	Depress central nervous system activity	Drowsiness, dizziness, headache, fatigue, lightheadedness
Mood Stabilizers	Bipolar disorder	Lithium, Depakote, Lamictal, Tegretol	Treat episodes of mania as well as depression	Excessive thirst, irregular heartbeat, itching/rash, swelling (face, mouth, and extremities), nausea, loss of appetite
Stimulants	ADHD	Adderall, Ritalin	Improve ability to focus on a task and maintain attention	Decreased appetite, difficulty sleeping, stomachache, headache

Table 16.2

Another biologically based treatment that continues to be used, although infrequently, is

electroconvulsive therapy (ECT) (formerly known by its unscientific name as electroshock therapy). It involves using an electrical current to induce seizures to help alleviate the effects of severe depression. The exact mechanism is unknown, although it does help alleviate symptoms for people with severe depression who have not responded to traditional drug therapy (Pagnin, de Queiroz, Pini, & Cassano, 2004). About 85% of people treated with ECT improve (Reti, n.d.). However, the memory loss associated with repeated administrations has led to it being implemented as a last resort (Donahue, 2000; Prudic, Peyser, & Sackeim, 2000). A more recent alternative is transcranial magnetic stimulation (TMS), a procedure approved by the FDA in 2008 that uses magnetic fields to stimulate nerve cells in the brain to improve depression symptoms; it is used when other treatments have not worked (Mayo Clinic, 2012).

> **DIG DEEPER**
>
> **Evidence-based Practice**
>
> A buzzword in therapy today is evidence-based practice. However, it's not a novel concept but one that has been used in medicine for at least two decades. Evidence-based practice is used to reduce errors in treatment selection by making clinical decisions based on research (Sackett & Rosenberg, 1995). In any case, evidence-based treatment is on the rise in the field of psychology. So what is it, and why does it matter? In an effort to determine which treatment methodologies are evidenced-based, professional organizations such as the American Psychological Association (APA) have recommended that specific psychological treatments be used to treat certain psychological disorders (Chambless & Ollendick, 2001). According to the APA (2005), "Evidence-based practice in psychology (EBPP) is the integration of the best available research with clinical expertise in the context of patient characteristics, culture, and preferences" (p. 1).
>
> The foundational idea behind evidence based treatment is that best practices are determined by research evidence that has been compiled by comparing various forms of treatment (Charman & Barkham, 2005). These treatments are then operationalized and placed in treatment manuals—trained therapists follow these manuals. The benefits are that evidence-based treatment can reduce variability between therapists to ensure that a specific approach is delivered with integrity (Charman & Barkham, 2005). Therefore, clients have a higher chance of receiving therapeutic interventions that are effective at treating their specific disorder. While EBPP is based on randomized control trials, critics of EBPP reject it stating that the results of trials cannot be applied to individuals and instead determinations regarding treatment should be based on a therapist's judgment (Mullen & Streiner, 2004).

16.3 Treatment Modalities

Learning Objectives

By the end of this section, you will be able to:
- Distinguish between the various modalities of treatment
- Discuss benefits of group therapy

Once a person seeks treatment, whether voluntarily or involuntarily, he has an **intake** done to assess his clinical needs. An intake is the therapist's first meeting with the client. The therapist gathers specific information to address the client's immediate needs, such as the presenting problem, the client's support system, and insurance status. The therapist informs the client about confidentiality, fees, and what to expect in treatment. **Confidentiality** means the therapist cannot disclose confidential communications to any third party unless mandated or permitted by law to do so. During the intake, the therapist and client will work together to discuss treatment goals. Then a treatment plan will be formulated, usually with specific measurable objectives. Also, the therapist and client will discuss how treatment success will be measured and the estimated length of treatment. There are several different modalities of treatment

(Figure 16.14): Individual therapy, family therapy, couples therapy, and group therapy are the most common.

(a) (b)

Figure 16.14 Therapy may occur (a) one-on-one between a therapist and client, or (b) in a group setting. (credit a: modification of work by Connor Ashleigh, AusAID/Department of Foreign Affairs and Trade)

INDIVIDUAL THERAPY

In **individual therapy**, also known as individual psychotherapy or individual counseling, the client and clinician meet one-on-one (usually from 45 minutes to 1 hour). These meetings typically occur weekly or every other week, and sessions are conducted in a confidential and caring environment (Figure 16.15). The clinician will work with clients to help them explore their feelings, work through life challenges, identify aspects of themselves and their lives that they wish to change, and set goals to help them work towards these changes. A client might see a clinician for only a few sessions, or the client may attend individual therapy sessions for a year or longer. The amount of time spent in therapy depends on the needs of the client as well as her personal goals.

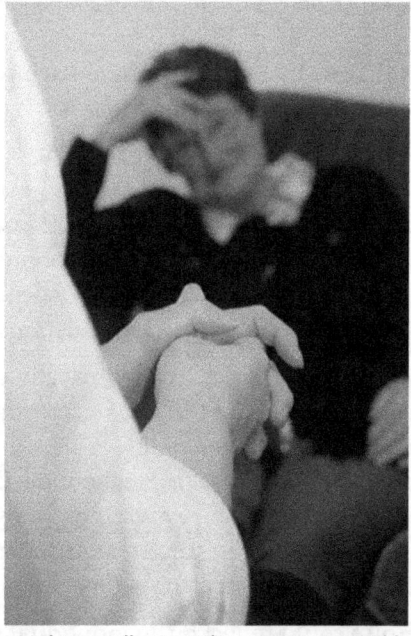

Figure 16.15 In an individual therapy session, a client works one-on-one with a trained therapist. (credit: Alan Cleaver)

GROUP THERAPY

In **group therapy**, a clinician meets together with several clients with similar problems (Figure 16.16). When children are placed in group therapy, it is particularly important to match clients for age and problems. One benefit of group therapy is that it can help decrease a client's shame and isolation about a problem while offering needed support, both from the therapist and other members of the group

(American Psychological Association, 2014). A nine-year-old sexual abuse victim, for example, may feel very embarrassed and ashamed. If he is placed in a group with other sexually abused boys, he will realize that he is not alone. A child struggling with poor social skills would likely benefit from a group with a specific curriculum to foster special skills. A woman suffering from post-partum depression could feel less guilty and more supported by being in a group with similar women.

Group therapy also has some specific limitations. Members of the group may be afraid to speak in front of other people because sharing secrets and problems with complete strangers can be stressful and overwhelming. There may be personality clashes and arguments among group members. There could also be concerns about confidentiality: Someone from the group might share what another participant said to people outside of the group.

Figure 16.16 In group therapy, usually 5–10 people meet with a trained therapist to discuss a common issue such as divorce, grief, an eating disorder, substance abuse, or anger management. (credit: Cory Zanker)

Another benefit of group therapy is that members can confront each other about their patterns. For those with some types of problems, such as sexual abusers, group therapy is the recommended treatment. Group treatment for this population is considered to have several benefits:

> Group treatment is more economical than individual, couples, or family therapy. Sexual abusers often feel more comfortable admitting and discussing their offenses in a treatment group where others are modeling openness. Clients often accept feedback about their behavior more willingly from other group members than from therapists. Finally, clients can practice social skills in group treatment settings. (McGrath, Cumming, Burchard, Zeoli, & Ellerby, 2009)

Groups that have a strong educational component are called psycho-educational groups. For example, a group for children whose parents have cancer might discuss in depth what cancer is, types of treatment for cancer, and the side effects of treatments, such as hair loss. Often, group therapy sessions with children take place in school. They are led by a school counselor, a school psychologist, or a school social worker. Groups might focus on test anxiety, social isolation, self-esteem, bullying, or school failure (Shechtman, 2002). Whether the group is held in school or in a clinician's office, group therapy has been found to be effective with children facing numerous kinds of challenges (Shechtman, 2002).

During a group session, the entire group could reflect on an individual's problem or difficulties, and others might disclose what they have done in that situation. When a clinician is facilitating a group, the focus is always on making sure that everyone benefits and participates in the group and that no one person is the focus of the entire session. Groups can be organized in various ways: some have an overarching theme or purpose, some are time-limited, some have open membership that allows people to come and go, and some are closed. Some groups are structured with planned activities and goals, while others are unstructured: There is no specific plan, and group members themselves decide how the group will spend its time and on what goals it will focus. This can become a complex and emotionally charged process, but it is also an opportunity for personal growth (Page & Berkow, 1994).

COUPLES THERAPY

Couples therapy involves two people in an intimate relationship who are having difficulties and are trying to resolve them (**Figure 16.17**). The couple may be dating, partnered, engaged, or married. The primary therapeutic orientation used in couples counseling is cognitive-behavioral therapy (Rathus & Sanderson, 1999). Couples meet with a therapist to discuss conflicts and/or aspects of their relationship that they want to change. The therapist helps them see how their individual backgrounds, beliefs, and actions are affecting their relationship. Often, a therapist tries to help the couple resolve these problems, as well as implement strategies that will lead to a healthier and happier relationship, such as how to listen, how to argue, and how to express feelings. However, sometimes, after working with a therapist, a couple will realize that they are too incompatible and will decide to separate. Some couples seek therapy to work out their problems, while others attend therapy to determine whether staying together is the best solution. Counseling couples in a high-conflict and volatile relationship can be difficult. In fact, psychologists Peter Pearson and Ellyn Bader, who founded the Couples Institute in Palo Alto, California, have compared the experience of the clinician in couples' therapy to be like "piloting a helicopter in a hurricane" (Weil, 2012, para. 7).

Figure 16.17 In couples counseling, a therapist helps people work on their relationship. (credit: Cory Zanker)

FAMILY THERAPY

Family therapy is a special form of group therapy, consisting of one or more families. Although there are many theoretical orientations in family therapy, one of the most predominant is the systems approach. The family is viewed as an organized system, and each individual within the family is a contributing member who creates and maintains processes within the system that shape behavior (Minuchin, 1985). Each member of the family influences and is influenced by the others. The goal of this approach is to enhance the growth of each family member as well as that of the family as a whole.

Often, dysfunctional patterns of communication that develop between family members can lead to conflict. A family with this dynamic might wish to attend therapy together rather than individually. In many cases, one member of the family has problems that detrimentally affect everyone. For example, a mother's depression, teen daughter's eating disorder, or father's alcohol dependence could affect all members of the family. The therapist would work with all members of the family to help them cope with the issue, and to encourage resolution and growth in the case of the individual family member with the problem.

With family therapy, the nuclear family (i.e., parents and children) or the nuclear family plus whoever lives in the household (e.g., grandparent) come into treatment. Family therapists work with the whole family unit to heal the family. There are several different types of family therapy. In **structural family therapy**, the therapist examines and discusses the boundaries and structure of the family: who makes the rules, who sleeps in the bed with whom, how decisions are made, and what are the boundaries within the family. In some families, the parents do not work together to make rules, or one parent may undermine the other, leading the children to act out. The therapist helps them resolve these issues and learn to communicate more effectively.

> **LINK TO LEARNING**
>
> Watch this video of a structural family session (http://openstax.org/l/Sfamily) to learn more.

In **strategic family therapy**, the goal is to address specific problems within the family that can be dealt with in a relatively short amount of time. Typically, the therapist would guide what happens in the therapy session and design a detailed approach to resolving each member's problem (Madanes, 1991).

16.4 Substance-Related and Addictive Disorders: A Special Case

Learning Objectives

By the end of this section, you will be able to:
- Recognize the goal of substance-related and addictive disorders treatment
- Discuss what makes for effective treatment
- Describe how comorbid disorders are treated

Addiction is often viewed as a chronic disease (Figure 16.18). The choice to use a substance is initially voluntary; however, because chronic substance use can permanently alter the neural structure in the prefrontal cortex, an area of the brain associated with decision-making and judgment, a person becomes driven to use drugs and/or alcohol (Muñoz-Cuevas, Athilingam, Piscopo, & Wilbrecht, 2013). This helps explain why relapse rates tend to be high. About 40%–60% of individuals **relapse**, which means they return to abusing drugs and/or alcohol after a period of improvement (National Institute on Drug Abuse [NIDA], 2008).

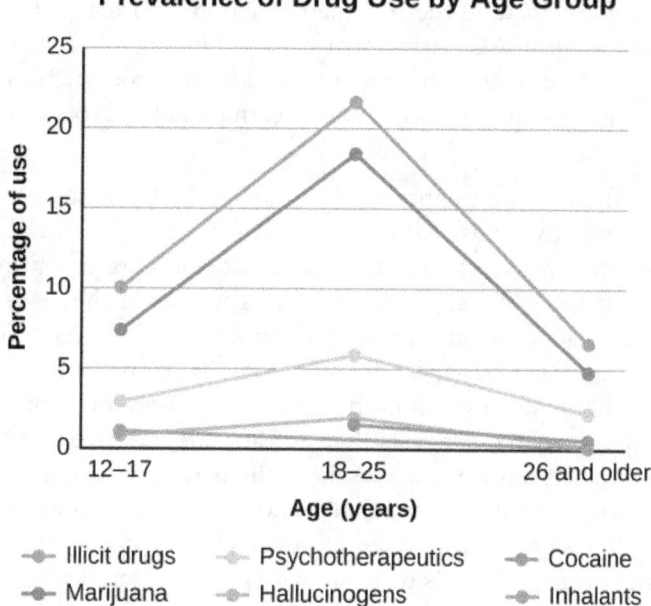

Figure 16.18 The National Survey on Drug Use and Health shows trends in prevalence of various drugs for ages 12–17, 18–25, and 26 or older.

The goal of substance-related treatment is to help a person with an addiction stop compulsive drug-seeking behaviors (NIDA, 2012). This means a person with addiction will need long-term treatment, similar to a person battling a chronic physical disease such as hypertension or diabetes. Treatment usually includes behavioral therapy and/or medication, depending on the individual (NIDA, 2012). Specialized therapies have also been developed for specific types of substance-related disorders, including alcohol, cocaine, and opioids (McGovern & Carroll, 2003). Substance-related treatment is considered much more cost-effective than incarceration or not treating those with addictions (NIDA, 2012) (Figure 16.19).

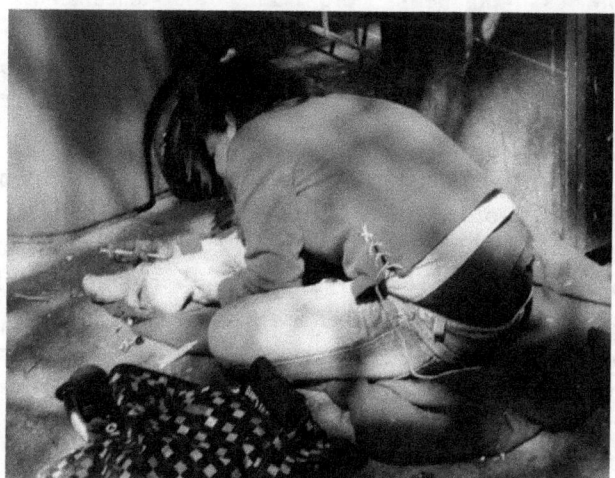

Figure 16.19 Substance use and abuse costs the United States over $600 billion a year (NIDA, 2012). This person with addiction is using heroin. (credit: "jellymc - urbansnaps"/Flickr)

WHAT MAKES TREATMENT EFFECTIVE?

Specific factors make substance-related treatment much more effective. One factor is duration of treatment. Generally, a person with addict needs to be in treatment for at least three months to achieve a positive outcome (Simpson, 1981; Simpson, Joe, & Bracy, 1982; NIDA, 2012). This is due to the psychological, physiological, behavioral, and social aspects of abuse (Simpson, 1981; Simpson et al., 1982; NIDA, 2012).

While in treatment, a person with addiction might receive behavior therapy, which can help motivate the person with addiction to participate in the treatment program and teach strategies for dealing with cravings and how to prevent relapse. Also, treatment needs to be holistic and address multiple needs, not just the drug addiction. This means that treatment will address factors such as communication, stress management, relationship issues, parenting, vocational concerns, and legal concerns (McGovern & Carroll, 2003; NIDA, 2012).

While individual therapy is used in the treatment of substance-related disorders, group therapy is the most widespread treatment modality (Weiss, Jaffee, de Menil, & Cogley, 2004). The rationale behind using group therapy for addiction treatment is that people with addiction are much more likely to maintain sobriety in a group format. It has been suggested that this is due to the rewarding and therapeutic benefits of the group, such as support, affiliation, identification, and even confrontation (Center for Substance Abuse Treatment, 2005). For teenagers, the whole family often needs to participate in treatment to address issues such as family dynamics, communication, and relapse prevention. Family involvement in teen drug addiction is vital. Research suggests that greater parental involvement is correlated with a greater reduction in use by teen substance abusers. Also, mothers who participated in treatment displayed better mental health and greater warmth toward their children (Bertrand et al., 2013). However, neither individual nor group therapy has been found to be more effective (Weiss et al., 2004). Regardless of the type of treatment service, the primary focus is on abstinence or at the very least a significant reduction in use (McGovern & Carroll, 2003).

Treatment also usually involves medications to detox a person with addiction safely after an overdose, to prevent seizures and agitation that often occur in detox, to prevent reuse of the drug, and to manage withdrawal symptoms. Getting off drugs often involves the use of drugs—some of which can be just as addictive. Detox can be difficult and dangerous.

LINK TO LEARNING

Watch this video about treating substance-related disorders using the biological, behavioral, and psychodynamic approaches (http://openstax.org/l/subdisorder) to learn more.

COMORBID DISORDERS

Frequently, a person with an addiction to drugs and/or alcohol has an additional psychological disorder. Saying a person has **comorbid disorders** means the individual has two or more diagnoses. This can often be a substance-related diagnosis and another psychiatric diagnosis, such as depression, bipolar disorder, or schizophrenia. These individuals fall into the category of mentally ill and chemically addicted (MICA)—their problems are often chronic and expensive to treat, with limited success. Compared with the overall population, substance abusers are twice as likely to have a mood or anxiety disorder. Drug abuse can cause symptoms of mood and anxiety disorders and the reverse is also true—people with debilitating symptoms of a psychiatric disorder may self-medicate and abuse substances.

In cases of comorbidity, the best treatment is thought to address both (or multiple) disorders simultaneously (NIDA, 2012). Behavior therapies are used to treat comorbid conditions, and in many cases, psychotropic medications are used along with psychotherapy. For example, evidence suggests that bupropion (trade names: Wellbutrin and Zyban), approved for treating depression and nicotine dependence, might also help reduce craving and use of the drug methamphetamine (NIDA, 2011). However, more research is needed to better understand how these medications work—particularly when combined in patients with comorbidities.

16.5 The Sociocultural Model and Therapy Utilization

Learning Objectives

By the end of this section, you will be able to:
- Explain how the sociocultural model is used in therapy
- Discuss barriers to mental health services among ethnic minorities

The sociocultural perspective looks at you, your behaviors, and your symptoms in the context of your culture and background. For example, José is an 18-year-old Hispanic male from a traditional family. José comes to treatment because of depression. During the intake session, he reveals that he is gay and is nervous about telling his family. He also discloses that he is concerned because his religious background has taught him that being gay is wrong. How does his religious and cultural background affect him? How might his cultural background affect how his family reacts if José were to tell them he is gay?

As our society becomes increasingly multiethnic and multiracial, mental health professionals must develop **cultural competence** (Figure 16.20), which means they must understand and address issues of race, culture, and ethnicity. They must also develop strategies to effectively address the needs of various populations for which Eurocentric therapies have limited application (Sue, 2004). For example, a counselor whose treatment focuses on individual decision making may be ineffective at helping a Chinese client with a collectivist approach to problem solving (Sue, 2004).

Multicultural counseling and therapy aims to offer both a helping role and process that uses modalities and defines goals consistent with the life experiences and cultural values of clients. It strives to recognize client identities to include individual, group, and universal dimensions, advocate the use of universal and culture-specific strategies and roles in the healing process, and balancs the importance of individualism and collectivism in the assessment, diagnosis, and treatment of client and client systems (Sue, 2001).

This therapeutic perspective integrates the impact of cultural and social norms, starting at the beginning of treatment. Therapists who use this perspective work with clients to obtain and integrate information about their cultural patterns into a unique treatment approach based on their particular situation (Stewart, Simmons, & Habibpour, 2012). Sociocultural therapy can include individual, group, family, and couples treatment modalities.

Figure 16.20 How do your cultural and religious beliefs affect your attitude toward mental health treatment? (credit "top-left": modification of work by Staffan Scherz; credit "top-left-middle": modification of work by Alejandra Quintero Sinisterra; credit "top-right-middle": modification of work by Pedro Ribeiro Simões; credit "top-right": modification of work by Agustin Ruiz; credit "bottom-left": modification of work by Czech Provincial Reconstruction Team; credit "bottom-left-middle": modification of work by Arian Zwegers; credit "bottom-right-middle": modification of work by "Wonderlane"/Flickr; credit "bottom-right": modification of work by Shiraz Chanawala)

> **LINK TO LEARNING**
>
> Watch this short **video about cultural competence and sociocultural treatments** (http://openstax.org/l/culturalcomp) to learn more.

BARRIERS TO TREATMENT

Statistically, ethnic minorities tend to utilize mental health services less frequently than White, middle-class Americans (Alegría et al., 2008; Richman, Kohn-Wood, & Williams, 2007). Why is this so? Perhaps the reason has to do with access and availability of mental health services. Ethnic minorities and individuals of low socioeconomic status (SES) report that barriers to services include lack of insurance, transportation, and time (Thomas & Snowden, 2002). However, researchers have found that even when income levels and insurance variables are taken into account, ethnic minorities are far less likely to seek out and utilize mental health services. And when access to mental health services is comparable across ethnic and racial groups, differences in service utilization remain (Richman et al., 2007).

In a study involving thousands of women, it was found that the prevalence rate of anorexia was similar across different races, but that bulimia nervosa was more prevalent among Hispanic and African American women when compared with non-Hispanic whites (Marques et al., 2011). Although they have similar or higher rates of eating disorders, Hispanic and African American women with these disorders tend to seek and engage in treatment far less than Caucasian women. These findings suggest ethnic disparities in access to care, as well as clinical and referral practices that may prevent Hispanic and African American women from receiving care, which could include lack of bilingual treatment, stigma, fear of not being understood, family privacy, and lack of education about eating disorders.

Perceptions and attitudes toward mental health services may also contribute to this imbalance. A recent study at King's College, London, found many complex reasons why people do not seek treatment: self-sufficiency and not seeing the need for help, not seeing therapy as effective, concerns about confidentiality, and the many effects of stigma and shame (Clement et al., 2014). And in another study, African Americans exhibiting depression were less willing to seek treatment due to fear of possible psychiatric hospitalization as well as fear of the treatment itself (Sussman, Robins, & Earls, 1987). Instead of mental health treatment, many African Americans prefer to be self-reliant or use spiritual practices (Snowden, 2001; Belgrave & Allison, 2010). For example, it has been found that the Black church plays a significant role as an alternative to mental health services by providing prevention and treatment-type programs designed to enhance the psychological and physical well-being of its members (Blank, Mahmood, Fox, & Guterbock, 2002).

Additionally, people belonging to ethnic groups that already report concerns about prejudice and discrimination are less likely to seek services for a mental illness because they view it as an additional stigma (Gary, 2005; Townes, Cunningham, & Chavez-Korell, 2009; Scott, McCoy, Munson, Snowden, & McMillen, 2011). For example, in one recent study of 462 older Korean Americans (over the age of 60) many participants reported suffering from depressive symptoms. However, 71% indicated they thought depression was a sign of personal weakness, and 14% reported that having a mentally ill family member would bring shame to the family (Jang, Chiriboga, & Okazaki, 2009).

Language differences are a further barrier to treatment. In the previous study on Korean Americans' attitudes toward mental health services, it was found that there were no Korean-speaking mental health professionals where the study was conducted (Orlando and Tampa, Florida) (Jang et al., 2009). Because of the growing number of people from ethnically diverse backgrounds, there is a need for therapists and psychologists to develop knowledge and skills to become culturally competent (Ahmed, Wilson, Henriksen, & Jones, 2011). Those providing therapy must approach the process from the context of the unique culture of each client (Sue & Sue, 2007).

DIG DEEPER

Treatment Perceptions

By the time a child is a senior in high school, 20% of his classmates—that is 1 in 5—will have experienced a mental health problem (U.S. Department of Health and Human Services, 1999), and 8%—about 1 in 12—will have attempted suicide (Centers for Disease Control and Prevention, 2014). Of those classmates experiencing mental disorders, only 20% will receive professional help (U.S. Public Health Service, 2000). Why?

It seems that the public has a negative perception of children and teens with mental health disorders. According to researchers from Indiana University, the University of Virginia, and Columbia University, interviews with over 1,300 U.S. adults show that they believe children with depression are prone to violence and that if a child receives treatment for a psychological disorder, then that child is more likely to be rejected by peers at school.

Bernice Pescosolido, author of the study, asserts that this is a misconception. However, stigmatization of psychological disorders is one of the main reasons why young people do not get the help they need when they are having difficulties. Pescosolido and her colleagues caution that this stigma surrounding mental illness, based on misconceptions rather than facts, can be devastating to the emotional and social well-being of our nation's children.

This warning played out as a national tragedy in the 2012 shootings at Sandy Hook Elementary. In her blog, Suzy DeYoung (2013), co-founder of Sandy Hook Promise (an organization parents and concerned others set up in the wake of the school massacre) speaks to treatment perceptions and what happens when children do not receive the mental health treatment they desperately need.

> I've become accustomed to the reaction when I tell people where I'm from.
>
> Eleven months later, it's as consistent as it was back in January.
>
> Just yesterday, inquiring as to the availability of a rental house this holiday season, the gentleman taking my information paused to ask, "Newtown, CT? Isn't that where that...that *thing* happened?
>
> A recent encounter in the Massachusetts Berkshires, however, took me by surprise.
>
> It was in a small, charming art gallery. The proprietor, a woman who looked to be in her 60s, asked where we were from. My response usually depends on my present mood and readiness for the inevitable dialogue. Sometimes it's simply, Connecticut. This time, I replied, Newtown, CT.
>
> The woman's demeanor abruptly shifted from one of amiable graciousness to one of visible agitation.
>
> "Oh my god," she said wide eyed and open mouthed. "Did you know her?"
>
> . . . .
>
> "Her?" I inquired
>
> That woman," she replied with disdain, "that woman that raised that monster."
>
> "That woman's" name was Nancy Lanza. Her son, Adam, killed her with a rifle blast to the head before heading out to kill 20 children and six educators at Sandy Hook Elementary School in Newtown, CT last December 14th.
>
> When Nelba Marquez Greene, whose beautiful 6-year-old daughter, Ana, was killed by Adam Lanza, was recently asked how she felt about "that woman," this was her reply:
>
> "She's a victim herself. And it's time in America that we start looking at mental illness with compassion, and helping people who need it.
>
> "This was a family that needed help, an individual that needed help and didn't get it. And what better can come of this, of this time in America, than if we can get help to people who really need it?" (pars. 1–7, 10–15)

Fortunately, we are starting to see campaigns related to the destigmatization of mental illness and an increase in public education and awareness. Join the effort by encouraging and supporting those around you to seek help if they need it. To learn more, visit the National Alliance on Mental Illness (NAMI) website (http://www.nami.org/). The nation's largest nonprofit mental health advocacy and support organization is NAMI.

Key Terms

asylum institution created for the specific purpose of housing people with psychological disorders

aversive conditioning counterconditioning technique that pairs an unpleasant stimulant with an undesirable behavior

behavior therapy therapeutic orientation that employs principles of learning to help clients change undesirable behaviors

biomedical therapy treatment that involves medication and/or medical procedures to treat psychological disorders

cognitive therapy form of psychotherapy that focuses on how a person's thoughts lead to feelings of distress, with the aim of helping them change these irrational thoughts

cognitive-behavioral therapy form of psychotherapy that aims to change cognitive distortions and self-defeating behaviors

comorbid disorder individual who has two or more diagnoses, which often includes a substance abuse diagnosis and another psychiatric diagnosis, such as depression, bipolar disorder, or schizophrenia

confidentiality therapist cannot disclose confidential communications to any third party, unless mandated or permitted by law

counterconditioning classical conditioning therapeutic technique in which a client learns a new response to a stimulus that has previously elicited an undesirable behavior

couples therapy two people in an intimate relationship, such as husband and wife, who are having difficulties and are trying to resolve them with therapy

cultural competence therapist's understanding and attention to issues of race, culture, and ethnicity in providing treatment

deinstitutionalization process of closing large asylums and integrating people back into the community where they can be treated locally

dream analysis technique in psychoanalysis in which patients recall their dreams and the psychoanalyst interprets them to reveal unconscious desires or struggles

electroconvulsive therapy (ECT) type of biomedical therapy that involves using an electrical current to induce seizures in a person to help alleviate the effects of severe depression

exposure therapy counterconditioning technique in which a therapist seeks to treat a client's fear or anxiety by presenting the feared object or situation with the idea that the person will eventually get used to it

family therapy special form of group therapy consisting of one or more families

free association technique in psychoanalysis in which the patient says whatever comes to mind at the moment

group therapy treatment modality in which 5–10 people with the same issue or concern meet together with a trained clinician

humanistic therapy therapeutic orientation aimed at helping people become more self-aware and accepting of themselves

individual therapy treatment modality in which the client and clinician meet one-on-one

intake therapist's first meeting with the client in which the therapist gathers specific information to address the client's immediate needs

involuntary treatment therapy that is mandated by the courts or other systems

nondirective therapy therapeutic approach in which the therapist does not give advice or provide interpretations but helps the person identify conflicts and understand feelings

play therapy therapeutic process, often used with children, that employs toys to help them resolve psychological problems

psychoanalysis therapeutic orientation developed by Sigmund Freud that employs free association, dream analysis, and transference to uncover repressed feelings

psychotherapy (also, psychodynamic psychotherapy) psychological treatment that employs various methods to help someone overcome personal problems, or to attain personal growth

rational emotive therapy (RET) form of cognitive-behavioral therapy

relapse repeated drug use and/or alcohol use after a period of improvement from substance abuse

Rogerian (client-centered therapy) non-directive form of humanistic psychotherapy developed by Carl Rogers that emphasizes unconditional positive regard and self-acceptance

strategic family therapy therapist guides the therapy sessions and develops treatment plans for each family member for specific problems that can addressed in a short amount of time

structural family therapy therapist examines and discusses with the family the boundaries and structure of the family: who makes the rules, who sleeps in the bed with whom, how decisions are made, and what are the boundaries within the family

systematic desensitization form of exposure therapy used to treat phobias and anxiety disorders by exposing a person to the feared object or situation through a stimulus hierarchy

token economy controlled setting where individuals are reinforced for desirable behaviors with tokens (e.g., poker chip) that be exchanged for items or privileges

transference process in psychoanalysis in which the patient transfers all of the positive or negative emotions associated with the patient's other relationships to the psychoanalyst

unconditional positive regard fundamental acceptance of a person regardless of what they say or do; term associated with humanistic psychology

virtual reality exposure therapy uses a simulation rather than the actual feared object or situation to help people conquer their fears

voluntary treatment therapy that a person chooses to attend in order to obtain relief from her symptoms

Summary

16.1 Mental Health Treatment: Past and Present
It was once believed that people with psychological disorders, or those exhibiting strange behavior, were

possessed by demons. These people were forced to take part in exorcisms, were imprisoned, or executed. Later, asylums were built to house the mentally ill, but the patients received little to no treatment, and many of the methods used were cruel. Philippe Pinel and Dorothea Dix argued for more humane treatment of people with psychological disorders. In the mid-1960s, the deinstitutionalization movement gained support and asylums were closed, enabling people with mental illness to return home and receive treatment in their own communities. Some did go to their family homes, but many became homeless due to a lack of resources and support mechanisms.

Today, instead of asylums, there are psychiatric hospitals run by state governments and local community hospitals, with the emphasis on short-term stays. However, most people suffering from mental illness are not hospitalized. A person suffering symptoms could speak with a primary care physician, who most likely would refer him to someone who specializes in therapy. The person can receive outpatient mental health services from a variety of sources, including psychologists, psychiatrists, marriage and family therapists, school counselors, clinical social workers, and religious personnel. These therapy sessions would be covered through insurance, government funds, or private (self) pay.

16.2 Types of Treatment

Psychoanalysis was developed by Sigmund Freud. Freud's theory is that a person's psychological problems are the result of repressed impulses or childhood trauma. The goal of the therapist is to help a person uncover buried feelings by using techniques such as free association and dream analysis.

Play therapy is a psychodynamic therapy technique often used with children. The idea is that children play out their hopes, fantasies, and traumas, using dolls, stuffed animals, and sandbox figurines.

In behavior therapy, a therapist employs principles of learning from classical and operant conditioning to help clients change undesirable behaviors. Counterconditioning is a commonly used therapeutic technique in which a client learns a new response to a stimulus that has previously elicited an undesirable behavior via classical conditioning. Principles of operant conditioning can be applied to help people deal with a wide range of psychological problems. Token economy is an example of a popular operant conditioning technique.

Cognitive therapy is a technique that focuses on how thoughts lead to feelings of distress. The idea behind cognitive therapy is that how you think determines how you feel and act. Cognitive therapists help clients change dysfunctional thoughts in order to relieve distress. Cognitive-behavioral therapy explores how our thoughts affect our behavior. Cognitive-behavioral therapy aims to change cognitive distortions and self-defeating behaviors.

Humanistic therapy focuses on helping people achieve their potential. One form of humanistic therapy developed by Carl Rogers is known as client-centered or Rogerian therapy. Client-centered therapists use the techniques of active listening, unconditional positive regard, genuineness, and empathy to help clients become more accepting of themselves.

Often in combination with psychotherapy, people can be prescribed biologically based treatments such as psychotropic medications and/or other medical procedures such as electro-convulsive therapy.

16.3 Treatment Modalities

There are several modalities of treatment: individual therapy, group therapy, couples therapy, and family therapy are the most common. In an individual therapy session, a client works one-on-one with a trained therapist. In group therapy, usually 5–10 people meet with a trained group therapist to discuss a common issue (e.g., divorce, grief, eating disorders, substance abuse, or anger management). Couples therapy involves two people in an intimate relationship who are having difficulties and are trying to resolve them. The couple may be dating, partnered, engaged, or married. The therapist helps them resolve their problems as well as implement strategies that will lead to a healthier and happier relationship. Family therapy is a special form of group therapy. The therapy group is made up of one or more families. The goal of this approach is to enhance the growth of each individual family member and the family as a whole.

16.4 Substance-Related and Addictive Disorders: A Special Case

Addiction is often viewed as a chronic disease that rewires the brain. This helps explain why relapse rates tend to be high, around 40%–60% (McLellan, Lewis, & O'Brien, & Kleber, 2000). The goal of treatment is to help an addict stop compulsive drug-seeking behaviors. Treatment usually includes behavioral therapy, which can take place individually or in a group setting. Treatment may also include medication. Sometimes a person has comorbid disorders, which usually means that they have a substance-related disorder diagnosis and another psychiatric diagnosis, such as depression, bipolar disorder, or schizophrenia. The best treatment would address both problems simultaneously.

16.5 The Sociocultural Model and Therapy Utilization

The sociocultural perspective looks at you, your behaviors, and your symptoms in the context of your culture and background. Clinicians using this approach integrate cultural and religious beliefs into the therapeutic process. Research has shown that ethnic minorities are less likely to access mental health services than their White middle-class American counterparts. Barriers to treatment include lack of insurance, transportation, and time; cultural views that mental illness is a stigma; fears about treatment; and language barriers.

Review Questions

1. Who of the following does not support the humane and improved treatment of mentally ill persons?
    a. Philippe Pinel
    b. medieval priests
    c. Dorothea Dix
    d. All of the above

2. The process of closing large asylums and providing for people to stay in the community to be treated locally is known as _____.
    a. deinstitutionalization
    b. exorcism
    c. deactivation
    d. decentralization

3. Joey was convicted of domestic violence. As part of his sentence, the judge has ordered that he attend therapy for anger management. This is considered _____ treatment.
    a. involuntary
    b. voluntary
    c. forced
    d. mandatory

4. Today, most people with psychological problems are not hospitalized. Typically they are only hospitalized if they _____.
    a. have schizophrenia
    b. have insurance
    c. are an imminent threat to themselves or others
    d. require therapy

5. The idea behind _____ is that how you think determines how you feel and act.
    a. cognitive therapy
    b. cognitive-behavioral therapy
    c. behavior therapy
    d. client-centered therapy

6. Mood stabilizers, such as lithium, are used to treat _____.
    a. anxiety disorders
    b. depression
    c. bipolar disorder
    d. ADHD

7. Clay is in a therapy session. The therapist asks him to relax and say whatever comes to his mind at the moment. This therapist is using _____, which is a technique of _____.
    a. active listening; client-centered therapy
    b. systematic desensitization; behavior therapy
    c. transference; psychoanalysis
    d. free association; psychoanalysis

8. A treatment modality in which 5–10 people with the same issue or concern meet together with a trained clinician is known as _____.
   a. family therapy
   b. couples therapy
   c. group therapy
   d. self-help group

9. What happens during an intake?
   a. The therapist gathers specific information to address the client's immediate needs such as the presenting problem, the client's support system, and insurance status. The therapist informs the client about confidentiality, fees, and what to expect in a therapy session.
   b. The therapist guides what happens in the therapy session and designs a detailed approach to resolving each member's presenting problem.
   c. The therapist meets with a couple to help them see how their individual backgrounds, beliefs, and actions are affecting their relationship.
   d. The therapist examines and discusses with the family the boundaries and structure of the family: For example, who makes the rules, who sleeps in the bed with whom, and how decisions are made.

10. What is the minimum amount of time addicts should receive treatment if they are to achieve a desired outcome?
    a. 3 months
    b. 6 months
    c. 9 months
    d. 12 months

11. When an individual has two or more diagnoses, which often includes a substance-related diagnosis and another psychiatric diagnosis, this is known as _____.
    a. bipolar disorder
    b. comorbid disorder
    c. codependency
    d. bi-morbid disorder

12. John was drug-free for almost six months. Then he started hanging out with his addict friends, and he has now started abusing drugs again. This is an example of _____.
    a. release
    b. reversion
    c. re-addiction
    d. relapse

13. The sociocultural perspective looks at you, your behaviors, and your symptoms in the context of your _____.
    a. education
    b. socioeconomic status
    c. culture and background
    d. age

14. Which of the following was *not* listed as a barrier to mental health treatment?
    a. fears about treatment
    b. language
    c. transportation
    d. being a member of the ethnic majority

Critical Thinking Questions

15. People with psychological disorders have been treated poorly throughout history. Describe some efforts to improve treatment, include explanations for the success or lack thereof.

16. Usually someone is hospitalized only if they are an imminent threat to themselves or others. Describe a situation that might meet these criteria.

17. Imagine that you are a psychiatrist. Your patient, Pat, comes to you with the following symptoms: anxiety and feelings of sadness. Which therapeutic approach would you recommend and why?

18. Compare and contrast individual and group therapies.

19. You are conducting an intake assessment. Your client is a 45-year-old single, employed male with cocaine dependence. He failed a drug screen at work and is mandated to treatment by his employer if he wants to keep his job. Your client admits that he needs help. Why would you recommend group therapy for him?

20. Lashawn is a 24-year-old African American female. For years she has been struggling with bulimia. She knows she has a problem, but she is not willing to seek mental health services. What are some reasons why she may be hesitant to get help?

Personal Application Questions

21. Do you think there is a stigma associated with mentally ill persons today? Why or why not?

22. What are some places in your community that offer mental health services? Would you feel comfortable seeking assistance at one of these facilities? Why or why not?

23. If you were to choose a therapist practicing one of the techniques presented in this section, which kind of therapist would you choose and why?

24. Your best friend tells you that she is concerned about her cousin. The cousin—a teenage girl—is constantly coming home after her curfew, and your friend suspects that she has been drinking. What treatment modality would you recommend to your friend and why?

25. What are some substance-related and addictive disorder treatment facilities in your community, and what types of services do they provide? Would you recommend any of them to a friend or family member with a substance abuse problem? Why or why not?

26. What is your attitude toward mental health treatment? Would you seek treatment if you were experiencing symptoms or having trouble functioning in your life? Why or why not? In what ways do you think your cultural and/or religious beliefs influence your attitude toward psychological intervention?

References

Introduction to Psychology

American Board of Forensic Psychology. (2014). *Brochure.* http://www.abfp.com/brochure.asp

American Psychological Association. (2014). www.apa.org

American Psychological Association. (2014). *Graduate training and career possibilities in exercise and sport psychology.* http://www.apadivisions.org/division-47/about/resources/training.aspx?item=1

American Psychological Association. (2019). *Maime Phipps Clark, PhD,* and *Kenneth Clark, PhD.* https://www.apa.org/pi/oema/resources/ethnicity-health/psychologists/clark

American Psychological Association. (2011). *Psychology as a career.* http://www.apa.org/education/undergrad/psych-career.aspx

Benjamin, L., Henry, K., & McMahon, L. (2005). Inez Beverly Prosser and the education of African Americans. *Journal of the History of the Behavioral Sciences, 41,* 43–62. https://onlinelibrary.wiley.com/doi/abs/10.1002/jhbs.20058

Betancourt, H., & López, S. R. (1993). The study of culture, ethnicity, and race in American psychology. *American Psychologist, 48,* 629–637.

Black, S. R., Spence, S. A., & Omari, S. R. (2004). Contributions of African Americans to the field of psychology. *Journal of Black Studies, 35,* 40–64.

Buss, D. M. (1989). Sex differences in human mate preferences: Evolutionary hypotheses tested in 37 cultures. *Behavioral and Brain Sciences, 12,* 1–49.

Calkins, M. W. (1906). A reconciliation between structural and functional psychology. *Psychological Review, 13,* 61–81.

Carlson, N. R. (2013). *Physiology of Behavior* (11th ed.). Pearson.

Confer, J. C., Easton, J. A., Fleischman, D. S., Goetz, C. D., Lewis, D. M. G., Perilloux, C., & Buss, D. M. (2010). Evolutionary psychology. Controversies, questions, prospects, and limitations. *American Psychologist, 65,* 100–126.

Crawford, M., & Marecek, J. (1989). Psychology reconstructs the female 1968–1988. *Psychology of Women Quarterly, 13,* 147–165.

Danziger, K. (1980). The history of introspection reconsidered. *Journal of the History of the Behavioral Sciences, 16,* 241–262.

Danziger, K. (1980). Wundt's psychological experiment in the light of his philosophy of science. *Psychological Research, 42,* 109–122.

Darwin, C. (1871). *The descent of man and selection in relation to sex.* John Murray.

Darwin, C. (1872). *The expression of the emotions in man and animals.* John Murray.

DeAngelis, T. (2010). Fear not. *gradPSYCH Magazine, 8,* 38.

Department of Health and Human Services. (n.d.). *Projected future growth of the older population.* http://www.aoa.gov/Aging_Statistics/future_growth/future_growth.aspx#age

Endler, J. A. (1986). *Natural Selection in the Wild.* Princeton University Press.

Fogg, N. P., Harrington, P. E., Harrington, T. F., & Shatkin, L. (2012). *College majors handbook with real career paths and payoffs* (3rd ed.). JIST Publishing.

Franko, D. L., et al. (2012). Racial/ethnic differences in adults in randomized clinical trials of binge eating disorder. *Journal of Consulting and Clinical Psychology, 80,* 186–195.

Friedman, H. (2008), Humanistic and positive psychology: The methodological and epistemological divide. *The Humanistic Psychologist, 36,* 113–126.

Gordon, O. E. (1995). *A brief history of psychology.* http://www.psych.utah.edu/gordon/Classes/Psy4905Docs/PsychHistory/index.html#maptop

Greengrass, M. (2004). 100 years of B.F. Skinner. *Monitor on Psychology, 35,* 80.

Guthrie, R. (1998). *Even the rat was white* (2nd edition). Allyn and Bacon.

Halonen, J. S. (2011). *White paper: Are there too many psychology majors?* Prepared for the Staff of the State University System of Florida Board of Governors. http://www.cogdop.org/page_attachments/0000/0200/FLA_White_Paper_for_cogop_posting.pdf

Hock, R. R. (2009). Social psychology. *Forty studies that changed psychology: Explorations into the history of psychological research* (pp. 308–317). Pearson.

Hoffman, C. (2012). *Careers in clinical, counseling, or school psychology; mental health counseling; clinical social work; marriage & family therapy and related professions.* http://www.indiana.edu/~psyugrad/advising/docs/Careers%20in%20Mental%20Health%20Counseling.pdf

Jang, K. L., Livesly, W. J., & Vernon, P. A. (1996). Heritability of the Big Five personality dimensions and their facets: A twin study. *Journal of Personality, 64,* 577–591.

Johnson, R., & Lubin, G. (2011). College exposed: What majors are most popular, highest paying and most likely to get you a job. *Business Insider.com.* http://www.businessinsider.com/best-college-majors-highest-income-most-employed-georgetwon-study-2011-6?op=1

Jones, M. C. (1924). A laboratory study of fear: The case of Peter. *Pedagogical Seminary, 31,* 308–315.

Knekt, P. P., et al. (2008). Randomized trial on the effectiveness of long- and short-term psychodynamic psychotherapy and solution-focused therapy on psychiatric symptoms during a 3-year follow-up. *Psychological Medicine: A Journal of Research In Psychiatry And The Allied Sciences, 38,* 689–703.

Landers, R. N. (2011, June 14). Grad school: Should I get a PhD or Master's in I/O psychology? http://neoacademic.com/2011/06/14/grad-school-should-i-get-a-ph-d-or-masters-in-io-psychology/#.UuKKLftOnGg

Macdonald, C. (2013). *Health psychology center presents: What is health psychology?* http://healthpsychology.org/what-is-health-psychology/

Madigan, S. & O'Hara, R. (1992). Short-term memory at the turn of the century: Mary Whiton Calkins's memory research. *American Psychologist, 47,* 170–174.

McCrae, R. R. & Costa, P. T. (2008). Empirical and theoretical status of the five-factor model of personality traits. In G. J. Boyle, G. Matthews, & D. H. Saklofske (Eds.), *The Sage handbook of personality theory and assessment. Vol. 1 Personality theories and models.* Sage.

Michalski, D., Kohout, J., Wicherski, M., & Hart, B. (2011). *2009 Doctorate Employment Survey.* APA Center for Workforce Studies. http://www.apa.org/workforce/publications/09-doc-empl/index.aspx

Miller, G. A. (2003). The cognitive revolution: A historical perspective. *Trends in Cognitive Sciences, 7,* 141–144.

Munakata, Y., McClelland, J. L., Johnson, M. H., & Siegler, R. S. (1997). Rethinking infant knowledge: Toward an adaptive process account of successes and failures in object permanence tasks. *Psychological Review, 104,* 689–713.

Mundasad, S. (2013). *Word-taste synaesthesia: Tasting names, places, and Anne Boleyn.* http://www.bbc.co.uk/news/health-21060207

Munsey, C. (2009). More states forgo a postdoc requirement. *Monitor on Psychology, 40,* 10.

National Association of School Psychologists. (n.d.). *Becoming a nationally certified school psychologist*

(NCSP). http://www.nasponline.org/CERTIFICATION/becomeNCSP.aspx

Nicolas, S., & Ferrand, L. (1999). Wundt's laboratory at Leipzig in 1891. *History of Psychology, 2*, 194–203.

Norcross, J. C. (n.d.) Clinical versus counseling psychology: What's the diff? http://www.csun.edu/~hcpsy002/Clinical%20Versus%20Counseling%20Psychology.pdf

Norcross, J. C., & Castle, P. H. (2002). Appreciating the PsyD: The facts. *Eye on Psi Chi, 7*, 22–26.

O'Connor, J. J., & Robertson, E. F. (2002). *John Forbes Nash.* http://www-groups.dcs.st-and.ac.uk/~history/Biographies/Nash.html

O'Hara, M. (n.d.). Historic review of humanistic psychology. http://www.ahpweb.org/index.php?option=com_k2&view=item&layout=item&id=14&Itemid=24

Person, E. S. (1980). Sexuality as the mainstay of identity: Psychoanalytic perspectives. *Signs, 5*, 605–630.

Pickren, W. & Rutherford, A. (2010). *A history of modern psychology in context*. Wiley.

Rantanen, J., Metsäpelto, R. L., Feldt, T., Pulkkinen, L., & Kokko, K. (2007). Long-term stability in the Big Five personality traits in adulthood. *Scandinavian Journal of Psychology, 48*, 511–518.

Riggio, R. E. (2013). What is industrial/organizational psychology? *Psychology Today*. http://www.psychologytoday.com/blog/cutting-edge-leadership/201303/what-is-industrialorganizational-psychology

Romo, R. (1986). George I. Sanchez and the civil rights movement: 1940–1960. *La Raza Law Journal, 1*, 342–362.

Sacks, O. (2007). A neurologists notebook: The abyss, music and amnesia. *The New Yorker*. http://www.newyorker.com/reporting/2007/09/24/070924fa_fact_sacks?currentPage=all

Shedler, J. (2010). The efficacy of psychodynamic psychotherapy. *American Psychologist, 65*(2), 98–109.

Soldz, S., & Vaillant, G. E. (1999). The Big Five personality traits and the life course: A 45-year longitudinal study. *Journal of Research in Personality, 33*, 208–232.

Thorne, B. M., & Henley, T. B. (2005). *Connections in the history and systems of psychology* (3rd ed.). Houghton Mifflin Company.

Tolman, E. C. (1938). The determiners of behavior at a choice point. *Psychological Review, 45*, 1–41.

U.S. Department of Education, National Center for Education Statistics. (2016). *The Condition of Education, 2016* (NCES 2016-144).

Weisstein, N. (1993). Psychology constructs the female: Or, the fantasy life of the male psychologist (with some attention to the fantasies of his friends, the male biologist and the male anthropologist). *Feminism and Psychology, 3*, 195–210.

Westen, D. (1998). The scientific legacy of Sigmund Freud, toward a psychodynamically informed psychological science. *Psychological Bulletin, 124*, 333–371.

Psychological Research

American Cancer Society. (n.d.). History of the cancer prevention studies. http://www.cancer.org/research/researchtopreventcancer/history-cancer-prevention-study

American Psychological Association. (2009). *Publication Manual of the American Psychological Association* (6th ed.). Author.

American Psychological Association. (n.d.). *Research with animals in psychology.* https://www.apa.org/research/responsible/research-animals.pdf

Arnett, J. (2008). The neglected 95%: Why American psychology needs to become less American. *American Psychologist, 63*(7), 602–614.

Aschwanden, C. (2018, December 6). Psychology's replication crisis has made the field better. *FiveThirtyEight*. https://fivethirtyeight.com/features/psychologys-replication-crisis-has-made-the-field-better/

Barnett, W. S. (2011). Effectiveness of early educational intervention. *Science, 333*(6045), 975–978. https://science.sciencemag.org/content/333/6045/975

Barton, B. A., Eldridge, A. L., Thompson, D., Affenito, S. G., Striegel-Moore, R. H., Franko, D. L., . . . Crockett, S. J. (2005). The relationship of breakfast and cereal consumption to nutrient intake and body mass index: The national heart, lung, and blood institute growth and health study. *Journal of the American Dietetic Association, 105*(9), 1383–1389. http://dx.doi.org/10.1016/j.jada.2005.06.003

Blann, L.E. (2005). Early intervention for children and families: With special needs. *MCN: The American Journal of Maternal Child Nursing, 30,* 263–67.

Chwalisz, K., Diener, E., & Gallagher, D. (1988). Autonomic arousal feedback and emotional experience: Evidence from the spinal cord injured. *Journal of Personality and Social Psychology, 54,* 820–828.

Dominus, S. (2011, May 25). Could conjoined twins share a mind? *New York Times Sunday Magazine*. http://www.nytimes.com/2011/05/29/magazine/could-conjoined-twins-share-a-mind.html?_r=5&hp&

Egnor, M. (2017, November 24). What the craniopagus twins teach us about the mind and the brain. *Evolution News & Science Today*. https://evolutionnews.org/2017/11/what-the-craniopagus-twins-teach-us-about-the-mind-and-the-brain/

Ethnicity and Health in America Series: Featured Psychologists (n.d.). *American Psychological Association*. https://www.apa.org/pi/oema/resources/ethnicity-health/psychologists/sumner-prosser

Fanger, S. M., Frankel, L. A., & Hazen, N. (2012). Peer exclusion in preschool children's play: Naturalistic observations in a playground setting. *Merrill-Palmer Quarterly, 58,* 224–254.

Fiedler, K. (2004). Illusory correlation. In R. F. Pohl (Ed.), *Cognitive illusions: A handbook on fallacies and biases in thinking, judgment and memory* (pp. 97–114). Psychology Press.

Frantzen, L. B., Treviño, R. P., Echon, R. M., Garcia-Dominic, O., & DiMarco, N. (2013). Association between frequency of ready-to-eat cereal consumption, nutrient intakes, and body mass index in fourth- to sixth-grade low-income minority children. *Journal of the Academy of Nutrition and Dietetics, 113*(4), 511–519.

Godoy, J. C., & Brussino, S. (2010). Psychology in Argentina. *The Corsini Encyclopedia of Psychology*. John Wiley & Sons.

Gunamudian David Boaz. (n.d.). *World Library*. http://www.worldlibrary.org/articles/Gunamudian_David_Boaz

Harper, J. (2013, July 5). Ice cream and crime: Where cold cuisine and hot disputes intersect. *The Times-Picaune*. http://www.nola.com/crime/index.ssf/2013/07/ice_cream_and_crime_where_hot.html

Jenkins, W. J., Ruppel, S. E., Kizer, J. B., Yehl, J. L., & Griffin, J. L. (2012). An examination of post 9-11 attitudes towards Arab Americans. *North American Journal of Psychology, 14,* 77–84.

Jones, J. M. (2013, May 13). Same-sex marriage support solidifies above 50% in U.S. *Gallup Politics*. http://www.gallup.com/poll/162398/sex-marriage-support-solidifies-above.aspx

Kobrin, J. L., Patterson, B. F., Shaw, E. J., Mattern, K. D., & Barbuti, S. M. (2008). *Validity of the SAT for predicting first-year college grade point average* (Research Report No. 2008-5). https://research.collegeboard.org/sites/default/files/publications/2012/7/researchreport-2008-5-validity-sat-predicting-first-year-college-grade-point-average.pdf

Lewin, T. (2014, March 5). A new SAT aims to realign with schoolwork. *New York Times*. http://www.nytimes.com/2014/03/06/education/major-changes-in-sat-announced-by-collegeboard.html.

Lowcock, E. C., Cotterchio, M., Anderson, L. N., Boucher, B. A., & El-Sohemy, A. (2013). High coffee intake, but not caffeine, is associated with reduced estrogen receptor negative and postmenopausal breast cancer risk with no effect modification by CYP1A2 genotype. *Nutrition and Cancer, 65*(3), 398–409. doi:10.1080/01635581.2013.768348

Lowry, M., Dean, K., & Manders, K. (2010). The link between sleep quantity and academic performance for the college student. *Sentience: The University of Minnesota Undergraduate Journal of Psychology, 3*(Spring), 16–19. http://www.psych.umn.edu/sentience/files/SENTIENCE_Vol3.pdf

Margaret Floy Washburn, PhD. (n.d.). *American Psychological Association.* https://www.apa.org/about/governance/president/bio-margaret-washburn.

Mary Whiton Calkins. (n.d.). *American Psychological Association.* https://www.apa.org/about/governance/president/bio-mary-whiton-calkins

Massimini, M., & Peterson, M. (2009). Information and communication technology: Affects of U.S. college students. *Cyberpsychology: Journal of Psychosocial Research on Cyberspace, 3*(1).

McKie, R. (2010, June 26). Chimps with everything: Jane Goodall's 50 years in the jungle. *The Guardian.* http://www.theguardian.com/science/2010/jun/27/jane-goodall-chimps-africa-interview

Narendra Nath Sen Gupta. (n.d.). *Veethi: The face of India.* https://www.veethi.com/india-people/narendra_nath_sen_gupta-profile-4893-16.htm

Neil, A. L., & Christensen, H. (2009). Efficacy and effectiveness of school-based prevention and early intervention programs for anxiety. *Clinical Psychology Review, 29,* 208–15.

Nobel Prize-winning scientist Frances Arnold retracts paper. (2020, January 3). *BBC News.* https://www.bbc.com/news/world-us-canada-50989423

Offit, P. (2008). *Autism's false prophets: Bad science, risky medicine, and the search for a cure.* Columbia University Press.

Patel, M., Lee, A. D., Clemmons, N. S., Redd, S. B., Poser, S., Blog, D., …Gastañaduy, P. A. (2019, October 11). National update on measles cases and outbreaks—United States, January 1–October 1, 2019. *Morbidity and Mortality Weekly Report, 68,* 893–96.

Perkins, H. W., Haines, M. P., & Rice, R. (2005). Misperceiving the college drinking norm and related problems: A nationwide study of exposure to prevention information, perceived norms and student alcohol misuse. *J. Stud. Alcohol, 66*(4), 470–478.

Peters-Scheffer, N., Didden, R., Korzilius, H., & Sturmey, P. (2011). A meta-analytic study on the effectiveness of comprehensive ABA-based early intervention programs for children with Autism Spectrum Disorders. *Research in Autism Spectrum Disorders, 5,* 60–69.

Rimer, S. (2008, September 21). College panel calls for less focus on SATs. *The New York Times.* http://www.nytimes.com/2008/09/22/education/22admissions.html?_r=0

Rothstein, J. M. (2004). College performance predictions and the SAT. *Journal of Econometrics, 121,* 297–317.

Rotton, J., & Kelly, I. W. (1985). Much ado about the full moon: A meta-analysis of lunar-lunacy research. *Psychological Bulletin, 97*(2), 286–306. doi:10.1037/0033-2909.97.2.286

Santelices, M. V., & Wilson, M. (2010). Unfair treatment? The case of Freedle, the SAT, and the standardization approach to differential item functioning. *Harvard Education Review, 80,* 106–134.

Sears, D. O. (1986). College sophomores in the laboratory: Influences of a narrow data base on social psychology's view of human nature. *Journal of Personality and Social Psychology, 51,* 515–530.

Shaw, C. M., & Tan, S. A. (2015). Integration of mobile technology in educational materials improves participation: Creation of a novel smartphone application for resident education. *Journal of Surgical*

Education, 72(4), 670–73. https://www.sciencedirect.com/science/article/abs/pii/S1931720415000318

Shrout, P. E., & Rodgers, J. L. (2018). Psychology, science, and knowledge construction: Broadening perspectives from the replication crisis. *Annual Review of Psychology, 69*, 487-510.

Strauss, V. (2019, March 19). Is it finally time to get rid of the SAT and ACT college admissions tests? *The Washington Post*. https://www.washingtonpost.com/education/2019/03/19/is-it-finally-time-get-rid-sat-act-college-admissions-tests/

Tuskegee University. (n.d.). *About the USPHS Syphilis Study*. http://www.tuskegee.edu/about_us/centers_of_excellence/bioethics_center/about_the_usphs_syphilis_study.aspx.

Women and Minorities in Psychology. (n.d.). *IResearch*. http://psychology.iresearchnet.com/history-of-psychology/women-and-minorities/

Biopsychology

Anderson, P. J., & Leuzzi, V. (2010). White matter pathology in phenylketonuria. *Molecular Genetics and Metabolism, 99*, S3–S9.

Arnst, C. (2003, November). Commentary: Getting rational about health-care rationing. *Bloomberg Businessweek Magazine*. http://www.businessweek.com/stories/2003-11-16/commentary-getting-rational-about-health-care-rationing

Azevedo, F. A., Carvalho, L. R., Grinberg, L. T., Farfel, J. M., Ferretti, R. E., Leite, R. E., ... & Herculano-Houzel, S. (2009). Equal numbers of neuronal and nonneuronal cells make the human brain an isometrically scaled-up primate brain. *Journal of Comparative Neurology, 513*(5), 532–541.

Banich, M. T., & Heller, W. (1998). Evolving perspectives on lateralization of function. *Current Directions in Psychological Science, 7*(1), 1–2.

Berridge, K. C., & Robinson, T. E. (1998). What is the role of dopamine in reward: Hedonic impact, reward learning, or incentive salience? *Brain Research Reviews, 28*, 309–369.

Chandola, T., Brunner, E., & Marmot, M. (2006). Chronic stress at work and the metabolic syndrome: A prospective study. *BMJ, 332*, 521–524.

Comings, D. E., Gonzales, N., Saucier, G., Johnson, J. P., & MacMurray, J. P. (2000). The DRD4 gene and the spiritual transcendence scale of the character temperament index. *Psychiatric Genetics, 10*, 185–189.

Confer, J. C., Easton, J. A., Fleischman, D. S., Goetz, C. D., Lewis, D. M. G, Perilloux, C., & Buss, D. M. (2010). Evolutionary psychology: Controversies, questions, prospects, and limitations. *American Psychologist, 65*, 110–126.

Connors, B. W., & Long, M. A. (2004). Electrical synapses in the mammalian brain. *Annual Review of Neuroscience, 27*, 393–418.

Ehret, G. (2006). Hemisphere dominance of brain function—which functions are lateralized and why?. 23 *Problems in Systems Neuroscience*, 44–61.

Fernandez, A. (2008, October 16). ABC reporter Bob Woodruff's incredible recovery from traumatic brain injury. *The Huffington Post*. https://www.huffpost.com/entry/abc-reporter-bob-woodruff_b_125863

Gaines, C. (2013, August). An A-Rod suspension would save the Yankees as much as $37.5 million in 2014 alone. *Business Insider*. http://www.businessinsider.com/an-a-rod-suspension-would-save-the-yankees-as-much-as-375-million-in-2014-2013-8

Gardner, E. L. (2011). Addiction and brain reward and antireward pathways. *Advances in Psychosomatic Medicine, 30*, 22–60.

Gazzaniga, M. S. (2005). Forty-five years of split-brain research and still going strong. *Nature Reviews Neuroscience, 6*(8), 653–659.

George, O., Le Moal, M., & Koob, G. F. (2012). Allostasis and addiction: Role of the dopamine and corticotropin-releasing factor systems. *Physiology & Behavior, 106*, 58–64.

Glaser, R., & Kiecolt-Glaser, J. K. (2005). Stress-induced immune dysfunction: Implications for health. *Nature Reviews Immunology, 5*, 243–251.

Gong, L., Parikh, S., Rosenthal, P. J., & Greenhouse, B. (2013). Biochemical and immunological mechanisms by which sickle cell trait protects against malaria. *Malaria Journal*. Advance online publication. doi:10.1186/1475-2875-12-317

Hardt, O., Einarsson, E. Ö., & Nader, K. (2010). A bridge over troubled water: Reconsolidation as a link between cognitive and neuroscientific memory research traditions. *Annual Review of Psychology, 61*, 141–167.

Herculano-Houzel, S. (2009). The human brain in numbers: a linearly scaled-up primate brain. *Frontiers in Human Neuroscience, 3*, 31.

Herculano-Houzel, S. (2012). The remarkable, yet not extraordinary, human brain as a scaled-up primate brain and its associated cost. *Proceedings of the National Academy of Sciences, 109*(Supplement 1), 10661–10668.

Huttenlocher, P. R. (2000). The neuropathology of phenylketonuria: human and animal studies. *European Journal of Pediatrics, 159*(2), S102–S106.

Macmillan, M. (1999). The Phineas Gage Information Page. http://www.uakron.edu/gage

March, J. S., Silva, S., Petrycki, S., Curry, J., Wells, K., Fairbank, J., … Severe, J. (2007). The treatment for adolescents with depression study (TADS): Long-term effectiveness and safety outcomes. *Arch Gen Psychiatry, 64*, 1132–1143.

Miguel, P. M., Pereira, L. O., Silveira, P. P., & Meaney, M. J. (2019). Early environmental influences on the development of children's brain structure and function. *Developmental Medicine and Child Neurology, 61*, 1127–33.

Mustanski, B. S., DuPree, M. G., Nievergelt, C. M., Bocklandt, S., Schork, N. J., & Hamer, D. H. (2005). A genome wide scan of male sexual orientation. *Human Genetics, 116*, 272–278.

National Institute on Drug Abuse. (2001, July). Anabolic steroid abuse: What are the health consequences of steroid abuse? *National Institutes of Health*. http://www.drugabuse.gov/publications/research-reports/anabolic-steroid-abuse/what-are-health-consequences-steroid-abuse

Short, A. K., and Baram, T. Z. (2019). Early-life adversity and neurological disease: Age-old questions and novel answers. *Nature Reviews Neurology, 15*, 657–69.

Squire, L. R. (2009). The legacy of patient H. M. for neuroscience. *Neuron, 61*, 6–9.

Tienari, P., Wynne, L. C., Sorri, A., et al. (2004). Genotype–environment interaction in schizophrenia spectrum disorder: long-term follow-up study of Finnish adoptees. *British Journal of Psychiatry, 184*, 216–222.

University of Utah Genetic Science Learning Center. (n.d.). What are genetic disorders? http://learn.genetics.utah.edu/content/disorders/whataregd/

Yudell, M., Roberts, D., DeSalle, R., & Tishkoff, S. (2016). Taking race out of human genetics. *Science, 351*(6273), 564–565.

States of Consciousness

Aggarwal, S. K., Carter, G. T., Sullivan, M. D., ZumBrunnen, C., Morrill, R., & Mayer, J. D. (2009). Medicinal use of cannabis in the United States: Historical perspectives, current trends, and future directions. *Journal of Opioid Management, 5*, 153–168.

Alhola, P. & Polo-Kantola, P. (2007). Sleep Deprivation: Impact on cognitive performance. *Neuropsychiatric*

Disease and Treatment, 3, 553–557.

Alladin, A. (2012). Cognitive hypnotherapy for major depressive disorder. *The American Journal of Clinical Hypnosis, 54,* 275–293.

American Psychiatric Association. (2013). *Diagnostic and statistical manual of mental disorders* (5th ed.). Author.

Aquina, C. T., Marques-Baptista, A., Bridgeman, P., & Merlin, M. A. (2009). Oxycontin abuse and overdose. *Postgraduate Medicine, 121,* 163–167.

Arnulf, I. (2012). REM sleep behavior disorder: Motor manifestations and pathophysiology. *Movement Disorders, 27,* 677–689.

Banks, S., & Dinges, D. F. (2007). Behavioral and physiological consequences of sleep restriction. *Journal of Clinical Sleep Medicine, 3,* 519–528.

Bartke, A., Sun, L. Y., & Longo, V. (2013). Somatotropic signaling: Trade-offs between growth, reproductive development, and longevity. *Physiological Reviews, 93,* 571–598.

Berkowitz, C. D. (2012). Sudden infant death syndrome, sudden unexpected infant death, and apparent life-threatening events. *Advances in Pediatrics, 59,* 183–208.

Berry, R. B., Kryger, M. H., & Massie, C. A. (2011). A novel nasal excitatory positive airway pressure (EPAP) device for the treatment of obstructive sleep apnea: A randomized controlled trial. *Sleep, 34,* 479–485.

Bixler, E. O., Kales, A., Soldatos, C. R., Kales, J. D., & Healey, S. (1979). Prevalence of sleep disorders in the Los Angeles metropolitan area. *American Journal of Psychiatry, 136,* 1257–1262.

Bostwick, J. M. (2012). Blurred boundaries: The therapeutics and politics of medical marijuana. *Mayo Clinic Proceedings, 87,* 172–186.

Brook, R. D., Appel, L. J., Rubenfire, M., Ogedegbe, G., Bisognano, J. D., Elliott, W. K., . . . Rajagopalan, S. (2013). Beyond medications and diet: Alternative approaches to lowering blood pressure: A scientific statement from the American Heart Association. *Hypertension, 61,* 1360–1383.

Broughton, R., Billings, R., Cartwright, R., Doucette, D., Edmeads, J., Edwardh, M., . . . Turrell, G. (1994). Homicidal somnambulism: A case report. *Sleep, 17,* 253–264.

Brown, L. K. (2012). Can sleep deprivation studies explain why human adults sleep? *Current Opinion in Pulmonary Medicine, 18,* 541–545.

Burgess, C. R., & Scammell, T. E. (2012). Narcolepsy: Neural mechanisms of sleepiness and cataplexy. *Journal of Neuroscience, 32,* 12305–12311.

Cai, D. J., Mednick, S. A., Harrison, E. M., Kanady, J. C., & Mednick, S. C. (2009). REM, not incubation, improves creativity by priming associative networks. *Proceedings of the National Academy of Sciences, USA, 106,* 10130–10134.

Caldwell, K., Harrison, M., Adams, M., Quin, R. H., & Greeson, J. (2010). Developing mindfulness in college students through movement based courses: Effects on self-regulatory self-efficacy, mood, stress, and sleep quality. *Journal of American College Health, 58,* 433–442.

Capellini, I., Barton, R. A., McNamara, P., Preston, B. T., & Nunn, C. L. (2008). Phylogenetic analysis of the ecology and evolution of mammalian sleep. *Evolution, 62,* 1764–1776.

Cartwright, R. (2004). Sleepwalking violence: A sleep disorder, a legal dilemma, and a psychological challenge. *American Journal of Psychiatry, 161,* 1149–1158.

Cartwright, R., Agargun, M. Y., Kirkby, J., & Friedman, J. K. (2006). Relation of dreams to waking concerns. *Psychiatry Research, 141,* 261–270.

Casati, A., Sedefov, R., & Pfeiffer-Gerschel, T. (2012). Misuse of medications in the European Union: A systematic review of the literature. *European Addiction Research, 18*, 228–245.

Chen, K. W., Berger, C. C., Manheimer, E., Forde, D., Magidson, J., Dachman, L., & Lejuez, C. W. (2013). Meditative therapies for reducing anxiety: A systematic review and meta-analysis of randomized controlled trials. *Depression and Anxiety, 29*, 545–562.

Chokroverty, S. (2010). Overview of sleep & sleep disorders. *Indian Journal of Medical Research, 131*, 126–140.

Christensen, A., Bentley, G. E., Cabrera, R., Ortega, H. H., Perfito, N., Wu, T. J., & Micevych, P. (2012). Hormonal regulation of female reproduction. *Hormone and Metabolic Research, 44*, 587–591.

CNN. (1999, June 25). 'Sleepwalker' convicted of murder. http://www.cnn.com/US/9906/25/sleepwalker.01/

Coe, W. C. (2009). Hypnosis as role enactment: The role demand variable. *American Journal of Clinical Hypnosis, 51*(4), 395–398. https://pdfs.semanticscholar.org/5afc/85bd66b3e05c38564963d57965b60955e71a.pdf

Coe, W. C., & Sarbin, T. R. (1966). An experimental demonstration of hypnosis as role enactment. *Journal of Abnormal Psychology, 71*(6), 400–406. https://psycnet.apa.org/doiLanding?doi=10.1037%2Fh0023920

Cropley, M., Theadom, A., Pravettoni, G., & Webb, G. (2008). The effectiveness of smoking cessation interventions prior to surgery: A systematic review. *Nicotine and Tobacco Research, 10*, 407–412.

De la Herrán-Arita, A. K., & Drucker-Colín, R. (2012). Models for narcolepsy with cataplexy drug discovery. *Expert Opinion on Drug Discovery, 7*, 155–164.

Del Casale, A., Ferracuti, S., Rapinesi, C., Serata, D., Sani, G., Savoja, V., . . . Girardi, P. (2012). Neurocognition under hypnosis: Findings from recent functional neuroimaging studies. *International Journal of Clinical and Experimental Hypnosis, 60*, 286–317.

Elkins, G., Johnson, A., & Fisher, W. (2012). Cognitive hypnotherapy for pain management. *The American Journal of Clinical Hypnosis, 54*, 294–310.

Ellenbogen, J. M., Hu, P. T., Payne, J. D., Titone, D., & Walker, M. P. (2007). Human relational memory requires time and sleep. *Proceedings of the National Academy of Sciences, USA, 104*, 7723–7728.

Fenn, K. M., Nusbaum, H. C., & Margoliash, D. (2003). Consolidation during sleep of perceptual learning of spoken language. *Nature, 425*, 614–616.

Ferini-Strambi, L. (2011). Does idiopathic REM sleep behavior disorder (iRBD) really exist? What are the potential markers of neurodegeneration in iRBD? *Sleep Medicine, 12*(2 Suppl.), S43–S49.

Fiorentini, A., Volonteri, L.S., Dragogna, F., Rovera, C., Maffini, M., Mauri, M. C., & Altamura, C. A. (2011). Substance-induced psychoses: A critical review of the literature. *Current Drug Abuse Reviews, 4*, 228–240.

Fogel, S. M., & Smith, C. T. (2011). The function of the sleep spindle: A physiological index of intelligence and a mechanism for sleep-dependent memory consolidation. *Neuroscience and Biobehavioral Reviews, 35*, 1154–1165.

Frank, M. G. (2006). The mystery of sleep function: Current perspectives and future directions. *Reviews in the Neurosciences, 17*, 375–392.

Freeman, M. P., Fava, M., Lake, J., Trivedi, M. H., Wisner, K. L., & Mischoulon, D. (2010). Complementary and alternative medicine in major depressive disorder: The American Psychiatric Association task force report. *The Journal of Clinical Psychiatry, 71*, 669–681.

Gold, D. R., Rogacz, S. R., Bock, N., Tosteson, T. D., Baum, T. M., Speizer, F. M., & Czeisler, C. A. (1992). Rotating shift work, sleep, and accidents related to sleepiness in hospital nurses. *American Journal of Public Health, 82*, 1011–1014.

Golden, W. L. (2012). Cognitive hypnotherapy for anxiety disorders. *The American Journal of Clinical*

Hypnosis, 54, 263–274.

Gómez, R. L., Bootzin, R. R., & Nadel, L. (2006). Naps promote abstraction in language-learning infants. *Psychological Science, 17,* 670–674.

Guilleminault, C., Kirisoglu, C., Bao, G., Arias, V., Chan, A., & Li, K. K. (2005). Adult chronic sleepwalking and its treatment based on polysomnography. *Brain, 128,* 1062–1069.

Guldenmund, P., Vanhaudenhuyse, A., Boly, M., Laureys, S., & Soddu, A. (2012). A default mode of brain function in altered states of consciousness. *Archives Italiennes de Biologie, 150,* 107–121.

Halász, P. (1993). Arousals without awakening—Dynamic aspect of sleep. *Physiology and Behavior, 54,* 795–802.

Han, F. (2012). Sleepiness that cannot be overcome: Narcolepsy and cataplexy. *Respirology, 17,* 1157–1165.

Hardeland, R., Pandi-Perumal, S. R., & Cardinali, D. P. (2006). Melatonin. *International Journal of Biochemistry & Cell Biology, 38,* 313–316.

Henry, D., & Rosenthal, L. (2013). "Listening for his breath:" The significance of gender and partner reporting on the diagnosis, management, and treatment of obstructive sleep apnea. *Social Science & Medicine, 79,* 48–56.

Hicks, R. A., Fernandez, C., & Pelligrini, R. J. (2001). The changing sleep habits of university students: An update. *Perceptual and Motor Skills, 93,* 648.

Hicks, R. A., Johnson, C., & Pelligrini, R. J. (1992). Changes in the self-reported consistency of normal habitual sleep duration of college students (1978 and 1992). *Perceptual and Motor Skills, 75,* 1168–1170.

Hilgard, E. R., & Hilgard, J. R. (1994). *Hypnosis in the Relief of Pain.* Brunner/Mazel.

Hishikawa, Y., & Shimizu, T. (1995). Physiology of REM sleep, cataplexy, and sleep paralysis. *Advances in Neurology, 67,* 245–271.

Herman, A., & Herman, A. P. (2013). Caffeine's mechanism of action and its cosmetic use. *Skin Pharmacology and Physiology, 26,* 8–14.

Hobson, J. A. (2002). *Dreaming: An introduction to the science of sleep.* Oxford University Press.

Hobson, J. A. (2009). REM sleep and dreaming: Towards a theory of protoconsciousness. *Nature Reviews Neuroscience, 10,* 803–814.

Horikawa, T., Tamaki, M., Miyawaki, Y. & Kamitani, Y. (2013). Neural Decoding of Visual Imagery During Sleep. *Science, 340*(6132), 639–642. doi:10.1126/science.1234330

Hossain, J. L., & Shapiro, C. M. (2002). The prevalence, cost implications, and management of sleep disorders: An overview. *Sleep and Breathing, 6,* 85–102.

Huang, L. B., Tsai, M. C., Chen, C. Y., & Hsu, S. C. (2013). The effectiveness of light/dark exposure to treat insomnia in female nurses undertaking shift work during the evening/night shift. *Journal of Clinical Sleep Medicine, 9,* 641–646.

Huber, R., Ghilardi, M. F., Massimini, M., & Tononi, G. (2004). Local sleep and learning. *Nature, 430,* 78–81.

Jayanthi, L. D., & Ramamoorthy, S. (2005). Regulation of monoamine transporters: Influence of psychostimulants and therapeutic antidepressants. *The AAPS Journal, 7,* E728–738.

Julien, R. M. (2005). Opioid analgesics. In *A primer of drug action: A comprehensive guide to the actions, uses, and side effects of psychoactive drugs* (pp. 461–500). Worth.

Kihlstrom, J. F. (2013). Neuro-hypnotism: Prospects for hypnosis and neuroscience. *Cortex, 49,* 365–374.

Killgore, W. D. S., Killgore, D. B., Day, L. M., Li, C., Kamimori, G. H., & Balkin, T. J. (2007). The effects of 53 hours of sleep deprivation on moral judgment. *Sleep: Journal of Sleep and Sleep Disorders Research, 30*(3), 345–352. https://academic.oup.com/sleep/article/30/3/345/2708190

Killgore, W. D. S., & Weber, M. (2014). Sleep deprivation and cognitive performance. In M. T. Bianchi (Ed.), *Sleep deprivation and disease: Effects on the body, brain and behavior*. (pp. 209–229). Springer Science + Business Media. https://link.springer.com/chapter/10.1007%2F978-1-4614-9087-6_16

Klein, D. C., Moore, R. Y., & Reppert, S. M. (Eds.). (1991). *Suprachiasmatic nucleus: The mind's clock*. Oxford University Press.

Kogan, N. M., & Mechoulam, R. (2007). Cannabinoids in health and disease. *Dialogues in Clinical Neuroscience, 9*, 413–430.

Kromann, C. B., & Nielson, C. T. (2012). A case of cola dependency in a woman with recurrent depression. *BMC Research Notes, 5*, 692.

LaBerge, S. (1990). Lucid dreaming: Psychophysiological studies of consciousness during REM sleep. In R. R. Bootzen, J. F. Kihlstrom, & D. L. Schacter (Eds.), *Sleep and cognition* (pp. 109–126). American Psychological Association.

Lang, A. J., Strauss, J. L., Bomeya, J., Bormann, J. E., Hickman, S. D., Good, R. C., & Essex, M. (2012). The theoretical and empirical basis for meditation as an intervention for PTSD. *Behavior Modification, 36*, 759–786.

Lesku, J. A., Roth, T. C., 2nd, Amlaner, C. J., & Lima, S. L. (2006). A phylogenetic analysis of sleep architecture in mammals: The integration of anatomy, physiology, and ecology. *The American Naturalist, 168*, 441–453.

Levitt, C., Shaw, E., Wong, S., & Kaczorowski, J. (2007). Systematic review of the literature on postpartum care: Effectiveness of interventions for smoking relapse prevention, cessation, and reduction in postpartum women. *Birth, 34*, 341–347.

Luppi, P. H., Clément, O., Sapin, E., Gervasoni, D., Peyron, C., Léger, L., . . . Fort, P. (2011). The neuronal network responsible for paradoxical sleep and its dysfunctions causing narcolepsy and rapid eye movement (REM) behavior disorder. *Sleep Medicine Reviews, 15*, 153–163.

Mage, D. T., & Donner, M. (2006). Female resistance to hypoxia: Does it explain the sex difference in mortality rates? *Journal of Women's Health, 15*, 786–794.

Mahowald, M. W., & Schenck, C. H. (2000). Diagnosis and management of parasomnias. *Clinical Cornerstone, 2*, 48–54.

Mahowald, M. W., Schenck, C. H., & Cramer Bornemann, M. A. (2005). Sleep-related violence. *Current Neurology and Neuroscience Reports, 5*, 153–158.

Mayo Clinic. (n.d.). *Sleep terrors (night terrors)*. http://www.mayoclinic.org/diseases-conditions/night-terrors/basics/treatment/con-20032552

Mather, L. E., Rauwendaal, E. R., Moxham-Hall, V. L., & Wodak, A. D. (2013). (Re)introducing medical cannabis. *The Medical Journal of Australia, 199*, 759–761.

Maxwell, J. C. (2006). *Trends in the abuse of prescription drugs. Gulf Coast Addiction Technology Transfer Center*. http://asi.nattc.org/userfiles/file/GulfCoast/PrescriptionTrends_Web.pdf

McCarty, D. E. (2010). A case of narcolepsy with strictly unilateral cataplexy. *Journal of Clinical Sleep Medicine, 15*, 75–76.

McDaid, C., Durée, K. H., Griffin, S. C., Weatherly, H. L., Stradling, J. R., Davies, R. J., . . . Westwood, M. E. (2009). A systematic review of continuous positive airway pressure for obstructive sleep apnoea-hypopnoea syndrome. *Sleep Medicine Reviews, 13*, 427–436.

McKim, W. A., & Hancock, S. D. (2013). *Drugs and behavior: An introduction to behavioral pharmacology, 7th edition*. Pearson.

Mignot, E. J. M. (2012). A practical guide to the therapy of narcolepsy and hypersomnia syndromes. *Neurotherapeutics, 9*, 739–752.

Miller, N. L., Shattuck, L. G., & Matsangas, P. (2010). Longitudinal study of sleep patterns of United States Military Academy cadets. *Sleep, 33*, 1623–1631.

Mitchell, E. A. (2009). SIDS: Past, present and future. *Acta Paediatrica, 98*, 1712–1719.

Montgomery, G. H., Schnur, J. B., & Kravits, K. (2012). Hypnosis for cancer care: Over 200 years young. *CA: A Cancer Journal for Clinicians, 63*, 31–44.

National Institute on Drug Abuse. (2019, January). *Opioid Overdose Crisis*. NIDA. https://www.drugabuse.gov/drugs-abuse/opioids/opioid-overdose-crisis

National Institute on Drug Abuse. (2019, October). *Methamphetamine: Overview*. NIDA. https://www.drugabuse.gov/publications/research-reports/methamphetamine/overview

National Institutes of Health. (n.d.). *Information about sleep*. http://science.education.nih.gov/supplements/nih3/sleep/guide/info-sleep.htm

National Research Council. (1994). *Learning, remembering, believing: Enhancing human performance*. The National Academies Press.

National Sleep Foundation. (n.d.). *How much sleep do we really need?* http://sleepfoundation.org/how-sleep-works/how-much-sleep-do-we-really-need

Ohayon, M. M. (1997). Prevalence of DSM-IV diagnostic criteria of insomnia: Distinguishing insomnia related to mental disorders from sleep disorders. *Journal of Psychiatric Research, 31*, 333–346.

Ohayon, M. M. (2002). Epidemiology of insomnia: What we know and what we still need to learn. *Sleep Medicine Reviews, 6*, 97–111.

Ohayon, M. M., Carskadon, M. A., Guilleminault, C., & Vitiello, M. V. (2004). Meta-analysis of quantitative sleep parameters from childhood to old age in healthy individuals: Developing normative sleep values across the human lifespan. *Sleep, 27*, 1255–1273.

Ohayon, M. M., & Roth, T. (2002). Prevalence of restless legs syndrome and periodic limb movement disorder in the general population. *Journal of Psychosomatic Research, 53*, 547–554.

Poe, G. R., Walsh, C. M., & Bjorness, T. E. (2010). Cognitive neuroscience of sleep. *Progress in Brain Research, 185*, 1–19.

Porkka-Heiskanen, T. (2011). Methylxanthines and sleep. *Handbook of Experimental Pharmacology, 200*, 331–348.

Presser, H. B. (1995). Job, family, and gender: Determinants of nonstandard work schedules among employed Americans in 1991. *Demography, 32*, 577–598.

Pressman, M. R. (2007). Disorders of arousal from sleep and violent behavior: The role of physical contact and proximity. *Sleep, 30*, 1039–1047.

Provini, F., Tinuper, P., Bisulli, F., & Lagaresi, E. (2011). Arousal disorders. *Sleep Medicine, 12*(2 Suppl.), S22–S26.

Rattenborg, N. C., Lesku, J. A., Martinez-Gonzalez, D., & Lima, S. L. (2007). The non-trivial functions of sleep. *Sleep Medicine Reviews, 11*, 405–409.

Raz, A. (2011). Hypnosis: A twilight zone of the top-down variety: Few have never heard of hypnosis but most know little about the potential of this mind-body regulation technique for advancing science. *Trends in Cognitive Sciences, 15*, 555–557.

Reiner, K., Tibi, L., & Lipsitz, J. D. (2013). Do mindfulness-based interventions reduce pain intensity? A critical review of the literature. *Pain Medicine, 14*, 230–242.

Restless Legs Syndrome Foundation. (n.d.). *Restless legs syndrome: Causes, diagnosis, and treatment for the patient living with Restless legs syndrome (RSL)*. www.rls.org

Rial, R. V., Nicolau, M. C., Gamundí, A., Akaârir, M., Aparicio, S., Garau, C., . . . Esteban, S. (2007). The trivial function of sleep. *Sleep Medicine Reviews, 11*, 311–325.

Reissig, C. J., Strain, E. C., & Griffiths, R. R. (2009). Caffeinated energy drinks—A growing problem. *Drug and Alcohol Dependence, 99*, 1–10.

Robson, P. J. (2014). Therapeutic potential of cannabinoid medicines. *Drug Testing and Analysis, 6*, 24–30.

Roth, T. (2007). Insomnia: Definition, prevalence, etiology, and consequences. *Journal of Clinical Sleep Medicine, 3*(5 Suppl.), S7–S10.

Rothman, R. B., Blough, B. E., & Baumann, M. H. (2007). Dual dopamine/serotonin releasers as potential medications for stimulant and alcohol addictions. *The AAPS Journal, 9*, E1–10.

Sánchez-de-la-Torre, M., Campos-Rodriguez, F., & Barbé, F. (2012). Obstructive sleep apnoea and cardiovascular disease. *The Lancet Respiratory Medicine, 1*, 31–72.

Savard, J., Simard, S., Ivers, H., & Morin, C. M. (2005). Randomized study on the efficacy of cognitive-behavioral therapy for insomnia secondary to breast cancer, part I: Sleep and psychological effects. *Journal of Clinical Oncology, 23*, 6083–6096.

Schicho, R., & Storr, M. (2014). Cannabis finds its way into treatment of Crohn's disease. *Pharmacology, 93*, 1–3.

Shukla, R. K, Crump, J. L., & Chrisco, E. S. (2012). An evolving problem: Methamphetamine production and trafficking in the United States. *International Journal of Drug Policy, 23*, 426–435.

Siegel, J. M. (2008). Do all animals sleep? *Trends in Neuroscience, 31*, 208–213.

Siegel, J. M. (2001). The REM sleep-memory consolidation hypothesis. *Science, 294*, 1058–1063.

Singh, G. K., & Siahpush, M. (2006). Widening socioeconomic inequalities in US life expectancy, 1980–2000. *International Journal of Epidemiology, 35*, 969–979.

Smedslund, G., Fisher, K. J., Boles, S. M., & Lichtenstein, E. (2004). The effectiveness of workplace smoking cessation programmes: A meta-analysis of recent studies. *Tobacco Control, 13*, 197–204.

Sofikitis, N., Giotitsas, N., Tsounapi, P., Baltogiannis, D., Giannakis, D., & Pardalidis, N. (2008). Hormonal regulation of spermatogenesis and spermiogenesis. *Journal of Steroid Biochemistry and Molecular Biology, 109*, 323–330.

Steriade, M., & Amzica, F. (1998). Slow sleep oscillation, rhythmic K-complexes, and their paroxysmal developments. *Journal of Sleep Research, 7*(1 Suppl.), 30–35.

Stickgold, R. (2005). Sleep-dependent memory consolidation. *Nature, 437*, 1272–1278.

Stone, K. C., Taylor, D. J., McCrae, C. S., Kalsekar, A., & Lichstein, K. L. (2008). Nonrestorative sleep. *Sleep Medicine Reviews, 12*, 275–288.

Suchecki, D., Tiba, P. A., & Machado, R. B. (2012). REM sleep rebound as an adaptive response to stressful situations. Frontiers in Neuroscience, 3. doi: 10.3389/fneur.2012.00041

Task Force on Sudden Infant Death Syndrome. (2011). SIDS and other sleep-related infant deaths: Expansion of recommendations for a safe infant sleeping environment. *Pediatrics, 128*, 1030–1039.

Taillard, J., Philip, P., Coste, O., Sagaspe, P., & Bioulac, B. (2003). The circadian and homeostatic modulation of sleep pressure during wakefulness differs between morning and evening chronotypes. *Journal of Sleep Research, 12*, 275–282.

Thach, B. T. (2005). The role of respiratory control disorders in SIDS. *Respiratory Physiology & Neurobiology, 149*, 343–353.

U.S. Food and Drug Administration. (2013, October 24). *Statement on Proposed Hydrocodone Reclassification from Janet Woodcock, M.D., Director, Center for Drug Evaluation and Research.* http://www.fda.gov/

drugs/drugsafety/ucm372089.htm

Vøllestad, J., Nielsen, M. B., & Nielsen, G. H. (2012). Mindfulness- and acceptance-based interventions for anxiety disorders: A systematic review and meta-analysis. *The British Journal of Clinical Psychology, 51*, 239–260.

Wagner, U., Gais, S., & Born, J. (2001). Emotional memory formation is enhanced across sleep intervals with high amounts of rapid eye movement sleep. *Learning & Memory, 8*, 112–119.

Wagner, U., Gais, S., Haider, H., Verleger, R., & Born, J. (2004). Sleep improves insight. *Nature, 427*, 352–355.

Walker, M. P. (2009). The role of sleep in cognition and emotion. *Annals of the New York Academy of Sciences, 1156*, 168–197.

Waterhouse. J., Fukuda, Y., & Morita, T. (2012). Daily rhythms of the sleep-wake cycle. *Journal of Physiological Anthropology, 31*(5). doi:10.1186/1880-6805-31-5

Welsh, D. K. Takahashi, J. S., & Kay, S. A. (2010). Suprachiasmatic nucleus: Cell autonomy and network properties. *Annual Review of Physiology, 72*, 551–577.

West, S., Boughton, M., & Byrnes, M. (2009). Juggling multiple temporalities: The shift work story of mid-life nurses. *Journal of Nursing Management, 17*, 110–119.

White, D. P. (2005). Pathogenesis of obstructive and central sleep apnea. *American Journal of Respiratory and Critical Care Medicine, 172*, 1363–1370.

Wickens, C. D., Hutchins, S. D., Laux, L., & Sebok, A. (2015). The impact of sleep disruption on complex cognitive tasks: A meta-analysis. *Human Factors, 57*(6), 930–946. https://journals.sagepub.com/doi/10.1177/0018720815571935

Williams, J., Roth, A., Vatthauer, K., & McCrae, C. S. (2013). Cognitive behavioral treatment of insomnia. *Chest, 143*, 554–565.

Williamson, A. M., & Feyer, A. M. (2000). Moderate sleep deprivation produces impairments in cognitive and motor performance equivalent to legally prescribed levels of alcohol intoxication. *Occupational and Environmental Medicine, 57*, 649–655.

Wolt, B. J., Ganetsky, M., & Babu, K. M. (2012). Toxicity of energy drinks. *Current Opinion in Pediatrics, 24*, 243–251.

Zangini, S., Calandra-Buonaura, G., Grimaldi, D., & Cortelli, P. (2011). REM behaviour disorder and neurodegenerative diseases. *Sleep Medicine, 12*(2 Suppl.), S54–S58.

Zeidan, F., Grant, J. A., Brown, C. A., McHaffie, J. G., & Coghill, R. C. (2012). Mindfulness meditation-related pain relief: Evidence for unique brain mechanisms in the regulation of pain. *Neuroscience Letters, 520*, 165–173.

Sensation and Perception

Aaron, J. I., Mela, D. J., & Evans, R. E. (1994). The influences of attitudes, beliefs, and label information on perceptions of reduced-fat spread. *Appetite, 22*, 25–37.

Abraira, V. E., & Ginty, D. D. (2013). The sensory neurons of touch. *Neuron, 79*, 618–639.

Animals in science/alternatives. *NEAVS*. https://www.navs.org/what-we-do/keep-you-informed/science-corner/alternatives/alternatives-to-animal-testing/#.XmsJ1qhKhPY

Ayabe-Kanamura, S., Saito, S., Distel, H., Martínez-Gómez, M., & Hudson, R. (1998). Differences and similarities in the perception of everyday odors: A Japanese-German cross-cultural study. *Annals of the New York Academy of Sciences, 855*, 694–700.

Birch, J. (2012). Worldwide prevalence of red-green color deficiency. *Journal of the Optical Society of America A, 29*, 313–320. https://www.osapublishing.org/josaa/abstract.cfm?uri=josaa-29-3-313

Chen, Q., Deng, H., Brauth, S. E., Ding, L., & Tang, Y. (2012). Reduced performance of prey targeting in pit vipers with contralaterally occluded infrared and visual senses. *PloS ONE, 7*(5), e34989. doi:10.1371/journal.pone.0034989

Comfort, A. (1971). Likelihood of human pheromones. *Nature, 230*, 432–479.

Correll, J., Park, B., Judd, C. M., & Wittenbrink, B. (2002). The police officer's dilemma: Using ethnicity to disambiguate potentially threatening individuals. *Journal of Personality and Social Psychology, 83*, 1314–1329.

Correll, J., Urland, G. R., & Ito, T. A. (2006). Event-related potentials and the decision to shoot: The role of threat perception and cognitive control. *The Journal of Experimental Social Psychology, 42*, 120–128.

Dunkle T. (1982). The sound of silence. *Science, 82*, 30–33.

Egeth, H., & Yantis, S. (1997). Visual attention: Control, representation, and time course. *Annual Review of Psychology, 48*, 269–297. https://www.researchgate.net/publication/14163796_Visual_Attention_Control_Representation_and_Time_Course

Fawcett, S. L., Wang, Y., & Birch, E. E. (2005). The critical period for susceptibility of human stereopsis. *Investigative Ophthalmology and Visual Science, 46*, 521–525.

Fine, M. S., & Minnery, B. S. (2009). Visual salience affects performance in a working memory task. *Journal of Neuroscience, 29*, 8016–8021. https://www.jneurosci.org/content/29/25/8016

Furlow, F. B. (1996, 2012). The smell of love. http://www.psychologytoday.com/articles/200910/the-smell-love

Galanter, E. (1962). Contemporary Psychophysics. In R. Brown, E.Galanter, E. H. Hess, & G. Mandler (Eds.), New directions in psychology. Holt, Rinehart & Winston.

Garland, E. L. (2012). Pain processing in the human nervous system: A selective review of nociceptive and biobehavioral pathways. *Primary Care, 39*, 561–571.

Goolkasian, P. & Woodbury, C. (2010). Priming effects with ambiguous figures. *Attention, Perception & Psychophysics, 72*, 168–178.

Grothe, B., Pecka, M., & McAlpine, D. (2010). Mechanisms of sound localization in mammals. *Physiological Reviews, 90*, 983–1012.

Hartline, P. H., Kass, L., & Loop, M. S. (1978). Merging of modalities in the optic tectum: Infrared and visual integration in rattlesnakes. *Science, 199*, 1225–1229.

Hubel, D. H., & Wiesel, T. N. (1959). Receptive fields of single neurones in the cat's striate cortex. *Journal of Physiology, 148*, 574–591. https://www.ncbi.nlm.nih.gov/pmc/articles/PMC1363130/

Hubel, D. H., & Wiesel, T. N. (1962). Receptive fields, binocular interaction and functional architecture in the cat's visual cortex. *Journal of Physiology, 160*, 106–154. https://www.ncbi.nlm.nih.gov/pmc/articles/PMC1359523/

Hubel, D. H., & Weisel, T. N. (1963). Single-cell responses in striate cortex of kittens deprived of vision in one eye. *Journal of Neurophysiology.* https://journals.physiology.org/doi/abs/10.1152/jn.1963.26.6.1003

Hubel, D. H., & Wiesel, T. N. (1970). The period of susceptibility to the physiological effects of unilateral eye closure in kittens. *The Journal of Physiology, 206*(2). https://physoc.onlinelibrary.wiley.com/doi/abs/10.1113/jphysiol.1970.sp009022

Kaiser, P. K. (1997). *The joy of visual perception: A web book.* http://www.yorku.ca/eye/noframes.htm

Khan, S., & Chang, R. (2013). Anatomy of the vestibular system: A review. *NeuroRehabilitation, 32*, 437–443.

Kinnamon, S. C., & Vandenbeuch, A. (2009). Receptors and transduction of umami taste stimuli. *Annals of the New York Academy of Sciences, 1170*, 55–59.

Kujawa, S. G., & Liberman, M. C. (2006). Acceleration of age-related hearing loss by early noise exposure: Evidence of a misspent youth. *Journal of Neuroscience, 26,* 2115–2123. https://www.jneurosci.org/content/26/7/2115

Kunst-Wilson, W. R., & Zajonc, R. B. (1980). Affective discrimination of stimuli that cannot be recognized. *Science, 207,* 557–558.

Lackner, J. R., & DiZio, P. (2005). Vestibular, proprioceptive, and haptic contributions to spatial orientation. *Annual Review of Psychology, 56,* 115–147.

Land, E. H. (1959). Color vision and the natural image. Part 1. *Proceedings of the National Academy of Science, 45*(1), 115–129.

Latham, S. (2012). U.S. law and animal experimentation: A critical primer. *The Hastings Center.* http://animalresearch.thehastingscenter.org/report/u-s-law-and-animal-experimentation-a-critical-primer/

Le, T. N., Straatman, L. V., Lea, J., & Westerberg, B. (2017). Current insights in noise-induced hearing loss: A literature review of the underlying mechanism, pathophysiology, asymmetry, and management options. *Journal of Otolaryngology - Head & Neck Surgery, 46*(1), 41. https://journalotohns.biomedcentral.com/articles/10.1186/s40463-017-0219-x

Liem, D. G., Westerbeek, A., Wolterink, S., Kok, F. J., & de Graaf, C. (2004). Sour taste preferences of children relate to preference for novel and intense stimuli. *Chemical Senses, 29,* 713–720.

Lodovichi, C., & Belluscio, L. (2012). Odorant receptors in the formation of olfactory bulb circuitry. *Physiology, 27,* 200–212.

Loersch, C., Durso, G. R. O., & Petty, R. E. (2013). Vicissitudes of desire: A matching mechanism for subliminal persuasion. *Social Psychological and Personality Science, 4*(5), 624–631.

Mack, A., & Rock, I. (1998). *Inattentional Blindness.* MIT Press.

Maffei, A., Haley, M., & Fontanini, A. (2012). Neural processing of gustatory information in insular circuits. *Current Opinion in Neurobiology, 22,* 709–716.

Miller, B. T., & D'Esposito, M. (2005). Searching for "the top" in top-down control. *Neuron, 48,* 535–538. https://www.sciencedirect.com/science/article/pii/S0896627305009360

Miller, E. K., & Cohen, J. D. (2001). An integrative theory of prefrontal cortex function. *Annual Review of Neuroscience, 24,* 167–202. https://www.annualreviews.org/doi/abs/10.1146/annurev.neuro.24.1.167

Milner, A. D., & Goodale, M. A. (2008). Two visual systems re-viewed. *Neuropsychological, 46,* 774–785.

Mizushige, T., Inoue, K., Fushiki, T. (2007). Why is fat so tasty? Chemical reception of fatty acid on the tongue. *Journal of Nutritional Science and Vitaminology, 53,* 1–4.

Most, S. B., Simons, D. J., Scholl, B. J., & Chabris, C. F. (2000). Sustained inattentional blindness: The role of location in the detection of unexpected dynamic events. *PSYCHE, 6*(14).

Nelson, M. R. (2008). The hidden persuaders: Then and now. *Journal of Advertising, 37*(1), 113–126.

Niimura, Y., & Nei, M. (2007). Extensive gains and losses of olfactory receptor genes in mammalian evolution. *PLoS ONE, 2,* e708.

Okawa, H., & Sampath, A. P. (2007). Optimization of single-photon response transmission at the rod-to-rod bipolar synapse. *Physiology, 22,* 279–286.

Payne, B. K. (2001). Prejudice and perception: The role of automatic and controlled processes in misperceiving a weapon. *Journal of Personality and Social Psychology, 81,* 181–192.

Payne, B. K., Shimizu, Y., & Jacoby, L. L. (2005). Mental control and visual illusions: Toward explaining race-biased weapon misidentifications. *Journal of Experimental Social Psychology, 41,* 36–47.

Peck, M. (2012, July 19). *How a movie changed one man's vision forever.* http://www.bbc.com/future/story/20120719-awoken-from-a-2d-world

Peterson, M. A., & Gibson, B. S. (1994). Must figure-ground organization precede object recognition? An assumption in peril. *Psychological Science, 5,* 253–259.

Petho, G., & Reeh, P. W. (2012). Sensory and signaling mechanisms of bradykinin, eicosanoids, platelet-activating factor, and nitric oxide in peripheral nociceptors. *Physiological Reviews, 92,* 1699–1775.

Proske, U. (2006). Kinesthesia: The role of muscle receptors. *Muscle & Nerve, 34,* 545–558.

Proske, U., & Gandevia, S. C. (2012). The proprioceptive senses: Their roles in signaling body shape, body position and movement, and muscle force. *Physiological Reviews, 92,* 1651–1697.

Purvis, K., & Haynes, N. B. (1972). The effect of female rat proximity on the reproductive system of male rats. *Physiology & Behavior, 9,* 401–407.

Radel, R., Sarrazin, P., Legrain, P., & Gobancé, L. (2009). Subliminal priming of motivational orientation in educational settings: Effect on academic performance moderated by mindfulness. *Journal of Research in Personality, 43*(4), 1–18.

Rauschecker, J. P., & Tian, B. (2000). Mechanisms and streams for processing "what" and "where" in auditory cortex. *Proceedings of the National Academy of Sciences, USA, 97,* 11800–11806.

Renier, L. A., Anurova, I., De Volder, A. G., Carlson, S., VanMeter, J., & Rauschecker, J. P. (2009). Multisensory integration of sounds and vibrotactile stimuli in processing streams for "what" and "where." *Journal of Neuroscience, 29,* 10950–10960.

Rensink, R. A. (2004). Visual sensing without seeing. *Psychological Science, 15,* 27–32.

Rock, I., & Palmer, S. (1990). The legacy of Gestalt psychology. *Scientific American, 262,* 84–90.

Roper, S. D. (2013). Taste buds as peripheral chemosensory receptors. *Seminars in Cell & Developmental Biology, 24,* 71–79.

Russell, M. J. (1976). Human olfactory communication. *Nature, 260,* 520–522.

Sachs, B. D. (1997). Erection evoked in male rats by airborne scent from estrous females. *Physiology & Behavior, 62,* 921–924.

Segall, M. H., Campbell, D. T., & Herskovits, M. J. (1963). Cultural differences in the perception of geometric illusions. *Science, 139,* 769–771.

Segall, M. H., Campbell, D. T., & Herskovits, M. J. (1966). *The influence of culture on visual perception.* Bobbs-Merrill.

Segall, M. H., Dasen, P. P., Berry, J. W., & Poortinga, Y. H. (1999). *Human behavior in global perspective* (2nd ed.). Allyn & Bacon.

Semaan, M. T., & Megerian, C. A. (2010). Contemporary perspectives on the pathophysiology of Meniere's disease: implications for treatment. *Current opinion in Otolaryngology & Head and Neck Surgery, 18*(5), 392–398.

Shamma, S. (2001). On the role of space and time in auditory processing. *Trends in Cognitive Sciences, 5,* 340–348.

Simons, D. J., & Chabris, C. F. (1999). Gorillas in our midst: Sustained inattentional blindness for dynamic events. *Perception, 28,* 1059–1074.

Spors, H., Albeanu, D. F., Murthy, V. N., Rinberg, D., Uchida, N., Wachowiak, M., & Friedrich, R. W. (2013). Illuminating vertebrate olfactory processing. *Journal of Neuroscience, 32,* 14102–14108.

Spray, D. C. (1986). Cutaneous temperature receptors. *Annual Review of Physiology, 48,* 625–638.

Strain, G. M. (2003). *How well do dogs and other animals hear?* http://www.lsu.edu/deafness/

HearingRange.html

Swets, J. A. (1964). Signal detection and recognition by human observers. *Psychological Bulletin, 60*, 429–441.

Ungerleider, L. G., & Haxby, J. V. (1994). 'What' and 'where' in the human brain. *Current Opinion in Neurobiology, 4,* 157–165.

U.S. Department of Health and Human Services, National Institutes of Health, & National Institute on Deafness and Other Communication Disorders (NIDCD). (2014). Noise-induced hearing loss. *NIH Publication No. 14-4233.* https://www.nidcd.nih.gov/health/noise-induced-hearing-loss

U.S. National Library of Medicine. (2013). Genetics home reference: Congenital insensitivity to pain. http://ghr.nlm.nih.gov/condition/congenital-insensitivity-to-pain

Vecera, S. P., & O'Reilly, R. C. (1998). Figure-ground organization and object recognition processes: An interactive account. *Journal of Experimental Psychology-Human Perception and Performance, 24,* 441–462.

Wakakuwa, M., Stavenga, D. G., & Arikawa, K. (2007). Spectral organization of ommatidia in flower-visiting insects. *Photochemistry and Photobiology, 83,* 27–34.

Weisel, T. N., & Hubel, D. H. (1963). Single-cell responses in striate cortex of kittens deprived of vision in one eye. *Journal of Neurophysiology.* https://journals.physiology.org/doi/abs/10.1152/jn.1963.26.6.1003

Weller, A. (1998). Human pheromones: Communication through body odour. *Nature, 392,* 126–127.

Wells, D. L. (2010). Domestic dogs and human health: An overview. *British Journal of Health Psychology, 12,* 145–156.

Wolfgang-Kimball, D. (1992). Pheromones in humans: myth or reality?. http://www.anapsid.org/pheromones.html

Wysocki, C. J., & Preti, G. (2004). Facts, fallacies, fears, and frustrations with human pheromones. *The Anatomical Record Part A: Discoveries in Molecular, Cellular, and Evolutionary Biology, 281,* 1201–1211.

Yantis, S., & Egeth, H. (1999). On the distinction between visual salience and stimulus-driven attentional capture. *Journal of Experimental Psychology: Human Perception and Performance, 25,* 661–676. https://psycnet.apa.org/doiLanding?doi=10.1037%2F0096-1523.25.3.661

Learning

Anderson, C. A., & Gentile, D. A. (2008). Media violence, aggression, and public policy. In E. Borgida & S. Fiske (Eds.), *Beyond common sense: Psychological science in the courtroom* (p. 322). Blackwell.

Anderson, C. A., Bushman, B. J., Donnerstein, E., Hummer, T. A., & Warburton, W. (2015). SPSSI research summary on media violence. *Analyses of Social Issues and Public Policy* (ASAP), 15(1), 4–19. https://doi.org/10.1111/asap.12093

Anderson, C. A., Shibuya, A., Ihori, N., Swing, E. L., Bushman, B. J., Sakamoto, A., Rothstein, H.R., & Saleem, M. (2010). Violent video game effects on aggression, empathy, and prosocial behavior in Eastern and Western countries: A meta-analytic review. *Psychological Bulletin,* 136(2), 151–173. HYPERLINK "https://psycnet.apa.org/doi/10.1037/a0018251"https://doi.org/10.1037/a0018251

Bandura, A., Ross, D., & Ross, S. A. (1961). Transmission of aggression through imitation of aggressive models. *Journal of Abnormal and Social Psychology, 63,* 575–582.

Bushman, B. J., Anderson, C. A., Donnerstein, E., Hummer, T. A., & Warburton, W. A. (2016). Reply to comments on SPSSI research summary on media violence by Cupit (2016), Gentile (2016), Glackin and Gray (2016), Gollwitzer (2016), and Krahé (2016). *Analyses of Social Issues and Public Policy* (ASAP), 16(1), 443–450. https://doi.org/10.1111/asap.12123

Cangi, K., & Daly, M. (2013). The effects of token economies on the occurrence of appropriate and inappropriate behaviors by children with autism in a social skills setting. *West Chester University:*

Journal of Undergraduate Research. http://www.wcupa.edu/UndergraduateResearch/journal/documents/cangi_S2012.pdf

Carlson, L., Holscher, C., Shipley, T., & Conroy Dalton, R. (2010). Getting lost in buildings. *Current Directions in Psychological Science, 19*(5), 284–289.

Chance, P. (2009). *Learning and behavior* (6th ed.). Wadsworth, Cengage Learning.

Chase, H. W., & Clark, L. (2010). Gambling severity predicts midbrain response to near-miss outcomes. *The Journal of Neuroscience, 30*(18), 6180–6187. https://www.jneurosci.org/content/30/18/6180.short

Cialdini, R. B. (2008). *Influence: Science and practice* (5th ed.). Pearson Education.

DeAngelis, T. (2010). 'Little Albert' regains his identity. *Monitor on Psychology, 41*(1), 10.

Ferguson, C. J. (2011). Video games and youth violence: A prospective analysis in adolescents. *Journal of Youth and Adolescence, 40*(4), 377–391. https://link.springer.com/article/10.1007/s10964-010-9610-x

Fryer, R. G., Jr. (2010, April). Financial incentives and student achievement: Evidence from randomized trials. *National Bureau of Economic Research [NBER] Working Paper, No. 15898.* http://www.nber.org/papers/w15898

Garcia, J., & Koelling, R. A. (1966). Relation of cue to consequence in avoidance learning. *Psychonomic Science, 4*, 123–124.

Garcia, J., & Rusiniak, K. W. (1980). What the nose learns from the mouth. In D. Müller-Schwarze & R. M. Silverstein (Eds.), *Chemical signals: Vertebrates and aquatic invertebrates* (pp. 141–156). Plenum Press.

Gentile, D. A. (2016). The evolution of scientific skepticism in the media violence "debate." *Analyses of Social Issues and Public Policy, 16*, 429–434.

Gershoff, E. T. (2002). Corporal punishment by parents and associated child behaviors and experiences: A meta-analytic and theoretical review. *Psychological Bulletin, 128*(4), 539–579. doi:10.1037//0033-2909.128.4.539

Gershoff, E.T., Grogan-Kaylor, A., Lansford, J. E., Chang, L., Zelli, A., Deater-Deckard, K., & Dodge, K. A. (2010). Parent discipline practices in an international sample: Associations with child behaviors and moderation by perceived normativeness. *Child Development, 81*(2), 487–502.

Hickock, G. (2010). The role of mirror neurons in speech and language processing. *Brain and Language, 112,* 1–2.

Holmes, S. (1993). Food avoidance in patients undergoing cancer chemotherapy. *Support Care Cancer, 1*(6), 326–330.

Hunt, M. (2007). *The story of psychology.* Doubleday.

Huston, A. C., Donnerstein, E., Fairchild, H., Feshbach, N. D., Katz, P. A., Murray, J. P., . . . Zuckerman, D. (1992). *Big world, small screen: The role of television in American society.* University of Nebraska Press.

Hutton, J. L., Baracos, V. E., & Wismer, W. V. (2007). Chemosensory dysfunction is a primary factor in the evolution of declining nutritional status and quality of life with patients with advanced cancer. *Journal of Pain Symptom Management, 33*(2), 156–165.

Jacobsen, P. B., Bovbjerg, D. H., Schwartz, M. D., Andrykowski, M. A., Futterman, A. D., Gilewski, T., . . . Redd, W. H. (1993). Formation of food aversions in cancer patients receiving repeated infusions of chemotherapy. *Behaviour Research and Therapy, 31*(8), 739–748.

Kirsch, SJ (2010). *Media and youth: A developmental perspective.* Wiley Blackwell.

Laskowski, C. S., Dorchak, D. L., Ward, K. M., Christensen, D. R., & Euston, D. R. (2019). Can slot-machine reward schedules induce gambling addiction in rats? *Journal of Gambling Studies, 35*(3), 887–914. https://www.ncbi.nlm.nih.gov/pubmed/31049772

Lefrançois, G. R. (2012). *Theories of human learning: What the professors said* (6th ed.). Wadsworth, Cengage Learning.

Miller, L. E., Grabell, A., Thomas, A., Bermann, E., & Graham-Bermann, S. A. (2012). The associations between community violence, television violence, intimate partner violence, parent-child aggression, and aggression in sibling relationships of a sample of preschoolers. *Psychology of Violence, 2(2)*, 165–78. doi:10.1037/a0027254

Murch, W. S., & Clark, L. (2016). Games in the brain: Neural substrates of gambling addiction. *The Neuroscientist, 22*(5), 534–545. https://www.ncbi.nlm.nih.gov/pubmed/26116634

Murrell, A., Christoff, K. & Henning, K. (2007) Characteristics of domestic violence offenders: associations with childhood exposure to violence. *Journal of Family Violence, 22*(7), 523-532.

Pavlov, I. P. (1927). *Conditioned reflexes: An investigation of the physiological activity of the cerebral cortex* (G. V. Anrep, Ed. & Trans.). Oxford University Press.

Potenza, M. N. (2013). Neurobiology of gambling behaviors. *Current Opinion in Neurobiology, 23*(4), 660–667. https://www.ncbi.nlm.nih.gov/pmc/articles/PMC3803105/

Rescorla, R. A., & Wagner, A. R. (1972). A theory of Pavlovian conditioning: Variations in the effectiveness of reinforcement and nonreinforcement. *Classical Conditioning II: Current Research and Theory, 2*, 64-99.

Rizzolatti, G., Fadiga, L., Fogassi, L., & Gallese, V. (2002). From mirror neurons to imitation: Facts and speculations. In A. N. Meltzoff & W. Prinz (Eds.), *The imitative mind: Development, evolution, and brain bases* (pp. 247–66). Cambridge University Press.

Rizzolatti, G., Fogassi, L., & Gallese, V. (2006, November). Mirrors in the mind. *Scientific American*, pp. 54–61.

Skinner, B. F. (1938). *The behavior of organisms: An experimental analysis*. Appleton-Century-Crofts.

Skinner, B. F. (1953). *Science and human behavior*. Macmillan.

Skinner, B. F. (1961). *Cumulative record: A selection of papers*. Appleton-Century-Crofts.

Skinner's utopia: Panacea, or path to hell? (1971, September 20). *Time*. http://www.wou.edu/~girodm/611/Skinner%27s_utopia.pdf

Skolin, I., Wahlin, Y. B., Broman, D. A., Hursti, U-K. K., Larsson, M. V., & Hernell, O. (2006). Altered food intake and taste perception in children with cancer after start of chemotherapy: Perspectives of children, parents and nurses. *Supportive Care in Cancer, 14*, 369–78.

Thorndike, E. L. (1911). Animal intelligence: An experimental study of the associative processes in animals. *Psychological Monographs, 8*.

Tolman, E. C., & Honzik, C. H. (1930). Degrees of hunger, reward, and non-reward, and maze performance in rats. *University of California Publications in Psychology, 4*, 241–256.

Tolman, E. C., Ritchie, B. F., & Kalish, D. (1946). Studies in spatial learning: II. Place learning versus response learning. *Journal of Experimental Psychology, 36*, 221–229. doi:10.1037/h0060262

Watson, J. B. & Rayner, R. (1920). Conditioned emotional reactions. *Journal of Experimental Psychology, 3*, 1–14.

Watson, J. B. (1919). *Psychology from the standpoint of a behaviorist*. J. B. Lippincott.

Yamamoto, S., Humle, T., & Tanaka, M. (2013). Basis for cumulative cultural evolution in chimpanzees: Social learning of a more efficient tool-use technique. *PLoS ONE, 8*(1): e55768. doi:10.1371/journal.pone.0055768

Thinking and Intelligence

Abler, W. (2013). Sapir, Harris, and Chomsky in the twentieth century. *Cognitive Critique, 7*, 29–48.

American Association on Intellectual and Developmental Disabilities. (2013). *Definition of intellectual disability*. http://aaidd.org/intellectual-disability/definition#.UmkR2xD2Bh4

American Psychological Association. (2013). In *Diagnostic and statistical manual of psychological disorders* (5th ed., pp. 34–36). American Psychological Association.

Aronson, E. (Ed.). (1995). Social cognition. In *The social animal* (p. 151). W.H. Freeman and Company.

Atkins v. Virginia, 00-8452 (2002).

Bartels, M., Rietveld, M., Van Baal, G., & Boomsma, D. I. (2002). Genetic and environmental influences on the development of intelligence. *Behavior Genetics, 32*(4), 237–238.

Bartlett, F. C. (1932). Remembering: A study in experimental and social psychology. Cambridge University Press.

Bayer, J. B., & Campbell, S. W. (2012). Texting while driving on automatic: Considering the frequency-independent side of habit. *Computers in Human Behavior, 28*, 2083–2090.

Barton, S. M. (2003). Classroom accommodations for students with dyslexia. *Learning Disabilities Journal, 13*, 10–14.

Berlin, B., & Kay, P. (1969). *Basic color terms: Their universality and evolution*. University of California Press.

Berninger, V. W. (2008). Defining and differentiating dysgraphia, dyslexia, and language learning disability within a working memory model. In M. Mody & E. R. Silliman (Eds.), *Brain, behavior, and learning in language and reading disorders* (pp. 103–134). The Guilford Press.

Blossom, M., & Morgan, J. L. (2006). Does the face say what the mouth says? A study of infants' sensitivity to visual prosody. In the 30th annual Boston University Conference on Language Development, Somerville, MA.

Boake, C. (2002, May 24). From the Binet-Simon to the Wechsler-Bellevue: Tracing the history of intelligence testing. *Journal of Clinical and Experimental Neuropsychology, 24*(3), 383–405.

Boroditsky, L. (2001). Does language shape thought? Mandarin and English speakers' conceptions of time. *Cognitive Psychology, 43*, 1–22.

Boroditsky, L. (2011, February). How language shapes thought. *Scientific American*, 63–65.

Bouchard, T. J., Lykken, D. T., McGue, M., Segal, N. L., & Tellegen, A. (1990). Sources of human psychological differences: The Minnesota Study of Twins Reared Apart. *Science, 250*, 223–228.

Buck v. Bell, 274 U.S. 200

Cairns Regional Council. (n.d.). Cultural greetings. http://www.cairns.qld.gov.au/__data/assets/pdf_file/0007/8953/CulturalGreetingExercise.pdf

Callero, P. L. (1994). From role-playing to role-using: Understanding role as resource. *Social Psychology Quarterly, 57*, 228–243.

Cattell, R. (1963). Theory of fluid and crystallized intelligence: A critical experiment. *Journal of Educational Psychology, 54*(1), 1–22.

Cianciolo, A. T., & Sternberg, R. J. (2004). *Intelligence: A brief history*. Blackwell Publishing.

Chomsky, N. (1965). *Aspects of the theory of syntax*. MIT Press

Corballis, M. C., & Suddendorf, T. (2007). Memory, time, and language. In C. Pasternak (Ed.), *What makes us human* (pp. 17–36). Oneworld Publications.

Cropley, A. (2006). In praise of convergent thinking. *Creativity Research Journal, 18*(3), 391–404.

Csikszentmihalyi, M., & Csikszentmihalyi, I. (1993). Family influences on the development of giftedness. *Ciba Foundation Symposium, 178*, 187–206.

Curtiss, S. (1981). Dissociations between language and cognition: Cases and implications. *Journal of Autism and Developmental Disorders, 11*(1), 15–30.

Cyclopedia of Puzzles. (n.d.) http://www.mathpuzzle.com/loyd/

Dates and Events. (n.d.). *Oprah Winfrey timeline.* http://www.datesandevents.org/people-timelines/05-oprah-winfrey-timeline.htm

Duncker, K. (1945). On problem-solving (L. S. Lees, Trans.) *Psychological Monographs, 58*(5), i–113. https://psycnet.apa.org/record/2011-16110-001

Fernández, E. M., & Cairns, H. S. (2011). *Fundamentals of psycholinguistics.* Wiley-Blackwell.

Flanagan, D., & Kaufman, A. (2004). *Essentials of WISC-IV assessment.* John Wiley and Sons, Inc.

Flynn, J., Shaughnessy, M. F., & Fulgham, S. W. (2012) Interview with Jim Flynn about the Flynn effect. *North American Journal of Psychology, 14*(1), 25–38.

Fox, M. (2012, November 1). Arthur R. Jensen dies at 89; Set off debate about I.Q. *New York Times*, p. B15.

Fromkin, V., Krashen, S., Curtiss, S., Rigler, D., & Rigler, M. (1974). The development of language in Genie: A case of language acquisition beyond the critical period. *Brain and Language, 1,* 81–107.

Furnham, A. (2009). The validity of a new, self-report measure of multiple intelligence. *Current Psychology: A Journal for Diverse Perspectives on Diverse Psychological Issues, 28,* 225–239.

Gardner, H. (1983). *Frames of mind: The theory of multiple intelligences.* Basic Books.

Gardner, H., & Moran, S. (2006). The science of multiple intelligences theory: A response to Lynn Waterhouse. *Educational Psychologist, 41,* 227–232.

German, T. P., & Barrett, H. C. (2005). Functional fixedness in a technologically sparse culture. *Psychological Science, 16,* 1–5.

Goad, B. (2013, January 25). *SSA wants to stop calling people 'mentally retarded.'* http://thehill.com/blogs/regwatch/pending-regs/279399-ssa-wants-to-stop-calling-people-mentally-retarded

Goldstone, R. L., & Kersten, A. (2003). Concepts and categorization. In A. F. Healy, R. W. Proctor, & I.B. Weiner (Eds.), *Handbook of psychology* (Volume IV, pp. 599–622). John Wiley & Sons, Inc.

Goleman, D. (1995). *Emotional intelligence; Why it can matter more than IQ.* Bantam Books.

Gordon, O. E. (1995). *Francis Galton (1822–1911).* http://www.psych.utah.edu/gordon/Classes/Psy4905Docs/PsychHistory/Cards/Galton.html

Gresham, F. M., & Witt, J. C. (1997). Utility of intelligence tests for treatment planning, classification, and placement decisions: Recent empirical findings and future directions. *School Psychology Quarterly, 12*(3), 249–267.

Guilford, J. P. (1967). *The nature of human intelligence.* McGraw Hill.

Heaton, S. (2004). Making the switch: Unlocking the mystery of the WISC-IV. *Case Conference.* University of Florida.

Jensen, J. (2011). Phoneme acquisition: Infants and second language learners. *The Language Teacher, 35*(6), 24–28.

Johnson, J. S., & Newport, E. L. (1989). Critical period effects in second language learning: The influence of maturational state on the acquisition of English as a second language. *Cognitive Psychology, 21,* 60–99.

Kahneman, D. (2011). *Thinking, fast and slow.* Farrar, Straus, and Giroux.

Kishyama, M. M., Boyce, W. T., Jimenez, A. M., Perry, L. M., & Knight, R. T. (2009). Socioeconomic disparities affect prefrontal function in children. *Journal of Cognitive Neuroscience, 21*(6), 1106–1115.

Klein, P. D. (1997). Multiplying the problems of intelligence by eight: A critique of Gardner's theory.

Canadian Journal of Education, 22, 377-94.

Ko, L. (2016). Unwanted sterilization and eugenics programs in the United States. *Independent Lens.* http://www.pbs.org/independentlens/blog/unwanted-sterilization-and-eugenics-programs-in-the-united-states/

Larry P v. Riles, C-71-2270 RFP. (1979).

Lenneberg, E. (1967). *Biological foundations of language.* Wiley.

Liptak, A. (2008, January 19). Lawyer reveals secret, toppling death sentence. *New York Times.* http://www.nytimes.com/2008/01/19/us/19death.html?_r=0

Locke, E. A. (2005, April 14). Why emotional intelligence is an invalid concept. *Journal of Organizational Behavior, 26,* 425–431.

Mayer, J. D., Salovey, P., & Caruso, D. (2004). Emotional intelligence: Theory, findings, and implications, *Psychological Inquiry, 15*(3), 197–215.

Modgil, S., & Routledge, C. M. (Eds.). (1987). *Arthur Jensen: Consensus and controversy.* Falmer Press.

Morgan, H. (1996). An analysis of Gardner's theory of multiple intelligence. *Roeper Review: A Journal on Gifted Education, 18,* 263–269.

Moskowitz, B. A. (1978). The acquisition of language. *Scientific American, 239,* 92–108. Petitto, L. A., Holowka, S., Sergio, L. E., Levy, B., & Ostry, D. J. (2004). Baby hands that move to the rhythm of language: Hearing babies acquiring sign languages babble silently on the hands. *Cognition, 93,* 43–73.

Neyfakh, L. (2013, October 7). "Why you can't stop checking your phone." http://www.bostonglobe.com/ideas/2013/10/06/why-you-can-stop-checking-your-phone/rrBJzyBGDAr1YlEH5JQDcM/story.html

Parker, J. D., Saklofske, D. H., & Stough, C. (Eds.). (2009). *Assessing emotional intelligence: Theory, research, and applications.* Springer.

Petitto, L. A., Holowka, S., Sergio, L. E., Levy, B., & Ostry, D. J. (2004). Baby hands that move to the rhythm of language: Hearing babies acquiring sign languages babble silently on the hands. Cognition, 93, 43–73.

Pickens, J. (1994). Full-term and preterm infants' perception of face-voice synchrony. *Infant Behavior and Development, 17,* 447–455.

Pratkanis, A. (1989). The cognitive representation of attitudes. In A. R. Pratkanis, S. J. Breckler, & A. G. Greenwald (Eds.), *Attitude structure and function* (pp. 71–98). Erlbaum.

Regier, T., & Kay, P. (2009). Language, thought, and color: Whorf was half right. *Trends in Cognitive Sciences, 13*(10), 439–446.

Riccio, C. A., Gonzales, J. J., & Hynd, G. W. (1994). Attention-deficit Hyperactivity Disorder (ADHD) and learning disabilities. *Learning Disability Quarterly, 17,* 311–322.

Richardson, K. (2002). What IQ tests test. *Theory & Psychology, 12*(3), 283–314.

Roberts, D. (2014, May 27). U.S. Supreme Court bars Florida from using IQ score cutoff for executions. *The Guardian.* http://www.theguardian.com/world/2014/may/27/us-supreme-court-iq-score-cutoff-florida-execution

Rushton, J. P., & Jensen, A. R. (2005). Thirty years of research on race differences in cognitive ability. *Psychology, public policy, and law, 11*(2), 235–294.

Rymer, R. (1993). *Genie: A Scientific Tragedy.* Harper Collins.

Sapir, E. (1964). *Culture, language, and personality.* University of California Press. (Original work published 1941)

Schlinger, H. D. (2003). The myth of intelligence. *The Psychological Record, 53*(1), 15–32.

Schneider, W. J., & McGrew, K. S. (2018). The Cattell-Horn-Carroll theory of cognitive abilities. In D. P. Flanagan & E. M. McDonough (Eds.), *Contemporary intellectual assessment: Theories, tests, and issues* (pp. 73–163). The Guilford Press.

Severson, K. (2011, December 9). Thousands sterilized, a state weighs restitution. *The New York Times.* http://www.nytimes.com/2011/12/10/us/redress-weighed-for-forcedsterilizations-in-north-carolina.html?pagewanted=all&_r=0

Singleton, D. M. (1995). Introduction: A critical look at the critical period hypothesis in second language acquisition research. In D.M. Singleton & Z. Lengyel (Eds.), *The age factor in second language acquisition: A critical look at the critical period hypothesis in second language acquisition research* (pp. 1–29). Multilingual Matters Ltd.

Skinner, B. F. (1957). *Verbal behavior.* Copley Publishing Group.

Smits-Engelsman, B. C. M., & Van Galen, G. P. (1997). Dysgraphia in children: Lasting psychomotor deficiency or transient developmental delay? *Journal of Experimental Child Psychology, 67*, 164–184.

Spelke, E. S., & Cortelyou, A. (1981). Perceptual aspects of social knowing: Looking and listening in infancy. In M.E. Lamb & L.R. Sherrod (Eds.), *Infant social cognition: Empirical and theoretical considerations* (pp. 61–83). Erlbaum.

Steitz, T. (2010). *Thomas A. Steitz – Biographical.* (K. Grandin, Ed.) http://www.nobelprize.org/nobel_prizes/chemistry/laureates/2009/steitz-bio.html

Sternberg, R. J. (1988). *The triarchic mind: A new theory of intelligence.* Viking-Penguin.

Terman, L. M. (1925). *Mental and physical traits of a thousand gifted children (I).* Stanford University Press.

Terman, L. M., & Oden, M. H. (1947). *The gifted child grows up: 25 years' follow-up of a superior group: Genetic studies of genius (Vol. 4).* Stanford University Press.

Terman, L. M. (1916). *The measurement of intelligence.* Houghton-Mifflin.

Tomasello, M., & Rakoczy, H. (2003). What makes human cognition unique? From individual to shared to collective intentionality. *Mind & Language, 18*(2), 121–147.

Tversky, A., & Kahneman, D. (1974). Judgment under uncertainty: Heuristics and biases. *Science, 185*(4157), 1124–1131.

van Troyer, G. (1994). Linguistic determinism and mutability: The Sapir-Whorf "hypothesis" and intercultural communication. *JALT Journal, 2*, 163–178.

Wechsler, D. (1958). *The measurement of adult intelligence.* Williams & Wilkins.

Wechsler, D. (1981). *Manual for the Wechsler Adult Intelligence Scale—revised.* Psychological Corporation.

Wechsler, D. (2002). *WPPSI-R manual.* Psychological Corporation.

Werker, J. F., & Lalonde, C. E. (1988). Cross-language speech perception: Initial capabilities and developmental change. *Developmental Psychology, 24*, 672–683.

Werker, J. F., & Tees, R. C. (1984). Cross-language speech perception: Evidence for perceptual reorganization during the first year of life. *Infant Behavior and Development, 7*, 49–63.

Whorf, B. L. (1956). *Language, thought and relativity.* MIT Press.

Williams, R. L., (1970). Danger: Testing and dehumanizing black children. *Clinical Child Psychology Newsletter, 9*(1), 5–6.

Zwicker, J. G. (2005). *Effectiveness of occupational therapy in remediating handwriting difficulties in primary students: Cognitive versus multisensory interventions.* Unpublished master's thesis, University of Victoria, Victoria, British Columbia, Canada). http://dspace.library.uvic.ca:8080/bitstream/handle/

1828/49/Zwicker%20thesis.pdf?sequence=1

Memory

Abel, M., & Bäuml, K.-H. T. (2013). Sleep can reduce proactive interference. *Memory, 22*(4), 332–339. doi:10.1080/09658211.2013.785570. http://www.psychologie.uni-regensburg.de/Baeuml/papers_in_press/sleepPI.pdf

Adams, J. K. (1957). Laboratory studies of behavior without awareness. *Psychological Bulletin, 54*, 383–405. https://psycnet.apa.org/record/1959-00483-001

Anderson, J. R., & Reder, L. M. (1999). The fan effect: New results and new theories. *Journal of Experimental Psychology: General, 128*, 186–197. https://psycnet.apa.org/record/1999-05245-004

Anderson, N. S. (1969). The influence of acoustic similarity on serial recall of letter sequences. *Quarterly Journal of Experimental Psychology, 21*(3), 248–255.

Anderson, R. C. (1984). Role of the reader's schema in comprehension, learning, and memory. In R. C. Anderson, J. Osborn, & R. J. Tierney (Eds.), *Learning to read in American schools: Basal Readers and Content Texts* (pp. 243–257). Erlbaum.

Atkinson, R. C., & Shiffrin, R. M. (1968). Human memory: A proposed system and its control processes. In K. W. Spence & J. T. Spence (Eds.), *The psychology of learning and motivation: Volume 2* (pp. 89–195). Academic Press.

Baddeley, A. (2004). *Your memory: A user's guide*. Firefly Books.

Baddeley, A. D. (2000). The episodic buffer: A new component of working memory? *Trends in Cognitive Sciences, 4*, 417–423. https://www.ncbi.nlm.nih.gov/pubmed/11058819

Baddeley, A. D., & Hitch, G. (1974). Working memory. In G. H. Bower (Ed.), *The psychology of learning and motivation: Advances in research and theory* (Vol. 8, pp. 47–89). Academic Press.

Bayley, P. J., & Squire, L. R. (2002). Medial temporal lobe amnesia: Gradual acquisition of factual information by nondeclarative memory. *Journal of Neuroscience, 22*, 5741–5748.

Bellezza, F. S. (1981). Mnemonic devices: Classification, characteristics and criteria. *Review of Educational Research, 51*, 247–275.

Benjamin N. Cardozo School of Law, Yeshiva University. (2009). Reevaluating lineups: Why witnesses make mistakes and how to reduce the chance of a misidentification. The Innocence Project website: http://www.innocenceproject.org/docs/Eyewitness_ID_Report.pdf

Blockland, A. (1996). Acetylcholine: A neurotransmitter for learning and memory? *Brain Research Reviews, 21*, 285–300.

Bodie, G. D., Powers, W. G., & Fitch-Hauser, M. (2006). Chunking, priming, and active learning: Toward an innovative approach to teaching communication-related skills. *Interactive Learning Environment, 14*(2), 119–135.

Bousfield, W. (1935). The occurrence of clustering in the recall of randomly arranged associates. *Journal of General Psychology, 49*, 229–240.

Bransford, J. D., & McCarrell, N. S. (1974). A sketch of a cognitive approach to comprehension. In W. B. Weimer & D. J. Palermo (Eds.), *Cognition and the symbolic processes* (pp. 189–229). Lawrence Erlbaum Associates.

Briere, J., & Conte, J. (1993). Self-reported amnesia for abuse in adults molested as children. *Journal of Traumatic Stress, 6*, 21–31.

Carli, L. (1999). Cognitive reconstruction, hindsight, and reactions to victims and perpetrators. *Personality and Social Psychology Bulletin, 25*(8), 966–979. doi:10.1177/01461672992511005

Ceci, S. J., & Bruck, M. (1993). Child witness: Translating research into policy. *Social Policy Report, 7*(3), 1–30.

Ceci, S. J., & Bruck, M. (1995). *Jeopardy in the courtroom: A scientific analysis of children's testimony*. American Psychological Association.

Cheit, R. E. (2007). *The recovered memory project*. http://blogs.brown.edu/recoveredmemory/.

Christianson, S. A. (1992). *The handbook of emotion and memory: Research and theory*. Erlbaum.

Clark, R. E., Zola, S. M., & Squire, L. R. (2000). Impaired recognition memory in rats after damage to the hippocampus. *The Journal of Neuroscience, 20*(23), 8853–8860.

Collins, A. M., & Loftus, E. F. (1975). A spreading-activation theory of semantic processing. *Psychological Review, 82*, 407–428. https://psycnet.apa.org/record/1976-03421-001

Corkin, S. (1965). Tactually-guided maze learning in man: Effects of unilateral cortical excisions and bilateral hippocampal lesions. *Neuropsychologia, 3*, 339–351.

Corkin, S. (1968). Acquisition of motor skill after bilateral medial temporal-lobe excision. *Neuropsychologia, 6*, 255–264.

Corkin, S., Amaral D. G., González, R. G., Johnson, K. A., & Hyman, B. T. (1997). H. M.'s medial temporal lobe lesion: Findings from magnetic resonance imaging. *Journal of Neuroscience, 17*(10), 3964–3979.

Cowan, N. (2010). The magical mystery tour: How is working memory capacity limited, and why? *Current Directions in Psychological Science, 19*, 51–57. https://www.ncbi.nlm.nih.gov/pmc/articles/PMC2864034/

Craik, F. I. M., & Lockhart, R. S. (1972). Levels of processing: A framework for memory research. *Journal of Verbal Learning and Verbal Behavior, 11*, 671–684.

Craik, F. I. M., Moroz, T. M., Moscovitch, M., Stuss, D. T., Winocur, G., Tulving, E., & Kapur, S. (1999). In search of the self: A positron emission tomography study. *Psychological Science, 10*(1), 26–34.

Craik, F. I. M., & Tulving, E. (1975). Depth of processing and the retention of words in episodic memory. *Journal of Experimental Psychology, 104*(3), 268–294.

Craik, F. I. M., & Watkins, M. J. (1973). The role of rehearsal in short-term memory. *Journal of Verbal Learning and Verbal Behavior, 12*, 599–607.

Green, J. T., & Woodruff-Pak, D. S. (2000). Eyeblink classical conditioning in aging animals. In D. S. Woodruff-Pak & J. E. Steinmetz (Eds.), *Eyeblink classical conditioning: Animal models* (Vol. 2, pp.155–178). Kluwer Academic.

Greenberg, D. L. (2004). President Bush's false [flashbulb] memory of 9/11/01. *Applied. Cognitive Psychology, 18*(3), 363–370. doi:10.1002/acp.1016

Devilly, G. J. (2007). If nothing happened why do I still hurt? An update on the memory wars. *InPsych, 29*(2), 16–18.

Ebbinghaus, H. (1964). *Memory: A contribution to experimental psychology* (H. A. Ruger & C. E. Bussenius, Trans.). Dover. (Original work published 1885)

Giddan, N. S., & Eriksen, C. W. (1959). Generalization of response biases acquired with and without verbal awareness. *Journal of Personality, 27*, 104–115. https://psycnet.apa.org/record/1960-03930-001

Goodman, G. S. (2006). Children's eyewitness memory: A modern history and contemporary commentary. *Journal of Social Issues, 62*, 811–832.

Greenspoon, J. (1955). The reinforcing effect of two spoken sounds on the frequency of two responses. *American Journal of Psychology, 68*, 409–416. https://psycnet.apa.org/record/1956-04488-001

Hassabis D., & Maguire E. A. (2007). Deconstructing episodic memory with construction. *Trends in Cognitive Sciences, 11*(7), 299–306.

Jacobs, J. (1887). Experiments on "prehension." *Mind, 12*, 75–79.

Jacoby, L. L. (1983). Perceptual enhancement: Persistent effects of an experience. *Journal of Experimental Psychology: Learning, Memory, and Cognition, 9,* 21–38. https://www.ncbi.nlm.nih.gov/pubmed/6220114

Jacoby, L. L., & Witherspoon, D. (1982). Remembering without awareness. *Canadian Journal of Psychology, 36,* 300–324. https://psycnet.apa.org/record/1983-04928-001

Johnson, K. E., & Mervis, C. B. (1997). Effects of varying levels of expertise on the basic level of categorization. *Journal of Experimental Psychology, General, 126,* 248–277. https://psycnet.apa.org/record/1997-05801-003

Johnson, K. E., & Mervis, C. B. (1998). Impact of intuitive theories on feature recruitment throughout the continuum of expertise. *Memory & Cognition, 26,* 382–401. https://link.springer.com/article/10.3758/BF03201148

Josselyn, J. A. (2010). Continuing the search for the engram: Examining the mechanism of fear memories. *Journal of Psychiatry Neuroscience, 35*(4), 221–228.

Kapur, S., Craik, F. I. M., Tulving, E., Wilson, A. A., Houle, S., & Brown, G. M. (1994). Neuroanatomical correlates of encoding in episodic memory: Levels of processing effect. *Proceedings of the National Academy of Sciences of the United States of America, 91*(6), 208–2011.

Keppel, G., & Underwood, B. J. (1962). Proactive inhibition in short-term retention of single items. *Journal of Verbal Learning & Verbal Behavior, 1,* 153–161. https://www.sciencedirect.com/science/article/abs/pii/S0022537162800231

Krieckhaus, E. E., & Eriksen, C. W. (1960). A study of awareness and its effects on learning and generalization. *Journal of Personality, 28,* 503–517. https://psycnet.apa.org/record/1961-04444-001

Lacey, J. L., & Smith, R. L. (1954). Conditioning and generalization of unconscious anxiety. *Science, 120,* 1045–1052. https://www.ncbi.nlm.nih.gov/pubmed/13216221

Lashley K. S. (1950). In search of the engram. *Society of Experimental Biology Symposium, 4: Psychological Mechanisms in Animal Behavior.* Cambridge University Press.

Lazarus, R. S., & McCleary, R. (1951). Autonomic discrimination without awareness: A study of subception. *Psychological Review, 58,* 113–122. https://www.ncbi.nlm.nih.gov/pubmed/14834294

Loftus, E. F., & Palmer, J. C. (1974). Reconstruction of auto-mobile destruction: An example of the interaction between language and memory. *Journal of Verbal Learning and Verbal Behavior, 13,* 585–589.

MacLeod, C. M., Gopie, N., Hourihan, K. L., Neary, K. R., & Ozubko, J. D. (2010). The production effect: Delineation of a phenomenon. *Journal of Experimental Psychology: Learning, Memory, and Cognition, 36*(3), 671–685.

Mayford, M., Siegelbaum, S. A., & Kandel, E. R. (2012). *Synapses and memory storage.* Cold Spring Harbor Perspectives in Biology, Cold Spring Harbor Laboratory Press.

McGaugh, J. L. (2003). *Memory and emotion: The making of lasting memories.* Columbia University Press.

McLeod, S. A. (2011). Anterograde amnesia. http://www.simplypsychology.org/anterograde-amnesia.html

Miller, G. A. (1956). The magical number seven, plus or minus two: Some limits on our capacity for processing information. *Psychological Review, 68,* 81–87.

Myhrer, T. (2003). Neurotransmitter systems involved in learning and memory in the rat: A meta-analysis based on studies of four behavioral tasks. *Brain Research Reviews, 41*(2–3), 268–287.

Newseum. (n.d.). G-men and journalists: D. C. sniper. http://www.newseum.org/exhibits-and-theaters/temporary-exhibits/g-men-and-journalists/sniper/

Nickerson, R. S., & Adams, M. J. (1979). Long-term memory for a common object. *Cognitive Psychology,*

11(3), 287–307.

Olson, M. A., & Fazio, R. H. (2001). Implicit attitude formation through classical conditioning. *Psychological Science, 12*, 413–417. https://www.ncbi.nlm.nih.gov/pubmed/11554676

Paivio, A. (1986). *Mental representations: A dual coding approach*. Oxford University Press.

Palmer, C. F., Jones, R. K., Hennessy, B. L., Unze, M. G., & Pick, A. D. (1989). How is a trumpet known? The "basic object level" concept and perception of musical instruments. *American Journal of Psychology, 102*, 17–37. https://www.jstor.org/stable/1423114?seq=1

Parker, E. S., Cahill, L., & McGaugh, J. L. (2006). A case of unusual autobiographical remembering. *Neurocase, 12*, 35–49.

Payne, B. K., Jacoby, L. L., & Lambert, A. J. (2004). Memory monitoring and the control of stereotype distortion. *Journal of Experimental Social Psychology, 40*, 52–64.

Peterson, L., & Peterson, M. J. (1959). Short-term retention of individual verbal items. *Journal of Experimental Psychology, 58*(3), 193–198. https://psycnet.apa.org/record/1960-05499-001

Pew Research Center (2011, September 1). *Ten years after 9/11: United in remembrance, divided over policies*. People Press.

Pipe, M.-E. (1996). Children's eyewitness memory. *New Zealand Journal of Psychology, 25*(2), 36–43.

Pipe, M.-E., Lamb, M., Orbach, Y., & Esplin, P. W. (2004). Recent research on children's testimony about experienced and witnessed events. *Developmental Review, 24*, 440–468.

Reber, A. S. (1976). Implicit learning of synthetic languages: The role of instructional set. *Journal of Experimental Psychology: Human Learning and Memory, 2*, 88–94. https://psycnet.apa.org/doiLanding?doi=10.1037%2F0278-7393.2.1.88

Roediger, H. L., III. (1990). Implicit memory: Retention without remembering. *American Psychologist, 45*, 1043–1056. https://www.ncbi.nlm.nih.gov/pubmed/2221571

Roediger, H. L., & DeSoto, K. A. (2015). The psychology of reconstructive memory. In J. Wright (Ed.), *International Encyclopedia of the Social and Behavioral sciences*, 2e. Elsevier.

Roediger, H. L., III, & McDermott, K. B. (2000). Tricks of memory. *Current Directions in Psychological Science, 9*, 123–127.

Rogers, T. B., Kuiper, N. A., & Kirker, W. S. (1977). Self-reference and the encoding of personal information. *Journal of Personal Social Psychology, 35*(9), 677–688.

Rosch, E., Mervis, C. B., Gray, W. D., Johnson, D. M., & Boyes-Braem, P. (1976). Basic objects in natural categories. *Cognitive Psychology, 8*(3), 382–439. https://psycnet.apa.org/record/1976-27194-001

Schacter, D. L. (1987). Implicit memory: History and current status. *Journal of Experimental Psychology: Learning, Memory, and Cognition, 13*, 501–551. https://pdfs.semanticscholar.org/8c35/06e3c78a987fb5a704bc60611680fcb5365b.pdf

Schacter, D. L. (1992). Priming and multiple memory systems: Perceptual mechanisms of implicit memory. *Journal of Cognitive Neuroscience 4*, 244–256. https://dash.harvard.edu/bitstream/handle/1/3627272/Schacter_PrimingMultiple.pdf?sequence=2

Schacter, D. (2001). *The seven sins of memory: How the mind forgets and remembers*. Houghton Mifflin.

Steinmetz, J. E. (1999). A renewed interest in human classical eyeblink conditioning. *Psychological Science, 10*, 24–25.

Tanaka, J. M., & Taylor, M. (1991). Object categories and expertise: Is the basic level in the eye of the beholder? *Cognitive Psychology, 23*, 457–482. http://citeseerx.ist.psu.edu/viewdoc/download?doi=10.1.1.320.9949&rep=rep1&type=pdf

Tigner, R. B. (1999). Putting memory research to good use. *College Teaching, 47*(4), 149–152.

Tulving, E. (1972). Episodic and semantic memory. In E. Tulving & W. Dolandson (Eds.), *Organization of memory* (pp. 381–403). Academic Press.

Tulving, E. (2002, February). Episodic memory: From mind to brain. *Annual Review of Psychology, 53*, 1–25. doi:10.1146/annurev.psych.53.100901.135114

van Praag, H. (2008). Neurogenesis and exercise: Past and future directions. *NeuroMolecular Medicine, 10*(2), 128–140.

Wells, G. L., & Quinlivan, D. S. (2009). Suggestive eyewitness identification procedures and the Supreme Court's reliability test in light of eyewitness science: 30 years later. *Law and Human Behavior, 33*, 1–24. doi:10.1007/s10979-008-9130-3

Wrubel, B. (Writer), & Spiller, M. (Director). (2010). The Old Wagon. In S. Levitan & C. Lloyd (Executive producers), *Modern Family*. 20th Century Fox Television.

Yang, J., Xu, X., Du, X., Shi, C., & Fang, F. (2011). Effects of unconscious processing on implicit memory for fearful faces. *PLoS One, 6*(2). https://journals.plos.org/plosone/article?id=10.1371/journal.pone.0014641

Yogo, M., & Fujihara, S. (2008). Working memory capacity can be improved by expressive writing: A randomized experiment in a Japanese sample. *British Journal of Health Psychology, 13*(1), 77–80. doi:10.1348/135910707X252440

Lifespan Development

Ainsworth, M. D. S., & Bell, S. M. (1970). Attachment, exploration, and separation: Illustrated by the behavior of one-year-olds in a strange situation. *Child Development, 41*, 49–67.

Ainsworth, M. D. S., Blehar, M. C., Waters, E., & Wall, S. (1978). *Patterns of attachment: A psychological study of the strange situation*. Erlbaum.

American Academy of Pediatrics. (2007). The importance of play in promoting healthy child development and maintaining strong parent-child bonds. *Pediatrics, 199*(1), 182–191.

American Psychological Association. (2019). *Ruth Howard, PhD*. https://www.apa.org/pi/oema/resources/ethnicity-health/psychologists/ruth-howard

Amsterdam, B. (1972). Mirror image reactions before age two. *Developmental Psychobiology, 5*, 297–305.

Archer, J. (1992). *Ethology and human development*. Harvester Wheatsheaf.

Arnett, J. (2000). Emerging adulthood: A theory of development from the late teens through the twenties. *American Psychologist, 55*(5), 469–480.

Arora, R., Mittal, A., & Kakkar, R. (2015). Alzheimer's disease: Recent advances. *Journal of Biochemistry and Molecular Biology Research, 1*, 87–104.

Ashley, S. J., Magnuson, S. I., Omnell, L. M., & Clarren, S. K. (1999). Fetal alcohol syndrome: Changes in craniofacial form with age, cognition, and timing of ethanol exposure in the macaque. *Teratology, 59*(3), 163–172.

Bahr, S. J., & Hoffman, J. P. (2010). Parenting style, religiosity, peers, and adolescent heavy drinking. *Journal of Studies on Alcohol and Drugs, 71*, 539–543.

Baillargeon, R. (2004). Infants' reasoning about hidden objects: Evidence for event-general and event-specific expectations. *Developmental Science, 7*(4), 391–424.

Baillargeon, R. (1987). Young infants' reasoning about the physical and spatial properties of a hidden object. *Cognitive Development, 2*(3), 179–200.

Baillargeon, R., Li, J., Gertner, Y., & Wu, D. (2011). How do infants reason about physical events. *The Wiley-Blackwell handbook of childhood cognitive development, 2*, 11–48.

Barber, B. K. (1994). Cultural, family, and person contexts of parent-adolescent conflict. *Journal of Marriage and the Family, 56*, 375–386.

Basseches, M. (1984). Dialectical thinking as metasystematic form of cognitive organization. In M. L. Commons, F. A. Richards, & C. Armon (Eds.), *Beyond formal operations: Late adolescent and adult cognitive development* (pp. 216–238). Praeger.

Baumrind, D. (1971). Current patterns of parental authority. *Developmental Psychology, 4*(1, Pt. 2), 1–103. doi:10.1037/h0030372

Baumrind, D. (1991). The influence of parenting style on adolescent competence and substance use. *Journal of Early Adolescence, 11*(1), 56–95.

Bayley, N., & Oden, M. H. (1955). The maintenance of intellectual ability in gifted adults. *Journal of Gerontology, 10*, 91–107.

Benjamin, L., Henry, K., & McMahon, L. (2005). Inez Beverly Prosser and the education of African Americans. *Journal of the History of the Behavioral Sciences, 41*, 43–62.

Bjorklund, D. F. (1987). A note on neonatal imitation. *Developmental Review, 7*, 86–92.

Blossom, M., & Morgan, J.L. (2006). Does the face say what the mouth says? A study of infants' sensitivity to visual prosody. In *30th anuual Boston University conference on language development, Somerville, MA*.

Bogartz, R. S., Shinskey, J. L., & Schilling, T. (2000). *Infancy, 1*(4), 403–428.

Bowlby, J. (1969). *Attachment and loss: Attachment* (Vol. 1). Basic Books.

Bowlby, J. (1988). *A secure base: Parent-child attachment and health human development*. Basic Books.

Bronfenbrenner, U. (1977). Toward an experimental ecology of human development. *American Psychologist, 32*, 513–531.

Brumley, R., Enquidanos, S., Jamison, P., Seitz, R., Morgenstern, N., Saito, S., . . . Gonzalez, J. (2007). Increased satisfaction with care and lower costs: Results of a randomized trial of in-home palliative care. *Journal of the American Geriatric Society, 55*(7), 993–1000.

Brumley, R. D., Enquidanos, S., & Cherin, D. A. (2003). Effectiveness of a home-based palliative care program for end-of-life. *Journal of Palliative Medicine, 6*(5), 715–724.

Callaghan, T. C., Rochat, P., Lillard, A., Claux, M.L., Odden, H., Itakura, S., . . . Singh, S. (2005). Synchrony in the onset of mental-state reasoning. *Psychological Science, 16*, 378–384.

Carel, J-C., Lahlou, N., Roger, M., & Chaussain, J. L. (2004). Precocious puberty and statural growth. *Human Reproduction Update, 10*(2), 135–147.

Carstensen, L. L. (1992). Social and emotional patterns in adulthood: Support for socioemotional selectivity. *Psychology and Aging, 7*(3), 331–338.

Case, R. (1985). *Intellectual development: Birth to Adulthood*. Academic.

Casey, B. J., Tottenham, N., Liston, C., & Durston, S. (2005). Imaging the developing brain: What have we learned about cognitive development? *TRENDS in Cognitive Sciences, 19*(3), 104–110.

Centers for Disease Control and Prevention. (2013). *Smoking during pregnancy*. http://www.cdc.gov/tobacco/basic_information/health_effects/pregnancy/

Chick, K., Heilman-Houser, R., & Hunter, M. (2002). The impact of child care on gender role development and gender stereotypes. *Early Childhood Education Journal, 29*(3), 149–154.

Chomsky, N. (1957). *Syntactic structures*. Mouton.

Clark, K. & Clark, M. (1950). Emotional factors in racial identification and preference in Negro children. *Journal of Negro Education, 19*, 341–350.

Clements, R. (2004). An investigation of the status of outdoor play. *Contemporary Issues in Early Childhood,*

5(1), 68–80.

Commons, M. L., & Bresette, L. M. (2006). Illuminating major creative scientific innovators with postformal stages. In C. Hoare (Ed.), *Handbook of adult development and learning* (pp. 255–280). Oxford University Press.

Connor, S. R., Pyenson, B., Fitch, K., Spence, C., & Iwasaki, K. (2007). Comparing hospice and nonhospice patient survival among patients who die within a three-year window. *Journal of Pain and Symptom Management, 33*(3), 238–246.

Courage, M. L., & Howe, M. L. (2002). From infant to child: The dynamics of cognitive change in the second year of life. *Psychological Bulletin, 128,* 250–277.

Curtiss, S. (1981). Dissociations between language and cognition: Cases and implications. *Journal of Autism and Developmental Disorders, 11*(1), 15–30.

Darling, N. (1999). *Parenting style and its correlates.* ERIC database (EDO-PS-99-3) http://ecap.crc.illinois.edu/eecearchive/digests/1999/darlin99.pdf

de Hevia, M. D., & Spelke, E. S. (2010). Number-space mapping in human infants. *Psychological Science, 21*(5), 653–660.

Dennett, D. (1987). *The intentional stance*. MIT Press.

Diamond, A. (2009). The interplay of biology and the environment broadly defined. *Developmental Psychology, 45*(1), 1–8.

Donenberg, G. R., Wilson, H. W., Emerson, E., Bryant, F. B. (2002). Holding the line with a watchful eye: The impact of perceived parental permissiveness and parental monitoring on risky sexual behavior among adolescents in psychiatric care. *AIDS Education Prevention, 14*(2), 138–157.

Dornbusch, S. M., Ritter, P. L., Leiderman, P. H., Roberts, D. F., & Fraleigh, M. J. (1987). The relation of parenting style to adolescent school performance. *Child Development, 58*(5), 1244–1257.

Duncan, G. J., & Magnuson, K. A. (2005). Can family socioeconomic resources account for racial and ethnic test score gaps? *The Future of Children, 15*(1), 35–54.

Erikson, E. H. (1963). *Childhood and Society* (2nd ed.). Norton.

Erikson, E. H. (1968). *Identity: Youth and crisis*. Norton.

Ferrer, M., & Fugate, A. (2003). *Helping your school-age child develop a healthy self-concept.* http://edis.ifas.ufl.edu/fy570#FOOTNOTE_2

Figdor, E., & Kaeser, L. (1998). Concerns mount over punitive approaches to substance abuse among pregnant women. *The Guttmacher Report on Public Policy 1*(5), 3–5.

Fischer, K. W., Yan, Z., & Stewart, J. (2003). Adult cognitive development: Dynamics in the developmental web. In J. Valsiner & K Connolly (Eds.), *Handbook of developmental psychology* (pp. 491–516). Sage Publications.

Flannery, D. J., Rowe, D. C., & Gulley, B. L. (1993). Impact of pubertal status, timing, and age on adolescent sexual experience and delinquency. *Journal of Adolescent Research, 8,* 21–40.

Forstmann, B., Tittgemeyer, M., Wagenmakers, E., Derrfuss, J., Imperati, D., & Brown, S. (2011). The speed-accuracy tradeoff in the elderly brain: A structural model-based approach. *Journal of Neuroscience, 31,* 17242–17249.

Freud, S. (1909). Analysis of a phobia in a five-year-old boy. In *Collected Papers: Volume 111, Case Histories (1949)* (pp. 149–289). Hogarth Press.

Fromkin, V., Krashen, S., Curtiss, S., Rigler, D., & Rigler, M. (1974). The development of language in Genie: A case of language acquisition beyond the critical period. *Brain and Language, 1,* 81–107.

Galambos, N. L., & Almeida, D. M. (1992). Does parent-adolescent conflict increase in early adolescence? *Journal of Marriage and the Family, 54*, 737–747.

Galvan, A., Hare, T., Voss, H., Glover, G., & Casey, B. J. (2007). Risk-taking and the adolescent brain: Who is at risk? *Developmental Science, 10*, F8–F14.

Ganger, J., & Brent, M.R. (2004). Reexamining the vocabulary spurt. *Developmental Psychology, 40*(4), 621–632.

Garcia-Betances, R., Jimenez-Mixco, V., Arredondo, M., & Cabrera-Umpierrez, M. (2015). Using virtual reality for cognitive training of the elderly. *American Journal of Alzheimer's Disease and Other Dementias, 30*, 49–54.

Ge, X., Conger, R. D., & Elder, G. H. (2001). Pubertal transition, stressful life events, and the emergence of gender differences in adolescent depressive symptoms. *Developmental Psychology, 37*, 404–417.

Gervai, J. (2009). Environmental and genetic influences on early attachment. *Child and Adolescent Psychiatry and Mental Health, 3*, 25.

Gesell, A. (1933). Maturation and the patterning of behavior. In C. Murchison (Ed.), *A handbook of child psychology* (2nd ed., pp. 209–235). Clark University Press.

Gesell, A. (1939). *Biographies of child development*. Paul B. Hoeber.

Gesell, A. (1940). *The first five years of life*. Harper.

Gesell, A., & Ilg, F. L. (1946). *The child from five to ten*. Harper.

Gilligan, C. (1982). *In a different voice: Psychological theory and women's development*. Harvard University Press.

Gleitman, L. R., & Newport, E. L. (1995). The invention of language by children: Environmental and biological influences on the acquisition of language. In L. R. Gleitman & M. Liberman (Eds.), *An invitation to cognitive science, Vol. 1: Language.* (2nd ed.) (pp. 1–24). MIT Press.

Godkin, M., Krant, M., & Doster, N. (1984). The impact of hospice care on families. *International Journal of Psychiatry in Medicine, 13*, 153–165.

Graber, J. A., Lewinsohn, P. M., Seeley, J. R., & Brooks-Gunn, J. (1997). Is psychopathology associated with the timing of pubertal development? *Journal of the Academy of Child and Adolescent Psychiatry, 36*, 1768–1776.

Hair, E. C., Moore, K. A., Garrett, S. B., Kinukawa, A., Lippman, L., & Michelson, E. (2005). The parent-adolescent relationship scale. In L. Lippman (Ed.), *Conceptualizing and Measuring Indicators of Positive Development: What Do Children Need to Fluorish?* (pp. 183–202). Kluwer Academic/Plenum Press.

Hall, G. S. (1904). *Adolescence*. Appleton.

Hall, S. S. (2004, May). The good egg. *Discover*, 30–39.

Harlow, H. (1958). The nature of love. *American Psychologist, 13*, 673–685.

Harris, J. R. (2009). *The nurture assumption: Why children turn out the way they do* (2nd ed.). Free Press.

Hart, B., & Risley, T. R. (2003). The early catastrophe: The 30 million word gap. *American Educator, 27*(1), 4–9.

Hatch, E. (1983). *Psycholinguistics: A second language perspective*. Newbury House.

Hertzog, C., Kramer, A. F., Wilson, R. S., & Lindenberger, U. (2009). Enrichment effects on adult cognitive development. *Psychological Science in the Public Interest, 9*(1), 1–65.

Hood, R. W., Jr., Spilka, B., Hunsberger, B., & Corsuch, R. (1996). *The psychology of religion: An empirical approach* (2nd ed.). Guilford.

Huebler, F. (2005, December 14). International education statistics. http://huebler.blogspot.com/2005/

12/age-and-level-of-education-in-nigeria.html

Hutchinson, N. (2011). A geographically informed vision of skills development. *Geographical Education, 24*, 15.

Huttenlocher, P. R., & Dabholkar, A. S. (1997). Regional differences in synaptogenesis in human cerebral cortex. *Journal of Comparative Neurology, 387*(2), 167–178.

Iverson, J.M., & Goldin-Meadow, S. (2005). Gesture paves the way for language development. *Psychological Science, 16*(5), 367–71.

Iyengar, S. S., Wells, R. E., & Schwartz, B. (2006). Doing better but feeling worse: Looking for the best job undermines satisfaction. *Psychological Science, 17*, 143–150.

John-Steiner, V. & Mahn, H. (1996). Sociocultural approaches to learning and development: A Vygotskian framework. *Educational Psychologist, 31*, 191–206.

Jos, P. H., Marshall, M. F., & Perlmutter, M. (1995). The Charleston policy on cocaine use during pregnancy: A cautionary tale. *The Journal of Law, Medicine & Ethics, 23*(2), 120–128.

Kaltiala-Heino, R. A., Rimpela, M., Rissanen, A., & Rantanen, P. (2001). Early puberty and early sexual activity are associated with bulimic-type eating pathology in middle adolescence. *Journal of Adolescent Health, 28*, 346–352.

Kaplan, H., & Dove, H. (1987). Infant development among the Aché of Eastern Paraguay. *Developmental Psychology, 23*, 190–198.

Karasik, L. B., Adolph, K. E., Tamis-LeMonda, C. S., & Bornstein, M. H. (2010). WEIRD Walking: Cross-cultural research on motor development. *Behavioral & Brain Sciences, 33*(2-3), 95–96.

Karnik, S., & Kanekar, A. (2012). Childhood obesity: A global public health crisis. *International Journal of Preventive Medicine, 3*(1), 1–7.

Kohlberg, L. (1969). Stage and sequence: The cognitive-developmental approach to socialization. In D. A. Goslin (Ed.), *Handbook of socialization theory and research* (p. 379). Rand McNally.

Kolb, B., & Whishaw, I. Q. (2009). *Fundamentals of human neuropsychology*. Worth.

Kübler-Ross, E. (1969). *On death and dying*. Macmillan.

Labouvie-Vief, G., & Diehl, M. (1999). Self and personality development. In J. C. Cavanaugh & S. K. Whitbourne (Eds.), *Gerontology: An interdisciplinary perspective* (pp. 238–268). Oxford University Press.

Larson, E. B., Wang, L., Bowen, J. D., McCormick, W. C., Teri, L., Crane, P., & Kukull, W. (2006). Exercise is associated with reduced risk for incident dementia among persons 65 years of age or older. *Annals of Internal Medicine, 144*, 73–81.

Lee, V. E., & Burkam, D. T. (2002). *Inequality at the starting gate: Social background differences in achievement as children begin school*. Economic Policy Institute.

Lobo, I. (2008) Environmental influences on gene expression. *Nature Education 1*(1), 39.

Loop, E. (2013). *Major milestones in cognitive development in early childhood*. http://everydaylife.globalpost.com/major-milestones-cognitive-development-early-childhood-4625.html

Maccoby, E. (1980). *Social development: Psychological growth and the parent-child relationship*. Harcourt Brace Jovanovich.

MacFarlane, A. (1978, February). What a baby knows. *Human Nature*, 74–81.

Maier, S. E., & West, J. R. (2001). Drinking patterns and alcohol-related birth defects. *Alcohol Research & Health, 25*(3), 168–174.

Main, M., & Solomon, J. (1990). Procedures for identifying infants as disorganized/disoriented during the

Ainsworth Strange Situation. In M. T. Greenberg, D. Cicchetti, & E. M. Cummings (Eds.), *Attachment in the Preschool Years* (pp. 121–160). University of Chicago Press.

Markus, H. R., Ryff, C. D., Curan, K., & Palmersheim, K. A. (2004). In their own words: Well-being at midlife among high school-educated and college-educated adults. In O. G. Brim, C. D. Ryff, & R. C. Kessler (Eds.), *How healthy are we? A national study of well-being at midlife* (pp. 273–319). University of Chicago Press.

McIntosh, D. N., Silver, R. C., & Wortman, C. B. (1993). Religion's role in adjustment to a negative life event: Coping with the loss of a child. *Journal of Personality and Social Psychology, 65*, 812–821.

McMillan, S. C., Small, B. J., Weitzner, M., Schonwetter, R., Tittle, M., Moody, L., & Haley, W. E. (2006). Impact of coping skills intervention with family caregivers of hospice patients with cancer. *Cancer, 106*(1), 214-222.

Miklikowska, M., Duriez, B., & Soenens, B. (2011). Family roots of empathy-related characteristics: The role of perceived maternal and paternal need support in adolescence. *Developmental Psychology, 47*(5), 1342–1352.

Mills, M., & Melhuish, E. (1974). Recognition of mother's voice in early infancy. *Nature, 252*, 123–124.

Mohr, R. D., & Zoghi, C. (2006). Is job enrichment really enriching? (U.S. Bureau of Labor Statistics Working Paper 389). Washington, DC: U.S. Bureau of Labor Statistics. http://www.bls.gov/ore/pdf/ec060010.pdf

Moore, K. A., Guzman, L., Hair, E. C., Lippman, L., & Garrett, S. B. (2004). Parent-teen relationships and interactions: Far more positive than not. *Child Trends Research Brief, 2004-25*. Child Trends.

National Institutes of Health. (2013). *What is prenatal care and why is it important?* http://www.nichd.nih.gov/health/topics/pregnancy/conditioninfo/Pages/prenatal-care.aspx

Neblett, E., Smalls, C., Ford, K., Nguyen, H., & Sellers, R. (2009). Racial socialization and racial identity: African American parents' messages about race as precursors to identity. *Journal of Youth and Adolescence, 38*, 189–203.

Newcombe, N. (2011). What is neoconstructivism? *Child Development Perspectives, 5*, 157–160.

Nolen-Hoeksema, S., & Larson, J. (1999). *Coping with loss*. Erlbaum.

Overman, W. H., Bachevalier, J., Turner, M., & Peuster, A. (1992). Object recognition versus object discrimination: Comparison between human infants and infant monkeys. *Behavioral Neuroscience, 106*, 15–29.

Paloutzian, R. F. (1996). *Invitation to the psychology of religion*. Allyn & Bacon.

Parent, J., Forehand, R., Merchant, M. J., Edwards, M. C., Conners-Burrow, N. A., Long, N., & Jones, D. J. (2011). The relation of harsh and permissive discipline with child disruptive behaviors: Does child gender make a difference in an at-risk sample? *Journal of Family Violence, 26*, 527–533.

Piaget, J. (1954). *The construction of reality in the child*. Basic Books.

Pickens, J. (1994). Full-term and preterm infants' perception of face-voice synchrony. *Infant Behavior and Development, 17*, 447–455.

Piaget, J. (1930). *The child's conception of the world*. Harcourt, Brace & World.

Piaget, J. (1932). *The moral judgment of the child*. Harcourt, Brace & World.

Podewils, L. J., Guallar, E., Kuller, L. H., Fried, L. P., Lopez, O. L., Carlson, M., & Lyketsos, C. G. (2005). Physical activity, APOE genotype, and dementia risk: Findings from the Cardiovascular Health Cognition Study. *American Journal of Epidemiology, 161*, 639–651.

Pollack, W., & Shuster, T. (2000). *Real boys' voices*. Random House.

Rhodes, R. L., Mitchell, S. L., Miller, S. C., Connor, S. R., & Teno, J. M. (2008). Bereaved family members' evaluation of hospice care: What factors influence overall satisfaction with services? *Journal of Pain and Symptom Management, 35*, 365–371.

Risley, T. R., & Hart, B. (2006). Promoting early language development. In N. F. Watt, C. Ayoub, R. H. Bradley, J. E. Puma, & W. A. LeBoeuf (Eds.), *The crisis in youth mental health: Early intervention programs and policies* (Vol. 4, pp. 83–88). Praeger.

Rogers, L. & Meltzoff, A. (2017). Is gender more important and meaningful than race? An analysis of racial and gender identity among black, white, and mixed-race children. *Cultural Diversity and Ethnic Minority Psychology, 23*, 323–334.

Rothbaum, R., Weisz, J., Pott, M., Miyake, K., & Morelli, G. (2000). Attachment and culture: Security in the United States and Japan. *American Psychologist, 55*, 1093–1104.

Ruggiero, G., D'Errico, O., & Iachini, T. (2016). Development of egocentric and allocentric spatial representations from childhood to elderly age. *Psychological Research, 80*, 259–272.

Russell, S. T., Crockett, L. J., & Chao, R. (Eds.). (2010). Asian American parenting and parent-adolescent relationships. In R. Levesque (Series Ed.), *Advancing responsible adolescent development*. Springer.

Ryff, C. D., & Singer, B. (2009). Understanding healthy aging: Key components and their integration. In V. L. Bengtson, D. Gans., N. M. Putney, & M. Silverstein. (Eds.), *Handbook of theories of aging* (2nd ed., pp. 117–144). Springer.

Samarel, N. (1991). *Caring for life after death*. Hemisphere.

Sanson, A., & Rothbart, M. K. (1995). Child temperament and parenting. In M. Bornstein (Ed.), *Applied and practical parenting* (Vol. 4, pp. 299–321). Lawrence Erlbaum.

Schechter, C., & Byeb, B. (2007). Preliminary evidence for the impact of mixed-income preschools on low-income children's language growth. *Early Childhood Research Quarterly, 22*, 137–146.

Shamay-Tsoory, S. G., Tomer, R., & Aharon-Peretz, J. (2005). The neuroanatomical basis of understanding sarcasm and its relationship to social cognition. *Neuropsychology, 19*(3), 288–300.

Shanahan, L., McHale, S. M., Osgood, D. W., & Crouter, A. C. (2007). Conflict frequency with mothers and fathers from middle childhood to late adolescence: Within and between family comparisons. *Developmental Psychology, 43*, 539–550.

Siegler, R. S. (2005). *Children's thinking* (4th ed). Erlbaum.

Siegler, R. S. (2006). Microgenetic analyses of learning. In D. Kuhn & R. S. Siegler (Eds.), *Handbook of child psychology: Cognition, perception, and language* (6th ed., Vol. 2). Wiley.

Sinnott, J. D. (1998). *The development of logic in adulthood: Postformal thought and its applications*. Springer.

Small, M. F. (1999). *Our babies, ourselves: How biology and culture shape the way we parent*. Anchor Books.

Spelke, E.S., & Cortelyou, A. (1981). Perceptual aspects of social knowing: Looking and listening in infancy. In M.E. Lamb & L.R. Sherrod (Eds.), *Infant social cognition: Empirical and theoretical considerations* (pp. 61–83). Erlbaum.

Spencer, M. B., Dupree, D., & Hartmann, T. (1997). A phenomenological variant of ecological systems theory (PVEST): A self-organization perspective in context. *Development and Psychopathology, 9*, 817–833.

Steinberg, L., & Morris, A. S. (2001). Adolescent development. *Annual Review of Psychology, 52*, 83–110.

Sterns, H. L., & Huyck, M. H. (2001). The role of work in midlife. In M. Lachman (Ed.), *The handbook of midlife development* (pp. 447–486). Wiley.

Steven L. Youngentob, et. al. (2007). Experience-induced fetal plasticity: The effect of gestational ethanol exposure on the behavioral and neurophysiologic olfactory response to ethanol odor in early postnatal and adult rats. *Behavioral Neuroscience, 121*(6), 1293–1305.

Stork, F. C., & Widdowson, D. A. (1974). *Learning about linguistics*. Hutchinson Ltd.

Streissguth, A. P., Bookstein, F. L., Barr, H. M., Sampson, P. D., O'Malley, K., & Young, J. K. (2004). Risk factors for adverse life outcomes in fetal alcohol syndrome and fetal alcohol effects. *Developmental and Behavioral Pediatrics, 25*(4), 228–238.

Striegel-Moore, R. H., & Cachelin, F. M. (1999). Body image concerns and disordered eating in adolescent girls: Risk and protective factors. In N. G. Johnson, M. C. Roberts, & J. Worell (Eds.), *Beyond appearance: A new look at adolescent girls*. American Psychological Association

Tanner, J. M. (1978). *Fetus into man: Physical growth from conception to maturity*. Harvard University Press.

Temel, J. S., Greer, J. A., Muzikansky, A., Gallagher, E. R., Admane, S., Jackson, V. A. . . . Lynch, T. J. (2010). Early palliative care for patients with metastic non-small-cell lung cancer. *New England Journal of Medicine, 363*, 733–742.

Thomas, A. (1984). Temperament research: Where we are, where we are going. *Merrill-Palmer Quarterly, 30*(2), 103–109.

Tran, T. D., & Kelly, S. J. (2003). Critical periods for ethanol-induced cell loss in the hippocampal formation. *Neurotoxicology and Teratology, 25*(5), 519–528.

Umberson, D., Pudrovska, T., & Reczek, C. (2010). Parenthood, childlessness, and well-being: A life course perspective. *Journal of Marriage and the Family, 72*(3), 612–629.

United Nations Educational, Scientific and Cultural Organization. (2013, June). *UIS Fact Sheet: Schooling for millions of children jeopardized by reductions in aid*. UNESCO Institute for Statistics.

Vaillant, G. E. (2002). *Aging well*. Little Brown & Co.

Van der Graaff, J., Branje, S., De Wied, M., Hawk, S., Van Lier, P., & Meeus, W. (2013). Perspective taking and empathetic concern in adolescence: Gender differences in developmental changes. *Developmental Psychology, 50*(3), 881.

van Ijzendoorn, M. H., & Sagi-Schwartz, A. (2008). Cross-cultural patterns of attachment: Universal and contextual dimensions. In J. Cassidy & P. R. Shaver (Eds.), *Handbook of attachment*. Guilford.

Vouloumanos, A., & Werker, J. F. (2004). Tuned to the signal: The privileged status of speech for young infants. *Developmental Science, 7*, 270–276.

Westermann, G., Mareschal, D., Johnson, M., Sirois, S., Spratling, M., & Thomas, M. (2007). Neuroconstructivism. *Developmental Science, 10*, 75–83.

WHO Multicentre Growth Reference Study Group. (2006). *WHO Child growth standards: Methods and development: Length/height-for-age, weight-for-age, weight-for-length, weight-for-height and body mass index-for-age*. World Health Organization.

Winerman, L. (2011). Closing the achievement gap. *Monitor of Psychology, 42*(8), 36.

Wortman, J. H., & Park, C. L. (2008). Religion and spirituality in adjustment following bereavement: An integrative review. *Death Studies*

Emotion and Motivation

Adelmann, P. K., & Zajonc, R. B. (1989). Facial efference and the experience of emotion. *Annual Review of Psychology, 40*, 249–280. https://www.annualreviews.org/doi/abs/10.1146/annurev.ps.40.020189.001341

Ahima, R. S., & Antwi, D. A. (2008). Brain regulation of appetite and satiety. *Endocrinology and Metabolism Clinics of North America, 37*, 811–823.

Aldao, A., & Dixon-Gordon, K. L. (2014). Broadening the scope of research on emotion regulation strategies and psychopathology. *Cognitive Behaviour Therapy, 43*(1), 22–33.

https://www.tandfonline.com/doi/abs/10.1080/16506073.2013.816769

Aldao, A., Nolen-Hoeksema, S., Schweizer, S. (2010). Emotion regulation strategies across psychopathology: A meta-analysis. *Clinical Psychology Review*, *30*, 217–237. https://www.ncbi.nlm.nih.gov/pubmed/20015584

Allen, L. S., & Gorski, R. A. (1992). Sexual orientation and the size of the anterior commissure in the human brain. *Proceedings of the National Academy of Sciences, USA*, *89*, 7199–7202.

American Psychiatric Association. (2013). *Feeding and eating disorders*. http://www.dsm5.org/documents/eating%20disorders%20fact%20sheet.pdf

Arnold, H. J. (1976). Effects of performance feedback and extrinsic reward upon high intrinsic motivation. *Organizational Behavior and Human Performance, 17*, 275–288.

Bailey, M. J., & Pillard, R. C. (1991). A genetic study of male sexual orientation. *Archives of General Psychiatry, 48*, 1089–1096.

Baldwin, J. D., & Baldwin, J. I. (1989). The socialization of homosexuality and heterosexuality in a non-western society. *Archives of Sexual Behavior, 18*, 13–29.

Bancroft, J. (2004). Alfred C. Kinsey and the politics of sex research. *Annual Review of Sex Research, 15*, 1–39.

Bandura, A. (1994). Self-efficacy. In V. S. Ramachandran (Ed.), *Encyclopedia of human behavior* (Vol. 4, pp. 71–81). Academic Press.

Barrett, L. F. (2017). The theory of constructed emotion: An active inference account of interoception and categorization. *Social Cognitive and Affective Neuroscience, 12*, 1–23. https://www.ncbi.nlm.nih.gov/pmc/articles/PMC5691871/

Bauminger, N. (2002). The facilitation of social-emotional understanding and social interaction in high-functioning children with autism: Intervention outcomes. *Journal of Autism and Developmental Disorders, 32*, 283–298.

Becker, J. B., Rudick, C. N., & Jenkins, W. J. (2001). The role of dopamine in the nucleus accumbens and striatum during sexual behavior in the female rat. *Journal of Neuroscience, 21*, 3236–3241.

Becker, J. M. (2012, April 25). Dr. Robert Spitzer apologizes to gay community for infamous "ex-gay" study. http://www.truthwinsout.org/news/2012/04/24542/

Beedie, C. J., Terry, P. C., Lane, A. M., & Devonport, T. J. (2011). Differential assessment of emotions and moods: Development and validation of the emotion and mood components of anxiety questionnaire. *Personality and Individual Differences, 50*, 228–233.

Bell, A. P., Weinberg, M. S., & Hammersmith, S. K. (1981). *Sexual preferences: Its development in men and women*. Indiana University Press.

Berlyne, D. E. (1960). Toward a theory of exploratory behavior: II. Arousal potential, perceptual curiosity, and learning. In (Series Ed.), *Conflict, arousal, and curiosity* (pp. 193–227). McGraw-Hill Book Company.

Bhasin, S., Enzlin, P., Coviello, A., & Basson, R. (2007). Sexual dysfunction in men and women with endocrine disorders. *The Lancet, 369*, 597–611.

Blackford, J. U., & Pine, D. S. (2012). Neural substrates of childhood anxiety disorders: A review of neuroimaging findings. *Child and Adolescent Psychiatric Clinics of North America, 21*, 501–525.

Boiger, M., & Mesquita, B. (2012). The construction of emotion in interactions, relationships, and cultures. *Emotion Review, 4*, 221–229. https://journals.sagepub.com/doi/10.1177/1754073912439765

Bremner, J. D., & Vermetten, E. (2004). Neuroanatomical changes associated with pharmacotherapy in posttraumatic stress disorder. *Annals of the New York Academy of Sciences, 1032*, 154–157.

Buck, R. (1980). Nonverbal behavior and the theory of emotion: The facial feedback hypothesis. *Journal of Personality and Social Psychology, 38*, 811–824.

Bullough, V. L. (1998). Alfred Kinsey and the Kinsey report: Historical overview and lasting contributions. *The Journal of Sex Research, 35*, 127–131.

Byne, W., Tobet, S., Mattiace, L. A., Lasco, M. S., Kemether, E., Edgar, M. A., . . . Jones, L. B. (2001). The interstitial nuclei of the human anterior hypothalamus: An investigation of variation with sex, sexual orientation, and HIV status. *Hormones and Behavior, 40*, 86–92.

Cameron, J., & Pierce, W. D. (1994). Reinforcement, reward, and intrinsic motivation: A meta-analysis. *Review of Educational Research, 64*, 363–423.

Capella, J. N. (1993). The facial feedback hypothesis in human interaction: Review and speculation. *Journal of Language and Social Psychology, 12*(12), 13–29. https://journals.sagepub.com/doi/10.1177/0261927X93121002

Carey, B. (2012, May 18). Psychiatry giant sorry for backing gay 'cure.' *The New York Times*. http://www.nytimes.com/2012/05/19/health/dr-robert-l-spitzer-noted-psychiatrist-apologizes-for-study-on-gay-cure.html?_r=0

Carter, C. S. (1992). Hormonal influences on human sexual behavior. In J. B. Becker, S. M. Breedlove, & D. Crews (Eds.), *Behavioral Endocrinology* (pp.131–142). MIT Press.

Cassidy, S. B., & Driscoll, D. J. (2009). Prader-Willi syndrome. *European Journal of Human Genetics, 17*, 3–13.

Centers for Disease Control and Prevention. (2012). *Overweight and obesity*. http://www.cdc.gov/obesity/index.html

Chwalisz, K., Diener, E., & Gallagher, D. (1988). Autonomic arousal feedback and emotional experience: Evidence from the spinal cord injured. *Journal of Personality and Social Psychology, 54*, 820–828.

Colapinto, J. (2000). *As nature made him: The boy who was raised as a girl.* Harper Collins.

Collier, D. A., & Treasure, J. L. (2004). The aetiology of eating disorders. *The British Journal of Psychiatry, 185*, 363–365.

Conrad, P. (2005). The shifting engines of medicalization. *Journal of Health and Social Behavior, 46*, 3–14.

Cornelius, R. R. (1991). Gregorio Marañon's two-factor theory of emotion. *Personality and Social Psychology Bulletin, 17*(1), 65–69. https://psycnet.apa.org/doi/10.1177/0146167291171010

Creighton, S. (2001). Surgery for intersex. *Journal of the Royal Society of Medicine, 94*, 218–220. https://journals.sagepub.com/doi/10.1177/014107680109400505

Cunha, C., Monfils, M. H., & LeDoux, J. E. (2010). GABA(C) receptors in the lateral amygdala: A possible novel target for the treatment of fear and anxiety disorders? *Frontiers in Behavioral Neuroscience, 4*, 6.

Daniel, T. L., & Esser, J. K. (1980). Intrinsic motivation as influenced by rewards, task interest, and task structure. *Journal of Applied Psychology, 65*, 566–573.

Darwin, C. (1872). *The expression of emotions in man and animals.* Appleton.

Davis, J. I., Senghas, A., & Ochsner, K. N. (2009). How does facial feedback modulate emotional experience? *Journal of Research in Personality, 43*, 822–829.

Deci, E. L. (1972). Intrinsic motivation, extrinsic reinforcement, and inequity. *Journal of Personality and Social Psychology, 22*, 113–120.

Deci, E. L., Koestner, R., & Ryan, R. M. (1999). A meta-analytic review of experiments examining the effects of extrinsic rewards on intrinsic motivation. *Psychological Bulletin, 125*, 627–668.

de Gelder, B. (2006). Towards the neurobiology of emotional body language. *Nature Reviews Neuroscience, 7*, 242–249.

Drazen, D. L., & Woods, S. C. (2003). Peripheral signals in the control of satiety and hunger. *Current Opinion in Clinical Nutrition and Metabolic Care, 5*, 621–629.

Druce, M.R., Small, C.J., & Bloom, S.R. (2004). Minireview: Gut peptides regulating satiety. *Endocrinology, 145*, 2660–2665.

Ekman, P. (1972). Universals and cultural differences in facial expressions of emotions. In J. Cole (Ed.), *Nebraska Symposium on Motivation* (pp. 207–282). University of Nebraska Press. https://1ammce38pkj41n8xkp1iocwe-wpengine.netdna-ssl.com/wp-content/uploads/2013/07/Universals-And-Cultural-Differences-In-Facial-Expressions-Of.pdf

Ekman, P., & Keltner, D. (1997). Universal facial expressions of emotion: An old controversy and new findings. In U. Segerstråle & P. Molnár (Eds.), *Nonverbal communication: Where nature meets culture* (pp. 27–46). Lawrence Erlbaum.

Everett, B. J. (1990). Sexual motivation: A neural and behavioural analysis of the mechanisms underlying appetitive and copulatory responses of male rats. *Neuroscience and Biobehavioral Reviews, 14*, 217–232.

Faris, E. (1921). Are instincts data or hypotheses? *American Journal of Sociology, 27*, 184–196.

Femenía, T., Gómez-Galán, M., Lindskog, M., & Magara, S. (2012). Dysfunctional hippocampal activity affects emotion and cognition in mood disorders. *Brain Research, 1476*, 58–70.

Fossati, P. (2012). Neural correlates of emotion processing: From emotional to social brain. *European Neuropsychopharmacology, 22*, S487–S491.

Fournier, J. C., Keener, M. T., Almeida, J., Kronhaus, D. M., & Phillips, M. L. (2013). Amygdala and whole-brain activity to emotional faces distinguishes major depressive disorder and bipolar disorder. *Bipolar Disorders*. Advance online publication. doi:10.1111/bdi.12106

Francis, N. H., & Kritsonis, W. A. (2006). A brief analysis of Abraham Maslow's original writing of *Self-Actualizing People: A Study of Psychological Health. Doctoral Forum National Journal of Publishing and Mentoring Doctoral Student Research, 3*, 1–7.

Frijda, N. H. (1988). The laws of emotion. *American Psychologist, 43*, 349–358. https://psycnet.apa.org/record/1988-28577-001

Gloy, V. L., Briel, M., Bhatt, D. L., Kashyap, S. R., Schauer, P. R., Mingrone, G., . . . Nordmann, A. J. (2013, October 22). Bariatric surgery versus non-surgical treatment for obesity: A systematic review and meta-analysis of randomized controlled trials. *BMJ, 347*. doi:http://dx.doi.org/10.1136/bmj.f5934

Golan, O., & Baron-Cohen, S. (2006). Systemizing empathy: Teaching adults with Asperger syndrome or high-functioning autism to recognize complex emotions using interactive multimedia. *Development and Psychopathology, 18*, 591–617.

Goosens, K. A., & Maren, S. (2002). Long-term potentiation as a substrate for memory: Evidence from studies of amygdaloid plasticity and Pavlovian fear conditioning. *Hippocampus, 12*, 592–599.

Graham, S., & Weiner, B. (1996). Theories and principles of motivation. In D. C. Berliner & R. C. Calfee (Eds.), *Handbook of educational psychology* (pp. 63–84). Routledge.

Greary, N. (1990). Pancreatic glucagon signals postprandial satiety. *Neuroscience and Biobehavioral Reviews, 14*, 323–328.

Gross, J. J. (1999). Emotion regulation: Past, present, and future. *Cognition & Emotion, 13*, 551–573. https://www.tandfonline.com/doi/abs/10.1080/026999399379186

Guastella, A. J., Einfeld, S. L., Gray, K. M., Rinehart, N. J., Tonge, B. J., Lambert, T. J., & Hickie, I. B. (2010). Intranasal oxytocin improves emotion recognition for youth with autism spectrum disorders. *Biological Psychiatry, 67*, 692–694.

Hall, J. A., & Kimura, D. (1994). Dermatoglyphic asymmetry and sexual orientation in men. *Behavioral Neuroscience, 108*(6), 1203–1206.

Hamer, D. H., Hu. S., Magnuson, V. L., Hu, N., & Pattatucci, A. M. (1993). A linkage between DNA markers on the X chromosome and male sexual orientation. *Science, 261*, 321-327.

Havas, D. A., Glenberg, A. M., Gutowski, K. A., Lucarelli, M. J., & Davidson, R. J. (2010). Cosmetic use of botulinum toxin-A affects processing of emotional language. *Psychological Science, 21*, 895–900.

Hobson, R. P. (1986). The autistic child's appraisal of expressions of emotion. *The Journal of Child Psychology and Psychiatry, 27*, 321–342.

Hock, R. R. (2008). Emotion and Motivation. In *Forty studies that changed psychology: Explorations into the history of psychological research* (6th ed.) (pp. 158–168). Pearson.

Hopp, H., Troy, A. S., & Mauss, I. B. (2011). The unconscious pursuit of emotion regulation: Implications for psychological health. *Cognition and Emotion, 25*, 532–545. https://www.ocf.berkeley.edu/~eerlab/pdf/papers/2011_Hopp_unconscious_pursuit_of_emotion_regulation.pdf

Hu, S. H., Wei, N., Wang, Q. D., Yan, L. Q., Wei, E.Q., Zhang, M. M., . . . Xu, Y. (2008). Patterns of brain activation during visually evoked sexual arousal differ between homosexual and heterosexual men. *American Journal of Neuroradiology, 29*, 1890–1896.

Hughes, I. A., Houk, C., Ahmed, S. F., Lee, P. A., LWPES Consensus Group, & ESPE Consensus Group. (2006). Consensus statement on management of intersex disorders. *Archives of Disease in Childhood, 91*, 554–563. https://www.ncbi.nlm.nih.gov/pmc/articles/PMC2082839/

Human Rights Campaign. (n.d.). *The lies and dangers of efforts to change sexual orientation or gender identity.* http://www.hrc.org/resources/entry/the-lies-and-dangers-of-reparative-therapy

Jenkins, W. J. (2010). Can anyone tell me why I'm gay? What research suggests regarding the origins of sexual orientation. *North American Journal of Psychology, 12*, 279–296.

Jenkins, W. J., & Becker, J. B. (2001). Role of the striatum and nucleus accumbens in paced copulatory behavior in the female rat. *Behavioural Brain Research, 121*, 19–28.

Kennedy, K. (2017). Coverage in transition: Considerations when expanding employer-provided health coverage to LGBTI employees and beneficiaries. *The John Marhsall Institutional Repository, 24*(1). https://repository.jmls.edu/cgi/viewcontent.cgi?article=1691&context=facpubs

Kinsey, A. C., Pomeroy, W. B., & Martin, C. E. (1948). *Sexual behavior in the human male.* W.B. Saunders Company.

Koltko-Rivera, M. E. (2006). Rediscovering the later version of Maslow's hierarchy of needs: Self-transcendence and opportunities for theory, research, and unification. *Review of General Psychology, 10*, 302–317.

Konturek, S. J., Pepera, J., Zabielski, K., Konturek, P. C., Pawlick, T., Szlachcic, A., & Hahn. (2003). Brain-gut axis in pancreatic secretion and appetite control. *Journal of Physiology and Pharmacology, 54*, 293–317.

Lang, P. J. (1994). The varieties of emotional experience: A meditation on James-Lange theory. *Psychological Review, 101*, 211–221.

Lazarus, R. S. (1991). Cognition and motivation in emotion. *American Psychologist, 46*, 352–367. https://psycnet.apa.org/record/1991-23402-001

Lazarus, R. S. (1991). *Emotion and adaptation.* Oxford University Press.

LeDoux, J. E. (1996). *The Emotional Brain: The Mysterious Underpinnings of Emotional Life.* Simon & Schuster.

LeDoux, J. E. (2002). *The synaptic self.* Macmillan.

Leonard, G. (1982). The failure of self-actualization theory: A critique of Carl Rogers and Abraham Maslow. *Journal of Humanistic Psychology, 22*, 56–73.

LeVay, S. (1991). A difference in the hypothalamic structure between heterosexual and homosexual men. *Science, 253*, 1034–1037.

LeVay, S. (1996). *Queer science: The use and abuse of research into homosexuality.* The MIT Press.

Levenson, R. W., Carstensen, L. L., Friesen, W. V., & Ekman, P. (1991). Emotion, physiology, and expression in old age. *Psychology and Aging, 6,* 28–35. https://psycnet.apa.org/record/1991-18170-001

Levy-Gigi, E., Szabó, C., Kelemen, O., & Kéri, S. (2013). Association among clinical response, hippocampal volume, and FKBP5 gene expression in individuals with posttraumatic stress disorder receiving cognitive behavioral therapy. *Biological Psychiatry, 74,* 793–800.

Lippa, R. A. (2003). Handedness, sexual orientation, and gender-related personality traits in men and women. *Archives of Sexual Behavior, 32,* 103–114.

Loehlin, J. C., & McFadden, D. (2003). Otoacoustic emissions, auditory evoked potentials, and traits related to sex and sexual orientation. *Archives of Sexual Behavior, 32,* 115–127.

Macdonald, H., Rutter, M., Howlin, P., Rios, P., Conteur, A. L., Evered, C., & Folstein, S. (1989). Recognition and expression of emotional cues by autistic and normal adults. *Journal of Child Psychology and Psychiatry, 30,* 865–877.

Malatesta, C. Z., & Haviland, J. M. (1982). Learning display rules: The socialization of emotion expression in infancy. *Child Development, 53,* 991–1003.

Maren, S., Phan, K. L., & Liberzon, I. (2013). The contextual brain: Implications for fear conditioning, extinction and psychopathology. *Nature Reviews Neuroscience, 14,* 417–428.

Martin-Gronert, M. S., & Ozanne, S. E. (2013). Early life programming of obesity. *Developmental Period Medicine, 17,* 7–12.

Maslow, A. H. (1943). A theory of human motivation. *Psychological Review, 50,* 370–396.

Matsumoto, D. (1990). Cultural similarities and differences in display rules. *Motivation and Emotion, 14,* 195–214.

Matsumoto, D., Yoo, S. H., & Nakagawa, S. (2008). Culture, emotion regulation, and adjustment. *Journal of Personality and Social Psychology, 94,* 925–937.

Mauss, I. B., & Robinson, M. D. (2009). Measures of emotion: A review. *Cognition and Emotion, 23,* 209–237. https://www.ncbi.nlm.nih.gov/pmc/articles/PMC2756702/

Mauss, I. B., Bunge, S. A., & Gross, J. J. (2007). Automatic emotion regulation. *Social and Personality Psychology Compass, 1,* 146–167. https://www.ocf.berkeley.edu/~eerlab/pdf/papers/2007_Mauss_Automatic%20Emotion%20Regulation.pdf

Mauss, I. B., Cook, C. L., & Gross, J. J. (2007). Automatic emotion regulation during anger provocation. *Journal of Experimental Social Psychology, 43,* 698–711. https://psycnet.apa.org/record/2007-12302-004

Mauss, I. B., Cook, C. L., Cheng, J. Y. J., & Gross, J. J. (2007). Individual differences in cognitive reappraisal: Experiential and physiological responses to an anger provocation. *International Journal of Psychophysiology, 66,* 116–124. https://www.ncbi.nlm.nih.gov/pubmed/17543404

Mauss, I. B., Levenson, R. W., McCarter, L., Wilhelm, F. H., & Gross, J. J. (2005). The tie that binds? Coherence among emotion experience, behavior, and physiology. *Emotion, 5,* 175–190. https://www.ncbi.nlm.nih.gov/pubmed/15982083

Mayo Clinic. (2012a). *Anorexia nervosa.* http://www.mayoclinic.com/health/anorexia/DS00606

Mayo Clinic. (2012b). *Bulimia nervosa.* http://www.mayoclinic.com/health/bulimia/DS00607

Mayo Clinic. (2013). *Gastric bypass surgery.* http://www.mayoclinic.com/health/gastric-bypass/MY00825

McAdams, D. P., & Constantian, C. A. (1983). Intimacy and affiliation motives in daily living: An experience sampling analysis. *Journal of Personality and Social Psychology, 45,* 851–861.

McClelland, D. C., & Liberman, A. M. (1949). The effect of need for achievement on recognition of need-related words. *Journal of Personality, 18,* 236–251.

McFadden, D., & Champlin, C. A. (2000). Comparisons of auditory evoked potentials in heterosexual, homosexual, and bisexual males and females. *Journal of the Association for Research in Otolaryngology, 1*, 89–99.

McFadden, D., & Pasanen, E. G. (1998). Comparisons of the auditory systems of heterosexuals and homosexuals: Clicked-evoked otoacoustic emissions. *Proceedings of the National Academy of Sciences, USA, 95*, 2709–2713.

McRae, K., Ochsner, K. N., Mauss, I. B., Gabrieli, J. J. D., & Gross, J. J. (2008). Gender differences in emotion regulation: An fMRI study of cognitive reappraisal. *Group Processes and Intergroup Relations, 11*, 143–162.

Miguel-Hidalgo, J. J. (2013). Brain structural and functional changes in adolescents with psychiatric disorders. *International Journal of Adolescent Medicine and Health, 25*, 245–256.

Money, J. (1962). *Cytogenic and psychosexual incongruities with a note on space-form blindness*. Paper presented at the 118th meeting of the American Psychiatric Association, Toronto, Canada.

Money, J. (1975). Ablatio penis: Normal male infant sex-reassigned as a girl. *Archives of Sexual Behavior, 4*, 65–71.

Moriceau, S., & Sullivan, R. M. (2006). Maternal presence serves as a switch between learning fear and attraction in infancy. *Nature Neuroscience, 9*, 1004–1006.

Murray, H. A., Barrett, W. G., Homburger, E., Langer, W. C., Mekeel, H. S., Morgan, C. D., . . . Wolf, R. E. (1938). *Explorations in personality: A clinical and experimental study of fifty men of college age*. Oxford University Press.

Niemiec, C. P., & Ryan, R. M. (2009). Autonomy, competence, and relatedness in the classroom: Applying self-determination theory to educational practice. *Theory and Research in Education, 7*, 133–144.

Nisbett, R. E., Peng, K., Choi, I., & Norenzayan, A. (2001). Culture and systems of thought: Holistic versus analytic cognition. *Psychological Review, 108*(2), 291–310. https://psycnet.apa.org/record/2001-17194-001

Novin, D., Robinson, K., Culbreth, L. A., & Tordoff, M. G. (1985). Is there a role for the liver in the control of food intake? *The American Journal of Clinical Nutrition, 42*, 1050–1062.

O'Connell, S. (Writer/Producer). (2004). Dr. Money and the boy with no penis. In *Horizon*. BBC.

Paramaguru, K. (2013, November). Boy, girl, or intersex? Germany adjusts to a third option at birth. *Time*. http://world.time.com/2013/11/12/boy-girl-or-intersex/

Pedersen, E. R. (2016). Using the solid research base on pregaming to begin intervention development: An epilogue to the special issue on pregaming. *Substance Use & Misuse, 51*(8), 1067–1073. https://www.tandfonline.com/doi/abs/10.1080/10826084.2016.1187533

Pessoa, L. (2010). Emotion and cognition and the amygdala: From "what is it?" to "what's to be done?" *Neuropsychologia, 48*, 3416–3429.

Pillard, R. C., & Bailey, M. J. (1995). A biologic perspective on sexual orientation. *The Psychiatric Clinics of North America, 18*(1), 71–84.

Pillard, R. C., & Bailey, M. J. (1998). Sexual orientation has a heritable component. *Human Biology, 70*, 347–365.

Ponseti, J., Bosinski, H. A., Wolff, S., Peller, M., Jansen, O., Mehdorn, H.M., . . . Siebner, H. R. (2006). A functional endophenotype for sexual orientation in humans. *Neuroimage, 33*(3), 825–833.

Prader-Willi Syndrome Association. (2012). *What is Prader-Willi Syndrome?* http://www.pwsausa.org/syndrome/index.htm

Qin, S., Young, C. B., Duan, X., Chen, T., Supekar, K., & Menon, V. (2013). Amygdala subregional structure and intrinsic functional connectivity predicts individual differences in anxiety during early childhood. *Biological Psychiatry.* Advance online publication. doi:10.1016/j.biopsych.2013.10.006

Rahman, Q., & Wilson, G. D. (2003a). Large sexual-orientation-related differences in performance on mental rotation and judgment of line orientation tasks. *Neuropsychology, 17,* 25–31.

Rahman, Q., & Wilson, G. D. (2003b). Sexual orientation and the 2nd to 4th finger length ratio: Evidence for organising effects of sex hormones or developmental instability? *Psychoneuroendocrinology, 28,* 288–303.

Raineki, C., Cortés, M. R., Belnoue, L., & Sullivan, R. M. (2012). Effects of early-life abuse differ across development: Infant social behavior deficits are followed by adolescent depressive-like behaviors mediated by the amygdala. *The Journal of Neuroscience, 32,* 7758–7765.

Rodriguez-Larralde, A., & Paradisi, I. (2009). Influence of genetic factors on human sexual orientation. *Investigacion Clinica, 50,* 377–391.

Roseman, I. J., and Smith, C. A. (2001). Appraisal theory: Overview, assumptions, varieties, controversies. In K. R. Scherer, A. Schorr, & T. Johnstone (Eds.), *Appraisal processes in emotion: Theory, methods, research,* (pp. 3–19). Oxford University Press.

Ross, M. W., & Arrindell, W. A. (1988). Perceived parental rearing patterns of homosexual and heterosexual men. *The Journal of Sex Research, 24,* 275–281.

Saxe, L., & Ben-Shakhar, G. (1999). Admissibility of polygraph tests: The application of scientific standards post-Daubert. *Psychology, Public Policy, and Law, 5,* 203–223.

Schachter, S., & Singer, J. E. (1962). Cognitive, social, and physiological determinants of emotional state. *Psychological Review, 69,* 379–399.

Shallcross, A. J., Troy, A. S., Boland, M., & Mauss, I. B. (2010). Let it be: Accepting negative emotional experiences predicts decreased negative affect and depressive symptoms. *Behaviour Research and Therapy, 48,* 921–929. https://www.ncbi.nlm.nih.gov/pubmed/20566191

Sherwin, B. B. (1988). A comparative analysis of the role of androgen in human male and female sexual behavior: Behavioral specificity, critical thresholds, and sensitivity. *Psychobiology, 16,* 416–425.

Smink, F. R. E., van Hoeken, D., & Hoek, H. W. (2012). Epidemiology of eating disorders: Incidence, prevalence, and mortality rates. *Current Psychiatry Reports, 14,* 406–414.

Soussignan, R. (2002). Duchenne smile, emotional experience, and autonomic reactivity: A test of the facial feedback hypothesis. *Emotion, 2,* 52–74. https://psycnet.apa.org/record/2002-18343-004

Speakman, J. R., Levitsky, D. A., Allison, D. B., Bray, M. S., de Castro, J. M., Clegg, D. J., . . . Westerterp-Plantenga, M. S. (2011). Set points, settling points and some alternative models: Theoretical options to understand how genes and environment combine to regulate body adiposity. *Disease Models & Mechanisms, 4,* 733–745.

Strack, F., Martin, L. & Stepper, S. (1988). Inhibiting and facilitating conditions of the human smile: A nonobtrusive test of the facial feedback hypothesis. *Journal of Personality and Social Psychology, 54,* 768–777.

Swaab, D. F., & Hofman, M. A. (1990). An enlarged suprachiasmatic nucleus in homosexual men. *Brain Research, 537,* 141–148.

Tamietto, M., Castelli, L., Vighetti, S., Perozzo, P., Geminiani, G., Weiskrantz, L., & de Gelder, B. (2009). Unseen facial and bodily expressions trigger fast emotional reactions. *Proceedings of the National Academy of Sciences,USA, 106,* 17661–17666.

Tangmunkongvorakul, A., Banwell, C., Carmichael, G., Utomo, I. D., & Sleigh, A. (2010). Sexual identities and lifestyles among non-heterosexual urban Chiang Mai youth: Implications for health. *Culture, Health, and Sexuality, 12,* 827–841.

Troy, A. S., Shallcross, A. J., & Mauss, I. B. (2013). A person–by–situation approach to emotion regulation: Cognitive reappraisal can either hurt or help, depending on the context. *Psychological Science, 12*, 2505–2514. https://www.ncbi.nlm.nih.gov/pubmed/24145331

Troy, A. S., Wilhelm, F. H., Shallcross, A. J., & Mauss, I. B. (2010). Seeing the silver lining: Cognitive reappraisal ability moderates the relationship between stress and depression. *Emotion, 10*, 783–795. https://www.ncbi.nlm.nih.gov/pmc/articles/PMC3278301/

Wang, Z., Neylan, T. C., Mueller, S. G., Lenoci, M., Truran, D., Marmar, C. R., . . . Schuff, N. (2010). Magnetic resonance imaging of hippocampal subfields in posttraumatic stress disorder. *Arch Gen Psychiatry, 67*(3), 296–303. doi:10.1001/archgenpsychiatry.2009.205

Weinsier, R. L., Nagy, T. R., Hunter, G. R., Darnell, B. E., Hensrud, D. D., & Weiss, H. L. (2000). Do adaptive changes in metabolic rate favor weight regain in weight-reduced individuals? An examination of the set-point theory. *The American Journal of Clinical Nutrition, 72*, 1088–1094.

Woods, S. C. (2004). Gastrointestinal satiety signals I. An overview of gastrointestinal signals that influence food intake. *American Journal of Physiology: Gastrointestinal and Liver Physiology, 286*, G7–G13.

Woods, S. C., & D'Alessio, D. A. (2008). Central control of body weight and appetite. *Journal of Clinical Endocrinology and Metabolism, 93*, S37–S50.

Yerkes, R. M., & Dodson, J. D. (1908). The relation of strength of stimulus to rapidity of habit-formation. *Journal of Comparative Neurology and Psychology, 18*, 459–482. doi:10.1002/cne.920180503

Zajonc, R. B. (1980). Feeling and thinking: Preferences need no inferences. *American Psychologist, 35*(2), 151–175.

Zajonc, R. B. (1998). Emotions. In D. T. Gilbert & S. T. Fiske (Eds.), *Handbook of social psychology* (4th ed., Vol. 1, pp. 591–632). McGraw-Hill.

Personality

Adler, A. (1930). Individual psychology. In C. Murchison (Ed.), *Psychologies of 1930* (pp. 395–405). Clark University Press.

Adler, A. (1937). A school girl's exaggeration of her own importance. *International Journal of Individual Psychology, 3*(1), 3–12.

Adler, A. (1956). *The individual psychology of Alfred Adler: A systematic presentation in selections from his writings.* (C. H. Ansbacher & R. Ansbacher, Eds.). Harper.

Adler, A. (1961). The practice and theory of individual psychology. In T. Shipley (Ed.), *Classics in psychology* (pp. 687–714). Philosophical Library

Adler, A. (1964). *Superiority and social interest.* Norton.

Akomolafe, M. J. (2013). Personality characteristics as predictors of academic performance of secondary school students. *Mediterranean Journal of Social Sciences, 4*(2), 657–664.

Allport, G. W. & Odbert, H. S. (1936). Trait-names: A psycho-lexical study. Psychological Review Company.

Anglim, J., & O'Connor, P. (2018). Measurement and research using Big Five, HEXACO, and narrow traits: A primer for researchers and practitioners. *Australian Journal of Psychology, 71*(1), 16–25. https://aps.onlinelibrary.wiley.com/doi/full/10.1111/ajpy.12202

Aronow, E., Weiss, K. A., & Rezinkoff, M. (2001). *A practical guide to the Thematic Apperception Test.* Brunner Routledge.

Bandura, A. (1977). Self-efficacy: Toward a unifying theory of behavioral change. *Psychological Review, 84*, 191–215.

Bandura, A. (1986). *Social foundations of thought and action: A social cognitive theory.* Prentice Hall.

Bandura, A. (1995). *Self-efficacy in changing societies*. Cambridge University Press.

Benassi, V. A., Sweeney, P. D., & Dufour, C. L. (1988). Is there a relation between locus of control orientation and depression? *Journal of Abnormal Psychology, 97*(3), 357.

Ben-Porath, Y., & Tellegen, A. (2008). *Minnesota Multiphasic Personality Inventory-2-RF*. University of Minnesota Press.

Benet-Martínez, V. & Karakitapoglu-Aygun, Z. (2003). The interplay of cultural values and personality in predicting life-satisfaction: Comparing Asian- and European-Americans. *Journal of Cross-Cultural Psychology, 34*, 38–61.

Benet-Martínez, V., & Oishi, S. (2008). Culture and personality. In O. P. John, R.W. Robins, L. A. Pervin (Eds.), *Handbook of personality: Theory and research*. Guildford Press.

Beutler, L. E., Nussbaum, P. D., & Meredith, K. E. (1988). Changing personality patterns of police officers. *Professional Psychology: Research and Practice, 19*(5), 503–507.

Bouchard, T., Jr. (1994). Genes, environment, and personality. *Science, 264*, 1700–1701.

Bouchard, T., Jr., Lykken, D. T., McGue, M., Segal, N. L., & Tellegen, A. (1990). Sources of human psychological differences: The Minnesota Study of Twins Reared Apart. *Science, 250*, 223–228.

Burger, J. (2008). *Personality* (7th ed.). Thompson Higher Education.

Buss, D. M. (2009). How can evolutionary psychology successfully explain personality and individual differences? *Perspectives on Psychological Science, 4*(4), 359–366. https://labs.la.utexas.edu/buss/files/2015/09/evolution-personality-and-individual-differences-2009.pdf

Carter, S., Champagne, F., Coates, S., Nercessian, E., Pfaff, D., Schecter, D., & Stern, N. B. (2008). *Development of temperament symposium*. Philoctetes Center, New York.

Cattell, R. B. (1946). *The description and measurement of personality*. Harcourt, Brace, & World.

Cattell, R. B. (1957). *Personality and motivation structure and measurement*. World Book.

Chamorro-Premuzic, T., & Furnham, A. (2008). Personality, intelligence, and approaches to learning as predictors of academic performance. *Personality and Individual Differences, 44*, 1596–1603.

Cheung, F. M., van de Vijver, F. J. R., & Leong, F. T. L. (2011). Toward a new approach to the study of personality in culture. *American Psychologist, 66*(7), 593–603.

Clark, A. L., & Watson, D. (2008). Temperament: An organizing paradigm for trait psychology. In O. P. John, R. W. Robins, & L. A. Previn (Eds.), *Handbook of personality: Theory and research* (3rd ed., pp. 265–286). Guilford Press.

Conrad, N. & Party, M.W. (2012). Conscientiousness and academic performance: A Mediational Analysis. International *Journal for the Scholarship of Teaching and Learning, 6* (1), 1–14.

Costantino, G. (1982). TEMAS: A new technique for personality research assessment of Hispanic children. Hispanic Research Center, Fordham University *Research Bulletin, 5*, 3–7.

Cramer, P. (2004). *Storytelling, narrative, and the Thematic Apperception Test*. Guilford Press.

Dana, R. H. (1986). Personality assessment and Native Americans. *Journal of Personality Assessment, 50*(3), 480–500.

Donnellan, M. B., & Lucas, R. E. (2008). Age differences in the big five across the life span: Evidence from two national samples. *Psychology and Aging, 23*(3), 558–566.

Duzant, R. (2005). *Differences of emotional tone and story length of African American respondents when administered the Contemporized Themes Concerning Blacks test versus the Thematic Apperception Test*. Unpublished doctoral dissertation, The Chicago School of Professional Psychology, Chicago, IL.

Exner, J. E. (2002). *The Rorschach: Basic foundations and principles of interpretation* (Vol. 1). Wiley.

Eysenck, H. J. (1990). An improvement on personality inventory. *Current Contents: Social and Behavioral Sciences, 22*(18), 20.

Eysenck, H. J. (1992). Four ways five factors are *not* basic. *Personality and Individual Differences, 13,* 667–673.

Eysenck, H. J. (2009). *The biological basis of personality* (3rd ed.). Transaction Publishers.

Eysenck, S. B. G., & Eysenck, H. J. (1963). The validity of questionnaire and rating assessments of extroversion and neuroticism, and their factorial stability. *British Journal of Psychology, 54,* 51–62.

Eysenck, H. J., & Eysenck, M. W. (1985*). Personality and individual differences: A natural science approach.* Plenum Press.

Eysenck, S. B. G., Eysenck, H. J., & Barrett, P. (1985). A revised version of the psychoticism scale. *Personality and Individual Differences, 6*(1), 21–29.

Fazeli, S. H. (2012). The exploring nature of the assessment instrument of five factors of personality traits in the current studies of personality. *Asian Social Science, 8*(2), 264–275.

Fancher, R. W. (1979). *Pioneers of psychology*. Norton.

Freud, S. (1920). Resistance and suppression. *A general introduction to psychoanalysis* (pp. 248–261). Horace Liveright.

Freud, S. (1923/1949). The ego and the id. Hogarth.

Freud, S. (1931/1968). Female sexuality. In J. Strachey (Ed. &Trans.), *The standard edition of the complete psychological works of Sigmund Freud* (Vol. 21). Hogarth Press.

Frewer, L., & Bleus A. V. (1991). Personality assessment in a collectivist culture. *South Pacific Journal of Psychology, 4,* 1–5.

Funder, D. C. (2001). Personality. *Annual Review of Psychology, 52,* 197–221.

Goldstein, M. L. "Projective personality assessment in child custody evaluations." n.d. https://www.drmarkgoldsteinphd.com/projective-personality-assessment-in-child-custody-evaluations

Hofstede, G. (2001). *Culture's consequences: Comparing values, behaviors, institutions, and organizations across nations* (2nd ed.). Sage.

Holaday, D., Smith, D. A., & Sherry, Alissa. (2010). Sentence completion tests: A review of the literature and results of a survey of members of the society for personality assessment. *Journal of Personality Assessment, 74*(3), 371–383.

Hothersall, D. (1995). *History of psychology*. McGraw-Hill.

Hoy, M. (1997). *Contemporizing of the Themes Concerning Blacks test (C-TCB)*. California School of Professional Psychology.

Hoy-Watkins, M., & Jenkins-Moore, V. (2008). The Contemporized-Themes Concerning Blacks Test (C-TCB). In S. R. Jenkins (Ed.), *A Handbook of Clinical Scoring Systems for Thematic Apperceptive Techniques* (pp. 659–698). Lawrence Erlbaum Associates.

Jang, K. L., Livesley, W. J., & Vernon, P. A. (1996). Heritability of the big five personality dimensions and their facts: A twin study. *Journal of Personality, 64*(3), 577–591.

Jang, K. L., Livesley, W. J., Ando, J., Yamagata, S., Suzuki, A., Angleitner, A., et al. (2006). Behavioral genetics of the higher-order factors of the Big Five. *Personality and Individual Differences, 41,* 261–272.

Judge, T. A., Livingston, B. A., & Hurst, C. (2012). Do nice guys-and gals- really finish last? The joint effects of sex and agreeableness on income. *Journal of Personality and Social Psychology, 102*(2), 390–407.

Jung, C. G. (1923). *Psychological types*. Harcourt Brace.

Jung, C. G. (1928). *Contributions to analytical psychology*. Harcourt Brace Jovanovich.

Jung, C. G. (1964). *Man and his symbols.* Doubleday and Company.

Jung, C., & Kerenyi, C. (1963). Science of mythology. In R. F. C. Hull (Ed. & Trans.), *Essays on the myth of the divine child and the mysteries of Eleusis.* Harper & Row.

Launer, J. (2005). Anna O. and the 'talking cure.' *QJM: An International Journal of Medicine, 98*(6), 465–466.

Lecci, L. B. & Magnavita, J. J. (2013). *Personality theories: A scientific approach.* Bridgepoint Education.

Lefcourt, H. M. (1982). *Locus of control: Current trends in theory and research* (2nd ed.). Erlbaum.

Lecci, L. B. & Magnavita, J. J. (2013). *Personality theories: A scientific approach.* Bridgepoint Education.

Likert, R. (1932). A technique for the measurement of attitudes. *Archives of Psychology, 140,* 1–55.

Lilienfeld, S. O., Wood, J. M., & Garb, H. N. (2000). The scientific status of projective techniques. *Psychological Science in the Public Interest, 1*(2), 27–66.

Maltby, J., Day, L., & Macaskill, A. (2007). *Personality, individual differences and intelligence* (3rd ed.). Pearson.

Maslow, A. H. (1970). *Motivation and personality.* Harper & Row.

Maslow, A. H. (1950). Self-actualizing people: A study of psychological health. In W. Wolff (Ed.), *Personality Symposia: Symposium 1 on Values* (pp. 11–34). Grune & Stratton.

McCrae, R. R., & Costa, P. T. (1997). Personality trait structure as a human universal. *American Psychologist, 52*(5), 509–516.

McCrae, R. R., et al. (2005). Universal features of personality traits from the observer's perspective: Data from 50 cultures. *Journal of Personality and Social Psychology, 88,* 547–561.

Mischel, W. (1993). *Introduction to personality* (5th ed.). Harcourt Brace Jovanovich.

Mischel, W., Ayduk, O., Berman, M. G., Casey, B. J., Gotlib, I. H., Jonides, J., et al. (2010). 'Willpower' over the life span: Decomposing self-regulation. *Social Cognitive and Affective Neuroscience, 6*(2), 252–256.

Mischel, W., Ebbesen, E. B., & Raskoff Zeiss, A. (1972). Cognitive and attentional mechanisms of delay in gratification. *Journal of Personality and Social Psychology, 21*(2), 204–218.

Mischel, W., & Shoda, Y. (1995). A cognitive-affective system theory of personality: Reconceptualizing situations, dispositions, dynamics, and invariance in personality structure. *Psychological Review, 102*(2), 246–268.

Mischel, W., Shoda, Y., & Rodriguez, M. L. (1989, May 26). Delay of gratification in children. *Science, 244,* 933-938.

Motley, M. T. (2002). Theory of slips. In E. Erwin (Ed.), *The Freud encyclopedia: Theory, therapy, and culture* (pp. 530–534). Routledge.

Noftle, E. E., & Robins, R. W. (2007). Personality predictors of academic outcomes: Big Five correlates of GPA and SAT scores. *Personality Processes and Individual Differences, 93,* 116–130.

Noga, A. (2007). *Passions and tempers: A history of the humors.* Harper Collins.

Oyserman, D., Coon, H., & Kemmelmier, M. (2002). Rethinking individualism and collectivism: Evaluation of theoretical assumptions and meta-analyses. *Psychological Bulletin, 128,* 3–72.

Piotrowski, Z. A. (1987). *Perceptanalysis: The Rorschach method fundamentally reworked, expanded and systematized.* Routledge.

Rentfrow, P. J., Gosling, S. D., Jokela, M., Stillwell, D. J., Kosinski, M., & Potter, J. (2013, October 14). Divided we stand: Three psychological regions of the United States and their political, economic, social, and health correlates. *Journal of Personality and Social Psychology, 105*(6), 996–1012.

Rentfrow, P. J., Jost, J. T., Gosling, S. D., & Potter, J. (2009). Statewide differences in personality predict voting patterns in 1996–2004 U.S. Presidential elections. In J. T. Jost, A. C. Kay, & H. Thorisdottir

(Eds.), *Series in political psychology: Social and psychological bases of ideology and system justification* (pp. 314–347). Oxford University Press.

Roesler, C. (2012). Are archetypes transmitted more by culture than biology? Questions arising from conceptualizations of the archetype. *Journal of Analytical Psychology, 57*(2), 223–246.

Rogers, C. (1980). *A way of being*. Houghton Mifflin.

Rothbart, M. K. (2011). *Becoming who we are: Temperament and personality in development*. Guilford Press.

Rothbart, M. K., Ahadi, S. A., & Evans, D. E. (2000). Temperament and personality: Origins and outcomes. *Journal of Personality and Social Psychology, 78*(1), 122–135.

Rothbart, M. K., & Derryberry, D. (1981). Development of individual differences in temperament. In M. E. Lamb & A. L. Brown (Eds.), *Advances in developmental psychology* (Vol. 1, pp. 37–86). Erlbaum.

Rothbart, M. K., Sheese, B. E., Rueda, M. R., & Posner, M. I. (2011). Developing mechanisms of self-regulation in early life. *Emotion Review, 3*(2), 207–213.

Rotter, J. (1966). Generalized expectancies for internal versus external control of reinforcements. *Psychological Monographs, 80,* 609.

Rotter, J. B., & Rafferty, J. E. (1950). *Manual the Rotter Incomplete Sentences Blank College Form*. The Psychological Corporation.

Schmitt, D. P., Allik, J., McCrae, R. R., & Benet-Martinez, V. (2007). The geographic distribution of Big Five personality traits: Patterns and profiles of human self-description across 56 nations. *Journal of Cross-Cultural Psychology, 38,* 173–212.

Scott, J. (2005). *Electra after Freud: Myth and culture*. Cornell University Press.

Segal, N. L. (2012). *Born together-reared apart: The landmark Minnesota Twin Study*. Harvard University Press.

Skinner, B. F. (1953). *Science and human behavior*. The Free Press.

Sotirova-Kohli, M., Opwis, K., Roesler, C., Smith, S. M., Rosen, D. H., Vaid, J., & Djnov, V. (2013). Symbol/meaning paired-associate recall: An "archetypal memory" advantage? *Behavioral Sciences, 3,* 541–561. http://www2.cnr.edu/home/araia/Myth_%20Body.pdf

Stelmack, R. M., & Stalikas, A. (1991). Galen and the humour theory of temperament. *Personal Individual Difference, 12*(3), 255–263.

Terracciano A., McCrae R. R., Brant L. J., Costa P. T., Jr. (2005). Hierarchical linear modeling analyses of the NEO-PI-R scales in the Baltimore Longitudinal Study of Aging. *Psychology and Aging, 20,* 493–506.

Thomas, A., & Chess, S. (1977). *Temperament and development*. Brunner/Mazel.

Tok, S. (2011). The big five personality traits and risky sport participation. *Social Behavior and Personality: An International Journal, 39*(8), 1105–1111.

Triandis, H. C. (1995). *Individualism and collectivism*. Westview.

Triandis, H. C., & Suh, E. M. (2002). Cultural influences on personality. *Annual Review of Psychology, 53,* 133–160.

Wagerman, S. A., & Funder, D. C. (2007). Acquaintance reports of personality and academic achievement: A case for conscientiousness. *Journal of Research in Personality, 41,* 221–229.

Watson, D., & Clark, L. A. (1984). Negative affectivity: The disposition to experience aversive emotional states. *Psychological Bulletin, 96,* 465–490.

Watts, T. W., Duncan, G. J., & Quan, H. (2018). Revisiting the marshmallow test: A conceptual replication investigating links between early delay of gratification and later outcomes. *Psychological Science 29*(7), 1159–1177. https://doi.org/10.1177/0956797618761661

Weiner, I. B. (2003). *Principles of Rorschach interpretation*. Lawrence Erlbaum.

Whyte, C. (1980). An integrated counseling and learning center. In K. V. Lauridsen (Ed.), *Examining the scope of learning centers* (pp. 33–43). Jossey-Bass.

Whyte, C. (1978). Effective counseling methods for high-risk college freshmen. *Measurement and Evaluation in Guidance, 6*(4), 198–200.

Whyte, C. B. (1977). High-risk college freshman and locus of control. *The Humanist Educator, 16*(1), 2–5.

Williams, R. L. (1972). Themes Concerning Blacks: Manual. Williams.

Wundt, W. (1874/1886). *Elements du psychologie, physiologique* (2ieme tome). [Elements of physiological psychology, Vol. 2]. (E. Rouvier, Trans.). Paris: Ancienne Librairie Germer Bailliere et Cie.

Yang, K. S. (2006). Indigenous personality research: The Chinese case. In U. Kim, K.-S. Yang, & K.-K. Hwang (Eds.), *Indigenous and cultural psychology: Understanding people in context* (pp. 285–314). Springer.

Young-Eisendrath, P. (1995). *Myth and body: Pandora's legacy in a post-modern world.* http://www2.cnr.edu/home/araia/Myth_%20Body.pdf

Social Psychology

Adams, H. E., Wright, L. W., Jr., & Lohr, B.A. (1996). Is homophobia associated with homosexual arousal? *Journal of Abnormal Psychology, 105*, 440–445.

Albarracín, D., & Wyer, R. S. (2001). Elaborative and nonelaborative processing of a behavior-related communication. *Personality and Social Psychology Bulletin, 27*, 691–705.

Alexander, M. (2001, August 22). Thirty years later, Stanford prison experiment lives on. *Stanford Report.* http://news.stanford.edu/news/2001/august22/prison2-822.html.

Allport, G. W. (1954). *The Nature of Human Prejudice.* Addison-Wesley.

American Psychological Association. (n.d.) Social psychology studies human interactions. https://www.apa.org/action/science/social/

American Psychological Association. (2010). Bullying: What parents, teachers can do to stop it. http://www.apa.org/news/press/releases/2010/04/bullying.aspx.

Aronson, E., & Mills, J. (1959). The effect of severity of initiation on liking for a group, *Journal of Abnormal and Social Psychology, 59*, 177–181.

Asch, S. E. (1955). Opinions and social pressure. *Scientific American, 193*, 31–35.

Batson, C. D. (1991). *The altruism question: Toward a social-psychological answer.* Erlbaum.

Bandura, A. (1999). Moral disengagement in the perpetration of inhumanities. *Personality and Social Psychology Review, 3*(3), 193–209. doi:10.1207/s15327957pspr0303_3.

Berkowitz, A. D. (2004). *The social norms approach: Theory, research and annotated bibliography.* http://www.alanberkowitz.com/articles/social_norms.pdf.

Berkowitz, L. (1993). *Aggression: Its causes, consequences, and control.* McGraw-Hill.

Betz, N. E. (2008). Women's career development. In F. Denmark & M. Paludi (Eds.), *Psychology of women: Handbook of issues and theories* (2nd ed., pp. 717–752). Praeger.

Blau, F. D., Ferber, M. A., & Winkler, A. E. (2010). *The economics of women, men, and work* (6th ed.). Prentice Hall.

Bond, C. F., & Titus, L. J. (1983). Social facilitation: A meta-analysis of 241 studies. *Psychological Bulletin, 94*, 265–292.

Bond, R., & Smith, P. B. (1996). Culture and conformity: A meta-analysis of studies using Asch's (1952b, 1956) line judgment task. *Psychological Bulletin, 119*(1), 111–137.

Bowen, L. (2011). Bullying may contribute to lower test scores. *Monitor on Psychology, 42*(9), 19.

Brown, R. (2010). *Prejudice: Its social psychology* (2nd ed.). Wiley-Blackwell.

Burger, J. (2009). Replicating Milgram: Would people still obey today? *American Psychologist, 64*, 1–11. https://www.ncbi.nlm.nih.gov/pubmed/19209958

Buss, D. M. (2004). *Evolutionary psychology: The new science of the mind* (2nd ed.). Allyn and Bacon.

Buss, D. M. (1989). Sex differences in human mate preferences: Evolutionary hypotheses tested in 37 cultures. *Behavioral and Brain Sciences, 12*, 1–49.

Ceci, S. J., & Williams, W. M. (2011). Understanding current causes of women's underrepresentation in science. *Proceedings of the National Academy of Sciences, 108*, 3157–3162.

Chang, E., Kannoth, S., Levy, S., Wang, S., Lee, J., & Levy, B. (2020). Global reach of ageism on older persons' health: A systematic review. *PLoS ONE, 15*, 1–24.

Choi, I., & Nisbett R. E. (1998). Situational salience and cultural differences in the correspondence bias and actor-observer bias. *Personality and Social Psychology Bulletin, 24*(9), 949–960. doi:10.1177/0146167298249003.

Cialdini, R. B. (2001). Harnessing the science of persuasion. *Harvard Business Review, 79*, 72–81.

Cialdini, R. B., Brown, S. L., Lewis, B. P., Luce, C., & Neuberg, S. L. (1997). Reinterpreting the empathy-altruism relationship: When one into one equals oneness. *Journal of Personality and Social Psychology, 73*, 481–494.

Colin Powell regrets Iraq war intelligence. (2011). http://www.aljazeera.com/news/americas/2011/09/20119116916873488.html.

Cozby, P. C. (1973). Self-disclosure: A literature review. *Psychological Bulletin, 79*, 73–91.

Crisp, R. J., & Turner, R. N. (2009). Can imagined interactions produce positive perceptions? Reducing prejudice through simulated social contact. *American Psychologist, 64*, 231–240.

Crowley, A. E., & Hoyer, W. D. (1994). An integrative framework for understanding two-sided persuasion. *Journal of Consumer Research, 20*(4), 561–574.

Croyle, R. T., & Cooper, J. (1983). Dissonance arousal: Physiological evidence. *Journal of Personality and Social Psychology, 45*, 782–791.

Cuddy, A. J., Norton, M. I., & Fiske, S. T. (2005). This old stereotype: The pervasiveness and persistence of the elderly stereotype. *Journal of Social Issues, 61*, 267–285.

Deutsch, M., & Gerard, H. (1955). A study of normative and informational social influences upon individual judgment. *Journal of Abnormal and Social Psychology, 51*, 629–636.

Devine, P. G. (1989). Stereotypes and prejudice: Their automatic and controlled components. *Journal of Personality and Social Psychology, 56*, 5–18.

Devine, P. G., & Elliot, A. J. (1995). Are racial stereotypes really fading? The Princeton trilogy revisited. *Personality and Social Psychology Bulletin, 21*, 1139–1150.

Dixon, T. L., & Linz D. (2000). Overrepresentation and underrepresentation of African Americans and Latinos as lawbreakers on television news. *Journal of Communication, 50*(2), 131–154.

Dodge, K. A., & Schwartz, D. (1997). Social information processing mechanisms in aggressive behavior. In D. M. Stoff and J. Breiling (Eds.), *Handbook of Antisocial Behavior* (pp. 171–180). John Wiley and Sons.

Doliński, D., Grzyb, T., Folwarczny, M., Grzybała, P., Krzyszycha, K., Martynowska, K., & Trojanowski, J. (2017). Would you deliver an electric shock in 2015? Obedience in the experimental paradigm developed by Stanley Milgram in the 50 years following the original studies. *Social Psychological and Personality Science, 8*(8), 927–933.

References

Dollard, J., Miller, N. E., Doob, L. W., Mowrer, O. H., & Sears, R. R. (1939). *Frustration and aggression.* Yale University Press.

Dovidio, J. F., & Gaertner, S. L. (2004). On the nature of contemporary prejudice. In P. S. Rothenberg, (Ed.), *Race, class, and gender in the United States: An integrated study* (6th ed., pp. 132–142). Worth.

Dovidio, J. F., Gluszek, A., John, M. S., Ditlmann, R., & Lagunes, P. (2010). Understanding bias toward Latinos: Discrimination, dimensions of difference, and experience of exclusion. *Journal of Social Issues, 66,* 59–78.

Eagly, A. H., & Chaiken, S. (1975). An attribution analysis of the effect of communicator characteristics on opinion change: The case of communicator attractiveness. *Journal of Personality and Social Psychology, 32,* 136–144.

Eagly, A. H., & Chaiken, S. (1993). *The psychology of attitudes.* Harcourt Brace Jovanovich College.

East Haven mayor suggests "he might have tacos" to repair relations with Latinos. (2012). https://www.youtube.com/watch?v=PCUwtfqF4wU.

Ehrlinger, J., Gilovich, T., & Ross, L. (2005). Peering into the bias blind spot: People's assessments of bias in themselves and others. *Personality and Social Psychology Bulletin, 31,* 680–692.

Festinger, L. (1957). *A theory of cognitive dissonance.* Stanford University Press.

Festinger, L., & Maccoby, N. (1964). On resistance to persuasive communications. *The Journal of Abnormal and Social Psychology, 68,* 359–366.

Festinger, L., Schachler, S., & Back, K. W. (1950). *Social pressures in informal groups: A study of human factors in housing.* Harper.

Fink, B., Neave, N., Manning, J. T., & Grammer, K. (2006). Facial symmetry and judgments of attractiveness, health and personality. *Personality and Individual Differences, 41,* 491–499.

Fiske, S. T., Cuddy, A. J., Glick, P., & Xu, J. (2002). A model of (often mixed) stereotype content: Competence and warmth respectively follow from perceived status and competition. *Journal of Personality and Social Psychology, 82*(6), 878–902.

Fiske, S. T., Gilbert, D. T., & Lindzey, G. (2010). *Handbook of social psychology* (5th ed.). Wiley.

Freedman, J. L., & Fraser, S. C. (1966). Compliance without pressure: The foot-in-the-door technique. *Journal of Personality and Social Psychology, 4,* 195–202.

Gaertner, S., Dovidio, J., Banker, B., Houlette, M., Johnson, K., & McGlynn, E. (2000). Reducing intergroup conflict: From superordinate goals to decategorization, recategorization, and mutual differentiation. *Group Dynamics: Theory, Research, and Practice, 4,* 98–114. https://psycnet.apa.org/doiLanding?doi=10.1037%2F1089-2699.4.1.98

Geen, R. G. (1989). Alternative conceptions of social facilitation. In P. B. Paulus (Ed.), *Psychology of group influence* (2nd ed., pp. 15–51). Lawrence Erlbaum.

Granström, K., Guvå, G., Hylander, I., & Rosander, M. (2009). *Riots and disturbances: How riots start and how order is secured.* Linköping University Electronic Press.

Greenberg, J., Schimel, J., & Martens, A. (2002). Ageism: Denying the face of the future. In T. D. Nelson (Ed.), *Ageism: Stereotyping and prejudice against older persons* (pp. 27–48). MIT Press.

Greenwald, A. G., McGhee, D. E., & Schwartz, J. L. (1998). Measuring individual differences in implicit cognition: The implicit association test. *Journal of Personality and Social Psychology, 74,* 1464–1480.

Greenwald, A. G., & Ronis, D. L. (1978). Twenty years of cognitive dissonance: Case study of the evolution of a theory. *Psychological Review, 85,* 53–57.

Grove, J. R., Hanrahan, S. J., & McInman, A. (1991). Success/failure bias in attributions across involvement categories in sport. *Personality and Social Psychology Bulletin, 17*(1), 93–97.

Gupta, P. B., & Lord, K. R. (1998). Product placement in movies: The effect of prominence and mode on recall. *Journal of Current Issues and Research in Advertising, 20*, 47–59.

Harding, L. (2018). Students of a feather "flocked" together: A group assignment method for reducing free-riding and improving group and individual learning outcomes. *Journal of Marketing Education, 40*, 117–127. https://journals.sagepub.com/doi/10.1177/0273475317708588

Hare, A. P. (2003). Roles, relationships, and groups in organizations: Some conclusions and recommendations. *Small Group Research, 34*, 123–154.

Harvard University, Department of Psychology. (2019). *Mary Whiton Calkins.* https://psychology.fas.harvard.edu/people/mary-whiton-calkins

Haugtvedt, C. P., & Wegener, D. T. (1994). Message order effects in persuasion: An attitude strength perspective. *Journal of Consumer Research, 21*, 205–218.

Hebl, M. R., Foster, J. B., Mannix, L. M., & Dovidio, J. F. (2002). Formal and interpersonal discrimination: A field study of bias toward homosexual applicants. *Personality and Social Psychology Bulletin, 28*(6), 815–825.

Heckert, T. M., Latier, A., Ringwald-Burton, A., & Drazen, C. (2006). Relations among student effort, perceived class difficulty appropriateness, and student evaluations of teaching: Is it possible to "buy" better evaluations through lenient grading? *College Student Journal, 40*(3), 588.

Herek, G. M., & McLemore, K. A. (2013). Sexual prejudice. *Annual Review of Psychology, 64*, 309–33. doi:10.1146/annurev-psych-113011-143826.

Heider, F. (1958). *The psychology of interpersonal relations.* Wiley.

Hinduja, S., & Patchin, J. W. (2010). Bullying, cyberbullying, and suicide. *Archives of Suicide Research, 14*(3), 206–221.

Hinduja, S. & Patchin, J. W. (2011). Cyberbullying research summary: Bullying, cyberbullying, and sexual orientation. Cyberbullying Research Center. http://www.cyberbullying.us/cyberbullying_sexual_orientation_fact_sheet.pdf.

Hodge, S. R., Burden, J. W., Jr., Robinson, L. E., & Bennett, R. A., III. (2008). Theorizing on the stereotyping of black male student-athletes. *Journal for the Study of Sports and Athletes in Education, 2*, 203–226.

Hoff, D. L., & Mitchell, S. N. (2009). Cyberbullying: Causes, effects, and remedies. *Journal of Education, 47*, 652–665.

Hovland, C. I., Janis, I. L. and Kelley, H. H. (1953). *Communications and persuasion: Psychological studies in opinion change.* Yale University Press.

Hovland, C.I., Weiss, W. (1951, Winter). The influence of source credibility on communication effectiveness. *Public Opinion Quarterly, 15*(4), 635–650.

Igou, E. R., & Bless, H. (2003). Inferring the importance of arguments: Order effects and conversational rules. *Journal of Experimental Social Psychology, 39*, 91–99.

Ito, T. A., & Urland, G. R., (2003). Race and gender on the brain: Electrocortical measures of attention to race and gender of multiply categorizable individuals. *Journal of Personality & Social Psychology, 85*, 616–626.

Iyengar, S., & Westwood, S. J. (2015). Fear and loathing across party lines: New evidence on group polarization. *American Journal of Political Science, 59*(3), 690–707.

Jackson, J. M., & Williams, K. D. (1985). Social loafing on difficult tasks: Working collectively can improve performance. *Journal of Personality and Social Psychology, 49*, 937–942.

Janis, I. L. (1972). *Victims of groupthink.* Houghton Mifflin.

Jones, E. E., & Nisbett, R. E. (1971). *The actor and the observer: Divergent perceptions of the causes of behavior.*

General Learning Press.

Jost, J. T., Banaji, M. R., & Nosek, B. A. (2004). A decade of system justification theory: Accumulated evidence of conscious and unconscious bolstering of the status quo. *Political Psychology, 25*, 881–919.

Jost, J. T., & Major, B. (Eds.). (2001). *The psychology of legitimacy: Emerging perspectives on ideology, justice, and intergroup relations*. Cambridge University Press.

Karau, S. J., & Williams, K. D. (1993). Social loafing: A meta-analytic review and theoretical integration. *Journal of Personality and Social Psychology, 65*, 681–706.

Kassin, S. (2017). The killing of Kitty Genovese: What else does this case tell us? *Perspectives on Psychological Science, 12*, 374–381. https://journals.sagepub.com/doi/abs/10.1177/1745691616679465

Krosnick, J. A., & Alwin, D. F. (1989). Aging and susceptibility to attitude change. *Journal of Personality and Social Psychology, 57*, 416–425.

Kumkale, G. T., & Albarracín, D. (2004). The sleeper effect in persuasion: A meta-analytic review. *Psychological Bulletin, 130*(1), 143–172. doi:10.1037/0033-2909.130.1.143.

Larsen, K. S. (1990). The Asch conformity experiment: Replication and transhistorical comparisons. *Journal of Social Behavior & Personality, 5*(4), 163–168.

Latané, B., & Darley, J. M. (1968). Group inhibition of bystander intervention in emergencies. *Journal of Personality and Social Psychology, 10*, 215–221.

Latané, B., Williams, K. and Harkins, S. G. (1979). Many hands make light the work: The causes and consequences of social loafing. *Journal of Personality and Social Psychology, 37*, 822–832.

Laurenceau, J.-P., Barrett, L. F., & Pietromonaco, P. R. (1998). Intimacy as an interpersonal process: The importance of self-disclosure, partner disclosure, and perceived partner responsiveness in interpersonal exchanges. *Journal of Personality and Social Psychology, 74*(5), 1238–1251. doi:10.1037/0022-3514.74.5.1238.

Lerner, M. J., & Miller, D. T. (1978). Just world research and the attribution process: Looking back and ahead. *Psychological Bulletin, 85*, 1030–1051.

Lumsdaine, A. A., & Janis, I. L. (1953). Resistance to "counterpropaganda" produced by one-sided and two-sided "propaganda" presentations. *Public Opinion Quarterly, 17*, 311–318.

Malle, B. F. (2006). The actor–observer asymmetry in attribution: A (surprising) meta-analysis. *Psychological Bulletin, 132*(6), 895–919. doi:10.1037/0033-2909.132.6.895.

Malloy, T. E., Albright, L., Kenny, D. A., Agatstein, F., & Winquist, L. (1997). Interpersonal perception and metaperception in non-overlapping social groups. *Journal of Personality and Social Psychology, 72*, 390–398.

Markus, H. R., & Kitayama, S. (1991). Culture and the self: Implications for cognition, emotion, and motivation. *Psychological Review, 98*, 224–253.

Martin, C. H., & Bull, P. (2008). Obedience and conformity in clinical practice. *British Journal of Midwifery, 16*(8), 504–509.

Masuda, T., & Nisbett, R. E. (2001). Attending holistically versus analytically: Comparing the context sensitivity of Japanese and Americans. *Journal of Personality and Social Psychology, 81*(5), 922–934. https://psycnet.apa.org/doiLanding?doi=10.1037%2F0022-3514.81.5.922

McPherson, M., Smith-Lovin, L., & Cook, J. M. (2001). Birds of a feather: Homophily in social networks. *Annual Review of Sociology, 27*, pp. 415–444. doi:10.1146/annurev.soc.27.1.415.

Milgram, S. (1963). Behavioral study of obedience. *Journal of Abnormal and Social Psychology, 67*, 371–378.

Milgram, S. (1965). Some conditions of obedience and disobedience to authority. *Human Relations, 18*, 57–76.

Miller, D. T., & Ross, M. (1975). Self-serving biases in the attribution of causality: Fact or fiction? *Psychological Bulletin, 82*, 213–225.

Miller, N., & Campbell, D. T. (1959). Recency and primacy in persuasion as a function of the timing of speeches and measurements. *The Journal of Abnormal and Social Psychology, 59*, 1–9.

Mischel, W. (1977). The interaction of person and situation. *Personality at the crossroads: Current issues in interactional psychology, 333*, 352.

Mitchell, D. H., & Eckstein, D. (2009). Jury dynamics and decision-making: A prescription for groupthink. *International Journal of Academic Research, 1*(1), 163–169.

Nelson, T. (Ed.). (2004). *Ageism: Stereotyping and prejudice against older persons*. The MIT Press.

Nisbett, R. E., Caputo, C., Legant, P., & Marecek, J. (1973). Behavior as seen by the actor and as seen by the observer. *Journal of Personality and Social Psychology, 27*, 154–164.

Nisbett, R. E., Peng, K., Choi, I., & Norenzayan, A. (2001). Culture and systems of thought: Holistic versus analytic cognition. *Psychological Review, 108*, 291–310.

Nosek, B. A. (2005). Moderators of the relationship between implicit and explicit evaluation. *Journal of Experimental Psychology: General, 134*(4), 565–584.

O'Keeffe, G. S., & Clarke-Pearson, K. (2011). The impact of social media on children, adolescents, and families. *Pediatrics, (127)*4, 800–4. doi:10.1542/peds.2011-0054.

Olson, M. A., & Fazio, R. H. (2003). Relations between implicit measures of prejudice what are we measuring? *Psychological Science, 14*, 636–639.

Olweus, D. (1993). *Bullying at school: What we know and what we can do*. Wiley-Blackwell.

Penton-Voak, I. S., Jones, B. C., Little, A. C., Baker, S., Tiddeman, B., Burt, D. M., & Perrett, D. I. (2001). Symmetry, sexual dimorphism in facial proportions and male facial attractiveness. *Proceedings of the Royal Society B: Biological Sciences, 268*, 1617–1623.

Petty, R. E., & Cacioppo, J. T. (1986). The elaboration likelihood model of persuasion. In *Communication and persuasion: Central and peripheral routes to attitude change* (pp. 1–24). Springer. doi:10.1007/978-1-4612-4964-1.

Petty, R. E., Wegener, D. T., & Fabrigar, L. R. (1997). Attitudes and attitude change. *Annual Review of Psychology, 48*, 609–647.

Pliner, P., Hart, H., Kohl, J., & Saari, D. (1974). Compliance without pressure: Some further data on the foot-in-the-door technique. *Journal of Experimental Social Psychology, 10*, 17–22.

Plant, E. A., & Devine, P. G. (1998). Internal and external motivation to respond without prejudice. *Journal of Personality and Social Psychology, 75*, 811–832.

Ramesh, A., & Gelfand, M. J. (2010). Will they stay or will they go? The role of job embeddedness in predicting turnover in individualistic and collectivistic cultures. *Journal of Applied Psychology, 95*(5), 807.

Raymer, M., Reid, M., Spiegel, M., & Purvanova, R. (2017). An examination of generational stereotypes as a path towards reverse ageism. *The Psychologist-Manager Journal, 20*, 148–175.

Regan, P. C., & Berscheid, E. (1997). Gender differences in characteristics desired in a potential sexual and marriage partner. *Journal of Psychology & Human Sexuality, 9*, 25–37.

Rhodes, N., & Wood, W. (1992). Self-esteem and intelligence affect influenceability: The mediating role of message reception. *Psychological Bulletin, 111*, 156–171.

Richard, F. D., Bond, C. F., Jr., & Stokes-Zoota, J. J. (2003). One hundred years of social psychology quantitatively described. *Review of General Psychology, 7*(4), 331–363. doi:10.1037/1089-2680.7.4.331.

References

Riggio, H. R., & Garcia, A. L. (2009). The power of situations: Jonestown and the fundamental attribution error. *Teaching of Psychology, 36*(2), 108–112. doi:10.1080/00986280902739636.

Rikowski, A., & Grammer, K. (1999). Human body odour, symmetry and attractiveness. *Proceedings of the Royal Society B: Biological Sciences, 266*(1422), 869–874. doi:10.1098/rspb.1999.0717.

Roesch, S. C., & Amirkham, J. H. (1997). Boundary conditions for self-serving attributions: Another look at the sports pages. *Journal of Applied Social Psychology, 27*, 245–261.

Rojek, J., Rosenfeld, R., & Decker, S. (2012). Policing race: The racial stratification of searches in police traffic stops. *Criminology, 50*, 993–1024.

Rosenberg, M. J., & Hovland, C. I. (1960). Cognitive, affective and behavioral components of attitudes. In *Attitude organization and change: An analysis of consistency among attitude components* (pp. 1–14). Yale University Press.

Rosenthal, R., & Jacobson, L. F. (1968). Teacher expectations for the disadvantaged. *Scientific American, 218*, 19–23.

Ross, L. (1977). The intuitive psychologist and his shortcomings: Distortions in the attribution process. *Advances in Experimental Social Psychology, 10*, 173–220.

Ross, L., Amabile, T. M., & Steinmetz, J. L. (1977). Social roles, social control, and biases in social-perception processes. *Journal of Personality and Social Psychology, 35*, 485–494.

Ross, L., & Nisbett, R. E. (1991). *The person and the situation: Perspectives of social psychology*. McGraw-Hill.

Rudman, L. A. (1998). Self-promotion as a risk factor for women: The costs and benefits of counterstereotypical impression management. *Journal of Personality and Social Psychology, 74*(3), 629–645.

Rusbult, C. E., & Van Lange, P. A. (2003). Interdependence, interaction, and relationships. *Annual Review of Psychology, 54*, 351–575.

Schank, R. C., Abelson, R. (1977). *Scripts, plans, goals, and understanding: An inquiry into human knowledge*. Lawrence Erlbaum Associates.

Shepperd, J. A., & Taylor, K. M. (1999). Social loafing and expectancy-value theory. *Personality and Social Psychology Bulletin, 25*, 1147–1158.

Sherif, M., Harvey, O. J., White, B. J., Hood, W. R., & Sherif, C. W. (1961). *Intergroup conflict and cooperation: The Robbers Cave experiment*. The University Book Exchange. http://livros01.livrosgratis.com.br/ps000162.pdf

Simms, A., & Nichols, T. (2014). Social loafing: A review of the literature. *Journal of Management Policy and Practice, 15*, 58–67.

Singh, D. (1993). Adaptive significance of female physical attractiveness: Role of waist-to-hip ratio. *Journal of Personality and Social Psychology, 65*, 293–307.

Sommers, S. R., & Ellsworth, P. C. (2000). Race in the courtroom: Perceptions of guilt and dispositional attributions. *Personality and Social Psychology Bulletin, 26*, 1367–1379.

Spears, B., Slee, P., Owens, L., & Johnson, B. (2009). Behind the scenes and screens: Insights into the human dimension of covert and cyberbullying. *Journal of Psychology, 217*(4), 189–196. doi:10.1027/0044-3409.217.4.189.

Sternberg, R. J. (1986). A triangular theory of love. *Psychological Review, 93*, 119–135.

Stewart, J. B. (2002). *Heart of a soldier*. Simon and Schuster.

Sutton, R.M. and Douglas, K.M. (2005). Justice for all, or just for me? More support for self-other differences in just world beliefs. Personality and Individual Differences, 9(3). pp. 637-645. ISSN 0191-8869.

Tajfel, H. (1974). Social identity and intergroup behaviour. *Social Science Information, 13*(2), 65–93.

Tajfel, H., & Turner, J. C. (1979). An integrative theory of intergroup conflict. In W. G. Austin & S. Worchel (Eds.), *The social psychology of intergroup relations* (pp. 33–48). Brooks-Cole.

Tavris, C., & Aronson, E. (2008). *Mistakes were made (but not by me): Why we justify foolish beliefs, bad decisions, and hurtful acts*. Houghton Mifflin Harcourt.

Taylor, L. S., Fiore, A. T., Mendelsohn, G. A., & Cheshire, C. (2011). "Out of my league": A real-world test of the matching hypothesis. *Personality and Social Psychology Bulletin, 37*(7), 942–954. doi:10.1177/0146167211409947.

Teger, A. I., & Pruitt, D. G. (1967). Components of group risk taking. *Journal of Experimental Social Psychology, 3*, 189–205.

Triandis, H. C. (2001). Individualism-collectivism and personality. *Journal of Personality, 69*, 907–924.

van Veen, V., Krug, M. K., Schooler, J. W., & Carter, C. S. (2009). Neural activity predicts attitude change in cognitive dissonance. *Nature Neuroscience, 12*, 1469–1474.

Vandebosch, H., & Van Cleemput, K. (2009). Cyberbullying among youngsters: Profiles of bullies and victims. *New media & Society, 11*(8), 1349–1371. doi:10.1177/1461444809341263.

Walker, I., & Crogan, M. (1998). Academic performance, prejudice, and the jigsaw classroom: New pieces to the puzzle. *Journal of Community and Applied Social Psychology, 8*, 381–393.

Walker, M. B., & Andrade, M. G. (1996). Conformity in the Asch task as a function of age. *The Journal of Social Psychology, 136*, 367–372.

Walster, E., & Festinger, L. (1962). The effectiveness of "overheard" persuasive communications. *Journal of Abnormal and Social Psychology, 65*, 395–402.

Wason, P. C., & Johnson-Laird, P. N. (1972). *The psychology of deduction: Structure and content*. Harvard University Press.

Weiner, B. (1979). A theory of motivation for some classroom experiences. *Journal of Educational Psychology, 71*(1), 3–25.

Wilson, M., & Daly, M. (1985). Competitiveness, risk taking, and violence: The young male syndrome. *Ethology and Sociobiology, 6*, 59–73.

Wilson, T. D., Lindsey, S., & Schooler, T. Y. (2000). A model of dual attitudes. *Psychological Review, 107*, 101–126.

Zajonc, R. B. (1965). Social facilitation. *Science, 149*(3681), 269–274. doi:10.1126/science.149.3681.269

Zhang, X., Fung, H. H., Stanley, J. T., Isaacowitz, D. M., & Zhang, Qi. (2014). Thinking more holistically as we grow older? Results from different tasks in two cultures. *Culture and Brain, 2*, 109–121. https://link.springer.com/article/10.1007%2Fs40167-014-0018-4

Zimbardo, P. G. (1969). The human choice: Individuation, reason, and order versus deindividuation, impulse, and chaos. In *Nebraska symposium on motivation*. University of Nebraska press.

Zimbardo, P. G. (2013). An end to the experiment. http://www.prisonexp.org/psychology/37.

Industrial-Organizational Psychology

ABC News. (2000, September 8). *Court OKs barring high IQs for Cops*. http://abcnews.go.com/US/court-oks-barring-high-iqs-cops/story?id=95836

Agerström, J., & Rooth, D.-O. (2011). The role of automatic obesity stereotypes in real hiring discrimination. *Journal of Applied Psychology, 96*, 790–805.

Allen, T. D., Eby, L. T., Poteet, M. L., Lentz, E., & Lima, L. (2004). Career benefits associated with mentoring for protégés: A meta-analysis. *Journal of Applied Psychology, 89*, 127–136.

Allen, T. D., Lentz, E., & Day, R. (2006). Career success outcomes associated with mentoring others: A comparison of mentors and nonmentors. *Journal of Career Development, 32*, 272–285.

American Civil Liberties Union. (n.d.). *Non-Discrimination Laws: State by State Information—Map*. https://www.aclu.org/maps/non-discrimination-laws-state-state-information-map

American National Standards Institute. (2000). *Control center ergonomic standards*. http://webstore.ansi.org/ergonomics/control_centre_ergonomics.aspx

American Psychological Association. (2016). Humanitarian work psychology. *Monitor on Psychology, 47*(4). https://www.apa.org/monitor/2016/04/humanitarian

Amiot, C. E., Terry, D. J., Jimmieson, N. L., & Callan, V. J. (2006). A longitudinal investigation of coping processes during a merger: Implications for job satisfaction and organizational identification. *Journal of Management, 32*, 552–574.

Arthur, W., Bennett, W., Edens, P. S., & Bell, S. T. (2003). Effectiveness of training in organizations: A meta-analysis of design and evaluation features. *Journal of Applied Psychology, 88*, 234–245.

Arthur, W., Woehr, D. J., & Graziano, W. G. (2001). Personality testing in employment settings: Problems and issues in the application of typical selection practices. *Personnel Review, 30*, 657–676.

Atkins, P. W. B., & Wood, R. E. (2002). Self-versus others' ratings as predictors of assessment center ratings: Validation evidence for 360-degree feedback programs. *Personnel Psychology, 55*, 871–904.

Badgett, M. V. L., Sears, B., Lau, H., & Ho, D. (2009). Bias in the workplace: Consistent evidence of sexual orientation and gender identity discrimination 1998–2008. *Chicago-Kent Law Review, 84*, 559–595.

Barrick, M. R., Swider, B. W., & Stewart, G. L. (2010). Initial evaluations in the interview: Relationships with subsequent interviewer evaluations and employment offers. *Journal of Applied Psychology, 95*, 1163–1172.

Bass, B. M. (1985). *Leadership and performance beyond expectations*. Free Press.

Bass, B. M., Avolio, B. J., & Atwater, L. (1996). The transformational and transactional leadership of men and women. *Applied Psychology: An International Review, 45*, 5–34.

Bauer, T. N., Erdogan, B., Liden, R. C., & Wayne, S. J. (2006). A longitudinal study of the moderating role of extraversion: Leader-member exchange, performance, and turnover during new executive development, *Journal of Applied Psychology, 91*(2), 298–310.

Bruno, T., & Abrahão, J. (2012). False alarms and incorrect rejections in an information security center: Correlation with the frequency of incidents. *Work, 41*, 2902–2907.

Buckingham, M., & Clifton, D. O. (2001). *Now, discover your strengths*. Free Press.

Bureau of Labor Statistics—U.S. Department of Labor. (2019). American time use survey—2018 results [Press release: USDL-19-1003]. https://www.bls.gov/news.release/pdf/atus.pdf

Bye, H. H., Horverak, J. G., Sandal, G. M., Sam, D. L., & Vijver, F. J. R. van de (2014). Cultural fit and ethnic background in the job interview. *International Journal of Cross Cultural Management, 14*, 7–26.

Carlson, D. S., Kacmar, K. M., & Williams, L. J. (2000). Construction and initial validation of a multidimensional measure of work–family conflict. *Journal of Vocational Behavior, 56*, 249–276.

Colligan, T. W., & Higgins, E. M. (2005). Workplace stress: Etiology and consequences. *Journal of Workplace Behavioral Health, 21*, 89–97.

Corbett, C., & Hill, C. (2012) *Graduating to a pay gap: The earnings of women and men one year after college graduation*. American Association of University Women.

DeGroot, T., & Gooty, J. (2009). Can nonverbal cues be used to make meaningful personality attributions in employment interviews? *Journal of Business Psychology, 24*, 179–192.

DeNisi, A. S., & Kluger, A. N. (2000). Feedback effectiveness: Can 360-degree appraisals be improved? *Academy of Management Executive, 14*, 129–139.

Dierdorff, E. C., & Wilson, M. A. (2003). A meta-analysis of job analysis reliability. *Journal of Applied Psychology, 88*, 635–646.

Eagly, A. H., Johannesen-Schmidt, M. C., & van Engen, M. L. (2003). Transformational, transactional, and laissez-faire leadership styles: A meta-analysis comparing women and men. *Psychological Bulletin, 129*, 569–591.

Eagly, A. H., & Johnson, B. T. (1990). Gender and leadership style: A meta-analysis. *Psychological Bulletin, 108*, 233–256.

Eby, L. T., Allen, T. D., Evans, S. C., Ng, T., & DuBois, D. (2008). Does mentoring matter? A multidisciplinary meta-analysis comparing mentored and non-mentored individuals. *Journal of Vocational Behavior, 72*, 254–267.

Eby, L. T., Durley, J. R., Evans, S. C., & Ragins, B. R. (2006). The relationship between short-term mentoring benefits and long-term mentor outcomes. *Journal of Vocational Behavior, 69*, 424–444.

Elmore, L. (2010, June). The workplace generation gaps. *Women in Business, 62*(2), 8–11.

Felfe, J., & Schyns, B. (2006). Personality and the perception of transformational leadership: The impact of extraversion, neuroticism, personal need for structure, and occupational self-efficacy. *Journal of Applied Social Psychology, 36*(3), 708–41.

Fletcher, C. (2001). Performance appraisal and management: The developing research agenda. *Journal of Occupational and Organizational Psychology, 74*, 473–487.

Gentry, W. A., Weber, T. J., & Sadri, G. (2008). Examining career-related mentoring and managerial performance across cultures: A multilevel analysis. *Journal of Vocational Behavior, 72*, 241–253.

Gibson, J. W., Greenwood, R. A., & Murphy, E. F. (2009). Generational differences in the workplace: Personal values, behaviors, and popular beliefs. *Journal of Diversity Management, 4*, 1–7.

Gilbreth, L. M. (1914). *The psychology of management: The function of the mind in determining, teaching, and installing methods of least waste*. Sturgis and Walton.

Gilbreth, L. M. (1998). *As I remember: An autobiography of Lillian Gilbreth*. Industrial Engineering and Management Press.

Gilmore, D. C., & Ferris, G. R. (1989). The effects of applicant impression management tactics on interviewer judgments. *Journal of Management,15*, 557–564.

Greenberg, J. (1993). Stealing in the name of justice: Informational and interpersonal moderators of theft reactions to underpayment inequity. *Organizational Behavior and Human Decision Processes, 54*, 81–103.

Greenberg, L., & Barling, J. (1999). Predicting employee agression against coworkers, subordinates and supervisors: The roles of person behaviors and perceived workplace factors. *Journal of Organizational Behavior, 20*, 897–913.

Greenhaus, J. H., & Beutell, N. J. (1985). Sources of conflict between work and family roles. *Academy of Management Review, 10*, 76–88.

Gyllensten, K., & Palmer, S. (2005). The role of gender in workplace stress: A critical literature review. *Health Education Journal, 64*, 271–288.

Hoogendoorn, S., Oosterbeek, H., & van Praag, M. (2013). The impact of gender diversity on the performance of business teams: Evidence from a field experiment. *Management Science, 59*, 1514–1528.

Hosoda, M., Stone-Romero, E., & Coats, G. (2003). The effects of physical attractiveness on job-related outcomes: A meta-analysis of experimental studies. *Personnel Psychology, 56*, 431–462.

Howard, J. L., & Ferris, G. R. (1996). The employment interview context: Social and situational influences on interviewer decisions. *Journal of Applied Social Psychology, 26*, 112–136.

Howell, W. C. (2003). Human factors and ergonomics. In W. C. Borman, D. R. Ilgen, R. J. Limoski, & I. B. Weiner (Eds.), *Handbook of psychology: Vol. 12: Industrial and organizational psychology* (pp. 565–593). Wiley.

Human Rights Campaign. (2013a). *Cities and counties with non-discrimination ordinances that include gender identity.* http://www.hrc.org/resources/entry/cities-and-counties-with-non-discrimination-ordinances-that-include-gender

Human Rights Campaign. (2013b). *Corporate equality index 2014: Rating American workplaces on lesbian, gay, bisexual and transgender equality.* http://www.hrc.org/campaigns/corporate-equality-index

Jordan v. New London, No. 99-9188, 2000 U.S. App. LEXIS 22195 (2d Cir. 2000) (unpublished). http://www.aele.org/apa/jordan-newlondon.html

Judge, T. A., & Kammeyer-Mueller, J. D. (2012). Job attitudes. *Annual Reviews of Psychology, 63*, 341–367.

Judge, T. A., Piccolo, R. F., Podsakoff, N. P., Shaw, J. C., & Rich, B. (2010). The relationship between pay and job satisfaction: A meta-analysis of the literature. *Journal of Vocational Behavior, 77*, 157–167.

Judge, T. A., & Watanabe, S. (1993). Another look at the job satisfaction–life satisfaction relationship. *Journal of Applied Psychology, 78*, 939–948.

Kaiser, R. B., & Overfield, D. V. (2011). Strengths, strengths overused, and lopsided leadership. *Consulting Psychology, 63*, 89–109.

Katzell, R. A., & Austin, J. T. (1992). From then to now: The development of industrial–organizational psychology in the United States. *Journal of Applied Psychology, 77*, 803–835.

Khanna, C., Medsker, G. J., & Ginter, R. (2012). *2012 income and employment survey results for the Society for Industrial and Organizational Psychology.* http://www.siop.org/2012SIOPIncomeSurvey.pdf

Koppes, L. L. (1997). American female pioneers of industrial and organizational psychology during the early years. *Journal of Applied Psychology, 82*, 500–515.

Lancaster, J. (2004). *Making time: Lillian Moller Gilbreth—A life beyond "Cheaper by the Dozen."* Northeastern University Press.

Lapierre, L. M., & Allen, T. D. (2006). Work-supportive family, family-supportive supervision, use of organizational benefits, and problem-focused coping: Implications for work–family conflict and employee well-being. *Journal of Occupational Health Psychology, 11*, 169–181.

Larson, C., & LaFasto, F. (1989). *Teamwork: What must go right / What can go wrong.* Sage.

Levine, S. P., & Feldman, R. S. (2002). Women and men's nonverbal behavior and self-monitoring in a job interview setting. *Applied Human Resources Management Research, 7*, 1–14.

Lewin, K., Lippitt, R., & White, R. K. (1939). Patterns of aggressive behavior in experimentally created "social climates." *Journal of Social Psychology, 10*, 271–301.

Liden, R. C., Martin, C. L., & Parsons, C. K. (1993). Interviewer and applicant behaviors in employment interviews. *Academy of Management Journal, 36*, 373–386.

Lips, H. (2013). The gender pay gap: Challenging the rationalizations. Perceived equity, discrimination, and the limits of human capital models. *Sex Roles, 68*, 169–185.

Locke, E. A. (1976). The nature and causes of job satisfaction. In M. D. Dunnette (Ed.), *Handbook of industrial and organizational psychology* (pp. 1297–1349). Rand McNally.

Manley, K. (2009). The BFOQ defense: Title VII's concession to gender discrimination. *Duke Journal of Gender Law & Policy, 16*, 169–210.

McCarney, R., Warner, J., Iliffe, S., van Haselen, R., Griffin, M., & Fisher, P. (2007). The Hawthorne effect:

A randomised, controlled trial. *BMC Medical Research Methodology, 7*, 30.

McDaniel, M. A., Whetzel, D. L., Schmidt, F. L., & Maurer, S. D. (1994). The validity of employment interviews: A comprehensive review and meta-analysis. *Journal of Applied Psychology, 79*, 599–616.

McGregor, D. (1960). *The human side of enterprise.* McGraw Hill.

McKeen, C., & Bujaki, M. (2007). Gender and mentoring. In B. R. Ragins & K. E. Kram (Eds.), *The handbook of mentoring at work: Theory, research and practice* (pp. 197–222). Sage Publications.

McMillan, S. K., Stevens, S., & Kelloway, E. K. (2009). History and development of industrial/organizational psychology in the Canadian forces personnel selection branch: 1938–2009. *Canadian Psychology, 50*, 283–291.

Meister, J. C., & Willyerd, K. (2010, May). Mentoring millennials. *Harvard Business Review*, 1–4.

Münsterberg, H. (1913). *Psychology and industrial efficiency.* Houghton Mifflin Company.

Myers, K. K., & Sadaghiani, K. (2010). Millennials in the workplace: A communication pespective on millennials organizational relationships and performance. *Journal of Business Psychology, 25*, 225–238.

Naquin, C., & Tynan, R. (2003). The team halo effect: Why teams are not blamed for their failures. *Journal of Applied Psychology, 88*, 332–340.

Occupational Safety & Health Administration. (2014). *Workplace violence*. United States Department of Labor. https://www.osha.gov/SLTC/workplaceviolence/

O'Keefe, J., & Bruyere, S. (1994). *Implications of the Americans with Disabilities Act for psychology.* Springer.

Ostroff, C., Kinicki, A. J., & Tamkins, M. M. (2003). Organizational culture and climate. In W. C. Borman, D. R. Ilgen, R. J. Klimoski, & I. B. Weiner (Eds.), *Handbook of psychology: Vol. 12: Industrial and organizational psychology* (pp. 145–158). Wiley.

Pettigrew, T. F., & Tropp, L. R. (2006). A meta-analytic test of intergroup contact theory. *Journal of Personality and Social Psychology, 90*, 751–783.

Phillips, A. S., & Bedeian, A. G. (1994). Leader-follower exchange quality: The role of personal and interpersonal attributes. *Academy of Management Journal, 37*(4), 990–1001.

Posig, M., & Kickul, J. (2004). Work-role expectation and work family conflict: Gender differences in emotional exhaustion. *Women in Management Review, 19*, 373–386.

Powell, A., Piccoli, G., & Ives, B. (2004). Virtual teams: A review of current literature and directions for future research. *The DATA BASE for Advances in Information Systems, 35*, 6–36.

Ragins, B. R., & Cotton, J. L. (1999). Mentor functions and outcomes: A comparison of men and women in formal and informal mentoring relationships. *Journal of Applied Psychology, 84*, 529–550.

Rakić, T., Steffens, M. C., & Mummendey, A. (2011). When it matters how you pronounce it: The influence of regional accents on job interview outcome. *British Journal of Psychology, 102*, 868–883.

Riley, M., Elgin, B., Lawrence, D., & Matlack, C. (2014, March 13). Missed alarms and 40 million stolen credit card numbers: How Target blew it. *Bloomberg Businessweek.* http://www.businessweek.com/articles/2014-03-13/target-missed-alarms-in-epic-hack-of-credit-card-data

Roethlisberg, F., & Dickson, W. (1939). *Management and the worker.* Harvard University Press.

Saad, L. (2012). U.S. workers least happy with their work stress and pay: Satisfaction is highest for safety conditions and relations with coworkers. *Gallup Economy.* http://www.gallup.com/poll/158723/workers-least-happy-work-stress-pay.aspx

Saari, L. M., & Judge, T. A. (2004). Employee attitudes and job satisfaction. *Human Resouce Management, 43*, 395–407.

Schraeder, M., Becton, J. B., & Portis, R. (2007). A critical examination of performance appraisals: An organization's friend or foe? *The Journal for Quality and Participation, 30*, 20–25.

Schyns, B., Kroon, B., & Moors, G. (2008). Follower characteristics and the perception of leader-member exchange. *Journal of Managerial Psychology, 23*(7), 772–788. https://www.emerald.com/insight/content/doi/10.1108/02683940810896330/full/html

Society for Industrial and Organizational Psychology (SIOP). (2014). What value does SIOP membership provide? http://www.siop.org/benefits/

Society for Occupational Health. (2020). History of OHP. http://sohp-online.org/field-of-ohp/history-of-ohp/

Taylor, F. W. (1911). *The principles of scientific management*. Harper & Brothers.

The New York Times. (1999, Sept. 9). *Metro news briefs: Connecticut—Judge rules that police can bar high IQ scores*. http://www.nytimes.com/1999/09/09/nyregion/metro-news-briefs-connecticut-judge-rules-that-police-can-bar-high-iq-scores.html

Tornow, W. W. (1993a). Editor's note: Introduction to special issue on 360-degree feedback. *Human Resource Management, 32*, 211–219.

Tornow, W. W. (1993b). Perceptions or reality: Is multi-perspective measurement a means or an end? *Human Resource Management, 32*, 221–229.

Toyota Motor Manufacturing. (2013). *Toyota production system terms*. http://www.toyotageorgetown.com/terms.asp

Ugboro, I. O. (2006). Organizational commitment, job redesign, employee empowerment and intent to quit among survivors of restructuring and downsizing. *Journal of Behavioral and Applied Management, 7*, 232–257.

United States Nuclear Regulatory Commission. (2013). *Backgrounder on the Three Mile Island accident*. http://www.nrc.gov/reading-rm/doc-collections/fact-sheets/3mile-isle.html

U.S. Equal Employment Opportunity Commission. (2014). *EEOC charge receipts by state (includes U.S. territories) and basis for 2013*. http://www1.eeoc.gov/eeoc/statistics/enforcement/state_13.cfm

U.S. Equal Employment Opportunity Commission. (n.d.). *Facts about sexual harassment*. http://www.eeoc.gov/eeoc/publications/fs-sex.cfm

Van De Water, T. (1997). Psychology's entrepreneurs and the marketing of industrial psychology. *Journal of Applied Psychology, 82*, 486–499.

van Knippenberg, D., van Knippenberg, B., Monden, L., & de Lima, F. (2002). Organizational identification after a merger: A social identity perspective. *British Journal of Social Psychology, 41*, 233–252.

Vinchur, A. J., & Koppes, L. L. (2014). Early contributors to the science and practice of industrial psychology. In L. L. Koppes, (Ed.), *Historical perspectives in industrial and organizational psychology* (pp. 37–58). Erlbaum.

Wagner, E. (2019a). Impasses Panel guts telework, official time for employees at Social Security Administration. *Government Executive*. https://www.govexec.com/management/2019/06/impasses-panel-guts-telework-official-time-employees-social-security-administration/157448/

Wagner, E. (2019b). Social Security ends telework program for 12,000 employees. *Government Executive*. https://www.govexec.com/pay-benefits/2019/10/social-security-ends-telework-program-12000-employees/160954/

Weiss, H. M. (2002). Deconstructing job satisfaction: Separating evaluations, beliefs and affective experiences. *Human Resouces Management Review, 12*, 173–194.

Stress, Lifestyle, and Health

Aboa-Éboulé, C., Brisson, C., Maunsell, E., Mâsse, B., Bourbonnais, R., Vézina, M., . . . Dagenais, G. R.

(2007). Job strain and risk for acute recurrent coronary heart disease events. *Journal of the American Medical Association, 298*, 1652–1660.

Abramson, L. Y., Seligman, M. E. P., & Teasdale, J. D. (1978). Learned helplessness in humans: Critique and reformulation. *Journal of Abnormal Psychology, 87*, 49–74.

Ader, R. & Cohen, N. (2001). Conditioning and immunity. In R. Ader, D. L. Felten & N. Cohen (Eds.), *Psychoneuroimmunology* (3rd ed., pp. 3–34). Academic Press.

Ader, R., & Cohen, N. (1975). Behaviorally conditioned immunosuppression. *Psychosomatic Medicine, 37*, 333–340.

Ahola, K., Honkonen, T., Isometsä, E., Kalimo, R., Nykyri, E., Aromaa, A., & Lönnqvist, J. (2005). The relationship between job-related burnout and depressive disorders—Results from the Finnish Health 2000 study. *Journal of Affective Disorders, 88*, 55–62.

Ahola, K., Honkonen, T., Kivamäki, M., Virtanen, M., Isometsä, E., Aromaa, A., & Lönnqvist, J. (2006). Contribution of burnout to the association between job strain and depression: The Health 2000 study. *Journal of Occupational and Environmental Medicine, 48*, 1023–1030.

Ajrouch, K. J., Reisine, S., Lim, S., Sohn, W., & Ismail, A. (2010). Perceived everyday discrimination and psychological distress: Does social support matter? *Ethnicity & Health, 15*(4), 417–434. https://www.tandfonline.com/doi/abs/10.1080/13557858.2010.484050

American Academy of Neurology. (2014). *Headache*. https://patients.aan.com/disorders/index.cfm?event=view&disorder_id=936

American Heart Association. (2012a). *What is angina?* http://www.heart.org/idc/groups/heart-public/@wcm/@hcm/documents/downloadable/ucm_300287.pdf

American Heart Association. (2012b). *Why blood pressure matters*. http://www.heart.org/HEARTORG/Conditions/HighBloodPressure/WhyBloodPressureMatters/Why-Blood-Pressure-Matters_UCM_002051_Article.jsp

American Heart Association. (2014, February 24). Depression as a risk factor for poor prognosis among patients with acute coronary syndrome: Systematic review and recommendations: A scientific statement from the American Heart Association. *Circulation*. http://circ.ahajournals.org/content/early/2014/02/24/CIR.0000000000000019.full.pdf+html

American Lung Association. (2010). *Asthma*. http://www.lung.org/assets/documents/publications/solddc-chapters/asthma.pdf

American Psychiatric Association. (2013). *Diagnostic and statistical manual of mental disorders* (5th ed.). Author.

Bandura, A. (1994). Self-efficacy. In V. S. Ramachandran (Ed.), *Encyclopedia of human behavior* (Vol. 4, pp. 71–81). Academic Press.

Bandura, A. (1997). *Self-efficacy: The exercise of control*. Freeman.

Bandura, A. (2004). Health promotion by social cognitive means. *Health Education & Behavior, 31*, 143–164.

Barefoot, J. C., & Schroll, M. S. (1996). Symptoms of depression, acute myocardial infarction, and total mortality in a community sample. *Circulation, 93*, 1976–1980.

Baron, R. S., & Kerr, N. L. (2003). *Group process, group decision, group action* (2nd ed.). Open University Press.

Baron, R. S., Cutrona, C. E., Hicklin, D., Russell, D. W., & Lubaroff, D. M. (1990). Social support and immune function among spouses of cancer patients. *Journal of Personality and Social Psychology, 59*, 344–352.

Baumeister, R. F., & Leary, M. R. (1995). The need to belong: Desire for interpersonal attachments as a fundamental human motivation. *Psychological Bulletin, 117*, 497–529.

Benson, H., & Proctor, W. (1994). *Beyond the relaxation response: How to harness the healing power of your personal beliefs*. Berkley Publishing Group.

Berkman, L. F., & Syme, L. (1979). Social networks, host resistance, and mortality: A nine-year follow-up study of Alameda County residents. *American Journal of Epidemiology, 109*, 186–204.

Blackburn, E. H., & Epel, E. S. (2012). Telomeres and adversity: Too toxic to ignore. *Nature, 490*(7419), 169–171.

Boehm, J. K., & Kubzansky, L. D. (2012). The heart's content: The association between positive psychological well-being and cardiovascular health. *Psychological Bulletin, 138*, 655–691.

Bolger, N., DeLongis, A., Kessler, R. C., & Schilling, E. A. (1989). Effects of daily stress on negative mood. *Journal of Personality and Social Psychology, 57*, 808–818.

Boyle, S. H., Michalek, J. E., & Suarez, E. C. (2006). Covariation of psychological attributes and incident coronary heart disease in U.S. Air Force veterans of the Vietnam War. *Psychosomatic Medicine, 68*, 844–850.

Brickman, P., & Campbell, D. T. (1971). Hedonic relativism and planning the good society. In M. H. Appley (Ed.), *Adaptation level theory: A symposium* (pp. 287–302). Academic Press.

Brickman, P., Coats, D., & Janoff-Bulman, R. (1978). Lottery winners and accident victims: Is happiness relative? *Journal of Personality and Social Psychology, 36*, 917–927.

Brummett, B. H., Barefoot, J. C., Siegler, I. C., Clapp-Channing, N. E., Lytle, B. L., Bosworth, H. B., . . . Mark, D. B. (2001). Characteristics of socially isolated patients with coronary artery disease who are at elevated risk for mortality. *Psychosomatic Medicine, 63*, 267–272.

Caceres, C., & Burns, J. W. (1997). Cardiovascular reactivity to psychological stress may enhance subsequent pain sensitivity. *Pain, 69*, 237–244.

Campeau, S., Nyhuis, T. J., Sasse, S. K., Kryskow, E. M., Herlihy, L., Masini, C. V., . . . Day, H. E. W. (2010). Hypothalamic pituitary adrenal axis responses to low-intensity stressors are reduced after voluntary wheel running in rats. *Journal of Neuroendocrinology, 22*, 872–888.

Cannon, W. B. (1932). *The wisdom of the body*. W. W. Norton.

Carroll, J. (2007). *Most Americans "very satisfied" with their personal lives*. Gallup. http://www.gallup.com/poll/103483/Most-Americans-Very-Satisfied-Their-Personal-Lives.aspx

Cathcart, S., Petkov, J., & Pritchard, D. (2008). Effects of induced stress on experimental pain sensitivity in chronic tension-type headache sufferers. *European Journal of Neurology, 15*, 552–558.

Centers for Disease Control and Prevention (CDC). (2006). *You can control your asthma: A guide to understanding asthma and its triggers*. http://www.cdc.gov/asthma/pdfs/asthma_brochure.pdf

Centers for Disease Control and Prevention (CDC). (2011). Million hearts: Strategies to reduce the prevalence of leading cardiovascular disease risk factors—United States, 2011. *Morbidity and Mortality Weekly Report [MMWR], 60*(36), 1248–1251. http://www.cdc.gov/mmwr/pdf/wk/mm6036.pdf

Centers for Disease Control and Prevention (CDC). (2013a). *Asthma's impact on the nation: Data from the CDC National Asthma Control Program*. http://www.cdc.gov/asthma/impacts_nation/AsthmaFactSheet.pdf

Centers for Disease Control and Prevention (CDC). (2013b). *Breathing easier*. http://www.cdc.gov/asthma/pdfs/breathing_easier_brochure.pdf

Center for Investigating Health Minds. (2013). *About*. http://www.investigatinghealthyminds.org/cihmCenter.html

Chandola, T., Britton, A., Brunner, E., Hemingway, H., Malik, M., Kumari, M., . . . Marmot, M. (2008). Work stress and coronary heart disease: What are the mechanisms? *European Heart Journal, 29*, 640–648.

Chang, E. C. (2001). Introduction: Optimism and pessimism and moving beyond the most fundamental questions. In E. C. Chang (Ed.), *Optimism and pessimism: Implications for theory, research, and practice* (pp. 3–12). American Psychological Association.

Chang, P. P., Ford, D. E., Meoni, L. A., Wang, N. Y., & Klag, M. J. (2002). Anger in young and subsequent premature cardiovascular disease. *Archives of Internal Medicine, 162,* 901–906.

Chida, Y., & Steptoe, A. (2009). The association of anger and hostility with future coronary heart disease: A meta-analytic review or prospective evidence. *Journal of the American College of Cardiology, 53,* 936–946.

Cohen, S., Frank, E., Doyle, W. J., Skoner, D. P., Rabin, B. S., & Gwaltney, J. M. J. (1998). Types of stressors that increase susceptibility to the common cold in healthy adults. *Health Psychology, 17,* 214–223.

Cohen, S., & Herbert, T. B. (1996). Health psychology: Psychological factors and physical disease from the perspective of human psychoneuroimmunology. *Annual Review of Psychology, 47,* 113–142.

Cohen, S., & Janicki-Deverts, D. (2012). Who's stressed? Distributions of psychological stress in the United States in probability samples in 1993, 2006, and 2009. *Journal of Applied Social Psychology, 42,* 1320–1334.

Cohen, S., Janicki-Deverts, D., & Miller, G. E. (2007). Psychological distress and disease. *Journal of the American Medical Association, 98,* 1685–1687.

Cohen, S., Doyle, W. J., Turner, R., Alper, C. M., & Skoner, D. P. (2003). Sociability and susceptibility to the common cold. *Psychological Science, 14,* 389–395.

Cohrs, J. C., Christie, D. J., White, M. P., & Das, C. (2013). Contributions of positive psychology to peace: Toward global well-being and resilience. *American Psychologist, 68,* 590–600.

Compton, W. C. (2005). *An introduction to positive psychology.* Thomson Wadsworth.

Cotton, D. H. G. (1990). *Stress management: An integrated approach to therapy.* Brunner/Mazel.

Craft, L. L., VanIterson, E. H., Helenowski, I. B., Rademaker, A. W., & Courneya, K. S. (2012). Exercise effects on depressive symptoms in cancer survivors: A systematic review and meta-analysis. *Cancer Epidemiology, Biomarkers & Prevention, 21,* 3–19.

Csikszentmihalyi, M. (1997). *Finding flow.* Basic Books.

Csikszentmihalyi, M. (1999). If we are so rich, why aren't we happy? *American Psychologist, 54,* 821–827.

D'Amato, G., Liccardi, G., Cecchi, L., Pellegrino, F., & D'Amato, M. (2010). Facebook: A new trigger for asthma? *The Lancet, 376,* 1740.

Davidson, K. W., Mostofsky, E., & Whang, W. (2010). Don't worry: be happy: Positive affect and reduced 10-year incident coronary heart disease: The Canadian Nova Scotia Health Survey. *European Heart Journal, 31,* 1065–1070.

de Kluizenaar, Y., Gansevoort, R. T., Miedema, H. M. E., & de Jong, P. E. (2007). Hypertension and road traffic noise exposure. *Journal of Occupational and Environmental Medicine, 49,* 484–492.

De Vogli, R., Chandola, T., & Marmot, M. G. (2007). Negative aspects of close relationships and heart disease. *Archives of Internal Medicine, 167,* 1951–1957.

DeLongis, A., Coyne, J. C., Dakof, G., Folkman, S., & Lazarus, R. S. (1982). Relationship of daily hassles, uplifts, and major life events to health status. *Health Psychology, 1,* 119–136.

Derogatis, L. R., & Coons, H. L. (1993). Self-report measures of stress. In L. Goldberger & S. Breznitz (Eds.), *Handbook of stress: Theoretical and clinical aspects* (2nd ed., pp. 200–233). Free Press.

Diehl, M., & Hay, E. L. (2010). Risk and resilience factors in coping with daily stress in adulthood: The role of age, self-concept incoherence, and personal control. *Developmental Psychology, 46,* 1132–1146.

Diener, E. (2012). New findings and future directions for subjective well-being research. *American Psychologist, 67,* 590–597.

Diener, E. (2013). The remarkable changes in the science of subjective well-being. *Perspectives on Psychological Science, 8*, 663–666.

Diener, E., & Biswas-Diener, R. (2002). Will money increase subjective well-being? A literature review and guide to needed research. *Social Indicators Research, 57*, 119–169.

Diener, E., Diener, M., & Diener, C. (1995). Factors predicting the subjective well-being of nations. *Journal of Personality and Social Psychology, 69*, 851–864.

Diener, E., Lucas, R., & Scollon, C. N. (2006). Beyond the hedonic treadmill: Revising the adaptation theory of well-being. *American Psychologist, 61*, 305–314.

Diener, E., Ng, W., Harter, J., & Arora, R. (2010). Wealth and happiness across the world: Material prosperity predicts life evaluation, whereas psychosocial prosperity predicts positive feelings. *Journal of Personality and Social Psychology, 99*, 52–61.

Diener, E., Oishi, S., & Ryan, K. L. (2013). Universals and cultural differences in the causes and structure of happiness: A multilevel review. In *Mental Well-Being* (pp. 153–176). Springer Netherlands.

Diener, E., Suh, E. M., Lucas, R. E., & Smith, H. L. (1999). Subjective well-being: Three decades of progress. *Psychological Bulletin, 125*, 276–302.

Diener, E., Tay, L., & Myers, D. (2011). The religion paradox: If religion makes people happy, why are so many dropping out? *Journal of Personality and Social Psychology, 101*, 1278–1290.

Diener, E., Tay, L., & Oishi, S. (2013). Rising income and the subjective well-being of nations. *Journal of Personality and Social Psychology, 104*, 267–276.

Diener, E., Wolsic, B., & Fujita, F. (1995). Physical attractiveness and subjective well-being. *Journal of Personality and Social Psychology, 69*, 120–129.

Dohrenwend, B. P. (2006). Inventorying stressful life events as risk factors for psychopathology: Toward resolution of the problem of intracategory variability. *Psychological Bulletin, 132*, 477–495.

Entringer, S., Epel, E. S., Kumsta, R., Lin, J., Hellhammer, D. H., Blackburn, E., Wüst, S., & Wadhwa, P. D. (2011). Stress exposure in intrauterine life is associated with shorter telomere length in young adulthood. *Proceedings of the National Academy of Sciences, USA, 108*, E513–E518.

Epel, E. S., Blackburn, E. H., Lin, J., Dhabhar, F. S., Adler, N. E., Morrow, J. D., & Cawthon, R. M. (2004). Accelerated telomere shortening in response to life stress. *Proceedings of the National Academy of Sciences, USA, 101*, 17312–17315.

Everly, G. S., & Lating, J. M. (2002). *A clinical guide to the treatment of the human stress response* (2nd ed.). Kluwer Academic/Plenum Publishing.

Falagas, M. E., Zarkadoulia, E. A., Ioannidou, E. N., Peppas, G., Christodoulou, C., & Rafailidis, P. I. (2007). The effect of psychosocial factors on breast cancer outcome: A systematic review. *Breast Cancer Research, 9*:R44. http://breast-cancer-research.com/content/pdf/bcr1744.pdf

Folkman, S., & Lazarus, R. S. (1980). An analysis of coping in a middle-aged community sample. *Journal of Health and Social Behavior, 21*, 219–239.

Fontana, A. M., Diegnan, T., Villeneuve, A., & Lepore, S. J. (1999). Nonevaluative social support reduces cardiovascular reactivity in young women during acutely stressful performance situations. *Journal of Behavioral Medicine, 22*, 75–91.

Friedman, H. S., & Booth-Kewley, S. (1987). The "disease-prone personality": A meta-analytic view of the construct. *American Psychologist, 42*, 539–555.

Friedman, M. (1977). Type A behavior pattern: Some of its pathophysiological components. *Bulletin of the New York Academy of Medicine, 53*, 593–604.

Friedman, M., & Rosenman, R. (1974). *Type A behavior and your heart*. Alfred A. Knopf.

Friedman, M., & Rosenman, R. H. (1959). Association of specific overt behavior pattern with blood and cardiovascular findings blood cholesterol level, blood clotting time, incidence of arcus senilis, and clinical coronary artery disease. *Journal of the American Medical Association, 169*(12), 1286–1296.

Fujita, F., & Diener, E. (2005). Life satisfaction set point: Stability and change. *Journal of Personality and Social Psychology, 88*, 158–164.

Fulmer, C. A., Gelfand, M. J., Kruglanski, A., Kim-Prieto, C., Diener, E., Pierro, A., & Higgins, E. T. (2010). On "feeling right" in cultural contexts: How person-culture match affects self-esteem and subjective well-being. *Psychological Science, 21*, 1563–1569.

Geoffroy, M. C., Hertzman, C., Li, L., & Power, C. (2013). Prospective association of morning salivary cortisol with depressive symptoms in mid-life: A life-course study. *PLoS ONE, 8*(11), 1–9.

Gerber, M., Kellman, M., Hartman, T., & Pühse, U. (2010). Do exercise and fitness buffer against stress among Swiss police and emergency response service officers? *Psychology of Sport and Exercise, 11*, 286–294.

Glaser, R., & Kiecolt-Glaser, J. K. (2005). Stress-induced immune dysfunction: Implications for health. *Nature Reviews Immunology, 5*, 243–251.

Glaser, R., Kiecolt-Glaser, J. K., Marucha, P. T., MacCallum, R. C., Laskowski, B. F., & Malarkey, W. B. (1999). Stress-related changes in proinflammatory cytokine production in wounds. *Archives of General Psychiatry, 56*, 450–456.

Glassman, A. H. (2007). Depression and cardiovascular comorbidity. *Dialogues in Clinical Neuroscience, 9*, 9–17.

Glassman, A. H., & Shapiro, P. A. (1998). Depression and the course of coronary artery disease. *American Journal of Psychiatry, 155*, 4–11.

Greenberg, J. S. (2006). *Comprehensive stress management* (9th ed.). McGraw-Hill.

Hackney, C. H., & Sanders, G. S. (2003). Religiosity and mental health: A meta-analysis of recent studies. *Journal for the Scientific Study of Religion, 42*, 43–55.

Hafeez, H., Zeshan, M., Tahir, M. A., Jahan, N., & Naveed, S. (2017). Health care disparities among lesbian, gay, bisexual, and transgender youth: A literature review. *Cureus, 9*(4). https://www.ncbi.nlm.nih.gov/pubmed/28638747

Hansen, T. (2012). Parenthood and happiness: A review of folk theories versus empirical evidence. *Social Indicators Research, 108*, 29–64.

Hare, D. L., Toukhsati, S. R., Johansson, P., & Jaarsma, T. (2013). Depression and cardiovascular disease: A clinical review. *European Heart Journal*. Advance online publication. doi:10.1093/eurheartj/eht462

Hatch, S. L., & Dohrenwend, B. P. (2007). Distribution of traumatic and other stressful life events by race/ethnicity, gender, SES, and age: A review of the research. *American Journal of Community Psychology, 40*, 313–332.

Haynes, S. G., Feinleib, M., & Kannel, W. B. (1980). The relationship of psychosocial factors to coronary disease in the Framingham study: III. Eight-year incidence of coronary heart disease. *American Journal of Epidemiology, 111*, 37–58.

Head, D., Singh, T., & Bugg, J. M. (2012). The moderating role of exercise on stress-related effects on the hippocampus and memory in later adulthood. *Neuropsychology, 26*, 133–143.

Helliwell, J., Layard, R., & Sachs, J. (Eds.). (2013). *World happiness report 2013*. United Nations Sustainable Development Solutions Network: http://unsdsn.org/wp-content/uploads/2014/02/WorldHappinessReport2013_online.pdf

Helson, H. (1964). Current trends and issues in adaptation-level theory. *American Psychologist, 19*, 26–38.

References

Holmes, T. H., & Masuda, M. (1974). Life change and illness susceptibility. In B. S. Dohrenwend & B. P. Dohrenwend (Eds.), *Stressful life events: Their nature and effects* (pp. 45–72). John Wiley & Sons.

Holmes, T. H., & Rahe, R. H. (1967). The social readjustment rating scale. *Journal of Psychosomatic Research, 11*, 213–218.

Holmes, T. S., & Holmes, T. H. (1970). Short-term intrusions into the life style routine. *Journal of Psychosomatic Research, 14*, 121–132.

Holt-Lunstad, J., Smith, T. B., & Layton, J. B. (2010). Social relationships and mortality risk: A meta-analytic review. *PLoS Medicine, 7*(7), e1000316.

Hunt, M. G., Marx, R., Lipson, C., & Young, J. (2018). No more FOMO: Limiting social media decreases loneliness and depression. *Journal and Social and Clinical Psychology, 37*(10), 751–768. https://guilfordjournals.com/doi/abs/10.1521/jscp.2018.37.10.751

Hupbach, A., & Fieman, R. (2012). Moderate stress enhances immediate and delayed retrieval of educationally relevant material in healthy young men. *Behavioral Neuroscience, 126*, 819–825.

Infurna, F. J., & Gerstorf, D. (2014). Perceived control relates to better functional health and lower cardiometabolic risk: The mediating role of physical activity. *Health Psychology, 33*, 85–94.

Infurna, F. J., Gerstorf, D., Ram, N., Schupp, J., & Wagner, G. G. (2011). Long-term antecedents and outcomes of perceived control. *Psychology and Aging, 26*, 559–575.

Johnson, W., & Krueger, R. F. (2006). How money buys happiness: Genetic and environmental processes linking finances and life satisfaction. *Journal of Personality and Social Psychology, 90*, 680–691.

Jonas, B. S., & Lando, J. F. (2000). Negative affect as a prospective risk factor for hypertension. *Psychosomatic Medicine, 62*, 188–196.

Jordan, H. T., Miller-Archie, S. A., Cone, J. E., Morabia, A., & Stellman, S. D. (2011). Heart disease among those exposed to the September 11, 2001 World Trade Center disaster: Results from the World Trade Center Health Registry. *Preventive Medicine: An International Journal Devoted to Practice and Theory, 53*, 370–376.

Kahneman, D. (2011). *Thinking fast and slow*. Farrar, Straus, & Giroux.

Kahneman, D., & Deaton, A. (2010). High income improves evaluation of life, but not emotional well-being. *Proceedings of the National Academy of Sciences, USA, 107*, 16489–16493.

Kanner, A. D., Coyne, J. C., Schaefer, C., & Lazarus, R. S. (1981). Comparison of two modes of stress measurement: Daily hassles and uplifts versus major life events. *Journal of Behavioral Medicine, 4*, 1–39.

Karasek, R., & Theorell, T. (1990). *Healthy work: Stress, productivity, and the reconstruction of working life*. Basic Books.

Kiecolt-Glaser, J. K. (2009). Psychoneuroimmunology: Psychology's gateway to the biomedical future. *Perspectives on Psychological Science, 4*, 367–369.

Kiecolt-Glaser, J. K., Glaser, R., Gravenstein, S., Malarkey, W. B., & Sheridan, J., (1996). Chronic stress alters the immune response to influenza virus vaccine in older adults. *Proceedings of the National Academy of Sciences, USA, 93*, 3043–3047.

Kiecolt-Glaser, J. K., McGuire, L., Robles, T. F., & Glaser, R. (2002). Psychoneuroimmunology and psychosomatic medicine: Back to the future. *Psychosomatic Medicine, 64*, 15–28.

Kiecolt-Glaser, J. K., McGuire, L., Robles, T. F., & Glaser, R. (2002).Psychoneuroimmunology: Psychological influences on immune function and health. *Journal of Consulting and Clinical Psychology, 70*, 537–547.

Kilpeläinen, M., Koskenvuo, M., Helenius, H., & Terho, E. O. (2002). Stressful life events promote the manifestation of asthma and atopic diseases. *Clinical and Experimental Allergy, 32*, 256–263.

Kivimäki, M., Head, J., Ferrie, J. E., Shipley, M. J., Brunner, E., Vahtera, J., & Marmot, M. G. (2006). Work stress, weight gain and weight loss. Evidence for bidirectional effects of body mass index in the Whitehall II study. *International Journal of Obesity, 30*, 982–987.

Klinnert, M. D., Nelson, H. S., Price, M. R., Adinoff, A. D., Leung, M., & Mrazek, D. A. (2001). Onset and persistence of childhood asthma: Predictors from infancy. *Pediatrics, 108*, E69.

Konnikova, M. (2015, January 14). Trying to cure depression, but inspiring torture. *The New Yorker*. https://www.newyorker.com/science/maria-konnikova/theory-psychology-justified-torture?verso=true

Kraus, M. W., Piff, P. K., Mendoza-Denton, R., Rheinschmidt, M. L., & Keltner, D. (2012). Social class, solipsism, and contextualism: How the rich are different from the poor. *Psychological Review, 119*, 546–572.

Krosnick, J. A. (1990). *Thinking about politics: Comparisons of experts and novices*. Guilford.

Krumboltz, M. (2014, February 18). Just like us? Elephants comfort each other when they're stressed out. *Yahoo News*. http://news.yahoo.com/elephants-know-a-thing-or-two-about-empathy-202224477.html

Lachman, M. E., & Weaver, S. L. (1998). The sense of control as a moderator of social class differences in health and well-being. *Journal of Personality and Social Psychology, 74*, 763–773.

Lavner, J. A., Karney, B. R., & Bradbury, T. N. (2013). Newlyweds' optimistic forecasts of their marriage: For better or for worse? *Journal of Family Psychology, 27*, 531–540.

Lazarus, R. P., & Folkman, S. (1984). *Stress, appraisal, and coping*. Springer.

Lee, M., & Rotheram-Borus, M. J. (2001). Challenges associated with increased survival among parents living with HIV. *American Journal of Public Health, 91*, 1303–1309.

Lehrer, P. M., Isenberg, S., & Hochron, S. M. (1993). Asthma and emotion: A review. *Journal of Asthma, 30*, 5–21.

Lepore, S. J. (1998). Problems and prospects for the social support-reactivity hypothesis. *Annals of Behavioral Medicine, 20*, 257–269.

Lichtman, J. H., Bigger, T., Blumenthal, J. A., Frasure-Smith, N., Kaufmann, P. G., Lespérance, F., . . . Froelicher, E. S. (2008). Depression and coronary heart disease: Recommendations for screening, referral, and treatment: A science advisory from the American Heart Association Prevention Committee of the Council on Cardiovascular Nursing, Council on Clinical Cardiology, Council on Epidemiology and Prevention, and Interdisciplinary Council on Quality of Care and Outcomes Research. *Circulation, 118*, 1768–1775.

Loerbroks, A., Apfelbacher, C. J., Thayer, J. F., Debling, D., & Stürmer, T. (2009). Neuroticism, extraversion, stressful life events and asthma: A cohort study of middle-aged adults. *Allergy, 64*, 1444–1450.

Logan H., Lutgendorf, S., Rainville, P., Sheffield, D., Iverson, K., & Lubaroff, D. (2001). Effects of stress and relaxation on capsaicin-induced pain. *The Journal of Pain, 2*, 160–170.

Lutter, M. (2007). Book review: Winning a lottery brings no happiness. *Journal of Happiness Studies, 8*, 155–160.

Lyon, B. L. (2012). Stress, coping, and health. In V. H. Rice (Ed.), *Handbook of stress, coping, and health: Implications for nursing research, theory, and practice* (2nd ed., pp. 2–20). Sage.

Lyubomirsky, S. (2001). Why are some people happier than others? The role of cognitive and motivational processes in well-being. *American Psychologist, 56*, 239–249.

Lyubomirsky, S., King, L., & Diener, E. (2005). The benefits of frequent positive affect: Does happiness lead to success? *Psychological Bulletin, 131*, 803–855.

Maier, S. F., Watkins, L. R., & Fleshner, M. (1994). Psychoneuroimmunology: The interface between behavior, brain, and immunity. *American Journal of Psychology 49*(12), 1004–1017.

Malzberg, B. (1937). Mortality among patients with involution melancholia. *American Journal of Psychiatry, 93*, 1231–1238.

Manuel, J. I. (2018). Racial/ethnic and gender disparities in health care use and access. *Health Services Research 53*(3), 1407–1429. https://www.ncbi.nlm.nih.gov/pmc/articles/PMC5980371/

Marmot, M. G., Bosma, H., Hemingway, H., & Stansfeld, S. (1997). Contribution of job control and other risk factors to social variations in coronary heart disease incidence. *The Lancet, 350*, 235–239.

Marmot, M. G. & Sapolsky, R. (2014). Of baboons and men: Social circumstances, biology, and the social gradient in health. In M. Weinstein, & M. A. Lane (Eds.), *Sociality, hierarchy, health: comparative biodemography, A collection of papers* (pp. 365–388). National Academies Press (US).

Martin, M. W. (2012). *Happiness and the good life*. Oxford University Press.

Maslach, C., & Jackson, S. E. (1981). The measurement of experienced burnout. *Journal of Occupational Behavior, 2*, 99–113.

McCarthy, J. (2020, January 10). Happiness not quite as widespread as usual in the U.S. *Gallup*. https://news.gallup.com/poll/276503/happiness-not-quite-widespread-usual.aspx

McEwan, B. (1998). Protective and damaging effects of stress mediators. *New England Journal of Medicine, 338*(3), 171–179.

McIntosh, J. (2014, July 28) What are headaches? What causes headaches? *Medical News Today*. http://www.medicalnewstoday.com/articles/73936.php

MedicineNet. (2013). *Headaches*. http://www.medicinenet.com/tension_headache/article.htm#what_causes_tension_headaches

Monat, A., & Lazarus, R. S. (1991). *Stress and coping: An anthology* (3rd ed.). Columbia University Press.

Myers, D. G. (2000). The funds, friends, and faith of happy people. *American Psychologist, 55*, 56–67.

Myers, T. C., Wittrock, D. A., & Foreman, G. W., (1998). Appraisal of subjective stress in individuals with tension-type headache: The influence of baseline measures. *Journal of Behavioral Medicine, 21*, 469–484.

Mykletun, A., Bjerkeset, O., Dewey, M., Prince, M., Overland, S., & Stewart, R. (2007). Anxiety, depression, and cause-specific mortality: The HUNT study. *Psychosomatic Medicine, 69*, 323–331.

Myrtek, M. (2001). Meta-analyses of prospective studies on coronary heart disease, type A personality, and hostility. *International Journal of Cardiology, 79*, 245–251.

Nabi, H., Kivimaki, M., De Vogli, R., Marmot, M. G., & Singh-Manoux, A. (2008). Positive and negative affect and risk of coronary heart disease: Whitehall II prospective cohort study. *British Medical Journal, 337*, a118.

National Institute of Arthritis and Musculoskeletal and Skin Diseases (NIAMS). (2012). *Understanding autoimmune diseases*. http://www.niams.nih.gov/Health_Info/Autoimmune/understanding_autoimmune.pdf

Nealey-Moore, J. B., Smith, T. W., Uchino, B. N., Hawkins, M. W., & Olson-Cerny, C. (2007). Cardiovascular reactivity during positive and negative marital interactions. *Journal of Behavioral Medicine, 30*, 505–519.

Neelakantan, S. (2013). Mind over myocardium. *Nature, 493*, S16–S17.

Neupert, S. D., Almeida, D. M., & Charles, S. T. (2007). Age differences in reactivity to daily stressors: The role of personal control. *Journal of Gerontology: Psychological Sciences, 62B*, P216–P225.

Nusair, M., Al-dadah, A., & Kumar, A. (2012). The tale of mind and heart: Psychiatric disorders and coronary heart disease. *Missouri Medicine, 109*, 199–203.

Office on Women's Health, U.S. Department of Health and Human Services. (2009). *Heart disease: Frequently asked questions.* http://www.womenshealth.gov/publications/our-publications/fact-sheet/heart-disease.pdf

Ong, A. D., Bergeman, C. S., & Bisconti, T. L. (2005). Unique effects of daily perceived control on anxiety symptomatology during conjugal bereavement. *Personality and Individual Differences, 38,* 1057–1067.

Ösby, U., Brandt, L., Correia, N., Ekbom, A., & Sparén, P. (2001). Excess mortality in bipolar and unipolar depression in Sweden. *Archives of General Psychiatry, 58,* 844–850.

Park, S. G., Kim, H. C., Min, J. Y., Hwang, S. H., Park, Y. S., & Min, K. B. (2011). A prospective study of work stressors and the common cold. *Occupational Medicine, 61,* 53–56.

Pascoe, E. A., & Smart Richman, L. (2009). Perceived discrimination and health: A meta-analytic review. *Psychological Bulletin, 135*(4), 531–554. https://www.ncbi.nlm.nih.gov/pmc/articles/PMC2747726/

Peterson, C., & Seligman, M. E. P. (1984). Causal explanations as a risk factor for depression: Theory and evidence. *Psychological Review, 91,* 347–374.

Peterson, C., & Steen, T. A. (2002). Optimistic explanatory style. In C. R. Snyder & S. J. Lopez (Eds.), *Handbook of positive psychology* (pp. 244–256). Oxford University Press.

Phillips, A. C. (2011). Blunted as well as exaggerated cardiovascular reactivity to stress is associated with negative health outcomes. *Japanese Psychological Research, 53,* 177–192.

Phillips, A. C., Gallagher, S., & Carroll, D. (2009). Social support, social intimacy, and cardiovascular reactions to acute psychological stress. *Annals of Behavioral Medicine, 37,* 38–45.

Pinquart, M., & Sörensen, S. (2000). Influence of socioeconomic status, social network, and competence on subjective well-being in later life. A meta-analysis. *Psychology and Aging, 15,* 187–224.

Ploubidis, G. B., & Grundy, E. (2009). Personality and all cause mortality: Evidence for indirect links. *Personality and Individual differences, 47,* 203–208.

Powell, J. (1996). *AIDS and HIV-related diseases: An educational guide for professionals and the public.* Insight Books.

Pressman, S. D., & Cohen, S. (2005). Does positive affect influence health? *Psychological Bulletin, 131,* 925–971.

Puterman, E., Lin, J., Blackburn, E., O'Donovan, A., Adler, N., & Epel, E. (2010). The power of exercise: Buffering the effect of chronic stress on telomere length. *PLoS ONE, 5*(5), e10837.

Quoidbach, J., Dunn, E. W., Petrides, K. V., & Mikolajczak, M. (2010). Money giveth, money taketh away: The dual effect of wealth on happiness. *Psychological Science, 21,* 759–763.

Rahe, R. H. (1974). The pathway between subjects' recent life changes and their near-future illness reports: Representative results and methodological issues. In B. S. Dohrenwend & B. P. Dohrenwend (Eds.), *Stressful life events: Their nature and effects* (pp. 73–86). Wiley & Sons.

Rahe, R. H., McKeen, J. D., & Arthur, R. J. (1967). A longitudinal study of life change and illness patterns. *Journal of Psychosomatic Research, 10,* 355–366.

Raney, J. D., & Troop-Gordon, W. (2012). Computer-mediated communication with distant friends: Relations with adjustment during students' first semester in college. *Journal of Educational Psychology, 104,* 848–861.

Rasmussen, H. N., & Wallio, S. C. (2008). The health benefits of optimism. In S. J. Lopez (Ed.), *Positive psychology: Exploring the best in people* (pp. 131–149). Praeger Publishers.

Rasmussen, H. N., Scheier, M. F., & Greenhouse, J. B. (2009). Optimism and physical health: A meta-analytic review. *Annals of Behavioral Medicine, 37,* 239–256.

Raymond, J. M., & Sheppard, K. (2018). Effects of peer mentoring on nursing students' perceived stress, sense of belonging, self-efficacy and loneliness. *Journal of Nursing Education and Practice, 8*(1), 16–23. https://pdfs.semanticscholar.org/ce60/8eca933ab45f3d608f9b5a1a505014dd2cb7.pdf

Ritz, T., Steptoe, A., Bobb, C., Harris, A. H. S., & Edwards, M. (2006). The asthma trigger inventory: Validation of a questionnaire for perceived triggers of asthma. *Psychosomatic Medicine, 68*, 956–965.

Rosengren, A., Hawken, S., Ounpuu, S., Sliwa, K., Zubaid, M., Almahmeed, W. A., . . . Yusuf, S. (2004). Association of psychosocial risk factors with risk of acute myocardial infarction in 11,119 cases and 13,648 controls from 52 countries (the INTERHEART study): Case-control study. *The Lancet, 364*, 953–962.

Rosenman, R. H., Brand, R. J., Jenkins, C. D., Friedman, M., Straus, R., & Wurm, M. (1975). Coronary heart disease in the Western Collaborative Group Study: Final follow-up experience of 8.5 years. *Journal of the American Medical Association, 223*, 872–877.

Rottenberg, J., Yaroslavsky, I., Carney, R. M., Freedland, K. E., George, C. J., Baki, I., Kovacs, M. (2014). The association between major depressive disorder and risk factors for cardiovascular disease in adolescence. *Psychosomatic Medicine, 76*, 122–127.

Salmon, P. (2001). Effects of physical exercise on anxiety, depression, and sensitivity to stress: A unifying theory. *Clinical Psychology Review, 21*, 33–61.

Saito, K., Kim, J. I., Maekawa, K., Ikeda, Y., & Yokoyama, M. (1997). The great Hanshin-Awaji earthquake aggravates blood pressure control in treated hypertensive patients. *American Journal of Hypertension, 10*, 217–221.

Salonen, P., Arola, H., Nygård, C., & Huhtala, H. (2008). Long-term associations of stress and chronic diseases in ageing and retired employees. *Psychology, Health, and Medicine, 13*, 55–62.

Sapolsky, R. M. (1998). *Why zebras don't get ulcers: An updated guide to stress, stress-related disease, and coping.* Freeman.

Sapolsky, R. M. (2004). Organismal stress and telomeric aging. An unexpected connection. *Proceedings of the National Academy of Sciences, USA, 101*, 17323–17324.

Schnall, P. L., & Landsbergis, P. A. (1994). Job strain and cardiovascular disease. *Annual Review of Public Health, 15*, 381–411.

Schwartz, B. S., Stewart, W. F., Simon, D., & Lipton, R. B. (1998). Epidemiology of tension-type headache. *Journal of the American Medical Association, 279*, 381–383.

Schwartz, N. M., & Schwartz, M. S. (1995). Definitions of biofeedback and applied physiology. In M. S. Schwartz & F. Andrasik (Eds.), *Biofeedback: A practitioners guide* (pp. 32–42). Guilford.

Scully, J. A., Tosi, H., & Banning, K. (2000). Life event checklists: Revisiting the Social Readjustment Rating Scale after 30 years. *Educational and Psychological Measurement, 60*, 864–876.

Segerstrom, S. C., & Miller, G. E. (2004). Psychological stress and the human immune system: A meta-analytic study of 30 years of inquiry. *Psychological Bulletin, 130*, 601–630.

Seligman, M. E., & Maier, S. F. (1967). Failure to escape traumatic shock. *Journal of Experimental Psychology, 74*, 1–9.

Seligman, M. E., Maier, S. F., & Geer, J. H. (1968). Alleviation of learned helplessness in the dog. *Journal of Abnormal Psychology, 3*, 256–262.

Seligman, M. E. P. (2002). *Authentic happiness: Using the new positive psychology to realize your potential for lasting fulfillment.* Free Press.

Seligman, M. E. P., Steen, T. A., Park, N., & Peterson, C. (2005). Positive psychology progress: Empirical validation of interventions. *American Psychologist, 60*, 410–421.

Seligman, M. P., & Csikszentmihalyi, M. (2000). Positive psychology: An introduction. *American*

Psychologist, 55, 5–14.

Selye, H. (1936). A syndrome produced by diverse nocuous agents. *Nature, 138*, 32–33.

Selye, H. (1974). *Stress without distress*. Lippencott.

Selye, H. (1976). *The stress of life* (Rev. ed.). McGraw-Hill.

Shalev, I., Moffitt, T. E., Sugden, K., Williams, B., Houts, R. M., Danese, A., . . . Caspi, A. (2013). Exposure to violence during childhood is associated with telomere erosion from 5 to 10 years of age: A longitudinal study. *Molecular Psychiatry, 18*, 576–581.

Shapiro, P. A. (2005). Heart disease. In J. L. Levenson (Ed.), *Textbook of psychosomatic medicine* (pp. 423–444). American Psychiatric Publishing.

Sims, M., Diez-Roux, A. V., Dudley, A., Gebreab, S., Wyatt, S. B., Bruce, M. A., . . . Taylor, H. A. (2012). Perceived discrimination and hypertension among African Americans in the Jackson Heart Study. *American Journal of Public Health, 102*(2 Suppl.), S258–S265.

Smyth, J. M., Soefer, M. H., Hurewitz, A., Kliment, A., & Stone, A. A. (1999). Daily psychosocial factors predict levels and diurnal cycles of asthma symptomatology and peak flow. *Journal of Behavioral Medicine, 22*, 179–193.

Sodergren, S. C., & Hyland, M. H. (1999). Expectancy and asthma. In I. Kirsch (Ed.), *How expectancies shape experience* (pp. 197–212). American Psychological Association.

Speck, R. M., Courneya, K. S., Masse, L. C., Duval, S., & Schmitz, K. H. (2010). An update of controlled physical activity trials in cancer survivors: A systematic review and meta-analysis. *Journal of Cancer Survivorship, 4*, 87–100.

Stansfeld, S. A., Shipley, M. J., Head, J., & Fuhrer, R. (2012). Repeated job strain and the risk of depression: Longitudinal analyses from the Whitehall II study. *American Journal of Public Health, 102*, 2360–2366.

Stein, F. (2001). Occupational stress, relaxation therapies, exercise, and biofeedback. *Work: Journal of Prevention, Assessment, and Rehabilitation, 17*, 235–246.

Steptoe, A., O'Donnell, K., Marmot, M., & Wardle, J. (2008). Positive affect and psychosocial processes related to health. *British Journal of Psychology, 99*, 211–227.

Stovner, L. J., Hagen, K., Jensen, R., Katsarava, Z., Lipson, R., Scher, A., . . . Zwart, J. (2007). The global burden of headache: A documentation of headache prevalence and disability worldwide. *Cephalalgia, 27*, 193–210.

Straub, R. O. (2007). *Health psychology: A biopsychosocial approach* (2nd ed.). Worth.

Stroebe, W., & Stroebe, M. (1996). The social psychology of social support. In E. T. Higgins & A. W. Kruglanski (Eds.), *Social psychology: Handbook of basic principles* (pp. 597–621). Guilford.

Stürmer, T., Hasselbach, P., & Amelang, M. (2006). Personality, lifestyle, and risk of cardiovascular disease and cancer: Follow-up of population based cohort. *British Medical Journal, 332*, 1359–1362.

Suls, J., & Bunde, J. (2005). Anger, anxiety, and depression as risk factors for cardiovascular disease: The problems and implications of overlapping affective dispositions. *Psychological Bulletin, 131*, 260–300.

Sulsky, L., & Smith, C. (2005). *Work stress*. Thomson Wadsworth.

Surtees, P. G., Wainwright, N. W. J., Luben, R., Wareham, N. J., Bingham, S. A., & Khaw, K.-T. (2010). Mastery is associated with cardiovascular disease mortality in men and women at apparently low risk. *Health Psychology, 29*, 412–420.

Tatris, T. W., Peeters, M. C. W., Le Blanc, P. M., Schreurs, P. J. G., & Schaufeli, W. B. (2001). From inequity to burnout: The role of job stress. *Journal of Occupational Health Psychology, 6*, 303–323.

Taylor, S. E. (1999). *Health psychology* (4th ed.). McGraw-Hill.

Theorell, T., Tsutsumi, A., Hallquist, J., Reuterwall, C., Hogstedt, C., Fredlund, P., . . . Johnson, J. V. (1998). Decision latitude, job strain, and myocardial infarction: A study of working men in Stockholm. *American Journal of Public Health, 88*, 382–388.

Thoits, P. A. (2010). Stress and health: Major findings and policy implications. *Journal of Health and Social Behavior, 51*(1 Suppl.), S41–S53.

Trudel, X., Brisson, C., & Milot, A. (2010). Job strain and masked hypertension. *Psychosomatic Medicine, 72*, 786–793.

Trueba, A. F., & Ritz, T. (2013). Stress, asthma, and respiratory infections: Pathways involving airway immunology and microbal endocrinology. *Brain, Behavior and Immunity, 29*, 11–27.

Uchino, B. N. (2009). Understanding the links between social support and physical health: A life-span perspective with emphasis on the separability of perceived and received support. *Perspectives on Psychological Science, 4*, 236–255.

Uchino, B. N., Vaughn, A. A., Carlisle, M., & Birmingham, W. (2012). Social support and immunity. In S. C. Segerstrom (Ed.), *The Oxford handbook of psychoneuroimmunology* (pp. 214–233). Oxford University Press.

Ukestad, L. K., and Wittrock, D. A. (1996). Pain perception and coping in recurrent headache. *Health Psychology, 15*, 65–68.

van der Schurr, W. A., Baumgartner, S. E., & Sumter, S. R. (2018). Social media use, social media stress, and sleep: Examining cross-sectional and longitudinal relationships in adolescents. *Health Communication, 34*(5), 552–559. https://www.tandfonline.com/doi/full/10.1080/10410236.2017.1422101

Vella, E. J., Kamarck, T. W., Flory, J. D., & Manuck, S. (2012). Hostile mood and social strain during daily life: A test of the transactional model. *Annals of Behavioral Medicine, 44*, 341–352.

Vines, A., Ward, J. B., Cordoba, E., & Black, K. Z. (2017). Perceived racial/ethnic discrimination and mental health: A review and future directions for social epidemiology. *Current Epidemiology Reports, 4*(2), 156–165. https://www.ncbi.nlm.nih.gov/pubmed/28920011

von Leupoldt, A., Ehnes, F., & Dahme, B. (2006). Emotions and respiratory function in asthma: A comparison of findings in everyday life and laboratory. *British Journal of Health Psychology, 11*, 185–198.

Watson, D., Clark, L. A., & Tellegen, A. (1988). Development and validation of brief measures of positive and negative affect: The PANAS scales. *Journal of Personality and Social Psychology, 54*, 1063–1070.

Weeke, A. (1979). Causes of death in manic-depressive. In M. Shou & M. Stromgren (Eds.), *Origin, prevention, and treatment of affective disorders* (pp. 289–299). Academic Press.

Whang, W., Kubzansky, L. D., Kawachi, I., Rexrod, K. M., Kroenke, C. H., Glynn, R. J., . . . Albert, C. M. (2009). Depression and risk of sudden cardiac death and coronary heart disease in women: Results from the Nurses' Health Study. *Journal of the American College of Cardiology, 53*, 950–958.

Wilson, T. D., & Gilbert, D. T. (2003). Affective forecasting. *Advances in Experimental Social Psychology, 35*, 345–411.

World Health Organization (WHO). (2013). *A global brief on hypertension: Silent killer, global public health crisis.* http://apps.who.int/iris/bitstream/10665/79059/1/WHO_DCO_WHD_2013.2_eng.pdf?ua=1

Wright, R. J., Rodriguez, M., & Cohen, S. (1998). Review of psychosocial stress and asthma: An integrated biopsychosocial approach. *Thorax, 53*, 1066–1074.

Wulsin, L. R., & Singal, B. M. (2003). Do depressive symptoms increase the risk for the onset of coronary disease? A systematic quantitative review. *Psychosomatic Medicine, 65*, 201–210.

Zacharie, R. (2009). Psychoneuroimmunology: A bio-psycho-social approach to health and disease. *Scandinavian Journal of Psychology, 50*, 645–651.

Psychological Disorders

Abela, J. R., & Hankin, B. L. (2011). Rumination as a vulnerability factor to depression during the transition from early to middle adolescence: A multiwave longitudinal study. *Journal of Abnormal Psychology, 120,* 259–271.

Abramowitz, J. S., & Siqueland, L. (2013). Obsessive-compulsive disorder. In L. G. Castonguay & T. F. Oltmanns (Eds.), *Psychopathology: From science to clinical practice* (pp. 143–171). Guilford Press.

Abramson, L. Y., Metalsky, G. I., & Alloy, L. B. (1989). Hopelessness depression: A theory- based subtype of depression. *Psychological Review, 96,* 358–372.

Afifi, T. O., Mather, A., Boman, J., Fleisher, W., Enns, M. W., MacMillan, H., & Sareen, J. (2010). Childhood adversity and personality disorder: Results from a nationally representative population-based survey. *Journal of Psychiatric Research, 45,* 814–822.

Agerbo, E., Nordentoft, M., & Mortensen, P. B. (2002). Familial, psychiatric, and socioeconomic risk factors for suicide in young people: Nested case-control study. *British Medical Journal, 325,* 74–77.

Aghukwa, C. N. (2012). Care seeking and beliefs about the cause of mental illness among Nigerian psychiatric patients and their families. *Psychiatric Services, 63,* 616–618.

Aikins, D. E., & Craske, M. G. (2001). Cognitive theories of generalized anxiety disorder. *Psychiatric Clinics of North America, 24,* 57–74.

Akinbami, L. J., Liu, X., Pastor, P., & Reuben, C. A. (2011, August). Attention deficit hyperactivity disorder among children aged 5–17 years in the United States, 1998–2009 (NCHS data brief No. 70). National Center for Health Statistics. http://www.cdc.gov/nchs/data/databriefs/db70.pdf

Al-Asadi, A. M., Klein, B., & Meyer, D. (2015). Multiple comorbidities of 21 psychological disorders and relationships with psychosocial variables: A study of the online assessment and diagnostic system within a web-based population. *Journal of Medical Internet Research, 17*(2), e55. https://www.ncbi.nlm.nih.gov/pubmed/25803420

Alden, L. E., & Bieling, P. (1998). Interpersonal consequences in the pursuit of safety. *Behaviour Research and Therapy, 36,* 53–64.

Alegria, A. A., Blanco, C., Petry, N. M., Skodol, A. E., Liu, S. M., & Grant, B. (2013). Sex differences in antisocial personality disorder: Results from the National Epidemiological Survey on Alcohol and Related Conditions. *Personality Disorders: Theory, Research, and Treatment, 4,* 214–222.

American Psychiatric Association. (2013). *Diagnostic and statistical manual of mental disorders* (5th ed.). Author.

American Psychological Association. (n.d.) *Forensic psychology.* https://www.apa.org/ed/graduate/specialize/forensic

Andreasen, N. C. (1987). The diagnosis of schizophrenia. *Schizophrenia Bulletin, 13,* 9–22.

Andréasson, S., Allbeck, P., Engström, A., & Rydberg, U. (1987). Cannabis and schizophrenia: A longitudinal study of Swedish conscripts. *Lancet, 330,* 1483–1486.

Asberg, M., Thorén, P., Träskman, L., Bertilsson, L., & Ringberger, V. (1976). "Serotonin depression"—a biochemical subgroup within the affective disorders? *Science, 191*(4226), 478–480. doi:10.1126/science.1246632

Asperger's syndrome dropped from psychiatrists' handbook the DSM: DSM-5, latest revision of Diagnostic and Statistical Manual, merges Asperger's with autism and widens dyslexia category. (2012, December 1). *The Guardian.* http://www.theguardian.com/society/2012/dec/02/aspergers-syndrome-dropped-psychiatric-dsm

Autism Genome Project Consortium. (2007). Mapping autism risk loci using genetic linkage and chromosomal rearrangements. *Nature Genetics, 39,* 319–328.

Baes, C. V. W., Tofoli, S. M. C., Martins, C. M. S., & Juruena, M. F. (2012). Assessment of the hypothalamic–pituitary–adrenal axis activity: Glucocorticoid receptor and mineralocorticoid receptor function in depression with early life stress—a systematic review. *Acta Neuropsychiatrica, 24*, 4–15.

Baio, J., Wiggins, L., Christensen, D. L., et al. (2018). Prevalence of Autism Spectrum Disorder among children aged 8 years — Autism and Developmental Disabilities Monitoring Network, 11 sites, United States, 2014. *Surveillance Summaries, 67*(6), 1–23. https://www.cdc.gov/mmwr/volumes/67/ss/ss6706a1.htm?s_cid=ss6706a1_w#suggestedcitation

Baker, L. A., Bezdjian, S., & Raine, A. (2006). Behavioral genetics: The science of antisocial behavior. *Law and Contemporary Problems, 69*, 7–46.

Barbaresi, W. J., Colligan, R. C., Weaver, A. L., Voigt, R. G., Killian, J. M., & Katusic, S. K. (2013). Mortality, ADHD, and psychosocial adversity in adults with childhood ADHD: A prospective study. *Pediatrics, 131*, 637–644.

Barker, P. (2010). *The legacy of Thomas Szasz*. http://www.centerforindependentthought.org/SzaszLegacy.html

Barkley, R. A. (2006). *Attention-deficit hyperactivity disorder: A handbook for diagnosis and treatment*. Guilford Press.

Barkley, R. A., Fischer, M., Smallish, L., & Fletcher, K. (2002). The persistence of attention-deficit/hyperactivity disorder into young adulthood as a function of reporting source and definition of disorder. *Journal of Abnormal Psychology, 111*, 279–289.

Battista, S. R., & Kocovski, N. L. (2010). Exploring the effect of alcohol on post-event processing specific to a social event. *Cognitive Behaviour Therapy, 39*, 1–10.

Baumeister, A. A., & Hawkins, M. F. (2004). The serotonin hypothesis of schizophrenia: A historical case study on the heuristic value of theory in clinical neuroscience. *Journal of the History of the Neurosciences, 13*, 277–291.

Beck, A. T. (1976). *Cognitive therapy and the emotional disorders*. International Universities Press.

Beck, A. T. (2008). The evolution of the cognitive model of depression and its neurobiological correlates. *American Journal of Psychiatry, 165*, 969–977.

Berman, A. L. (2009). School-based suicide prevention: Research advances and practice implications. *School Psychology Review, 38*, 233–238.

Bettelheim, B. (1967). *The empty fortress: Infantile autism and the birth of the self*. Free Press.

Beucke, J. C., Sepulcre, J., Talukdar, T., Linnman, C., Zschenderlein, K., Endrass, T., ... Kathman, N. (2013). Abnormally high degree connectivity of the orbitofrontal cortex in obsessive-compulsive disorder. *JAMA Psychiatry, 70*, 619–629.

Biederman, J., Faraone, S. V., Hirshfeld-Becker, D. R., Friedman, D., Robin, J. A., & Rosenbaum, J. F. (2001). Patterns of psychopathology and dysfunction in high-risk children of parents with panic disorder and major depression. *American Journal of Psychiatry, 158*, 49–57.

Boland, R. J., & Keller, M. B. (2009). Course and outcome of depression. In I. H. Gotlib & C. L. Hammen (Eds.), *Handbook of depression* (pp. 23–43). Guilford Press.

Bolton, D., Rijsdijk, F., O'Connor, T. G., Perrin, S., & Eley, T. C. (2007). Obsessive-compulsive disorder, tics and anxiety in 6-year-old twins. *Psychological Medicine, 37*, 39–48.

Bourguignon, E. (1970). Hallucinations and trance: An anthropologist's perspective. In W. Keup (Ed.), *Origins and mechanisms of hallucination* (pp. 183–190). Plenum Press.

Bouton, M. E., Mineka, S., & Barlow, D. H. (2001). A modern learning theory perspective on the etiology of panic disorder. *Psychological Review, 108*, 4–32.

Bramsen, I., Dirkzwager, A. J. E., & van der Ploeg, H. M. (2000). Predeployment personality traits and exposure to trauma as predictors of posttraumatic stress symptoms: A prospective study of former peacekeepers. *American Journal of Psychiatry, 157*, 1115–1119.

Bregman, J. D. (2005). Definitions and characteristics of the spectrum. In D. Zager (Ed.), *Autism spectrum disorders: Identification, education, and treatment* (3rd ed., pp. 3–46). Erlbaum.

Brewin, C. R., Andrews, B., & Valentine, J. D. (2000). Meta-analysis of risk factors for posttraumatic stress disorder in trauma-exposed adults. *Journal of Consulting and Clinical Psychology, 68*, 748–756.

Bremner, J. D., Krystal, J. H., Southwick, S. M., & Charney, D. S. (1996). Noradrenergic mechanisms in stress and anxiety: I. preclinical studies. *Synapse, 23*, 28–38.

Brown, A. S., Begg, M. D., Gravenstein, S., Schaefer, C. A., Wyatt, R. J., Breshnahan, M., . . . Susser, E. S. (2004). Serologic evidence of prenatal influenza in the etiology of schizophrenia. *Archives of General Psychiatry, 61*, 774–780.

Brent, D. A., & Bridge, J. (2003). Firearms availability and suicide: A review of the literature. *American Behavioral Scientist, 46*, 1192–1210.

Brown, G. W., & Harris, T. O. (1989). Depression. In G. W. Brown and T. O. Harris (Eds.), *Life events and illness* (pp. 49–93). Guilford Press.

Brown, G. W., Ban, M., Craig, T. J. K., Harris, T. O., Herbert, J., & Uher, R. (2013). Serotonin transporter length polymorphism, childhood maltreatment, and chronic depression: A specific gene-environment interaction. *Depression and Anxiety, 30*, 5–13.

Buchanan-Barker, P., Barker, P. (2009, February). The convenient myth of Thomas Szasz. *Journal of Psychiatric and Mental Health Nursing, 16*(1): 87–95. doi:10.1111/j.1365-2850.2008.01310.x

Buchsbaum, M. S., Nuechterlein, K. H., Haier, R. J., Wu, J., Sicotte, N., Hazlett, E., . . . Guich, S. (1990). Glucose metabolic rate in normal and schizophrenics during the continuous performance test assessed by positron emission tomography. *British Journal of Psychiatry, 156*, 216–227.

Burt, S. A. (2009). Rethinking environmental contributions to child and adolescent psychopathology: A meta-analysis of shared environmental influences. *Psychological Bulletin, 135*, 608–637.

Butler, L. D., & Nolen-Hoeksema, S. (1994). Gender differences in responses to depressed mood in a college sample. *Sex Roles, 30*, 331–346.

Byrd, R. (2002, October 17). Report to the legislature on the principal findings from the epidemiology of autism in California: A comprehensive pilot study. http://www.dds.ca.gov/Autism/MindReport.cfm

Cadoret, R., Yates, W., Ed., T., Woodworth, G., & Stewart, M. (1995). Genetic environmental interactions in the genesis of aggressivity and conduct disorders. *Archives of General Psychiatry, 52*, 916–924.

Cannon, M., Jones, P. B., & Murray, R. M. (2002). Obstetric complications and schizophrenia: Historical and meta-analytic review. *American Journal of Psychiatry, 159*, 1080–1092.

Casadio, P., Fernandes, C., Murray, R. M., & Di Forti, M. (2011). Cannabis use in young people: The risk for schizophrenia. *Neuroscience and Biobehavioral Reviews, 35*, 1779–1787.

Cardeña, E., & Gleaves, D. H. (2006). Dissociative disorders. In M. Hersen, S. M. Turner, & D. C. Beidel (Eds.), *Adult psychopathology and diagnosis* (pp. 473–503). John Wiley & Sons.

Caspi, A., Sugden, K., Moffitt, T. E., Taylor, A., Craig, I. W., Harrington, H., Poulton, R. (2003). Influence of life stress on depression: Moderation by a polymorphism in the 5-HTT gene. *Science, 301*(5631), 386–389.

Centers for Disease Control and Prevention. (2010, November 12). Increasing prevalence of parent-reported attention-deficit/hyperactivity disorder among children, United States, 2003–2007. *Morbidity and Mortality Weekly Report, 59*(44), 1439–1443.

Centers for Disease Control and Prevention. (2012). Suicide: Facts at a glance. http://www.cdc.gov/ViolencePrevention/pdf/Suicide_DataSheet-a.pdf

Centers for Disease Control and Prevention. (2012, March 30). Prevalence of autism spectrum disorders—autism and developmental disabilities monitoring network, 14 sites, United States, 2008. *Morbidity and Mortality Weekly Report: Surveillance Summaries, 61*(3), 1–19. http://www.cdc.gov/mmwr/pdf/ss/ss6103.pdf

Centers for Disease Control and Prevention. (2013a). *Definitions: Self-directed violence.* http://www.cdc.gov/violenceprevention/suicide/definitions.html.

Centers for Disease Control and Prevention. (2013b). *National suicide statistics at a glance: Trends in suicide rates among both sexes, by age group, United States, 1991–2009.* http://www.cdc.gov/violenceprevention/suicide/statistics/trends02.html

Charney, D. S., Woods, S. W., Nagy, L. M., Southwick, S. M., Krystal, J. H., & Heninger, G. R. (1990). Noradrenergic function in panic disorder. *Journal of Clinical Psychiatry, 51*, 5–11.

Clark, D. M. (1996). Panic disorder: From theory to therapy. In R. M. Rapee (Ed.), *Current controversies in the anxiety disorders* (pp. 318–344). Guilford Press.

Clauss, J. A., & Blackford, J. U. (2012). Behavioral inhibition and risk for developing social anxiety disorder: A meta-analytic study. *Journal of the American Academy of Child and Adolescent Psychiatry, 51*(10), 1066–1075.

Clegg, J. W. (2012). Teaching about mental health and illness through the history of the DSM. *History of Psychology, 15*, 364–370.

Compton, W. M., Conway, K. P., Stinson, F. S., Colliver, J. D., & Grant, B. F. (2005). Prevalence, correlates, and comorbidity of DSM-IV antisocial personality syndromes and alcohol and specific drug use disorders in the United States: Results from the national epidemiologic survey on alcohol and related conditions. *Journal of Clinical Psychiatry, 66*, 677–685.

Cook, M., & Mineka, S. (1989). Observational conditioning of fear to fear-relevant versus fear-irrelevant stimuli in rhesus monkeys. *Journal of Abnormal Psychology, 98*, 448–459.

Craske, M. G. (1999). *Anxiety disorders: Psychological approaches to theory and treatment.* Westview Press.

Crego, C., & Widiger, T. A. (2014). Psychopathy and the DSM. *Journal of Personality.* http://www.sakkyndig.com/psykologi/artvit/crego2014.pdf

Crosby, A. E., Ortega, L., & Melanson, C. (2011). *Self-directed violence surveillance: Uniform definitions and recommended data elements, version 1.0.* http://www.cdc.gov/violenceprevention/pdf/self-directed-violence-a.pdf

Dalenberg, C. J., Brand, B. L., Gleaves, D. H., Dorahy, M. J., Loewenstein, R. J., Cardeña, E., . . . Spiegel, D. (2012). Evaluation of the evidence for the trauma and fantasy models of dissociation. *Psychological Bulletin, 138*, 550–588.

Dancing mania. (2011, July 2). *Sometimes interesting: Weird, forgotten, and sometimes interesting things.* https://sometimes-interesting.com/2011/07/02/dancing-mania/

Davidson, R. J., Pizzagalli, D. A., & Nitschke, J. B. (2009). Representation and regulation of emotional depression: Perspectives from cognitive neuroscience. In I. H. Gotlib & C. L. Hammen (Eds.), *Handbook of depression* (pp. 218–248). Guilford Press.

Davis, K. L., Kahn, R. S., Ko., G., & Davidson, M. (1991). Dopamine in schizophrenia: A review and reconceptualization. *American Journal of Psychiatry, 148*, 1474–1486.

Demos, J. (1983). *Entertaining Satan: Witchcraft and the culture of early New England.* Oxford University Press.

Dempsey, A. F., Schaffer, S., Singer, D., Butchart, A., Davis, M., & Freed, G. L. (2011). Alternative vaccination schedule preferences among parents of young children. *Pediatrics, 128*, 848–856.

DeStefano, F., Price, C. S., & Weintraub, E. S. (2013). Increasing exposures to antibody-stimulating proteins and polysaccharides in vaccines is not associated with risk of autism. *The Journal of Pediatrics, 163,* 561–567.

DiGrande, L., Perrin, M. A., Thorpe, L. E., Thalji, L., Murphy, J., Wu, D., . . . Brackbill, R. M. (2008). Posttraumatic stress symptoms, PTSD, and risk factors among lower Manhattan residents 2–3 years after the September 11, 2001 terrorist attacks. *Journal of Traumatic Stress, 21,* 264–273.

DNA project aims to count Scots redheads. (2012, November 7). *British Broadcast Corporation [BBC].* http://www.bbc.com/news/uk-scotland-20237511

Downs, M. (2008, March 31). Autism-vaccine link: Evidence doesn't dispel doubts. www.webmd.com/brain/autism/searching-for-answers/vaccines-autism

Dozois, D. J. A., & Beck, A. T. (2008). Cognitive schemas, beliefs and assumptions. In K. S. Dobson & D. J. A. Dozois (Eds.), *Risk factors in depression* (pp. 121–143). Academic Press.

Drevets, W. C., Bogers, W. U., & Raichle, M. E. (2002). Functional anatomical correlates of antidepressant drug treatment assessed using PET measures of regional glucose metabolism. *European Neuropsychopharmacology, 12,* 527–544.

Ehlers, A., & Clark, D. M. (2000). A cognitive model of posttraumatic stress disorder. *Behaviour Research and Therapy, 38,* 319–345.

Etzersdorfer, E., Voracek, M., & Sonneck, G. (2004). A dose-response relationship between imitational suicides and newspaper distribution. *Archives of Suicide Research, 8,* 137–145.

Fabrega, H. (2007). How psychiatric conditions were made. *Psychiatry, 70,* 130–153.

Facer-Irwin, E., Blackwood, N. J., Bird, A., Dickson, H., McGlade, D., Alves-Costa, F., & MacManus, D. (2019, Sept 26). PTSD in prison settings: A systematic review and meta-analysis of comorbid mental disorders and problematic behaviours. *PLOS ONE, 14*(9). https://journals.plos.org/plosone/article?id=10.1371/journal.pone.0222407

Fitzgerald, P. B., Laird, A. R., Maller, J., & Daskalakis, Z. J. (2008). A meta-analytic study of changes in brain activation in depression. *Human Brain Mapping, 29,* 683–695.

Fields, T. (2010). Postpartum depression effects on early interactions, parenting, and safety practices: A review. *Infant Behavior and Development, 33,* 1–6.

Fisher, C. (2010, February 11). DSM-5 development process included emphasis on gender and cultural sensitivity. http://www.bmedreport.com/archives/9359

Fleischman, A., Bertolote, J. M., Belfer, M., & Beautrais, A. (2005). Completed suicide and psychiatric diagnoses in young people: A critical examination of the evidence. *American Journal of Orthopsychiatry, 75,* 676–683.

Foote, B., Smolin, Y., Kaplan, M., Legatt, M. E., & Lipschitz, D. (2006). Prevalence of dissociative disorders in psychiatric outpatients. *American Journal of Psychiatry, 163,* 623–629.

Fox, N. A., Henderson, H. A., Marshall, P. J., Nichols, K. E., & Ghera, M. M. (2005). Behavioral inhibition: Linking biology and behavior within a developmental framework. *Annual Review of Psychology, 56,* 235–262.

Frances, A. (2012, December 2). DSM 5 is guide not bible—ignore its ten worst changes. http://www.psychologytoday.com/blog/dsm5-in-distress/201212/dsm-5-is-guide-not-bible-ignore-its-ten-worst-changes

Freeman, A., Stone, M., Martin, D., & Reinecke, M. (2005). A review of borderline personality disorder. In A. Freeman, M. Stone, D. Martin, & M. Reinecke (Eds.), *Comparative treatments for borderline personality disorder* (pp. 1–20). Springer.

Fung, M. T., Raine, A., Loeber, R., Lynam, D. R., Steinhauer, S. R., Venables, P. H., & Stouthamer-Loeber,

M. (2005). Reduced electrodermal activity in psychopathy-prone adolescents. *Journal of Abnormal Psychology, 114*, 187–196.

Fusar-Poli, P., Borgwardt, S., Bechdolf, A., Addington, J., Riecher-Rössler, A., Schultze-Lutter, F., . . . Yung, A. (2013). The psychosis high-risk state: A comprehensive state-of-the-art review. *Archives of General Psychiatry, 70*, 107–120.

Gauthier, J., Siddiqui, T. J., Huashan, P., Yokomaku, D., Hamdan, F. F., Champagne, N., . . . Rouleau, G.A. (2011). Truncating mutations in NRXN2 and NRXN1 in autism spectrum disorders and schizophrenia. *Human Genetics, 130*, 563–573.

Gizer, I. R., Ficks, C., & Waldman, I. D. (2009). Candidate gene studies of ADHD: A meta-analytic review. *Human Genetics, 126*, 51–90.

Goldstein, A. J., & Chambless, D. L. (1978). A reanalysis of agoraphobia. *Behavior Therapy, 9*, 47–59.

Goldstein, J. M., Buka, S. L., Seidman, L. J., & Tsuang, M. T. (2010). Specificity of familial transmission of schizophrenia psychosis spectrum and affective psychoses in the New England family study's high-risk design. *Archives of General Psychiatry, 67*, 458–467.

Good, B. J., & Hinton, D. E. (2009). Panic disorder in cross-cultural and historical perspective. In D. E. Hinton & B. J. Good (Eds.), *Culture and panic disorder* (pp. 1–28). Stanford University Press.

Goodman, S. H., & Brand, S. R. (2009). Depression and early adverse experiences. In I. H. Gotlib & C. L. Hammen (Eds.), *Handbook of depression* (pp. 249–274). Guilford Press.

Gotlib, I. H., & Joormann, J. (2010). Cognition and depression: Current status and future directions. *Annual Review of Clinical Psychology, 6*, 285–312.

Gottesman, I. I. (2001). Psychopathology through a life span-genetic prism. *American Psychologist, 56*, 867–878.

Graybiel, A. N., & Rauch, S. L. (2000). Toward a neurobiology of obsessive-compulsive disorder. *Neuron, 28*, 343–347.

Green, M. F. (2001). *Schizophrenia revealed: From neurons to social interactions*. W. W. Norton.

Hackmann, A., Clark, D. M., & McManus, F. (2000). Recurrent images and early memories in social phobia. *Behaviour Research and Therapy, 38*, 601–610.

Halligan, S. L., Herbert, J., Goodyer, I., & Murray, L. (2007). Disturbances in morning cortisol secretion in association with maternal postnatal depression predict subsequent depressive symptomatology in adolescents. *Biological Psychiatry, 62*, 40–46.

Hare, R. D. (1965). Temporal gradient of fear arousal in psychopaths. *Journal of Abnormal Psychology, 70*, 442–445.

Hasin, D. S., Fenton, M. C., & Weissman, M. M. (2011). Epidemiology of depressive disorders. In M. T. Tsuang, M. Tohen, & P. Jones (Eds.), *Textbook of psychiatric epidemiology* (pp. 289–309). John Wiley & Sons.

Herek, G. M. (2012). *Facts about homosexuality and mental health*. Sexual orientation: Science, education, and policy. https://psychology.ucdavis.edu/rainbow/html/facts_mental_health.html

Herman, J. (1997). *Trauma and recovery: The aftermath of violence—from domestic abuse to political terror*. Basic Books.

Herrenkohl, T. I., Maguin, E., Hill, K. G., Hawkins, J. D., Abbott, R. D., & Catalano, R. (2000). Developmental risk factors for youth violence. *Journal of Adolescent Health, 26*, 176–186.

Heston, L. L. (1966). Psychiatric disorders in foster home reared children of schizophrenic mothers. *British Journal of Psychiatry, 112*, 819–825.

Hettema, J. M., Neale, M. C., & Kendler, K. S. (2001). A review and meta-analysis of the genetic epidemiology of anxiety disorders. *The American Journal of Psychiatry, 158*, 1568–1578.

Holsboer, F., & Ising, M. (2010). Stress hormone regulation: Biological role and translation into therapy. *Annual Review of Psychology, 61*, 81–109.

Hopwood, C. J., Schade, N., Krueger, R. F., Wright, A. G. C., & Markon, K. E. (2012). Connecting DSM-5 personality traits and pathological beliefs: Toward a unifying model. *Journal of Psychopathology and Behavioral Assessment, 35*(2). https://www.ncbi.nlm.nih.gov/pmc/articles/PMC3833658/

Howes, O. D., & Kapur, S. (2009). The dopamine hypothesis of schizophrenia: Version III—The final common pathway. *Schizophrenia Bulletin, 35*, 549–562.

Hoza, B., Mrug, S., Gerdes, A. C., Hinshaw, S. P., Bukowski, W. M., Gold, J. A., . . . Arnold, L. E. (2005). What aspects of peer relationships are impaired in children with ADHD? *Journal of Consulting and Clinical Psychology, 73*, 411–423.

Hughes, V. (2007). Mercury rising. *Nature Medicine, 13*, 896–897.

Jaegers, L. A., Matthieu, M. M., Vaughn, M. G., Werth, P., Katz I. M., & Ahmad, S. O. (2019, June). Posttraumatic stress disorder and job burnout among jail officers. *Journal of Occupational and Environmental Medicine, 61*(6), 505–510. https://journals.lww.com/joem/Citation/2019/06000/Posttraumatic_Stress_Disorder_and_Job_Burnout.9.aspx

Jellinek, M. S., & Herzog, D. B. (1999). The child. In A. M. Nicholi, Jr. (Ed.), *The Harvard guide to psychiatry* (pp. 585–610). The Belknap Press of Harvard University.

Johnson, J. G., Cohen, P., Kasen, S., & Brook, J. S. (2006). Dissociative disorders among adults in the community, impaired functioning, and axis I and II comorbidity. *Journal of Psychiatric Research, 40*, 131–140.

Joormann, J. (2009). Cognitive aspects of depression. In I. H. Gotlib & C. L. Hammen (Eds.), *Handbook of depression* (pp. 298–321). Guilford Press.

Joyce, P. R., McKenzie, J. M., Luty, S. E., Mulder, R. T., Carter, J. D., Sullivan, P. F., & Cloninger, C. R. (2003). Temperament, childhood environment, and psychopathology as risk factors for avoidant and borderline personality disorders. *Australian and New Zealand Journal of Psychiatry, 37*, 756–764.

Judd, L. L. (2012). Dimensional paradigm of the long-term course of unipolar major depressive disorder. *Depression and Anxiety, 29*, 167–171.

Kagan, J., Reznick, J. S., & Snidman, N. (1988). Biological bases of childhood shyness. *Science, 240*, 167–171.

Katzelnik, D. J., Kobak, K. A., DeLeire, T., Henk, H. J., Greist, J. H., Davidson, J. R. T., . . . Helstad, C. P. (2001). Impact of generalized social anxiety disorder in managed care. *The American Journal of Psychiatry, 158*, 1999–2007.

Kendler, K. S., Hettema, J. M., Butera, F., Gardner, C. O., & Prescott, C. A. (2003). Life event dimensions of loss, humiliation, entrapment, and danger in the prediction of onsets of major depression and generalized anxiety. *Archives of General Psychiatry, 60*, 789–796.

Kennedy, A., LaVail, K., Nowak, G., Basket, M., & Landry, S. (2011). Confidence about vaccines in the United States: Understanding parents' perceptions. *Health Affairs, 30*, 1151–1159.

Kessler, R. C. (1997). The effects of stressful life events on depression. *Annual Review of Psychology, 48*, 191–214.

Kessler, R. C. (2003). Epidemiology of women and depression. *Journal of Affective Disorders, 74*, 5–13.

Kessler, R. C., Berglund, P., Demler, O., Jin, R., Merikangas, K. P., & Walters, E. F. (2005). Lifetime prevalence and age-of-onset distributions of DSM-IV disorders in the National Comorbidity Survey Replication. *Archives of General Psychiatry, 62*, 593–602.

Kessler, R. C., Chiu, W. T., Jin, R., Ruscio, A. M., Shear, K., & Walters, E. (2006). The epidemiology of panic attacks, panic disorder, and agoraphobia in the National Comorbidity Survey Replication. *Archives of General Psychiatry, 63,* 415–424.

Kessler, R. C., Galea, S., Gruber, M. J., Sampson, N. A., Ursano, R. J., & Wessely, S. (2008). Trends in mental illness and suicidality after Hurricane Katrina. *Molecular Psychiatry, 13,* 374–384.

Kessler, R. C., Ruscio, A. M., Shear, K., & Wittchen, H. U. (2009). Epidemiology of anxiety disorders. In M. B. Stein & T. Steckler (Eds.), *Behavioral neurobiology of anxiety and its treatment* (pp. 21–35). Springer.

Kessler, R. C. Sonnega, A., Bromet, E., Hughes, M., & Nelson, C. B. (1995). Posttraumatic stress disorder in the National Comorbidity Survey. *Archives of General Psychiatry, 52,* 1048–1060.

Kessler, R. C., & Wang, P. S. (2009). Epidemiology of depression. In I. H. Gotlib & C. L. Hammen (Eds.), *Handbook of depression* (pp. 5–22). Guilford Press.

Khashan, A. S., Abel, K. M., McNamee, R., Pedersen, M. G., Webb, R., Baker, P., . . . Mortensen, P. B. (2008). Higher risk of offspring schizophrenia following antenatal maternal exposure to severe adverse life events. *Archives of General Psychiatry, 65,* 146–152.

Kilpatrick, D. G., Badour, C. L., & Resnick, H. S. (2017). Trauma and posttraumatic stress disorder prevalence and sociodemographic characteristics. In S. N. Gold (Ed.), *APA handbook of trauma psychology: Foundations in knowledge: Volume 1* (pp. 63–85). American Psychological Association.

Kinney, D. K., Barch, D. H., Chayka, B., Napoleon, S., & Munir, K. M. (2009). Environmental risk factors for autism: Do they help or cause de novo genetic mutations that contribute to the disorder? *Medical Hypotheses, 74,* 102–106.

Kleim, B., Gonzalo, D., & Ehlers, A. (2011). The Depressive Attributions Questionnaire (DAQ): Development of a short self-report measure of depressogenic attributions. *Journal of Psychopathology and Behavioral Assessment, 33,* 375–385.

Klein, R. G., Mannuzza, S., Olazagasti, M. A. R., Roizen, E., Hutchison, J. A., Lashua, E. C., & Castellanos, F. X. (2012). Clinical and functional outcome of childhood attention-deficit/hyperactivity disorder 33 years later. *Archives of General Psychiatry, 69,* 1295–1303.

Koenen, K. C., Stellman, J. M., Stellman, S. D., & Sommer, J. F. (2003). Risk factors for course of posttraumatic stress disorder among Vietnam veterans: A 14-year follow-up of American Legionnaires. *Journal of Consulting and Clinical Psychology, 71,* 980–986.

Kopell, B. H., & Greenberg, B. D. (2008). Anatomy and physiology of the basal ganglia: Implications for DBS in psychiatry. *Neuroscience and Biobehavioral Reviews, 32,* 408–422.

Large, M., Sharma, S., Compton, M. T., Slade, T., & Nielssen, O. (2011). Cannabis use and earlier onset of psychosis: A systematic meta-analysis. *Archives of General Psychiatry, 68,* 555–561.

Lasalvia, A., Zoppei, S., Van Bortel, T., Bonetto, C., Cristofalo, D., Wahlbeck, K., Thornicroft, G. (2013). Global pattern of experienced and anticipated discrimination reported by people with major depressive disorder: A cross-sectional survey. *The Lancet, 381,* 55–62.

Lawrie, S. M., & Abukmeil, S. S. (1998). Brain abnormality in schizophrenia: A systematic and quantitative review of volumetric magnetic resonance imaging studies. *British Journal of Psychiatry, 172,* 110–120.

LeMoult, J., Castonguay, L. G., Joormann, J., & McAleavey, A. (2013). Depression. In L. G. Castonguay & T. F. Oltmanns (Eds.), *Psychopathology: From science to clinical practice* (pp. 17–61). Guilford Press.

Lezenweger, M. F., Lane, M. C., Loranger, A. W., & Kessler, R. C. (2007). DSM-IV personality disorders in the National Comorbidity Survey Replication. *Biological Psychiatry, 62,* 553–564.

Lilienfeld, S. O., & Marino, L. (1999). Essentialism revisited: Evolutionary theory and the concept of mental disorder. *Journal of Abnormal Psychology, 108,* 400–411.

Linnet, K. M., Dalsgaard, S., Obel, C., Wisborg, K., Henriksen, T. B., Rodriquez, A., . . . Jarvelin, M. R. (2003). Maternal lifestyle factors in pregnancy risk of attention deficit hyperactivity disorder and associated behaviors: A review of current evidence. *The American Journal of Psychiatry, 160*, 1028–1040.

Livesley, J. (2008). Toward a genetically-informed model of borderline personality disorder. *Journal of Personality Disorders, 22*, 42–71.

Livesley, J., & Jang, K. L. (2008). The behavioral genetics of personality disorders. *Annual Review of Clinical Psychology, 4*, 247–274.

Loe, I. M., & Feldman, H. M. (2007). Academic and educational outcomes of children with ADHD. *Journal of Pediatric Psychology, 32*, 643–654.

Luxton, D. D., June, J. D., & Fairall, J. M. (2012, May). Social media and suicide: A public health perspective. *American Journal of Public Health, 102*(S2), S195–S200. doi:10.2105/AJPH.2011.300608

Mackin, P., & Young, A. H. (2004, May 1). The role of cortisol and depression: Exploring new opportunities for treatments. *Psychiatric Times*. http://www.psychiatrictimes.com/articles/role-cortisol-and-depression-exploring-new-opportunities-treatments

Maher, W. B., & Maher, B. A. (1985). Psychopathology: I. from ancient times to the eighteenth century. In G. A. Kimble & K. Schlesinger (Eds.), *Topics in the history of psychology: Volume 2* (pp. 251–294). Erlbaum.

Mann, J. J., (2003). Neurobiology of suicidal behavior. *Nature Reviews Neuroscience, 4*, 819–828.

Marker, C. D. (2013, March 3). Safety behaviors in social anxiety: Playing it safe in social anxiety. http://www.psychologytoday.com/blog/face-your-fear/201303/safety-behaviors-in-social-anxiety

Martens, E. J., de Jonge, P., Na, B., Cohen, B. E., Lett, H., & Whooley, M. A. (2010). Scared to death? Generalized anxiety disorder and cardiovascular events in patients with stable coronary heart disease. *Archives of General Psychiatry, 67*, 750–758.

Mataix-Cols, D., Frost, R. O., Pertusa, A., Clark, L. A., Saxena, S., Leckman, J. F., . . . Wilhelm, S. (2010). Hoarding disorder: A new diagnosis for DSM-V? *Depression and Anxiety, 27*, 556–572.

Mayes, R., & Horowitz, A. V. (2005). DSM-III and the revolution in the classification of mental illness. *Journal of the History of the Behavioral Sciences, 41*, 249–267.

Mazure, C. M. (1998). Life stressors as risk factors in depression. *Clinical Psychology: Science and Practice, 5*, 291–313.

Marshal, M. P., & Molina, B. S. G. (2006). Antisocial behaviors moderate the deviant peer pathway to substance use in children with ADHD. *Journal of Clinical Child and Adolescent Psychology, 35*, 216–226.

McCabe, K. (2010, January 24). Teen's suicide prompts a look at bullying. *Boston Globe*. http://www.boston.com

McCabe, R. E., Antony, M. M., Summerfeldt, L. J., Liss, A., & Swinson, R. P. (2003). Preliminary examination of the relationship between anxiety disorders in adults and self-reported history of teasing or bullying experiences. *Cognitive Behaviour Therapy, 32*, 187–193.

McCann, D., Barrett, A., Cooper, A., Crumpler, D., Dalen, L., Grimshaw, K., . . . Stevenson, J. (2007). Food additives and hyperactive behaviour in 3-year-old and 8/9-year-old children in the community: A randomised, double-blinded, placebo-controlled trial. *The Lancet, 370*(9598), 1560–1567.

McEwen, B. S. (2005). Glucocorticoids, depression, and mood disorders: Structural remodeling in the brain. *Metabolism: Clinical and Experimental, 54*, 20–23.

McNally, R. J. (2003). *Remembering trauma*. Harvard University Press.

Meek, S. E., Lemery-Chalfant, K., Jahromi, L. D., & Valiente, C. (2013). A review of gene-environment correlations and their implications for autism: A conceptual model. *Psychological Review, 120*, 497–521.

Mental health myths and facts. (2017, August 29). MentalHealth.gov. https://www.mentalhealth.gov/basics/mental-health-myths-facts

Merikangas, K. R., & Tohen, M. (2011). Epidemiology of bipolar disorder in adults and children. In M. T. Tsuang, M. Tohen, & P. Jones (Eds.), *Textbook of psychiatric epidemiology* (pp. 329–342). John Wiley & Sons.

Merikangas, K. R., Jin, R., He, J. P., Kessler, R. C., Lee, S., Sampson, N. A., Zarkov, Z. (2011). Prevalence and correlates of bipolar spectrum disorder in the World Mental Health Survey Initiative. *Archives of General Psychiatry, 68*, 241–251.

Mezzich, J. E. (2002). International surveys on the use of ICD-10 and related diagnostic systems. *Psychopathology, 35*, 72–75.

Michaud, K., Matheson, K., Kelly, O., & Anisman, H. (2008). Impact of stressors in a natural context on release of cortisol in healthy adult humans: A meta-analysis. *Stress, 11*, 177–197.

Mineka, S., & Cook, M. (1993). Mechanisms involved in the observational conditioning of fear. *Journal of Experimental Psychology: General, 122*, 23–38.

Moffitt, T. E., Caspi, A., Harrington, H., Milne, B. J., Melchior, M., Goldberg, D., & Poulton, R. (2007). Generalized anxiety disorder and depression: Childhood risk factors in a birth cohort followed to age 32. *Psychological Medicine, 37*, 441–452.

Moitra, E., Beard, C., Weisberg, R. B., & Keller, M. B. (2011). Occupational impairment and social anxiety disorder in a sample of primary care patients. *Journal of Affective Disorders, 130*, 209–212.

Molina, B. S. G., & Pelham, W. E. (2003). Childhood predictors of adolescent substance abuse in a longitudinal study of children with ADHD. *Journal of Abnormal Psychology, 112*, 497–507.

Moore, T. H., Zammit, S., Lingford-Hughes, A., Barnes, T. R., Jones, P. B., Burke, M., & Lewis, G. (2007). Cannabis use and risk of psychotic or affective mental health outcomes. *Lancet, 370*, 319–328.

Morris, E. P., Stewart, S. H., & Ham, L. S. (2005). The relationship between social anxiety disorder and alcohol use disorders: A critical review. *Clinical Psychology Review, 25*, 734–760.

Mowrer, O. H. (1960). *Learning theory and behavior.* John Wiley & Sons.

Nader, K. (2001). Treatment methods for childhood trauma. In J. P. Wilson, M. J. Friedman, & J. D. Lindy (Eds.), *Treating psychological trauma and PTSD* (pp. 278–334). Guilford Press.

Nanni, V., Uher, R., & Danese, A. (2012). Childhood maltreatment predicts unfavorable course of illness and treatment outcome in depression: A meta-analysis. *American Journal of Psychiatry, 169*, 141–151.

Nathan, D. (2011). *Sybil exposed: The extraordinary story behind the famous multiple personality case.* Free Press.

National Comorbidity Survey. (2007). *NCS-R lifetime prevalence estimates.* http://www.hcp.med.harvard.edu/ncs/index.php

National Institute on Drug Abuse (NIDA). (2007, October). *Comorbid drug use and mental illness: A research update from the National Institute on Drug Abuse.* http://www.drugabuse.gov/sites/default/files/comorbid.pdf

National Institute on Drug Abuse (NIDA). (2018, February). *Common comorbidities with substance use disorders.* https://www.drugabuse.gov/node/pdf/1155/common-comorbidities-with-substance-use-disorders

Nelson, A. J. (2014, Nov. 8). Teen was insane when he killed child, judge rules. *Omaha World-Herald.* https://www.omaha.com/eedition/sunrise/articles/teen-was-insane-when-he-killed-child-judge-rules/article_d680d09b-be8e-55c3-992f-22da28e60bf8.html

Nestadt, G., Samuels, J., Riddle, M., Bienvenu, J., Liang, K. Y., LaBuda, M., . . . Hoehn-Saric, R. (2000). A family study of obsessive-compulsive disorder. *Archives of General Psychiatry, 57*, 358–363.

Newman, C. F. (2004). Suicidality. In S. L. Johnson & R. L. Leahy (Eds.), *Psychological treatment of bipolar disorder* (pp. 265–285). Guilford Press.

Nikolas, M. A., & Burt, S. A. (2010). Genetic and environmental influences on ADHD symptom dimensions of inattention and hyperactivity: A meta-analysis. *Journal of Abnormal Psychology, 119*, 1–17.

Nolen-Hoeksema, S. (1987). Sex differences in unipolar depression: Evidence and theory. *Psychological Bulletin, 101*, 259–282.

Nolen-Hoeksema, S. (1991). Responses to depression and their effects on the duration of depressive episodes. *Journal of Abnormal Psychology, 100*, 569–582.

Nolen-Hoeksema, S. & Hilt, L. M. (2009). Gender differences in depression. In I. H. Gotlib & C. L. Hammen (Eds.), *Handbook of depression* (pp. 386–404). Guilford Press.

Nolen-Hoeksema, S., Larson, J., & Grayson, C. (1999). Explaining the gender difference in depressive symptoms. *Journal of Personality and Social Psychology, 77*, 1061–1072.

Norberg, M. M., Calamari, J. E., Cohen, R. J., & Riemann, B. C. (2008). Quality of life in obsessive-compulsive disorder: An evaluation of impairment and a preliminary analysis of the ameliorating effects of treatment. *Depression and Anxiety, 25*, 248–259.

Novella, S. (2008, April 16). The increase in autism diagnoses: Two hypotheses. http://www.sciencebasedmedicine.org/the-increase-in-autism-diagnoses-two-hypotheses/

Novick, D. M., Swartz, H. A., & Frank, E. (2010). Suicide attempts in bipolar I and bipolar II disorder: A review and meta-analysis of the evidence. *Bipolar Disorders, 12*, 1–9.

Noyes, R. (2001). Comorbidity in generalized anxiety disorder. *Psychiatric Clinics of North America, 24*, 41–55.

O'Connor, R. C., Smyth, R., Ferguson, E., Ryan, C., & Williams, J. M. G. (2013). Psychological processes and repeat suicidal behavior: A four-year prospective study. *Journal of Consulting and Clinical Psychology*. Advance online publication. doi:10.1037/a0033751

Öhman, A., & Mineka, S. (2001). Fears, phobias, and preparedness: Toward an evolved module of fear and fear learning. *Psychological Review, 108*, 483–552.

Oliver, J. (2006, Summer). The myth of Thomas Szasz. *The New Atlantis, 13*. http://www.thenewatlantis.com/docLib/TNA13-Oliver.pdf

Olsson, A., & Phelps, E. A. (2007). Social learning of fear. *Nature Neuroscience, 10*, 1095–1102.

Oltmanns, T. F., & Castonguay, L. G. (2013). General issues in understanding and treating psychopathology. In L. G. Castonguay & T. F. Oltmanns (Eds.), *Psychopathology: From science to clinical practice* (pp. 1–16). Guilford Press.

Orr, S. P., Metzger, L. J., Lasko, N. B., Macklin, M. L., Peri, T., & Pitman, R. K. (2000). De novo conditioning in trauma-exposed individuals with and without posttraumatic stress disorder. *Journal of Abnormal Psychology, 109*, 290–298.

Owens, D., Horrocks, J., & House, A. (2002). Fatal and non-fatal repetition of self-harm: Systematic review. *British Journal of Psychiatry, 181*, 193–199.

Ozer, E. J., Best, S. R., Lipsey, T. L., & Weiss, D. S. (2003). Predictors of posttraumatic stress disorder and symptoms in adults: A meta-analysis. *Psychological Bulletin, 129*, 52–73.

Parker-Pope, T. (2013, May 2). Suicide rates rise sharply in U.S. *The New York Times*. http://www.nytimes.com.

Patterson, M. L., Iizuka, Y., Tubbs, M. E., Ansel, J., Tsutsumi, M., & Anson, J. (2007). Passing encounters east and west: Comparing Japanese and American pedestrian interactions. *Journal of Nonverbal Behavior, 31*, 155–166.

Pauls, D. L. (2010). The genetics of obsessive-compulsive disorder: A review. *Dialogues in Clinical Neuroscience, 12*, 149–163.

Paykel, E. S. (2003). Life events and affective disorders. *Acta Psychiatrica Scandinavica, 108*(S418), 61–66.

Pazain, M. (2010, December 2). To look or not to look? Eye contact differences in different cultures. http://www.examiner.com/article/to-look-or-not-to-look-eye-contact-differences-different-cultures

Phan, K. L., Fitzgerald, D. A., Nathan, P. J., Moore, G. J., Uhde, T. W., & Tancer, M. E. (2005). Neural substrates for voluntary suppression of negative affect: A functional magnetic resonance imaging study. *Biological Psychiatry, 57*, 210–219.

Phillips, D. P. (1974). The influence of suggestion on suicide: Substantive and theoretical implications of the Werther Effect. *American Sociological Review, 39*, 340–354.

Phillips, K. (2005). *The broken mirror: Understanding and treating body dysmorphic disorder*. Oxford University Press.

Piper, A., & Merskey, H. (2004). The persistence of folly: A critical examination of dissociative identity disorder: Part I: The excesses of an improbable concept. *Canadian Journal of Psychiatry, 49*, 592–600.

Pittman, R. K. (1988). Post-traumatic stress disorder, conditioning, and network theory. *Psychiatric Annals, 18*, 182–189.

Pompili, M., Serafini, G., Innamorati, M., Möller-Leimkühler, A. M., Guipponi, G., Girardi, P., Tatarelli, R., & Lester, D. (2010). The hypothalamic-pituitary-adrenal axis and serotonin abnormalities: A selective overview of the implications of suicide prevention. *European Archives of Psychiatry and Clinical Neuroscience, 260*, 583–600.

Pope, H. G., Jr., Barry, S. B., Bodkin, A., & Hudson, J. I. (2006). Tracking scientific interest in the dissociative disorders: A study of scientific publication output 1984–2003. *Psychotherapy and Psychosomatics, 75*, 19–24.

Pope, H. G., Jr., Hudson, J. I., Bodkin, J. A., & Oliva, P. S. (1998). Questionable validity of 'dissociative amnesia' in trauma victims: Evidence from prospective studies. *British Journal of Psychiatry, 172*, 210–215.

Pope, H. G., Jr., Poliakoff, M. B., Parker, M. P., Boynes, M., & Hudson, J. I. (2006). Is dissociative amnesia a culture-bound syndrome? Findings from a survey of historical literature. *Psychological Medicine, 37*, 225–233.

Postolache, T. T., Mortensen, P. B., Tonelli, L. H., Jiao, X., Frangakis, C., Soriano, J. J., & Qin, P. (2010). Seasonal spring peaks of suicide in victims with and without prior history of hospitalization for mood disorders. *Journal of Affective Disorders, 121*, 88–93.

Putnam, F. W., Guroff, J. J., Silberman, E. K., Barban, L., & Post, R. M. (1986). The clinical phenomenology of multiple personality disorder: A review of 100 recent cases. *Journal of Clinical Psychiatry, 47*, 285–293.

Rachman, S. (1977). The conditioning theory of fear acquisition: A critical examination. *Behaviour Theory and Research, 15*, 375–387.

Regier, D. A., Kuhl, E. A., & Kupfer, D. A. (2012). DSM-5: Classification and criteria changes. *World Psychiatry, 12*, 92–98.

Rhee, S. H., & Waldman, I. D. (2002). Genetic and environmental influences on antisocial behavior: A meta-analysis of twin and adoption studies. *Psychological Bulletin, 128*, 490–529.

Robinson, M. S., & Alloy, L. B. (2003). Negative cognitive styles and stress-reactive rumination interact to predict depression: A prospective study. *Cognitive Therapy and Research, 27*, 275–292.

Roche, T. (2002, March 18). Andrea Yates: More to the story. *Time*. http://content.time.com/time/nation/article/0,8599,218445,00.html.

Root, B. A. (2000). *Understanding panic and other anxiety disorders*. University Press of Mississippi.

Ross, C. A., Miller, S. D., Reagor, P., Bjornson, L., Fraser, G. A., & Anderson, G. (1990). Structured interview data on 102 cases of multiple personality disorder from four centers. *The American Journal of Psychiatry, 147*, 596–601.

Rothschild, A. J. (1999). Mood disorders. In A. M. Nicholi, Jr. (Ed.), *The Harvard guide to psychiatry* (pp. 281–307). The Belknap Press of Harvard University.

Ruder, T. D., Hatch, G. M., Ampanozi, G., Thali, M. J., & Fischer, N. (2011). Suicide announcement on Facebook. *Crisis, 35*, 280–282.

Ruscio, A. M., Stein, D. J., Chiu, W. T., & Kessler, R. C. (2010). The epidemiology of obsessive-compulsive disorder in the National Comorbidity Survey Replication. *Molecular Psychiatry, 15*, 53–63.

Rushworth, M. F., Noonan, M. P., Boorman, E. D., Walton, M. E., & Behrens, T. E. (2011). Frontal cortex and reward-guided learning and decision-making. *Neuron, 70*, 1054–1069.

Rotge, J. Y., Guehl, D., Dilharreguy, B., Cuny, E., Tignol, J., Biolac, B., ... Aouizerate, B. (2008). Provocation of obsessive-compulsive symptoms: A quantitative voxel-based meta-analysis of functional neuroimaging studies. *Journal of Psychiatry and Neuroscience, 33*, 405–412.

Saxena, S., Bota, R. G., & Brody, A. L. (2001). Brain-behavior relationships in obsessive- compulsive disorder. *Seminars in Clinical Neuropsychiatry, 6*, 82–101.

Schwartz, T. (1981). *The hillside strangler: A murderer's mind*. New American Library.

Seligman, M. E. P. (1971). Phobias and preparedness. *Behavioral Therapy, 2*, 307–320.

Shih, R. A., Belmonte, P. L., & Zandi, P. P. (2004). A review of the evidence from family, twin, and adoption studies for a genetic contribution to adult psychiatric disorders. *International Review of Psychiatry, 16*, 260–283.

Siegle, G. J., Thompson, W., Carter, C. S., Steinhauer, S. R., & Thase, M. E. (2007). Increased amygdala and decreased dorsolateral prefrontal BOLD responses in unipolar depression: Related and independent features. *Biological Psychiatry, 61*, 198–209.

Silverstein, C. (2009). The implications of removing homosexuality from the DSM as a mental disorder. *Archives of Sexual Behavior, 38*, 161–163.

Simon, D., Kaufmann, C., Müsch, K., Kischkel, E., & Kathmann, N. (2010). Fronto-striato-limbic hyperactivation in obsessive-compulsive disorder during individually tailored symptom provocation. *Psychophysiology, 47(4)*, 728–738. doi:10.1111/j.1469-8986.2010.00980.x

Snyder, S. H. (1976). The dopamine hypothesis of schizophrenia: Focus on the dopamine receptor. *The American Journal of Psychiatry, 133*, 197–202.

Spinaris, C. G., Denhof, M. D., & Kellaway, J. A. (2012). *Posttraumatic stress disorder in United States corrections professionals: Prevalence and impact on health and functioning*. Desert Waters Correctional Outreach. http://desertwaters.com/wp-content/uploads/2013/09/PTSD_Prev_in_Corrections_09-03-131.pdf

Stack, S. (2000). Media impacts on suicide: A quantitative review of 243 findings. *Social Science Quarterly, 81*, 957–971.

Stanley, B., Molcho, A., Stanley, M., Winchel, R., Gameroff, M. J., Parson, B., & Mann, J. J. (2000). Association of aggressive behavior with altered serotonergic function in patients who are not suicidal. *American Journal of Psychiatry, 157*, 609–614.

Stein, M. B., & Kean, Y. M. (2000). Disability and quality of life in social phobia: Epidemiological findings. *The American Journal of Psychiatry, 157*, 1606–1613.

Steinmetz, J. E., Tracy, J. A., & Green, J. T. (2001). Classical eyeblink conditioning: Clinical models and applications. *Integrative Physiological and Behavioral Science, 36*, 220–238.

Stuppy-Sullivan, A., & Baskin-Sommers, A. (2019). Evaluating dysfunction in cognition and reward among offenders with antisocial personality disorder. *Personality Disorders Theory, Research, and Treatment.* https://modlab.yale.edu/sites/default/files/files/StuppySullivanBaskinSommers_reward_2019.pdf

Surguladze, S., Brammer, M. J., Keedwell, P., Giampietro, V., Young, A. W., Travis, M. J., . . . Phillips, M. L. (2005). A differential pattern of neural response toward sad versus happy facial expressions in major depressive disorder. *Biological Psychiatry, 57,* 201–209.

Szasz, T. S. (1960). The myth of mental illness. *American Psychologist, 15,* 113–118.

Szasz, T. S. (2010). *The myth of mental illness: Foundations of a theory of personal conduct.* HarperCollins (Original work published 1961)

Szasz, T. S. (1965). Legal and moral aspects of homosexuality. In J. Marmor (Ed.), *Sexual inversion: The multiple roots of homosexuality* (pp. 124–139). Basic Books.

Swanson, J. M., Kinsbourne, M., Nigg, J., Lanphear, B., Stephanatos, G., Volkow, N., . . . Wadhwa, P. D. (2007). Etiologic subtypes of attention-deficit/hyperactivity disorder: Brain imaging, molecular genetic and environmental factors and the dopamine hypothesis. *Neuropsychology Review, 17,* 39–59.

Thakur, G. A., Sengupta, S. M., Grizenko, N., Schmitz, N., Pagé, V., & Joober, R. (2013). Maternal smoking during pregnancy and ADHD: A comprehensive clinical and neurocognitive characterization. *Nicotine and Tobacco Research, 15,* 149–157.

Thase, M. E. (2009). Neurobiological aspects of depression. In I. H. Gotlib & C. L. Hammen (Eds.), *Handbook of depression* (pp. 187–217). Guilford Press.

The Associated Press. (2013, May 15). New psychiatric manual, DSM-5, faces criticism for turning "normal" human problems into mental illness. http://www.nydailynews.com/life-style/health/shrinks-critics-face-new-psychiatric-manual-article-1.1344935

Thompson, A., Molina, B. S. G., Pelham, W., & Gnagy, E. M. (2007). Risky driving in adolescents and young adults with childhood ADHD. *Journal of Pediatric Psychology, 32,* 745–759.

Thornicroft, G. (1990). Cannabis and psychosis: Is there epidemiological evidence for an association? *British Journal of Psychiatry, 157,* 25–33.

Tienari, P., Wynne, L. C., Sorri, A., Lahti, I., Lasky, K., Moring, J., . . . Wahlberg, K. (2004). Genotype-environment interaction in schizophrenia spectrum disorder. *British Journal of Psychiatry, 184,* 216–222.

Trezza V., Cuomo, V., & Vanderschuren, L. J. (2008). Cannabis and the developing brain: Insights from behavior. *European Journal of Pharmacology, 585,* 441–452.

Tsuang, M. T., Farone, S. V., & Green, A. I. (1999). Schizophrenia and other psychotic disorders. In A. M. Nicholi, Jr. (Ed.), *The Harvard guide to psychiatry* (pp. 240–280). The Belknap Press of Harvard University Press.

van Praag, H. M. (2005). Can stress cause depression?. *The World Journal of Biological Psychiatry, 6*(S2), 5–22.

Victor, T. A., Furey, M. L., Fromm, S. J., Öhman, A., & Drevets, W. C. (2010). Relationship between amygdala responses to masked faces and mood state and treatment in major depressive disorder. *Archives of General Psychiatry, 67,* 1128–1138.

Volkow N. D., Fowler J. S., Logan J., Alexoff D., Zhu W., Telang F., . . . Apelskog-Torres K. (2009). Effects of modafinil on dopamine and dopamine transporters in the male human brain: clinical implications. *Journal of the American Medical Association*, 301, 1148–1154.

Wakefield, J. C. (1992). The concept of mental disorder: On the boundary between biological facts and social values. *American Psychologist, 47,* 373–388.

Waller, J. (2009a). Looking back: Dancing plagues and mass hysteria. *The Psychologist, 22*(7), 644–647.

Waller, J. (2009b, February 21). A forgotten plague: Making sense of dancing mania. *The Lancet, 373*(9664),

624–625. doi:10.1016/S0140-6736(09)60386-X

Weiser, E. B. (2007). The prevalence of anxiety disorders among adults with Asthma: A meta-analytic review. *Journal of Clinical Psychology in Medical Settings, 14,* 297–307.

White, C. N., Gunderson, J. G., Zanarani, M. C., & Hudson, J. I. (2003). Family studies of borderline personality disorder: A review. *Harvard Review of Psychiatry, 11,* 8–19.

Whooley, M. A. (2006). Depression and cardiovascular disease: Healing the broken-hearted. *Journal of the American Medical Association, 295,* 2874–2881.

Wilcox, H. C., Conner, K. R., & Caine, E. D. (2004). Association of alcohol and drug use disorders and completed suicide: An empirical review of cohort studies. *Drug and Alcohol Dependence, 76,* S11–S19.

Wing, L., Gould, J., & Gillberg, C. (2011). Autism spectrum disorders in the DSM-V: Better or worse than the DSM IV? *Research in Developmental Disabilities, 32,* 768–773.

Wisner, K. L., Sit, D. K. Y., McShea, M. C., Rizzo, D. M., Zoretich, R. A., Hughes, C. L., Hanusa, B. H. (2013). Onset timing, thoughts of self-harm, and diagnoses in postpartum women with screen-positive depression findings. *JAMA Psychiatry, 70,* 490–498.

Wolraich, M. L., Wilson, D. B., & White, J. W. (1995). The effect of sugar on behavior or cognition in children. *Journal of the American Medical Association, 274,* 1617–1621.

World Health Organization (WHO). (2013). *International classification of diseases (ICD).* http://www.who.int/classifications/icd/en/

Wyatt, W. J., & Midkiff, D. M. (2006). Biological psychiatry: A practice in search of a science. *Behavior and Social Issues, 15,* 132–151.

Xie, P., Kranzler, H. R., Poling, J., Stein, M. B., Anton, R. F., Brady, K., Gelernter, J. (2009). Interactive effect of stressful life events and the serotonin transporter *5-HTTLPR* genotype on posttraumatic stress disorder diagnosis in 2 independent populations. *Archives of General Psychology, 66,* 1201–1209.

Zachar, P., & Kendler, K. S. (2007). Psychiatric disorders: A conceptual taxonomy. *The American Journal of Psychiatry, 16,* 557–565.

Zuckerman, M. (1999). *Vulnerability to psychopathology: A biosocial model.* American Psychological Association.

Therapy and Treatment

Abbass, A., Kisely, S., & Kroenke, K. (2006). Short-term psychodynamic psychotherapy for somatic disorders: Systematic review and meta-analysis of clinical trials. *Psychotherapy and Psychosomatics, 78,* 265–274.

Ahmed, S., Wilson, K. B., Henriksen, R. C., & Jones, J. W. (2011). What does it mean to be a culturally competent counselor? *Journal for Social Action in Counseling and Psychology, 3*(1), 17–28.

Alavi, A., Sharifi, B., Ghanizadeh, A., & Dehbozorgi, G. (2013). Effectiveness of cognitive-behavioral therapy in decreasing suicidal ideation and hopelessness of the adolescents with previous suicidal attempts. *Iranian Journal of Pediatrics, 23*(4), 467–472.

Alegría, M., Chatterji, P., Wells, K., Cao, Z., Chen, C. N., Takeuchi, D., . . . Meng, X. L. (2008). Disparity in depression treatment among racial and ethnic minority populations in the United States. *Psychiatric Services, 59*(11), 1264–1272.

American Psychological Association. (2005). *Policy statement on evidence-based practice in psychology.* http://www.apapracticecentral.org/ce/courses/ebpstatement.pdf

American Psychological Association. (2014). *Can psychologists prescribe medications for their patients?* http://www.apa.org/news/press/releases/2004/05/louisiana-rx.aspx

American Psychological Association. (2014). *Psychotherapy: Understanding group therapy.*

http://www.apa.org/helpcenter/group-therapy.aspx

Beck, A. T., Rush, A. J., Shaw, B. F., & Emery, G. (1979). *Cognitive therapy of depression*. The Guilford Press.

Beck Institute for Cognitive Behavior Therapy. (n.d.). *History of cognitive therapy*. http://www.beckinstitute.org/history-of-cbt/

Beck, J. S. (2011). *Cognitive behavior therapy: Basics and beyond* (2nd ed.). The Guilford Press.

Belgrave, F., & Allison, K. (2010). *African-American psychology: From Africa to America* (2nd ed.). Sage Publications.

Bertrand, K., Richer, I., Brunelle, N., Beaudoin, I., Lemieux, A., & Ménard, J-M. (2013). Substance abuse treatment for adolescents: How are family factors related to substance use change? *Journal of Psychoactive Drugs, 45*(1), 28–38.

Blank, M. B., Mahmood, M., Fox, J. C., & Guterbock, T. (2002). Alternative mental health services: The role of the black church in the South. *American Journal of Public Health, 92,* 1668–1672.

Blumberg, J. (2007, October 24). A brief history of the Salem witch trials. *Smithsonian.com*. http://www.smithsonianmag.com/history-archaeology/brief-salem.html?c=y&page=2

Butlera, A. C., Chapmanb, J. E., Formanc, E. M., & Becka, A. T. (2006). The empirical status of cognitive-behavioral therapy: A review of meta-analyses. *Clinical Psychology Review, 26,* 17–31.

Center for Substance Abuse Treatment. (2005). *Substance Abuse Treatment: Group Therapy*. Treatment Improvement Protocol (TIP) Series 41. DHHS Publication No. (SMA) 05-3991. Substance Abuse and Mental Health Services Administration.

Centers for Disease Control and Prevention. (2014). *Suicide prevention: Youth suicide*. http://www.cdc.gov/violenceprevention/pub/youth_suicide.html

Chambless, D. L., & Ollendick, T. H. (2001). Empirically supported psychological interventions: Controversies and evidence. *Annual Review of Psychology, 52,* 685–716.

Charman, D., & Barkham, M. (2005). Psychological treatments: Evidence-based practice and practice-based evidence. *InPsych Highlights*. www.psychology.org.au/publications/inpsych/treatments

Chorpita, B. F., Daleiden, E. L., Ebesutani, C., Young, J., Becker, K. D., Nakamura, B. J., . . . Starace, N. (2011), Evidence-based treatments for children and adolescents: An updated review of indicators of efficacy and effectiveness. *Clinical Psychology: Science and Practice, 18,* 154–172.

Clement, S., Schauman, O., Graham, T., Maggioni, F., Evans-Lacko, S., Bezborodovs, N., . . . Thornicroft, G. (2014, February 25). What is the impact of mental health-related stigma on help-seeking? A systematic review of quantitative and qualitative studies. *Psychological Medicine,* 1–17.

Cuijpers, P., Sijbrandij, M. Koole, S. L., Andersson, G., Beekman, A. T., & Reynolds, C. F. (2014). Adding psychotherapy to antidepressant medication in depression and anxiety disorders: a meta-analysis. *World Psychiatry, 13*(1), 56–67.

Daniel, D. (n.d.). *Rational emotive in behavior therapy the context of modern psychlogical research*. albertellis.org/rebt-in-the-context-of-modern-psychological-research

Davidson, W. S. (1974). Studies of aversive conditioning for alcoholics: A critical review of theory and research methodology. *Psychological Bulletin, 81*(9), 571–581.

DeRubeis, R. J., Hollon, S. D., Amsterdam, J. D., Shelton, R. C., Young, P. R., Salomon, R. M., . . . Gallop, R. (2005). Cognitive Therapy vs medications in the treatment of moderate to severe depression. *Archives of General Psychiatry, 62*(4), 409–416.

DeYoung, S. H. (2013, November 14). The woman who raised that monster. http://www.huffingtonpost.com/suzy-hayman-deyoung/the-woman-who-raised-that_b_4266621.html

Dickerson, F. B., Tenhula, W. N., & Green-Paden, L. D. (2005). The token economy for schizophrenia: Review of the literature and recommendations for future research. *Schizophrenia Research, 75*(2), 405–416.

Donahue, A. B. (2000). Electroconvulsive therapy and memory loss: A personal journey. *The Journal of ECT, 162*, 133–143.

Elkins, R. L. (1991). An appraisal of chemical aversion (emetic therapy) approaches to alcoholism treatment. *Behavior Research and Therapy, 29*(5), 387–413.

Gary, F. A. (2005). Stigma: Barrier to mental health care among ethnic minorities. *Issues in Mental Health Nursing, 26*(10), 979–999.

Gerardi, M., Cukor, J., Difede, J., Rizzo, A., & Rothbaum, B. O. (2010). Virtual reality exposure therapy for post-traumatic stress disorder and other anxiety disorders. *Current Psychiatry Reports, 12*(298), 299–305.

Harter, S. (1977). A cognitive-developmental approach to children's expression of conflicting feelings and a technique to facilitate such expression in play therapy. *Journal of Consulting and Clinical Psychology, 45*(3), 417–432.

Hemphill, R. E. (1966). Historical witchcraft and psychiatric illness in Western Europe. *Proceedings of the Royal Society of Medicine, 59*(9), 891–902.

Ivey, S. L., Scheffler, R., & Zazzali, J. L. (1998). Supply dynamics of the mental health workforce: Implications for health policy. *Milbank Quarterly, 76*(1), 25–58.

Jang, Y., Chiriboga, D. A., & Okazaki, S. (2009). Attitudes toward mental health services: Age group differences in Korean American adults. *Aging & Mental Health, 13*(1), 127–134.

Jones, M. C. (1924). A laboratory study of fear: The case of Peter. *Pedagogical Seminary, 31*, 308–315.

Kalff, D. M. (1991). Introduction to sandplay therapy. *Journal of Sandplay Therapy, 1*(1), 9.

Leblanc, M., & Ritchie, M. (2001). A meta-analysis of play therapy outcomes. *Counselling Psychology Quarterly, 14*(2), 149–163.

Lovaas, O. I. (1987). Behavioral treatment and normal educational and intellectual functioning in young autistic children. *Journal of Consulting & Clinical Psychology, 55*, 3–9.

Lovaas, O. I. (2003). *Teaching individuals with developmental delays: Basic intervention techniques*. Pro-Ed.

Lowinger, R. J., & Rombom, H. (2012). The effectiveness of cognitive behavioral therapy for PTSD in New York City Transit Workers. *North American Journal of Psychology, 14*(3), 471–484.

Madanes, C. (1991). Strategic family therapy. In A. S. Gurman and D. P. Kniskern (Eds.), *Handbook of Family Therapy, Vol. 2*. (pp. 396–416). Brunner/Mazel.

Marques, L., Alegría, M., Becker, A. E., Chen, C. N., Fang, A., Chosak, A., & Diniz, J. B. (2011). Comparative prevalence, correlates of impairment, and service utilization for eating disorders across US ethnic groups: Implications for reducing ethnic disparities in health care access for eating disorders. *International Journal of Eating Disorders, 44*(5), 412–420.

Martin, B. (2007). *In-Depth: Cognitive behavioral therapy*. http://psychcentral.com/lib/in-depth-cognitive-behavioral-therapy/000907

Mayo Clinic. (2012). *Tests and procedures: Transcranial magnetic stimulation*. http://www.mayoclinic.org/tests-procedures/transcranial-magnetic-stimulation/basics/definition/PRC-20020555

McGovern, M. P., & Carroll, K. M. (2003). Evidence-based practices for substance use disorders. *Psychiatric Clinics of North America, 26*, 991–1010.

McGrath, R. J., Cumming, G. F., Burchard, B. L., Zeoli, S., & Ellerby, L. (2009). *Current practices and emerging trends in sexual abuser management: The safer society North American survey*. The SaferSociety Press.

McLellan, A. T., Lewis, D. C., O'Brien, C. P., & Kleber, H. D. (2000). Drug dependence, a chronic medical illness: Implications for treatment, insurance, and outcomes evaluation. *JAMA, 284*(13), 1689–1695.

Minuchin, P. (1985). Families and individual development: Provocations from the field of family therapy. *Child Development, 56*(2), 289–302.

Mullen, E. J., & Streiner, D. L. (2004). The evidence for and against evidence-based practice. *Brief Treatment and Crisis Intervention, 4*(2), 111–121.

Muñoz-Cuevas, F. J., Athilingam, J., Piscopo, D., & Wilbrecht, L. (2013). Cocaine-induced structural plasticity in frontal cortex correlates with conditioned place preference. *Nature Neuroscience, 16*, 1367–1369.

National Association of Cognitive-Behavioral Therapists. (2009). History of cognitive behavioral therapy. http://nacbt.org/historyofcbt.htm.

National Institute of Mental Health. (2017). *Any disorder among children.* http://www.nimh.nih.gov/statistics/1ANYDIS_CHILD.shtml

National Institute of Mental Health. (n.d.). *Use of mental health services and treatment among children.* http://www.nimh.nih.gov/statistics/1NHANES.shtml

National Institutes of Health. (2013, August 6). *Important events in NIMH history.* http://www.nih.gov/about/almanac/organization/NIMH.htm

National Institute on Drug Abuse. (2008). *Addiction science: From Molecules to managed care.* http://www.drugabuse.gov/publications/addiction-science/relapse

National Institute on Drug Abuse. (2011). *Drug facts: Comorbidity: Addiction and other mental disorders.* http://www.drugabuse.gov/publications/drugfacts/comorbidity-addiction-other-mental-disorders

National Institute on Drug Abuse. (2012). *Principles of drug addiction treatment: A research-based guide* (3rd ed.). http://www.drugabuse.gov/publications/principles-drug-addiction-treatment-research-based-guide-third-edition/principles-effective-treatment

Nelson, P. (1993). Autobiography in Five Short Chapters. In *There's a Hole in my Sidewalk: The Romance of Self-Discovery*. Beyond Words Publishing.

O'Connor, K. J. (2000). *The play therapy primer* (2nd ed.). Wiley.

Page, R. C., & Berkow, D. N. (1994). *Unstructured group therapy: Creating contact, choosing relationship.* Jossey Bass.

Pagnin, D., de Queiroz, V., Pini, S., & Cassano, G. B. (2004). Efficacy of ECT in depression: A meta-analytic review. *Journal of ECT, 20*, 13–20.

Prins, S. J., & Draper, L. (2009). *Improving outcomes for people with mental illnesses under community corrections supervision: A guide to research-informed policy and practice.* Council of State Governments Justice Center.

Prochaska, J. O., & Norcross, J. C. (2010). *Systems of psychotherapy* (7th ed.). Wadsworth.

Prudic, J., Peyser, S., & Sackeim, H. A. (2000). Subjective memory complaints: A review of patient self-assessment of memory after electroconvulsive therapy. *The Journal of ECT, 16*(2), 121–132.

Rathus, J. H., & Sanderson, W. C. (1999). *Marital distress: Cognitive behavioral treatments for couples.* Jason Aronson.

Reti, I. R. (n.d.). *Electroconvulsive therapy today.* Johns Hopkins Medicine. http://www.hopkinsmedicine.org/psychiatry/specialty_areas/brain_stimulation/docs/DepBulletin407_ECT_extract.pdf

Richman, L. S., Kohn-Wood, L. P., & Williams, D. R. (2007). The role of discrimination and racial identity for mental health service utilization. *Journal of Social and Clinical Psychology, 26*(8), 960–981.

Rizzo, A., Newman, B., Parsons, T., Difede, J., Reger, G., Holloway, K., . . . Bordnick, P. (2010). Development and clinical results from the Virtual Iraq exposure therapy application for PTSD. *Annals of the New York Academy of Sciences, 1208*, 114–125.

Rogers, C. (1951). *Client-centered psychotherapy*. Houghton-Mifflin.

Sackett, D. L., & Rosenberg, W. M. (1995). On the need for evidence-based medicine. *Journal of Public Health, 17*, 330–334.

Sallows, G. O., & Graupner, T. D. (2005). Intensive behavioral treatment for children with autism: Four-year outcome and predictors. *American Journal of Mental Retardation, 110*(6), 417–438.

Scott, L. D., McCoy, H., Munson, M. R., Snowden, L. R., & McMillen, J. C. (2011). Cultural mistrust of mental health professionals among Black males transitioning from foster care. *Journal of Child and Family Studies, 20*, 605–613.

Shechtman, Z. (2002). Child group psychotherapy in the school at the threshold of a new millennium. *Journal of Counseling and Development, 80*(3), 293–299.

Shedler, J. (2010). The efficacy of psychodynamic psychotherapy. *American Psychologist, 65*, 98–109.

Simpson D. D. (1981). Treatment for drug abuse. *Archives of General Psychiatry, 38*, 875–880.

Simpson D. D, Joe, G. W., & Bracy, S. A. (1982). Six-year follow-up of opioid addicts after admission to treatment. *Archives General Psychiatry, 39*, 1318–1323.

Snowden, L. R. (2001). Barriers to effective mental health services for African Americans. *Mental Health Services Research, 3*, 181–187.

Stensland, M., Watson, P. R., & Grazier, K. L. (2012). An examination of costs, charges, and payments for inpatient psychiatric treatment in community hospitals. *Psychiatric Services, 63*(7), 66–71.

Stewart, S. M., Simmons, A., & Habibpour, E. (2012). Treatment of culturally diverse children and adolescents with depression. *Journal of Child and Adolescent Psychopharmacology, 22*(1), 72–79.

Streeton, C., & Whelan, G. (2001). Naltrexone, a relapse prevention maintenance treatment of alcohol dependence: A meta-analysis of randomized controlled trials. *Alcohol and Alcoholism, 36*(6), 544–552.

Sue, D. W. (2001). Multidimensional facets of cultural competence. *Counseling Psychologist, 29*(6), 790–821.

Sue, D. W. (2004). Multicultural counseling and therapy (MCT). In J. A. Banks and C. Banks (Eds.), *Handbook of research on multicultural education* (2nd ed., pp. 813–827). Jossey-Bass.

Sue, D. W., & Sue, D. (2007). *Counseling the culturally different: Theory and practice* (5th ed.). Wiley.

Sussman, L. K., Robins, L. N., & Earls, F. (1987). Treatment–seeking for depression by Black and White Americans. *Social Science & Medicine, 24*, 187–196.

Szasz, T. S. (1960). The Myth of Mental Illness. *American Psychologist, 15*, 113–118.

Thomas, K. C., & Snowden, L. R. (2002). Minority response to health insurance coverage for mental health services. *Journal of Mental Health Policy and Economics, 4*, 35–41.

Tiffany, F. (2012/1891). *Life of Dorothea Lynde Dix* (7th ed.). Houghton, Mifflin.

Torrey, E. F. (1997). *Out of the shadows: Confronting America's mental illness crisis*. Wiley.

Torrey, E. F., Zdanowicz, M. T., Kennard, A. D., Lamb, H. R., Eslinger, D. F., Biasotti, M. C., & Fuller, D. A. (2014, April 8). *The treatment of persons with mental illness in prisons and jails: A state survey*. Treatment Advocacy Center. http://tacreports.org/storage/documents/treatment-behind-bars/treatment-behind-bars.pdf

Townes D. L., Cunningham N. J., & Chavez-Korell, S. (2009). Reexaming the relationships between racial identity, cultural mistrust, help-seeking attitudes, and preference for a Black counselor. *Journal of Counseling Psychology, 56*(2), 330–336.

U.S. Department of Agriculture. (2013, December 10). USDA announces support for mental health facilities in rural areas [Press release No. 0234.13]. http://www.usda.gov/wps/portal/usda/usdahome?contentid=2013/12/0234.xml

U.S. Department of Health and Human Services. (1999). *Mental health: A report of the Surgeon General*. Rockville, MD: U.S. Department of Health and Human Services, Substance Abuse and Mental Health Services Administration, Center for Mental Health Services, National Institutes of Health, National Institute of Mental Health.

U.S. Department of Health and Human Services, Health Resources and Services Administration, Office of Rural Health Policy. (2005). *Mental health and rural America: 1984-2005*. ftp://ftp.hrsa.gov/ruralhealth/RuralMentalHealth.pdf

U.S. Department of Health and Human Services, Substance Abuse and Mental Health Services Administration, Center for Behavioral Health Statistics and Quality. (2017). *Results from the 2016 National Survey on Drug Use and Health: Mental Health Findings*. https://www.samhsa.gov/data/sites/default/files/NSDUH-DetTabs-2016/NSDUH-DetTabs-2016.pdf

U.S. Department of Health and Human Services, Substance Abuse and Mental Health Services Administration, Center for Behavioral Health Statistics and Quality. (2011, September). *Results from the 2010 National Survey on Drug Use and Health: Summary of National Findings* (NSDUH Series H-41, HHS Publication No. [SMA] 11-4658). http://www.samhsa.gov/data/NSDUH/2k10ResultsRev/NSDUHresultsRev2010.htm

U.S. Department of Health and Human Services, Substance Abuse and Mental Health Services Administration, Center for Behavioral Health Statistics and Quality. (2013, September). *Results from the 2012 National Survey on Drug Use and Health: Summary of National Findings* (NSDUH Series H-46, HHS Publication No. [SMA] 13-4795). http://www.samhsa.gov/data/NSDUH/2012SummNatFindDetTables/NationalFindings/NSDUHresults2012.htm#ch2.2

U.S. Department of Housing and Urban Development, Office of Community Planning and Development. (2011). *The 2010 Annual Homeless Assessment Report to Congress*. http://www.hudhre.info/documents/2010HomelessAssessmentReport.pdf

U.S. Department of Labor. (n.d.). *Mental health parity*. http://www.dol.gov/ebsa/mentalhealthparity/

U.S. Public Health Service. (2000). *Report of the Surgeon General's conference on children's mental health: A national action agenda*. Department of Health and Human Services.

Wagenfeld, M. O., Murray, J. D., Mohatt, D. F., & DeBruiynb, J. C. (Eds.). (1994). *Mental health and rural America: 1980–1993* (NIH Publication No. 94-3500). U.S. Government Printing Office.

Wampold, B. E. (2007). Psychotherapy: The humanistic (and effective) treatment. *American Psychologist, 62*, 857–873. doi:10.1037/0003-066X.62.8.857

Weil, E. (2012, March 2). Does couples therapy work? *The New York Times*. http://www.nytimes.com/2012/03/04/fashion/couples-therapists-confront-the-stresses-of-their-field.html?pagewanted=all&_r=0

Weiss, R. D., Jaffee, W. B., de Menil, V. P., & Cogley, C. B. (2004). Group therapy for substance abuse disorders: What do we know? *Harvard Review of Psychiatry, 12*(6), 339–350.

Willard Psychiatric Center. (2009). *Echoes of Willard*. http://www.echoesofwillard.com/willard-psychiatric-centre/

Wolf, M., & Risley, T. (1967). Application of operant conditioning procedures to the behavior problems of an autistic child: A follow-up and extension. *Behavior Research and Therapy, 5*(2), 103–111.

Wolpe, J. (1958). *Psychotherapy by reciprocal inhibition*. Stanford University Press.

Index

A

absentmindedness, 283, 290

Absolute threshold, 156

absolute threshold, 183

Accommodation, 304

accommodation, 334

acoustic encoding, 265, 290

acquisition, 198, 219

action potential, 86, 87, 107

actor-observer bias, 425, 461

Adler, 389

Adolescence, 325

adolescence, 334

adrenal gland, 107

adrenal glands, 105

adrenarche, 325, 334

advance directive, 333, 334

afterimage, 169, 183

ageism, 449, 461

aggression, 453, 461

agonist, 107

Agonists, 88

agoraphobia, 576, 618

Alarm reaction, 519

alarm reaction, 556

algorithm, 235, 256

all-or-none, 87, 107

allele, 78, 107

alpha wave, 147

alpha waves, 125

Altruism, 456

altruism, 461

American Psychiatric Association, 567

American Psychological Association (APA), 19, 32, 477

Americans with Disabilities Act, 506

Americans with Disabilities Act (ADA), 491

Amnesia, 276

amnesia, 290

amplitude, 160, 183

amygdala, 98, 107, 273, 368

anal stage, 388, 413

Analytical intelligence, 243

analytical intelligence, 256

analytical psychology, 391, 413

anchoring bias, 239, 256

anger, 536

animal research, 65

Anorexia nervosa, 353

anorexia nervosa, 373

antagonist, 88, 107

anterograde amnesia, 276, 290

antisocial, 217

antisocial personality disorder, 614, 618

anxiety disorder, 618

Anxiety disorders, 575

archetype, 413

archetypes, 392

archival research, 49, 67

arousal theory, 274, 290

artificial concept, 228, 256

Asch, 439

Asch effect, 439, 440, 461

Asperger's, 608

assimilation, 304, 334

Associative learning, 192

associative learning, 219

Asthma, 539

asthma, 556

asylum, 659

Asylums, 631

Atkinson, 266

Atkinson-Shiffrin model, 290

Attachment, 319

attachment, 334

attention deficit/hyperactivity disorder, 618

attention deficit/hyperactivity disorder (ADHD), 605

Attitude, 432

attitude, 461

attribution, 426, 461

attrition, 51, 67

atypical, 564, 618

auditory cortex, 97, 107

authoritarian parenting style, 334

authoritarian style, 324

authoritative parenting style, 334

authoritative style, 323

autism spectrum disorder, 608, 618

automatic processing, 264, 290

autonomic nervous system, 90, 107

availability heuristic, 240, 256

Aversive conditioning, 639

aversive conditioning, 659

avoidant attachment, 321, 334

avoidant personality disorder, 611

axon, 84, 107

B

Bandura, 215, 346, 395

Bariatric surgery, 351

bariatric surgery, 373

basilar membrane, 172, 183

basolateral complex, 368, 373

Beck, 642

behavior therapy, 639, 659

behavioral genetics, 78

behaviorism, 13, 32

bias, 284, 290

binaural, 173

binaural cue, 183

Binge eating disorder, 353

binge eating disorder, 373

binocular, 170

binocular cue, 183

binocular disparity, 170, 183

biofeedback, 548, 556

biological clock, 117

biological perspective, 88, 107

biological rhythm, 147

Biological rhythms, 116

Biomedical therapy, 636

biomedical therapy, 645, 659

biopsychology, 20, 32

biopsychosocial model, 26, 32

Bipolar and related disorders, 589

bipolar and related disorders, 618

bipolar disorder, 591, 618

bisexual, 356, 373

blind spot, 165, 183

blocking, 290

BMI, 350

body dysmorphic disorder, 582, 618

Body language, 371

body language, 373

body mass index, 350

bona fide occupational qualification (BFOQ), 506

bona fide occupational qualifications (BFOQs), 492

borderline personality disorder, 613, 618

Bottom-up processing, 157

bottom-up processing, 183

brain imaging, 101

Broca's area, 95, 107

bulimia nervosa, 352, 373

Bullying, 453

bullying, 454, 461

bystander effect, 455, 461

C

caffeine, 140

Cannon, 517

Cannon-Bard theory, 365

Cannon-Bard theory of emotion, 373

cardiovascular disorders, 533, 556

case study, 45

cataplexy, 133, 147

catatonic behavior, 618

catatonic behaviors, 599

cause and effect, 53

cause-and-effect relationship, 67

central nervous system (CNS), 89, 107

central nucleus, 368, 373

central route, 437

central route persuasion, 461

central sleep apnea, 132, 147

cerebellum, 100, 107, 274

cerebral cortex, 93, 107

checklist, 503, 506

Chomsky, 230

chromosome, 107

Chromosomes, 78

chunking, 286, 290

circadian rhythm, 117, 147

classical conditioning, 194, 219, 576, 580, 584

cleft chin, 79

client-centered therapy, 644

clinical, 45

clinical or case study, 67

Clinical psychology, 26

clinical psychology, 32

closure, 181, 183

cochlea, 171, 183

cochlear implant, 183

Cochlear implants, 174

Codeine, 141

codeine, 147

cognition, 226, 256

Index

Cognitive development, 296

cognitive development, 334

cognitive dissonance, 432, 433, 435, 461

Cognitive empathy, 326

cognitive empathy, 334

cognitive map, 213, 219

cognitive psychology, 21, 32, 256

Cognitive psychology, 226

cognitive script, 229, 256

Cognitive therapy, 642

cognitive therapy, 659

Cognitive-behavioral therapy, 130

cognitive-behavioral therapy, 147, 659

Cognitive-behavioral therapy (CBT), 643

cognitive-mediational theory, 366, 373

collective unconscious, 128, 147, 392, 413

collectivist culture, 461

collectivistic culture, 424

color vision, 167

comorbid disorder, 659

comorbid disorders, 654

comorbidity, 569, 618, 654

Companionate love, 459

companionate love, 461

Compliance, 445

components of emotion, 363, 373

Compulsions, 582

computerized tomography (CT) scan, 101, 107

concept, 256

Conception, 310

conception, 334

Concepts, 227

concrete operational stage, 306, 334

conditioned response (CR), 195, 219

conditioned stimulus (CS), 194, 219

conditioning, 194

conductive hearing loss, 173, 183

cone, 183

cones, 164

confederate, 439, 461

Confidentiality, 648

confidentiality, 659

confirmation bias, 55, 67, 239, 256, 451, 461

Conformity, 439, 445

conformity, 461

confounding variable, 53, 67

congenital analgesia, 178

congenital deafness, 173, 183

congenital insensitivity to pain, 178

congenital insensitivity to pain (congenital analgesia), 183

congruence, 399, 413

conscious, 383, 413

Consciousness, 116

consciousness, 147

conservation, 306, 334

construction, 277, 290

consummate love, 459, 461

Contemporized-Themes Concerning Blacks Test (C-TCB), 412, 413

continuity, 181

Continuous development, 298

continuous development, 334

continuous positive airway pressure (CPAP), 132, 147

continuous reinforcement, 209, 219

control group, 56, 67

convergent thinking, 245, 256

Coping, 541

coping, 556

cornea, 164, 183

corpus callosum, 94, 107

Correlation, 52

correlation, 67

correlation coefficient, 52, 67

correlational research, 54, 525

correlations, 253

Cortisol, 521

cortisol, 556

Counseling psychology, 26

counseling psychology, 32

counterconditioning, 639, 659

Couples therapy, 651

couples therapy, 659

Creative intelligence, 243

creative intelligence, 256

Creativity, 245

creativity, 256

critical (sensitive) period, 334

critical or sensitive period, 314

cross-sectional research, 50, 67

Crystallized intelligence, 242

crystallized intelligence, 256

cues, 170

cultural competence, 655, 659

cultural display rule, 370, 373

cultural intelligence, 244, 256

culture, 17, 297, 406, 406, 413, 565, 655

cultures, 159, 182

Cyberbullying, 454

cyberbullying, 461

D

Daily hassles, 525

daily hassles, 556

dancing mania, 572

deaf culture, 175

Deafness, 173

deafness, 183

debriefing, 64, 67

Deception, 64

deception, 67

decibel (dB), 183

decibels (dB), 162

declarative memory, 290

deductive reasoning, 41, 67

defense mechanism, 413

defense mechanisms, 385

Deindividuation, 445

deinstitutionalization, 633, 659

delta wave, 147

delta waves, 126

delusion, 618

Delusions, 599

dendrite, 107

dendrites, 84

deoxyribonucleic acid (DNA), 78, 107

dependent personality disorder, 611

dependent variable, 58, 67

depersonalization, 603

Depersonalization/derealization disorder, 603

depersonalization/derealization disorder, 618

depressant, 136, 147

depression, 537, 589

depressive disorder, 618

Depressive disorders, 589

depth perception, 169, 183

Derealization, 603

developmental milestone, 334

developmental milestones, 297

Developmental psychology, 22

developmental psychology, 32

diabetes, 105, 107

diagnosis, 568, 618

Diagnostic and Statistical Manual of Mental Disorders, 134

Diagnostic and Statistical Manual of Mental Disorders (DSM-5), 568

Diagnostic and Statistical Manual of Mental Disorders, Fifth Edition (DSM-5), 618

diathesis-stress model, 574, 618

diathesis-stress models, 595

difference threshold, 156

Diffusion of responsibility, 455

diffusion of responsibility, 461

discontinuous, 298

discontinuous development, 334

Discrimination, 447, 447

discrimination, 448, 449, 449, 450, 450, 461, 489

disorganized attachment, 321, 334

Disorganized or abnormal motor behavior, 599

Disorganized thinking, 599

disorganized thinking, 618

disorganized/abnormal motor behavior, 618

displacement, 387, 413

dispositionism, 423, 461

dissertation, 28, 32

dissociative amnesia, 603, 619

Dissociative disorders, 603

dissociative disorders, 619

dissociative fugue, 603, 619

dissociative identity disorder, 604, 619

distorted body image, 353, 373

distress, 515, 556

divergent thinking, 245, 256

Diversity training, 501

diversity training, 506

Dix, 632

Do Not Resuscitate (DNR), 333

do not resuscitate (DNR), 334

dominant allele, 79, 107

dopamine hypothesis, 601, 619

double-blind study, 57, 67

Downsizing, 495

downsizing, 506

dream analysis, 637, 659

drive theory, 344, 373

Dyscalculia, 255

dyscalculia, 256

dysgraphia, 255, 256

dyslexia, 255, 256

E
Ebbinghaus, 283

effortful processing, 264, 290

ego, 385, 413

egocentrism, 306, 334

elaboration likelihood model, 437

elaborative rehearsal, 287, 290

electroconvulsive therapy (ECT), 648, 659

Electroencephalography (EEG), 103

electroencephalography (EEG), 107

electromagnetic spectrum, 160, 183

embryo, 311, 335

emerging adulthood, 327, 335

emotion, 362, 373

emotion-focused coping, 541

Emotional intelligence, 244

emotional intelligence, 256

Empathy, 456

empathy, 461

empirical, 38, 67

empirical method, 8, 32

encoding, 264, 290

endocrine system, 104, 107

engram, 272, 290

epigenetics, 82, 107

Episodic memory, 269

episodic memory, 290

equipotentiality hypothesis, 272, 290

Erikson, 301, 390

etiology, 564, 619

euphoric high, 139, 147

eustress, 515, 556

event schema, 229, 256

evolutionary psychology, 20, 78, 147

Evolutionary psychology, 123

excitement, 357, 373

exercise, 547

experiment, 55

experimental design, 59

experimental group, 56, 67

Experimenter bias, 57

experimenter bias, 67

Explicit memories, 268

explicit memory, 290

exposure therapy, 639, 659

Extinction, 199

extinction, 219

extrinsic, 342

extrinsic motivation, 373

Eysenck, 402

F
facial feedback hypothesis, 373

fact, 67

Facts, 40

false memory syndrome, 280, 290

falsifiable, 43, 67

Family therapy, 651

family therapy, 659

fight or flight, 91

fight or flight response, 91, 108

fight-or-flight response, 518, 556

figure-ground relationship, 179, 183

Fine motor skills, 316

fine motor skills, 335

Five Factor model, 23

Five Factor Model, 404, 413

fixed interval reinforcement schedule, 210, 219

fixed ratio reinforcement schedule, 210, 219

flashback, 619

flashbacks, 585

flashbulb memory, 274, 290

flight of ideas, 591, 619

Flow, 555

flow, 556

Fluid intelligence, 242

fluid intelligence, 256

Flynn effect, 247, 256

foot-in-the-door technique, 438, 462

forebrain, 94, 98, 108

Forensic psychology, 27

forensic psychology, 32

Forgetting, 281

forgetting, 290

formal operational stage, 306, 335

fovea, 164, 183

fraternal twins, 82, 108

free association, 637, 659

Frequency, 160

frequency, 183

Freud, 11, 43, 128, 301, 382, 383, 581, 637

frontal lobe, 95, 108

frustration aggression theory, 453

Functional fixedness, 238

functional fixedness, 256

Functional magnetic resonance imaging (fMRI), 102

functional magnetic resonance imaging (fMRI), 108

functionalism, 10, 32

fundamental attribution error, 423, 462

G

Gage, 95, 96

Galen, 380

Gender dysphoria, 359

gender dysphoria, 373

Gender identity, 359

gender identity, 373

gene, 108

general adaptation syndrome, 519, 556

generalize, 68

generalized anxiety disorder, 580, 619

Generalizing, 46

genes, 78

Genes, 82

genetic environmental correlation, 81, 108

genital stage, 389, 413

genotype, 78, 108

Gestalt, 12

Gestalt psychology, 179, 183

Ghraib, 431

Gilbreth, 480, 503

glial cell, 108

Glial cells, 83

gonad, 108

gonadarche, 325, 335

gonads, 105

good continuation, 181, 183

Goodall, 47

Grammar, 230

grammar, 256

grandiose delusion, 619

grandiose delusions, 599

Gross motor skills, 316

gross motor skills, 335

Group polarization, 443, 445

group polarization, 462

group therapy, 649, 659

Groupthink, 442, 445

groupthink, 462

gyri, 93

gyrus, 108

H

habit, 344, 373

hair cell, 184

hair cells, 172

hallucination, 598, 619

hallucinogen, 142, 147

happiness, 549, 553, 556

harassment, 501

harmful dysfunction, 566, 619

Hawthorne effect, 478, 506

health care proxy, 333, 335

Health psychology, 26

health psychology, 516, 556

hearing, 173

heart disease, 537, 556

hemisphere, 108

hemispheres, 93

Henner, 271

heritability, 252, 413, 573

Heritability, 400

hertz (Hz), 160, 184

heterosexual, 356, 373

heterozygous, 79, 108

heuristic, 235, 256

hierarchy of needs, 346, 373

higher-order conditioning, 196, 219

hindbrain, 100, 108

Hindsight bias, 239

hindsight bias, 257

hippocampus, 98, 108, 273, 369

histrionic personality disorder, 611

hoarding disorder, 583, 619

Holmes, 523

Homeostasis, 90, 117

homeostasis, 108, 147

Homophily, 457

homophily, 462

homophobia, 450, 450, 462

homosexual, 356, 373

homozygous, 79, 108

hopelessness theory, 595, 619

hormone, 108

hormones, 104

Horney, 393

hospice, 331, 335

Hostile aggression, 453

hostile aggression, 462

Hovland, 436

Human factors psychology, 472

human factors psychology, 506

Humanism, 14

humanism, 32, 399

humanistic therapy, 644, 659

hunger, 348

hypertension, 534, 556

hyperthymesia, 271

Hypnosis, 143

hypnosis, 147

hypothalamic-pituitary-adrenal (HPA) axis, 520, 556

hypothalamus, 98, 108

hypothesis, 42, 55, 68

I

id, 384, 413

ideal self, 399, 413

identical twins, 82, 108

illusory correlation, 68

Illusory correlations, 54

imitation, 215

immune system, 521, 530, 557

immunosuppression, 530, 557

immutable characteristic, 506

immutable characteristics, 491

Implicit memories, 269

implicit memory, 290

in-group, 451, 462

in-group bias, 452, 462

Inattentional blindness, 158

inattentional blindness, 184

incongruence, 399, 413

incus, 171, 184

independent variable, 58, 68

individual psychology, 389, 413

individual therapy, 649, 660

individualistic culture, 424, 462

inductive reasoning, 41, 68

Industrial and organizational (I-O) psychology, 472

industrial and organizational (I-O) psychology, 506

Industrial psychology, 472

industrial psychology, 506

Industrial-Organizational psychology, 25

inferiority complex, 389, 413

inflammatory pain, 177, 184

informational social influence, 440, 462

Informational social influence, 445

informed consent, 64, 68

initiation, 434

Innocence Project, 278

insomnia, 118, 147

instinct, 219, 344, 374

instincts, 192

Institutional Animal Care and Use Committee (IACUC), 66, 68

institutional review board (IRB), 64

Institutional Review Board (IRB), 68

instrumental aggression, 453, 462

intake, 648, 660

intelligence quotient, 245, 257

inter-rater reliability, 48, 68

Interaural level difference, 173

interaural level difference, 184

Interaural timing difference, 173

interaural timing difference, 184

internal factor, 423, 462

International Classification of Diseases (ICD), 570, 619

Interpersonal, 422

Intrapersonal, 422

intrinsic, 342

intrinsic motivation, 374

introspection, 9, 32

Involuntary treatment, 635

involuntary treatment, 660

iris, 164, 184

J

James, 10, 344

James-Lange theory, 364

James-Lange theory of emotion, 374

Jet lag, 118

jet lag, 147

job analysis, 481, 506

job burnout, 527, 557

job interview, 485

Job satisfaction, 493

job satisfaction, 506

job strain, 527, 557

Johnson, 357

Jung, 128, 391

just noticeable difference, 184

just noticeable difference (jnd), 156

just-world hypothesis, 427, 462

justification of effort, 434, 462

K

K-complex, 126, 147

kinesthesia , 179, 184

Kinsey, 356

Kohlberg, 308

L

Language, 230

language, 257

latency period, 389, 413

Latent content, 128

latent content, 147

latent learning, 213, 219

lateralization, 93, 108

law of effect, 204, 219

learned helplessness, 543

learning, 192, 219, 395

lens, 164, 184

leptin, 348, 374

levels of processing, 288, 290

Lexicon, 230

lexicon, 257

lifespan development, 429

limbic system, 98, 108, 367

Linear perspective, 170

linear perspective, 184

living will, 333, 335

locus coeruleus, 580, 619

locus of control, 397, 413

Long-Term Memory, 266

Long-term memory (LTM), 268

long-term memory (LTM), 291

longitudinal fissure, 93, 108

Longitudinal research, 50

longitudinal research, 68

lucid dream, 147

Lucid dreams, 129

lymphocytes, 531, 557

M

magnetic resonance imaging (MRI), 102, 108

major depressive disorder, 589, 619

malleus, 171, 184

Mania, 589

mania, 619

manic depression, 591

manic episode, 591, 620

Manifest content, 128

manifest content, 148

marijuana, 601

Maslow, 14, 346, 399

Masters, 357

Meditation, 145

meditation, 148, 547

medulla, 100, 109

Meissner's corpuscle, 184

Meissner's corpuscles, 177

melatonin, 118, 148

membrane potential, 85, 109

Memory, 264

memory, 291

memory-enhancing strategies, 286

memory-enhancing strategy, 291

menarche, 325, 335

Ménière's disease, 174, 184

mental set, 238, 257

Merkel's disk, 184

Merkel's disks, 177

meta-analysis, 121, 148

metabolic rate, 349, 374

Methadone, 141

methadone, 148

methadone clinic, 148

Methadone clinics, 141

Methamphetamine, 139

methamphetamine, 148

midbrain, 99, 109

Milgram, 24, 441, 442

Minnesota Multiphasic Personality Inventory (MMPI), 409, 413

Minnesota Study of Twins Reared Apart, 400

Misattribution, 284

misattribution, 291

Mischel, 397

misinformation effect paradigm, 279, 291

mitosis, 310, 335

mnemonic device, 291

Mnemonic devices, 287

model, 219

modeling, 576

models, 214

Molaison, 99

monaural, 173

monaural cue, 184

monocular cue, 184

monocular cues, 170

Mood, 362

mood disorder, 620

Mood disorders, 588

Morbid obesity, 350

morbid obesity, 374

morpheme, 257

morphemes, 230

Motivation, 342

motivation, 374

motor cortex, 95, 109

Motor skills, 316

motor skills, 335

Müller-Lyer, 159

Multiple Intelligences Theory, 243, 257

mutation, 80, 109

myelin sheath, 84, 109

N

narcissistic personality disorder, 611

narcolepsy, 133, 148

natural concept, 257

Natural concepts, 227

natural selection, 123

naturalistic observation, 46, 68

nature, 299, 335

Negative affectivity, 537

negative affectivity, 557

negative correlation, 52, 68

negative punishment, 205, 219

negative reinforcement, 205, 219

negative symptom, 620

Negative symptoms, 599

nervous system, 83, 89

neurodevelopmental disorder, 620

neurodevelopmental disorders, 605

neuron, 85, 109

Neurons, 83, 83

neuropathic pain, 178, 184

neuroplasticity, 93, 109

neurosis, 385, 414

neurotransmitter, 109, 274

neurotransmitters, 84, 88

neutral stimulus (NS), 194, 219

newborn reflexes, 314, 335

nicotine, 140

night terror, 148

Night terrors, 132

nociception, 177, 184

Nodes of Ranvier, 84, 109

non-REM (NREM), 125, 148

nondirective therapy, 644, 660

normative approach, 297, 335

normative social influence, 440, 462

Normative social influence, 445

Norming, 246

norming, 257

nurture, 299, 335

O

O*Net, 482

Obedience, 441, 445

obedience, 462

obese, 350, 374

object permanence, 305, 335

observational learning, 214, 219

observer bias, 48, 68

obsessions, 582

Obsessive-compulsive and related disorders, 581

obsessive-compulsive and related disorders, 620

obsessive-compulsive disorder, 620

obsessive-compulsive disorder (OCD), 581

obsessive-compulsive personality disorder, 611

Obstructive sleep apnea, 132

obstructive sleep apnea, 148

occipital lobe, 97, 109

olfactory bulb, 176, 184

Olfactory receptor, 176

olfactory receptor, 184

ology, 32

operant conditioning, 203, 219, 584

operational definition, 56, 68

opiate/opioid, 148

opiates, 140

opinion, 68

opinions, 40

opioid, 140

opponent-process theory, 169

opponent-process theory of color perception, 184

optic chiasm, 165, 184

optic nerve, 165, 184

optimism, 554, 557

oral stage, 388, 414

orbitofrontal cortex, 583, 620

Organizational culture, 500

organizational culture, 506

Organizational psychology, 472

organizational psychology, 493, 506

Orgasm, 357

orgasm, 374

ossicles, 171

out-group, 451, 462

overgeneralization, 232, 257

overweight, 350, 374

P

Pacinian corpuscle, 184

Pacinian corpuscles, 177

pancreas, 105, 109

panic attack, 579, 620

panic disorder, 579, 620

paranoid delusion, 620

paranoid delusions, 599

paranoid personality disorder, 611

parasomnia, 130

parasympathetic nervous system, 90, 109

parietal lobe, 96, 109

parinsomnia, 148

partial reinforcement, 209, 219

Participants, 58

participants, 68

pattern perception, 182, 185

Pavlov, 12, 193

peak, 185

peer-reviewed journal article, 68

peer-reviewed journal articles, 60

Perceived control, 542

perceived control, 557

perception, 21, 185

Perception, 157

perceptual hypotheses, 182

perceptual hypothesis, 185

performance appraisal, 506

Performance appraisals, 487

peripartum onset, 591, 620

peripheral nervous system (PNS), 89, 109

peripheral route, 437

peripheral route persuasion, 462

permissive parenting style , 335

permissive style, 324

persistence, 285, 291

persistent depressive disorder, 591, 620

Personality, 380

personality, 414

personality disorder , 620

personality disorders, 611

Personality psychology, 23

personality psychology, 32

personality trait, 32

personality traits, 23

Persuasion, 435

persuasion, 462

phallic stage, 388, 414

PhD, 27, 32

Phenotype, 78

phenotype, 109

phenylketonuria, 79

pheromone, 185

pheromones, 177

phobia, 575

phoneme, 230, 257

photoreceptor, 164, 185

Physical dependence, 134

physical dependence, 148

Physical development, 296

physical development , 335

Piaget, 22, 303

pineal gland, 118, 148

Pinel, 632

pinna, 171, 185

pitch, 161, 185

pituitary gland, 104, 109

place theory, 172

place theory of pitch perception, 185

placebo effect, 57, 68

placenta, 311, 335

plateau, 357, 374

Play therapy, 638

play therapy, 660

polygenic, 80, 109

polygraph, 366, 374

pons, 100, 109

population, 48, 68

positive affect, 554, 557

positive correlation, 52, 68

positive psychology, 553, 557

positive punishment, 205, 219

positive reinforcement, 205, 220

Positron emission tomography (PET), 102

positron emission tomography (PET) scan, 109

postdoctoral training program, 32

postdoctoral training programs, 29

postpartum depression, 591

posttraumatic stress disorder (PTSD), 585, 620

Practical intelligence, 242

practical intelligence, 257

Prader-Willi Syndrome, 351

prefrontal cortex, 95, 109

prejudice, 182, 448, 449, 449, 450, 462

Prejudice, 446, 447, 450

prenatal care, 312, 335

prenatal development, 310

preoperational stage, 305, 335

primary appraisal, 512, 557

primary reinforcer, 207, 220

Primary sexual characteristics, 325

primary sexual characteristics, 335

principle of closure, 181, 185

proactive interference, 285, 291

problem-focused coping, 541

problem-solving strategy, 234, 257

Procedural justice, 502

procedural justice, 506

procedural memory, 270, 291

prodromal symptom, 620

prodromal symptoms, 602

projection, 387, 414

Projective test, 414

projective testing, 410

proprioception, 179, 185

prosocial, 217

prosocial behavior, 456, 462

prototype, 227, 257

proximity, 180, 185

psychoanalysis, 639, 660

Psychoanalytic theory, 11

psychoanalytic theory, 32

psychodynamic, 638

psychological dependence, 134, 148

psychological disorder, 564, 620

Psychology, 8

psychology, 32

Psychoneuroimmunology, 531

psychoneuroimmunology, 557

Psychopathology, 564

psychopathology, 620

psychophysiological disorders, 529, 557

psychosexual development, 301, 335

psychosexual stage of development, 387

psychosexual stages of development, 414

Psychosocial development, 296

psychosocial development, 301, 336, 336

Psychotherapy, 636

psychotherapy, 660

psychotropic medication, 109

Psychotropic medications, 88

PsyD, 29, 32

punishment, 205, 220

Punnett square, 79, 80

pupil, 164, 185

R

Racism, 448

racism, 462

radical behaviorism, 212, 220

Rahe, 523

random assignment, 59, 68

random sample, 59, 69

Range of reaction, 81

range of reaction, 109, 257

Range of Reaction, 253

Rapid eye movement (REM), 125

rapid eye movement (REM) sleep, 148

rational emotive therapy (RET), 643, 660

rationalization, 387, 414

reaction formation, 387, 414

real self, 399, 414

Recall, 272

recall, 291

receptor, 109

Receptors, 84

recessive allele, 79, 110

reciprocal determinism, 395, 414

Reciprocity, 457

reciprocity, 462

Recognition, 272

recognition, 291

reconstruction, 277, 291

reflex, 220

Reflexes, 192

refractory period, 357, 374

regression, 387, 414

Rehearsal, 267

rehearsal, 286, 291

reinforcement, 220

relapse, 652, 660

relaxation response technique, 547, 557

relearning, 272, 291

Reliability, 62

reliability, 69

REM sleep behavior disorder (RBD), 131, 148

replicate, 61, 69

Representative bias, 239

representative bias, 257

representative sample, 248, 257

repressed, 387

repression, 414

resistant attachment, 321, 336

Resolution, 357

resolution, 374

resting potential, 85, 110

restless leg syndrome, 132, 148

reticular formation, 99, 110

retina, 164, 185

retrieval, 271, 291

Retroactive interference, 285

retroactive interference, 291

Retrograde amnesia, 277

retrograde amnesia, 291

reuptake, 87, 110

reversibility, 306, 336

rod, 185

Rods, 164

Rogerian, 644

Rogerian (client-centered therapy), 660

Rogers, 15, 644

role schema, 228, 257

Romantic love, 459

romantic love, 462

Rorschach Inkblot Test, 410, 414

Rotating shift work, 119

rotating shift work, 148

Rotter, 397

Rotter Incomplete Sentence Blank (RISB), 411, 414

Ruffini corpuscle, 185

Ruffini corpuscles, 177

Rumination, 596

rumination, 620

S

safety behavior, 621

safety behaviors, 577

sample, 48, 69

satiation, 348, 374

Scapegoating, 452

scapegoating, 463

Schachter-Singer two-factor theory, 365

Schachter-Singer two-factor theory of emotion, 374

schema, 228, 257, 336

Schemata, 304

Schiavo, 101

schizoid personality disorder, 611

schizophrenia, 82, 621

Schizophrenia, 598

schizotypal personality disorder, 611

scientific management, 497, 506

scientific method, 41

Scott, 477

script, 430, 463

seasonal pattern, 591, 621

second-order conditioning, 196

secondary appraisal, 513, 557

secondary reinforcer, 207, 220

Secondary sexual characteristics, 325

secondary sexual characteristics, 336

secure attachment, 321, 336

secure base, 320, 336

selective migration, 407, 414

self-concept, 399, 414

Self-disclosure, 457

self-disclosure, 463

Self-efficacy, 346, 396

self-efficacy, 374, 414

self-fulfilling prophecy, 451, 463

self-reference effect, 266, 291

Self-serving bias, 426

self-serving bias, 463

Seligman, 553

Selye, 512, 519

semantic encoding, 265, 291

Semantic memory, 269

semantic memory, 291

Semantics, 230

semantics, 257

semipermeable membrane, 83, 110

sensation, 21, 156, 185

sensorimotor, 305

sensorimotor stage, 336

sensorineural hearing loss, 174, 185

sensory adaptation, 157, 185

Sensory Memory, 266

sensory memory, 267, 291

serotonin, 594, 597

set point theory, 374

set-point theory, 349

Sexism, 449

sexism, 463

sexual harassment, 502, 506

sexual orientation, 356, 374

sexual response cycle, 357, 374

shaping, 206, 220

Shiffrin, 266

Short-Term Memory, 266

Short-term memory (STM), 267

short-term memory (STM), 291

signal detection theory, 158, 185

similarity, 180, 185

single-blind study, 57, 69

Situationism, 423

situationism, 463

Skinner, 13, 203, 230, 395

Skinner box, 14

Sleep, 116

sleep, 148

Sleep apnea, 132

sleep apnea, 149

sleep debt, 119, 149

Sleep rebound, 122

sleep rebound, 149

Sleep regulation, 118

sleep regulation, 149

sleep spindle, 126, 149

sleepwalking, 131, 149

Smart, 279

smell, 175

Social anxiety disorder, 577

social anxiety disorder, 621

social exchange theory, 459, 463

Social facilitation, 445

social facilitation, 463

Social loafing, 444, 445

social loafing, 463

social norm, 429, 463

Social psychology, 24, 422

social psychology, 463

Social Readjustment Rating Scale (SRRS), 523, 557

social role, 428, 463

Social support, 544

social support, 557

social-cognitive theory, 395, 414

Society for Industrial and Organizational Psychology (SIOP), 481

socioemotional selectivity theory, 330, 336

sodium-potassium pump, 85

soma, 84, 110

somatic delusion, 599, 621

somatic nervous system, 90, 110

somatosensory cortex, 96, 110

specific phobia, 575, 621

spermarche, 325, 336

spinal cord, 92

spontaneous recovery, 200, 220

sport and exercise psychology, 26, 33

Stage 1 sleep, 125

stage 1 sleep, 149

stage 2 sleep, 126, 149

Stage 3, 126

stage 3 sleep, 149

stage 4 sleep, 149

stage of exhaustion, 520, 557

stage of moral reasoning, 336

stage of resistance, 520, 557

stages of moral reasoning, 308

standard deviation, 257

Standard deviations, 249

Standardization, 246

standardization, 257

Stanford prison experiment, 430

stanford prison experiment, 463

stapes, 171, 185

statistical analysis, 60, 69

stereotype, 447, 451, 463

Stereotype, 447

stereotypes, 182

stimulant, 149

Stimulants, 137

stimulus discrimination, 200, 220

stimulus generalization, 201, 220

Storage, 266

storage, 291

strategic family therapy, 652,

660

stress, 495, 512, 512, 522, 528, 541, 548, 557

stressor, 522

stressors, 512, 558

structural family therapy, 652, 660

structuralism, 10, 33

sublimation, 387, 414

subliminal message, 185

subliminal messages, 156

substantia nigra, 99, 110

sudden infant death syndrome (SIDS), 133, 149

Suggestibility, 277

suggestibility, 291

suicidal ideation, 590, 621

Suicide, 596

suicide, 621

sulci, 93

sulcus, 110

superego, 384, 414

supernatural, 571, 621

suprachiasmatic nucleus (SCN), 117, 149

survey, 69

Surveys, 48

sympathetic nervous system, 90, 110, 520

synaptic cleft, 84, 110

synaptic vesicle, 110

synaptic vesicles, 84

Syntax, 230

syntax, 257

systematic desensitization, 640, 660

T

taste, 175

Taste aversion, 199

taste bud, 185

Taste buds, 175

Taylor, 479

Telecommuting, 497

telecommuting, 506

telomere, 532

TEMAS Multicultural Thematic Apperception Test, 412, 415

Temperament, 324

temperament , 336, 402, 415

temporal lobe, 97, 110

temporal theory, 172

temporal theory of pitch perception, 185

teratogen, 313, 336

terminal button, 110

terminal buttons, 84

thalamus, 98, 110

Thematic Apperception Test (TAT), 410, 415

theory, 42, 69

theory of evolution by natural selection, 77, 110

Theory X, 497, 506

Theory Y, 497, 507

therapy, 26

thermoception, 177, 185

theta wave, 149

Theta waves, 125

Thorndike, 204

threshold of excitation, 86, 110

thyroid, 110

thyroid gland, 105

Timbre, 163

timbre, 185

token economy, 642, 660

Tolerance, 135

tolerance, 149

top-down processing, 157, 185

traits, 401, 415

transactional leadership, 498

transactional leadership style, 507

transduction, 156, 186

transference, 637, 660

transformational leadership, 498

transformational leadership style, 507

transgender hormone therapy, 359, 374

transience, 282, 291

trial and error, 234, 257

triangular theory of love, 458, 463

triarchic theory of intelligence, 242, 257

trichromatic theory of color perception, 186

trichromatic theory of color vision, 167

trough, 186

Tuskegee Syphilis Study, 65

tympanic membrane, 171, 186

Type A, 535, 558

Type B, 535, 558

U

U.S. Equal Employment Opportunity Commission (EEOC), 489, 507

Umami, 175

umami, 186

unconditional positive regard, 644, 660

unconditioned response (UCR), 194, 220

unconditioned stimulus (UCS), 194, 220

unconscious, 383, 415

uninvolved parenting style, 336

uninvolved style, 324

universal emotions, 370

V

vaccinations, 609

validity, 47, 69

Validity, 63

variable interval reinforcement schedule, 210, 220

variable ratio reinforcement schedule, 211, 220

ventral tegmental area (VTA), 99, 110

ventricle, 621

ventricles, 601

vertigo, 174, 186

vestibular sense, 178, 186

vicarious punishment, 216, 220

vicarious reinforcement, 216, 220

virtual reality exposure therapy, 641, 660

visible spectrum, 160, 186

vision, 164

Visual encoding, 265

visual encoding, 292

Voluntary treatment, 635

voluntary treatment, 660

W

Wakefulness, 116

wakefulness, 149

Watson, 13, 201

Wavelength, 160

wavelength, 186

Wernicke's area, 97, 110

withdrawal, 135, 149

work team, 507

work teams, 500

work-family balance, 496

Working backwards, 235

working backwards, 258

Workplace violence, 502

workplace violence, 507

work–family balance, 507

Wundt, 9, 381

Y

Yale attitude change approach, 436

Yerkes-Dodson law, 345, 374

Z

Zimbardo, 430

Zimmerman, 421

zygote, 310, 336